Lecture Notes in Computer Science 13748

More information about this series at https://link.springer.com/bookseries/558

Eike Kiltz · Vinod Vaikuntanathan (Eds.)

Theory of Cryptography

20th International Conference, TCC 2022
Chicago, IL, USA, November 7–10, 2022
Proceedings, Part II

Editors
Eike Kiltz (ID)
Ruhr University Bochum
Bochum, Germany

Vinod Vaikuntanathan (ID)
Massachusetts Institute of Technology
Cambridge, MA, USA

ISSN 0302-9743   ISSN 1611-3349 (electronic)
Lecture Notes in Computer Science
ISBN 978-3-031-22364-8   ISBN 978-3-031-22365-5 (eBook)
https://doi.org/10.1007/978-3-031-22365-5

This Springer imprint is published by the registered company Springer Nature Switzerland AG
The registered company address is: Gewerbestrasse 11, 6330 Cham, Switzerland

Preface

The 20th Theory of Cryptography Conference (TCC 2022) was held during November 7–10, 2022, at the University of Chicago, USA. It was sponsored by the International Association for Cryptologic Research (IACR). The general chair of the conference was David Cash.

The conference received 139 submissions, of which the Program Committee (PC) selected 60 for presentation giving an acceptance rate of 43%. Each submission was reviewed by at least three PC members in a single-blind process. The 44 PC members (including PC chairs), all top researchers in our field, were helped by 116 external reviewers, who were consulted when appropriate. These proceedings consist of the revised version of the 60 accepted papers. The revisions were not reviewed, and the authors bear full responsibility for the content of their papers.

We are extremely grateful to Kevin McCurley for providing fast and reliable technical support for the HotCRP review software whenever we had any questions. We made extensive use of the interaction feature supported by the review software, where PC members could anonymously interact with authors. This was used to ask specific technical questions, such as those about suspected bugs or unclear connections to prior work. We believe this approach improved our understanding of the papers and the quality of the review process. We also thank Kay McKelly for her fast and meticulous help with the conference website.

This was the eighth year that TCC presented the Test of Time Award to an outstanding paper that was published at TCC at least eight years ago, making a significant contribution to the theory of cryptography, preferably with influence also in other areas of cryptography, theory, and beyond. This year, the Test of Time Award Committee selected the following paper, published at TCC 2011: "Perfectly secure oblivious RAM without random oracles" by Ivan Damgård, Sigurd Meldgaard, and Jesper Buus Nielsen. The award committee recognized this paper for "the first perfectly secure unconditional Oblivious RAM scheme and for setting the stage for future Oblivious RAM and PRAM schemes". The authors were invited to deliver a talk at TCC 2022. The conference also featured two other invited talks, by Rahul Santhanam and by Eran Tromer.

This year, TCC awarded a Best Young Researcher Award for the best paper authored solely by young researchers. The award was given to the paper "A Tight Computational Indistinguishability Bound of Product Distributions" by Nathan Geier.

We are greatly indebted to the many people who were involved in making TCC 2022 a success. A big thanks to the authors who submitted their papers and to the PC members and external reviewers for their hard work, dedication, and diligence in reviewing the papers, verifying their correctness, and discussing the papers in depth. We thank the University of Chicago Computer Science department, Google Research, Algorand Foundation, NTT Research, and Duality Technologies for their generous sponsorship of the conference. A special thanks goes to the general chair David Cash, and to Brian LaMacchia, Kevin McCurley, Kay McKelly, Sandry Quarles, Douglas Stebila, and the

TCC Steering Committee. Finally, we are thankful to the thriving and vibrant community of theoretical cryptographers. Long Live TCC!

September 2022

Eike Kiltz
Vinod Vaikuntanathan

Organization

General Chair

David Cash — University of Chicago, USA

Program Committee Chairs

Eike Kiltz — Ruhr-Universität Bochum, Germany
Vinod Vaikuntanathan — MIT, USA

Steering Committee

Jesper Buus Nielsen — Aarhus University, Denmark
Krzysztof Pietrzak — Institute of Science and Technology, Austria
Huijia (Rachel) Lin — UCSB, USA
Yuval Ishai — Technion, Israel
Tal Malkin — Columbia University, USA
Manoj M. Prabhakaran — IIT Bombay, India
Salil Vadhan — Harvard University, USA

Program Committee

Gilad Asharov — Bar-Ilan University, Israel
Marshall Ball — New York University, USA
Amos Beimel — Ben Gurion University, Israel
Fabrice Benhamouda — Algorand Foundation, USA
Nir Bitansky — Tel Aviv University, Israel
Zvika Brakerski — Weizmann Institute of Science, Israel
Anne Broadbent — University of Ottawa, Canada
Yilei Chen — Tsinghua University, China
Ran Cohen — Reichman University, Israel
Geoffroy Couteau — CNRS, IRIF, Université Paris Cité, France
Nils Fleischhacker — Ruhr University Bochum, Germany
Rishab Goyal — University of Wisconsin-Madison, USA
Siyao Guo — NYU Shanghai, China
Dennis Hofheinz — ETH Zurich, Switzerland
Gabe Kaptchuk — Boston University, USA
Jonathan Katz — University of Maryland, USA

Dakshita Khurana	UIUC, USA
Susumu Kiyoshima	NTT Research, USA
Karen Klein	ETH Zurich, Switzerland
Venkata Koppula	Indian Institute of Technology Delhi, India
Eyal Kushilevitz	Technion, Israel
Alex Lombardi	University of California, Berkeley, USA
Julian Loss	CISPA Helmholtz Center for Information Security, Germany
Fermi Ma	Simons Institute and UC Berkeley, USA
Mohammad Mahmoody	University of Virginia, USA
Ryo Nishimaki	NTT Corporation, Japan
Adam O'Neill	University of Massachusetts Amherst, USA
Emmanuela Orsini	KU Leuven, Belgium
Omer Paneth	Tel Aviv University, Israel
Alon Rosen	Bocconi University, Italy
Lior Rotem	The Hebrew University, Israel
Ron Rothblum	Technion, Israel
Peter Scholl	Aarhus University, Denmark
Sruthi Sekar	UC Berkeley, USA
Katerina Sotiraki	UC Berkeley, USA
Nicholas Spooner	University of Warwick, UK
Noah Stephens-Davidowitz	Cornell University, USA
Stefano Tessaro	University of Washington, USA
Prashant Vasudevan	National University of Singapore, Singapore
David Wu	University of Texas at Austin, USA
Yu Yu	Shanghai Jiao Tong University, China
Mark Zhandry	NTT Research and Princeton University, USA

Additional Reviewers

Damiano Abram
Amit Agarwal
Shweta Agrawal
Nicolas Alhaddad
Benedikt Auerbach
Renas Bacho
Christian Badertscher
Saikrishna Badrinarayanan
James Bartusek
Gabrielle Beck
Alexander Bienstock
Dung Bui
Suvradip Chakraborty

Rohit Chatterjee
Arka Rai Choudhuri
Kelong Cong
Hongrui Cui
Eric Culf
Dana Dachman-Soled
Pratish Datta
Lalita Devadas
Nico Döttling
Thomas Espitau
Jaiden Fairoze
Oriol Farràs
Weiqi Feng

Ben Fisch
Danilo Francati
Tore Frederiksen
Cody Freitag
Rachit Garg
Romain Gay
Nicholas Genise
Suparno Ghoshal
Aarushi Goel
Eli Goldin
Shai Halevi
Mathias Hall-Andersen
Dominik Hartmann

Alexandra Henzinger
Martin Hirt
Viet Tung Hoang
Charlotte Hoffmann
Justin Holmgren
James Hulett
Yuval Ishai
Palak Jain
Ruta Jawale
Zhengzhong Jin
Daniel Jost
Chethan Kamath
Martti Karvonen
Julia Kastner
Shuichi Katsumata
Fuyuki Kitagawa
Sabrina Kunzweiler
Ulysse Lechine
Derek Leung
Hanjun Li
Baiyu Li
Xiao Liang
Yao-Ting Lin
Tianren Liu
Qipeng Liu
Chen-Da Liu-Zhang

Sébastien Lord
George Lu
Takahiro Matsuda
Pierre Meyer
Pratyush Mishra
Tamer Mour
Marta Mularczyk
Alice Murphy
Varun Narayanan
Hai Nguyen
Maciej Obremski
Michele Orrù
Hussien Othman
Tapas Pal
Giorgos Panagiotakos
Dimitris Papachristoudis
Guillermo Pascual Perez
Anat Paskin-Cherniavsky
Robi Pedersen
Luowen Qian
Willy Quach
Nicholas Resch
Lawrence Roy
Yusuke Sakai
Pratik Sarkar
Benjamin Schlosser

Akash Shah
Yixin Shen
Omri Shmueli
Min Jae Song
Fang Song
Pratik Soni
Shravan Srinivasan
Igors Stepanovs
Dominique Unruh
Neekon Vafa
Benedikt Wagner
Hendrik Waldner
Mingyuan Wang
Hoeteck Wee
Ke Wu
Zhiye Xie
Sophia Yakoubov
Takashi Yamakawa
Eylon Yogev
Peter Yuen
Rachel Zhang
Jiaheng Zhang
Vassilis Zikas
Leo de Castro
Akin Ünal

Contents – Part II

Anonymity, Verifiability and Robustness

Encryption

Encryption

Forward-Secure Encryption with Fast Forwarding

Yevgeniy Dodis[1], Daniel Jost[1(✉)] ⓘ, and Harish Karthikeyan[2]

[1] New York University, New York, USA
{dodis,daniel.jost}@cs.nyu.edu
[2] J.P. Morgan AI Research, New York, USA
harish.karthikeyan@jpmchase.com

Abstract. Forward-secure encryption (FSE) allows communicating parties to refresh their keys across epochs, in a way that compromising the current secret key leaves all prior encrypted communication secure. We investigate a novel dimension in the design of FSE schemes: fast-forwarding (FF). This refers to the ability of a stale communication party, that is "stuck" in an old epoch, to efficiently "catch up" to the newest state, and frequently arises in practice. While this dimension was not explicitly considered in prior work, we observe that one can augment prior FSEs—both in symmetric- and public-key settings—to support fast-forwarding which is sublinear in the number of epochs. However, the resulting schemes have disadvantages: the symmetric-key scheme is a security parameter slower than any conventional stream cipher, while the public-key scheme inherits the inefficiencies of the HIBE-based forward-secure PKE.

To address these inefficiencies, we look at the common real-life situation which we call the *bulletin board model*, where communicating parties rely on some infrastructure—such as an application provider—to help them store and deliver ciphertexts to each other. We then define and construct FF-FSE in the bulletin board model, which addresses the above-mentioned disadvantages. In particular,

- Our FF-stream-cipher in the bulletin-board model has: (a) *constant* state size; (b) *constant* normal (no fast-forward) operation; and (c) *logarithmic* fast-forward property. This essentially matches the efficiency of non-fast-forwardable stream ciphers, at the cost of constant communication complexity with the bulletin board per update.
- Our public-key FF-FSE avoids HIBE-based techniques by instead using so-called updatable public-key encryption (UPKE), introduced in several recent works (and more efficient than public-key FSEs). Our UPKE-based scheme uses a novel type of "update graph" that we construct in this work. Our graph has constant in-degree, logarithmic diameter, and logarithmic "cut property" which is essential for the efficiency of our schemes. Combined with recent UPKE schemes, we get two FF-FSEs in the bulletin board model, under DDH and LWE.

Y. Dodis—Partially supported by gifts from VMware Labs and Algorand Foundation, and NSF grants 1815546 and 2055578.
D. Jost—Research supported by the Swiss National Science Foundation (SNF) via Fellowship no. P2EZP2_195410.
H. Karthikeyan—Work done while at New York University, New York, USA.

E. Kiltz and V. Vaikuntanathan (Eds.): TCC 2022, LNCS 13748, pp. 3–32, 2022.
https://doi.org/10.1007/978-3-031-22365-5_1

1   Introduction

Forward Secrecy. Encryption is the fundamental building block of cryptography designed to protect the confidentiality of data such as messages. The security of encryption is, however, confined by its requirement to secretly store the keys. Indeed, leaking an encryption scheme's secret key material typically means that all security is forgone. With cryptographic applications nowadays also typically running on a wide variety of different (and often poorly maintained) devices, alongside other software outside of the control of the cryptographic engineer, such key exposures pose a very real threat scenario.

This risk can be partially mitigated by *forward security*, which refers to the concept that the corruption of a system at some point should not adversely affect the security of prior operations. While initially proposed as a concept for key exchange [20, 32] it soon got broadened to incorporate a variety of non-interactive cryptographic primitives, such as forward-secure public-key encryption [16] and forward-secure signatures [6, 40]. Roughly speaking, the non-interactive notions share the idea that they divide time into *epochs* with the objective that leaking the secret state at epoch i does not endanger the security properties of past epochs $j < i$.

Fast-Forwarding. In this work, we investigate a novel dimension of the price—in terms of computational and storage overhead—of forward-secure encryption: *fast-forwarding*. The term fast-forwarding refers to the ability of a stale communication party, that is "stuck" in an old epoch, to efficiently "catch up" to the newest state. Such a situation, for instance, might occur if the user has a device that is only sporadically used and has consequently been turned off over a prolonged period.

Indeed, for many applications recovering the latest (or a recent) state seems of intrinsically higher priority than recovering the intermediate states. For example, in an email or a group chat it is often the case that messages sent weeks or months ago might simply no longer be relevant while replying to a recent conversation might be urgent. Moreover, in many communication protocols *sending* messages requires first obtaining (reasonably) up-to-date key material, further motivating the need for fast-forwarding. An example would be secure group messaging (such as MLS) where the group maintains a shared symmetric key that is distributed using public-key cryptography, which is then used to symmetrically encrypt and authenticate messages. It has been proposed to strengthen MLS' forward secrecy [3] by replacing the PKE used for distributing those group keys with a variant of FS-PKE (called UPKE). One of the main drawbacks of that proposal, however, was the lack of fast-forwarding, resulting in a party stuck in an old state having to restore the latest group keys in linear time before being able to send any message. While sequentially downloading old messages might be fine, being unable to send messages—until that process is completed—could trigger an assortment of problems.

1.1 Basic Solutions and a New Dimension

The functionality of forward-secure encryption—either symmetric- or public-key—automatically ensures that one can (fast-)forward from period i to period $j \gg i$ in time proportional to $(j-i)$. In this work, we will call such solutions *linear* and ask if one can build forward-secure encryption with a *sublinear* fast-forward property. To the best of our knowledge, this question was not explicitly considered in the literature. However, one can look at existing techniques for ensuring forward security and come up with some initial observations and solutions.

Symmetric Encryption: Stream Ciphers. Forward-secure symmetric-key encryption is typically achieved using basic stream ciphers, constructed from iteratively evaluating a pseudorandom generator (PRG) [7]. While this construction is efficient, as it only requires a constant size state and a constant number of cryptographic operations to encrypt the next message, it does not allow fast-forwarding: if the receiver last decrypted ciphertext i and now gets ciphertext $j \gg i$, then they need to advance the underlying PRG by $(j - i)$ steps. The existence of an efficient fast-forwarding method would be highly surprising for any widely used stream cipher, as they are not based on number theory.[1]

Instead, we can observe that the Goldreich-Goldwasser-Micali (GGM) construction can be turned into a forward-secure PRG with the fast-forwarding property. More concretely, one can adapt the template for building forward-secure signature schemes [6,40], where the PRG outputs correspond to the GGM tree's leaves and store the current leaf's right sibling path, i.e., the set of nodes from which exactly all leaves to the right of the current leaf can be deduced. We outline this in more detail in the full version [21].

Lemma 1 (Informal). *The template [6,40] (for building forward-secure signature schemes) can be adapted to the Goldreich-Goldwasser-Micali (GGM) construction [30] to build a forward-secure PRG with the fast-forward property. If n denotes the maximal number of epochs, then the scheme stores $\mathcal{O}(\log(n))$ seeds as local state, and sequential updating as well as fast-forwarding from epoch i to $j > i$ take $\mathcal{O}(\log(n))$ PRG expansions.*

While practically efficient, this folklore construction comes at the cost of worst-case logarithmic sequential evaluations, logarithmic local state, as well as a priori bounded number of overall evaluations. While some of those restrictions can be circumvented using more elaborate constructions—such as growing trees or potentially a cleverly designed amortized evaluation strategy—at least logarithmic-sized storage seems inherent. Thus, wearing a theoretician's hat, the first question we ask is:

Question 1. Can one have a model that allows for fast-forward stream ciphers simultaneously having: (a) *constant* state size; (b) *constant* sequential (no fast-forward) operation; and (c) sublinear (ideally, *logarithmic*) fast-forward property?

---

[1] The number-theoretic Blum-Blum-Shub PRG [8] can be modified to allow sublinear (in fact, logarithmic) fast-forwarding by additionally keeping the factorization of $N = pq$. Doing so, however, loses forward security.

Forward-Secure Public-Key Encryption. In the public-key setting, Canetti, Halevi, and Katz [16] introduced the notion of *forward-secure public-key encryption* (FS-PKE) and presented a generic construction of FS-PKE from hierarchical identity-based encryption (HIBE). Their construction essentially mirrors the simple logarithmic construction of the fast-forward PRG mentioned above, but replaces the "GGM tree" with the "HIBE tree." As a result, we observe that this construction allows us to fast-forward from any epoch i to any epoch $j > i$ using $\mathcal{O}(\log j)$ many HIBE secret-key expansions, needs logarithmic-sized storage of HIBE keys (which, in turn, might be long, depending on the HIBE used) and does worst-case logarithmic many secret-key expansions to just proceed to the next epoch.

As of today, this generic construction from HIBE remains the only non-trivial FS-PKE known. Unfortunately, while HIBE schemes from various assumptions exist [9,10,15,18,25,26], they are all either built from primitives not readily available in widespread cryptographic libraries (e.g., bilinear maps) or are primarily theoretical. To the best of our knowledge, this plays a significant role in why FS-PKE has never gained significant adoption in the real world. Hence, we ask:

Question 2. Can one have a meaningful model for fast-forward public-key encryption that potentially enables more efficient schemes than the generic HIBE-based solution mentioned above?

Bulletin Board Model. To address our motivating questions above, we notice that most secure real-world communication applications critically rely on the existence of some centralized server, whose job is to store and appropriately route encrypted messages to the corresponding participants. In other words, since communicating parties might not all be online, or might not have direct communication channels among them, one anyway has to implement some mechanism where old ciphertexts will be delivered to parties when those parties come online and request them. In practice, those servers often perform additional tasks such as helping people discover each other's keys, verifying the authenticity of the keys, serializing the order of concurrently received messages, etc.

End-to-end (E2E) security means that this centralized infrastructure is treated as untrusted, ensuring that a breach or a subpoena cannot affect the users' security. For most applications, however, the server's collaboration is required for correctness.[2] Generally speaking, for such server-assisted protocols, one requires that the most harm a malicious server can inflict is a denial of service (DoS) attack. This is typically deemed an acceptable risk, as a DoS attack is against the service provider's economic incentives.

In our work, we assume the existence of such a server and abstract it as a *bulletin board* functionality. Intuitively (see Sect. 3.1), this functionality allows

---

[2] Indeed, many secure messaging systems are designed for the rather peculiar model where the server is assumed to be somewhat-but-not-fully trusted. For instance, MLS aims to provide E2E security, yet exhibits weaknesses if the server does not consistently order messages.

all the parties to append some data to a public board, in a way that this data is automatically serialized (so that everybody reads it in the same order), and cannot disappear. Moreover, while the size of the bulletin board is allowed to grow linearly with the number of epochs, it does not "count" toward any of the parties' storage. However, it is also not completely "free", as any party's reading/appending to the bulletin board counts toward the efficiency of this party. More concretely, for primitives using this bulletin-board model, we consider the communication complexity (both in the size of transmitted messages as well as required rounds) as part of the respective efficiency notion but choose to disregard the server's storage requirements. This is motivated by real-world communication applications often treating server storage as essentially free (at least for "short" messages such as control messages or text messages, but not necessarily multi-media content) while paying close attention to the efficiency constraints of end-user devices. While disregarding server storage is an oversimplification, we remark that purging could be done in practice, at a potential functionality loss.[3] We can now make our Questions 1 and 2 more precise. Namely, we will ask (and answer) them *in the bulletin-board model*:

Question 3. Assuming the existence of a bulletin board, can we design forward-secure fast-forward stream ciphers and public-key encryption schemes satisfying the efficiency requirements stated in Questions 1 and 2, respectively?

It is prudent to point out that regular forward-secure stream ciphers are already extremely efficient. The bulletin board, however, will help us achieve the fast-forward property whose study we initiate. Even with fast-forwarding, however, the bulletin board model may be primarily of theoretical interest, as the adapted GGM construction is most likely efficient enough for all practical purposes, and the communication latency with the bulletin board likely outweighs the reduced local storage requirement. Nevertheless, we view Question 1 as an interesting open theoretical problem, as even a solution with fast-forwarding and either constant storage or constant sequential updates is an open problem.

In contrast, in the public-key setting there exists no truly practical[4] FS-PKE. It also appears that the bulletin board does not offer any benefit for the HIBE-based FS-PKE schemes. However, for its variant known as *Updatable Public-Key Encryption* (UPKE) [3,36], the bulletin board provides some critical functionality support. We discuss this in more detail below to motivate our new notion of *fast-forward UPKE*.

1.2   Our Contributions

Modeling. We provide a simple yet powerful formalization of the *bulletin board model* capturing a central server offering shared untrusted storage to assist the

---

[3] These concerns are interesting but orthogonal to our contributions.

[4] Despite some remarkable progress in the construction of pairing-based HIBE (e.g. [10]) over the last decades, those solutions have never gained any widespread adoption, partially for their omission from popular cryptographic libraries.

protocol execution. Our model entirely avoids complications such as interactive models of computation, is carefully designed to ensure that it does not introduce any side-effects such as the access pattern leaking secret information, and allows to easily capture bandwidth constraints.

We then provide rigorous definitions of two forward-secure encryption primitives in the bulletin board model, using a common template: *fast-forwardable stream cipher* and *fast-forwardable updatable public-key encryption* (FF-UPKE). We define correctness as well as IND-CPA security for both notions. We stress that our notions are the first formalization of the fast-forwarding property: while we observe that GGM-PRF and HIBE-based FS-PKE happen to allow for such an operation, none of the respective notions mandates/formalizes it.

Fast-Forwardable Stream Cipher. As a first scheme, we present a fast-forwardable stream cipher, in the bulletin board model, that requires *constant* (in the number of epochs) storage and a *constant* number of cryptographic operations to sequentially advance to the next epoch while allowing to fast-forward to any epoch j in $\mathcal{O}(\log j)$ cryptographic operations. The communication bandwidth of each operation also coincidences with the number of cryptographic operations mentioned above. Thus, we answer the first part of Question 3 affirmatively. Our construction is based on carefully adapting the GGM-based forward-secure stream cipher to:

(1) avoid the logarithmic worst-case computational complexity by appropriate amortization;
(2) offload most of the local storage to the bulletin board without compromising forward secrecy.

Roughly speaking, our scheme expands two GGM nodes per sequential update to ensure that whenever we need a leaf it has already been expanded. As this leads to linearly many expanded but not yet consumed seeds, we have to properly outsource to the bulletin board. This is achieved by encrypting them under independent keys associated with the GGM nodes (also derived from the parent seed), over time forming a linked list among the leaves in increasing order. In the meantime, forward-secrecy is preserved as all encryptions obey the tree's preorder, i.e., we only encrypt a node v's seed under nodes with a smaller preorder index. Let us briefly remark on the potential use-cases of such a solution. Compared to the folklore GGM-based solution, in most settings, trading logarithmic local computation and storage overhead for the need for communication appears to be highly undesirable. However, when used e.g. in the context of secure messaging, the party has to communicate with the server anyway, and as such our construction does not incur a cost in terms of round-trips but merely bandwidth. In such cases, trading a small bandwidth overhead for a logarithmic computation gain could be worthwhile.

One might attempt to apply the same techniques to the HIBE-based FS-PKE construction. We observe, however, that they do not directly translate over, as the senders cannot help the (typically single) receiver. As a result, while the respective solution inherently does support logarithmic fast-forwarding (without even using the bulletin board) supporting constant-time sequential updates does not work in the same way as in the symmetric setting. Concretely, when using a bulletin board to amortize sequential updates (by outsourcing encryptions of secret keys) only receivers knowing those secret keys can upload the respective ciphertexts. This has two major drawbacks. First, for a setting with a single receiver, once the receiver fast-forwards to obtain the decryption key of an epoch $j \gg i$, they would be "stuck" there and have to make up the missed $(j-i)$ sequential operations to "complete" the bulletin board before being able to sequentially update in a constant number of operations again. Second, for certain applications where all receivers are assumed to be only sporadically online, having receivers to maintain the bulletin board is generally undesirable. We thus focus on the slightly different primitive of updatable public-key encryption—which is well-suited for the bulletin-board model—instead.

Detour: Updatable Public-Key Encryption. Motivated by various applications to secure messaging, forward-secure PKE in a setting where an untrusted server provides synchronization among parties has been considered under the name UPKE in the literature [3, 36]. The idea of UPKE is that one can use ciphertexts—conveniently serialized and placed on the bulletin board (abstracting the messaging server)—to also contain information on how to move from the old (pk, sk) tuple, into a new (pk', sk'), in a way that: (a) new messages will be encrypted by pk' and decrypted by sk'; (b) exposure of sk' does not help to decrypt prior ciphertexts (including the one just sent under pk); (c) the person preparing ciphertext helps to "move" from sk to sk' without knowing either secret key but pk only. To show the potential of the bulletin board, the work of [36] provided a very simple and efficient UPKE (in the random oracle model) that has similar efficiency to the underlying ElGamal encryption. Recently, [22] also built two standard model UPKE schemes from the DDH and LWE assumptions, which were again much more efficient than their HIBE-based counterparts based on either DDH or LWE.

These constructions further validated the intuition that UPKE may be a significantly cheaper alternative compared to regular FS-PKE. They, however, eschew the inherent fast-forwarding property the generic HIBE-based FS-PKE enjoys. It thus remained an open problem whether it is possible to build a truly efficient fast-forwardable PKE primitive. In this work, we provide a partially affirmative answer for FF-UPKE. While not truly practical, our constructions are again more efficient when compared to their HIBE counterparts from the same assumptions. Specifically, the LWE-based construction is significantly simpler and more efficient than the best-known post-quantum secure FS-PKE scheme (see Sect. 1.3). Moreover, our novel approach initiates the study in this new dimension and hopefully serves as a launchpad for improved construction. Critically, we propose a generic FF-UPKE construction (much like the original FS-PKE scheme) that is not tethered to any particular assumption. In this process, we introduce a new primitive, whose instantiation directly implies FF-UPKE.

Our Work: FF-UPKE. We define *FF-UPKE*. As with standard UPKE, the sender can create special ciphertexts which do not encrypt messages,[5] but can help move from the current tuple $(\mathsf{pk}_i, \mathsf{sk}_i)$ for epoch i to the next tuple $(\mathsf{pk}_{i+1}, \mathsf{sk}_{i+1})$ for epoch $(i + 1)$. To support fast-forwarding from epoch i to epoch j, we introduce a special "leaping" algorithm. This algorithm can help a receiver[6] who currently holds sk_i to get to the latest key sk_j, by only reading a sublinear (in $(j-i)$) number of messages from the bulletin board, and performing a sublinear number of cryptographic operations. See Definition 4.

Aside from solving the practical problem of allowing an offline receiver to quickly catch up with the current messages, FF-UPKE also weakens the strictly sequential requirement of standard UPKE, that receiver should read and process every previous key update message. Indeed, the sublinear efficiency requirement of FF-UPKE means that the receiver has multiple "opportunities" to catch up, even if it cannot access some of the key update messages.[7]

FF-UPKE Construction. We also present a novel FF-UPKE scheme. To this end, we observe that all existing UPKE schemes refresh the secret key by having the sender choose an "update secret" δ that is then sent encrypted under the current public key pk_i. After decrypting δ using sk_i, the next secret key $\mathsf{sk}_{i+1} = \mathsf{sk}_i + \delta$ (using appropriate group operation $+$), while the sender can compute the next public key pk_{i+1} using only the current public key pk_i and the value δ. Our generic FF-UPKE construction is built around the idea of so-called *cumulative updates* using any so-called *update-homomorphic* UPKE scheme—a notion we introduce to formalize that multiple such update messages can be homomorphically combined. (See Definition 6 for the precise formalization of this requirement.)

As in prior UPKE schemes, in our construction, the sender for epoch i will choose update secret δ_{i+1}, and we will have the invariant that $\mathsf{sk}_j = \mathsf{sk}_i + \Delta[i, j]$, where $\Delta[i, j] := (\delta_{i+1} + \ldots + \delta_j)$, for any $j > i$. Now, however, senders can use the update homomorphism to create encryptions $\mathsf{up}_{i,j}$ that "cumulatively encrypt" $\Delta[i, j]$ under pk_i, for certain carefully chosen pairs $i < j$. Those encryption are then stored in the bulletin board to allow the receiver to fast-forward.

Finally, we show that with minor modifications the standard model DDH/LWE UPKE schemes of Dodis et al. [22] both satisfy the above homomorphism.[8]

---

[5] For the highest security, these can be sent after every regular ciphertext encrypting a message, but we do not require this to allow for the most flexibility.

[6] Of course, a new sender who "fell behind" other senders, can trivially "catch up" by retrieving the latest public key from the bulletin board.

[7] Of course, the sender for epoch i should still be able to get the current key pk_i.

[8] Interestingly, the most efficient random-oracle based scheme [3,36] does not appear to be update-homomorphic, and will not be enough for our purposes.

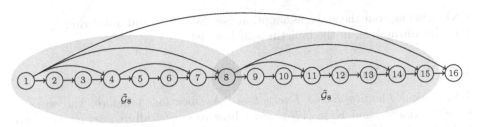

Fig. 1. The update graph $\tilde{\mathcal{G}}_{16}$, consists of two subgraphs $\tilde{\mathcal{G}}_8$ and an extra node.

Technical Tool: Update Graph. As one can see, the efficiency of our cumulative update scheme for building FF-UPKE from update-homomorphic UPKE critically depends on the properties of what we call an *update graph* $\mathcal{G}$, which will govern the collection of edges (i, j) for which parties need to maintain update ciphertexts $\mathsf{up}_{i,j}$. As it turns out (see Definition 8), three such parameters will be essential for understanding the efficiency of our construction:

- The *maximum in-degree* $\alpha(n)$ of any vertex $j \leq n$;
- The *diameter* $\beta(n)$ of the sub-graph of the first n vertices;
- The cardinality $\gamma(n)$ of the *active set* that includes all vertices $i < n$ which have at least one edge (i, j) with $j > n$ in $\mathcal{G}$.

We call such graphs $(\alpha(n), \beta(n), \gamma(n))$-*update graphs*. To the best of our knowledge, while many related notions of dynamic graphs are known in the literature (e.g., see [42] and references therein), including graphs having small in-degree and diameter, the exact notion of update graph we need for our construction is new.

We build a nearly optimal $(2, \mathcal{O}(\log n), \mathcal{O}(\log n))$-update graph. Our construction is inspired by the simple family of spanner graphs that recursively join two consecutive graphs of an equal number of nodes with an overarching edge spanning from the first to the last node. We observe that this results in a graph with logarithmic diameter but also logarithmic indegree. To circumvent the growing indegree, we modify this construction slightly and, in each recursive step, add one additional node at the end, to which the overarching edge connects. We call this graph $\tilde{\mathcal{G}}_n$, where n denotes its number of nodes. See Fig. 1 for the example of $\tilde{\mathcal{G}}_{16}$.

As we will see, using this graph $\tilde{\mathcal{G}}$ results in our final FF-UPKE scheme having logarithmic overhead for key update and fast-forwarding, and no overhead for public-key size, encryption, and decryption, as compared to the underlying update-homomorphic UPKE.

Putting it All Together. Instantiating our generic cumulative update scheme with our update graph and the two homomorphic-update UPKE scheme from DDH and LWE, we get two concrete FF-UPKE schemes from DDH and LWE, respectively, achieving greater efficiency than the best-known HIBE-based FS-

PKE scheme from the same assumption (see Sect. 1.3) and answering Question 2 in the affirmative, in the bulletin board model.

1.3   Related Work

Hierarchical Identity Based Encryption. As mentioned before, the work of Canetti, Halevi, and Katz [17] showed how to generically construct Forward-Secure Public Key Encryption from Hierarchical Identity Based Encryption [29,33]. Indeed, over time, various HIBE schemes have been proposed under an assortment of assumptions such as LWE [2,18], CDH/DDH [15,25,26], and pairing-based Diffie-Hellman Assumptions [9,10], among others. However, despite the beautiful theory, HIBE-based schemes have not found much adoption in practice, either due to the reluctance of practitioners to use pairings, or because the constructions are rather impractical. For example, the CDH/DDH-based constructions [15,25,26], while giving us constructions of FS-PKE in the standard model, rely on garbled circuits. More formally, if κ is the security parameter, it relies on a chain of $\mathcal{O}(\kappa)$ such circuits, and the blow-up of the public key operations performed by the circuits is significant. HIBE constructions based on LWE [2,18] rely on either lattice trapdoors or GPV-style pre-image sampling [28] which are inefficient and quite complex. Additionally, all of these HIBE constructions suffer from overhead of $\mathcal{O}(\kappa)$ to support an unbounded number of time periods in the FS-PKE construction built from HIBE. Thus, while our new DDH/LWE schemes are not yet as practical as PKEs from the same assumption (and we also did not try to optimize all the constants in our constructions for the elegance of presentation), they certainly are more efficient than the corresponding HIBE-based FS-PKEs, even taking into account the reliance on the bulletin board model.

Forward-Secure Signatures. Anderson [4] first proposed the idea of Forward-Secure signatures. The idea was that the compromise of a secret key at a time i should not allow for the forgery of messages at a time $j < i$. Construction of this primitive was proposed by Bellare and Miner [6] and later extended and improved by Malkin *et al.* [40]. There are still other constructions that are secure in the random oracle model [1,34,38].

Key Evolving Encryption Schemes. Two recent works - Jaeger and Stepanovs [35] and Poettering and Rössler [41] - proposed a scheme that was secure even when the key updates were labeled by arbitrary (even adversarially chosen) strings. This is a stronger setting than even FS-PKE and unsurprisingly, these constructions were realized from HIBE Schemes.

Updatable Public Key Encryption. The work of Jost *et al.* [36] and Alwen *et al.* [3] formally introduced the primitive and presented constructions that were secure in the random oracle model. The work of Dodis *et al.* [22] explored constructions that were secure in the standard model. In addition, they also considered extensions of the simpler CPA-based security definition to stronger definitions.

Updatable Encryption. Updatable Encryption [11,12,14,27,37,39], vastly different from the idea of UPKE, explores the orthogonal problem of updating the ciphertext that was encrypted under a key at a time i to be consistent, i.e., decryptable by the key at a time $j > i$. This primitive, however, is for the *symmetric key* setting. Informally, the construction produces different ciphertexts for the same messages under different keys. The goal is to produce tokens that help update the ciphertext without revealing any information about the underlying message.

Key Insulated Public Key Cryptosystems. Key Insulated Public Key Cryptosystems [23,24], though motivated for other purposes, achieves the feature of fast-forwardability. They do this by offering random-access key updates which help move from the current period i to any other period j. However, the constructions and indeed the setting assume that there is a party that is trusted, resistant to exposure/leakage, and has a secure channel to the secret key owner.

Puncturable (Public Key) Encryption. Puncturable Encryption [5,43] and Puncturable PKE [19,31,44] achieve forward secrecy on a per ciphertext basis. That is, puncturing has to work purely based on received ciphertexts, rather than dividing time into epochs, with senders not having to "target" a certain epoch or obtain an updated (public) key. Hence, puncturable PKE solves a much more difficult problem than FS-PKE or fast-forwardable UPKE, leading to *significantly less efficient* solutions.

Puncturable PRFs. Our fast-forwardable PRG construction is quite similar to some of the constructions of puncturable PRFs based on the GGM construction [13]. We remark, however, that the (standard) *notion* of a puncturable PRF is quite different and, for example, lacks the iterative aspect of "continuously re-puncturing" which we require for our notion.

2 Preliminaries

We write $\mathbb{N} := \{1, 2, \ldots\}$ and for $x \in \mathbb{N}$ we write $[x] := \{1, 2, \ldots, x\}$. We write $x \leftarrow a$ to assign the value a to the variable x. Moreover, for a set S we write $x \leftarrow_\$ S$ to denote sampling an element from S uniformly at random or according. For a probabilistic algorithm A, we write $A(\cdot; r)$ to denote that A is run with explicit randomness r. The security parameter is denoted by κ.

A directed graph $\mathcal{G} = (V, E)$ consists of a vertices set V and an edge set $E \subseteq V^2$. For an edge $(u, v) \in E$, we call u the *tail* and v the *head*. For a node $w \in V$, we denote by $E_\mathcal{G}^{in}(w) := \{(u, v) \in E \mid v = w\}$ the set of incoming edges, and by $E_\mathcal{G}^{out}(w) := \{(u, v) \in E \mid u = w\}$ the set of outgoing edges, respectively. Moreover, we denote by $\deg_\mathcal{G}^{in}(w) := |E_\mathcal{G}^{in}(w)|$ and $\deg_\mathcal{G}^{out}(w) := |E_\mathcal{G}^{out}(w)|$ the in- and outdegrees, respectively. We often omit to specify the graph for these functions when the context is clear. For $u, v \in V$ we say that edges $((v_1, v_2), (v_2, v_3), \ldots, (v_n, v_{n+1})) \in E^n$ is a *path* of length n from v_1 to v_{n+1}. If the concrete path is not of relevance, we sometimes use $u \rightsquigarrow v$ as a shorthand notation for and refer by $|u \rightsquigarrow v|$ to its length. Additionally, we refer to $d(u, v)$ as the minimum length of all paths from u to v (or ∞ if no such path exists). Finally, the diameter of the graph $\mathcal{G}$ refers to the maximal distance between any nodes u and v for which a path exists, i.e., $\mathrm{diam}(\mathcal{G}) := \max\{d(u, v) \mid u, v \in V \wedge d(u, v) \neq \infty\}$.

Cryptographic Primitives. We make use of a *pseudo-random generator* with expansion factor 4, which is a function $\mathsf{PRG.Expand}: \{0, 1\}^\kappa \to \{0, 1\}^{4\kappa}$ such that the two distribution ensembles $\{\mathsf{PRG.Expand}(\mathsf{s}) \mid \mathsf{s} \leftarrow_{\$} \{0, 1\}^\kappa\}_{\kappa \in \mathbb{N}}$ and $\{\mathsf{k} \leftarrow_{\$} \{0, 1\}^{4\kappa}\}_{\kappa \in \mathbb{N}}$ are computationally indistinguishable.

Moreover, we use a *nonce-based symmetric encryption scheme*, which is a tuple of deterministic algorithms $(\mathsf{SE.Enc}, \mathsf{SE.Dec})$, such that for any encryption $\mathsf{c} \leftarrow \mathsf{SE.Enc}(\mathsf{k}, \mathsf{m}, \mathsf{n})$, the corresponding decryption recovers the correct message $\mathsf{m} \leftarrow \mathsf{SE.Dec}(\mathsf{k}, \mathsf{c}, \mathsf{n})$. We require the scheme to satisfy standard IND-CPA security as long as the nonce n is not reused.

3 Fast-Forwarding in the Bulletin Board Model

3.1 Bulletin Board

In this work, we consider a setting where parties can make use of an append-only bulletin board BB to store and retrieve (shared) information, reducing their storage and computation costs. Intuitively, BB can be thought of as an associative array where for an index $\mathsf{idx} \in \mathcal{I}$ they can retrieve a value $v \leftarrow \mathsf{BB}[\mathsf{idx}]$ either returning the previously stored value v or a special error symbol $\perp$. Along the same lines, $\mathsf{BB}[\mathsf{idx}] \leftarrow v'$ sets the value to v' if it has been previously undefined, or ignores the new value.

We formalize this by using a partial function $\mathsf{BB}: \mathcal{I} \rightharpoonup \mathcal{V}$. Moreover, we define two additional operators on the bulletin board: restriction and appending. For a subset of possible indices I, $\mathsf{BB}\!\upharpoonright_I$ denotes the modified bulletin board only defined for those indices. We will use this operation as a convenient way to handle a party "fetching" a subset of the values of the bulletin board alongside the associated indices. The append operations append another bulletin board to the existing one while ignoring all already defined values. We will use this operation to represent a party "uploading" new values to the bulletin board.

Definition 1. *For an index space $\mathcal{I}$ and a value space $\mathcal{V}$, we call a partial function* $\mathsf{BB}: \mathcal{I} \rightharpoonup \mathcal{V}$ *a bulletin board. That is,* $\mathsf{BB} \subset \mathcal{I} \times \mathcal{V}$ *such that for all* $\mathsf{idx} \in \mathcal{I}$ *and* $v_1, v_2 \in \mathcal{V}$, $(\mathsf{idx}, v_1) \in \mathsf{BB}$ *and* $(\mathsf{idx}, v_2) \in \mathsf{BB}$ *implies* $v_1 = v_2$. *For a set of indices* $\mathrm{I} \subseteq \mathcal{I}$, *we denote by* $\mathsf{BB}\!\upharpoonright_\mathrm{I}$ *function restriction. That is,* $\mathsf{BB}\!\upharpoonright_\mathrm{I} := \{(\mathsf{idx}, v) \in \mathsf{BB} \mid \mathsf{idx} \in \mathrm{I}\}$. *Moreover, for bulletin boards* BB_1 *and* BB_2, *we define* $\mathsf{BB}_1 +\!\!\!+ \mathsf{BB}_2 := \mathsf{BB}_1 \cup \mathsf{BB}_2\!\upharpoonright_{\mathcal{I}\setminus\mathrm{dom}(\mathsf{BB}_1)}$, *where* dom *denotes the domain.*

3.2 Fast-Forwardable Stream Ciphers

We investigate the construction of fast-forwardable forward-secure stream ciphers in the bulletin-board model. It is easy to see that the folklore stream cipher construction from a PRG yields this as long as the PRG is both forward secure and fast forwardable. We, thus, focus on fast-forwardable PRGs[9] instead.

Definition 2. *A* Fast-Forwardable PRG (FF-PRG) *consists of the deterministic algorithms* (Init, Update, Update-Idx, Leap, Leap-Idx), *where:*

- *The* $(\mathsf{st}_1, \mathsf{R}_1, \mathsf{BB}_{init}) \leftarrow$ Init(key) *algorithm takes* key $\in \{0,1\}^\kappa$ *and produces an initial state* st_1, *output* R_1, *and initial bulletin board state* BB_{init}.
- *The* $(\mathsf{st}_{i+1}, \mathsf{R}_{i+1}, \mathsf{BB}_{up}) \leftarrow$ Update$(\mathsf{st}_i, \mathsf{BB}\lceil_{\mathrm{I}_i})$ *algorithm takes a state and parts of the bulletin board as inputs, and produces the updated state and the next output, as well as content to upload to the bulletin board. The corresponding update-index algorithm* $\mathrm{I}_i \leftarrow$ Update-Idx(i) *determines the part of the bulletin board required for this operation.*
- *The* $(\mathsf{st}_j, \mathsf{R}_j) \leftarrow$ Leap$(\mathsf{st}_i, j, \mathsf{BB}\lceil_{\mathrm{I}_{i,j}})$ *algorithm takes a state* st_i, *the target epoch* $j > i$, *and parts of the bulletin board as inputs, to leap to the* j-*th state and output. The indices are determined by* $\mathrm{I}_{i,j} \leftarrow$ Leap-Idx(i,j).

Efficiency. For an FF-PRG scheme to be non-trivial we require fast-forwarding to be of sub-linear complexity in $j - i$, concerning both running time and communication complexity. More specifically, we require the output size of Leap-Idx to be bounded by fixed polynomials of the security parameter κ, i.e., to be independent of $j - i$. This in turn also implies that the running time of Leap is bounded by a fixed polynomial in κ.

Correctness and Security. For correctness, we intuitively expect that fast-forwarding results in the same output and state as sequentially advancing throughout the epochs. Note, however, that fast-forwarding is meant to be a "catching up" mechanism. Thus, we require fast-forwarding only to work whenever some other party (using the same bulletin board) has already reached the target epoch. A formal description of the correctness game is presented in the full version [21].

The key indistinguishability game of an FF-PRG formalizes that R_i look indistinguishable from fresh uniform random outputs. Forward security moreover asserts that for past outputs this holds even once the state is leaked. Note that for defining security, fast-forwarding is irrelevant, as Leap does not write to the bulletin board and, by correctness, results in the same state as sequential updates.

Definition 3 (Security). *A FF-PRG is secure, if every PPT adversary $\mathcal{A}$ has negligible advantage (i.e.,* $2 \Pr[\text{Key-Indist}_\mathcal{A} = \mathsf{true}] - 1$) *in winning the key indistinguishability game depicted in Fig. 2.*

We remark that having explicit indexing algorithms Update-Idx and Leap-Idx that depend on public information only, guarantees that the *access pattern* to the bulletin board does not leak confidential information about a party's state.

---

[9] For simplicity, we henceforth omit explicitly mentioning forward secrecy as part of each primitive's name.

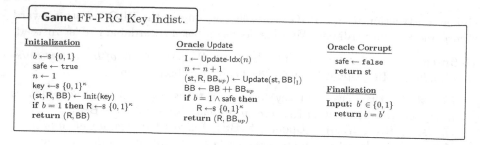

Fig. 2. The security game of FF-PRGs.

Constructions. In Sect. 4, we present an FF-PRG scheme with the following properties: First, Init and Update perform a constant number of cryptographic operations and output a constant number of elements to be uploaded to the bulletin board, i.e., $|\mathsf{BB}_{init}|, |\mathsf{BB}_{up}| \in \mathcal{O}(1)$. Second, Update only requires a constant number of elements from the bulletin board, i.e., $|\mathsf{Update\text{-}Idx}(i)| \in \mathcal{O}(1)$. Third, all elements on the bulletin board are of size $\mathcal{O}(\kappa)$ (such as a key or an encryption). Finally, $\mathsf{Leap}(\mathsf{st}_i, j, \mathsf{BB}_{in})$ performs at most $\mathcal{O}(\log j)$ operations and $\mathsf{Leap\text{-}Idx}(i, j)$ is of cardinality at most $\mathcal{O}(\log j)$.

Recall from Sect. 1.2 that while introducing additional communication might often be undesirable there are settings where communication with a centralized server anyways occurs, such as the symmetric ratcheting layer of Signal. There, switching this to our protocol would not add communication latency, but only slightly increased bandwidth. Moreover, our scheme is *concretely efficient* and for 2^T epochs reduces the secret storage compared to the GGM tree by roughly a factor of $T/7$. For example, for $T = 20$ under standard parameter choices of 128 bit seeds we go from 320 bytes to 122 bytes (and the bulletin board material after 2^{20} epochs will be under 50 MB).

3.3 Fast-Forwardable Updatable Public-Key Encryption

We now proceed to formalize fast-forwardable UPKE in the bulletin board model.

Definition 4. *A Fast-Forwardable Updatable Public-Key Encryption scheme is a tuple of PPT algorithms* FF-UPKE := (KeyGen, Encrypt, Decrypt, UpdatePK, UpdatePK-Idx, UpdateSK, UpdateSK-Idx, LeapSK, LeapSK-Idx), *defined as follows:*

- *The* $(\mathsf{pk}_1, \mathsf{sk}_1, \mathsf{BB}_{init}) \leftarrow \mathsf{KeyGen}(1^\kappa)$ *algorithm outputs an initial secret/ public key pair* sk_1 *and* pk_1 *and an initial state of the bulletin board.*
- *The* $\mathsf{c} \leftarrow \mathsf{Encrypt}(\mathsf{pk}_i, \mathsf{m})$ *algorithm encrypts* m *under the public key* pk_i *and the deterministic* $\mathsf{m} \leftarrow \mathsf{Decrypt}(\mathsf{sk}_i, \mathsf{c})$ *algorithm decrypts* c *using the corresponding secret key.*
- *The* $(\mathsf{pk}_{i+1}, \mathsf{BB}_{up}) \leftarrow \mathsf{UpdatePK}(\mathsf{pk}_i, \mathsf{BB}\!\restriction_{\mathsf{I}_i})$ *algorithm takes a public key and parts of the bulletin board as input, and outputs the updated public key and content to be upload to the bulletin board.*

- *The deterministic* $\mathsf{sk}_{i+1} \leftarrow \mathsf{UpdateSK}(\mathsf{sk}_i, \mathsf{BB}\lceil_{\mathrm{I}_i})$ *algorithm takes a secret key and parts of the bulletin board as inputs, and outputs the updated secret key.*
- *The deterministic* $\mathsf{sk}_j \leftarrow \mathsf{LeapSK}(\mathsf{sk}_i, j, \mathsf{BB}\lceil_{\mathrm{I}_{i,j}})$ *algorithm takes a secret key* sk_i, *the target epoch* $j > i$, *and parts of the bulletin board as inputs.*

The deterministic algorithms $\mathrm{I}_i \leftarrow \mathsf{UpdatePK\text{-}Idx}(i)$, $\mathrm{I}_i \leftarrow \mathsf{UpdateSK\text{-}Idx}(i)$, *and* $\mathrm{I}_{i,j} \leftarrow \mathsf{LeapSK\text{-}Idx}(i, j)$ *determine the part of the bulletin board required for the respective operations.*

Modeling and Efficiency. One of the key properties of UPKE is that UpdatePK may be probabilistic. It is thus assumed that multiple senders coordinate on the advancing of epochs, with only one party executing UpdatePK and then distributing the updated public key to the other senders. (Indeed, this synchronization requirement seems to be what gives UPKE a significant performance lead over FS-PKE.) While in practice this might be achieved by storing the public key on the bulletin board, passing around an explicit public key allows us to easily model that during an epoch parties do not need to access the bulletin board.

Moreover, UpdateSK does not write any information to the bulletin board for the following reasons: First, there is typically only one receiver (per key pair) in a public-key setting, so there is no need to upload information that might help other receivers. Second, if the receiver had to somehow assist senders, this would introduce additional online requirements contradicting the asynchronous nature of public-key communication. (The synchronization among senders to prevent conflicting updates does not require all or any particular of them to be online.)

We require all algorithms except LeapSK to run in polynomial time independent of the epoch i. The LeapSK is allowed to run in time sublinear in $j - i$ (non-triviality). However, we stress that LeapSK-Idx must have a running time, and thus output size, of a fixed polynomial independent of $j - i$, meaning that LeapSK has communication complexity at most $\mathsf{poly}(\log j)$.

Correctness and Security. In a nutshell, there are two ways for an adversary to break correctness: (1) he breaks the correctness of the encryption, i.e., comes up with a message such that its encryption does not decrypt properly, or (2) he breaks the correctness of the fast-forwarding mechanism. For simplicity, we require from an FF-UPKE scheme that fast-forwarding from epoch i to j results in the same secret key sk_j as would have resulted from sequentially updating. Note that since FF-UPKE is designed for a setting where parties might use bad randomness, the correctness game allows the adversary to choose all randomness. A formal definition of correctness can be found in the full version [21].

Security is formalized as an IND-CPA game, depicted in Fig. 3. The game allows the adversary to make a single challenge from which he must decide whether he received encryption of m_0 or m_1. Ahead, he can make an arbitrary number of updates to the public key, potentially supplying the randomness. Moreover, to formalize forward secrecy, he can corrupt the receiver's state to

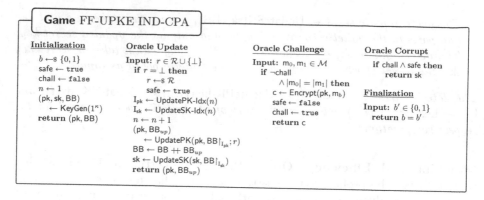

Fig. 3. The IND-CPA game of FF-UPKE.

obtain the secret key—once at least one is secure, i.e., not with adversarially chosen randomness, an update has been applied. Similar to the FF-PRG notion, we observe that the LeapSK algorithm is irrelevant for security.

Definition 5 (Security). *An FF-UPKE is said to be IND-CPA secure, if every PPT adversary $\mathcal{A}$ has a negligible advantage in winning the IND-CPA game depicted in Fig. 3.*

Constructions. In Sect. 5, we present a generic FF-UPKE scheme where public and secret keys do not grow with the epoch number i, the UpdatePK algorithm reads and writes $\mathcal{O}(\log i)$ positions on the bulletin board, UpdateSK reads $\mathcal{O}(1)$ positions, and LeapSK accesses $\mathcal{O}(\log j)$ position to fast-forward from epoch i to j. The construction makes use of a so-called Update-Homomorphic UPKE scheme as a building block. In the full version [21] we provide two concrete instantiations of this building block, based off minor modifications the standard-model UPKE schemes introduced in the recent work of Dodis et al. [22]. Both lead two bulletin board values of the order of $\mathcal{O}(\kappa^2)$ many cryptographic elements.

4   Constructing a Fast-Forwardable PRNG

In this section, we present a construction of a fast-forwardable PRNG. We first introduce the basic variant supporting a bounded number of epochs. We then extend this construction in Sect. 4.2 to an unbounded number of epochs.

4.1   The Basic Construction

Our construction is based on the GGM construction. To this end, we first observe that in a GGM tree of height h, and thus 2^h leaves, there are a total of $2^h - 1$ inner nodes to expand. Hence, the amortized number of expansions over the course of the $2^h - 1$ many possible updates in this tree is just one. In the following, we will show that if for each update we do *two* expansions, then at the time we need a new leaf it has already been derived.

Implemented naively, this would of course make a party's state grow linearly in the number of updates, which is where the outsourcing to the bulletin board comes into play. Roughly speaking, rather than keeping all the expanded seeds in the local state, we encrypt them under an appropriate key to outsource. Those encryption keys are derived from the GGM tree as well. To this end, we modify the expansion step of a node v's seed as follows:

$$(s_{v_{\text{left}}}, k_{v_{\text{left}}}, s_{v_{\text{right}}}, k_{v_{\text{right}}}) \leftarrow \text{PRG.Expand}(s_v),$$

where k_v is an encryption key associated with v. Using this key, we can then encrypt another node's seed s_u and key k_u using nonce-based symmetric encryption, i.e., $c \leftarrow \text{SE.Enc}(k_v, (s_u, k_u), n)$. Concretely, we use the index u as nonce, $n = u$, and store this ciphertext at index (v, u) in the bulletin board.

To ensure forward secrecy, only certain such links can be stored. Recall to this end that when using the GGM construction as a forward-secure PRNG, one expands the tree's nodes according to the *preorder traversal* and keeps the nodes from the copath (sometimes called sibling path) that are right children as a state. Hence, to preserve forward secrecy, we maintain the following invariant:

I1. Whenever the bulletin board stores an encryption $c \leftarrow \text{SE.Enc}(k_v, (s_u, k_u), u)$
    for nodes u and v, then $\text{preorderIdx}(v) < \text{preorderIdx}(u)$,

where $\text{preorderIdx}(v)$ returns v's index according to the preorder traversal.

Initialization. Let us now turn our attention towards which such links we want to outsource. Initially Init(key) first derives a seed s and outsourcing key k for the root (e.g., $(s, k, \cdot, \cdot) \leftarrow \text{PRG.Expand}(key)$ and then proceeds to expand the leftmost path in the GGM. The copath is outsourced to the bulletin board by encrypting each node under the previous when traversing the copath from the leaf to the root. Additionally, we encrypt the first copath node under its left sibling, i.e., the first epoch's leaf. All of those encryptions satisfy Invariant 1.

See Fig. 4 for the example of GGM$_4$, the GGM tree of height 4, at the end of the Init operation. For clarity, we labeled each node with its preorder index. White nodes represent inner nodes that have already been expanded, black nodes those for which the seeds are currently known, and gray nodes are currently beyond the expansion horizon. The dotted arrows represent the outsourced encryptions, i.e., a dotted arrow from node v to u means that we store $\text{SE.Enc}(k_v, (s_u, k_u), u)$ at position (v, u) in the bulletin board.

The Init algorithm outputs the seed $R_1 = s_{h+1}$ (of the leftmost leaf) and a state containing the following values: the key k_i and the seeds and keys of the thirst three nodes on i's right copath, starting at its right sibling. We call those three nodes the initial frontier, which we discuss in a moment. In our example of GGM$_4$, this is s_5 and (s_j, k_j) for $j \in \{6, 7, 10\}$.

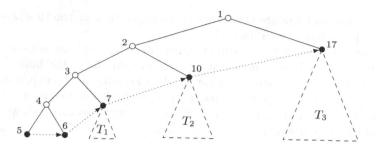

Fig. 4. The tree GGM_4 after the Init algorithm. Dotted arrows represent encryptions outsourced to the bulletin board.

Expanding the Tree. The nodes are expanded according to their preorder index. We call the first not yet expanded node the *frontier*. In our example of GGM_4, the initial frontier is node 7, which is then expanded into nodes 8 and 9. In this step, Update "replaces" (they remain on the bulletin board but are no longer needed for this party) the links $(6,7)$ and $(7,10)$ with the following ones: $(6,8)$, $(8,9)$, and $(9,10)$. (All those newly added encryptions satisfy Invariant 1.) The new frontier is now 10. When later expanding node 10 into nodes 11 and 14, we upload links $(9,11)$, $(11,14)$, and $(14,17)$, replacing the existing links $(9,10)$ and $(10,17)$. See Fig. 5 for the state of the tree after the expansion of $f = 10$. More generally, when expanding f, we consider the following two additional nodes

- $f^- := \mathsf{prevLeaf}(f)$ denoting the the largest leaf index $f^- < f$ that is not a descendent of f.
- $f^+ := \mathsf{rCoPath}(f)$ denoting the first node on f's right copath,

and replace the links (f^-, f) and (f, f^+) by link

- $(f^-, \mathrm{leftChild}(f))$,
- $(\mathrm{leftChild}(f), \mathrm{rightChild}(f))$,
- $(\mathrm{rightChild}(f), f^+)$.

We observe that by definition $\mathsf{rCoPath}(\mathrm{rightChild}(f)) = \mathsf{rCoPath}(f) = f^+$ and $\mathsf{rCoPath}(\mathrm{leftChild}(f)) = \mathrm{rightChild}(f)$. Thus, storing those additional links maintains the first of the following invariant that will become crucial for fast forwarding.

I2. For any v not on the leftmost path, if s_v has been computed, then the link $(v, \mathsf{rCoPath}(v))$, i.e., $\mathsf{SE.Enc}(k_v, (s_{\mathsf{rCoPath}(v)}, k_{\mathsf{rCoPath}(v)}), \mathsf{rCoPath}(v))$, has been added to the bulletin board.
I3. For any leaf v except the leftmost one, if s_v has been computed, then the link $(\mathsf{prevLeaf}(v), v)$ has been added to the bulletin board.

To be able to efficiently create those links described above, our algorithm keeps at any point in time the index, seed, and key of the f, f^-, and f^+ as part of the state. After the expansion, those pointers of course have to be adjusted and the respective seeds and keys locally stored.

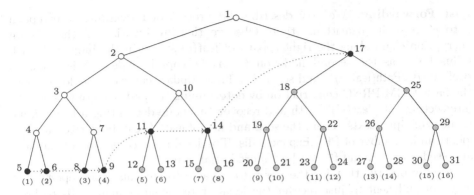

Fig. 5. A visualization of the node expansion in the enhanced GGM construction.

- If leftChild(f) is not a leaf, then f' becomes this node. The new f^+ is thus is the right sibling that we also just derived and f^- remains unchanged.
- If leftChild(f) is a leaf, then this node becomes the new f^-. The new f gets the old f^+. Its first right copath node becomes the new f^+. While for the latter we do not have seed or key readily stored, we know from Invariant 2 that there is a link from the old to the new f^+ stored in the bulletin board that we can use to retrieve those values.

Sequential Updates. For each sequential update from epoch e to $e + 1$, the Update algorithm has to output the seed of the $(e+1)$-th leaf, which we denote by leaf$(e+1)$. For this to be done in a constant number of cryptographic operations, the algorithm relies on a link (leaf(e), leaf$(e+1)$) is readily stored in the bulletin board. Recall from Invariant 3 that such a link exists as long as the seed leaf$(e+1)$ has been derived at this point, meaning that Update just needs to expand the frontier sufficiently fast.

We achieve this by doing two expansions per invocation of Update, as long as there are still nodes to expand. Consider the inner nodes on the copath of the leftmost leaf. Those node root $h - 1$ trees $T_1, \ldots T_{h-1}$ of increasing height that still need to be expanded after Init, as shown in Fig. 4. During the first update, i.e., when moving to node 6 in our example of GGM_4, we can expand T_1. More generally, we observe that T_j has 2^j leaves and T_{j+1} has 2^j inner nodes that need to be expanded. Hence, doing two expansion steps per Update invocation maintains the following invariant:

I4. By the time the epoch advances from T_j to T_{j+1}, i.e., when transitioning from epoch e to $e + 1$ such that leaf$(e) \in T_j$ and leaf$(e + 1) \in T_{j+1}$, the tree T_{j+1} has already been fully expanded.

In summary, our algorithm achieves sequential updating using at most three elements from the bulletin board (one to derive the new epoch's output and two for the tree expansion) and two PRG expansion and uploading at most six new elements to the bulletin board.

Fast Forwarding. We now describe the process of forwarding from epoch e to $e' \gg e$ in logarithmic time. Observe that by Invariant 2 there is an encryption chain along the right copath of $\mathsf{leaf}(e)$ stored in the bulletin board. (This holds as the second node on the right copath of $\mathsf{leaf}(e)$ is equal to $\mathsf{rCoPath}(\mathsf{rCoPath}(\mathsf{leaf}(e)))$ and so forth.) Thus, Update can work analogously to the basic GGM-PRNG construction by determining the first node of this copath intersecting with $\mathsf{leaf}(e')$'s path and recover this node decrypting a logarithmic number of ciphertexts. Then, the seed and key of $\mathsf{leaf}(e')$ can be derived using a logarithmic number of PRG.Expand calls. The local state consisting of the keys and seeds of f^-, f, and f^+ can be restored analogously.

Finally observe that for the party to be able to continue from epoch e' it may not sufficient to just recover the local state, as subsequent calls to both Update and Leap require certain links to be stored in the bulletin board. For our setting, where we assume that Leap is only used to catch up with other parties, this is not an issue, however. For each epoch between e and e' the first party reaching it must have done so using a sequential update, uploading all necessary encryptions as part of this process.

Efficiency. Let n denote the maximal number of epochs, i.e., $n = 2^h$. Then, the Init algorithm performs $\mathcal{O}(\log(n))$ many cryptographic operations and uploads this many elements to the bulletin board. Afterwards, Update requires at most $3 = \mathcal{O}(1)$ elements from the bulletin board and performs $\mathcal{O}(1)$ cryptographic operations and uploads at most $6 = \mathcal{O}(1)$ elements. So far we have glossed over how the $\mathsf{UpdateSK\text{-}Idx}(e)$ algorithm works. In short, it needs to be able to compute $\mathsf{leaf}(e)$, the f corresponding to $\mathsf{leaf}(e)$, $\mathsf{rCoPath}(\mathsf{f})$ and $\mathsf{prevLeaf}(\mathsf{f})$. Each of them can be easily computed in time $\mathcal{O}(\log n)$ given that f advances at the predictable double speed compared to $\mathsf{leaf}(e)$. Finally, Leap requires $\mathcal{O}(\log n)$ elements from the bulletin board and performs $\mathcal{O}(\log n)$ computation. In addition, $\mathsf{Leap\text{-}Idx}(e, e')$ needs to compute the elements of the right copath of $\mathsf{leaf}(e)$ that are ancestors of $\mathsf{leaf}(e')$, the corresponding frontier f', and $\mathsf{prevLeaf}(\mathsf{f}')$. It then outputs the corresponding paths to recover e', $\mathsf{prevLeaf}(\mathsf{f}')$, f', and $\mathsf{rCoPath}(\mathsf{f}')$, where the latter can be directly recovered from f'. All of those computations can be done in $\mathcal{O}(\log n)$ as well.

Correctness and Security. Let us briefly summarize the main results of this section, which is that our modifications to the forward-secure GGM-based PRNG do not affect either correctness or security. A proof of the follow theorem is presented in the full version [21].

Theorem 1. *The scheme outlined in Sect. 4.1 is correct and secure FF-PRNG, for a bounded number of at most 2^h epochs.*

4.2 Supporting an Unbounded Number of Epochs

In this section, we now briefly outline how our construction can be extended to support an unbounded number of epochs, and in the process reduce the running time of Init to $\mathcal{O}(1)$.

In a nutshell, we can apply the idea of a sequence of GGM trees of growing height, as used in [40]. Their roots can be derived using a forward-secure PRNG, such as the folklore construction from PRG.Expand. Recall from Invariant 4 that within a tree GGM_t, Update is done expanding before the epoch reaches the subtree T_{t-1} (cf. Figure 4). As this subtree has 2^{t-1} more leaves, we can spend this time initializing the next tree GGM_{t+1} instead, deriving its leftmost path and storing encryptions of its copath on the bulletin board.

We refer to the full version of the paper [21] for a more detailed description of the scheme.

5 Fast-Forwardable Updatable Public-Key Encryption

Our generic FF-UPKE uses any update-homomorphic UPKE (H-UPKE) and is built around the idea of so-called *cumulative updates*, i.e., update ciphertexts that aggregate a sequence of individual updates. We use an *update graph* to govern which cumulative updates are produced, to balance the senders' overhead with the receiver's ability to fast forward. (For instance, the complete update graph would allow the receiver to update in constant time while imposing an undesirable linear overhead on each sender, while the empty update graph results in a plain UPKE without fast-forwarding.)

5.1 Update-Homomorphic UPKE

As a building block—to allow for cumulative updates—our construction makes use of an update-homomorphic UPKE scheme, constituting a special case of updatable public-key encryption.

In brief, in addition to a key-generation algorithm $(\mathsf{pk}_1, \mathsf{sk}_1, \mathsf{pp}) \leftarrow \mathsf{KeyGen}(1^\kappa)$, and respective message encryption and decryption algorithms $\mathsf{c} \leftarrow \mathsf{Encrypt}(\mathsf{pk}_i, \mathsf{m})$ and $\mathsf{m} \leftarrow \mathsf{Decrypt}(\mathsf{sk}_i, \mathsf{c})$, an update-homomorphic UPKE scheme provides the following structure:

(1) update ciphertext consist of an encrypted update message, i.e., $\mathsf{up}_{i+1} \leftarrow \mathsf{UpdEnc}(\mathsf{pk}_i, \delta_{i+1})$, sampled using $\delta_{i+1} \leftarrow \mathsf{UpdGen}(\mathsf{pp})$ based on the public parameters pp;
(2) update messages are elements from the secret-key space which forms a group under some operator $\star$;
(3) the secret keys are updated according to $\mathsf{sk}_{i+1} = \mathsf{sk}_i \star \delta_{i+1}$;
(4) UpdEnc is message homomorphic, i.e., there is an algorithm $\mathsf{Upd\text{-}Comb}(\mathsf{up}, \mathsf{up}')$ homomorphically combining two updates encrypted under the same public key pk_i.

Using the shorthand notation $\Delta_{[j,\ell]} := (\delta_{j+1} \star \cdots \star \delta_\ell)$, the homomorphism property thus ensures that we can compute an encryption that is equivalent to $\mathsf{Up}^i_{[j,\ell]} \leftarrow \mathsf{UpdEnc}(\mathsf{pk}_i, \Delta_{[j,\ell]})$ from two partial updates $\mathsf{Up}^i_{[j,k]}$ and $\mathsf{Up}^i_{[k,\ell]}$, for any $j < k < \ell$. More formally, we define update-homomorphic UPKE schemes as follows.

Definition 6. *An* update-homomorphic UPKE (H-UPKE) *scheme is a tuple of algorithms* (KeyGen, Encrypt, Decrypt, UpdGen, UpdEnc, UpdDec, UpdatePK, Upd-Comb) *for which the secret-key space* $\mathcal{SK}$ *forms a semigroup (i.e., is associative with respect to some operator* $\star$*) and the algorithms are defined as follows:*

- *the* key-generation *algorithm* $(\mathsf{pk}_1, \mathsf{sk}_1, \mathsf{pp}) \leftarrow \mathsf{KeyGen}(1^\kappa)$*, which outputs an initial key pair* sk_1 *and* pk_1*, as well as public parameters* pp*;*
- *the* encryption *algorithm* $\mathsf{c} \leftarrow \mathsf{Encrypt}(\mathsf{pk}_i, \mathsf{m})$ *and the and deterministic decryption algorithm* $\mathsf{m} \leftarrow \mathsf{Decrypt}(\mathsf{sk}_i, \mathsf{c})$*, respectively;*
- *the* update-sample *algorithm* $\delta_{i+1} \leftarrow \mathsf{UpdGen}(\mathsf{pp})$ *producing* $\delta_{i+1} \in \mathcal{SK}$*;*
- *the deterministic* public-key update *algorithm* $\mathsf{pk}_{i+1} \leftarrow \mathsf{UpdatePK}(\mathsf{pk}_i, \delta_{i+1})$*, which given a public key and an update message produces an updated one;*
- *the* update-encryption *algorithm* $\mathsf{up}^i_j \leftarrow \mathsf{UpdEnc}(\mathsf{pk}_i, \delta_j)$*, for* $j > i$*;*
- *the* update-combination *algorithm* $\mathsf{Up}^i_{[j,\ell]} \leftarrow \mathsf{Upd\text{-}Comb}(\mathsf{Up}^i_{[j,k]}, \mathsf{Up}^i_{[k,\ell]})$*, merging two updates encrypted under the same public key* pk_i*.*
- *the and deterministic* update-decryption $\Delta^i_{[j,\ell]} \leftarrow \mathsf{UpdDec}(\mathsf{sk}_i, \mathsf{Up}^i_{[j,\ell]})$*;*

Correctness and Security. We formalize correctness using two separate properties. The first property essentially demands that the pairs (Encrypt, Decrypt) and (UpdEnc, UpdDec) represent correct pairs of encryption and decryption algorithms for their respective message spaces—analogously to the standard UPKE definition. This is formalized in the game on the left side of Fig. 6. To account for the evolving sequence of public and secret keys, as well as the use of bad randomness, the game allows the adversary to update the keys an arbitrary number of periods under his randomness before submitting a challenge message to be encrypted. The adversary wins if either the ciphertext or one of the update messages gets decrypted incorrectly. The second property concerns homomorphism and is, thus, unique to update-homomorphic UPKE. It requires that the output of Upd-Comb must correctly decrypt to the multiplication of the underlying update secrets (for the group operator $\star$), i.e., that

$$\Delta_{[j,k]} \star \Delta_{[k,\ell]}$$
$$= \mathsf{UpdDec}\Big(\mathsf{sk}_i, \mathsf{Upd\text{-}Comb}\big(\mathsf{UpdEnc}(\mathsf{pk}_i, \Delta_{[j,k]}), \mathsf{UpdEnc}(\mathsf{pk}_i, \Delta_{[k,\ell]})\big)\Big).$$

Finally, we require IND-CPA security. The IND-CPA game is essentially the same as for regular UPKE, when accounting for the imposed special structure of the updating mechanism, via the sender invoking

1. $\delta \leftarrow \mathsf{UpdGen}(\mathsf{pp})$
2. $\mathsf{up} \leftarrow \mathsf{UpdEnc}(\mathsf{pk}, \delta)$
3. $\mathsf{pk}' \leftarrow \mathsf{UpdatePK}(\mathsf{pk}, \delta)$,

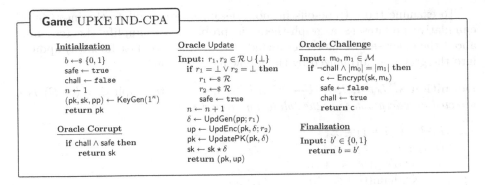

Fig. 6. The IND-CPA game of Update-Homomorphic Updatable Public-Key Encryption (H-UPKE).

and on the other side the receiver using $\delta \leftarrow \mathsf{UpdDec}(\mathsf{sk}, \mathsf{up})$ and $\mathsf{sk}' \leftarrow \mathsf{sk} \star \delta$. A formal description of the resulting IND-CPA game can be found on the right hand side of Fig. 6.

Definition 7 (Security). *A UPKE scheme is said to be IND-CPA secure if any PPT adversary $\mathcal{A}$ has a negligible probability of winning the game depicted in Fig. 6.*

Schemes. In the full version [21] we show that with minor modifications the standard-model UPKE schemes of Dodis et al. [22] do lend themselves to an update-homomorphic UPKE scheme, resulting in instantiations under either the DDH or the LWE assumption. We remark that both constructions have some (different) caveats: the LWE-based scheme supports a bounded number of homomorphic operations, supporting aggregation of at most q atomic updates (but q can be chosen superpolynomially large at the expense of slightly larger other parameters) while the DDH-based construction supports an a priori unbounded number of aggregations but decryption of an aggregated update takes local computation time $\mathcal{O}(\sqrt{n})$ in the number of underlying updates n.

5.2 Update Graphs

A crucial part of our construction will be deciding which cumulative updates to generate. If, on the one hand, we insert too few such cumulative updates, then $\mathsf{LeapSK\text{-}Idx}(i, j) \approx j - i$ loses the fast-forward property. If, on the other hand, we insert too many—e.g., all of them—then both $\mathsf{UpdatePK}$ will need both to read and write linearly many elements from the bulletin board. Indeed, such a solution would represent in many aspects the trivial dual solution to no fast-forwarding, as the former requires linear bandwidth for the receiver whereas the latter requires linear bandwidth for all the senders.

To examine those trade-offs in more detail, we reformulate the insertion of cumulative updates as a graph-theoretic problem. To simplify the reasoning about the index set, we moreover include the atomic (non fast-forward) updates into the graph, as formalized by the following definition.

Definition 8. *Let $\alpha, \beta, \gamma\colon \mathbb{N} \to \mathbb{N}$. An (α, β, γ)-update graph $\mathcal{G} = (\mathbb{N}, E)$ is a directed acyclic graph with the following properties:*

1. *$\forall i \in \mathbb{N} : (i, i+1) \in E$,*
2. *$\forall (i, j) \in E : i < j$,*
3. *$\forall n \in \mathbb{N} : \deg_{\mathcal{G}}^{in}(n) \le \alpha(n)$,*
4. *$\forall n \in \mathbb{N} : \mathrm{diam}(\mathcal{G}_n) \le \beta(n)$,*
5. *$\forall n \in \mathbb{N} : |\mathrm{active}_{\mathcal{G}}(n)| \le \gamma(n)$,*

where $\mathrm{active}_{\mathcal{G}}(n) := \{i \in [n-1] \mid \exists j > n : (i, j) \in E\}$, and $(\mathcal{G}_n)_{n \in \mathbb{N}}$ with $\mathcal{G}_n := ([n], E_n)$ and $E_n := E \cap [n]^2$ denotes the sequence of prefix graphs.

Looking slightly ahead, let us briefly consider how the different parameters will affect the efficiency of our construction. First, the number of update messages required by LeapSK is bounded by $\beta(j)$. Second, $\mathrm{active}_{\mathcal{G}(n)} \le \gamma(n)$ corresponds to the set of cumulative updates that need to be extended when a sender initiates the i-th epoch using UpdatePK. Finally, the indegree represents the number of "finalized" updates for the respective epoch. This mainly becomes of relevance if the FF-UPKE scheme is deployed in a single-sender setting.

To be of use for our construction, we need that a given update graph can be efficiently computed. Specifically, our construction will need to compute the sets $E_{\mathcal{G}}^{in}(i)$ and $\mathrm{active}_{\mathcal{G}}(i)$ for each node i, as well as computing short paths between any nodes i and j.

Definition 9. *We say that an (α, β, γ)-update graph $\mathcal{G} = (\mathbb{N}, E)$ is implemented by a pair of deterministic algorithms $(\mathcal{G}.\mathsf{Eval}, \mathcal{G}.\mathsf{Path})$ if:*

- *$\mathcal{G}.\mathsf{Eval}(n)$ outputs $E^{in}(n)$ and $\mathrm{active}(n)$ in $\mathcal{O}(\mathrm{poly}(\log n))$ time;*
- *$\mathcal{G}.\mathsf{Path}(i, j)$ outputs a path e from node i to j such that $|e| \le \beta(j)$ in $\mathcal{O}(\mathrm{poly}(\beta(j) \cdot j))$.*

5.3   A Generic Construction

We now construct a Fast-Forwardable UPKE scheme based on an Update-Homomorphic UPKE scheme and an update graph. The basic idea is very simple: When the sender j chooses the corresponding update secret δ_{j+1}, in addition to updating pk_j to pk_{j+1}, they will also

(1) produce fresh ciphertext $\mathsf{Up}_{[j,j+1]}$ encrypting δ_{j+1} under pk_j; and
(2) for every $i \in \mathrm{active}(j+1) \cup E^{in}(j+1)$, fetch $\mathsf{Up}_{[i,j]}$ from the bulletin board, and use the update-homomorphic property of the UPKE to compute ciphertexts $\mathsf{Up}_{[i,j+1]}$ to be published in the bulletin board.

On the receiving side, if the receiver knows key sk_i, and wishes to jump to some key sk_j for $j > i$, it will:

(1) compute a short "leap path" $i = i_0 \to i_i \to \cdots \to i_d = j$ in the update graph;
(2) retrieve d ciphertexts $\{\mathsf{Up}_{[i_k, i_{k+1}]}\}$ from the bulletin board;
(3) decrypt Up_{i_0, i_1} using $\mathsf{sk}_i = \mathsf{sk}_{i_0}$ to get $\Delta_{[i_0, i_1]}$;
(4) compute $\mathsf{sk}_{i_1} := \mathsf{sk}_{i_0} \star \Delta_{[i_0, i_1]}$;
(5) iterate steps (3)–(4) d times to finally "catch up" with $\mathsf{sk}_j = \mathsf{sk}_{i_d}$.

A formal description of the scheme is presented in Fig. 7.

A Single-Sender Variant. When deployed in a single-sender setting, such as a two-party secure messaging scheme (considered as the original motivation for UPKE by Jost et al. [36]) the scheme can be slightly tweaked for a different storage/bandwidth trade-off. To this end, we observe that in our scheme the receiver will never access the temporary "ongoing" update messages but only ever use an element (i, j) if $(i, j) \in E$. As a consequence, the sender may choose to upload only the elements from $E^{\mathsf{in}}(n)$ while keeping the ongoing cumulative updates as part of his local state.

This works nicely since the sender does not need arbitrary $\gamma(n) + \alpha(n)$ many of the $\mathcal{O}(n)$ so far uploaded elements, but in each step we have

$$\mathrm{active}(n) \cup E^{\mathsf{in}}(n) \subseteq \mathrm{active}(n-1) \cup \{n-1\},$$

implying that $\mathcal{O}(\gamma + \alpha(n))$ storage suffices. Additionally, this variant has the distinct advantage that $\mathsf{UpdatePK}$ does not need to read anything from the bulletin board, i.e., $\mathsf{UpdatePK\text{-}Idx}(n) = \varnothing$, potentially reducing latency.

The corresponding protocol is depicted in Fig. 7 as well using the dashed boxes. For simplicity, we model the local state as the public key containing a "local" bulletin board.

Correctness and Efficiency. Correctness of the construction follows essentially directly from the correctness of the underlying Update-Homomorphic UPKE scheme, which is formalized in parts of the correctness of a regular UPKE scheme plus the correctness condition of the homomorphism. Moreover, by the construction the various parameters of the update graph directly translate to the efficiency of the scheme, yielding the following result.

Theorem 2. *The FF-UPKE schemes presented in Fig. 7 are correct if the underlying scheme H-UPKE is correct and update homomorphic as formalized via the games from Fig. 6.*

Moreover, the regular scheme has public and secret keys of roughly the same size, and encryption and decryption of the same efficiency, as the underlying H-UPKE scheme. Using an (α, β, γ)-update graph, yields the following efficiency:

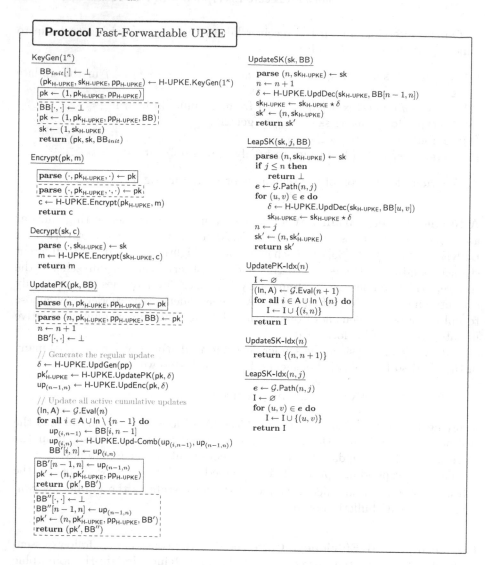

Fig. 7. The FF-UPKE protocols are built from an Update-Homomorphic UPKE scheme H-UPKE and an update graph $\mathcal{G}$. Lines enclosed in solid boxes belong to the regular multi-sender protocol, whereas lines enclosed in dashed boxes represent the single-sender variant.

- UpdatePK: $|\text{UpdatePK-Idx}(n)| \leq \gamma(n+1)$ and $|BB_{up}| \leq \gamma(n+1)+1$. Moreover, UpdatePK needs $\mathcal{O}(\gamma(n+1))$ as many cryptographic operations as the underlying scheme.
- UpdateSK: $|\text{UpdateSK-Idx}(n)| = 1$ and UpdateSK uses $\mathcal{O}(1)$ as many cryptographic operations as the underlying scheme.

- LeapSK: $|\mathsf{LeapSK}\text{-}\mathsf{Idx}(n,j)| \leq \beta(j)$ and LeapSK uses $\mathcal{O}(\beta(j))$ as many cryptographic operations as the underlying scheme.

The single-sender scheme has a secret key of roughly the same size as the underlying H-UPKE scheme, and a public key size of roughly $\gamma(n)$ as big as the underlying scheme (modeling local storage) and the same efficiency except that $|\mathsf{UpdatePK}\text{-}\mathsf{Idx}(n)| = 0$ and $|\mathsf{BB}_{up}| \leq \alpha(n+1)$.

A proof is presented in the full version of the paper [21].

Security. Security also follows directly from the security of the underlying Update-Homomorphic UPKE scheme, as intuitively the cumulative updates represent a computation on public data.

Theorem 3. *The FF-UPKE schemes presented in Fig. 7 are IND-CPA secure, according to Definition 5, if the underlying scheme H-UPKE is IND-CPA secure according to Definition 7.*

A proof can be found in the full version [21] of this document.

6   Conclusions and Open Problems

We identified *fast-forwarding* as a compelling property of forward-secure encryption, and have shown that in the practically relevant *bulletin-board model* fast-forwarding can be obtained at little additional cost. First, we have constructed a fast-forwardable stream cipher that maintains a constant local state and has a constant running time per update operation. This essentially matches the efficiency of non-fast-forwardable stream ciphers at the cost of constant communication complexity with the bulletin board per update.

Second, we presented a generic construction of a fast-forwardable updatable public-key encryption scheme from a novel primitive of an update-homomorphic UPKE scheme. This bridges the gap between forward-secure PKE, for which fast-forwardability is the norm, and its more efficient cousin UPKE, where none of the existing schemes were fast-forwardable. As a feasibility result, we presented instantiations based on the DDH and LWE assumptions, respectively.

While neither instantiation is truly practical, we believe that our novel construction of FF-UPKE could ultimately lead to constructions significantly outperforming those of forward-secure PKE, resolving the dilemma of practical public-key encryption to having to choose between forward-secrecy and fast-forwarding. Accordingly, this leaves the construction of efficient update-homomorphic UPKE schemes as an intriguing problem, demonstrating that while highly practical UPKE schemes are known to exist in the ROM, the search for efficient schemes in the standard model may be of interest for the sake of exhibiting homomorphic properties typically unknown to ROM constructions.

Acknowledgments. We would like to thank Michael Elkin for a useful discussion about update graphs and bringing [42] to our attention.

References

1. Abdalla, M., Reyzin, L.: A new forward-secure digital signature scheme. In: Okamoto, T. (ed.) ASIACRYPT 2000. LNCS, vol. 1976, pp. 116–129. Springer, Heidelberg (2000). https://doi.org/10.1007/3-540-44448-3_10
2. Agrawal, S., Boneh, D., Boyen, X.: Efficient lattice (H)IBE in the standard model. In: Gilbert, H. (ed.) EUROCRYPT 2010. LNCS, vol. 6110, pp. 553–572. Springer, Heidelberg (2010). https://doi.org/10.1007/978-3-642-13190-5_28
3. Alwen, J., Coretti, S., Dodis, Y., Tselekounis, Y.: Security analysis and improvements for the IETF MLS standard for group messaging. In: Micciancio, D., Ristenpart, T. (eds.) CRYPTO 2020. LNCS, vol. 12170, pp. 248–277. Springer, Cham (2020). https://doi.org/10.1007/978-3-030-56784-2_9
4. Anderson, R.: Invited lecture. In: Fourth Annual Conference on Computer and Communications Security. ACM (1997)
5. Aviram, N., Gellert, K., Jager, T.: Session resumption protocols and efficient forward security for TLS 1.3 0-RTT. J. Cryptol. **34**(3), 1–57 (2021). https://doi.org/10.1007/s00145-021-09385-0
6. Bellare, M., Miner, S.K.: A forward-secure digital signature scheme. In: Wiener, M. (ed.) CRYPTO 1999. LNCS, vol. 1666, pp. 431–448. Springer, Heidelberg (1999). https://doi.org/10.1007/3-540-48405-1_28
7. Bellare, M., Yee, B.: Forward-security in private-key cryptography. In: Joye, M. (ed.) CT-RSA 2003. LNCS, vol. 2612, pp. 1–18. Springer, Heidelberg (2003). https://doi.org/10.1007/3-540-36563-X_1
8. Blum, L., Blum, M., Shub, M.: Comparison of two pseudo-random number generators. In: Chaum, D., Rivest, R.L., Sherman, A.T. (eds.) CRYPTO'82, pp. 61–78. Plenum Press, New York (1982)
9. Boneh, D., Boyen, X.: Efficient selective-id secure identity-based encryption without random oracles. In: Cachin, C., Camenisch, J.L. (eds.) EUROCRYPT 2004. LNCS, vol. 3027, pp. 223–238. Springer, Heidelberg (2004). https://doi.org/10.1007/978-3-540-24676-3_14
10. Boneh, D., Boyen, X., Goh, E.-J.: Hierarchical identity based encryption with constant size ciphertext. In: Cramer, R. (ed.) EUROCRYPT 2005. LNCS, vol. 3494, pp. 440–456. Springer, Heidelberg (2005). https://doi.org/10.1007/11426639_26
11. Boneh, D., Eskandarian, S., Kim, S., Shih, M.: Improving speed and security in updatable encryption schemes. In: Moriai, S., Wang, H. (eds.) ASIACRYPT 2020. LNCS, vol. 12493, pp. 559–589. Springer, Cham (2020). https://doi.org/10.1007/978-3-030-64840-4_19
12. Boneh, D., Lewi, K., Montgomery, H., Raghunathan, A.: Key homomorphic PRFs and their applications. In: Canetti, R., Garay, J.A. (eds.) CRYPTO 2013. LNCS, vol. 8042, pp. 410–428. Springer, Heidelberg (2013). https://doi.org/10.1007/978-3-642-40041-4_23
13. Boneh, D., Waters, B.: Constrained pseudorandom functions and their applications. In: Sako, K., Sarkar, P. (eds.) ASIACRYPT 2013. LNCS, vol. 8270, pp. 280–300. Springer, Heidelberg (2013). https://doi.org/10.1007/978-3-642-42045-0_15
14. Boyd, C., Davies, G.T., Gjøsteen, K., Jiang, Y.: Fast and secure updatable encryption. In: Micciancio, D., Ristenpart, T. (eds.) CRYPTO 2020. LNCS, vol. 12170, pp. 464–493. Springer, Cham (2020). https://doi.org/10.1007/978-3-030-56784-2_16

15. Brakerski, Z., Lombardi, A., Segev, G., Vaikuntanathan, V.: Anonymous IBE, leakage resilience and circular security from new assumptions. In: Nielsen, J.B., Rijmen, V. (eds.) EUROCRYPT 2018. LNCS, vol. 10820, pp. 535–564. Springer, Cham (2018). https://doi.org/10.1007/978-3-319-78381-9_20
16. Canetti, R., Halevi, S., Katz, J.: A forward-secure public-key encryption scheme. In: Biham, E. (ed.) EUROCRYPT 2003. LNCS, vol. 2656, pp. 255–271. Springer, Heidelberg (2003). https://doi.org/10.1007/3-540-39200-9_16
17. Canetti, R., Halevi, S., Katz, J.: Chosen-ciphertext security from identity-based encryption. In: Cachin, C., Camenisch, J.L. (eds.) EUROCRYPT 2004. LNCS, vol. 3027, pp. 207–222. Springer, Heidelberg (2004). https://doi.org/10.1007/978-3-540-24676-3_13
18. Cash, D., Hofheinz, D., Kiltz, E., Peikert, C.: Bonsai trees, or how to delegate a lattice basis. J. Cryptol. 25(4), 601–639 (2011). https://doi.org/10.1007/s00145-011-9105-2
19. Derler, D., Jager, T., Slamanig, D., Striecks, C.: Bloom filter encryption and applications to efficient forward-secret 0-RTT key exchange. In: Nielsen, J.B., Rijmen, V. (eds.) EUROCRYPT 2018. LNCS, vol. 10822, pp. 425–455. Springer, Cham (2018). https://doi.org/10.1007/978-3-319-78372-7_14
20. Diffie, W., van Oorschot, P.C., Wiener, M.J.: Authentication and authenticated key exchanges. Des. Codes Cryptogr. 2(2), 107–125 (1992)
21. Dodis, Y., Jost, D., Karthikeyan, H.: Forward-secure encryption with fast forwarding. Cryptology ePrint Archive, Paper 2022/1233 (2022). https://eprint.iacr.org/2022/1233, full version of this report
22. Dodis, Y., Karthikeyan, H., Wichs, D.: Updatable public key encryption in the standard model. In: Nissim, K., Waters, B. (eds.) TCC 2021. LNCS, vol. 13044, pp. 254–285. Springer, Cham (2021). https://doi.org/10.1007/978-3-030-90456-2_9
23. Dodis, Y., Katz, J., Xu, S., Yung, M.: Key-insulated public key cryptosystems. In: Knudsen, L.R. (ed.) EUROCRYPT 2002. LNCS, vol. 2332, pp. 65–82. Springer, Heidelberg (2002). https://doi.org/10.1007/3-540-46035-7_5
24. Dodis, Y., Katz, J., Xu, S., Yung, M.: Strong key-insulated signature schemes. In: Desmedt, Y.G. (ed.) PKC 2003. LNCS, vol. 2567, pp. 130–144. Springer, Heidelberg (2003). https://doi.org/10.1007/3-540-36288-6_10
25. Döttling, N., Garg, S.: From selective IBE to full IBE and selective HIBE. In: Kalai, Y., Reyzin, L. (eds.) TCC 2017. LNCS, vol. 10677, pp. 372–408. Springer, Cham (2017). https://doi.org/10.1007/978-3-319-70500-2_13
26. Döttling, N., Garg, S.: Identity-based encryption from the diffie-hellman assumption. In: Katz, J., Shacham, H. (eds.) CRYPTO 2017. LNCS, vol. 10401, pp. 537–569. Springer, Cham (2017). https://doi.org/10.1007/978-3-319-63688-7_18
27. Everspaugh, A., Paterson, K., Ristenpart, T., Scott, S.: Key rotation for authenticated encryption. In: Katz, J., Shacham, H. (eds.) CRYPTO 2017. LNCS, vol. 10403, pp. 98–129. Springer, Cham (2017). https://doi.org/10.1007/978-3-319-63697-9_4
28. Gentry, C., Peikert, C., Vaikuntanathan, V.: Trapdoors for hard lattices and new cryptographic constructions. In: Ladner, R.E., Dwork, C. (eds.) 40th ACM STOC, pp. 197–206. ACM Press (2008). https://doi.org/10.1145/1374376.1374407
29. Gentry, C., Silverberg, A.: Hierarchical ID-based cryptography. In: Zheng, Y. (ed.) ASIACRYPT 2002. LNCS, vol. 2501, pp. 548–566. Springer, Heidelberg (2002). https://doi.org/10.1007/3-540-36178-2_34
30. Goldreich, O., Goldwasser, S., Micali, S.: How to construct random functions. J. ACM 33(4), 792–807 (1986)

31. Green, M.D., Miers, I.: Forward secure asynchronous messaging from puncturable encryption. In: 2015 IEEE Symposium on Security and Privacy, pp. 305–320. IEEE Computer Society Press (2015). https://doi.org/10.1109/SP.2015.26

32. Günther, C.G.: An identity-based key-exchange protocol. In: Quisquater, J.-J., Vandewalle, J. (eds.) EUROCRYPT 1989. LNCS, vol. 434, pp. 29–37. Springer, Heidelberg (1990). https://doi.org/10.1007/3-540-46885-4_5

33. Horwitz, J., Lynn, B.: Toward hierarchical identity-based encryption. In: Knudsen, L.R. (ed.) EUROCRYPT 2002. LNCS, vol. 2332, pp. 466–481. Springer, Heidelberg (2002). https://doi.org/10.1007/3-540-46035-7_31

34. Itkis, G., Reyzin, L.: Forward-secure signatures with optimal signing and verifying. In: Kilian, J. (ed.) CRYPTO 2001. LNCS, vol. 2139, pp. 332–354. Springer, Heidelberg (2001). https://doi.org/10.1007/3-540-44647-8_20

35. Jaeger, J., Stepanovs, I.: Optimal channel security against fine-grained state compromise: the safety of messaging. In: Shacham, H., Boldyreva, A. (eds.) CRYPTO 2018. LNCS, vol. 10991, pp. 33–62. Springer, Cham (2018). https://doi.org/10.1007/978-3-319-96884-1_2

36. Jost, D., Maurer, U., Mularczyk, M.: Efficient ratcheting: almost-optimal guarantees for secure messaging. In: Ishai, Y., Rijmen, V. (eds.) EUROCRYPT 2019. LNCS, vol. 11476, pp. 159–188. Springer, Cham (2019). https://doi.org/10.1007/978-3-030-17653-2_6

37. Klooß, M., Lehmann, A., Rupp, A.: (R)CCA secure updatable encryption with integrity protection. In: Ishai, Y., Rijmen, V. (eds.) EUROCRYPT 2019. LNCS, vol. 11476, pp. 68–99. Springer, Cham (2019). https://doi.org/10.1007/978-3-030-17653-2_3

38. Kozlov, A., Reyzin, L.: Forward-secure signatures with fast key update. In: Cimato, S., Persiano, G., Galdi, C. (eds.) SCN 2002. LNCS, vol. 2576, pp. 241–256. Springer, Heidelberg (2003). https://doi.org/10.1007/3-540-36413-7_18

39. Lehmann, A., Tackmann, B.: Updatable encryption with post-compromise security. In: Nielsen, J.B., Rijmen, V. (eds.) EUROCRYPT 2018. LNCS, vol. 10822, pp. 685–716. Springer, Cham (2018). https://doi.org/10.1007/978-3-319-78372-7_22

40. Malkin, T., Micciancio, D., Miner, S.: Efficient generic forward-secure signatures with an unbounded number of time periods. In: Knudsen, L.R. (ed.) EUROCRYPT 2002. LNCS, vol. 2332, pp. 400–417. Springer, Heidelberg (2002). https://doi.org/10.1007/3-540-46035-7_27

41. Poettering, B., Rösler, P.: Towards bidirectional ratcheted key exchange. In: Shacham, H., Boldyreva, A. (eds.) CRYPTO 2018. LNCS, vol. 10991, pp. 3–32. Springer, Cham (2018). https://doi.org/10.1007/978-3-319-96884-1_1

42. Solomon, S., Elkin, M.: Balancing degree, diameter and weight in euclidean spanners. In: de Berg, M., Meyer, U. (eds.) ESA 2010. LNCS, vol. 6346, pp. 48–59. Springer, Heidelberg (2010). https://doi.org/10.1007/978-3-642-15775-2_5

43. Sun, S., et al.: Practical backward-secure searchable encryption from symmetric puncturable encryption. In: Lie, D., Mannan, M., Backes, M., Wang, X. (eds.) ACM CCS 2018, pp. 763–780. ACM Press (2018). https://doi.org/10.1145/3243734.3243782

44. Wei, J., Chen, X., Wang, J., Hu, X., Ma, J.: Forward-secure puncturable identity-based encryption for securing cloud emails. In: Sako, K., Schneider, S., Ryan, P.Y.A. (eds.) ESORICS 2019. LNCS, vol. 11736, pp. 134–150. Springer, Cham (2019). https://doi.org/10.1007/978-3-030-29962-0_7

Rate-1 Incompressible Encryption from Standard Assumptions

Pedro Branco[1]([✉]), Nico Döttling[2]⍾, and Jesko Dujmović[2,3]⍾

[1] Johns Hopkins University, Baltimore, MD 21218, USA
pedrodemelobranco@gmail.com
[2] Helmholtz Center for Information Security (CISPA), 66123 Saarbrücken, Germany
{doettling,jesko.dujmovic}@cispa.de
[3] Saarland University, 66123 Saarbrücken, Germany

Abstract. Incompressible encryption, recently proposed by Guan, Wichs and Zhandry (EUROCRYPT'22), is a novel encryption paradigm geared towards providing strong long-term security guarantees against adversaries with *bounded long-term memory*. Given that the adversary forgets just a small fraction of a ciphertext, this notion provides strong security for the message encrypted therein, even if, at some point in the future, the entire secret key is exposed. This comes at the price of having potentially very large ciphertexts. Thus, an important efficiency measure for incompressible encryption is the message-to-ciphertext ratio (also called the rate). Guan et al. provided a low-rate instantiation of this notion from standard assumptions and a rate-1 instantiation from indistinguishability obfuscation (iO). In this work, we propose a simple framework to build rate-1 incompressible encryption from standard assumptions. Our construction can be realized from, e.g. the DDH and additionally the DCR or the LWE assumptions.

1 Introduction

Incompressible Cryptography. [19,26,27,32,34,42] is a flourishing paradigm trying to leverage memory limitations of adversaries to achieve strong security goals. While traditionally, the goal of cryptography in the bounded storage model [40] is to minimize the need for computational assumptions or even obtain information-theoretically secure constructions, incompressible cryptography is geared more toward mitigating the consequences of key exfiltration and key exposure attacks. In this work, we focus on the notion of *incompressible encryption* [26,32][1] recently coined by Guan et al. [32]. An incompressible encryption scheme produces large, incompressible ciphertexts and guarantees that any adversary who *forgets* even a small fraction of the ciphertext data will learn nothing about the encrypted data, even if he is later given the corresponding secret key!

---

[1] Dziembowski [26] introduced this concept under the name *forward-secure storage* in the symmetric key setting.

E. Kiltz and V. Vaikuntanathan (Eds.): TCC 2022, LNCS 13748, pp. 33–69, 2022.
https://doi.org/10.1007/978-3-031-22365-5_2

One motivation for incompressible encryption is to hamper adversaries conducting a mass-surveillance operation by forcing them to store massive amounts of ciphertext data even if they are just interested in a tiny fraction of the encrypted data. In a similar scenario, an adversary trying to exfiltrate information encrypted under an incompressible encryption scheme from a data-center will have to exfiltrate massive amounts of data, even if his exfiltration target is just a small piece of information.

An orthogonal notion to incompressible encryption is encryption in the *bounded-retrieval model* [3,4,8,9,22,25,36,42] where the goal is to make the secret key large and incompressible (to make it hard to exfiltrate) while keeping all other system parameters small, such as the sizes of public keys and ciphertexts, as well as the overhead of encryption and decryption.

Encryption with High Rate. An important efficiency measure of encryption schemes is their ciphertext expansion or rate. The rate of an encryption scheme is the ratio between plaintext size and ciphertext size. The closer the rate is to 1, the more efficient a scheme manages to pack information into a ciphertext. Conversely, the closer the rate is to 0, the less information is encoded in potentially large ciphertexts. For incompressible encryption, achieving a high rate (ideally converging to 1), especially if we think of the data center application above, where a small rate would also put a massive burden on the data center.

Guan et al. [32] provided two constructions of incompressible encryption.

- A construction from the minimal assumption of public-key encryption which has ciphertext-rate approaching 0.
- A construction from indistinguishability obfuscation (iO) [6,28,37] which achieves ciphertext-rate approaching 1.

We remark that their rate-1 construction relies on non-black-box techniques and iO, which gives this result a strong feasibility flavor.

Given this state of affairs, this work is motivated by the following question:

Can we build a rate-1 incompressible encryption scheme based on standard assumptions while only making black-box use of cryptographic primitives?

1.1   Our Results

In this work, we build a rate-1 incompressible encryption scheme from standard assumptions while only using black-box techniques. Our result uses what we call programmable hash proof systems (HPS) (which are a variant of standard HPS [16,17] with some additional properties), plain-model incompressible encodings [42] and a pseudorandom generator (PRG). In particular, we prove the following theorem.

Theorem 1 (Informal). *Let S be the storage capacity of the adversary and let n be the size of the encrypted messages. Assuming programmable HPS, incompressible encodings and PRGs exist, there is an incompressible encryption scheme fulfilling the following properties:*

1. *Ciphertexts are of size $n + n^\varepsilon \cdot \mathsf{poly}(\lambda)$ for some $\varepsilon > 0$.*
2. *The public key is of size $n^{\varepsilon'} \cdot \mathsf{poly}(\lambda)$ for some $\varepsilon' > 1/2$.*
3. *Moreover, the size of ciphertexts is only slightly larger than the adversary's storage space, that is, $S + \mathsf{poly}(\lambda)$.*

The ciphertext rate $n/(n + n^\varepsilon \cdot \mathsf{poly}(\lambda))$ approaches 1 for large enough messages. Additionally, the public key is sublinear in the size of the encrypted message.

In terms of assumptions, incompressible encodings can be based on either decisional composite residuosity (DCR) or learning with errors (LWE). The PRG can be based on any one-way function. We also show that programmable HPS can be instantiated from the decisional Diffie-Hellman (DDH) assumption by tweaking the famous HPS by Cramer and Shoup [17]. Consequently, our final incompressible encryption scheme can be based solely on standard assumptions.

Streaming Encryption. Streaming encryption/decryption is a property of incompressible encryption schemes which allows the honest encryptor/decryptor to perform operations with very low storage capacity. It is easy to see that streaming decryption is an inherently conflicting property with high rate ciphertexts [32]. This is because the honest decryptor needs storage at least as large as the size of the message. Otherwise, an adversary can essentially mimic the decryptor and learn something about the encrypted message (e.g., the most significant bit).

However, we note that our scheme has *stream encryption*, i.e., the honest encryptor does not need much space to perform encryption. This follows from the fact that the incompressible encodings construction of [42] has stream encoding.

Extension to CCA Security. In the security experiment for incompressible encryption presented in [32] the adversary is never allowed to query a decryption oracle. In other words, their work only considered IND-CPA incompressible encryption. In this work, we also give the adversary access to an decryption oracle extending incompressible encryption to IND-CCA2 incompressible encryption. We stress that IND-CCA2 security is usually considered the *right* security definition to use in practice. We show that our construction is, in fact, is IND-CCA2 incompressible secure.

1.2 Comparison with Previous Work

[32] presented two incompressible encryption schemes. The first one is based only on the minimal assumption of PKE. However, the ciphertext rate is very far from 1. The second one achieves rate-1 but is based on i$\mathcal{O}$. We compare these schemes in Table 1.

Table 1. Comparison with previous work. Here, n denotes the size of the encrypted messages and ε' is any constant between 1/2 and 1.

	Ciphertext rate	Public key size	Hardness assumption	Security
[32]	$1/\mathsf{poly}(\lambda)$	$\mathsf{poly}(\lambda)$	PKE	IND-CPA
[32]	1	$\mathsf{poly}(\lambda)$	$i\mathcal{O}$	IND-CPA
Our result	1	$n^{\varepsilon'} \cdot \mathsf{poly}(\lambda)$	DDH $\wedge$ (DCR $\vee$ LWE)	IND-CCA2

Other Related Work. Some recent works made significant progress in the area of incompressible cryptography. The works of [19,27,42] proposed constructions for incompressible encodings either in the random oracle model or in the CRS model. The work of [34] used the BSM together with computational assumptions to propose constructions of primitives that are not known just from computational assumptions, such as virtual grey-box obfuscation.

Incompressible cryptography is closely related to the bounded storage model (BSM) [39]. However, most works in the BSM (e.g. [5,13,24,33,45]) focus on achieving unconditional security for primitives that are already known from computational assumptions such as public-key encryption and oblivious transfer.

Open Problems. We leave the open problem of developing an incompressible encryption scheme that combines concretely short public keys with small ciphertexts. A possible approach for this would be to find a programmable hash proof system where the size of the public key is essentially independent of the size of the encapsulated key.

Full Version. In the full version [11], we justify focusing on the plain model by providing a simple incompressible encryption scheme that is secure in the random oracle model but is broken for any instantiation of the random oracle. This provides another uninstantiability for the random oracle in the vein of [7,10,12,14,21,29,31,41].

The full version also contains a programmable HPS based on isogeny-based assumptions with worse parameters than the DDH programmable HPS and a programmable HPS based on the hardness of LWE with superpolynomial modulus-to-noise ratio with better parameters than the DDH programmable HPS. The LWE construction, however, only results in incompressible IND-CPA security.

2   Technical Overview

In this technical overview, we sketch the main techniques to build an IND-CPA incompressible scheme. We later argue how these techniques can be tweaked to obtain a scheme that is IND-CCA2 incompressible secure.

Security Notion. The syntax and correctness notions for incompressible encryption are identical to standard public-key encryption (PKE). The main difference is in the security definition. Since the security notion of incompressible encryption is relatively new, we will briefly detail its security experiment here. Consider the following security game between a challenger $\mathcal{C}$ and a 3-stage PPT adversary $\mathcal{A} = (\mathcal{A}_1, \mathcal{A}_2, \mathcal{A}_3)$.

1. $\mathcal{C}$ creates a pair of public and secret keys pk, sk.
2. Given pk, the first stage $\mathcal{A}_1$ chooses two messages $\mathsf{m}_0, \mathsf{m}_1$.
3. $\mathcal{C}$ chooses $b \leftarrow_\$ \{0, 1\}$ uniformly at random and encrypts $\mathsf{ct} \leftarrow \mathsf{Enc}(\mathsf{pk}, \mathsf{m}_b)$.
4. Given the ciphertext ct and the state of $\mathcal{A}_1$, the second stage $\mathcal{A}_2$ produces a state st of size $S < |\mathsf{ct}|$. That is, the state st should be somewhat smaller than ct.
5. Now, the third stage $\mathcal{A}_3$ receives as input the state st (produced by $\mathcal{A}_2$) and the secret key sk. The goal of $\mathcal{A}_3$ is to guess the bit b.

We say that an incompressible encryption is secure if, for any adversary, $\mathcal{A}$ the advantage of winning the following game is negligible in the security parameter λ.

2.1   The Scheme of GWZ

Before we provide an outline of our construction, we will briefly discuss the underlying ideas of the low-rate incompressible encryption scheme constructed in [32]. At the very core is the following idea: The ciphertext essentially consists of a very long truly random random string R and a short payload part $c = (c_1, c_2)$, where c_1 is an encryption of a seed k for a randomness extractor Ext, and $c_2 = \mathsf{Ext}(k, R) \oplus \mathsf{m}$ is essentially a one-time-pad encryption of the message m under the key $\mathsf{Ext}(k, R)$. Clearly, if c_1 was *not* part of the ciphertext, then security of this scheme follows routinely by the following observations:

- In the view of the third stage $\mathcal{A}_3$ of the adversary R has high min-entropy, as R is uniformly random and the state st is significantly shorter than R.
- Furthermore, as we assume c_1 is not part of the ciphertext, st is independent of k
- Hence by the extraction property of Ext the string $\mathsf{Ext}(k, R)$ is uniformly random in the adversary's view, and therefore m_b is statistically hidden.

Now, the main idea of [32] to make this approach work even though c_1 is part of the ciphertext is to encrypt k in such a way that c_1 *can be made independent* of the extractor seed k. This is achieved by choosing a suitable encryption scheme for which c_1 can be chosen independently of k, and a suitable secret key which decrypts c_1 to k can be chosen *after the fact*, i.e. after the leakage st has been computed. [32] provide an elegant construction of such a scheme from non-compact single-key functional encryption, which can be built from any public key encryption scheme [30].

2.2   The Big Picture

While our construction departs significantly from the blueprint of [32] we use the same high-level concept of an encryption scheme that allows delaying secret-key generation in the security proof. Rather than constructing incompressible PKE directly, we first tackle the intermediate and simpler task of realizing a rate-1 *incompressible symmetric-key encryption*. In a second step, we will then transform *any* incompressible SKE scheme into an incompressible PKE scheme in a rate-preserving way. It turns out that even constructing a rate-1 incompressible SKE from standard assumptions is a non-trivial task and does not follow, e.g. from the (low-rate) public-key construction of [32].

Since our two steps are independent of one another, improvements of either in future work will lead to better incompressible encryption schemes. For simplicity, in the following outline, we will focus only on CPA security, whereas in the main body, we present a CCA secure construction (Fig. 1).

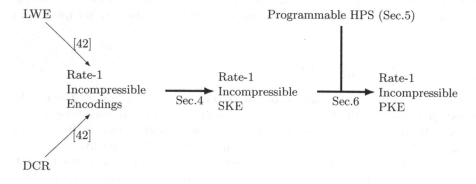

Fig. 1. Overview of the results in this work, bold arrows are contributions of this work.

2.3   Rate-1 Incompressible Symmetric-Key Encryption

In the symmetric-key setting, the syntax and correctness of incompressible SKE are pretty much that of standard symmetric-key encryption, whereas the security notion is similar to that of incompressible PKE, just with the difference that the first stage $\mathcal{A}_1$ of the adversary is not given a public key (as there is none). Thus, the security notion we consider here is the incompressible encryption-analogue of security against an eavesdropper (IND-EAV).

Failed Naive Attempts. As a (failed) very first attempt, one may try "make work" an incompressible SKE construction from the One-Time-Pad (OTP), i.e. the secret key k is a random bit-string as long as the message m and the ciphertext is $c = k \oplus m$. However, the obvious issue with this is that such a ciphertext c *decomposes* into many one-bit ciphertexts $c_i = k_i \oplus m_i$, and it is enough for $\mathcal{A}_2$ to leak a few bits of c to enable $\mathcal{A}_3$ to partially decrypt c and thus distinguish encryptions of m_0 from encryptions of m_1. As a next idea, one may try the following: Encryption chooses a (fresh) pseudorandom generator (PRG) seed s, encrypt m into $\hat{m} = m \oplus \mathsf{PRG}(s)$, use k to encrypt the seed s into a *header ciphertext* c, i.e. the encryption of m is $(\mathsf{Enc}(k, s), m \oplus \mathsf{PRG}(s))$. While this approach does look promising, we observe that it is stuck at either *leakage-rate* $1/2$ or ciphertext-rate $1/2$, that is as soon as $\mathcal{A}_3$ learns $\mathsf{Enc}(k, s)$ in its entirety and a few bits of $m_b \oplus \mathsf{PRG}(s)$, he will be able to distinguish encryptions of m_0 from m_1.

Introducing Circularity. Clearly, we need some kind of mechanism to *glue* the two ciphertexts components together, i.e. we want to make it such that if some parts of $\hat{m}$ are missing, then c will be useless (and vice versa). As a first, heuristic "hands-on" approach to achieve this, we can try to use $\hat{m}$ as a source of randomness from which we extract a key to mask the seed s. Thus, let $\mathsf{Ext}(\cdot, \cdot)$ be a *seeded* randomness extractor. We compute a ciphertext $(c, \hat{m})$ by first computing $\hat{m} = m \oplus \mathsf{PRG}(s)$ for a random seed s as before, but then encrypt s into c via $c = s \oplus \mathsf{Ext}(k, \hat{m})$, i.e. we use k as an extractor seed to extract a one-time-pad key $\mathsf{Ext}(k, \hat{m})$ from $\hat{m}$. Clearly, given k and a ciphertext $(c, \hat{m})$, we can decrypt by first computing $s = c \oplus \mathsf{Ext}(k, \hat{m})$ and then $m = \hat{m} \oplus \mathsf{PRG}(s)$. The rationale for why we hope this construction to be secure is that as soon as a significant fraction of the bits of $\hat{m}$ are lost, the output of the extractor $\mathsf{Ext}(k, \hat{m})$ should look uniform, and thus $\hat{m} = m \oplus \mathsf{PRG}(s)$ should hide m by the pseudorandomness of PRG. However, this circularity backfires when trying to establish security of this construction just from the pseudorandomness of PRG and the randomness-extraction property of Ext: In order to use pseudorandomness of PRG, we first need to *remove* the s from the view of the adversary, but $c = s \oplus \mathsf{Ext}(k, \hat{m})$ is correlated with s given k. On the other hand, in order to use the randomness extraction property of Ext we need that $\hat{m}$ has high entropy given st. But all the entropy of $\hat{m} = m \oplus \mathsf{PRG}(s)$ comes from the seed s, which is very small. Hence $\approx \lambda$ bits of $\hat{m}$ suffice to information-theoretically determine s.

Consequently, while heuristically, this construction seems secure, it seems unlikely the individual security properties of PRG and Ext suffice to *prove* this construction secure.

Breaking Circularity. Hence, what we need is a mechanism to break the circularity, which we have just introduced. Looking at where establishing security of the above construction gets stuck, a natural point to start is to make it such that $\hat{m}$ looks like it has a large amount of real entropy once a few bits of $\hat{m}$ are missing, i.e. $L(\hat{m})$ being computationally indistinguishable from $L(\hat{r})$ for a high-entropy distribution $\hat{r}$ for any efficiently computable leakage function $L(\cdot)$[2].

Incompressible Encodings. Fortunately, an encoding mechanism achieving this notion called *incompressible encodings* was just recently introduced and constructed by Moran and Wichs [42]. As a technical tool, they introduced the

---

[2] In our case the leakage function L is described by the adversary's second stage $\mathcal{A}_2$.

notion of *HILL-entropic encoding* in their work, which will be sufficient, if not to say ideally suited for our construction. Such a scheme consists of an encoding algorithm En and a decoding algorithm De, both of which rely on a (large) common random string $\text{crs} \leftarrow_\$ \{0,1\}^t$:

- The encoding algorithm $\text{En}_{\text{crs}}(m)$ is a *randomized algorithm* which takes a message m and produces an encoding $\hat{m}$
- The decoding algorithm $\text{De}_{\text{crs}}(\hat{m})$ is a deterministic algorithm which takes an encoding $\hat{m}$ and returns a message m.

In terms of correctness, one naturally requires that encoding followed by decoding leads to the original message. Security-wise, we require that there exists a simulator Sim which on input a message m produces a pair $(\text{crs}', \tilde{m})$, which is computationally indistinguishable from a real pair of crs and encoding of m, i.e.

$$(\text{crs}, \text{En}_{\text{crs}}(m)) \approx_c \text{Sim}(m),$$

where $\text{crs} \leftarrow_\$ \{0,1\}^t$. Additionally, we require that if $(\text{crs}', \tilde{m}) \leftarrow \text{Sim}(m)$, then $\tilde{m}$ has almost full *true* min-entropy given crs', i.e. $\tilde{H}_\infty(\tilde{m}|\text{crs}') \geq (1-\epsilon)n$, where $\tilde{H}_\infty$ is the average conditional min-entropy. The (very) high level idea how this can be achieved is that in simulation the common random string and the encoded message *switch roles*, in the sense that the simulated common random string crs' encodes the message m, whereas the encoding $\tilde{m}$ now has room to have (very) high entropy.

Moran and Wichs [42] provide two instantiations of their construction, one from DCR and one from LWE. These constructions achieve rate-1, i.e., the encoding is only slightly larger than the encoded message. The conceptual idea behind the construction is rather elegant: The encoding function $\text{En}_{\text{crs}}(m)$ generates a pair of public key and trapdoor (pk, td) of *preimage-sampleable surjective lossy function* F (for which we have efficient constructions from DCR or LWE) and sets x to be a randomly sampled preimage of $m \oplus \text{crs}$, i.e. $x = F_{\text{td}}^{-1}(m \oplus \text{crs})$, and sets $\hat{m} = (\text{pk}, x)$. To decode $\hat{m}$, one computes $m = F_{\text{pk}}(x) \oplus \text{crs}$. The simulator Sim chooses a *highly lossy public key* $\tilde{\text{pk}}$, chooses x uniformly at random, and sets $\text{crs}' = m \oplus F_{\tilde{\text{pk}}}(x)$ and $\tilde{m} = (\tilde{\text{pk}}, x)$. Given that F_{pk} is *regular* for surjective keys pk, meaning that if x is uniform then $F_{\text{pk}}(x)$ is also (statisticalluy close to) uniform, we can routinely establish that real pairs $(\text{crs}, \hat{m})$ are computationally indistinguishable from simulated $(\text{crs}', \tilde{m})$ using the indistinguishability of surjective public keys pk and highly lossy public keys $\tilde{\text{pk}}$. Moreover, for simulated pairs $(\text{crs}' = m \oplus F_{\tilde{\text{pk}}}(x), \tilde{m} = (\tilde{\text{pk}}, x))$ we can easily argue that x (and hence $\tilde{m}$) has high min-entropy given $\text{crs}' = m \oplus F_{\tilde{\text{pk}}}(x)$, as $F_{\tilde{\text{pk}}}$ is highly lossy and hence x has high min entropy given $F_{\tilde{\text{pk}}}(x)$.

Moran and Wichs [42] go on to show that for any incompressible encoding/HILL-entropic encoding, the common random string crs must be as long as the message, if one wants to establish security from a *falsifiable assumption* [43] under a black-box reduction.

The Full Construction. We will now provide our complete construction of incompressible SKE and sketch the security proof. For our scheme, the secret key

K is a uniformly random bit-string of suitable length which will be parsed as $K = (\text{crs}, k)$, where crs is the common random string for a HILL-entropic encoding (En, De), and k is the seed for a randomness extractor Ext. Encryption and decryption work as follows.

- $\text{Enc}(K = (\text{crs}, k), m)$: Choose a uniformly random PRG seed $s \leftarrow_\$ \{0,1\}^\lambda$ and compute $\hat{m} = \text{En}_{\text{crs}}(m \oplus \text{PRG}(s))$. Compute $c = s \oplus \text{Ext}(k, \hat{m})$ and output the ciphertext $\text{ct} = (c, \hat{m})$.
- $\text{Dec}(K = (\text{crs}, k), \text{ct} = (c, \hat{m}))$: Compute $s = c \oplus \text{Ext}(k, \hat{m})$ and output $m = \text{De}_{\text{crs}}(\hat{m}) \oplus \text{PRG}(s)$.

Correctness of this scheme follows routinely.

Security of this scheme is established along the following lines. First we rely on the security of the HILL-entropic encoding to replace $(\text{crs}, \hat{m})$ with a *simulated pair* $(\text{crs}', \tilde{m}) = \text{Sim}(m \oplus \text{PRG}(s))$. By the security of the HILL-entropic encoding, this modification is (computationally) unnoticeable to the adversary. However, now the encoding $\tilde{m}$ has true high min-entropy given crs'. Thus, using a min-entropy chain rule (e.g. by [23]) we can argue that $\tilde{m}$ still has sufficiently high min-entropy given both crs' and a leak $L(\tilde{m})$. Hence, the randomness extraction property guarantees that $\text{Ext}(k, \tilde{m})$ will extract uniform randomness (given crs' and $L(\tilde{m})$). To establish this we need a mild extra property of the extractor Ext that given a (uniformly random) extractor output y and $\tilde{m}$ we can sample a key k' *after the fact* such that $(k', y) \approx (k, \text{Ext}(k, \tilde{m}))$. Hence in the next hybrid modification, we can thus replace $c = s \oplus \text{Ext}(k, \tilde{m})$ with a uniformly random and independent string c'. Now that c' is independent of s, we can use the pseudorandomness property of PRG to replace $m \oplus \text{PRG}(s)$ in $(\text{crs}', \tilde{m}) = \text{Sim}(m \oplus \text{PRG}(s))$ with a uniformly random string u, i.e. $(\text{crs}', \tilde{m}) = \text{Sim}(u)$. We have finally arrived at an experiment where the ciphertext $\text{ct} = (c', \tilde{m})$ is independent of the message m, and hence the adversary's advantage is 0.

Concerning the rate of this scheme, note that a ciphertext $\text{ct} = (c, \hat{m})$ has rate 1, as c is just of size $\text{poly}(\lambda)$ (independent of the message length n), and the HILL-entropic encoding $\hat{m}$ is rate 1.

2.4 From Symmetric-Key to Public-Key Incompressible Encryption via Hash Proof Systems

Now that we have a construction of incompressible SKE, we need a way to establish a *long* key K between the sender and receiver. This is a job for a *key encapsulation mechanism* (KEM) [18]. A key-encapsulation mechanism consists of:

- A key-encapsulation mechanism consists of a key-generation algorithm KeyGen which produces a pair of public and secret keys (pk, sk).
- An encapsulation algorithm which takes a public key pk and produces a symmetric key K and a ciphertext header c_0 *encapsulating* K.
- A decapsulation algorithm Dec which takes a secret key sk and a ciphertext header c_0 and outputs a key K.

The correctness requirement is the obvious one, whereas the standard security requirement is that K is pseudorandom given pk and c_0. A symmetric key K generated via a KEM can now be used to encrypt a message m into a payload ciphertext c_1 using a symmetric key encryption scheme. The full ciphertext is $c = (c_0, c_1)$.

However, to transform an incompressible SKE into an incompressible PKE *not just any key encapsulation mechanism will do*. The simple reason is that in the incompressible (public key) encryption security game, the adversary gets to see the secret key sk in the end, which will allow him to decapsulate the (short) ciphertext header c_0 into the symmetric key K. But the standard security notion of KEMs discussed above does not require that the encapsulated key K follows a uniform distribution. Indeed, e.g. for simple PRG-based KEMs, the encapsulated key is statistically far from uniform. However, recall that in our construction of incompressible SKE above, we made critical use of the fact that the key K follows a uniform distribution and that the security reduction can *program* it in a suitable way.

Thus, we need a KEM which we can switch into a mode in which the ciphertext header c_0 encapsulates a truly uniform key K. As we need the ciphertext header c_0 to be substantially shorter than the encapsulated key K, the entropy of K in this mode *must* come from the secret key sk.

Enter Hash Proof Systems. This is where hash proof systems (HPS) [17] come into play[3]. Recall that HPS are defined relative to an NP-language $\mathcal{L} \subseteq \{0,1\}^k$. We have a key-generation algorithm KeyGen which generates a public or *projected* key pk, and a secret or *hashing* key sk. The hashing or decapsulation algorithm Decap takes the secret key sk and *any* $x \in \{0,1\}^k$ and produces a hash value K. The restricted hashing or encapsulation algorithm Encap takes a public key pk, an $x \in \mathcal{L}$ and a witness w (with respect to a fixed NP-relation for $\mathcal{L}$) for membership of x in $\mathcal{L}$ and produces a hash-value K.

In terms of correctness or completeness, we require that Decap and Encap agree on $\mathcal{L}$, i.e. if $x \in \mathcal{L}$ and w is a valid witness for x, then it holds that $\mathsf{Decap}(\mathsf{sk}, x) = \mathsf{Encap}(\mathsf{pk}, x, w)$.

In terms of security, we require *smoothness*, namely given that $x \notin \mathcal{L}$, it holds that $\mathsf{Decap}(\mathsf{sk}, x)$ is statistically close to uniform *given* pk.

HPS are especially useful for sparse pseudorandom languages $\mathcal{L}$, such as the decisional Diffie-Hellman (DDH) language) [17]. We define this language with respect to a pair of (randomly chosen) generators $g, h \in \mathbb{G}$, where $\mathbb{G}$ is a cryptographic group of prime order p. A pair $x = (g', h')$ is in $\mathcal{L}$, if there exists an $r \in \mathbb{Z}_p$ such that $g' = g^r$ and $h' = h^r$. The DDH assumption states that a random element in $\mathcal{L}$, i.e. a pair (g^r, h^r) is computationally indistinguishable from a pair of uniformly random group elements (u, v)[4].

---

[3] HPS have been instrumental in many prior works on leakage resilience cryptography e.g. [3,36].

[4] Note that such a pair is not in $\mathcal{L}$, except with negligible probability $1/p$.

In the Cramer-Shoup [17] scheme, the secret key $\mathsf{sk} = (\alpha, \beta)$ consists of two uniformly random values $\alpha, \beta \in \mathbb{Z}_p$, and the public key pk is computed as $\mathsf{pk} = g^\alpha h^\beta$. Given a public key pk an instance $c_0 = (g^r, h^r)$ with witness r, we compute a key $\mathsf{K} = \mathsf{pk}^r$. Given a secret key $\mathsf{sk} = (\alpha, \beta)$ and an instance $c_0 = (g', h')$ we compute a key $\mathsf{K} = g'^\alpha h'^\beta$. It follows routinely that encapsulation and decapsulation agree on $\mathcal{L}$. Moreover, for a $(g^*, h^*) \notin \mathcal{L}$ it holds $\mathsf{K}^* = g^{*\alpha} h^{*\beta}$ is uniformly random given $\mathsf{pk} = g^\alpha h^\alpha$ by a simple linear algebra argument.

Hash Proof Systems, and in particular the Cramer-Shoup HPS (almost) give us a KEM with the desired properties. Namely, given pk and (g, h), to encapsulate a key k we choose a uniformly random $r \in \mathbb{Z}_p$ and compute $c_0 = (g^r, h^r)$ and $\mathsf{K} = \mathsf{pk}^r$. To decapsulate K from $c_0 = (g', h')$ given $\mathsf{sk} = (\alpha, \beta)$, we compute $\mathsf{K} = g'^\alpha h'^\beta$.

A typical proof-strategy using HPS lets a reduction compute the encapsulated key (on the sender's side) via the decapsulation algorithm using the secret key. Correctness of the HPS ensures that this does not change K. Hence this modification will not be detected by an adversary. Now we don't need the witness r anymore. We can replace c_0 with a uniformly random c_0' and argue that this modification is computationally undetectable by the adversary, thanks to the DDH assumption. Since now c_0' is outside of $\mathcal{L}$ w.o.p, it holds that K is uniform even given pk, as desired.

However, this is still not enough to make our security reduction go through. It turns out we not only have to ensure that K is uniform given pk, but also that for *any given* K and fixed pk and c_0 we can find a secret key sk (compatible with pk) such that $\mathsf{Decap}(\mathsf{sk}, c_0) = \mathsf{K}$. Realizing this property using the Cramer-Shoup HPS directly seems hard, as in order to sample an $\mathsf{sk} = (\alpha, \beta)$ with $\mathsf{K} = g'^\alpha h'^\beta$ we would need to compute a discrete logarithm of K.

Programmable Hash Proof Systems. For this purpose, we will consider a notion of *programmable* hash proof systems, which obey a stronger smoothness notion. In short, such an HPS has the following property. Given a public key pk, a (fake) ciphertext header c_0^* (not in $\mathcal{L}$) and secret auxiliary information aux depending on both pk and c_0, we can sample a uniformly random secret key sk^* such that $\mathsf{Decap}(\mathsf{sk}^*, c_0^*) = \mathsf{K}$, for which it holds that $(\mathsf{pk}, c_0^*, \mathsf{sk}^*) \approx_s (\mathsf{pk}, c_0^*, \mathsf{sk})$ if K is chosen uniformly random.

Our idea to achieve this is simple: We will concatenate Decap (and also Encap) with a *balanced small range* hash function $\mathsf{HC} : \mathbb{G} \to \{0, 1\}$, i.e. we have $\mathsf{Decap}'(\mathsf{sk}, c_0) = \mathsf{HC}(\mathsf{Decap}(\mathsf{sk}, c_0))$ and $\mathsf{Encap}'(\mathsf{pk}, c_0, r) = \mathsf{HC}(\mathsf{Encap}(\mathsf{pk}, c_0, r))$. Here balanced means that if $h \in \mathbb{G}$ is a uniformly random group element, then $\mathsf{HC}(h)$ is statistically close to a uniformly random bit. While there exist deterministic constructions of such extractors for certain groups (e.g. [15]) we can find such an HC for any group via the leftover-hash lemma [35]. For such a hash function, we can efficiently sample a uniformly random pre-image $h \in \mathbb{G}$ of K for which we *do know* the discrete logarithm (with respect to a generator $g \in \mathbb{G}$). We achieve this via rejection sampling: Given a bit $\mathsf{K} \in \{0, 1\}$, choose a uniformly random $z \in \mathbb{Z}_p$ and test whether $\mathsf{HC}(g^z) = \mathsf{K}$ (which happens with probability $1/2$), and reject and resample if the test fails.

Now let $h = g^y$, $\mathsf{pk} = g^t$ and $c_0^* = (g' = g^r, h' = g^s)$ be a public key and (fake) ciphertext, for which the auxiliary information is (y, t, r, s), i.e. the discrete logarithms of pk and c_0^*. Given a key $\mathsf{K} \in \{0, 1\}$, we first sample a uniformly random $z \in \mathbb{Z}_p$ such that $\mathsf{HC}(g^z) = \mathsf{K}$. Now we have 2 linear constraints (over $\mathbb{Z}_p$) on $\mathsf{sk} = (\alpha, \beta) \in \mathbb{Z}_p^2$, namely

$$t = \alpha + \beta \cdot y$$

from $\mathsf{pk} = g^\alpha \cdot h^\beta$ and

$$z = \alpha r + \beta s$$

from $\mathsf{HC}(g^z) = \mathsf{HC}(g'^\alpha \cdot h'^\beta)$. Since we now have two equations and two unknowns α and β, we can solve for α and β using basic linear algebra.

We do pay a price to get programmability: Instead of getting $\log(|\mathbb{G}|)$ key bits per public key pk, we only get a single bit. Naturally, this can be improved up to $\log(\lambda)$ key-bits while keeping the above rejection sampling procedure expected polynomial time.

The Full Construction. We are now ready to present our fully-fledged construction. This construction will have a large public key. We will later discuss how the size of the public key can be reduced.

Assume thus that $(\mathsf{Enc}, \mathsf{Dec})$ is an incompressible SKE scheme, and that $(\mathsf{KeyGen}, \mathsf{Encap}, \mathsf{Decap})$ is a programmable HPS for a decision-membership-hard language $\mathcal{L}$, for concreteness assume the DDH language. Our incompressible PKE construction is given by the following algorithms.

- The key-generation algorithm KeyGen' generates random group elements $g, h \in \mathbb{G}$ and n pairs of public and secret keys $(\mathsf{pk}_1, \mathsf{sk}_1), \ldots, (\mathsf{pk}_n, \mathsf{sk}_n)$ using KeyGen (on g, h) and set $\mathsf{PK} = (g, h, \mathsf{pk}_1, \ldots, \mathsf{pk}_n)$ and $\mathsf{SK} = (\mathsf{sk}_1, \ldots, \mathsf{sk}_n)$.
- The encryption algorithm Enc' proceeds as follows, given a public key $\mathsf{PK} = (g, h, \mathsf{pk}_1, \ldots, \mathsf{pk}_n)$ and a message m. First, generate a random DDH instance $c_0 = (g' = g^r, h' = h^r)$ using a random $r \leftarrow_\$ \mathbb{Z}_p$. Now compute the key-bits $\mathsf{K}_1 = \mathsf{Encap}(\mathsf{pk}_1, c_0, r), \ldots, \mathsf{K}_n = \mathsf{Encap}(\mathsf{pk}_n, c_0, r)$ and set $\mathsf{K} = (\mathsf{K}_1, \ldots, \mathsf{K}_n)$. Next, we use K to encrypt m using the incompressible SKE scheme, i.e. we compute $c_1 = \mathsf{Enc}(\mathsf{K}, m)$ and output the ciphertext $c = (c_0, c_1)$.
- The decryption algorithm Dec' takes a secret key $\mathsf{SK} = (\mathsf{sk}_1, \ldots, \mathsf{sk}_n)$ and a ciphertext $c = (c_0, c_1)$, and proceeds as follows. First, it decapsulates the key $\mathsf{K} = (\mathsf{K}_1, \ldots, \mathsf{K}_n)$ by computing $\mathsf{K}_1 = \mathsf{Decap}(\mathsf{sk}, c_0), \ldots, \mathsf{K}_n = \mathsf{Decap}(\mathsf{sk}_n, c_0)$. Next, it decrypts c_1 to m via $m = \mathsf{Dec}(\mathsf{K}, c_1)$.

Correctness of this scheme follows routinely from the correctness of its components.

Note that if the incompressible SKE scheme $(\mathsf{Enc}, \mathsf{Dec})$ is rate-1, then so is our public-key scheme $(\mathsf{KeyGen}', \mathsf{Enc}', \mathsf{Dec}')$, as the only additional information in ciphertexts $c = (c_0, c_1)$ is the header c_0, which consists of just two group elements. On the other hand, note that the size of the public key of this scheme scales with the size n of the symmetric key K, which in our symmetric-key construction scales with the size of the message m.

Security of the Full Construction. We will now turn to sketching the security proof for the main construction. In the first hybrid step (somewhat expectedly), we use the HPS Decap algorithm instead of the Encap algorithm to compute the key-bits K_i *in the encryption of the challenge ciphertext*. That is, in the encryption of the challenge ciphertext we replace $K_i = \mathsf{Encap}(\mathsf{pk}_i, c_0, r)$ with $K_i = \mathsf{Decap}(\mathsf{sk}_i, c_0)$ for all $i = 1, \ldots, n$. Due to the correctness property of the HPS, this modification does not change the distribution of K. Hence this hybrid change goes unnoticed by the adversary. In the second hybrid step, since we don't need r anymore, we replace $c_0 = (g^r, h^r)$ with a uniformly random c_0'. We can use the DDH assumption to argue that this modification goes unnoticed.

The next hybrid step is the critical one: We choose g, h, the pk_i and c_0' with auxiliary information, i.e. together with their discrete logarithms with respect to g, choose $K \leftarrow\!\!\$\ \{0, 1\}^n$ uniformly at random and sample each sk_i such that $K_i = \mathsf{Decap}'(\mathsf{sk}_i, c_0')$ using the programming algorithm of the programmable HPS. We can argue statistical indistinguishability using the programmability property of HPS. The crucial observation now is that the public key $\mathsf{PK} = (g, h, \mathsf{pk}_1, \ldots, \mathsf{pk}_n)$ and the ciphertext header c_0 are computed *independently* of K and SK, and in fact we choose SK depending on K, i.e. we can choose SK after everything else.

This now allows us to turn an adversary $\mathcal{A}$ with non-negligible advantage in this hybrid experiment into an adversary $\mathcal{A}'$ with the same advantage against the incompressible SKE scheme. $\mathcal{A}'$ first generates PK as in the hybrid experiment and provides PK to the first stage $\mathcal{A}_1$ of $\mathcal{A}$, which will output m_0, m_1. Now the second stage $\mathcal{A}_2'$ gets to see a symmetric-key encryption c_1 of m_b, and turns this into a public-key encryption by setting $c = (c_0, c_1)$, where c_0 computed as in the hybrid experiment. This ciphertext c is then given $\mathcal{A}_2$, which outputs a state/leak st, and $\mathcal{A}_2'$ outputs the same state st.

Finally, $\mathcal{A}_3'$ given a symmetric key K and the state st proceeds as follows. Using the auxiliary information aux[5]. and the key K, it samples a secret key $\mathsf{SK} = (\mathsf{sk}_1, \ldots, \mathsf{sk}_n)$ such that for all $i = 1, \ldots, n$ it holds that $K_i = \mathsf{Decap}'(\mathsf{sk}_i, c_0)$, as in the hybrid experiment. Then, $\mathcal{A}_3'$ runs $\mathcal{A}_3$ on SK and st and outputs whatever $\mathcal{A}_3$ outputs.

It is not hard to see that from the view of $\mathcal{A}$, $\mathcal{A}'$ simulates the hybrid experiment perfectly. Hence, the advantage of $\mathcal{A}'$ against the incompressible symmetric-key security experiment is the same as that of $\mathcal{A}$ against the hybrid experiment, and we derive the desired contradiction.

---

[5] There is a technical subtlety in the security definition of incompressible SKE which we omitted before: We allow the first stage $\mathcal{A}_1'$ of a symmetric-key adversary $\mathcal{A}'$ to produce a large state (i.e. scaling with the message size), which is provided to *both* $\mathcal{A}_2'$ and $\mathcal{A}_3'$. This is to *communicate* a potentially large public key PK from $\mathcal{A}_1$ to $\mathcal{A}_3$ without putting a burden on the leakage-budget of the leaker-stage $\mathcal{A}_2'$. One could consider an alternative definition where this communication from $\mathcal{A}_1'$ to $\mathcal{A}_3'$ is not allowed. In such a setting we could still prove our construction secure by *compressing* the auxiliary information aux from which PK and c_0 are generated using a PRG.

Reducing the Public-Key-Size. As mentioned above, the construction we discussed in the last two paragraphs has a near-optimal ciphertext size (i.e. increasing the size of the symmetric-key ciphertext only by two group elements). In contrast, it has a very large public key which scales *linearly* with the size of the encrypted messages/the ciphertexts.

We will now discuss a tradeoff which achieves a better balance between ciphertext size and public key size. Concretely, we will provide a tradeoff which achieves a ciphertext size of $n + n^\epsilon \mathsf{poly}(\lambda)$ for an $0 < \epsilon < 1$ and public key size $n^{\epsilon'} \mathsf{poly}(\lambda)$ for an $1/2 < \epsilon' < 1$. I.e. we achieve ciphertext rate $1 - n^{\epsilon-1}\mathsf{poly}(\lambda)$, which approaches 1 for sufficiently large n, while having a key of sublinear size.

In order to declutter the presentation, we will switch from multiplicative notation of group operations in $\mathbb{G}$ to additive notion in the following discussion. That is we will denote group elements g^x by $[x]$, and write $\alpha \cdot [x]$ instead of $(g^x)^\alpha$. Furthermore, we will consider vectors and matrices of group elements, i.e. if $\mathbf{x} \in \mathbb{Z}_p^k$ is a vector, then $[\mathbf{x}]$ is its element-wise encoding in the group $\mathbb{G}$. Likewise, we write an encoding of a matrix $\mathbf{A} \in \mathbb{Z}_p^{k \times l}$ as $[\mathbf{A}]$.

In our discussion above we considered a HPS for the *two-dimensional* DDH language, i.e. the language consisting of all $r \cdot [\mathbf{v}]$ given two $[\mathbf{v}]$, where $\mathbf{v} \in \mathbb{Z}_p^2$ is a randomly chosen 2-dimensional vector over $\mathbb{Z}_p$.

Thus let $\mathbf{v} \in \mathbb{Z}_p^k$ be a randomly chosen k-dimensional vector. The goal of the k-dimensional DDH problem is to distinguish $([\mathbf{v}], t \cdot [\mathbf{v}])$ from $([\mathbf{v}], [\mathbf{u}])$, where $\mathbf{v}$ and $\mathbf{u}$ are chosen uniformly random from $\mathbb{Z}_p^k$ and r is chosen uniformly from $\mathbb{Z}_p$. It follows routinely via a standard rerandomization argument that the k-dimensional DDH problem is hard, given that the 2-dimensional DDH problem is hard.

We can construct an HPS for k-DDH analogously to the 2-dimensional case: Fix a vector $[\mathbf{v}] \in \mathbb{G}^k$. The secret key sk is a random vector $\boldsymbol{\alpha} \in \mathbb{Z}_p^k$, whereas the public key is given by $[\mathsf{pk}] = \boldsymbol{\alpha}^\top[\mathbf{v}]$, i.e. the inner product of $\boldsymbol{\alpha}$ and $[\mathbf{v}]$. Given a vector $[\mathbf{w}] = r \cdot [\mathbf{v}]$ and a witness r, the Encap algorithm computes $[\mathsf{K}] = r \cdot [\mathsf{pk}]$. On the other hand, given any vector $[\mathbf{w}] \in \mathbb{G}^k$ and a secret key $\mathsf{sk} = \boldsymbol{\alpha}$, the Decap algorithm computes $\boldsymbol{\alpha}^\top \cdot [\mathbf{w}]$. Arguing correctness and smoothness are again simple exercises in linear algebra. Furthermore, this HPS satisfies a stronger notion of $k - 1$-smoothness: Given uniformly random $[\mathbf{w}_1], \ldots, [\mathbf{w}_{k-1}]$, it holds that

$$(\mathsf{pk}, \boldsymbol{\alpha}^\top[\mathbf{w}_1], \ldots, \boldsymbol{\alpha}^\top[\mathbf{w}_{k-1}]) \approx_s (\mathsf{pk}, [u_1], \ldots, [u_{k-1}]),$$

where the $[u_1], \ldots, [u_{k-1}]$ are uniformly random in $\mathbb{G}$. Establishing this is again routine linear algebra.

We will first briefly discuss how the HPS can be made programmable. In essence, we follow the same idea as above: We take a balance function $\mathsf{HC} : \mathbb{G} \to \{0, 1\}$ and define the Decap algorithm to compute $\mathsf{HC}(\boldsymbol{\alpha}^\top[\mathbf{w}])$. We claim this construction is $k - 1$-programmable. That is, given $[\mathbf{v}]$, $[\mathsf{pk}] = [t]$, uniformly random $[\mathbf{w}_1], \ldots [\mathbf{w}_{k-1}]$ together with the witnesses $\mathbf{v}$, t and $\mathbf{w}_1, \ldots, \mathbf{w}_{k-1}$, and a random $\mathsf{K} = (\mathsf{K}_1, \ldots, \mathsf{K}_{k-1}) \in \{0, 1\}^{k-1}$, we can efficiently sample a uniformly random $\boldsymbol{\alpha} \in \mathbb{Z}_p^k$ such that $t = \boldsymbol{\alpha}^\top \mathbf{v}$ and $\mathsf{K}_i = \mathsf{HC}(\boldsymbol{\alpha}^\top[\mathbf{w}_i])$ for $i = 1, \ldots, n$. We proceed as above: First we choose uniformly random $z_i \in \mathbb{Z}_p$ such that $\mathsf{K}_i = \mathsf{HC}([z_i])$ for all i. Then we get the linear equation system

$$\boldsymbol{\alpha}^\top \mathbf{v} = t$$
$$\boldsymbol{\alpha}^\top \mathbf{w}_1 = z_1$$
$$\vdots$$
$$\boldsymbol{\alpha}^\top \mathbf{w}_{k-1} = z_{k-1}.$$

Since the $\mathbf{w}_i$ are chosen uniformly random, this system has full rank w.o.p., and hence we can find a matching secret key $\boldsymbol{\alpha}$ via simple linear algebra.

Now, plugging this programmable HPS into our construction of incompressible PKE, we obtain the following parameters.

- A single public pk consisting of one group element can be used to encapsulate k key bits. Hence, to encapsulate n key bits we need n/k public keys amounting to n/k group elements.
- The ciphertext header now contains $k \cdot (k-1) \leq k^2$ group elements (in the above notation the vectors $[\mathbf{w}_1], \ldots, [\mathbf{w}_{k-1}]$).

Hence, if we want to strike a balance where the (additive) ciphertext overhead is of the same size as the public key, we obtain the relation

$$\frac{n}{k} = k^2,$$

which yields to $k = n^{1/3}$. Hence, for this choice of parameters the public key consists of a $n^{2/3}$ group elements (which is sublinear), and the size of the ciphertext is $n + n^{2/3}\log(|\mathbb{G}|) = n(1 - n^{-1/3}\log(|\mathbb{G}|))$ bits, which approaches rate 1.

2.5   Extension to CCA Security

The scheme described so far achieves IND-CPA incompressible security. This work also considers an IND-CCA2 incompressible security definition where the adversary gets oracle access to a decryption oracle.

To achieve IND-CCA2 security, we follow the framework of [17]. We add a second hash proof system that acts as integrity proof for ciphertexts. The second hash proof system does not need to be programmable but universal$_2$ [17] or 2-smooth [1]. It allows the decryption oracle to only answer queries to honestly generated ciphertexts. This mechanism ensures that the decryption oracle does not give up entropy of the programmable HPS's secret key.

In the main body of this work, we provide the full construction that achieves this level of security.

3 Preliminaries

The acronym PPT denotes "probabilistic polynomial time". Throughout this work, λ denotes the security parameter. By $\mathsf{negl}(\lambda)$, we denote a negligible function in λ, that is, a function that vanishes faster than any inverse polynomial in λ. Let $n \in \mathbb{N}$. Then, $[n]$ denotes the set $\{1, \ldots, n\}$. If $\mathcal{A}$ is an algorithm, we denote by $y \leftarrow \mathcal{A}(x)$ the output y after running $\mathcal{A}$ on input x. If S is a (finite) set, we denote by $x \leftarrow_\$ S$ the experiment of sampling uniformly at random an element x from S. If D is a distribution over S, we denote by $x \leftarrow_\$ D$ the element x sampled from S according to D.

For two probability distributions X, Y, we use the notation $X \approx_s Y$ to state that the distributions are statistically indistinguishable and $X \approx_c Y$ to state that the distributions are computationally indistinguishable.

For ease of notation, in any of our constructions we assume public parameters p are known to every algorithm and every secret key sk also contains the corresponding public key pk.

We present some information-theoretical notions and results that will be instrumental throughout this work.

Definition 1 (Average Min-Entropy [23]). *For two jointly distributed random variables (X, Y), the average min-entropy of X conditioned on Y is defined as*

$$\tilde{H}_\infty(X|Y) = -log(\mathbb{E}_{y \leftarrow_\$ Y}[max_x \Pr[X = x | Y = y]]).$$

Lemma 1 (Lemma 2.2 b) of [23]). *For random variables X, Y, Z where Y is supported over a set of size T, we have*

$$\tilde{H}_\infty(X|(Y, Z)) \geq \tilde{H}_\infty((X, Y)|Z) - log(T) \geq \tilde{H}_\infty(X|Z) - log(T).$$

Definition 2 (Average-Case Extractor [23]). *Let $n, d, m \in \mathbb{N}$. A function $\mathsf{Ext} : \{0,1\}^n \times \{0,1\}^d \to \{0,1\}^m$ is a (k, ϵ) strong average-case min-entropy extractor if, for all random variables (X, Y) where X takes values in $\{0,1\}^n$ and $\tilde{H}_\infty(X|Y) \geq k$, we have that $(U_d, \mathsf{Ext}(X, U_d), Y)$ is ϵ-close to (U_d, U_m, Y), where U_d and U_m are independent uniformly random strings of length d and m respectively.*

Lemma 2 (Generalized Leftover Hash Lemma 2.4 of [23]). *Let $n, m \in \mathbb{N}$. Let $\{H_r : \{0,1\}^n \to \{0,1\}^m\}_{r \in R}$ be a family of universal hash functions, then $\mathsf{Ext}(x, r) \mapsto H_r(x)$ is an average-case (k, ϵ)-strong extractor whenever $m \leq k - 2log(\frac{1}{\epsilon}) + 2$.*

Definition 3 (Pseudorandom Generator). *Let $n, m = \mathsf{poly}(\lambda)$. A function $G : \{0,1\}^n \to \{0,1\}^m$ is a pseudorandom generator if, for uniformly random $\mathsf{s} \leftarrow_\$ \{0,1\}^n$ and $r \leftarrow_\$ \{0,1\}^m$, we have*

$$G(\mathsf{s}) \approx_c r.$$

Definition 4 (Collision-Resitant Hash Function). *Let $n, m, l = \mathsf{poly}(\lambda)$. A collision-resistant hash function is a seeded function $\mathsf{CRHF} : \{0,1\}^n \times \{0,1\}^m \to \{0,1\}^l$ with the property that for all PPT adversaries $\mathcal{A}$, random seed $\mathsf{s} \in \{0,1\}^n$ we have $\mathcal{A}(\mathsf{s})$ outputs x, x' with $x \neq x'$ and $\mathsf{CRHF}_\mathsf{s}(x) = \mathsf{CRHF}_\mathsf{s}(x')$ with negligible probability.*

3.1 Decisional Diffie-Hellman Assumption

In the following, let $\mathcal{G}$ be a (prime-order) *group generator*, that is, $\mathcal{G}$ is an algorithm that takes as an input a security parameter 1^λ and outputs $(\mathbb{G}, p, g)$, where $\mathbb{G}$ is the description of a multiplicative cyclic group, p is the order of the group which is always a prime number unless differently specified, and g is a generator of the group. Sometimes we denote the size of the group by $|\mathbb{G}|$.

We denote by $[a]$ be value g^a. Similarly, if $\mathbf{A} \in \mathbb{Z}_p^{n \times m}$ is a matrix with entries $a_{i,j}$ then $[\mathbf{A}]$ denotes the matrix where each (i, j)-entry is the value $g^{a_{i,j}}$. Note that given $\mathbf{x} \in \mathbb{Z}_p^n$, $\mathbf{y} \in \mathbb{Z}_p^m$ and $[\mathbf{A}]$, we can compute $\mathbf{x}^T[\mathbf{A}] = [\mathbf{x}^T\mathbf{A}]$ and $[\mathbf{A}]\mathbf{y} = [\mathbf{A}\mathbf{y}]$.

In the following we state the decisional version of the Diffie-Hellman (DDH) assumption.

Definition 5 (Decisional Diffie-Hellman Assumption). *Let $(\mathbb{G}, p, g) \leftarrow_\$ \mathcal{G}(1^\lambda)$. We say that the DDH assumption holds (with respect to $\mathcal{G}$) if for any PPT adversary $\mathcal{A}$*

$$|\Pr[1 \leftarrow \mathcal{A}((\mathbb{G}, p, g), ([a], [b], [ab]))] - \Pr[1 \leftarrow \mathcal{A}((\mathbb{G}, p, g), ([a], [b], [c]))]| \leq \mathsf{negl}(\lambda)$$

where $a, b, c \leftarrow_\$ \mathbb{Z}_p$.

3.2 Public-Key Encryption

Definition 6 (Public-Key Encryption). *A public-key encryption (PKE) scheme is a triple of PPT algorithms*

$(\mathsf{pk}, \mathsf{sk}) \leftarrow \mathsf{KeyGen}(1^\lambda)$: *Given the security parameter λ the key-generation algorithm outputs a public key pk and a secret key sk.*

$c \leftarrow \mathsf{Enc}(\mathsf{pk}, \mathsf{m})$: *Given a public key pk and a message m encryption outputs a ciphertext c.*

$\mathsf{m} \leftarrow \mathsf{Dec}(\mathsf{sk}, c)$: *Given a secret key sk and a ciphertext c decryption outputs a message m.*

Correctness. For all $\lambda, S \in \mathbb{N}$, messages m and $(\mathsf{pk}, \mathsf{sk})$ in the range of KeyGen we have that $\mathsf{m} = \mathsf{Dec}(\mathsf{sk}, \mathsf{Enc}(\mathsf{pk}, \mathsf{m}))$.

IND-CPA Security. For all $\lambda \in \mathbb{N}$ and all adversaries $\mathcal{A} = (\mathcal{A}_1, \mathcal{A}_2)$ we have that

$$\Pr\left[b \leftarrow \mathcal{A}_2(\mathsf{st}, c) : \begin{array}{c} (\mathsf{pk}, \mathsf{sk}) \leftarrow \mathsf{KeyGen}(1^\lambda) \\ (\mathsf{m}_0, \mathsf{m}_1, \mathsf{st}) \leftarrow \mathcal{A}_1(\mathsf{pk}) \\ b \leftarrow_\$ \{0,1\} \\ c \leftarrow \mathsf{Enc}(\mathsf{pk}, \mathsf{m}_b) \end{array}\right] \leq \frac{1}{2} + \mathsf{negl}(\lambda).$$

3.3　HILL-Entropic Encodings

We recall the notion of HILL-entropic encodings from [42].

Definition 7 (HILL-Entropic Encodings [42]). *An (α, β)-HILL-entropic encoding scheme with selective security in the CRS setting consists of two PTT algorithms:*

- $c \leftarrow \mathsf{En}_{\mathsf{crs}}(1^\lambda, \mathsf{m})$: *An encoding algorithm that takes a common random string* crs *and a message* m *producing an encoding* c.
- $m \leftarrow \mathsf{De}_{\mathsf{crs}}(c)$: *A decoding algorithm that takes a common random string* crs *and an encoding* c *and produces a message* m.

Correctness. There is some negligible μ such that for all $\lambda \in \mathbb{N}$ and all $m \in \{0,1\}^*$ we have
$$\Pr[\mathsf{De}_{\mathsf{crs}}(\mathsf{En}_{\mathsf{crs}}(1^\lambda, \mathsf{m})) = \mathsf{m}] = 1 - \mu(\lambda).$$

α-Expansion. For all $\lambda, k \in \mathbb{N}$ and all $\mathsf{m} \in \{0,1\}^k$ we have $|\mathsf{En}_{\mathsf{crs}}(1^\lambda, \mathsf{m})| \leq \alpha(\lambda, k)$.

β-HILL-Entropy. There exists an algorithm SimEn s.t. for any polynomial $k = k(\lambda)$ and any ensamble of messages $\mathsf{m} = \{\mathsf{m}_\lambda\}$ of length $|\mathsf{m}_\lambda| = k(\lambda)$, consider the following "real" experiment:

- $\mathsf{crs} \leftarrow_\$ \{0,1\}^{t(\lambda, k)}$
- $c \leftarrow \mathsf{En}_{\mathsf{crs}}(1^\lambda, \mathsf{m}_\lambda)$

and let CRS, C denote the random variables for the corresponding values in the "real" experiment. Also consider the following "simulated" experiment:

- $(\mathsf{crs}', c') \leftarrow \mathsf{SimEn}(1^\lambda, \mathsf{m}_\lambda)$

and let CRS', C' denote the random variables for the corresponding values in the "simulated" experiment. We require that $(CRS, C) \approx_c (CRS', C')$ and $\tilde{H}_\infty(C'|CRS') \geq \beta(\lambda, k)$.

We call a (α, β)-HILL-entropic encoding good if $\alpha(\lambda, k) = k(1+o(1))+\mathsf{poly}(\lambda)$ and $\beta(\lambda, k) = k(1 - o(1)) - \mathsf{poly}(\lambda)$. Moran and Wichs [42] provide good HILL-entropic encodings from DCR [20,44] or LWE [46] in the CRS model. They also show that the CRS must be as big as the encoded message.

4　Incompressible Symmetric-Key Encryption

In this section, we define incompressible symmetric-key encryption (SKE) and give a construction from entropic encodings.

4.1   Definition

First, we recall the notion of forward-secure storage [26] under the name of incompressible symmetric-key encryption. For our purposes we only need IND-EAV style security but this could be extended similar to what we did with incompressible public-key encryption.

Definition 8 (Incompressible SKE). *An incompressible symmetric-key encryption scheme is a tuple of PPT algorithms using uniformly random keys* k

$c \leftarrow$ Enc(k, m)**:** *Given a symmetric key* k *and a message* m *encryption it outputs a ciphertext* c.
$m \leftarrow$ Dec(sk, c)**:** *Given a symmetric key* k *and a ciphertext* c *decryption it outputs a message* m.

We require size of message space, size of key space, and size of ciphertext space to be polynomials over the security parameter λ and the space bound S; that is, $n = n(\lambda, S)$, $k = k(\lambda, S)$, and $l = l(\lambda, S)$ respectively.

Correctness. For all $\lambda, S \in \mathbb{N}$, messages m and keys $k \in \{0, 1\}^k$ we have that $m = $ Dec$(k,$ Enc$(k, m))$

Security. For security parameter λ and space bound S, a symmetric-key encryption scheme (Enc, Dec) has incompressible SKE security if for all PPT adversaries $\mathcal{A} = (\mathcal{A}_1, \mathcal{A}_2, \mathcal{A}_3)$ the probability of winning the following experiment is $\leq \frac{1}{2} + $ negl(λ).

Dist$_{\mathcal{A}, \Pi}^{\text{IncomSKE}}(\lambda, S)$ **Experiment:**
- Run the adversary $(m_0, m_1, st_1) \leftarrow \mathcal{A}_1(1^\lambda)$ to receive two messages m_0 and m_1
- Sample a bit $b \leftarrow_{\$} \{0, 1\}$ uniformly at random
- Sample $k \leftarrow_{\$} \{0, 1\}^{n(\lambda, S)}$ uniformly at random
- Run $c \leftarrow$ Enc(k, m_b) to encrypt m_b
- Run the adversary $st_2 \leftarrow \mathcal{A}_2(st_1, c)$ to produce a state st_2 smaller than S
- Run the final adversary $b' \leftarrow \mathcal{A}_3(k, st_1, st_2, m_0, m_1)$
- The adversary wins if $b = b'$

4.2   Construction

Now we show how to build incompressible symmetric-key encryption using HILL-entropic encodings, extractors, and pseudorandom generators.

Construction 1. *Let λ be the security parameter, S be the space bound of the adversary and n be the size of the message space. Let (En, De) be an (α, β)-HILL-entropic encoding,* Ext $: \{0, 1\}^{\alpha(\lambda, n)} \times \{0, 1\}^{d(\lambda)} \rightarrow \{0, 1\}^\lambda$ *be a $(\beta(\lambda, n) - S, $ negl$(\lambda))$ strong average-case min-entropy extractor where $d(\lambda)$ is a polynomial and $G : \{0, 1\}^\lambda \rightarrow \{0, 1\}^n$ be a PRG.*

Enc(k, m):
  - *Parse* $k = (k_1, k_2, crs)$.
  - *Sample* $s \leftarrow_\$ \{0,1\}^\lambda$ *uniformly at random.*
  - *Let* $c_1 \leftarrow En_{crs}(1^\lambda, G(s) \oplus m)$.
  - *Let* $c_2 \leftarrow s \oplus Ext(c_1, k_1) \oplus k_2$.
  - *Return* $c = (c_1, c_2)$.
Dec(k, c):
  - *Parse* $k = (k_1, k_2, crs)$.
  - *Parse* $c = (c_1, c_2)$.
  - *Let* $s \leftarrow Ext(c_1, k_1) \oplus c_2 \oplus k_2$.
  - *Return* $De_{crs}(c_1) \oplus G(s)$.

Parameters. The ciphertexts are of size $\lambda + \alpha(\lambda, n)$. The keys are of size $d(\lambda) + t(\lambda, n)$, where $t(\lambda, n)$ is the size of the encoding's crs. Notice that the extractor exists if $\beta(\lambda, n) - S - 2\log\left(\frac{1}{negl(\lambda)} + 2\right) \geq \lambda$ according to Lemma 2. So, the adversary is allowed a leakage of size $S \leq \beta(\lambda, n) - \lambda - 2\log\left(\frac{1}{negl(\lambda)} + 2\right)$.

Therefore, if we choose a "good" entropic encoding we get a rate of $\frac{n}{n(1+o(1))+poly(\lambda)}$, allowed leakage of $S = n(1 - o(1)) - poly(\lambda)$, and keysize of $k = n(1 + o(1)) + poly(\lambda)$.

Correctness. By the correctness of the entropic encoding $De_{crs}(En_{crs}(1^\lambda, G(s) \oplus m)) = G(s) \oplus m$. Since Ext is deterministic under a fixed key k_1 then $Ext(c_1, k_1) \oplus c_2 \oplus k_2 = Ext(c_1, k_1) \oplus s \oplus Ext(c_1, k_1) = s$. Therefore, $De_{crs}(c_1) \oplus G(s) = m$.

Theorem 2 (Security). *The incompressible SKE presented in Construction 1 has incompressible SKE security if (En,De) is an (α, β)-HILL-entropic encoding, Ext is a $(\beta(\lambda, n) - S, negl(\lambda))$ strong average-case min-entropy extractor, and G is a pseudorandom generator each with the listed parameters.*

Proof. We prove security via hybrids. First we list the hybrid and then argue their indistinguishability. In each hybrid we highlight the changes compared to the previous one.

H_0:
  - Run the adversary $m_0, m_1, st_1 \leftarrow \mathcal{A}_1(1^\lambda)$ to receive two messages m_0 and m_1.
  - Sample bit $b \leftarrow_\$ \{0,1\}$ uniformly at random.
  - Sample $k \leftarrow_\$ \{0,1\}^n$ uniformly at random.
  - Run $c \leftarrow Enc(k, m_b)$ to encrypt m_b.
  - Run the adversary $st_2 \leftarrow \mathcal{A}_2(st_1, c)$ to produce a state st_2 smaller than S.
  - Run the final adversary $b' \leftarrow \mathcal{A}_3(k, st_1, st_2, m_0, m_1)$.
  - The adversary wins if $b = b'$.

In H_1 we explicitly represent what happens in Enc.

H_1:

- Run the adversary $m_0, m_1, st_1 \leftarrow \mathcal{A}_1(1^\lambda)$ to receive two messages m_0 and m_1.
- Sample bit $b \leftarrow_\$ \{0,1\}$ uniformly at random.
- Sample $k_1 \leftarrow_\$ \{0,1\}^{d(\lambda,n)}$ uniformly at random.
- Sample $k_2 \leftarrow_\$ \{0,1\}^\lambda$ uniformly at random.
- Sample crs $\leftarrow_\$ \{0,1\}^{t(\lambda,n)}$ uniformly at random.
- Sample $s \leftarrow_\$ \{0,1\}^\lambda$ uniformly at random.
- Let $c_1 \leftarrow \mathsf{En}_{crs}(1^\lambda, G(s) \oplus m_b)$.
- Let $c_2 \leftarrow s \oplus \mathsf{Ext}(c_1, k_1) \oplus k_2$.
- Let $c \leftarrow (c_1, c_2)$ and $k \leftarrow (k_1, k_2, crs)$.
- Run the adversary $st_2 \leftarrow \mathcal{A}_2(st_1, c)$ to produce a state st_2 smaller than S.
- Run the final adversary $b' \leftarrow \mathcal{A}_3(k, st_1, st_2, m_0, m_1)$.
- The adversary wins if $b = b'$

In H_2 we switch the entropic encoding to the simulated code that has a lot of entropy.

H_2:

- Run the adversary $m_0, m_1, st_1 \leftarrow \mathcal{A}_1(1^\lambda)$ to receive two messages m_0 and m_1.
- Sample bit $b \leftarrow_\$ \{0,1\}$ uniformly at random.
- Sample $k_1 \leftarrow_\$ \{0,1\}^{d(\lambda,n)}$ uniformly at random.
- Sample $k_2 \leftarrow_\$ \{0,1\}^\lambda$ uniformly at random.
-
- Sample $s \leftarrow_\$ \{0,1\}^\lambda$ uniformly at random.
- Let $(crs, c_1) \leftarrow \mathsf{SimEn}(1^\lambda, G(s) \oplus m_b)$.
- Let $c_2 \leftarrow s \oplus \mathsf{Ext}(c_1, k_1) \oplus k_2$.
- Let $c \leftarrow (c_1, c_2)$ and $k \leftarrow (k_1, k_2, crs)$.
- Run the adversary $st_2 \leftarrow \mathcal{A}_2(st_1, c)$ to produce a state st_2 smaller than S.
- Run the final adversary $b' \leftarrow \mathcal{A}_3(k, st_1, st_2, m_0, m_1)$.
- The adversary wins if $b = b'$.

I H_3 we switch the order in which we sample c_2 and k_2.

H_3:

- Run the adversary $m_0, m_1, st_1 \leftarrow \mathcal{A}_1(1^\lambda)$ to receive two messages m_0 and m_1.
- Sample bit $b \leftarrow_\$ \{0,1\}$ uniformly at random.
- Sample $k_1 \leftarrow_\$ \{0,1\}^{d(\lambda,n)}$ uniformly at random.

- Sample $s \leftarrow_\$ \{0,1\}^\lambda$ uniformly at random.
- Let $(\mathsf{crs}, c_1) \leftarrow \mathsf{SimEn}(1^\lambda, G(\mathsf{s}) \oplus \mathsf{m}_b)$.
- Sample $c_2 \leftarrow_\$ \{0,1\}^\lambda$ uniformly at random.
- Let $c \leftarrow (c_1, c_2)$.
- Run the adversary $\mathsf{st}_2 \leftarrow \mathcal{A}_2(\mathsf{st}_1, c)$ to produce a state st_2 smaller than S.
- Let $\mathsf{k}_2 \leftarrow c_2 \oplus \mathsf{Ext}(c_1, \mathsf{k}_1) \oplus \mathsf{s}$.
- Let $\mathsf{k} \leftarrow (\mathsf{k}_1, \mathsf{k}_2, \mathsf{crs})$.
- Run the final adversary $b' \leftarrow \mathcal{A}_3(\mathsf{k}, \mathsf{st}_1, \mathsf{st}_2, \mathsf{m}_0, \mathsf{m}_1)$.
- The adversary wins if $b = b'$.

In H_4 we replace the output of the extractor Ext by a uniformly random value.

H_4:
- Run the adversary $\mathsf{m}_0, \mathsf{m}_1, \mathsf{st}_1 \leftarrow \mathcal{A}_1(1^\lambda)$ to receive two messages m_0 and m_1.
- Sample bit $b \leftarrow_\$ \{0,1\}$ uniformly at random.
- Sample $\mathsf{k}_1 \leftarrow_\$ \{0,1\}^{d(\lambda,n)}$ uniformly at random.
- Sample $s \leftarrow_\$ \{0,1\}^\lambda$ uniformly at random.
- Let $(\mathsf{crs}, c_1) \leftarrow \mathsf{SimEn}(1^\lambda, G(\mathsf{s}) \oplus \mathsf{m}_b)$.
- Sample $c_2 \leftarrow_\$ \{0,1\}^\lambda$ uniformly at random.
- Let $c \leftarrow (c_1, c_2)$.
- Run the adversary $\mathsf{st}_2 \leftarrow \mathcal{A}_2(\mathsf{st}_1, c)$ to produce a state st_2 smaller than S.
- Sample $\mathsf{k}_2 \leftarrow_\$ \{0,1\}^\lambda$ uniformly at random.
- Let $\mathsf{k} \leftarrow (\mathsf{k}_1, \mathsf{k}_2, \mathsf{crs})$.
- Run the final adversary $b' \leftarrow \mathcal{A}_3(\mathsf{k}, \mathsf{st}_1, \mathsf{st}_2, \mathsf{m}_0, \mathsf{m}_1)$.
- The adversary wins if $b = b'$.

Finally we replace the output of $G(\mathsf{s})$ by a uniformly random value.

H_5:
- Run the adversary $\mathsf{m}_0, \mathsf{m}_1, \mathsf{st}_1 \leftarrow \mathcal{A}_1(1^\lambda)$ to receive two messages m_0 and m_1.
- Sample bit $b \leftarrow_\$ \{0,1\}$ uniformly at random.
- Sample $\mathsf{k}_1 \leftarrow_\$ \{0,1\}^{d(\lambda,n)}$ uniformly at random.
- Sample $s \leftarrow_\$ \{0,1\}^\lambda$ uniformly at random.
- Sample $r \leftarrow_\$ \{0,1\}^n$ uniformly at random.
- Let $(\mathsf{crs}, c_1) \leftarrow \mathsf{SimEn}(1^\lambda, r)$.
- Sample $c_2 \leftarrow_\$ \{0,1\}^\lambda$ uniformly at random.
- Let $c \leftarrow (c_1, c_2)$.
- Run the adversary $\mathsf{st}_2 \leftarrow \mathcal{A}_2(\mathsf{st}_1, c)$ to produce a state st_2 smaller than S.
- Sample $\mathsf{k}_2 \leftarrow_\$ \{0,1\}^\lambda$ uniformly at random.
- Let $\mathsf{k} \leftarrow (\mathsf{k}_1, \mathsf{k}_2; \mathsf{crs})$.

- Run the final adversary $b' \leftarrow \mathcal{A}_3(\mathsf{k}, \mathsf{st}_1, \mathsf{st}_2, \mathsf{m}_0, \mathsf{m}_1)$.
- The adversary wins if $b = b'$.

$H_0 \approx H_1$:

The differences between H_0 and H_1 are purely syntactical. In H_1 we just show more detail of Enc.

$H_1 \approx_c H_2$:

Instead of sampling the common random string for the entropic encoding uniformly at random and then encoding $G(\mathsf{s}) \oplus \mathsf{m}$ we simulate both steps using SimEn. Assume there exists a PPT adversary $\mathcal{A} = (\mathcal{A}_1, \mathcal{A}_2, \mathcal{A}_3)$ that can distinguish the two hybrids H_1 and H_2 with a non-negligible advantage of ϵ. From this we construct a PPT adversary $\mathcal{A}' = (\mathcal{A}'_1, \mathcal{A}'_2)$ that can break the β-HILL-entropy of (En, De) with advantage ϵ.

$\mathcal{A}'_1(1^\lambda)$:

- Run the adversary $\mathsf{m}_0, \mathsf{m}_1, \mathsf{st}_1 \leftarrow \mathcal{A}_1(1^\lambda)$ to receive two messages m_0 and m_1
- Sample bit $b \leftarrow_\$ \{0, 1\}$ uniformly at random
- Sample $\mathsf{k}_1 \leftarrow_\$ \{0, 1\}^{d(\lambda, n)}$ uniformly at random
- Sample $\mathsf{s} \leftarrow_\$ \{0, 1\}^\lambda$ uniformly at random
- Return $G(\mathsf{s}) \oplus \mathsf{m}_b$

$\mathcal{A}'_2(\mathsf{crs}, c_1)$:

- Let $c_2 \leftarrow \mathsf{s} \oplus \mathsf{Ext}(c_1, \mathsf{k}_1)$
- Let $c \leftarrow (c_1, c_2)$
- Run the adversary $\mathsf{st}_2 \leftarrow \mathcal{A}_2(\mathsf{st}_1, c)$ to produce a state st_2 smaller than S
- Run the final adversary $b' \leftarrow \mathcal{A}_3(\mathsf{k}, \mathsf{st}_1, \mathsf{st}_2, \mathsf{m}_0, \mathsf{m}_1)$
- Return b'

If $\mathcal{A}$ can distinguish H_1 from H_2 then $\mathcal{A}'$ can distinguish a uniformly random $\mathsf{crs} \leftarrow_\$ \{0, 1\}^{t(\lambda, n)}$ and $c_1 \leftarrow \mathsf{En}(1^\lambda, G(\mathsf{s}) \oplus \mathsf{m}_b)$ from $(\mathsf{crs}, c_1) \leftarrow \mathsf{SimEn}(1^\lambda, G(\mathsf{s}) \oplus \mathsf{m}_b)$ as it perfectly simulates H_2 in the case that $(\mathsf{crs}, c_1) \leftarrow \mathsf{SimEn}(1^\lambda, G(\mathsf{s}) \oplus \mathsf{m}_b)$ and perfectly simulates H_1 in the other case.

$H_2 \approx H_3$:

In H_3 we switch the order in which we sample c_2 and k_2. From the view of the adversary this is statistically identical.

$H_3 \approx_s H_4$:

Let $C_1, C_2, CRS, K_1, K_2,$ and ST_2 denote the random variables for the corresponding values in the experiment and U_λ independent uniform randomness of length λ. By the β-HILL entropy of the entropic encoding we know that $\tilde{H}_\infty(C_1|CRS) \geq \beta$. Using Lemma 1 we deduce that

$$\tilde{H}_\infty(C_1|(CRS, K_2, ST_2, C_2)) \geq \beta - 2\lambda - log(S)$$

Therefore, the extractor gives us that $(K_1, K_2, CRS, ST_2, U_\lambda)$ and $(K_1, K_2, CRS, ST_2, \mathsf{Ext}(C_1, K_1))$ are statistically close.

$H_3 \approx_c H_4$:

In H_4 we encode a uniformly random string instead of $G(\mathsf{s}) \oplus \mathsf{m}_b$. Assume there exists a PPT adversary $\mathcal{A} = (\mathcal{A}_1, \mathcal{A}_2, \mathcal{A}_3)$ that can distinguish the two hybrids H_3 and H_4 with a non-negligible advantage of ϵ. From this we construct a PPT adversary $\mathcal{A}'$ that can break the pseudorandomness of G with advantage ϵ.

$\mathcal{A}'(r')$:

- Run the adversary $\mathsf{m}_0, \mathsf{m}_1, \mathsf{st}_1 \leftarrow \mathcal{A}_1(1^\lambda)$ to receive two messages m_0 and m_1
- Sample bit $b \leftarrow_\$ \{0, 1\}$ uniformly at random
- Sample $\mathsf{k}_1 \leftarrow_\$ \{0, 1\}^{d(\lambda, n)}$ uniformly at random
- Sample $\mathsf{s} \leftarrow_\$ \{0, 1\}^\lambda$ uniformly at random
- Sample $r \leftarrow r' \oplus \mathsf{m}_b$ uniformly at random
- Let $(\mathsf{crs}, c_1) \leftarrow \mathsf{SimEn}(1^\lambda, r)$
- Sample $c_2 \leftarrow_\$ \{0, 1\}^\lambda$ uniformly at random
- Let $c \leftarrow (c_1, c_2)$
- Run the adversary $\mathsf{st}_2 \leftarrow \mathcal{A}_2(\mathsf{st}_1, c)$ to produce a state st_2 smaller than S
- Run the final adversary $b' \leftarrow \mathcal{A}_3(\mathsf{k}, \mathsf{st}_1, \mathsf{st}_2, \mathsf{m}_0, \mathsf{m}_1)$
- Return b'

If $\mathcal{A}$ can distinguish H_3 from H_4 then $\mathcal{A}'$ can distinguish $G(\mathsf{s})$ with uniformly random $\mathsf{s} \leftarrow_\$ \{0, 1\}^\lambda$ from uniformly random $r' \leftarrow_\$ \{0, 1\}^n$ as it perfectly simulates H_3 in the case that $r' \leftarrow G(\mathsf{s})$ and perfectly simulates H_4 in the other case.

H_4:

In H_4 the winning probability of the adversary is $\frac{1}{2}$ as it gets no information about b at all.

5   Programmable Hash Proof Systems

In this work we think of a hash proof systems as a key encapsulation mechanism where the encapsulated key is independent of the public key and the ciphertext under certain conditions. This allows us to later resample the secret key in the incompressibility experiments.

For our construction we need two different hash proof systems. One that is Y-programmable and one that is 2-smooth both using the same language.

5.1   Definitions

First we define hash proof system that we will use as a mask in our encryption scheme.

Definition 9 (Y-Programmable Hash Proof System [17,38]). *A Y-programmable hash proof system is defined over a NP language $\mathcal{L} \subset X$, where each element x in the language $\mathcal{L}$ has a witness w. Additionally there exist a subset $Y \subset X \setminus \mathcal{L}$ and efficient ways to sample a language $\mathcal{L}$ with a corresponding trapdoor $\mathsf{td}_\mathcal{L}$, an $x \in \mathcal{L}$ with its witness w and an $x \in Y$ with a corresponding trapdoor td_x*

- $(\mathsf{p}, \mathsf{td}_{\mathcal{L}}) \leftarrow \mathsf{Gen}(1^{\lambda}, 1^k)$: *Given the security parameter λ, the encapsulated key size k the language generation algorithm that outputs public parameters p defining a language $\mathcal{L}$ and a trapdoor $\mathsf{td}_{\mathcal{L}}$ to that language.*
- $(x \in \mathcal{L}, w) \leftarrow \mathsf{samp}\mathcal{L}(\mathsf{p})$: *Given the public parameters, it outputs an element $x \in \mathcal{L}$ with the corresponding witness w.*
- $(x \in Y, \mathsf{td}_x) \leftarrow \mathsf{samp}Y(\mathsf{p}, \mathsf{td}_{\mathcal{L}})$: *Given the public parameters and a trapdoor $\mathsf{td}_{\mathcal{L}}$, it outputs $x \in Y$ and the corresponding trapdoor td_x.*

The hash proof system itself consists of these algorithms:

- $(\mathsf{pk}, \mathsf{sk}) \leftarrow \mathsf{KeyGen}(\mathsf{p})$: *Given the public parameters, the key generation algorithm outputs a public key pk and a secret key sk.*
- $\mathsf{k} \leftarrow \mathsf{Encap}(\mathsf{pk}, x, w)$: *Given the public lye pk, en element x and a witness w. the key encapsulation algorithm outputs an encapsulated key k.*
- $\mathsf{k} \leftarrow \mathsf{Decap}(\mathsf{sk}, x)$: *Given the secret key sk and any $x \in X$, the key decapsulation algorithm outputs an encapsulated key. k. Notice x can be outside $\mathcal{L}$.*
- $\mathsf{sk}' \leftarrow \mathsf{Program}(\mathsf{td}_{\mathcal{L}}, \mathsf{td}_x, \mathsf{sk}, x, \mathsf{k})$ *Given two trapdoors $\mathsf{td}_{\mathcal{L}}, \mathsf{td}_x$, a secret key sk, an element $x \in Y$, and an encapsulated key k, the programming algorithm outputs a new secret key sk'.*

Correctness. For all $\lambda, k \in \mathbb{N}$, $(\mathsf{p}, \mathsf{td}_{\mathcal{L}})$ in the range of $\mathsf{Gen}(1^{\lambda}, 1^k)$, $(\mathsf{pk}, \mathsf{sk})$ in the range of $\mathsf{KeyGen}(\mathsf{p})$, $x \in \mathcal{L}$ and for $\mathsf{k} \leftarrow \mathsf{Encap}(\mathsf{pk}, x, w)$, we have $\mathsf{k} = \mathsf{Decap}(\mathsf{sk}, x)$ with $|\mathsf{k}| = k$.

Language Indistinguishability. For all $\lambda, k \in \mathbb{N}$ if we sample $(\mathsf{p}, \mathsf{td}_{\mathcal{L}}) \leftarrow \mathsf{Gen}(1^{\lambda}, 1^k)$, $\mathcal{L} \ni x \leftarrow \mathsf{samp}\mathcal{L}(\mathsf{p})$, and $(x^* \in Y, \mathsf{td}_{x^*}) \leftarrow \mathsf{samp}Y(\mathsf{p}, \mathsf{td}_{\mathcal{L}})$, we have the computational indistinguishability: $x \approx_c x^*$.

Programmability. For all $\lambda, k \in \mathbb{N}$, $(\mathsf{p}, \mathsf{td}_{\mathcal{L}})$ in the range of $\mathsf{samp}\mathcal{L}(1^{\lambda}, 1^k)$, $(\mathsf{pk}, \mathsf{sk})$ in the range of $\mathsf{KeyGen}(\mathsf{p})$, $\mathsf{k} \in \{0, 1\}^m$, and for (x, td_x) in the range of $\mathsf{samp}Y(\mathsf{p}, \mathsf{td}_{\mathcal{L}})$, $\mathsf{sk}' \leftarrow \mathsf{Program}(\mathsf{td}_{\mathcal{L}}, \mathsf{td}_x, \mathsf{sk}, x, \mathsf{k})$, we have $\mathsf{Decap}(\mathsf{sk}', x) = \mathsf{k}$.

Y-Programmable Smoothness. For all $\lambda, k \in \mathbb{N}$, $(\mathsf{p}, \mathsf{td}_{\mathcal{L}})$ in the range of $\mathsf{Gen}(1^{\lambda}, 1^k)$, $(\mathsf{pk}, \mathsf{sk})$ in the range of $\mathsf{KeyGen}(\mathsf{p})$, (x, td_x) in the range of $\mathsf{samp}Y(\mathsf{p}, \mathsf{td}_{\mathcal{L}})$, $\mathsf{k} \in \{0, 1\}^m$, and $\mathsf{sk}' \leftarrow \mathsf{Program}(\mathsf{td}_{\mathcal{L}}, \mathsf{td}_x, \mathsf{sk}, x, \mathsf{k})$ we have statistical indistinguishability $(\mathsf{pk}, \mathsf{sk}, x) \approx_s (\mathsf{pk}, \mathsf{sk}', x)$.

Notice, if $Y = X \setminus \mathcal{L}$ then Y-programmable smoothness implies smoothness. Next we recall 2-smooth hash proof systems with our adjusted notation.

Definition 10 (2-Smooth Hash Proof System [1,17]). *A 2-smooth hash proof system is defined over a NP language $\mathcal{L} \subset X$ as above The hash proof system itself consists of the following algorithms:*

- $(\mathsf{pk}, \mathsf{sk}) \leftarrow \mathsf{KeyGen}(\mathsf{p})$: *Given the public parameters, the key generation algorithm that outputs a public key pk and a secret key sk.*
- $\mathsf{k} \leftarrow \mathsf{Encap}(\mathsf{pk}, x, w, \tau)$: *Given public key pk, an element of the language $x \in \mathcal{L}$, its witness w, and a tag τ, the key encapsulation algorithm outputs an encapsulated key k.*

– k ← Decap(sk, x, τ): *Given the secret key* sk, *any* $x \in X$, *and a tag* τ. *the key decapsulation algorithm outputs an encapsulated key* k. *Notice x can be outside* $\mathcal{L}$.

Correctness. For all $\lambda, k \in \mathbb{N}$, (p, td$_\mathcal{L}$) in the range of Gen($1^\lambda, 1^k$), (pk, sk) in the range of KeyGen(p), $x \in \mathcal{L}$, tags τ, and for k ← Encap(pk, x, w, τ), we have k = Decap(sk, x, τ) with $|k| = k$.

Language Indistinguishability. Exactly as above.

2-Smoothness. For all $\lambda, k \in \mathbb{N}$, (p, td$_\mathcal{L}$) in the range of Gen($1^\lambda, 1^k$), $x, x' \in X \setminus \mathcal{L}$, two tags τ, τ' such that $(x, \tau) \neq (x', \tau')$, let (pk, sk) ← KeyGen(p) and sample k ←$\$$ $\{0, 1\}^k$ we have computational indistinguishability between (pk, Decap(sk, x, τ), Decap(sk, x', τ')) and (pk, Decap(sk, x, τ), k).

5.2   Programmable Hash Proof System from DDH

In our protocols we need programmable HPS with a big encapsulated key space (for classic notation [17] this would be called the hash space).

Some smooth hash proof systems are easily transformed into programmable HPS with big encapsulated keys by generating more public keys and using them on the same $x \in X$. These HPS include the one from weak pseudorandom effective group actions [2]. That transformation causes the public key size to scale linearly with the size of the encapsulated key and leave the size of the ciphertext indepent of the encapsulated key size. We provide more details about this in the full version [11].

We present a variant of the original [17] HPS with an interesting trade off. Here both public key size and ciphertext size scale in the 2/3-power with k, the size of the encapsulated key.

Construction 2. *Let* HC : $\mathbb{G} \times \{0, 1\}^{log(|\mathbb{G}|)} \to \{0, 1\}$ *denote a 1-bit randomness extractor over a group element; if this function is applied over a matrix of group elements, then it means that the function is applied entry-wise with the same randomness. In the following let $\ell, s \in \mathbb{N}$ such that $\ell \cdot s = k$. We get an interesting tradeoff for our application when $\ell = k^{1/3}$ and $s = k^{2/3}$.*

Gen($1^\lambda, 1^k$) :
- $(\mathbb{G}, p, g) \leftarrow\$ \mathcal{G}(1^\lambda)$.
- *Sample* $\mathbf{h} \leftarrow\$ \mathbb{Z}_p^\ell \setminus \{\mathbf{0}\}$ *uniformly at random.*
- *Return* p $= (\mathbb{G}, p, g, [\mathbf{h}])$ *and* td$_\mathcal{L}$ = $\mathbf{h}$.

samp$\mathcal{L}$(p) :
- *Parse* p $= (\mathbb{G}, p, g, [\mathbf{h}])$.
- *Sample* $\mathbf{y} \leftarrow\$ \mathbb{Z}_p^{\ell-1}$ *uniformly at random.*
- *Return* $x = [\mathbf{y}]$ *and* $w = \mathbf{y}$.

sampY (p, td$_\mathcal{L}$) :
- *Parse* p $= (\mathbb{G}, p, g, [\mathbf{h}])$.

- *Let* $\text{td}_\mathcal{L} = \mathbf{h}$.
- *Sample* $\mathbf{E} \leftarrow_\$ \mathbb{Z}_p^{\ell \times (\ell-1)}$ *such that* $(\mathbf{h}\ \mathbf{E})$ *is invertible uniformly at random.*
- *Return* $x = [\mathbf{E}]$ *and* $w = \mathbf{E}$.

KeyGen(p):
- *Parse* $\mathsf{p} = (\mathbb{G}, p, g, [\mathbf{h}])$.
- *Sample* $r \leftarrow_\$ \{0,1\}^{\log(|\mathbb{G}|)}$ *the public randomness for a extractor.*
- *Sample* $\mathbf{A} \leftarrow_\$ \mathbb{Z}_p^{s \times \ell}$ *uniformly at random.*
- *Return* $\mathsf{pk} = (\mathbf{A}[\mathbf{h}], r)$ *and* $\mathsf{sk} = \mathbf{A}$.

Encap $(\mathsf{pk}, c = [\mathbf{h}\mathbf{y}^t], w = \mathbf{y})$:
- *Parse* $\mathsf{p} = (\mathbb{G}, p, g, [\mathbf{h}] \in \mathbb{G}^\ell)$.
- *Parse* $\mathsf{pk} = ([\mathbf{f}] \in \mathbb{G}^s, r)$.
- *Let* $\mathbf{K} \leftarrow \mathsf{HC}([\mathbf{f}]\mathbf{y}^t, r)$ *the component-wise extractor of the outer product between* $\mathbf{f}$ *and* $\mathbf{y}$.
- *Return* $\mathsf{k} = \mathbf{K}$.

Decap $(\mathsf{sk}, x = [\mathbf{E}] \in \mathbb{G}^{\ell \times (\ell-1)})$:
- *Parse* $\mathsf{pk} = ([\mathbf{f}], r)$
- *Parse* $\mathsf{sk} = \mathbf{A} \in \mathbb{Z}_p^{s \times \ell}$.
- *Let* $\mathbf{K} \leftarrow \mathsf{HC}(\mathbf{A}[\mathbf{E}], r)$ *the component-wise extractor of the product between* $\mathbf{A}$ *and* $[\mathbf{E}]$.
- *Return* $\mathsf{k} = \mathbf{K}$.

Program$(\text{td}_\mathcal{L}, \text{td}_x, \mathsf{sk}, x, \mathsf{k})$:
- *Parse* $\mathsf{pk} = ([\mathbf{f}], r)$, $\text{td}_\mathcal{L} = \mathbf{h} \in \mathbb{Z}_p^\ell$, $\text{td}_x = \mathbf{E} \in \mathbb{Z}_p^{\ell \times (\ell-1)}$, $\mathsf{sk} = \mathbf{A}$, *and* $\mathsf{k} = \mathbf{K} \in \{0,1\}^{s \times (\ell-1)}$.
- *For each* $i \in [\ell-1], j \in [s]$ *sample* $B_{i,j} \leftarrow_\$ \mathbb{Z}_p$ *such that* $K_{i,j} = \mathsf{HC}([B_{i,j}], r)$ *via rejection sampling.*
- *Set* $\mathbf{B} = (B)_{i,j}$. *Let* $\mathbf{A}' \leftarrow (\mathbf{A}\mathbf{h}\ \mathbf{B})(\mathbf{h}\ \mathbf{E})^{-1}$.
- *Return* $\mathsf{sk}' = \mathbf{A}'$.

Correctness. For any $(\mathsf{p} = (\mathbb{G}, p, g, [\mathbf{h}]), \text{td}_\mathcal{L})$ in the range of Gen, $(\mathsf{pk} = ([\mathbf{A}\mathbf{h}], r), \mathsf{sk} = \mathbf{A})$ in the range of KeyGen, and $[\mathbf{h}\mathbf{y}^t] \in \mathcal{L}$ we have $\mathsf{Encap}(\mathsf{pk}, [\mathbf{h}\mathbf{y}^t])$ outputs $\mathsf{k} = \mathsf{HC}([\mathbf{A}\mathbf{h}]\mathbf{y}^t, r) = \mathsf{HC}([\mathbf{A}\mathbf{h}\mathbf{y}^t], r)$. Decapsulation then outputs $\mathsf{k} = \mathsf{HC}(\mathbf{A}[\mathbf{h}\mathbf{y}^t], r) = \mathsf{HC}([\mathbf{A}\mathbf{h}\mathbf{y}^t], r)$.

Programmability. Since we choose $\mathbf{h}$ and $\mathbf{E}$ s.t. $(\mathbf{h}\ \mathbf{E})$ is invertible Program always outputs a matrix $\mathbf{A}'$ with the property that $\mathbf{A}'\mathbf{E} = \mathbf{B}$ and $\mathsf{k} = \mathsf{HC}([\mathbf{B}], r)$.

Programmable Smoothness. If we first sample k uniformly random and then program for the key k Program$(\text{td}_\mathcal{L}, \text{td}_x, \mathsf{sk}, x, \mathsf{k})$ the resulting distribution over $\mathbf{B}$ will be uniformly random. And because $(\mathbf{h}\ \mathbf{E})$ is invertible then $\mathbf{A}'$ is a uniformly random under the condition that $\mathbf{A}'\mathbf{h} = \mathbf{A}\mathbf{h}$. The same holds for $\mathbf{A}$. Therefore, $(\mathsf{pk}, \mathsf{sk} = \mathbf{A}, x)$ and $(\mathsf{pk}, \mathsf{sk}' = \mathbf{A}', x)$ are identically distributed.

Theorem 3 (Language Indistinguishability). *If DDH is hard for* $\mathcal{G}$ *then elements from the language* $\mathcal{L} = \{[\mathbf{h}]\mathbf{y}^t | \mathbf{y} \in \mathbb{Z}_p^{\ell-1}\}$ *and* $Y = \{[\mathbf{E}] | \mathbf{E} \in \mathbb{Z}_p^{\ell \times (\ell-1)} \wedge (\mathbf{h}\ \mathbf{E})$ *is invertible} of Construction 2 are indistinguishable.*

Proof. We prove security via hybrids. First we list the hybrids and then argue their indistinguishability. In each hybrid we highlight the changes compared to the previous one.

H_0:

- Let $(\mathsf{p}, \mathsf{td}_{\mathcal{L}}) \leftarrow \mathsf{Gen}(1^{\lambda}, 1^{k})$.
- Let $(\mathsf{pk}, \mathsf{sk}) \leftarrow \mathsf{KeyGen}(\mathsf{p})$.
- Let $(x, w) \leftarrow \mathsf{samp}\mathcal{L}(\mathsf{p})$.
- Let $\mathsf{k} \leftarrow \mathsf{Encap}(\mathsf{pk}, x, w)$.
- Run the adversary $\mathcal{A}(\mathsf{pk}, \mathsf{sk}, x)$.

H_1:

- Sample a group $(\mathbb{G}, p, g) \leftarrow_{\$} \mathcal{G}(1^{\lambda})$.
- Sample $r \leftarrow_{\$} \{0, 1\}^{log(|\mathbb{G}|)}$ the randomness for the extractor .
- Sample $\mathbf{h} \leftarrow_{\$} \mathbb{Z}_p^{\ell} \setminus \{\mathbf{0}\}$ uniformly at random .
- Sample $\mathbf{A} \leftarrow_{\$} \mathbb{Z}_p^{s \times \ell}$ uniformly at random .
- Let $\mathsf{p} = (\mathbb{G}, p, g, [\mathbf{h}])$.
- Let $\mathsf{pk} = ([\mathbf{Ah}], r)$ and $\mathsf{sk} = \mathbf{A}$.
- Sample $\mathbf{y} \leftarrow_{\$} \mathbb{Z}_p^{\ell-1}$ uniformly at random .
- Let $x = [\mathbf{hy}^t] = [\mathbf{C}]$.
- Run the adversary $\mathcal{A}(\mathsf{pk}, \mathsf{sk}, x)$.

$H_{2,i}$:

- Sample a group $(\mathbb{G}, p, g) \leftarrow_{\$} \mathcal{G}(1^{\lambda})$.
- Sample $r \leftarrow_{\$} \{0, 1\}^{log(|\mathbb{G}|)}$ the randomness for the extractor.
- Sample $\mathbf{h} \leftarrow_{\$} \mathbb{Z}_p^{\ell} \setminus \{\mathbf{0}\}$ uniformly at random.
- Sample $\mathbf{A} \leftarrow_{\$} \mathbb{Z}_p^{s \times \ell}$ uniformly at random.
- Let $\mathsf{p} = (\mathbb{G}, p, g, [\mathbf{h}])$.
- Let $\mathsf{pk} = ([\mathbf{Ah}], r)$ and $\mathsf{sk} = \mathbf{A}$.
- Sample $\mathbf{y} \leftarrow_{\$} \mathbb{Z}_p^{\ell-1}$ uniformly at random.
- Let $[\mathbf{C}] = [\mathbf{hy}^t]$.
- Sample $\mathbf{E} \leftarrow_{\$} \mathbb{Z}_p^{l \times (l-1)}$ uniformly at random .
- Replace the first i entries of $[\mathbf{C}]$ by the first i entries in $[\mathbf{E}]$.
- Let $x = [\mathbf{C}]$.
- Run the adversary $\mathcal{A}(\mathsf{pk}, \mathsf{sk}, x)$.

H_3:

- Sample a group $(\mathbb{G}, p, g) \leftarrow_{\$} \mathcal{G}(1^{\lambda})$.
- Sample $r \leftarrow_{\$} \{0, 1\}^{log(|\mathbb{G}|)}$ the randomness for the extractor.
- Sample $\mathbf{h} \leftarrow_{\$} \mathbb{Z}_p^{\ell} \setminus \{\mathbf{0}\}$ uniformly at random.
- Sample $\mathbf{A} \leftarrow_{\$} \mathbb{Z}_p^{s \times \ell}$ uniformly at random.
- Let $\mathsf{p} = (\mathbb{G}, p, g, [\mathbf{h}])$.

- Let $\mathsf{pk} = ([\mathbf{Ah}], r)$ and $\mathsf{sk} = \mathbf{A}$.
- Sample $\mathbf{E} \leftarrow_\$ \mathbb{Z}_p^{l \times (l-1)}$ uniformly   at   random   such that $(\mathbf{h} \; \mathbf{E})$ is invertible .
- Let $x = [\mathbf{E}]$.
- Run the adversary $\mathcal{A}(\mathsf{pk}, \mathsf{sk}, x)$.

$H_0 \approx H_1$:

The differences between H_0 and H_1 are purely syntactical. In H_1 we just show more detail of Gen and Encap.

$H_1 \approx H_{2,0}$:

The differences between H_1 and $H_{2,0}$ are purely syntactical.

$H_{2,i} \approx_c H_{2,i+1}$:

In $H_{2,i+1}$ we replace the $n + 1$st element of $\mathbf{C}$ by a random one. Assume there exists a PPT adversary $\mathcal{A}$ that can distinguish the two hybrids $H_{2,i}$ and $H_{2,i+1}$ with a non-negligible advantage of ϵ. From this we construct a PPT adversary $\mathcal{A}'$ that can break DDH with advantage ϵ.

$\mathcal{A}' \, ((\mathbb{G}, p, g), ([a], [b], [\rho]))$:

- Let $u \leftarrow i \mod l$
- Let $v \leftarrow \lfloor i/l \rfloor$
- Sample $r \leftarrow_\$ \{0, 1\}^{\log(|\mathbb{G}|)}$ the randomness for the extractor
- Sample $\mathbf{h} \leftarrow_\$ \mathbb{Z}_p^\ell \setminus \{\mathbf{0}\}$ uniformly at random
- Replace $[x_u]$ by $[a]$
- Sample $\mathbf{A} \leftarrow_\$ \mathbb{Z}_p^{s \times \ell}$ uniformly at random
- Let $\mathsf{p} = (\mathbb{G}, p, g, [\mathbf{h}])$
- Let $\mathsf{pk} = ([\mathbf{Ah}], r)$ and $\mathsf{sk} = \mathbf{A}$
- Sample $\mathbf{y} \leftarrow_\$ \mathbb{Z}_p^{\ell-1}$ uniformly at random
- For $u' \in [l]$ and $v' \in [l-1]$ let $C_{u',v'} \leftarrow \begin{cases} [\rho] & \text{if } u' = u, v' = v \\ [b]x_{u'} & \text{if } u' \neq u, v' = v \\ [x_{u'}]y_{v'} & \text{else} \end{cases}$

- Sample $\mathbf{E} \leftarrow_\$ \mathbb{Z}_p^{l \times (l-1)}$
- Replace the first i entries of $[\mathbf{C}]$ by the first i entries in $[\mathbf{E}]$
- Let $x = [\mathbf{C}]$
- Run the adversary $b' \leftarrow \mathcal{A}(\mathsf{pk}, \mathsf{sk}, x)$
- Return b'

If $\mathcal{A}$ distinguishes between $H_{2,i}$ and $H_{2,i+1}$ then $\mathcal{A}'$ distinguishes between $\rho = ab$ and ρ being uniformly random as $\mathcal{A}'$ perfectly simulates $H_{2,i}$ in the case that $\rho = ab$ and $H_{2,i+1}$ if r is uniformly random.

$H_{2,m} \approx_s H_3$:

$H_{2,m}$ is statistically close to H_3 because with probability $1 - \mathsf{negl}(\lambda)$ we have $(\mathbf{h} \; \mathbf{E})$ is invertible.

Parameters. For an encapsulated key of size k this scheme roughly gets us public parameters of size $k^{1/3} \cdot \mathsf{poly}(\lambda)$, public key of size $k^{2/3} \cdot \mathsf{poly}(\lambda)$ and elements from X of size $k^{2/3} \cdot \mathsf{poly}(\lambda)$.

5.3   2-Smooth Hash Proof System from DDH

The above hash proof system only is programmable if $x \in Y$. To make our encryption scheme CCA secure we need a efficient way to check whether $x \in \mathcal{L}$ or $x \in X \setminus \mathcal{L}$. To do this we construct the 2-smooth hash proof system below that is defined over the same language.

Construction 3. *We construct a 2-smooth hash proof system with a output size of λ using an extractor* $\mathsf{Ext} : \mathbb{G}^{\ell-1} \times \{0,1\}^p \to \{0,1\}^\lambda$ *and a collision resistant hash function* CRHF *that maps into* $\mathbb{Z}_p$*. As a language description we use the same as in Construction 2.*

KeyGen(p):
- *Parse* $\mathsf{p} = (\mathbb{G}, p, g, [\mathbf{h}])$.
- *Sample* $r \leftarrow_\$ \{0,1\}^{log(|\mathbb{G}|)}$ *uniformly at random.*
- *Sample* $\mathsf{s} \leftarrow_\$ \{0,1\}^\lambda$ *uniformly at random.*
- *Sample* $\mathbf{a}, \mathbf{b} \leftarrow_\$ \mathbb{Z}_p^\ell$ *uniformly at random.*
- *Return* $\mathsf{pk} = (\mathbf{a}^t[\mathbf{h}], \mathbf{b}^t[\mathbf{h}], r, \mathsf{s})$ *and* $\mathsf{sk} = (\mathbf{a}, \mathbf{b})$.

Encap $(\mathsf{pk}, x = [\mathbf{h}\mathbf{y}^t] \in \mathbb{G}^{\ell \times (\ell-1)}, w = \mathbf{y} \in \mathbb{Z}_p^{\ell-1}, \tau)$:
- *Parse* $\mathsf{p} = (\mathbb{G}, p, g, [\mathbf{h}] \in \mathbb{G}^\ell)$ *and* $\mathsf{pk} = ([f], [f'] \in \mathbb{G}, r, \mathsf{s})$.
- *Let* $[\mathbf{d}] = ([f]\mathbf{y}) + (\mathsf{CRHF}_\mathsf{s}(x, \tau)[f']\mathbf{y})$.
- *Return* $\mathsf{k} = \mathsf{Ext}([\mathbf{d}^t], r)$.

Decap $(\mathsf{sk}, x = [\mathbf{E}] \in \mathbb{G}^{\ell \times (\ell-1)}, \tau)$:
- *Parse* $\mathsf{p} = (\mathbb{G}, p, g, [\mathbf{h}] \in \mathbb{G}^\ell)$ *and* $\mathsf{pk} = ([f], [f'] \in \mathbb{G}, r, \mathsf{s})$.
- *Parse* $\mathsf{sk} = (\mathbf{a} \in \mathbb{Z}_p^\ell, \mathbf{b} \in \mathbb{Z}_p^\ell)$.
- *Parse* $x = [\mathbf{E}] \in \mathbb{G}^{\ell \times (\ell-1)}$.
- *Return* $\mathsf{k} = \mathsf{Ext}(\mathbf{a}^t[\mathbf{E}] + \mathsf{CRHF}_\mathsf{s}(x, \tau)\mathbf{b}^t[\mathbf{E}], r)$.

Correctness. For any $(\mathsf{p} = (\mathbb{G}, p, g, [\mathbf{h}]), \mathsf{td}_\mathcal{L})$ in the range of Gen, $(\mathsf{pk} = (\mathbf{a}^t[\mathbf{h}], \mathbf{b}^t[\mathbf{h}], r, \mathsf{s}), \mathsf{sk} = (\mathbf{a}, \mathbf{b}))$ in the range of KeyGen, and $[\mathbf{h}\mathbf{y}^t] \in \mathcal{L}$ we have $\mathsf{Encap}(\mathsf{pk}, [\mathbf{h}\mathbf{y}^t])$ outputs

$$\mathsf{k} = \mathsf{Ext}\left((([f]\mathbf{y}) + ([f]\mathsf{CRHF}_\mathsf{s}(x, \tau)\mathbf{y}))^t, r\right) = \mathsf{Ext}\left([(\mathbf{a}^t\mathbf{h})\mathbf{y}^t + \mathsf{CRHF}_\mathsf{s}(x, \tau)(\mathbf{b}^t\mathbf{h})\mathbf{y}^t], r\right).$$

On the other hand, decapsulation outputs

$$\mathsf{k} = \mathsf{Ext}(\mathbf{a}^t[\mathbf{h}\mathbf{y}^t] + \mathsf{CRHF}_\mathsf{s}(x, \tau)\mathbf{b}^t[\mathbf{h}\mathbf{y}^t], r) = \mathsf{Ext}\left([(\mathbf{a}^t\mathbf{h})\mathbf{y}^t + \mathsf{CRHF}_\mathsf{s}(x, \tau)(\mathbf{b}^t\mathbf{h})\mathbf{y}^t], r\right)$$

Language Indistinguishability. Since we use the same language as in Construction 2 the language indistinguishability holds by the same argument.

2-Smoothness. For all $\lambda, n \in \mathbb{N}$, $(\mathsf{p}, \mathsf{td}_\mathcal{L})$ in the range of $\mathsf{Gen}(p)$, $x, x' \in X \setminus \mathcal{L}$, two tags τ, τ' such that $(x, \tau) \neq (x', \tau')$, let $(\mathsf{pk}, \mathsf{sk}) \leftarrow \mathsf{KeyGen}(p)$ and sample $\mathsf{k} \leftarrow_\$ \{0,1\}^m$. Let $\gamma \leftarrow \mathsf{CRHF}_\mathsf{s}(x, \tau)$ and $\gamma' \leftarrow \mathsf{CRHF}_\mathsf{s}(x', \tau')$. Using $(x, \tau) \neq (x', \tau')$ and the collision resistance of CRHF we can assume that $\gamma \neq \gamma'$.

In the following let $\mathbf{d} = \mathbf{a}^t[\mathbf{E}] + \gamma \mathbf{b}^t[\mathbf{E}]$ (computed in $\mathsf{Decap}(\mathsf{sk}, x, \tau)$) and $\mathbf{d}' = \mathbf{a}^t[\mathbf{E}'] + \gamma'\mathbf{b}^t[\mathbf{E}']$ (computed in $\mathsf{Decap}(\mathsf{sk}, x', \tau')$). Then the following equation holds:

$$(f \ f' \ \mathbf{d}^t \ \mathbf{d}'^t) = (\mathbf{a}^t \ \mathbf{b}^t) \begin{pmatrix} \mathbf{h} & 0 & \mathbf{E} & \mathbf{E}' \\ 0 & \mathbf{h} & \gamma\mathbf{E} & \gamma'\mathbf{E}' \end{pmatrix}$$

If $x, x' \in X \setminus \mathcal{L}$ then there exists a column $\mathbf{z}$ with index i in $\mathbf{E}$ s.t. $\mathbf{z}$ is linearly independent of $\mathbf{h}$ and $\mathbf{z}'$ with index i' in $\mathbf{E}'$ s.t. $\mathbf{z}'$ is l.i. of $\mathbf{h}$. Then the following equation also holds:

$$(f \ f' \ d_i \ d'_{i'}) = (\mathbf{a}^t \ \mathbf{b}^t) \begin{pmatrix} \mathbf{h} & 0 & \mathbf{z} & \mathbf{z}' \\ 0 & \mathbf{h} & \gamma\mathbf{z} & \gamma'\mathbf{z}' \end{pmatrix}$$

Now, we argue that the matrix on the right side has rank 4. We have that $\begin{pmatrix} \mathbf{h} \\ 0 \end{pmatrix}$ and $\begin{pmatrix} 0 \\ \mathbf{h} \end{pmatrix}$ are linearly independent. Moreover, $\begin{pmatrix} \mathbf{z} \\ \gamma\mathbf{z} \end{pmatrix}$ is outside the span of $\begin{pmatrix} \mathbf{h} \\ 0 \end{pmatrix}$ and $\begin{pmatrix} 0 \\ \mathbf{h} \end{pmatrix}$ because $\mathbf{h}$ and $\mathbf{z}$ are linearly independent. Finally, $\begin{pmatrix} \mathbf{z}' \\ \gamma'\mathbf{z}' \end{pmatrix}$ is outside the span of $\begin{pmatrix} \mathbf{z} \\ \gamma\mathbf{z} \end{pmatrix}, \begin{pmatrix} \mathbf{h} \\ 0 \end{pmatrix}$, and $\begin{pmatrix} 0 \\ \mathbf{h} \end{pmatrix}$. To see this, assume that this is not the case, i.e., that there exists a linear combination

$$\begin{pmatrix} \mathbf{z}' \\ \gamma'\mathbf{z}' \end{pmatrix} = c_1 \begin{pmatrix} \mathbf{z} \\ \gamma\mathbf{z} \end{pmatrix} + c_2 \begin{pmatrix} \mathbf{h} \\ 0 \end{pmatrix} + c_3 \begin{pmatrix} 0 \\ \mathbf{h} \end{pmatrix}.$$

Assume there exist $c_1, c_2, c_3 \in \mathbb{N}^+$ such that $\mathbf{z}' = c_1\mathbf{z} + c_2\mathbf{h}$ and $\gamma'\mathbf{z}' = c_1\gamma\mathbf{z} + c_3\mathbf{h}$. Then we replace $\mathbf{z}'$ in the second equation

$$\gamma'(c_1\mathbf{z} + c_2\mathbf{h}) = c_1\gamma\mathbf{z} + c_3\mathbf{h}$$
$$\Leftrightarrow (\gamma' - \gamma)c_1\mathbf{z} = (c_3 - \gamma'c_2)\mathbf{h}$$

This however can only be true if $\gamma' - \gamma = 0$ because $\mathbf{z}$ is linearly independent of $\mathbf{h}$.

Since $\mathbf{a}$ and $\mathbf{b}$ are chosen uniformly at random then so are f, f', d_i, and d'_i. If d_i and d'_i are uniformly random then $\mathsf{Decap}(\mathsf{sk}, x, \tau) = \mathsf{Ext}(\mathbf{d}^t, r)$ and $\mathsf{Decap}(\mathsf{sk}, x', \tau') = \mathsf{Ext}(\mathbf{d}'^t, r)$ are statistically close to uniformly random by the extractor property.

Parameters. For the same language as in Construction 2 with public parameters of size $k^{1/3} \cdot \mathsf{poly}(\lambda)$ and elements of $k^{2/3} \cdot \mathsf{poly}(\lambda)$ Construction 3 roughly results in public keys of size $2k^{1/3} \cdot \mathsf{poly}(\lambda)$ and an encapsulated key of size λ.

6 Incompressible PKE from Incompressible SKE and HPS

First we extend the incompressible encryption security notion [32] to the chosen ciphertext scenario and then we show a new construction paradigm using hash proof systems and incompressible symmetric-key encryption.

6.1 CCA Incompressible Encryption

We use the definition of incompressible encryption by Guan et al. [32]. It defines a public-key encryption scheme where the adversary has to know most of the ciphertext to decrypt it even with access to the secret key.

Definition 11 (Incompressible PKE). *An incompressible public-key encryption scheme is a triple of PPT algorithms*

$(\mathsf{pk}, \mathsf{sk}) \leftarrow \mathsf{KeyGen}(1^\lambda, 1^S)$: *Given the security parameter λ and a space bound S the key-generation algorithm outputs a public key* pk *and a secret key* sk.
$c \leftarrow \mathsf{Enc}(\mathsf{pk}, \mathsf{m})$: *Given a public key* pk *and a message* m *the encryption algorithm outputs a ciphertext c.*
$\mathsf{m} \leftarrow \mathsf{Dec}(\mathsf{sk}, c)$: *Given a secret key* sk *and a ciphertext c the decryption algorithm outputs a message* m.

Both size of message space and size of ciphertext space are polynomials over security parameter λ and space bound S, that is, $n = n(\lambda, S)$ and $l = l(\lambda, S)$ respectively.

Correctness. For all $\lambda, S \in \mathbb{N}$, messages m and $(\mathsf{pk}, \mathsf{sk})$ in the range of KeyGen we have that $\mathsf{m} = \mathsf{Dec}(\mathsf{sk}, \mathsf{Enc}(\mathsf{pk}, \mathsf{m}))$.

CCA Incompressible Security. Similar to standard IND-CCA (sometimes referred to as IND-CCA2) security we extend incompressible encryption such that the adversary has access to an encryption oracle.

For security parameter λ and space bound S, a public key encryption scheme (KeyGen, Enc, Dec) has incompressible CCA PKE security if for all PPT adversaries $\mathcal{A} = (\mathcal{A}_1, \mathcal{A}_2, \mathcal{A}_3)$ wins the following experiment with probability $\leq \frac{1}{2} + \mathsf{negl}(\lambda)$.

$\mathsf{Dist}_{\mathcal{A}, \Pi}^{\mathsf{CCAIncomPKE}}(\lambda, S)$ **Experiment:**
  - Run key generation algorithm $\mathsf{KeyGen}(1^\lambda, 1^S)$ to obtain $(\mathsf{pk}, \mathsf{sk})$.
  - Run the adversary $\mathsf{m}_0, \mathsf{m}_1, \mathsf{st}_1 \leftarrow \mathcal{A}_1^{\mathsf{Dec}_{\mathsf{sk}}}(\mathsf{pk})$ on public key pk with oracle access to $\mathsf{Dec}(\mathsf{sk}, \cdot)$ to receive two messages $\mathsf{m}_0, \mathsf{m}_1$ and state st_1.
  - Sample bit $b \leftarrow_\$ \{0, 1\}$ uniformly at random.
  - Run $c \leftarrow \mathsf{Enc}(\mathsf{pk}, \mathsf{m}_b)$ to encrypt m_b.
  - Run the adversary $\mathsf{st}_2 \leftarrow \mathcal{A}_2^{\mathsf{Dec}_{\mathsf{sk}}}(\mathsf{pk}, c, \mathsf{st}_1)$ with oracle access to $\mathsf{Dec}(\mathsf{sk}, \cdot)$ for all inputs but c to produce a state st_2 smaller than S.
  - Run the final adversary $b' \leftarrow \mathcal{A}_3(\mathsf{sk}, \mathsf{st}_1, \mathsf{st}_2, \mathsf{m}_0, \mathsf{m}_1)$.
  - The adversary wins if $b = b'$.

Rate. We define the rate by $\frac{|\mathsf{m}|}{|\mathsf{Enc}(\mathsf{pk}, \mathsf{m})|}$ the size of a message divided by a ciphertext encrypting the message. We say a scheme has rate-1 when the rate is $1 - o(1)$.

6.2 Construction

We construct a encryption scheme that very much resembles the classic Cramer-Shoup [17] scheme. Instead of masking the ciphertext with the randomness that comes out of the hash proof system we use it as a key for an incompressible symmetric-key encryption scheme.

Construction 4 (Incompressible PKE). *Given security parameter λ, space bound S, and message length n let (KeyGen$'$, Encap$'$, Decap$'$, Program$'$) be a Y-programmable hash proof system for a language $\mathcal{L} \subset X$ (where you can sample x with according witness from $\mathcal{L}$ and sample x with according trapdoor from Y) where the representation size of X is $p(\lambda, S, n)$ and encapsulated keys of size $k(\lambda, S_{\mathsf{sym}}, n)$, (KeyGen$''$, Encap$''$, Decap$''$) is a 2-smooth hash proof system for the same language with encapsulation key size of λ and public key size $p'(\lambda, S, n)$, and (Enc$_{\mathsf{sym}}$, Dec$_{\mathsf{sym}}$) be an incompressible SKE with messages of size n, keys of size $k(\lambda, S_{\mathsf{sym}}, n)$ and ciphertexts of size $l(\lambda, S_{\mathsf{sym}}, n)$ with incompressible SKE adversary being allowed to leak a state of size $S_{\mathsf{sym}} = S + p(\lambda, S, n) + p'(\lambda, S, n)$.*

KeyGen($1^\lambda, 1^S$):
- *Generate language and corresponding trapdoor* $(\mathsf{p}, \mathsf{td}_\mathcal{L}) \leftarrow \mathsf{Gen}(1^\lambda, 1^n)$.
- *Let* $(\mathsf{pk}', \mathsf{sk}') \leftarrow \mathsf{KeyGen}'(\mathsf{p})$.
- *Let* $(\mathsf{pk}'', \mathsf{sk}'') \leftarrow \mathsf{KeyGen}''(\mathsf{p})$.
- *Return* $\mathsf{pk} = (\mathsf{pk}', \mathsf{pk}'')$ *and* $\mathsf{sk} = (\mathsf{sk}', \mathsf{sk}'')$.

Enc(pk, m):
- *Parse* $\mathsf{pk} = (\mathsf{pk}', \mathsf{pk}'')$
- *Let* $(x, w) \leftarrow \mathsf{samp}\mathcal{L}(\mathsf{p})$.
- *Let* $\mathsf{k} \leftarrow \mathsf{Encap}'(\mathsf{pk}', x, w)$.
- *Let* $c_{\mathsf{sym}} \leftarrow \mathsf{Enc}_{\mathsf{sym}}(\mathsf{k}, \mathsf{m})$.
- *Let* $\pi \leftarrow \mathsf{Encap}''(\mathsf{pk}'', x, w, c_{\mathsf{sym}})$.
- *Return* $c = (x, c_{\mathsf{sym}}, \pi)$.

Dec(sk, c):
- *Parse* $\mathsf{sk} = (\mathsf{sk}', \mathsf{sk}'')$.
- *Parse* $c = (x, c_{\mathsf{sym}}, \pi)$.
- *If* $\pi = \mathsf{Decap}''(\mathsf{sk}'', x, c_{\mathsf{sym}})$
  - *Let* $\mathsf{k} \leftarrow \mathsf{Decap}'(\mathsf{sk}', x)$
  - *Return* $\mathsf{m} = \mathsf{Dec}_{\mathsf{sym}}(\mathsf{k}, c_{\mathsf{sym}})$.
- *Return* $\perp$.

Parameters. (KeyGen, Enc, Dec) is an incompressible PKE with messages of size n, ciphertexts of size $l(\lambda, S_{\mathsf{sym}}, n) + p(\lambda, S, n) + p'(\lambda, S, n)$, the adversary is allowed a leak of size $S = S_{\mathsf{sym}} - p(\lambda, S, n) - p'(\lambda, S, n)$, and the public key is of size $p(\lambda, S, n) + p'(\lambda, S, n)$.

When instantiating the two hash proof systems with Constructions 2, 3 and the incompressible SKE with Construction 1 then (KeyGen, Enc, Dec) is an incompressible PKE with messages of size n, ciphertexts of size $(n + n^{2/3}\mathsf{poly}(\lambda))(1 + o(1))$, the adversary is allowed a leak of size $S = n(1 - o(1)) - \mathsf{poly}(\lambda)(n(1 + o(1)))^{2/3}$, the public key is of size $n^{2/3}(1 + o(1))\mathsf{poly}(\lambda)$, and the secret key is of size $n(1 + o(1))\mathsf{poly}(\lambda)$.

Correctness. Follows from the correctness of (KeyGen′, Encap′, Decap′, Program′), (KeyGen″, Encap″, Decap″), and (Enc$_{sym}$, Dec$_{sym}$).

Theorem 4 (Security). *The PKE Construction 4 has incompressible CCA PKE security if (KeyGen′, Encap′, Decap′, Program′) is a programmable hash proof system with the listed parameters, (KeyGen″, Encap″, Decap″) is a 2-smooth hash proof system with the listed parameters, and (Enc$_{sym}$, Dec$_{sym}$) is an incompressible secure SKE with the listed parameters.*

The proof of this theorem can be found in the full version [11] of this paper.

Acknowledgement. We would like to thank Stefan Dziembowski, Daniel Wichs, and the anonymous reviewers of TCC for discussions and comments.

Nico Döttling is funded by the European Union. Views and opinions expressed are however those of the author(s) only and do not necessarily reflect those of the European Union or the European Research Council Executive Agency. Neither the European Union nor the granting authority can be held responsible for them. (ERC-2021-STG 101041207 LACONIC).

Part of the work of Pedro Branco was done while at IST University of Lisbon.

References

1. Abdalla, M., Benhamouda, F., Pointcheval, D.: Disjunctions for hash proof systems: new constructions and applications. In: Oswald, E., Fischlin, M. (eds.) Advances in Cryptology - EUROCRYPT 2015, Part II. LNCS, vol. 9057, pp. 69–100. Springer, Heidelberg (2015). https://doi.org/10.1007/978-3-662-46803-6_3
2. Alamati, N., De Feo, L., Montgomery, H., Patranabis, S.: Cryptographic group actions and applications. In: Moriai, S., Wang, H. (eds.) Advances in Cryptology - ASIACRYPT 2020, Part II. LNCS, vol. 12492, pp. 411–439. Springer, Heidelberg (2020). https://doi.org/10.1007/978-3-030-64834-3_14
3. Alwen, J., Dodis, Y., Naor, M., Segev, G., Walfish, S., Wichs, D.: Public-key encryption in the bounded-retrieval model. In: Gilbert, H. (ed.) Advances in Cryptology - EUROCRYPT 2010. LNCS, vol. 6110, pp. 113–134. Springer, Heidelberg (2010). https://doi.org/10.1007/978-3-642-13190-5_6
4. Alwen, J., Dodis, Y., Wichs, D.: Leakage-resilient public-key cryptography in the bounded-retrieval model. In: Halevi, S. (ed.) Advances in Cryptology - CRYPTO 2009. LNCS, vol. 5677, pp. 36–54. Springer, Heidelberg (2009). https://doi.org/10.1007/978-3-642-03356-8_3
5. Aumann, Y., Rabin, M.O.: Information theoretically secure communication in the limited storage space model. In: Wiener, M.J. (ed.) Advances in Cryptology - CRYPTO 2099. LNCS, vol. 1666, pp. 65–79. Springer, Heidelberg (1999). https://doi.org/10.1007/3-540-48405-1_5
6. Barak, B., et al.: On the (im)possibility of obfuscating programs. In: Kilian, J. (ed.) Advances in Cryptology - CRYPTO 2001. LNCS, vol. 2139, pp. 1–18. Springer, Heidelberg (2001). https://doi.org/10.1007/3-540-44647-8_1
7. Bellare, M., Boldyreva, A., Palacio, A.: An uninstantiable random-oracle-model scheme for a hybrid-encryption problem. In: Cachin, C., Camenisch, J. (eds.) Advances in Cryptology - EUROCRYPT 2004. LNCS, vol. 3027, pp. 171–188. Springer, Heidelberg (2004). https://doi.org/10.1007/978-3-540-24676-3_11

8. Bellare, M., Dai, W.: Defending against key exfiltration: efficiency improvements for big-key cryptography via large-alphabet subkey prediction. In: Thuraisingham, B.M., Evans, D., Malkin, T., Xu, D. (eds.) ACM CCS 2017: 24th Conference on Computer and Communications Security, pp. 923–940. ACM Press, Dallas, TX, USA (2017). https://doi.org/10.1145/3133956.3133965

9. Bellare, M., Kane, D., Rogaway, P.: Big-key symmetric encryption: resisting key exfiltration. In: Robshaw, M., Katz, J. (eds.) Advances in Cryptology - CRYPTO 2016, Part I. LNCS, vol. 9814, pp. 373–402. Springer, Heidelberg (2016). https://doi.org/10.1007/978-3-662-53018-4_14

10. Black, J.: The ideal-cipher model, revisited: an uninstantiable blockcipher-based hash function. In: Robshaw, M.J.B. (ed.) Fast Software Encryption - FSE 2006. LNCS, vol. 4047, pp. 328–340. Springer, Heidelberg (2006). https://doi.org/10.1007/11799313_21

11. Branco, P., Döttling, N., Dujmovic, J.: Rate-1 incompressible encryption from standard assumptions. IACR Cryptol. ePrint Arch. 697 (2022). https://eprint.iacr.org/2022/697

12. Brzuska, C., Farshim, P., Mittelbach, A.: Random-oracle uninstantiability from indistinguishability obfuscation. In: Dodis, Y., Nielsen, J.B. (eds.) TCC 2015: 12th Theory of Cryptography Conference, Part II. LNCS, vol. 9015, pp. 428–455. Springer, Heidelberg (2015). https://doi.org/10.1007/978-3-662-46497-7_17

13. Cachin, C., Maurer, U.: Unconditional security against memory-bounded adversaries. In: Kaliski, B.S. (ed.) CRYPTO 1997. LNCS, vol. 1294, pp. 292–306. Springer, Heidelberg (1997). https://doi.org/10.1007/BFb0052243

14. Canetti, R., Goldreich, O., Halevi, S.: The random oracle methodology, revisited. J. ACM **51**(4), 557–594 (2004). https://doi.org/10.1145/1008731.1008734

15. Chevalier, C., Fouque, P.A., Pointcheval, D., Zimmer, S.: Optimal randomness extraction from a Diffie-Hellman element. In: Joux, A. (ed.) Advances in Cryptology - EUROCRYPT 2009. LNCS, vol. 5479, pp. 572–589. Springer, Heidelberg (2009). https://doi.org/10.1007/978-3-642-01001-9_33

16. Cramer, R., Shoup, V.: A practical public key cryptosystem provably secure against adaptive chosen ciphertext attack. In: Krawczyk, H. (ed.) CRYPTO 1998. LNCS, vol. 1462, pp. 13–25. Springer, Heidelberg (1998). https://doi.org/10.1007/BFb0055717

17. Cramer, R., Shoup, V.: Universal hash proofs and a paradigm for adaptive chosen ciphertext secure public-key encryption. In: Knudsen, L.R. (ed.) Advances in Cryptology - EUROCRYPT 2002. LNCS, vol. 2332, pp. 45–64. Springer, Heidelberg (2002). https://doi.org/10.1007/3-540-46035-7_4

18. Cramer, R., Shoup, V.: Design and analysis of practical public-key encryption schemes secure against adaptive chosen ciphertext attack. SIAM J. Comput. **33**(1), 167–226 (2003)

19. Damgård, I., Ganesh, C., Orlandi, C.: Proofs of replicated storage without timing assumptions. In: Boldyreva, A., Micciancio, D. (eds.) Advances in Cryptology - CRYPTO 2019, Part I. LNCS, vol. 11692, pp. 355–380. Springer, Heidelberg (2019). https://doi.org/10.1007/978-3-030-26948-7_13

20. Damgård, I., Jurik, M.: A generalisation, a simplification and some applications of Paillier's probabilistic public-key system. In: Kim, K. (ed.) PKC 2001: 4th International Workshop on Theory and Practice in Public Key Cryptography. LNCS, vol. 1992, pp. 119–136. Springer, Heidelberg (2001). https://doi.org/10.1007/3-540-44586-2_9

21. Dent, A.W.: Adapting the weaknesses of the random oracle model to the generic group model. In: Zheng, Y. (ed.) Advances in Cryptology - ASIACRYPT 2002. LNCS, vol. 2501, pp. 100–109. Springer, Heidelberg (2002). https://doi.org/10.1007/3-540-36178-2_6

22. Di Crescenzo, G., Lipton, R.J., Walfish, S.: Perfectly secure password protocols in the bounded retrieval model. In: Halevi, S., Rabin, T. (eds.) TCC 2006: 3rd Theory of Cryptography Conference. LNCS, vol. 3876, pp. 225–244. Springer, Heidelberg (2006). https://doi.org/10.1007/11681878_12

23. Dodis, Y., Ostrovsky, R., Reyzin, L., Smith, A.: Fuzzy extractors: How to generate strong keys from biometrics and other noisy data. SIAM J. Comput. 38(1), 97–139 (2008). https://doi.org/10.1137/060651380, https://doi.org/10.1137/060651380

24. Dodis, Y., Quach, W., Wichs, D.: Speak much, remember little: cryptography in the bounded storage model, revisited. Cryptology ePrint Archive, Report 2021/1270 (2021). https://eprint.iacr.org/2021/1270

25. Dziembowski, S.: Intrusion-resilience via the bounded-storage model. In: Halevi, S., Rabin, T. (eds.) TCC 2006: 3rd Theory of Cryptography Conference. LNCS, vol. 3876, pp. 207–224. Springer, Heidelberg (2006). https://doi.org/10.1007/11681878_11

26. Dziembowski, S.: On forward-secure storage (extended abstract). In: Dwork, C. (ed.) Advances in Cryptology - CRYPTO 2006. LNCS, vol. 4117, pp. 251–270. Springer, Heidelberg (2006). https://doi.org/10.1007/11818175_15

27. Garg, R., Lu, G., Waters, B.: New techniques in replica encodings with client setup. In: Pass, R., Pietrzak, K. (eds.) TCC 2020: 18th Theory of Cryptography Conference, Part III. LNCS, vol. 12552, pp. 550–583. Springer, Heidelberg (2020). https://doi.org/10.1007/978-3-030-64381-2_20

28. Garg, S., Gentry, C., Halevi, S., Raykova, M., Sahai, A., Waters, B.: Candidate indistinguishability obfuscation and functional encryption for all circuits. In: 54th Annual Symposium on Foundations of Computer Science, pp. 40–49. IEEE Computer Society Press, Berkeley, CA, USA (2013). https://doi.org/10.1109/FOCS.2013.13

29. Goldwasser, S., Kalai, Y.T.: On the (in)security of the Fiat-Shamir paradigm. In: 44th Annual Symposium on Foundations of Computer Science, pp. 102–115. IEEE Computer Society Press, Cambridge, MA, USA (2003). https://doi.org/10.1109/SFCS.2003.1238185

30. Gorbunov, S., Vaikuntanathan, V., Wee, H.: Functional encryption with bounded collusions via multi-party computation. In: Safavi-Naini, R., Canetti, R. (eds.) Advances in Cryptology - CRYPTO 2012. LNCS, vol. 7417, pp. 162–179. Springer, Heidelberg (2012). https://doi.org/10.1007/978-3-642-32009-5_11

31. Goyal, R., Koppula, V., Waters, B.: Lockable obfuscation. In: Umans, C. (ed.) 58th Annual Symposium on Foundations of Computer Science, pp. 612–621. IEEE Computer Society Press, Berkeley, CA, USA (2017). https://doi.org/10.1109/FOCS.2017.62

32. Guan, J., Wichs, D., Zhandry, M.: Incompressible cryptography. In: Dunkelman, O., Dziembowski, S. (eds.) Advances in Cryptology - EUROCRYPT 2022, Part I. LNCS, vol. 13275, pp. 700–730. Springer, Heidelberg (2022). https://doi.org/10.1007/978-3-031-06944-4_24

33. Guan, J., Zhandry, M.: Simple schemes in the bounded storage model. In: Ishai, Y., Rijmen, V. (eds.) Advances in Cryptology - EUROCRYPT 2019, Part III. LNCS, vol. 11478, pp. 500–524. Springer, Heidelberg (2019). https://doi.org/10.1007/978-3-030-17659-4_17

34. Guan, J., Zhandry, M.: Disappearing cryptography in the bounded storage model. In: Nissim, K., Waters, B. (eds.) TCC 2021: 19th Theory of Cryptography Conference, Part II. LNCS, vol. 13043, pp. 365–396. Springer, Heidelberg (2021). https://doi.org/10.1007/978-3-030-90453-1_13

35. Håstad, J., Impagliazzo, R., Levin, L.A., Luby, M.: A pseudorandom generator from any one-way function. SIAM J. Comput. **28**(4), 1364–1396 (1999)

36. Hazay, C., López-Alt, A., Wee, H., Wichs, D.: Leakage-resilient cryptography from minimal assumptions. In: Johansson, T., Nguyen, P.Q. (eds.) Advances in Cryptology - EUROCRYPT 2013. LNCS, vol. 7881, pp. 160–176. Springer, Heidelberg (2013). https://doi.org/10.1007/978-3-642-38348-9_10

37. Jain, A., Lin, H., Sahai, A.: Indistinguishability obfuscation from well-founded assumptions. In: STOC, pp. 60–73. ACM (2021)

38. Kalai, Y.T.: Smooth projective hashing and two-message oblivious transfer. In: Cramer, R. (ed.) Advances in Cryptology - EUROCRYPT 2005. LNCS, vol. 3494, pp. 78–95. Springer, Heidelberg(2005). https://doi.org/10.1007/11426639_5

39. Maurer, U.: Conditionally-perfect secrecy and a provably-secure randomized cipher. J. Cryptol. **5**(1), 53–66 (1992)

40. Maurer, U.M.: Protocols for secret key agreement by public discussion based on common information. In: Brickell, E.F. (ed.) Advances in Cryptology - CRYPTO 1992. LNCS, vol. 740, pp. 461–470. Springer, Heidelberg (1993). https://doi.org/10.1007/3-540-48071-4_32

41. Maurer, U.M., Renner, R., Holenstein, C.: Indifferentiability, impossibility results on reductions, and applications to the random oracle methodology. In: Naor, M. (ed.) TCC 2004: 1st Theory of Cryptography Conference. LNCS, vol. 2951, pp. 21–39. Springer, Heidelberg (2004). https://doi.org/10.1007/978-3-540-24638-1_2

42. Moran, T., Wichs, D.: Incompressible encodings. In: Micciancio, D., Ristenpart, T. (eds.) Advances in Cryptology - CRYPTO 2020, Part I. LNCS, vol. 12170, pp. 494–523. Springer, Heidelberg (2020). https://doi.org/10.1007/978-3-030-56784-2_17

43. Naor, M.: On cryptographic assumptions and challenges (invited talk). In: Boneh, D. (ed.) Advances in Cryptology - CRYPTO 2003. LNCS, vol. 2729, pp. 96–109. Springer, Heidelberg 2003). https://doi.org/10.1007/978-3-540-45146-4_6

44. Paillier, P.: Public-key cryptosystems based on composite degree residuosity classes. In: Stern, J. (ed.) Advances in Cryptology - EUROCRYPT 19 LNCS, vol. 1592, pp. 223–238. Springer, Heidelberg 1999). https://doi.org/10.1007/3-540-48910-X_16

45. Raz, R.: A time-space lower bound for a large class of learning problems. In: Umans, C. (ed.) 58th Annual Symposium on Foundations of Computer Science,pp. 732–742. IEEE Computer Society Press, Berkeley, CA, USA (2017). https://doi.org/10.1109/FOCS.2017.73

46. Regev, O.: On lattices, learning with errors, random linear codes, and cryptography. In: Gabow, H.N., Fagin, R. (eds.) 37th Annual ACM Symposium on Theory of Computing, pp. 84–93. ACM Press, Baltimore, MA, USA (2005). https://doi.org/10.1145/1060590.1060603

Achievable **CCA2** Relaxation
for Homomorphic Encryption

Adi Akavia[1]([✉])(iD), Craig Gentry[2], Shai Halevi[3](iD), and Margarita Vald[4](iD)

[1] University of Haifa, Haifa, Israel
adi.akavia@gmail.com
[2] TripleBlind, New York City, USA
[3] Algorand Foundation, New York City, USA
shaih@alum.mit.edu
[4] Intuit Inc., Petah Tikva, Israel
margarita.vald@cs.tau.ac.il

Abstract. Homomorphic encryption (HE) protects data in-use, but can be computationally expensive. To avoid the costly bootstrapping procedure that refreshes ciphertexts, some works have explored client-aided outsourcing protocols, where the client intermittently refreshes ciphertexts for a server that is performing homomorphic computations. But is this approach secure against malicious servers?

We present a CPA-secure encryption scheme that is completely insecure in this setting. We define a new notion of security, called *funcCPA*, that we prove is sufficient. Additionally, we show:

- Homomorphic encryption schemes that have a certain type of circuit privacy – for example, schemes in which ciphertexts can be "sanitized" – are funcCPA-secure.
- In particular, assuming certain existing HE schemes are CPA-secure, they are also funcCPA-secure.
- For certain encryption schemes, like Brakerski-Vaikuntanathan, that have a property that we call oblivious secret key extraction, funcCPA-security implies circular security – i.e., that it is secure to provide an encryption of the secret key in a form usable for bootstrapping (to construct fully homomorphic encryption).

Namely, funcCPA-security lies strictly between CPA-security and CCA2-security (under reasonable assumptions), and has an interesting relationship with circular security, though it is not known to be equivalent.

1 Introduction

Homomorphic encryption (HE) supports computing over encrypted data without access to the secret key. HE is a prominent approach to safeguarding data and

The first author thanks the Israel Science Foundation (grant 3380/19) and Israel National Cyber Directorate via the Haifa, BIU and Tel-Aviv cyber centers for their support. The fourth author thanks Yaron Sheffer for helpful discussions. Pre-prints for preliminary versions of this works appeared in [2,3,7].

E. Kiltz and V. Vaikuntanathan (Eds.): TCC 2022, LNCS 13748, pp. 70–99, 2022.
https://doi.org/10.1007/978-3-031-22365-5_3

minimizing the impact of potential breaches, especially useful for outsourcing of computations over sensitive data, as required by the industry cloud-based architecture.

The security notion achievable for HE schemes is security against chosen-plaintext attack (CPA-security), whereas it is well known that security against chosen-ciphertext attack (CCA2-security) is not achievable due to the inherent malleability of HE schemes. However, CPA-security is not always sufficient for securing protocols, as it considers only honestly generated ciphertexts and has no guarantees in settings where an adversary is allowed to inject its own maliciously crafted ciphertexts into an honest system (see e.g. [40], Chap. 10). Therefore, relying on CPA-security typically secures protocols only against semi-honest adversaries e.g. in [1, 4, 6, 8, 25, 29, 42] (unless further cryptographic tools are employed to enhance security).

In practice however security against malicious adversaries is desired to combat real-life attacks. A natural question therefore is the following:

Is there a relaxation of CCA2-security that is achievable for HE schemes and secures protocols against malicious attackers?

Our Contribution. In this work we answer affirmatively the above question by providing a new security notion, showing it is achievable for HE schemes and that it guarantees privacy against malicious adversaries for a wide and natural family of protocols.

The new security notion, named *function-chosen-plaintext-attack* (funcCPA-security), is a relaxation of CCA2 security for public key encryption schemes. Concretely, while CCA2 security captures resiliency against adversaries that receive decryptions of ciphertexts of their choice, funcCPA guarantees resiliency only against adversaries that receive re-encryptions of the underlying cleartext values of ciphertexts of their choice (or, more generally, encryptions of the result of a computation on those values); See Definition 6. That is, in funcCPA the adversary sees only ciphertexts, no cleartext values; nonetheless, the adversary has full control on the computation performed on the underlying values, even without knowing them, and can inject maliciously crafted ciphertexts.

We note that funcCPA-security is clearly implied by CCA2, moreover, we show it is a strict weakening of CCA2 by showing it is achievable for HE schemes (where CCA2-security is not). Furthermore, funcCPA-security implies CPA-security, but not vice-versa. To prove the latter, we provide: (1) a security proof showing, for a wide and natural family of outsourcing protocols (named, *client-aided outsourcing protocols*), that they preserve privacy when instantiated with any funcCPA-secure encryption scheme; and (2) an attack that breaks privacy in these protocols when instantiated with a (carefully crafted) CPA-secure encryption scheme. This shows that funcCPA-security lies strictly between CPA and CCA2 security.

To prove that funcCPA is achievable for HE schemes we show how to construct funcCPA-secure HE schemes from any CPA-secure HE scheme equipped with a sanitization algorithm, including the HE schemes of Gentry [23], Brakerski-Vaikuntanathan [12] and Ducas and Micciancio [19] (where sanitization is as defined in [20], see Definition 3).

Theorem 1 (funcCPA-secure HE scheme achievability, informal). *Every CPA-secure HE scheme with a sanitization algorithm can be transformed into a funcCPA-secure HE scheme.*

To further motivate the definition of funcCPA-security we note that many secure outsourcing protocols in the literature provide the server with the capability of seeing re-encryptions of ciphertexts of its choice, and even encrypted results of computations performed on the underlying values of such ciphertexts. For example, in [42] the client provides the server with re-encryptions for ciphertexts of the server's choice, with the goal of avoiding costly bootstrapping at the server's side. Likewise, in [1,4,6,8,25,29] the server obtains, via interaction with the client, the encrypted results of applying various computations on the underlying cleartext values of ciphertexts of its choice, including computing comparisons [8], minima [1,4], linear equations solutions [6,25], ReLU [29].

To capture and generalize secure outsourcing protocols such as discussed above [1,4,6,8,25,29], we define a natural family of protocols named: *client-aided outsourcing protocols*. This family consists of all protocols where a client generates keys and uploads encrypted data to a server; the server executes computations over the encrypted data and sends encrypted results to the client; moreover, the server may send the client (typically few and lightweight) queries of the form $(\mathbf{e}, G)$, for $\mathbf{e}$ a vector of ciphertexts and G a function, so that the client computes G on the underlying cleartext values and sends the server the encrypted result $\mathbf{e}' \leftarrow \mathsf{Enc}_{pk}(G(\mathsf{Dec}_{sk}(\mathbf{e})))$.

We prove that client-aided outsourcing protocols instantiated with funcCPA-secure schemes preserve privacy against malicious servers.

Theorem 2 (privacy against malicious servers, informal). *Client-aided outsourcing protocols instantiated with any funcCPA-secure scheme preserve privacy against malicious servers.*

Conversely, the attack we exhibit exemplifies that CPA-security does not provide privacy against malicious servers for this class of protocols.

Theorem 3 (attack, informal). *There exist CPA-secure HE schemes so that for client-aided outsourcing protocols instantiated with these schemes, there is an attack by the server that recovers the client's input.*

Achievability by existing schemes of funcCPA-security. To avoid the performance overhead incurred due to using sanitization we examine the achievability of func-CPA-security for popular HE schemes. We prove that the leveled HE schemes of BV [12], BGV [11] and B/FV [10,21] are leveled-funcCPA-secure (based on their CPA-security). That is, they satisfy a natural adaptation of funcCPA to leveled settings, where the funcCPA oracle answers queries with ciphertexts for the next level.[1] Our security proof requires essentially no modifications to the schemes

---

[1] This leveled-funcCPA oracle is useful, for example, in applications where the oracle is employed to replace deep homomorphic computations that will consume many levels of the scheme by a query to the oracle that consumes only a single level.

(other than a slight change in their evaluation keys generation that has little influence on performance) and without any extra security assumptions.

Theorem 4 (leveled HE are leveled-funcCPA-secure, informal). *The leveled HE schemes of BV, BGV, B/FV are leveled-funcCPA-secure.*

More generally, the above holds for every leveled HE scheme with keys generated independently for each level (as specified in Definition 9).

In contrast, for the homomorphic schemes of BV and BGV we show that func-CPA-security implies (weak) circular security. Concretely, we show that the func-CPA oracle enables generating from the public key an encryption of the secret key (in the encoding required for bootstrapping), and thus funcCPA-security eliminates the need for the weak circular security assumption. This can be interpreted as a barrier on proving funcCPA-security for these schemes, as it would resolve the long standing open problem on the necessity of circular security assumption (see e.g. Question 11 in Peikert's survey [37]).

Theorem 5 (funcCPA vs. circular security, informal). *If the homomorphic encryption scheme of BV or BGV is funcCPA-secure, then it is weakly circular secure.*

On the necessity of funcCPA against semi-honest adversaries. To further study the funcCPA-security notion, we examine its necessity against semi-honest adversaries. We prove that for client-aided outsourcing protocols satisfying a natural property, CPA-security suffices against semi-honest adversaries. The property we require is that the protocol is *cleartext computable* in the sense that the client's input determines the underlying cleartext values of the ciphertexts transmitted throughout the protocol. This captures the fact that the encryption in the protocol is an external wrapping of the cleartext values, used merely for achieving privacy against the server, and does not affect the underlying cleartext computation. This property is natural in outsourcing protocols, where the server does not contribute any input to the computation but rather it is only a vessel for storing and processing encrypted data on behalf of the client.

Theorem 6 (privacy against semi-honest servers, informal). *Cleartext-computable client-aided outsourcing protocols using a CPA-secure encryption scheme preserve privacy against semi-honest servers.*

Our Techniques. Our definition of funcCPA (Definition 6) extends CPA by granting the adversary in the CPA experiment access to an $\mathsf{Enc}_{pk}(\mathcal{G}(\mathsf{Dec}_{sk}(\cdot)))$ oracle for a family of functions $\mathcal{G}$. Namely, the adversary can submit (possibly, adaptive) queries $(\mathbf{e}, G)$, for ciphertexts $\mathbf{e}$ and a function $G \in \mathcal{G}$ of its choice, and receive an encrypted result $\mathbf{e}' \leftarrow \mathsf{Enc}_{pk}(G(\mathsf{Dec}_{sk}(\mathbf{e})))$.

To prove achievability of funcCPA for sanitized HE schemes (Theorem 1), we first define the notion of circuit-privacy$^+$ that lies between the semi-honest and malicious definitions of circuit privacy in allowing maliciously formed ciphertexts but requiring honestly generated keys. We then show how to transform CPA-secure schemes with a sanitization algorithm into CPA-secure circuit-private$^+$ schemes (Lemma 2). Finally, we prove that CPA-secure circuit-private$^+$ schemes are funcCPA-secure.

For our attack proving the insufficiency of CPA-security (Theorem 3) we first show that every CPA-secure scheme can be slightly modified to yield a punctured CPA-secure scheme with which our attack is applicable. The attack uses a single query $\mathbf{e}' \leftarrow \mathsf{Enc}_{pk}(G(\mathsf{Dec}_{sk}(\mathbf{e})))$, where $\mathbf{e}$ is a concatenation of the client's encrypted input with a special "trapdoor" ciphertexts planted in the public-key. The query $\mathbf{e}$ hits the puncturing of the scheme so that the result $\mathbf{e}'$ reveals the client's input. The encryption scheme remains CPA secure, despite the puncturing, because the trapdoor ciphertext is infeasible to generate honestly i.e. by encrypting an efficiently samplable message.

Related Work. *Several CCA relaxations* were previously considered. Relaxing CCA2 by forbidding querying the decryption oracle on any ciphertext that decrypt to the same message as the challenge ciphertext (or extensions of this notion) was proposed in [13,38,41]. However, for HE this is unachievable (because the adversary can produce ciphertexts that decrypt to related messages, query the decryption oracle on those, and consequently recover the message in the challenge ciphertext).

CCA1-secure HE schemes were constructed in a line of work including [31,33]. This however seems insufficient for privacy against malicious servers in client-aided outsourcing protocols, because CCA1 does not guarantee security if non-trivial queries are submitted after the challenge. Moreover, CCA1 is known to be unachievable for *fully* homomorphic encryption schemes that follow Gentry's blueprint (because they provide an encryption of the secret key for the purpose of bootstrapping, and querying the CCA1 oracle on this ciphertext would recover the secret key and break security); and even when deviating from Gentry's blueprint, CCA1 is only known to be achievable from non-standard assumptions [14]: indistinguishability obfuscation (iO) or succinct non-interactive arguments of knowledge (SNARKs).

In contrast, we show that funcCPA-security is: (1) sufficient for guaranteeing privacy against malicious servers in client-aided outsourcing protocols; (2) achievable for HE schemes, even fully homomorphic ones that follow Gentry's blueprint; and (3) achievable from standard assumptions.

Insufficiency of CPA-security for protocols utilizing homomorphic encryption was considered by Li and Micciancio [32]. They show that protocols instantiated with the CPA-secure approximate HE schemes of CKKS [16] are insecure when the protocol exposes decryptions to the attacker, even for semi-honest adversaries. In contrast, our attack applies both to exact and approximate schemes and even when no decryptions are provided (albeit with a malicious adversary).

Prior versions of this work. Preliminary versions of this work appeared in [2,3,7]: The notion of funcCPA-security and its implication to privacy against malicious servers (Theorem 2) was introduced in [3], in the context of presenting new privacy preserving machine learning protocols. We remark that these protocols were published in [4,5], albeit with security only against semi-honest servers. The study of funcCPA was extended in [7] by introducing the generic construction of funcCPA-secure encryption from sanitization (Theorem 1); proving the insufficiency of CPA-security for privacy against malicious servers (Theorem 3); and proving the sufficiency of CPA-security for privacy against semi-honest servers in cleartext computable client-aided outsourcing protocols (Theorem 6). Open problems presented in [7] were addressed in [2], where we proved that leveled HE schemes are (leveled) funcCPA-secure (Theorem 4), and introduced connections between funcCPA and circular-security (Theorem 5). In addition, [2] introduced the observation that funcCPA w.r.t the identity function (i.e., with an oracle that can only refresh ciphertexts) implies funcCPA w.r.t an oracle that can compute all the circuits for which the scheme is homomorphic (Lemma 1).

Follow-up Work. A follow-up work by Nuida [35] proposed a different definition of funcCPA (albeit, using the same name funcCPA). It was shown in [35] that their definition does not guarantee privacy in client-aided outsourcing protocols, and the thrust of that work was to study several possible treatments of invalid ciphertexts.

We stress that the results from [35] have no bearing on our funcCPA definition, in particular we show in Theorem 2 that our definition does imply privacy for client-aided protocols. We note that our results hold regardless of how invalid ciphertexts are treated (as long as funcCPA holds wrt an oracle that uses the same treatment as the client in the protocol). See Remark 2. We also note that [35, Theorems 3 and 5] are special cases of [7, Theorem 7].

Paper organization. Preliminary definitions are given in Sect. 2. Our results on funcCPA definition, sufficiency and achievability in Sect. 3. Our result on the insufficiency of CPA against malicious adversaries in Sects. 4, and on its sufficiency against semi-honest ones for natural protocols in Sect. 5. We conclude in Sect. 6.

2 Preliminaries

We briefly specify standard definitions. See details in our full version [2].

Terminology and notations. For $n \in \mathbb{N}$, we denote by $[n]$ the set $\{1, \ldots, n\}$. We use standard definitions (see e.g. Goldreich [26]) for *negligible* and *polynomial* functions with respect to the security parameter λ, denoted $\mathsf{neg}(\lambda)$ and $\mathsf{poly}(\lambda)$; *probabilistic polynomial time* algorithms, denoted ppt; *random variables*; *probability ensembles*; *computationally indistinguishability*; *statistical distance* denoted by $\Delta(\cdot, \cdot)$; and *(strong) one-way function*.

CPA-secure public key encryption. We use the standard definition for public key encryption (PKE) scheme $\mathcal{E} = (\mathsf{Gen}, \mathsf{Enc}, \mathsf{Dec})$ and its properties of *correctness*,

CPA-indistinguishability experiment against an adversary $\mathcal{A}$ denoted $\mathsf{EXP}_{\mathcal{A},\mathcal{E}}^{cpa}(\lambda)$, and *CPA-security* for single and multiple messages. A scheme is *fully decryptable* if applying the decryption algorithm on any ciphertext in the ciphertext space returns an element from the message space (and requiring, in addition, that the ciphertext space is efficiently recognizable). See the formal definitions in [30].

Homomorphic encryption. A homomorphic public-key encryption scheme (HE) is a public-key encryption scheme equipped with an additional ppt algorithm called Eval that supports "homomorphic evaluations" on ciphertexts. The correctness requirement is extended to hold with respect to any sequence of homomorphic evaluations performed on ciphertexts. A fully homomorphic encryption scheme must satisfy an additional property called *compactness* requiring that the size of the ciphertext does not grow with the complexity of the sequence of homomorphic operations.

Definition 1 (Homomorphic encryption (HE)). *A homomorphic public-key encryption (HE) scheme* $\mathcal{E}$ = (Gen, Enc, Dec, Eval) *with message space* $\mathcal{M}$ *is a tuple of ppt algorithms as follows:* (Gen, Enc, Dec) *is a correct PKE. Eval (homomorphic evaluation) takes as input the public key* pk, *a circuit* $C\colon \mathcal{M}^\ell \to \mathcal{M}$, *and ciphertexts* $c_1, \ldots, c_\ell$, *and outputs a ciphertext* $\widehat{c} \leftarrow \mathsf{Eval}_{pk}(C, c_1, \ldots, c_\ell)$.

The scheme is secure *if it is a CPA-secure PKE;* compact *if its decryption circuit is of polynomial size (in the security parameter);* C-homomorphic *for a circuit family* C *if for all* $C \in \mathcal{C}$ *and all inputs* $x_1, \ldots, x_\ell$ *to* C, *letting* $(pk, sk) \leftarrow$ $\mathsf{Gen}(1^\lambda)$ *and* $c_i \leftarrow \mathsf{Enc}(pk, x_i)$ *it holds that:*

$$\Pr[\mathsf{Dec}_{sk}(\mathsf{Eval}_{pk}(C, c_1, \ldots, c_\ell)) \neq C(x_1, \ldots, x_\ell)] \leq \mathsf{neg}(\lambda)$$

where the probability is taken over all the randomness in the experiment; and fully homomorphic *if it is compact and* C-homomorphic *for* C *the class of all circuits.*

A C-homomorphic encryption scheme is *bootstrappable* if it supports homomorphic evaluation of all circuits composed from copies of its decryption circuit connected by a single gate from the set of gates (see [22, Definitions 4.1.2–4.1.3]).

A HE scheme is *leveled* (leveled HE) if for each $L \in \mathbb{Z}^+$ given as an extra parameter to Gen, denoted $(pk, sk) \leftarrow \mathsf{Gen}(1^\lambda, 1^L)$, the scheme compactly evaluates all circuits of depth at most L. The complexity of its algorithms is polynomial in L on top of λ. CPA-security for leveled HE is defined similarly to the standard CPA definition except for the capability of the adversary to choose the level to which the challenge ciphertext is encrypted (to guarantee security of the scheme for all the levels). More formally,

The CPA indistinguishability experiment $\mathsf{EXP}_{\mathcal{A},\mathcal{E}}^{cpa}(\lambda, L)$ *for* leveled HE is parameterized by the security parameter λ and number of levels L, and executed between a challenger Chal and an adversary $\mathcal{A}$ as follows:

1. $\mathsf{Gen}(1^\lambda, 1^L)$ is run by Chal to obtain keys $(pk_\ell, sk_\ell)_{\ell \in \{0,\ldots,L\}}$ (we consider the public key pk_ℓ to include the evaluation key evk_ℓ if exists).
2. Chal provides the adversary $\mathcal{A}$ with $(pk_\ell)_{\ell \in \{0,\ldots,L\}}$. $\mathcal{A}$ sends to Chal two messages $x_0, x_1 \in \mathcal{M}$ s.t. $|x_0| = |x_1|$ and $\ell \in \{0, \ldots, L\}$.

3. Chal chooses a random bit $b \in \{0, 1\}$, computes a ciphertext $c \leftarrow \mathsf{Enc}_{pk_\ell}(x_b)$ and sends c to $\mathcal{A}$. We call c the challenge ciphertext.
4. $\mathcal{A}$ outputs a bit b'.
5. The output of the experiment is defined to be 1 if $b' = b$ (0 otherwise).

Definition 2 (CPA security for leveled HE). *A leveled HE scheme* $\mathcal{E} =$ (Gen, Enc, Dec, Eval) *is* CPA-secure *if for every* ppt *adversary* $\mathcal{A}$, *there exists a negligible function* neg *such that for all sufficiently large* λ *and every* L *polynomial in* λ,

$$\Pr[\mathsf{EXP}^{cpa}_{\mathcal{A},\mathcal{E}}(\lambda, L) = 1] < \frac{1}{2} + \mathsf{neg}(\lambda)$$

where the probability is over all randomness in the experiment.

Sanitization. A ciphertext *sanitization* algorithm for a homomorphic encryption re-randomizes ciphertexts to make them statistically close to other (sanitized) ciphertexts decrypting to the same plaintext. Sanitization algorithms exists for most contemporary HE schemes [20].

Definition 3 (Sanitization algorithm [20]). *A Sanitize algorithm for a homomorphic public-key encryption scheme* $\mathcal{E} =$ (Gen, Enc, Dec, Eval) *is a* ppt *algorithm that takes a public key* pk *and a ciphertext* c *and returns a ciphertext, so that with probability* $\geq 1 - \mathsf{neg}(\lambda)$ *over the choice of* $(pk, sk) \leftarrow$ Gen(1^λ) *the following holds:*

- *(Message-preservation)* $\forall c$ *in the ciphertext space:*
  $\mathsf{Dec}_{sk}(\mathsf{Sanitize}_{pk}(c)) = \mathsf{Dec}_{sk}(c)$.
- *(Sanitization)* $\forall c, c'$ *in the ciphertext space s.t.* $\mathsf{Dec}_{sk}(c) = \mathsf{Dec}_{sk}(c')$:

$$\Delta\left((\mathsf{Sanitize}_{pk}(c), (pk, sk)), (\mathsf{Sanitize}_{pk}(c'), (pk, sk))\right) \leq \mathsf{neg}(\lambda).$$

Interactive client-server protocols. The protocols considered in this work involve two-parties, client and server, denoted by Clnt and Srv respectively, where the client has input and output, the server has no input and no output, and both receive the security parameter λ. The client and server interact in an interactive protocol denoted by $\pi = \langle \mathsf{Clnt}, \mathsf{Srv} \rangle$. The server's view in an execution of π, on client's input x, no server's input (denoted by $\bot$), and security parameter λ, is a random variable $\mathsf{view}^\pi_{\mathsf{Srv}}(x, \bot, \lambda)$ capturing what the server has learned, and defined by $\mathsf{view}^\pi_{\mathsf{Srv}}(x, \bot, \lambda) = (r, m_1, \ldots, m_t)$ where r is the random coins of Srv, and $m_1, \ldots, m_t$ are the messages Srv received during the protocol's execution. The client's output in the execution is denoted by $\mathsf{out}^\pi_{\mathsf{Clnt}}(x, \bot, \lambda)$. The protocol preserves privacy if the views of any server on (same length) inputs are computationally indistinguishable [27, Definition 2.6.2 Part 2]:[2]

---

[2] The server has no input or output, so we do not require security against the client.

Definition 4 (Correctness and privacy). *An interactive client-server protocol* $\pi = \langle \mathsf{Clnt}, \mathsf{Srv} \rangle$ *for computing* $F : \mathsf{A} \to \mathsf{B}$, *where the server has no input or output is said to be:*

Correct: *if* Srv *and* Clnt *are ppt and for all* $x \in \mathsf{A}$,
$$\Pr[out^{\pi}_{\mathsf{Clnt}}(x, \bot, \lambda) = F(x)] > 1 - \mathsf{neg}(\lambda).$$
Private: *if for every ppt server* Srv^* *and every ppt distinguisher* $\mathcal{D}$ *that chooses* $x_0, x_1 \in \mathsf{A}$ *s.t.* $|x_0| = |x_1|$, *there exists a negligible function* $\mathsf{neg}(\cdot)$ *such that for every* $\lambda \in \mathbb{N}$, *it holds that:*

$$|\Pr[\mathcal{D}(view^{\pi}_{\mathsf{Srv}^*}(x_0, \bot, \lambda)) = 1] - \Pr[\mathcal{D}(view^{\pi}_{\mathsf{Srv}^*}(x_1, \bot, \lambda)) = 1]| \leq \mathsf{neg}(\lambda)$$

where the probability is taken over the random coins of Clnt *and* Srv^*.

Definition 4 captures malicious adversaries, but can be relaxed to semi-honest ones by quantifying only over the prescribed Srv rather than every ppt Srv^*. We call the former *privacy against malicious servers* and the latter *privacy against semi-honest servers*.

Client-aided outsourcing protocols. We formally define the family of *client-aided outsourcing protocols*, or $(\mathcal{E}, \mathcal{G})$-*aided outsourcing protocols*, parameterized by a PKE scheme $\mathcal{E}$ with message space $\mathcal{M}$ and a family of functions $\mathcal{G} = \{G_n : \mathcal{M} \to \mathcal{M}\}_{n \in \mathbb{N}}$. We note that $\mathcal{E}$ can be any PKE scheme (i.e., not necessarily an HE scheme).

Definition 5 ($(\mathcal{E}, \mathcal{G})$-aided outsourcing protocol). *Let* $\mathcal{E} = (\mathsf{Gen}, \mathsf{Enc}, \mathsf{Dec})$ *be a public-key encryption scheme with message space* $\mathcal{M}$, *and* $\mathcal{G} = \{G_n : \mathcal{M} \to \mathcal{M}\}_{n \in \mathbb{N}}$ *a family of functions. An interactive client-server protocol* $\pi = \langle \mathsf{Clnt}, \mathsf{Srv} \rangle$ *for computing a function* $F : \mathsf{A} \to \mathsf{B}$ *is called an* $(\mathcal{E}, \mathcal{G})$-*aided outsourcing protocol if it has the following three stage structure:*

1. **Client's input outsourcing phase (on input** $x \in \mathsf{A}$**):** Clnt *runs* $(pk, sk) \leftarrow \mathsf{Gen}(1^{\lambda})$, *encrypts its input* $\mathbf{c} \leftarrow \mathsf{Enc}_{pk}(x)$, *and sends* $\mathbf{c}$ *and* pk *to* Srv.
2. **Server's computation phase:** Srv *performs some computation and in addition may interact (multiple times) with* Clnt *by sending it pairs* $(\mathbf{e}, n)$, *for* $\mathbf{e}$ *a vector of ciphertexts and* $n \in \mathbb{N}$, *receiving in response* $\mathsf{Enc}_{pk}(G_n(\mathsf{Dec}_{sk}(\mathbf{e})))$.
3. **Client's output phase:** Srv *sends to* Clnt *the last message of the protocol; upon receiving this message,* Clnt *produces an output.*

Remark 1 (multiple inputs and outputs). The query $\mathbf{e}$ and response $\mathbf{e}'$ can be vectors of ciphertexts, with decryption and encryption in $\mathsf{Enc}_{pk}(G_n(\mathsf{Dec}_{sk}(\mathbf{e})))$ computed entry-by-entry. Throughout the paper we slightly abuse notations and denote by $\mathcal{M}$, Dec, Enc, $\mathbf{e}$ and $\mathbf{e}'$ also their extension to vectors.

3 A Sufficient and Achievable Relaxation of CCA2

In this section we formally define funcCPA-security and prove that client-aided protocols instantiated with a funcCPA-secure scheme preserve privacy against malicious adversaries (Sect. 3.1); Show that funcCPA-secure HE is achievable from any HE equipped with a sanitization algorithm (Sect. 3.2); Prove that funcCPA-security is satisfied by all leveled schemes satisfying a natural property, e.g., the leveled HE schemes of BV [12], BGV [11] and B/FV [10,21] (Sect. 3.3); Conversely, show that funcCPA-security for homomorphic schemes with (another) natural property, e.g., the schemes of BV [12] and BGV [11], implies weak circular security (Sect. 3.4).

3.1 funcCPA-Security: A Sufficient Relaxation of CCA2

We define the *function-chosen-plaintext attack* (funcCPA-security) security notion of public-key encryption, and show that $(\mathcal{E}, \mathcal{G})$-aided outsourcing protocols preserve privacy against malicious servers if $\mathcal{E}$ is funcCPA-secure. We remark that $\mathcal{E}$ may be a PKE that is not necessarily a HE.

The definition captures a weaker adversary than the standard CCA2 adversary in the sense that the adversary has access to a "decrypt-function-encrypt" oracle, specified with respect to a family of functions, where the adversary may submit a ciphertext together with a function identifier and receive in response a ciphertext that is produced as follows. The submitted ciphertext is first decrypted, then the requested function is calculated on the plaintext and the result is encrypted and returned to the adversary.

More formally, we define funcCPA-security via a funcCPA-experiment specified for a public-key encryption scheme $\mathcal{E} = (\mathsf{Gen}, \mathsf{Enc}, \mathsf{Dec})$ with message space $\mathcal{M}$, a family of functions $\mathcal{G} = \{G_n \colon \mathcal{M} \rightarrow \mathcal{M}\}_{n \in \mathbb{N}}$, and an adversary $\mathcal{A}$, as follows:

The funcCPA indistinguishability experiment $\mathsf{EXP}^{Fcpa}_{\mathcal{A}, \mathcal{E}, \mathcal{G}}(\lambda)$:

1. $\mathsf{Gen}(1^{\lambda})$ is run to obtain a key-pair (pk, sk)
2. The adversary $\mathcal{A}$ is given pk and access to a decrypt-function-encrypt oracle, denoted $\mathsf{Enc}_{pk}(\mathcal{G}(\mathsf{Dec}_{sk}(\cdot)))$, defined as follows: queries to $\mathsf{Enc}_{pk}(\mathcal{G}(\mathsf{Dec}_{sk}(\cdot)))$ are pairs consisting of a ciphertext $\mathbf{e}$ and a function index n, and the response is $\mathbf{e}' \leftarrow \mathsf{Enc}_{pk}(G_n(\mathsf{Dec}_{sk}(\mathbf{e})))$.
3. $\mathcal{A}$ outputs a pair of messages $x_0, x_1 \in \mathcal{M}$ with $|x_0| = |x_1|$.
4. A random bit $b \in \{0, 1\}$ is chosen, and the ciphertext $c \leftarrow \mathsf{Enc}_{pk}(x_b)$ is computed and given to $\mathcal{A}$. We call c the challenge ciphertext. $\mathcal{A}$ continues to have access to the $\mathsf{Enc}_{pk}(\mathcal{G}(\mathsf{Dec}_{sk}(\cdot)))$ oracle.
5. The adversary $\mathcal{A}$ outputs a bit b'. The experiment's output is defined to be 1 if $b' = b$, and 0 otherwise.

Definition 6 (funcCPA). *A PKE scheme $\mathcal{E} = (\mathsf{Gen}, \mathsf{Enc}, \mathsf{Dec})$ with message space $\mathcal{M}$ is* funcCPA-secure *w.r.t. a family of functions $\mathcal{G} = \{G_n \colon \mathcal{M} \rightarrow \mathcal{M}\}_{n \in \mathbb{N}}$ (funcCPA-secure w.r.t. $\mathcal{G}$) if for all ppt adversaries $\mathcal{A}$, there exists a negligible function* $\mathsf{neg}(\cdot)$ *such that for all sufficiently large λ,*

$$\Pr[\mathsf{EXP}^{Fcpa}_{\mathcal{A}, \mathcal{E}, \mathcal{G}}(\lambda) = 1] \leq \frac{1}{2} + \mathsf{neg}(\lambda)$$

where the probability is taken over the random coins used by $\mathcal{A}$, as well as the random coins used to generate (pk, sk), choose b, and encrypt.

Remark 2 (Handling decryption errors). In Definitions 5 and 6 we do not include an explicit discussion of how decryption errors are treated. This is because our theorem showing that funcCPA implies privacy (Theorem 7) holds with any treatment of errors, as long as errors are treated identically by both the client in the client-aided outsourcing protocol and the oracle in the funcCPA-experiment. An example of a possible treatment of errors follows: if decryption fails on a query $(\mathbf{e}, n)$ submitted to the client or oracle, they return $\mathsf{Enc}_{pk}(G_n(m))$ for an arbitrary message $m \in \mathcal{M}$. Another example is provided in our preprint [3].

Theorem 7 (funcCPA implies privacy). *Let $\mathcal{E}$ be a PKE with message space $\mathcal{M}$ and $\mathcal{G} = \{G_n \colon \mathcal{M} \to \mathcal{M}\}_{n \in \mathbb{N}}$ a family of functions. If $\mathcal{E}$ is funcCPA-secure w.r.t. $\mathcal{G}$, then every $(\mathcal{E}, \mathcal{G})$-aided outsourcing protocol preserves privacy against malicious servers.*

Proof. Let π be a $(\mathcal{E}, \mathcal{G})$-aided outsourcing protocol for a function $F : \mathsf{A} \to \mathsf{B}$. Assume by contradiction that privacy does not hold for π. That is, there exists a ppt distinguisher $\mathcal{D}$ that chooses $x_0, x_1 \in \mathsf{A}$ with $|x_0| = |x_1|$, a malicious ppt server Srv^*, and a polynomial $p(\cdot)$ such that for infinitely many $\lambda \in \mathbb{N}$:

$$\Pr[\mathcal{D}(\mathsf{view}^\pi_{\mathsf{Srv}^*}(x_1, \bot, \lambda)) = 1] - \Pr[\mathcal{D}(\mathsf{view}^\pi_{\mathsf{Srv}^*}(x_0, \bot, \lambda)) = 1] \geq \frac{1}{p(\lambda)} \quad (1)$$

We show that given $\mathcal{D}$ and Srv^* we can construct an adversary $\mathcal{A}$ that violates the funcCPA security of $\mathcal{E}$ with respect to the family $\mathcal{G}$.

The adversary $\mathcal{A}$ participates in $\mathsf{EXP}^{Fcpa}_{\mathcal{A}, \mathcal{E}, \mathcal{G}}$ as follows:

1. Upon receiving pk, $\mathcal{A}$ outputs x_0, x_1 (as computed by $\mathcal{D}$).
2. Upon receiving $\mathbf{c}_x \leftarrow \mathsf{Enc}_{pk}(x_b)$ from the challenger, $\mathcal{A}$ internally executes Srv^* and behaves as the Clnt in the execution of the protocol π: in the client's input outsourcing phase of π, $\mathcal{A}$ sends $(\mathbf{c}_x, pk)$ to Srv^*; in the server's computation phase of π, every incoming message $(\mathbf{e}, n)$ to Clnt is redirected to the oracle $\mathsf{Enc}_{pk}(\mathcal{G}(\mathsf{Dec}_{sk}(\cdot)))$ and the response is sent to Srv^* as if it were coming from Clnt.
3. $\mathcal{A}$ runs the distinguisher $\mathcal{D}$ on $\mathsf{view}_{\mathsf{Srv}^*}$ (Srv^*'s view in $\mathcal{A}$ during Step 2) and outputs whatever $\mathcal{D}$ outputs.

The adversary $\mathcal{A}$ is ppt due to Srv^* and $\mathcal{D}$ being ppt. Note that π is perfectly simulated.

We denote by $\mathsf{view}^{\mathsf{EXP}^{Fcpa}}_{\mathsf{Srv}^*}(x_b, \bot, \lambda)$ the view of Srv^*, simulated by $\mathcal{A}$, in the execution of $\mathsf{EXP}^{Fcpa}_{\mathcal{A}, \mathcal{E}, \mathcal{G}}$ with bit b being selected by the challenger. Since $\mathcal{A}$ behaves exactly as Srv^* in π, it holds that for every $b \in \{0, 1\}$,

$$\Pr[\mathcal{D}(\mathsf{view}^\pi_{\mathsf{Srv}^*}(x_b, \bot, \lambda)) = 1] = \Pr[\mathcal{D}(\mathsf{view}^{\mathsf{EXP}^{Fcpa}}_{\mathsf{Srv}^*}(x_b, \bot, \lambda)) = 1] \quad (2)$$

From Eqs. 1 and 2 it follows that:

$$\Pr[\mathcal{D}(\text{view}_{\text{Srv}^*}^{\text{EXP}^{Fcpa}}(x_1, \bot, \lambda)) = 1] - \Pr[\mathcal{D}(\text{view}_{\text{Srv}^*}^{\text{EXP}^{Fcpa}}(x_0, \bot, \lambda)) = 1] \geq \frac{1}{p(\lambda)}$$

(3)

Therefore, we obtain that:

$\Pr[\text{EXP}_{\mathcal{A},\mathcal{E},\mathcal{G}}^{Fcpa}(\lambda) = 1]$

$= \frac{1}{2} \cdot \left(\Pr[\text{EXP}_{\mathcal{A},\mathcal{E},\mathcal{G}}^{Fcpa}(\lambda) = 1 | b = 1] + \Pr[\text{EXP}_{\mathcal{A},\mathcal{E},\mathcal{G}}^{Fcpa}(\lambda) = 1 | b = 0] \right)$

$= \frac{1}{2} \cdot \left(\Pr[\mathcal{D}(\text{view}_{\text{Srv}^*}^{\text{EXP}^{Fcpa}}(x_1, \bot, \lambda)) = 1] + \Pr[\mathcal{D}(\text{view}_{\text{Srv}^*}^{\text{EXP}^{Fcpa}}(x_0, \bot, \lambda)) = 0] \right)$

$= \frac{1}{2} + \frac{1}{2} \cdot \left(\Pr[\mathcal{D}(\text{view}_{\text{Srv}^*}^{\text{EXP}^{Fcpa}}(x_1, \bot, \lambda)) = 1] - \Pr[\mathcal{D}(\text{view}_{\text{Srv}^*}^{\text{EXP}^{Fcpa}}(x_0, \bot, \lambda)) = 1] \right)$

$\geq \frac{1}{2} + \frac{1}{2} \cdot \frac{1}{p(\lambda)}$

where the last inequality follows from Eq. 3. Combining this with $\mathcal{A}$ being ppt we derive a contradiction to $\mathcal{E}$ being funcCPA secure. This concludes the proof.
□

We observe that for fully decryptable $\mathcal{C}$-homomorphic schemes, it suffices to prove funcCPA-security w.r.t the identity function $\mathcal{I}$ to obtain funcCPA-security w.r.t $\mathcal{C}$. We note that full decryption holds for well-known schemes including [10, 11, 17, 19, 24, 39].

Lemma 1. *Let* $\mathcal{E} = (\text{Gen}, \text{Enc}, \text{Dec}, \text{Eval})$ *be a fully decryptable[3] $\mathcal{C}$-homomorphic PKE scheme. If $\mathcal{E}$ is funcCPA-secure w.r.t the identity function $\mathcal{I}$ then it is funcCPA-secure w.r.t $\mathcal{C}$.*

Proof. Let $\mathcal{E} = (\text{Gen}, \text{Enc}, \text{Dec}, \text{Eval})$ be a fully decryptable $\mathcal{C}$-homomorphic encryption scheme with message space $\mathcal{M}$ and ciphertext $\mathcal{T}$ that is funcCPA-secure w.r.t the identity function $\mathcal{I} : \mathcal{M} \to \mathcal{M}$. For any ppt adversary $\mathcal{A}$ that participates in $\text{EXP}_{\mathcal{A},\mathcal{E},\mathcal{C}}^{Fcpa}$ we construct an adversary $\mathcal{B}$ for $\text{EXP}_{\mathcal{B},\mathcal{E},\mathcal{I}}^{Fcpa}$ that behaves as follows: The adversary $\mathcal{B}$ runs $\mathcal{A}$ internally while relaying messages between the challenger and $\mathcal{A}$, with the exception that $\text{Enc}_{pk}(\mathcal{C}(\text{Dec}_{sk}(\cdot)))$ queries are treated as follows: first the queried ciphertext is forwarded to the challenger that returns a fresh ciphertext of the encrypted value, then Eval is executed over this fresh ciphertext and the result ciphertext is forwarded again to the challenger that returns a fresh ciphertext for its underlying value. That is, $\mathcal{B}$ does the following:

---

[3] We note that the fully decryptable requirement addresses decryption errors. This requirement can be replaced by including in Definition 6 the following treatment of errors: in case of a decryption error, the funcCPA oracle returns an encryption of the queried function on an arbitrary message in the message space.

- Upon receiving pk from challenger, forward it to $\mathcal{A}$.
- Answer queries $(\mathbf{e}, n)$ to $\mathsf{Enc}_{pk}(\mathcal{C}(\mathsf{Dec}_{sk}(\cdot)))$ by sending $(\mathbf{e}, \mathcal{I})$ to the challenger and obtaining a fresh ciphertext $\mathbf{e}'$ (and $\bot$ if $\mathbf{e} \notin \mathcal{T}$), computing $\mathbf{e}'' \leftarrow \mathsf{Eval}_{pk}(C_n, \mathbf{e}')$ and sending $(\mathbf{e}'', \mathcal{I})$ to the challenger. The response to the second query is given to $\mathcal{A}$.
- Once $\mathcal{A}$ generates x_0, x_1 forward them to the challenger and return the response $c \leftarrow \mathsf{Enc}_{pk}(x_b)$ to $\mathcal{A}$.
- Output the b' that $\mathcal{A}$ outputs.

The adversary $\mathcal{B}$ is ppt (due to $\mathcal{A}$ and Eval being ppt), and all the interaction of $\mathcal{A}$ is perfectly simulated by $\mathcal{B}$ due to $\mathcal{E}$ being fully decryptable together with $\mathcal{C}$-homomorphic. More formally, letting $(pk, sk) \leftarrow \mathsf{Gen}(1^\lambda)$, for all $C \in \mathcal{C}$ and $c_1, \ldots c_\ell \in \mathcal{T}$ it holds that:

$$\Pr\left[\begin{matrix}\mathsf{Dec}_{sk}(\mathsf{Eval}_{pk}(C, \mathsf{Enc}_{pk}(\mathsf{Dec}_{sk}(c_1)), \ldots, \mathsf{Enc}_{pk}(\mathsf{Dec}_{sk}(c_\ell)))) \\ \neq \\ C(\mathsf{Dec}_{sk}(c_1), \ldots, \mathsf{Dec}_{sk}(c_\ell))\end{matrix}\right] \leq \mathsf{neg}(\lambda)$$

(if $\mathcal{A}$ submits a ciphertext not in $\mathcal{T}$ then the challenger's response is $\bot$ in both executions). Since the number of queries of $\mathcal{A}$ is polynomial in λ the indistinguishability of $\mathsf{EXP}^{Fcpa}_{\mathcal{A},\mathcal{E},\mathcal{C}}(\lambda)$ and $\mathsf{EXP}^{Fcpa}_{\mathcal{B},\mathcal{E},\mathcal{I}}(\lambda)$ follows. Finally, from the funcCPA-security of $\mathcal{E}$ w.r.t $\mathcal{I}$ we conclude that

$$\Pr[\mathsf{EXP}^{Fcpa}_{\mathcal{A},\mathcal{E},\mathcal{C}}(\lambda) = 1] \leq \frac{1}{2} + \mathsf{neg}(\lambda)$$

as required.

$\square$

3.2   Sanitized HE Schemes are funcCPA-Secure

We show how to transform any HE scheme $\mathcal{E}$ that has a sanitization algorithm into a sanitized HE scheme, denoted $\mathcal{E}^{\mathsf{santz}}$, so that if $\mathcal{E}$ is CPA-secure, then $\mathcal{E}^{\mathsf{santz}}$ is funcCPA-secure.

Definition 7 (Sanitized scheme $\mathcal{E}^{santz}$). *Let $\mathcal{E} = (\mathsf{Gen}, \mathsf{Enc}, \mathsf{Dec}, \mathsf{Eval})$ be HE scheme with message space $\mathcal{M}$ and a sanitization algorithm $\mathsf{Sanitize}$. We define its sanitized scheme $\mathcal{E}^{santz} = (\mathsf{Gen}, \mathsf{Enc}^{santz}, \mathsf{Dec}, \mathsf{Eval}^{santz})$ as follows: Gen and Dec are as in $\mathcal{E}$; Enc^{santz} takes a public key pk and a message $m \in \mathcal{M}$ and outputs:*

$$\mathsf{Enc}^{santz}_{pk}(m) = \mathsf{Sanitize}_{pk}(\mathsf{Enc}_{pk}(m));$$

Eval^{santz} takes pk, a circuit C, and ciphertexts $c_1, \ldots, c_\ell$ and outputs:

$$\mathsf{Eval}^{santz}_{pk}(C, c_1, \ldots, c_\ell) = \mathsf{Sanitize}_{pk}(\mathsf{Eval}_{pk}(C, \mathsf{Sanitize}_{pk}(c_1), \ldots, \mathsf{Sanitize}_{pk}(c_\ell))).$$

We note that $\mathcal{E}^{\mathsf{santz}}$ inherits the compactness, security and correctness properties of $\mathcal{E}$ (in particular, correctness holds due to correctness of $\mathcal{E}$ and the message-preservation property of $\mathsf{Sanitize}$). The homomorphism of $\mathcal{E}^{\mathsf{santz}}$ may, in general, hold with respect to a subset of the circuits for which $\mathcal{E}$ is homomorphic. Nonetheless, when employing the sanitization algorithm of Ducas and Stehlé [20] both $\mathcal{E}$ and $\mathcal{E}^{\mathsf{santz}}$ are fully homomorphic.

Theorem 8 ($\mathcal{E}^{santz}$ is funcCPA-secure). *Let $\mathcal{E}$ be a fully decryptable CPA-secure HE scheme with a sanitization algorithm; $\mathcal{E}^{santz}$ its sanitized scheme. If $\mathcal{E}^{santz}$ is C-homomorphic, then it is funcCPA-secure w.r.t. C.*[4]

Proof. To prove the theorem we first enhance the definition of circuit privacy to *circuit-privacy$^+$* (cf. Definition 8 below); then show that the sanitized scheme $\mathcal{E}^{santz}$ satisfies circuit-privacy$^+$ for C (cf. Lemma 2 below); and show that if a C-homomorphic CPA-secure encryption scheme satisfies circuit-privacy$^+$ for C, then it is funcCPA-secure w.r.t. C (cf. Lemma 3 below). We conclude that $\mathcal{E}^{santz}$ is funcCPA-secure w.r.t. C.   □

Circuit-privacy$^+$. Our definition of circuit-privacy$^+$ addresses maliciously generated ciphertexts by quantifying over all ciphertexts in the ciphertext space, rather than only over ciphertexts that were properly formed by applying the encryption algorithm on a message. Prior definitions of circuit privacy either considered the semi-honest settings where both the keys and the ciphertext are properly formed [9,23,28], or considered settings where both keys and ciphertexts may be maliciously formed [18,28,34,36]. In contrast, in our settings the keys are properly formed whereas the ciphertexts may be maliciously formed.

Definition 8 (Circuit-privacy$^+$). *A C-homomorphic PKE scheme $\mathcal{E} =$ (Gen, Enc, Dec, Eval) is circuit-private$^+$ for C if the following holds with probability $\geq 1 - \mathsf{neg}(\lambda)$ over the choice of $(pk, sk) \leftarrow$ Gen(1^λ): For every circuit $C \in C$ over ℓ inputs and ciphertexts $c_1, \ldots, c_\ell$ in the ciphertext space of $\mathcal{E}$ the following distributions are statistically close:*

$$\Delta\left(\mathsf{Enc}_{pk}\left(C\left(\mathsf{Dec}_{sk}(c_1), \ldots, \mathsf{Dec}_{sk}(c_\ell)\right)\right), \mathsf{Eval}_{pk}\left(C, c_1, \ldots, c_\ell\right)\right) \leq \mathsf{neg}(\lambda)$$

where the distributions are over the random coins of Enc and Eval.

We prove that the sanitized scheme $\mathcal{E}^{santz}$ is circuit-private$^+$.

Lemma 2 ($\mathcal{E}^{santz}$ is circuit-private$^+$). *Let $\mathcal{E}$ be a fully decryptable HE scheme with a sanitization algorithm, and $\mathcal{E}^{santz}$ its sanitized scheme. If $\mathcal{E}^{santz}$ is C-homomorphic, then it is circuit-private$^+$ for C.*

Proof. We highlight the key steps; the formal details appear in Appendix A.

To prove that $\mathcal{E}^{santz}$ is circuit-private$^+$ we show that ciphertexts resulting from homomorphic evaluation *over maliciously crafted ciphertexts* are statistically close to those resulting from first decrypting then computing in cleartext and then encrypting the output. Sanitizing these ciphertexts (as done in $\mathcal{E}^{santz}$) is aimed for guaranteeing this statistical closeness. However, the sanitization guarantee holds only if these ciphertexts *decrypt to the same message*; proving the latter is the heart of our proof.

We cannot rely on homomorphism to argue the latter, because correct evaluation is guaranteed only on "fresh" encryptions (cf. *maliciously* crafted ciphertexts

---

[4] We slightly abuse notations and allow funcCPA with respect to a circuit family.

as in our scenario). To address this issue we introduce a "hybrid" experiment, where we *decrypt-and-then-encrypt* the ciphertexts given as input to Eval, which guarantees that they are fresh encryptions. (We rely on full decryption to ensure that decryption yields some element in the message space.) In this hybrid experiment correct evaluation indeed holds.

To guarantee that correct evaluation holds even without re-encryption, we rely on the fact that in $\mathcal{E}^{\text{santz}}$ we *sanitize also the input* to Eval and not just its output. This "inner" sanitization guarantees that the sanitized input ciphertexts are *statistically close* to those in the hybrid experiment (since they decrypt to the same message); from this (together with their statistical independent due to injecting fresh randomness in each sanitization) we derive that the ciphertext produced by the homomorphic evaluation is statistically close to the one produced in the hybrid experiment. This in turn implies that they decrypt to the same message.   □

Circuit-privacy$^+$ *implies funcCPA.* We prove that a HE scheme is funcCPA-secure if it is CPA-secure and circuit-private$^+$.

Lemma 3 (circuit-privacy$^+$ implies funcCPA). *Let $\mathcal{E}$ be a CPA-secure PKE. If $\mathcal{E}$ is $\mathcal{C}$-homomorphic and circuit-private$^+$ for $\mathcal{C}$, then $\mathcal{E}$ is funcCPA-secure w.r.t. $\mathcal{C}$.*

Proof. The main proof idea is to carefully replace $\text{Enc}_{pk}(\mathcal{G}(\text{Dec}_{sk}(\cdot)))$ oracle calls with Eval operations; details follow.

Let $\mathcal{E} = (\text{Gen}, \text{Enc}, \text{Dec}, \text{Eval})$ be a CPA-secure $\mathcal{C}$-homomorphic encryption scheme with message space $\mathcal{M}$ that is circuit-private$^+$ for $\mathcal{C}$. For any ppt adversary $\mathcal{A}$ that participates in $\text{EXP}_{\mathcal{A},\mathcal{E},\mathcal{C}}^{Fcpa}$ we construct an adversary $\mathcal{B}$ for $\text{EXP}_{\mathcal{B},\mathcal{E}}^{cpa}$ that behaves as follows: The adversary $\mathcal{B}$ runs $\mathcal{A}$ internally while relaying messages between the challenger and $\mathcal{A}$, with the exception that $\text{Enc}_{pk}(\mathcal{C}(\text{Dec}_{sk}(\cdot)))$ queries are answered using Eval. That is, $\mathcal{B}$ does the following:

- Upon receiving pk from challenger, forward it to $\mathcal{A}$.
- Answer queries $(\mathbf{e}, n)$ to $\text{Enc}_{pk}(\mathcal{C}(\text{Dec}_{sk}(\cdot)))$ by $\mathbf{e}' \leftarrow \text{Eval}_{pk}(C_n, \mathbf{e})$.
- Once $\mathcal{A}$ generates x_0, x_1 forward them to the challenger and return the response $\mathbf{c} \leftarrow \text{Enc}_{pk}(x_b)$ to $\mathcal{A}$.
- Output the b' that $\mathcal{A}$ outputs.

The adversary $\mathcal{B}$ is ppt (due to $\mathcal{A}$ and Eval being ppt), and all the interaction of $\mathcal{A}$ is perfectly simulated by $\mathcal{B}$ except for the responses to queries to $\text{Enc}_{pk}(\mathcal{C}(\text{Dec}_{sk}(\cdot)))$ that are simulated using Eval. Circuit privacy$^+$ of $\mathcal{E}$ guarantees that these responses are indistinguishable from decrypting, applying C_n and encrypting the result.

More formally, we define a series of hybrid executions that gradually move between $\text{EXP}_{\mathcal{A},\mathcal{E},\mathcal{C}}^{Fcpa}$ experiment (where $\text{Enc}_{pk}(\mathcal{C}(\text{Dec}_{sk}(\cdot)))$ oracle is used) to $\text{EXP}_{\mathcal{B},\mathcal{E}}^{cpa}$ experiment (where Eval is used). Let q denote an upper bound on the number of queries done by $\mathcal{A}$, we define $q + 1$ hybrids as follows:

Hybrid H_0 is defined as the execution of $\text{EXP}_{\mathcal{A},\mathcal{E},\mathcal{C}}^{Fcpa}$.

Hybrid H_i is defined for $i \in [q]$. The hybrid H_i is defined as $EXP^{Fcpa}_{\mathcal{A}_i, \mathcal{E}, \mathcal{C}}$, where $\mathcal{A}_i$'s last i queries are answered using Eval instead of oracle $Enc_{pk}(\mathcal{C}(Dec_{sk}(\cdot)))$.

Note that H_q is equivalent to the CPA-experiment $EXP^{cpa}_{\mathcal{B}, \mathcal{E}}$, and hence,

$$\Pr[EXP^{cpa}_{\mathcal{B}, \mathcal{E}}(\lambda) = 1] = \Pr[EXP^{Fcpa}_{\mathcal{A}_q, \mathcal{E}, \mathcal{C}}(\lambda) = 1] \tag{4}$$

In each pair of adjacent hybrids H_{i-1} and H_i the difference is that in H_i the $(q - i + 1)$'th query is done using Eval instead $Enc_{pk}(\mathcal{C}(Dec_{sk}(\cdot)))$ oracle. In this case the indistinguishability follows from $\mathcal{E}$ being circuit private[+] for $\mathcal{C}$. Namely,

$$| \Pr[EXP^{Fcpa}_{\mathcal{A}_i, \mathcal{E}, \mathcal{C}}(\lambda) = 1] - \Pr[EXP^{Fcpa}_{\mathcal{A}_{i-1}, \mathcal{E}, \mathcal{C}}(\lambda) = 1]| \leq neg(\lambda).$$

Since q is polynomial in λ, by the hybrid argument the indistinguishability of $EXP^{Fcpa}_{\mathcal{A}, \mathcal{E}, \mathcal{C}}$ and $EXP^{cpa}_{\mathcal{B}, \mathcal{E}}$ follows. Finally, from the CPA-security of $\mathcal{E}$ and Eq. 4 we conclude that

$$\Pr[EXP^{Fcpa}_{\mathcal{A}, \mathcal{E}, \mathcal{C}}(\lambda) = 1] \leq \frac{1}{2} + neg(\lambda)$$

As required.   □

3.3   funcCPA Security of leveled HE Schemes

We show that CPA implies funcCPA for leveled HE schemes satisfying a natural property. This property is satisfied, e.g., by BV [12], BGV [11] and B/FV [10,21] (with a slight modification of their evaluation key), see Corollary 1.

Concretely, we address leveled HE schemes where each level is associated with a set of keys (usually, public, secret and evaluation keys), each ciphertext is associated with a (efficiently recognizable) level corresponding to the keys used for this ciphertext, and the scheme has independent level keys in the sense that the public and secret key pair can be sampled independently for each level, and the evaluation key for each level can be efficiently generated from the secret key for the current level and the public key for the next level.

Definition 9 (independent level keys). *We say that a leveled HE scheme $\mathcal{E} = (Gen, Enc, Dec, Eval)$ has* independent level keys *if Gen (level key generation) takes as input the security parameter 1^λ and a number of levels 1^L, uses ppt algorithms GenKey and GenEvKey, and outputs for each level $\ell \in \{0, \ldots, L\}$ a public key, secret key, and an evaluation key defined by: $(pk_\ell, sk_\ell) \leftarrow GenKey(1^\lambda)$ and $evk_\ell \leftarrow GenEvKey(sk_\ell, pk_{\ell-1})$ denoted: $(pk_\ell, evk_\ell, sk_\ell,)_{\ell \in [L]} \leftarrow Gen(1^\lambda, 1^L)$*

We reformulate the definition of funcCPA to capture security for leveled HE schemes (leveled-funcCPA) as follows: the adversary can choose the level to which the challenge ciphertext is encrypted, and the "decrypt-function-encrypt" oracle is modified to return a ciphertext for the next level. That is, to answer a query on a ciphertext of level ℓ, the ciphertext is first decrypted using sk_ℓ, then the requested function is calculated on the plaintext and the result is encrypted under the public-key for the next level $pk_{\ell-1}$ and returned to the adversary, see Definition 10.

The leveled-funcCPA indistinguishability experiment $\mathsf{EXP}_{\mathcal{A},\mathcal{E},\mathcal{G}}^{Fcpa}(\lambda, L)$ *for leveled* HE is parameterized by the security parameter λ and number of levels L, and executed between a challenger Chal and an adversary $\mathcal{A}$:

1. $\mathsf{Gen}(1^\lambda, 1^L)$ is run to obtain keys $(pk_\ell, sk_\ell)_{\ell \in \{0,\dots,L\}}$ (we consider the public key pk_ℓ to include the evaluation key evk_ℓ if it exists).
2. The adversary $\mathcal{A}$ is given $(pk_\ell)_{\ell \in \{0,\dots,L\}}$ and access to a decrypt-function-encrypt oracle, denoted $\{\mathsf{Enc}_{pk_{\ell-1}}(\mathcal{G}(\mathsf{Dec}_{sk_\ell}(\cdot)))\}_{\ell \in [L]}$, defined as follows: the queries to this oracle are pairs $(\mathbf{e}_\ell, n)$ consisting of a ciphertext $\mathbf{e}_\ell$ of some level $\ell \in [L]$ (where the level is efficiently identifiable given the ciphertext) and a function index n, and the response is $\mathbf{e}' \leftarrow \mathsf{Enc}_{pk_{\ell-1}}(G_n(\mathsf{Dec}_{sk_\ell}(\mathbf{e}_\ell)))$.[5]
3. $\mathcal{A}$ outputs a pair of messages $x_0, x_1 \in \mathcal{M}$ s.t. $|x_0| = |x_1|$ and $\ell \in \{0, \dots, L\}$.
4. A random bit $b \in \{0, 1\}$ is chosen, and the ciphertext $c \leftarrow \mathsf{Enc}_{pk_\ell}(x_b)$ is computed and given to $\mathcal{A}$. We call c the challenge ciphertext. $\mathcal{A}$ continues to have access to the oracle.
5. The adversary $\mathcal{A}$ outputs a bit b'. The experiment's output is defined to be 1 if $b' = b$ (0 otherwise).

Definition 10 (funcCPA for leveled HE). *A leveled HE scheme* $\mathcal{E} =$ (Gen, Enc, Dec, Eval) *with message space* $\mathcal{M}$ *is leveled-funcCPA-secure with respect to a family of functions* $\mathcal{G} = \{G_n \colon \mathcal{M} \to \mathcal{M}\}_{n \in \mathbb{N}}$ *(leveled-funcCPA-secure w.r.t.* $\mathcal{G}$*) if for all ppt adversaries* $\mathcal{A}$*, there exists a negligible function* $\mathsf{neg}(\cdot)$ *such that for all sufficiently large* λ *and every* L *polynomial in* λ,

$$\Pr[\mathsf{EXP}_{\mathcal{A},\mathcal{E},\mathcal{G}}^{Fcpa}(\lambda, L) = 1] < \frac{1}{2} + \mathsf{neg}(\lambda)$$

where the probability is taken over all random coins of the experiment.

We prove that CPA-secure leveled HE schemes with independent level keys are funcCPA-secure w.r.t any admissible family $\mathcal{G}$. *Admissible* here says that all $G_n \in \mathcal{G}$ are polynomial-time computable and have fixed output length $|G_n(x_0)| = |G_n(x_1)|$ for all $x_0, x_1 \in \mathcal{M}$. (We note that the latter trivially holds when $\mathcal{G}$ is a family of circuits.)

Theorem 9 (leveled HE is funcCPA). *Let* $\mathcal{E}$ *be a leveled HE scheme with independent level keys. If* $\mathcal{E}$ *is CPA-secure, then* $\mathcal{E}$ *is leveled-funcCPA-secure w.r.t. any admissible family* $\mathcal{G}$.

Proof. Let $\mathcal{E} = $ (Gen, Enc, Dec, Eval) be a CPA-secure public-key leveled HE scheme with message space $\mathcal{M}$. Assume by contradiction that there exists an admissible family of functions $\mathcal{G} = \{G_n \colon \mathcal{M} \to \mathcal{M}\}_{n \in \mathbb{N}}$ over $\mathcal{M}$ such that $\mathcal{E}$

---

[5] In case of an error, compute $\mathbf{e}' \leftarrow \mathsf{Enc}_{pk_{\ell-1}}(G_n(m))$ for an arbitrary $m \in \mathcal{M}$.

is not funcCPA-secure w.r.t $\mathcal{G}$. That is, there exists a ppt adversary $\mathcal{A}$ and a polynomial $p(\cdot)$ such that for infinity many λ and L it holds that:

$$\Pr[\mathsf{EXP}^{Fcpa}_{\mathcal{A},\mathcal{E},\mathcal{G}}(\lambda, L) = 1] > \frac{1}{2} + \frac{1}{p(\lambda)} \tag{5}$$

We show below that given $\mathcal{A}$ we can construct an adversary $\mathcal{B}$ that wins in $\mathsf{EXP}^{cpa}_{\mathcal{B},\mathcal{E}}(\lambda, L)$ with non-negligible advantage, violating the CPA security of $\mathcal{E}$.

The adversary $\mathcal{B}$ executes $\mathcal{A}$, relaying messages between the challenger and $\mathcal{A}$, while responding to any query $(\mathbf{e}_\ell, n)$ from $\mathcal{A}$ with an encryption using $pk_{\ell-1}$ of G_n on an arbitrary message $m \in \mathcal{M}$. That is $\mathcal{B}$ does the following,

- Upon receiving $(pk_\ell)_{\ell \in \{0,...,L\}}$ from challenger, forward it to $\mathcal{A}$.
- Answer queries $(\mathbf{e}_\ell, n)$ for a ciphertext $\mathbf{e}_\ell$ of level ℓ by $\mathbf{e}' \leftarrow \mathsf{Enc}_{pk_{\ell-1}}(G_n(m))$ for an arbitrary $m \in \mathcal{M}$.
- Once $\mathcal{A}$ generates x_0, x_1 and ℓ forward them to the challenger and return the response $c \leftarrow \mathsf{Enc}_{pk_\ell}(x_b)$ to $\mathcal{A}$.
- Output the b' that $\mathcal{A}$ outputs.

The adversary $\mathcal{B}$ is ppt due to adversary $\mathcal{A}$ being ppt and admissibility of $\mathcal{G}$. Moreover all the interaction of $\mathcal{A}$ is perfectly simulated by $\mathcal{B}$ except for the responses to queries to $\{\mathsf{Enc}_{pk_{\ell-1}}(\mathcal{G}(\mathsf{Dec}_{sk_\ell}(\cdot)))\}_{\ell \in [L]}$ that are simulated using encryption of the image of G_n on an arbitrary message.

Let $\mathsf{EXP}^{Fcpa^\#}$ experiment denote this variant of EXP^{Fcpa} that is simulated by $\mathcal{A}$, namely $\mathsf{EXP}^{Fcpa^\#}$ is an experiment identical to EXP^{Fcpa} except that each query $(\mathbf{e}_\ell, n)$ to Chal is answered by the encryption of $G_n(m)$ under $pk_{\ell-1}$ for arbitrary $m \in \mathcal{M}$.

By definition of $\mathsf{EXP}^{Fcpa^\#}$ it holds that,

$$\Pr[\mathsf{EXP}^{Fcpa^\#}_{\mathcal{A},\mathcal{E},\mathcal{G}}(\lambda, L) = 1] = \Pr[\mathsf{EXP}^{cpa}_{\mathcal{B},\mathcal{E}}(\lambda, L) = 1] \tag{6}$$

Furthermore, the CPA security and independent level keys of $\mathcal{E}$ guarantees (as shown in Lemma 4 below) that $\mathcal{A}$'s winning probability in $\mathsf{EXP}^{Fcpa^\#}$ and EXP^{Fcpa} is computationally indistinguishable. In particular,

$$\begin{aligned} |\Pr[\mathsf{EXP}^{Fcpa^\#}_{\mathcal{A},\mathcal{E},\mathcal{G}}(\lambda, L) = 1] \\ - \Pr[\mathsf{EXP}^{Fcpa}_{\mathcal{A},\mathcal{E},\mathcal{G}}(\lambda, L) = 1]| \leq \mathsf{neg}(\lambda)\ . \end{aligned} \tag{7}$$

Putting Eq. 7 together with Eqs. 5–6 it follows that

$$\Pr[\mathsf{EXP}^{cpa}_{\mathcal{B},\mathcal{E}}(\lambda, L) = 1] \geq \frac{1}{2} + \frac{1}{p(\lambda)} - \mathsf{neg}(\lambda). \tag{8}$$

Combining this with $\mathcal{A}$ being ppt we derive a contradiction to $\mathcal{E}$ being CPA secure. This concludes the proof. $\qquad\square$

Let $\mathsf{EXP}^{Fcpa^\#}$ be as defined in the proof of Theorem 9, i.e., it is identical to EXP^{Fcpa} except that Chal, upon receiving queries $(\mathbf{e}_\ell, n)$, instead of responding as in step 2 in Definition 10, responds by sending the encryption under $pk_{\ell-1}$ of $G_n(m)$ for an arbitrary message $m \in \mathcal{M}$ (rather then $m = \mathsf{Dec}_{sk_\ell}(\mathbf{e}_\ell)$). We show that the adversary is indifferent to the correctness of answers it receives from the Chal in the sense that its output distribution in EXP^{Fcpa} and $\mathsf{EXP}^{Fcpa^\#}$ is indistinguishable.

Lemma 4. *Let $\mathcal{E} = (\mathsf{Gen}, \mathsf{Enc}, \mathsf{Dec}, \mathsf{Eval})$ be a CPA-secure leveled HE scheme with a message space $\mathcal{M}$. Let $\mathcal{G} = \{G_n : \mathcal{M} \to \mathcal{M}\}_{n \in \mathbb{N}}$ be a family of admissible functions. If $\mathcal{E}$ has independent level keys then for any ppt adversary $\mathcal{A}$, there exists a negligible function $\mathsf{neg}(\cdot)$ such that for all sufficiently large λ and every L polynomial in λ the following holds:*

$$|\Pr[\mathsf{EXP}^{Fcpa^\#}_{\mathcal{A},\mathcal{E},\mathcal{G}}(\lambda, L) = 1] - \Pr[\mathsf{EXP}^{Fcpa}_{\mathcal{A},\mathcal{E},\mathcal{G}}(\lambda, L) = 1]| \le \mathsf{neg}(\lambda)$$

Proof. The proof relies on keys independence; details appear in the full version [2]. □

Schemes with independent level keys. In BV, BGV and B/FV, for example, indeed each ciphertext is associated with a level and there are independent encryption and decryption keys (pk_ℓ, sk_ℓ) for each level ℓ. Moreover, the evaluation key evk_ℓ (called key switching in BV, BGV and B and re-linearization keys in FV) is essentially the encryption of an efficiently computable function of the secret key sk_ℓ of the current level (concretely, the encryption of $sk'_\ell = \mathsf{Powersof2}(sk_\ell \otimes sk_\ell)$) under the public key $pk_{\ell-1}$ for the next level.

More accurately, to generate evk_ℓ they use a *fresh* public key $pk'_{\ell-1}$ with which they mask sk'_ℓ. This is important when instantiating their scheme as a fully homomorphic encryption, i.e., when there's a single key tuple (pk, evk, sk) used for all levels, in which case using pk (rather than pk') to encryt a function of sk would require a circular security assumption. In contrast, when using these schemes as a leveled HE, as we do, then anyhow the keys (pk_ℓ, sk_ℓ) are sampled independently from $(pk_{\ell-1}, sk_{\ell-1})$, and so encrypting sk'_ℓ under $pk_{\ell-1}$ requires no circular security assumption. Therefore, their generation of the evaluation keys can be modified to output the encryption of sk'_ℓ under $pk_{\ell-1}$, without harming correctness or security.[6] With this slight modification indeed these scheme satisfy Definition 9.

Proposition 1. *The leveled HE schemes of BV, BGV and B/FV [10–12, 21] (with the aforementioned evaluation key) have independent level keys.*

Corollary 1. *The leveled HE schemes of BV, BGV and B/FV [10–12, 21] (with the aforementioned evaluation key) are leveled-funcCPA-secure.*

---

[6] We remark that the noise in the modified evaluation keys is slightly larger: the noise of a fresh ciphertext, rather than a sample from the error distribution; nonetheless, this makes essentially no difference when using the scheme.

3.4   Barriers on Proving funcCPA for Existing HE Schemes

In this section we prove that if the homomorphic encryption scheme of BV [12] or BGV [11] is funcCPA-secure, then it is (weakly) circular secure. More generally, we show the above holds for all schemes satisfying a property we call *oblivious secret key extraction (ObvSK)*. In the following we first formally define weak circular security and ObvSK; then prove that for schemes supporting ObvSK, funcCPA-security w.r.t a proper family $\mathcal{F}$ implies weak circular security; and conclude by showing that the schemes of BV and BGV support ObvSK.

Circular security extends CPA-security to capture security of public key encryption schemes against adversaries seeing an encryption of the secret key [15, Definition 2.5].

Circular security is required by all fully homomorphic encryption schemes following Gentry's [22] blueprint, as they publish an encryption of the secret key to be used during bootstrapping (where bootstrapping [22] is the process of homomorphically evaluating the scheme's decryption circuit with a hardwired ciphertext on an encrypted secret key as input). Specifically, they require security to hold against adversaries seeing an encryption of the secret key in the encoding by which it is specified as input to the decryption circuit (see [12, Definition 3.8]).

Weak circular security is formally stated, for a public key encryption scheme $\mathcal{E} = (\text{Gen}, \text{Enc}, \text{Dec})$, using the following experiment between a challenger Chal and an adversary $\mathcal{A}$ (where sk denotes the secret key when specified in the encoding as required for the decryption circuit):

The weak circular indistinguishability experiment $\text{EXP}_{\mathcal{A},\mathcal{E}}^{wc}(\lambda)$:

1. Chal computes $(pk, sk) \leftarrow \text{Gen}(1^{\lambda})$ and $\mathbf{c}_{sk} \leftarrow \text{Enc}_{pk}(\text{sk})$, and sends $(pk, \mathbf{c}_{sk})$ to $\mathcal{A}$.
2. $\mathcal{A}$ sends to Chal two messages x_0, x_1 s.t. $|x_0| = |x_1|$.
3. Chal chooses a random bit $b \in \{0,1\}$, computes a ciphertext $c \leftarrow \text{Enc}_{pk}(x_b)$ and sends c to $\mathcal{A}$. We call c the challenge ciphertext.
4. $\mathcal{A}$ outputs a bit b'.
5. The output of the experiment is defined to be 1 if $b' = b$ (0 otherwise).

Definition 11 (weak circular security). *A PKE scheme $\mathcal{E} = (\text{Gen}, \text{Enc}, \text{Dec})$ is weakly circular secure if for every ppt adversary $\mathcal{A}$, there exists a negligible function* $\text{neg}(\cdot)$ *such that for all sufficiently large λ,*

$$\Pr[\text{EXP}_{\mathcal{A},\mathcal{E}}^{wc}(\lambda) = 1] \leq \frac{1}{2} + \text{neg}(\lambda)$$

where the probability is taken over the random coins of $\mathcal{A}$ and Chal.

Oblivious secret key extraction captures the ability to generate, from the public key, ciphertexts encrypting data related to the secret key, so that from their decryption one can efficiently compute the secret key in the encoding as required for the decryption circuit.

Definition 12 (oblivious secret key extraction (ObvSK)). *Let $\mathcal{E} = ($Gen, Enc, Dec$)$ be a PKE scheme with message space $\mathcal{M}$, and $\mathcal{F} = \{F_n \colon \mathcal{M} \to \mathcal{M}\}_{n \in \mathbb{N}}$ be a family of functions. We say that $\mathcal{E}$ supports oblivious secret key extraction (ObvSK) w.r.t $\mathcal{F}$ if there exists a ppt algorithm Alg that takes a public key pk and outputs $n = n(\lambda)$ ciphertexts under pk, so that the following holds. There exists a negligible function $\mathsf{neg}(\cdot)$ such that for all $\lambda \in \mathbb{N}$ the following holds:*

$$\Pr\left[\begin{array}{c} (pk,sk)\leftarrow\mathsf{Gen}(1^\lambda) \\ (c_1,\ldots,c_n)\leftarrow\mathsf{Alg}(pk) \\ F_n(\mathsf{Dec}_{sk}(c_1),\ldots,\mathsf{Dec}_{sk}(c_n))=sk \end{array} \right] \geq 1 - \mathsf{neg}(\lambda) \tag{9}$$

where the secret key sk outputted by F_n is in the encoding required for the decryption circuit, and where the probability is taken over the randomness in Gen and Alg.

funcCPA-security for schemes supporting ObvSK implies weak circular security. Next we show that if a public key encryption scheme $\mathcal{E}$ support ObvSK w.r.t $\mathcal{F}$ and is funcCPA-secure w.r.t $\mathcal{G}$ that contains $\mathcal{F}$, then $\mathcal{E}$ is weakly circular secure.

Theorem 10. *Let $\mathcal{E} = ($Gen, Enc, Dec$)$ be a PKE scheme that is funcCPA-secure w.r.t a family of functions $\mathcal{G}$. If $\mathcal{E}$ is ObvSK w.r.t $\mathcal{F}$ and $\mathcal{F} \subseteq \mathcal{G}$ then $\mathcal{E}$ is weakly circular-secure.*

Proof. The proof idea is, given pk, to first use Alg (from the ObvSK property) to get encrypted data related to sk; then use $\mathsf{Enc}_{pk}(\mathcal{G}(\mathsf{Dec}_{sk}(\cdot)))$ (from the funcCPA property) to transform them to ciphertexts $\mathbf{c}_{sk}$ encrypting sk (in the encoding for the decryption circuit); finally show that –if the scheme is not circular secure– then using $\mathbf{c}_{sk}$ we can break funcCPA-security. The formal details follow.

Suppose by contradiction that $\mathcal{E}$ is not circular-secure, i.e., there exists a ppt adversary $\mathcal{A}$ that wins $\mathsf{EXP}^{wc}_{\mathcal{A},\mathcal{E}}$ with non-negligible advantage over a random guess. We construct an adversary $\mathcal{B}$ that runs $\mathcal{A}$ internally and breaks funcCPA-security of the scheme.

The adversary $\mathcal{B}$ participates in the funcCPA-security experiment as follows. First, given pk from Chal, $\mathcal{B}$ computes $(c_1, \ldots, c_n) \leftarrow \mathsf{Alg}(pk)$ (for Alg as guaranteed by the ObvSK property), sends a query $((c_1, \ldots, c_n), n)$ to the $\mathsf{Enc}_{pk}(\mathcal{G}(\mathsf{Dec}_{sk}(\cdot)))$ oracle (provided as part of the funcCPA experiment), and receives in response (the vector of ciphertexts)

$$\mathbf{c}_{sk} = \mathsf{Enc}_{pk}(F_n(\mathsf{Dec}_{sk}(c_1), \ldots, \mathsf{Dec}_{sk}(c_n))),$$

which is an encryption of the secret key sk in the encoding as needed for bootstrapping with $1 - \mathsf{neg}(\lambda)$ probability (by the ObvSK property). Next $\mathcal{B}$, internally runs $\mathcal{A}$, while providing to it $\mathbf{c}_{sk}$ together with pk, relaying messages between $\mathcal{A}$ and Chal, and outputting the guess b' outputted by $\mathcal{A}$.

The view of $\mathcal{A}$ in $\mathsf{EXP}^{Fcpa}_{\mathcal{B},\mathcal{E}}$ is identical to its view in $\mathsf{EXP}^{wc}_{\mathcal{A},\mathcal{E}}$ (except with a $\mathsf{neg}(\lambda)$ probability, for the case of failure in the ObvSK). Implying (by the contradiction assumption)

$$\Pr[\mathrm{EXP}_{\mathcal{B},\mathcal{E}}^{Fcpa}(\lambda) = 1] > \frac{1}{2} + \frac{1}{p(\lambda)}$$

for some polynomial $p(\cdot)$, in contradiction to the funcCPA-security of $\mathcal{E}$.   □

As a corollary from Theorem 10 we conclude that for bootstrappable ObvSK schemes, funcCPA-security implies full homomorphism without relying on any circular security assumption.

Corollary 2. *Let $\mathcal{E} = (\mathsf{Gen}, \mathsf{Enc}, \mathsf{Dec}, \mathsf{Eval})$ be a bootstrappable HE scheme that supports ObvSK w.r.t $\mathcal{F}$. If $\mathcal{E}$ is funcCPA-secure w.r.t $\mathcal{G}$ and $\mathcal{F} \subseteq \mathcal{G}$ then $\mathcal{E}$ is fully homomorphic.*

Proof. The proof is derived by combining the following two facts. First, by Theorem 4.3.2 in [22], bootstrappable HE schemes that are weakly circular secure are fully homomorphic. Second, by Theorem 10, if $\mathcal{E}$ support ObvSK w.r.t $\mathcal{F}$ and it is funcCPA-secure w.r.t $\mathcal{G}$ that contains $\mathcal{F}$, then $\mathcal{E}$ is weakly circular secure. Combining the above, we conclude that $\mathcal{E}$ is fully homomorphic.   □

Schemes supporting ObvSK. BV and BGV are examples of schemes supporting ObvSK. More generally, we show that ObvSK is supported by all public key encryption schemes $\mathcal{E} = (\mathsf{Gen}, \mathsf{Enc}, \mathsf{Dec})$ satisfying the following:

1. The secret key $sk = (1, s)$ and ciphertext c are from the ring:
   - LWE-based schemes: $\mathbb{Z}_q^{n+1}$
   - RLWE-based schemes: R_q^2 for $R_q = \mathbb{Z}_q[x]/F[X]$
   where q, n, d are positive integers, d a power of 2, $F[X] = X^d + 1$, and s has small coefficients in the sense that decryption correctness holds on ciphertexts encrypting each coefficient of s.
2. Decryption is via inner-product (with messages encoded in the least significant bits): $\mathsf{Dec}_{sk}(c) = \left[[\langle c, sk \rangle]_q\right]_p$ where $[z]_x$ is the remainder of z in division by x and p a positive integer.

In the following let $\mathcal{F}^{LWE} = \{F_n^{LWE} \colon \mathbb{Z}_q^n \to \{0,1\}^{n \cdot \lceil \log q \rceil}\}_{q,n}$ denote a family of functions that given $(s_1, \ldots, s_n) \in \mathbb{Z}_q^n$ outputs $sk = (1, s) \in \mathbb{Z}_q^{n+1}$ in the encoding as required by the decryption circuit in LWE-based schemes satisfying the above properties. Similarly, let $\mathcal{F}^{RLWE} = \{F_d^{RLWE} \colon R_q \to R_q^2\}_{q,d}$ denote a family of functions that given $(s'_{d-1}, \ldots, s'_0) \in R_q$ outputs $sk = (1, (-s'_0, s'_{d-1}, \ldots, s'_1)) \in R_q^2$ in the encoding as required by the decryption circuit in the RLWE-based schemes satisfying the above properties. (Here $(s'_{d-1}, \ldots, s'_0)$ is a vector of coefficients specifying a polynomial $s'(X) \in R_q$, and 1 denotes the unit element in R_q.) Moreover, for a scheme $\mathcal{E}$ satisfying the above properties, either in the LWE-based or RLWE-based form, we use the short hand notation of denoting by $\mathcal{F}^{GLWE}$ the family $\mathcal{F}^{LWE}$ in case $\mathcal{E}$ is LWE-based, and $\mathcal{F}^{RLWE}$ otherwise.

Proposition 2. *Suppose $\mathcal{E} = (\mathsf{Gen}, \mathsf{Enc}, \mathsf{Dec})$ satisfies (1)–(2) above. Then $\mathcal{E}$ supports ObvSK w.r.t to $\mathcal{F}^{GLWE}$.*

Proof. The proof appears in the full version [2].

As an immediate corollary from Proposition 2 we obtain that the addressed schemes support ObvSK.

Corollary 3 (BV and BGV support ObvSK). *The HE schemes from BV [12] and BGV [11] support ObvSK w.r.t to $\mathcal{F}^{GLWE}$.*

Since these schemes are known to be bootstrappable, then combining Corollary 3 with Corollary 2 we derive that if they are funcCPA-secure then they are fully homomorphic.

Corollary 4. *If BV [12] or BGV [11] is funcCPA-secure w.r.t to $\mathcal{G}$ containing $\mathcal{F}^{GLWE}$, then it is fully homomorphic.*

4   CPA Insufficiency Against Malicious Adversaries

We show that CPA-security is insufficient for guaranteeing privacy in client-aided outsourcing protocols. For this purpose we construct a CPA-secure PKE scheme and exhibit an input-recovery attack that completely breaks privacy in client-aided outsourcing protocols instantiated with our scheme. In fact, we can transform any CPA-secure encryption scheme $\mathcal{E}$ with message space $\mathcal{M}$ of super polynomial size, using a one-way function f and any function G, into a CPA-secure encryption scheme $\mathcal{E}^f$ for which our attack works on any $(\mathcal{E}^f, \mathcal{G})$-aided outsourcing protocol for any $\mathcal{G}$ containing G . Moreover, if $\mathcal{E}$ was an HE scheme then so is $\mathcal{E}^f$. For simplicity of the presentation we concentrate on G being the identity function $\mathcal{I}$ for the construction of $\mathcal{E}^f$. The scheme $\mathcal{E}^f$ is similar to $\mathcal{E}$, except for the key difference that its encryption and decryption are "punctured" on a random point $m^* \in \mathcal{M}$, where its public key implicitly specifies m^* by augmenting it with $f(m^*)$ and $\mathsf{Enc}_{pk}(m^*)$.[7] See our construction in Fig. 1 and Theorem 11. Our attack breaks security in the strong sense that the server is able to completely recover the client's input; See Theorem 12.

Theorem 11 (properties of $\mathcal{E}^f$). *For every PKE scheme $\mathcal{E}$ and one-way function f over the message-space of $\mathcal{E}$, the scheme $\mathcal{E}^f$ (cf. Figure 1) is a PKE scheme satisfying the following. If $\mathcal{E}$ is CPA-secure, compact, and $\mathcal{C}$-homomorphic, then $\mathcal{E}^f$ is CPA-secure, compact, and $\mathcal{C} \times \mathcal{C}$-homomorphic.*[8]

Proof. Correctness, compactness and homomorphism of $\mathcal{E}^f$ follow directly from the properties of $\mathcal{E}$. The CPA-security of $\mathcal{E}^f$ follows from the CPA-security of $\mathcal{E}$ and the one-wayness of f: the encryption in $\mathcal{E}^f$ is identical to encrypting pairs

---

[7] In case our $\mathcal{G}$ of interest does not contain the identity function, we slightly modify $\mathcal{E}^f$ by replacing each occurrence of $\mathsf{Enc}_{pk}(m^*)$ and $f(m^*)$ in Fig. 1 with $\mathsf{Enc}_{pk}(G(m^*))$ and $f(G(m^*))$ respectively for an efficiently computable $G \in \mathcal{G}$, and slightly modify the proof by replacing each occurrence of $\mathcal{I}$ by G.

[8] We note that a $\mathcal{C} \times \mathcal{C}$-homomorphic encryption scheme is also $\mathcal{C}$-homomorphic, as we can embed $\mathcal{C}$ in $\mathcal{C} \times \mathcal{C}$, e.g., by mapping every $C \in \mathcal{C}$ into $(C, C) \in \mathcal{C} \times \mathcal{C}$.

$\mathsf{Gen}^f(1^\lambda)$: Given 1^λ, output (pk^f, sk^f) computed as follows. Let $(pk, sk) \leftarrow \mathsf{Gen}(1^\lambda)$ and sample a uniformly random $m^* \in \mathcal{M}$. Set

$$pk^f := (pk, \mathsf{Enc}_{pk}(m^*), f(m^*)) \text{ and } sk^f := (sk, f(m^*)).$$

$\mathsf{Enc}^f_{pk^f}(m)$: Given $m = (m_1, m_2) \in \mathcal{M} \times \mathcal{M}$, if $f(m_2) = f(m^*)$ then output (m_1, m_2), else output

$$(\mathsf{Enc}_{pk}(m_1), \mathsf{Enc}_{pk}(m_2)).$$

$\mathsf{Dec}^f_{sk^f}(c)$: Given $c = (c_1, c_2)$, if $f(c_2) = f(m^*)$ then output (c_1, c_2), else output

$$(\mathsf{Dec}_{sk}(c_1), \mathsf{Dec}_{sk}(c_2)).$$

$\mathsf{Eval}^f_{pk^f}(C, c_1, ..., c_\ell)$: Given a circuit $C = C_1 \times C_2$ over ℓ inputs, and ℓ ciphertexts $c_i = (c_{i,1}, c_{i,2})$ for $i \in [\ell]$, do the following. For each $i \in [\ell]$, if $f(c_{i,2}) = f(m^*)$ then set $c'_i = (\mathsf{Enc}_{pk}(c_{i,1}), \mathsf{Enc}_{pk}(c_{i,2}))$, else set $c'_i = c_i$. Output

$$(\mathsf{Eval}_{pk}(C_1, c'_{1,1}, ..., c'_{\ell,1}), \mathsf{Eval}_{pk}(C_2, c'_{1,2}, ..., c'_{\ell,2})).$$

Fig. 1. The construction of the scheme $\mathcal{E}^f = (\mathsf{Gen}^f, \mathsf{Enc}^f, \mathsf{Dec}^f, \mathsf{Eval}^f)$ from a PKE scheme $\mathcal{E} = (\mathsf{Gen}, \mathsf{Enc}, \mathsf{Dec}, \mathsf{Eval})$ with message space $\mathcal{M}$ and ciphertext space $\mathcal{T}$ and a one-way function f over $\mathcal{M}$. The message-space and ciphertext-space of $\mathcal{E}^f$ are $\mathcal{M} \times \mathcal{M}$ and $(\mathcal{T} \times \mathcal{T}) \cup (\mathcal{M} \times \mathcal{M})$ respectively.

(m_1, m_2) of messages under $\mathcal{E}$, except if m_2 is a pre-image of $f(m^*)$, but the latter occurs with no more than a negligible probability due to f being a one-way function and m^* being a random message. See formal details in the full version [2]. $\qquad \square$

We present our attack in which the server recovers the client's input in any $(\mathcal{E}^f, \mathcal{G})$-aided outsourcing protocol for $\mathcal{G}$ containing the identity function $\mathcal{I}$. We remark that our attack is applicable from every PKE $\mathcal{E}$, regardless of whether it is a HE scheme.

Theorem 12 (CPA-security does not imply privacy). *For every PKE scheme $\mathcal{E}$ with message-space $\mathcal{M}$ and every one-way function f over $\mathcal{M}$, there exists a CPA-secure PKE scheme $\mathcal{E}^f$ so that for every family of functions $\mathcal{G} = \{G_n \colon \mathcal{M} \to \mathcal{M}\}_{n \in \mathbb{N}}$ containing the identity function $\mathcal{I}$ and every $(\mathcal{E}^f, \mathcal{G})$-aided outsourcing protocol there is a server's strategy that recovers the client's input.*

Proof. Denote $\mathcal{E} = (\mathsf{Gen}, \mathsf{Enc}, \mathsf{Dec})$. Set $\mathcal{E}^f = (\mathsf{Gen}^f, \mathsf{Enc}^f, \mathsf{Dec}^f)$ to be the encryption scheme constructed from $\mathcal{E}$ and f in Fig. 1.

Our active input-recovery attack is applicable on any $(\mathcal{E}^f, \mathcal{G})$-aided outsourcing protocol $\pi = \langle \mathsf{Clnt}, \mathsf{Srv} \rangle$ as follows.

1. Clnt executes phase 1 of π. That is, it runs $(pk^f, sk^f) \leftarrow \mathsf{Gen}^f(1^\lambda)$ to obtain a public key $pk^f = (pk, \mathsf{Enc}_{pk}(m^*), f(m^*))$, encrypts its input x by computing $\mathbf{c}_x \leftarrow \mathsf{Enc}^f_{pk^f}(x, x)$ and sends $\mathbf{c}_x$ and pk^f to Srv.

2. Upon receiving $c_x = (c_1, c_2)$ and pk^f, Srv generates a new ciphertext $e = (c_1, \text{Enc}_{pk}(m^*))$, where $\text{Enc}_{pk}(m^*)$ is taken from pk^f, and sends $(e, \mathcal{I})$ to Clnt.
3. Clnt sends $(c'_1, c'_2) \leftarrow \text{Enc}^f_{pk^f}(\mathcal{I}(\text{Dec}^f_{sk^f}(e)))$ to Srv.
4. Upon receiving the client's response (c'_1, c'_2), Srv outputs c'_1.

The attack recovers the client's input x because $c'_1 = x$ as explained next. Observe that $\mathcal{I}(\text{Dec}^f_{sk^f}(e)) = (x, m^*)$ is a message where the encryption algorithms $\text{Enc}^f_{pk^f}$ is punctured, implying that

$$\text{Enc}^f_{pk^f}(\mathcal{I}(\text{Dec}^f_{sk^f}(e))) = (x, m^*).$$

Namely, $(c'_1, c'_2) = (x, m^*)$ in Step 3, and so $c'_1 = x$. □

5   CPA Implies Privacy Against Semi-honest Adversaries

We define a natural property for $(\mathcal{E}, \mathcal{G})$-aided outsourcing protocols (called *cleartext computable*), and show that for protocols satisfying this property, CPA-security guarantees privacy against semi-honest servers; See Theorem 13.

Cleartext computable protocols. A protocol is cleartext computable if the messages whose encryption constitutes the client's responses to the server's queries are efficiently computable given only the client's input. To formalize this we first define the client's cleartext response. Let $\pi = \langle \text{Clnt}, \text{Srv} \rangle$ be an $(\mathcal{E}, \mathcal{G})$-aided outsourcing protocol (cf. Definition 5). The client's *cleartext response* in an execution of π on client's input x and randomness r_{Clnt}, server's randomness r_{Srv}, and security parameter $\lambda \in \mathbb{N}$, is defined by:

$$\text{clear-res}^\pi((x, r_{\text{Clnt}}), r_{\text{Srv}}, \lambda) = (G_{n_1}(\text{Dec}_{sk}(e_1)), \ldots, G_{n_q}(\text{Dec}_{sk}(e_q)))$$

where $(sk, pk) \leftarrow \text{Gen}(1^\lambda)$ is the key pair generated by the client in Phase 1 of π; q is the number of queries sent from server to client in Phase 2 of π; and for each $j \in [q]$, (e_j, n_j) and $\text{Enc}_{pk}(G_{n_j}(\text{Dec}_{sk}(e_j)))$ are the jth server's query and the corresponding client's response respectively with $G_{n_j}(\text{Dec}_{sk}(e_j))$ being the underlying cleartext response message.

Definition 13 (cleartext computable). *An $(\mathcal{E}, \mathcal{G})$-aided outsourcing protocol $\pi = \langle \text{Clnt}, \text{Srv} \rangle$ for computing a function $F : A \to B$ is cleartext computable if Srv is ppt and there exists a ppt function h such that for all inputs $x \in A$, all client and server randomness r_{Clnt} and r_{Srv}, respectively, and all $\lambda \in \mathbb{N}$*

$$\text{clear-res}^\pi((x, r_{\text{Clnt}}), r_{\text{Srv}}, \lambda) = h(x)$$

CPA-security implies privacy for cleartext computable protocols. We show that for cleartext computable $(\mathcal{E}, \mathcal{G})$-aided outsourcing protocols, CPA-security of $\mathcal{E}$ implies that the protocol preserves privacy against semi-honest servers.

Similarly to Theorem 9, the family $\mathcal{G}$ should be admissible in the sense that all $G_n \in \mathcal{G}$ are polynomial-time computable (in the security parameter) and have fixed output length, i.e., $|G_n(x_0)| = |G_n(x_1)|$ for all $x_0, x_1 \in \mathcal{M}$.

Theorem 13 (privacy of cleartext computable protocols). *Every cleartext computable $(\mathcal{E}, \mathcal{G})$-aided outsourcing protocol preserves privacy against semi-honest servers, provided that $\mathcal{E}$ is CPA-secure and $\mathcal{G}$ is admissible.*

Proof. We show that for cleartext computable protocols, when instantiated with a CPA-secure encryption scheme, a semi-honest server cannot distinguish encrypted response of correct or random values, and hence privacy follows. The formal proof appears in the full version [2].

6   Conclusions

In this work we introduce the notion of funcCPA, which is a strict relaxation of CCA2-security, show it is achievable for HE schemes (unlike CCA2) and sufficient for ensuring privacy against malicious servers for the wide an natural family of client-aided outsourcing protocols (unlike CPA, as we prove). In contrast, against semi-honest adversaries, we prove that CPA-security suffices for ensuring privacy in all cleartext computable client-aided outsourcing protocols.

A   Proof of Lemma 2

We prove Lemma 2 showing that for every fully decryptable HE scheme $\mathcal{E}$ that has a sanitization algorithm Sanitize, if its sanitized version $\mathcal{E}^{\mathsf{santz}}$ is $\mathcal{C}$-homomorphic, then it is circuit-private$^+$ for $\mathcal{C}$.

Proof (of Lemma 2). Let $\mathcal{E} = (\mathsf{Gen}, \mathsf{Enc}, \mathsf{Dec}, \mathsf{Eval})$ be a fully decryptable HE scheme with a sanitization algorithm Sanitize. Denote by $\mathcal{E}^{\mathsf{santz}} = (\mathsf{Gen}, \mathsf{Enc}^{\mathsf{santz}}, \mathsf{Dec}, \mathsf{Eval}^{\mathsf{santz}})$ its sanitized version as specified in Definition 7. Let $\mathcal{C}$ be the set of circuits so that $\mathcal{E}^{\mathsf{santz}}$ is $\mathcal{C}$-homomorphic. We show that $\mathcal{E}^{\mathsf{santz}}$ is circuit-private$^+$ for $\mathcal{C}$.

Fix a circuit $C \in \mathcal{C}$ over ℓ inputs, ciphertexts $c_1, \ldots, c_\ell$, a security parameter λ. To prove circuit-privacy$^+$ holds we need to show the two ciphertexts $\mathsf{Enc}_{pk}^{\mathsf{santz}}(C(\mathsf{Dec}_{sk}(c_1), \cdots, \mathsf{Dec}_{sk}(c_\ell)))$ and $\mathsf{Eval}_{pk}^{\mathsf{santz}}(C, c_1, \ldots, c_\ell)$ are statistically close, with overwhelming probability over the choice of $(pk, sk) \leftarrow \mathsf{Gen}(\lambda)$.

By definition of $\mathcal{E}^{\mathsf{santz}}$,

$$\mathsf{Enc}_{pk}^{\mathsf{santz}}(C(\mathsf{Dec}_{sk}(c_1), \cdots, \mathsf{Dec}_{sk}(c_\ell)))$$

$$= \mathsf{Sanitize}_{pk}(\mathsf{Enc}_{pk}(C(\mathsf{Dec}_{sk}(c_1), \ldots, \mathsf{Dec}_{sk}(c_\ell)))) \tag{10}$$

and

$$\mathsf{Eval}_{pk}^{\mathsf{santz}}(C, c_1, \ldots, c_\ell)$$

$$= \mathsf{Sanitize}_{pk}(\mathsf{Eval}_{pk}(C, \mathsf{Sanitize}_{pk}(c_1), \ldots, \mathsf{Sanitize}_{pk}(c_\ell))) \tag{11}$$

By the sanitization property of Sanitize, if two ciphertexts decrypt to the same plaintext then their sanitized version is statistically close. Therefore it is sufficient to show that the corresponding ciphertexts in the above two equations (i.e., $\mathsf{Enc}_{pk}\left(C\left(\mathsf{Dec}_{sk}(c_1),\ldots,\mathsf{Dec}_{sk}(c_\ell)\right)\right)$ and $\mathsf{Eval}_{pk}(C,\mathsf{Sanitize}_{pk}(c_1),\ldots,$ $\mathsf{Sanitize}_{pk}(c_\ell))$) decrypt to the same plaintext.

The correctness property of $\mathcal{E}$ together with it being fully decryptable ensures that for every $(pk,sk)\leftarrow\mathsf{Gen}(1^\lambda)$:

$$\forall i \in [\ell] : \Pr[\mathsf{Dec}_{sk}(\mathsf{Enc}_{pk}(\mathsf{Dec}_{sk}(c_i))) = \mathsf{Dec}_{sk}(c_i)] \geq 1 - \mathsf{neg}(\lambda) \qquad (12)$$

and

$$\Pr\left[\begin{smallmatrix}\mathsf{Dec}_{sk}(\mathsf{Enc}_{pk}(C(\mathsf{Dec}_{sk}(c_1),\ldots,\mathsf{Dec}_{sk}(c_\ell))))\\=C(\mathsf{Dec}_{sk}(c_1),\ldots,\mathsf{Dec}_{sk}(c_\ell))\end{smallmatrix}\right] \geq 1 - \mathsf{neg}(\lambda) \qquad (13)$$

where the probabilities are taken over the random coins of the encryption algorithm.

From Eq. 12 together with the sanitization property of $\mathsf{Sanitize}$, we obtain that, for each $i \in [\ell]$, with probability $\geq 1 - \mathsf{neg}(\lambda)$ over the choice of $(pk,sk) \leftarrow \mathsf{Gen}(1^\lambda)$:

$$\Delta\left(\left(\mathsf{Sanitize}_{pk}(\mathsf{Enc}_{pk}(\mathsf{Dec}_{sk}(c_i))),(pk,sk)\right),\left(\mathsf{Sanitize}_{pk}(c_i),(pk,sk)\right)\right) \leq \mathsf{neg}(\lambda)$$

Moreover, with probability $\geq 1 - \mathsf{neg}(\lambda)$, the above holds for all $i \in [\ell]$ simultaneously (by union bound).

Since $\mathsf{Sanitize}$ uses independent randomness for each $i \in [\ell]$, its output on distinct i's is statistically independent. So the joint distribution over all $i \in [\ell]$ is likewise negligible (since the statistical distance of the joint distribution of independent random variables is the sum of their statistical distances, and the number of random variables is $\ell = \mathsf{poly}(\lambda)$). Namely,

$$\Delta\left(\begin{smallmatrix}(\mathsf{Sanitize}_{pk}(\mathsf{Enc}_{pk}(\mathsf{Dec}_{sk}(c_1))),\ldots,\mathsf{Sanitize}_{pk}(\mathsf{Enc}_{pk}(\mathsf{Dec}_{sk}(c_\ell))),(pk,sk)),\\(\mathsf{Sanitize}_{pk}(c_1),\ldots,\mathsf{Sanitize}_{pk}(c_\ell),(pk,sk))\end{smallmatrix}\right) \leq \mathsf{neg}(\lambda) \quad (14)$$

The $\mathcal{C}$-homomorphism of $\mathcal{E}^{\mathsf{santz}}$ guarantees that $\mathcal{E}^* = (\mathsf{Gen},\mathsf{Enc}^{\mathsf{santz}},\mathsf{Dec},\mathsf{Eval})$ is likewise $\mathcal{C}$-homomorphic (due to the message-preservation property of $\mathsf{Sanitize}$), and hence for every $(pk,sk) \leftarrow \mathsf{Gen}(1^\lambda)$ it holds that,

$$\Pr\left[\begin{smallmatrix}\mathsf{Dec}_{sk}(\mathsf{Eval}_{pk}(C,\mathsf{Sanitize}_{pk}(\mathsf{Enc}_{pk}(\mathsf{Dec}_{sk}(c_1))),\ldots,\mathsf{Sanitize}_{pk}(\mathsf{Enc}_{pk}(\mathsf{Dec}_{sk}(c_\ell)))))\\=C(\mathsf{Dec}_{sk}(c_1),\ldots,\mathsf{Dec}_{sk}(c_\ell))\end{smallmatrix}\right] \geq 1 - \mathsf{neg}(\lambda) \quad (15)$$

Combining Eqs. 14–15 we guarantee correctness of Eval on the sanitized $c_1,\ldots,c_\ell$. That is, for every $(pk,sk) \leftarrow \mathsf{Gen}(1^\lambda)$ it holds that,

$$\Pr\left[\begin{smallmatrix}\mathsf{Dec}_{sk}(\mathsf{Eval}_{pk}(C,\mathsf{Sanitize}_{pk}(c_1),\ldots,\mathsf{Sanitize}_{pk}(c_\ell)))\\=C(\mathsf{Dec}_{sk}(c_1),\ldots,\mathsf{Dec}_{sk}(c_\ell))\end{smallmatrix}\right] \geq 1 - \mathsf{neg}(\lambda)$$

Using the correctness property of $\mathcal{E}$ as stated in Eq. 13 we obtain that for every $(pk,sk) \leftarrow \mathsf{Gen}(1^\lambda)$ it holds that with probability $\geq 1 - \mathsf{neg}(\lambda)$ over the random coins of the experiment,

$$\mathsf{Dec}_{sk}\left(\mathsf{Eval}_{pk}\left(C,\mathsf{Sanitize}_{pk}(c_1),\ldots,\mathsf{Sanitize}_{pk}(c_\ell)\right)\right)$$

$$=\mathsf{Dec}_{sk}\left(\mathsf{Enc}_{pk}\left(C\left(\mathsf{Dec}_{sk}(c_1),\ldots,\mathsf{Dec}_{sk}(c_\ell)\right)\right)\right)$$

This concludes the proof as by the sanitization property of Sanitize, we obtain that with probability $\geq 1 - \mathsf{neg}(\lambda)$ over the choice of $(pk, sk) \leftarrow \mathsf{Gen}(1^\lambda)$ and the random coins in Enc and Eval the following distributions are statistically close,

$$\mathsf{Sanitize}_{pk}\left(\mathsf{Enc}_{pk}\left(C\left(\mathsf{Dec}_{sk}(c_1), \ldots, \mathsf{Dec}_{sk}(c_\ell)\right)\right)\right)$$

and

$$\mathsf{Sanitize}_{pk}\left(\mathsf{Eval}_{pk}\left(C, \mathsf{Sanitize}_{pk}(c_1), \ldots, \mathsf{Sanitize}_{pk}(c_\ell)\right)\right)$$

as desired.   □

References

1. Akavia, A., Feldman, D., Shaul, H.: Secure search on encrypted data via multi-ring sketch. In: Lie, D., Mannan, M., Backes, M., Wang, X., eds Proceedings of the 2018 ACM SIGSAC Conference on Computer and Communications Security, CCS 2018, Toronto, ON, Canada, October 15–19, 2018, pages 985–1001. ACM (2018)
2. Akavia, A., Gentry, C., Halevi, S., Vald, M.: Achievable CCA2 relaxation for homomorphic encryption. Cryptology ePrint Archive, Paper 2022/282 (2022). https://eprint.iacr.org/2022/282
3. Akavia, A., Leibovich, M., Resheff, Y.S., Ron, R., Shahar, M., Vald, M.: Privacy-preserving decision tree training and prediction against malicious server. Cryptology ePrint Archive, Paper 2019/1282 (2019). https://eprint.iacr.org/2019/1282
4. Akavia, A., Leibovich, M., Resheff, Y.S., Ron, R., Shahar, M., Vald, M.: Privacy-preserving decision trees training and prediction. In: Hutter, F., Kersting, K., Lijffijt, J., Valera, I. (eds.) ECML PKDD 2020. LNCS (LNAI), vol. 12457, pp. 145–161. Springer, Cham (2021). https://doi.org/10.1007/978-3-030-67658-2_9
5. Akavia, A., Leibovich, M., Resheff, Y.S., Ron, R., Shahar, M., Vald, M.: Privacy-preserving decision trees training and prediction. ACM Trans. Priv. Secur. **25**(3), 1–30 (2022)
6. Akavia, A., Shaul, H., Weiss, M., Yakhini, Z.: Linear-regression on packed encrypted data in the two-server model. In: Brenner, M., Lepoint, T., Rohloff, K., eds Proceedings of the 7th ACM Workshop on Encrypted Computing & Applied Homomorphic Cryptography, WAHC@CCS 2019, London, UK, November 11–15, 2019, pp. 21–32. ACM (2019)
7. Akavia, A., Vald, M.: On the privacy of protocols based on CPA-secure homomorphic encryption. Cryptology ePrint Archive, Report 2021/803 (2021). https://ia.cr/2021/803
8. Bost, R., Popa, R.A., Tu, S., Goldwasser, S.: Machine learning classification over encrypted data. In: NDSS, vol. 4324, p. 4325 (2015)
9. Bourse, F., Del Pino, R., Minelli, M., Wee, H.: FHE circuit privacy almost for free. In: Robshaw, M., Katz, J. (eds.) CRYPTO 2016. LNCS, vol. 9815, pp. 62–89. Springer, Heidelberg (2016). https://doi.org/10.1007/978-3-662-53008-5_3
10. Brakerski, Z.: Fully homomorphic encryption without modulus switching from classical gapSVP. In: Advances in Cryptology - CRYPTO 2012–32nd Annual Cryptology Conference, Santa Barbara, CA, USA, August 19–23, 2012, pp. 868–886. Proceedings (2012)
11. Brakerski, Z., Gentry, C., Vaikuntanathan, V.: (Leveled) fully homomorphic encryption without bootstrapping. In: Innovations in Theoretical Computer Science 2012, Cambridge, MA, USA, January 8–10, 2012, pages 309–325 (2012)

12. Brakerski, Z., Vaikuntanathan, V.: Efficient fully homomorphic encryption from (standard) LWE. SIAM J. Comput. **43**(2), 831–871 (2014)
13. Canetti, R., Krawczyk, H., Nielsen, J.B.: Relaxing chosen-ciphertext security. In: Boneh, D. (ed.) CRYPTO 2003. LNCS, vol. 2729, pp. 565–582. Springer, Heidelberg (2003). https://doi.org/10.1007/978-3-540-45146-4_33
14. Canetti, R., Raghuraman, S., Richelson, S., Vaikuntanathan, V.: Chosen-ciphertext secure fully homomorphic encryption. In: Fehr, S. (ed.) PKC 2017. LNCS, vol. 10175, pp. 213–240. Springer, Heidelberg (2017). https://doi.org/10.1007/978-3-662-54388-7_8
15. Cash, D., Green, M., Hohenberger, S.: New definitions and separations for circular security. In: Fischlin, M., Buchmann, J., Manulis, M. (eds.) PKC 2012. LNCS, vol. 7293, pp. 540–557. Springer, Heidelberg (2012). https://doi.org/10.1007/978-3-642-30057-8_32
16. Cheon, J.H., Kim, A., Kim, M., Song, Y.: Homomorphic encryption for arithmetic of approximate numbers. In: Takagi, T., Peyrin, T. (eds.) ASIACRYPT 2017. LNCS, vol. 10624, pp. 409–437. Springer, Cham (2017). https://doi.org/10.1007/978-3-319-70694-8_15
17. Chillotti, I., Gama, N., Georgieva, M., Izabachène, M.: TFHE: fast fully homomorphic encryption over the torus. J. Cryptol. **33**, 34–91 (2019)
18. Chongchitmate, W., Ostrovsky, R.: Circuit-private multi-key FHE. In: Fehr, S. (ed.) PKC 2017. LNCS, vol. 10175, pp. 241–270. Springer, Heidelberg (2017). https://doi.org/10.1007/978-3-662-54388-7_9
19. Ducas, L., Micciancio, D.: FHEW: bootstrapping homomorphic encryption in less than a second. In: Oswald, E., Fischlin, M. (eds.) EUROCRYPT 2015. LNCS, vol. 9056, pp. 617–640. Springer, Heidelberg (2015). https://doi.org/10.1007/978-3-662-46800-5_24
20. Ducas, L., Stehlé, D.: Sanitization of FHE ciphertexts. In: Fischlin, M., Coron, J.-S. (eds.) EUROCRYPT 2016. LNCS, vol. 9665, pp. 294–310. Springer, Heidelberg (2016). https://doi.org/10.1007/978-3-662-49890-3_12
21. Fan, J., Vercauteren, F.: Somewhat practical fully homomorphic encryption. IACR Cryptol. ePrint Arch. **2012**, 144 (2012)
22. Gentry, C.: A fully homomorphic encryption scheme. Ph. D thesis, Stanford University (2009). https://crypto.stanford.edu/craig
23. Gentry, C.: Fully homomorphic encryption using ideal lattices. In: Proceedings of the 41st Annual ACM Symposium on Theory of Computing, STOC '09, pp. 169–178. Association for Computing Machinery, (2009)
24. Gentry, C., Sahai, A., Waters, B.: Homomorphic encryption from learning with errors: conceptually-simpler, asymptotically-faster, attribute-based. In: Canetti, R., Garay, J.A. (eds.) CRYPTO 2013. LNCS, vol. 8042, pp. 75–92. Springer, Heidelberg (2013). https://doi.org/10.1007/978-3-642-40041-4_5
25. Giacomelli, I., Jha, S., Joye, M., Page, C.D., Yoon, K.: Privacy-preserving ridge regression with only linearly-homomorphic encryption. In: Preneel, B., Vercauteren, F. (eds.) ACNS 2018. LNCS, vol. 10892, pp. 243–261. Springer, Cham (2018). https://doi.org/10.1007/978-3-319-93387-0_13
26. Goldreich, O.: The Foundations of Cryptography - Basic Techniques, vol. 1. Cambridge University Press, Cambridge (2001)
27. Hazay, C., Lindell, Y.: Efficient Secure Two-Party Protocols. ISC, Springer, Heidelberg (2010). https://doi.org/10.1007/978-3-642-14303-8
28. Ishai, Y., Paskin, A.: Evaluating branching programs on encrypted data. In: Vadhan, S.P. (ed.) TCC 2007. LNCS, vol. 4392, pp. 575–594. Springer, Heidelberg (2007). https://doi.org/10.1007/978-3-540-70936-7_31

29. Juvekar, C., Vaikuntanathan, V., Chandrakasan, A.: Gazelle: a low latency framework for secure neural network inference. In: Proceedings of the 27th USENIX Conference on Security Symposium, SEC'18, pp. 1651–1668. USENIX Association (2018)

30. Katz, J., Lindell, Y.: Introduction to Modern Cryptography (Chapman & Hall/CRC Cryptography and Network Security Series). Chapman & Hall/CRC (2007)

31. Lai, J., Deng, R.H., Ma, C., Sakurai, K., Weng, J.: CCA-Secure Keyed-Fully Homomorphic Encryption. In: Cheng, C.-M., Chung, K.-M., Persiano, G., Yang, B.-Y. (eds.) PKC 2016. LNCS, vol. 9614, pp. 70–98. Springer, Heidelberg (2016). https://doi.org/10.1007/978-3-662-49384-7_4

32. Li, B., Micciancio, D.: On the security of homomorphic encryption on approximate numbers. IACR Cryptology ePrint Archive **2020**, 1533 (2020)

33. Loftus, J., May, A., Smart, N.P., Vercauteren, F.: On CCA-secure somewhat homomorphic encryption. In: Miri, A., Vaudenay, S. (eds.) SAC 2011. LNCS, vol. 7118, pp. 55–72. Springer, Heidelberg (2012). https://doi.org/10.1007/978-3-642-28496-0_4

34. Malavolta, G.: Circuit privacy for quantum fully homomorphic encryption. IACR Cryptol. ePrint Arch. **2020**, 1454 (2020)

35. Nuida, K.: How to handle invalid queries for malicious-private protocols based on homomorphic encryption. In: Proceedings of the 9th ACM on ASIA Public-Key Cryptography Workshop, APKC '22, pp. 15–25, New York, NY, USA (2022). Association for Computing Machinery

36. Ostrovsky, R., Paskin-Cherniavsky, A., Paskin-Cherniavsky, B.: Maliciously circuit-private FHE. In: Garay, J.A., Gennaro, R. (eds.) CRYPTO 2014. LNCS, vol. 8616, pp. 536–553. Springer, Heidelberg (2014). https://doi.org/10.1007/978-3-662-44371-2_30

37. Peikert, C.: A decade of lattice cryptography. Found. Trends Theor. Comput. Sci. **10**(4), 283–424 (2016)

38. Prabhakaran, M., Rosulek, M.: Homomorphic encryption with CCA security. In: Aceto, L., Damgård, I., Goldberg, L.A., Halldórsson, M.M., Ingólfsdóttir, A., Walukiewicz, I. (eds.) ICALP 2008. LNCS, vol. 5126, pp. 667–678. Springer, Heidelberg (2008). https://doi.org/10.1007/978-3-540-70583-3_54

39. Regev, O.: On lattices, learning with errors, random linear codes, and cryptography. J. ACM **56**(6), 84–93 (2009)

40. Rosulek, M.: The joy of cryptography. http://joyofcryptography.com

41. Shoup, V.: A proposal for an ISO standard for public key encryption. IACR Cryptol. ePrint Arch., p. 112 (2001)

42. Wang, W., et al.: Toward scalable fully homomorphic encryption through light trusted computing assistance. CoRR abs/1905.07766 (2019)

Multi-party Computation I

Round-Optimal Honest-Majority MPC in Minicrypt and with Everlasting Security
(Extended Abstract)

Benny Applebaum[1] , Eliran Kachlon[1](✉) , and Arpita Patra[2]

[1] Tel-Aviv University, Tel-Aviv, Israel
benny.applebaum@gmail.com, elirn.chalon@gmail.com
[2] Indian Institute of Science, Bangalore, India
arpita@iisc.ac.in

Abstract. We study the round complexity of secure multiparty computation (MPC) in the challenging model where full security, including guaranteed output delivery, should be achieved at the presence of an active rushing adversary who corrupts up to half of parties. It is known that 2 rounds are insufficient in this model (Gennaro et al. Crypto 2002), and that 3 round protocols can achieve computational security under public-key assumptions (Gordon et al. Crypto 2015; Ananth et al. Crypto 2018; and Badrinarayanan et al. Asiacrypt 2020). However, despite much effort, it is unknown whether public-key assumptions are inherently needed for such protocols, and whether one can achieve similar results with security against computationally-unbounded adversaries.

In this paper, we use Minicrypt-type assumptions to realize 3-round MPC with full and active security. Our protocols come in two flavors: for a small (logarithmic) number of parties n, we achieve an optimal resiliency threshold of $t \leq \lfloor (n-1)/2 \rfloor$, and for a large (polynomial) number of parties we achieve an almost-optimal resiliency threshold of $t \leq 0.5n(1 - \epsilon)$ for an arbitrarily small constant $\epsilon > 0$. Both protocols can be based on sub-exponentially hard injective one-way functions in the plain model.

If the parties have an access to a collision resistance hash function, we can derive *statistical everlasting security* for every NC1 functionality, i.e., the protocol is secure against adversaries that are computationally bounded during the execution of the protocol and become computationally unlimited after the protocol execution.

As a secondary contribution, we show that in the strong honest-majority setting ($t < n/3$), every NC1 functionality can be computed in 3 rounds with everlasting security and complexity polynomial in n based on one-way functions. Previously, such a result was only known based on collision-resistance hash function.

1 Introduction

Interaction is a valuable and expensive resource in cryptography and distributed computation. Consequently, a huge amount of research has been devoted towards

---

A full version of this paper appears in [AKP21].

© The Author(s), under exclusive license to Springer Nature Switzerland 2022
E. Kiltz and V. Vaikuntanathan (Eds.): TCC 2022, LNCS 13748, pp. 103–120, 2022.
https://doi.org/10.1007/978-3-031-22365-5_4

characterizing the amount of interaction, typically measured via round complexity, that is needed for various distributed tasks (e.g., Byzantine agreement [LF82, DR85, FM85], coin flipping [Cle86, MNS16], and zero-knowledge proofs [GK96, CKPR01]) under different security models. In this paper, we focus on the problem of general secure-multiparty-computation (MPC) in the challenging setting of *full security* (including guaranteed output delivery) with *maximal resiliency*. That is, even an active (aka Byzantine or malicious) adversary that controls a minority (up to half) of the parties should not be able to violate privacy or to prevent the honest parties from receiving a valid output. In this setting, originally presented in the classical work of Rabin and Ben-Or [RB89], we assume that each pair of parties is connected by a secure and authenticated point-to-point channel and that all parties have access to a common broadcast channel, which allows each party to send a message to all parties and ensures that the received message is identical.

The round complexity of honest-majority fully-secure MPC protocols was extensively studied. The lower-bound of [GIKR02, GLS15] shows that two rounds are insufficient for this task even when the parties are given access to a common reference string (CRS). In [AJL+12], a 5-round protocol was constructed based on Threshold Fully-Homomorphic Encryption (TFHE) and Non-Interactive Zero-Knowledge proofs (NIZK). An optimal round complexity of three, was later obtained by [GLS15] in the CRS model by relying on a stronger variant of TFHE that can be based on the learning with errors (LWE) assumption. Later in [BJMS20] the CRS was removed, and in [ACGJ18] LWE was replaced by weaker public-key primitives like general public-key encryption (PKE) and two-round witness indistinguishable proofs (Zaps). (The latter can be based on primitives like trapdoor permutations [DN07] and indistinguishability obfuscation [BP15], or on intractability assumptions related to bilinear groups [GOS12] and LWE [BFJ+20, GJJM20].)

The above results may give the impression that public-key assumptions are essential for honest-majority fully-secure MPC. However, if one puts no restriction on the round complexity, then, as shown by Rabin and Ben-Or [RB89], one can obtain unconditional results and no assumptions are needed at all! Specifically, every efficiently computable function can be securely computed with statistical security against computationally-unbounded adversaries.[1] Constant-round versions of this protocol are known either with an exponential dependency in the circuit-depth (or space-complexity) of the underlying function [IK00], or with computational security under the weakest-known cryptographic assumption: the existence of one-way functions [BMR90, DI05]. Moreover, for the special case of 3 parties (and single corruption), 3-round protocols were constructed by [PR18] based on injective one-way functions.

This leaves an intriguing *gap* between general-purpose *optimal-round* protocols to protocols with larger round complexity, both in terms of the underlying assumptions and with respect to the resulting security notion. We therefore ask:

---

[1] Interestingly, perfect security is impossible to achieve in this setting as it requires a strong honest-majority of $2n/3$ [BGW88].

Q1: Are public-key assumptions inherently needed for 3-round fully-secure honest-majority MPC? Is it possible to replace these assumptions with symmetric-key assumptions?

Q2: Is it possible to obtain 3-round fully-secure honest-majority MPC with some form of unconditional security against computationally-unbounded adversaries?

We answer these questions to the affirmative. We show that 3-round MPC with full security at the presence of honest-majority can be realized based on Minicrypt-type assumptions without relying on PKE, and present variants of our protocol that achieve *statistical everlasting security*. To the best of our knowledge, this is the first construction of everlasting-secure protocol in this setting *regardless of the underlying assumptions*. We continue with a detailed description of our results.

1.1 Our Contribution

1.1.1 Round-Optimal MPC in Minicrypt

We present the first 3-round general MPC protocol under Minicrypt assumptions. In fact, our protocol consists of 1 offline (input-independent) round, and 2 online rounds. To obtain our main result, we reveal a strong connection between round-optimal MPC and round-optimal protocols for functionalities whose output depends on the input of a single party, aka *single input functionalities* (SIF). In particular, we prove the following theorem.

Theorem 1. *Assuming the existence of non-interactive commitment scheme, there exists a compiler that takes a protocol* sif *with 1 offline round and 1 online round for single input functionalities, and outputs a protocol with 1 offline round and 2 online rounds for general MPC, with the same resiliency as* sif.

In a recent result by the same authors [AKP22], a round-optimal SIF protocol was presented based on the existence of injective one-way functions with sub-exponential hardness. The protocol has optimal resiliency when the number of parties n is logarithmic in the security parameter, and almost-optimal resiliency when the number of parties is polynomial in the security parameter. Since injective one-way function implies the existence of perfectly-binding non-interactive commitment scheme [Blu81, Yao82, GL89], we obtain the following theorem by plugging the protocol of [AKP22] in Theorem 1.

Theorem 2. *Assuming the existence of injective one-way functions with sub-exponential hardness, for every $\epsilon > 0$, every efficiently-computable functionality can be realized in 1 offline round and 2 online rounds in the plain model, with full security against an active rushing adversary, under one of the following conditions.*

- *(Optimal resiliency for small number of parties) The number of parties n is at most logarithmic in the security parameter, and the adversary corrupts less than $n/2$ parties.*

– (Almost-optimal resiliency for polynomially-many parties) *The number of parties n is allowed to be polynomial in the security parameter, and the adversary corrupts less than $n \cdot (\frac{1}{2} - \epsilon)$ parties.*

In concrete terms, for an n-party functionality given by a boolean circuit C, and for security parameter κ, we derive (a) an honest majority protocol with complexity $\mathrm{poly}(|C|, \kappa)2^{O(n)}$ which is $\mathrm{poly}(\kappa)$ when $n = O(\log \kappa)$ and $|C| = \mathrm{poly}(\kappa)$; and (b) $t = n \cdot (\frac{1}{2} - \epsilon)$ resilient protocol of complexity $\mathrm{poly}(n, \kappa, |C|, 2^{1/\epsilon^2})$ which simplifies to $\mathrm{poly}(\kappa)$ when $|C| = \mathrm{poly}(\kappa)$ and $\epsilon > 0$ is an arbitrarily small constant. In fact, even if ϵ mildly *decreases* with κ, e.g., $\epsilon = \Omega(\frac{1}{\sqrt{\log \kappa}})$, the overall complexity remains polynomial. (See also the discussion in [AKP22].)

Let us further mention that two-round SIF protocols with optimal resiliency and polynomially many parties can be obtained if one is willing to make stronger assumptions (e.g., random oracle or correlation intractable functions), or if the adversary is non-rushing [AKP22]. These results extend to the MPC setting via Theorem 1.

1.1.2 Round-Optimal MPC with Everlasting Security in Minicrypt

The notion of statistical everlasting security [MU10] can be viewed as a hybrid version of statistical and computational security. During the run-time, the adversary is assumed to be computationally-bounded (e.g., cannot find collisions in the hash function) but after the protocol terminates, the adversary hands its view to a computationally-unbounded analyst who can apply arbitrary computations in order to extract information on the inputs of the honest parties. This feature is one of the main advantages of information-theoretic protocols: after-the-fact secrecy holds regardless of technological advances and regardless of the time invested by the adversary.

We show that Theorem 1 yields a round-optimal MPC protocol with everlasting security when it is instantiated with statistically-hiding commitments and everlasting secure round-optimal SIF protocol. Such a SIF protocol was also realized in [AKP22] based on collision-resistant hash functions. Since the latter are known to imply statistically-hiding commitments [DPP98, HM96], we derive the following theorem.

Theorem 3. *Given access to a collision resistant hash function, every* $\mathbf{NC}^1$ *functionality can be realized in 1 offline round and 2 online rounds, with full everlasting security against an active rushing adversary, under the same conditions of Theorem 2.*

Remark 1 (On the use of hash function). Similarly to the everlasting SIF protocol from [AKP22], our protocol assumes that all parties are given an access to a collision resistance hash function h, and we (implicitly) prove that any adversary that violates the security of the protocol can be efficiently compiled into an adversary that finds collisions in the hash function h. Theoretically speaking, such a function should be chosen from a family of functions $\mathcal{H}$ in order to defeat non-uniform adversaries.[2] One may assume that h is chosen *"once and for all"* by some simple set-up mechanism. In particular, this set-up mechanism can be realized distributively by a single round of public-coin messages by letting each party sample randomness r_i that specifies a hash function h_i and then taking h to be the concatenated hash function [Her09]. This simple set-up protocol remains secure even against an active rushing adversary that may corrupt all the participants except for a single one. Alternatively, the choice of the hash function can be abstracted by a CRS functionality, or even, using the multi-string model of [GO14] with a single honestly-generated string. It should be emphasized that this CRS is being used in a very *weak* way: It is "non-programmable" (the simulator receives h as an input) and it can be sampled once and for all by using the above trivial public-coin mechanism. Finally, even if one counts this extra set-up step as an additional round, to the best of our knowledge, our protocol remains the only known solution that achieves everlasting security, regardless of the underlying assumptions.

Remark 2 (On $\mathbf{NC}^1$ functionalities). All our everlasting-security protocols are restricted to $\mathbf{NC}^1$. More generally, the computational complexity of these protocols grows exponentially with the depth or space of the underlying function. This is expected since even for strictly-weaker notions of security (e.g., passive statistical security against a single corrupted party), it is unknown how to construct *efficient constant-round* protocols for functions beyond $\mathbf{NC}^1$ and log-space. (In fact, this is a well-known open problem that goes back to [BFKR90].)

The difference between everlasting and computational security is *fundamental* and is analogous to the difference between statistical commitments and computational commitments or statistical ZK arguments vs. computational ZK arguments (see, e.g., the discussions in [BCC88, NOVY98]). In both the former cases, we get computational security against "online cheating" and statistical security against after-the-fact attacks.

We note that all previous protocols inherently fail to achieve everlasting security. Indeed, for technical reasons (that will be discussed later in Sect. 2), previous constructions emulate private channels over a broadcast channel via the use of PKE. Furthermore, the (encrypted) information that is delivered over this channel fully determines the inputs. Thus, an analyst that collects the broadcast messages and later breaks the secrecy of the PKE (e.g., via brute-force) can learn all the private inputs of the parties.

1.1.3 Round-Optimal MPC for $t < n/3$ with Everlasting Security from OWF

For strong honest-majority, where $t < n/3$, we provide a 3-round protocol for general MPC with everlasting security *in the plain model* based on the existence of one-way functions. This protocol is round-optimal by the lower bound of [GIKR02].

---

[2] In a uniform setting, one could use a keyless hash function; see also the discussion of Rogaway [Rog06].

Theorem 4. *Assuming the existence of one-way functions, every* $\mathbf{NC}^1$ *functionality can be realized in the plain model by a 3-round protocol that provides everlasting security against an active rushing adversary corrupting* $t < n/3$ *of the parties. If we are willing to compromise to computational security, we obtain a secure protocol for every efficiently computable functionality.*

Known round-optimal protocols in this regime, all appear in [AKP20], either achieve (1) statistical security but with running time exponential in n, or (2) everlasting security from collision resistant hash-functions and a CRS as a trusted setup, or (3) computational security from injective one-way function in the plain model. Therefore, our construction can be seen as the first round-optimal construction that efficiently achieves some form of security against unbounded adversaries in the plain model. Moreover, it does so only based on one-way functions. As a primary tool, we design a verifiable secret sharing (VSS) with everlasting security in 2 rounds from OWFs. Known VSS protocols in this regime either achieve (1) statistical security but with running time exponential in n with $t < n/3$ [AKP20], (2) everlasting security from collision resistant hash-functions and a CRS as a trusted setup with $t < n/2$ [BKP11], or (3) computational security from non-interactive commitments schemes with $t < n/2$ [BKP11].

1.1.4 Summary of the Results

We summarize our results in the honest-majority regime in Table 1 and compare them to the existing results. In Table 2 we summarize our results in the strong honest-majority regime, and compare them to the existing results.

Table 1. Comparison of our work with the state-of-the-art relevant results

Ref.	Rounds	Threshold	Setup plain/CRS	Security it/es/cs[†]	Cryptographic assumptions
[RB89]	circuit-depth	$t < n/2$	Plain	it	–
[IK00]*	constant > 3	$t < n/2$	Plain	it	–
[BMR90,DI05]	constant > 3	$t < n/2$	Plain	cs	OWF
[PR18]	3	$n = 3, t = 1$	Plain	cs	Injective OWF
[GLS15]	3	$t < n/2$	CRS	cs	threshold multi-key FHE
[BJMS20]	3	$t < n/2$	Plain	cs	LWE
[ACGJ18]	3	$t < n/2$	Plain	cs	PKE, Zaps
This	3	$t < n(\frac{1}{2} - \epsilon)^{\S}$	Plain	cs	sub-exponential injective OWF
This*	3	$t < n(\frac{1}{2} - \epsilon)^{\S}$	CRS	es	collision resistant hash function

[†] it: information-theoretic, es: everlasting security, cs: computational security.
* For $\mathbf{NC}^1$ circuits
$\S$ We achieve $t < n/2$ when n is logarithmic in the security parameter.

Previous Unpublished Version and a Sibling Paper. A previous version of this paper contained a weak form of some of the current results together with 2-round SIF protocols based on the Fiat-Shamir heuristic. The SIF protocols were

Table 2. Comparison of our work with the state-of-the-art relevant results for $t < n/3$

Ref.	Rounds	Threshold	Setup plain/CRS	Security it/es/cs[†]	Cryptographic assumptions	Complexity in terms of n
[AKP20]*	3	$t < n/3$	Plain	it	–	Exponential
[AKP20]	3	$t < n/3$	Plain	cs	injective OWF	Polynomial
[AKP20]*	3	$t < n/3$	CRS	es	collision-resistant hash-function	Polynomial
This*	3	$t < n/3$	Plain	es	OWF	Polynomial
This	3	$t < n/3$	Plain	cs	OWF	Polynomial

[†] it: information-theoretic, es: everlasting security, cs: computational security.
* For $\mathbf{NC}^1$ circuits

strengthened and were fully moved to [AKP22], and the derivation of the 3-round MPC protocols was significantly changed and modularized, leading to the new compiler (Theorem 1). Theorem 4 is also new and did not appear in previous versions. Overall, the current version of this writeup and [AKP22] contain a disjoint sets of results that together fully subsume the previous versions of this paper.

2   Technical Overview

In this section, we give a detailed overview of our constructions while emphasizing the main novelties. Section 2.1 is devoted to the proof of the main theorem (Theorem 1) and Sect. 2.2 is devoted to the strong honest-majority result (Theorem 4). Throughout, we assume that there are n parties, $P_1, \ldots, P_n$, of which at most t are corrupt, where we assume two settings: $t < n/2$ for Sect. 2.1 and $t < n/3$ for Sect. 2.2. We assume that the parties communicate over secure point-to-point channels and over a broadcast channel.

2.1   Main Theorem

Our goal is to prove our main Theorem 1, that states that assuming the existence of non-interactive commitments we can transform any sif protocol with 1 offline round and 1 online round into a 3 round protocol for general MPC with the same resiliency as sif. Following previous works [GLS15, ACGJ18], we prove Theorem 1 by using the following outline: (1) We start with a 2 round protocol Π^{sm} with security against *semi-malicious* adversary that is allowed to choose its input and randomness, but other than that plays honestly; (2) We upgrade the security of the protocol to hold against a *first-round fail-stop* adversary that, in addition to choosing its input and randomness, is allowed to abort a corrupted party during the first round of the protocol; (3) We compile the protocol to a new protocol with an extra offline round that achieves security against a *fully fail-stop* adversary that is allowed to abort a corrupted party at any round; (4) We transform the protocol for fail-stop adversaries to a protocol for malicious adversaries. Jumping ahead, previous constructions employed Zaps/NIZK for the last step and PKE/threshold homomorphic encryption both for steps (3) and (4). We will show how to relax these assumptions.

The Initial Protocol Π^{sm}. Our starting point is a 2-round protocol Π^{sm} that is secure against a rushing semi-malicious adversary that corrupts a minority of the parties. For concreteness, we use the protocol of [ABT18], though any other protocol could be used. This protocol provides *perfect security* for $\mathbf{NC}^1$ functionalities and *computational security* for $\mathbf{P}$/poly functionalities, assuming the existence of one-way functions. The protocol is fully describe in the full version of this paper [AKP21]. The first round of the protocol consists only of private messages, and the second round consists of broadcast messages. (In fact, using standard techniques we can transform any 2-round protocol to a protocol that satisfies this property, see e.g., [GIKR01].) We denote the first-round private message from P_i to P_j by a_{ij}, and the second-round broadcast of P_i by b_i.

2.1.1   Coping with First-Round Aborts

Roughly speaking, when an adversary aborts, we let the other parties emulate her role for the remaining rounds. The emulation is relatively simple when the abort happens in the first round of Π^{sm} since the parties have a chance to respond to the abort in the second round. Specifically, suppose that P_i aborts in the first round. Then the other parties face 2 problems: (1) P_i did not send her first round messages; and (2) the first-round messages that were *directed* to P_i were lost and will be missing later during the reconstruction of output. The first issue is solved by letting each party to locally generate the outgoing messages of P_i by running P_i on the all-zero input and the all-zero random tape.[3] To solve the second issue, we modify the protocol so that each first round message from P_j to P_i is also being shared among all other parties. That is, in the first round, every P_j shares each of its first-round outgoing messages $a_{j1}, \ldots, a_{jn}$ via Shamir's secret sharing, using degree-t polynomials. If P_i aborts during the first round then in the second round, the parties reconstruct all the 1st round incoming messages of P_i. After the second round, the parties have enough information to locally continue the emulation of P_i (with respect to the all-zero inputs) and generate her second round broadcast messages. We note that in previous works (e.g., [ACGJ18]) first-round aborts are handled differently by adding an additional "function-delayed" requirement on the initial protocol Π^{sm}, and that this property is not required for our compiler.

2.1.2   Coping with Second-Round Aborts

Second-round aborts are trickier to handle: When the honest parties send their second-round messages, they do not know which other parties are about to abort. Accordingly, one has to support "silent emulation", that is, any subset of $n - t$

---

[3] Here, among other places, we use the fact that Π^{sm} is secure against a semi-malicious adversary.

second-round messages should suffice for emulating all other second-round messages. In previous works, the implementation of this mechanism employs heavy tools (threshold homomorphic encryption in [GLS15] and PKE plus garbled circuits in [ACGJ18]) and requires an additional offline round. We review these ideas and present an information-theoretic variant of them.

Ananth et al. [ACGJ18] (ACGJ) first use PKE to ensure that all the communication between the parties will be over the broadcast channel. That is, in a preprocessing round (denoted Round 0), every P_i generates keys $(\mathsf{pk}_i, \mathsf{sk}_i)$ for PKE, and broadcasts pk_i. In the following rounds, the private channel from P_j to P_i is emulated by letting P_j broadcast her message encrypted under the public key pk_i of P_i. After this modification, we can write the second-round message of party P_i as a function f_i that given

(1) the encrypted messages $(A_{ji})_{j \in \{1,\ldots,n\}}$ that P_i receives in Round 1,
(2) the input $\mathbf{x}(i)$ and randomness r_i of P_i in the simulation of Π^{sm}, and
(3) the secret key sk_i,

outputs the public broadcast message b_i that P_i sends in the second round. (That is, f_i decrypts the messages A_{ji} using sk_i in order to obtain a_{ji}, and then computes the second round broadcast b_i of P_i in Π^{sm} based on $(\mathbf{x}(i), r_i, (a_{ji})_{j \in \{1,\ldots,n\}})$.) Observe that f_i depends on private inputs (items 2, 3) and on some public values (item 1) that will be broadcasted during the first round. The key observation is that the private inputs are already known before the first round begins. This fact will be exploited to delegate the computation of f_i.

Specifically, at the beginning of the first round, we let every P_i generate a *garbled circuit* for a function f_i. During the first round, P_i broadcasts the garbled circuit together with the labels of $(\mathbf{x}(i), r_i)$ and sk_i. In addition, P_i secret-shares all the labels that correspond to *every potential* ciphertext value $(A_{ji})_{j \in [n]}$. The actual ciphertexts, $(A_{ji})_{j \in \{1,\ldots,n\}}$, are broadcasted concurrently during the first round by the corresponding parties, and so, in the second round, all the non-aborted parties publish the shares of the corresponding labels. Consequently, after this round, everyone can recover the correct labels via secret reconstruction of the secret sharing, and hence obtain the broadcast b_i of P_i. To make the proof go through, ACGJ assume that the garbled circuit is *adaptively* private [BHR12] in the sense that privacy holds even if the adversary first gets to see the garbled circuit, and only then chooses the inputs to the circuit and receive the corresponding labels.

We note that the same approach can be applied without relying on any computational assumptions. First, instead of using PKE, we let the parties exchange one-time pads during the offline round. That is, in Round 0 we let every P_i sample random pads $\eta_i = (\eta_{i1}, \ldots, \eta_{in})$ and send the pad ("key") η_{ij} to P_j by using a *private channel*. Now a first-round message a_{ji} from P_j to P_i can be broadcasted in an encrypted form $A_{ji} := a_{ji} + \eta_{ij}$. (For technical reasons that will be explained later, we encrypt the message under the receiver's key.) The garbled circuits can also be instantiated with an information-theoretic garbled circuits, aka perfect randomized encodings. (The second-message function of Π^{sm} is now "simple enough" to allow such a realization.) Furthermore, we avoid the need for adaptive garbled circuits, by sharing the garbled circuit together with the labels of $(\mathbf{x}(i), r_i)$ and η_i among all the other parties; these shares are later revealed during the second round.[4] We note that the above description is over-simplified and, in order to handle second-round aborts *together* with first-round aborts, we need to slightly modify the function f_i. (See the full version of this paper [AKP21] for full details.)

2.1.3 From Fail-Stop to Malicious Adversary

To obtain a protocol with security against a malicious adversary, we follow the GMW paradigm and ask each party to prove in zero-knowledge that she followed the protocol. Ignoring for now the exact details of the zero-knowledge proof, the basic idea is that a malicious deviation from the protocol will be caught due to the soundness properties of the proof, and will be treated as if the cheater aborted the computation. Crucially, here too one must assume that the underlying protocol works over a *broadcast* channel. As discussed in [ACGJ18], if the underlying semi-malicious protocol uses private channels, then a party may need to prove different statements to different parties in order to establish honest behavior, which may lead to inconsistent views regarding her "abort" status. Indeed, [GLS15, ACGJ18] make here another use of PKE in order to make sure that the protocol's messages are delivered over a broadcast channel. In fact, this usage of PKE dates back to the GMW compiler [GMW87].

Generating Public Committing Transcript. We can use the previous maneuver to shift all private messages to Round 0 via one-time pads, however, the resulting protocol is still not ready for "zero-knowledge compilation". Indeed, even if we add a zero-knowledge layer, the adversary can cheat either by "claiming that she received different messages" (i.e., changing the keys that correspond to her incoming messages) or by "claiming that she sent different messages". Intuitively, the problem is that our information-theoretic solution is non-committing. We solve this problem via the use of non-interactive commitment (NICOM). Details follow.

In the preprocessing round (Round 0), we let each party P_i broadcast a vector of commitments, $(C_{i1}, \ldots, C_{in})$ to all her private keys, $(\eta_{i1}, \ldots, \eta_{in})$, for the one-time pads, and send o_{ij}, the opening of C_{ij}, to P_j over the private channel. In addition, we let all parties commit to their inputs and randomness for the fail-stop protocol in Round 1 just like in the standard GMW transform. (We emphasize that Round 0 is still input-independent.) Next, we employ some zero-knowledge primitive (to be discussed below) to prove that a party P_i computes

---

[4] We note that [ACGJ18] implicitly shared the garbled circuit as well. Indeed, recall that they (a) shared the "input labels" and (b) employed the adaptively secure garbled circuit from [BHR12]. The latter is obtained by taking a standard garbled circuit and encrypting the offline part under a one-time pad that is released as part of the online input. The combination of these two steps, (a) and (b), indirectly induces (a somewhat complicated) secret sharing of the garbled circuit and the input labels.

a message properly with respect to the public commitments. Specifically, in the first round party P_i can prove that the garbled circuit for f_i was generated properly with respect to her committed randomness, committed input, and with respect to the one-time keys, $\eta_{1i}, \ldots, \eta_{ni}$, that he received from all other parties in the preprocessing round. For the last part we exploit the fact that P_i also received a witness, o_{ji}, that connects the keys to their commitments.

This approach almost works. The only problem is that a party P_j may cheat in Round 0 by sending to P_i a "bad" pair of key/opening (η_{ji}, o_{ji}) that are inconsistent with the public commitment C_{ij}. Fortunately, there is a simple round-efficient solution: If the key is malformed, we simply send the messages from P_i to P_j in the clear un-encrypted. Formally, in Round 1, P_i broadcasts a list L_i of all parties that sent *invalid* openings in Round 0. If P_i needs to send a private message a_{ij} to a party P_j according to Π^{sm}, for $P_j \notin L_i$, then P_i simply sends the encrypted message $a_{ij} + \eta_{ji}$ over the broadcast channel. For a party $P_j \in L_i$, we simply let P_i send the message a_{ij} *unencrypted* over the broadcast channel. We also use the same mechanism for additional private messages that the parties have to exchange, that are not necessarily a part of the protocol Π^{sm} (e.g., sending private shares for the garbled circuit). As before, we only use encryption in Round 1, while Round 2 consists only of public unencrypted messages. This modification does not violate privacy since messages from P_i to P_j will be sent unencrypted only if one of these parties is corrupted, which means that the adversary is supposed to learn the message anyway.

Instantiating the Zero-Knowledge Layer. Finally, we have to instantiate the zero-knowledge layer in a round-preserving way. Previous works either make use of NIZK at the expense of adding a CRS [AJL+12, GLS15] or exploited the offline round to set-up some multi-party variant of ZK [GOS12, ACGJ18]. In terms of assumptions both approaches rely on NIZK/Zaps which are known to be equivalent assuming one-way functions [DN07]. We strongly exploit the existence of honest majority, and observe that these primitives can be replaced by a SIF protocol. Given a relation R, define the single input functionality that (1) takes the statement x and witness w from the prover, and (2) if $R(x, w) = 1$ it returns x to all parties, and if not, it returns a failure symbol $\perp$ to all parties. We can therefore realize a round-efficient variant of multi-verifier zero-knowledge proof (MVZK) based on SIF with 1 offline round and 1 online round. We emphasize that the security of SIF protocols is formulated via an MPC-based definition by relating the protocol to an *ideal SIF functionality*. This leads to security guarantees that are stronger than those achieved by standalone versions of the MVZK primitive (e.g., the SIF protocol provides *knowledge-extraction*).

Summary. Overall, the SIF is being employed as follows. In Round 0, the parties execute the offline round of the SIF protocol, exchange one-time pads and publish their commitments. In Round 1, we let every P_i commit to its input and randomness, and let P_i prove via SIF that (1) for every $P_j \notin L_i$, the public encrypted message from P_i to P_j is consistent with the committed input and randomness of P_i, and it is encrypted with the committed random pad η_{ji}; (2)

for every $P_j \in L_i$, the public unencrypted message from P_i to P_j is consistent with the committed input and randomness of P_i. Similarly, in Round 2 every P_i proves via SIF that its public broadcast is consistent with (1) its committed input and randomness; (2) the unencrypted public incoming message from P_j, for every P_j for which $P_i \in L_j$; and (3) the decrypted incoming message from P_j, where the decryption used the committed random pad η_{ij}, for every P_j for which $P_i \notin L_j$.

Remark 3 (Everlasting security). All the components, except for the NICOM and SIF, are information-theoretic. As a result, we derive the everlasting security version of the protocol by plugging-in NICOM and SIF with everlasting security guarantees. The protocol remains the same and the proof of security is given in a unified way.

Remark 4 (Reusing the preprocessing round). Recall that the preprocessing round consists of exchanging committed one-time pads, and initializing the SIF protocol. If one does not care about everlasting security, the one-time pads can be replaced with (committed) pairwise private-keys for a symmetric encryption scheme, and in this case the same keys can be used for many invocations of the protocol. Under this modification, we can reuse the preprocessing step (Round 0) or even treat it as a private-key infrastructure provided that the preprocessing step of the SIF is also reusable. While the construction from [AKP22] does not satisfy this property, other SIF constructions (e.g., based on NIZK) can be used to achieve this property. We remark that, even if one employs NIZK-based SIF, our approach is beneficial since it bypasses the need for PKE. Indeed, the Fiat-Shamir heuristic [FS86] suggests that NIZK can be based on strong symmetric-key assumptions like correlated robust hash functions [CGH04], and may not require PKE-based assumptions. (See [CCH+19] for further discussion and references).

Remark 5 (On non black-box use of the commitment scheme). Observe that our compiler uses the underlying commitment scheme in a non black-box way. This is a common characteristic of GMW-type compilers, where the zero-knowledge proofs use the underlying cryptographic primitives in a non black-box way, and it occurs in previous round-optimal protocols as well, including [ACGJ18].

2.2   Strong Honest-Majority MPC with Everlasting Security from OWF

We continue with an overview of the 3-round MPC protocol that provides everlasting security in the plain model for strong honest-majority, $t < n/3$. In [AKP20] it is shown that such a protocol follows from a 2-round protocol for *verifiable secret sharing* (VSS) that provides everlasting security. We design such a protocol based on digital signatures whose existence is equivalent to the existence of one-way functions [Rom90].

The VSS Functionality. We will need the following variant of VSS.[5] The functionality receives a symmetric bivariate polynomial $F(x,y)$ of degree at most t in each variable from a distinguished party D, called the *dealer*, and delivers to each party P_i the univariate polynomial $f_i(x) := F(x,i)$. The use of symmetric bivariate polynomials can be seen as an extension of the standard Shamir's t-out-of-n secret sharing, that allow us to make a consistency-check between any pair of parties P_i and P_j, since $f_i(j) = F(j,i) = F(i,j) = f_j(i)$.

2-Round VSS Protocol. In the first round, we let D generate a signature-key and a verification-key for a digital signature scheme, and broadcast the verification-key. In addition, we let D send $f_i(x)$ to P_i, together with a signature on the *tuples* $(i,j,f_i(j))_{j \in \{1,...,n\}}$. At the end of the first round, a party is *happy* with D if all the signatures it received are valid, and it is *unhappy* with D otherwise. Observe that if D is honest then all honest parties are happy. The second round of the protocol consists of (1) consistency check for happy parties, and (2) public recovery of the shares of unhappy parties. We elaborate on these two issues in the next subsections.

2.2.1 Consistency Check

The goal of the consistency check is to ensure that (a) there are at least $t+1$ happy honest parties, and that (b) all of them are consistent with each other, i.e., $f_i(j) = f_j(i)$ for every happy and honest P_i and P_j. Looking forward, this will imply that the shares of the happy honest parties fully determine a symmetric bivariate polynomial $F(x,y)$ of degree at most t in each variable, where for an honest D the polynomial $F(x,y)$ is the input polynomial of D.

It is not hard to achieve (a). In Round 2, each party declares, via broadcast, whether she is happy or not, and we discard the dealer if there are more than t unhappy parties. This guarantees that an honest dealer will never be discarded (since all honest parties are happy) and a corrupt dealer must gain the support of at least $(n-t)-t \geq t+1$ happy honest parties in order to remain undiscarded.

2-Wise Consistency via Reveal-if-Not-Equal Gadget. Pair-wise consistency (item b) is being handled via a special comparison gadget that takes from each pair of happy parties (P_i, P_j) the points $m_A = f_i(j), m_B = f_j(i)$ and their corresponding signatures s_A, s_B, and broadcasts an equality bit that indicates whether $m_A = m_B$ and in case of inequality releases the points and their signatures (m_A, s_A, m_B, s_B). When P_i and P_j are honest, a disagreement accompanied with valid signatures certifies that D is corrupted. Of course, when $m_A = m_B$, we do not want any information about m_A, m_B to be revealed to the other parties. If 3 rounds are allowed then we can easily realize the gadget by letting P_i and P_j compare their values privately on the second round (by exchanging messages

---

[5] Previous works on VSS [CGMA85] usually define VSS as a standalone primitive that satisfies a set of requirements (see, e.g., [KKK09,BKP11]). Following [AKP20] (see also [AL17]) we consider VSS as an *ideal functionality*. We mention that any VSS that satisfies the ideal-functionality definition also satisfies the standalone definition.

over the private channel) and then announcing the result at the next round. We avoid this overhead by making an additional observation: When one of the parties, say P_i, is corrupt we do not care about the privacy nor the correctness of the gadget. Privacy does not matter since the adversary already knows $m_B = f_j(i)$. As for correctness, even if the "gadget misbehaves", an honest dealer is protected against a disqualification by the security of the signatures.

We realize the gadget with the aid of garbled circuits (or perfect randomized encodings). Let g be a function that takes (m_A, m_B, s_A, s_B), returns 1 if $m_A = m_B$, and returns (m_A, m_B, s_A, s_B) otherwise. In the first round, we let Alice (P_i) generate a garbled circuit G for g, and send the randomness used to generate G to Bob (P_j). Conveniently, g is "simple enough" (i.e., an $\mathbf{NC}^1$ function) so we can obtain an *information-theoretic* garbled circuit G. In the second round, Alice broadcasts G, together with the labels corresponding to her inputs in G, and Bob broadcasts the labels corresponding to his inputs in G. It is not hard to see that the properties of the protocol follow directly from the correctness and security of the garbled circuit. Based on this gadget, after the second round everyone learns whether Alice and Bob are in agreement, and, in case they disagree, whether the dealer should be discarded due to a conflicting pair of valid signatures. If the dealer was not discarded in any consistency check of a pair (P_i, P_j), we conclude that all happy honest parties are consistent.

2.2.2 Handling Unhappy Parties

It remains to explain how to help unhappy (honest) parties to recover a share that is consistent with all the happy honest parties. The main idea is to let every unhappy P_i ask from every other P_j to publicly reveal all the common information, i.e., the value $f_j(i)$ and the corresponding signature. Since we have only 1 additional round, we design an additional gadget with 1 offline round and 1 online round similarly to the reveal-if-not-equal gadget.[6] In this gadget, Alice inputs a bit flag_A, while Bob inputs some secret s_B. When Alice and Bob are honest, if $\mathsf{flag}_A = 0$ then the listeners learn no information about s_B, while if $\mathsf{flag}_A = 1$ they learn s_B. As before, when one of the parties is corrupt there are no security guarantees.

We use this mechanism for every pair (P_i, P_j), where P_i takes the role of Alice and P_j takes the role of Bob. We let P_i input $\mathsf{flag}_A = 1$ if P_i is unhappy, and $\mathsf{flag}_i = 0$ otherwise; in addition, P_j sets s_B to be the share $f_j(i)$ together with the corresponding signature. Observe that if both P_i and P_j are honest and happy, then the adversary learns no information about their common point; however, if P_i is unhappy and P_j is happy, then *all the parties* learn the point $f_j(i)$ together with a valid signature.

An honest unhappy P_i will be able to reveal all evaluations $f_j(i)$ from happy honest parties P_j, together with valid signatures. We let *all* parties interpolate over all values whose corresponding signatures were valid, in order to obtain $f_i(x)$. Since there are at least $t + 1$ happy honest parties, we are promised that $f_i(x)$ is either consistent with the polynomial $F(x, y)$ defined by the shares of

---

[6] In fact, in our construction we merge the two gadgets.

the happy honest parties, or has degree more than t, in which case *all* the parties reject the dealer. Finally, for an honest D and a corrupt unhappy P_i, the values that are revealed with valid signatures must be consistent with $F(x, y)$, so the interpolated polynomial will have degree at most t, and D will not be discarded.

Acknowledgements. B. Applebaum and E. Kachlon are supported by the Israel Science Foundation grant no. 2805/21. A. Patra would like to acknowledge financial support from DST National Mission on Interdisciplinary Cyber-Physical Systems (NM-ICPS) 2020–2025 and SERB MATRICS (Theoretical Sciences) Grant 2020–2023.

References

[ABT18] Applebaum, B., Brakerski, Z., Tsabary, R.: Perfect secure computation in two rounds. In: Theory of Cryptography - 16th International Conference, TCC 2018, Panaji, India, 11–14 November 2018, Proceedings, Part I, pp. 152–174 (2018)

[ACGJ18] Ananth, P., Choudhuri, A.R., Goel, A., Jain, A.: Round-optimal secure multiparty computation with honest majority. In: Shacham, H., Boldyreva, A. (eds.) CRYPTO 2018. LNCS, vol. 10992, pp. 395–424. Springer, Cham (2018). https://doi.org/10.1007/978-3-319-96881-0_14

[AJL+12] Asharov, G., Jain, A., López-Alt, A., Tromer, E., Vaikuntanathan, V., Wichs, D.: Multiparty computation with low communication, computation and interaction via threshold FHE. In: Pointcheval, D., Johansson, T. (eds.) EUROCRYPT 2012. LNCS, vol. 7237, pp. 483–501. Springer, Heidelberg (2012). https://doi.org/10.1007/978-3-642-29011-4_29

[AKP20] Applebaum, B., Kachlon, E., Patra, A.: The resiliency of MPC with low interaction: the benefit of making errors (extended abstract). In: Pass, R., Pietrzak, K. (eds.) TCC 2020. LNCS, vol. 12551, pp. 562–594. Springer, Cham (2020). https://doi.org/10.1007/978-3-030-64378-2_20

[AKP21] Applebaum, B., Kachlon, E., Patra, A.: Round-optimal honest-majority MPC in minicrypt and with everlasting security. IACR Cryptol. ePrint Arch. **2021**, 346 (2021). https://eprint.iacr.org/2021/346

[AKP22] Applebaum, B., Kachlon, E., Patra, A.: Verifiable relation sharing and multi-verifier zero-knowledge in two rounds: trading NIZKs with honest majority. Cryptol. ePrint Arch. **2022**, 167 (2022). https://ia.cr/2022/167, To appear in CRYPTO 2022

[AL17] Asharov, G., Lindell, Y.: A full proof of the BGW protocol for perfectly secure multiparty computation. J. Cryptol. **30**(1), 58–151 (2017). https://doi.org/10.1007/s00145-015-9214-4

[BCC88] Brassard, G., Chaum, D., Crépeau, C.: Minimum disclosure proofs of knowledge. J. Comput. Syst. Sci. **37**(2), 156–189 (1988)

[BFJ+20] Badrinarayanan, S., Fernando, R., Jain, A., Khurana, D., Sahai, A.: Statistical ZAP arguments. In: Canteaut, A., Ishai, Y. (eds.) EUROCRYPT 2020. LNCS, vol. 12107, pp. 642–667. Springer, Cham (2020). https://doi.org/10.1007/978-3-030-45727-3_22

[BFKR90] Beaver, D., Feigenbaum, J., Kilian, J., Rogaway, P.: Security with low communication overhead. In: Menezes, A.J., Vanstone, S.A. (eds.) CRYPTO 1990. LNCS, vol. 537, pp. 62–76. Springer, Heidelberg (1991). https://doi.org/10.1007/3-540-38424-3_5

[BGW88]   Ben-Or, M., Goldwasser, S., Wigderson, A.: Completeness theorems for non-cryptographic fault-tolerant distributed computation (extended abstract). In: Proceedings of the 20th Annual ACM Symposium on Theory of Computing, 2–4 May 1988, Chicago, Illinois, pp. 1–10 (1988)

[BHR12]   Bellare, M., Hoang, V.T., Rogaway, P.: Adaptively secure garbling with applications to one-time programs and secure outsourcing. In: Wang, X., Sako, K. (eds.) ASIACRYPT 2012. LNCS, vol. 7658, pp. 134–153. Springer, Heidelberg (2012). https://doi.org/10.1007/978-3-642-34961-4_10

[BJMS20] Badrinarayanan, S., Jain, A., Manohar, N., Sahai, A.: Secure MPC: laziness leads to GOD. In: Moriai, S., Wang, H. (eds.) ASIACRYPT 2020. LNCS, vol. 12493, pp. 120–150. Springer, Cham (2020). https://doi.org/10.1007/978-3-030-64840-4_5

[BKP11]   Backes, M., Kate, A., Patra, A.: Computational verifiable secret sharing revisited. In: Lee, D.H., Wang, X. (eds.) ASIACRYPT 2011. LNCS, vol. 7073, pp. 590–609. Springer, Heidelberg (2011). https://doi.org/10.1007/978-3-642-25385-0_32

[Blu81]   Blum, M.: Coin flipping by telephone. In: Advances in Cryptology: A Report on CRYPTO 81, CRYPTO 81, IEEE Workshop on Communications Security, Santa Barbara, California, 24–26 August 1981, pp. 11–15 (1981)

[BMR90]   Beaver, D., Micali, S., Rogaway, P.: The round complexity of secure protocols (extended abstract). In: Proceedings of the 22nd Annual ACM Symposium on Theory of Computing, 13–17 May 1990, Baltimore, Maryland, pp. 503–513 (1990)

[BP15]   Bitansky, N., Paneth, O.: ZAPs and non-interactive witness indistinguishability from indistinguishability obfuscation. In: Dodis, Y., Nielsen, J.B. (eds.) TCC 2015. LNCS, vol. 9015, pp. 401–427. Springer, Heidelberg (2015). https://doi.org/10.1007/978-3-662-46497-7_16

[CCH+19] Canetti, R., et al.: Fiat-Shamir: from practice to theory. In: Charikar, M., Cohen, E. (eds.) Proceedings of the 51st Annual ACM SIGACT Symposium on Theory of Computing, STOC 2019, Phoenix, AZ, USA, 23–26 June 2019, pp. 1082–1090. ACM (2019)

[CGH04]   Canetti, R., Goldreich, O., Halevi, S.: The random oracle methodology, revisited. J. ACM 51(4), 557–594 (2004)

[CGMA85] Chor, B., Goldwasser, S., Micali, S., Awerbuch, B.: Verifiable secret sharing and achieving simultaneity in the presence of faults (extended abstract). In: 26th Annual Symposium on Foundations of Computer Science, Portland, Oregon, USA, 21–23 October 1985, pp. 383–395 (1985)

[CKPR01] Canetti, R., Kilian, J., Petrank, E., Rosen, A.: Black-box concurrent zero-knowledge requires omega~(log n) rounds. In: Proceedings on 33rd Annual ACM Symposium on Theory of Computing, 6–8 July 2001, Heraklion, Crete, pp. 570–579 (2001)

[Cle86]   Cleve, R.: Limits on the security of coin flips when half the processors are faulty (extended abstract). In: Proceedings of the 18th Annual ACM Symposium on Theory of Computing, 28–30 May 1986, Berkeley, California, pp. 364–369 (1986)

[DI05]   Damgård, I., Ishai, Y.: Constant-round multiparty computation using a black-box pseudorandom generator. In: Shoup, V. (ed.) CRYPTO 2005. LNCS, vol. 3621, pp. 378–394. Springer, Heidelberg (2005). https://doi.org/10.1007/11535218_23

[DN07] Dwork, C., Naor, M.: Zaps and their applications. SIAM J. Comput. **36**(6), 1513–1543 (2007)

[DPP98] Damgård, I., Pedersen, T.P., Pfitzmann, B.: Statistical secrecy and multibit commitments. IEEE Trans. Inf. Theory **44**(3), 1143–1151 (1998)

[DR85] Dolev, D., Reischuk, R.: Bounds on information exchange for byzantine agreement. J. ACM **32**(1), 191–204 (1985)

[FM85] Feldman, P., Micali, S.: Byzantine agreement in constant expected time (and trusting no one). In: 26th Annual Symposium on Foundations of Computer Science, Portland, Oregon, USA, 21–23 October 1985, pp. 267–276 (1985)

[FS86] Fiat, A., Shamir, A.: How to prove yourself: practical solutions to identification and signature problems. In: Odlyzko, A.M. (ed.) CRYPTO 1986. LNCS, vol. 263, pp. 186–194. Springer, Heidelberg (1987). https://doi.org/10.1007/3-540-47721-7_12

[GIKR01] Gennaro, R., Ishai, Y., Kushilevitz, E., Rabin, T.: The round complexity of verifiable secret sharing and secure multicast. In: Proceedings on 33rd Annual ACM Symposium on Theory of Computing, 6–8 July 2001, Heraklion, Crete, pp. 580–589 (2001)

[GIKR02] Gennaro, R., Ishai, Y., Kushilevitz, E., Rabin, T.: On 2-round secure multiparty computation. In: Yung, M. (ed.) CRYPTO 2002. LNCS, vol. 2442, pp. 178–193. Springer, Heidelberg (2002). https://doi.org/10.1007/3-540-45708-9_12

[GJJM20] Goyal, V., Jain, A., Jin, Z., Malavolta, G.: Statistical zaps and new oblivious transfer protocols. In: Canteaut, A., Ishai, Y. (eds.) EUROCRYPT 2020. LNCS, vol. 12107, pp. 668–699. Springer, Cham (2020). https://doi.org/10.1007/978-3-030-45727-3_23

[GK96] Goldreich, O., Krawczyk, H.: On the composition of zero-knowledge proof systems. SIAM J. Comput. **25**(1), 169–192 (1996)

[GL89] Goldreich, O., Levin, L.A.: A hard-core predicate for all one-way functions. In: Proceedings of the 21st Annual ACM Symposium on Theory of Computing, 14–17 May 1989, Seattle, Washington, USA, pp. 25–32 (1989)

[GLS15] Dov Gordon, S., Liu, F.-H., Shi, E.: Constant-round MPC with fairness and guarantee of output delivery. In: Gennaro, R., Robshaw, M. (eds.) CRYPTO 2015. LNCS, vol. 9216, pp. 63–82. Springer, Heidelberg (2015). https://doi.org/10.1007/978-3-662-48000-7_4

[GMW87] Goldreich, O., Micali, S., Wigderson, A.: How to solve any protocol problem. In: Proc. of STOC (1987)

[GO14] Groth, J., Ostrovsky, R.: Cryptography in the multi-string model. J. Cryptol. **27**(3), 506–543 (2014)

[GOS12] Groth, J., Ostrovsky, R., Sahai, A.: New techniques for noninteractive zero-knowledge. J. ACM **59**(3), 1–35 (2012)

[Her09] Herzberg, A.: Folklore, practice and theory of robust combiners. J. Comput. Secur. **17**(2), 159–189 (2009)

[HM96] Halevi, S., Micali, S.: Practical and provably-secure commitment schemes from collision-free hashing. In: Koblitz, N. (ed.) CRYPTO 1996. LNCS, vol. 1109, pp. 201–215. Springer, Heidelberg (1996). https://doi.org/10.1007/3-540-68697-5_16

[IK00] Ishai, Y., Kushilevitz, E.: Randomizing polynomials: a new representation with applications to round-efficient secure computation. In: 41st Annual Symposium on Foundations of Computer Science, FOCS 2000, 12–14 November 2000, Redondo Beach, California, pp. 294–304 (2000)

[KKK09] Katz, J., Koo, C.-Y., Kumaresan, R.: Improving the round complexity of VSS in point-to-point networks. Inf. Comput. **207**(8), 889–899 (2009)

[LF82]   Lamport, L., Fischer, M.: Byzantine generals and transaction commit protocols. Technical Report 62, SRI International (1982)

[MNS16] Moran, T., Naor, M., Segev, G.: An optimally fair coin toss. J. Cryptol. **29**(3), 491–513 (2016). https://doi.org/10.1007/s00145-015-9199-z

[MU10]   Müller-Quade, J., Unruh, D.: Long-term security and universal composability. J. Cryptol. **23**(4), 594–671 (2010). https://doi.org/10.1007/s00145-010-9068-8

[NOVY98] Naor, M., Ostrovsky, R., Venkatesan, R., Yung, M.: Perfect zero-knowledge arguments for NP using any one-way permutation. J. Cryptol. **11**(2), 87–108 (1998). https://doi.org/10.1007/s001459900037

[PR18]   Patra, A., Ravi, D.: On the exact round complexity of secure three-party computation. In: Advances in Cryptology - CRYPTO 2018–38th Annual International Cryptology Conference, Santa Barbara, CA, 19–23 August 2018, Proceedings, Part II, pp. 425–458 (2018)

[RB89]   Rabin, T., Ben-Or, M.: Verifiable secret sharing and multiparty protocols with honest majority (extended abstract). In: Proceedings of the 21st Annual ACM Symposium on Theory of Computing, 14–17 May 1989, Seattle, Washigton, pp. 73–85 (1989)

[Rog06] Rogaway, P.: Formalizing human ignorance: collision-resistant hashing without the keys. IACR Cryptol. ePrint Arch. 281 (2006)

[Rom90] Rompel, J.: One-way functions are necessary and sufficient for secure signatures. In: Ortiz, H. (ed.) Proceedings of the 22nd Annual ACM Symposium on Theory of Computing, 13–17 May 1990, Baltimore, Maryland, pp. 387–394. ACM (1990)

[Yao82] Yao, A.C.: Theory and applications of trapdoor functions (extended abstract). In: 23rd Annual Symposium on Foundations of Computer Science, Chicago, Illinois, USA, 3–5 November 1982, pp. 80–91 (1982)

Sublinear Secure Computation from New Assumptions

Elette Boyle[1,2], Geoffroy Couteau[3], and Pierre Meyer[1,3(✉)]

[1] Reichman University, Herzliya, Israel
eboyle@alum.mit.edu
[2] NTT Research, Sunnyvale, USA
[3] Université Paris Cité, IRIF, CNRS, Paris, France
{couteau,pierre.meyer}@irif.fr

Abstract. Secure computation enables mutually distrusting parties to jointly compute a function on their secret inputs, while revealing nothing beyond the function output. A long-running challenge is understanding the required communication complexity of such protocols—in particular, when communication can be *sublinear* in the circuit representation size of the desired function. For certain functions, such as Private Information Retrieval (PIR), this question extends to even sublinearity in the input size.

We develop new techniques expanding the set of computational assumptions for sublinear communication in both settings:

- **Circuit size.** We present sublinear-communication protocols for secure evaluation of general layered circuits, given any 2-round rate-1 batch oblivious transfer (OT) protocol with a particular "decomposability" property. In particular, this condition can be shown to hold for the recent batch OT protocols of (Brakerski et al. Eurocrypt 2022), in turn yielding a new sublinear secure computation feasibility: from Quadratic Residuosity (QR) together with polynomial-noise-rate Learning Parity with Noise (LPN).

  Our approach constitutes a departure from existing paths toward sublinear secure computation, all based on fully homomorphic encryption or homomorphic secret sharing.

- **Input size.** We construct single-server PIR based on the Computational Diffie-Hellman (CDH) assumption, with *polylogarithmic* communication in the database input size n. Previous constructions from CDH required communication $\Omega(n)$. In hindsight, our construction comprises of a relatively simple combination of existing tools from the literature.

Keywords: Foundations · Private information retrieval · Secure multiparty computation

1 Introduction

Secure computation enables mutually distrusting parties to jointly compute a function on their secret inputs, while revealing nothing beyond the function

© The Author(s), under exclusive license to Springer Nature Switzerland 2022
E. Kiltz and V. Vaikuntanathan (Eds.): TCC 2022, LNCS 13748, pp. 121–150, 2022.
https://doi.org/10.1007/978-3-031-22365-5_5

output. We focus on the case of two-party computation with semi-honest (passive) security. Since the seminal feasibility results of the 1980s [Yao86, GMW87, BGW88, CCD88], a major challenge in the area of secure computation has been if and when it is possible to break the "circuit-size barrier." This barrier refers to the fact that all classical techniques for secure computation required a larger amount of communication than the size of a boolean circuit representing the function to be computed. In contrast, insecure computation only requires exchanging the inputs, which are usually considerably smaller than the entire circuit.

Early positive results with sublinear communication either required exponential computation [BFKR91, NN01], or (as discussed later) were limited to very simple functions such as point functions [CGKS95, KO97, CG97] or constant-depth circuits [BI05].

Beyond the Circuit-Size Barrier. This situation changed with the breakthrough result of Gentry [Gen09] on *fully homomorphic encryption* (FHE). FHE is a powerful primitive supporting computation on encrypted data, which can be used to build optimal-communication protocols in the computational setting [DFH12, AJL+12], by having parties perform the desired computation *locally* on encrypted inputs without additional communication. However, despite significant efforts, the set of assumptions under which we know how to build FHE is very narrow. Standard approaches are restricted to lattice-based assumptions, such as Learning With Errors (LWE), and in particular do not include any of the traditional assumptions which were used in the 20th century. Very recent developments in indistinguishability obfuscation imply results based on an alternative (relatively exotic) bundle of assumptions [CLTV15, JLS22].[1]

The work of [BGI16] first showed that secure computation with communication sublinear in the circuit size could also be based on assumptions not known to imply FHE, via a new primitive of *homomorphic secret sharing* (HSS). HSS can be viewed as a relaxation of FHE, where homomorphic evaluation can be distributed among two parties who do not interact with each other. More concretely, from the Decisional Diffie-Hellman (DDH) assumption, [BGI16] constructed a form of HSS for branching programs (including NC^1), implying secure computation for the corresponding function class with asymptotically optimal communication. In turn, this was shown to yield secure computation for general layered circuits[2] of size s with sublinear communication $O(s/\log s)$, by evaluating in $(\log s)$-depth blocks, and communicating only between blocks.

Since then, the HSS-based approach and variations have resulted in sublinear-communication secure protocols from an additional assortment of assumptions. Following the [BGI16] blueprint, the works of [FGJI17, OSY21, RS21] were able to replace the DDH assumption with Decision Composite Residuosity (DCR).

---

[1] Namely, subexponential security of the combination of: Learning Parity with Noise, plus polynomial-stretch pseudorandom generators in NC^0, plus the Decision Linear assumption on symmetric bilinear groups of prime order [JLS22].

[2] A depth-d circuit is layered if it can be divided into d layers such that any wire connects adjacent layers.

The framework was recently abstracted and extended to further algebraic structures, including a class of assumptions based on class groups of imaginary quadratic fields [ADOS22]. In addition, the work of [CM21] built HSS for log log-depth circuits (yielding $O(s/\log\log s)$ communication secure computation for layered circuits) based on a strong flavor of the Learning Parity with Noise (LPN) assumption: with a small number of samples, but assuming super-polynomial hardness, with inverse-superpolynomial noise rate.

To date, these two approaches—FHE and HSS—still comprise the only known paths to sublinear-communication secure computation for general circuit classes, without resorting to superpolynomial computation or setup assumptions such as correlated randomness [IKM+13, DNNR17, Cou19]. It remains a motivated research agenda not only to continue expanding the set of distinct computational assumptions upon which sublinear secure computation can be built, but additionally of exploring new types of approaches toward this goal.

Private Information Retrieval. As mentioned, one exception to the above treatment is the special case of specific simple functionalities: most prominently, the task of Private Information Retrieval (PIR) [CGKS95, KO97]. A (single-server) PIR protocol roughly amounts to a secure computation protocol (with one-sided privacy) for the specific function $f(x, i) = x_i$ with $x \in \{0, 1\}^n$ and $i \in [n]$. Unlike the case of general computation (where the communication complexity of the underlying function may be $\Omega(n)$ even without security), PIR can admit secure protocols with communication *sublinear (even polylogarithmic) in the input size.*

For many years, protocols for PIR with polylogarithmic communication in n were known only from the Decisional Composite Residuosity (DCR), Learning with Errors (LWE), or Phi-hiding assumptions [CMS99, Cha04, Lip05, OS07]. More recently, such constructions were achieved from Quadratic Residuosity (QR), or Decisional Diffie-Hellman (DDH) [DGI+19].

1.1   Our Results

We present new approaches and techniques for both of the above settings, ultimately extending the set of computational assumptions under which we can achieve sublinear-communication secure computation protocols.

Our results fall within two primary categories:

- We obtain (slightly) sublinear secure two-party computation for general layered circuits, through a new path of low-communication batch oblivious transfer.
- We explore the specific goal of Private Information Retrieval (PIR), and provide a new construction with polylogarithmic communication based on *Computational* Diffie-Hellman (CDH).

We emphasize that our protocols execute in polynomial runtime, and do not rely on any correlated randomness assumptions.

Sublinear 2PC for Layered Circuits. We present a new approach toward secure two-party computation protocols for general layered circuits, with communication complexity that scales sublinearly in the circuit size. As opposed to building FHE or HSS, our approach begins with protocols for "batch Oblivious Transfer" with low communication.

Oblivious Transfer (OT) is an atomic functionality in which sender and receiver parties begin with inputs $m_0, m_1 \in \{0, 1\}$ and $b \in \{0, 1\}$, respectively; at the conclusion the receiver learns the selected message m_b; and neither party learns further information about one another's inputs. OT was shown to be a complete functionality for general secure computation [Kil00], where OT protocol execution(s) take place for each nonlinear gate of the corresponding circuit.

OT protocols are known from a number of standard assumptions, in just two rounds of communication (i.e., one message from receiver to sender, and one message in return); but, the communication complexity for all such solutions is (inherently) significantly larger than the input size. Very recently, it was shown by Brakerski et al. [BBDP22] how to achieve a *batched* version of OT, still in two rounds, and with *rate-1* communication. That is, for a collection of message pairs $(\{m_0^{(i)}, m_1^{(i)}\})_{i \in [k]}$ and selection bits $(b^{(i)})_{i \in [k]}$, a sender and receiver could perform k parallel batched executions of OT in communication roughly k.

We prove that any such protocol which satisfies an additional *decomposability* property suffices to imply secure computation protocols for general layered circuits with sublinear communication complexity. To define decomposability, consider the communication structure of any 2-round rate-1 batch OT protocol. In the first round, the receiver sends $k + o(k)$ bits to the sender,[3] somehow encoding its selection bits $b^{(i)}$. In response, the sender performs some computation as a function of its message pairs $\{m_0^{(i)}, m_1^{(i)}\}$, and returns $k + o(k)$ bits in response, somehow encoding the k selected messages, $m_{b^{(i)}}^{(i)}$. For the constructions of [BBDP22], the sender's message size is just $k + \mathsf{polylog}(k)$.

We say that the (2-round, rate-1) batch OT protocol is *decomposable* if for any agreed subset $S \subset [k]$ of indices, the sender can choose a corresponding subset of $|S| + \mathsf{polylog}(k)$ of its return message bits, such that sending this partial sender response reveals *exactly* the corresponding subset of selected messages $(m_{b^{(i)}}^{(i)})_{i \in S}$ to the receiver. Namely, given the partial response, these $|S|$ messages can be recovered, and no information is revealed about $m_{b^{(i)}}^{(i)}$ for $i \notin S$.

Theorem 1 (Sublinear 2PC from Decomposable Batch OT - informal). *Assume existence of 2-round rate-1 batch OT with the above "decomposability" property. Then for any k, we can securely compute layered (synchronous) circuits of depth d and size s using $\mathsf{poly}(2^{2^k}, s)$ computation and $O(2^{2^k} \cdot d \cdot \mathsf{poly}(\lambda) + s/k)$ communication.*

In particular, for $k = O(\log \log s)$, we obtain communication $O(s/\log \log s + d^{1/3} \cdot s^{2(1+\varepsilon)/3} \cdot \mathsf{poly}(\lambda))$, for an arbitrary small constant ε. The latter is sublinear in s whenever $d = o(s^{1-\varepsilon}/\mathsf{poly}(\lambda))$, i.e., the circuit is not too "tall and skinny".

---

[3] Our construction can actually handle arbitrary *constant* client-to-server upload rate, as long as the sender-to-receiver download rate is 1.

This decomposability property is not simply hypothetical, but rather was inspired by the batch-OT protocols of Brakerski et al. [BBDP22], which we show to satisfy the requirement. At a high level, the sender's message in their protocols consists of an encryption of the selected message bits (computed homomorphically as a function of receiver-sent ciphertexts of its selection bits, together with the message pairs $\{m_0^{(i)}, m_1^{(i)}\}$), compressed à la [DGI+19] to rate 1. The resulting rate-1 ciphertexts have the structure of a $\mathsf{polylog}(k)$-size "header" string, independent of the messages, together with a *single bit* of information for each encrypted message bit. Decomposability thus follows (pseudo)directly, by simply omitting those information bits corresponding to encrypted messages the sender wishes to drop (i.e., $[k]\backslash S$).[4]

In turn, we obtain the following corollary.

Corollary 2 (Sublinear 2PC from QR+LPN - informal). *The conclusion of Theorem 1 holds based on Quadratic Residuosity (QR) and Learning Parity with Noise (LPN) for any inverse-polynomial noise rate.*

Our result is summarized on Table 1, where we also recall the state of the art in sublinear secure computation. We remark that while sublinear $O(s/\log\log s)$-communication protocols were known from a variant of LPN from [CM21], their result must assume superpolynomial hardness of LPN with a small inverse-superpolynomial error rate. In contrast, our result requires only polynomial hardness of LPN, with any inverse-polynomial error rate (as inherited by the construction of [BBDP22]).

We finally mention that this result is also not implied by the constructions of pseudorandom correlation functions (PCF) [BCG+20] from QR+LPN of [OSY21] (or in fact any of the line of work on pseudorandom correlation generators (PCG) [BCG+19]). While PCG/PCFs enable the generation of large quantities of *random* instances of OT with sublinear communication, the best known approaches for utilizing these random correlations within an actual secure computation protocol require communication that scales linearly with the circuit size.

Private Information Retrieval. Motivated by the goal of building decomposable rate-1 batch OT from new assumptions, we then turn to a deeper exploration of one of the required underlying components from the [BBDP22] batch OT construction: (single-server) Private Information Retrieval (PIR).

We succeed in constructing PIR with polylogarithmic communication from the *Computational Diffie-Hellman* assumption. While this is only one subcomponent required to obtain the necessary batch OT from LPN+CDH,[5] this provides one step toward this direction. But, more importantly, it constitutes a new feasibility result of its own right. From CDH, previously no PIR protocol was known with communication $o(n)$.

---

[4] We are of course sweeping details under the rug here, and refer the reader to the main body for a more complete treatment.

[5] Indeed, the approach of [BBDP22] requires also a form of homomorphic encryption compressible to rate 1.

Table 1. Existing protocols for secure computation with sublinear communication under various assumptions, in the computational setting.

	Assumptions	Circuit class	Sublinearity[a]
[Gen09]	LWE	P/poly	$O(n + m)$
[BGI16]	DDH	Layered circuits	$O(n + m + s/\log s)$
[OSY21, RS21]	DCR	Layered circuits	$O(n + m + s/\log s)$
[CM21]	Superpoly LPN[b]	Layered circuits	$O(n + m + s/\log\log s)$
[ADOS22]	Class groups	Layered circuits	$O(n + m + s/\log s)$
This work	LPN + QR[c]	Layered circuits	$O\left(n + m + d^{1/3} \cdot s^{2(1+\varepsilon)/3} \cdot \mathsf{poly}(\lambda) + \frac{s}{\log\log s}\right)$

[a] We use n for input size, m for output size, s for circuit size, and d for circuit depth.
[b] [CM21] assumes the superpolynomial hardness of the LPN assumption with dimension N, $O(N)$ samples, and noise rate $N^{o(1)-1}$.
[c] We assume the polynomial hardness of LPN with dimension N, $\mathsf{poly}(N)$ samples, and inverse-polynomial noise rate.

Theorem 3 (PIR from CDH - informal). *Based on the Computational Diffie-Hellman (CDH) assumption, there exists single-server PIR on n-bit databases with communication* $\mathsf{polylog}(n)$ *and* $\mathcal{O}(\log(n))$ *rounds.*

In hindsight, our construction forms a surprisingly simple and clean combination of two existing tools from the literature. Along the way, we identify an improved procedure for converting between a weak form of "semi-PIR" as considered in [BIP18], which reveals the client's queried index with some probability, to full-blown secure PIR. We refer the reader to the Technical Overview for more details.

2 Technical Overview

We assume familiarity with standard cryptographic assumptions such as QR, LPN, CDH, and DDH, and refer the reader to the full version for a formal statement of these assumptions.

2.1 Sublinear 2PC for Layered Circuits from Decomposable Batch OT

We consider Boolean circuits over any base of gates with fan-in two.

Toward our sublinear 2PC result for layered circuits, we begin by focusing on circuits of low depth k (e.g., think of $k = \log\log\log s$), and devise a secure protocol with communication $n + m + (2^{2^k} \cdot \mathsf{poly}(\lambda))$, for input size n, output size m, circuit size s, and security parameter λ. Given such a tool, we can appropriately divide a larger layered circuit into depth-k blocks where the sum of all block input and output sizes is s/k, and then iteratively compute (secret shares of) each layer output via the sub-protocol. Combined, this yields a secure computation for the layered circuit with overall communication $O(s/k + 2^{2^k} \cdot d \cdot \mathsf{poly}(\lambda))$, as desired.

Starting Point: An SPIR Viewpoint. Consider a circuit with input size n, output size m, and low depth k. Given fan-in 2, each output bit is computed as a function of at most 2^k input bits. We may thus view the circuit output as dictated by m separate truth tables, each of size 2^{2^k}, indexed by the values of the corresponding relevant 2^k input bits. More concretely, think of one party as holding the (partially collapsed) truth tables incorporating its known inputs, and the second party as holding its own input string, dictating the relevant position of each truth table. We will refer to the first party as "sender" and second as "receiver".

Given this perspective, protocols for (Symmetric) Private Information Retrieval (SPIR) immediately come to mind. An SPIR protocol is a strengthened version of PIR, where the client additionally learns nothing beyond its queried value of the database. Secure computation of our circuit precisely amounts to m instances of SPIR, where the receiver party learns exactly the desired indexed values of the m truth tables.

However, the situation is not so simple: Even the best known (S)PIR protocols have communication polylogarithmic in the database size. Applying m instances of SPIR for the m outputs would thus yield communication $\mathsf{polylog}(2^k) \cdot m \in \Omega(km)$, killing sublinearity.

In order to obtain sublinear communication, we must somehow leverage that the m SPIR instances are not completely independent, but rather are made with *correlated* queries. That is, although there are m instances each with (2^k)-bit index values, the $m \cdot 2^k$ selection bits have several repeats, collectively coming from different subsets of only $n < m \cdot 2^k$ input bits.

Toward Batch SPIR with Correlated Queries. Our task becomes precisely to construct such an object: m-instance batch SPIR, with significantly lower communication complexity given correlated queries.

For purposes of discussion, suppose there existed a 2-round rate-1 protocol for oblivious transfer, where each sender and receiver (magically) sends only a single bit. Given access to such a tool, then by leveraging ideas from the literature (e.g., achieving PIR from linearly homomorphic encryption [KO97]), we would be set. Indeed, the receiver would simply send 1 bit for each input bit, corresponding to the first OT message using this value as a selector bit. These first messages could then be *reused* by the sender in multiple, recursive executions.

More concretely, suppose the server holds a database of N bits and that the receiver wants to retrieve the element stored at index $x = (x_1, \ldots, x_{\log N})$. If the receiver sends a message otr_1 generated as its first-round OT-receiver message for the first bit x_1 of the desired index, the server can take the database, pair up elements whose indices differ only on the first bit, then apply the OT-server computation with respect to otr_1 on each pair in order to retrieve a single-bit response for each, creating a new "database" of half the number of elements, each corresponding to a 1-bit sender answer message. If instead the receiver sends messages $(\mathsf{otr}_1, \ldots, \mathsf{otr}_{\log N})$, one for each bit of the desired index, the server can now iteratively compress the database down to a single bit by building a "Merkle tree" where in each recursive iteration corresponding to input index bit x_i, the new "database" is split into pairs of messages whose indices differ only in this index, and performing the OT-server computation on each pair produces a new list of 1-bit sender answer messages of again half the length. At the conclusion, the server will be left with a single message value remaining, which by construction precisely enables the receiver to recover the target value stored at index x. This approach extends directly for m distinct databases with the *same* total receiver message $(\mathsf{otr}_1, \ldots, \mathsf{otr}_{\log N})$, since the corresponding OT-receiver messages can be used independently in any mix and match format across databases. In turn, the sender would need to send only m total bits response, one bit for each database query.

Of course, unfortunately, we do not have such a strong rate-1 OT. We thus turn to the next closest alternative which does exist: 2-round rate-1 *batch* OT, as recently achieved by Brakerski et al. [BBDP22]. Batch OT considers a collection of ℓ message pairs $(\{m_0^{(i)}, m_1^{(i)}\})_{i \in [\ell]}$ and selection bits $(b^{(i)})_{i \in [\ell]}$, and enables a sender and receiver to perform ℓ parallel batched executions of OT with communication roughly ℓ. Attempting to apply the above strategy with rate-1 batch OT, however, poses significant challenges.

- The batching structure restricts the "mix and match" abilities of the sender when using the receiver's OT message. The sender must respond to the *entire* batched vector of receiver's selection bits at any stage, without freely accessing subsets of selection bits. Instead, the above approach involves using each selection bit $b^{(i)}$ within a *different* number $(N/2^i)$ of message pairs.
- Even worse, the sender's (batch) response in general is only defined given *all* ℓ *pairs of messages* to be selected by the bits $b^{(1)}, \ldots, b^{(\ell)}$. In contrast, the above approach crucially relies on the ability to choose the message pairs for selection bit $b^{(i)}$ *dynamically* as a function of the server's responses given the previous selection bits $b^{(1)}, \ldots, b^{(i-1)}$.
- Finally, it is no longer the case that for each selected message the sender has a *single* corresponding response bit. In fact, rate 1 here does not even mean that for ℓ instances that exactly ℓ bits are sent in each direction, but rather just asymptotically $\ell + o(\ell)$. This means that in each recursive OT execution, the sender's messages (and thus "database entry" size) may grow, leading to large growth and ultimately large communication upon further recursions.

Decomposable Batch OT. With this motivation, we introduce the notion of *decomposable (2-round, rate-1) batch oblivious transfer*, which can be seen as a strengthening of two-round batch OT with constant upload-rate (*i.e.* the size of the receiver message is linear in the batch size ℓ) and download-rate asymptotically one (*i.e.* the size of the sender message is $\ell + o(\ell)$). The differences boil down to a notion of *decomposability* which we impose on the sender message.

At a high level, what we want to capture is the fact that the receiver should be able to retrieve the ith selected message in the batch if and only it also has access to the ith bit of the sender message (using its own internal state saved from generating the receiver message). More generally, given only a subset of the bits of the sender message, the receiver should able to retrieve the corresponding subset of selected messages in the batch.

Slightly more formally, we say that the (2-round, rate-1) batch OT protocol is *decomposable* if for any agreed subset $S \subset [\ell]$ of indices, the sender can choose a corresponding subset of $|S| + \mathsf{polylog}(\ell)$ of its return message bits, such that sending this partial sender response reveals *exactly* the corresponding subset of selected messages $(m_{b(i)}^{(i)})_{i \in S}$ to the receiver. Namely, given the partial response, these $|S|$ messages can be recovered, and no information is revealed about $m_{b(i)}^{(i)}$ for $i \notin S$.

For our purposes, it will suffice to consider a relaxation of the notion we just described, and allow the sender message to have some small overhead rather than having a one-to-one correspondence between the bits on the sender message and the ℓ selected messages. In this relaxed form, we require that the sender message be comprised of two parts: a "reusable" part (of size $o(\ell)$), and a "decomposable" part (of size ℓ). On its own, the reusable part should reveal nothing about the messages, but can be used to "decode" each bit of the decomposable part so as to retrieve (exactly) the corresponding selected message in the batch. Among other benefits of this relaxation, it allows us to consider constructions whose download-rate is only asymptotically one.

This decomposability property is not only enough for our needs, but perhaps more importantly, is *achievable*, in fact achieved by the batch OT constructions of [BBDP22]. Roughly speaking, the sender message in their construction is composed of a rate-1 encryption of the vector of requested message bits, with structure consisting of a short "header" independent of the message bits, together with a single ciphertext bit encoding each message bit separately. Decomposability can then be achieved by sending only those ciphertext bits encoding the desired subset of messages.

Slightly more accurately, this describes the situation for all but an inverse-polynomial fraction of message bits (corresponding to noisy coordinates of an LPN ciphertext sent by the receiver), which actually encode the *incorrect* messages. In order to separately address these values, they employ a "co-PIR" (or "punctured OT" [BGI17]) to efficiently mask out the undesired values from the receiver, and a separate PIR to learn the correct values for these positions. The separate PIR query responses appear as part of the short "header" information of the server's response, which may sound like an issue, as this portion should not reveal information directly about any message bits. However, this problem does not occur, because the extra PIR queries are set up to actually reveal the *difference* between the masked-out incorrect message $(r_i \oplus m_{1-b})$ and the target message m_b. Because of the mask, this difference value (revealed in the header) provides no information about any message in the absence of the corresponding value $(r_i \oplus m_{1-b})$ from the payload portion of the ciphertext, as required by decomposability. We refer the reader to Sect. 3.2 for further details.

Sublinear 2PC from Decomposable Batch OT. This decomposability property directly allows us to address one of the above challenges of batch OT: we will not have issues with exponential growth of the database entry size in the recursive OT executions. Instead, the result of one iteration of the batch OT on n inputs will result in a short $o(n)$-size header together with n bits that each provide information about a distinct queried message. The header string we will put to the side (ultimately we will send the collection of all the headers, which is still sufficiently short). The remaining n bits induce the recursive sender-message database that, as desired, consists of exactly 1 bit per message.

In fact, if we temporarily suppose that the assignment graph structure of n input bits to $m = n$ output bits can be decomposed as the disjoint union of 2^k matchings, then we have a solution. Each disjoint matching will correspond directly to a different instance of n-input batch OT, where each of the n inputs is simultaneously used to index a different database. Applying the recursive solution as above, the sender will ultimately compute a single bit for each output, as well as a collection of header strings from each of the batch OT executions.

The remaining challenge is that general circuits do *not* have such nice regular structure, instead with inputs appearing in different numbers of output computations, with inconvenient correlations, demanding a stronger form of "mix and match" of batched OT queries beyond a direct approach.

To address this issue, we modify the structure of batch OT receiver queries, effectively extending the batch size (say from n to $2n$), and employing a careful choice of how to pack extra copies of more highly influential input bits into the queried vector, so that the overall total number of batch OT instances remains sufficiently small that the overhead of extra header strings does not negatively impact the final communication complexity. We refer the reader to the technical body for a detailed treatment of this procedure.

2.2   Polylogarithmic PIR from CDH

We now turn our attention to our second contribution: private information retrieval with polylogarithmic communication from the computational Diffie-Hellman assumption. A private information retrieval (PIR) is a two party protocol between a server S holding a string z (the database) and a client C holding an integer i. At the end of the interaction, the client should learn z_i, without revealing i to the server. A polylogarithmic PIR is a PIR where the total communication is $\mathsf{poly}(\lambda, \log |z|)$, where λ is the security parameter.

Below, we sketch our approach to building polylogarithmic PIR from CDH. In hindsight, our construction is in fact relatively straightforward, and follows from an elegant combination of two recent results. We outline the sequence of implications below.

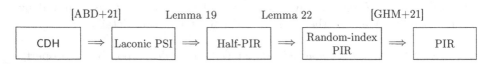

Laconic PSI. A private set intersection protocol is a two-party protocol allowing a receiver to securely compute the intersection of its input set S_R with the set S_S of a sender: at the end of the protocol, the receiver learns $S_R \cap S_S$ and nothing more. A *laconic* PSI protocol, introduced in [ABD+21], additionally enforces that the protocol is two-round (receiver to sender, then sender to receiver), and both the total communication and the sender runtime are bounded by $\mathsf{poly}(\lambda, \log|S_R|, |S_S|)$. The work of [ABD+21] showed that laconic PSI can be constructed from anonymous hash encryption, a primitive that can be constructed (in particular) from the CDH assumption [DG17b, DG17a, BLSV18].

From Laconic PSI to Half-PIR. Given a laconic PSI protocol, we exhibit a construction of polylogarithmic-communication PIR, using in addition a pseudorandom function. However, our construction only achieves a very weak form of security: it only guarantees that the index i is kept hidden from the server with probability $1/2$. This notion, which we call half-PIR, has been introduced in [BIP18] (under the name $\mathsf{Rand}\frac{1}{2}\mathsf{PIR}$). It was shown in [BIP18] that polylogarithmic half-PIR already suffices to construct *slightly sublinear* PIR (with communication $O(|z|/\log|z|)$); looking ahead, we will provide a stronger reduction and show that it actually implies polylogarithmic PIR.

Our construction of half-PIR proceeds as follows: the client and the server agree on a PRF key K. The server with input z builds the set $S_R = \{F_K(1||z_1), \cdots, F_K(|z|||z_{|z|})\}$, and the client with input i builds the set $S_S = \{F_K(i||b)\}$, where b is a uniformly random bit. The core properties that this achieves are:

- If $b = z_i$, then $|S_R \cap S_S| = 1$ (note that $|S_S| = 1$), and
- If $b \neq z_i$, then $|S_R \cap S_S| = 0$ with high probability.

To show the second property, we rely on the security of the PRF to argue that a collision between PRF evaluations on distinct inputs is highly unlikely (provided the PRF outputs are large enough). Note, therefore, that we rely on the PRF *security* to argue the *correctness* of the construction (while this is slightly unusual, this kind of arguments has been used a few times in the literature).

Now, the server and the client execute a laconic PSI, which has total communication $\mathsf{poly}(\lambda, \log|z|)$ (since $|S_S| = 1$). At the end of the protocol, the server, who plays the role of the receiver, sends $|S_R \cap S_S|$ to the client. Note that $|S_R \cap S_S| = (1 - b) \oplus z_i$, hence the client can decode z_i from this information. Yet, whenever $|S_R \cap S_S| = 0$, the security of the laconic PSI implies that the server actually learns nothing about i: this guarantees client security with probability $1/2$. When $|S_R \cap S_S| = 1$, however, the server learns the intersection $S_R \cap S_S = F_K(i||z_i)$, and can in particular retrieve i easily.

From Half-PIR to PIR. We now turn to constructing a polylogarithmic PIR from a polylogarithmic half-PIR. Here, our construction is mostly a simple observation: half-PIR implies random-index PIR via a straightforward construction. A random-index PIR, introduced in [GHM+21], is a PIR protocol where the client has no input, and receives (i, z_i) where the index i is picked uniformly at random between 1 and $|z|$. Given a half-PIR, building a random-index PIR is almost immediate: the client and the server execute λ parallel instances of a half-PIR protocol, where the client uses uniformly random independent indices in each instance. With overwhelming probability, at least one of these instances will be secure (in the sense that the server does not learn the index); the client simply outputs (i^*, z_{i^*}) where i^* is the index used in the first such execution.

Eventually, random-index PIR was recently shown in [GHM+21] to imply full-fledged PIR, with a $\log|z|$ blowup in communication and round complexity. The key observation underlying this reduction is that a single invocation of a random-index PIR, together with sending $\log|z|$ bits, allows to reduce the task of executing a PIR on a size-$|z|$ database to that of executing a PIR on a size-$|z|/2$ database. The construction follows by recursively invoking this construction (we provide a more detailed description of this construction in Sect. 4.3). Combining all these building blocks together leads to a logarithmic-round, polylogarithmic-communication PIR from the CDH assumption.

3   Sublinear Computation for $\log\log$-Depth Circuits

3.1   Decomposable Two-Round Batch Oblivious Transfer

We introduce the notion of *decomposable two-round batch oblivious transfer* (Definition 4), which can be seen as a strengthening of two-round batch OT with constant upload-rate and download-rate asymptotically one. The differences boil down to a notion of *decomposability* which we impose on the sender message, which should be comprised of a (small) *reusable part* and a linear-size *decomposable part*: the receiver should be able to retrieve the ith selected message in the batch if and only it also has access to the ith bit of the decomposable part of the sender message (along with the reusable part).

Definition 4 (Decomposable Two-Round Batch Oblivious Transfer). *Let $k \in \mathbb{N}^*$ and $\alpha(\cdot) = o(n)$. A semi-honest two-round decomposable batch OT protocol with $\alpha(\cdot)$-overhead between a sender and a receiver is defined as a triple of PPT algorithms* dec-OT $=$ (dec-OTR, dec-OTS, dec-OTD) *with the following syntax and properties:*

- **Syntax.**
    dec-OTR : *On input the security parameter 1^λ and a vector of selection bits $\vec{b} = (b_1, \ldots, b_k) \in \{0,1\}^k$,* dec-OTR *outputs a receiver message* otr $\in \{0,1\}^{\mathcal{O}(k)}$ *and an internal state* st; *without loss of generality we assume that* st *contains all the random coins used by* dec-OTR *as well as $\vec{b}$.*

    dec-OTS : *On input the security parameter 1^λ, a receiver message* otr, *and a database* $((m_0^{(i)}, m_1^{(i)}))_{i \in [k]} \in \{0,1\}^{2k}$ *comprised of k pairs of bits,* dec-OTS *outputs a sender message* ots $=$ (ots*, ots^{dec}), *which is comprised of a reusable part* ots$^\star \in \{0,1\}^{\alpha(k)}$ *and a decomposable part* ots$^{\text{dec}} \in \{0,1\}^k$.

    dec-OTD : *On input a batch subset $K \subseteq [k]$, a partial sender message* ots$' \in \{0,1\}^{\alpha(k)+|K|}$, *and an internal state* st, dec-OTD *outputs a vector of messages* $(\widetilde{m}_i)_{i \in K} \in \{0,1\}^{|K|}$.

- **Decomposable Correctness.** *For every* $\lambda \in \mathbb{N}^*$, $K \subseteq [k]$, *every* $\vec{b} = (b_1, \ldots, b_k) \in \{0,1\}^k$, *and every* $\vec{m} = ((m_0^{(i)}, m_1^{(i)}))_{i \in [k]} \in \{0,1\}^{2k}$,

$$
\Pr \left[(\tilde{m}_1, \ldots, \tilde{m}_{|K|}) = (m_{b_i}^{(i)})_{i \in K} : \begin{array}{l} (\mathsf{otr}, \mathsf{st}) \xleftarrow{\$} \mathsf{dec\text{-}OTR}(1^\lambda, \vec{b}) \\ (\mathsf{ots}^\star, \mathsf{ots}^{\mathcal{DB}}) \xleftarrow{\$} \mathsf{dec\text{-}OTS}(1^\lambda, \mathsf{otr}, \vec{m}) \\ (\tilde{m}_1, \ldots, \tilde{m}_{|K|}) \xleftarrow{\$} \mathsf{dec\text{-}OTD}(K, (\mathsf{ots}^\star, [\mathsf{ots}^{\mathsf{dec}}]_K), \mathsf{st}) \end{array} \right] = 1.
$$

- **Receiver Security (against Semi-Honest Sender).** *There exists an expected polynomial time simulator* Sim_S *such that for every* $\lambda \in \mathbb{N}^*$ *and every* $\vec{b} = (b_1, \ldots, b_k) \in \{0,1\}^k$,

$$
\left\{ \mathsf{otr} : (\mathsf{otr}, \mathsf{st}) \xleftarrow{\$} \mathsf{dec\text{-}OTR}(1^\lambda, \vec{b}) \right\} \stackrel{c}{\approx} \left\{ \mathsf{Sim}_S(1^\lambda) \right\}.
$$

- **Decomposable Sender Security (against Semi-Honest Receiver).** *There exists an expected polynomial time simulator* Sim_R *such that for every* $\lambda \in \mathbb{N}^*$, *every* $K \subseteq [k]$, *every* $\vec{b} = (b_1, \ldots, b_k) \in \{0,1\}^k$, *and every* $\vec{m} = ((m_0^{(i)}, m_1^{(i)}))_{i \in [k]} \in \{0,1\}^{2k}$,

$$
\left\{ (\mathsf{ots}^\star, [\mathsf{ots}^{\mathsf{dec}}]_K, \mathsf{otr}, \mathsf{st}) : \begin{array}{l} (\mathsf{otr}, \mathsf{st}) \xleftarrow{\$} \mathsf{dec\text{-}OTR}(1^\lambda, \vec{b}) \\ (\mathsf{ots}^\star, \mathsf{ots}^{\mathcal{BD}}) \xleftarrow{\$} \mathsf{dec\text{-}OTS}(1^\lambda, \mathsf{otr}, \vec{m}) \end{array} \right\} \stackrel{c}{\approx}
$$

$$
\left\{ (\mathsf{sim}^\star, \mathsf{sim}^{\mathsf{dec}}, \mathsf{otr}, \mathsf{st}) : \begin{array}{l} (\mathsf{otr}, \mathsf{st}) \xleftarrow{\$} \mathsf{dec\text{-}OTR}(1^\lambda, \vec{b}) \\ (\mathsf{sim}^\star, \mathsf{sim}^{\mathsf{dec}}) \xleftarrow{\$} \mathsf{Sim}_R(1^\lambda, K, (m_{b_i}^{(i)})_{i \in K}, \vec{b}, \mathsf{otr}, \mathsf{st}) \end{array} \right\}.
$$

3.2 Instantiation Under QR + LPN, Adapted from [BBDP22]

As noted previously, two-round decomposable batch oblivious transfer can be seen as a strengthening of two-round batch OT with constant upload-rate and download-rate asymptotically one. As a matter of fact, the construction of batch OT with optimal rate from [BBDP22] natively satisfies the extra requirements and can be cast as two-round decomposable batch OT with sublinear overhead.

Theorem 5 (Corollary of [BBDP22, Sect. 7]). *Assume the* QR *assumption and the binary LPN assumption* $\mathsf{LPN}(\mathsf{dim}, \mathsf{num}, \rho)$ *with dimension* $\mathsf{dim} = \mathsf{poly}(\lambda)$, *number of samples* $\mathsf{num} = \mathsf{dim}^c$ *(for any constant* $c > 1$*), and noise rate* $\rho = \mathsf{num}^{\varepsilon - 1}$ *(for some constant* $\varepsilon < 1$*). Then for any* $\ell = \ell(\lambda)$*, there exists a decomposable two-round batch oblivious transfer for batch size* $k = \ell \cdot \mathsf{num}$ *where*

- *The receiver message* otr *has size* $(\ell^2 \cdot \mathsf{dim} + \ell \cdot \mathsf{num}^\varepsilon) \cdot \mathsf{poly}(\lambda) + k$
- *The sender message* $\mathsf{ots} = (\mathsf{ots}^\star, \mathsf{ots}^{\mathsf{dec}})$ *has size* $|\mathsf{ots}^\star| = (\mathsf{num} + \ell \cdot \mathsf{num}^\varepsilon) \cdot \mathsf{poly}(\lambda)$ *and* $|\mathsf{ots}^{\mathsf{dec}}| = k$.

In particular, for appropriate parameters (sufficiently large ℓ, and num sufficiently larger than ℓ), $|\mathsf{otr}| = k + o(k)$, and $|\mathsf{ots}^\star| = o(k)$.

The proof of Theorem 5 is deferred to the full version of this paper. Note that the construction of batch OT in [BBDP22] from LPN plus DDH or LPN plus polynomial-modulus LWE can similarly be shown to be decomposable. However, two-party sublinear secure computation is already known under these assumptions, via HSS for NC^1 [BGI16, BKS19].

3.3 Bounded Query Repetitions

At a high level the goal of this section is to show how a receiver message of dec-OT can be re-used, possibly with imbalances in how many times each selection bit in the batch is re-used, while asymptotically preserving upload- and download-rate.

Definition 6 (Decomposable Two-Round Batch Oblivious Transfer with Bounded Query Repetitions). *Let $k \in \mathbb{N}^\star$ and $\alpha = o(n)$. A semi-honest two-round decomposable batch OT protocol with $\alpha(\cdot)$-overhead and T-bounded query repetitions between a sender and a receiver can be defined as a triple of PPT algorithms $\mathsf{rep\text{-}OT} = (\mathsf{rep\text{-}OTR}, \mathsf{rep\text{-}OTS}, \mathsf{rep\text{-}OTD})$ with the following syntax and properties:*

- **Syntax.**
  - $\mathsf{rep\text{-}OTR}$: *On input the security parameter 1^λ and a vector of selection bits $\vec{b} = (b_1, \ldots, b_k) \in \{0,1\}^k$, $\mathsf{rep\text{-}OTR}$ outputs a receiver message $\mathsf{otr} \in \{0,1\}^{\mathcal{O}(k)}$ and an internal state st; without loss of generality we assume that st contains all the random coins used by $\mathsf{rep\text{-}OTR}$ as well as $\vec{b}$.*
  - $\mathsf{rep\text{-}OTS}$: *On input the security parameter 1^λ, a query otr, a database $((m_0^{(i)}, m_1^{(i)}))_{i \in [k']} \in \{0,1\}^{2k'}$ (where $k \le k' \le k \cdot T$), and a vector of repetitions $\mathsf{rep} = (\mathsf{rep}_1, \ldots, \mathsf{rep}_k) \in [0, T]^k$ such that $\sum_{i=1}^k \mathsf{rep}_i = k'$, $\mathsf{rep\text{-}OTS}$ outputs a sender message $\mathsf{ots} = (\mathsf{ots}^\star, \mathsf{ots}^{\mathsf{dec}})$, which is comprised of a reusable part $\mathsf{ots}^\star \in \{0,1\}^{\alpha(k)}$ and a decomposable part $\mathsf{ots}^{\mathsf{dec}} \in \{0,1\}^{k'}$, as well as rep.*
  - $\mathsf{rep\text{-}OTD}$: *On input a batch subset $K \subseteq [k']$, a partial sender message $\mathsf{ots}' \in \{0,1\}^{\alpha(k)+|K|}$, a vector of repetitions $\mathsf{rep} = (\mathsf{rep}_1, \ldots, \mathsf{rep}_k) \in [0,T]^k$ such that $\sum_{i=1}^k \mathsf{rep}_i = k'$, and an internal state st, $\mathsf{rep\text{-}OTD}$ outputs a vector of messages $(\widetilde{m}_i)_{i \in K} \in \{0,1\}^{|K|}$.*
- **Decomposable Correctness.** *For every $\lambda \in \mathbb{N}^\star$, $K \subseteq [k']$, every $\vec{b} = (b_1, \ldots, b_k) \in \{0,1\}^k$, and every $\vec{m} = ((m_0^{(i)}, m_1^{(i)}))_{i \in [k']} \in \{0,1\}^{2k'}$,*

$$\Pr\left[(\widetilde{m}_1, \ldots, \widetilde{m}_{|K|}) = (m_{\sigma_i}^{(i)})_{i \in K} : \begin{array}{l} (\mathsf{otr}, \mathsf{st}) \xleftarrow{\$} \mathsf{rep\text{-}OTR}(1^\lambda, \vec{b}) \\ ((\mathsf{ots}^\star, \mathsf{ots}^{\mathsf{dec}}), \mathsf{rep}) \xleftarrow{\$} \mathsf{rep\text{-}OTS}(1^\lambda, \mathsf{otr}, \vec{m}, \mathsf{rep}) \\ (\widetilde{m}_1, \ldots, \widetilde{m}_{|K|}) \xleftarrow{\$} \mathsf{rep\text{-}OTD}(K, (\mathsf{ots}^\star, [\mathsf{ots}^{\mathsf{dec}}]_K), \mathsf{rep}, \mathsf{st}) \end{array} \right] = 1,$$

$$\text{where } \sigma_i := b_{\max\{j : (\sum_{j' < j} \mathsf{rep}_{j'}) \le i\}}.$$

– **Receiver Security (against Semi-Honest Sender).** *There exists an expected polynomial time simulator* Sim_S *such that for every* $\lambda \in \mathbb{N}^*$ *and every* $\vec{b} = (b_1, \ldots, b_k) \in \{0,1\}^k$,

$$\left\{ \text{otr} \colon (\text{otr}, \text{st}) \xleftarrow{\$} \text{rep-OTR}(1^\lambda, \vec{b}) \right\} \stackrel{c}{\approx} \left\{ \text{Sim}_S(1^\lambda) \right\} .$$

– **Decomposable Sender Security (against Semi-Honest Receiver).** *There exists an expected polynomial time simulator* Sim_R *such that for every* $\lambda \in \mathbb{N}^*$, *every* $\text{rep} = (\text{rep}_1, \ldots, \text{rep}_k) \in [0,T]^k$ *such that* $\|\text{rep}\|_1 = k'$, *every* $K \subseteq [k']$, *every* $\vec{b} = (b_1, \ldots, b_k) \in \{0,1\}^k$, *and every* $\vec{m} = ((m_0^{(i)}, m_1^{(i)}))_{i \in [k']} \in \{0,1\}^{2k'}$,

$$\left\{ (\text{ots}^\star, [\text{ots}^{\text{dec}}]_K, \text{otr}, \text{st}) \colon \begin{array}{c} (\text{otr}, \text{st}) \xleftarrow{\$} \text{rep-OTR}(1^\lambda, \vec{b}) \\ (\text{ots}^\star, \text{ots}^{\text{dec}}) \xleftarrow{\$} \text{rep-OTS}(1^\lambda, \text{otr}, \vec{m}, \text{rep}) \end{array} \right\} \stackrel{c}{\approx}$$

$$\left\{ (\text{sim}^\star, \text{sim}^{\text{dec}}, \text{otr}, \text{st}) \colon \begin{array}{c} (\text{otr}, \text{st}) \xleftarrow{\$} \text{rep-OTR}(1^\lambda, \vec{b}) \\ (\text{sim}^\star, \text{sim}^{\text{dec}}) \xleftarrow{\$} \text{Sim}_R(1^\lambda, K, (m_{\sigma_i}^{(i)})_{i \in K}, \vec{b}, \text{rep}, \text{otr}, \text{st}) \end{array} \right\}$$

$$\text{where } \sigma_i := b_{\max\{j \colon (\sum_{j' < j} \text{rep}_{j'}) \le i\}} .$$

Lemma 7 (From dec-OT **to** rep-OT**).** *If* dec-OT *is a semi-honest two-round decomposable batch OT protocol with* α *overhead, then the construction* rep-OT *from Fig. 1 is a semi-honest two-round decomposable batch OT protocol with* $\alpha \cdot T$ *overhead and* T-*bounded repetitions.*

The proof of Lemma 7 is deferred to the full version of this paper.

3.4   Two-Round Batch SPIR with Correlated Queries

We next introduce and achieve a notion of batch symmetric PIR with correlated queries. This corresponds to batch SPIR where the queries are not independent; rather, the total entropy w used to describe the queries is small, and the queried indices can be reconstructed via a public function that "mixes and matches" the individual bits of entropy $\vec{\alpha} = (\alpha_1, \ldots, \alpha_w)$ in a public manner. This will allow us to compress k size-N databases each down to a single bit—achieving batch SPIR—using batch OT on the selection bit vector $\vec{\alpha}$, by building a "Merkle-like forest" (seeing each 1-out-of-2 OT in the batch as a roughly length-halving hash function): the correlation in the queries across different databases is what allows the nodes of the Merkle forest to be batched.

In more detail, if the w bits of entropy are $\alpha_1, \ldots, \alpha_w$, "mixing and matching" means that each of the $(n = \log N)$-bit queries to a single database can be obtained by concatenating n of the bits α_i, possibly permuted. In the notation below, the jth query is given by vector $(\alpha_{s_{j,1}}, \ldots, \alpha_{s_{j,n}})$. We will be interested in how many times a given α_i appears within the k queries (counted by the

---

Decomposable Two-Round Batch Oblivious Transfer with Bounded Query Repetition

Parameters: Batch number k, Repetition bound T.

Requires: A two-round decomposable batch dec-OT protocol dec-OT = (dec-OTR, dec-OTS, dec-OTD) with α-overhead such that $\alpha(k) = o(k/T)$.

rep-OTR: On input the security parameter 1^λ and a vector of selection bits $\vec{b} = (b_1, \ldots, b_k) \in \{0,1\}^k$:

1. Compute $(\mathsf{otr}, \mathsf{st}) \xleftarrow{\$} \mathsf{dec\text{-}OTR}(1^\lambda, \vec{b})$.
2. Output $(\mathsf{otr}, \mathsf{st})$.

rep-OTS: On input the security parameter 1^λ, a receiver message otr, a database $\vec{m} \in \{0,1\}^{2k'}$, and a vector of repetitions $\mathsf{rep} = (\mathsf{rep}_1, \ldots, \mathsf{rep}_k) \in [0,T]^k$ such that $\|\mathsf{rep}\|_1 = k'$:

1. Parse $\vec{m}$ as $((m_0^{(j,i)}, m_1^{(j,i)}))_{j \in [k], i \in [\mathsf{rep}_j]}$.
2. For $j \in [k]$ and $i \in [\mathsf{rep}_j + 1, T]$, set $(m_0^{(j,i)}, m_1^{(j,i)}) \leftarrow (0,0)$.
3. For $i \in [T]$ set $\vec{m}_i := ((m_0^{(j,i)}, m_1^{(j,i)}))_{j \in [k]}$.
4. For $j = 1 \ldots T$:
   $\quad$ Compute $(\mathsf{ot}_{S,j}^\star, \mathsf{ot}_{S,j}^{\mathsf{dec}}) \xleftarrow{\$} \mathsf{dec\text{-}OTS}(1^\lambda, \mathsf{otr}, \vec{m}_j)$.
5. Set $\quad \mathsf{ots}^\star \quad \leftarrow \quad \mathsf{ot}_{S,1}^\star \| \ldots \| \mathsf{ot}_{S,T}^\star \quad$ and $\quad \mathsf{ot}_S^{\mathsf{dec}} \quad \leftarrow$
   $([\mathsf{ot}_{S,1}^{\mathsf{dec}}]_1 \| \ldots \| [\mathsf{ot}_{S,\mathsf{rep}_1}^{\mathsf{dec}}]_1) \| \ldots \| ([\mathsf{ot}_{S,1}^{\mathsf{dec}}]_k \| \ldots \| [\mathsf{ot}_{S,\mathsf{rep}_k}^{\mathsf{dec}}]_k)$.
6. Output $(\mathsf{ot}_S^\star, \mathsf{ot}_S^{\mathsf{dec}})$.

rep-OTD: On input a sender message ots, a vector of repetitions $\mathsf{rep} = (\mathsf{rep}_1, \ldots, \mathsf{rep}_k) \in [0,T]^k$ such that $\|\mathsf{rep}\|_1 = k'$, and an internal state st:

1. Parse ots as $(\mathsf{ot}_S^\star, \mathsf{ot}_S^{\mathsf{dec}})$.
2. Parse $\mathsf{ot}_S^\star$ as $\mathsf{ot}_{S,1}^\star \| \ldots \| \mathsf{ot}_{S,T}^\star$.
3. Parse $\mathsf{ot}_S^{\mathsf{dec}}$ as $([\mathsf{ot}_{S,1}^{\mathsf{dec}}]_1 \| \ldots \| [\mathsf{ot}_{S,\mathsf{rep}_1}^{\mathsf{dec}}]_1) \| \ldots \| ([\mathsf{ot}_{S,1}^{\mathsf{dec}}]_k \| \ldots \| [\mathsf{ot}_{S,\mathsf{rep}_k}^{\mathsf{dec}}]_k)$.

4. For $i = 1 \ldots T$:
   (a) Set $K_i := \{j : j \in [k], \mathsf{rep}_j \leq i\}$, ordered according to the natural order on $\mathbb{N}$.
   (b) Set $\vec{v}_i \leftarrow \big\|_{j \in K_i} [\mathsf{ot}_{S,i}^{\mathsf{dec}}]_j$.
   (c) Compute $(\widetilde{m}_{i,j})_{j \in K_i} \xleftarrow{\$} \mathsf{dec\text{-}OTD}(K_i, (\mathsf{ot}_{S,i}^\star, v_i), \mathsf{st})$.
5. Output $(\widetilde{m}_{1,1}, \ldots, \widetilde{m}_{\mathsf{rep}_1,1}, \widetilde{m}_{1,2}, \ldots, \widetilde{m}_{\mathsf{rep}_2,2}, \ldots, \widetilde{m}_{\mathsf{rep}_k,k})$.

Fig. 1. From dec-OT with α overhead to rep-OT with $\alpha \cdot T$ overhead.

occurrence function t_i below), as well as how many times it appears in specific position $j' \in [n]$ within the k queries (denoted below by $t_{i,j'}$). If all $t_{i,j'}$ are bounded by T, then for each level $j' \in [n]$ in the "Merkle forest" we can achieve the desired length-halving compression by using at most T batch OT sender computations on the original batch OT selection vector $\vec{\alpha}$.

Definition 8 ("Mix and Match" Functions). *A "mix and match" function* MixAndMatch: $\{0,1\}^w \to [N]^k$ *is one parameterised by* k *ordered subsets of* $n :=$ $\log N$ *elements of* $[w]$, $S_j = (s_{j,1}, \ldots, s_{j,n}) \in [w]^n$ *for* $j \in [k]$ *such that:*

$$\forall \vec{\alpha} = (\alpha_1, \ldots, \alpha_w) \in \{0,1\}^w, \mathsf{MixAndMatch}(\alpha_1, \ldots, \alpha_w) := (x_1, \ldots, x_k),$$
$$\text{with } x_j := \alpha_{s_{j,1}} \cdots \alpha_{s_{j,n}} \in [N].$$

Such a function is associated with an occurrence function, which counts the occurrences of each input position in the outputs:

$$t. : [w] \to [k]$$
$$i \mapsto t_i = \sum_{j=1}^{k} \mathbb{1}_{i \in S_j}$$

Each t_i *(*$i \in [w]$*) can be decomposed as* $t_i = t_{i,1} + \cdots + t_{i,n}$, *where* $t_{i,j'}$ *is equal to the number of values of* $j \in [k]$ *such that* $s_{j,j'} = i$.

- *MixAndMatch is said to be* T-*balanced if* $\forall i \in [w], \forall j' \in [n], t_{i,j'} \leq T$.
- *MixAndMatch is said to be* T-*balanceable if it can be expressed as the function* MixAndMatch = (MixAndMatch' $\circ$ replicate), *where* MixAndMatch: $\{0,1\}^{w'} \to$ $[N]^k$ *is a* T-*balanced mix-and-match function and* replicate *is defined as:*

$$\text{replicate:} \quad \{0,1\}^w \quad \to \{0,1\}^{w'} \qquad \qquad \text{where } w' := \sum_{i \in [w]} \lceil t_i/T \rceil.$$
$$(b_1, \ldots, b_w) \mapsto (b_1^{\| \lceil t_1/T \rceil} \| \ldots \| b_w^{\| \lceil t_w/T \rceil})$$

Lemma 9. *Let* $w, n \in \mathbb{N}$ *be a sufficiently large integers. For any family of unordered subsets* $S_1, \ldots, S_k \in \binom{[w]}{n}$ *there exists an ordering of each subset* S_j *such that the mix-and-match function induced by the resulting* $(\tilde{S}_j)_{j \in [k]}$ *is* polylog(w)-*balanceable.*
Furthermore, such orderings can be found in expected constant time.

The proof of Lemma 9 is deferred to the full version of this paper.

Definition 10 Two-Round Batch Computational Batch SPIR with Correlated "Mix and Match" Queries). *A semi-honest two-round batch SPIR protocol with correlated "mix and match" queries between a sender and a receiver can be defined as a triple of PPT algorithms* corrSPIR = (corrSPIR$_R$, corrSPIR$_S$, corrSPIR$_D$) *parameterised by a public* T-*balanceable "mix and match" function (Definition 8)* MixAndMatch: $\{0,1\}^w \to [N]^k$ *with the following syntax and properties:*

- **Syntax.**

- corrSPIR$_R$: *On input the security parameter* 1^λ *and a vector of selection bits* $\vec{b} = (b_1, \dots, b_w) \in \{0,1\}^w$, corrSPIR$_R$ *outputs a receiver message* spir$_R \in \{0,1\}^{\mathcal{O}(w)}$ *and an internal state* st; *without loss of generality, we assume* st *contains all the coins used by* corrSPIR$_R$ *as well as* $\vec{b}$.
- corrSPIR$_S$: *On input the security parameter* 1^λ, *a receiver message* spir$_R$, *and* k *N-bit databases* $\vec{m}_1, \dots, \vec{m}_k \in \{0,1\}^N$, corrSPIR$_S$ *outputs a sender message* spir$_S \in \{0,1\}^{\mathcal{O}(k)}$.
- corrSPIR$_D$: *On input a sender message* spir$_S$ *and an internal state* st, corrSPIR$_D$ *outputs a vector of messages* $(\widetilde{m}_1, \dots, \widetilde{m}_k) \in \{0,1\}^k$.

- **Correctness.**

$$\forall \vec{b} = (b_1, \dots, b_w) \in \{0,1\}^w, \forall \vec{M} = (\vec{m}_1, \dots, \vec{m}_k) \in \{0,1\}^{N \cdot k},$$

$$\Pr\left[(\widetilde{m}_1, \dots, \widetilde{m}_k) = (\vec{m}_1[x_1], \dots, \vec{m}_k[x_k]) : \begin{matrix} (\text{spir}_R, \text{st}) \xleftarrow{\$} \text{corrSPIR}_R(1^\lambda, \vec{b}) \\ \text{spir}_S \xleftarrow{\$} \text{corrSPIR}_S(1^\lambda, \text{spir}_R, \vec{M}) \\ (\widetilde{m}_1, \dots, \widetilde{m}_k) \xleftarrow{\$} \text{corrSPIR}_D(\text{spir}_S, \text{st}) \end{matrix} \right] = 1$$

$$where \ (x_1, \dots, x_k) := \text{MixAndMatch}(\vec{b}).$$

- **Security.** *The following protocol securely realises* $\mathcal{F}_{\text{corrSPIR}}$ *(Fig. 2) in the presence of a semi-honest adversary: the receiver computes* $(\text{spir}_R, \text{st}) \xleftarrow{\$}$ corrSPIR$_R(1^\lambda, \vec{b})$ *and sends* spir$_R$ *to the sender, who in turn computes* spir$_S \xleftarrow{\$}$ corrSPIR$_S(1^\lambda, \text{spir}_R, \vec{M})$ *and returns* spir$_S$; *finally, the receiver computes and outputs* $(\widetilde{m}_1, \dots, \widetilde{m}_k) \xleftarrow{\$}$ corrSPIR$_D(\text{spir}_S, \text{st})$.

Functionality $\mathcal{F}_{\text{corrSPIR}}$

The functionality $\mathcal{F}_{\text{corrSPIR}}$ is parameterised by the number k of SPIRs in the batch, the size N of each database, and the number w of selection bits. Furthermore, it is parameterised by a public T-balanceable "mix and match" function (definition 8) MixAndMatch: $\{0,1\}^w \to [N]^k$. $\mathcal{F}_{\text{corrSPIR}}$ interacts with an ideal sender **S** and an ideal receiver **R** via the following queries.

1. On input (**sender**, $\vec{M} = (\vec{m}_i)_{i \in [k]}$) from **S**, with $\vec{m}_i = (m_{i,j})_{j \in [N]} \in \{0,1\}^N$ store $\vec{M}$.
2. On input (**receiver**, $(b_j)_{j \in [w]}$) from **R**, check if a tuple of inputs $\vec{M}$ has already been recorded; if so, compute $(x_1, \dots, x_k) :=$ MixAndMatch$(b_1, \dots, b_w) \in [N]^k$, send $(m_{i,x_i})_{i \in [k]}$ to **R**, and halt.

If the functionality receives an incorrectly formatted input, it aborts.

Fig. 2. Ideal functionality $\mathcal{F}_{\text{corrSPIR}}$ for batch SPIR with correlated "Mix and Match" queries

Theorem 11. *Assume that* rep-OT *is a semi-honest two-round decomposable batch OT protocol with* $\alpha(\cdot)$-*overhead and* T-*bounded query repetitions. Then construction* (corrSPIR$_R$, corrSPIR$_S$, corrSPIR$_D$) *from Fig. 3 is a two-round batch SPIR protocol with correlated "mix and match" queries. Furthermore the size of the receiver message is linear in* $w + k \cdot n/T$ *and the size of the sender message is upper bounded by* $k + (\log N) \cdot (N-1) \cdot \alpha(w + k \cdot n/T)$ *(where* k *is the batch number and* N *is the size of each of the* k *databases).*

3.5   Sublinear Computation of log log-Depth Circuits from corrSPIR

In this section Theorem 12 shows how to build sublinear secure computation for shallow (roughly log log-depth) circuits from corrSPIR, with an explicit protocol provided in Fig. 4. Main Theorem 1 combines all of the previous theorems and shows that sublinear secure computation for shallow circuits can be based on QR + LPN.

Theorem 12. *If* corrSPIR *is a two-round batch* SPIR *protocol with correlated "mix and match" queries, then* Π_{2PC} *from Fig. 4 securely computes the randomized functionality* $(\vec{x}_0, \vec{x}_1) \mapsto \{(\vec{r}, C(\vec{x}_0 \oplus \vec{x}_1) \oplus \vec{r}): \vec{r} \overset{\$}{\leftarrow} \{0,1\}^m\}$ *in the presence of a semi-honest adversary corrupting (at most) one of the two parties.*

The proof of Theorem 12 is deferred to the full version of this paper.

Our first main theorem follows from the combination of Theorem 5—which instantiates dec-OT from QR + LPN—, Lemma 7—which provides a construction of rep-OT from dec-OT—, Theorem 11—which provides a construction of corrSPIR from rep-OT, and Theorem 12 —which provides a secure computation protocol from corrSPIR.

Main Theorem 1 (Sublinear Secure Computation from QR + LPN). *Assume the* QR *assumption and the binary* LPN *assumption* LPN(dim, num, ρ) *with dimension* dim = poly(λ), *number of samples* num = $(n + m)^{1/3} \cdot$ poly(λ), *and noise rate* $\rho = $ num$^{\varepsilon - 1}$ *(for some constant* $\varepsilon < 1$). *Then for any* n-*input* m-*output boolean circuit* C *of size* s *and depth* k, *there is a two-party protocol for*

Batch SPIR with Correlated "Mix and Match" Queries

Parameters: k, N, $n := \log N$, w, T, a T-balanceable MixAndMatch: $\{0,1\}^w \rightarrow [N]^k$ (parameterised by subsets $S_j = (s_{j,1}, \ldots, s_{j,n}) \in [w]^n$ for $j \in [k]$) and an associated list of number of occurrences $(t_1, \ldots, t_w)$ with $t_i = t_{i,1} + \cdots + t_{i,n}$, a two-round batch rep-OT protocol rep-OT = (rep-OTR, rep-OTS, rep-OTD).

corrSPIR$_R$: On input the security parameter 1^λ and a vector of selection bits $\vec{b} = (b_1, \ldots, b_w) \in \{0,1\}^w$:

Fig. 3. corrSPIR from rep-OT.

1. Set $\vec{b}' \leftarrow b_1^{\|\lceil t_1/T\rceil} \| \cdots \| b_w^{\|\lceil t_w/T\rceil}$.
2. Compute $(\mathsf{spir}_R, \mathsf{st}) \stackrel{\$}{\leftarrow} \mathsf{OTR}(1^\lambda, \vec{b}')$, and output $(\mathsf{spir}_R, \mathsf{st}\|\vec{b})$.

$\mathsf{corrSPIR}_S$: On input the security parameter 1^λ, a receiver message spir_R, and k databases $\vec{m}_1, \ldots, \vec{m}_k \in [N]$:

1. Set $(\mathsf{DB}_{1,1}, \ldots, \mathsf{DB}_{1,k}) := (\vec{m}_1, \ldots, \vec{m}_k)$.
2. For $d = 1, \ldots, n$:
   (a) For $i = 1, \ldots, w$:
   $$\text{Set } \mathsf{rep}_{d,i} \leftarrow \begin{cases} T^{\|\lceil t_{i,d}/T\rceil}\|0^{\|\lceil t_i/T\rceil - \lceil t_{i,d}/T\rceil} & \text{if } T | t_{i,d} \\ T^{\|\lfloor t_{i,d}/T\rfloor}\|t_{i,d}\%T\|0^{\|\lceil t_i/T\rceil - \lceil t_{i,d}/T\rceil} & \text{if } T \nmid t_{i,d} \end{cases}$$
   (b) Set $\mathsf{rep}_d \leftarrow \mathsf{rep}_{d,1}\| \cdots \|\mathsf{rep}_{d,w}$.
   (c) Initialise $X_d \leftarrow \varnothing$.
   (d) For $j = 1, \ldots, k$:
       For $x = 0, \ldots, N/2^d - 1$:
       $X_d.\mathsf{append}(((\mathsf{DB}_{d,j}[2x], \mathsf{DB}_{d,j}[2x+1]), s_{j,d}, x, j))$.
   (e) Sort X_d according to the lexicographic order which first sorts by increasing fourth element (the "$j \in [k]$") and then, in case of equality, by increasing third element (the "$x \in [0, N/2^d - 1]$").
   (f) Greedily partition X_d as $X_d = X_{d,1} \sqcup \cdots \sqcup X_{d,(N/2^d)}$ such that for each $\ell \in [N/2^d]$ and each $i \in [w]$, $X_{d,\ell}$ contains (up to) $t_{i,d}$ elements of the form $((\cdot, \cdot), i, \cdot, \cdot)$; "greedily" is here taken to mean that the first $t_{i,d}$ elements of the form $((\cdot, \cdot), i, \cdot, \cdot)$ are placed in $X_{d,1}$, the next $t_{i,d}$ in $X_{d,2}$, and so on.
   (g) For $\ell = 1, \ldots, N/2^d$:
       – Sort $X_{d,\ell}$ according to the second element in increasing order, breaking ties with the fourth, and then if necessary the third element of the 4-tuples.
       – Set $\mathsf{DB}'_{d,\ell} \leftarrow (S_{d,\ell}[0].\mathsf{first}, \ldots, S_{d,\ell}[(\sum_{i=1}^w t_{i,d}) - 1].\mathsf{first}) \in \{0,1\}^{2|S_{d,\ell}|}$.
       – Set $(\mathsf{ots}^\star_{d,\ell}, \mathsf{ots}^{\mathsf{dec}}_{d,\ell}) \stackrel{\$}{\leftarrow} \mathsf{rep\text{-}OTS}(1^\lambda, \mathsf{spir}_R, \mathsf{DB}'_{d,\ell}, \mathsf{rep}_d)$.
   (h) If $d < n$:
       – For $j = 1, \ldots, k$:
           Initialise $\mathsf{DB}_{d+1,j} \leftarrow 0^{\|N/2^d}$.
       – For $\ell = 1, \ldots, N/2^d$:
           For $\ell' = 0, \ldots, (\sum_{i=1}^w t_{i,d}) - 1$:
               Parse $X_{d,\ell}[\ell']$ as $((\cdot, \cdot), \cdot, x, j)$, with $x \in [N/2^d]$ and $j \in [k]$.
               Set $\mathsf{DB}_{d+1,j}[x] \leftarrow \mathsf{ots}^{\mathsf{dec}}_{d,\ell}[\ell']$.
   (i) Set $\mathsf{ots}^\star_d \leftarrow (\mathsf{ots}^\star_{d,1}, \ldots, \mathsf{ots}^\star_{d,N/2^d})$.
3. Set $\mathsf{spir}_S := ((\mathsf{ots}^\star_1, \ldots, \mathsf{ots}^\star_n), \mathsf{ots}^{\mathsf{dec}}_n)$, and output spir_S.

$\mathsf{corrSPIR}_D$: On input a sender message spir_S and an internal state st:

Fig. 3. (*continued*)

---

1. Parse spir_S as $\mathsf{spir}_S = ((\mathsf{ots}_1^\star, \ldots, \mathsf{ots}_n^\star), \mathsf{ots}_n^{\mathsf{dec}})$, and parse st as $\mathsf{st}' \| \vec{b}$.
2. Set $(y_1, \ldots, y_k) \leftarrow \mathsf{MixAndMatch}(\vec{b})$ (*i.e.* $y_j \leftarrow b_{s_{j,1}} \ldots b_{s_{j,n}}$ for $j \in [n]$).
3. Initialise $(\widetilde{m}_1, \ldots, \widetilde{m}_k) \leftarrow \mathsf{ots}_n^{\mathsf{dec}}$.
4. For $d = 1, \ldots, n$:
   (a) Initialise $X_d \leftarrow \varnothing$.
   (b) Initialise $X_d \leftarrow ((\bot, \; s_{j,d}, \; x, \; j))_{j \in [k], x \in [0, N/2^d - 1]}$
   (c) Sort X_d according to the lexicographic order which first sorts by increasing fourth element (the "$j \in [k]$") and then, in case of equality, by increasing third element (the "$x \in [0, N/2^d - 1]$").
   (d) Greedily partition X_d as $X_d = X_{d,1} \sqcup \cdots \sqcup X_{d,N/2^d}$ such that for each $\ell \in [N/2^d]$ and each $i \in [w]$, $X_{d,\ell}$ contains exactly $t_{i,d}$ elements of the form $(\cdot, i, \cdot, \cdot)$; "greedily" is here taken to mean that the first $t_{i,d}$ elements of the form $(\cdot, i, \cdot, \cdot)$ are placed in $X_{d,1}$, the next $t_{i,d}$ in $X_{d,2}$, and so on.
   (e) For $\ell = 1, \ldots, N/2^d$:
       Sort $X_{d,\ell}$ according to the second element in increasing order, breaking ties with the fourth, and then if necessary the third element of the 4-tuples.
   (f) Parse $\mathsf{ots}_d^\star$ as $\mathsf{ots}_d^\star = (\mathsf{ots}_{d,1}^\star, \ldots, \mathsf{ots}_{d,N/2^d}^\star)$
   (g) For $j = 1, \ldots, k$:
       – Set $\ell_{j,d}$ to be the unique $\ell \in [N/2^d]$ such that $(\bot, \; s_{j,d}, \; (b_{s_{j,n}} \ldots b_{s_{j,d}}), \; j) \in X_{d,\ell}$.
       – Set $\mathsf{ind}_{j,d}$ to be the index of $(\bot, \; s_{j,d}, \; (b_{s_{j,n}} \ldots b_{s_{j,d}}), \; j)$ in $X_{d,\ell}$.
       – Update $\widetilde{m}_j \leftarrow \mathsf{rep\text{-}OTD}(\{\mathsf{ind}_{j,d}\}, (\mathsf{ots}_{d,\ell_{j,d}}^\star, \widetilde{m}_j), \mathsf{rep}, \mathsf{st})$
5. Output $(\widetilde{m}_1, \ldots, \widetilde{m}_k)$.

Fig. 3. (*continued*)

securely computing C using only $\mathcal{O}(n + m + 2^{k+2^k} \cdot \mathsf{polylog}(n) \cdot \mathsf{poly}(\lambda) \cdot ((n + m)^{2/3} + (n+m)^{(1+2\varepsilon)/3}))$ bits of communication, and computation $\mathsf{poly}(\lambda, 2^{2^k})$.

The discussion on the parameters is deferred to the full version of this paper.

Corollary 13 (Sublinear Secure Computation of $\log\log$**-Depth Circuits).** *Assume the* QR *assumption and the binary* LPN *assumption* $\mathsf{LPN}(\mathsf{dim}, \mathsf{num}, \rho)$ *with dimension* $\mathsf{dim} = \mathsf{poly}(\lambda)$, *number of samples* $\mathsf{num} = (n+m)^{1/3} \cdot \mathsf{poly}(\lambda)$, *and noise rate* $\rho = \mathsf{num}^{-1/2}$. *Then for any n-input m-output boolean circuit C of polynomial size s and depth $\log\log s/4$, there is a two-party protocol for securely computing C using only* $\mathcal{O}(n + m + \sqrt{s} \cdot \mathsf{poly}(\lambda) \cdot (n+m)^{2/3})$ *bits of communication, and polynomial computation.*

3.6 Extension to Layered Circuits

Layered circuits are boolean circuits whose gates can be arranged into layers such that any wire connects adjacent layers. It is well-known from previ-

---

Protocol Π_{2PC}

Functionality:

- **Parameters:** $C\colon \{0,1\}^n \to \{0,1\}^m$ is a boolean circuit of depth k. For $j \in [m]$, $S_j = \{s_{j,1},\ldots,s_{j,2^k}\}$ is the subset[a] of the inputs on which depends the jth output of f, and for $i \in [n]$ we denote t_i the number of outputs of C on which the ith variable depends. $(\pi_j)_{j\in[m]} \in (\mathfrak{S}_{2^k})^m$ is a family of m permutations on $[2^k]$, such that the following is a $(T = \mathrm{polylog}(n))$-balanced "mix and match" function:

$$\mathsf{MixAndMatch}_C\colon \quad \{0,1\}^w \quad \to \quad\quad\quad [2^k]^m$$
$$(x_1,\ldots,x_w) \mapsto (x_{s_{j,\pi_j(1)}}\|\ldots\|x_{s_{j,\pi_j(2^k)}})_{j\in[m]}$$

- **Inputs:** Parties P_0 and P_1 hold additive shares $(\vec{x}_0, \vec{x}_1)$ of an input $\vec{x} \in \{0,1\}^n$.
- **Outputs:** The parties output $C(\vec{x})$.
- **Requires:** $\mathsf{corrSPIR} = (\mathsf{corrSPIR}_R, \mathsf{corrSPIR}_S, \mathsf{corrSPIR}_D)$ is a two-round batch SPIR protocol with correlated "mix and match" queries.

Protocol:

1. P_0 samples $\vec{y}_0 \xleftarrow{\$} \{0,1\}^m$ and for $j \in [m]$ sets $\mathsf{DB}_j \in \{0,1\}^{2^{2^k}}$ to be the truth table of the following function:

$$g_j\colon \quad \{0,1\}^{2^k} \quad \to \quad\quad\quad\quad\quad \{0,1\}$$
$$(X_1,\ldots,X_{2^k}) \mapsto C_j((X_{\pi_j(1)} \oplus \vec{x}_0[\pi_j(1)]\|\ldots\|X_{\pi_j(2^k)} \oplus \vec{x}_0[\pi_j(2^k)])) \oplus \vec{y}_0[j]$$
$$\text{where } C_j \text{ is the } j^{th} \text{ output of } C.$$

2. P_1 sets $\vec{x}'_1 \leftarrow (\vec{x}_1[1])^{\|\lceil t'_1/T\rceil}\|\ldots\|b_w^{\|\lceil t'_w/T\rceil}$.
3. P_1 samples $(\mathsf{spir}_R, \mathsf{st}) \xleftarrow{\$} \mathsf{corrSPIR}_R(1^\lambda, \vec{x}_1)$ and sends spir_R to P_0.
4. P_0 samples $\mathsf{spir}_S \xleftarrow{\$} \mathsf{corrSPIR}_S(1^\lambda, \mathsf{spir}_R, (\mathsf{DB}_j)_{j\in[m]})$ and sends $(\mathsf{spir}_S, \vec{y}_0)$ to P_1.
5. P_1 recovers $\vec{y}_1 \leftarrow \mathsf{corrSPIR}_D(\mathsf{spir}_S, \mathsf{st})$.
6. P_1 sets $\vec{y} \leftarrow \vec{y}_0 \oplus \vec{y}_1$, and sends $\vec{y}$ to P_0.
7. Each party P_σ outputs $\vec{y}$.

---

[a] Because C has depth k and each of its gate has fan-in at most 2, each output value only depends on at most 2^k inputs. Without loss of generality we can assume each output depends on exactly 2^k (by allowing for trivial "dependencies").

Fig. 4. Secure computation of low-depth circuits from corrSPIR

ous works [BGI16, Cou19, CM21] that sublinear protocols for low-depth circuits translate to sublinear protocols for general layered circuits: the parties simply cut the layered circuit into low-depth "chunks", and securely evaluate it chunk-by-chunk. We refer to the full version of this paper for the extension of our protocol to layered circuits.

4   Polylogarithmic PIR from CDH

A private information retrieval is a two-party protocol between a server S holding a string z (the database) and a client C holding an integer i, where only the client receives an output. The security parameter λ and the length $n(\lambda) = \mathsf{poly}(\lambda) = |z|$ of the server database are a common (public) input. We let $\mathsf{View}_S(\lambda, z, i)$ denote the view of S during its interaction with C on respective inputs (z, i) with common input $(\lambda, n = |z|)$, and by $\mathsf{Out}_C(\lambda, z, i)$ the output of C after the interaction.

Definition 14 (Private Information Retrieval). *A private information retrieval for database size $n = n(\lambda)$ (n-PIR) is an interactive protocol between a PPT server S holding a string $z \in \{0, 1\}^n$ and a PPT client C holding an index $i \leq n$ which satisfies the following properties:*

- **Correctness:** *there exists a negligible function μ such that for every $\lambda \in \mathbb{N}$, $z \in \{0, 1\}^n$, $i \in [n]$:*

$$\Pr[\mathsf{Out}_C(\lambda, z, i) = z_i] \geq 1 - \mu(\lambda).$$

- **Security:** *there exists a negligible function μ such that for every PPT adversary $\mathcal{A}$, large enough $\lambda \in \mathbb{N}$, $(i, j) \in [n]^2$, and $z \in \{0, 1\}^n$:*

$$|\Pr[\mathcal{A}(1^{\lambda+n}, \mathsf{View}_S(\lambda, z, i)) = 1] - \Pr[\mathcal{A}(1^{\lambda+n}, \mathsf{View}_S(\lambda, z, j)) = 1]| \leq \mu(\lambda, n).$$

- **Efficiency:** *A PIR is* polylogarithmic *if its communication complexity $c(\lambda, n)$, measured as the worst-case number of bits exchanged between S and C (over their inputs (z, i) and their random coins), satisfies $c(\lambda, n) = \mathsf{poly}(\lambda, \log n)$.*

Main Theorem 2. *Assuming the hardness of the computational Diffie-Hellman assumption against $\mathsf{poly}(n)$-time adversaries, there exists a polylogarithmic n-PIR protocol, with polylogarithmic client computation, and $O(\log n)$ rounds.*

4.1   Laconic Private Set Intersection

Definition 15 (Laconic PSI [ABD+21]). *An ℓPSI scheme* $\mathsf{LPSI} = (\mathsf{Setup}, \mathsf{R}_1, \mathsf{S}, \mathsf{R}_2)$ *is defined as follows:*

- $\mathsf{Setup}(1^\lambda)$: *Take as input a security parameter 1^λ and outputs a common reference string* crs.

- $R_1(crs, S_R)$: *takes as input a* crs *and a receiver set* S_R. *Outputs a first PSI message* psi_1 *and a state* st.
- $S(crs, S_S, psi_1)$: *takes as input a* crs, *a sender set* S_S, *and a first PSI message* psi_1. *Outputs a second PSI message* psi_2.
- $R_2(crs, st, psi_2)$: *takes as input a* crs, *a state* st, *and a second PSI message* psi_2. *Outputs a set* $\mathcal{X}$.

An ℓPSI protocol satisfies the following properties:

- *Correctness: for every sets* (S_R, S_S), *given* crs $\xleftarrow{\$}$ Setup(1^λ), $(psi_1, st) \xleftarrow{\$}$ $R_1(crs, S_R)$, $psi_2 \xleftarrow{\$} S(crs, S_S, psi_1)$, *and* $\mathcal{X} \xleftarrow{\$} R_2(crs, st, psi_2)$, *it holds that* $\mathcal{X} = S_R \cap S_S$ *with probability 1.*
- *Security: the two-round protocol defined by* LPSI $=$ (Setup, R_1, S, R_2) *implements the PSI functionality given on Fig. 5 in the semi-honest model.*
- *Efficiency: there exists a fixed polynomial* poly *such that both the length of* psi_1 *and the running time of* S *are bounded by* poly(λ, log $|S_R|$).

Functionality $\mathcal{F}_{psi}$

Parameters: The PSI functionality $\mathcal{F}_{psi}$ is parameterised with a universe $\mathcal{U}$.

Setup Phase: The functionality waits until it receives S_R with $S_R \subseteq \mathcal{U}$ from R. Ignores subsequent messages from R.

Send Phase: The functionality waits until it receives S_S with $S_S \subseteq \mathcal{U}$ from S. Sends $S_R \cap S_S$ to R. Ignores subsequent messages from R.

Fig. 5. PSI functionality $\mathcal{F}_{psi}$

Lemma 16 (ℓPSI from CDH [ABD+21]). *Assuming the security of the computational Diffie-Hellman assumption against* poly(n)*-time adversaries, there exists an ℓPSI protocol for receiver sets of size n with statistical receiver security and computational (semi-honest) sender security.*

4.2   From Laconic PSI to Half-PIR

We define the notion of half-PIR, first introduced in [BIP18] (under the name Rand$\frac{1}{2}$PIR). Informally, a half-PIR behaves as a regular PIR with probability 1/2; otherwise, correctness and security might not hold. The receiver gets notified when the scheme successfully worked as intended.

Definition 17. *A half-PIR protocol is defined as an n-PIR (Definition 14) where the correctness and security properties are modified as follows:*

- **Correctness:** *there exists a negligible function* μ *such that for every* $\lambda \in \mathbb{N}$, $z \in \{0,1\}^n$, $i \in [n]$:

$$\Pr[\mathsf{Out}_C(\lambda, z, i) = (z_i, \mathsf{success})] \geq 1/2 - \mu(\lambda).$$

- **Security:** *there exists a negligible function μ such that for every PPT adversary $\mathcal{A}$, large enough $\lambda \in \mathbb{N}$, $(i,j) \in [n]^2$, and $z \in \{0,1\}^n$, it holds that $|p_i - p_j| \leq \mu(n, \lambda)$, where for an integer $k \in [n]$, p_k denotes the* conditional *probability $\Pr[\mathcal{A}(1^{\lambda+n}, \mathrm{View}_S(\lambda, z, k)) = 1 \mid \mathrm{Out}_C(\lambda, z, k)_2 = \mathrm{success}]$.*

Below, we recall the definition of pseudorandom functions (PRFs), first introduced in the seminal work of [GGM84]. For simplicity, we restrict our attention to PRFs with key length and output length equal to the security parameter λ.

Definition 18 (Pseudorandom function [GGM84, NR95]). *A pseudorandom function with input size m is syntactically defined by a function family $\mathcal{F} = \{F_K : \{0,1\}^{m(\lambda)} \mapsto \{0,1\}^\lambda\}_{\lambda \in \mathbb{N}, K \in \{0,1\}^\lambda}$, where the output $F_K(x)$ can be computed from (K, x) in polynomial time, and which satisfies the following security property: for every $\lambda \in \mathbb{N}$ and every oracle PPT attacker $\mathcal{A}$, it holds that*

$$\left| \Pr_K[\mathcal{A}(1^\lambda)^{F_K(\cdot)} = 1] - \Pr_R[\mathcal{A}(1^\lambda)^{R(\cdot)} = 1] \right| \leq \mathrm{negl}(\lambda),$$

where $K \xleftarrow{\$} \{0,1\}^\lambda$, and $R \colon \{0,1\}^m \mapsto \{0,1\}^\lambda$ is a truly random function. Furthermore, we say that the PRF is $T(\lambda)$-secure if the above inequality still holds when $\mathcal{A}$ is additionally given 1^T as input.

For a high-level intuition of the protocol provided in Fig. 6, we refer to the full version of this paper.

Half-PIR from Laconic PSI and PRF.

Parameters: The protocol is parameterised with a security parameter λ, and a database size $n = n(\lambda) \leq 2^\lambda \cdot \mathrm{negl}(\lambda)$. $\{F_K\}_{K \in \{0,1\}^\lambda}$ is a family of $n(\lambda)$-secure PRFs with input size $m = \log n + 1$. The protocol operates in the $\mathcal{F}_{\mathsf{psi}}$-hybrid model, where the universe $\mathcal{U}$ is defined as $\{0,1\}^\lambda$. The server holds an input string $z \in \{0,1\}^n$ and a the client holds an index $i \leq n$.

Protocol: The protocol operates in three steps.

1. The server picks a random PRF key $K \xleftarrow{\$} \{0,1\}^\lambda$ and sends it to the client. The client samples a uniformly random bit $b \xleftarrow{\$} \{0,1\}$, and sets $y \leftarrow F_K(i \| b)$.
2. The server constructs the set $S_R = \{F_K(1 \| z_1), \cdots, F_K(n \| z_n)\}$, and queries (sid, S_R) to $\mathcal{F}_{\mathsf{psi}}$, playing the role of the receiver. The client constructs the set $S_S = \{y\}$ and queries S_S to $\mathcal{F}_{\mathsf{psi}}$, playing the role of the sender. The server receives $S_R \cap S_S$.
3. The server indicates whether $S_R \cap S_S$ is empty by sending a bit to the client. If $S_R \cap S_S$ is empty, the client outputs $(1 - b, \mathsf{success})$; otherwise, the client outputs (b, fail).

Fig. 6. Half-PIR from Laconic PSI and PRF.

Security Analysis. The security analysis is deferred to the full version of this paper.

Instantiating the Functionalities. Pseudorandom functions can be constructed from one-way functions [GGM84]. Instantiating the functionality $\mathcal{F}_{\mathsf{psi}}$ with the CDH-based laconic PSI protocol of [ABD+21] involves communication and client computation $\mathsf{poly}(\lambda, \log |S_R|) = \mathsf{poly}(\lambda, \log n)$ (since $|S_R| = n$). Summing up, we have:

Lemma 19. *Assuming the hardness of the computational Diffie-Hellman assumption against $\mathsf{poly}(n)$-time adversaries, there exists a (constant-round) polylogarithmic half-PIR protocol for databases of size n (where the client computation is also polylogarithmic).*

4.3 From Polylogarithmic Half-PIR to Polylogarithmic PIR

We now describe a simple generic transformation from Half-PIR to PIR.

Random-Index PIR. First, we recall the definition of *random-index* PIR from [GHM+21]:

Definition 20 (Random-Index PIR). *A random-index PIR for database of size n is a two-party protocol between a server and a client which implements the random-index PIR functionality given on Fig. 7 in the semi-honest model.*

Interestingly, random-index PIR was recently shown to imply full-fledged PIR, with only a logarithmic (in n) blowup in communication and rounds, in [GHM+21]:

Functionality $\mathcal{F}_{\mathsf{rpir}}$

Parameters: The functionality is parameterised with a database size n.
Server Message: The functionality waits until it receives $z \in \{0,1\}^n$ from the server.
Output: If the client is honest, sample $i \xleftarrow{\$} [n]$ and output (i, z_i) to the client. Otherwise, output z to the client.

Fig. 7. Random-index PIR functionality $\mathcal{F}_{\mathsf{rpir}}$.

Lemma 21. *If there exists a random-index PIR protocol for databases of size n with communication complexity $c(\lambda, n)$ and round complexity $r(\lambda, n)$, then there exists an n-PIR protocol with communication complexity $O(c(\lambda, n) \cdot \log n)$ and round complexity $O(r(\lambda, n) \cdot \log n)$.*

We refer to the full version of this paper for a high-level explanation, and to [GHM+21] for a formal proof of Lemma 21.

From Half-PIR to Random-Index PIR. By the above, constructing PIR from half-PIR is reduced to constructing random-index PIR from half-PIR. The latter, however, is straightforward: the client and the server can simply execute a half-PIR, where the client picks its input uniformly at random. At the end of the protocol, if the client receives fail, both parties simply restart the protocol. By the correctness of the half-PIR, a successful execution will happen after an expected $O(1)$ number of restarts. Below, we describe a slight variant of this where the client runs λ half-PIRs in parallel, and outputs the lexicographically first successful output.

Random-Index PIR from Half-PIR.

Parameters: The protocol is parameterised with a security parameter λ, and a database size $n = n(\lambda) \leq 2^\lambda \cdot \mathsf{negl}(\lambda)$. The server holds an input string $z \in \{0,1\}^n$; the client has no input.

Protocol: The client samples λ uniformly random integers $(i_1, \cdots, i_\lambda) \xleftarrow{\$} [n]^\lambda$. The client and the server run in parallel λ instances of a half-PIR protocol with respective client inputs i_j and server input z. The client receives outputs $\mathsf{Out}_C(\lambda, z, i_j)$.

Output: The client sets j^* to be the lexicographically first j such that $\mathsf{Out}_C(\lambda, z, i_j) = (z_j, \mathsf{success})$ for some bit z_j. The client outputs $(z_{j^*}, \mathsf{success})$. If there is no such j, the client outputs $\perp$ instead.

The security analysis is deferred to the full version of this paper. Combining this protocol with Lemma 21, we get:

Lemma 22. *If there exists a half-PIR protocol for databases of size n with communication complexity $c(\lambda, n)$ and round complexity $r(\lambda, n)$, then there exists an n-PIR protocol with communication complexity $O(\lambda \cdot c(\lambda, n) \cdot \log n)$ and round complexity $O(r(\lambda, n) \cdot \log n)$.*

Putting together Lemmas 19 and 22 finishes the proof of Theorem 2.

Acknowledgments. Elette Boyle and Pierre Meyer were supported by AFOSR Award FA9550-21-1-0046, a Google Research Award, and ERC Project HSS (852952). Geoffroy Couteau was supported by the ANR SCENE.

References

[ABD+21] Alamati, N., Branco, P., Döttling, N., Garg, S., Hajiabadi, M., Pu, S.: Laconic private set intersection and applications. In: Nissim, K., Waters, B. (eds.) TCC 2021. LNCS, vol. 13044, pp. 94–125. Springer, Cham (2021). https://doi.org/10.1007/978-3-030-90456-2_4

[ADOS22] Abram, D., Damgård, I., Orlandi, C., Scholl, P.: An algebraic framework for silent preprocessing with trustless setup and active security. Cryptol. ePrint Arch. (2022)

[AJL+12] Asharov, G., Jain, A., López-Alt, A., Tromer, E., Vaikuntanathan, V., Wichs, D.: Multiparty computation with low communication, computation and interaction via threshold FHE. In: Pointcheval, D., Johansson, T. (eds.) EUROCRYPT 2012. LNCS, vol. 7237, pp. 483–501. Springer, Heidelberg (2012). https://doi.org/10.1007/978-3-642-29011-4_29

[BBDP22] Brakerski, Z., Branco, P., Döttling, N., Pu, S.: Batch OT with optimal rate. In: Dunkelman, O., Dziembowski, S. (eds.) EUROCRYPT 2022. Lecture Notes in Computer Science, vol. 13276, pp. 157–186. Springer, Cham (2022). https://doi.org/10.1007/978-3-031-07085-3_6

[BCG+19] Boyle, E., Couteau, G., Gilboa, N., Ishai, Y., Kohl, L., Scholl, P.: Efficient pseudorandom correlation generators: silent OT extension and more. In: Boldyreva, A., Micciancio, D. (eds.) CRYPTO 2019, Part III. LNCS, vol. 11694, pp. 489–518. Springer, Cham (2019). https://doi.org/10.1007/978-3-030-26954-8_16

[BCG+20] Boyle, E., Couteau, G., Gilboa, N., Ishai, Y., Kohl, L., Scholl, P.: Correlated pseudorandom functions from variable-density LPN. In: 61st FOCS, pp. 1069–1080. IEEE Computer Society Press (2020)

[BFKR91] Beaver, D., Feigenbaum, J., Kilian, J., Rogaway, P.: Security with low communication overhead. In: Menezes, A.J., Vanstone, S.A. (eds.) CRYPTO 1990. LNCS, vol. 537, pp. 62–76. Springer, Heidelberg (1991). https://doi.org/10.1007/3-540-38424-3_5

[BGI16] Boyle, E., Gilboa, N., Ishai, Y.: Breaking the circuit size barrier for secure computation under DDH. In: Robshaw, M., Katz, J. (eds.) CRYPTO 2016, Part I. LNCS, vol. 9814, pp. 509–539. Springer, Heidelberg (2016). https://doi.org/10.1007/978-3-662-53018-4_19

[BGI17] Boyle, E., Gilboa, N., Ishai, Y.: Group-based secure computation: optimizing rounds, communication, and computation. In: Coron, J.-S., Nielsen, J.B. (eds.) EUROCRYPT 2017, Part II. LNCS, vol. 10211, pp. 163–193. Springer, Cham (2017). https://doi.org/10.1007/978-3-319-56614-6_6

[BGW88] Ben-Or, M., Goldwasser, S., Wigderson, A.: Completeness theorems for non-cryptographic fault-tolerant distributed computation (extended abstract). In: 20th ACM STOC, pp. 1–10. ACM Press (1988)

[BI05] Barkol, O., Ishai, Y.: Secure computation of constant-depth circuits with applications to database search problems. In: Shoup, V. (ed.) CRYPTO 2005. LNCS, vol. 3621, pp. 395–411. Springer, Heidelberg (2005). https://doi.org/10.1007/11535218_24

[BIP18] Boyle, E., Ishai, Y., Polychroniadou, A.: Limits of Practical Sublinear Secure Computation. In: Shacham, H., Boldyreva, A. (eds.) CRYPTO 2018, Part III. LNCS, vol. 10993, pp. 302–332. Springer, Cham (2018). https://doi.org/10.1007/978-3-319-96878-0_11

[BKS19] Boyle, E., Kohl, L., Scholl, P.: Homomorphic secret sharing from lattices without FHE. In: Ishai, Y., Rijmen, V. (eds.) EUROCRYPT 2019, Part II. LNCS, vol. 11477, pp. 3–33. Springer, Cham (2019). https://doi.org/10.1007/978-3-030-17656-3_1

[BLSV18] Brakerski, Z., Lombardi, A., Segev, G., Vaikuntanathan, V.: Anonymous IBE, leakage resilience and circular security from new assumptions. In: Nielsen, J.B., Rijmen, V. (eds.) EUROCRYPT 2018, Part I. LNCS, vol.

10820, pp. 535–564. Springer, Cham (2018). https://doi.org/10.1007/978-3-319-78381-9_20

[CCD88] Chaum, D., Crépeau, C., Damgård, I.: Multiparty unconditionally secure protocols (extended abstract). In: 20th ACM STOC, pp. 11–19. ACM Press (1988)

[CG97] Chor, B., Gilboa, N.: Computationally private information retrieval (extended abstract). In: 29th ACM STOC, pp. 304–313. ACM Press (1997)

[CGKS95] Chor, B., Goldreich, O., Kushilevitz, E., Sudan, M.: Private information retrieval. In: 36th FOCS, pp. 41–50. IEEE Computer Society Press (1995)

[Cha04] Chang, Y.-C.: Single database private information retrieval with logarithmic communication. In: Wang, H., Pieprzyk, J., Varadharajan, V. (eds.) ACISP 2004. LNCS, vol. 3108, pp. 50–61. Springer, Heidelberg (2004). https://doi.org/10.1007/978-3-540-27800-9_5

[CLTV15] Canetti, R., Lin, H., Tessaro, S., Vaikuntanathan, V.: Obfuscation of probabilistic circuits and applications. In: Dodis, Y., Nielsen, J.B. (eds.) TCC 2015, Part II. LNCS, vol. 9015, pp. 468–497. Springer, Heidelberg (2015). https://doi.org/10.1007/978-3-662-46497-7_19

[CM21] Couteau, G., Meyer, P.: Breaking the circuit size barrier for secure computation under quasi-polynomial LPN. In: Canteaut, A., Standaert, F.-X. (eds.) EUROCRYPT 2021, Part II. LNCS, vol. 12697, pp. 842–870. Springer, Cham (2021). https://doi.org/10.1007/978-3-030-77886-6_29

[CMS99] Cachin, C., Micali, S., Stadler, M.: Computationally private information retrieval with polylogarithmic communication. In: Stern, J. (ed.) EUROCRYPT 1999. LNCS, vol. 1592, pp. 402–414. Springer, Heidelberg (1999). https://doi.org/10.1007/3-540-48910-X_28

[Cou19] Couteau, G.: A note on the communication complexity of multiparty computation in the correlated randomness model. In: Ishai, Y., Rijmen, V. (eds.) EUROCRYPT 2019, Part II. LNCS, vol. 11477, pp. 473–503. Springer, Cham (2019). https://doi.org/10.1007/978-3-030-17656-3_17

[DFH12] Damgård, I., Faust, S., Hazay, C.: Secure two-party computation with low communication. In: Cramer, R. (ed.) TCC 2012. LNCS, vol. 7194, pp. 54–74. Springer, Heidelberg (2012). https://doi.org/10.1007/978-3-642-28914-9_4

[DG17a] Döttling, N., Garg, S.: From selective IBE to full IBE and selective HIBE. In: Kalai, Y., Reyzin, L. (eds.) TCC 2017, Part I. LNCS, vol. 10677, pp. 372–408. Springer, Cham (2017). https://doi.org/10.1007/978-3-319-70500-2_13

[DG17b] Döttling, N., Garg, S.: Identity-based encryption from the Diffie-Hellman assumption. In: Katz, J., Shacham, H. (eds.) CRYPTO 2017, Part I. LNCS, vol. 10401, pp. 537–569. Springer, Cham (2017). https://doi.org/10.1007/978-3-319-63688-7_18

[DGI+19] Döttling, N., Garg, S., Ishai, Y., Malavolta, G., Mour, T., Ostrovsky, R.: Trapdoor hash functions and their applications. In: Boldyreva, A., Micciancio, D. (eds.) CRYPTO 2019, Part III. LNCS, vol. 11694, pp. 3–32. Springer, Cham (2019). https://doi.org/10.1007/978-3-030-26954-8_1

[DNNR17] Damgård, I., Nielsen, J.B., Nielsen, M., Ranellucci, S.: The TinyTable protocol for 2-party secure computation, or: gate-scrambling revisited. In: Katz, J., Shacham, H. (eds.) CRYPTO 2017, Part I. LNCS, vol. 10401, pp. 167–187. Springer, Cham (2017). https://doi.org/10.1007/978-3-319-63688-7_6

[FGJI17] Fazio, N., Gennaro, R., Jafarikhah, T., Skeith, W.E.: Homomorphic secret sharing from paillier encryption. In: Okamoto, T., Yu, Y., Au, M.H., Li, Y. (eds.) ProvSec 2017. LNCS, vol. 10592, pp. 381–399. Springer, Cham (2017). https://doi.org/10.1007/978-3-319-68637-0_23

[Gen09] Gentry, C.: Fully homomorphic encryption using ideal lattices. In: Mitzenmacher, M. (eds.) 41st ACM STOC, pp. 169–178. ACM Press (2009)

[GGM84] Goldreich, O., Goldwasser, S., Micali, S.: How to construct random functions. In: 25th FOCS, pp. 464–479. IEEE Computer Society Press (1984)

[GHM+21] Gentry, C., Halevi, S., Magri, B., Nielsen, J.B., Yakoubov, S.: Randomindex PIR and applications. In: Nissim, K., Waters, B. (eds.) TCC 2021. LNCS, vol. 13044, pp. 32–61. Springer, Cham (2021). https://doi.org/10.1007/978-3-030-90456-2_2

[GMW87] Goldreich, O., Micali, S., Wigderson, A.: How to play any mental game or a completeness theorem for protocols with honest majority. In: Aho, A. (eds.) 19th ACM STOC, pp. 218–229. ACM Press (1987)

[IKM+13] Ishai, Y., Kushilevitz, E., Meldgaard, S., Orlandi, C., Paskin-Cherniavsky, A.: On the power of correlated randomness in secure computation. In: Sahai, A. (ed.) TCC 2013. LNCS, vol. 7785, pp. 600–620. Springer, Heidelberg (2013). https://doi.org/10.1007/978-3-642-36594-2_34

[JLS22] Jain, A., Lin, H., Sahai, A.: Indistinguishability obfuscation from LPN over $\mathbb{F}_p$, DLIN, and PRGs in NC^0. In: Eurocrypt 2022 (2022, to appear)

[Kil00] Kilian, J.: More general completeness theorems for secure two-party computation. In: 32nd ACM STOC, pp. 316–324. ACM Press (2000)

[KO97] Kushilevitz, E., Ostrovsky, R.: Replication is NOT needed: SINGLE database, computationally-private information retrieval. In: 38th FOCS, pp. 364–373. IEEE Computer Society Press (1997)

[Lip05] Lipmaa, H.: An oblivious transfer protocol with log-squared communication. In: Zhou, J., Lopez, J., Deng, R.H., Bao, F. (eds.) ISC 2005. LNCS, vol. 3650, pp. 314–328. Springer, Heidelberg (2005). https://doi.org/10.1007/11556992_23

[NN01] Naor, M., Nissim, K.: Communication preserving protocols for secure function evaluation. In: 33rd ACM STOC, pp. 590–599. ACM Press (2001)

[NR95] Naor, M., Reingold, O.: Synthesizers and their application to the parallel construction of pseudo-random functions. In: 36th FOCS, pp. 170–181. IEEE Computer Society Press (1995)

[OS07] Ostrovsky, R., Skeith, W.E.: A survey of single-database private information retrieval: techniques and applications. In: Okamoto, T., Wang, X. (eds.) PKC 2007. LNCS, vol. 4450, pp. 393–411. Springer, Heidelberg (2007). https://doi.org/10.1007/978-3-540-71677-8_26

[OSY21] Orlandi, C., Scholl, P., Yakoubov, S.: The rise of paillier: homomorphic secret sharing and public-key silent OT. In: Canteaut, A., Standaert, F.-X. (eds.) EUROCRYPT 2021, Part I. LNCS, vol. 12696, pp. 678–708. Springer, Cham (2021). https://doi.org/10.1007/978-3-030-77870-5_24

[RS21] Roy, L., Singh, J.: Large message homomorphic secret sharing from DCR and applications. In: Malkin, T., Peikert, C. (eds.) CRYPTO 2021. LNCS, vol. 12827, pp. 687–717. Springer, Cham (2021). https://doi.org/10.1007/978-3-030-84252-9_23

[Yao86] Yao, A.C.-C.: How to generate and exchange secrets (extended abstract). In: 27th FOCS, pp. 162–167. IEEE Computer Society Press (1986)

How to Obfuscate MPC Inputs

Ian McQuoid(✉), Mike Rosulek, and Jiayu Xu

Oregon State University, Corvallis, OR 97331, USA
{mcquoidi,rosulekm,xujiay}@oregonstate.edu

Abstract. We introduce the idea of input obfuscation for secure two-party computation (io2PC). Suppose Alice holds a private value x and wants to allow clients to learn $f(x, y_i)$, for their choice of y_i, via a secure computation protocol. The goal of io2PC is for Alice to encode x so that an adversary who compromises her storage gets only oracle access to the function $f(x, \cdot)$. At the same time, there must be a 2PC protocol for computing $f(x, y)$ that takes only this encoding (and not the plaintext x) as input.

We show how to achieve io2PC for functions that have virtual black-box (VBB) obfuscation in either the random oracle model or generic group model. For functions that can be VBB-obfuscated in the random oracle model, we provide an io2PC protocol by replacing the random oracle with an oblivious PRF. For functions that can be VBB-obfuscated in the generic group model, we show how Alice can instantiate a "personalized" generic group. A personalized generic group is one where only Alice can perform the algebraic operations of the group, but where she can let others perform operations in that group via an oblivious interactive protocol.

1 Introduction

Alice has invested significant resources into training a machine-learning classifier. She decides to capitalize on her investment by creating a service where customers can pay her to classify inputs of their choice. The classifier itself is sensitive, and so are the inputs of Alice's clients, so her service uses secure two-party computation (2PC) to perform these classifications. She deploys a server that repeatedly runs the 2PC protocol with customers. This server is a high-value target for attackers, since it must store the details of Alice's proprietary classifier. If a hacker compromises Alice's server it is unavoidable that he learns her classifier... or is it?

Input Obfuscation for 2PC. Abstractly, Alice has an input x and she wants to use a 2PC protocol to allow customers to repeatedly learn $f(x, y_i)$ for any y_i of their choice. An attacker who compromises her computer can gain oracle access to the function $f(x, \cdot)$ by running the 2PC protocol in its head, playing the role of Alice using her private state information which was compromised. In this work, we investigate whether compromising Alice's computer can leak *no more than* oracle access to $f(x, \cdot)$. **Input obfuscation for 2PC (io2PC)** refers to (1) a way for Alice to encode her input x, along with (2) a 2PC protocol for computing functions of x that takes this encoding—not x—as input. The encoding itself should leak only oracle access to the function $f(x, \cdot)$.

Why isn't This Trivial? If knowledge of Alice's encoded input is equivalent to having oracle access to $f(x, \cdot)$, then her encoded input is actually a **virtual-black-box (VBB)** obfuscation. So a natural approach is to use a 2PC protocol that takes the obfuscation from Alice, and the input y from Bob evaluates the obfuscation on y and gives the result to Bob.

Unfortunately, this natural approach does not work. The reason is that we require a strong definition of VBB described in Sect. 2.2 which precludes known constructions of non-trivial functions in the standard model as these obfuscations rely on weakened definitions of VBB [7,9,25]. It *is* possible to construct VBB for trivial functions such as the constant function, but all (non-trivial) instances of VBB to our knowledge are in an *idealized* model such as the random oracle model [21], the generic group model [2], or the generic graded encodings model [5]. As the algorithm that evaluates a VBB obfuscation on an input will call the ideal model's oracle, this algorithm cannot be implemented inside of a 2PC protocol.

One way to think about io2PC is designing a 2PC protocol for obliviously evaluating an obfuscated program, even if the obfuscation scheme requires an idealized model.

1.1   Overview of Our Results

We first formally define io2PC, and then show how to achieve it for certain classes of functions.

Inspiration from saPAKE. In io2PC we are interested in allowing a server to encode a function in such a way that even on compromise, the adversary only obtains oracle access to the underlying function. This kind of security property is similar to one found in the definition of **strong asymmetric password-authenticated key exchange (saPAKE)** [19]. In saPAKE, a server wants to authenticate clients using passwords and stores only "digests" of the passwords so that when an adversary steals the server's storage, the adversary gains only oracle access to a password-checking functionality (*i.e.* it can submit a password guess and learn whether that guess is correct). In other words, the adversary gains oracle access to a *point function* for each user, with the distinguished point being the user's password. It is therefore natural to think of saPAKE as a special case of io2PC, considering only point functions.

Although the oracle saPAKE protocols provide on compromise is a point function, saPAKE protocols are much stronger than pure point functions as they allow for joint key establishment. To simplify, we can consider lighter VBB obfuscations of point functions in the random oracle model [21]. An obfuscation of the point function $f(x, \cdot)$ simply consists of the value $\mathcal{O}_x = H(x)$, for random oracle H, where the obfuscation can be "evaluated" on y by computing $H(y)$ and comparing it to $\mathcal{O}_x$. As we will see in Sect. 3, this simple construction doesn't meet the security requirements for io2PC as it allows the oracle interaction in the obfuscation to take place before server compromise. This is exactly the issue that OPAQUE [19] set out to solve for asymmetric PAKE (aPAKE) protocols. Jareki, Krawczyk, and Xu present a compiler which augments an aPAKE protocol by replacing the client's input with the output of an **oblivious pseudo-random function (OPRF)** on the client's input. Roughly, an OPRF is a two-party protocol for evaluating a PRF F on a client's input x and a server's key k where the client learns the PRF output $F(k, x)$ and the server learns nothing. We discuss modeling this primitive in further detail in Sect. 4.1. The OPAQUE technique allows the server to gatekeep the oracle behind an interactive protocol. This prevents the adversary from evaluating the oracle call locally until the server is compromised. It is tempting to apply the OPAQUE compiler directly to our VBB point function, and generally this idea underlying the OPAQUE compiler serves as valid intuition for the techniques used in our compilers.

Our Result for Random-Oracle VBB Obfuscations. Our main constructions develop and extend the analogy of applying the OPAQUE compiler directly to VBB obfuscations. We construct io2PC for a function f, if the related class of functions $\mathcal{C}_f = \{f(x, \cdot) \mid x \in \{0, 1\}^n\}$ has a VBB obfuscation in the random oracle model. The obfuscation scheme consists of algorithms Obf and ObfEval satisfying the following:

- Correctness: $\mathsf{ObfEval}^H(\mathsf{Obf}^H(x), y) = f(x, y)$
- Virtual black box: For any probabilistic polynomial-time (PPT) adversary $\mathcal{A}$, there exists a PPT simulator $\mathcal{S}$ such that $\mathcal{A}^H(\mathsf{Obf}^H(x))$'s view can be simulated by $\mathcal{S}$ given only black-box access to $f(x, \cdot)$.

In our io2PC protocol Alice chooses and stores an OPRF key k and uses the keyed OPRF in place of a random oracle to compute $\mathcal{O}_x = \mathsf{Obf}^{\mathsf{OPRF}(k, \cdot)}(x)$. She then stores $\mathcal{O}_x$ instead of x for future interactions. As in the OPAQUE protocol, we require an OPRF protocol where knowledge of the key k only gives oracle access to $F(k, \cdot)$. Thus, even when an adversary steals the encoding $\mathcal{O}_x$, the OPRF still acts as a random oracle, in terms of observability and programmability, to the simulator. This is what allows us to reduce to VBB security and argue that $\mathcal{O}_x$ leaks no more than oracle access to $f(x, \cdot)$. It is indeed possible to realize such an OPRF protocol in the random oracle model; in this case, the OPRF algorithm itself makes calls to the random oracle. Since our simulator must be efficient, but reduces to the simulator for the VBB obfuscation, our results do not immediately generalize to virtual *grey*-box (VGB) obfuscations. This is because VGB simulators can be inefficient and would not be simulatable under our restrictions.

When a client wants to interactively evaluate $f(x, y)$, the goal is to instead run $\mathsf{ObfEval}^{\mathsf{OPRF}(k, \cdot)}(\mathcal{O}_x, y)$, since Alice holds only $\mathcal{O}_x$ instead of x. However, the two cannot simply run this computation as a 2PC protocol, since OPRF involves calls to the random oracle. Instead, Alice can send $\mathcal{O}_x$ to the client, who runs $\mathsf{ObfEval}^?(\mathcal{O}_x, y)$. The parties can then run an OPRF protocol each time $\mathsf{ObfEval}$ makes an oracle query.

Our Result for Generic-Group Obfuscation. In our random-oracle result, we can think of the OPRF as a "personalized" random oracle. It is a random function that only Alice, holding the OPRF key, can evaluate and her evaluations of this function are visible and programmable to the simulator. She can also allow a client to evaluate this function (without leaking the input to Alice) using the OPRF protocol.

Suppose we have a VBB obfuscation now in the generic group model. What is the analogy of a "personalized" generic group? How can Alice instantiate a group, for which only she has the key, which acts as a generic group with respect to the simulator, and yet she can grant access to the group operations via an oblivious protocol? We formalize a personalized generic group as an ideal functionality, and then show how to realize such a functionality. Of course, our protocol is in the generic group model, just as the OPRF ("personalized random oracle") protocol is in the random oracle model.

We show that our main io2PC technique also applies to VBB obfuscations in the generic group model. In other words, Alice can obfuscate her input, replacing the generic group with her personalized group during the obfuscation process. The client can evaluate the obfuscated program, deferring group operations to the oblivious personalized generic group protocol.

Additionally, we provide example applications of our personalized protocols and show that the hyperplane-membership obfuscation of [10] is indeed a VBB obfuscation in the generic group model. Previously, the obfuscation was proven VBB with an inefficient simulator, under the Strong DDH assumption. Using this hyperplane obfuscation in our main protocol, we achieve an io2PC for hyperplane membership.

We conjecture that io2PC is possible for functions that are VBB-obfuscatable in the generic graded encoding model (*i.e.* all circuits [6]); however, we leave this result for future work.

1.2 Related Work

Upon server compromise, an adversary learns no more than oracle access to some residual function. Specific instances of this kind of property have been considered previously: in the context of [strong] asymmetric password-authenticated key exchange (aPAKE) [4,19], where server compromise should reveal no more than an equality-test oracle; and by Thomas *et al.* [24], where server compromise should reveal no more than a set-membership oracle. Our study of io2PC systematizes security properties and constructions of this kind, which have previously been studied in an *ad hoc* way.

Beyond the context of server compromise, the more general idea of leaking oracle access appears in some MPC models: In both *non-interactive multiparty computation (NIMPC)* [3] and the one-pass computation model [15], each party speaks only once in the protocol, with the difference in models being the communication pattern (star topology vs path topology). In these models, it is inevitable that certain types of corruption allow the adversary to re-execute the protocol on different inputs an unlimited number of times. Such an adversary can thereby learn the output of the function on many inputs of its choice, with the honest parties' inputs being fixed. Therefore, the *best possible* security in these models is if the protocol leaks no more than oracle access to this residual function.

Beyond this similarity of defining best-possible security with respect to a residual functino oracle, there are important differences between these prior works and ours. In the NIMPC protocols of [3] and one-pass protocols of [13,15], the residual functions are completely learnable from oracle queries, either by virtue of being over a small domain, or by being algebraically simple. Our work is meant to be used with unlearnable residual functions—for example, we instantiate our framework with point functions and hyperplane membership queries.

More fundamentally, prior works like [14] in the NIMPC model define security in the style of *indistinguishability obfuscation (iO)*—if two vectors of inputs for honest parties result in *functionally identical* residual functions, then the protocol must hide which input vector the honest parties use. This kind of definition for MPC is not conducive to composable security. By contrast, we explicitly require a virtual black-box (VBB) style of security, and define security in the UC framework. Our VBB-style definition also models the fact that, after compromising the server, the adversary must expend some effort each time it wants to evaluate the residual function.

2 Preliminaries

Let κ be the security parameter. We assume that all algorithms have 1^κ as input and do not explicitly write it.

2.1 Idealized Models

In an idealized model, all parties have oracle access to some exponentially large random object. In the *random oracle model*, the random object is a function $H : \{0,1\}^* \to \{0,1\}^n$. In the *ideal permutation model*, the random object is a pair of functions $\Pi, \Pi^{-1} : X \to X$ where Π and Π^{-1} are inverses.

We also consider the generic group model, which we discuss in more detail in Sect. 5.1.

Immediately below, we define VBB obfuscation in an idealized model, making the definition agnostic with respect to the actual choice of idealized model. We simply let all algorithms have oracle access to some idealized oracle Ora, which may be a random oracle or a generic group.

2.2 Obfuscation

Definition 1. *Let $C_f = \{f(x, \cdot) \mid x \in \{0,1\}^*\}$ be a class of functions. An **obfuscation** for C_f (in the Ora-idealized model) is a tuple of polynomial-time algorithms* $(\mathsf{Obf}, \mathsf{ObfEval})$, *where*

- $\mathsf{Obf}^{\mathsf{Ora}}(x)$ *outputs an **obfuscated program** $\mathcal{O}_x$;*
- $\mathsf{ObfEval}^{\mathsf{Ora}}(\mathcal{O}_x, y)$ *outputs a value z in the range of f.*

The obfuscation satisfies correctness if for all x, y, we have $\mathsf{ObfEval}^{\mathsf{Ora}}(\mathsf{Obf}^{\mathsf{Ora}}(x), y) = f(x, y)$ *with overwhelming probability.*

We often omit explicitly writing Ora if it is clear from the context.

Looking ahead, we replace the idealized oracle in ObfEval with an interactive protocol. Hence, we must require that the number of oracle queries does not depend on the input.

Definition 2. *An obfuscation* $(\mathsf{Obf}, \mathsf{ObfEval})$ *for C_f has **input-independent** query complexity if there is a polynomial function c such that for all x, y,* $\mathsf{ObfEval}^{\mathsf{Ora}}(\mathcal{O}_x, y)$ *makes $c(\kappa)$ queries to its Ora oracle. Throughout the paper, we then refer to an obfuscation with this property as a triple* $(\mathsf{Obf}, \mathsf{ObfEval}, c)$.

Virtual black-box (VBB) security means that holding an obfuscated program is equivalent to having oracle access to the function being obfuscated. In our io2PC protocol, we need to explicitly relate the number of queries an adversary makes to its idealized oracle, and the number of queries the simulator makes to its function oracle.

Definition 3. *An obfuscation* $(\mathsf{Obf}, \mathsf{ObfEval}, c)$ *has **virtual black-box (VBB) security with simulation rate** r if there exists a polynomial-time simulator* $\mathsf{Sim} = (\mathsf{Sim}_0, \mathsf{Sim}_1)$ *such that for any polynomial-time adversary $\mathcal{A}$ and any x, the distributions*

$$\{\mathcal{O}_x \leftarrow \mathsf{Obf}^{\mathsf{Ora}}(x); \mathcal{A}^{\mathsf{Ora}}(\mathcal{O}_x)\} \qquad (\textit{real interaction})$$

$$\{(\mathcal{O}_x, \textit{state}) \leftarrow \mathsf{Sim}_1(); \mathcal{A}^{\mathsf{Sim}_2^{f(x, \cdot)}(\textit{state})}(\mathcal{O}_x)\} \qquad (\textit{ideal interaction})$$

are indistinguishable, and furthermore in the ideal interaction $Q_S \le r \cdot \frac{Q_A}{c}$, where Q_S is the number of queries Sim_2 makes to its function oracle, and Q_A is the number of queries $\mathcal{A}$ makes to its oracle interface.

We also need the following extractability property of obfuscation to handle the case where a corrupt server generates an obfuscated program in our io2PC protocol.

Definition 4. *A VBB obfuscation* $(\mathsf{Obf}, \mathsf{ObfEval}, c)$ *for C_f is **extractable** if for any polynomial-time adversary $\mathcal{A}$, there is a polynomial-time algorithm* $\mathsf{Extract}$ *such that*

$$\Pr\left[\mathsf{ObfEval}^{\mathsf{Ora}}(\mathcal{O}, y) \ne f(x, y) : \begin{array}{l} (y, \mathcal{O}) \leftarrow \mathcal{A}^{\mathsf{Ora}} \\ x := \mathsf{Extract}(\mathcal{O}, \mathcal{H}) \end{array}\right]$$

is negligible, where $\mathcal{H}$ is the list of $\mathcal{A}$'s queries.

In Sect. 6 we describe examples of obfuscation schemes that satisfy these definitions.

Standard Model VBB. Recall that at least trivial VBB obfuscations are possible in the standard model. Even in an idealized model, if ObfEval never queries its oracle, then we have a VBB obfuscation in the standard model. However, our constructions need something slightly stronger than VBB. In particular, Definition 3 and Definition 4 require an idealized model for non-trivial functions. A standard-model VBB allows the evaluator to learn $f(x, \cdot)$ on an unbounded number of inputs, for the cost of 0 oracle queries, making the simulation rate for Definition 3 infinite. A similar observation has been made in the context of asymmetric PAKE [16]: aPAKE seems impossible to achieve in the standard model, as measuring the time of an offline dictionary attack requires counting the adversary's oracle queries. In Definition 4, the simulator's only advantage over a regular adversary is that it can observe the obfuscator's idealized oracle queries.

So our protocol paradigm is incompatible with (at least non-trivial) standard-model VBB. But the spirit of io2PC is possible for standard-model VBB. The server stores an obfuscation $\mathcal{O}_x$ of $f(x, \cdot)$. The parties can do a standard 2PC protocol computing $(\mathcal{O}_x, y) \to \mathsf{ObfEval}(\mathcal{O}_x, y)$, which is possible because ObfEval is a standard-model program. Upon compromising the server, an adversary learns only $\mathcal{O}_x$ which is equivalent to oracle access to $f(x, \cdot)$ by the VBB property. This protocol does not achieve our specific io2PC functionality, though, because the simulator cannot perform the necessary extractions of x from $\mathcal{O}_x$, and of an adversary's oracle queries to $f(x, \cdot)$ after compromising the server to learn $\mathcal{O}_x$.

3   Defining io2PC

In this section, we formally define io2PC. The ideal functionality is presented in Fig. 1. In $\mathcal{F}_{\mathsf{iO2PC}}$ and future functionalities, we leverage the universal composability framework's ability to analyze a single protocol instance by providing unique session and subsession identifiers $(sid, ssid)$.

Intuitively, io2PC can be thought of as an extension of VBB obfuscation to an interactive setting where the server may store its obfuscated input for long periods. This setting has been studied in the context of (strong) asymmetric PAKE [12,19], where the server stores a "password file" (e.g., the hash of its password) instead of the plain password. Similar to the asymmetric PAKE functionality, this is modeled as follows: In the initialization phase, the server sends its input to $\mathcal{F}_{\mathsf{iO2PC}}$ who stores it. After that, the functionality provides an interface for the adversary to compromise the server—the Compromise query—which corresponds to stealing the server's long-term storage in the real world. This allows the adversary to perform *offline evaluations*, in which it evaluates the function primed on the server's input, without any online interaction.

In an *online evaluation*, the server can use the stored input, or use a replacement input if the server is corrupt. This is meant to model the real-world scenario where a corrupt server executes the protocol on fresh input instead of using

Parameters:
– client C, server S, and ideal adversary $\mathcal{A}^*$

Storage:
– three maps, status, budget and input

On command (Init, sid, x) from S:
1. If status[sid] is defined: ignore the message.
2. Set status[sid] := active.
3. Set input[sid] := x.
4. Set budget[sid] := 0.
5. Send (Init, sid, S) to $\mathcal{A}^*$.

On command (Compromise, sid) from $\mathcal{A}^*$:
6. Set status[sid] := compromised.

On command (OfflineEval, sid, y) from party $P \in \{\mathcal{A}^*, S\}$:
7. If $P = \mathcal{A}^*$, and either status[sid] $\neq$ compromised or S is honest: ignore the message.
8. If status[sid] is undefined: send (IOEval, $sid, \bot$) to P.
9. Otherwise, retrieve $x :=$ input[sid] and send (OfflineEval, $sid, f(x,y)$) to P.

On command (IOEval, $sid, ssid, x'$) from S:
10. If S is honest, retrieve $x :=$ input[sid], otherwise, set $x := x'$.
11. Send (IOEval, $sid, ssid$, S) to $\mathcal{A}^*$.
12. If C is corrupt: set budget[sid] := budget[sid] $+ r$.
13. Wait for (IOEval, $sid, ssid, y$) from C or (Abort, $sid, ssid$) from $\mathcal{A}^*$.
14. If honest C sends (IOEval, $sid, ssid, y$): send (IOEval, $sid, ssid, f(x,y)$) to C.
15. If corrupt C sends (IOEval, $sid, ssid, y$):
    – Set budget[sid] := budget[sid] $- 1$ and send (IOEval, $sid, ssid, f(x,y)$) to C.
16. If $\mathcal{A}^*$ sends (Abort, $sid, ssid$):
    – If S is corrupt, send (IOEval, $sid, \bot$) to C.

On command (Redeem, $sid, ssid, y$) from $\mathcal{A}^*$:
17. If status[sid] is undefined: ignore the message.
18. Retrieve $x :=$ input[sid].
19. If budget[sid] $= 0$, send (IOEval, $sid, ssid, \bot$) to $\mathcal{A}^*$.
20. Otherwise set budget[sid] := budget[sid] -1 and send (IOEval, $sid, ssid, f(x,y)$) to $\mathcal{A}^*$.

Fig. 1. The functionality $\mathcal{F}_{\mathrm{iO2PC}}$ computing $\mathcal{C}_f$ with simulation rate r

stored input. Finally, the client may query against the functionality and receive the function result on the client and server's inputs.

3.1   Simulation Rate

Our eventual io2PC protocol has the following interesting property. A corrupt client may perform k different IOEval sessions in such a way that it eventually learns (only) k outputs of the function, but the simulator cannot extract *any* of the client's inputs until after the kth session.[1] We handle this issue in $\mathcal{F}_{iO2PC}$ with a *ticketing* mechanism. During each IOEval the client need not immediately learn the output of f. Rather, the functionality grants a ticket that entitles the client to one evaluation of f, and this evaluation of f can be redeemed at any later point.

More generally, the functionality can grant r tickets for a single IOEval. Intuitively, think of IOEval as granting some resources to the client, which it can use to evaluate f. But there may be "cheap" inputs to f which require r times fewer resources than the worst case, in which case one session of IOEval may provide enough resources for a corrupt client to learn r outputs of the function.

3.2   Server Compromise and Offline Evaluation

Following the treatment of server compromise in aPAKE [12,19], our functionality separates Byzantine server **corruption** and server **compromise**. Upon being compromised, the server only leaks its long-term storage to the adversary but *remains honest*; in other words, a Compromise query does not allow the server to be controlled by the adversary. On the other hand, server corruption not only leaks the entire state of the server to the adversary, but additionally allows for complete control of the server. We consider the *static corruption* model, but crucially, we allow the adversary to *adaptively compromise* an honest server. This is reflected in our $\mathcal{F}_{iO2PC}$ functionality: the adversary can compromise the server via a Compromise message at any time, which marks the status of the current session compromised, after which the adversary can perform offline evaluations. However, in subsequent online evaluations, a compromised server is still treated as honest.

Furthermore, similar to the (strong) aPAKE functionality, we require that both Compromise and OfflineEval messages be accounted for by the environment. In particular, this means that the ideal adversary (simulator) cannot take certain actions without some corresponding real-world event caused by the real adversary: the ideal adversary cannot send Compromise unless the real adversary compromises the server, and it cannot send OfflineEval unless the real adversary performs some "work" (in the form of random oracle or generic group queries) that corresponds to evaluating f. The rationale is similar to why Byzantine corruptions are accounted for by the environment in the UC framework: to prevent the simulator from corrupting all parties and making the simulation trivial. Indeed, the Compromise and OfflineEval messages can be formally modeled as a special form of corruption—see [8,16] for a detailed description.

---

[1] Essentially, our protocol for IOEval simply allows the client to make some fixed number of OPRF queries. Instead of using those OPRF queries for k *sequential* evaluations of the function, the client can schedule the OPRF queries in parallel— e.g., the first query in all k evaluations, then the second query in all k evaluations, etc.

3.3 Preventing Precomputation

We require that OfflineEval commands sent by a corrupt client are accounted for by the environment, and can only be issued by the environment if the real-world adversary does some observable "work". Crucially, that "work" must happen *after* server compromise. This requirement means that the client cannot "precompute" work before compromise that permits the simulator to send many OfflineEval commands instantly upon server compromise.

This feature is analogous to the definition of **strong** aPAKE. In non-strong aPAKE, an adversary can learn all parties' stored passwords *instantly* upon compromise of the password file. In strong aPAKE, an adversary can only make password guesses after compromise, and these password guesses must be accounted for by the environment—*i.e.* they must correspond to observable work performed *after compromise* by the adversary. In this sense, our $\mathcal{F}_{\mathsf{iO2PC}}$ functionality is analogous to the *strong* flavor of aPAKE.

4 io2PC for Random-Oracle-Model Obfuscation

In this section, we describe a compiler for realizing io2PC from functions that have VBB obfuscation in the random oracle model. Let us first recall the OPAQUE compiler [19] from aPAKE to saPAKE. The OPAQUE compiler works by replacing the input password pw to the starting aPAKE protocol with the evaluation $\mathsf{OPRF}(pw)$. This compiler serves as a source of intuition for an intermediate compiler for io2PC which takes a VBB obfuscation in the random oracle model and replaces the input x to each random oracle evaluation with $\mathsf{OPRF}(x)$.

Recall the point function obfuscation $\mathcal{O}_x = H(x)$ for random oracle H, with evaluation $H(\cdot) \stackrel{?}{=} \mathcal{O}_x$ [21]. Applying this compiler, we arrive at the io2PC protocol in which the server stores $\mathcal{O}'_x = H(\mathsf{OPRF}(x))$ and interactively evaluates $H(\mathsf{OPRF}(\cdot)) \stackrel{?}{=} \mathcal{O}'_x$ by sending $\mathcal{O}'_x$ to the client then acting as the server in an OPRF protocol. This intuitive compiler is not far from the truth, as for random oracle H, $H(\mathsf{OPRF}(\cdot))$ is itself an OPRF, so we simplify slightly by instead replacing all random oracle invocations directly with OPRF invocations. Indeed, with a small modification replacing the OPRF in this compiler with a verifiable OPRF (VOPRF), we achieve the compiler described in Sect. 4.2.

4.1 Oblivious PRF

An Oblivious Pseudorandom Function (OPRF) [11] for a Pseudorandom Function (PRF) family $F_{(\cdot)}$ is, generally, a two-party protocol for realizing the functionality where a server who holds a key k and a client who holds an input x evaluate $F_k(x)$ with output $(\epsilon, F_k(x))$. Namely, the client learns $F_k(x)$ and the server learning nothing about the input x or the output $F_k(x)$. OPRFs have found many applications and have been extended to support verification of client and server inputs [18,20].

Our functionality $\mathcal{F}_{\text{VOPRF}}$, in Fig. 2, for a verifiable OPRF (VOPRF) with active compromise closely follows the functionality of Jarecki, Krawczyk, and Xu [19].

Parameters:
- client C, server S, and ideal adversary $\mathcal{A}^*$

Storage:
- two maps, status and F

On command (VOPRFInit, sid) from S:
1. If status[sid] is defined: ignore the message.
2. Set status[sid] := active.
3. Send (VOPRFInit, sid, S) to $\mathcal{A}^*$.

On command (Compromise, sid) from $\mathcal{A}^*$:
4. Set status[sid] := compromised.

On command (OfflineEval, sid, x) from party P $\in \{\mathcal{A}^*, \text{S}\}$:
5. If status[sid] $\neq$ compromised or S is not corrupted, and P $\neq$ S: ignore the message.
6. If status[sid] is undefined: send (VOPRFEval, $sid, \perp$) to P.
7. Otherwise, if $F[x]$ is undefined, set $F[x] \leftarrow \mathbf{H}$, and send (OfflineEval, $sid, F[x]$) to P.

On command (VOPRFEval, $sid, ssid, x$) from C:
8. If status[sid] is undefined: send (VOPRFEval, $sid, \perp$) to C.
9. Send (VOPRFEval, $sid, ssid, $ C) to $\mathcal{A}^*$, (VOPRFEval, $sid, ssid$) to S, and wait for (SComplete, $sid, ssid$) from S.
10. Send (SComplete, $sid, ssid, $ S) to $\mathcal{A}^*$ and wait for either (Deliver, $sid, ssid$) or (Abort, $sid, ssid$) from $\mathcal{A}^*$.
11. If $\mathcal{A}^*$ sends (Abort, $sid, ssid$):
    - If $F[x]$ is undefined, set $F[x] \leftarrow \mathbf{H}$ and send (VOPRFEval, $sid, F[x]$) to C.
12. If $\mathcal{A}^*$ instead sends (Abort, $sid, ssid$):
    - If S is corrupt, send (VOPRFEval, $sid, \perp$) to C.

Fig. 2. The functionality $\mathcal{F}_{\text{VOPRF}}$ for evaluating random function F with range $\mathbf{H}$

The main difference between the functionality in Fig. 2 and the comparable OPRF functionality [19] is the addition of the Abort query. $\mathcal{F}_{\text{VOPRF}}$ is *verifiable* in the sense that it allows for a client to abort in the face of a corrupt server who may, for example, commit to a PRF key through a public key and use a different PRF key during evaluation. Instead of presenting multiple tables indexed by a function parameter as in previous functionalities [18], $\mathcal{F}_{\text{VOPRF}}$ uses a single key provided during initialization and then exposes Abort. This verifiability also models the client's ability to verify consistent key usage between various OPRF interactions with a given server. The client will be assured that all interactions compute the same underlying PRF or else the client can abort.

Our VOPRF functionality Fig. 2 differs from others in the literature (*e.g.*, [1]). Our definition requires that the outputs of the VOPRF are pseudorandom even to the server. This requirement is related to the fact that io2PC (like asymmetric PAKE) requires programmability of outputs from the simulator, even for the server's *non-interactive* evaluations of the OPRF [16]. In particular, this means that to provide input obfuscation to non-trivial functions we must rely on some assumption with stronger programmability than afforded by a CRS. As such, we cannot achieve this functionality outside a *strongly* programmable model such as the random oracle model or the generic group model.

The requirement that the outputs of the VOPRF are pseudorandom even to the server is necessary to realize the intuition that a corrupt client can only gain *oracle access* to the underlying PRF on server compromise. We like to think of such a (V)OPRF as a "personalized" Random Oracle which the server can let another party evaluate, privately, on some input. When an honest server is compromised by a corrupt client, the client gains the ability to evaluate this personal random function at will; however, since the outputs of the function are pseudorandom to the server they are also pseudorandom to a client who compromises the server's storage. To meet the idea of oracle access, these evaluations must also be observable. With these two properties, we can see that the exposed oracle is analogous to a personalized random oracle.

Jarecki, Kiayias, and Krawczyk [18] provide an efficient UC instantiation of a VOPRF in the random oracle model under a one-more Gap DH assumption. We recall that protocol—called 2HashDH-NIZK therein for its eponymous entry and exit hashes—in Fig. 3.

Similar to previous results for the 2HashDH-NIZK protocol [18] in Fig. 3 and its non-verifiable derivative [19], we know that 2HashDH-NIZK satisfies our requirements for adaptive compromise, and relative to S's public key, 2HashDH-NIZK satisfies our verifiability requirements. The inclusion of a NIZK does not significantly modify the proof for adaptive compromise, and we may consider the existence of an authenticated channel, mediated through the authenticated channel functionality $\mathcal{F}_{\text{AUTH}}$ to provide the server's public key to the client. In situations where the public key of the server is known a-priori to the client, we may drop the need for an authenticated channel; however, in the cases we consider for io2PC, the existence of an authenticated channel is already assumed.

4.2   io2PC Protocol

We present our OPRF-based io2PC protocol in Fig. 4. In the initialization phase, the server computes an obfuscation of its input x, with the random oracle queries made via evaluating the random function in $\mathcal{F}_{\text{VOPRF}}$ offline. Crucially, after computing the obfuscated input $\mathcal{O}_x$, the server only stores $\mathcal{O}_x$ and *erases the original input* x. In online evaluation, the server sends its storage $\mathcal{O}_x$ to the client, who then runs the obfuscation evaluation procedure to compute the function result with the random oracle queries made via evaluating the random function in $\mathcal{F}_{\text{VOPRF}}$ online (so the client runs evaluation with $\mathcal{F}_{\text{VOPRF}}$ c times).

Parameters:
Generator g of cyclic group of order q
Random Oracles $H_1(\cdot), H_2(\cdot), H_3(\cdot)$
Client C and Server S
KeyGen:
  S samples $k \leftarrow \mathbb{Z}_q$.
  S stores k and returns public key g^k.
Compromise:
  S returns stored key k.
Offline Evaluation:
  On input x, S returns $H_2(g^k, x, H_1(x)^k)$

Online Evaluation:
  C, on input x, samples $r \leftarrow \mathbb{Z}_p$ and
  sends $(H_1(x))^r$ to S.
  S, on message b from C sends $h = g^k$,
  b^k, and $\mathsf{NIZK}^{H_3}(b, b^k, g, g^k)$ to C.
  C, on message h, c, π from S, verifies
  π is a valid proof then returns
  $H_2(h, x, c^{1/r})$.

Fig. 3. VOPRF protocol 2HashDH-NIZK

Our protocol bears a resemblance to the OPAQUE strong aPAKE protocol [19], where the client evaluates an OPRF on its password and obtains a point obfuscation of the password (called the "randomized password" in [19]), receives, from the server, an encryption of the client's authenticated key exchange (AKE) credentials under the randomized password, decrypts and learns its credentials, and then runs an AKE protocol with the server. However, since our goal here is not key exchange, our protocol is significantly simpler than OPAQUE: the server only needs to send the obfuscation (the randomized password) to the client, and no AKE protocol is run between the client and the server.

Using Verifiable OPRF. Our io2PC protocol requires a *verifiable* OPRF, meaning that the client should be convinced that the server uses a consistent OPRF key. The alert reader may notice that OPAQUE does not require a verifiable OPRF. However, OPAQUE corresponds to a variant of io2PC for the special case of point functions, and some situations arise in the special case of io2PC which are not present in that special case.

First, point-function obfuscation (and hence OPAQUE) requires only a *single* call to the OPRF/random oracle. In the general case, if multiple random oracle queries are required to evaluate an obfuscation, and these oracle queries are replaced by OPRF calls, what should happen if a corrupt server changes its OPRF key between those calls? This is not just a hypothetical question—in the obfuscation presented in Sect. 6.2, the evaluation algorithm should make some "dummy queries" to its oracle so that the total number of queries does not depend on the input. But the choice of which queries are "dummies" depends on the input. A corrupt server could therefore observe whether changing its OPRF key in an instance leads to any change in the client's output, thereby deducing whether a query is a dummy or not.

Second, point function obfuscation is special because the effect of substituting the "wrong" OPRF key can be easily simulated. Using the wrong OPRF key for a point function makes the point function output false with overwhelming probability, and this can be simulated by the corrupt server simply choosing a random target point for the point function. But in general, it is not immediate that selectively changing the OPRF key is equivalent to choosing a different obfuscated input.

Theorem 1. *Suppose* (Obf, ObfEval, c) *is a VBB obfuscation for C_f with simulation rate r, in the random oracle model. Then the io2PC protocol (Fig. 4) realizes the $\mathcal{F}_{\text{io2PC}}$ functionality computing C_f with simulation rate r (Fig. 1) in the $\mathcal{F}_{\text{VOPRF}}$-hybrid world.*

Parameters:
  - Obfuscation (Obf, ObfEval, c) for the class of functions $C_f = \{f(x, \cdot) \mid x \in \{0,1\}^*\}$, in the random oracle model.
  - Client C and server S.

On command (Init, sid, x) for S:
  1. S: Send (VOPRFInit, sid) to $\mathcal{F}_{\text{VOPRF}}$
  2. S: Run $\mathcal{O}_x \leftarrow \text{Obf}^?(x)$, where each time Obf queries its oracle at q:
      - Send (OfflineEval, $sid, ssid, q$) to $\mathcal{F}_{\text{VOPRF}}$
      - Receive response (OfflineEval, $sid, ssid, r$)
      - Give r to Obf as the response to its oracle query
  3. S: Store $\mathcal{O}_x$.

On command (Compromise, sid) from $\mathcal{A}^*$:
  4. $\mathcal{A}^*$ must also send (Compromise, sid) to $\mathcal{F}_{\text{VOPRF}}$
  5. $\mathcal{A}^*$ learns $\mathcal{O}_x$.

On command (IOEval, $sid, ssid$) for S:
  6. S: Send ($sid, ssid, \mathcal{O}_x$) to C.
  7. Both parties set $i := 0$.
  8. C: Await command (IOEval, $sid, ssid, y$).
  9. C: Run $z := \text{ObfEval}^?(\mathcal{O}_x, y)$, where each time ObfEval queries its oracle at q:
      - C: Send (VOPRFEval, $sid, ssid\|i, q$) to $\mathcal{F}_{\text{VOPRF}}$
      - S: Await (VOPRFEval, $sid, ssid\|i$) from $\mathcal{F}_{\text{VOPRF}}$
      - Both: set $i := i + 1$
      - S: If $i > c$: abort. Otherwise, send (SComplete, $sid, ssid\|i$) to $\mathcal{F}_{\text{VOPRF}}$
      - C: Await response (VOPRFEval, $sid, ssid\|i, r$) from $\mathcal{F}_{\text{VOPRF}}$
      - C: Give r to Obf as the response to its oracle query
  10. C: Output (IOEval, $sid, ssid, z$)

Fig. 4. The io2PC protocol for computing function f, based on a VBB obfuscation in the random oracle model.

We provide the main ideas for the simulator here and provide a proof of this theorem in the full version of this paper.

In the Case that S *is Corrupt.* Sim simulates $\mathcal{F}_{\text{VOPRF}}$ and keeps track of all queries the corrupt server makes to the functionality. Upon receiving (IOEval, $sid, ssid,$ C) from $\mathcal{F}$, and $(sid, ssid, \mathcal{O}_x)$ from the corrupt server, Sim makes dummy OPRF evaluations VOPRFEval and receives Deliver, until it receives a total number of c Deliver messages from $\mathcal{A}$. Finally, Sim calculates $x := \text{Extract}(\mathcal{O}_x, \mathcal{H})$ and sends (IOEval, $sid, ssid, x$) to $\mathcal{F}$. In this case, we write S* for the server to stress the fact that it is corrupt. The simulator Sim behaves as follows:

In the Case that C *is Corrupt.* On Init from $\mathcal{F}$, Sim runs $\mathcal{O}_x := \text{SimObf}_1()$, the first phase of the VBB simulator for (Obf, ObfEval). When $\mathcal{A}$ compromises the server and $\mathcal{F}_{\text{VOPRF}}$, Sim sends $\mathcal{O}_x$ to $\mathcal{A}$.[2] When $\mathcal{A}$ queries its offline OPRF oracle on input p after compromise, Sim runs $\text{SimObf}_2()$ with the adversary querying $H(p)$. When SimObf_2 makes a query y to its oracle $f(x, \cdot)$, Sim sends (OfflineEval, y) to $\mathcal{F}$, and on $\mathcal{F}$'s response (OfflineEval, z), Sim sends z to SimObf_2 as the response to its query. Finally, when SimObf_2 outputs q as the response to the adversary's $H(p)$ query, Sim sends q to $\mathcal{A}$ as the OPRF output. On IOEval from $\mathcal{F}$, Sim sends $\mathcal{O}_x$ to the corrupt client. If $\mathcal{A}$ queries the OPRF on input p, Sim runs $\text{SimObf}_2()$ with the adversary querying $H(p)$ until c queries are made. Finally, when SimObf_2 makes a query y to its function oracle $f(x, \cdot)$:

- If this is the first such query since the last (IOEval, S) from $\mathcal{F}$, Sim sends (IOEval, y) to $\mathcal{F}$.
- Otherwise, Sim sends (Redeem, y) to $\mathcal{F}$.

On $\mathcal{F}$'s response (IOEval, z), Sim sends z to SimObf_2 as the response to its query. Finally, when both of the following happen: (1) SimObf_2 outputs q as the response to the adversary's $H(p)$ query, and (2) $\mathcal{A}$ sends Deliver aimed at $\mathcal{F}_{\text{VOPRF}}$, Sim sends (VOPRFEval, q) to the corrupt client.

5   io2PC for Generic-Group Obfuscations

5.1   Generic Groups

Generic groups were introduced by Shoup [23] as a way to model an idealized cyclic group where the only allowable operations are the standard group operations. Consider an encoding $\sigma : \mathbb{Z}_p \to \{0,1\}^*$ of group elements (without loss of generality, the cyclic group of order p) into strings. The group operation (on encoded elements) is defined by the function $\text{mult}_\sigma(\sigma(x), \sigma(y)) = \sigma(x+y \bmod p)$. In Shoup's generic group model, parties have access to an oracle for mult_σ for a *uniformly chosen* encoding σ, along with an encoding of the group generator. Under such a random encoding, the encoding of a group element leaks nothing about that item's "identity" (*i.e.* its discrete log).

---

[2] Following *e.g.*, [19], we assume that $\mathcal{A}$ always sends a Compromise message to S and $\mathcal{F}_{\text{VOPRF}}$ simultaneously. These two actions correspond to a single action in the real protocol, *i.e.* compromising the server.

Maurer [22] proposed a slightly different model of generic groups, where the encoding of elements is not bijective; *i.e.* each group element may have many valid encodings. In this model, a stateful oracle maintains a mapping $D : \{0,1\}^* \to \mathbb{Z}_p$, where an abstract *handle* h represents the group element $D[h] \in \mathbb{Z}_p$. A party can query its oracle to multiply handles h_1, h_2—to do this, the oracle chooses a new handle h_3 and records $D[h_3] = D[h_1] + D[h_2] \bmod p$.

In Shoup's generic group model, every group element x has a unique encoding $\sigma(x)$, which means that it is trivial to test equality of group elements. In Maurer's model, the oracle must provide an equality-test function—*i.e.* given handles h_1, h_2 the oracle returns $D[h_1] \stackrel{?}{=} D[h_2]$.

The two generic group models are equivalent in terms of algorithmic power (*e.g.*, the discrete log problem is equally difficult in both models) [17]. However, the distinction is important when incorporating generic groups into a larger cryptographic system. For example, in the Shoup model one may compute a hash of a group element's encoding, so that anyone who can compute the same group element can also compute the same hash. In the Maurer model, two parties may compute two different handles for the "same" group element, so one must be more careful about the distinction between handles and the group elements they represent.

In this work we use a generic group model more similar to Maurer's model. The details are given in Fig. 5. Group elements may be represented by many handles, and the oracle must therefore provide an explicit equality test feature. Without loss of generality, we provide a zero-test feature as it is simpler.

In Maurer's model, the handles can be sequential numbers—*i.e.* the ith oracle query is given handle "i". This suffices to reason about non-interactive algorithms. In our setting, the generic group oracle is a common resource shared among many parties (similar to a random oracle), and in that case sequence numbers would reveal how many group operations other parties have performed. Our generic group oracle therefore chooses new handles uniformly at random.

Conventions. Although technically a generic group is modeled as an oracle, it becomes too cumbersome to notate all group operations as oracle calls. Instead, we use standard (multiplicative) group notation to denote operations in the group, as is standard.

A group requires both a group operation and inverses. Since we always consider groups of known order p, inverses can be computed by raising to the $p - 1$ power, which can be done with the group-multiplication oracle, so we do not provide a separate explicit group-inverse oracle.

Our generic group formulation assumes that every handle represents *some* group element. Any handle not specifically generated by the oracle corresponds to a uniformly chosen group element. Hence, parties can generate [handles of] random group elements at any time.

Standard Concepts. The generic group oracle uses a map dlog to keep track of the discrete log of every handle. The discrete log of a group element is of course

---

dlog := empty map
$g^* \leftarrow \{0,1\}^{2\kappa}$
$\text{dlog}[g^*] := 1$

ZeroTest(g_1):
   if dlog[g_1] undefined: dlog[g_1] $\leftarrow \mathbb{Z}_p$
   return dlog[g_1] $\overset{?}{=} 0$

Mult(g_1, g_2):
   if dlog[g_1] undefined: dlog[g_1] $\leftarrow \mathbb{Z}_p$
   if dlog[g_2] undefined: dlog[g_2] $\leftarrow \mathbb{Z}_p$
   $g_3 \leftarrow \{0,1\}^{2\kappa}$
   dlog[g_3] := dlog[g_1] + dlog[g_2] mod p
   return g_3

gen():
   return g^*

Fig. 5. A generic group oracles for group of order p, with handles of length 2κ

an element of $\mathbb{Z}_p$. A common proof technique in the generic group model is to keep track of discrete logs *symbolically*.

We use the mathbb font to denote formal variables like $\mathbb{K}, \mathbb{R}$. Then we extend the contents of dlog to contain not only scalars from $\mathbb{Z}_p$ but rational functions in these formal variables—*i.e.* dlog[·] $\in \mathbb{Z}_p(\mathbb{K}, \mathbb{R}, \ldots)$. When multiplying group elements, the new handle's dlog value is still recorded as dlog[g_3] = dlog[g_1] + dlog[g_2], but now addition denotes (symbolic) addition of functions over the formal variables.

In our security proofs, we write an expression like "$g^{a\mathbb{K}+b}$" to indicate that the simulator generates a new group handle whose dlog value is the symbolic expression $a\mathbb{K} + b$. Our convention is that lowercase letters like a, b will denote scalars from $\mathbb{Z}_p$.

In a standard generic-group security proof, a random group element like g^r will be replaced by a symbolic one $g^{\mathbb{R}}$. After an adversary performs group operations, other group elements may have dlog-values that are expressions including $\mathbb{R}$. A zero-test on such a group element is performed by checking whether the dlog of that group element is *identically (symbolically) zero*. A standard argument shows that symbolic zero-tests are indistinguishable from real/concrete zero-test, provided that all symbolic dlog expressions have bounded degree, and the dlog formal variables take the place of uniformly chosen (concrete) discrete log values.

5.2 Personalized Generic Group

In the previous sections, we saw that we can convert a VBB obfuscation into an io2PC protocol by replacing a random oracle with an oblivious PRF. We like to think of an OPRF as a kind of "personalized" random oracle. It is a random function, to which only the server has the key; yet the server can allow the client to evaluate the function on a private input. Even if the server's key to the OPRF is stolen, the adversary's access to the random function is observable/programmable to the simulator.

In this section we extend this analogy from random oracles to generic groups. A **personalized generic group (PGG)** is a group to which only the server has the key; yet the server can allow the client to perform the group operation on private inputs. If the server's key to the group is stolen, the adversary's access to the group is analogous to a true generic group.

We formally define a personalized generic group as an ideal functionality $\mathcal{F}_{pgg}$ in Fig. 6. The functionality maintains a map DLog associating discrete logs with handles, similar to a standard generic group. The server can perform group operations at any time by sending appropriate commands (OfflineMult, OfflineZeroTest) to the functionality. The client can perform group operations, but only interactively (OnlineMult, OnlineZeroTest) and only with approval from the server. These group operations are oblivious—the server does not learn which group elements the client is operating on. Only after designating the session as compromised can a corrupt client also gain the ability to perform the group operations unilaterally.

We point out some other notable aspects of the definition: There are a few things that a client can do non-interactively, *i.e.* without the server's assistance and approval. A client can freely "clone" a handle, resulting in another handle with the same DLog value. In our eventual PGG protocol, this is indeed possible, but does not seem to give obvious advantage to the client. The client can also generate a handle representing a random group element since by default, all handles correspond to uniform group elements.

A corrupt server can learn all discrete logs of all handles. This makes the simulation considerably easier, but does not seem to represent any issues with our usage of the functionality. Note that if the server is honest but a corrupt client compromises the session, the client cannot learn discrete logs. This helps reflect the fact that the corrupt client can obtain at most oracle access to a generic group upon compromising the session. It is likely that our PGG protocol could be proven secure without letting the simulator for a corrupt server learn all discrete logs, but at the cost of increased proof complexity.

The OnlineMult and OfflineMult commands are not analogous. OfflineMult is more powerful than OnlineMult, since it allows the caller (either the server or a client after the session is compromised) to perform arbitrary linear combinations of group elements, not just a single group operation between two elements. We could define the PGG ideal functionality so that OnlineMult is more powerful than a single group operation, and our protocol could achieve this feature in a natural way. We have chosen to model only the minimal functionality of OnlineMult.

The simulator for a $\mathcal{F}_{pgg}$ protocol should only call OfflineMult at most once for each multiplication made (after compromise) in the common group by the corrupt client; and it should call OfflineZeroTest at most once for each zero-test made in the common group by the corrupt client. *i.e.* an adversary must expend new effort for each OfflineMult and OfflineZeroTest, and furthermore that effort must be expended *after compromise*. However, recall that an OfflineMult is more powerful than a single multiplication. A corrupt client could perform a single multiplication in the common group that is as powerful as a single OfflineMult (which performs a more powerful linear combination of group elements) in the personalized group.[3] For this reason, it is much **more important to measure an adversary's effort in terms of zero-tests and not group multiplications,** since the simulator does not precisely preserve the number of group multiplications between the common group and personalized group. Only the zero-tests are preserved exactly.

5.3   Protocol for Personalized Generic Groups

In this section we describe our protocol for a personalized generic group. The protocol is in the ideal permutation model and uses a generic group itself. This leads to a high potential for confusion. We differentiate between the **common group** and the **personalized group**:

The common group is the generic group that is used by the protocol. Both parties have unrestricted oracle access to the operations of this group. Group element handles are associated with their discrete log via a map that we call dlog. In the security proof, the simulator finds it useful to play the role of this generic group and maintain the dlog map differently (e.g., with symbolic expressions rather than scalars from $\mathbb{Z}_p$).

The personalized group is one that is realized by the protocol. In the ideal functionality for this personalized group, handles are associated with their discrete log via a map that we call DLog. The goal of this personalized group is to carefully restrict the client's access to the operations that involve DLog, via an interactive protocol.

Main Idea. In our protocol, a "key" for a personalized generic group consists of a key k to a strong PRP F, with forward and inverse evaluation denoted F^+ and F^- respectively, and a random generator $\widehat{g}$ (of the common group). An element in the personalized group with discrete log x is represented by a handle of the form $(F_k(m), \widehat{g}^x g^m)$ for $m \in \mathbb{Z}$ providing a multiplicative blind g^m. This kind of encoding can be motivated as follows:

A client who doesn't know the "key" to the personalized group can only create handles of random elements, because the action of $F_k^{\pm}$ is unpredictable.

After compromising the server and learning the "key" $(k, \widehat{g})$, an adversary can invert the PRP to obtain m, then remove the g^m blinding term to obtain simply $\widehat{g}^x$. In other words, after compromising the server, the handle becomes equivalent to knowing $\widehat{g}^x$. The adversary can now perform group operations on these unblinded values of the form $\widehat{g}^x$, without the server's help. But since we are in a generic group, the simulator can continue to observe the adversary's group operations on these values.

With the help of the server, it is possible for the client to perform group operations on two of these handles:

1. Consider two handles of the form (c_1, g_1) and (c_2, g_2), where $c_1 = F_k(m_1), c_2 = F_k(m_2)$ and $g_1 = \widehat{g}^{x_1} g^{m_1}, g_2 = \widehat{g}^{x_2} g^{m_2}$. The client can perform

---

[3] This is indeed possible in our protocol but would be mitigated if the common-group oracle had a group-multiplication feature exactly as powerful as OfflineMult of $\mathcal{F}_{\mathsf{pgg}}$.

$g_3 = g_1 g_2 = \widehat{g}^{x_1+x_2} g^{m_1+m_2}$. This is half of a valid handle for the element with discrete log $x_1 + x_2$. If the client can obtain an encryption of $F_k(m_1 + m_2)$, they will be able to construct a complete and correct handle.

2. The client and server run a 2PC protocol, where the client provides c_1, c_2, and the server provides k, and the client learns $F_k(m_1 + m_2)$. The server learns nothing. Note that this 2PC protocol involves no group operations in the common generic group – it merely involves arithmetic on exponents and PRP evaluation.

Similarly, the client can perform a zero-test with the server's help:

1. Given a handle (c_1, g_1) the client wants to know whether these have the form $c_1 = F_k(m_1)$ and $g_1 = \widehat{g}^0 g^{m_1} = g^{m_1}$. In other words, the client should learn whether c_1 encrypts the discrete log of g_1.

2. Our approach again involves enlisting the help of a 2PC protocol. The client provides c_1 and the server provides k, so m_1 can be obtained inside the 2PC functionality. The functionality provides two basic functions: First, it chooses a random s and lets the client learn $g^{s \cdot m_1}$ using the value of m_1 that it computed. Next, it allows the client to raise any group element of its choice to the s power. Assuming the client chooses to compute g_1^s, the result equals $g^{s \cdot m_1}$ if and only if $g_1 = g^{m_1}$. We discuss exactly how this is done below.

Details and Fine Print. The full details of our protocol are given in Fig. 8, where the separate 2PC functionality invoked by the parties is described in Fig. 7. This "helper functionality" is a typical reactive functionality that can be securely realized by any standard 2PC protocol. The preceding outline captures the main intuition of our protocol, but there are several necessary modifications required for technical reasons.

First, the handles are "wrapped" in an ideal permutation $\Pi^\pm$—*i.e.* a valid handle is h of the form $\Pi(c_1, g_1)$ where c_1, g_1 are as described above, and Π is an ideal permutation. By enlisting the ideal permutation, the simulator can observe every time a new handle is generated or an existing handle is "unpacked" into its two components.

In our outline, the parties run an oblivious protocol that allows a client, who holds handles $\Pi(F_k(m_1), \widehat{g}^{x_1} g^{m_1})$ and $\Pi(F_k(m_2), \widehat{g}^{x_2} g^{m_2})$, to obtain a new handle $\Pi(F_k(m_1 + m_2), \widehat{g}^{x_1+x_2} g^{m_1+m_2})$. However, this new handle would leak its "history" to anyone who holds k, which would be undesirable. The new handle should instead have a fresh mask m_3, rather than a mask $m_1 + m_2$ derived from its parent handles. When the parties run a 2PC to let the client learn its new ciphertext, the client should instead learn $F_k(m_3)$ for a fresh m_3. Then the client needs to learn a correction term $\Delta = g^{m_3 - m_1 - m_2}$ so it can complete the handle as $\Pi(F_k(m_3), (g_1 \cdot g_2 \cdot \Delta) = \widehat{g}^{x_1+x_2} g^{m_3})$. Since the 2PC functionality itself cannot generate group elements (this would require contacting the generic group oracle for the common group), it delegates this task to the server. *i.e.* it gives $m_3 - m_1 - m_2$ to the server, who generates and sends $\Delta = g^{m_3 - m_1 - m_2}$ to the client.

Parameters:
- group order p
- handle length ℓ
- client C and server S

Storage:
- map DLog; our convention is uninitialized entries of DLog are sampled uniformly from $\mathbb{Z}_p$ before being used.
- map status

On input $(\mathsf{Init}, sid, h \in \{0,1\}^\ell)$ from server S:
1. If status$[sid]$ already defined: abort.
2. Set status$[sid] :=$ active.
3. Send $(\mathsf{Init}, sid, \mathsf{S}, h)$ to C.
4. Set DLog$[h] := 1$.

On $(\mathsf{Compromise}, sid)$ from $\mathcal{A}^*$:
5. Set status$[sid] :=$ compromised.

On input $(\mathsf{OnlineMult}, sid, ssid, h_1, h_2)$ from C:
6. Give $(\mathsf{OnlineMult}, sid, ssid)$ to S and await response $(\mathsf{Deliver}, sid, ssid)$
7. Sample $h_3 \leftarrow \{0,1\}^\ell$.
8. Set DLog$[h_3] :=$ DLog$[h_1] +$ DLog$[h_2] \bmod p$.
9. Give $(\mathsf{OnlineMult}, sid, ssid, h_3)$ to P.

On input $(\mathsf{OfflineMult}, sid, ssid, u_0, (u_1, h_1), \ldots, (u_n, h_n))$ from party $P \in \{\mathsf{S}, \mathcal{A}^*\}$:
10. If status$[sid] \neq$ compromised and $P = \mathcal{A}^*$: do nothing.
11. Sample $h' \leftarrow \{0,1\}^\ell$.
12. Set DLog$[h'] := u_0 + u_1$DLog$[h_1] + \cdots + u_n$DLog$[h_n] \bmod p$.
13. Give $(\mathsf{OfflineMult}, sid, ssid, h')$ to P.

On input $(cmd \in \{\mathsf{OnlineZeroTest}, \mathsf{OfflineZeroTest}\}, sid, ssid, h)$ from party $P \in \{\mathcal{A}^*, \mathsf{S}\}$:
14. If status$[sid] \neq$ compromised and $cmd = \mathsf{OnlineZeroTest}$ and $P = \mathcal{A}^*$: do nothing.
15. If $cmd = \mathsf{OnlineZeroTest}$:
    Give $(\mathsf{OnlineZeroTest}, sid, ssid)$ to S and await response $(\mathsf{Deliver}, sid, ssid)$
16. Give $(cmd, sid, ssid, [\mathsf{DLog}[h] \overset{?}{=} 0])$ to P.

On input $(\mathsf{Identify}, h)$ from corrupt S:
17. Give DLog$[h]$ to S

On input $(\mathsf{Register}, v)$ from corrupt S:
18. $h \leftarrow \{0,1\}^\ell$
19. DLog$[h] := v$
20. Give h to C

On input $(\mathsf{CloneHandle}, h)$ from corrupt C:
21. $h' \leftarrow \{0,1\}^\ell$
22. DLog$[h'] :=$ DLog$[h]$
23. Give h' to C

Fig. 6. The personalized generic group functionality $\mathcal{F}_{\mathsf{pgg}}$.

However, the server may cheat and send a different group element than the functionality intended. To prevent this, the functionality authenticates the group element with a one-time MAC. The functionality gives random MAC key α, β to the client, and gives s and its one-time MAC $\mu = \alpha s + \beta$ to the server. Now the server can send both g^s and g^μ to the client, who can check the MAC in the exponent via $(g^s)^\alpha \cdot g^\beta \overset{?}{=} (g^\mu)$.

There are two conceptual steps in the zero-test protocol which are more complicated than our high-level outline. First, the 2PC helper functionality wants the client to learn the group element $g^{m_1 s}$. It delegates this to the server, using the same method above with one-time MACs, so that the client can be sure that it receives the intended group element. Actually, we must blind the exponent $m_1 s$ from the server (since it also learns s below, and it should not learn m_1 which is tied to this particular handle)—so the functionality gives a random z to the client, and asks the server to deliver $g^{m_1 s + z}$. The client can unblind by multiplying with g^{-z}.

Second, the 2PC functionality gives s to the server so that the server can take part in a blind exponentiation protocol (raising a group element of the client's choice to the s power). It is important to ensure that the server raises the client's element to the correct power, since otherwise the server could easily cause a zero-test to fail even when it should correctly succeed. For this, we (1) have the functionality deliver the value g^s to the client (via delegating to the server), and (2) have the server run a simple *verifiable* exponentiation protocol, where the client can be convinced that its group element was indeed raised to the s power.

Security. In the full version of this paper we prove the following:

Theorem 2. *The protocol in Fig. 8 UC-securely realizes $\mathcal{F}_{\mathsf{pgg}}$ (Fig. 6) in the generic group and ideal-permutation model, when F is a strong PRP.*

We provide a sketch of the main ideas here. The case of a corrupt server is considerably easier. It is easy to see that the server's view during OnlineMult, OnlineZeroTest gives no information about the client's choice of handles, since all the communication is mediated through the helper functionality $\mathcal{F}_{\mathsf{helper}}$. The $\mathcal{F}_{\mathsf{pgg}}$ functionality allows a corrupt server to both learn the discrete log for any handle, and also directly register a handle with a chosen discrete log. The simulator can use these features to intercept all of the adversary's $\Pi^\pm$ oracle queries and relay discrete log information between the functionality and the actual group elements used for $h = \Pi(\cdot, g_1)$.

The case of a corrupt client is considerably more complex, but the main idea is as follows. In the real world, handles have the form $h = \Pi(c, \hat{g}^{\mathsf{DLog}[h]} g^{F_k^{-1}(c)})$. We use the technique of symbolic discrete logs (described in Sect. 5.1) to model the adversary's ignorance of certain values. The adversary does not know the discrete log of $\hat{g}$, so we represent it by a formal variable $\mathbb{K}$. Before the session is compromised, the adversary does not know $F_k^{-1}(c)$ for any c, so we represent this value by formal variable $\mathbb{M}_c$. The adversary initially does not know anything about the $\mathsf{DLog}[h]$ values, so we represent them by formal variables $\mathbb{D}_h$.

Parameters:
- modulus p
- strong PRP $F^{\pm} : \{0,1\}^{\kappa} \times \mathbb{Z}_p \to \mathbb{Z}_p$
- client C and server S

Storage: value k, initially sampled as $k \leftarrow \{0,1\}^{\kappa}$

On command (HelpInit, sid) from S:

1. Sample $\alpha, \beta, c, s \leftarrow \mathbb{Z}_p$
2. $\mu = \alpha s + \beta$ // one-time MAC of s under key (α, β)
3. Send (HelpInit, sid, α, β, c) to C and send (HelpInit, sid, s, μ, c, k) to S.

On command (HelpMult, $sid, ssid, c_1, c_2$) from C:

4. Send (HelpMult, $sid, ssid$) to S await response (Deliver, $sid, ssid$).
5. $m_1 := F_k^{-1}(c_1); \ m_2 := F_k^{-1}(c_2)$.
6. $\alpha, \beta, m_3 \leftarrow \mathbb{Z}_p$.
7. $c_3 = F_k(m_3)$.
8. $s = m_3 - m_1 - m_2 \bmod p$.
9. $\mu = \alpha s + \beta \bmod p$. // one-time MAC of s under key (α, β)
10. Give (HelpMult, $sid, ssid, \alpha, \beta, c_3$) to C and give (HelpMult, $sid, ssid, s, \mu$) to S

On command (HelpZeroTest, $sid, ssid, c$) from C:

11. Send (HelpZeroTest, $sid, ssid$) to S and await response (Deliver, $sid, ssid$)
12. $m := F_k^{-1}(c)$.
13. $\alpha, \beta, \gamma, s, z \leftarrow \mathbb{Z}_p$.
14. $t := sm + z$
15. $\mu = \alpha s + \beta t + \gamma \bmod p$. // one-time MAC of (s, t) under key (α, β, γ)
16. Give (HelpZeroTest, $sid, ssid, \alpha, \beta, \gamma, z$) to C and give (HelpZeroTest, $sid, ssid, s, t, \mu$) to S

Fig. 7. Helper functionality $\mathcal{F}_{\mathsf{helper}}$ for our personalized generic group protocol.

The adversary can only gain information about group elements (in the common group) through a zero-test. When the adversary makes such a zero-test, the simulator observes it and checks the dlog value of that group element. This dlog is a symbolic expression over the formal variables. Formal variables $\mathbb{M}_c$ and $\mathbb{K}$ represent values that are random from the adversary's point a view, so if the dlog expression is not symbolically equal to zero as a function of those variables, then the zero test in the real world would succeed only with negligible probability. Hence the simulator can simply claim that the zero-test fails. However, the dlog expression may contain $\mathbb{D}_h$ terms which represent concrete DLog[h] values, and depending on the actual values in DLog[h] the dlog expression may or may not be identically zero as a function of the other formal variables. In that case, the simulator must know whether the concrete DLog values make the dlog expression identically zero. We carefully analyze what kinds of expressions are possible in dlog, and show that this situation only happens when the simulator needs to know whether a single DLog[h] value is zero, and then only after the adversary has done an OnlineZeroTest on h. In all other cases, the concrete values in DLog

Parameters:
- generic group $\langle g \rangle$ of prime order p, with handles of length 2κ
- strong PRP $F^{\pm}$
- ideal permutation $\Pi^{\pm} : (\mathbb{Z}_p \times \{0,1\}^{2\kappa}) \rightarrow (\mathbb{Z}_p \times \{0,1\}^{2\kappa})$
- client C and server S

On input (Init, sid) for server S:
1. S: Send (HelpInit, sid) to $\mathcal{F}_{\mathsf{helper}}$
2. C: Receive (HelpInit, sid, α, β, c) from $\mathcal{F}_{\mathsf{helper}}$
3. S: Receive (HelpInit, sid, s, μ, c, k) from $\mathcal{F}_{\mathsf{helper}}$
4. S: Store $(\widehat{g} := g^{s-m}, k)$, where $m := F_k^{-1}(c)$.
5. S: Send $(S = g^s, M = g^\mu)$ to C.
6. C: If $S^\alpha \cdot g^\beta \neq M$: abort.
7. C: Output (Init, $sid, h = \Pi(c, S)$)

On input (**Compromise**, sid) from $\mathcal{A}^*$:
8. $\mathcal{A}^*$ should learn $(k, \widehat{g})$

On input (**OnlineMult**, $sid, ssid, h_1, h_2$) for C:
9. C: $(c_1, g_1) = \Pi^{-1}(h_1)$; $(c_2, g_2) = \Pi^{-1}(h_2)$.
10. C: Send (HelpMult, $sid, ssid, c_1, c_2$) to $\mathcal{F}_{\mathsf{helper}}$
11. S: Await (Deliver, $sid, ssid$) from environment and forward it to $\mathcal{F}_{\mathsf{helper}}$
12. C: Receive (HelpMult, $sid, ssid, \alpha, \beta, c_3$) from $\mathcal{F}_{\mathsf{helper}}$
13. S: Receive (HelpMult, $sid, ssid, s, \mu$) from $\mathcal{F}_{\mathsf{helper}}$
14. S: Send $(S = g^s, M = g^\mu)$ to C.
15. C: If $S^\alpha \cdot g^\beta \neq M$: abort.
16. C: Output (OnlineMult, $sid, ssid, h_3 = \Pi(c_3, g_1 \cdot g_2 \cdot S)$)

On input (**OnlineZeroTest**, $sid, ssid, h_1$) for C:
17. C: $(c_1, g_1) = \Pi^{-1}(h_1)$.
18. C: Send (HelpZeroTest, $sid, ssid, c_1$) to $\mathcal{F}_{\mathsf{helper}}$
19. S: Await (Deliver, $sid, ssid$) from environment and forward it to $\mathcal{F}_{\mathsf{helper}}$
20. C: Receive (HelpZeroTest, $sid, ssid, \alpha, \beta, \gamma, z$) from $\mathcal{F}_{\mathsf{helper}}$
21. S: Receive (HelpZeroTest, $sid, ssid, s, t, \mu$) from $\mathcal{F}_{\mathsf{helper}}$
22. S: Send $(S = g^s, T = g^t, M = g^\mu)$ to C.
23. C: If $S^\alpha \cdot T^\beta \cdot g^\gamma \neq M$: abort.
24. C: $a, b, c \leftarrow \mathbb{Z}_p$; $A := g_1^a \cdot g^b$; $C := g_1^c$; send (A, C) to S.
25. S: Send $A' = A^s$ and $C' = C^s$ to C
26. C: If $(A')^c \neq (C')^a \cdot S^{bc}$: abort
27. C: Output (OnlineZeroTest, $sid, ssid, [(C')^{1/c} \overset{?}{=} T \cdot g^{-z}]$)

On input (**OfflineMult**, $sid, ssid, u_0, (u_1, h_1), \ldots, (u_n, h_n)$) for S:
28. S: For each $i \in [n]$ do: $(c_i, g_i) = \Pi^{-1}(h_i)$; $m_i := F_k^{-1}(c_i)$
29. S: $m^* \leftarrow \mathbb{Z}_p$; $c^* := F_k(m^*)$; $h^* = \Pi(c^*, \widehat{g}^{u_0} \prod_i g_i^{u_i} \cdot g^{m^* - \sum_i m_i})$
30. S: Output (OfflineMult, $sid, ssid, h^*$)

On input (**OfflineZeroTest**, $sid, ssid, h_1$) for S:
31. S: $(c_1, g_1) = \Pi^{-1}(h_1)$; $m_1 := F_k^{-1}(c_1)$
32. S: Output (OfflineZeroTest, $sid, ssid, [g_1 \overset{?}{=} g^{m_1}]$)

Fig. 8. Our personalized generic group protocol.

have no bearing on whether a dlog expression is symbolically zero (at least before session compromise).

When the adversary compromises the session, it learns the PRP key k. This makes the $F_k^{-1}(c)$ values no longer uncertain from the adversary's point of view. We model this by having the simulator replace every formal variable $\mathbb{M}_c$ with a concrete value $F_k^{-1}(c)$, after compromise. This changes what kinds of expressions the adversary is able to make appear in dlog. After the compromise, there are more situations where the concrete values in $\mathsf{DLog}[h]$ have a bearing on whether a dlog expression is symbolically zero. In those cases, the simulator can use OfflineMult, OfflineZeroTest to learn the relevant information about those DLog values.

5.4   io2PC Protocol for Generic-Group Obfuscation

Finally, with a personalized generic group, we can realize io2PC for any function that has a suitable VBB obfuscation in the generic group model. The protocol is essentially the same as our io2PC for random-oracle obfuscation (Fig. 4), but we replace the OPRF with a personalized generic group. We give the details in Fig. 9.

Theorem 3. *Suppose* (Obf, ObfEval, c) *is a VBB obfuscation for* $\mathcal{C}_f$ *with simulation rate* r, *in the generic group model. Then the io2PC protocol (Fig. 9) realizes the* $\mathcal{F}_{\text{iO2PC}}$ *functionality computing* $\mathcal{C}_f$ *with simulation rate* r *(Fig. 1) in the* $\mathcal{F}_{\text{pgg}}$*-hybrid world.*

The proof is essentially identical to that of Theorem 1, with the obvious changes replacing the random oracle/OPRF with generic group/personalized group.

6   Compatible Obfuscations

In this section we discuss obfuscations that are compatible with our io2PC approach, namely those that are input-independent, virtual black-box, and extractable.

6.1   Point Functions

For the point function, *i.e.* the function family $\mathcal{C}_f$ where $f(x,y) = (x \overset{?}{=} y)$, there is a simple obfuscation in the random oracle model. We only sketch the scheme and its security argument: given a random oracle H with range $\mathbf{H}$, let $\mathsf{Obf}(x)$ output $H(x)$, and $\mathsf{ObfEval}(\mathcal{O}_x, y)$ output $(H(y) \overset{?}{=} \mathcal{O}_x)$. Clearly, this scheme is correct and input-independent with query rate $c = 1$. The VBB simulator chooses $\mathcal{O}_x \leftarrow \mathbf{H}$ and answers the adversary's $H(y)$ queries as follows: it learns whether $y = x$ via querying $f(x,y)$, and if so, it returns $\mathcal{O}_x$; otherwise it returns a random element in $\mathbf{H}$. The simulation rate is 1 as $Q_S = Q_A$.

Parameters:
- Obfuscation $(\mathsf{Obf}, \mathsf{ObfEval}, c)$ for the class of functions $\mathcal{C}_f = \{f(x, \cdot) \mid x \in \{0,1\}^*\}$, in the generic-group model.
- Client C and server S.

On command (Init, sid, x), S for S:
1. S: Send (Init, sid) to $\mathcal{F}_{\mathsf{pgg}}$
2. S: Receive response (Init, sid, h)
3. S: Run $\mathcal{O}_x \leftarrow \mathsf{Obf}^?(x)$, where each time Obf queries its oracle:
   - If the query is of the form $\mathsf{Mult}(h_1, h_2)$:
     - Send $(\mathsf{OfflineMult}, sid, ssid, 0, (1, h_1), (1, h_2))$ to $\mathcal{F}_{\mathsf{pgg}}$
     - Receive response $(\mathsf{OfflineMult}, sid, ssid, h_3)$
     - Give h_3 to Obf as the response to its oracle query
   - If the query is of the form $\mathsf{ZeroTest}(h_1)$:
     - Send $(\mathsf{OfflineZeroTest}, sid, ssid, h_1)$ to $\mathcal{F}_{\mathsf{pgg}}$
     - Receive response $(\mathsf{OfflineZeroTest}, sid, ssid, b)$
     - Give b to Obf as the response to its oracle query
4. S: Store $\mathcal{O}_x$.

On command $(\mathsf{Compromise}, sid)$ from $\mathcal{A}^*$:
5. $\mathcal{A}^*$ must also send $(\mathsf{Compromise}, sid)$ to $\mathcal{F}_{\mathsf{pgg}}$
6. $\mathcal{A}^*$ learns $\mathcal{O}_x$.

On command $(\mathsf{IOEval}, sid, ssid)$ for S:
7. S: Send $(sid, ssid, \mathcal{O}_x)$ to C.
8. Both parties set $i := 0$
9. C: Await command $(\mathsf{IOEval}, sid, ssid, y)$.
10. C: Run $z := \mathsf{ObfEval}^?(\mathcal{O}_x, y)$, where each time $\mathsf{ObfEval}$ queries its oracle:
    - If the query is of the form $\mathsf{Mult}(h_1, h_2)$:
      - C: Send $(\mathsf{OnlineMult}, sid, ssid\|i, h_1, h_2)$ to $\mathcal{F}_{\mathsf{pgg}}$
      - S: Await $(\mathsf{OnlineMult}, sid, ssid\|i)$ from $\mathcal{F}_{\mathsf{pgg}}$
      - S: Send $(\mathsf{Deliver}, sid, ssid\|i)$ to $\mathcal{F}_{\mathsf{pgg}}$
      - C: Await response $(\mathsf{OnlineMult}, sid, ssid\|i, h_3)$ from $\mathcal{F}_{\mathsf{pgg}}$
      - C: Give h_3 to Obf as the response to its oracle query
    - If the query is of the form $\mathsf{ZeroTest}(h_1)$:
      - C: Send $(\mathsf{OnlineZeroTest}, sid, ssid\|i, q)$ to $\mathcal{F}_{\mathsf{pgg}}$
      - S: Await $(\mathsf{OnlineZeroTest}, sid, ssid\|i)$ from $\mathcal{F}_{\mathsf{pgg}}$
      - Both: set $i := i + 1$
      - S: If $i > c$: abort. Otherwise, send $(\mathsf{Deliver}, sid, ssid\|i)$ to $\mathcal{F}_{\mathsf{pgg}}$
      - C: Await response $(\mathsf{OnlineZeroTest}, sid, ssid\|i, b)$ from $\mathcal{F}_{\mathsf{pgg}}$
      - C: Give b to Obf as the response to its oracle query
11. C: Output $(\mathsf{IOEval}, sid, ssid, z)$

Fig. 9. The io2PC protocol for computing function f, based on a VBB obfuscation in the generic group model.

For the extractability property, $\mathsf{Extract}(\mathcal{O}, \mathcal{H})$ checks if there is an $x \in \mathcal{H}$ such that $H(x) = \mathcal{O}$. If there is more than one such x, $\mathsf{Extract}$ aborts; if there is exactly one such x, it outputs x; if there is no such x, it outputs $\perp$. It is not hard to see that the probability of the bad event in the definition of extractability is negligible (it happens only if $\mathcal{A}$ finds a collision in H, or finds $\mathcal{O}, y$ with $\mathcal{O} = H(y)$ without querying $H(y)$).

6.2   Hyperplane Membership

Extending the idea of point-function obfuscation above, we may consider the same function in higher dimensional spaces. In this section, we provide a new proof for a hyperplane membership protocol in the generic group model.

Let p be a prime with $||p|| = \kappa$ and $d = \mathsf{poly}(\kappa)$. For $\boldsymbol{x} \in \mathbb{Z}_p^d$, define function $F_{\boldsymbol{x}} : \mathbb{Z}_p^d \to \{\text{FALSE}, \text{TRUE}\}$ as

$$F_{\boldsymbol{x}}(\boldsymbol{y}) = \begin{cases} \text{TRUE} & \text{if } \langle \boldsymbol{x}, \boldsymbol{y} \rangle = 0 \\ \text{FALSE} & \text{otherwise} \end{cases}$$

i.e. $F_{\boldsymbol{x}}$ computes membership in the subspace of $\mathbb{Z}_p^d$ containing all vectors orthogonal to $\boldsymbol{x}$. We use $\mathcal{F}_p^d$ to denote the function family $\{F_{\boldsymbol{x}}\}$. Obfuscation of $\mathcal{F}_p^d$ has been considered previously [10], and we recall the construction below.

Obfuscation. The obfuscation in Fig. 10 is due to Canetti, Rothblum, and Varia [10] whose proof is based on strong DDH assumption proven in the GGM, but the proof constructs an inefficient simulator in the dimension of the ambient space. We reconsider the protocol and prove for an efficient simulator with access to a global GGM.

Parameters:
Generic group G with handle space $\mathbf{H}$.
Public generator g of prime order p. $\mathsf{ObfEval}(\mathcal{O}_x, \boldsymbol{y})$:
Ambient space dimension d.   Interpret $\mathcal{O}_x$ as $(o_i)_{i \in [d]} \in \mathbf{H}^d$.
$\mathsf{Obf}(\boldsymbol{x})$:   Return $\prod_i o_i^{x_i} \overset{?}{=} g^0$
   Sample a generator γ of G.
   Return $\mathcal{O}_x = (\gamma^{x_i})_{i \in [d]}$.

Fig. 10. VBB hyperplane membership obfuscation

On input $\boldsymbol{x} = (x_i)_{i \in [d]} \in \mathbb{Z}_p^d$ and input $\boldsymbol{y} = (y_i)_{i \in [d]} \in \mathbb{Z}_p^d$, correctness is immediately evident as $\mathsf{ObfEval}(\mathsf{Obf}(\boldsymbol{x}), \boldsymbol{y})$ computes $\prod_i (\gamma^{x_i})^{y_i} = \gamma^{\langle \boldsymbol{x}, \boldsymbol{y} \rangle} \overset{?}{=} \gamma^0$. The obfuscation algorithm $\mathsf{Obf}(\boldsymbol{x})$ must be careful about optimizing its generic group operations, however. Even if $x_i = x_j$ for distinct i, j, the obfuscation algorithm must ensure that distinct handles are generated for γ^{x_i} and γ^{x_j}; e.g., by separately multiplying by g^0. Finally, note that depending on how Fig. 10 is implemented, the number of multiplication queries that ObfEval makes is data dependent. Specifically, when evaluating exponentiation through squaring ObfEval will compute g^2 with one query while computing g^{127} will require 12 queries. To make the total number of multiplication queries a constant, we may simply require a constant-time exponentiation algorithm.

In our previous definition for simulation rate, we stated that for an obfuscation to have simulation rate r, it must hold that $Q_S \leq r \cdot \frac{Q_A}{c}$. However, the GGM oracle has two interfaces for queries: the multiplication query Mult and the zero test query ZeroTest. As we stated earlier (see Sect. 5.2), it is much more important to measure an adversary's effort in terms of zero-tests and not group multiplications. If we only count ZeroTest queries, the obfuscation scheme is indeed limited by a single query with $Q_S = Q_A$. In the theorem below, the statements about query rate and simulation rate refer only to ZeroTest queries.

Virtual Black-Box Property

Theorem 4. *The scheme in Fig. 10 is a VBB obfuscation Definition 3 for F in the Generic Group Model, with query rate $c = 1$ and simulation rate $r = 1$.*

Proof Sketch:
The simulator Sim replaces the obfuscation $\mathcal{O}_x$ with uniformly sampled handles $\mathcal{O} \leftarrow \mathbf{H}^d$ and then plays the role of the two GG oracles Mult and ZeroTest. In the real world, the obfuscation uses a sampled generator γ with uniform discrete logarithm and since this value is outside the adversary's view, we represent it with the formal variable $\mathbb{K}$. Sim then catalogs the symbolic discrete logarithms of all multiplications the adversary makes relative to handles $\{o_i\}_{i \in [d]}$, comprising $\mathcal{O}$, and the public generator g. As the adversary can only gain information about relations between group elements through a zero-test, it can't tell if $\mathcal{O}$ was replaced until it interacts with the ZeroTest oracle. When the adversary makes such a zero-test, Sim checks the discrete logarithm of that group element. By construction, the discrete logarithm of these queries will take on the form of a polynomial $\mathbb{K}(\sum_i a_i x_i) + z$, for coefficients $a_i, z \in \mathbb{Z}_p$, relative to base g. Noting that $\sum_i a_i x_i$ is exactly $\langle x, a \rangle$, Sim may then check if this combination is zero by querying the function oracle $f(x, a)$. But since the simulator does not need to know the x_i to make the query, the simulator may run agnostic of the input x.

A full proof of this property and the security of the construction is given in the full version of this paper.

Extractability. The construction in Fig. 10 is extractable (Definition 4) through the following algorithm:

- Extract on input $(\mathcal{O}, \mathcal{H})$ iterates through all handles in $\mathcal{H}$ and catalogs their discrete logarithms relative to g in a list DL.
  - If any handles h were sampled by $\mathcal{A}$, Extract samples a uniform discrete logarithm $DL[h] \leftarrow \mathbb{Z}_p$.

- Extract, interprets $\mathcal{O}$ as $(o_i)_{i\in[d]} \in \mathbf{H}^d$, and for each o_i:
  - If $DL[o_i]$ is defined, Extract sets $x_i := DL[o_i]$.
  - Otherwise, Extract samples $x_i \leftarrow \mathbb{Z}_p$.
- Extract finally returns $\boldsymbol{x} = (x_i)_{i\in[d]}$.

A proof of this property is given in the full version of this paper.

References

1. Albrecht, M.R., Davidson, A., Deo, A., Smart, N.P.: Round-optimal verifiable oblivious pseudorandom functions from ideal lattices. In: Garay, J.A. (ed.) PKC 2021, Part II. LNCS, vol. 12711, pp. 261–289. Springer, Cham (2021). https://doi.org/10.1007/978-3-030-75248-4_10
2. Bartusek, J., Lepoint, T., Ma, F., Zhandry, M.: New Techniques for Obfuscating Conjunctions. In: Ishai, Y., Rijmen, V. (eds.) EUROCRYPT 2019, Part III. LNCS, vol. 11478, pp. 636 666. Springer, Cham (2019). https://doi.org/10.1007/978-3-030-17659-4_22
3. Beimel, A., Gabizon, A., Ishai, Y., Kushilevitz, E., Meldgaard, S., Paskin-Cherniavsky, A.: Non-Interactive Secure Multiparty Computation. In: Garay, J.A., Gennaro, R. (eds.) CRYPTO 2014, Part II. LNCS, vol. 8617, pp. 387–404. Springer, Heidelberg (2014). https://doi.org/10.1007/978-3-662-44381-1_22
4. Bellovin, S.M., Merritt, M.: Augmented encrypted key exchange: a password-based protocol secure against dictionary attacks and password file compromise. In: Denning, D.E., Pyle, R., Ganesan, R., Sandhu, R.S., Ashby, V. (eds.) ACM CCS 1993, pp. 244–250. ACM Press (1993)
5. Brakerski, Z., Rothblum, G.N.: Obfuscating conjunctions. In: Canetti, R., Garay, J.A. (eds.) CRYPTO 2013, Part II. LNCS, vol. 8043, pp. 416 434. Springer, Heidelberg (2013). https://doi.org/10.1007/978-3-642-40084-1_24
6. Brakerski, Z., Rothblum, G.N.: Virtual black-box obfuscation for all circuits via generic graded encoding. In: Lindell, Y. (ed.) TCC 2014. LNCS, vol. 8349, pp. 1–25. Springer, Heidelberg (2014). https://doi.org/10.1007/978-3-642-54242-8_1
7. Canetti, R.: Towards realizing random oracles: hash functions that hide all partial information. In: Kaliski, B.S. (ed.) CRYPTO 1997. LNCS, vol. 1294, pp. 455–469. Springer, Heidelberg (1997). https://doi.org/10.1007/BFb0052255
8. Canetti, R.: Universally composable security: a new paradigm for cryptographic protocols. In: 42nd FOCS, pp. 136–145. IEEE Computer Society Press (2001)
9. Canetti, R., Dakdouk, R.R.: Obfuscating point functions with multibit output. In: Smart, N. (ed.) EUROCRYPT 2008. LNCS, vol. 4965, pp. 489–508. Springer, Heidelberg (2008). https://doi.org/10.1007/978-3-540-78967-3_28
10. Canetti, R., Rothblum, G.N., Varia, M.: Obfuscation of hyperplane membership. In: Micciancio, D. (ed.) TCC 2010. LNCS, vol. 5978, pp. 72–89. Springer, Heidelberg (2010). https://doi.org/10.1007/978-3-642-11799-2_5
11. Freedman, M.J., Ishai, Y., Pinkas, B., Reingold, O.: Keyword search and oblivious pseudorandom functions. In: Kilian, J. (ed.) TCC 2005. LNCS, vol. 3378, pp. 303–324. Springer, Heidelberg (2005). https://doi.org/10.1007/978-3-540-30576-7_17
12. Gentry, C., MacKenzie, P., Ramzan, Z.: A method for making password-based key exchange resilient to server compromise. In: Dwork, C. (ed.) CRYPTO 2006. LNCS, vol. 4117, pp. 142–159. Springer, Heidelberg (2006). https://doi.org/10.1007/11818175_9

13. Gordon, S.D., Malkin, T., Rosulek, M., Wee, H.: Multi-party computation of polynomials and branching programs without simultaneous interaction. In: Johansson, T., Nguyen, P.Q. (eds.) EUROCRYPT 2013. LNCS, vol. 7881, pp. 575–591. Springer, Heidelberg (2013). https://doi.org/10.1007/978-3-642-38348-9_34

14. Halevi, S., Ishai, Y., Jain, A., Komargodski, I., Sahai, A., Yogev, E.: Non-Interactive Multiparty Computation Without Correlated Randomness. In: Takagi, T., Peyrin, T. (eds.) ASIACRYPT 2017, Part III. LNCS, vol. 10626, pp. 181–211. Springer, Cham (2017). https://doi.org/10.1007/978-3-319-70700-6_7

15. Halevi, S., Lindell, Y., Pinkas, B.: Secure computation on the web: computing without simultaneous interaction. In: Rogaway, P. (ed.) CRYPTO 2011. LNCS, vol. 6841, pp. 132–150. Springer, Heidelberg (2011). https://doi.org/10.1007/978-3-642-22792-9_8

16. Hesse, J.: Separating symmetric and asymmetric password-authenticated key exchange. In: Galdi, C., Kolesnikov, V. (eds.) SCN 2020. LNCS, vol. 12238, pp. 579–599. Springer, Cham (2020). https://doi.org/10.1007/978-3-030-57990-6_29

17. Jager, T., Schwenk, J.: On the equivalence of generic group models. In: Baek, J., Bao, F., Chen, K., Lai, X. (eds.) ProvSec 2008. LNCS, vol. 5324, pp. 200–209. Springer, Heidelberg (2008). https://doi.org/10.1007/978-3-540-88733-1_14

18. Jarecki, S., Kiayias, A., Krawczyk, H.: Round-optimal password-protected secret sharing and T-PAKE in the password-only model. In: Sarkar, P., Iwata, T. (eds.) ASIACRYPT 2014, Part II. LNCS, vol. 8874, pp. 233–253. Springer, Heidelberg (2014). https://doi.org/10.1007/978-3-662-45608-8_13

19. Jarecki, S., Krawczyk, H., Xu, J.: OPAQUE: an asymmetric PAKE protocol secure against pre-computation attacks. In: Nielsen, J.B., Rijmen, V. (eds.) EUROCRYPT 2018, Part III. LNCS, vol. 10822, pp. 456–486. Springer, Cham (2018). https://doi.org/10.1007/978-3-319-78372-7_15

20. Jarecki, S., Liu, X.: Efficient oblivious pseudorandom function with applications to adaptive OT and Secure Computation of Set Intersection. In: Reingold, O. (ed.) TCC 2009. LNCS, vol. 5444, pp. 577–594. Springer, Heidelberg (2009). https://doi.org/10.1007/978-3-642-00457-5_34

21. Lynn, B., Prabhakaran, M., Sahai, A.: Positive results and techniques for obfuscation. In: Cachin, C., Camenisch, J.L. (eds.) EUROCRYPT 2004. LNCS, vol. 3027, pp. 20–39. Springer, Heidelberg (2004). https://doi.org/10.1007/978-3-540-24676-3_2

22. Maurer, U.M.: Abstract models of computation in cryptography (invited paper). In: Smart, N.P. (ed.) Cryptography and Coding 2005. LNCS, vol. 3796, pp. 1–12. Springer, Heidelberg (2005). https://doi.org/10.1007/11586821_1

23. Shoup, V.: Lower bounds for discrete logarithms and related problems. In: Fumy, W. (ed.) EUROCRYPT 1997. LNCS, vol. 1233, pp. 256–266. Springer, Heidelberg (1997). https://doi.org/10.1007/3-540-69053-0_18

24. Thomas, K., et al.: Protecting accounts from credential stuffing with password breach alerting. In: 28th USENIX Security Symposium (USENIX Security 19), Santa Clara, CA, pp. 1556–1571. USENIX Association (2019)

25. Wee, H.: On obfuscating point functions. In: Gabow, H.N., Fagin, R. (eds.) 37th ACM STOC, pp. 523–532. ACM Press (2005)

Statistical Security in Two-Party Computation Revisited

Saikrishna Badrinarayanan[1], Sikhar Patranabis[2], and Pratik Sarkar[3(✉)]

[1] Snap, Seattle, USA
[2] IBM Research India, Bangalore, India
sikhar.patranabis@ibm.com
[3] Department of Computer Science, Boston University, Boston, USA
pratik93@bu.edu

Abstract. We present a new framework for building round-optimal one-sided statistically secure two party computation (2PC) protocols in the plain model. We demonstrate that a relatively weak notion of oblivious transfer (OT), namely a three round elementary oblivious transfer eOT with statistical receiver privacy, along with a non-interactive commitment scheme suffices to build a one-sided statistically secure two party computation protocol with black-box simulation. Our framework enables the first instantiations of round-optimal one-sided statistically secure 2PC protocols from the CDH assumption and certain families of isogeny-based assumptions.

As part of our compiler, we introduce the following new one-sided statistically secure primitives in the pre-processing model that might also be of independent interest:

1. Three round statistically sender private random-OT where only the last OT message depends on the receiver's choice bit and the sender receives random outputs generated by the protocol.
2. Four round delayed-input statistically sender private conditional disclosure of secrets where the first two rounds of the protocol are independent of the inputs of the parties.

The above primitives are directly constructed from eOT and hence we obtain their instantiations from the same set of assumptions as our 2PC.

1 Introduction

Secure two party computation (2PC) enables two mutually distrusting parties to compute a function on their private inputs without revealing anything

---

S. Badrinarayanan—Work done while the author was affiliated with Visa Research USA.

S. Patranabis—Most of the work was done while the author was affiliated with Visa Research USA.

P. Sarkar—Supported by NSF Awards 1931714, 1414119, and the DARPA SIEVE program.

E. Kiltz and V. Vaikuntanathan (Eds.): TCC 2022, LNCS 13748, pp. 181–210, 2022.
https://doi.org/10.1007/978-3-031-22365-5_7

beyond their output. An important question in the study of secure computation has been designing protocols in minimal rounds. The phenomenal work of Katz and Ostrovsky [KO04] showed that four rounds are necessary when one party receives the output and five rounds are necessary if both parties wish to receive output. Starting with [KO04], there has been a large body of work in designing round-optimal protocols in the plain model, secure against a probabilistic polynomial time (PPT) malicious adversary, in the two-party setting [ORS15, COSV17, CCG+21] and the multi-party setting with dishonest majority [GMPP16, BHP17, ACJ17, BGJ+18, HHPV18, CCG+20].

Statistical Security. A natural question to ask is can we obtain round optimal protocols when the parties are computationally unbounded? For the specific problem of zero knowledge proofs/arguments, this question has been well studied [GMW91, Nao91, GK96, BJY97, NOVY98, HNO+09]. In particular, assuming collision resistant hash functions: (i) Statistical zero knowledge arguments for NP, where soundness is computational and zero knowledge is statistical, are known in four rounds (round optimal) with black-box simulation [BJY97] and (ii) Computational zero knowledge proofs for NP, that satisfy statistical soundness and computational zero knowledge, are known in five rounds (round optimal) with black-box simulation [GK96]. There has also been work on building round-optimal (two rounds) statistically secure protocols for weaker functionalities like ZAPs and witness indistinguishable proofs/arguments [DN07, KKS18, BFJ+20, GJJM20].

Handling computationally unbounded adversaries for general two party functionalities is more challenging. For instance, Katz [Kat08] proved that it is impossible to obtain four round zero knowledge (ZK) proofs. This immediately rules out statistical security in four rounds for a two party secure computation protocol where only one party (denoted as the receiver) wishes to learn the output and the other party (denoted as the sender) is computationally unbounded. Therefore, the best possible security that one can hope for in four rounds is security against a computationally unbounded receiver and a PPT sender. This was termed as *one-sided statistical security* by Khurana and Mughees [KM20]. The works of [OPP14, CO17, KKS18] considered weaker notions such as one-sided statistical security with respect to super-polynomial time simulation. However, the question of obtaining one-sided statistically secure protocols with (standard) polynomial-time black-box simulation remained elusive for a long time. Only recently, this question was addressed by the work of [KM20]. They constructed round-optimal one-sided statistically secure two-party computation protocols with black-box simulation-based security against malicious adversaries:

- A four round statistically sender private (SSP) protocol where the receiver obtains the output at the end of fourth round,
- A five round statistically sender private protocol where the receiver obtains the output at the end of fourth round and the sender obtains the output at the end of fifth round.

The underlying building blocks in [KM20] are two-round statistically sender private OT ($\mathsf{SSP_{OT}}$) [BD18, NP01, HK12] and a non-interactive commitment

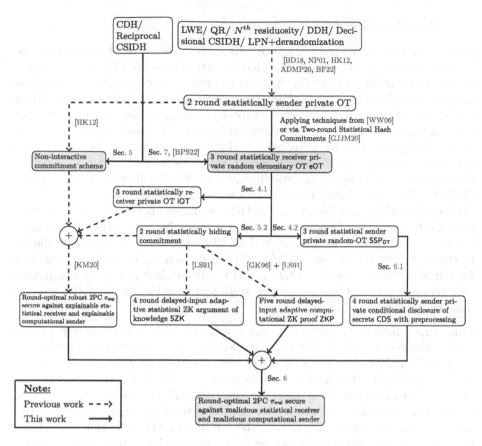

Fig. 1. Roadmap of our compiler

scheme. They instantiate the above protocol based on Learning with Errors (LWE), Decisional Diffie Hellman (DDH) or Quadratic Residuosity (QR). However, it was left as an open problem in their work to study the minimal assumptions required to obtain round-optimal 2PC protocols with one-sided statistical security, following similar investigations on assumptions versus round complexity in zero knowledge arguments/proofs with statistical security. For instance, it is unknown whether we can build round-optimal one-sided statistically secure 2PC protocols from other standard assumptions such as the Computational Diffie-Hellman (CDH) or the newer class of isogeny-based assumptions. In this work, we ask the following question:

Can we construct round-optimal one-sided statistically secure 2PC protocols with black-box simulation in the plain model from a wider class of assumptions?

1.1   Our Contributions

We answer the above question in the affirmative. We establish a general compiler to achieve round-optimal one-sided statistically secure 2PC protocols that
relies on potentially weaker (or "less structured") cryptographic primitives as
compared to those used by [KM20]. These primitives can be instantiated from
essentially *all* commonly used cryptographic assumptions, including new instantiations from the CDH assumption and certain isogeny-based assumptions such
as the Reciprocal CSIDH assumption (which were not known before and are
contributions of this work), as well as instantiations from LWE, LPN (+ derandomization techniques)[1], Quadratic Residuosity, N^{th} Residuosity, and decisional
CSIDH (all of which follow from existing works). In particular, the new instantiations from CDH and Reciprocal CSIDH are enabled precisely by the usage of
potentially weaker (or "less structured") cryptographic primitives in our framework as compared to those used by [KM20]. Our approach is conceptually similar
to that taken by the authors of [AMPS21] to weaken the underlying primitives
for round-optimal secure computation (MPC) protocols which are secure against
adaptive corruption of parties, but the techniques used by our compiler are fundamentally different.

Our Ingredients. We introduce the notion of statistically receiver private
(SRP) elementary OT in the plain model following the work of Dottling et
al. [DGH+20]. We denote it as eOT^2 throughout the paper. It is a three round
OT protocol, where the sender, with no input, sends the first message that can
be viewed as a pre-processing phase, the receiver sends the second message based
on its choice bit, and then, the sender computes random outputs (which can be
viewed as its two input messages in the traditional OT definition) and sends
the final OT message. Elementary security ensures that a maliciously corrupt
receiver is unable to compute both sender outputs. Statistical receiver privacy
implies that the choice bit is statistically hidden from a maliciously corrupt
sender, with unbounded computational power. We show that such an OT protocol combined with a non-interactive commitment scheme suffices for one-sided
statistical security. This yields a four-round 2PC protocol where the receiver
obtains the output at the end of the fourth round, and a five-round protocol
where both parties obtain the output. Our contributions are summarized in
Theorem 1 and has been depicted in Fig. 1.

Theorem 1 (Informal). *Assuming a non-interactive commitment scheme and
a three round statistically-receiver private elementary OT, denoted as eOT, there
exists:*

---

[1] Throughout this paper, when we refer to the LPN assumption, we refer to the
"extremely low-noise" variant of LPN with noise parameters in the $O\left((\log n)^2 / n\right)$
regime, as used in many recent works, including [BF22].

[2] We consider that our eOT protocol provides statistical receiver privacy, as opposed to
the elementary OT protocol defined in [DGH+20] which only provides computational
receiver privacy.

- A four-round 2PC protocol where the receiver obtains the output at the end of the protocol,
- A five-round 2PC protocol where both parties obtain the output.

Both our protocols achieve statistical security against a malicious receiver and computational security against a malicious sender in the plain model[3] and require black-box simulation.

We demonstrate that a two-round SSP_{OT} implies eOT and a non-interactive commitment scheme, hence re-obtaining the results of [KM20] through our compiler. Instantiating the SSP_{OT} from LPN+Nissan Wigderson style derandomization [BF22] and isogeny-based assumption, like decisional CSIDH [ADMP20], we obtain new instantiations of our compiler. In addition, we also build eOT and non-interactive commitments from CDH and other isogeny based assumptions like reciprocal[4] CSIDH [LGdSG21]. This gives us one-sided statistical 2PC from CDH and reciprocal CSIDH which was not known before. Combining the above results, we obtain one-sided statistical 2PC from most well-studied assumptions in cryptography.

Theorem 2 (Informal). *Assuming CDH, LWE, LPN (+derandomization techniques), QR, N^{th} Residuosity, or isogeny-based assumptions (decisional CSIDH or Reciprocal CSIDH), there exists:*

- A four-round 2PC protocol where the receiver obtains the output at the end of the protocol,
- A five-round 2PC protocol where both parties obtain the output.

Both our protocols achieve statistical security against a malicious receiver and computational security against a malicious sender in the plain model and require black-box simulation.

As part of our building blocks, we introduce the notion of statistically sender private conditional disclosure of secrets CDS in the preprocessing model and demonstrate that eOT (and information theoretic garbling for NC1 circuits) suffices for its construction. This is a weakening of two-round statistically sender private conditional disclosure of secrets which is built from two-round SSP_{OT}. Our primitive could be of independent interest, especially in constructing one-sided statistically secure MPC protocols from different assumptions. Formally,

Theorem 3. *Assuming a three round statistically-receiver private elementary OT, there exists a four-round statistically sender private conditional disclosure of secrets CDS for NC1 circuits in the pre-processing model, where the first two rounds of CDS are input-independent.*

---

[3] For the five round protocol, receiver is the party that obtains output first (at the end of round four) and sender is the party that obtains output at the end of round five.

[4] Reciprocal CSIDH is quantum equivalent to computational CSIDH, which is weaker than decisional CSIDH. However, reciprocal CSIDH and decisional CSIDH assumptions are incomparable in the classical setting.

Instantiating eOT from the above assumptions, we obtain the CDS from most well-studied assumptions as follows.

Theorem 4. *Assuming CDH, LWE, LPN (+derandomization techniques), QR, N^{th} Residuosity, or isogeny-based assumptions (decisional CSIDH or Reciprocal CSIDH), there exists a four-round statistically sender private conditional disclosure of secrets CDS for NC1 circuits in the pre-processing model, where the first two rounds of CDS are input-independent.*

The information theoretic garbling [Kol05] for NC1 circuits is used to construct the above CDS for NC1 circuits. The above CDS for NC1 circuits suffice for one-sided statistical 2PC for all circuits.

Roadmap. We provide a detailed overview of our protocols in Sect. 2. Then we define our building blocks in Sect. 3. We define other OT protocols in Sect. 4 and construct them from eOT. These OTs protocol would be instrumental in our final compiler. We construct our round optimal one-sided statistically secure 2PC protocol π_{exp} against explainable parties in Sect. 5. Finally, we compile π_{exp} to obtain a round optimal one-sided statistically secure 2PC protocol π_{mal} which is secure against malicious corruptions in Sect. 6. In the same section we construct statistically sender private CDS in preprocessing model. Finally, we provide instantiations of eOT from different assumptions in Sect. 7.

2   Technical Overview

In this section we demonstrate that a three round statistically receiver private elementary OT, denoted as eOT, and a non-interactive commitment scheme suffices to obtain a five round (which is round optimal) 2PC protocol that obtains security against a computationally unbounded receiver and a PPT sender. Then we instantiate eOT and the commitment scheme from various assumptions. Along the way, we introduce new primitives of independent interest - statistical conditional disclosure of secrets CDS in the preprocessing model and a three round random SSP-OT, and instantiate them from various assumptions.

2.1   One-Sided Statistical Two-Party Computation Protocol

Our compiler builds upon the compiler of [KM20] by weakening the underlying primitives in their compiler. We recall their protocol for completeness. [KM20] constructed a five round 2PC protocol against malicious adversaries. The first party, denoted as the receiver, is computationally unbounded and obtains the output at the end of fourth round. The second party, called the sender, is computationally bounded and obtains the output at the end of fifth round. The protocol proceeds through two transformations- where [KM20] first constructs a protocol which is secure against explainable adversaries and then compiles it (interactive proofs) to obtain security against malicious adversaries.

Robust 2PC Secure Against Explainable Adversaries. As the first step, [KM20] considered explainable adversaries[5] which generates protocol messages in the support of the distribution of all honestly generated transcripts, and the simulator needs to extract the input and randomness of the adversarial party from the transcript. In this setting, the classical garbled circuit based approach of [Yao86], where the receiver is the evaluator and sender is the garbler, fails since the receiver is computationally unbounded and information theoretically private garbling scheme is known only for NC1 circuits.

Reversing the Roles. [KM20] takes a different approach where the receiver garbles the circuit and sender evaluates it. The sender obtains the wire labels corresponding to its input through a statistical receiver private OT, hence hiding its input against an unbounded corrupt receiver. The OT protocol takes three rounds, starting from the receiver (acting as the sender of the OT), and the garbled circuit is sent in the third round by the receiver.

Simulating against Explainable Parties. The simulator needs to simulate against explainable adversaries by extracting their inputs. To enable extraction of the corrupt sender's input the sender is also required to commit to its input using a four round statistically hiding and computationally binding extractable commitment scheme. Similarly, the receiver commits to its input and randomness using a three round statistically binding and computationally hiding extractable commitment scheme. These commitments allow a simulator to extract the input and randomness of the explainable adversarial parties. The simulator against a corrupt sender's extracts the sender's input at the end of fourth round from the commitment scheme and obtains the correct output only at the end of fourth round. However, the receiver is required to send the garbled circuit in the third round. This creates a problem in simulation since a corrupt sender, evaluating the garbled circuit, distinguishes an interaction with an honest receiver from an interaction with the simulated receiver based on the garbled circuit output.

One Last Modification. To avoid this, the receiver garbles a different circuit so that the garbled circuit computes an encryption of the output. The sender obtains the garbled circuit at the end of third round, evaluates it to obtain the encrypted output and then sends it to the receiver in the fourth round. The receiver decrypts the output and sends it to the sender in the fifth round. In the ideal world the simulator sends a simulated garbled circuit which outputs an encryption of 0 to the corrupt sender, hence providing correct simulation in the ideal world. [KM20] also ensured that the first two rounds of the protocol are robust - i.e. if the parties behave maliciously in the first 2 rounds of the protocol then they can influence the protocol output but they would fail to infer any

---

[5] It is different from the notion of semi-malicious security [MW16] where the adversary in addition to generating the the protocol messages in the support of the distribution of all honestly generated transcripts, also outputs the input and randomness that was used, on a special tape.

information about the honest party's input. The robustness property is crucial when we upgrade to security against malicious adversaries.

Summary. To summarize the result of [KM20] they obtain a robust 5-round secure two-party computation protocol π_{exp} with black-box simulation against unbounded explainable receivers and PPT explainable senders, where the receiver obtains its output at the end of fourth round and the sender obtains its output at the end of the fifth round. Their underlying primitives are as follows:

1. Three round oblivious transfer with statistical privacy for a receiver and computational privacy for a sender,
2. Three round statistically binding and computationally hiding commitment scheme satisfying extractability.
3. Four round statistically hiding and computationally binding commitment scheme satisfying extractability.
4. Information theoretic garbled circuits for NC1 circuits (used by [KM20] to validate a specific NC1 relation as part of their statistically secure two-round CDS protocol – we expand more on this subsequently).

Overview of Our Contributions. We demonstrate that an elementary OT protocol (denoted simply as eOT in rest of the paper) and a non-interactive commitment scheme suffices to instantiate the above primitives and hence yield the protocol π_{exp} from eOT and a non-interactive commitment scheme.

1. The three round SRP-OT protocol, denoted as iOT, that satisfies indistinguishability based sender security is built from eOT in Sect. 4.1 in a round preserving manner. We discuss it in Sect. 2.2.
2. The three round statistically binding and computationally hiding commitment scheme can be constructed [PRS02] from any non-interactive commitment scheme.
3. The four round statistically hiding and computationally binding commitment scheme satisfying extractability can be obtained [KM20] by replacing the non-interactive commitment scheme in [PRS02] with a two round statistically hiding commitment scheme. We build the two round statistically hiding commitment scheme from SRP iOT in Sect. 5.2 and we briefly discus about it in Sect. 2.2.
4. Garbled circuits can be obtained [Yao86, LP07] from one way functions.

The Final Compiler. Next, the security of π_{exp} is uplifted such that it is secure against malicious adversaries using zero knowledge protocols as follows.

Tackling a Malicious Sender. The sender is required to prove that it generated the second and fourth round messages of π_{exp} correctly. This is performed using a four round delayed-input statistical zero knowledge protocol SZK where the input statement is chosen by the sender (behaving as the prover) in the last round of SZK. SZK is run in parallel to π_{exp} and the robustness of the first two rounds of π_{exp} ensures that the input of an honest receiver is not leaked even if a corrupt sender constructs the second round message of π_{exp} maliciously. We also require SZK to be an argument of knowledge for reasons, discussed later. SZK can be built [LS91] from two round statistically hiding commitment scheme.

Tackling a Malicious Receiver. Similar to the sender, the receiver is required to prove that it generated the first, third and fifth round messages of π_{exp} correctly. This is performed using a five round delayed-input zero knowledge proof ZKP where the input statement is chosen by the receiver (behaving as the prover) in the last round of ZKP. ZKP is run in parallel to π_{exp} and the robustness of the first two rounds of π_{exp} ensures that the input of an honest sender is not leaked even if a corrupt receiver constructs the first round message of π_{exp} maliciously. ZKP can be built [LS91]+ [GK96] from two round statistically hiding commitment scheme. However, a maliciously constructed third round message of π_{exp} could leak an honest sender's input when the sender sends the fourth round message of π_{exp}. ZKP fails to address this issue since it takes five rounds to complete and an honest sender could detect the malicious behavior of a corrupt receiver only at the end of the fifth round. This leaks the honest sender's inputs.

Conditional Disclosure of Secrets. [KM20] addresses the above situation by using a two round conditional disclosure of secrets CDS where the receiver sends the public key for the CDS alongwith the third round message of π_{exp}. The sender encrypts the fourth round message of π_{exp} under the CDS public key and input statement - the first and third round message of π_{exp} is constructed in an explainable manner by the receiver. The receiver successfully decrypts the fourth round message of π_{exp} if it produces a witness attesting to the fact that the first and third round message of π_{exp} is explainable. If the receiver fails to produce such a witness, then the CDS plaintext (fourth round message of π_{exp}) remains statistically hidden. The CDS protocol requires soundness against a statistical receiver and witness privacy against a semi-honest computationally bounded sender. In the final protocol, the sender is required to prove in the fourth round that it constructed the CDS sender message correctly using SZK since the CDS provides security guarantees against a semi-honest sender. We require the SZK to be argument of knowledge so that the simulator (against a corrupt sender) is able to extract the encrypted CDS plaintext, which is the fourth round message of π_{exp}, in order to generate the final message of the protocol.

Note that [KM20] constructs an NC1 circuit which checks the validity of receiver's witness. The authors of [KM20] then proceed to construct a (two-round) CDS protocol with statistical security for the class of relations that are verifiable by NC1 circuits by combining two round statistically sender private OT with information-theoretic garbled circuits for NC1. In fact, it can be shown (via dashed lines in Fig. 1) that two-round statistically sender private OT suffices to instantiate the 2PC protocol of [KM20]. However, two-round statistically sender private OT is a relatively strong primitive and is not known from many well-studied assumptions, like CDH.

Our Proposal. We shift our starting point to presumably weaker primitives - a three round SRP eOT protocol where only the second OT message depends on the receiver's input and the sender's outputs are random. We show that eOT suffices for compiling π_{exp} to our final protocol π_{mal} which provides statistical security against a malicious receiver and computational security against a malicious sender as follows:

1. By applying round-preserving transformations on eOT we obtain a three round delayed-input statistical sender private OT protocol SSP_{OT} - where only the last OT message depends on the receiver's input and the sender's outputs are random. Combining SSP_{OT} with information theoretic garbling for NC1 we obtain a four round statistical CDS protocol where the first two rounds, aka preprocessing phase, are independent of the input statement and the witness. This new primitive suffices for conditional disclosure of secrets in the above 2PC protocol since the first two rounds can be used for the preprocessing phase of the SSP_{OT} and the last two rounds can be used to run the input-dependent phase of CDS.
2. The four round delayed-input statistical zero knowledge SZK can be built [LS91] from two round statistically hiding commitment.
3. The five round delayed-input zero knowledge proof ZKP can be obtained [LS91]+ [GK96] from two round statistically hiding commitment.
4. The first two rounds of iOT implies a two round statistically hiding commitment scheme.

Previously, we have shown that π_{exp} can be obtained from a non-interactive commitment scheme and eOT. Combining the two results, we obtain our one-sided 2PC protocol from a non-interactive commitment scheme and eOT.

Instantiations. We demonstrate that a two-round statistical sender private OT implements eOT (by applying OT reversal techniques [WW06]) and the first message of the two-round statistical sender private OT is a non-interactive commitment scheme. Hence, our result generalizes the work of [KM20] and we obtain instantiations from LWE, QR, N^{th} residuosity, DDH, Decisional CSIDH and LPN+Nissan Wigderson derandomization by instantiating [BD18, NP01, HK12, HK12, ADMP20, BF22] the underlying two-round statistical sender private OT from the above assumptions. Furthermore, we build eOT and the non-interactive commitment scheme from CDH and reciprocal CSIDH [LGdSG21] assumptions. This was not previously known from [KM20]. To summarize, our proposed framework enables one-sided statistical 2PC from essentially all well-studied cryptographic assumptions.

2.2   Constructing Our Ingredients from eOT

Next, we briefly introduce our ingredient primitives and discuss their constructions. A roadmap explaining our framework based on these ingredients can be found in Fig. 1.

Three Round Statistically Receiver Private eOT. We introduce the notion of statistically receiver private elementary OT in plain model following the work of [DGH+20]. It is a three round OT protocol where the sender sends the first message as a preprocessing phase, the receiver sends the second message based on its choice bit, and the sender sends the third message. The sender obtains random outputs. The elementary security ensures that a maliciously corrupt receiver is unable to compute both sender outputs. Statistical receiver privacy implies that the choice bit is statistically hidden from a maliciously corrupt sender. We show that a two round statistically sender private OT can be used to build eOT through OT reversal techniques [WW06], hence obtaining instantiations from a wide variety of assumptions (namely LWE, QR, N^{th} residuosity, DDH, Decisional CSIDH and LPN+Nissan Wigderson derandomization). We also construct eOT from CDH by building upon the two-round CDH based protocol of [DGH+20] in the crs model. In the CDH-based eOT instantiation, the sender sends the crs of the CDH based protocol of [DGH+20] as the OT first message and then their two-round CDH based protocol is run between the parties using the first message as the crs. We also provide the first construction of eOT based on reciprocal CSIDH assumption.[6]

Three Round Statistically Receiver Private iOT. We uplift the security of eOT to construct iOT such that it obtains indistinguishability based security against a malicious receiver. If the receiver's choice bit is γ then $m_{1-\gamma}$ is computationally indistinguishable from a random string to a malicious receiver. We perform this in a round-preserving way by applying the elementary OT (via search OT) to indistinguishability-based security OT transformations from [DGH+20] based on Goldreich-Levin hash function. This yields iOT from the same set of assumptions as eOT.

Three Round Delayed-Input Statistically Sender Private SSP_{OT}. Next, we introduce the notion of delayed-input statistically sender private SSP_{OT}, where only the last OT message depends on the receiver's choice bit γ. It is a three round OT protocol where the receiver sends the first message as a receiver preprocessing phase, the sender sends the second message as a sender preprocessing phase, and the receiver sends the third message based on γ. The sender obtains random output strings. We carefully apply OT reversal techniques on three-round SRP iOT in a round-preserving way to obtain a version of SSP_{OT} where the sender obtains random output bits. Then we combine multiple such bit SSP_{OT} protocol with a randomness extractor to obtain the final SSP_{OT} protocol. This yields SSP_{OT} from the same set of assumptions as iOT (and eOT).

Statistically Sender Private CDS with Preprocessing. We introduce the notion of conditional disclosure of secrets CDS in the preprocessing phase. The first two rounds of CDS are input-independent. The receiver sends the third message which depends on the statement-witness pair. The sender encrypts the plaintext under the statement and sends the ciphertext as the fourth message.

For our 2PC protocol, we require security against a maliciously corrupted statistical receiver and a computationally bounded semi-honest sender. We con-

---

[6] Reciprocal CSIDH assumption is quantum equivalent to computational CSIDH and it is incomparable to decisional CSIDH.

struct an NC1 circuit which checks the validity of receiver's witness by relying on the result of [KM20]. Then we proceed to combine our three round delayed-input $\mathsf{SSP_{OT}}$ protocol with information theoretic garbling scheme [Kol05] for NC1 circuit to construct our CDS, where the first two rounds of CDS are the preprocessing phases of $\mathsf{SSP_{OT}}$. In the third round of the CDS the receiver inputs the witness bits as the choice bit of the $\mathsf{SSP_{OT}}$ protocol. Upon obtaining the $\mathsf{SSP_{OT}}$ third round messages, the semi-honest sender garbles an NC1 circuit outputs the plaintext if verification of the receiver's witness succeeds corresponding to the input statement. The sender sends a mapping between the random outputs of $\mathsf{SSP_{OT}}$ to the wire labels corresponding to the witness bits. The receiver decrypts the wire labels corresponding to the witness bits and evaluates the garbled circuit to obtain the plaintext. This yields our CDS protocol from $\mathsf{SSP_{OT}}$ and one way functions, obtaining the CDS protocol from the same set of assumptions as eOT.

Two Round Statistically Hiding Commitment. We show that the first two rounds of eOT is a two round statistically hiding commitment where the verifier (acting as the eOT sender) sends the first message as the setup phase. The committer (acting as the eOT receiver) commits to bit γ using the OT second message. Statistical receiver privacy of eOT ensures that statistical hiding of γ. If a corrupt committer breaks binding of the commitment scheme with two valid decommitments corresponding to bits 0 and 1, then those decommitments can be used to break computational sender privacy of eOT by recovering both sender messages of eOT. This yields two round statistically hiding commitments from the same set of assumptions as eOT.

3   Preliminaries

We present our notations and discuss the building blocks in this section.

3.1   Notations

We denote by $a \leftarrow D$ a uniform sampling of an element a from a distribution D. The set of elements $\{1, \ldots, n\}$ is represented by $[n]$. We denote the computational security parameter by κ and statistical security parameter by μ respectively. Let $\mathbb{Z}_q$ denote the field of order q, where $q = \frac{p-1}{2}$ and p are primes. Let G be the multiplicative group corresponding to $\mathbb{Z}_p^*$ with generator g, where CDH assumption holds. We denote a field of size $\mathcal{O}(2^\mu)$ as $\mathbb{F}$. For a bit $b \in \{0,1\}$, we denote $1 - b$ by $\bar{b}$. In our paper we consider one-sided statistical 2PC protocol against explainable parties and also against malicious corruption of parties. We refer to the paper of [KM20] for the one-sided statistical security model against explainable parties and against malicious adversaries for the sake of completeness.

3.2   Oblivious Transfer Protocols

We define our OT notions - eOT, iOT and $\mathsf{SSP_{OT}}$, as follows.

Elementary OT with Statistical Receiver Privacy (eOT). We denote a three round OT protocol, where sender sends the first message and the sender receives random outputs, by a tuple of four algorithms defined as follows:

- $OT^{(1)}_{S\to R}(1^\kappa)$: The sender computes ot_1 as the OT sender message and sends it to the receiver.
- $OT^{(2)}_{R\to S}(1^\kappa, \gamma, ot_1)$: The receiver computes the OT receiver message ot_2 and internal state st_R based on choice bit γ and ot_1. The receiver sends ot_2 to the sender.
- $OT^{(3)}_{S\to R}(1^\kappa, ot_2)$: The sender computes (ot_3, m_0, m_1). The sender sends ot_3 as the OT sender message and outputs $(m_0, m_1) \in \{0,1\}$.
- $OT_R(st_R, ot_3)$: The receiver computes m' and outputs it.

Correctness. The above three-round OT protocol is said to be correct if for any security parameter $\kappa \in \mathbb{N}$ and any bit $\gamma \in \{0,1\}$, letting

$$ot_1 \leftarrow OT^{(1)}_{S\to R}(1^\kappa), \quad (ot_2, st_R) \leftarrow OT^{(2)}_{R\to S}(1^\kappa, \gamma, ot_1),$$

$$(ot_3, m_0, m_1) \leftarrow OT^{(3)}_{S\to R}(1^\kappa, ot_2), \quad m' \leftarrow OT_R(st_R, ot_3),$$

we have $m' = m_\gamma$ with overwhelming probability.

Statistical Receiver Privacy. The above OT protocol satisfies statistical receiver privacy if the two tuples are statistically close.

$$\{OT^{(2)}_{R\to S}(1^\kappa, 0, ot_1), ot_1\} \overset{s}{\approx} \{OT^{(2)}_{R\to S}(1^\kappa, 1, ot_1), ot_1\},$$

where $ot_1 \leftarrow \mathcal{A}(1^\kappa)$ is generated by an adversary $\mathcal{A}$ who maliciously corrupts the sender.

Elementary Sender Security. The work of [DGH+20] introduced the notion of elementary sender security in the crs model. It is the weakest security notion against a malicious receiver. We extend their notion to the plain model. Let $\mathcal{A} = (\mathcal{A}_1, \mathcal{A}_2)$ denote a non-uniform adversary who maliciously corrupts the receiver. To break elementary security the adversary is required to output both strings m_0 and m_1. This is formalized by the following experiment. $\underline{\mathsf{Exp}^\kappa_{eOT}(\mathcal{A})}$:

1. Run $ot_1 \leftarrow OT^{(1)}_{S\to R}(1^\kappa)$.
2. Obtain $(ot_2, st_{\mathcal{A}}) \leftarrow \mathcal{A}_1(1^\kappa, ot_1)$.
3. Run $(ot_3, m_0, m_1) \leftarrow OT^{(3)}_{S\to R}(1^\kappa, ot_2)$.
4. Obtain $(m_0^*, m_1^*) \leftarrow \mathcal{A}_2(st_{\mathcal{A}}, ot_3)$ and output 1 iff $(m_0^*, m_1^*) == (m_0, m_1)$.

We say that the OT protocol satisfies elementary sender security if $\Pr[\mathsf{Exp}^\kappa_{eOT}(\mathcal{A}) = 1] = \mathsf{neg}(\kappa)$.

Definition 1. *We denote a three-round OT protocol with the above algorithms as eOT if it satisfies sender elementary security and statistical receiver privacy.*

Indistinguishability OT with Statistical Receiver Privacy (iOT). We denote a three round OT protocol, where sender sends the first message and the parties have chosen inputs, by a tuple of four algorithms defined as follows:

- $OT_{S\to R}^{(1)}(1^\kappa)$: The sender computes ot_1 as the OT sender message and sends it to the receiver.
- $OT_{R\to S}^{(2)}(1^\kappa, \gamma, ot_1)$: The receiver computes the OT receiver message ot_2 and internal state st_R based on choice bit γ and ot_1. The receiver sends ot_2 to the sender.
- $OT_{S\to R}^{(3)}(1^\kappa, (m_0, m_1), ot_2)$: The sender computes ot_3 based on ot_2 and its inputs $(m_0, m_1) \in \{0, 1\}$. The sender sends ot_3 as the OT sender message.
- $OT_R(st_R, ot_3)$: The receiver computes m' and outputs it.

Correctness. The above three-round OT protocol is said to be correct if for any security parameter $\kappa \in \mathbb{N}$ and any bit $\gamma \in \{0, 1\}$, letting

$$ot_1 \leftarrow OT_{S\to R}^{(1)}(1^\kappa), \quad (ot_2, st_R) \leftarrow OT_{R\to S}^{(2)}(1^\kappa, \gamma, ot_1),$$

$$ot_3 \leftarrow OT_{S\to R}^{(3)}(1^\kappa, (m_0, m_1), ot_2), \quad m' \leftarrow OT_R(st_R, ot_3),$$

we have $m' = m_\gamma$ with overwhelming probability.

Statistical Receiver Privacy. The above OT protocol satisfies statistical receiver privacy if the two tuples are statistically close.

$$\{OT_{R\to S}^{(2)}(1^\kappa, 0, ot_1), ot_1\} \overset{s}{\approx} \{OT_{R\to S}^{(2)}(1^\kappa, 1, ot_1), ot_1\},$$

where $ot_1 \leftarrow \mathcal{A}(1^\kappa)$ is generated by an adversary $\mathcal{A}$ who maliciously corrupts the sender.

Indistinguishability-Based Sender Security. Sender's indistinguishability security was defined in [DGH+20] in the crs model. We extend it to the plain model via an experiment $\mathsf{Exp}_{iOT}^{crs, r, w, b}(\mathcal{A})$ between a non-uniform PPT adversary $\mathcal{A} = (\mathcal{A}_1, \mathcal{A}_2)$ and a challenger, where the experiment is parameterized by random coins $r \in \{0, 1\}^\kappa$, a bit $w \in \{0, 1\}$, and a bit $b \in \{0, 1\}$:

$\underline{\mathsf{Exp}_{iOT}^{w, b}(\mathcal{A}):}$

1. Run $ot_1 \leftarrow OT_{S\to R}^{(1)}(1^\kappa)$.
2. Run $(m_0, m_1, ot_2, st_\mathcal{A}) \leftarrow \mathcal{A}_1(1^\kappa, ot_1; r)$.
3. If $b = 0$, compute $ot_3 \leftarrow OT_{S\to R}^{(3)}(1^\kappa, (m_0, m_1), ot_2)$.
4. If $b = 1$, compute $ot_3 \leftarrow OT_{S\to R}^{(3)}(1^\kappa, (m_0', m_1'), ot_2)$ where $m_w' \leftarrow \{0, 1\}$ and $m_{1-w}' := m_{1-w}$.
5. Output $s \leftarrow \mathcal{A}_2(st_\mathcal{A}, ot_3)$.

We say that iOT satisfies sender's indistinguishability security if for any PPT adversary $\mathcal{A}$, the following holds where the probability is taken over $r \leftarrow \{0, 1\}^\kappa$.

$$|\Pr[\mathsf{Exp}_{iOT}^{crs, r, w, 0}(\mathcal{A}) = 1] - \Pr[\mathsf{Exp}_{iOT}^{crs, r, w, 1}(\mathcal{A}) = 1]| \leq \mathsf{neg}(\kappa).$$

Definition 2. *We denote a three-round OT protocol with the above algorithms as iOT if it satisfies indistinguishability-based sender security and statistical receiver privacy.*

Statistically Sender Private Random OT ($\mathsf{SSP_{OT}}$). We denote a three-round OT protocol, where the receiver sends the first message and the sender obtains random outputs, by a tuple of four algorithms defined as follows:

- $\mathsf{OT}^{(1)}_{R \to S}(1^\kappa)$: The receiver computes ot_1 as the OT receiver message and $\mathsf{st_R}$ as the internal state. The receiver sends ot_1 to the sender and stores $\mathsf{st_R}$ as the internal receiver state.
- $\mathsf{OT}^{(2)}_{S \to R}(1^\kappa, \mathsf{ot}_1)$: Given the OT message ot_1, the sender outputs a message ot_2 and secret internal state $\mathsf{st_S}$.
- $\mathsf{OT}^{(3)}_{R \to S}(\mathsf{st_R}, \gamma, \mathsf{ot}_2)$: Given a secret state $\mathsf{st_R}$, choice bit γ and a message ot_2, the receiver computes $\mathsf{m}' \in \{0,1\}^\ell$ and the OT message ot_3. The receiver sends ot_3 to the sender and outputs m'.
- $\mathsf{OT_S}(\mathsf{st_S}, \mathsf{ot}_3)$: Given the secret state $\mathsf{st_S}$ and a message ot_3, it outputs two string-messages $(\mathsf{m}_0, \mathsf{m}_1) \in \{0,1\}^\ell$.

Remark. Note that the receiver's choice bit γ is not included in the first algorithm $\mathsf{OT}^{(1)}_{R \to S}$ and is only used in the algorithm $\mathsf{OT}^{(3)}_{R \to S}$ thereby allowing the protocol to enjoy a "delayed-input" feature.

Correctness. The above protocol is said to be correct if for any $\kappa \in \mathbb{N}$ and any bit $\gamma \in \{0,1\}$, letting

$$(\mathsf{ot}_1, \mathsf{st_R}) \leftarrow \mathsf{OT}^{(1)}_{R \to S}(1^\kappa), \quad (\mathsf{ot}_2, \mathsf{st_S}) \leftarrow \mathsf{OT}^{(2)}_{S \to R}(1^\kappa, \mathsf{ot}_1),$$
$$(\mathsf{ot}_3, \mathsf{m}') \leftarrow \mathsf{OT}^{(3)}_{R \to S}(\mathsf{st_R}, \gamma, \mathsf{ot}_2), \quad (\mathsf{m}_0, \mathsf{m}_1) \leftarrow \mathsf{OT_S}(\mathsf{st_S}, \mathsf{ot}_3),$$

we have $\mathsf{m}' = \mathsf{m}_\gamma$ with overwhelming probability.

Computational Receiver Privacy. The above protocol satisfies computational receiver privacy if for any $\kappa \in \mathbb{N}$, any $b \in \{0,1\}$, and any non-uniform PPT adversary $\mathcal{A} = (\mathcal{A}_1, \mathcal{A}_2)$, letting $\beta = \mathsf{Exp}^{\kappa,b}(\mathcal{A})$, we have

$$|\Pr[\beta = 0] - \Pr[\beta = 1]| \leq \mathsf{negl}(\kappa),$$

where the experiment $\mathsf{Exp}^{\kappa,b}(\mathcal{A})$ is defined as follows:
   $\mathsf{Exp}^{\kappa,b}(\mathcal{A})$:

1. $(\mathsf{ot}_1, \mathsf{st_R}) \leftarrow \mathsf{OT}^{(1)}_{R \to S}(1^\kappa)$.
2. $(\mathsf{ot}_2, \mathsf{st}) \leftarrow \mathcal{A}_1(1^\kappa, \mathsf{ot}_1)$.
3. $(\mathsf{ot}_3, \mathsf{m}') \leftarrow \mathsf{OT}^{(3)}_{R \to S}(\mathsf{st_R}, b, \mathsf{ot}_2)$.
4. $b' \leftarrow \mathcal{A}_2(\mathsf{ot}_3, \mathsf{st})$.
5. If $b = b'$, output 0. Else, output 1.

Statistical Sender Privacy. Consider an execution of the above three round protocol involving an honest sender and an (unbounded, non-uniform) malicious adversary $\mathcal{A} = (\mathcal{A}_1, \mathcal{A}_2)$:

$$(\mathsf{ot}_1, \mathsf{st}_\mathsf{R}) \leftarrow \mathcal{A}_1(1^\kappa), \quad (\mathsf{ot}_2, \mathsf{st}_\mathsf{S}) \leftarrow \mathsf{OT}^{(2)}_{\mathsf{S} \to \mathsf{R}}(1^\kappa, \mathsf{ot}_1),$$

$$(\mathsf{ot}_3, \mathsf{st}) \leftarrow \mathcal{A}_2(\mathsf{st}_\mathsf{R}, \gamma, \mathsf{ot}_2), \quad (\mathsf{m}_0, \mathsf{m}_1) \leftarrow \mathsf{OT}_\mathsf{S}(\mathsf{st}_\mathsf{S}, \mathsf{ot}_3).$$

Let $\mathsf{View}^\kappa(\mathcal{A})$ denote the view of the adversary $\mathcal{A} = (\mathcal{A}_1, \mathcal{A}_2)$ in the above protocol execution. A three-round SSP-string-sROT protocol is said to satisfy statistical sender privacy if for any $\kappa \in \mathbb{N}$ and any (unbounded, non-uniform) adversary $\mathcal{A} = (\mathcal{A}_1, \mathcal{A}_2)$, there exists a bit $\beta \in \{0, 1\}$ such that the following two distributions are statistically indistinguishable:

$$(\mathsf{View}^\kappa(\mathcal{A}), \mathsf{m}_\beta) \stackrel{s}{\approx} (\mathsf{View}^\kappa(\mathcal{A}), \mathsf{U}),$$

where $\mathsf{U} \leftarrow \{0, 1\}^{|\mathsf{m}_\beta|}$ denotes a random bit string of size $|\mathsf{m}_\beta|$.

Definition 3. *We denote a three-round OT protocol with the above algorithms as* SSP_{OT} *if it satisfies statistical sender privacy and computational receiver privacy.*

3.3 Additional Preliminaries

In this section, we briefly describe some cryptographic primitives that we use for our constructions.

Garbling Schemes. A garbling scheme [Yao86,LP09,BHR12] consists of the following algorithms: Gb takes a circuit $\mathcal{C}$ as input and outputs a garbled circuit GC, encoding information Keys, and decoding information d. En takes an input x and encoding information Keys and outputs a garbled input X. Ev takes a garbled circuit and garbled input X and outputs a garbled output Y. Finally, De takes a garbled output Y and decoding information and outputs a plain circuit-output (or an error, $\perp$). There is an additional verification algorithm Ve in the garbling scheme which when accepts a given (GC, Keys, d) signifies that the GC is correct, and that the garbled output corresponding to any clear output can be extracted. The garbling scheme used in our protocols need to satisfy several properties such as *correctness, privacy, verifiability and reconstructability*. We refer to the full version of our paper [BPS22] for formal definitions.

We are interested in a class of garbling schemes referred to as *projective* in [BHR12]. When garbling a circuit $\mathcal{C} : \{0, 1\}^n \mapsto \{0, 1\}^m$, a projective garbling scheme produces encoding information of the form $\mathsf{Keys} = \left(\mathsf{Keys}_i^0, \mathsf{Keys}_i^1\right)_{i \in [n]}$, and the encoded input X corresponding to $x = (x_i)_{i \in [n]}$ can be interpreted as $\mathsf{X} = \mathsf{En}(x, \mathsf{Keys}) = \left(\mathsf{Keys}_i^{x_i}\right)_{i \in [n]}$. Information-theoretic Garbled circuits for NC1 circuits with information theoretic privacy can be built from one way functions [Yao86,LP09] based on one-way functions satisfies.

Zero-Knowledge Proofs and Arguments for NP [KM20]. An n-round delayed-input interactive protocol for deciding a language L corresponding to a relation $\mathcal{R}$ is denoted by $\langle \mathsf{P}, \mathsf{V} \rangle$ and it proceeds as follows:

- At the beginning of the protocol, P and V receive the size of the instance and execute the first $n - 1$ rounds.
- At the start of the last round, P receives input $(x, w) \in \mathcal{R}$ and V receives x. Upon receiving the last round message from P, V outputs 0 or 1.

For our protocols, we rely on proofs and arguments for NP that satisfy delayed-input completeness, adaptive soundness and adaptive ZK. We again refer to the full version of our paper [BPS22] for formal definitions. We point out that four round delayed-input statistical zero knowledge arguments can be obtained from [LS91] by relying on two round statistically hiding commitments, while five round delayed-input zero knowledge proofs can be obtained by relying on [GK96], where the instance is adaptively chosen in the last round by the combining techniques from [LS91]. The proof system can be instantiated from two round statistically hiding commitments.

Low Depth-Proof Systems [KM20]. The authors of [KM20] described how any computation that is verifiable by a family of polynomial sized circuits can be transformed into a proof that is verifiable by a family of circuits in NC1. The works of [GGH+13] and [KM20] presented a simple construction of a low-depth non-interactive proof for any NP-verification circuit. The prover P executes the NP-verification circuit on the witness and generates the proof as the sequential concatenation (in some specified order) of the bit values assigned to the individual wires of the circuit. The verifier V proceeds by checking consistency of the values assigned to the internal wires of the circuit for each gate. In particular for each gate in the NP-verification circuit the verifier checks if the wire vales provided in the proof represent a correct evaluation of the gate. Since the verification corresponding to each gate can be done independent of every other gate and in constant depth, we have that V itself is constant depth. We again refer to the full version of our paper [BPS22] for formal definitions.

4   Three Round Oblivious Transfer Protocols

In this section, we describe our statistically sender private $\mathsf{SSP_{OT}}$ construction from eOT which satisfies statistical receiver privacy. First, we build iOT from eOT and then we build $\mathsf{SSP_{OT}}$ from iOT. All our protocols are round preserving in nature. The corresponding definitions of the OT protocols can be found in Sect. 3.2. Our $\mathsf{SSP_{OT}}$ protocol enjoys a delayed-input feature since only the last OT protocol message depends on the receiver's input. This will be useful later on in obtaining statistically sender private CDS in the preprocessing model and also our one-sided statistical 2PC.

4.1   Statistically Receiver Private Indistinguishability-Based OT

We denote an elementary OT protocol as $\mathsf{eOT} = (\mathsf{eOT.OT}^{(1)}_{\mathsf{S \to R}}, \mathsf{eOT.OT}^{(2)}_{\mathsf{R \to S}}, \mathsf{eOT.OT}^{(3)}_{\mathsf{S \to R}}, \mathsf{eOT.OT_R})$. We construct our indistinguishability based SRP-bit OT protocol, denoted as iOT, as follows:

- $OT_{S \to R}^{(1)}(1^\kappa)$: The sender obtains $eOT.ot_1 \leftarrow eOT.OT_{S \to R}^{(1)}(1^\kappa)$. The sender sends $ot_1 = eOT.ot_1$ as the OT sender message.
- $OT_{R \to S}^{(2)}(1^\kappa, \gamma, ot_1)$: The receiver computes the OT receiver message as $(eOT.ot_2, eOT.st_R) \leftarrow eOT.OT_{R \to S}^{(2)}(1^\kappa, \gamma, ot_1)$. It sends $ot_2 = eOT.ot_2$ to the sender and stores $st_R = eOT.st_R$.
- $OT_{S \to R}^{(3)}(1^\kappa, (m_0, m_1), ot_2)$: The sender performs the following:
  - The sender runs eOT sender protocol for κ times on ot_2 to compute

  $$\{eOT.ot_{3,i}, (eOT.m_{0,i}, eOT.m_{1,i})\} = eOT.OT_{S \to R}^{(3)}(1^\kappa, ot_2),$$

  for $i \in [\kappa]$.
  - Sender computes $eOT.m_\alpha = (eOT.m_{\alpha,1}, \ldots eOT.m_{\alpha,\kappa})$ for $\alpha \in \{0,1\}$.
  - Denote the length of $eOT.m_0$ and $eOT.m_1$ as $n = n(\kappa)$ where $n = |eOT.m_0| = |eOT.m_1|$.
  - The sender samples $s_0, s_1 \leftarrow \{0,1\}^n$ as the description of the Goldreich-Levin Hash function.
  - The sender computes $p_\alpha = m_\alpha \oplus \langle eOT.m_\alpha, s_\alpha \rangle$ for $\alpha \in \{0,1\}$.

  The sender sends $ot_3 = (\{eOT.ot_{3,i}\}_{i \in [\kappa]}, s_0, s_1, p_0, p_1)$.
- $OT_R(st_R, ot_3)$: The receiver performs the following:
  - The receiver runs eOT decryption algorithm for κ times to compute

  $$\{eOT.m_{\gamma,i}\} = eOT.OT_R(eOT.st_R, eOT.ot_{3,i}),$$

  for $i \in [\kappa]$.
  - The receiver sets $eOT.m_\gamma = (eOT.m_{\gamma,1}, \ldots, eOT.m_{\gamma,\kappa})$.
  - The receiver outputs $m_\gamma = p_\gamma \oplus \langle eOT.m_\gamma, s_\gamma \rangle$.

Correctness. It can be verified in a straightforward manner.

Lemma 1. *The above protocol satisfies perfect receiver's privacy if eOT satisfies perfect receiver privacy.*

Proof. The receiver's choice bit γ is perfectly hidden in OT message $ot_2 = eOT.ot_2$ if $eOT.ot_2$ perfectly hides γ.

Lemma 2. *The above protocol satisfies sender's indistinguishability based security if eOT satisfies computational sender's elementary security.*

Proof. The work of [DGH+20] showed that the above transformation converts an elementary OT to an iOT OT protocol (via search OT). By combining Theorems 5.2 and 5.3 of [DGH+20] we prove the above theorem. We refer to their paper for more details regarding the proof steps.   □

4.2   Three Round Statistically Sender Private OT

Our $\mathsf{SSP_{OT}}$ construction relies on randomness extractors and the leftover hash lemma. We briefly define them as follows for completeness.

Definition 4. *(Randomness Extractor.)* $\mathsf{Ext} : \{0,1\}^n \times \{0,1\}^d \rightarrow \{0,1\}^\ell$ *is a strong (k, ϵ) randomness extractor if for every k-source $X \in \{0,1\}^n$ the following holds:*

$$\{U_d, \mathsf{Ext}(X, U_d)\} \overset{\epsilon}{\approx} \{U_d, U_\ell\},$$

where U_d and U_ℓ are uniformly sampled d-bit and ℓ-bit strings respectively.

Definition 5. *(Leftover Hash Lemma.)* *If* $\mathsf{H} = \{h : \{0,1\}^n \rightarrow \{0,1\}^\ell\}$ *is a pairwise independent hash family of hash function where $\ell = k - 2\log_2(\frac{1}{\epsilon})$, then* $\mathsf{Ext}(x, h) \overset{def}{=} h(x)$ *is a strong (k, ϵ) extractor.*

Construction. We denote an iOT protocol as $\mathsf{iOT} = (\mathsf{iOT.OT}^{(1)}_{\mathsf{S \rightarrow R}}, \mathsf{iOT.OT}^{(2)}_{\mathsf{R \rightarrow S}}, \mathsf{iOT.OT}^{(3)}_{\mathsf{S \rightarrow R}}, \mathsf{iOT.OT_R})$. We define our SSP-OT $\mathsf{SSP_{OT}}$ as a tuple of four algorithms defined as follows:

- $\mathsf{OT}^{(1)}_{\mathsf{R \rightarrow S}}(1^\kappa)$:
    - The receiver runs iOT protocol for n times by computing $\{\mathsf{iOT.ot}_{1,i}\} = \mathsf{iOT.OT}^{(1)}_{\mathsf{S \rightarrow R}}(1^\kappa)$ for $i \in [n]$.
    - The receiver sends $\mathsf{ot}_1 = \{\mathsf{iOT.ot}_{1,i}\}_{i \in [n]}$ as the OT receiver message.
- $\mathsf{OT}^{(2)}_{\mathsf{S \rightarrow R}}(1^\kappa, \mathsf{ot}_1)$: The sender performs the following for $i \in [n]$:
    - The sender samples $\gamma_i \leftarrow \{0,1\}$.
    - The sender computes $(\mathsf{iOT.ot}_{2,i}, \mathsf{iOT.st}_{R,i}) = \mathsf{iOT.OT}^{(2)}_{\mathsf{R \rightarrow S}}(1^\kappa, \gamma_i, \mathsf{iOT.ot}_{1,i})$ with choice bit set to γ_i.
    - The sender samples a mapping $\mathsf{Map}_i \leftarrow \{0,1\}$.
    - The sender samples a pairwise independent hash function $h \leftarrow \mathsf{H}_\kappa$.

    The sender sends $\mathsf{ot}_2 = (h, \{\mathsf{iOT.ot}_{2,i}, \mathsf{Map}_i\}_{i \in [n]})$ as the OT sender message and stores $\mathsf{st_S} = \{\mathsf{iOT.st}_{R,i}, \mathsf{Map}_i, \gamma_i\}_{i \in [n]}$ as the internal state.
- $\mathsf{OT}^{(3)}_{\mathsf{R \rightarrow S}}(1^\kappa, b, \mathsf{ot}_2)$:
    - The receiver samples $\mathsf{p}_{0,i} \leftarrow \{0,1\}$ and sets $\mathsf{p}_{1,i} = b \oplus \mathsf{p}_{0,i}$ for every $i \in [n]$.
      The receiver computes $\mathsf{iOT.ot}_{3,i} = \mathsf{iOT.OT}^{(3)}_{\mathsf{S \rightarrow R}}(1^\kappa, (\mathsf{p}_{0,i}, \mathsf{p}_{1,i}), \mathsf{iOT.ot}_{2,i})$ for every $i \in [n]$.
    - The receiver sets $\mathsf{t}_{b,i} = \mathsf{Map}_i \oplus \mathsf{p}_{0,i}$.
    - The receiver sets $\mathsf{t}_b = (\mathsf{t}_{b,1}, \ldots, \mathsf{t}_{b,n})$.
    - The receiver computes $\mathsf{m}_b = H(\mathsf{t}_b)$.

    The receiver sends $\mathsf{ot}_3 = \{\mathsf{iOT.ot}_{3,i}\}_{i \in [n]}$ as the OT receiver message and outputs m_b as the output.
- $\mathsf{OT_S}(\mathsf{st_S}, \mathsf{ot}_3)$:
    - The sender computes $\mathsf{a}_i = \mathsf{iOT.OT_R}(\mathsf{iOT.st}_{R,i}, \mathsf{iOT.ot}_{3,i})$ for $i \in [n]$.
    - The sender computes $\mathsf{t}_{i,0} = \mathsf{Map}_i \oplus \mathsf{a}_i$ and $\mathsf{t}_{i,1} = \gamma_i \oplus \mathsf{t}_{i,0}$.
    - For $\alpha \in \{0,1\}$, the sender sets $\mathsf{t}_\alpha = (\mathsf{t}_{\alpha,1}, \ldots, \mathsf{t}_{\alpha,n})$.
    - For $\alpha \in \{0,1\}$, the sender computes $\mathsf{m}_\alpha = H(\mathsf{t}_\alpha)$.

    The sender outputs $(\mathsf{m}_0, \mathsf{m}_1)$.

Correctness. The sender computes p_{i,γ_i} from the ith iOT run. The sender sets $t_{0,i} = \mathsf{Map}_i \oplus a_i = \mathsf{Map}_i \oplus p_{\gamma_i,i}$ and $t_{1,i} = \gamma_i \oplus t_{0,i} = \gamma_i \oplus \mathsf{Map}_i \oplus p_{\gamma_i,i}$. The receiver computes the following from the ith OT:

$$
\begin{aligned}
(b', t'_{b_i}) &= (p_{0,i} \oplus p_{1,i}, \mathsf{Map}_i \oplus p_{0,i}) \\
&= (p_{0,i} \oplus p_{1,i}, \mathsf{Map}_i \oplus p_{\gamma_i,i} \oplus (p_{0,i} \oplus p_{1,i}) \cdot \gamma_i) \\
&= (b, \mathsf{Map}_i \oplus p_{\gamma_i,i} \oplus b \cdot \gamma_i) \\
&= (b, t_{0,i} \oplus b \cdot \gamma_i) \\
&= (b, t_{b,i}).
\end{aligned}
$$

The sender outputs $m_\alpha = H(t_\alpha)$ for $\alpha \in \{0,1\}$. And the receiver outputs $m_b = H(t_b)$ thus proving correctness.

Lemma 3. *The above protocol satisfies statistical sender privacy if iOT satisfies statistical receiver privacy and H is a $(\lceil \frac{n}{2} \rceil, \epsilon)$-randomness extractor.*

Proof. The sender's secret input γ_i to the ith iOT remains hidden due to statistical receiver privacy of iOT. Without loss of generality, assuming a corrupt receiver obtains atmost $\lceil \frac{n}{2} \rceil$ bits of t_0 and $\lfloor \frac{n}{2} \rfloor$ bits of t_1 simultaneously by setting $b == 0$ for $\frac{n}{2}$ runs of iOT and setting $b == 1$ for the rest $\frac{n}{2}$ runs of iOT. In such a case, $\lceil \frac{n}{2} \rceil$ bits of t_1 remains hidden and is uniformly distributed. Thus the input space of the hash function H has an entropy of $k = \lceil \frac{n}{2} \rceil$ and $\ell = \lceil \frac{n}{2} \rceil - 2\log_2(\frac{1}{\epsilon})$. Applying the leftover hash lemma we argue that H behaves as a (k, ϵ) randomness extractor and thus statistically hiding m_1. The same argument holds for statistically hiding m_0 if the receiver sets $b == 1$ in $\lceil \frac{n}{2} \rceil$ runs of iOT. $\square$

Lemma 4. *The above protocol satisfies computational receiver privacy if iOT satisfies computational sender privacy.*

Proof. We demonstrate that execution of the protocol with choice bit $b == 0$ is indistinguishable from the execution of the protocol with choice bit $b == 1$ through a sequence of $(n + 1)$ hybrids. We defer the detailed description of the hybrids and the corresponding indistinguishability arguments to the full version of our paper [BPS22]. $\square$

5   One-Sided Statistically Secure 2PC Against Explainable Parties

We describe our one-sided statistically secure 2PC protocol π_{exp} secure against explainable parties in this section. High level overview can be found in Sect. 2.1.

5.1   Protocol π_{exp}

The work of [KM20] built a 2PC protocol against explainable parties given: (i) a three round statistically binding and computationally hiding commitment scheme satisfying extractability, (ii) a four round statistically hiding and computationally binding commitment scheme satisfying extractability, (iii) information theoretic garbled circuits for NC1 circuits, and (iv) a three round OT protocol with statistical privacy for a receiver and computational privacy for a sender (see [KM20] for the formal theorem statement). We demonstrate that our elementary OT protocol (with statistical receiver privacy) and a non-interactive commitment/public key encryption scheme with perfect decryption suffices to instantiate the primitives used by their construction:

1. Three round statistically binding and computationally hiding commitments can be based on any non-interactive commitment scheme [PRS02], which can itself be based on any public-key encryption [LS19] (satisfying perfect correctness) or injective one-way function [Blu81].
2. Four round statistically hiding and computationally binding commitment scheme satisfying extractability can be obtained from two round statistically hiding commitment schemes which we build from iOT in Sect. 5.2.
3. Garbled circuits can be obtained [Yao86] from one way functions.
4. The three round SRP-OT protocol is instantiated using the iOT protocol from Sect. 4.1.

5.2 Two Round Statistically Hiding Commitment

We denote an iOT protocol as $\mathsf{iOT} = (\mathsf{iOT.OT}^{(1)}_{S \rightarrow R}, \mathsf{iOT.OT}^{(2)}_{R \rightarrow S}, \mathsf{iOT.OT}^{(3)}_{S \rightarrow R}, \mathsf{iOT.OT}_R)$. We define a two round statistically hiding commitment Com as tuple of three algorithms $(\mathsf{Com}_1, \mathsf{Com}_2, \mathsf{Decom})$ between a sender and a receiver as follows:

- $\mathsf{Com}_1(1^\kappa)$: The receiver computes $c_1 = \mathsf{iOT.ot}_1 = \mathsf{iOT.OT}^{(1)}_{S \rightarrow R}(1^\kappa)$. The receiver sends c_1 as the first message of the commitment scheme.
- $\mathsf{Com}_2(1^\kappa, c_1, b)$: The sender computes $(c_2, d) = \mathsf{iOT.OT}^{(2)}_{R \rightarrow S}(1^\kappa, b, c_1)$. The sender sends c_2 as the commitment and stores $\mathsf{st} = (b, d)$ as the decommitment.
- $\mathsf{Decom}(\mathsf{st}, (c_1, c_2))$: The sender sends $\mathsf{st} = (b, d)$ as the decommitment. The receiver performs the following for $i \in [\kappa]$:
  - Computes $(\mathsf{iOT.ot}_3^i, (m_0^i, m_1^i)) = \mathsf{iOT.OT}^{(3)}_{S \rightarrow R}(1^\kappa, c_1)$.
  - The receiver aborts if $\mathsf{iOT.OT}_R(\mathsf{st}, \mathsf{iOT.ot}_3^i) \neq m_b^i$.
  The receiver outputs accept if the above checks pass.

Theorem 5. $\mathsf{Com} = (\mathsf{Com}_1, \mathsf{Com}_2, \mathsf{Decom})$ *is a two round statistically hiding commitment scheme with computational binding if iOT satisfies statistical receiver privacy and computational sender security.*

Proof. We argue hiding and binding of Com as follows:

- The sender's committed bit b remains statistically hidden in c_2 since c_2 is the output of $\mathsf{iOT.OT}^{(2)}_{R \rightarrow S}$ algorithm and c_2 statistically hides b due to statistical receiver privacy of iOT.

- If a corrupt receiver breaks binding of the protocol by producing two valid openings $(0, d_0)$ and $(1, d_1)$ then it breaks sender privacy of the iOT protocol. m_0^i (resp. m_1^i) can be correctly decrypted using $(0, d_0)$ (resp. $(1, d_1)$) as the receiver's decryption randomness. □

6   One-Sided Statistically Secure 2PC Against Malicious Corruptions

We describe our one-sided statistically secure 2PC protocol π_{mal} secure against malicious corruption of parties in this section. We rely on the following primitives for our protocol.

1. Five round one-sided statistically secure 2PC protocol against explainable parties where both parties get the output. We instantiate it using π_{exp} based on eOT (Sect. 5.1) and non-interactive commitments.
2. Four round statistically sender private Conditional Disclosure of Secrets, denoted as CDS, in the preprocessing phase where the first two rounds are input-independent.
3. Four round delayed-input statistical zero knowledge SZK. This can be built [LS91] from two round statistically hiding commitment.
4. The five round delayed-input zero knowledge proof ZKP. This can be obtained [LS91]+ [GK96] from two round statistically hiding commitment.
5. Four round statistically sender private Conditional Disclosure of Secrets, denoted as CDS, in the preprocessing phase where the first two rounds are input-independent.

The two round statistically hiding commitment is built from eOT (via iOT) in Sect. 5.2. Next, we formally define and construct the CDS protocol before proceeding to the construction of π_{mal}.

6.1   Conditional Disclosure of Secrets in the Preprocessing Model

We denote a Conditional Disclosure of Secrets in preprocessing model as a tuple of five algorithms $\mathsf{CDS} = (\mathsf{CDS}_1, \mathsf{CDS}_2, \mathsf{CDS}_3, \mathsf{CDS}_4, \mathsf{CDS}_5)$ defined as follows:

- $\mathsf{CDS}_1(1^\kappa)$: The receiver computes $(\mathsf{cds}_1, \mathsf{st}_R)$ in the preprocessing phase. The receiver sends cds_1 and stores st_R as the internal state.
- $\mathsf{CDS}_2(1^\kappa, \mathsf{cds}_1)$: The sender computes $(\mathsf{cds}_2, \mathsf{st}_S)$ in the preprocessing phase. The sender sends cds_2 and stores st_S as internal state.
- $\mathsf{CDS}_3(1^\kappa, (x, w), \mathsf{st}_R, \mathsf{cds}_2)$: The receiver computes $(\mathsf{cds}_3, \mathsf{st}_R)$ based on the statement x, witness w and cds_2. The receiver sends cds_3 and updates st_R as the internal state.
- $\mathsf{CDS}_4(1^\kappa, (x, \mathsf{ptxt}), \mathsf{st}_S, \mathsf{cds}_3)$: The sender encrypts plaintext ptxt based on statement x and cds_3 to compute cds_4. The sender sends cds_4.
- $\mathsf{CDS}_5(\mathsf{st}_R, \mathsf{cds}_4)$: The receiver outputs ptxt' as the decrypted message.

The above algorithms should satisfy the following properties:

Correctness. For any $(x, w) \in \mathcal{L}$, and message $\mathsf{ptxt} \in \{0, 1\}^*$ the following holds:

$$\Pr\Big[\mathsf{CDS}_5(\mathsf{st_R}, \mathsf{cds}_4) == \mathsf{ptxt} | (\mathsf{cds}_1, \mathsf{st_R}) \leftarrow \mathsf{CDS}_1(1^\kappa), (\mathsf{cds}_2, \mathsf{st_S}) \leftarrow \mathsf{CDS}_2(1^\kappa, \mathsf{cds}_1),$$

$$(\mathsf{cds}_3, \mathsf{st_R}) \leftarrow \mathsf{CDS}_3(1^\kappa, (x, w), \mathsf{st_R}, \mathsf{cds}_2), \mathsf{cds}_4 \leftarrow \mathsf{CDS}_4(1^\kappa, (x, \mathsf{ptxt}), \mathsf{st_S}, \mathsf{cds}_3)\Big] = 1.$$

Message Indistinguishability. For any $x \notin \mathcal{L}$, $\mathsf{cds}_3^* \in \{0, 1\}^*$ and any two equal-length messages ptxt_0, ptxt_1, the following distributions are statistically indistinguishable:

$$\mathsf{CDS}_4(1^\kappa, (x, \mathsf{ptxt}_0), \mathsf{st_S}, \mathsf{cds}_3^*) \overset{s}{\approx} \mathsf{CDS}_4(1^\kappa, (x, \mathsf{ptxt}_1), \mathsf{st_S}, \mathsf{cds}_3^*).$$

Receiver Simulation. There exists a simulator $\mathsf{Sim} = (\mathsf{Sim}_1, \mathsf{Sim}_2)$ such that for any PPT distinguisher $\mathcal{D} = (\mathcal{D}_1, \mathcal{D}_2)$, such that for any $x \in \mathcal{L}$, with $\mathcal{R}(x, w) = 1$ the following holds:

$$\Big| \Pr[\mathcal{D}_2(\mathsf{CDS}_3(1^\kappa, (x, w), \mathsf{st_R}, \mathsf{cds}_2), \mathsf{st}_\mathcal{D}) - 1 | (\mathsf{cds}_1, \mathsf{st_R}) \leftarrow \mathsf{CDS}_1(1^\kappa),$$

$$(\mathsf{cds}_2, \mathsf{st}_\mathcal{D}) \leftarrow \mathcal{D}_1(1^\kappa)] - \Pr[\mathcal{D}_2(\mathsf{Sim}_2(x, \mathsf{st_{Sim}}), \mathsf{st}_\mathcal{D}) = 1 | (\mathsf{cds}_1, \mathsf{st_{Sim}}) \leftarrow \mathsf{Sim}_1(1^\kappa),$$

$$(\mathsf{cds}_2, \mathsf{st}_\mathcal{D}) \leftarrow \mathcal{D}_1(1^\kappa)] \Big| \leq \mathsf{neg}(\kappa).$$

It can be observed that cds_1 and cds_2 are independent of x and hence can be performed offline in a preprocessing phase.

Construction. We denote an $\mathsf{SSP_{OT}}$ protocol as $\mathsf{SSP_{OT}} = (\mathsf{SSP_{OT}}.\mathsf{OT}^{(1)}_{\mathsf{R} \to \mathsf{S}}, \mathsf{SSP_{OT}}.\mathsf{OT}^{(2)}_{\mathsf{S} \to \mathsf{R}}, \mathsf{SSP_{OT}}.\mathsf{OT}^{(3)}_{\mathsf{R} \to \mathsf{S}}, \mathsf{SSP_{OT}}.\mathsf{OT_S})$.

- $\mathsf{CDS}_1(1^\kappa)$: For $i \in [n]$, the receiver computes $\mathsf{cds}_1^i = \mathsf{ot}_1^i = \mathsf{SSP_{OT}}.\mathsf{OT}^{(1)}_{\mathsf{R} \to \mathsf{S}}(1^\kappa)$. The receiver sends $\mathsf{cds}_1 = \{\mathsf{cds}^i\}_{i \in [n]}$ to the sender and stores $\mathsf{st_R} = \perp$ as the internal state.

- $\mathsf{CDS}_2(1^\kappa, \mathsf{cds}_1)$: For $i \in [n]$, the sender performs the following: $(\mathsf{cds}_2^i, \mathsf{SSP_{OT}}.\mathsf{st}_\mathsf{S}^i) = \mathsf{SSP_{OT}}.\mathsf{OT}^{(2)}_{\mathsf{S} \to \mathsf{R}}(1^\kappa, \mathsf{cds}_1^i)$. The sender sends $\mathsf{cds}_2 = \{\mathsf{cds}_2^i\}_{i \in [n]}$ to the receiver and stores $\mathsf{st_S} = \{\mathsf{SSP_{OT}}.\mathsf{st}_\mathsf{S}^i\}$ as the internal sender's state.

- $\mathsf{CDS}_3(1^\kappa, (x, w), \mathsf{st_R}, \mathsf{cds}_2)$: The receiver denotes $w = \{w_i\}_{i \in [n]}$. It computes $(\mathsf{cds}_3^i, \mathsf{m}_i') = \mathsf{OT}_{\mathsf{R} \to \mathsf{S}}(1^\kappa, w_i, \mathsf{cds}_2^i)$ for $i \in [n]$. The receiver sends $\mathsf{cds}_3 = \{\mathsf{cds}_3^i\}_{i \in [n]}$ to sender and stores $\mathsf{st_R} = (w, \{\mathsf{m}_i'\}_{i \in [n]})$ as internal state.

- $\mathsf{CDS}_4(1^\kappa, (x, \mathsf{ptxt}), \mathsf{st_S}, \mathsf{cds}_3)$: The sender performs the following:

  1. Computes the following circuit C:

$$C(x, w, \mathsf{ptxt}) = \mathsf{ptxt} \text{ iff } (\mathcal{R}(x, w) == 1)$$
$$= 0, \text{ otherwise}$$

x is hardcoded in the circuit, $w \in \{0,1\}^n$ and $\mathsf{ptxt} \in \{0,1\}^\ell$ are inputs to the circuit. The sender garbles circuit $\mathcal{C}$ as $(\mathrm{GC}, \mathbf{lab}) \leftarrow \mathsf{Garble.Gb}(1^\kappa, \mathcal{C})$. The computes

2. For $i \in [n]$, it computes $(\mathsf{m}_0^i, \mathsf{m}_1^i) = \mathsf{SSP_{OT}.OT_S}(\mathsf{SSP_{OT}.st_S^i}, \mathsf{cds}_3^i)$.

3. Parse $\mathbf{lab} = \{\mathsf{lab}_i^0, \mathsf{lab}_i^1\}_{i \in [n+\ell]}$. For $i \in [n], \alpha \in \{0,1\}$, the sender computes $y_i^\alpha = \mathsf{m}_i^\alpha \oplus \mathsf{lab}_i^\alpha$. Set $\mathbf{y} = \{y_i^0, y_i^1\}_{i \in [n]}$.

4. Compute the wire labels corresponding to input $\mathsf{ptxt} \in \{0,1\}^\ell$ as follows $(\mathsf{L}_i = \mathsf{Garble.En}(\mathsf{ptxt}_i, \{\mathsf{lab}_{n+i}^0, \mathsf{lab}_{n+i}^1\}))$ for $i \in [\ell]$.
The sender sends $\mathsf{cds}_4 = (\mathrm{GC}, \mathbf{y}, \{\mathsf{L}_i\}_{i \in [\ell]})$ to the receiver.

- $\mathsf{CDS}_5(\mathsf{st_R}, \mathsf{cds}_4)$: For $i \in [n]$, the receiver computes $\mathsf{lab}_i' = \mathsf{m}_i' \oplus y_i^{w_i}$. The receiver sets $\mathsf{lab}_{n+i}' = \mathsf{L}_i$ for $i \in [\ell]$. The receiver evaluates the garbled circuit to obtain $\mathsf{ptxt}' = \mathsf{Garble.Ev}(\mathrm{GC}, \{\mathsf{lab}_i'\}_{i \in [n+\ell]})$. The receiver outputs ptxt' as the decrypted message.

Correctness. The receiver obtains $\mathsf{lab}_i' = \mathsf{lab}_i^{w_i}$ for $i \in [n]$ from the ith OT protocol corresponding to witness bit w_i. It evaluates the garbled circuit GC to obtain the message $\mathsf{ptxt}' == \mathsf{ptxt}$ if $\mathcal{R}(x,w) = 1$.

Theorem 6. *Assuming $\mathsf{SSP_{OT}}$ is a four round OT protocol with statistical sender privacy against a malicious receiver and computational receiver privacy against a semi-honest sender, and Garble is an information theoretic garbling scheme for NC1 circuits, then CDS is a conditional disclosure of secrets for statements $x \in \mathcal{L}$ which are verifiable by relations $\mathcal{R}(x, \cdot)$ that can be computed by NC1 circuits. Moreover, it provides receiver simulation against a malicious receiver and message indistinguishability against a semi-honest sender.*

Proof. We defer the detailed proof to the full version of our paper [BPS22]. □

6.2   Protocol π_{mal}

We compile the 2PC protocol π_{exp} of [KM20] (Sect. 5.1), which is secure against unbounded explainable receiver and PPT explainable sender, to be secure against malicious corruptions. Our protocol π_{mal} can be found below and the security is summarized in Theorem 7. High level overview can be found in Sect. 2.1.

Construction. The receiver R has input A and sender S has input B. We present our compiler $\pi_{\mathsf{mal}} = (\mathsf{R}_1, \mathsf{S}_1, \mathsf{R}_2, \mathsf{S}_2, \mathsf{R}_3, \mathsf{S}_3)$ as follows:

- $\mathsf{R}_1(1^\kappa, \mathsf{A})$: The receiver performs the following:
  1. Sample $r_\mathsf{R} \leftarrow \{0,1\}^*$ and compute $\pi_{\mathsf{exp}}^1 = \pi_{\mathsf{exp}}.\mathsf{R}_1(\mathsf{A}; r_\mathsf{R})$ according to the explainable protocol.
  2. Set $(z_1, \mathsf{st_{ZKP,P}}) \leftarrow \mathsf{ZKP.P}(1^\kappa)$ and $(z_1', \mathsf{st_{SZK,V}}) \leftarrow \mathsf{SZK.V}_1(1^\kappa)$ as the first messages of the ZK proof with R as prover, and SZK argument with R as verifier, respectively.
  3. Set $(\mathsf{cds}_1, \mathsf{st_{CDS,R}}) = \mathsf{CDS.CDS}_1(1^\kappa)$ as the first message of the CDS scheme as receiver.

4. Send $\pi^1_{mal} = (\pi^1_{exp}, z_1, z'_1, cds_1)$.
5. Store $st_R = (A, r_R, st_{ZKP,P}, st_{SZK,V}, st_{CDS,R})$.

- $S_1(1^\kappa, B, \pi^1_{mal})$: The sender performs the following:
  1. Sample $r_S \leftarrow \{0,1\}^*$ and set $\pi^2_{exp} = \pi_{exp}.S_1(\pi^1_{exp}, B; r_S)$ according to the explainable protocol.
  2. Set $(z_2, st_{ZKP,V}) \leftarrow ZKP.V_1(z_1, 1^\kappa)$, $(z'_2, st_{SZK,P}) \leftarrow SZK.P_1(z'_1)$ as the second message of the ZKPproof with S as verifier, and SZK argument with sender as prover, respectively.
  3. Sample $r^{CDS}_S \leftarrow \{0,1\}^*$ and compute $(cds_2, st_{CDS,S}) = CDS.CDS_2(r^{CDS}_S, cds_1)$ as the second message of the CDS scheme as sender.
  4. Send $\pi^2_{mal} = (\pi^2_{exp}, z_2, z'_2, cds_2)$.
  5. Store $st_S = (B, r_S, st_{ZKP,V}, st_{SZK,P}, st_{CDS,S})$.
- $R_2(st_R, \pi^2_{mal})$: The receiver performs the following:
  1. Compute $\pi^3_{exp} = \pi_{exp}.R_2(\pi^2_{exp}, A; r_R)$. Set statement $x_{CDS} = (\pi^1_{exp}, \pi^2_{exp}, \pi^3_{exp})$ and witness $w_{CDS} = (A, r_R, ldp)$ where ldp is a low-depth proof of

$$(\pi^1_{exp} = \pi_{exp}.R_1(A; r_R) \wedge \pi^3_{exp} = \pi_{exp}.R_2(\pi^2_{exp}, A; r_R)).$$

  2. Compute $(cds_3, st_{CDS,R}) \leftarrow CDS.CDS_3(1^\kappa, (x_{CDS}, w_{CDS}), st_{CDS,R}, cds_2)$.
  3. Compute $(z_3, st_{ZKP,P}) \leftarrow ZKP.P_2(z_2, st_{ZKP,P})$ and $(z'_3, st_{SZK,V}) \leftarrow SZK.V_2(z'_2, st_{SZK,V})$.
  4. Send $\pi^3_{mal} = (\pi^3_{exp}, z_3, z'_3, cds_3)$.
  5. Update $st_R = (A, r_R, st_{ZKP,P}, st_{SZK,V}, st_{CDS,R})$.
- $S_2(st_S, \pi^3_{mal})$: The sender performs the following:
  1. Set $\pi^4_{exp} = \pi_{exp}.S_2(\pi^3_{exp}, B; r_S)$.
  2. Set statement $x_{CDS} = (\pi^1_{exp}, \pi^2_{exp}, \pi^3_{exp})$. Compute CDS response

$$cds_4 \leftarrow CDS.CDS_4(r^{CDS}_S, (x_{CDS}, \pi^4_{exp}), st_{CDS,S}, cds_3).$$

  3. Compute $(z_4, st_{ZKP,V}) \leftarrow ZKP.V_2(z_3, st_{ZKP,V})$.
  4. Set the statement $x_{SZK} = (cds^1, cds_2, cds_3, cds_4, x_{CDS})$ for witness $w_{SZK} = (B, r^{CDS}_S, r_S, \pi^4_{exp})$ and set $z'_4 \leftarrow SZK.P_2(z'_3, x_{SZK}, st_{SZK,P})$.
  5. Send $\pi^4_{mal} = (cds_4, z_4, z'_4)$.
  6. Update $st_S = (B, r_S, st_{ZKP,V}, st_{SZK,P})$
- $R_3(st_R, \pi^4_{mal})$: The receiver performs the following:
  1. Set the statement as $x_{SZK} = (cds^1, cds_2, cds_3, cds_4, x_{CDS})$. The receiver aborts if the verification fails as $SZK.V_3(z'_4, x_{SZK}, st_{SZK,V}) = 0$. Otherwise, decrypt $\pi^5_{exp} = CDS.CDS_5(st_{CDS,R}, cds_4)$ and compute the final message as $(\pi^5_{exp}, out) = \pi_{exp}.R_3(\pi^4_{exp}, A; r_R)$.
  2. Set $x_{ZKP} = (\pi^1_{exp}, \pi^2_{exp}, \pi^3_{exp}, \pi^4_{exp}, \pi^5_{exp})$, $w_{ZKP} = (A, r_R)$ and compute the ZKP proof as $z_5 = ZKP.P_3(z_4, x_{ZKP}, st_{ZKP,P})$.
  3. Send $\pi^5_{mal} = (\pi^5_{exp}, z_5)$ to the sender and output out.
- $S_3(st_S, \pi^5_{mal})$: Set statement $x_{ZKP} = (\pi^1_{exp}, \pi^2_{exp}, \pi^3_{exp}, \pi^4_{exp}, \pi^5_{exp})$ for ZKP proof. If $ZKP.V_3(z_5, x_{ZKP}, st_{ZKP,V}) == 0$ then abort. Else, output $\pi_{exp}.S_3(\pi^5_{exp}, B; r_S)$.

We denote the statement for the CDS as follows:

$$L_{CDS} = \{(\pi_{exp}^1, \pi_{exp}^2, \pi_{exp}^3) : \exists(A, r_R, \mathsf{ldp}) \text{ s.t. } \mathsf{ldp} \text{ is a low depth proof of}$$

$$\pi_{exp}^1 = \pi_{exp}.R_1(A; r_R) \wedge \pi_{exp}^3 = \pi_{exp}.R_2(\pi_{exp}^2, A; r_R)\}$$

The SZK statement proven by the sender is as follows:

$$L_{SZK} = \{(cds_1, cds_2, cds_3, cds_4, x_{CDS}) : \exists(B, r_S^{CDS}, r_S, \pi_{exp}^4) \text{ s.t. } \pi_{exp}^2 = S_1(\pi_{exp}^1, B; r_S) \wedge$$

$$(cds_2, st_{CDS,S}) = CDS.CDS_2(r_S^{CDS}) \wedge cds_4 = CDS.CDS_4(r_S^{CDS}, (x_{CDS}, \pi_{exp}^4), st_{CDS,S}, cds_3)\}.$$

We denote the ZKP statement proven by the receiver as follows:

$$L_{ZKP} = \{(\pi_{exp}^1, \pi_{exp}^2, \pi_{exp}^3, \pi_{exp}^4, \pi_{exp}^5) \exists(A, r_R) \text{ s.t. } \pi_{exp}^1 = \pi_{exp}.R_1(A; r_R)$$

$$\wedge \pi_{exp}^3 = \pi_{exp}.R_2(\pi_{exp}^2, A; r_R) \wedge \pi_{exp}^5 = \pi_{exp}.R_3(\pi_{exp}^4, A; r_R)\}.$$

Theorem 7. *Assuming the following holds:*

1. *Four round delayed-input adaptive statistical zero-knowledge arguments of knowledge* SZK $= (V_1, P_1, V_2, P_2, V_3)$ *with adaptive soundness,*
2. *Five round delayed-input adaptive computational zero-knowledge proofs* ZKP $= (P_1, V_1, P_2, V_2, P_3, V_3)$ *with adaptive soundness,*
3. *Four round statistical Conditional Disclosure of Secrets CDS = (CDS$_1$, CDS$_2$, CDS$_3$, CDS$_4$, CDS$_5$) for NP relations verifiable by NC1 circuits with two rounds of preprocessing phase and two rounds of input-dependent phase,*
4. *Five round robust two-party secure computation protocol $\pi_{exp} = (R_1, S_1, R_2, S_2, R_3, S_3)$ against unbounded explainable receiver and PPT explainable sender*

there exists a robust 5-round secure two-party computation protocol $\pi_{mal} = (R_1, S_1, R_2, S_2, R_3, S_3)$ with black-box simulation against unbounded malicious receivers and PPT malicious senders, where the receiver obtains its output at the end of fourth round and the sender obtains its output at the end of the fifth round.

Proof. We defer the detailed proof to the full version of our paper [BPS22]. □

7 Instantiations of eOT

We instantiate eOT from CDH, reciprocal CSIDH assumption and two-round SSP$_{OT}$. Due to lack of space, we only describe the CDH-based instantiation here. We refer to the full version of our paper [BPS22] for the instantiations based on the reciprocal CSIDH assumption and two-round SSP$_{OT}$.

CDH-Based Instantiation. We define our elementary OT protocol eOT $= (OT_{S \to R}^{(1)}, OT_{R \to S}^{(2)}, OT_{S \to R}^{(3)}, OT_R)$ as a tuple of four algorithms defined as follows:

- $\mathsf{OT}_{\mathsf{S}\to\mathsf{R}}^{(1)}(1^\kappa)$: The sender samples $Q \leftarrow G$. The sender sends $\mathsf{ot}_1 = Q$ as the OT sender message.
- $\mathsf{OT}_{\mathsf{R}\to\mathsf{S}}^{(2)}(1^\kappa, \gamma, \mathsf{ot}_1)$: The receiver performs the following with input choice bit γ as follows:
  - Sample $\mathsf{sk} \leftarrow \mathbb{Z}_q$.
  - Set $\mathsf{pk}_\gamma = g^{\mathsf{sk}}$ and set $\mathsf{pk}_{1-\gamma} = \frac{Q}{\mathsf{pk}_\gamma}$.

  The receiver sends $\mathsf{ot}_2 = \mathsf{pk}_0$ as the OT receiver message and sets $\mathsf{st}_\mathsf{R} = (\gamma, \mathsf{sk})$.
- $\mathsf{OT}_{\mathsf{S}\to\mathsf{R}}^{(3)}(1^\kappa, \mathsf{ot}_2)$: The sender computes following:
  - Generate $\mathsf{pk}_1 = \frac{Q}{\mathsf{pk}_0}$.
  - Sample $r \leftarrow \mathbb{Z}_q$. Compute $R = g^r$.
  - Compute $\mathsf{m}_0 = \mathsf{pk}_0^r$ and $\mathsf{m}_1 = \mathsf{pk}_1^r$.

  The sender sends $\mathsf{ot}_3 = R$ as the OT sender message and outputs $(\mathsf{m}_0, \mathsf{m}_1)$ as the output.
- $\mathsf{OT}_\mathsf{R}(\mathsf{st}_\mathsf{R}, \mathsf{ot}_3)$: The receiver computes $\mathsf{m}_\gamma = R^{\mathsf{sk}}$ and outputs m_γ.

Correctness. The sender outputs $(\mathsf{m}_0, \mathsf{m}_1)$. The receiver outputs $\mathsf{m}_\gamma = R^{\mathsf{sk}} = g^{r\mathsf{sk}} = \mathsf{pk}_\gamma^r$ corresponding to bit γ.

Lemma 5. *The above protocol satisfies perfect receiver's elementary security.*

Proof. The distribution of pk_0 is randomly distributed over G irrespective of the value of γ. □

Lemma 6. *The above protocol satisfies computational sender's elementary security based on the CDH assumption.*

Proof. Let $\mathcal{A}$ be an adversary breaking sender privacy of the above OT protocol, then we build an adversary $\mathcal{B}$ breaking the CDH assumption. Recall that $\mathcal{A}$ receives $Q = g^q$ from the sender (for an uniformly sampled $q \leftarrow \mathbb{Z}_q$), sends pk_0 to the sender, receives $R = g^r$ from the sender (for an uniformly sampled $r \leftarrow \mathbb{Z}_q$) and wins if it outputs $\mathsf{m}_0 = \mathsf{pk}_0^r$ and $\mathsf{m}_1 = \mathsf{pk}_1^r$. The CDH adversary $\mathcal{B}$ (acting as the sender) receives $(g, X = g^x, Y = g^y)$ as the CDH challenge. $\mathcal{B}$ sets $Q = X$ and sends it to $\mathcal{A}$. Upon receiving pk_0 from $\mathcal{A}$, $\mathcal{B}$ sends $R = Y$ to $\mathcal{A}$. If $\mathcal{A}$ succeeds then it outputs $\mathsf{m}_0 = \mathsf{pk}_0^y$ and $\mathsf{m}_1 = \mathsf{pk}_1^y$. $\mathcal{B}$ outputs $\mathsf{m}_0 \cdot \mathsf{m}_1$ to the CDH challenger. Recall that $\mathsf{pk}_0 \cdot \mathsf{pk}_1 = Q = X$. If $\mathcal{A}$ succeeds then $\mathcal{B}$ breaks CDH since the following holds:

$$\mathsf{m}_0 \cdot \mathsf{m}_1 = \mathsf{pk}_0^y \cdot \mathsf{pk}_1^y = (\mathsf{pk}_0 \cdot \mathsf{pk}_1)^y = X^y$$

□

References

[ACJ17] Ananth, P., Choudhuri, A.R., Jain, A.: A new approach to round-optimal secure multiparty computation. In: Katz, J., Shacham, H. (eds.) CRYPTO 2017, Part I. LNCS, vol. 10401, pp. 468–499. Springer, Cham (2017). https://doi.org/10.1007/978-3-319-63688-7_16

[ADMP20] Alamati, N., De Feo, L., Montgomery, H., Patranabis, S.: Cryptographic group actions and applications. In: Moriai, S., Wang, H. (eds.) ASIACRYPT 2020, Part II. LNCS, vol. 12492, pp. 411–439. Springer, Cham (2020). https://doi.org/10.1007/978-3-030-64834-3_14

[AMPS21] Alamati, N., Montgomery, H., Patranabis, S., Sarkar, P.: Two-round adaptively secure MPC from isogenies, LPN, or CDH. In: Tibouchi, M., Wang, H. (eds.) ASIACRYPT 2021. LNCS, vol. 13091, pp. 305–334. Springer, Cham (2021). https://doi.org/10.1007/978-3-030-92075-3_11

[BD18] Brakerski, Z., Döttling, N.: Two-message statistically sender-private OT from LWE. In: Beimel, A., Dziembowski, S. (eds.) TCC 2018, Part II. LNCS, vol. 11240, pp. 370–390. Springer, Cham (2018). https://doi.org/10.1007/978-3-030-03810-6_14

[BF22] Bitansky, N., Freizeit, S.: Statistically sender-private OT from LPN and derandomization. Cryptology ePrint Archive, Report 2022/185 (2022). https://ia.cr/2022/185

[BFJ+20] Badrinarayanan, S., Fernando, R., Jain, A., Khurana, D., Sahai, A.: Statistical ZAP arguments. In: Canteaut, A., Ishai, Y. (eds.) EUROCRYPT 2020, Part III. LNCS, vol. 12107, pp. 642–667. Springer, Cham (2020). https://doi.org/10.1007/978-3-030-45727-3_22

[BGJ+18] Badrinarayanan, S., Goyal, V., Jain, A., Kalai, Y.T., Khurana, D., Sahai, A.: Promise zero knowledge and its applications to round optimal MPC. In: Shacham, H., Boldyreva, A. (eds.) CRYPTO 2018, Part II. LNCS, vol. 10992, pp. 459–487. Springer, Cham (2018). https://doi.org/10.1007/978-3-319-96881-0_16

[BHP17] Brakerski, Z., Halevi, S., Polychroniadou, A.: Four round secure computation without setup. In: Kalai, Y., Reyzin, L. (eds.) TCC 2017, Part I. LNCS, vol. 10677, pp. 645–677. Springer, Cham (2017). https://doi.org/10.1007/978-3-319-70500-2_22

[BHR12] Bellare, M., Hoang, V.T., Rogaway, P.: Foundations of garbled circuits. In: Yu, T., Danezis, G., Gligor, V.D. (eds.) ACM CCS 2012, pp. 784–796. ACM Press (2012)

[BJY97] Bellare, M., Jakobsson, M., Yung, M.: Round-optimal zero-knowledge arguments based on any one-way function. In: Fumy, W. (ed.) EUROCRYPT 1997. LNCS, vol. 1233, pp. 280–305. Springer, Heidelberg (1997). https://doi.org/10.1007/3-540-69053-0_20

[Blu81] Blum, M.: Coin flipping by telephone. In: Gersho, A. (ed.) CRYPTO 1981, vol. ECE Report 82–04, pp. 11–15. University of California, Santa Barbara, Department of Electrical and Computer Engineering (1981)

[BPS22] Badrinarayanan, S., Patranabis, S., Sarkar, P.: Statistical security in two-party computation revisited. Cryptology ePrint Archive, Paper 2022/1190 (2022). https://eprint.iacr.org/2022/1190

[CCG+20] Rai Choudhuri, A., Ciampi, M., Goyal, V., Jain, A., Ostrovsky, R.: Round optimal secure multiparty computation from minimal assumptions. In: Pass, R., Pietrzak, K. (eds.) TCC 2020,Part II. LNCS, vol. 12551, pp. 291–319. Springer, Cham (2020). https://doi.org/10.1007/978-3-030-64378-2_11

[CCG+21] Choudhuri, A.R., Ciampi, M., Goyal, V., Jain, A., Ostrovsky, R.: Oblivious transfer from trapdoor permutations in minimal rounds. In: Nissim, K., Waters, B. (eds.) TCC 2021, Part II. LNCS, vol. 13043, pp. 518–549. Springer, Cham (2021). https://doi.org/10.1007/978-3-030-90453-1_18

[CO17]   Chongchitmate, W., Ostrovsky, R.: Circuit-private multi-key FHE. In: Fehr, S. (ed.) PKC 2017, Part II. LNCS, vol. 10175, pp. 241–270. Springer, Heidelberg (2017). https://doi.org/10.1007/978-3-662-54388-7_9

[COSV17] Ciampi, M., Ostrovsky, R., Siniscalchi, L., Visconti, I.: Round-optimal secure two-party computation from trapdoor permutations. In: Kalai, Y., Reyzin, L. (eds.) TCC 2017, Part I. LNCS, vol. 10677, pp. 678–710. Springer, Cham (2017). https://doi.org/10.1007/978-3-319-70500-2_23

[DGH+20] Döttling, N., Garg, S., Hajiabadi, M., Masny, D., Wichs, D.: Two-round oblivious transfer from CDH or LPN. In: Canteaut, A., Ishai, Y. (eds.) EUROCRYPT 2020, Part II. LNCS, vol. 12106, pp. 768–797. Springer, Cham (2020). https://doi.org/10.1007/978-3-030-45724-2_26

[DN07]   Dwork, C., Naor, M.: Zaps and their applications. SIAM J. Comput. (2007)

[GGH+13] Garg, S., Gentry, C., Halevi, S., Raykova, M., Sahai, A., Waters, B.: Candidate indistinguishability obfuscation and functional encryption for all circuits. In: 54th FOCS, pp. 40–49. IEEE Computer Society Press (2013)

[GJJM20] Goyal, V., Jain, A., Jin, Z., Malavolta, G.: Statistical zaps and new oblivious transfer protocols. In: Canteaut, A., Ishai, Y. (eds.) EUROCRYPT 2020, Part III. LNCS, vol. 12107, pp. 668–699. Springer, Cham (2020). https://doi.org/10.1007/978-3-030-45727-3_23

[GK96]   Goldreich, O., Kahan, A.: How to construct constant-round zero-knowledge proof systems for NP. J. Cryptol. 9(3), 167–190 (1996)

[GMPP16] Garg, S., Mukherjee, P., Pandey, O., Polychroniadou, A.: The exact round complexity of secure computation. In: Fischlin, M., Coron, J.-S. (eds.) EUROCRYPT 2016, Part II. LNCS, vol. 9666, pp. 448–476. Springer, Heidelberg (2016). https://doi.org/10.1007/978-3-662-49896-5_16

[GMW91]   Goldreich, O., Micali, S., Wigderson, A.: Proofs that yield nothing but their validity for all languages in NP have zero-knowledge proof systems. J. ACM (1991)

[HHPV18] Halevi, S., Hazay, C., Polychroniadou, A., Venkitasubramaniam, M.: Round-optimal secure multi-party computation. In: Shacham, H., Boldyreva, A. (eds.) CRYPTO 2018, Part II. LNCS, vol. 10992, pp. 488–520. Springer, Cham (2018). https://doi.org/10.1007/978-3-319-96881-0_17

[HK12]   Halevi, S., Kalai, Y.T.: Smooth projective hashing and two-message oblivious transfer. J. Cryptol. 25(1), 158–193 (2012)

[HNO+09] Haitner, I., Nguyen, M.-H., Ong, S.J., Reingold, O., Vadhan, S.P.: Statistically hiding commitments and statistical zero-knowledge arguments from any one-way function. SIAM J. Comput. (2009)

[Kat08]   Katz, J.: Which languages have 4-round zero-knowledge proofs? In: Canetti, R. (ed.) TCC 2008. LNCS, vol. 4948, pp. 73–88. Springer, Heidelberg (2008). https://doi.org/10.1007/978-3-540-78524-8_5

[KKS18]   Kalai, Y.T., Khurana, D., Sahai, A.: Statistical witness indistinguishability (and more) in two messages. In: Nielsen, J.B., Rijmen, V. (eds.) EUROCRYPT 2018, Part III. LNCS, vol. 10822, pp. 34–65. Springer, Cham (2018). https://doi.org/10.1007/978-3-319-78372-7_2

[KM20]   Khurana, D., Mughees, M.H.: On statistical security in two-party computation. In: Pass, R., Pietrzak, K. (eds.) TCC 2020, Part II. LNCS, vol. 12551, pp. 532–561. Springer, Cham (2020). https://doi.org/10.1007/978-3-030-64378-2_19

[KO04]   Katz, J., Ostrovsky, R.: Round-optimal secure two-party computation. In: Franklin, M. (ed.) CRYPTO 2004. LNCS, vol. 3152, pp. 335–354. Springer, Heidelberg (2004). https://doi.org/10.1007/978-3-540-28628-8_21

[Kol05]   Kolesnikov, V.: Gate evaluation secret sharing and secure one-round two-party computation. In: Roy, B. (ed.) ASIACRYPT 2005. LNCS, vol. 3788, pp. 136–155. Springer, Heidelberg (2005). https://doi.org/10.1007/11593447_8

[LGdSG21] Lai, Y.-F., Galbraith, S.D., Delpech de Saint Guilhem, C.: Compact, efficient and UC-secure isogeny-based oblivious transfer. In: Canteaut, A., Standaert, F.-X. (eds.) EUROCRYPT 2021. LNCS, vol. 12696, pp. 213–241. Springer, Cham (2021). https://doi.org/10.1007/978-3-030-77870-5_8

[LP07]   Lindell, Y., Pinkas, B.: An efficient protocol for secure two-party computation in the presence of malicious adversaries. In: Naor, M. (ed.) EUROCRYPT 2007. LNCS, vol. 4515, pp. 52–78. Springer, Heidelberg (2007). https://doi.org/10.1007/978-3-540-72540-4_4

[LP09]   Lindell, Y., Pinkas, B.: A proof of security of Yao's protocol for two-party computation. J. Cryptol. 22(2), 161–188 (2009)

[LS91]   Lapidot, D., Shamir, A.: Publicly verifiable non-interactive zero-knowledge proofs. In: Menezes, A.J., Vanstone, S.A. (eds.) CRYPTO 1990. LNCS, vol. 537, pp. 353–365. Springer, Heidelberg (1991). https://doi.org/10.1007/3-540-38424-3_26

[LS19]   Lombardi, A., Schaeffer, L.: A note on key agreement and non-interactive commitments. IACR Cryptology ePrint Archive, p. 279 (2019)

[MW16]   Mukherjee, P., Wichs, D.: Two round multiparty computation via multi-key FHE. In: Fischlin, M., Coron, J.-S. (eds.) EUROCRYPT 2016, Part II. LNCS, vol. 9666, pp. 735–763. Springer, Heidelberg (2016). https://doi.org/10.1007/978-3-662-49896-5_26

[Nao91]   Naor, M.: Bit commitment using pseudorandomness. J. Cryptol. (1991)

[NOVY98] Naor, M., Ostrovsky, R., Venkatesan, R., Yung, M.: Perfect zero-knowledge arguments for NP using any one-way permutation. J. Cryptol. (1998)

[NP01]   Naor, M., Pinkas, B.: Efficient oblivious transfer protocols. In: Rao Kosaraju, S. (ed.) 12th SODA, pp. 448–457. ACM-SIAM (2001)

[OPP14]   Ostrovsky, R., Paskin-Cherniavsky, A., Paskin-Cherniavsky, B.: Maliciously circuit-private FHE. In: Garay, J.A., Gennaro, R. (eds.) CRYPTO 2014, Part I. LNCS, vol. 8616, pp. 536–553. Springer, Heidelberg (2014). https://doi.org/10.1007/978-3-662-44371-2_30

[ORS15]   Ostrovsky, R., Richelson, S., Scafuro, A.: Round-optimal black-box two-party computation. In: Gennaro, R., Robshaw, M. (eds.) CRYPTO 2015, Part II. LNCS, vol. 9216, pp. 339–358. Springer, Heidelberg (2015). https://doi.org/10.1007/978-3-662-48000-7_17

[PRS02]   Prabhakaran, M., Rosen, A., Sahai, A.: Concurrent zero knowledge with logarithmic round-complexity. In: 43rd FOCS, pp. 366–375. IEEE Computer Society Press (2002)

[WW06]   Wolf, S., Wullschleger, J.: Oblivious transfer is symmetric. In: Vaudenay, S. (ed.) EUROCRYPT 2006. LNCS, vol. 4004, pp. 222–232. Springer, Heidelberg (2006). https://doi.org/10.1007/11761679_14

[Yao86]   Yao, A.C.-C.: How to generate and exchange secrets (extended abstract). In: 27th FOCS, pp. 162–167. IEEE Computer Society Press (1986)

Protocols: Key Agreement and Commitments

On the Worst-Case Inefficiency of CGKA

Alexander Bienstock[1]([✉]), Yevgeniy Dodis[1], Sanjam Garg[2,3],
Garrison Grogan[5], Mohammad Hajiabadi[4], and Paul Rösler[1][ID]

[1] New York University, New York, USA
{abienstock,dodis,paul.roesler}@cs.nyu.edu
[2] UC Berkeley, Berkeley, USA
sanjamg@berkeley.edu
[3] NTT Research, East Palo Alto, USA
[4] University of Waterloo, Waterloo, Canada
mdhajiabadi@uwaterloo.ca
[5] Berkeley, USA

Abstract. Continuous Group Key Agreement (CGKA) is the basis of
modern Secure Group Messaging (SGM) protocols. At a high level, a
CGKA protocol enables a group of users to continuously compute a
shared (evolving) secret while members of the group add new members,
remove other existing members, and perform state updates. The state
updates allow CGKA to offer desirable security features such as forward
secrecy and post-compromise security.

CGKA is regarded as a practical primitive in the real-world. Indeed,
there is an IETF Messaging Layer Security (MLS) working group devoted
to developing a standard for SGM protocols, including the CGKA protocol at their core. Though known CGKA protocols seem to perform
relatively well when considering natural sequences of performed group
operations, there are no formal guarantees on their efficiency, other than
the $O(n)$ bound which can be achieved by trivial protocols, where n
is the number of group numbers. In this context, we ask the following
questions and provide negative answers.

1. *Can we have CGKA protocols that are efficient in the worst case?* We
   start by answering this basic question in the negative. First, we show
   that a natural primitive that we call Compact Key Exchange (CKE)
   is at the core of CGKA, and thus tightly captures CGKA's worst-case
   communication cost. Intuitively, CKE requires that: first, n users
   non-interactively generate key pairs and broadcast their public keys,

The full version [10] of this article is available in the IACR eprint archive as article
2022/1237.

Y. Dodis—Partially supported by gifts from VMware Labs and Algorand Foundation,
and NSF grants 1815546 and 2055578.

S. Garg—This research is supported in part by DARPA under Agreement No.
HR00112020026, AFOSR Award FA9550-19-1-0200, NSF CNS Award 1936826, and
research grants by the Sloan Foundation, and Visa Inc. Any opinions, findings and
conclusions or recommendations expressed in this material are those of the author(s)
and do not necessarily reflect the views of the United States Government or DARPA.
M. Hajiabadi—Work supported by an NSERC Discovery Grant RGPIN/03270-2022.

E. Kiltz and V. Vaikuntanathan (Eds.): TCC 2022, LNCS 13748, pp. 213–243, 2022.
https://doi.org/10.1007/978-3-031-22365-5_8

then, some other *special* user securely communicates to these n users a shared key. Next, we show that CKE with communication cost $o(n)$ by the special user *cannot* be realized in a black-box manner from public-key encryption, thus implying the same for CGKA, where n is the corresponding number of group members.

2. *Can we realize one CGKA protocol that works as well as possible in all cases?* Here again, we present negative evidence showing that no such protocol based on black-box use of public-key encryption exists. Specifically, we show two distributions over sequences of group operations such that no CGKA protocol obtains optimal communication costs on both sequences.

1 Introduction

Secure Group Messaging (SGM) platforms such as Signal Messenger, Facebook Messenger, WhatsApp, etc., are used by billions of people worldwide. SGM has received lots of attention recently, including from the IETF Messaging Layer Security (MLS) working group [8], which is creating an eponymous standard for SGM protocols. While these protocols' security properties are well documented, understanding their *efficiency* properties remains a central research question.

Continuous Group Key Agreement (CGKA) is at the core of SGM protocols. First formalized in [3], CGKA allows a group of users to continuously compute a shared (evolving) symmetric key. This shared group key is re-computed as users asynchronously add (resp. remove) others to (resp. from) the group, as well as execute periodic state refreshes. CGKA provides very robust security guarantees: it not only requires privacy of group keys from non-members, including the facilitating delivery server (which users send CGKA ciphertexts to, in case other group members are offline), but much more. Even in the event of a state compromise in which a user's secret state is leaked to an adversary, group keys should shortly become private again through ordinary protocol state refreshes. Furthermore, in face of such a state compromise, past group keys should remain secure. The former security requirement is referred to as *post-compromise security* (PCS), while the latter is referred to as *forward secrecy* (FS).

Ideally, for use in practice, CGKA protocols should use simple, well-established, and efficient cryptographic primitives and have $O(\log n)$ communication per operation (or at most sub-linear), where n is the number of group members. Indeed, many CGKA protocols in the literature described below claim to have "fair-weather" $O(\log n)$ communication, meaning that when conditions are *good*, communication cost per operation is $O(\log n)$. Such informal claims have pleased practitioners and supported their beliefs that CGKA can be used in the real-world. However, no such formal efficiency guarantees, nor any non-trivial definitions of such *good* conditions have ever been established. Indeed, as elaborated upon below, there are no formal analyses showing that a CGKA protocol can do any better than the trivial $O(n)$ communication cost per operation, on any non-trivial sequence of operations.

CGKA Protocols in the Literature. Many CGKA protocols have been introduced in the literature to provide the above security properties. The largest portion of these are based on a basic tree structure, as in the Asynchronous Ratchet Tree (ART) protocol [21] and the TreeKEM family of protocols [1,3–6,9,11], the simplest of which is currently used in MLS [8]. Most of these tree-based protocols are of the same approximate form (although they have slightly different efficiency profiles; see [6] for a comparison based on simulations): each node contains a Public Key Encryption (PKE) key pair, users are assigned to the leaves and only store the secret keys on the path from their leaf to the root, and the root is the group secret. When a user executes an operation, they refresh the secret keys along the path(s) of one (or more) leaves to the root, encrypting these secrets to the siblings along the path(s). Thus, in *very specific* good conditions, communication can easily be seen to be $O(\log n)$. However, due to PCS requirements (elaborated on below), the trees in all of these protocols may periodically *degrade*, resulting in $\Omega(n)$ communication complexity in the worst case, even amortized over many operations.

Instead of using a tree structure, Weidner *et al.* suggest using pairwise channels of the Continuous Key Agreement scheme derived from the famous two-party Signal Secure Messaging protocol [2,14,18,20,26,28,32]. However, this trivial construction of course requires $\Omega(n)$ communication per operation.

In summary, all known CGKA protocols (based on public-key encryption) achieve the same worst-case efficiency as the trivial protocol.

1.1   Our Results

In this paper, we work towards understanding the possible efficiency guarantees that *any* CGKA protocol can achieve in the worst-case, i.e., in cases when the conditions are *not good*. We start by asking the following question:

Can we construct a CGKA protocol that does better than the trivial CGKA protocol in the worst-case?

We provide a negative answer to the above question. In particular, we show that every CGKA (from PKE) has large $\Omega(n)$ worst-case communication cost. Although one can hope that this worst-case will not occur often in practice, until there are better, well-defined assumptions on the structure of operation sequences under which practitioners hope that good efficiency bounds can be proven, there is always a danger of bad efficiency in some cases. As the first step of this lower bound, we show that a natural primitive which we call *Compact Key Exchange* (CKE) is at the core of CGKA, and in fact tightly captures the worst-case communication cost of CGKA. The heart of our negative result is then a black-box separation showing that PKE are insufficient for efficiently realizing CKE. Finally, using the above equivalence, we translate this result into the aforementioned lower bound on CGKA.

Given that no CGKA protocol can be efficient in the worst case, we ask:

Can we realize one CGKA protocol that works as well as possible in all cases?

Here again, we present negative evidence showing that no such protocol based on black-box use of PKE exists. Specifically, we show two distributions over sequences of group operations such that no single CGKA protocol making only black-box use of PKE obtains optimal communication costs on both sequences. That is, any CGKA protocol which acts well on one distribution of operations must have much worse $\Omega(n)$ communication cost on the other distribution; otherwise, it violates our CKE lower bound.

1.2   Compact Key Exchange

To prove our CGKA lower bound, we first isolate and define *Compact Key Exchange* (CKE), a novel primitive that captures one type of scenario that results in large CGKA communication. CKE is related to Multi-Receiver Key Encapsulation Mechanisms [30]. It involves n users who each non-interactively broadcasts a public key, and another special user who sends those n users an encryption of a symmetric key, which only the n users can decrypt. As explained below, we will show that CKE is *equivalent* to CGKA, in terms of worst-case communication complexity.

1.3   Standard Security of Continuous Group Key Agreement

Our CGKA lower bound focuses on the efficiency ramifications of post-compromise security (PCS). The standard form of PCS required for CGKA in the literature [1,3,6,21] is in fact quite strong. Informally, it requires the following two properties:

1. *Double-join prevention.* A malicious user may memorize randomness used in operations they execute. If they are removed from the group at a later time, they must be prevented from using this memorized randomness to *re-join* the group without invitation.
2. *Resilience to randomness leakage.* An honest user's malfunctioning device may continuously leak randomness which the user samples for CGKA operations (e.g., due to implementation flaws or an installed virus). Once the leakage is stopped (due to updating the implementation or removing the virus) and the user performs a state update, the adversary must be prevented from using the previously leaked randomness to obtain future group secrets.

Thus, once a user is removed, all group secrets should be independent of any randomness sampled by them. Similarly, if a user executes a state refresh, all new group secrets should be independent of any randomness *previously* sampled by them.

We emphasize that while the two properties above are rather strong, weakening PCS to exclude them (i.e., where we assume randomness is never leaked and securely deleted after each operation) yields many trivial CGKA protocols (from any PKE) with $O(\log n)$ worst-case communication. For example, one can simply use Tainted TreeKEM (TTKEM) [6] *without taints*. In all these protocols honest parties need to sample secrets for other parties, and are then trusted to delete them once communicated (encrypted) to these other parties. Clearly, most real-world implementations should not be comfortable with this level of trust, and should especially strive for property 1 above instead. Indeed, from very early on in the MLS standardization initiative, requiring property 1 was deemed important[1] and ultimately prioritized over efficiency[2] in the version of TreeKEM used by MLS [8, §13.1]. This protocol, as well as other existing protocols, such as TTKEM, explicitly prevent double-joins (e.g., by sometimes *blanking* or *tainting* nodes that are not on the path to the root from the leaf of a user that is executing an operation) at great efficiency cost; $\Omega(n)$ in the worst-case. Moreover, even though property 2 may seem especially strong, all CGKA definitions in the literature require both properties [1,3,6,21], and our lower bound holds for both (in isolation). Nevertheless, we leave it as an interesting topic for future work to study what kind of efficiency guarantees can be obtained in a more restricted setting, where property 2 is not required.

1.4   Equivalence of CKE and CGKA Worst-Case Communication Complexity

The first step in proving our $\Omega(n)$ CGKA lower bound (from PKE) is showing that CKE and CGKA with the standard PCS notion detailed above are equivalent, both in terms of implication and worst-case communication complexity. It is important to note that in all our definitions of CKE and CGKA, we specify the weakest correctness and security requirements under which our lower bounds hold. This only *strengthens* our lower bound. For example, we only consider non-adaptive, passive adversaries.

CKE is at the Core of CGKA. In Sect. 3, we show that CGKA implies CKE and furthermore that the worst-case communication complexity of CKE from black-box PKE lower bounds that of CGKA from the same primitives. The intuition is as follows. Consider a CGKA group with n members at a certain time during its lifetime. To ensure that our lower bound is meaningful, we allow for any sequence of operations to be executed up until this point. Now, consider the situation in which user A adds k new users. If the CGKA protocol only uses PKE, then each added user only stores secrets (besides their own) that were generated by user A.[3] If user B removes user A as the next operation, then due

---

[1] First proposal of the TreeKEM design with a discussion about the double-join problem: https://mailarchive.ietf.org/arch/msg/mls/e3ZKNzPC7Gxrm3Wf0q96ds LZoD8/.

[2] Proposal to prevent double-joins in TreeKEM, resulting in linear complexity in the worst-case: https://mailarchive.ietf.org/arch/msg/mls/Zzw2tqZC1FCbVZA9LKE RsMIQXik/.

[3] Note: for any CGKA protocol, it could be that each of the added k users may share secrets with all of the current group members, derived from non-interactive key exchange using key-bundles stored on a server. However, these shared secrets are only between pairs of users, and thus do not seem useful for establishing the group secret (since secure communication between pairs of users can already be achieved via PKE).

to PCS, every secret which the k added users shared with any of the current group members cannot be re-used; user A must have generated all of them and thus could potentially (maliciously) re-join the group without being added if one of the secrets is reused. Thus, as part of the remove operation, user B must communicate the new group key to each of the other k added users, with only the knowledge of their (independent) public keys. This is exactly the setting of CKE. Indeed if $k = \Omega(n)$, and additionally we can show that the ciphertext size for CKE must be $\Omega(n)$, then we can show the same for when user B removes user A in CGKA above. Furthermore, if user C then removes user B, we are in the same situation again, and thus this ciphertext must also be $\Omega(n)$. We can repeat this scenario *ad infinitum*, where after a user executes a remove in the sequence, they add a new user, such that even amortized over a long sequence of operations, the communication cost is $\Omega(n)$. We in fact further generalize this result in Sect. 3 to intuitively show that if α users add the k new users then execute ℓ rounds of sequential state refreshes, the combined communication cost of each round is $\Omega(k)$.

A bit more formally, we show how to construct CKE for k users from CGKA in a manner such that if the CGKA ciphertext is small for the above operation and the CGKA protocol only uses PKE in a black-box manner, then the corresponding CKE ciphertext is small, contradicting our lower bound for CKE, discussed below.

Difference from Lower Bound of [11]. It is important to mention that our CGKA communication complexity lower bound already holds for fully synchronous, non-concurrent CGKA executions. Hence, the lower bound by Bienstock *et al.* [11] that uses symbolic proof techniques to show a communication lower bound for concurrently initiated operations in CGKA executions (with required fast PCS recovery[4]) is entirely independent with respect to our employed methods and resulting statement.

CKE Tightly Implies CGKA. For completeness, in the full version [10] we also show that one can use CKE to construct a CGKA protocol where the worst-case communication complexity of the CGKA protocol is proportional to that of the used CKE protocol. The CGKA protocol simply lets the user, executing a given CGKA operation, run the CKE algorithm of the special CKE user to communicate a fresh group key to the public keys of all current CGKA group members. Therefore, CGKA and CKE are surprisingly equivalent in terms of both cryptographic strength *and* worst-case (communication) complexity; f one could construct CKE efficiently, they could also construct CGKA efficiently, and vice versa.

1.5   Black-Box Compact Key Exchange Lower Bound

In order to prove the CGKA lower bounds discussed above, we need a lower bound on the underlying CKE primitive. Therefore, in Sect. 4, we prove a black-

---

[4] Unlike in [1] who circumvent the [11] lower bound by allowing for slower PCS recovery.

box separation showing that all CKE protocols that make black-box use of public-key encryption (PKE) require the ciphertext sent from the special user to the n users to have size $\Omega(n)$, *irrespective of the sizes of the public keys* that the n users have sent to the special user. Our impossibility holds even if the scheme comes with a CRS, of arbitrary size. Ruling out schemes that allow for a CRS will help us with our CGKA lower bounds.

Intuitively, since the n public keys are generated *independently* from each other, our result implies that there is no non-trivial "compression" operation that the special user can do to save over the trivial protocol: choosing a key and separately encrypting the key to each user independently.

Relations to Broadcast Encryption. We note that the notion of CKE is incomparable to that of broadcast encryption, at least in an ostensible sense. Recall that a broadcast encryption scheme is a type of attribute-based encryption that allows for broadcasting a message to a subset of users, in a way that the resulting ciphertext is compact. One crucial difference between broadcast encryption and CKE is that under CKE, users have independent secret keys, while under broadcast encryption, user secret keys are correlated, all obtained via a master secret key.

Relations to Other Black-Box Impossibility Results. The work of Boneh et al. [15] shows that identity-based encryption (IBE) is black-box impossible from trapdoor permutations (TDPs). A striking similarity between IBE and CKE is that both deal with some form of compactness: that of public parameters (PP) for IBE and of ciphertexts in CKE. The techniques of [15] crucially rely on the number of identities being much larger than the number of queries required to generate a public parameter. In our setting, this is no longer the case: the number of queries made by the encryption algorithm to generate a compact ciphertext may be much larger than n, and hence the techniques of [15] do not work in our setting. In addition, we allow the CRS to grow with the number of identities.

Extensions and Limitations of Our Impossibility Results. We believe that out impossibility should extend quite naturally to separate CKE from trapdoor permutations (TDPs), though we have not worked out the details. Our impossibility results have no bearing on the base primitive being used in a non-black-box way, and indeed by using strong tools such as indistinguishability obfuscation (which inherently results in non-black-box constructions), one might be able to build compact CKE.

Overview. Our impossibility result is proved relative to a random PKE oracle $O := (g, e, d)$. We give an attack against any CKE protocol (CRSGen, Init, Comm, Derive) (Definition 7) instantiated with O. To give some intuition about the attack, suppose e is an encryption oracle, whose output length (i.e., the ciphertext length) is sufficiently larger than its input length (i.e., the length of (pk, m, r)). This in particular implies that in order to get a valid (pk, c)—one under which there exists some m and r such that $e(pk, m, r) = c$—one has to call the e oracle first. Now if a CKE ciphertext for n users has length $o(n)$, this means that one can "embed" at most $o(n)$ valid e-ciphertexts into C. Say the ciphertexts are $c_1, \ldots, c_t$ with corresponding public keys $\mathsf{pk}_1, \ldots, \mathsf{pk}_t$, where $t \in o(n)$. This means that we need at most t effective trapdoors (with respect to $\mathbf{O}$) to decrypt C, namely the trapdoors that correspond to $(\mathsf{pk}_1, \ldots, \mathsf{pk}_t)$. Also, since C should be decryptable by each user, the set of "effective" trapdoors for each user (those required to decrypt C) should be a subset of all these t trapdoors. Now since $t = o(n)$, there exists a user whose effective trapdoors are a subset of all other users. But since the CKE secret keys for all users are generated independently and with no correlations, if we run the CKE key generation algorithm many times, we should be able to recover all the required trapdoors, for at least one user. This is the main idea of the proof.

The above overview is overly simplistic, omitting many subtleties. For example, an e-ciphertext that is decrypted may come from one of the public keys $\mathsf{PK}_1, \ldots, \mathsf{PK}_n$ (which can be arbitrarily large), and not from C itself. Second, the notion of "embedded ciphertexts" in C is not clear. We will formalize all these subtleties in Sect. 4 and will give a more detailed overview there, after establishing some notation.

New Techniques. Our proofs introduce some techniques that may be of independent interest. Firstly, our proofs involve oracle sampling steps (a technique also used in many other papers), but one novel thing in our proofs is that we need to make sure that the sampled oracles do not contain a certain set of query/response pairs. In comparison, prior oracle sampling techniques involve choosing oracles that agree with a set of query/answer pairs. This technique of making certain query/response pairs off-limits, and the implications proved, might find applications in proving other impossibility results. Moreover, our proofs use theorems about non-uniform attacks against random oracles [19,22] to argue that an $o(n)$ CKE ciphertext cannot embed n ciphertexts; we find this connection novel.

In Sect. 4, we will give an overview (and the proof) for the restricted construction setting in which oracle access is of the form (CRSGen[g], Init[g], Comm[e], Derive[d]). This will capture most of the ideas that go into the full proof. We will then give a proof for the general construction case in the full version [10].

1.6 No *Single* Optimal CGKA Protocol Exists

In Sect. 5, we present another negative result for CGKA protocols that make black-box use of PKE. Naturally, CGKA protocols proceed in an online manner such that users do not know which operations will be executed next. Therefore, users have to make choices when executing operations that may result in unnecessary communication. We leverage this situation to show that there does not exist any *single* CGKA protocol that makes black-box use of PKE and that has optimal communication costs for every sequence that may be executed. More specifically, for every CGKA protocol Π, there exists some distribution of CGKA operations Seq and some other CGKA protocol Π' such that Π has much higher communication costs than Π' when executing Seq.

Our driving example is as follows: suppose again that starting with a CGKA group in arbitrary state, k users are added by user A and remain offline. Next, α users (including user A) execute state refreshes. In this case, some protocols might use a strategy which, through these state refreshes, create and communicate extra redundant secrets for the k added users, while others may use a strategy which simply relies on those secrets communicated by user A. For the former strategy, if the k added users afterwards come online and execute their own state refreshes, then the communication of these extra secrets will have been unnecessary, and a protocol which follows the latter strategy will have much lower communication cost. However, for the latter strategy, if one of the $\alpha - 1$ users, user j, who only communicated a small amount ($o(k)$) in their state refresh thereafter remains offline while the other $\alpha - 1$ users execute rounds of sequential state refreshes, then we know from what we prove in Sect. 3 that each of the rounds will have $\Omega(k)$ communication cost. This is intuitively because the k added users mostly share secrets with the $\alpha - 1$ users excluding user j, and thus when these $\alpha - 1$ users perform state refreshes, they must re-communicate secrets to the k added users. On the other hand, a protocol that follows the former strategy can have much lower communication cost if the state refresh ciphertext of user j *alone* was large ($\Omega(k)$). This is intuitively because the k added users still share enough secrets with user j, so that when the other $\alpha - 1$ users execute their state refreshes, they do not need to communicate much new to the added users.

1.7   Lessons Learned for Practice

Our results show that the execution of a CGKA protocol causes impractical communication overhead amongst the group members if (1) the CGKA protocol is built from PKE only, (2) the CGKA protocol achieves the weakest accepted notion of security, and (3) group members of the protocol execution initiate certain non-trivial operation sequences. We note that, on an intuitive level, PKE are essentially the only building blocks of all practical CGKA constructions. Furthermore, all of the non-trivial operation sequences employed for our lower bounds are legitimate, and *could* happen in practice. Consequently, impractical worst-case communication overheads seem to be inevitable. However, in order to avoid such impractical communication overheads, one could (a) try to find suitable practical building blocks *other* than PKE to circumvent the lower bound, (b) lower the security requirements for CGKA (which we strongly advise against!), or (c) identify *all problematic* operation sequences and then forbid their execution. We believe that (a) finding better constructions and (c) identifying all such problematic operation sequences are interesting questions that we leave open for future work. However, for (a), we emphasize that one would ultimately need to circumvent our CKE lower bound. Although one may be able to do so using strong primitives such as indistinguishability obfuscation (as in the multi-party non-interactive key exchange of [16]), we view it as a challenging problem to do so from *practical* tools other than PKE.

We provide some further consequences of our lower bound in practice below.

CGKA with Two Administrators. Many real-world SGM systems in production may impose membership policies on users. That is, it could be that there are only a few "administrators" that are allowed to add and remove others from the group, while everyone else can only update their state and send messages. As shown by [12], for the setting in which there is only ever *one* administrator, CGKA boils down to the classical setting of Multicast Encryption [13,17,24,25,29,31,33]. Since there is only one administrator in Multicast, $O(\log n)$ communication complexity is easily achieved even with security property 1 above [12] (however, security property 2 already results in $\Omega(n)$ complexity for the administrator in Multicast). This is due to the fact that the sole administrator is never removed and executes all operations; thus she can use a tree as in some of the aforementioned CGKA protocols, and never allow it to degrade.

Therefore, a natural question is: In the setting of two administrators that can replace one another with new administrators, and where only property 1, but not property 2, is required for the administrators; can we retain $O(\log n)$ communication?[5] One can observe that our above lower bound answers this question in the negative. Indeed, there only ever need to be two administrators in the group. If so, then as above, one administrator can add k users, then the second administrator can replace the first with a new third administrator, then the third administrator can replace the second administrator, and so on. Thus, the jump from one to two administrators in the worst case requires communication to increase from $O(\log n)$ to $\Omega(n)$ per operation, if security property 1 (and not 2) is required.

MLS Propose-and-Commit Framework. The latest MLS protocol draft (version 14) [8], uses the "propose-and-commit" framework for CGKA. In this framework, users can publish many messages that *propose* different group operations (adding/removing others or updating their state), and a new group key is not established until some user subsequently publishes a *commit* message. The motivation behind this design is to allow for greater concurrency of CGKA operations: In prior drafts of MLS, users would attempt to establish a new group key with each operation. If many users desired to execute an operation at the same time and published corresponding CGKA ciphertexts, the delivery server would have to choose one such ciphertext to deliver to all group members (and thus only one of the group operations would be executed). With propose-and-commit, the delivery server still has to choose between commit messages, but many proposed group operations can be combined inside a single commit.

We however observe that we can still apply our above CGKA lower bound to this framework. Indeed, consider the scenario wherein one user (resp. administrator) A proposes to add k users, then publishes a commit for these additions. Thereafter, some other user (resp. administrator) B can replace A in a new proposal, then publish a commit for this replacement. Again, replacements can be repeated *ad infinitum*, and it can easily be seen that each such commit will

---

[5] If neither administrator is removed, of course $O(\log n)$ communication can be retained if they share a multicast tree.

still cost $\Omega(n)$ communication. Hence, our result of Sect. 3 naturally holds in the propose-and-commit framework.

2   Definitions

In this section, we define syntax and non-adaptive, one-way notions of security for Continuous Group Key Agreement and Compact Key Exchange. First, we introduce some notation.

Notation. For algorithm A, $y \leftarrow A(x; r)$ means that A on input x with randomness r outputs y. If r is not made explicit, it is assumed to be sampled uniformly at random, and we use notation $y \leftarrow_\$ A(x)$. We will also use the notation $x \leftarrow_\$ X$ to denote uniformly random sampling from set X. We will use dictionaries for our CGKA security game. The value stored with key x in dictionary D is denoted by $D[x]$. The statement $D[*] \leftarrow v$ initializes a dictionary D in which the default value for each key is v.

2.1   Continuous Group Key Agreement

In the simple, restricted form that we consider here, *Continuous Group Key Agreement* (CGKA) allows a dynamic set of users to continuously establish symmetric group keys. For participating in a group, a user first generates a public key and a secret state via algorithm Gen. With the secret state, a user can add or remove users to or from a group via algorithms Add and Rem. Furthermore, each user can update the secrets in their state from time to time to recover from adversarial state corruptions via algorithm Up. We call the latter three actions *group operations*. After all users process a group operation via algorithm Proc, they share the same group key. In order to analyze the *most efficient* form of CGKA, we assume a central bulletin board **B** to which public information on the current group structure is posted (initially empty) Thus, newly added users can obtain the relevant information about the group (which intuitively may be of size $\Omega(n)$ anyway, where n is the current number of group members) from **B**, instead of receiving it explicitly from the adding user. Note: the MLS protocol specification indeed suggests the added user can obtain the group tree of the protocol (size $\Omega(n)$) from a bulletin board (the delivery server) in this manner [8].

In the following, the added user simply downloads the *entire* board. Of course, in practice, this would be very inefficient, but this only strengthens our lower bound on the amount of communication sent between *current* group members (as opposed to the amount of information retrieved from the bulletin board by added users).

Definition 1. *A* Continuous Group Key Agreement *scheme* CGKA = (Gen, Add, Rem, Up, Proc) *consists of the following algorithms:*[6]

- Gen *is a PPT algorithm that outputs* (ST, PK).
- Add *is a PPT algorithm that takes in* (ST, PK), *where* ST *is the secret state of the user invoking the algorithm and* PK *is the public key of the added user, and outputs* (ST', K, C), *where* ST' *is the updated secret state of the invoking user,* K *is the new shared group key, and* C *is the ciphertext that is sent to (and then processed by) the group members. For efficiency purposes,* $C = (C_G, C_B)$ *consists of a share* C_G *that is sent to all group members directly and a share* C_B *that is posted to the central bulletin board* **B**.
- Rem *is a PPT algorithm that takes in* (ST, PK), *where* ST *is the secret state of the user invoking the algorithm and* PK *is the public key of the removed user, and outputs* (ST', K, C) *as above.*
- Up *is a PPT algorithm that takes in secret state* ST *of the user invoking the algorithm and outputs* (ST', K, C) *as above.*
- Proc *is a deterministic, polynomial time algorithm that takes in* (ST, C_G), *where* ST *is the secret state of the user invoking the algorithm and* C_G *is the ciphertext directly received for an operation, and outputs updated state and group key* (ST', K). *For users that were just added to the group,* Proc *additionally takes in bulletin board* **B**. *If the operation communicated via* C *removes the processing user from the group,* K *is set to a special symbol* ⊥.

Correctness and Security. We define correctness and security of CGKA via games that are played by an adversary $\mathcal{A}$, in which $\mathcal{A}$ controls an execution of the CGKA protocol. For simplicity and clarity, we only consider a *non-adaptive* protocol execution in a *single group*. The games are specified in Fig. 1.

Before either game starts, the adversary specifies the sequence of queries to the oracles **Gen**(), **Add**(), **Rem**(), **Up**(), and **Corr**() that will be executed. **Gen**() allows the adversary to initialize a new user, from which it receives the corresponding public key PK. The other oracles allow the adversary to execute group operations, i.e., to add, remove, and update users, respectively. Additionally, for the security game, the adversary beforehand specifies the *epoch* t which it will attack, i.e., for which it will guess the group key. The game starts in epoch $t = 0$, then increments t each time a group operation oracle is queried. The game forces the adversary to first query **Add**() to initialize the group. It keeps track of group members for each epoch using dictionary G. For simplicity, in each group operation query, the game immediately uses each current group member's state to process the resulting ciphertext directly sent to them, C_G, along with the

---

[6] For the sake of comprehensible communication analysis, we do not provide an explicit Create(ST, $PK_1, \ldots, PK_n$) algorithm (for which in practice, $\Omega(n)$ ciphertext size could be tolerated). Instead, we require the group creator to one-by-one add $PK_1, \ldots PK_n$, which allows us to prove a more meaningful lower bound on just Add, Rem, and Up operations.

Initialization: Set (i) $t = 0$; (ii) **WeakEpochs, WeakUsers** $= \emptyset$; and (iii) $\mathbf{G}[*], \mathbf{Rand}[*], \mathbf{ST}[*], \mathbf{K}[*] \leftarrow \perp$.

- **Gen()** executes $(\mathsf{ST}, \mathsf{PK}) \leftarrow_{\$} \mathsf{Gen}()$, sets $\mathbf{ST}[\mathsf{PK}] \leftarrow \mathsf{ST}$, and returns PK.
- **Add**(PK, PK*) first aborts if (i) $\mathsf{PK} = \mathsf{PK}^*$; (ii) $t \neq 0$ and $\mathsf{PK} \notin \mathbf{G}[t]$; or (iii) $\mathsf{PK}^* \in \mathbf{G}[t]$. Otherwise it:
  1. For randomly sampled r, sets $\mathbf{Rand}[\mathsf{PK}, t + 1] \leftarrow r$ and executes $(\mathbf{ST}[\mathsf{PK}], \mathbf{K}[t+1, \mathsf{PK}], (C_G, C_B)) \leftarrow \mathsf{Add}(\mathbf{ST}[\mathsf{PK}], \mathsf{PK}^*; r)$.
  2. Sets $\mathbf{G}[t + 1] \leftarrow \mathbf{G}[t] \cup \{\mathsf{PK}, \mathsf{PK}^*\}$.
  3. For every $\mathsf{PK}' \in \mathbf{G}[t] \setminus \{\mathsf{PK}\}$, executes $(\mathbf{ST}[\mathsf{PK}'], \mathbf{K}[t + 1, \mathsf{PK}']) \leftarrow \mathsf{Proc}(\mathbf{ST}[\mathsf{PK}'], C_G)$. Also executes $(\mathbf{ST}[\mathsf{PK}^*], \mathbf{K}[t + 1, \mathsf{PK}^*]) \leftarrow \mathsf{Proc}(\mathbf{ST}[\mathsf{PK}^*], C_G, \mathbf{B})$.
  4. If $(\mathbf{WeakUsers} \cap \mathbf{G}[t + 1]) \neq \emptyset$, sets $\mathbf{WeakEpochs} \leftarrow \mathbf{WeakEpochs} \cup \{t + 1\}$.
  5. Increments $t \leftarrow t + 1$ and returns (C_G, C_B).
- **Rem**(PK, PK*) first aborts if (i) $t = 0$; (ii) $\mathsf{PK} = \mathsf{PK}^*$; (iii) $\mathsf{PK} \notin \mathbf{G}[t]$; or (iv) $\mathsf{PK}^* \notin \mathbf{G}[t]$. Otherwise, it:
  1. For randomly sampled r, sets $\mathbf{Rand}[\mathsf{PK}, t + 1] \leftarrow r$ and executes $(\mathbf{ST}[\mathsf{PK}], \mathbf{K}[t+1, \mathsf{PK}], (C_G, C_B)) \leftarrow \mathsf{Rem}(\mathbf{ST}[\mathsf{PK}], \mathsf{PK}^*; r)$.
  2. Sets $\mathbf{G}[t + 1] \leftarrow \mathbf{G}[t] \setminus \{\mathsf{PK}^*\}$.
  3. For every $\mathsf{PK}' \in \mathbf{G}[t] \setminus \{\mathsf{PK}\}$, executes $(\mathbf{ST}[\mathsf{PK}'], \mathbf{K}[t + 1, \mathsf{PK}']) \leftarrow \mathsf{Proc}(\mathbf{ST}[\mathsf{PK}'], C_G)$.
  4. If $(\mathbf{WeakUsers} \cap \mathbf{G}[t + 1]) \neq \emptyset$, sets $\mathbf{WeakEpochs} \leftarrow \mathbf{WeakEpochs} \cup \{t + 1\}$.
  5. Increments $t \leftarrow t + 1$ and returns (C_G, C_B).
- **Up**(PK) first aborts if (i) $t = 0$; or (ii) $\mathsf{PK} \notin \mathbf{G}[t]$. Otherwise, it:
  1. For randomly sampled r, sets $\mathbf{Rand}[\mathsf{PK}, t + 1] \leftarrow r$ and executes $(\mathbf{ST}[\mathsf{PK}], \mathbf{K}[t+1, \mathsf{PK}], (C_G, C_B)) \leftarrow \mathsf{Up}(\mathbf{ST}[\mathsf{PK}]; r)$.
  2. Sets $\mathbf{G}[t + 1] \leftarrow \mathbf{G}[t]$ and $\mathbf{WeakUsers} \leftarrow \mathbf{WeakUsers} \setminus \{\mathsf{PK}\}$.
  3. For every $\mathsf{PK}' \in \mathbf{G}[t + 1] \setminus \{\mathsf{PK}\}$, executes $(\mathbf{ST}[\mathsf{PK}'], \mathbf{K}[t + 1, \mathsf{PK}']) \leftarrow \mathsf{Proc}(\mathbf{ST}[\mathsf{PK}'], C_G)$.
  4. If $(\mathbf{WeakUsers} \cap \mathbf{G}[t + 1]) \neq \emptyset$, sets $\mathbf{WeakEpochs} \leftarrow \mathbf{WeakEpochs} \cup \{t + 1\}$.
  5. Increments $t \leftarrow t + 1$ and returns (C_G, C_B).

- **Corr**(PK) first sets **WeakUsers** $\leftarrow$ **WeakUsers** $\cup \{\mathsf{PK}\}$ and **WeakEpochs** $\leftarrow$ **WeakEpochs** $\cup \{t' \leq t : \mathsf{PK} \in \mathbf{G}[t']\}$. Then it returns $\mathbf{ST}[\mathsf{PK}]$ and $\mathbf{Rand}[\mathsf{PK}, t']$, for every $t' \leq t$.

Fig. 1. The CGKA correctness and security games.

current bulletin board **B**, in the case of an added user. Dictionary **K** keeps track of the group key that each user computes for each epoch. Each group operation oracle returns $C = (C_G, C_B)$ to the adversary.

Definition 2. *A CGKA scheme* CGKA *is* correct *if for every adversary* $\mathcal{A}$ *against the correctness game defined by Fig. 1, and for all t and* PK, PK$' \in$ **G**$[t]$: Pr $\left[\mathbf{K}[t, \mathsf{PK}] = \mathbf{K}[t, \mathsf{PK}']\right] = 1$.

Our notion of security is slightly weakened compared to the standard definition in the CGKA literature, which only strengthens our lower bound. That is, the corruption of a user may affect the security of those keys that were established in the past while this user was a group member. Thus, forward secrecy is not captured. Also, we do not consider authenticity.[7] However, our notion still captures basic security requirements plus standard PCS requirement (mentioned in the introduction), as explained below.

We first explain the importance of dictionary **Rand**, in addition to sets **WeakEpochs** and **WeakUsers**, which allow the game to capture this security. **Rand** keeps track of the randomness the users sample to execute the operations of each epoch. Intuitively, **WeakEpochs** and **WeakUsers** keep track of those epochs and users that are insecure, respectively. When the adversary queries oracle **Corr**(PK), the game returns the corresponding user's secret state, as well as the randomness which she used to execute *all* of her past group operations. Thus, the game adds PK to **WeakUsers** and since we do not require forward secrecy, it also adds to **WeakEpochs** every past epoch in which the corresponding user was in the group. Now, for every **Up**(PK) query, the game removes PK from **WeakUsers**. This in part captures PCS: in every group operation query, if there are still weak users in the group (i.e., (**WeakUsers** $\cap$ G$[t+1]) \neq \emptyset$), then the game adds the new epoch $t + 1$ to **WeakEpochs**. So, if there is a member of the group that was corrupted and did not since update their state, the epoch is deemed weak. Conversely, as soon as every group member updates their state or is removed after a corruption, epochs are no longer deemed weak.

After receiving all return values of the pre-specified sequence's queries to these oracles, the adversary outputs a key K. This key K is a guess for the actual group key established in epoch t, where t is the pre-specified attack epoch. Note that this recoverability definition is weaker than standard indistinguishability definitions, which strengthens our lower bound.

Definition 3. *A CGKA scheme* CGKA *is* secure *if for every PPT adversary* $\mathcal{A} = (\mathcal{A}_1, \mathcal{A}_2)$ *against the security game defined by Fig. 1:*

$$\Pr\left[K \leftarrow_{\$} \mathcal{A}_2(\omega, \mathsf{Trans}) : K = \mathbf{K}[t, \mathsf{PK}^*]; t \notin \mathbf{WeakEpochs};\right.$$
$$\left.\mathsf{PK}^* \in \mathsf{G}[t]; (\omega, \mathsf{Seq}, t) \leftarrow_{\$} \mathcal{A}_1(1^\lambda)\,\right] \leq \mathsf{negl}(\lambda),$$

where $\mathcal{A}_1$ non-adaptively specifies the sequence of oracle queries Seq *and the attacked epoch t, and $\mathcal{A}_2$ guesses the attacked key when obtaining the transcript of oracle return values* Trans.

---

[7] Analyzing the effect of required authenticity under weak randomness [7] on (communication) complexity in the group setting [27], as well as of extended security goals such as anonymity [23] remains an interesting open question.

2.2 Compact Key Exchange

We can now define Compact Key Exchange with access to a common reference string (CRS). Such protocols allow some users $1, \ldots, n$ to sample independent (across users) key pairs $(\mathsf{SK}_1, \mathsf{PK}_1), \ldots, (\mathsf{SK}_n, \mathsf{PK}_n)$, then publicly broadcast $\mathsf{PK}_1, \ldots, \mathsf{PK}_n$. Upon reception of these public keys, special user 0 generates a key K and message C, and broadcasts C. Finally, upon reception of C, every user $i \in [n]$ uses SK_i, the set of public keys $\{\mathsf{PK}_j\}_{j \in [n]}$, and C to derive K.

Definition 4. *A* Compact Key Exchange *scheme* CKE $=$ (CRSGen, Init, Comm, Derive) *in the standard model with common reference string* CRS $\in \mathcal{CRS}$ *consists of the following algorithms:*

- Init *is a PPT algorithm that takes in* CRS $\leftarrow_\$ \mathrm{CRSGen}(1^\lambda)$ *and outputs* $(\mathsf{SK}, \mathsf{PK})$.
- Comm *is a PPT algorithm that takes in* CRS *and set* $\{\mathsf{PK}_i\}_{i \in [n]}$ *and outputs* (K, C).
- Derive *is a deterministic, polynomial time algorithm that takes in* CRS, SK_i, *where* $i \in [n]$, *set* $\{\mathsf{PK}_j\}_{j \in [n]}$, *and* C, *and outputs* K.

For correctness, we require that for any n, and for every $i \in [n]$:

$$\Pr\left[K \leftarrow \mathrm{Derive}\left(\mathsf{CRS}, \mathsf{SK}_i, \{\mathsf{PK}_j\}_{j\in[n]}, C\right) : (K, C) \leftarrow_\$ \mathrm{Comm}\left(\mathsf{CRS}, \{\mathsf{PK}_j\}_{j\in[n]}\right) ; \right.$$
$$\forall j \in [n], (\mathsf{SK}_j, \mathsf{PK}_j) \leftarrow_\$ \mathrm{Init}(\mathsf{CRS});$$
$$\left. \mathsf{CRS} \leftarrow_\$ \mathrm{CRSGen}(1^\lambda)\right] = 1.$$

For security, we require that for every PPT adversary $\mathcal{A}$ that specifies $n = \mathsf{poly}(\lambda)$:

$$\Pr\left[K \leftarrow_\$ \mathcal{A}\left(\mathsf{CRS}, \{\mathsf{PK}_i\}_{i\in[n]}, C\right) : (K, C) \leftarrow_\$ \mathrm{Comm}\left(\mathsf{CRS}, \{\mathsf{PK}_i\}_{i\in[n]}\right) ; \right.$$
$$\forall i \in [n], (\mathsf{SK}_i, \mathsf{PK}_i) \leftarrow_\$ \mathrm{Init}(\mathsf{CRS});$$
$$\left. \mathsf{CRS} \leftarrow_\$ \mathrm{CRSGen}(1^\lambda)\right] \leq \mathsf{negl}(\lambda).$$

Ideally, $|C|$ should be a small function (perhaps independent) of n.

Remark 1. Of course, there is a simple CKE protocol (without CRS) from PKE scheme PKE $=$ (Gen, Enc, Dec), where $|C| = O(\lambda \cdot n)$: Init() simply samples sk $\leftarrow_\$ \{0,1\}^\lambda$, then computes pk $\leftarrow$ Gen(sk) and outputs (sk, pk). Comm($\{\mathsf{pk}_i\}_{i\in[n]}$) samples $K \leftarrow_\$ \{0,1\}^\lambda$, and for each $i \in [n]$ computes $c_i \leftarrow_\$ \mathrm{Enc}(\mathsf{pk}_i, K)$. It then outputs (K, C), where $C = (c_1, \ldots, c_n)$. Finally, Derive($\mathsf{sk}_i, \{\mathsf{pk}_j\}_{j\in[n]}, C$) computes $K \leftarrow \mathrm{Dec}(\mathsf{sk}_i, c_i)$ and outputs K. Correctness and security follow trivially.

3 From CGKA to CKE Tightly

In this section, we show that CKE is at the core of CGKA, both in terms of cryptographic strength and *worst-case* communication complexity, by providing a *tight* construction of the former from the latter. Due to space constraints, the simpler counter direction—building CGKA from CKE, tightly—is provided in the full version [10]. From these two reductions, we show that the worst-case communication complexity of CGKA operations is asymptotically equivalent to the size of CKE ciphertexts. That is, we show that the best possible size of a CKE ciphertext implies 1. a lower bound on the worst-case communication complexity of CGKA operations; and 2. an upper bound for the same. With this result, we additionally prove that the communication overhead in a CGKA group is necessarily increased if group members remain offline after they were added to the group. Indeed, based on our $\Omega(n)$ lower bound on CKE ciphertext size for protocols that make black-box use of PKE from Sect. 4, we show that worst-case communication overhead for CGKA protocols that make black-box use of PKE is $\Omega(k)$, where k is the number of added users who remain inactive after being added to the group. Furthermore, we show that this holds even for (unboundedly) many consecutive operations.

To illustrate our proof idea, consider the following execution of a CGKA protocol: Let users A and B be members of an existing CGKA group. User A adds k new users to this group before user B removes A from the group and B finally conducts a state update. After A is removed and B updates his state, the group must share a key that is secure even if A is corrupted after he is removed or B was corrupted before his update, and there were no other corruptions. (Note that these corruptions of A and B must be harmless w.r.t. security because A was removed and B updated his state to recover according to PCS.) We observe that the only information received by the k new users so far were A's add-ciphertexts and B's remove- and update-ciphertexts. Since A may have been corrupted (which reveals the randomness she used for adding the k users), the add-ciphertexts may contain no confidential payload. Similarly, B might have been corrupted until he updated his state. Hence, B's ciphertext that updates his state is the only input from which the k users can derive a secure group key. This update ciphertext intuitively corresponds to a CKE ciphertext that establishes a key with the k newly added users. In our proof, we generalize this intuition to show that, as long as k new group members remain passive, a recurring linear communication overhead in $\Omega(k)$ cannot be avoided when active group members repeatedly update the group's key material.

3.1   Embedding CGKA Ciphertexts in CKE Ciphertexts

With our proof that CGKA implies CKE, we directly lift the communication-cost lower bound for CKE from Sect. 4 to certain *bad* sequences in a CGKA execution. That means, our proof implies that such bad sequences in a CGKA execution lead to a linear communication overhead in the number of *affected* users. For this, we build a CKE construction that embeds specific CGKA ciphertexts in its CKE ciphertexts. Thus, a CGKA scheme that achieves sub-linear communication costs in the number of affected group members for these embedded ciphertexts results in a CKE with compact ciphertexts, which contradicts our lower bound from Sect. 4.

Components of Bad Sequences. Intuitively, a *bad CGKA sequence* is an operation sequence in a CGKA session during which k *passive users* are added to the group that stay offline while (few) other members actively conduct CGKA operations continuously. A CGKA session that contains such a sequence can be split into (1) a *pre-add phase* that ends when the first of these k passive users is added and (2) the subsequent *bad sequence* itself. The *bad sequence* contains (2.a) the *add operations* due to which the passive users become group members as well as (2.c) multiple, potentially overlapping, iterations of *collective update assistances*. With these *collective update assistances*, the active users update key material for the newly added passive users, which causes the communication overhead in $\Omega(k)$. From the perspective of each *collective update assistance*, the remaining operations in a *bad sequence* can be categorized into (2.b) *ineffective pre-assistance operations* and (2.d) an *irrelevant end*. (The numbering in the above enumeration reflects the order of these components within the bad sequence)

Let sequence $\mathsf{Seq} = (\mathsf{Op}_1, \ldots, \mathsf{Op}_n)$ be the execution schedule of a CGKA session, where each Op_t is a tuple that refers to an executed group operation with the following format: $\mathsf{Op}_t = (\mathsf{Up}, \mathsf{PK}, \bot)$ means that PK updates their state; $\mathsf{Op}_t = (\mathsf{Add}, \mathsf{PK}, \mathsf{PK}^*)$ means that PK adds PK^*; $\mathsf{Op}_t = (\mathsf{Rem}, \mathsf{PK}, \mathsf{PK}^*)$ means that PK removes PK^*; see Sect. 2.1 for more details. Further, let $PU, |PU| = k$, be the public key set of the k passive users, such that for every $\mathsf{PK}^* \in PU$ there exists an operation $(\mathsf{Add}, \cdot, \mathsf{PK}^*)$ but neither an operation $(\mathsf{Rem}, \cdot, \mathsf{PK}^*)$ nor an operation $(\cdot, \mathsf{PK}^*, \cdot)$ in sequence Seq.

(1) The *pre-add phase* starts at the beginning of the entire sequence and ends with the $t_1^A - 1$th operation, where $\mathsf{Op}_{t_1^A} = (\mathsf{Add}, \cdot, \mathsf{PK}^*)$ is the *first* operation that adds a user $\mathsf{PK}^* \in PU$ to the group. **(2.a)** The *add operations*, starting with operation $\mathsf{Op}_{t_1^A}$, end with the *last* operation $\mathsf{Op}_{t_k^A} = (\mathsf{Add}, \cdot, \mathsf{PK}^*)$ that adds a user $\mathsf{PK}^* \in PU$ to the group. (Also operations other than adding passive users can be contained in this phase.)

(2.c) The first *collective update assistance* ends when all active users conducted their first update after the add operations. During such a *collective update assistance*, the active users both propagate new *own key material* but also collectively establish and communicate new *key material for the passive users*. We define AU_{t^*} as the public key set of *users* who are *active* between the t_1^Ath and t^*th operation. That means $\mathsf{PK}^* \in AU_{t^*}$ iff there exists at least one operation $\mathsf{Op}_t = (\cdot, \mathsf{PK}^*, \cdot)$ but no operation $\mathsf{Op}_t = (\mathsf{Rem}, \cdot, \mathsf{PK}^*)$ for $t_1^A \leq t \leq t^*$ in sequence Seq. Every *collective update assistance* by active users in set AU_{t^*} is determined by its final operation $\mathsf{Op}_{t^*}, t^* > t_k^A$, for which it must hold that all users $\mathsf{PK}^* \in AU_{t^*}$ conducted an update operation between the $t_k^A + 1$th and t^*th operation. Such a *collective update assistance* consists of a set of *effective operations* EO_{t^*} from sequence Seq. These *effective operations* establish key material with the passive users and, in total, have a communication overhead of $\Omega(k)$ as we will prove. **(2.b)** Operations executed prior to the t^*th operation that are not in set EO_{t^*} are called *ineffective pre-assistance operations*. **(2.d)** The remaining sequence after the t^*th operation is the *irrelevant end*. In summary, a bad sequence from the perspective of one (out of potentially many) *collective update assistances* is structured as follows: (2.a) *add operations* between the t_1^Ath and t_k^Ath operation, (2.b) *ineffective pre-assistance operations* between the $t_k^A + 1$th and $t^* - 1$th operation, (2.c) *effective operations* between the $t_k^A + 1$th and t^*th operation that constitute this *collective update assistance*, and (2.d) *irrelevant end* after the t^*th operation.

The *effective operations* consist of all active users' operations since their respective most recent update operation. That means, for each active user public key $\mathsf{PK} \in AU_{t^*}$, the set of *effective operations* EO_{t^*} in a *collective update assistance* contains all operations $\mathsf{Op}_{t'} = (\cdot, \mathsf{PK}, \cdot)$ that were initiated since the most recent update operation $\mathsf{Op}_{t_\mathsf{PK}} = (\mathsf{Up}, \mathsf{PK}, \cdot)$ by user PK, where $t_\mathsf{PK} \le t' \le t^*$ with maximal t_PK, respectively.

Intuition for a Bad Sequence. Active users establish secret key material for passive users in *collective update assistances*. The communication overhead in $\Omega(k)$ that is induced by such a *collective update assistance* can be distributed among all corresponding *effective operations*. That means, active users can trade the work of establishing key material and the corresponding necessary communication overhead within each *collective update assistance*. However, it is important to emphasize that operations only establish key material to passive users *effectively* if the involved active users are not corrupted at that point. Hence, from the perspective of a CGKA group key computed with the t^*th operation, prior operations only contribute effectively to its secure computation if the involved users were able to recover from a potential earlier corruption. Such a recovery from a corruption is achieved via an update operation. This is the reason why the *effective operations* are defined as each active user's last operations since their most recent state update. During and after these state updates, the active users collectively assist the passive users in securely deriving the same CGKA group key in the t^*th operation.

Based on the above terminology, we formulate our communication overhead lower bound in the following theorem:

Theorem 1 (CGKA Lower Bound). *Let* Seq *be an execution schedule of a CGKA session during which k passive users are added to the group until the t_k^Ath operation. Let t^* determine the last operation of any subsequent* collective update *assistance such that all active users in set AU_{t^*} conduct an update between the $t_k^A + 1$th and t^*th operation. Finally, let EO_{t^*} be the corresponding set of* effective *operations that consist of all active users' most recent update and subsequent operations until the t^*th operation. The total size of ciphertexts sent by operations in set EO_{t^*} is $\Omega(k)$ for every CGKA construction that makes black-box use of PKE.*

The proof of Theorem 1 is provided in the full version [10].

In Corollary 1 we formulate a simpler, more specific variant of bad sequences that is directly implied by Theorem 1. Consider a sequence Seq in which the active users, after adding the passive users, only conduct state update operations.

Then, the *effective operations* of each *collective update assistance* in sequence Seq are simply the most recent state updates by each active user.

Corollary 1 (Effective Update Operations). *Let* Seq *be an execution schedule of a CGKA session during which* k *passive users are added to the group until the* t_k^A*th operation. Let* t^* *determine the last operation of any subsequent collective update assistance such that all active users in set* AU_{t^*} *conduct an update between the* $t_k^A + 1$*th and* t^**th operation. If all operations after the* t_k^A*th operation are state updates, then the total size of ciphertexts sent due to the most recent updates by each active user in set* AU_{t^*} *is* $\Omega(k)$ *for every CGKA construction that makes black-box use of PKE, where* $|AU_{t^*}| = |EO_{t^*}|$.

Overlapping Collective Update Assistances. We want to point out that *effective operations* of different *collective update assistances* may overlap. For example, an active user A may update their state during the sequence Seq precisely once after the passive users were added. The remaining active users B and C may repeatedly perform new updates until the end of the sequence. In this case, the *effective operations* of all *collective update assistances* in sequence Seq will include the single update operation by A and always the most recent operations of B and C since their respective latest update in this sequence. As we will show in Sect. 5, there exists no optimal strategy to exploit the fact that effective operations of *different* collective update assistances can *overlap*. For example, one cannot successfully predict which *single* effective operations are in *several* collective update assistances and thus make these *single* operations have large communication overhead, so that large costs are not repeated several times.

Continuous Update Assistances. We finally come back to our motivating example CGKA execution schedule. In this schedule, only one user A adds the k passive users, and another user B removes A thereafter. In order to show that adding k passive users can induce a *continuous* communication overhead, we extend this execution schedule: after adding the k passive users, l active users replace each other, one after another. More precisely, first a user A adds k users as well as a second user B, then user B removes A and adds a new user C, then C replaces user B by a new user D, and so on. Each of these active users additionally performs a state update after replacing their predecessor. The effect of this cascade of replace-update sequences is that each contained update operation constitutes a single ~~collective~~ update assistance, individually inducing a communication overhead of $\Omega(k)$.[8] As a result, the entire schedule induces a communication overhead of $\Omega(k \cdot l)$. We formally define this CGKA execution schedule in Definition 5 and give the corresponding Corollary 2.

Definition 5 (Continuous Update Assistance). *Let* Seq *be an operation schedule of a CGKA session during which user* PK_0 *adds* k *passive users to the group until the* t_k^A*th operation. Schedule* Seq *contains a* Continuous Update

---

[8] We strike out "collective" because each update assistance is conducted by a single active user in this execution schedule.

Assistance *of length l after the* $t_k^A th$ *operation if* Seq *proceeds after the* $t_k^A th$ *operation with l repetitions of operation sequences* $(\mathsf{Op}_{i,A}, \mathsf{Op}_{i,R}, \mathsf{Op}_{i,U}), i \in [l]$, *where* $\mathsf{Op}_{i,A} = (\mathsf{Add}, \mathsf{PK}_i, \mathsf{PK}_{i+1})$, $\mathsf{Op}_{i,R} = (\mathsf{Rem}, \mathsf{PK}_{i+1}, \mathsf{PK}_i)$, *and* $\mathsf{Op}_{i,U} = (\mathsf{Up}, \mathsf{PK}_{i+1}, \bot)$ *for independent users* $\mathsf{PK}_j, j \in [l+1]$.

Corollary 2 (Continuous Communication Overhead). *For every CGKA execution schedule* Seq *that contains a* Continuous Update Assistance *of length l after the* $t_k^A th$ *operation, the total size of ciphertexts output by the* $3l$ *operations after the* $t_k^A th$ *operation is* $\Omega(k \cdot l)$ *for every CGKA construction that makes black-box use of PKE.*

The proof of Corollary 2 is a direct application of Theorem 1 via a simple hybrid argument that considers each replace-update sequence in Seq as a ~~collective~~ update assistance.

4   CKE Lower Bound from PKE

Before showing our lower bound for CKE from PKE, we need to define the model in which we prove it.

Preliminaries. For a function f we write $f(*) = y$ to indicate $f(x) = y$ for some input x. We generalize this notation for the case in which some part of the input is fixed, writing $f(a_1, *) = y$, interpreted in the natural way. Due to space limitations, many other preliminaries are deferred to the full version [10].

CKE in the Ψ-Model. The model for our proof gives the protocol and adversary access to an oracle distribution, defined as follows:

Definition 6. *We define an oracle distribution* Ψ *that produces oracles* $(\mathbf{O}, \mathbf{u}, \mathbf{v})$*, where* $\mathbf{O} = (\mathbf{g}, \mathbf{e}, \mathbf{d})$*. The distribution is parameterized over a security parameter* λ*, but we keep it implicit for better readability.*

- $\mathbf{g}$: $\{0,1\}^\lambda \mapsto \{0,1\}^{3\lambda}$ *is a random length-tripling function, mapping a secret key to a public key.*
- $\mathbf{e}$: $\{0,1\}^{3\lambda} \times \{0,1\} \times \{0,1\}^\lambda \mapsto \{0,1\}^{3\lambda}$: *is a random function satisfying the following: for every* $\mathsf{pk} \in \{0,1\}^{3\lambda}$*, the function* $\mathbf{e}(\mathsf{pk}, \cdot, \cdot)$ *is injective; i.e., if* $(m, r) \neq (m', r')$*, then* $\mathbf{e}(\mathsf{pk}, m, r) \neq \mathbf{e}(\mathsf{pk}, m', r')$.
- $\mathbf{d}$: $\{0,1\}^\lambda \times \{0,1\}^{3\lambda} \mapsto \{0,1\}$ *is the decryption oracle, where* $\mathbf{d}(\mathsf{sk}, c)$ *outputs* $m \in \{0,1\}$ *if* $\mathbf{e}(\mathbf{g}(\mathsf{sk}), m, *) = c$*; otherwise,* $\mathbf{d}(\mathsf{sk}, c) = \bot$.
- $\mathbf{v}$: $\{0,1\}^{3\lambda} \times \{0,1\}^{3\lambda} \mapsto \{\bot, \top\}$*, is a ciphertext-validity checking oracle:* $\mathbf{v}(\mathsf{pk}, c)$ *outputs* $\top$ *if* c *is in the range of* $\mathbf{e}(\mathsf{pk}, \cdot, \cdot)$ *(that is,* $c := \mathbf{e}(\mathsf{pk}, *, *)$*); otherwise, it outputs* $\bot$.
- $\mathbf{u}$: $\{0,1\}^{3\lambda} \times \{0,1\}^{3\lambda} \mapsto \{0,1\} \cup \{\bot\}$*, is an oracle that decrypts wrt invalid public keys; given* (pk, c)*, if there exists* sk *such that* $\mathbf{g}(sk) = \mathsf{pk}$*, then* $\mathbf{u}(\mathsf{pk}, c) = \bot$*; otherwise, if there exists a message* $m \in \{0,1\}$ *such that* $\mathbf{e}(\mathsf{pk}, m, *) = c$*, return* m*; else, return* $\bot$.

Now, we can define CKE in the Ψ-model.

Definition 7. *A* Compact Key Exchange *scheme in the Ψ-model is defined equivalently as in Definition 4, except that each of the CKE algorithms and the adversary additionally have access to the Ψ oracles. We denote such access using Ψ as a superscript in the corresponding algorithms, e.g.,* $\mathsf{Init}^{\Psi}(\mathsf{CRS})$. *All other syntax and security requirements stay the same.*

4.1 Proof Outline

Our lower bound is derived from the following two lemmas. The first lemma shows a random $(\mathbf{g}, \mathbf{e}, \mathbf{d})$ constitutes an ideally-secure PKE protocol, even against adversaries that have access to the oracles $(\mathbf{u}, \mathbf{v})$, in addition to $(\mathbf{g}, \mathbf{e}, \mathbf{d})$. The second lemma shows that the security of any proposed CKE protocol $(\mathsf{CRSGen}, \mathsf{Init}, \mathsf{Comm}, \mathsf{Derive})$, instantiated with a random $\mathbf{O} := (\mathbf{g}, \mathbf{e}, \mathbf{d})$, may be broken by an adversary making at most a polynomial number of queries to $(\mathbf{O}, \mathbf{u}, \mathbf{v})$. The black-box separation will then follow.

Lemma 1 (O is secure against $(\mathbf{O}, \mathbf{u}, \mathbf{v})$). *For any polynomial-query adversary A:* $\Pr[\mathsf{A}^{\mathbf{O}, \mathbf{u}, \mathbf{v}}(\mathsf{pk}, c) = b] \leq 1/2 + \frac{1}{2^{\lambda/2}}$, *where* $(\mathbf{g}, \mathbf{e}, \mathbf{d}, \mathbf{u}, \mathbf{v}) \leftarrow_\$ \Psi$, $\mathbf{O} := (\mathbf{g}, \mathbf{e}, \mathbf{d})$, $b \leftarrow_\$ \{0,1\}$, $\mathsf{sk} \leftarrow_\$ \{0,1\}^{\lambda}$, $\mathsf{pk} = \mathbf{g}(\mathsf{sk})$, $r \leftarrow_\$ \{0,1\}^{\lambda}$ *and* $c - \mathbf{e}(\mathsf{pk}, b; r)$.

The following lemma shows how to break compact CKE constructions relative to the PKE oracles. The lemma shows that even for encrypting single-bit keys (i.e., $|K| = 1$), a CKE ciphertext cannot be sub-linear in n.

Lemma 2 (Breaking CKE relative to $(\mathbf{O}, \mathbf{u}, \mathbf{v})$). *Let* $(\mathsf{CRSGen}, \mathsf{Init}, \mathsf{Comm}, \mathsf{Derive})$ *be a candidate black-box construction of CKE, where for any CKE ciphertext C, $|C| \leq \frac{3\lambda(n-1)}{2}$. For any constant c, there exists a polynomial-query adversary $\mathsf{Brk}^{\mathbf{O}, \mathbf{u}, \mathbf{v}}$ such that* $\Pr[\mathsf{Brk}^{\mathbf{O}, \mathbf{u}, \mathbf{v}}(\mathsf{PK}_1, \ldots, \mathsf{PK}_n, C) = K] \geq 1 - \frac{1}{\lambda^c}$, *where* $(\mathbf{g}, \mathbf{e}, \mathbf{d}, \mathbf{u}, \mathbf{v}) \leftarrow_\$ \Psi$, $\mathbf{O} := (\mathbf{g}, \mathbf{e}, \mathbf{d})$, $\mathsf{CRS} \leftarrow_\$ \mathsf{CRSGen}^{\mathbf{O}}(1^{\lambda})$, $(\mathsf{PK}_i, *) \leftarrow_\$ \mathsf{Init}^{\mathbf{O}}(\mathsf{CRS})$ *for* $i \in [n]$, *and* $(K, C) \leftarrow_\$ \mathsf{Comm}^{\mathbf{O}}(\mathsf{CRS}, \mathsf{PK}_1, \ldots, \mathsf{PK}_n)$.

Roadmap. Lemma 1 is proved in a straightforward way (hence omitted), given the random nature of the oracles. The proof of Lemma 2 is the main technical bulk of our paper, consisting of the description of an attacker and attack analysis. We first describe the attacker for the case $(\mathsf{Init}^{\mathbf{g}}, \mathsf{Comm}^{\mathbf{e}}, \mathsf{Derive}^{\mathbf{d}})$ in Sect. 4.2, and will then describe an attack against general constructions in the full version [10]. Lemma 2 will follow similarly from the below simpler attack. We may now obtain the following from Lemmas 1, 2, proved via standard black-box separation techniques.

Theorem 2. *There exists no fully-black-box construction of CKE schemes from PKE schemes with CKE ciphertext size $o(n)|c|$, where $|c|$ denotes the ciphertext size of the base PKE scheme.*

4.2   Attack for $(\text{CRSGen}^g, \text{Init}^g, \text{Comm}^e, \text{Derive}^d)$

We will show an attack for the case in which oracle access is of the form $(\text{CRSGen}^g, \text{Init}^g, \text{Comm}^e, \text{Derive}^d)$. This already captures the main ideas behind the impossibility result. We will then show how to relax this assumption.

Attack Overview. Let $(\text{PK}_1, \ldots, \text{PK}_n, C)$ be the public keys and the ciphertext. We show an impossibility as long as $|C| \leq \frac{3\lambda(n-1)}{2}$, where recall that 3λ is the size of a base ciphertext as per oracles generated by Ψ (Definition 6). This particular choice for the size of C will ensure that C can "embed" at most $n-1$ base ciphertexts, in a sense we will later describe.

For simplicity, in this overview we assume that the scheme does not have a CRS. The attack is based on the following high-level idea. During the generation of each $(\text{PK}_i, \text{SK}_i) \leftarrow_\$ \text{Init}^g(1^\lambda)$ a set of g-type query/answer pairs made. Let $\text{KPair}_i = \{(\text{pk}_{i,1}, \text{sk}_{i,1}), \ldots, (\text{pk}_{i,t}, \text{sk}_{i,t})\}$ be the set of public/secret key pairs produced during the generation of PK_i. These public keys are in someway encoded in PK_i, and the ability to decrypt with respect to these base $\text{pk}_{i,j}$ public keys is the only advantage that the ith party, who has SK_i, has over an adversary.

Consider a random execution of $(K, C) \leftarrow_\$ \text{Comm}^e(\text{PK}_1, \ldots, \text{PK}_n)$, and let $Q = \{(\text{pk}_1, b_i, r_i, c_i) \mid i \in [f]\}$ contain the set of all query/answer pairs, and let $Q_c = \{c_1, \ldots, c_f\}$. Since the ciphertext C is compact, C can embed at most $(n-1)$ ciphertexts c_i from the set Q_c. By embedding we mean anyone, including the legitimate users, given only C can extract at most $n-1$ valid pairs (pk_i, c_i) without querying e.

Now for each user consider its local decryption execution. Each user performing decryption will need to decrypt pairs of the form (pk, c), in order to recover a shared K. We focus on those pairs which are valid, meaning that c is in the range of $e(\text{pk}, \cdot, \cdot)$. Looking ahead, the reason for this is that for invalid pairs for which the answer is $\perp$, an adversary can already simulate the answer by calling u. Let S_i' be the set of valid pairs that come up during decryption performed by user i. Since C embeds at most $n-1$ valid pairs (pk, c), for some user h: $S_h' \subseteq S_1' \cup \ldots S_{h-1}'$. In other words, the set of base trapdoors needed to decrypt S_h' is a subset of those for $S_1' \cup \ldots S_{h-1}'$. Moreover, in order for any user to be able to decrypt some (pk, c), the user should have observed a query/answer pair (pk, sk) during its execution of $\text{Init}^g(1^\lambda)$. Thus, recalling KPair_h, the set of base secret keys needed to decrypt elements in S_h' is a subset of $\text{KPair}_1 \cup \ldots, \cup \text{KPair}_{h-1}$. But each of these KPair_i sets (for $i \in [n]$) is obtained by running $\text{Init}^g(1^\lambda)$ on a security parameter, and so if an adversary runs $\text{Init}^g(1^\lambda)$ many times and collects all query/answer pairs in a set Freq, the adversary with high probability will collect all the trapdoors needed to successfully decrypt for at least one user.

How to Perform Simulated Decryption? So far, the discussion above says that an adversary can collect a set Freq which with high probability contains all (pk, sk) pairs needed to decrypt with respect to at least one user. But even given Freq, it is unclear how to perform decryption for any user. The adversary cannot simply "look at" Freq and somehow decrypt C — the adversary will need a secret key

SK to be able to run Derive(SK, ·). The solution is to let the adversary sample a "fake" secret keys for users, in a manner consistent with query-answer knowledge of Freq.

We make the following assumption for the construction (CRSGen^g, Init^g, Comm^e, Derive^d) that we want to prove an impossibility for. The assumption is made only for ease of exposition.

Assumption 3. We assume for any oracle $(g, e, d) \leftarrow_\$ \Psi$ picked as in Definition 6, each algorithm in (CRSGen^g, Init^g, Comm^e, Derive^d) makes only a security parameter λ number of queries.

Definition 8 (Partial oracles and consistency). *We say a partial oracle O_1 (defined only on a subset of all points) is Ψ-valid if for some $O_2 \in$ Supp(Ψ): $O_1 \subseteq O_2$, where* Supp *denotes the support of a distribution. We say an oracle (g, e, d) is PKE-valid if it satisfies PKE completeness. A partial PKE-valid oracle is one which is a subset of a PKE-valid oracle. Note that any Ψ-valid oracle is PKE-valid as well. We say a partial oracle O_1 is consistent with a set of query/response pairs S if $O_1 \cup S$ is PKE-valid.*

We also need to define the notion of a partial oracle forbidding a set of query/response pairs. This technique of forbidding a set of query/answer pairs will be used extensively in our constructions, and to the best of our knowledge, no previous impossibility results deal with this technique.

Definition 9 (Forbidding queries). *Let* Forbid *consists of "wildcard" queries/ responses, of the form $(q \xrightarrow{z} *)$ or $(* \xrightarrow{z} u)$, where $z \in \{g, e\}$. We say that a partial oracle $O_1 = (\tilde{g}, \tilde{e})$ forbids* Forbid *if (a) for any $(q \xrightarrow{z} *) \in$ Forbid the oracle $\tilde{z}$ is not defined on input q and (b) for any $(* \xrightarrow{z} u)$ the oracle $\tilde{z}$ is not defined on any input point with a corresponding output u (i.e., y is not in the set of output points defined under $\tilde{z}$).*

The attacker will first perform many random executions of Init^g(CRS) to collect all likely query/response pairs: those that appear during a random execution with a high-enough probability. This will allow the adversary to learn the secret keys for all likely base pk's that might be embedded to more than one user's CKE public key. Once this step is done, the attacker will sample partial oracles that are consistent with the set of collected query/answer pairs. Recall that by Assumption 3 any execution of Init^g(CRS) makes exactly λ queries. We say a partial oracle **O'** (defined only on a subset of points) is minimal for an execution Init$^{O'}$(CRS; R), if the execution makes queries only to those points defined in **O'**, and nothing else. This means in particular that **O'** is defined only on λ points. In the definition below, we talk about sampling *minimal* partial oracles **O'** that agree with some set of query/answer pairs.

Definition 10 (Sampling partial oracles). *We define the procedure* ConsOrc. *In this definition we assume that the algorithm* Init^{g,e} *makes both g and e queries (as opposed to g only), since this definition will also be used for the general attack.*

- **Input:** $(\mathsf{CRS}, \mathsf{PK}, \mathsf{Freq}, \mathsf{Forbid})$: *A CRS* CRS, *public key* PK, *and set of query/answer pairs* Freq *and a set of query/answer pairs* Forbid. *The set* Forbid *consists of "wildcard" forbidden queries/responses, of the form* $(q \xrightarrow{z} *)$ *or* $(* \xrightarrow{z} u)$, *where* $z \in \{\mathbf{g}, \mathbf{e}\}$.
- **Output:** $(\mathsf{SK}, \mathbf{O}')$ *or* $\perp$, *produced as follows. Sample a partial Ψ-generated* $\mathbf{O}' = (\mathbf{g}', \mathbf{e}')$ *defined only on* λ *queries (see Assumption 3), sample randomness* R *and a resultant* SK *uniformly at random subject to the conditions that (a)* $\mathbf{O}'$ *is consistent with* Freq; *(b)* $\mathbf{O}'$ *forbids* Forbid *(Definition 9) (c)* $\mathrm{Init}^{\mathbf{O}'}(\mathsf{CRS}; R) = (\mathsf{PK}, \mathsf{SK})$ *and (d)* $\mathbf{O}'$ *is R-minimal: the execution of* $\mathrm{Init}^{\mathbf{O}'}(\mathsf{CRS}; R)$ *makes only queries to those in* $\mathbf{O}'$, *and nothing else. If no such* $(\mathsf{SK}, \mathbf{O}')$ *exists, output* $\perp$.[9]

In our attack, the adversary will try performing simulated decryptions for different parties. The adversary will do so by sampling a simulated secret key $\widetilde{\mathsf{SK}}$ for that party, along with a partial oracle $\mathbf{g}'$ relative to which $\widetilde{\mathsf{SK}}$ is a secret key for that party's public key PK (i.e., $(\mathsf{PK}, \widetilde{\mathsf{SK}}) \leftarrow_\$ \mathrm{Init}^{\mathbf{g}'}(\mathsf{CRS})$). The adversary will then perform decryption with respect to an oracle $\mathbf{g}' \Diamond^* \mathbf{O}$ that is the result of superimposing $\mathbf{g}'$ on the real oracle $\mathbf{O}$. We will define the superimposed oracle below. Essentially, the superimposed oracle is defined in a way so that it agrees with $\mathbf{g}'$, it is a valid PKE oracle, and also agrees with the real oracle as much as possible. In the definition below we define this superimposing process, but note that we are not claiming that the output of $\mathbf{g}' \Diamond^* \mathbf{O}$ on a given query can be necessarily obtained by making a polynomial number of queries to $\mathbf{O}$.

As notation we use $(\mathsf{sk}_1 \xrightarrow{\mathbf{g}} \mathsf{pk}_1)$ to denote a query/answer pair of $\mathbf{g}$-type. We use similar notation for other types of queries. If L is a set of query/answer pairs, we use $\mathsf{Query}(\mathsf{L})$ to denote the query parts of the elements of L.

Definition 11 (Composed Oracles $\Diamond^*$). *Let* $\mathbf{O} := (\mathbf{g}, \mathbf{e}, \mathbf{d})$ *be a Ψ-valid oracle (a possible output of Ψ) and let*

$$\mathbf{g}' := \{(\mathsf{sk}_1 \xrightarrow{\mathbf{g}} \mathsf{pk}_1), \dots, (\mathsf{sk}_w \xrightarrow{\mathbf{g}} \mathsf{pk}_w)\}$$

be a partial Ψ-valid oracle consisting of only $\mathbf{g}$-type queries. We define a composed oracle $\mathbf{g}' \Diamond^* \mathbf{O} := (\widetilde{\mathbf{g}}, \mathbf{e}, \widetilde{\mathbf{d}})$ *as follows.*

- $\widetilde{\mathbf{g}}(\cdot)$: *for a given* sk, *let* $\widetilde{\mathbf{g}}(\mathsf{sk}) \stackrel{\Delta}{=} \mathsf{pk}_i$ *if* $\mathsf{sk} = \mathsf{sk}_i$ *for* $i \in [w]$; *otherwise,* $\widetilde{\mathbf{g}}(\mathsf{sk}) \stackrel{\Delta}{=} \mathbf{g}(\mathsf{sk})$.
- $\widetilde{\mathbf{d}}(\cdot, \cdot)$: *for a given pair* (sk, c), *define* $\widetilde{\mathbf{d}}(\mathsf{sk}, c)$ *as follows. Assuming* $\mathsf{pk} = \widetilde{\mathbf{g}}(\mathsf{sk})$, *if there exists* $m \in \{0, 1\}$ *such that* $c = \mathbf{e}(\mathsf{pk}, m, *)$, *return* m; *otherwise, return* $\perp$.

In the definition above notice that the resulting oracle $(\widetilde{\mathbf{g}}, \mathbf{e}, \widetilde{\mathbf{d}})$ is Ψ-valid (i.e., and hence a valid PKE oracle, satisfying PKE completeness) as long as $\mathbf{O}$ and $\mathbf{g}'$ are Ψ-valid. Thus, we have the following lemma.

---

[9] This can happen because of the presence of forbidding queries in Forbid.

Lemma 3. *Assuming* $\mathbf{O}$ *and* $\mathbf{g'}$ *are* Ψ-*valid,* $(\widetilde{\mathbf{g}}, \mathbf{e}, \widetilde{\mathbf{d}})$, *obtained as in Definition 11, is* Ψ-*valid, and hence PKE-valid.*

Due to space limitations, we formally define and analyze the attack in the full version [10].

5   No *Single* Optimal CGKA Protocol Exists

In this section, we will show that there is no *single best* CGKA protocol. More precisely, for any CGKA protocol Π, there is a distribution of CGKA sequences and some other CGKA protocol Π' such that on sequences drawn from this distribution, Π' has much lower expected amortized communication cost than Π. We make the same restriction on protocols that we have throughout the paper: the protocols are only allowed to use PKE.

The main intuition behind this section is the following: As we saw from Corollary 1 of Theorem 1, if starting with a group of n users with public keys $\mathsf{PK}_1, \ldots \mathsf{PK}_n$ in any state (for example, every user has just executed an update),

1. k users are added to the group and then remain offline (i.e., do not execute any operations),
2. Then the α users (w.l.o.g., users $1, \ldots, \alpha$ with public keys $\mathsf{PK}_1, \ldots \mathsf{PK}_\alpha$) that have been online since the first of the above users was added all update,

the combined size of their ciphertexts must be $\Omega(k)$. Now, consider the scenario in which user 1 adds all of the k new users, then updates, and then users $2, \ldots, \alpha$ all execute updates. While adding the k new users, user 1 may or may not have built some structure for group members to communicate with them until they come online (for example, in TTKEM user 1 would have sampled and communicated key pairs for all nodes that are on the paths from the k users' leaves to the root). The protocol Π is then left with a choice regarding the updates of users $2, \ldots, \alpha$. Roughly, either:

a. Each of the users $2, \ldots, \alpha$ rebuild complete structure themselves (say, sample and communicate their own key pairs for nodes on the paths from the k users' leaves to the root, as user 1 would have done when adding them in TTKEM) to communicate with the k newly added users; or
b. At least one such user i does not (i.e., they only rebuild asymptotically incomplete structure themselves) and thus relies on some asymptotically non-trivial amount of structure created by the users that have executed operations before them to communicate with the k added users.

We will however show that both (a) and (b) can be losing strategies; i.e., no matter if a protocol Π chooses strategy (a) or (b) (or probabilistically favors one over the other), it can be starkly outperformed by another protocol Π' when executing certain sequences (by the same amount in both cases). In the case of (a), if after users $2, \ldots, \alpha$ execute their updates, the k added users come online and execute their own updates, then users $2, \ldots, \alpha$ all rebuilt complete structure themselves unnecessarily – the k added users can themselves create structure which allows others to communicate with them thereafter using $O(\log n)$ communication each (for example, in TTKEM, they would just sample key pairs for their paths). Therefore if all subsequent operations are updates, the communication of the protocol can easily stay low. So, if Π chose (a) then it communicated a factor of $\Omega(k/\log n)$ more than it had to during the updates of Step 2; or $\Omega(n/\log n)$ if $k = \Omega(n)$. In Sect. 5.1, we formally define the distribution containing such sequences as ActiveBad and in Sect. 5.2 formally prove the statement of the previous sentence. (Technically, for fairness reasons when comparing with the result of the next paragraph, we also account for the communication of a certain number of updates after Step 2. So the result, while qualitatively the same, is quantitatively not as stark.)

In the case of (b) consider the scenario in which (i) one of the α active users, user j, is randomly selected to become *passive* for the remainder of the sequence, i.e., they never execute another operation, then (ii) the other $\alpha - 1$ active users perform ℓ rounds of taking turns executing updates. If Π chose strategy (b) and user j is the one who only rebuilt asymptotically incomplete structure themselves, then according to Corollary 1, each of the ℓ rounds of Step (ii) will have high $\Omega(k)$ communication each. However, if strategy (a) had been chosen by Π (and user 1 built complete structure as well) then the communication of user j would allow for the ℓ rounds of Step (ii) to be executed with low communication: $O(\alpha \log n)$ (using TTKEM-like updates; we explain more later). So if Π chose (b) then in expectation, it communicated a factor of $\Omega(\ell k/(\alpha \cdot (k\alpha + \ell\alpha \log n)))$ more than it had to; or $\Omega(n/\log n)$ if $k = \Omega(n)$, $\ell = \Theta(n/\log n)$, and $\alpha = O(1)$. In Sect. 5.1, we formally define the distribution containing such sequences as LazyBad and in Sect. 5.2 formally prove the statement of the previous sentence (albeit with slightly different concrete parameters for k, ℓ, and α).

5.1   Bad Sequences of Operations

We first formally define the two distributions of sequences, LazyBad and ActiveBad, such that for any CGKA protocol Π, we can choose one of these distributions and it will be the case that there is some Π′ which has much lower expected communication than Π on that distribution. Both LazyBad and ActiveBad are parameterized by:

- n: The number of users in the group before user 1 adds the new users;
- PreAddSeq: The operations of the pre-add phase, i.e., the sequence of *valid* operations (the first operation is Add to create the group, only users that are not in the group are added by users in the group, only users in the group are removed by other users in the group, only users in the group can execute an update, and at the end of Seq the group has n members) to be executed before the k adds and subsequent operations of ActiveBad or LazyBad.
- k: The number of users added by user 1;
- α: the number of active users after the first of the k users is added; and

– ℓ: For LazyBad, the number of rounds of updates in which one of the originally active users is passive. We use ℓ in ActiveBad only to ensure that on input the same parameters, the two types of sequences have the same length (for fairness reasons).

We define both types of sequences as distributions, even though ActiveBad(n, PreAddSeq, k, α, ℓ) is just one sequence (i.e., that sequence is drawn from the distribution ActiveBad(n, PreAddSeq, k, α, ℓ) with probability 1). In the following, we will assume that both n and k are powers of 2, for simplicity. Also, we will often make the parameters n, k, α, and ℓ implicit and simply refer to ActiveBad(n, PreAddSeq, k, α, ℓ) as ActiveBad(PreAddSeq) and LazyBad(n, PreAddSeq, k, α, ℓ) as LazyBad(PreAddSeq). We first define LazyBad(PreAddSeq):

Definition 12. *A sequence* Seq *of CGKA operations drawn from distribution* LazyBad(n, PreAddSeq, k, α, ℓ) *consists of the following phases:*

- **Phase** P0: *The pre-add phase, i.e., the operations* $\mathsf{Op}_1, \ldots, \mathsf{Op}_{t_1^A - 1}$ *of* PreAddSeq.
- **Phase** P1: *For* $i \in [k]$ *operations* $\mathsf{Op}_{1,i} = (\mathrm{Add}, \mathsf{PK}_1, \mathsf{PK}_{n+i})$. *Then operation* $\mathsf{Op}_{1,k+1} = (\mathrm{Up}, \mathsf{PK}_1, \bot)$.
- **Phase** P2: *For* $i \in [\alpha - 1]$ *operations* $\mathsf{Op}_{2,i} = (\mathrm{Up}, \mathsf{PK}_{i+1}, \bot)$.
- **Phase** P3: *Let* $j \leftarrow_\$ [\alpha]$. *Then, for each* $m \in [\ell]$: *for every* $i < j$ *(resp.* $i > j$), $\mathsf{Op}_{3,(m-1)(\alpha-1)+i} = (\mathrm{Up}, \mathsf{PK}_i, \bot)$ *(resp.* $\mathsf{Op}_{3,(m-1)(\alpha-1)+i-1} = (\mathrm{Up}, \mathsf{PK}_i, \bot)$), *where* PK_i *is the most recent public key of user* i.

Next, we define ActiveBad(PreAddSeq), which has the same phases $0 - 2$ as LazyBad(PreAddSeq), but differs in phase 3 as described above:

Definition 13. *A sequence* Seq *of CGKA operations drawn from distribution* ActiveBad(n, PreAddSeq, k, α, ℓ) *consists of the same phases P0-P2 as above then:*

- **Phase** P3: *For* $i \in [\ell \cdot (\alpha - 1)]$: $\mathsf{Op}_{3,i} = (\mathrm{Up}, \mathsf{PK}_{n+1+(i \bmod \alpha)}, \bot)$, *where* $\mathsf{PK}_{n+1+(i \bmod \alpha)}$ *is the most recent public key of user* $n + 1 + (i \bmod \alpha)$.

Note that by Theorem 1, for every CGKA protocol it must be that update $\mathsf{Op}_{1,k+1} = (\mathrm{Up}, \mathsf{PK}_1, \bot)$ in Phase P1 of either distribution requires $\Omega(k)$ communication, no matter what the operations of PreAddSeq were and what structure the adds of user 1 in Phase P1 created. Since with $O(k)$ communication, user 1 can in this update create full structure with which other users in the group can communicate with the added $\mathsf{PK}_{n+1} \ldots, \mathsf{PK}_{n+\alpha}$ thereafter (as in TTKEM), it is intuitively the best choice for a protocol to use this behavior for user 1. Thus, since we aim to define these two distributions in a way that emphasizes the different choices protocols can make to minimize communication, user 1's first update is included in Phase P1 and we define the communication complexity of a protocol executing a sequence drawn from one of these two distributions to include only the communication costs of the operations in Phase P2 and P3:

Definition 14. *Let* Seq *be a sequence of CGKA operations drawn from distribution*
LazyBad(PreAddSeq) *(resp.* ActiveBad(PreAddSeq)*) and* $CC_\Pi[Op]$ *be the communication cost of a CGKA protocol* Π *executing operation* Op *of* Seq *after executing all preceding operations of* Seq *in order. Then:*

1. *The* amortized communication complexity *of a protocol* Π *that executes* Seq *is* $\mathbf{CC}_\Pi[\text{Seq}] := (\sum_{Op \in P2 \cup P3} CC_\Pi[Op])/((\alpha - 1) \cdot (\ell + 1))$, *where* P2 *and* P3 *are the corresponding phases in* Seq *of* LazyBad(PreAddSeq) *(resp.* ActiveBad(PreAddSeq)*).*
2. *The* expected amortized communication complexity *of a protocol* Π *on random* Seq *drawn from* LazyBad(PreAddSeq) *(resp.* ActiveBad(PreAddSeq)*) is*

$$\mathbf{CC}_\Pi(\mathsf{LazyBad}(\mathsf{PreAddSeq})) := \mathbb{E}_{\mathsf{Seq} \leftarrow_\$ \mathsf{LazyBad}(\mathsf{PreAddSeq})}[\mathbf{CC}_\Pi[\mathsf{Seq}]]$$

$$(\mathit{resp.} \mathbf{CC}_\Pi(\mathsf{ActiveBad}(\mathsf{PreAddSeq})) := \mathbb{E}_{\mathsf{Seq} \leftarrow_\$ \mathsf{ActiveBad}(\mathsf{PreAddSeq})}[\mathbf{CC}_\Pi[\mathsf{Seq}]]),$$

where the randomness is over the choice of Seq *and the random coins of* Π.

5.2   Suboptimality of All CGKA Protocols

We now state and prove our Theorem showing that all CGKA protocols must have suboptimal expected amortized communication complexity on either LazyBad(PreAddSeq) or ActiveBad(PreAddSeq). First, we define a specific PreAddSeq which intuitively leaves the CGKA group in a *full* state:

Definition 15. *Valid sequence of CGKA operations* Full_n *contains the following operations in order:* $(\mathrm{Add}, \mathsf{PK}_1, \mathsf{PK}_2), (\mathrm{Add}, \mathsf{PK}_1, \mathsf{PK}_3), \ldots, (\mathrm{Add}, \mathsf{PK}_1, \mathsf{PK}_n),$ $(\mathrm{Up}, \mathsf{PK}_1, \bot), (\mathrm{Up}, \mathsf{PK}_2, \bot), \ldots, (\mathrm{Up}, \mathsf{PK}_n, \bot).$

Theorem 4. *Let* $\ell = O(k/\log n)$. *Then for every CGKA protocol* Π *and every* PreAddSeq, *there exists some other protocol* Π' *such that either*

$$\mathbf{CC}_\Pi(\mathsf{LazyBad}(\mathsf{PreAddSeq})) \geq \mathbf{CC}_{\Pi'}(\mathsf{LazyBad}(\mathsf{Full}_n)) \cdot \Omega(\ell/\alpha^2), \ \mathit{or}$$

$$\mathbf{CC}_\Pi(\mathsf{ActiveBad}(\mathsf{PreAddSeq})) \geq \mathbf{CC}_{\Pi'}(\mathsf{ActiveBad}(\mathsf{Full}_n)) \cdot \Omega(k/\ell \log n).$$

Note that PreAddSeq can be any *valid* sequence that results in a group with n members, including (but not limited to) Full_n. As will be seen, our results combine general lower bounds for the considered protocol Π on any PreAddSeq, with upper bounds for protocols Π' on specifically Full_n.

Before proving the Theorem, we separate CGKA protocols Π into two classes based on their expected behavior in phase P2 of a sequence drawn from LazyBad(PreAddSeq) or ActiveBad(PreAddSeq). The first class of protocols are more likely than not to have some *lazy* user in phase P2: i.e., a user whose update operation $Op_{2,i} = (\mathrm{Up}, \mathsf{PK}_{i+1}, \bot)$ in phase P2 has communication cost $CC_\Pi[Op] = o(k)$. The other class of protocols are the opposite – they are more likely than not to have only *heavy* users in phase P2: i.e., all users have update operations $Op_{2,i} = (\mathrm{Up}, \mathsf{PK}_{i+1}, \bot)$ in phase P2 with communication cost $CC_\Pi[Op] = \Omega(k)$.

Definition 16. *CGKA protocol* Π *is* Lazy *if* $\Pr[\exists i \in [\alpha - 1] : \mathbf{CC}_\Pi[\mathsf{Op}_{2,i}] = o(k)] > 1/2$. *Otherwise,* Π *is* Active.

Proof of Theorem 4. The following lemmas, proved in the full version [10] due to space limitations, and which intuitively follow from the descriptions of this section, allow us to prove Theorem 4. □

Lemma 4. *There is a protocol* Π_{Active} *that has expected amortized communication cost* $\mathbf{CC}_{\Pi_{\mathsf{Active}}}(\mathsf{LazyBad}(\mathsf{Full}_n)) = O(k/\ell + \log n)$ *on random* Seq *drawn from* $\mathsf{LazyBad}(n, \mathsf{Full}_n, k, \alpha, \ell)$.

Lemma 5. *For every protocol* Π *that is* Lazy *and every* PreAddSeq, *the expected total communication cost* $\mathbf{CC}_\Pi(\mathsf{LazyBad}(\mathsf{PreAddSeq})) = \Omega(k/\alpha^2)$ *on random* Seq *drawn from* $\mathsf{LazyBad}(n, \mathsf{PreAddSeq}, k, \alpha, \ell)$.

Lemma 6. *There is a protocol* Π_{Lazy} *that has expected total communication cost* $\mathbf{CC}_{\Pi_{\mathsf{Lazy}}}(\mathsf{ActiveBad}(\mathsf{Full}_n)) = O(\log n)$ *on random* Seq *drawn from* $\mathsf{ActiveBad}(n, \mathsf{Full}_n, k, \alpha, \ell)$.

Lemma 7. *For every protocol* Π *that is* Active *and every* PreAddSeq, *its expected total communication cost* $\mathbf{CC}_\Pi(\mathsf{ActiveBad}(\mathsf{PreAddSeq})) = \Omega(k/\ell)$ *on random* Seq *drawn from* $\mathsf{ActiveBad}(n, \mathsf{PreAddSeq}, k, \alpha, \ell)$.

The following corollary thus easily follows:

Corollary 3. *Let* $k = \Omega(n)$, $\ell = \Theta(\sqrt{n})$, *and* $\alpha = O(\sqrt{\log n})$. *Then for every protocol* Π, *there exists some other protocol* Π' *such that either on a random sequence drawn from* $\mathsf{ActiveBad}(\mathsf{Full}_n)$, *or from* $\mathsf{LazyBad}(\mathsf{Full}_n)$, Π' *has a factor of* $\Omega(\sqrt{n}/\log n)$ *better amortized communication in expectation than* Π *does.*

References

1. Alwen, J., et al.: CoCoA: concurrent continuous group key agreement. In: Dunkelman, O., Dziembowski, S. (eds.) EUROCRYPT 2022. LNCS, vol. 13276, pp. 815–844. Springer, Cham (2022). https://doi.org/10.1007/978-3-031-07085-3_28
2. Alwen, J., Coretti, S., Dodis, Y.: The double ratchet: security notions, proofs, and modularization for the signal protocol. In: Ishai, Y., Rijmen, V. (eds.) EUROCRYPT 2019, Part I. LNCS, vol. 11476, pp. 129–158. Springer, Cham (2019). https://doi.org/10.1007/978-3-030-17653-2_5
3. Alwen, J., Coretti, S., Dodis, Y., Tselekounis, Y.: Security analysis and improvements for the IETF MLS standard for group messaging. In: Micciancio, D., Ristenpart, T. (eds.) CRYPTO 2020, Part I. LNCS, vol. 12170, pp. 248–277. Springer, Cham (2020). https://doi.org/10.1007/978-3-030-56784-2_9
4. Alwen, J., Coretti, S., Jost, D., Mularczyk, M.: Continuous group key agreement with active security. In: Pass, R., Pietrzak, K. (eds.) TCC 2020, Part II. LNCS, vol. 12551, pp. 261–290. Springer, Cham (2020). https://doi.org/10.1007/978-3-030-64378-2_10
5. Alwen, J., Jost, D., Mularczyk, M.: On the insider security of MLS. Cryptology ePrint Archive, Report 2020/1327 (2020). https://eprint.iacr.org/2020/1327

6. Alwen, J., et al.: Keep the dirt: tainted treekem, adaptively and actively secure continuous group key agreement. In: 2021 IEEE Symposium on Security and Privacy (SP). IEEE (2021)
7. Balli, F., Rösler, P., Vaudenay, S.: Determining the core primitive for optimally secure ratcheting. In: Moriai, S., Wang, H. (eds.) ASIACRYPT 2020, Part III. LNCS, vol. 12493, pp. 621–650. Springer, Cham (2020). https://doi.org/10.1007/978-3-030-64840-4_21
8. Barnes, R., Beurdouche, B., Robert, R., Millican, J., Omara, E., Cohn-Gordon, K.: The Messaging Layer Security (MLS) Protocol. Internet-Draft draft-ietf-mls-protocol-14, Internet Engineering Task Force (2022). https://datatracker.ietf.org/doc/html/draft-ietf-mls-protocol-14. Work in Progress
9. Bhargavan, K., Barnes, R., Rescorla, E.: TreeKEM: Asynchronous Decentralized Key Management for Large Dynamic Groups (2018). pubs/treekem.pdf https://mailarchive.ietf.org/arch/msg/mls/e3ZKNzPC7Gxrm3Wf0q96dsLZoD8
10. Bienstock, A., Dodis, Y., Garg, S., Grogan, G., Hajiabadi, M., Rösler, P.: On the worst-case inefficiency of CGKA. Cryptology ePrint Archive (2022)
11. Bienstock, A., Dodis, Y., Rösler, P.: On the price of concurrency in group ratcheting protocols. In: Pass, R., Pietrzak, K. (eds.) TCC 2020, Part II. LNCS, vol. 12551, pp. 198–228. Springer, Cham (2020). https://doi.org/10.1007/978-3-030-64378-2_8
12. Bienstock, A., Dodis, Y., Tang, Y.: Multicast key agreement, revisited. In: Galbraith, S.D. (ed.) CT-RSA 2022. LNCS, vol. 13161, pp. 1–25. Springer, Cham (2022). https://doi.org/10.1007/978-3-030-95312-6_1
13. Bienstock, A., Dodis, Y., Yeo, K.: Forward secret encrypted RAM: lower bounds and applications. In: Nissim, K., Waters, B. (eds.) TCC 2021. LNCS, vol. 13044, pp. 62–93. Springer, Cham (2021). https://doi.org/10.1007/978-3-030-90456-2_3
14. Bienstock, A., Fairoze, J., Garg, S., Mukherjee, P., Raghuraman, S.: A more complete analysis of the signal double ratchet algorithm. Cryptology ePrint Archive, Report 2022/355 (2022). https://ia.cr/2022/355
15. Boneh, D., Papakonstantinou, P.A., Rackoff, C., Vahlis, Y., Waters, B.: On the impossibility of basing identity based encryption on trapdoor permutations. In: 49th FOCS, pp. 283–292. IEEE Computer Society Press (2008)
16. Boneh, D., Zhandry, M.: Multiparty key exchange, efficient traitor tracing, and more from indistinguishability obfuscation. In: Garay, J.A., Gennaro, R. (eds.) CRYPTO 2014, Part I. LNCS, vol. 8616, pp. 480–499. Springer, Heidelberg (2014). https://doi.org/10.1007/978-3-662-44371-2_27
17. Canetti, R., Garay, J., Itkis, G., Micciancio, D., Naor, M., Pinkas, B.: Multicast security: a taxonomy and some efficient constructions. In: IEEE INFOCOM 1999. Conference on Computer Communications. Proceedings. Eighteenth Annual Joint Conference of the IEEE Computer and Communications Societies. The Future is Now (Cat. No.99CH36320), vol. 2, pp. 708–716 (1999)
18. Canetti, R., Jain, P., Swanberg, M., Varia, M.: Universally composable end-to-end secure messaging. Cryptology ePrint Archive, Report 2022/376 (2022). https://ia.cr/2022/376
19. Chung, K.M., Lin, H., Mahmoody, M., Pass, R.: On the power of nonuniformity in proofs of security. In: Kleinberg, R.D. (ed.) ITCS 2013, pp. 389–400. ACM (2013)
20. Cohn-Gordon, K., Cremers, C., Dowling, B., Garratt, L., Stebila, D.: A formal security analysis of the signal messaging protocol. In: 2017 IEEE European Symposium on Security and Privacy (EuroS P), pp. 451–466 (2017)
21. Cohn-Gordon, K., Cremers, C., Garratt, L., Millican, J., Milner, K.: On ends-to-ends encryption: asynchronous group messaging with strong security guarantees.

In: Lie, D., Mannan, M., Backes, M., Wang, X. (eds.) ACM CCS 2018, pp. 1802–1819. ACM Press (2018)

22. Coretti, S., Dodis, Y., Guo, S., Steinberger, J.: Random oracles and non-uniformity. In: Nielsen, J.B., Rijmen, V. (eds.) EUROCRYPT 2018, Part I. LNCS, vol. 10820, pp. 227–258. Springer, Cham (2018). https://doi.org/10.1007/978-3-319-78381-9_9

23. Dowling, B., Hauck, E., Riepel, D., Rösler, P.: Strongly anonymous ratcheted key exchange. In: ASIACRYPT 2022. LNCS (2022)

24. Harney, H., Muckenhirn, C.: RFC2093: Group key management protocol (GKMP) specification (1997)

25. Mittra, S.: Iolus: a framework for scalable secure multicasting. In: Proceedings of the ACM SIGCOMM 1997 Conference on Applications, Technologies, Architectures, and Protocols for Computer Communication, SIGCOMM 1997, pp. 277–288. Association for Computing Machinery, New York (1997). https://doi.org/10.1145/263105.263179

26. Perrin, T., Marlinspike, M.: The double ratchet algorithm (2016). https://signal.org/docs/specifications/doubleratchet/

27. Poettering, B., Rösler, P., Schwenk, J., Stebila, D.: SoK: game-based security models for group key exchange. In: Paterson, K.G. (ed.) CT-RSA 2021. LNCS, vol. 12704, pp. 148–176. Springer, Cham (2021). https://doi.org/10.1007/978-3-030-75539-3_7

28. Rösler, P., Mainka, C., Schwenk, J.: More is less: on the end-to-end security of group chats in signal, Whatsapp, and Threema. In: 2018 IEEE European Symposium on Security and Privacy, EuroS&P 2018 (2018)

29. Sherman, A.T., McGrew, D.A.: Key establishment in large dynamic groups using one-way function trees. IEEE Trans. Softw. Eng. 29(5), 444–458 (2003)

30. Smart, N.P.: Efficient key encapsulation to multiple parties. In: Blundo, C., Cimato, S. (eds.) SCN 2004. LNCS, vol. 3352, pp. 208–219. Springer, Heidelberg (2005). https://doi.org/10.1007/978-3-540-30598-9_15

31. Wallner, D., Harder, E., Agee, R.: RFC2627: key management for multicast: issues and architectures (1999)

32. Weidner, M., Kleppmann, M., Hugenroth, D., Beresford, A.R.: Key agreement for decentralized secure group messaging with strong security guarantees. In: Vigna, G., Shi, E. (eds.) ACM CCS 2021, pp. 2024–2045. ACM Press (2021)

33. Wong, C.K., Gouda, M., Lam, S.S.: Secure group communications using key graphs. In: Proceedings of the ACM SIGCOMM 1998 Conference on Applications, Technologies, Architectures, and Protocols for Computer Communication, SIGCOMM 1998, pp. 68–79. Association for Computing Machinery, New York (1998). https://doi.org/10.1145/285237.285260

Adaptive Multiparty NIKE

Venkata Koppula[1]([✉]), Brent Waters[2,3], and Mark Zhandry[2,4]

[1] IIT Delhi, Delhi, India
kvenkata@cse.iitd.ac.in
[2] NTT Research, Sunnyvale, USA
[3] UT Austin, Austin, USA
bwaters@cs.utexas.edu
[4] Princeton University, Princeton, USA

Abstract. We construct adaptively secure multiparty non-interactive key exchange (NIKE) from polynomially-hard indistinguishability obfuscation and other standard assumptions. This improves on all prior such protocols, which required sub-exponential hardness. Along the way, we establish several compilers which simplify the task of constructing new multiparty NIKE protocols, and also establish a close connection with a particular type of constrained PRF.

1 Introduction

Non-interactive key exchange (NIKE) is a fundamental application in public key cryptography. In a G-party NIKE protocol, a group of G users simultaneously publish individual public keys to a bulletin board, keeping individual secret keys to themselves. Then just by reading the bulletin board and using their individual private keys but no further interaction, the G users can arrive at a common key hidden to anyone outside the group.

In this work, we build multiparty NIKE attaining *adaptive* security under polynomially-hard non-interactive assumptions. Our assumptions are indistinguishability obfuscation (iO) and standard assumptions on cryptographic groups[1]. The main restriction is that we must bound the number of users that can be adaptively corrupted. The number of honest users, and even the number of adversarially generated users, can be unbounded; only the number of users that were initially honest and later corrupted must be bounded. This improves on prior standard-model adaptively secure schemes [BZ14,Rao14], which all bound the *total* number of users, and also required either *interactive* or *sub-exponential* assumptions. Along the way, we several compilers to simplify the design process of iO-based multiparty NIKE. We also explore adaptive security for constrained PRFs, giving a new construction for "one symbol fixing" constraints, and show a close connection to multiparty NIKE.

---

[1] We note two uses of the term "group": the group of users establishing a shared key, and the cryptographic group used as a tool. Which use should be clear from context.

© The Author(s), under exclusive license to Springer Nature Switzerland 2022
E. Kiltz and V. Vaikuntanathan (Eds.): TCC 2022, LNCS 13748, pp. 244–273, 2022.
https://doi.org/10.1007/978-3-031-22365-5_9

1.1 Prior Work and Motivation

NIKE has a long history, with the 2-party case dating back to the foundational work of Diffie and Hellman [DH76], and the multiparty case already referred to as "a long-standing open problem" in 2002 [BS02]. Joux gave a 3-party protocol from pairings [Jou00]. The first protocol for $G \geq 4$ used multilinear maps [GGH13], though the only protocols directly based on multilinear maps that have not been attacked are limited to a *constant* number of users [MZ18]. Currently, the only known solutions for a super-constant number of users are built from indistinguishability obfuscation (iO). The first such construction for polynomially-many users was due to Boneh and Zhandry [BZ14] (using punctured programming techniques [SW14]), with a number of follow-up works [Rao14, KRS15, HJK+16, MZ17, GPSZ17, BGK+18].

Multiparty NIKE remains a fascinating object: the central feature of *non-interactive* key exchange (as opposed to protocols requiring multiple interaction rounds) is that public keys can be re-used across many groups, simplifying key management and significantly reducing communication. This feature makes NIKE an important tool with many applications. Multiparty NIKE in particular is a useful tool for group key management [STW96] and broadcast encryption with small parameters [BZ14]. Multiparty NIKE is also interesting from a foundational perspective, being perhaps the simplest cryptographic object which currently is *only* known via obfuscation[2].

Adaptive Security. The re-use of public keys in a NIKE protocol, on the other hand, opens the door to various *active* attacks. For example, if a shared key for one group is accidentally leaked, it should not compromise the shared key of other groups, including those that may intersect. Worse, an adversary may participate in certain groups using maliciously generated public keys, or may be able to corrupt certain users. Finally, decisions about which groups' shared keys to compromise, how the adversary devises its own malicious public keys, which users to corrupt, and even which set of users to ultimately attack, can all potentially be made *adaptively*.

Adaptive security is an important goal in cryptography generally, being the focus of hundreds if not thousands of papers. Numerous works have considered adaptive NIKE. In the 2-party case, adaptive security can often be obtained *generically* by guessing the group that the adversary will attack. If there are a total of N users in the system, the reduction loss is N^2, a polynomial. The focus of works in the 2-party case (e.g. [CKS08, FHKP13, BJLS16, HHK18, HHKL21]) has therefore been *tight* reductions, which still remains unresolved.

The situation becomes more critical in the multiparty case, where the generic guessing reduction looses a factor of $\binom{N}{G} \approx N^G$, which is exponential for polynomial group size G. In order to make this generic reduction work, one must assume the (sub)exponential hardness of the underlying building blocks and scale up the security parameter appropriately. This results in qualitatively stronger underlying computational assumptions. A couple works have attempted to improve

---

[2] Multiparty NIKE can also be built via functional encryption [GPSZ17], which is equivalent to iO [BV15a, AJ15] under sub-exponential reductions.

on this reduction, achieving security in the random oracle model [HJK+16], or under *interactive* assumptions [BZ14,Rao14][3]. In fact, Rao [Rao14] argues that exponential loss or interactive assumption is likely necessary, giving a black box impossibility of a polynomial reduction to non-interactive assumptions. This impossibility will be discussed in more depth momentarily. We also note existing standard-model adaptively secure schemes all limit the *total* number of users, including both honest *and* dishonest users, to an a priori polynomial bound.

Constrained PRFs. A constrained PRF is a pseudorandom function which allows the key holder to produce *constrained* keys k_C corresponding to functions C. The key k_C should allow for evaluating the PRF on any input x where $C(x) = 1$, but the output should remain pseudorandom if $C(x) = 0$. First proposed in three concurrent works [BW13,KPTZ13,BGI14], constrained PRFs have become a fundamental concept in cryptography, with many follow-up works (e.g. [BV15b,BFP+15,CRV16,DKW16,CC17,BTVW17,AMN+18]). A particularly interesting class of constrained PRFs are those for *bit-fixing* constraints, which give secret key broadcast encryption [BW13], for example.

Adaptivel secure constrained PRFs of of particular interest [Hof14,FKPR14, HKW15,HKKW14,DKN+20]. Unfortunately, with one exception, all known adaptively secure constrained PRFs require random oracles, super-polynomial hardness, or a constant collusion resistance bound. The one exception is [HKW15] for simple puncturing constraints, where C contains a list of polynomially-many points, and accepts all inputs not in the list. Even with such simple constraints, the construction requires iO, algebraic tools, and a non-trivial proof.

1.2   Technical Challenges

Rao's Impossibility. Rao [Rao14] proves that multiparty NIKE protocols with standard model proofs relative to non-interactive assumptions (including iO) must incur an exponential loss. The proof follows a meta-reduction, which runs the reduction until the reduction receives the challenge from the underlying non-interactive assumption. At this point, Rao argues that the adversary need not commit to the group it will attack. Now, we split the reduction into two branches:

- In the first branch, choose and corrupt an arbitrary honest user i, obtaining secret key sk_i. Then abort the branch.
- In the second branch, choose the group S to attack such that (1) S contains only honest users for this branch, and (2) $i \in S$. User i is honest in this branch since it was never corrupted here, despite being corrupted in the other branch. Use sk_i to compute the shared group key.

From the view of the reduction, the second branch appears to be a valid adversary. Hence, by the guarantees of the reduction, it must break the underlying hard problem, a contradiction. Hence, no such reduction could exist.

---

[3] Note that multiparty NIKE itself is an interactive assumption.

Rao's proof is quite general, and handles reductions that may rewind the adversary or run it many times concurrently. It also works in the more restricted setting where there is an upper bound on the total number of users in the system.

There is *one* way in which Rao's result does not completely rule out a construction: in order to guarantee that the second branch is successful, one needs that the shared key derived from sk_i must match the shared key in the second branch. This would seem to follow from correctness, as i is a member of the group S. However, correctness only holds with respect to honestly generated public and secret keys. The reduction may, however, give out malformed public or secret keys that are indistinguishable from the honest keys. In this case, it may be that sk_i actually computes the wrong shared key, causing the meta-reduction to fail.

Rao therefore considers "admissible reductions" where, roughly, the public keys of users outputted by the reduction, even if not computed honestly, uniquely determine the shared key. Analogous lower bounds have been shown for tight reductions in the 2-party setting [BJLS16,HHK18,HHKL21], making similar restrictions on the reduction referred to as "committing reductions".

All existing reductions for multiparty NIKE from iO are admissible. A closer look reveals that all such schemes derive the shared key from a constrained PRF applied to the public values of the users. While the secret key is used to compute this value, the value itself is not dependent on the secret key, only the public key. Therefore, Rao's impossibility captures all the existing techniques, and new ideas are required to achieve adaptive security from static polynomial assumptions.

Dual System Methodology? The situation is reminiscent of HIBE and ABE, where Lewko and Waters [LW14] showed that adaptive security cannot be proved under polynomially hard non-interactive assumptions, using reductions that always output secret keys which decrypt consistently. Solutions overcoming this barrier were already known, say based on dual system encryption [Wat09,LOS+10]. The point of [LW14] was to explain necessary features of those proofs.

The multiparty NIKE setting appears much more challenging. HIBE and ABE benefit from a central authority which issues keys. In the proof, the reduction provides the adversary with all of the keys, which will have a special structure that allows for decrypting some ciphertexts and not others. In the NIKE setting, the adversary is allowed to introduce *his own* users. This presents many challenges as we cannot enforce any dual system structure on such users. It also gives the adversary a lot more power to distinguish the *reduction's* keys from honestly generated keys, as the adversary can request the shared keys of groups containing both honest and malicious users.

Recently, Hesse et al. [HHKL21] circumvent the above barriers in the 2-party setting. However there is no obvious analog to the multiparty setting.

Another Barrier: Adaptive Constrained PRFs. Looking ahead, we will show that adaptive multiparty NIKE implies adaptive constrained PRFs for a "one symbol fixing" functionality (1-SF-PRF). Here, inputs are words over a polynomial-sized alphabet Σ, and constrains have the form $(?, ?, \cdots , ?, s, ?, \ldots)$, constraining only a single position to some character. The resulting PRFs are fully collusion resistant. 1-SF-PRFs can be seen as a special case of bit-fixing PRFs, where only a single contiguous block of bits can be fixed. Adaptive constrained PRFs for even very simple functionalities have remained a very challenging open question. In particular, no prior standard-model construction from polynomial hardness achieves functionalities that have a superpolynomial number of both accepting and rejecting inputs. Any adaptive multiparty NIKE construction would along the way imply such a functionality, representing another barrier.

1.3 Result Summary

- We give several compilers, allowing us to simplify the process of designing multiparty NIKE schemes. One compiler shows how to generically remove a common setup from multiparty NIKE (assuming iO). We note that many iO-based solutions could be tweaked to remove setup, but the solutions were ad hoc and in the adaptive setting often required significant effort; we accomplish this generically.

  Another compiler shows that it suffices to ignore the case where the adversary can compromise the security of shared keys for a different groups of users. That is, we show how to generically compile any scheme that is secure against adversaries that *cannot* compromise shared keys into one that is secure even if the adversary *can*.
- We show a close connection between multiparty NIKE and 1-SF-PRFs:
  - Adaptively secure multiparty NIKE implies adaptively secure one-symbol-fixing PRF.
  - One-symbol-fixing PRFs, together with iO, imply a multiparty NIKE protocol with a bounded number of honest users (and hence also corruption queries) and group size, but an unbounded number of malicious users. This result starts by constructing a weaker NIKE protocol, and then applying our compilers.
- We construct adaptively secure 1-SF-PRFs from iO and DDH, thus obtaining multiparty NIKE from the same assumptions with bounded honest users.
- We give a direct construction of multiparty NIKE from iO and standard assumptions on groups, allowing for an unbounded number of honest users. The construction roughly follows the path above, but opens up the abstraction layers and makes crucial modifications to attain the stronger security notion. The main limitation is that there is still a bound on the number of users that the adversary can adaptively corrupt, as well as on the group size.

1.4 Technical Overview

We first briefly recall the types of queries an adversary can make:

- **Corrupt User.** The adversary selects an honest user's public key, and learns the secret key.
- **Shared Key.** The adversary selects a list of public keys, which may contain both honest users adversarially-generated users, and learns the shared key for the group of users. Since the adversary's public keys may be malformed, different users may actually arrive at different shared keys. So the query specifies which of the users' version of the shared key is revealed.

– **Challenge.** Here, the adversary selects a list of honest public keys, and tries to distinguish the shared key from random.

Upgrading NIKE. In addition to providing the first iO-based NIKE, Boneh and Zhandry [BZ14] also construct the first NIKE without a trusted setup, or crs. Their basic idea is to first design an iO-based protocol *with* a crs, but where the resulting crs is only needed to generate the shared keys, but not the individual public keys. Then they just have every user generate their own crs; when it comes time to compute the shared key for a group, the group arbitrarily selects a "leader" and uses the leader's crs.

The above works in the selective setting. However, in the adaptive setting, problems arise. The crs contains an obfuscated program that is run on the user's secret key. The adversary could therefore submit a Shared Key query on an adversarial public key containing a malicious crs. If that malicious user is selected as the leader for the group, honest users' secret keys will be fed into the malicious program, the output being revealed to the adversary, leading to simple attacks. Worse, in Rao's basic scheme with setup, the users need to know the crs in order to generate their public key. So in the setup-less scheme, each user would need to wait until the leader outputs their crs before they can publish their public key, resulting in an interactive protocol. Boneh and Zhandry and later Rao [Rao14] therefore devised more sophisticated techniques to remove the trusted setup.

Our first result sidesteps the above difficulties, by considering the setting where Shared Key queries are not allowed. In this setting, we can make the above strategy of having each party run their own trusted setup fully generic. To accommodate the case where the public keys may depend on the trusted setup, we actually have each user produce an obfuscation of a program that takes as input the crs, and samples a public key. In order to prove security, we also have the secret key for a user be an obfuscated program, which is analogous to the public key program except that is samples the corresponding secret key. In the reduction, this allows us to adaptively embed information in the secret key, which is needed to get the proof to work. See Sect. 3.2 for details.

Then we show how to generically lift any NIKE scheme that does not support Shared Key queries into one that does support them, without any additional assumptions. Combined with the previous compiler, we therefore eliminate the crs *and* add Shared Key queries to any scheme. The high-level idea is to give the reduction a random subset of the secret keys for honest users. The hope is that these keys will be enough to answer all Shared Key queries, while *not* allowing the reduction to answer the Challenge query. This requires care, as this will not be possible if some of the Shared Key queries have too much overlap with the Challenge query. See Sect. 3.3 for details.

Connection to Constrained PRFs. Multi-party NIKE already had a clear connection to constrained PRFs, with all iO-based NIKE crucially using constrained PRFs. In Sect. 4, we make this precise, showing that one symbol fixing (1-SF) PRFs are *equivalent* to NIKE, assuming iO.

One direction is straightforward: to build a 1-SF PRF from multiparty NIKE, create $n \times |\Sigma|$ users, which are arranged in an $|\Sigma| \times n$ grid. Each input in Σ^n then selects a single user from each column, and the value of the PRF is the shared key for the resulting set of n users. To constrain the ith symbol to be σ, simply reveal the secret key for user σ in column i.

The other direction is more complicated, and requires additionally assuming iO. The high-level idea is that the shared key for a group of users will be a PRF evaluated on the list of the users' public keys. If we pretend for the moment that user public keys come from a polynomial-sized set Σ, we could imagine using a 1-SF PRF for this purpose.

Following most iO-based NIKE protocols, we will then have a crs be an obfuscated program which takes as input the list of public keys, together with one of the users secret keys, and evaluates the PRF if the secret key is valid. Our novelty is how we structure the proof to attain adaptive security. Observe that user σ's secret key allows them to evaluate the PRF on any input that contains at least one σ. This is the union of the inputs that can be computed by keys that constrain symbol i to σ, as i ranges over all input positions.

We therefore switch to a hybrid where user σ has the aforementioned constrained keys covertly embedded in their secret key. In this hybrid, we crucially allow the reduction to generate the user's public key without knowing the constrained keys, and only later when the adversary makes a corruption query will it query for the constrained keys and construct the user's secret key. This strategy is our first step to overcoming Rao's impossibility result: the shared key is no longer information-theoretically determined by the public keys, and is only determined once the secret key with the embedded constrained key is specified. We note, however, that a version of Rao's impossibility still applies to the underlying adaptively secure constrained PRFs, which we will have to overcome later when constructing our PRF.

Moving to this hybrid is accomplished using a simplified version of delayed backdoor programming [HJK+16]. After switching the secret keys for each user, we switch the crs program to use the embedded constrained keys to evaluate the PRF, rather than the master key. At this point, adaptive NIKE security follows directly from adaptive 1-SF PRF security.

Of course, NIKE protocols cannot have public keys in a polynomial-sized set. Our actual protocol first generically compiles a 1-SF PRF into a more sophisticated constrained PRF where now Σ is exponentially large. By adapting the above sketch to this special kind of constrained PRF, we obtain the full proof. See Sect. 4 for details.

Constructing 1-SF PRFs. We turn to constructing a 1-SF PRF. As mentioned above, a version of Rao's impossibility result still applies even to constrained PRFs. Namely, an "admissible" reduction would commit at the beginning of the experiment to the PRF functionality it provides to the adversary. Such an admissible reduction cannot be used to prove adaptive security for constrained PRFs, for almost identical reasons as with Rao's impossibility. This means our reduction must actually have the PRF seen by the adversary be specified dynamically, where its outputs are actually dependent on prior queries made by the adversary.

One may be tempted to simply obfuscate a puncturable PRF. Boneh and Zhandry [BZ14] show that this gives a constrained PRF for any constraint, though only with selective security. Unfortunately, it appears challenging to to get adaptively secure constrained PRFs with this strategy. In particular, the punctured PRF specifies the value of the PRF at all points but one, which is problematic given that we need to dynamically determine the PRF function in order to circumvent Rao's impossibility.

We will instead use algebraic tools to achieve an adaptively secure construction. Our PRF will be Naor-Reingold [NR97], but adapted from a binary alphabet to a polynomial-sized alphabet. The secret key contains $n \times |\Sigma|$ random values $e_{j,\sigma}$, and the PRF on input $(x_1, \ldots, x_n) \in \Sigma^n$ outputs

$$\mathsf{F}(k, x) = h^{\prod_{i=1}^{n} e_{i,x_i}},$$

where h is a random generator of a cryptographic group. Without using any computational assumptions, F is already readily seen to be a 1-SF constrained PRF for *a single constrained key*. To constrain position i to σ, simply give out $e_{i,\sigma}$ and $e_{j,x}$ for all $x \in \Sigma$ and all $j \neq i$.

However, we immediately run into trouble even for two constrained keys, since constrained keys for two different i immediately yield the entire secret key. Instead, we constrain keys in this way, except that we embed the constrained keys in an obfuscated program. While this is the natural approach to achieve many-key security, it is a priori unclear how to actually prove security.

We show that obfuscating the constrained keys does in fact upgrade the single-key security of the plain scheme to many-time security. The proof is quite delicate. Essentially, we move to a hybrid where each constrained key uses its own independent h. The main challenge is that, since multiple keys will be able to compute the PRF at the same point, we need to ensure consistency between the keys. Our proof has each constrained key only use its particular h for inputs that cannot be computed by previous constrained keys. For outputs that can be computed by previous keys, the new constrained key will use the h for those keys.

Interestingly, this means that keys in this hybrid must actually contain the h's of all previous constrained keys, and the evaluation of the PRF will actually depend on the order constrained keys are queried. The salient point is that, when the ith constrained key query is made, we only commit to the structure of the PRF on the points that can be evaluated by the first i queries, but the PRF on the remaining part of the domain is unspecified. Structuring the proof in this way is the main insight that allows us to circumvent Rao's impossibility and prove adaptive security.

By careful iO arguments, we show that we are able to move to such a setting where the h for different pieces are random independent bases. The challenge query is guaranteed to be in its own piece, using a different h than all the constrained keys. Therefore, once we move to this setting the constrained keys do not help evaluate the challenge, and security follows. See the Sect. 5 for details. By combining with our compilers, we obtain the following:

Theorem 1 (Informal). *Assuming polynomial iO and DDH, there exist an adaptively secure multiparty NIKE where the number of honestly generated users is a priori bounded, but where the number of maliciously generated users is unbounded.*

In addition to improving to only polynomial hardness, the above improves on existing works by enhancing the security definition to allow an unbounded number of malicious users.

Our Final Construction. Finally, we give another NIKE construction which further improves on the security attained in Theorem 1, at the cost of a slightly stronger group-based assumption:

Theorem 2 (Informal). *Assuming polynomial iO and the DDH-powers assumption, there exist an adaptively secure multiparty NIKE where the group size and number of corruptions is bounded, but otherwise the number of honest and malicious users unbounded.*

We note that bounding the number of corruptions is very natural, and has arisen in many cryptographic settings under the name "bounded collusions." Examples include traitor tracing [CFN94], Broadcast encryption [FN94], identity-based encryption [DKXY02] and its generalizations to functional encryption [GVW12], to name a few. Bounded collusions are often seen as a reasonable relaxation, and in many cases are stepping-stones to achieving full security. We view bounded collusion security for NIKE similarly, except that in some ways, bounded corruptions for NIKE is even stronger than bounded collusions, in that we allow the NIKE adversary to control an *unbounded* number of users, only limiting the number of users that can be corrupted adaptively.

In our construction, we no longer go through 1-SF-PRFs explicitly, but instead open up the layers of abstraction that gave Theorem 1 and make several crucial modifications to the overall protocol. The main technical challenge is that, in our proof of security for 1-SF-PRFs, we must hard-code all prior queries into each secret key. In the obtained NIKE scheme, this means hard-coding all the keys of users generated by the challenger. But as the number of hard-coded users can never be more than the bit-length of the secret key, this limits the number of honest users.

In our solution, we no longer explicitly hardcode the challenger-generated users, but switch to a hybrid where they are generated with a trigger. Only the obfuscated programs can detect this trigger so that they look like honestly generated users, and it moreover is impossible for the adversary to generate users with the trigger. By a delicate hybrid argument, we are able to mimic the security proof above using these triggers instead of the explicitly hardcoded public keys. See the Full Version [KWZ22] for details.

Note that the DDH-powers assumption is a q-type assumption, but this can be proved from a single assumption in the composite order setting, assuming appropriate subgroup decision assumptions [CM14].

1.5 Organization

Section 2 covers the definitions of multiparty NIKE and constrained PRFs that we will study. Section 3 gives our compilers for enhancing multiparty NIKE. Section 4 demonstrates the equivalence of 1-SF-PRFs and multiparty NIKE in the iO setting. Section 5 gives our construction of 1-SF-PRFs from iO. Due to lack of space, the proof of Theorem 2 removing the bound on the number of honest users is deferred to the Full Version [KWZ22].

2 Preliminaries

2.1 Multiparty NIKE

Here, we define the version of NIKE that we will be considering.

Definition 1 (Multiparty NIKE, Syntax). *A multiparty NIKE scheme with bounded honest users is a pair* (Pub, KeyGen) *with the following syntax:*

- Pub$(1^\lambda, 1^\ell, 1^n, 1^c)$ *takes as input the security parameter λ, an upper bound n on the number of honest users, an upper bound ℓ on the number of users in a set, and an upper bound c on the number of corruptions. It outputs a public key* pk *and secret key* sk.
- KeyGen(U, sk) *takes as input a list U of $t \leq \ell$ public keys, plus the secret key for one of the public keys. It outputs a shared key. We have the following correctness guarantee: for any $\ell, n, c > 0, t \in [\ell]$ and any $i, j \in [t]$,*

$$\Pr[\text{KeyGen}(\{\text{pk}_1, \ldots, \text{pk}_t\}, \text{sk}_i) = \text{KeyGen}(\{\text{pk}_1, \ldots, \text{pk}_t\}, \text{sk}_j)] \geq 1 - \text{negl}$$

where the probability is over $(\text{pk}_i, \text{sk}_i) \leftarrow \text{Gen}(1^\lambda, 1^\ell, 1^n, 1^c)$ *for $i = 1, \ldots, t$.*

Enhanced Correctness Notions. As a technical part of our compilers, we will also consider stronger variants of correctness. The first is *perfect correctness*, where the probability above is exactly 1. The second notion is *adversarial correctness*, which is defined via the following experiment with an adversary $\mathcal{A}$:

- On input 1^λ, $\mathcal{A}$ computes $1^\ell, 1^n, 1^c$.
- The challenger runs $(\text{pk}_b, \text{sk}_b) \leftarrow \text{Pub}(1^\lambda, 1^\ell, 1^n, 1^c)$ for $b = 0, 1$, and sends pk_0, pk_1 to $\mathcal{A}$
- $\mathcal{A}$ then computes a set U of public keys such that $|U| \leq \ell$ and $\text{pk}_0, \text{pk}_1 \in U$.
- The challenger computes $k_b = \text{KeyGen}(U, \text{sk}_b)$ for $b = 0, 1$. $\mathcal{A}$ wins if and only if $k_0 \neq k_1$.

A NIKE scheme is adversarially correct if, for all PPT adversaries $\mathcal{A}$, there exists a negligible function ϵ such that the $\mathcal{A}$ wins with probability at most ϵ.

Definition 2 (Multiparty NIKE, Adaptive Security). *Consider the following experiment with an adversary $\mathcal{A}$:*

- *The challenger initializes empty tables T and U. T will contain records $(\mathsf{pk}, \mathsf{sk}, b)$ where pk, sk are the public key and secret key for a user, and b is a flag bit indicating if the user is honest (0) or corrupted (1). We will maintain that if the flag bit is 0, then $\mathsf{sk} \neq \bot$. U will contain sets of public keys. The challenger also stores a set S^*, initially set to $\bot$.*
- *$\mathcal{A}$ receives 1^λ, replies with $1^\ell, 1^n, 1^c$, and then makes several kinds of queries:*
  - **Register Honest User.** *Here, $\mathcal{A}$ sends nothing. The challenger runs $(\mathsf{pk}, \mathsf{sk}) \leftarrow \mathsf{Pub}(1^\lambda, 1^\ell, 1^n, 1^c)$. If there is a record containing pk in T, the challenger replies with $\bot$. Otherwise, it adds $(\mathsf{pk}, \mathsf{sk}, 0)$ to T, and sends pk to $\mathcal{A}$. The total number of such queries is not allowed to exceed n.*
  - **Corrupt User.** *Here, $\mathcal{A}$ sends an pk. The challenger finds a record $(\mathsf{pk}, \mathsf{sk}, 0)$ in the table T. If no such record is found, or if a record is found but with flag bit set to 1, the challenger replies with $\bot$. Otherwise it replies with sk. It then updates the record in T to $(\mathsf{pk}, \mathsf{sk}, 1)$. The total number of such queries is not allowed to exceed c.*
  - **Register Malicious User.** *Here, $\mathcal{A}$ sends a public key pk. If there is no record in T containing pk, the challenger adds to T the record $(\mathsf{pk}, \bot, 1)$. There is no limit to the number of such queries.*
  - **Shared Key.** *The adversary sends an unordered set $S = (\mathsf{pk}_1, \ldots, \mathsf{pk}_t)$ of up to $t \leq \ell$ distinct public keys, as well as an index $i \in [t]$. If $S^* \neq \bot$ and $S = S^*$, then the challenger replies with $\bot$. Otherwise, the challenger checks for each $j \in [t]$ if there is a $(\mathsf{pk}_j, \mathsf{sk}_j, b_j) \in T$. Moreover, it checks that $\mathsf{sk}_i \neq \bot$. If any of the checks fail, the challenger replies with $\bot$. If all the checks pass, the challenger replies with $\mathsf{KeyGen}(S, \mathsf{sk}_i)$. It adds the list S to U. There is no limit to the number of such queries.*
  - **Challenge.** *The adversary makes a single challenge query on an unordered list $S = (\mathsf{pk}_1^*, \ldots, \mathsf{pk}_t^*)$ of up to $t \leq \ell$ distinct public keys. The challenger sets $S^* = S$. The challenger then checks for each $j \in [t]$ that there is a record $(\mathsf{pk}_j^*, \mathsf{sk}_j^*, b_j^*)$ in T such that $b_j^* = 0$. The challenger also checks that S^* is not in U. If any of the checks fails, the challenger immediately aborts and outputs a random bit.*

    If the checks pass, the challenger chooses a random bit $b^* \in \{0,1\}$ and replies with k_{b^*} where $k_0 \leftarrow \mathsf{KeyGen}(S^*, \mathsf{sk}_1)$ and k_1 is uniformly random.
- *$\mathcal{A}$ produces a guess b' for b^*. The challenger outputs 1 iff $b' = b^*$.*

A Multiparty NIKE is adaptively secure if, for all PPT adversaries $\mathcal{A}$, there exists a negligible function ϵ such that the challenger outputs 1 with probability at most $\frac{1}{2} + \epsilon$.

Other security notions. We can also consider multiparty NIKE with *unbounded honest users*, where the input 1^n is ignored in Pub, and there is no limit to the number of Register Honest User. We can similarly consider multiparty NIKE with *unbounded corruptions* where there is no limit to the number of Corrupt

User queries, and *unbounded set size*, where there is no limit to the set size t that can be inputted to KeyGen or queried in Shared Key or Challenger queries.

We can also consider NIKE that is "secure with out X queries", which means that security holds against all adversaries that do not make any type X queries.

Common Reference String. We can also consider a crs model, where there is a setup algorithm crs ← Setup($1^\lambda, 1^\ell, 1^n, 1^c$). Then Pub is changes to have the syntax (pk, sk) ← Pub(crs). In the adaptive security experiment, we have the challenger run crs ← Setup($1^\lambda, 1^\ell, 1^n, 1^c$) and give crs to $\mathcal{A}$. It then uses the updated Pub algorithm when registering honest users.

2.2   Constrained PRFs

A Special Case of Bit-Fixing PRFs. Here, we define a type of bit-fixing PRF.

Definition 3 (1-Symbol-Fixing PRF, Syntax). *1-SF-PRF is a tuple* (Gen, Eval, Constr, EvalC) *with the following syntax:*

- Gen($1^\lambda, 1^{|\Sigma|}, 1^\ell$) *takes as input a security parameter* λ, *an alphabet size* $|\Sigma|$, *and an input length* ℓ, *all represented in unary. It outputs a key* k.
- Eval(k, x) *is the main evaluation algorithm, which is deterministic and takes as input a key* k *and* $x \in \Sigma^\ell$, *and outputs a string.*
- Constr(k, i, z) *is a potentially randomized algorithm that takes as input a key* k, *index* $i \in [\ell]$, *and symbol* $z \in \Sigma$. *It outputs a constrained key* $k_{i,z}$.
- EvalC($k_{i,z}, x$) *takes as input a constrained key* $k_{i,z}$ *for an index/symbol pair* (i, z), *and an input* x. *It outputs a string. We have the correctness guarantee:*

$$\text{EvalC}(k_{i,z}, x) = \begin{cases} \perp & \text{if } x_i \neq z \\ \text{Eval}(k, x) & \text{if } x_i = z \end{cases}$$

Definition 4 (1-SF-PRF, Adaptive Security). *Consider the following experiment with an adversary* $\mathcal{A}$:

- $\mathcal{A}$ *on input* 1^λ, *produces* $1^{|\Sigma|}, 1^\ell$. *The challenger runs* $k \leftarrow \text{Gen}(1^\lambda, 1^{|\Sigma|}, 1^\ell)$. *It returns nothing to* $\mathcal{A}$.
- *Then* $\mathcal{A}$ *can adaptively make the following types of queries:*
  - **Constrain.** $\mathcal{A}$ *sends* i, z, *and receives* $k_{i,z} \leftarrow \text{Constr}(k, i, z)$. *The challenger records each* (i, z) *in a table* C. *There is no limit to the number of constrain queries.*
  - **Eval.** $\mathcal{A}$ *sends an input* x, *and receives* Eval(k, x). *The challenger records each* x *in a table* E. *There is no limit to the number of Eval queries.*
  - **Challenge.** $\mathcal{A}$ *can make a* single *challenge query on an input* $x^* \in \Sigma^\ell$. *The challenger flips a random bit* $b \in \{0, 1\}$ *and replies with* $y^* = y_b$ *where* $y_0 = \text{Eval}(k, x)$ *and* y_1 *is sampled uniformly and independently.*
  If at any time, $x_i^* = z$ *for some* $(i, z) \in C$ *or* $x^* \in E$, *the challenger immediately aborts and outputs a random bit.*
- *The adversary outputs bit* b'. *The challenger outputs 1 if* $b = b'$, *0 otherwise.*

A 1-SF-PRF is adaptively secure *if, for all PPT adversaries $\mathcal{A}$, there exists a negligible function ϵ such that the challenger outputs 1 with probability at most $\frac{1}{2} + \epsilon$. It is* adaptively secure without Eval queries *if this holds for all $\mathcal{A}$ that make no Eval queries.*

A 1-SF-PRF *scheme is said to be* adaptively secure against unique-query adversaries *if the above holds for any adversary $\mathcal{A}$ that makes unique constrained key queries to the challenger.*

3   Enhancing Multi-party NIKE

Here give some compilers for multi-party NIKE, which allow for simplifying the task of designing new NIKE protocols built from iO. Our ultimate goal is to show that one can safely ignore Shared Key and Register Malicious User queries, and also employ a trusted setup. Our compilers then show how to lift such a scheme into one secure under all types of queries and without a trusted setup.

3.1   Achieving Adversarial Correctness

First, we convert any NIKE that is perfectly correct into one with adversarial correctness. While adversarial correctness is not a particular design goal in multiparty NIKE, this step will be needed in order to apply our later compilers.

Theorem 3. *Assume there exists a multi-party NIKE with perfect correctness, potentially in the crs model. Assume additionally there exists a NIZK. Then there exists a multi-party NIKE with both perfect and adversarial correctness in the crs model. If the perfectly correct scheme has unbounded honest users, corruptions, and/or set size, then so does the resulting adversarially correctscheme.*

Theorem 3 follows from a standard application of NIZKs, and is similar to a theorem used in the context of two-party NIKE by [HHK18]. The proof is given in the Full Version [KWZ22].

3.2   Removing the CRS

Next, we use iO to remove the common reference string (crs) from any multiparty NIKE. A side-effect of this transformation, however, is that we only achieve security without Register Malicious User queries.

Theorem 4. *Assuming there exists iO an adaptively secure multi-party NIKE in the common reference string (crs) model, then there also exists adaptively multi-party NIKE in the plain model that is secure without Register Malicious User queries. If the crs scheme has unbounded honest users, corruptions, and/or set size, or has perfect and/or adversarial correctness, or only has secure without X queries for some X, then the same is true of the resulting plain model scheme.*

Proof. Theorem 4 formalizes the ad hoc techniques for removing the CRS in iO-based constructions starting from Boneh and Zhandry [BZ14]. The proofs of the bounded/unbounded cases and perfect/adversarial correctness cases are essentially the same, so we focus on the case where everything is bounded. We will let (Setup, Pub', KeyGen') be a multi-party NIKE with setup.

Let F be a puncturable PRF. F can be constructed from any one-way function, which are in turn implied by any NIKE scheme. We construct a new mutliparty NIKE (Pub, KeyGen) without setup as follows:

- Pub($1^\lambda, 1^\ell, 1^n, 1^c$): Run crs $\leftarrow$ Setup($1^\lambda, 1^\ell, 1^n, 1^c$). Sample a random PRF key k for F. Let $\mathsf{PKey}_k, \mathsf{SKey}_k$ be the programs in Figs. 1 and 2, and let $\widehat{\mathsf{PKey}} = \mathrm{iO}(\mathsf{PKey}_k), \widehat{\mathsf{SKey}} = \mathrm{iO}(\mathsf{SKey}_k)$. pk $= (\mathsf{crs}, \widehat{\mathsf{PKey}})$ and sk $= \widehat{\mathsf{SKey}}$.
- KeyGen(S, sk_i): Let pk$^* \in S$ be the minimal pk $\in S$ according to some ordering; we will call pk* the distinguished public key.
  Write pk$^* = (\mathsf{crs}^*, \widehat{\mathsf{PKey}}^*)$. Let S' be derived from S, where for each pk $= (\mathsf{crs}, \widehat{\mathsf{PKey}}) \in S$, we include pk$' = \widehat{\mathsf{PKey}}(\mathsf{crs}^*)$ in S'. Also let $\mathsf{sk}_i = \widehat{\mathsf{SKey}}_i$, and run $\mathsf{sk}_i' = \widehat{\mathsf{SKey}}_i(\mathsf{crs}^*)$. Then run and output KeyGen'($\mathsf{crs}, S', \mathsf{sk}_i'$).

Inputs: crs	Inputs: crs
Constants: k	Constants: k
1. (pk', sk') $\leftarrow$ Pub'(crs; F(k, crs))	1. (pk', sk') $\leftarrow$ Pub'(crs; F(k, crs))
2. Output pk'	2. Output sk'

Fig. 1. The program PKey_k.   **Fig. 2.** The program SKey_k.

Correctness: Correctness follows from the correctness of the underlying scheme:

$$\mathsf{KeyGen}(S, \mathsf{sk}_i) = \mathsf{KeyGen}'(\mathsf{crs}, S', \mathsf{sk}_i') = \mathsf{KeyGen}'(\mathsf{crs}, S', \mathsf{sk}_j')$$
$$= \mathsf{KeyGen}(S, \mathsf{sk}_j)$$

Security: Security is proved in the Full Version [KWZ22], following a careful application of iO techniques.

3.3 Adding Shared Key Queries

The final compiler generically convert a NIKE scheme whose security does *not* support shared key queries into one that does.

Theorem 5. *Assume there exists a multi-party NIKE with adversarial correctness and adaptive security without Shared Key or Register Malicious User queries. Then there exists a multi-party NIKE with adversarial correctness and adaptive security (with Shared Key and Register Malicious User queries). If the* *original scheme is also perfectly correct, then so is the resulting scheme. If the original scheme has unbounded honest users, corruptions, and/or set size, then so does the resulting scheme. The resulting scheme is in the CRS model if and only if the original scheme is.*

Note the requirement that the underlying NIKE protocol have adversarial correctness. The proof of Theorem 5 exploits the structure of multiparty NIKE, together with combinatorial tricks, to ensure that the reduction can answer all Shared Key queries (even on sets involving malicious users) while not being able to answer the challenge query.

In slightly more detail, the rough idea is to randomly give the reduction some of the secret keys for users. We give the reduction enough secret keys so that with non-negligible probability it will be able to answer all shared key queries, while simultaneously being *unable* to answer the challenge query.

The main challenge is that shared key queries can be very "close" to the challenge query, potentially differing in only a single user. In order to be able to answer the shared key query but not the challenge query, we must give out the secret key for exactly the differing user, which we do not know in advance. In our solution, every user will actually contain many sub-users. The shared key for a group of users is then the shared key for some collection of the sub-users. The collections of sub-users will be chosen so that the collections for each group are "far" apart. The proof is given in the Full Version [KWZ22].

3.4 Putting It All Together

We can combine Theorems 3, 4, and 5 together, to get the following corollary:

Corollary 1. *Assume there exists iO and perfectly correct multi-party NIKE in the crs model with adaptive security without Shared Key or Register Malicious User queries. Then there exists perfectly correct (and also adversarially correct) multi-party NIKE in the plain model with adaptive security (under both Shared Key and Register Malicious User queries). If the original scheme has unbounded honest users, corruptions, and/or set size, then so does the resulting scheme.*

Corollary 1 shows that, for multiparty NIKE from iO, it suffices to work in the CRS model and ignore Shared Key and Register Malicious User queries.

4   The Equivalence of Multiparty NIKE and 1-SF-PRF

In this section, we show that NIKE is equivalent to a 1-SF-PRF. In the Full Version [KWZ22], we show that NIKE implies 1-SF-PRF, following a simple combinatorial construction. Here, we focus on the other direction.

4.1   From 1-SF-PRF to Special Constrained PRF

Here, we define an intermediate notion of constrained PRF, which enhances a 1-SF-PRF. The idea is that the symbol space Σ is now exponentially large.

However, at the beginning a polynomial-sized set S is chosen, and a punctured key is revealed that allows for evaluating the PRF on any point *not* in S. The points in S then behave like the symbol space for a plain 1-SF-PRF, where it is possible to generate keys that fix any given position to some symbol in S.

Looking ahead to our NIKE construction, the set S will correspond to the public keys of the honest users of the system, while the rest of Σ will correspond to maliciously-generated keys. The abstraction of our special constrained PRF in this section is the missing link to formalize the connection between 1-SF-PRFs and NIKE as outlined in Sect. 1.

Definition 5 (Special Constrained PRF, Syntax). *SC-PRF is a tuple of algorithms* (Gen, Eval, Punc, EvalP, Constr, EvalC) *with the following syntax:*

- Gen$(1^\lambda, |\Sigma|, 1^\ell, 1^n)$ *takes as input a security parameter λ, an alphabet size $|\Sigma|$, an input length ℓ, and a maximal set size n. Here, $|\Sigma|$ is represented in binary (thus allowing exponential-sized Σ), but everything else in unary.*
- Eval(k, x) *is the main evaluation algorithm, which is deterministic and takes as input a key k and $x \in \Sigma^\ell$, and outputs a string.*
- Punc(k, S) *is a randomized puncturing algorithm that takes as input a key k and set $S \subseteq \Sigma$ of size at most n. It outputs a punctured key k_S.*
- EvalP(k_S, x) *takes as input an $x \in \Sigma^\ell$, and outputs a value such that*

$$\mathsf{EvalP}(k_S, x) = \begin{cases} \bot & \text{if } x \in S^n \\ \mathsf{Eval}(k, x) & \text{if } x \notin S^n \end{cases}$$

- Constr(k, S, i, z) *is a potentially randomized constraining algorithm that takes as input a set S, a key k, an index $i \in [\ell]$, and symbol $z \in S$. It outputs a constrained key $k_{S,i,z}$.*
- EvalC$(k_{S,i,z}, x)$ *takes as input a constrained key $k_{S,i,z}$ for a set/index/symbol triple (S, i, z), and input x. It outputs a string. The correctness guarantee is:*

$$\mathsf{EvalC}(k_{S,i,z}, x) = \begin{cases} \bot & \text{if } x_i \neq z \\ \mathsf{Eval}(k, x) & \text{if } x_i = z \end{cases}$$

Definition 6 (Special Constrained PRF, Adaptive Security). *Consider the following experiment with an adversary $\mathcal{A}$:*

- *$\mathcal{A}$ on input 1^λ, outputs $|\Sigma|, 1^\ell, 1^n$, and set S of size at most n. The challenger runs $k \leftarrow \mathsf{Gen}(1^\lambda, |\Sigma|, 1^\ell, 1^n)$ and $k_S \leftarrow \mathsf{Punc}(k, S)$. It sends k_S to $\mathcal{A}$.*
- *Then $\mathcal{A}$ can adaptively make the following types of queries:*
  - **Constrain.** *$\mathcal{A}$ sends i, z, and receives $k_{S,i,z} \leftarrow \mathsf{Constr}(k, S, i, z)$. The challenger records each (i, z) in a table C.*
  - **Eval.** *$\mathcal{A}$ sends an input x, and receives $\mathsf{Eval}(k, x)$. The challenger records each x in a table E. There is no limit to the number of Eval queries.*
  - **Challenge.** *$\mathcal{A}$ can make a single challenge query on an input $x^* \in S^\ell$. The challenger flips a random bit $b \in \{0, 1\}$ and replies with $y^* = y_b$ where $y_0 = \mathsf{Eval}(k, x)$ and y_1 is sampled uniformly and independently.*

If at any time, $x_i^* = z$ for some $(i, z) \in C$ or $x^* \in E$, the challenger immediately aborts and outputs a random bit.
- The adversary outputs bit b'. The challenger outputs 1 if $b = b'$, 0 otherwise.

A Special Constrained PRF is adaptively secure if, for all PPT adversaries $\mathcal{A}$, there exists a negligible function ϵ such that the challenger outputs 1 with probability at most $\frac{1}{2} + \epsilon$.

Theorem 6. *If 1-SF-PRFs exist, then so do Special Constrained PRFs.*

The proof of Theorem 6 use purely combinatorial techniques. The idea is to set the symbol space Σ for the Special Constrained PRF to be codewords over the symbol space for the 1-SF-PRF, where the code is an error correcting code with certain properties. We defer the details to the Full Version [KWZ22].

4.2   From Special Constrained PRF to Multiparty NIKE with Setup

As a warm up, we construct multiparty NIKE in the common reference string model. We will need the following ingredients:

Definition 7. *A* single-point binding (SPB) signature *is a quadruple of algorithms* (Gen, Sign, Ver, GenBind) *where* Gen, Sign, Ver *satisfy the usual syntax of a signature scheme. Additionally, we have the following:*

- $(\text{vk}, \sigma) \leftarrow \text{GenBind}(1^\lambda, m)$ *takes as input a message m, and produces a verification key* vk *and signature σ.*
- *For any messages $m, m' \neq m$, with overwhelming probability over the choice of $(\text{vk}, \sigma) \leftarrow \text{GenBind}(1^\lambda, m)$, $\text{Ver}(\text{vk}, m', \sigma') = \bot$ for any σ'. That is, there is no message $m' \neq m$ where there is a valid signature of m' relative to* vk.
- *For any m, $\text{GenBind}(1^\lambda, m)$ and $(\text{vk}, \text{Sign}(\text{sk}, m))$ are indistinguishable, where $(\text{vk}, \text{sk}) \leftarrow \text{Gen}(1^\lambda)$. Note that this property implies that $\text{Ver}(\text{vk}, m, \sigma)$ accepts, when $(\text{vk}, \sigma) \leftarrow \text{GenBind}(1^\lambda, m)$.*

Definition 8. *A* multi-point binding (MPB) hash function *is a triple of algorithms* (Gen, H, GenBind) *where:*

- $\text{Gen}(1^\lambda, 1^n)$ *takes as input the security parameter λ, and an upper bound n on the number of inputs to bind. It produces a hashing key* hk.
- $H(\text{hk}, x)$ *deterministically produces a hash h.*
- $\text{GenBind}(1^\lambda, 1^n, S^*)$ *takes as input λ, n, and also a set S^* of inputs of size at most n. It produces a hashing key* hk *with the property that, with overwhelming probability over the choice of* hk $\leftarrow \text{GenBind}(1^\lambda, 1^n, S^*)$, *for any $x \in S^*$ and any $x' \neq x$ (which may or may not be in S^*), $H(\text{hk}, x) \neq H(\text{hk}, x')$.*
- *For any n and any set S^* of size at most n, $(S^*, \text{Gen}(1^\lambda, 1^n))$ is computationally indistinguishable from $(S^*, \text{GenBind}(1^\lambda, 1^n, S^*))$.*

A single-point *binding (SPB) hash function is as above, except we fix $n = 1$.*

We will rely on the following Lemmas of Guan, Wichs, and Zhandry [GWZ22]:

Lemma 1 ([GWZ22]). *Assuming one-way functions exist, so do single-point binding signatures.*

[GWZ22] show how to construct single-point binding hash functions. We adapt their construction to multi-point binding hashes:

Lemma 2. *Assuming one-way functions and iO exist, then so do multi-point binding hash functions.*

This lemma is proved in the Full Version [KWZ22], following almost identical ideas to the proof as [GWZ22].

We use multi-point binding hash functions in order to statistically bind to a set of inputs S^* with a hash that is much smaller than the inputs. Such hash functions will contain many collisions, but the point binding guarantee means that there is no collision with S^*. The SPB signature is used for similar reasons.

Our NIKE Construction. We don't bound collusion queries c (that is, the number of corruption queries), but bound the number of honest users, which implicitly bounds the collusion queries at n.

- Setup($1^\lambda, 1^\ell, 1^n$): Run hk $\leftarrow$ Gen$_{Hash}(1^\lambda, 1^\ell)$. Let $\mathcal{Y}$ be the range of H. Also sample $k \leftarrow$ Gen$_{PRF}(1^\lambda, |\mathcal{Y}|, 1^\ell, 1^n)$. Let KGen$_{hk,k}$ be the program given in Fig. 3, padded to the maximum size of the programs in Figs. 3 and 4, and let $\widehat{\text{KGen}} = \text{iO}(\text{KGen}_{hk,k})$. Output crs $= \widehat{\text{KGen}}$.
- Pub(crs): Sample a random message m and run $(\text{vk}, \sigma) \leftarrow$ GenBind$_{Sig}(1^\lambda, m)$. Output pk $=$ vk and sk $= (m, \sigma)$.
- KeyGen(crs, pk$_1, \ldots,$ pk$_\ell, i,$ sk$_i$): assume the pk$_j$ are sorted in order of increasing pk according to some fixed ordering; if the pk$_j$ are not in order sort them, and change i accordingly. Write crs $= \widehat{\text{KGen}}$, pk$_j =$ vk$_j$ and sk$_i = (m_i, \sigma_i)$. Then output $\widehat{\text{KGen}}(\text{vk}_1, \ldots, \text{vk}_\ell, i, m_i, \sigma_i)$.

Inputs: vk$_1, \ldots,$ vk$_\ell, i, m_i, \sigma_i$
Constants: hk, k

1. If the vk$_i$ are not sorted in increasing order, immediately abort and output $\perp$.
2. If Ver(vk$_i, m_i, \sigma_i$) rejects, immediately abort and output $\perp$.
3. For each $t \in [\ell]$, let $u_t = H(\text{hk}, \text{vk}_t)$.
4. Output Eval$_{PRF}(k, u_1 || u_2 || \ldots || u_\ell)$

Fig. 3. The program KGen$_{hk,k}$.

Correctness. We need for any n and $i, j \in [\ell]$, that KeyGen(crs, $\{\text{pk}_j\}_j, i,$ sk$_i$) outputs a value equal to KeyGen(crs, $\{\text{pk}_1, \ldots, \text{pk}_\ell\}, j,$ sk$_j$) with overwhelming probability. This follows from the correctness of the signature scheme. With overwhelming probability, Ver(vk$_i, m_i, \sigma_i$) $=$Ver(vk$_j, m_j, \sigma_j$) $= 1$. Once the signature check passes, the outputs are identical.

Security. We will prove security via a sequence of hybrid experiments.

- Game$_{\text{real}}$: This corresponds to the security game.

- **Setup Phase:**
  The challenger samples $\mathsf{hk} \leftarrow \mathsf{Gen}_{Hash}(1^\lambda, 1^\ell)$.
  Next, it samples $k \leftarrow \mathsf{Gen}_{PRF}(1^\lambda, |\mathcal{Y}|, 1^\ell, 1^n)$.
  The challenger computes $\widehat{\mathsf{KGen}} = \mathsf{iO}(\mathsf{KGen}_{\mathsf{hk},k})$ and sends $\mathsf{crs} = \widehat{\mathsf{KGen}}$ to the adversary. It also maintains a table T which is initially empty.
- **Pre-challenge Queries** The adversary makes the following queries:
  * *Honest user registration query*: For the ith registration query, the challenger chooses m_i^*, computes $(\mathsf{vk}_i^*, \sigma_i^*) \leftarrow \mathsf{GenBind}_{Sig}(1^\lambda, m_i^*)$, sets vk_i^* as the public key and (m_i^*, σ_i^*) as the secret key. It adds $(\mathsf{vk}_i^*, (m_i^*, \sigma_i^*), 0)$ to the table T.
  * *Corruption query*: On receiving a corruption query for vk_i^*, the challenger sends (m_i^*, σ_i^*) to the adversary, and updates the ith entry in T to $(\mathsf{vk}_i^*, (m_i^*, \sigma_i^*), 1)$.
  * *Registering Malicious user*: On receiving pk, the challenger adds $(\mathsf{pk}, \perp, 1)$ to T.
- **Challenge Query** On receiving $(\mathsf{vk}_1, \ldots, \mathsf{vk}_\ell)$, the challenger checks the table T contains a $(\mathsf{vk}_i, (m_i, \sigma_i), 0)$ for each $i \in [\ell]$. If so, it chooses a random bit $b \leftarrow \{0,1\}$. If $b = 0$, it sends $\mathsf{Eval}_{PRF}(k, u_1 || \ldots || u_\ell)$, where $u_i = H(\mathsf{hk}, \mathsf{vk}_i)$. Else it sends a uniformly random string.
- **Post-challenge Queries** Same as pre-challenge queries.
- **Guess** Finally, the adversary sends its guess b', and wins if $b = b'$.

- Game$_1$: This experiment is identical to Game$_0$, except that the challenger chooses the n pairs $(\mathsf{vk}^*, \sigma^*)$ and m^* during setup. These are used to answer registration queries. The distribution of all components is identical to that in the previous experiment.
- Game$_2$: In this experiment, the challenger uses the honest users' verification keys to sample a hash key that is binding to all the verification keys. That is, it replaces $\mathsf{hk} \leftarrow \mathsf{Gen}_{Hash}(1^\lambda, 1^\ell)$ in Game$_0$ and Game$_1$ with $\mathsf{hk} \leftarrow \mathsf{GenBind}_{Hash}\left(1^\lambda, \{\mathsf{vk}_i^*\}_{i \in [n]}\right)$.
- Game$_3$: In this game, the challenger uses a different (but functionally identical) program (KGenAlt, defined in Fig. 4) for computing the CRS. The Setup phase is now the following, with the changes from Game$_2$ in yellow:
  - **Setup Phase:**
    For $j \in [n]$, sample m_j^* and $(\mathsf{vk}_j^*, \sigma_j^*) \leftarrow \mathsf{GenBind}_{Sig}(1^\lambda, m_j^*)$.
    The challenger samples $\mathsf{hk} \leftarrow \mathsf{GenBind}_{Hash}\left(1^\lambda, \{\mathsf{vk}_j^*\}_{j \in [n]}\right)$.
    Next, it samples $k \leftarrow \mathsf{Gen}_{PRF}(1^\lambda, |\mathcal{Y}|, 1^\ell, 1^n)$.
    The challenger computes $u_j^* = H(\mathsf{hk}, \mathsf{vk}_j^*)$ and sets $S = \{u_j^*\}_{j \in [n]}$.
    It computes $K_S \leftarrow \mathsf{Punc}(k, S)$ and constrained keys
    $K_j^* = \left(\mathsf{Constr}(k, S, t, u_j^*)\right)_{t \in [\ell]}$. It sets $v_j^* = m_j^* \oplus K_j^*$ for each $j \in [n]$.
    The challenger computes $\widehat{\mathsf{KGenAlt}} = \mathsf{iO}\left(\mathsf{KGenAlt}_{\mathsf{hk}, \{u_j^*, v_j^*, K_j^*\}, K_S}\right)$ and sends $\mathsf{crs} = \widehat{\mathsf{KGenAlt}}$ to the adversary. It also maintains a table T which is initially empty.

Inputs: $\mathsf{vk}_1, \ldots, \mathsf{vk}_\ell, i, m_i, \sigma_i$
Constants: Hash key hk

$$S = \{u_j^*\}_{j \in [n]}$$

$$\{v_j^*\}_{j \in [n]}$$

Punctured key K_S

1. If the vk_i are not sorted in increasing order, immediately abort and output $\bot$.
2. If $\mathsf{Ver}(\mathsf{vk}_i, m_i, \sigma_i)$ rejects, immediately abort and output $\bot$.
3. For each $t \in [\ell]$, let $u_t = H(\mathsf{hk}, \mathsf{vk}_t)$.
4. If $u_i \in \{u_j^*\}_{j \in [n]}$, compute $K_j^* = \left(K_{j,t}^* \right)_{t \in [\ell]} = m_i \oplus v_i^*$,

   then output $\mathsf{EvalC}(K_{j,i}^*, u_1 || u_2 || \ldots || u_\ell)$. Else output $\mathsf{EvalP}(K_S, u_1 || u_2 || \ldots || u_\ell)$.

Fig. 4. The program $\mathsf{KGenAlt}_{\mathsf{hk}, \{u_j^*, v_j^*, K_j^*\}, K_S}$. (Color figure online)

- Game$_4$: In this experiment, during setup, the challenger replaces $(\mathsf{vk}_j^*, \sigma_j^*) \leftarrow \mathsf{GenBind}_{Sig}(1^\lambda, m^*)$ from Game$_3$ with $(\mathsf{sk}_j^*, \mathsf{vk}_j^*) \leftarrow \mathsf{Gen}_{Sig}(1^\lambda)$ and $\sigma_j^* \leftarrow \mathsf{Sign}(\mathsf{sk}_j^*, m_j^*)$.
- Game$_5$: This game represents a syntactic change. Instead of choosing m_j^* first and then computing v_j^*, the challenger chooses uniformly random v_j^*, and sets $m_j^* = v_j^* \oplus K_j^*$. In terms of the adversary's view, this experiment is identical to the previous one.
  Now the constrained keys are not needed during setup, and can instead be generated adaptively during the corruption queries, which are now answered as follows (changes from Game$_4$ in yellow): On receiving a corruption query for vk_i^*, the challenger computes $K_i^* = \left(\mathsf{Constr}(k, S, t, u_j^*) \right)_{t \in [\ell]}$. It then computes $m_j^* = v_j^* \oplus K_j^*$ and sends (m_i^*, σ_i^*) to the adversary, and updates the ith entry in T to $(\mathsf{vk}_i^*, (m_i^*, \sigma_i^*), 1)$.

In the Full Version [KWZ22], we analyse the adversary's advantage in each of these experiments, showing these games are computationally indistinguishable.

5   Construction of 1-SF-PRFs

The previous section worked to distill adaptively secure NIKE to the more basic primitive of constrained PRFs for one symbol fixing. While these transformations simplify the problem, the central barriers to proving adaptive security still remain. In this section we address these head on.

We review the main issues for adaptivity. Consider an adversary $\mathcal{A}$ that first makes several constrained key queries $(\mathsf{index}_1, \mathsf{sym}_1), \ldots, (\mathsf{index}_Q, \mathsf{sym}_Q)$. Next the $\mathcal{A}$ submits a challenge input x^* such that $x_i^* \neq z$ for any pre-challenge key query (i, z) and receives back the challenge output from the challenger. Before submitting its guess, $\mathcal{A}$ will first perform some consistency checks on the constrained keys it received. For example, it can run the evaluation algorithm on multiple points that are valid for different sets of constrained keys and verify that it receives the same output from each. If not, it aborts and makes no guess.

Dealing with such an attacker is difficult for multiple reasons. First, a reduction cannot simply guess x^* or which index/symbol pairs will be queried without an exponential loss. Second, it cannot issue constrained keys that are deviate much from each other less this be detected by $\mathcal{A}$'s consistency checks.

We overcome these issues by having the challenger gradually issues constrained keys that deviate from a canonical PRF which is used to evaluate on the challenge input. However, we endeavor to keep all subsequent issued keys consistent with any introduced deviation so that this will avoid being detected.

Diving deeper our construction will use constrained keys which are obfuscated programs. Initially, the obfuscated program will simply check if an input x is consistent with the single symbol fixing of the key. If so, it evaluates the canonical PRF which is a Naor-Reingold style PRF.

The proof will begin by looking at the first key that is issued by the challenger for some query $(\mathsf{index}_1, \mathsf{sym}_1)$. For this key the obfuscated program will branch off and evaluate any inputs x where $x_{\mathsf{index}_1} = \mathsf{sym}_1$ in a different, but functionally equivalent way to the canonical PRF. By the security of iO this will not be detected. Moreover, this alternative evaluation for when $x_{\mathsf{index}_1} = \mathsf{sym}_1$ will be adopted by all further issued keys. Once this alternative pathway is set for all keys, we can change the evaluation on such inputs to be inconsistent with the canonical PRF, but mutually consistent with all issued keys. This follows from the DDH assumption. The proof can then proceed to the transforming the second issued key in a similar way such that there is a separate pathway for all inputs x where $x_{\mathsf{index}_2} = \mathsf{sym}_2$. The one exception is that the second and all future keys will give prioritization to the first established pathway whenever we have an input x where both $x_{\mathsf{index}_1} = \mathsf{sym}_1$ and $x_{\mathsf{index}_2} = \mathsf{sym}_2$.

The proof continues on in this way where each new key issued will establish an alternative evaluation which will be used except when it is pre-empted by an earlier established alternative. In this manner the constrained keys issued will always be mutually consistent on inputs, even while they gradually deviate from the canonical PRF. Finally, at the end of the proof all issued keys will use some alternative pathway for *all* evaluations. At this point we can use indistinguishability obfuscation again to remove information about the canonical PRF from the obfuscated programs since it is never used. With this information removed no attacker can distinguish a canonical PRF output from a random value.

We remark that in order to execute our proof strategy, our initial obfuscated program must be as large as any program used in the proof. In particular, it must be large enough to contain an alternative evaluation programming for all corrupted keys. Thus our constrained PRF keys must grow in size proportional to $\ell \cdot |\Sigma|$ and our resulting NIKE is parameterized for a set number of collusions.

5.1   Construction

- Gen($1^\lambda, \Sigma, 1^\ell$): The key generation algorithm first runs $\mathcal{G}(1^\lambda)$ to compute $(p, \mathbb{G})$. Next, it chooses $v \leftarrow \mathbb{G}$, exponents $e_{j,w} \leftarrow \mathbb{Z}_p$ for each $j \in [\ell]$, $w \in \Sigma$. The PRF key K consists of $(v, \{e_{j,w}\})$.
- Eval(K, x): Let K $= (v, \{e_{j,w}\})$ and $x = (x_1, \ldots, x_\ell) \in \Sigma^\ell$. The PRF evaluation on input x is v^t, where $t = \left(\prod_{j \le n} e_{j,x_j}\right)$.
- Constr(K, i, z) : The constrained key is an obfuscation of the program ConstrainedKey$_{K,i,z}$ (defined in Fig. 5). The program is sufficiently padded to ensure that it is of the same size as the programs ConstrainedKeyAlt, ConstrainedKeyAlt$'$ (defined in Fig. 6, 7) as well as an additional program that is used in the security proof. This additional program is specified in the Full Version [KWZ22].

  It outputs $K_{i,z} \leftarrow iO(1^\lambda, \mathsf{ConstrainedKey}_{K,i,z})$ as the constrained key.

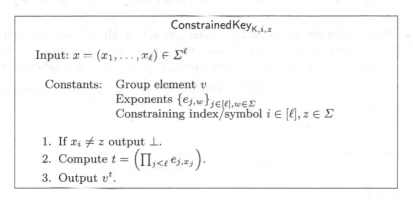

Fig. 5. Program ConstrainedKey

- EvalC($K_{i,z}, x$): The constrained key $K_{i,z}$ is an obfuscated program. The evaluation algorithm outputs $K_{i,z}(x)$.

5.2   Security Proof

We will prove that the above construction satisfies security against unique-query adversaries, via a sequence of hybrid games. The first game corresponds to the original security game (security against *unique query adversary*). Next, we define Q hybrid games $\{\mathsf{Game}_y\}_{y \in [Q]}$, where Q is a bound on the total number of constrained key queries by the adversary.

- Game$_{\mathrm{real}}$:
  - **Setup Phase:** The challenger chooses $v \leftarrow \mathbb{G}$, $e_{j,w} \leftarrow \mathbb{Z}_p$ for each $j \in [\ell], w \in \Sigma$. Let K $= (v, (e_{j,w})_{j,w})$.

    The challenger also maintains an ordered list L of (index, sym) pairs. This list is initially empty, and for each (new) query, the challenger adds a tuple to L.

- **Pre-challenge queries:** Next, the challenger receives pre-challenge constrained key queries. Let $(\text{index}_j, \text{sym}_j)$ be the jth constrained key query. The challenger adds $(\text{index}_j, \text{sym}_j)$ to L.
  The challenger computes the constrained key $\mathsf{K}_j \leftarrow \text{iO}(1^\lambda, \mathsf{ConstrainedKey}_{\mathsf{K},\text{index}_j,\text{sym}_j})$ and sends K_j to the adversary.
- **Challenge Phase:** Next, the adversary sends a challenge x^* such that $x_i^* \neq z$ for any pre-challenge key query (i, z). The challenger chooses $b \leftarrow \{0, 1\}$. If $b = 0$, the challenger computes $t = \prod_i e_{i,x_i^*}$ and sends v^t. If $b = 1$, the challenger sends a uniformly random group element in $\mathbb{G}$.
- **Post-challenge queries:** The post-challenge queries are handled similar to the pre-challenge queries.
- **Guess:** Finally, the adversary sends the guess b' and wins if $b = b'$.
- Game$_y$: In this game, the challenger uses an altered program for the first y constrained keys. It makes the following changes to Game$_{\text{real}}$:
  - **Setup Phase:** The challenger additionally samples $h_j \leftarrow \mathbb{G}$ for all $j \in [y]$. Let $H = (h_j)_{j \in [y]}$.
  - **Pre-challenge queries:** Let $(\text{index}_j, \text{sym}_j)$ be the jth constrained key query. The challenger adds $(\text{index}_j, \text{sym}_j)$ to L. Let $s = \min(y, j)$, and let L_s (resp. H_s) denote the first s entries in L (resp. H). The challenger computes the key $\boxed{\mathsf{K}_j \leftarrow \text{iO}(1^\lambda, \mathsf{ConstrainedKeyAlt}_{s,L_s,H_s,v,(e_{j,w}),\text{index}_j,\text{sym}_j})}$ and sends K_j to the adversary.

$$\mathsf{ConstrainedKeyAlt}_{s,L_s,H_s,v,(e_{j,w}),i,z}$$

Input: $x = (x_1, \ldots, x_\ell) \in \Sigma^\ell$

Constants: $\boxed{s \in \ell \cdot |\Sigma|}$

$\boxed{\text{List } L_s = \big((\text{index}_j, \text{sym}_j)\big)_{j \in [s]}}$

$\boxed{H_s = (h_j)_{j \in [s]}}$
Group element v,
Exponents $(e_{j,w})_{j,w}$,
Constraining index/symbol $i \in [\ell], z \in \Sigma$

1. If $x_i \neq z$ output $\perp$.
2. Compute $t = \left(\prod_{j \leq \ell} e_{j,x_j}\right)$.
3. Find the smallest $j \in [s]$ such that $x_{\text{index}_j} = \text{sym}_j$.
   (a) If such j exists, then output $\boxed{h_j^t}$.
   (b) Else output v^t.

Fig. 6. Program ConstrainedKeyAlt (Color figure online)

Analysis. We will now show that $\mathsf{Game}_{\mathsf{real}}$ and Game_y are computationally indistinguishable for all $y \in [Q]$. Finally, we will show that no polynomial time adversary has non-negligible advantage in Game_Q, showing that the scheme is secure against *unique query adversaries*. For any adversary $\mathcal{A}$, let $\mathsf{adv}_{\mathcal{A},\mathsf{real}}$ denote $\mathcal{A}$'s advantage in $\mathsf{Game}_{\mathsf{real}}$, and let $\mathsf{adv}_{\mathcal{A},y}$ denote $\mathcal{A}$'s advantage in Game_y.

Lemma 3. *Assuming* iO *is secure, for any PPT adversary $\mathcal{A}$, there exists a negligible function* negl *such that for all λ, $|\mathsf{adv}_{\mathcal{A},\mathsf{real}} - \mathsf{adv}_{\mathcal{A},0}| \leq \mathsf{negl}(\lambda)$.*

Proof. For $y = 0$, the lists L_y and H_y are empty, and as a result, the programs are functionally identical. On any input x, both programs output v^t. Therefore, their obfuscations are computationally indistinguishable.

Lemma 4. *Fix any $y \in [Q]$. Assuming* DDH *and security of* iO, *for any PPT adversary $\mathcal{A}$ making at most Q queries, there exists a negligible function* negl *such that for all λ, $|\mathsf{adv}_{\mathcal{A},y} - \mathsf{adv}_{\mathcal{A},y+1}| \leq \mathsf{negl}(\lambda)$.*

Proof. We will define hybrid games to show that Game_y and Game_{y+1} are computationally indistinguishable. The main difference in the two games is with regard to the last $Q - y$ constrained key queries. Note that the first y constrained keys are identical in both experiments. For each of the last $Q - y$ constrained keys, if (i, z) is the constrained key query, then the adversary receives an obfuscation of

- $P_{y,i,z} \equiv \mathsf{ConstrainedKeyAlt}_{y,L_y,H_y,v,(e_{j,w}),i,z}$ in Game_y,
- $P_{y+1,i,z} \equiv \mathsf{ConstrainedKeyAlt}_{y+1,L_{y+1},H_{y+1},v,(e_{j,w}),i,z}$ in Game_{y+1}

Note that the programs $P_{y,i,z}$ and $P_{y+1,i,z}$ only differ on inputs x where $x_i = z$ (in one case the output is v^t, while in the other case the output is h_{y+1}^t). We will prove that these two hybrid games are indistinguishable, using a sequence of sub-hybrid experiments defined below.

- $\mathsf{Game}_{y,a}$: This security game is similar to Game_y, except that the challenger guesses the $(y + 1)^{\mathrm{th}}$ query in the setup phase.
  - **Setup Phase:** The challenger chooses $v \leftarrow \mathbb{G}$, $h_j \leftarrow \mathbb{G}$ for all $j \in [y]$ and $e_{j,w} \leftarrow \mathbb{Z}_p$ for all $j \in [\ell], w \in \Sigma$. Let $H_y = (h_j)_{j \in [y]}$.
    The challenger maintains an ordered list L of (index, sym) pairs which is initially empty.
    The challenger also chooses $(\mathsf{index}_{y+1}, \mathsf{sym}_{y+1}) \leftarrow [\ell] \times \Sigma$.
  - **Pre-challenge queries:** Next, the challenger receives pre-challenge constrained key queries. Let $(\mathsf{index}_q, \mathsf{sym}_q)$ be the qth constrained key query. The challenger adds $(\mathsf{index}_q, \mathsf{sym}_q)$ to L.
    If the $(y + 1)^{\mathrm{th}}$ query is not $(\mathsf{index}_{y+1}, \mathsf{sym}_{y+1})$, then the challenger aborts. The adversary wins with probability $1/2$.
    Let $s = min(y, q)$, and let L_s denote the first s entries in L. The challenger computes the constrained key $K_q \leftarrow \mathsf{iO}(1^\lambda, \mathsf{ConstrainedKeyAlt}_{s,L_s,H_s,v,(e_{j,w}),\mathsf{index}_q,\mathsf{sym}_q})$ and sends K_q to the adversary.

- **Challenge Phase:** Next, the adversary sends a challenge x^* such that $x_i^* \neq z$ for any pre-challenge key query (i, z). The challenger chooses $b \leftarrow \{0, 1\}$. If $b = 0$, the challenger computes $t = \prod_i e_{i, x_i^*}$ and sends v^t. If $b = 1$, the challenger sends a uniformly random group element in $\mathbb{G}$.
- **Post-challenge queries:** The post-challenge queries are handled similar to the pre-challenge queries.
- **Guess:** Finally, the adversary sends the guess b' and wins if $b = b'$.

- $\mathsf{Game}_{y,b}$: This security game is similar to $\mathsf{Game}_{y,a}$, except that the challenger chooses the h_j constants and one of the $e_{j,w}$ exponents differently. However, the distribution of these components is identical to their distribution in the previous game.

  - **Setup Phase:** The challenger chooses $g \leftarrow \mathbb{G}$, $b \leftarrow \mathbb{Z}_p$, $c_j \leftarrow \mathbb{Z}_p$ for all $j \in [y]$. It sets $v = g^b$, $h_j = g^{c_j}$.

    It chooses $e_{j,w} \leftarrow \mathbb{Z}_p$ for all $j \in [n]$, $w \in \Sigma$, $(j, w) \neq (\mathsf{index}_{y+1}, \mathsf{sym}_{y+1})$.

    It chooses $a \leftarrow \mathbb{Z}_p$ and sets $e_{\mathsf{index}_{y+1}, \mathsf{sym}_{y+1}} = a$, $A = g^a$ and $T = v^a$.

    Note that the terms A and T are not used in this experiment; they will be used in some of the following hybrid experiments. Let $H_y = (h_j)_{j \in [y]}$.

- $\mathsf{Game}_{y,c}$: In this security game, the challenger computes the constrained keys differently. Instead of sending an obfuscation of ConstrainedKeyAlt (with appropriate hardwired constants), the challenger computes an obfuscation of ConstrainedKeyAlt' (with appropriate hardwired constants). The program ConstrainedKeyAlt' is defined in Fig. 7, and is padded to be of the same size as ConstrainedKey, ConstrainedKeyAlt and ConstrainedKeyEnd.

  The main difference is that ConstrainedKeyAlt' does not contain the exponent $e_{\mathsf{index}_{y+1}, \mathsf{sym}_{y+1}}$ (recall $(\mathsf{index}_{y+1}, \mathsf{sym}_{y+1})$ is the $(y+1)^{\text{th}}$ constrained key query, and the challenger guesses this query during setup). Instead, the program contains $g^{e_{\mathsf{index}_{j+1}, \mathsf{sym}_{j+1}}}$ and $v^{e_{\mathsf{index}_{j+1}, \mathsf{sym}_{j+1}}}$. As a result, the final output is computed differently (although the outputs are identical).

  We will show that the two programs are functionally identical, and therefore their obfuscations are computationally indistinguishable.

  - **Pre-challenge queries:** Let $(\mathsf{index}_q, \mathsf{sym}_q)$ be the qth constrained key query. The challenger adds $(\mathsf{index}_q, \mathsf{sym}_q)$ to L. Let L_j denote the first j entries in L.

    If $q \leq y$, the challenger computes $\mathsf{K}_q \leftarrow \mathrm{iO}(1^\lambda, \mathsf{ConstrainedKeyAlt}_{q, L_q, H_q, v, (e_{j,w}), \mathsf{index}_q, \mathsf{sym}_q})$ and sends K_q to the adversary.

    If the $(y+1)^{\text{th}}$ query is not $(\mathsf{index}_{y+1}, \mathsf{sym}_{y+1})$,[4] then the challenger aborts. The adversary wins with probability $1/2$.

    If $q > y$, the challenger sends an obfuscation of the program:

    $\mathsf{ConstrainedKeyAlt'}_{y, L_y, (\mathsf{index}_{y+1}, \mathsf{sym}_{y+1}), \{c_y\}, g, v, B, T, (e_{j,w})_{(j,w)}, \mathsf{index}_q, \mathsf{sym}_q}$

---

[4] Recall $(\mathsf{index}_{y+1}, \mathsf{sym}_{y+1})$ is chosen during the setup phase.

ConstrainedKeyAlt′

Input: $x = (x_1, \ldots, x_\ell) \in \Sigma^\ell$

Constants: $y \in [\, \ell \cdot |\Sigma| \,]$
List of first y queries $L_y = \big((\mathsf{index}_j, \mathsf{sym}_j)\big)_{j \in [y]}$
$(y+1)^{\text{th}}$ query $(\mathsf{index}_{y+1}, \mathsf{sym}_{y+1})$
exponents for computing $(h_j)_j : (c_j)_{j \in [y]}$
Group elements g, v, A, T
PRF eval exponents $= (e_{j,w})_{(j,w) \neq (\mathsf{index}_{y+1}, \mathsf{sym}_{y+1})}$
Constraining index/symbol $i \in [\ell], z \in \Sigma$

1. If $x_i \neq z$ output $\perp$.
2. Compute t as follows:
   (a) If $x_{\mathsf{index}_{y+1}} = \mathsf{sym}_{y+1}$ then set $t = \left(\prod_{j \neq \mathsf{index}_{y+1}} e_{j,x_j}\right)$
   (b) Else $t = \left(\prod_j e_{j,x_j}\right)$
3. Find the smallest $j \in [y]$ such that $x_{\mathsf{index}_j} = \mathsf{sym}_j$.
   (a) If such j exists and $x_{\mathsf{index}_{y+1}} = \mathsf{sym}_{y+1}$ then output $(A)^{t \cdot c_j}$
   (b) If such j exists and $x_{\mathsf{index}_{y+1}} \neq \mathsf{sym}_{y+1}$ then output $\left(g_j^c\right)^t$
   (c) Else if no such j exists and $x_{\mathsf{index}_{y+1}} = \mathsf{sym}_{y+1}$ output $(T)^t$.
   (d) Else if no such j exists and $x_{\mathsf{index}_{y+1}} \neq \mathsf{sym}_{y+1}$ output v^t.

Fig. 7. Program ConstrainedKeyAlt′

- $\mathsf{Game}_{y,d}$: In this security game, the challenger sets T to be a uniformly random element in $\mathbb{G}$ instead of $T = v^a$.
- $\mathsf{Game}_{y,e}$: This security game represents a syntactic change. We choose $h_{j+1} \leftarrow \mathbb{G}$ and set $T = h_{j+1}^a$. The element h_{j+1} is not used anywhere else.
- $\mathsf{Game}_{y,f}$: In this experiment, the challenger uses ConstrainedKeyAlt for the last $Q - y$ constrained key queries. On receiving query (i, z), the challenger sends an obfuscation of $\mathsf{ConstrainedKeyAlt}_{y+1, L_{y+1}, H_{y+1}, v, (e_{k,w}), i, z}$. Here L_{y+1} and H_{y+1} are defined as in $\mathsf{Game}_{y,e}$.
- $\mathsf{Game}_{y,g}$: This security game is identical to $\mathsf{Game}_{y,f}$, and the changes in this game are syntactic. Instead of sampling exponents c_j and setting $h_j = g^{c_j}$, the challenger chooses $h_j \leftarrow \mathbb{G}$. Similarly, the challenger samples $v \leftarrow \mathbb{G}$, and samples all the exponents $e_{j,w} \leftarrow \mathbb{Z}_p$. Note that this experiment is identical to Game_{y+1}, except that the challenger guesses $(\mathsf{index}_{y+1}, \mathsf{sym}_{y+1})$ in the setup phase.

Claim 1. *For any $y \in [Q]$, and any adversary $\mathcal{A}$ making at most Q constrained key queries, $|\mathsf{adv}_{\mathcal{A},y} - \mathsf{adv}_{\mathcal{A},y+1}| = \frac{1}{\ell \cdot |\Sigma|} \left(|\mathsf{adv}_{\mathcal{A},y,a} - \mathsf{adv}_{\mathcal{A},y,g}|\right).$*

Proof. Note that the only difference between $\mathsf{Game}_{y,a}$ and Game_y is that the challenger guesses the $(y+1)^{\text{th}}$ constrained key query in the setup phase. Similarly, the only difference between $\mathsf{Game}_{y,g}$ and Game_{y+1} is that the challenger guesses the $(y+1)^{th}$ constrained key query. This guess is correct with probability $1/(\ell \cdot |\Sigma|)$, and therefore $|\mathsf{adv}_{\mathcal{A},y} - \mathsf{adv}_{\mathcal{A},y+1}| = \frac{1}{\ell \cdot |\Sigma|} (|\mathsf{adv}_{\mathcal{A},y,a} - \mathsf{adv}_{\mathcal{A},y,g}|)$.

Therefore, it suffices to show that $\mathsf{Game}_{y,a}, \ldots, \mathsf{Game}_{y,g}$ are computationally indistinguishable. This is proved in the Full Version [KWZ22]. Proving the indistinguishability of these hybrids completes the proof of Lemma 4.

Acknowledgements. We thank Rachit Garg and George Lu for helpful feedback on an earlier draft of our work.

References

[AJ15] Ananth, P., Jain, A.: Indistinguishability obfuscation from compact functional encryption. In: Gennaro, R., Robshaw, M. (eds.) CRYPTO 2015, Part I. LNCS, vol. 9215, pp. 308–326. Springer, Heidelberg (2015). https://doi.org/10.1007/978-3-662-47989-6_15

[AMN+18] Attrapadung, N., Matsuda, T., Nishimaki, R., Yamada, S., Yamakawa, T.: Constrained PRFs for NC^1 in traditional groups. In: Shacham, H., Boldyreva, A. (eds.) CRYPTO 2018, Part II. LNCS, vol. 10992, pp. 543–574. Springer, Cham (2018). https://doi.org/10.1007/978-3-319-96881-0_19

[BFP+15] Banerjee, A., Fuchsbauer, G., Peikert, C., Pietrzak, K., Stevens, S.: Key-homomorphic constrained pseudorandom functions. In: Dodis, Y., Nielsen, J.B. (eds.) TCC 2015, Part II. LNCS, vol. 9015, pp. 31–60. Springer, Heidelberg (2015). https://doi.org/10.1007/978-3-662-46497-7_2

[BGI14] Boyle, E., Goldwasser, S., Ivan, I.: Functional signatures and pseudorandom functions. In: Krawczyk, H. (ed.) PKC 2014. LNCS, vol. 8383, pp. 501–519. Springer, Heidelberg (2014). https://doi.org/10.1007/978-3-642-54631-0_29

[BGK+18] Boneh, D., et al.: Multiparty non-interactive key exchange and more from isogenies on elliptic curves. J. Math. Cryptol. **14**, 5–14 (2018)

[BJLS16] Bader, C., Jager, T., Li, Y., Schäge, S.: On the impossibility of tight cryptographic reductions. In: Fischlin, M., Coron, J.-S. (eds.) EUROCRYPT 2016, Part II. LNCS, vol. 9666, pp. 273–304. Springer, Heidelberg (2016). https://doi.org/10.1007/978-3-662-49896-5_10

[BS02] Boneh, D., Silverberg, A.: Applications of multilinear forms to cryptography. Contemp. Math. **324**, 71–90 (2002)

[BTVW17] Brakerski, Z., Tsabary, R., Vaikuntanathan, V., Wee, H.: Private constrained PRFs (and more) from LWE. In: Kalai, Y., Reyzin, L. (eds.) TCC 2017, Part I. LNCS, vol. 10677, pp. 264–302. Springer, Cham (2017). https://doi.org/10.1007/978-3-319-70500-2_10

[BV15a] Bitansky, N., Vaikuntanathan, V.: Indistinguishability obfuscation from functional encryption. In: Guruswami, V. (ed.) 56th FOCS, pp. 171–190. IEEE Computer Society Press (2015)

[BV15b] Brakerski, Z., Vaikuntanathan, V.: Constrained key-homomorphic PRFs from standard lattice assumptions. In: Dodis, Y., Nielsen, J.B. (eds.) TCC 2015, Part II. LNCS, vol. 9015, pp. 1–30. Springer, Heidelberg (2015). https://doi.org/10.1007/978-3-662-46497-7_1

[BW13]   Boneh, D., Waters, B.: Constrained Pseudorandom Functions and Their
          Applications. In: Sako, K., Sarkar, P. (eds.) ASIACRYPT 2013, Part II.
          LNCS, vol. 8270, pp. 280–300. Springer, Heidelberg (2013). https://doi.
          org/10.1007/978-3-642-42045-0_15

[BZ14]   Boneh, D., Zhandry, M.: Multiparty key exchange, efficient traitor tracing,
          and more from indistinguishability obfuscation. In: Garay, J.A., Gennaro,
          R. (eds.) CRYPTO 2014, Part I. LNCS, vol. 8616, pp. 480–499. Springer,
          Heidelberg (2014). https://doi.org/10.1007/978-3-662-44371-2_27

[CC17]   Canetti, R., Chen, Y.: Constraint-hiding constrained PRFs for NC^1 from
          LWE. In: Coron, J.-S., Nielsen, J.B. (eds.) EUROCRYPT 2017, Part I.
          LNCS, vol. 10210, pp. 446–476. Springer, Cham (2017). https://doi.org/
          10.1007/978-3-319-56620-7_16

[CFN94]   Chor, B., Fiat, A., Naor, M.: Tracing traitors. In: Desmedt, Y.G. (ed.)
          CRYPTO 1994. LNCS, vol. 839, pp. 257–270. Springer, Heidelberg (1994).
          https://doi.org/10.1007/3-540-48658-5_25

[CKS08]   Cash, D., Kiltz, E., Shoup, V.: The twin Diffie-hellman problem and appli-
          cations. In: Smart, N. (ed.) EUROCRYPT 2008. LNCS, vol. 4965, pp.
          127–145. Springer, Heidelberg (2008). https://doi.org/10.1007/978-3-540-
          78967-3_8

[CM14]   Chase, M., Meiklejohn, S.: Déjà Q: using dual systems to revisit q-type
          assumptions. In: Nguyen, P.Q., Oswald, E. (eds.) EUROCRYPT 2014.
          LNCS, vol. 8441, pp. 622–639. Springer, Heidelberg (2014). https://doi.
          org/10.1007/978-3-642-55220-5_34

[CRV16]   Chandran, N., Raghuraman, S., Vinayagamurthy, D.: Reducing depth in
          constrained PRFs: from bit-fixing to NC^1. In: Cheng, C.-M., Chung, K.-
          M., Persiano, G., Yang, B.-Y. (eds.) PKC 2016, Part II. LNCS, vol. 9615,
          pp. 359–385. Springer, Heidelberg (2016). https://doi.org/10.1007/978-3-
          662-49387-8_14

[DH76]   Diffie, W., Hellman, M.E.: New directions in cryptography. IEEE Trans.
          Inf. Theory **22**(6), 644–654 (1976)

[DKN+20] Davidson, A., Katsumata, S., Nishimaki, R., Yamada, S., Yamakawa, T.:
          Adaptively secure constrained pseudorandom functions in the standard
          model. In: Micciancio, D., Ristenpart, T. (eds.) CRYPTO 2020, Part I.
          LNCS, vol. 12170, pp. 559–589. Springer, Cham (2020). https://doi.org/
          10.1007/978-3-030-56784-2_19

[DKW16]   Deshpande, A., Koppula, V., Waters, B.: Constrained pseudorandom func-
          tions for unconstrained inputs. In: Fischlin, M., Coron, J.-S. (eds.) EURO-
          CRYPT 2016, Part II. LNCS, vol. 9666, pp. 124–153. Springer, Heidelberg
          (2016). https://doi.org/10.1007/978-3-662-49896-5_5

[DKXY02] Dodis, Y., Katz, J., Xu, S., Yung, M.: Key-insulated public key cryptosys-
          tems. In: Knudsen, L.R. (ed.) EUROCRYPT 2002. LNCS, vol. 2332, pp.
          65–82. Springer, Heidelberg (2002). https://doi.org/10.1007/3-540-46035-
          7_5

[FHKP13] Freire, E.S.V., Hofheinz, D., Kiltz, E., Paterson, K.G.: Non-interactive
          key exchange. In: Kurosawa, K., Hanaoka, G. (eds.) PKC 2013. LNCS,
          vol. 7778, pp. 254–271. Springer, Heidelberg (2013). https://doi.org/10.
          1007/978-3-642-36362-7_17

[FKPR14] Fuchsbauer, G., Konstantinov, M., Pietrzak, K., Rao, V.: Adaptive secu-
          rity of constrained PRFs. In: Sarkar, P., Iwata, T. (eds.) ASIACRYPT
          2014, Part II. LNCS, vol. 8874, pp. 82–101. Springer, Heidelberg (2014).
          https://doi.org/10.1007/978-3-662-45608-8_5

[FN94] Fiat, A., Naor, M.: Broadcast encryption. In: Stinson, D.R. (ed.) CRYPTO 1993. LNCS, vol. 773, pp. 480–491. Springer, Heidelberg (1994). https://doi.org/10.1007/3-540-48329-2_40

[GGH13] Garg, S., Gentry, C., Halevi, S.: Candidate multilinear maps from ideal lattices. In: Johansson, T., Nguyen, P.Q. (eds.) EUROCRYPT 2013. LNCS, vol. 7881, pp. 1–17. Springer, Heidelberg (2013). https://doi.org/10.1007/978-3-642-38348-9_1

[GPSZ17] Garg, S., Pandey, O., Srinivasan, A., Zhandry, M.: Breaking the subexponential barrier in obfustopia. In: Coron, J.-S., Nielsen, J.B. (eds.) EUROCRYPT 2017, Part III. LNCS, vol. 10212, pp. 156–181. Springer, Cham (2017). https://doi.org/10.1007/978-3-319-56617-7_6

[GVW12] Gorbunov, S., Vaikuntanathan, V., Wee, H.: Functional encryption with bounded collusions via multi-party computation. In: Safavi-Naini, R., Canetti, R. (eds.) CRYPTO 2012. LNCS, vol. 7417, pp. 162–179. Springer, Heidelberg (2012). https://doi.org/10.1007/978-3-642-32009-5_11

[GWZ22] Guan, J., Wichs, D., Zhandry, M.: Incompressible cryptography. In: Dunkelman, O., Dziembowski, S. (eds.) EUROCRYPT 2022, Part I. LNCS, vol. 13275, pp. 700–730. Springer, Cham (2022). https://doi.org/10.1007/978-3-031-06944-4_24

[HHK18] Hesse, J., Hofheinz, D., Kohl, L.: On tightly secure non-interactive key exchange. In: Shacham, H., Boldyreva, A. (eds.) CRYPTO 2018. LNCS, vol. 10992, pp. 65–94. Springer, Cham (2018). https://doi.org/10.1007/978-3-319-96881-0_3

[HHKL21] Hesse, J., Hofheinz, D., Kohl, L., Langrehr, R.: Towards tight adaptive security of non-interactive key exchange. In: Nissim, K., Waters, B. (eds.) TCC 2021, Part III. LNCS, vol. 13044, pp. 286–316. Springer, Cham (2021). https://doi.org/10.1007/978-3-030-90456-2_10

[HJK+16] Hofheinz, D., Jager, T., Khurana, D., Sahai, A., Waters, B., Zhandry, M.: How to generate and use universal samplers. In: Cheon, J.H., Takagi, T. (eds.) ASIACRYPT 2016, Part II. LNCS, vol. 10032, pp. 715–744. Springer, Heidelberg (2016). https://doi.org/10.1007/978-3-662-53890-6_24

[HKKW14] Hofheinz, D., Kamath, A., Koppula, V., Waters, B.: Adaptively secure constrained pseudorandom functions. Cryptology ePrint Archive, Report 2014/720 (2014). https://eprint.iacr.org/2014/720

[HKW15] Hohenberger, S., Koppula, V., Waters, B.: Adaptively secure puncturable pseudorandom functions in the standard model. In: Iwata, T., Cheon, J.H. (eds.) ASIACRYPT 2015, Part I. LNCS, vol. 9452, pp. 79–102. Springer, Heidelberg (2015). https://doi.org/10.1007/978-3-662-48797-6_4

[Hof14] Hofheinz, D.: Fully secure constrained pseudorandom functions using random oracles. Cryptology ePrint Archive, Report 2014/372 (2014). https://eprint.iacr.org/2014/372

[Jou00] Joux, A.: A one round protocol for tripartite Diffie–Hellman. In: Bosma, W. (ed.) ANTS 2000. LNCS, vol. 1838, pp. 385–393. Springer, Heidelberg (2000). https://doi.org/10.1007/10722028_23

[KPTZ13] Kiayias, A., Papadopoulos, S., Triandopoulos, N., Zacharias, T.: Delegatable pseudorandom functions and applications. In: Sadeghi, A.-R., Gligor, V.D., Yung, M. (eds.) ACM CCS 2013, pp. 669–684. ACM Press (2013)

[KRS15] Khurana, D., Rao, V., Sahai, A.: Multi-party key exchange for unbounded parties from indistinguishability obfuscation. In: Iwata, T., Cheon, J.H.

(eds.) ASIACRYPT 2015, Part I. LNCS, vol. 9452, pp. 52–75. Springer, Heidelberg (2015). https://doi.org/10.1007/978-3-662-48797-6_3

[KWZ22] Koppula, V. Waters, B., Zhandry, M.: Adaptive multiparty NIKE (full version) (2022)

[LOS+10] Lewko, A., Okamoto, T., Sahai, A., Takashima, K., Waters, B.: Fully secure functional encryption: attribute-based encryption and (hierarchical) inner product encryption. In: Gilbert, H. (ed.) EUROCRYPT 2010. LNCS, vol. 6110, pp. 62–91. Springer, Heidelberg (2010). https://doi.org/10.1007/978-3-642-13190-5_4

[LW14] Lewko, A., Waters, B.: Why proving HIBE systems secure is difficult. In: Nguyen, P.Q., Oswald, E. (eds.) EUROCRYPT 2014. LNCS, vol. 8441, pp. 58–76. Springer, Heidelberg (2014). https://doi.org/10.1007/978-3-642-55220-5_4

[MZ17] Ma, F., Zhandry, M.: Encryptor combiners: a unified approach to multiparty NIKE, (H)IBE, and broadcast encryption. Cryptology ePrint Archive, Report 2017/152 (2017). https://eprint.iacr.org/2017/152

[MZ18] Ma, F., Zhandry, M.: The MMap strikes back: obfuscation and new multilinear maps immune to CLT13 zeroizing attacks. In: Beimel, A., Dziembowski, S. (eds.) TCC 2018, Part II. LNCS, vol. 11240, pp. 513–543. Springer, Cham (2018). https://doi.org/10.1007/978-3-030-03810-6_19

[NR97] Naor, M., Reingold, O.: Number-theoretic constructions of efficient pseudo-random functions. In: 38th FOCS, pp. 458–467. IEEE Computer Society Press (1997)

[Rao14] Rao, V.: Adaptive multiparty non-interactive key exchange without setup in the standard model. Cryptology ePrint Archive, Report 2014/910 (2014). https://eprint.iacr.org/2014/910

[STW96] Steiner, M., Tsudik, G., Waidner, M.: Diffie-Hellman key distribution extended to group communication. In: Gong, L., Stern, J. (eds.) ACM CCS 96, pp. 31–37. ACM Press (1996)

[SW14] Sahai, A., Waters, B.: How to use indistinguishability obfuscation: deniable encryption, and more. In: Shmoys, D.B. (ed.) Symposium on Theory of Computing, STOC 2014, New York, NY, USA, 31 May–03 June 2014, pp. 475–484. ACM (2014)

[Wat09] Waters, B.: Dual system encryption: realizing fully secure IBE and HIBE under simple assumptions. In: Halevi, S. (ed.) CRYPTO 2009. LNCS, vol. 5677, pp. 619–636. Springer, Heidelberg (2009). https://doi.org/10.1007/978-3-642-03356-8_36

On the Impossibility of Algebraic Vector Commitments in Pairing-Free Groups

Dario Catalano[1], Dario Fiore[2], Rosario Gennaro[3],
and Emanuele Giunta[2,4(✉)]

[1] University of Catania, Catania, Italy
catalano@dmi.unict.it
[2] IMDEA Software Institute, Madrid, Spain
{dario.fiore,emanuele.giunta}@imdea.org
[3] Protocol Labs., New York, USA
rosario.gennaro@protocol.ai
[4] Universidad Politecnica de Madrid, Madrid, Spain

Abstract. Vector Commitments allow one to (concisely) commit to a vector of messages so that one can later (concisely) open the commitment at selected locations. In the state of the art of vector commitments, *algebraic* constructions have emerged as a particularly useful class, as they enable advanced properties, such as stateless updates, subvector openings and aggregation, that are for example unknown in Merkle-tree-based schemes. In spite of their popularity, algebraic vector commitments remain poorly understood objects. In particular, no construction in standard prime order groups (without pairing) is known.

In this paper, we shed light on this state of affairs by showing that a large class of concise algebraic vector commitments in pairing-free, prime order groups are impossible to realize.

Our results also preclude any cryptographic primitive that implies the algebraic vector commitments we rule out, as special cases. This means that we also show the impossibility, for instance, of succinct polynomial commitments and functional commitments (for all classes of functions including linear forms) in pairing-free groups of prime order.

1 Introduction

Vector commitments [9,27] (VC) are a class of commitment schemes that allow a sender to commit to a vector $\mathbf{v}$ of n messages, in such a way that she can later open the commitment at selected positions. Namely, the sender can convince anyone that the i-th message in the committed vector is v_i. A secure scheme shall satisfy *position binding*, i.e. generating valid openings to different values $v_i \neq v_i'$ for the same position i is computationally infeasible.

The distinguishing feature of vector commitments is that commitments and openings must be *succinct*. In the original notion of [9,27], this means that their size is independent of n, the length of the vector, but a relaxed notion allowing a logarithmic dependence in n may be considered, as in the case of the celebrated Merkle tree construction [29].

E. Kiltz and V. Vaikuntanathan (Eds.): TCC 2022, LNCS 13748, pp. 274–299, 2022.
https://doi.org/10.1007/978-3-031-22365-5_10

Mainly thanks to their succinctness property, vector commitments have been shown to be a useful building block in several applications, such as zero-knowledge sets [9,27,31], verifiable databases [3,9], succinct arguments [4,22,25,30], proofs of retrievability [12,20], and stateless blockchains [4,10].

Analyzing the state of the art of VC schemes, we see that VC constructions are based on two main approaches.

On one side, we have tree-based VCs, notably Merkle trees [29] and their generalizations [24]. These constructions have the advantage of being realizable from collision resistant hash functions, and thus can be based on the hardness of virtually any cryptographic problem including factoring, discrete logarithm, SIS and many more. In fact, we notice that VCs with logarithmic-size openings are *equivalent* to collision-resistant hash functions. The main drawback of tree-based schemes is that their openings are of size $O(\log n)$. Additionally, the tree-based approach seems to inherently impede the realization of properties such as subvector openings [4,25] and aggregation [8], that turn useful in both theoretical and practical applications of VCs.

On the other side, we have *algebraic* vector commitments, notably based on bilinear pairings [9,21,27], groups of unknown order [9], and lattices [34,35]. Roughly speaking, an algebraic VC is one in which the commitment and verification algorithm only use algebraic operations over the group that underlies the construction (this rules out hashing group elements for example). The main advantage of these constructions is that they admit openings of constant size,[1] that are virtually optimal – a single group element in most constructions. Moreover, algebraic schemes naturally achieve useful properties such as (additive) homomorphism, stateless updatability [9], subvector openings [4,25] and aggregation [8]. Yet, the powerful versatility of existing VCs with constant-size openings contrasts with the limited theoretical understanding of their foundations.

We see two main open questions related to algebraic VCs. The first one concerns the minimal general assumption that implies them. While tree-based schemes with logarithmic openings are well understood, being de facto equivalent to collision-resistant hash functions[2], we have no generic recipe to build algebraic VCs with constant-size openings.[3] The second question is whether algebraic VCs can be built from "standard" prime-order groups without pairings. In this setting, known constructions rely either on the tree-based approach (e.g., building a Merkle tree on top of Pedersen hash function), or on inner-product arguments in the random oracle model [6,7]. Both these approaches entail logarithmic-size openings and a non-algebraic verification.

---

[1] We include lattice-based schemes in the 'algebraic' category although they do not perfectly fit our notion of using a group in a black box way; also, existing schemes still need (poly) logarithmic-size openings.

[2] A Merkle tree is a VC with logarithm openings that can be realized from any CRHF. Conversely, in any non trivial VC the commitment procedure has to be shrinking and collision resistant, from which CRHF can be built.

[3] The only generic construction with constant size opening is the folklore one that combines a hash function and a constant-size SNARK; yet this is non-algebraic due to the need of encoding the hash computation in the SNARK's constraint system.

We believe that settling these two questions would improve our understanding of vector commitments. In this work, we focus on the second question for two important reasons: (i) on the theoretical front, studying algebraic VCs in this minimal setting helps us understand conceptually what are the "ingredients" needed to build them; (ii) on the practical side, pairing-free groups of known order are the simplest and most efficient cryptographic setting, and yet we know of no construction of algebraic VCs there.

Our results are negative: we show that a broad class of VC schemes in this setting cannot both be succinct and satisfy position binding.

1.1   Our Results

We informally call a vector commitment built on top of a group $\mathbb{G}$ of prime order q "algebraic" if all its procedures use $\mathbb{G}$ in a black box way, i.e. without relying on the representation of group elements. We show the following two main results.

Impossibility of Algebraic VCs with Linear Verification. We start by looking at the class of algebraic VC schemes in which the verification algorithm is a set of linear equations over $\mathbb{G}$. Specifically, for a message m and position i the verification consists of checking that

$$A(\mathbf{z}, m, i) \cdot \mathbf{X} \stackrel{?}{=} B(\mathbf{z}, m, i) \cdot \mathbf{Y} \tag{1}$$

where $\mathbf{X} = (\mathbf{X}_1, \mathbf{X}_2)$ are the group elements appearing respectively in the public parameters and the commitment, openings are of the form $(\mathbf{Y}, \mathbf{z})$ with $\mathbf{Y}$ being a vector of group elements and $\mathbf{z}$ of field elements, and A, B are functions defining matrices with coefficients in $\mathbb{F}_q$.

We believe this to be the simplest and most natural form of verification using only group operations. However we show that whenever A depends affinely on $\mathbf{z}, m$ and B is independent from them (we say such a scheme has *strictly* linear verification), then it is impossible to achieve both position binding and succinctness. More specifically we prove that if a scheme has position binding, commitments of bit-length ℓ_c and opening proofs of bit-length ℓ_π, then asymptotically their product is lower bounded by the length of the vector we are committing to, i.e. $\ell_c \cdot \ell_\pi = \Omega(n)$. Thus either $\ell_c = \Omega(\sqrt{n})$ or $\ell_\pi = \Omega(\sqrt{n})$. Interestingly, this family of schemes captures generalizations of Pedersen commitments [2] which, as we show in the full version, achieve this lower bound.

Next, we investigate how crucial are our requirements on the dependence of $A(\cdot)$ and $B(\cdot)$ on $\mathbf{z}, m$. We show they are necessary. Indeed, if we allow either A to depend quadratically, or B affinely, on $\mathbf{z}, m$ then there exist succinct VC constructions whose verification can be written in the above form over a group $\mathbb{G}$. We provide examples in the full version. The schemes we find however rely on arithmetization techniques to encode arbitrary circuits as constraint systems of degree 2 over a finite field [13]. This for instance means that, for proper choice of A and B, it is possible to express, using an algebraic verification equation as

(1), computations like the validity tests for a Merkle tree path, or any arbitrary VC verification algorithm.

Despite being secure and succinct, VC schemes built this way do not satisfactorily answer our question in a positive way, as they appear to bypass the underlying group as their source of hardness. Indeed, either their security comes from problems unrelated to $\mathbb{G}$, or if they depend on $\mathbb{G}$, they must do it in a non-black-box way[4].

Impossibility of Algebraic VCs with Generic Group Verification. Motivated by these findings, we investigate whether VCs can be built given *only* black-box access to a cryptographic group. To study this case, we just assume the VC (which we call *algebraic with generic verification*) to use the underlying group generically, without any further constraint on its verification procedure.

Eventually we provide a black-box separation in Maurer's Generic Group Model [28]. This informally implies that any VC using $\mathbb{G}$ generically and whose position binding reduces to a hard problem in $\mathbb{G}$ (such as DLP or CDH) cannot be succinct, as it must hold $\ell_c \cdot \ell_\pi = \Omega(n)$.

1.2 Our Techniques

Our strategy to prove our impossibility results on algebraic vector commitments consists of two main steps. (A) We show that from a VC it is possible to construct a class of signature schemes. In particular, if the VC is algebraic with linear (resp. generic) verification, the resulting signature scheme's verification has analogous algebraic properties. (B) We prove the insecurity of this class of signature schemes in pairing-free groups of known order. To achieve the latter result we build on, and extend, the recent techniques of [11], that provide negative results for a somewhat smaller family of algebraic signatures.

In what follows we give an overview on each step.

From VCs to Signatures. Given a VC scheme for vectors of length n our transformation produces a signature scheme with polynomially bounded message space $\{1, \ldots, n\}$. In a nutshell, the public key is a commitment c to a vector of n random values $(s_1, \ldots, s_n)$. The signature on the message $i \in [n]$ is the pair (s_i, π_i) where π_i is the VC opening proof that c opens to s_i at position i. Verification simply runs the VC verification algorithm to check that the opening is valid.

Conveniently, this transformation maps algebraic VCs with linear/generic verification to signature schemes with the analogous property, which we then call algebraic signatures with linear/generic verification. This happens since the verification algorithm is essentially the same in both primitives.

The resulting signature however may not be proved existentially unforgeable if it comes from a VC satisfying only position binding. Indeed the latter property does not imply that every opening proof is hard to compute. However, assuming

---

[4] For example, one may consider a Merkle-tree of Pedersen commitments which must use the group representation to go from one level to another.

that the scheme is also succinct, an adversary who produces 'many' correct openings should have to correctly guess the value of several messages s_i used to generate the commitment. This can be shown to be information-theoretically hard if the commitment and opening proofs provided have significantly smaller bit-length than the min-entropy of those messages.

For this reason we introduce a relaxed security notion, called ϑ-unforgeability, where an adversary must provide not only one but at least more than ϑ-many[5] forgeries for non-queried messages. Setting ϑ as a proper function of the number of queries made by the adversary, we prove that signatures from VCs are ϑ-unforgeable.

Impossibility of Algebraic Signatures, Revisited. To conclude our impossibility result for VCs, we finally provide an impossibility result and a black-box separation for algebraic signatures with strictly linear and generic verification respectively. In particular, we show in both cases that the message space in a ϑ-unforgeable construction is upper-bounded by $n + \vartheta$ with n being the number of group elements in the verification key. We also show this to be tight by providing a construction that achieves this bound in the full version.

Notice that similar results were already proved in [11]. In their work signatures are assumed to be of the form $(\mathbf{Y}, t)$ with $\mathbf{Y}$ a vector of group elements and $t \in \{0, 1\}^\kappa$. Moreover the verification procedure is assumed to consist of a linear check as in Eq. 1. For this class of signatures, which can be shown equivalent to our notion of *algebraic with linear verification*, they provide an attack running in time $O(2^\kappa \cdot \mathsf{poly}(\lambda))$.

Thus their adversary is efficient only when $t = O(\log \lambda)$, whereas our impossibility result applies to schemes with strictly linear verification, where signatures may contain several field elements. Likewise, their black-box separation only captures schemes with *linear verification*, while we extend it to signatures where all procedures are simply required to be generic. To show that this class of schemes is indeed more general we provide examples in the full version.

We finally stress that, as in [11], our results hold in Maurer's Generic Group Model [28]. For a comparison with other models of generic computation, such as Shoup's Generic Group Model [40], we refer to the discussion in [42].

1.3   Interpretation of Our Impossibility and Further Implications

As mentioned earlier, both our impossibility results specify precise bounds and conditions under which VCs cannot be built generically in pairing-free groups. The bottom line is that, whenever a position-binding VC scheme uses the group in a black box way (and relies on it for security), then it cannot be succinct, which we recall is the distinguishing feature of this primitive.

Another interesting aspect of our impossibility results is that they imply analogous impossibilities for any primitive that allows one to construct algebraic VCs (with either strictly linear or generic-group verification) in pairing-free groups. Notably, our impossibility applies to polynomial commitments [21],

---

[5] Where ϑ may depend on the public parameters as well as the number of queries.

and functional commitments [26] supporting any class of functions that includes projections, i.e., $C_i(\mathbf{v}) = v_i$ (already captured by linear forms). Indeed, each of these primitives allows one to build a VC with exactly the same succinctness and type of verification.[6] Therefore we obtain that any secure functional commitment or polynomial commitment using a pairing-free group in a black-box way cannot be succinct (or, more precisely, they must satisfy $\ell_c \cdot \ell_\pi = \Omega(n)$).

Our impossibility for algebraic signatures instead can be shown to imply analogous results for verifiable random functions [32] and identity-based encryption [5,39], the latter through the Naor-trick reduction, as observed in [11]. In this way our black-box separation for signatures yield a simpler argument for the tight result in [38].

An interesting question left open by our work is understanding if our results can imply the impossibility of further cryptographic primitives via a connection to the classes of algebraic signatures and vector commitments that we rule out. Another open question concerns the minimal assumptions required to describe a VC with constant-size commitment and openings. We notice that our impossibility for VCs with generic verification holds in Maurer's generic group model [28]. When using Shoup's GGM [40], our results may not hold as one could use the group oracle as a random oracle [43], e.g., to build a Merkle tree of Pedersen hashes (see a similar discussion for signatures in [11]). However, to the best of our knowledge all these techniques would in the best case lead to schemes with logarithmic-size openings.

1.4 Related Work

The study of impossibility results about the construction of cryptographic primitives in restricted models is an important area of research that provides insights on the foundations of a cryptographic problem. Starting with the seminal paper of Impagliazzo and Rudich [19], a line of works study the (in)feasibility of constructing cryptographic primitives in a black-box way from general assumptions, such as one-way functions or trapdoor permutations (e.g. [14–17,23,41]).

Another line of works (more closely related to ours), initiated by Papakonstantinou, Rackoff and Vahlis [33], considers the problem of proving impossibility of cryptographic primitives that make black-box use of a cryptographic group without pairings. Specifically, [33] prove that identity-based encryption (IBE) algorithms built in this model of computation cannot be secure. Following [33], more recent works study the impossibility, in generic group models for pairing-free groups of known order, of other cryptographic primitives, such as verifiable delay functions [36], identity-based encryption (with a result tighter than [33]) [38] and signature schemes [11]. In addition to proving impossibility for algebraic signatures with generic-group algorithms, [11] also prove the generic impossibility of a class of algebraic signatures whose verification is a system of linear equations over a group.

---

[6] These constructions are trivial/folklore and we do not elaborate further on them.

In [37], Schul-Ganz and Segev prove a lower bound on the number of group operations needed to verify batch membership proofs in accumulators that make black-box use of a cryptographic group. Their lower bound applies analogously to the verification of subvector openings in vector commitments. Despite the result and the techniques of [37] differ from ours, both [37] and our work show certain limitations of constructing VCs in prime order groups.

Finally, we mention the work of Abe, Haralambiev and Ohkubo [1] that also considers a question related to constructing vector commitments. Following a research line on structure-preserving cryptography, Abe et al. [1] investigate if it is possible to construct commitment schemes in bilinear groups in which messages, keys, commitments, and decommitments are elements of bilinear groups, and whose openings are verified by pairing product equations. For this class of schemes, they prove that the commitment cannot be shrinking. Implicitly this result also implies the impossibility of constructing succinct vector commitments in this structure-preserving setting in bilinear groups.

1.5 Organization of the Paper

In Sect. 3 we define algebraic VCs and show our transformation to ϑ-unforgeable signatures. Section 4 presents the definition of algebraic signatures and our impossibility results for strictly linear verification and generic group verification. Finally, in Sect. 5 we illustrate how to relate the parameters of our VC-to-signatures transformation with those needed by the impossibility of algebraic signatures.

2   Preliminaries

Notation. We denote the security parameter by λ and negligible functions with $\mathsf{negl}(\lambda)$. We say that an algorithm is PPT if it runs in probabilistic polynomial time. For a positive integer n, $[n]$ denotes the set $\{1, \ldots, n\}$. We use $(\mathbb{G}, +)$ to denote a group of known prime order q with canonical generator G, and $\mathbb{F}_q$ for the field of order q. The identity (or zero) element is denoted as $0 \in \mathbb{G}$. Given a vector $\mathbf{x} \in \mathbb{F}_q^n$, we denote $\mathbf{x} \cdot G = (x_1 G, \ldots, x_n G)$.

$\mathbb{F}_q^{n,m}$ is the space of matrices A with m columns and n rows and entries in $\mathbb{F}_q$. $\mathrm{rk}\, A$ denotes the rank of A, i.e. the maximum number of linearly independent rows. $A^\top$ is the transposed of A. All $\mathbf{x} \in \mathbb{F}_q^n$ are assumed to be column vectors, whereas row vectors are denoted as $\mathbf{x}^\top$.

In what follows 'GGM' stands for Maurer's Generic Group Model [28] for a group of known prime order q. This model can be defined through two stateful oracles $\mathcal{O}_{\mathsf{add}}$ and $\mathcal{O}_{\mathsf{eq}}^0$ such that: group element are labeled with progressively increasing indices, the first being associated to the canonical generator G, $\mathcal{O}_{\mathsf{add}}(X, Y)$ associate the next index to the element $X + Y$ and $\mathcal{O}_{\mathsf{eq}}^0(X)$ returns 1 if X equals the identity element, 0 otherwise.

2.1 Vector Commitments

We recall the definition of vector commitments from [9].

Definition 1 (VC). *A Vector Commitment scheme is a tuple of algorithms* (VC.Setup, VC.Com, VC.Open, VC.Vfy) *and a message space* VC.M *such that*

- VC.Setup(1^λ) $\overset{\$}{\to}$ pp *generates the public parameters.*
- VC.Com(pp, $m_1, \ldots, m_n$) $\overset{\$}{\to}$ c, aux *produce a commitment to* $m_1, \ldots, m_n \in$ VC.M *together with some auxiliary information.*
- VC.Open(pp, m, i, aux) $\overset{\$}{\to}$ π *return an opening proof that the i-th entry of a given commitment is m_i.*
- VC.Vfy(pp, c, m, i, π) $\to 0/1$ *verifies the opening proof's correctness.*

We require a vector commitment scheme to satisfy *perfect correctness*, that is, given public parameters pp $\overset{\$}{\leftarrow}$ VC.Setup(1^λ), commitment c, aux $\overset{\$}{\leftarrow}$ VC.Com(pp, $m_1, \ldots, m_n$) for any $m_i \in$ VC.M, and opening $\pi \overset{\$}{\leftarrow}$ VC.Open(pp, m_i, i, aux), it holds

$$\Pr\left[\text{VC.Vfy(pp, } c, m, i, \pi) \to 1\right] = 1$$

Moreover, to avoid trivial cases, in this paper we assume $|\text{VC.M}| \geq 2$.

The main security property for a vector commitments is the so called *position binding*, which informally states that no adversary can open the same position of a given commitment to two different values. Formally

Definition 2 (Position binding). *A vector commitment scheme satisfies position binding if for any* PPT *adversary* $\mathcal{A}$ *there exists a negligible function* $\varepsilon(\lambda)$ *such that*

$$\Pr\left[\begin{array}{l} \text{VC.Vfy(pp, } c, m, i, \pi) \to 1 \\ \text{VC.Vfy(pp, } c, m', i, \pi') \to 1 \\ m \neq m' \end{array} \middle| \begin{array}{l} \text{pp} \overset{\$}{\leftarrow} \text{VC.Setup}(1^\lambda) \\ \mathcal{A}(\text{pp}) \to (c, m, m', i, \pi, \pi') \end{array}\right] \leq \varepsilon(\lambda).$$

The property that distinguishes VCs from classical binding commitments is *succinctness* Following [9,27], a VC scheme is said succinct if there is a fixed $p(\lambda) = \text{poly}(\lambda)$ such that for any n the size of honestly generated commitments and openings is bounded by $p(\lambda)$. One may also consider weaker notions where the size may be bounded by $p(\lambda) \log n$ or $p(\lambda, \log n)$.

Since in our work we are interested in understanding the feasibility of VCs based on their level of succinctness, we consider a parametric notion. We say that a VC has succinctness (ℓ_c, ℓ_π) if for any $m_1, \ldots, m_n \in$ VC.M, commitment c, aux $\overset{\$}{\leftarrow}$ VC.Com(pp, $m_1, \ldots, m_n$) and opening $\pi \overset{\$}{\leftarrow}$ VC.Open(pp, m_i, i, aux) for any $i \in [n]$, we have that c (resp. π) has bit-length $\ell_c(\lambda, n)$ (resp. $\ell_\pi(\lambda, n)$).

2.2   Digital Signatures

Definition 3. *A signature scheme is a tuple of* PPT *algorithms* (S.Setup, S.Sign, S.Vfy) *and a message space set* S.M *such that*

- S.Setup(1^λ) $\xrightarrow{\$}$ (sk, vk) *generates the secret and verification keys*
- S.Sign(sk, m) $\xrightarrow{\$}$ σ *returns the signature of a message* $m \in$ S.M
- S.Vfy(vk, m, σ) $\rightarrow 0/1$ *verifies the signature* σ *for a message* $m \in$ S.M

We further require a signature scheme to satisfy *perfect correctness*, meaning that if (sk, vk) $\leftarrow^\$$ S.Setup(1^λ) and $\sigma \leftarrow^\$$ S.Sign(sk, m) for any $m \in$ S.M then the verification algorithm accepts always, i.e.

$$\Pr\left[\text{S.Vfy}(\text{vk}, m, \sigma) \rightarrow 1\right] = 1.$$

3   Algebraic Vector Commitments

In this paper we focus on vector commitments built on a pairing-free group of known order, using it in a black box way. We start by introducing a notion of algebraic vector commitments where the verification algorithm only consists of a system of linear equations.

Definition 4 (Algebraic VCs with linear verification). *A vector commitment scheme is said to be* algebraic with linear verification *if the message space is* VC.M $= \mathbb{F}_q$ *and*

- VC.Setup(1^λ) $\xrightarrow{\$}$ pp *such that* pp $= (\mathbf{X}_1, s_1) \in \mathbb{G}^{\nu_1} \times \{0,1\}^*$.
- VC.Com(pp, $m_1, \ldots, m_n$) $\xrightarrow{\$}$ c, aux *such that* $c = (\mathbf{X}_2, s_2) \in \mathbb{G}^{\nu_2} \times \{0,1\}^*$.
- VC.Open(pp, m, i, aux) $\rightarrow \pi$ *such that* $\pi = (\mathbf{Y}, \mathbf{z})$ *with* $\mathbf{Y} \in \mathbb{G}^k$ *and* $\mathbf{z} \in \mathbb{F}_q^h$.
- *There exist* $A : \mathbb{F}_q^{h+1} \times [n] \times \{0,1\}^* \rightarrow \mathbb{F}_q^{\ell,n}$ *and* $B : \mathbb{F}_q^{h+1} \times [n] \times \{0,1\}^* \rightarrow \mathbb{F}_q^{\ell,k}$ *matrices such that* VC.Vfy(pp, c, m, i, π) $\rightarrow 1$ *if and only if, calling* $\mathbf{X} = \mathbf{X}_1 || \mathbf{X}_2$ *and* $s = s_1 || s_2$

$$A(\mathbf{z}, m, i, s) \cdot \mathbf{X} = B(\mathbf{z}, m, i, s) \cdot \mathbf{Y}.$$

For the ease of presentation we will omit s in A and B when clear from the context. Notice that the definition imposes linearity only with respect to group elements while it allows procedures A, B to depend non-linearly on the field vector element $\mathbf{z}$.

As we shall see, our first impossibility result states that whenever A is an affine function of $\mathbf{z}, m$ and B does not depends on $\mathbf{z}, m$, then the resulting scheme cannot be both "succinct" and position binding. We call these schemes *strictly linear* since their verification equations depend linearly both in $\mathbf{z}$ and $\mathbf{Y}$.

Definition 5 (Algebraic VCs with strictly linear verification). *A vector commitment is said to be* algebraic with strictly linear verification *if it satisfies Definition 4, $A(\mathbf{z}, m, i)$ is an affine function[7] of $\mathbf{z}, m$ and $B(i)$ does not depends on $\mathbf{z}, m$.*

---

[7] i.e. $A(\mathbf{z}, m, i) = A_0(i) + z_1 A_1(i) + \ldots + z_h A_h(i) + m A_{h+1}(i)$.

However, if we allow A to depend quadratically, or B linearly, on $\mathbf{z}, m$ then we could use arithmetization techniques, such as R1CS, to encode a circuit representing for example a Merkle tree verification into the verification equation of Definition 4. This means that we can construct algebraic VC schemes with linear verification that are succinct and position binding. Explicit examples of such schemes are provided in the full version.

This technique however either bypasses the underlying group and may reduce security to external problems, or rely on non-black-box usage of the group. An example of the latter comes by encoding a Merkle tree built using an hash function whose collision resistance is based on discrete logarithm over the same group $\mathbb{G}$, such as Pedersen hash. Note that this construction would not retain algebraic properties from the underlying group. For this reason, following an approach similar to [11,33], we study whether in the Generic Group Model (GGM) the security of a VC can be reduced to hard problems on the underlying group. To this aim we provide the following more general definition.

Definition 6 (Algebraic VCs with generic verification). *A vector commitment scheme is said to be* algebraic *with generic verification if, in the GGM, the algorithms* VC.Setup, VC.Com, VC.Open, VC.Vfy *are oracle machines with access to* $\mathcal{O}_{\mathsf{add}}$ *and* $\mathcal{O}_{\mathsf{eq}}^{0}$.

3.1 Generic Transformation from VCs to Signatures

The strategy we adopt to show our impossibility results is to establish a connection between vector commitments and signatures, providing a way to construct the latter from the former generically. This way we will be able to bridge extensions of the impossibility results in [11] for algebraic signatures to algebraic vector commitments.

More specifically, for a given VC (not necessarily algebraic) our transformation produces a signature scheme with polynomially bounded message space $\{1, \ldots, n\}$. The high-level idea is to compute a commitment c to random messages $m_1, \ldots, m_n$, and use (pp, c) as the verification key and the auxiliary information aux as the secret key. In order to sign a message $i \in \{1, \ldots, n\}$, the signer returns m_i and π, the message and opening proof for the i-th position, while verification is performed by checking the correctness of π. A formal description of the transformation is presented in Fig. 1.

3.2 ϑ-Unforgeability

In terms of security the transformation in Fig. 1 fails in general to realize a UF-CMA-secure signature scheme. Informally, the problem is that position binding and succinctness do not imply, per se, that every opening proof is hard to compute, after having seen other openings. Indeed the latter property could be easily violated, for example, by a VC where VC.Open attaches to every opening the proof (m_1, π_1) for position 1. Notice that one could modify any VC to do so without violating succinctness nor position binding. Yet starting from such a

$S_{VC}.\text{Setup}(1^\lambda)$:

1 : $\text{VC.Setup}(1^\lambda) \to \text{pp}$

2 : $m_1, \ldots, m_n \xleftarrow{\$} \text{VC.M}$

3 : $c, \text{aux} \xleftarrow{\$} \text{VC.Com}(\text{pp}, m_1, \ldots, m_n)$

4 : $\text{vk} \leftarrow (\text{pp}, c) \ \text{sk} \leftarrow (\text{aux}, \{m_i\}_{i=1}^n)$

5 : Return vk, sk

$S_{VC}.\text{Sign}(\text{sk}, i)$:

1 : Parse $\text{sk} = (\text{aux}, \{m_i\}_{i=1}^n)$

2 : $\pi \leftarrow \text{VC.Open}(\text{pp}, m_i, i, \text{aux})$

3 : $\sigma \leftarrow (m_i, \pi)$

4 : Return σ

$S_{VC}.\text{Vfy}(\text{vk}, i, \sigma)$:

1 : Parse $\text{vk} = (\text{pp}, c)$ and $\sigma = (m_i, \pi)$.   Return $\text{VC.Vfy}(\text{pp}, c, m_i, i, \pi)$

Fig. 1. Generic transformation from VCs to signature schemes

VC would allow an adversary to easily forge a signature for message 1 in the scheme in Fig. 1.

Observe that, informally, if the VC scheme were *hiding*, meaning that no information about messages in unopened positions is leaked, and |VC.M| is large enough, then the associated signature would be secure, since an adversary would have to guess the right message in the i-th position. This intuition can be extended to general VC assuming that the scheme is *succinct*. Indeed, even though the commitment c or its openings π may leak information about unopened messages among $m_1, \ldots, m_n$, if their bit length is significantly smaller than n, no adversary can produce "too many" forgeries given only a few openings, as correctly guessing these message would be information-theoretically hard.

For this reason we introduce a relaxed notion of unforgeability for signatures, called ϑ-unforgeability, which is enough for our purposes. In a nutshell, it requires a winning adversary to produce at least ϑ forgeries on *distinct* messages, with ϑ being a function of the queries performed and the public parameters. Next, using the intuition above, we prove that signature schemes obtained through the transformation in Fig. 1 satisfy this weaker notion.

Definition 7 (ϑ-UF). *Given a function $\vartheta : \{0, 1\}^* \to \mathbb{N}$ and a signature scheme we define the ϑ-Unforgeability Experiment as in Fig. 2. The advantage of an adversary $\mathcal{A}$ is defined as*

$$\text{Adv}^{\vartheta\text{-UF}}(\mathcal{A}) = \Pr\left[\text{Exp}_{\mathcal{A}}^{\vartheta\text{-UF}} = 1\right].$$

A scheme is ϑ-Unforgeable if any PPT adversary has negligible advantage.

To provide more intuition about this notion we observe that setting $\vartheta = 0$ yields the classic unforgeability under chosen message attacks (UF-CMA) [18] security definition. For higher values of ϑ we obtain progressively weaker definitions until $\vartheta(\text{vk}, Q) = |\text{S.M}|$, which is trivially true for any scheme. The notion

---

$\mathsf{Exp}_{\mathcal{A}}^{\vartheta\text{-}\mathsf{UF}}$ **with adversary** $\mathcal{A}$:

1 :   Initialize $Q \leftarrow \varnothing$, generate $\mathsf{sk}, \mathsf{vk} \leftarrow^{\$} \mathsf{S.Setup}(1^{\lambda})$ and send $\mathcal{A} \leftarrow \mathsf{vk}$

2 :   **When** $\mathcal{A} \to m \in \mathsf{S.M}$:

3 :   Sign $\sigma \leftarrow^{\$} \mathsf{S.Sign}(\mathsf{sk}, m)$, store $Q \leftarrow Q \cup (m, \sigma)$ and send $\mathcal{A} \leftarrow \sigma$

4 :   **When** $\mathcal{A} \to F$:

5 :   Return 1 if the following conditions are satisfied:

6 :   For all $(m, \sigma) \in F$, the signature is correct, i.e. $\mathsf{S.Vfy}(\mathsf{vk}, m, \sigma) \to 1$

7 :   Messages in F were not queried, i.e. $(m, \sigma) \in F \;\Rightarrow\; (m, \cdot) \notin Q$

8 : $|\{m \;:\; (m, \cdot) \in F\}| > \vartheta(\mathsf{vk}, Q)$

9 :   Else return 0

Fig. 2. ϑ-Unforgeability Experiment for a given signature scheme

of t-time security is also captured by our definition setting

$$\vartheta(\mathsf{vk}, Q) = \begin{cases} 0 & \text{If } |Q| \leq t \\ |\mathsf{S.M}| & \text{If } |Q| > t \end{cases}$$

Finally we can show that a signature scheme obtained from a "succinct" VC satisfy this notion. A proof appears in the full version.

Theorem 1. *Given a Vector Commitment with commitments of bit-length $\ell_c = \ell_c(n, \lambda)$ and opening proofs of bit-length $\ell_{\pi} = \ell_{\pi}(n, \lambda)$, then there exists a* PPT *black box reduction $\mathcal{R}$ of ϑ-UF for the derived signature scheme described in Fig. 1 to the position binding property, where*

$$\vartheta(\mathsf{vk}, Q) = \frac{\lambda + \ell_c + |Q| \cdot (\ell_{\pi} + \log |\mathsf{VC.M}|)}{\log |\mathsf{VC.M}|}.$$

In particular for any position binding VC, the resulting signature is ϑ-UF with ϑ as specified above.

4   Algebraic Signatures

Having established a connection between VC and signatures we now provide the analogous of algebraic VC with (strictly) linear/generic verification in the signature setting. The first one is equivalent to the notion of *algebraic signature* in [11] and simply constrain the verification procedure to test a system of linear equations, albeit with a minor addition: as these signatures may come in our case from a VC, we split S.Setup in a CRS-generator S.SetupCRS which returns the public parameters (a list of group elements $\mathbf{X}_1$) and the actual key generation algorithm S.SetupKey($\mathbf{X}_1$) which produces vk and sk. Note there is no loss of generality assuming this structure as S.SetupCRS may return an empty vector which could then be ignored by S.SetupKey.

Definition 8. *A signature scheme* (S.Setup, S.Sign, S.Vfy) *is said to be algebraic with linear verification if*

- S.Setup *is divided into two algorithms* S.SetupCRS *and* S.SetupKey *such that* S.SetupCRS$(1^\lambda) \overset{\$}{\to} (\mathbf{X}_1, s_1) \in \mathbb{G}^{n_1}$ *and* S.SetupKey$(1^\lambda, \mathbf{X}_1, s_1) \overset{\$}{\to}$ sk, vk *with*

$$\text{vk} = (\mathbf{X}, s) \in \mathbb{G}^n \times \{0,1\}^* \quad : \quad \mathbf{X} = \mathbf{X}_1 \| \mathbf{X}_2, \qquad \mathbf{X}_2 \in \mathbb{G}^{n_2}, \qquad s = s_1 \| s_2.$$

- S.Sign(sk, m) $\overset{\$}{\to} \sigma$ *where* $\sigma = (\mathbf{Y}, \mathbf{z})$ *with* $\mathbf{Y} \in \mathbb{G}^k$ *and* $\mathbf{z} \in \mathbb{F}_q^h$.
- *There exist* $A : \mathbb{F}_q^h \times$ S.M $\times \{0,1\}^* \to \mathbb{F}_q^{\ell,n}$ *and* $B : \mathbb{F}_q^h \times$ S.M $\times \{0,1\}^* \to \mathbb{F}_q^{\ell,k}$ *matrices such that* S.Vfy(vk, m, σ) $\to 1$ *if and only if* $\sigma = (\mathbf{z}, \mathbf{Y})$ *and*

$$A(\mathbf{z}, m, s)\mathbf{X} = B(\mathbf{z}, m, s)\mathbf{Y}.$$

Furthermore the scheme is said to have strictly linear verification if $A(\mathbf{z}, m, s)$ *is an affine function of* $\mathbf{z}$ *and* $B(m, s)$ *does not depend on* $\mathbf{z}$.

When clear from the context we will omit for clarity the argument s in the matrices A, B above. Next we provide an analogous for algebraic vector commitments with generic verification. As in the previous definition we split the setup algorithm into a procedure that prepares the CRS and another one that uses the CRS, oblivious to any trapdoor information about it, to compute the secret and verification keys.

Definition 9. *A signature scheme* (S.Setup, S.Sign, S.Vfy) *is said to be algebraic with generic verification if, in the GGM, all algorithms have access to* $\mathcal{O}_{\text{add}}$ *and* $\mathcal{O}_{\text{eq}}^0$. *Furthermore we require* S.Setup *to be divided into two algorithms* S.SetupCRS *and* S.SetupKey *such that* S.SetupCRS$(1^\lambda) \overset{\$}{\to} (\mathbf{X}_1, s_1) \in \mathbb{G}^{n_1} \times \{0,1\}^*$ *and* S.SetupKey$(1^\lambda, \mathbf{X}_1, s_1) \overset{\$}{\to}$ sk, vk *with*

$$\text{vk} = (\mathbf{X}, s) \in \mathbb{G}^n \times \{0,1\}^* \quad : \quad \mathbf{X} = \mathbf{X}_1 \| \mathbf{X}_2, \qquad \mathbf{X}_2 \in \mathbb{G}^{n_2}, \qquad s = s_1 \| s_2.$$

4.1 Attack to Schemes with Strictly Linear Verification

We now provide an attack for algebraic signatures with strictly linear verification. The same notation of Definition 8 will be used below without further reference.

Theorem 2. *Given a signature scheme with strictly linear verification, for any* ϑ *polynomially bounded such that* $n_2 + \vartheta \leq |\text{S.M}|$ *there exists a* PPT *algorithm* $\mathcal{A}$ *that in the unforgeability experiment in Fig. 2 performs at most* n_2 *queries and produces* ϑ *distinct forgeries with significant probability.*

Proof. For the sake of presentation we build $\mathcal{A}$ describing first a subroutine $\mathcal{B}$ which could break security by doing potentially more signing queries that n_2. Next, we show how $\mathcal{A}$ can use $\mathcal{B}$ in a black-box way to realize the full attack with n_2 queries.

Similarly to the attack described in [11], upon receiving the verification key $(\mathbf{X}, s)$, the subroutine $\mathcal{B}$ (described formally in Fig. 3) keeps track of all possible exponents of $\mathbf{X}$ in an affine space $L \subseteq \mathbb{F}_q^n$. Then for each message m_i either a forgery can be produced or a new condition on $\mathbf{X}$ is found, thus decreasing $\dim L$, at the cost of a signature query. This is done by checking if the system $A(\mathbf{z}, m)\mathbf{x} = B(m)\mathbf{y}$ can be solved for a given $\mathbf{z} \in \mathbb{F}_q^h$ and all $\mathbf{x} \in L$. More specifically we define $S(L, m)$, the *solutions* set, as the collection of all those $\mathbf{z}$ for which any $\mathbf{x} \in L$ makes the systems solvable, formally

$$S(L, m) = \{\mathbf{z} \in \mathbb{F}_q^h : A(\mathbf{z}, m) \cdot L \subseteq \operatorname{Im} B(m)\}.$$

If $S(L, m)$ is easy to compute, a strategy for $\mathcal{B}$ is to check whether $S(L, m) \neq \varnothing$ and in this case to get any $\mathbf{z} \in S(L, m)$ and find, using pseudo-inverses or Gaussian elimination, a vector $\mathbf{Y} \in \mathbb{G}^k$ such that $A(\mathbf{z}, m)\mathbf{X} = B(m)\mathbf{Y}$. Conversely, if $S(L, m) = \varnothing$, $\mathcal{B}$ may request a signature $(\mathbf{Y}, \mathbf{z})$, which implies that the exponent $\mathbf{x}$ of $\mathbf{X}$ satisfies the condition $A(\mathbf{z}, m)\mathbf{x} \in \operatorname{Im} B(m)$. Notice that, unlike the attack presented in [11], $\mathcal{B}$ is required to be PPT and thus computing $S(L, m)$ efficiently is essential in our argument. This will follow as we assumed the verification to be strictly linear, implying that $S(L, m)$ is an affine space.

Although $\mathcal{B}$ effectively breaks security, we can only upper bound the number of signatures queried by $n_1 + n_2$, i.e. one for each group element in the CRS $\mathbf{X}_1$ and verification key $\mathbf{X}_2$, since initially $L = \mathbb{F}_q^{n_1+n_2}$ with dimension $n_1 + n_2$. In order to reduce the requested signatures to be at most n_2 we introduce a preprocessing phase to find as many linear relations among group elements of the CRS as possibile and then run $\mathcal{B}$ providing as input a refined space L. Informally, if $\mathcal{B}$ is unable to find new relations among the elements of $\mathbf{X}_1$, then $\dim L$ can at most decrease by n_2, yielding the desired upper bound.

To conclude we then need to describe how the preprocessing is carried out: The core idea is to initialize the set of possible exponents $V = \mathbb{F}_q^{n_1}$ and execute several times $\mathcal{B}(\mathsf{vk}^*, V)$ replying to signing queries with $\mathsf{S.Sign}(\mathsf{sk}^*, \cdot)$ where $\mathsf{vk}^*, \mathsf{sk}^* \xleftarrow{\$} \mathsf{S.SetupKey}(1^\lambda, \mathbf{X}_1, s_1)$ is freshly sampled each time. If in some of those executions $\mathcal{B}$ is able to find a new relation among the group elements, then V is updated accordingly (lowering its dimension by at least 1), and a new round of simulations is run. Conversely if $\mathcal{B}(\mathsf{vk}^*, V)$ fails to find new relations several times in this simulated environment, then it is executed one last time with the real verification key vk and signing oracle. If no new relation is found in this last execution, $\mathcal{A}$ concludes by returning the forgeries found by $\mathcal{B}$. Otherwise $\mathcal{A}$ aborts.

Informally $\mathcal{A}$ aborts with low probability since the simulated and real executions are identically distributed from $\mathcal{B}$ perspective and in particular since no relation is found among the many simulated executions, it is unlikely this will happen in the real one. Finally we remark that simulating the signature challenger in this preprocessing phase is crucial. In this way the only signature queries performed by $\mathcal{A}$ are those requested by the last execution of $\mathcal{B}$.

Having provided the intuition behind the attacker $\mathcal{A}$ built on top of $\mathcal{B}$, we now proceed to prove the theorem through a sequence of claims. We begin by

Adversary $\mathcal{B}(\mathsf{vk}, V)$:

1:    Set $L \leftarrow V \times \mathbb{F}_q^{n_2} \subseteq \mathbb{F}_q^{n_1 + n_2}$

2:    Initialize the set of forgeries $F \leftarrow \varnothing$ and call $\theta \leftarrow n_2 + \vartheta$

3:    Sample $m_1, \ldots, m_\theta \leftarrow^\$ $ S.M distinct messages

4:    **For** $i \in \{1, \ldots, \theta\}$:

5:      **If** $S(L, m_i) \neq \varnothing$:

6:        Get a vector $\mathbf{z} \in S(L, m_i)$

7:        Find a solution $\mathbf{Y} \in \mathbb{G}^k$ such that $A(\mathbf{z}, m_i)\mathbf{X} = B(m_i)\mathbf{Y}$

8:        Set $\sigma \leftarrow (\mathbf{Y}, \mathbf{z})$ and store $F \leftarrow F \cup \{(m_i, \sigma)\}$

9:      **Else:**

10:       Query m_i to the challenger and get $\sigma = (\mathbf{Y}, \mathbf{z})$

11:       Update $L \leftarrow L \cap \{\mathbf{x} \in \mathbb{F}_q^n : A(\mathbf{z}, m_i)\mathbf{x} \in \mathrm{Im}\, B(m_i)\}$

12:    Return F, L

Fig. 3. $\mathcal{B}$ breaking ϑ-UF of an algebraic signature with strictly linear verification.

stating the following properties about $\mathcal{B}(\mathsf{vk}, V)$ where we denote $\mathsf{vk} = (\mathbf{X}, s)$ with $\mathbf{X} = \mathbf{X}_1 \| \mathbf{X}_2$, $\mathbf{x}_1$ the discrete logarithm of $\mathbf{X}_1$ and $\mathbf{x}$ the discrete logarithm of $\mathbf{X}$. Finally we denote $\pi : \mathbb{F}_q^{n_1} \times \mathbb{F}_q^{n_2} \to \mathbb{F}_q^{n_1}$ the projection on first component, i.e. $\pi(\mathbf{x}_1, \mathbf{x}_2) = \mathbf{x}_1$.

Claim 1. *If L is an affine space, $S(L, m)$ is an affine space. Moreover an affine base for $S(L, m)$ can be computed in polynomial time.*

Claim 2. *If $\mathbf{x}_1 \in V$ then at any step of $\mathcal{B}(\mathsf{vk}, V)$, $\mathbf{x} \in L$.*

Claim 3. *If $\mathbf{x}_1 \in V$, $\mathcal{B}$ is* PPT *and upon returning (F, L), F is a set of valid forgeries.*

Claim 4. *For a given m_i, if the condition at step 5 is not satisfied, i.e. $S(L, m_i) = \varnothing$, then after step 11 the dimension of L decreases strictly.*

Claim 5. *After the execution of line 1, Fig 3, $\dim L = n_2 + \dim V$ and if $\mathcal{B}(\mathsf{vk}, V)$ returns (F, L) with $\pi(L) = V$ then $\dim L \geq \dim V$.*

Next we state the following properties about $\mathcal{A}$

Claim 6. *$\mathcal{A}$ is* PPT.

Claim 7. *At any step of $\mathcal{A}$ execution, $\mathbf{x}_1 \in V$.*

Claim 8. *$\mathcal{A}$ fails with probability $\Pr[\mathcal{A}(\mathsf{vk}) \to \mathsf{fail}] \leq 1/2$.*

First we observe these claims imply the thesis. Indeed by Claim 8, with probability greater than $1/2$, $\mathcal{A}$ does not return fail. By construction, this implies that in the last execution $\mathcal{B}(\mathsf{vk}, V)$ returns (F, L) with $\pi(L) = V$. Thus by

Adversary $\mathcal{A}^{\text{S.Sign(sk, } \cdot \text{)}}(\text{vk})$:

---

1 :   Parse $\text{vk} = (\mathbf{X}, s)$ with $\mathbf{X} = \mathbf{X}_1 \| \mathbf{X}_2$ and $s = s_1 \| s_2$

2 :   Initialize $V \leftarrow \mathbb{F}_q^{n_1}$ the space of potential exponents of $\mathbf{X}_1$

3 :   **Do:**

4 :   **For** $2n_1 + 1$ times:

5 : $\text{vk}^*, \text{sk}^* \leftarrow^{\$} \text{S.SetupKey}(1^\lambda, \mathbf{X}_1, s_1)$

6 :   Execute $F^*, L^* \leftarrow^{\$} \mathcal{B}^{\text{S.Sign(sk}^*, \cdot \text{)}}(\text{vk}^*, V)$

7 :   Set $V^* \leftarrow \{\mathbf{x}_1 : \exists \mathbf{x}_2 : \mathbf{x}_1 \| \mathbf{x}_2 \in L^*\}$ the projection of L^* on $\mathbb{F}_q^{n_1}$

8 :   **If** $V^* \neq V$:

9 :   Update $V \leftarrow V^*$, **break**

10 :   **Until** the for-cycle ends without interruptions

11 :   Execute $F, L \leftarrow^{\$} \mathcal{B}^{\text{S.Sign(sk, } \cdot \text{)}}(\text{vk}, V)$

12 :   Compute V^* as the projection of L on $\mathbb{F}_q^{n_1}$

13 :   **If** $V^* \neq V$: Return fail

14 :   **Else:** Return F

Fig. 4. $\mathcal{A}$ breaking the ϑ-UF of an algebraic signature using as subroutine an algorithm $\mathcal{B}$, which is that of Fig. 3 in the case of schemes with strictly linear verification, or that of Fig. 5 in the case of schemes with generic verification.

Claim 5 $n_2 + \dim V \geq L \geq \dim V$ at any step of $\mathcal{B}$ during its last execution. As a consequence $\dim L$ can decrease at most n_2 times. Applying Claim 4 we conclude that $S(L, m_i) = \varnothing$ can happen at most n_2 times because each time this occurs, $\dim L$ decreases. It follows then that for at least $\theta - n_2 = \vartheta$ messages, the condition $S(L, m_i) \neq \varnothing$ is satisfied, meaning that $\mathcal{B}$ adds a new signature to the set F, which in the end will have cardinality $|F| \geq \vartheta$. Finally, since $\mathbf{x} \in V$ by Claim 7, we can apply Claim 3 to conclude that F is a valid set of forgeries, implying that $\mathcal{A}$ breaks ϑ-UF.

Next, we provide a proof for each of these claims:

Proof of Claim 1. We start observing that if L is any set and $\mathbf{x}_1, \ldots, \mathbf{x}_d \in L$ is a base for the linear span of L then $S(L, m) = \bigcap_{i=1}^{d} S(\mathbf{x}_i, m)$. By construction, $\mathbf{x}_i \in L$ implies $S(L, m) \subseteq S(\mathbf{x}_i, m)$, and in particular $S(L, m) \subseteq \bigcap_{i=1}^{d} S(\mathbf{x}_i, m)$. Conversely let $\mathbf{z}$ be a vector in the intersection of all $S(\mathbf{x}_i, m)$. We can find vectors $\mathbf{u}_i \in \mathbb{F}_q^k$ such that $A(\mathbf{z}, m)\mathbf{x}_i = B(m)\mathbf{u}_i$. Since $\mathbf{x}_1, \ldots, \mathbf{x}_d$ is a base for the linear span of L, for any $\mathbf{x} \in L$ we can express it as a linear combination $\alpha_1 \mathbf{x}_1 + \ldots + \alpha_d \mathbf{x}_d$. In conclusion

$$A(\mathbf{z}, m)\mathbf{x} = \sum_{i=1}^{d} \alpha_i A(\mathbf{z}, m)\mathbf{x}_i = \sum_{i=1}^{d} \alpha_i B(m)\mathbf{u}_i = B(m) \sum_{i=1}^{d} \alpha_i \mathbf{u}_i.$$

Thus $A(\mathbf{z}, m)\mathbf{x} \in \text{Im } B(m)$ and in particular $\mathbf{z} \in S(L, m)$.

In order to show that $S(L, m)$ is efficiently computable it suffices to show that $S(\mathbf{x}, m)$ can be computed in polynomial time for any point $\mathbf{x}$. To this aim let $f_{\mathbf{x}} : \mathbb{F}_q^h \to \mathbb{F}_q^\ell$ be such that $f(\mathbf{z}) = A(\mathbf{z}, m)\mathbf{x}$. Since the scheme has strictly linear verification (Definition 8) $A(\cdot, m)$ is an affine map and so is f. Furthermore by construction $S(\mathbf{x}, m) = f_{\mathbf{x}}^{-1}(\mathrm{Im}\, B(m))$ since $\mathbf{z} \in S(\mathbf{x}, m)$ if and only if $A(\mathbf{z}, m)\mathbf{x} \in \mathrm{Im}\, B(m)$. This concludes the argument as the preimage through an affine map of a linear space is an affine space which can be computed in polynomial time.

Proof of Claim 2. If $\mathbf{x}_1 \in V$ then $\mathbf{x} = \mathbf{x}_1 \| \mathbf{x}_2 \in V \times \mathbb{F}_q^{n_2}$ which by construction implies that, when L is initialized, $\mathbf{x} \in L$. Next assume by induction $\mathbf{x} \in L$ in all previous steps. The only instruction in $\mathcal{B}$ that may modify L is in step 11 and when this is executed, since $\sigma = (\mathbf{Y}, \mathbf{z})$ is a valid signature by perfect correctness, we have

$$A(\mathbf{z}, m_i)\mathbf{X} = B(m_i)\mathbf{Y} \quad \Rightarrow \quad A(\mathbf{z}, m_i)\mathbf{x} \in \mathrm{Im}\, B(m_i).$$

Proof of Claim 3. To prove that $\mathcal{B}$ is a PPT algorithm, observe that the for-loop is executed $\theta = n_2 + \vartheta$, that is polynomially bounded, times. Inside the loop, checking $S(L, m_i) \neq \varnothing$ and possibly computing a $\mathbf{z} \in S(L, m_i)$ can be done efficiently from Claim 1 by computing a base for it. Next, calling $\mathbf{x}$ the discrete logarithm of $\mathbf{X}$, we have that $A(\mathbf{z}, m_i)\mathbf{x} \in \mathrm{Im}\, B(m_i)$ because

$$\mathbf{z} \in S(L, m_i) \quad \Rightarrow \quad A(\mathbf{z}, m_i) \cdot L \subseteq \mathrm{Im}\, B(m_i) \quad \Rightarrow \quad A(\mathbf{z}, m_i)\mathbf{x} \in \mathrm{Im}\, B(m_i)$$

where the last implication follows as $\mathbf{x} \in L$ by Claim 2 and the assumption $\mathbf{x}_1 \in V$. Thus, calling H a weak-inverse[8] of $B(m_i)$, which can be computed efficiently, the vector $\mathbf{Y}$ can be set as $H \cdot A(\mathbf{z}, m_i)\mathbf{X}$. Indeed, as $A(\mathbf{z}, m_i)\mathbf{X} \in \mathrm{Im}\, B(m_i)$ there exists a vector $\mathbf{Z} \in \mathbb{G}^k$ such that $A(\mathbf{z}, m_i)\mathbf{X} = B(m_i)\mathbf{Z}$ and in particular

$$B(m_i)\mathbf{Y} = B(m_i)HA(\mathbf{z}, m_i)\mathbf{X} = B(m_i)HB(m_i)\mathbf{Z} = B(m_i)\mathbf{Z} = A(\mathbf{z}, m_i)\mathbf{X}.$$

Finally, given the bases of two affine spaces, a base of their intersection can be computed efficiently. This conclude the proof that $\mathcal{B}$ is PPT.

For the second part, by construction each entry in F is of the form $(m_i, \mathbf{Y}, \mathbf{z})$ such that

$$A(\mathbf{z}, m_i)\mathbf{X} = B(m_i)\mathbf{Y}.$$

Therefore, by our definition of signatures with linear verification scheme, the verifier accepts $(m_i, \mathbf{Y}, \mathbf{z})$. The claim is thus proven.

Proof of Claim 4. Since the condition at step 5 is not satisfied, $S(L, m_i) = \varnothing$ and in particular $\mathbf{z} \notin S(L, m_i)$ implying that $A(\mathbf{z}, m_i)\mathbf{x} \notin \mathrm{Im}\, B(m_i)$ for some $\mathbf{x} \in L$. Therefore L is not contained in the space of all $\mathbf{x}$ such that $A(\mathbf{z}, m_i)\mathbf{x} \in \mathrm{Im}\, B(m_i)$ and in particular its dimension decreases after the execution of step 11

---

[8] H is the weak-inverse of A if $A \cdot H \cdot A = A$.

Proof of Claim 5. The first part follow as L is initially $V \times \mathbb{F}_q^{n_2}$ of dimension $\dim V + n_2$. The second part follows by linear algebra since $\dim L \geq \dim \pi(L) = \dim V$.

Proof of Claim 6. Since S.SetupKey, S.Sign and $\mathcal{B}$ are PPT algorithm, by Claim 3 in the last case, each step in the loop can be computed efficiently. In particular, as $2n_1 + 1$ is polynomially bounded, each for-loop in $\mathcal{A}$ can be performed efficiently.

Next we show that the procedure inside the Do-Until loop is repeated at most $n_1 + 1$ times. The key observation is that during the execution of $\mathcal{B}$, the space L forms a monotone decreasing sequence, implying that when $\mathcal{B}(\mathsf{vk}^*, V) \to (F^*, L^*)$ then $L^* \subseteq V \times \mathbb{F}_q^{n_2}$. In particular this implies that $\pi(L^*) \subseteq \pi(V \times \mathbb{F}_q^{n_2}) = V$. Thus if at any point the for-loop is halted, $\pi(L^*) = V^* \neq V$ implies $V^* \subsetneq V$. Hence the dimension of V strictly decreases, and since initially $\dim(V) = n_1$, the foor-loop can be halted at most n_1 times.

Finally, using again that $\mathcal{B}$ is an efficient algorithm, computing F, L can be done in polynomial time. It follows that $\mathcal{A}$ is PPT.

Proof of Claim 7. We proceed by induction. Initially $V = \mathbb{F}_q^{n_1}$ implies $\mathbf{x}_1 \in V$. Next we observe that the value of V is only changed if, within the for-loop, $V^* \neq V$ (see step 8, Fig. 4). Assume by induction that before this step is executed $\mathbf{x}_1 \in V$. Then, when this happens, $\mathcal{B}(\mathsf{vk}^*, V) \to (F^*, L^*)$ had been executed with $\mathbf{x}_1 \in V$. By Claim 2 this implies that $\mathbf{x} \in L^*$ and in particular $\mathbf{x}_1 = \pi(\mathbf{x}) \in \pi(L^*) = V^*$. Thus when $\mathcal{A}$ sets $V \leftarrow V^*$, $\mathbf{x}_1 \in V$.

Proof of Claim 8. Define the following events:

- $\mathcal{E}_{i,j}$ = "During the i-th iteration of the Do-Until loop, and the j-th iteration of the for loop, $\mathcal{B}^{\mathsf{S.Sign}(\mathsf{sk}^*, \cdot)}(\mathsf{vk}^*, V)$ returns (F^*, L^*) such that $\pi(L^*) = V$".
- $\mathcal{E}_{\mathsf{last}}$ = "$\mathcal{B}^{\mathsf{S.Sign}(\mathsf{sk}, \cdot)}(\mathsf{vk}, V)$ returns F, L with $\pi(L) = V$".

Furthermore let $I \sim \{1, \ldots, n_1 + 1\}$ be the random variable such that $\mathcal{A}$ terminates the Do-Until loop after the I-th execution. Then we observe that, conditioned on $\mathbf{X}_1, s_1$ and the V at iteration i, the event $\mathcal{E}_{i,j}$ depends only on the random coins used for $\mathcal{B}$, S.SetupKey and S.Sign which are chosen independently at each execution of $\mathcal{B}$. In particular, for a fixed i, the events $\{\mathcal{E}_{i,j}\}_j$ are independent and, since for $\mathcal{E}_{i,j}, \mathcal{E}_{i,k}$ with $j \neq k$ the procedure $\mathcal{B}$ is invoked with the same input

$$\Pr[\mathcal{E}_{i,j}] = \Pr[\mathcal{E}_{i,k}].$$

We may therefore define $p_i = \Pr[\mathcal{E}_{i,1}]$ as the success probability of each execution of $\mathcal{B}$ during the i-th loop. Similarly, if $I = i$, the vector space V given in input to $\mathcal{B}$ is by construction equal to the one used during the i-th execution of the Do-Until loop. In particular

$$p_i = \Pr[\mathcal{E}_{\mathsf{last}} | I = i].$$

To conclude we show that

$$\Pr\left[\mathcal{A} \to \mathsf{fail}\right] = \Pr\left[\neg\mathcal{E}_{\mathsf{last}}\right] = \sum_{i=1}^{n_1+1} \Pr\left[\neg\mathcal{E}_{\mathsf{last}}|I=i\right] \cdot \Pr\left[I=i\right]$$

$$\leq \sum_{i=1}^{n_1+1} \Pr\left[\neg\mathcal{E}_{\mathsf{last}}|I=i\right] \cdot \Pr\left[\mathcal{E}_{i,1} \wedge \ldots \wedge \mathcal{E}_{i,2n_1+1}\right]$$

$$= \sum_{i=1}^{n_1+1} \Pr\left[\neg\mathcal{E}_{\mathsf{last}}|I=i\right] \cdot \prod_{j=1}^{2n_1+1} \Pr\left[\mathcal{E}_{i,j}\right]$$

$$= \sum_{i=1}^{n_1+1} (1-p_i) \cdot p_i^{2n_1+1}$$

$$\leq \sum_{i=1}^{n_1+1} \frac{1}{2n_1+2} = \frac{n_1+1}{2n_1+2} = \frac{1}{2}.$$

where the first inequality comes from the fact that $I = i$ implies $\mathcal{E}_{i,j}$ for all $j \in \{1, \ldots, 2n_1 + 1\}$, while the second inequality comes from the fact that the function $f_t(x) = (1-x)x^t$ is upper bounded by $1/(t+1)$ when $x \in [0,1]$. Indeed $f_t(0) = f_t(1) = 0$ and its derivative vanishes only at $t/(t+1)$, which has to be the maximum point, implying that

$$(1-x) \cdot x^t \leq \left(1 - \frac{t}{t+1}\right) \cdot \left(\frac{t}{t+1}\right)^t \leq \frac{1}{t+1}.$$

4.2   Attack to Schemes with Generic Verification

Theorem 3. *Given an algebraic signature scheme with generic verification, for any ϑ such that $n_2 + \vartheta \leq |\mathsf{S.M}|$ there exists an adversary $\mathcal{A}$ that in the unforgeability experiment in Fig. 2 performs at most n_2 signature queries and produces ϑ distinct forgeries.*

Moreover, calling κ an upper bound on the signature bit-length, and χ an upper bound on the number of queries S.Vfy performs to $\mathcal{O}_{\mathsf{eq}}^0$, then $\mathcal{A}$ runs in time $O(\vartheta \cdot 2^\kappa \cdot 2^\chi \cdot \mathsf{poly}(\lambda))$ and performs $O(\vartheta \cdot \mathsf{poly}(\lambda))$ queries to $\mathcal{O}_{\mathsf{add}}$ and $\mathcal{O}_{\mathsf{eq}}^0$.

Proof. As done in Theorem 4 we begin by providing an attack $\mathcal{B}$ which breaks the scheme but performs potentially $n_1 + n_2$ signature queries.

At a high level $\mathcal{B}$, given the verification key $\mathsf{vk} = (\mathbf{X}, s)$, will keep track of all possible exponents of $\mathbf{X}$ in a set L and for each message m either the dimension of L decreases by one or $\mathcal{B}$ finds a forgery. Assume without loss of generality that signatures are of the form $(\mathbf{Y}', t')$ with $\mathbf{Y}' \in \mathbb{G}^k$ and $t' \in \{0,1\}^\kappa$.

For any m, our adversary attempts to produce a forgery as follows: For all possible $t \in \{0,1\}^\kappa$, it executes the verification algorithm by simulating a generic group $\widetilde{\mathbb{G}}$ with oracles $\widetilde{\mathcal{O}}_{\mathsf{add}}$ and $\widetilde{\mathcal{O}}_{\mathsf{eq}}^0$. More specifically, since S.Vfy requires as input the verification key $(\mathbf{X}, s)$, the message m and the signatures $(\mathbf{Y}, t)$, $\mathcal{B}$

reproduces all the group elements involved by assigning dummy indexes for $\widetilde{\mathbf{X}}$, $\widetilde{\mathbf{Y}}$ and runs S.Vfy$((\widetilde{\mathbf{X}}, s), m, (\widetilde{\mathbf{Y}}, t))$. During the execution, each query to $\widetilde{\mathcal{O}}_{\mathsf{add}}$ is emulated by simply returning new incremental indexes, while to emulate $\widetilde{\mathcal{O}}_{\mathsf{eq}}^0$, χ bits $\beta_1, \ldots, \beta_\chi$ are chosen at the beginning of the execution so that the answer to the i-th query will be β_i. Note that each element T_i the verifier queries to $\widetilde{\mathcal{O}}_{\mathsf{eq}}^0$ has to be a linear combination of the initial group elements he received, i.e. $T_i = \mathbf{a}_i^\top \widetilde{\mathbf{X}} - \mathbf{b}_i^\top \widetilde{\mathbf{Y}} - c_i \cdot \widetilde{G}$ obtained though $\widetilde{\mathcal{O}}_{\mathsf{add}}$, and $\mathcal{B}$ can extract these coefficients.

Repeating the execution of S.Vfy for different values of $\beta_1, \ldots, \beta_\chi$ implicitly defines a tree of height χ in which paths are determined by the replies $\mathcal{B}$ gave at the i-th query to $\widetilde{\mathcal{O}}_{\mathsf{eq}}^0$. If at some point a path $\beta_1, \ldots, \beta_\chi$ that makes the verifier accept is found, $\mathcal{B}$ can try to find a vector $\mathbf{Y}$ in the real GGM, such that the i-query S.Vfy would do to $\mathcal{O}_{\mathsf{eq}}^0$ will be answered with β_i. If such a $\mathbf{Y}$ is found, then $(\mathbf{Y}, t)$ will be a valid forgery for m.

Recalling that the i-th query has the form $T_i = \mathbf{a}_i \widetilde{\mathbf{X}} - \mathbf{b}_i \widetilde{\mathbf{Y}} - c_i \cdot G$, then $\mathcal{B}$ needs to find a vector $\mathbf{Y}$ such that for all $i \in \{1, \ldots, \chi\}$

$$\mathbf{a}_i^\top \mathbf{X} = \mathbf{b}_i^\top \mathbf{Y} + c_i \cdot G \text{ when } \beta_i = 1, \qquad \mathbf{a}_i^\top \mathbf{X} \neq \mathbf{b}_i^\top \mathbf{Y} + c_i \cdot G \text{ when } \beta_i = 0$$

Regarding the equations on the left side, they can be packed up into a system $A\mathbf{X} = B\mathbf{Y} + \mathbf{c} \cdot G$. Through pseudo-inverses or Gaussian elimination is easy to check if solutions exists for all $\mathbf{x} \in L$ (as in the proof of Theorem 2). If this is not the case $\mathcal{B}$ simply discards this path and continues its brute-force search. However, even if the previous condition is satisfied, for some of the points $\mathbf{x}$ in L it may be the case that any vector $\mathbf{y}$ satisfying $A\mathbf{x} = B\mathbf{y} + \mathbf{c}$ fails to satisfy some of the inequalities above $\mathbf{a}_i^\top \mathbf{x} \neq \mathbf{b}_i^\top \mathbf{y} + c_i$, implying that no solution $\mathbf{Y} \in \mathbb{G}^k$ can be found if $\mathbf{x}$ is the discrete logarithm of $\mathbf{X}$. We call these points $\mathbf{x} \in L$ *faulty* and, more specifically, the set of faulty points is defined as

$$\mathcal{F}_{\mathbf{a},b,c}^{A,B,\mathbf{c}} = \{\mathbf{x} : A\mathbf{x} \in \operatorname{Im} B + \mathbf{c}, \ \forall \mathbf{y} \in \mathbb{F}_q^m \ A\mathbf{x} = B\mathbf{y} + \mathbf{c} \Rightarrow \mathbf{a}^\top \mathbf{x} = \mathbf{b}^\top \mathbf{y} + c\}.$$

Three possible cases may occur now:

- If all points in L are faulty with respect to some inequality constraint, then $\mathcal{B}$ gives up on the path as the solution $\mathbf{Y}$ does not exist.

- If not all points are faulty $\mathcal{B}$ attempts to solve the system, which requires expensive queries to $\mathcal{O}_{\mathsf{add}}, \mathcal{O}_{\mathsf{eq}}^0$: if a solution $\mathbf{Y}$ satisfying all constraints is found, this is a valid forgery.

- If not all points are faulty, but no solution can be found, it means that $\mathbf{x}$, the discrete log of $\mathbf{X}$, has to be a faulty point. This information reduces the dimension of L as not all points in L are faulty.

Finally, if no solution can be found for any $t \in \{0,1\}^\kappa$ and path $\beta_1, \ldots, \beta_\chi$, $\mathcal{B}$ queries a signature for m and uses this information to reduce the dimension of L. As for the proof of Theorem 2, $\mathcal{B}$ might overall query $n_1 + n_2$ signatures (as opposed to the desired n_1) since initially it has no information on the exponents

Adversary $B(\mathsf{vk}, V)$:

1 :   Initialize $F \leftarrow \varnothing$ the set of forgeries
2 :   Call $L = V \times \mathbb{F}_q^{n_2}$ the set of possible exponents of $\mathbf{X}$
3 :   Call $\theta = n + \vartheta$ and sample $m_1, \ldots, m_\theta \leftarrow^{\$} \mathsf{S.M}$ distinct messages
4 :   **For** $m \in {-m_1, \ldots, m_\theta}$":
5 :   **For** $t \in {-0,1}^{"\kappa}$ and $(\beta_1, \ldots, \beta_\chi) \in {-0,1}^{"\chi}$:
6 :   Simulate a Generic Group $\widetilde{\mathbb{G}}$ with generator $\widetilde{G}$ and oracles $\widetilde{O}_{\mathsf{add}}$ and $\widetilde{O}_{\mathsf{eq}}^0$
7 :   Assign indices for two vectors $\widetilde{\mathbf{X}} \in \widetilde{\mathbb{G}}^n$ and $\widetilde{\mathbf{Y}} \in \widetilde{\mathbb{G}}^k$
8 :   Run $\mathsf{S.Vfy}((\widetilde{\mathbf{X}}, s), m, (\widetilde{\mathbf{Y}}, t))$ using $\widetilde{\mathbb{G}}$
9 :   **When** $\mathsf{S.Vfy}$ queries $\widetilde{O}_{\mathsf{add}}(T, S)$:
10 :   Store a way to express $T + S$ as a linear combination of $\widetilde{\mathbf{X}}$, $\widetilde{\mathbf{Y}}$ and $\widetilde{G}$
11 :   Return to $\mathsf{S.Vfy}$ a label for $T + S$
12 :   **When** $\mathsf{S.Vfy}$ queries $\widetilde{O}_{\mathsf{eq}}^0(T_i)$ the i-th time:
13 :   Store $\mathbf{a}_i \in \mathbb{F}_q^n$, $\mathbf{b}_i \in \mathbb{F}_q^k$ and $c_i \in \mathbb{F}_q$ such that $T_i = \mathbf{a}_i^\top \widetilde{\mathbf{X}} - \mathbf{b}_i^\top \widetilde{\mathbf{Y}} - c_i \cdot \widetilde{G}$
14 :   Return β_i to $\mathsf{S.Vfy}$
15 :   **When** $\mathsf{S.Vfy}$ halts and returns $b \in {-0,1}$":
16 :   Let $A = (\mathbf{a}_i : \beta_i = 1)$, $B = (\mathbf{b}_i : \beta_i = 1)$ and $\mathbf{c} = (c_i : \beta_i = 1)$
17 :   **If** $b = 0$:
18 :   **Continue** cycle in line 5
19 :   **Elif** $A \cdot L \not\subseteq \mathrm{Im}\, B + \mathbf{c}$:
20 :   **Continue** cycle in line 5
21 :   **Elif** $\exists i : \beta_i = 0$ and $L \subseteq F_{\mathbf{a}_i, \mathbf{b}_i, c_i}^{A, B, \mathbf{c}}$:
22 :   **Continue** cycle in line 5
23 :   **Elif** $\exists i : \beta_i = 0$ and $\mathbf{X} \in F_{\mathbf{a}_i, \mathbf{b}_i, c_i}^{A, B, \mathbf{c}} \cdot G$:
24 :   Update $L \leftarrow L \cap F_{\mathbf{a}_i, \mathbf{b}_i, c_i}^{A, B, \mathbf{c}}$
25 :   **Break** cycle in line 5
26 :   **Else:**
27 :   Find $\mathbf{Y} \in \mathbb{G}^k$ s.t. $A\mathbf{X} = B\mathbf{Y} + \mathbf{c}G$ and $\mathbf{a}_i^\top \mathbf{X} \neq \mathbf{b}_i^\top \mathbf{Y} + c_i G$ for $\beta_i = 0$
28 :   Store $\sigma \leftarrow (\mathbf{Y}, t)$ and $F \leftarrow F \cup {-(m, \sigma)}$"
29 :   **Break** cycle in line 5
30 :   **If** the cycle ended without interruptions:
31 :   Query a signature for m and wait for $(\mathbf{Y}, t)$
32 :   Reconstruct $A, B, \mathbf{c}$ as in step 16 using $(\mathbf{X}, s, m, \mathbf{Y}, t)$ and the group $\mathbb{G}$
33 :   Update $L \leftarrow L \cap {-\mathbf{x} \in \mathbb{F}_q^n : A\mathbf{x} \in \mathrm{Im}\, B + \mathbf{c}}$"
34 :   Return F, L

Fig. 5. B breaking security of an algebraic signature scheme with generic verification.

of $\mathbf{X}$, i.e. $\dim L = n_1 + n_2$, and each signature query may reveal only one new linear combination among these group elements. To address this issue we use the same strategy presented in Theorem 2, that is, we use $\mathcal{B}$ in a black-box way inside the algorithm $\mathcal{A}$, formally described in Fig. 4. The main idea is again that $\mathcal{A}$ initially extracts linear combinations among CRS elements that could be found by $\mathcal{B}$, and finally executes $\mathcal{B}$ providing the retrieved information as input. In this way $\mathcal{B}$ will, with significant probability, only find relations among elements of $\mathbf{X}_2$, thus requesting at most n_2 signatures.

A detailed description of $\mathcal{A}$ appears in Fig. 5, while a more detailed proof of the Theorem appears in the full version.

5 Conclusions

5.1 Impossibility of Algebraic Vector Commitments

Using both the negative results provided in the previous sections for algebraic signatures and Theorem 1 connecting the efficiency of a VC to the security of the associated signature scheme, we obtain two lower bounds for algebraic vector commitments

Theorem 4. *Given a position binding algebraic VC with strictly linear verification, let $\ell_c = \ell_c(n)$ and $\ell_\pi = \ell_\pi(n)$ be respectively the commitment and opening bit length to commit to a vector of n entries. Then*

$$\nu_2 + \frac{\lambda + \ell_c + \nu_2 \cdot (\ell_\pi + \log|\mathsf{VC.M}|)}{\log|\mathsf{VC.M}|} \geq n.$$

Proof. Assume there exists an algebraic VC with strictly linear verification contradicting the above inequality and satisfying position binding. Then by Theorem 1 the signature scheme obtained through the transformation in Fig. 1 would satisfy ϑ-UF with

$$\vartheta(\mathsf{vk}, Q) = \frac{\lambda + \ell_c + |Q| \cdot (\ell_\pi + \log|\mathsf{VC.M}|)}{\log|\mathsf{VC.M}|}$$

and its message space would have size $|\mathsf{S_{VC}.M}| = n$. Since vk contains ν_2 group elements excluding those that belong to the CRS, i.e. the public parameters of the original Vector Commitment, the attacker $\mathcal{A}$ from Theorem 2 can produce at least $n - \nu_2$ forgeries performing at most ν_2 queries. Called Q the set of queries performed by $\mathcal{A}$ we would have that

$$\vartheta(\mathsf{vk}, Q) \leq \frac{\lambda + \ell_c + \nu_2 \cdot (\ell_\pi + \log|\mathsf{VC.M}|)}{\log|\mathsf{VC.M}|} < n - \nu_2$$

where we use the fact that $|Q| \leq \nu_2$ in the first inequality. This is then a contradiction since $\mathcal{A}$ would breaks the ϑ-UF of the derived signature, implying that the given vector commitment was not binding.

Theorem 5. *Given an algebraic VC with generic verification that is position binding against unbounded adversaries performing polynomially bounded queries to the GGM oracles $\mathcal{O}_{add}$, $\mathcal{O}_{eq}^0$, using the same notation of Theorem 4, then*

$$\nu_2 + \frac{\lambda + \ell_c + \nu_2 \cdot (\ell_\pi + \log |\mathsf{VC.M}|)}{\log |\mathsf{VC.M}|} \geq n.$$

Proof. Assuming again by contradiction that the above inequality is not satisfied, Theorem 1 implies that the associated signature scheme is ϑ-UF against any unbounded adversary $\mathcal{C}$ making at most polynomially many signature and group operations queries, or otherwise $\mathcal{R}^{\mathcal{C}}$ would break position binding with significant advantage. Notice that since $\mathcal{R}$ is PPT, $\mathcal{R}^{\mathcal{C}}$ still performs polynomially many generic group operations. As in the proof of Theorem 4 then, our initial assumption implies $\vartheta \leq n - \nu_2$. Since the adversary $\mathcal{A}$ of Theorem 3 returns $n - \nu_2$ signatures performing at most ν_2 queries, this contradicts the ϑ-UF of the associated signature against this adversary.

Corollary 1. *Given an algebraic vector commitment with strictly linear verification, then $\ell_c \cdot \ell_\pi = \Omega(n)$. Analogously, given an algebraic vector commitment with generic verification position binding against unbounded adversary performing at most polynomially many queries to the GGM oracles, $\ell_c \cdot \ell_\pi = \Omega(n)$.*

Note that this lower bound implies in both cases that either $\ell_c = \Omega(\sqrt{n})$ or $\ell_\pi = \Omega(\sqrt{n})$.

5.2   Impossibility of Algebraic Signatures

As a by-product of our study on VC we also obtain the following two impossibility results for algebraic signatures which extend the one presented in [11] to a broader family of schemes.

Theorem 6. *For any UF-CMA algebraic signature scheme with strictly linear verification, $n_1 \geq |\mathsf{S.M}|$.*

Theorem 7. *For any algebraic signature scheme with generic verification UF-CMA secure against any unbounded adversary performing at most polynomially many queries to the GGM oracles, $n_1 \geq |\mathsf{S.M}|$.*

Acknowledgements. This work has received funding in part from the European Research Council (ERC) under the European Union's Horizon 2020 research and innovation program under project PICOCRYPT (grant agreement No. 101001283), by the Spanish Government under projects SCUM (ref. RTI2018-102043-B-I00), RED2018-102321-T, and SECURING (ref. PID2019-110873RJ-I00), by the Madrid Regional Government under project BLOQUES (ref. S2018/TCS-4339), by a research grant from Nomadic Labs and the Tezos Foundation, by the Programma ricerca di ateneo UNICT 35 2020-22 linea 2 and by research gifts from Protocol Labs.

References

1. Abe, M., Haralambiev, K., Ohkubo, M.: Group to group commitments do not shrink. In: Pointcheval, D., Johansson, T. (eds.) EUROCRYPT 2012. LNCS, vol. 7237, pp. 301–317. Springer, Heidelberg (2012). https://doi.org/10.1007/978-3-642-29011-4_19
2. Bayer, S., Groth, J.: Efficient zero-knowledge argument for correctness of a shuffle. In: Pointcheval, D., Johansson, T. (eds.) EUROCRYPT 2012. LNCS, vol. 7237, pp. 263–280. Springer, Heidelberg (2012). https://doi.org/10.1007/978-3-642-29011-4_17
3. Benabbas, S., Gennaro, R., Vahlis, Y.: Verifiable delegation of computation over large datasets. In: Rogaway, P. (ed.) CRYPTO 2011. LNCS, vol. 6841, pp. 111–131. Springer, Heidelberg (2011). https://doi.org/10.1007/978-3-642-22792-9_7
4. Boneh, D., Bünz, B., Fisch, B.: Batching techniques for accumulators with applications to IOPs and stateless blockchains. In: Boldyreva, A., Micciancio, D. (eds.) CRYPTO 2019. LNCS, vol. 11692, pp. 561–586. Springer, Cham (2019). https://doi.org/10.1007/978-3-030-26948-7_20
5. Boneh, D., Franklin, M.: Identity-based encryption from the Weil pairing. In: Kilian, J. (ed.) CRYPTO 2001. LNCS, vol. 2139, pp. 213–229. Springer, Heidelberg (2001). https://doi.org/10.1007/3-540-44647-8_13
6. Bootle, J., Cerulli, A., Chaidos, P., Groth, J., Petit, C.: Efficient zero-knowledge arguments for arithmetic circuits in the discrete log setting. In: Fischlin, M., Coron, J.-S. (eds.) EUROCRYPT 2016. LNCS, vol. 9666, pp. 327–357. Springer, Heidelberg (2016). https://doi.org/10.1007/978-3-662-49896-5_12
7. Bünz, B., Bootle, J., Boneh, D., Poelstra, A., Wuille, P., Maxwell, G.: BulletProofs: short proofs for confidential transactions and more. In: 2018 IEEE Symposium on Security and Privacy, pp. 315–334. IEEE Computer Society Press, May 2018. https://doi.org/10.1109/SP.2018.00020
8. Campanelli, M., Fiore, D., Greco, N., Kolonelos, D., Nizzardo, L.: Incrementally aggregatable vector commitments and applications to verifiable decentralized storage. In: Moriai, S., Wang, H. (eds.) ASIACRYPT 2020. LNCS, vol. 12492, pp. 3–35. Springer, Cham (2020). https://doi.org/10.1007/978-3-030-64834-3_1
9. Catalano, D., Fiore, D.: Vector commitments and their applications. In: Kurosawa, K., Hanaoka, G. (eds.) PKC 2013. LNCS, vol. 7778, pp. 55–72. Springer, Heidelberg (2013). https://doi.org/10.1007/978-3-642-36362-7_5
10. Chepurnoy, A., Papamanthou, C., Zhang, Y.: Edrax: a cryptocurrency with stateless transaction validation. Cryptology ePrint Archive, Report 2018/968 (2018). https://eprint.iacr.org/2018/968
11. Döttling, N., Hartmann, D., Hofheinz, D., Kiltz, E., Schäge, S., Ursu, B.: On the impossibility of purely algebraic signatures. In: Nissim, K., Waters, B. (eds.) TCC 2021. LNCS, vol. 13044, pp. 317–349. Springer, Cham (2021). https://doi.org/10.1007/978-3-030-90456-2_11
12. Fisch, B.: PoReps: proofs of space on useful data. Cryptology ePrint Archive, Report 2018/678 (2018). https://eprint.iacr.org/2018/678
13. Gennaro, R., Gentry, C., Parno, B., Raykova, M.: Quadratic span programs and succinct NIZKs without PCPs. In: Johansson, T., Nguyen, P.Q. (eds.) EUROCRYPT 2013. LNCS, vol. 7881, pp. 626–645. Springer, Heidelberg (2013). https://doi.org/10.1007/978-3-642-38348-9_37
14. Gennaro, R., Gertner, Y., Katz, J.: Lower bounds on the efficiency of encryption and digital signature schemes. In: 35th ACM STOC, pp. 417–425. ACM Press, June 2003. https://doi.org/10.1145/780542.780604

15. Gennaro, R., Trevisan, L.: Lower bounds on the efficiency of generic cryptographic constructions. In: 41st Annual Symposium on Foundations of Computer Science, FOCS 2000, 12–14 November 2000, Redondo Beach, California, USA, pp. 305–313. IEEE Computer Society (2000)
16. Gertner, Y., Kannan, S., Malkin, T., Reingold, O., Viswanathan, M.: The relationship between public key encryption and oblivious transfer. In: 41st Annual Symposium on Foundations of Computer Science, FOCS 2000, 12–14 November 2000, Redondo Beach, California, USA, pp. 325–335. IEEE Computer Society (2000)
17. Gertner, Y., Malkin, T., Reingold, O.: On the impossibility of basing trapdoor functions on trapdoor predicates. In: 42nd FOCS, pp. 126–135. IEEE Computer Society Press, October 2001. https://doi.org/10.1109/SFCS.2001.959887
18. Goldwasser, S., Micali, S., Rivest, R.L.: A digital signature scheme secure against adaptive chosen-message attacks. SIAM J. Comput. **17**(2), 281–308 (1988)
19. Impagliazzo, R., Rudich, S.: Limits on the provable consequences of one-way permutations. In: 21st ACM STOC, pp. 44–61. ACM Press, May 1989. https://doi.org/10.1145/73007.73012
20. Juels, A., Kaliski Jr., B.S.: PORs: proofs of retrievability for large files. In: Ning, P., De Capitani di Vimercati, S., Syverson, P.F. (eds.) ACM CCS 2007, pp. 584–597. ACM Press, October 2007. https://doi.org/10.1145/1315245.1315317
21. Kate, A., Zaverucha, G.M., Goldberg, I.: Constant-size commitments to polynomials and their applications. In: Abe, M. (ed.) ASIACRYPT 2010. LNCS, vol. 6477, pp. 177–194. Springer, Heidelberg (2010). https://doi.org/10.1007/978-3-642-17373-8_11
22. Kilian, J.: On the complexity of bounded-interaction and noninteractive zero-knowledge proofs. In: 35th FOCS, pp. 466–477. IEEE Computer Society Press, November 1994. https://doi.org/10.1109/SFCS.1994.365744
23. Kim, J.H., Simon, D.R., Tetali, P.: Limits on the efficiency of one-way permutation-based hash functions. In: 40th Annual Symposium on Foundations of Computer Science, FOCS 1999, 17–18 October 1999, pp. 535–542. IEEE Computer Society, New York (1999)
24. Kuszmaul, J.: Verkle trees (2018). https://math.mit.edu/research/highschool/primes/materials/2018/Kuszmaul.pdf
25. Lai, R.W.F., Malavolta, G.: Subvector commitments with application to succinct arguments. In: Boldyreva, A., Micciancio, D. (eds.) CRYPTO 2019. LNCS, vol. 11692, pp. 530–560. Springer, Cham (2019). https://doi.org/10.1007/978-3-030-26948-7_19
26. Libert, B., Ramanna, S.C., Yung, M.: Functional commitment schemes: from polynomial commitments to pairing-based accumulators from simple assumptions. In: Chatzigiannakis, I., Mitzenmacher, M., Rabani, Y., Sangiorgi, D. (eds.) ICALP 2016. LIPIcs, vol. 55, pp. 30:1–30:14. Schloss Dagstuhl (2016). https://doi.org/10.4230/LIPIcs.ICALP.2016.30
27. Libert, B., Yung, M.: Concise mercurial vector commitments and independent zero-knowledge sets with short proofs. In: Micciancio, D. (ed.) TCC 2010. LNCS, vol. 5978, pp. 499–517. Springer, Heidelberg (2010). https://doi.org/10.1007/978-3-642-11799-2_30
28. Maurer, U.: Abstract models of computation in cryptography. In: Smart, N.P. (ed.) Cryptography and Coding 2005. LNCS, vol. 3796, pp. 1–12. Springer, Heidelberg (2005). https://doi.org/10.1007/11586821_1
29. Merkle, R.C.: A digital signature based on a conventional encryption function. In: Pomerance, C. (ed.) CRYPTO 1987. LNCS, vol. 293, pp. 369–378. Springer, Heidelberg (1988). https://doi.org/10.1007/3-540-48184-2_32

30. Micali, S.: CS proofs (extended abstracts). In: 35th FOCS, pp. 436–453. IEEE Computer Society Press, November 1994. https://doi.org/10.1109/SFCS.1994.365746

31. Micali, S., Rabin, M.O., Kilian, J.: Zero-knowledge sets. In: 44th FOCS, pp. 80–91. IEEE Computer Society Press, October 2003. https://doi.org/10.1109/SFCS.2003.1238183

32. Micali, S., Rabin, M.O., Vadhan, S.P.: Verifiable random functions. In: 40th FOCS, pp. 120–130. IEEE Computer Society Press, October 1999. https://doi.org/10.1109/SFFCS.1999.814584

33. Papakonstantinou, P.A., Rackoff, C., Vahlis, Y.: How powerful are the DDH hard groups? Electron. Colloquium Comput. Complex, 167 (2012). https://eccc.weizmann.ac.il/report/2012/167

34. Papamanthou, C., Shi, E., Tamassia, R., Yi, K.: Streaming authenticated data structures. In: Johansson, T., Nguyen, P.Q. (eds.) EUROCRYPT 2013. LNCS, vol. 7881, pp. 353–370. Springer, Heidelberg (2013). https://doi.org/10.1007/978-3-642-38348-9_22

35. Peikert, C., Pepin, Z., Sharp, C.: Vector and functional commitments from lattices. In: Nissim, K., Waters, B. (eds.) TCC 2021. LNCS, vol. 13044, pp. 480–511. Springer, Cham (2021). https://doi.org/10.1007/978-3-030-90456-2_16

36. Rotem, L., Segev, G., Shahaf, I.: Generic-Group Delay Functions Require Hidden-Order Groups. In: Canteaut, A., Ishai, Y. (eds.) EUROCRYPT 2020. LNCS, vol. 12107, pp. 155–180. Springer, Cham (2020). https://doi.org/10.1007/978-3-030-45727-3_6

37. Schul-Ganz, G., Segev, G.: Accumulators in (and Beyond) generic groups: nontrivial batch verification requires interaction. In: Pass, R., Pietrzak, K. (eds.) TCC 2020. LNCS, vol. 12551, pp. 77–107. Springer, Cham (2020). https://doi.org/10.1007/978-3-030-64378-2_4

38. Schul-Ganz, G., Segev, G.: Generic-group identity-based encryption: a tight impossibility result. In: Tessaro, S. (ed.) 2nd Conference on Information-Theoretic Cryptography (ITC 2021). Leibniz International Proceedings in Informatics (LIPIcs), vol. 199, pp. 26:1–26:23. Schloss Dagstuhl - Leibniz-Zentrum für Informatik, Dagstuhl (2021). https://doi.org/10.4230/LIPIcs.ITC.2021.26. https://drops.dagstuhl.de/opus/volltexte/2021/14345

39. Shamir, A.: Identity-based cryptosystems and signature schemes. In: Blakley, G.R., Chaum, D. (eds.) CRYPTO 1984. LNCS, vol. 196, pp. 47–53. Springer, Heidelberg (1985). https://doi.org/10.1007/3-540-39568-7_5

40. Shoup, V.: Lower bounds for discrete logarithms and related problems. In: Fumy, W. (ed.) EUROCRYPT 1997. LNCS, vol. 1233, pp. 256–266. Springer, Heidelberg (1997). https://doi.org/10.1007/3-540-69053-0_18

41. Simon, D.R.: Finding collisions on a one-way street: can secure hash functions be based on general assumptions? In: Nyberg, K. (ed.) EUROCRYPT 1998. LNCS, vol. 1403, pp. 334–345. Springer, Heidelberg (1998). https://doi.org/10.1007/BFb0054137

42. Zhandry, M.: To label, or not to label (in generic groups). Cryptology ePrint Archive, Report 2022/226 (2022). https://eprint.iacr.org/2022/226

43. Zhandry, M., Zhang, C.: The relationship between idealized models under computationally bounded adversaries. Cryptology ePrint Archive, Report 2021/240 (2021). https://eprint.iacr.org/2021/240

Four-Round Black-Box Non-malleable Schemes from One-Way Permutations

Michele Ciampi[1]([✉])([iD]), Emmanuela Orsini[2]([iD]), and Luisa Siniscalchi[3,4]([iD])

[1] The University of Edinburgh, Edinburgh, UK
michele.ciampi@ed.ac.uk
[2] imec-COSIC, KU Leuven, Leuven, Belgium
emmanuela.orsini@kuleuven.be
[3] Department Computer Science, Aarhus University, Aarhus, Denmark
lsiniscalchi@cs.au.dk
[4] Concordium Blockchain Research Center, Aarhus, Denmark

Abstract. We construct the first four-round non-malleable commitment scheme based solely on the black-box use of one-to-one one-way functions. Prior to our work, all non-malleable commitment schemes based on black-box use of polynomial-time cryptographic primitives require more than 16 rounds of interaction.

A key tool for our construction is a proof system that satisfies a new definition of security that we call *non-malleable zero-knowledge with respect to commitments*. In a nutshell, such a proof system can be safely run in parallel with any (potentially interactive) commitment scheme. We provide an instantiation of this tool using the MPC-in-the-Head approach in combination with BMR.

1 Introduction

Starting from the pioneering work of Dolev et al. [15], a long line of works has focused on constructing new non-malleable commitment schemes with improved characteristics, both in terms of efficiency and assumptions. Given the strong connection of non-malleable commitments with secure multi-party computation [3,44], improvements in the area of non-malleable commitments have a big impact on the multi-party computation (MPC) landscape. In particular, recent developments on the round complexity of non-malleable commitments led to the first round-optimal MPC protocols in the plain model [1,7,10,26].

The round complexity of commitment schemes based on polynomial-time hardness assumptions in the stand-alone setting is nowadays well understood. Non-interactive commitments can be constructed assuming the existence of 1-to-1 one-way functions (OWFs) [19] and 2-round commitments can be constructed assuming the existence of OWFs only. Moreover, non-interactive commitments do not exist if one relies on the black-box use of OWFs only [34]. Recently many progress have been made also for the case of *non-malleable* (NM) commitments[1].

---

[1] In this paper we will consider only NM commitments w.r.t. commitments. For the case of NM w.r.t. decommitments see [4,14,21,35,39,41].

© The Author(s), under exclusive license to Springer Nature Switzerland 2022
E. Kiltz and V. Vaikuntanathan (Eds.): TCC 2022, LNCS 13748, pp. 300–329, 2022.
https://doi.org/10.1007/978-3-031-22365-5_11

Indeed, the long sequence of very exciting positive results [2,8,9,20,22,24,31–33,37–43] led to the work of Khurana [29] in which the authors showed how to obtain a 3-round (which is optimal for the case of polynomial-time assumptions [36]) non-malleable commitment scheme based on specific number-theoretic assumptions, and to [23] where the authors proposed a round optimal scheme based on one-to-one OWFs.

Black-Box (BB) Constructions. While these recent results show round-optimal constructions, they make non-black-box use of cryptography. Constant round BB schemes are known [20,22,31,43], but their round complexity is far to be optimal. More specifically, Goyal et al. [22] give a black-box NM commitment protocol only based on the existence of one-way functions, but this construction requires more than 16 rounds. In another work, Goyal et al. [24] mention that combining their protocol with ideas from [22] would could to a 6-round protocol but no explicit construction was given. Therefore the following question remained open.

> *Does it exist a non-malleable commitment scheme that makes black-box use of standard polynomial-time cryptographic primitives where the commitment phase consists of less than 16 rounds?*

In this work, we provide a positive answer, by proposing a 4-round non-malleable commitment scheme that only makes black-box use of one-to-one one-way functions. Whether it is possible to achieve the same result in three rounds remains a fascinating open question.

1.1   Our Contributions

The state-of-the-art in constructing non-malleable commitments based on minimal assumptions shows a significant gap in the round complexity of black-box and non-black-box protocols. In this work, we almost close this gap by describing the first 4-round non-malleable commitment that makes black-box use of the underlying primitives and is based on the almost minimal assumption of injective one-way functions.[2] In particular, we prove the following theorem.

Theorem (Informal). *Assuming one-to-one OWFs, there exists a 4-round non-malleable commitment scheme that makes black-box use of the OWFs.*

Our 4-round non-malleable commitment crucially relies on a novel 3-round public-coin proof system that is zero-knowledge against honest verifiers (HVZK), and such that the statement to be proven can be specified in the last round (*delayed-input property*). In particular, our protocol enjoys *adaptive-soundness* and *adaptive-HVZK* [11,12,27]. These properties guarantee that HVZK and

---

[2] Our BB 4-round non-malleable commitment scheme satisfies the notion of standalone (or one-one) non-malleability. Obtaining a concurrent (or many-many) BB non-malleable commitment scheme in just 4 rounds, or less, still remains an open question.

soundness hold even against an adversary that decides the statement to be proven (and the witness for the HVZK case) adaptively on the first two rounds of the protocol. A protocol that satisfies such properties and that also makes black-box use of the underlying cryptographic primitives is proposed in [27]. What makes our scheme different is that it also enjoys a special form of non-malleability that we call *non-malleable HVZK with respect to commitment (NMZKC)*.

In a nutshell, this notion allows us to safely compose the proof system in parallel with any type of commitment scheme. In more detail, we consider the following setting. There is a man-in-the-middle (MiM) adversary that interacts (acting as the verifier) with an honest prover of a proof system Π_{AI} (where AI stands for adaptive-input). In the right session instead, the MiM acts as the sender for a (potentially interactive) commitment scheme Π_{com}, with an honest receiver. The notion of NMZKC guarantees that the distribution of the messages committed by the MiM in the right session is independent of whether the messages of Π_{AI} are generated honestly (i.e., using the witness for some NP statement x), or are computed using the simulator.

We believe that this tool and notion can be of independent interest. Indeed, NMZKC proof systems might be used in place of *rewind secure* schemes. A rewind secure proof system guarantees that the zero-knowledge property holds even if an adversarial verifier is allowed to rewind the prover a bounded number of times (this can be seen as a mild form of resettability). The reason why the notion of rewind security has gained a lot of attention recently is exactly that it simplifies the composition of proof systems with other primitives. For example, it simplifies the composition of a proof system with extractable commitments. The high-level idea is that in the security proof it is possible to extract from the commitment without harming the zero-knowledge property of the proof system. Hence, it is possible to check whether the distribution of the committed messages changes depending on whether the messages of the proof system are simulated or are generated honestly. This proof technique has been exploited in many recent works [7,13,23]. And, more interestingly, it was used also to construct the first one-one non-malleable commitment [24][3]. As we will discuss in the technical overview, we will replace the rewind secure proof system proposed in [24] (that inherently makes non-black-box use of the underlying primitives) with our NMZKC proof system.

We believe that NMZKC in some scenarios can replace the use of rewind secure primitives, and this might be particularly helpful given that our protocol is completely black-box in the use of the underlying cryptographic primitives. To the best of our knowledge, no black-box rewind secure three-round HVZK protocol is currently available. In summary, we prove the following theorem.

---

[3] In Sect. 8 we propose a comparison between the approach based on rewind-secure primitives of [24] and the one we propose in this work. In particular, we explain why and how we can rely on a simpler underlying weak-non-malleable commitment scheme compared to the one used in [24].

Theorem (Informal). *Assuming one-to-one OWFs, then there exists a 3-round delayed-input public-coin adaptive-input proof system that also is NMZKC and it makes black-box use of the OWFs.*

2   Overview of Techniques

We first describe how to construct the main tool required for our construction, which is a commit-and-prove proof system that satisfies the definition of non-malleable HVZK with respect to commitment. Then we show how to use this tool to construct our four-round non-malleable commitment protocol.

2.1   Our NMZKC Protocol and New Commitment Schemes

We start this section by recalling how to turn an MPC protocol into a proof system for any $\mathcal{NP}$-relation Rel following the *MPC-in-the-head* approach of [28]. Let Π_{MPC} be an n-party MPC protocol that is secure against up to t semi-honest corruptions. First, the prover secret-shares the witness w using an additive secret-sharing, while f will be a verification function that outputs 1 iff w is a valid witness, i.e., $f(x, w_1, \ldots, w_n) = 1 \iff (x, w_1 \oplus \cdots \oplus w_n) \in \mathsf{Rel}$. Then, it simulates all n parties running the protocol locally and sends the verifier commitments to each parties' views. Later, the verifier randomly chooses t of the parties' commitments to be opened, and checks that the committed messages are consistent with an honest execution of the MPC protocol according to the opened views. Since only t parties are opened, the verifier learns nothing about the secret input w, while the random choice of the opened parties ensures that enough views have been computed honestly, ensuring soundness.[4]

Unfortunately, this scheme is inherently non-delayed input since the prover needs both statement and witness to generate the views that must be committed in the first round. To overcome this limitation, we consider a specific class of two-phase MPC protocols. In particular, we require protocols with an input-independent offline phase, where the parties only produce correlated randomness that will be used to speed up the second phase. In the second phase (the online phase) the input is required and used to compute the output of the function. We denote such protocols by $\Pi_{\mathsf{MPC}} := (\Pi_{\mathsf{MPC}}^{\mathsf{off}}, \Pi_{\mathsf{MPC}}^{\mathsf{on}})$, where the two algorithms $\Pi_{\mathsf{MPC}}^{\mathsf{off}}$ and $\Pi_{\mathsf{MPC}}^{\mathsf{on}}$ denote respectively the offline and the online phase of Π_{MPC}.

Equipped with such an MPC protocol, we can modify the approach of [28] as follows. The prover only simulates $\Pi_{\mathsf{MPC}}^{\mathsf{off}}$, and commits to the individual views. Then the verifier, as described before, selects a random subset of parties to be opened. After receiving the challenge, the prover opens the requested commitments and additionally runs $\Pi_{\mathsf{MPC}}^{\mathsf{on}}$ to obtain the entire views of the parties requested by the verifier. At the end of this process, the verifier holds complete

---

[4] This sketch protocol gives a noticeable probability of cheating to the prover, typically the soundness of the protocol can be easily amplified via parallel repetition.

views for all the parties it requested and can check their consistency as previously described.

Intuitively, (non-adaptive input) HVZK comes again from the hiding of the commitments and the (semi-honest) security of the MPC protocol. However, it is clear that this approach fails completely against malicious provers. Indeed, they might easily generate online messages in a malicious way for all the parties the verifier did not ask to open. Note that in this case, Π_{MPC} is secure against t corrupted parties, but the adversary might generate ill-formed online messages for the remaining $n - t$. To work around this problem, we require Π_{MPC} to enjoy a stronger notion of security that we call *robustness*. In a nutshell, this notion requires that, when the offline phase of Π_{MPC} has been honestly computed, then it is always possible to check if a message received during the online phase has been honestly generated or not. In this way, robustness allows to prove soundness also w.r.t. a malicious prover that specifies the inputs in the last round (i.e. adaptive-input soundness).

The above approach guarantees that the protocol enjoys delayed-input completeness and adaptive-input soundness. However, it is not clear how to argue that the protocol is adaptive-input HVZK given that Π_{MPC} is only semi-honest secure. The reason is that we would like to rely on the security of the underlying MPC protocol thus committing to simulated views in the first round. However, to simulate these views the MPC simulator needs to know the input of the corrupted parties. We recall that such input consists of a share of the witness (which is easy to simulate) and the theorem to be proven. This is problematic since the adaptive-input HVZK simulator needs to generate the first round without knowing the theorem, hence, we cannot run the MPC simulator of the underlying protocol.

To circumvent this issue, we make use of a special type of commitment scheme, that we call *ambiguous* commitment[5]. Compared to a standard commitment scheme, they can be opened in two modes: binding and equivocal. If the commitment is computed using the binding mode then the commitment is binding, otherwise, it can be equivocated to any message the sender wants.

Using ambiguous commitments, we modify our protocol as follows. The prover generates the views of Π_{MPC} as before, but it creates a 2-out-of-2 secret sharing of each of these views and commits to them using the ambiguous commitment scheme in biding mode (i.e., two commitments per view are generated). Then, the verifier challenges the prover asking to open a random subset of views as before. In addition, for each of the opened views, the verifier asks to see the randomness used to generate one of the two commitments and rejects if it notices that a commitment has not been computed using the binding procedure. The rest of the protocol proceeds as before.

The adaptive-input HVZK simulator, which we recall needs to generate the first round without knowing the theorem, works as follows. On input the challenge it can compute one commitment in equivocal mode (the one for which the simulator will not need to disclose its randomness), and one in binding mode. The

---

[5] Such commitments are sometimes called *equivocal* or *trapdoor* commitments.

binding commitments simply contain a random string. The set of commitments computed in the described way constitutes the first round.

Upon receiving the theorem, the adaptive-input HVZK simulator runs the MPC simulator of Π_{MPC}. At this point, the simulator computes the xor of the i-th view with the random string committed in the i-th binding commitment and opens the equivocal commitment to the obtained value.

The soundness still holds because, intuitively, the verifier performs a cut-and-choose to make sure that the commitments are all computed in binding mode. Clearly, an adversary has still a non-negligible probability of cheating, but by repeating the protocol we obtain a sound protocol.

Non-malleable HVZK with Respect to Commitment. So far we have only argued that our protocol, that we denote with Π_{AI}, is adaptive HVZK and adaptive sound. We also want to argue that our protocol is non-malleable HVZK with respect to commitment. We recall that in this security notion, there is a MiM adversary that on the left session acts as the adversary for the adaptive HVZK security game, and in the right session it acts as the sender for a commitment scheme. In more detail, the adversary picks a challenge and sends it to the left session (that acts as a challenger for the experiment). The challenger tosses a coin b, and if $b = 0$ then it computes the first round of Π_{AI} using the honest prover procedure, otherwise it computes it using the adaptive HVZK simulator. The adversary now picks a statement x and a witness w and sends those to the challenger. If $b = 0$, the challenger runs the honest prover of Π_{AI} on input (x, w) to compute a third-round message, if $b = 1$ instead the challenger runs the HVZK on input x (and the previous state of the simulator), thus obtaining the third message. The challenger then sends this third message to the MiM in the left session and stops.

While the MiM is acting as described in the left session, it concurrently sends a commitment in the right session. We say that Π_{AI} is non-malleable HVZK with respect to commitment, if the distribution of the messages committed on the right session by the MiM does not depend on b.

We prove that Π_{AI} is non-malleable HVZK with respect to any extractable commitment Π_{com}. The idea is to use an adversary to the NMZKC property to construct an adversary for the adaptive-HVZK property. That is, we let the MiM to interact with the adaptive HVZK challenger while at the same time we run the extractor of the commitment scheme to check how the distribution of the committed messages changes. Unfortunately, this simple idea has a major flaw. The rewinds made by the extractor of the commitment might also rewind the challenger of the HVZK security game. Indeed in each rewind made by the extractor, the MiM could send a new theorem-witness pair, and ask for a new third round of Π_{AI}.

To prove that Π_{AI} can cope with such an adversarial behavior, we exploit how our HVZK simulator works. We note that once the challenge is known, then the simulator knows what commitments will be opened to honestly and what commitments will be equivocated. If an adversary during the rewinds samples new theorem-witness, we simply need to run multiple times the simulator of the underlying MPC protocol and equivocate the commitments accordingly. Hence, we can reduce the adversary that wins in the non-malleable HVZK with respect to commitment experiment to an adversary that either breaks the security of our commitment or the security of the underlying MPC protocol.

Σ-*Commitment.* In this work, we also consider a class of three-round public commitment schemes that we call Σ-commitment. A Σ-commitment is hiding against honest receiver (HRH), and in addition, it is extractable. To realize a Σ-commitment $\Sigma = (\mathcal{S}^\Sigma, \mathcal{R}^\Sigma)$, we use the approach of Goyal et al. [22], which makes use of an information-theoretic verifiable secret sharing protocol Π^{vss}. The protocol works as follows. To commit to a message w, the sender $\mathcal{S}^\Sigma$ runs "in its head" the sharing phase of Π^{vss}, with input a message m. Then the sender commits to the views (obtained by the execution of sharing phase of Π^{vss}) of each player separately using a statistical binding commitment scheme Π^{com}. The receiver, upon receiving these commitments, samples a random set $I \subset [n]$, with $|I| \leq t$, and sends it to the sender. Finally, the sender replies by decommitting the views corresponding to the challenge I.

The property of HRH comes from the fact that, if the challenge I is known in advance, then we can commit to a random message and simulate the openings of the commitment. We can prove that a simulated transcript is indistinguishable from the transcript generated by an honest committed with input m via a simple reduction to the security of the statistically binding commitments.

Putting Together Σ and Π_{AI} to Realize a Commit-and-Prove Protocol Π. We use Σ and Π_{AI} to realize a black-box commit-and-prove protocol, which will be the main building block we use to construct our non-malleable commitment scheme. Our commit-and-prove protocol Π works as follows. The prover commits λ-times to the witness w running Σ and proving, using Π_{AI}, that each committed message w satisfies some relation Rel^6. The statement to be proven can be postponed to the last round since Π_{AI} is delayed-input complete.

To make sure that the same message is committed in all these executions, we use a technique proposed by Khurana et al. in [30]. Namely, in each execution of Σ, instead of committing to w, we commit to $w||r$, for some random value r. Then, we use the protocol Π_{AI} to prove that $a = w + r\alpha$, where α is chosen as part of the challenge, and a is sent in the third round from the prover.

As argued in [30], since r is global across all the executions, if $w \neq w'$ then $w + r\alpha \neq w' + r\alpha$ with overwhelming probability due to the Schwartz-Zippel lemma. Therefore, if the committed messages are different across the (multiple) executions, then the statement proven by Π_{AI} must be false, and the soundness of Π_{AI} guarantees that the verifier rejects. The adaptive-input SHVZK follows from the adaptive-input SHVZK of Π_{AI} and the HRH property of Σ.

---

[6] Π_{AI} works for any type of secret sharing scheme, and in our case Π_{AI} is parametrized by the reconstruction algorithm of the verifiable secret sharing Π^{vss} (i.e., the prover of Π_{AI} expects to receive n views generated using the sharing algorithm of Π^{vss}). We note that given that Π^{vss} is information-theoretic, then Π_{AI} still makes black-box use of the underlying cryptographic primitives.

Concrete Instantiation for Robust MPC. As we mentioned, one of the main tool we rely on is a robust MPC protocol. We recall that a robust MPC protocol allows the prover to initially commit only to the offline views, which are input-independent, and only in the last round to "complete the proof" with the online views. The robustness property guarantees that the commitments generated in the first round univocally specify the actual MPC evaluation so that the online steps only consist of an input-distribution phase and deterministic computations. In this way, even if the prover already knows which views are going to be opened, it cannot force the evaluation to output 1 unless $\mathsf{Rel}(x, w) = 1$, except with negligible probability.

Although robustness seems a very strong requirement, we show that a minor modification of the standard BMR protocols leads to an efficient robust MPC scheme. We recall that BMR [3] is a two-phase protocol consisting of an input-independent phase, also called *garbling*, and an online evaluation. In the garbling step, all parties $\mathsf{P}_1, \ldots, \mathsf{P}_n$ involved in the protocol generate a sharing of the garbled circuit according to some fixed secret sharing scheme $\langle \cdot \rangle$ with t-privacy. As in any other garbled-circuit based scheme, to garble a Boolean circuit each wire is assigned two random keys $\boldsymbol{k}_{w,0}, \boldsymbol{k}_{w,1}$ encoding, respectively, the 0-value and 1-value. The goal of the process is to generate four ciphertexts for each gate according to the gate function, such that each output-wire key is encrypted according to all combinations of input-wire keys which evaluate that output wire key. During the online evaluation, these encrypted truth tables, are revealed to all parties so to allow local evaluation of the circuit. Intuitively, it is clear that upon collecting all the input keys, parties can start evaluating the circuit. At this point, this evaluation is completely deterministic and does not require any interaction. For this reason, assuming that the garbling phase is correctly generated and the input-keys corresponding to the input-wires of the circuit are correct, namely, they correspond to the keys generated in the offline phase, the online views generated by each party correspond to a correct evaluation of the garbled circuit and cannot lead to an incorrect result. In the full version, we recall the basics of BMR-style protocols and explain the robustness property in more detail.

2.2   4-Round Non-malleable Commitment Π_{nmc}

We are finally ready to describe how our non-malleable commitment scheme works. Our starting point is the 3-round public-coin commitment scheme of Goyal et al. [24]. This commitment scheme, which we denote with Π_{wnmc}, is non-malleable against adversaries that never commit to $\perp$ (i.e., the adversary always generates well-formed commitments). To lift the security of such a commitment and build a fully non-malleable commitment scheme, [24] run, in parallel to Π_{wnmc}, a zero-knowledge proof.

As noted in [9,24], a standard ZK proof does not suffice since the commitment and the zero-knowledge proof might not be composed in parallel. As such, and as we have already anticipated, in [24] the authors rely on a ZK proof that is rewind-secure. We also note that the statement to be proven by the ZK is fully-formed only in the last round (since Π_{wnmc} consists of 3 rounds.) This inherently requires the ZK protocol to be delayed-input. To the best of our knowledge, the only protocols that satisfy all these properties are that proposed in [23,24], which, unfortunately, make non-black-box use of the underlying primitives. In [9], the authors propose a ZK proof that can be composed in parallel with the weak-non-malleable commitment of Goyal et al., but this approach requires non-black-box access to the commitment scheme.

The idea is to use our commit-and-prove protocol Π, and argue that it can be safely composed in parallel with Π_{wnmc} due to the property of NMZKC. Unfortunately, Π is only honest-verifier zero-knowledge, and here we need a zero-knowledge proof that is secure against any type of adversaries.

To lift the security of our protocol, we rely on the FLS-trick [16] (with some modifications). More concretely, we construct a 4-round zero-knowledge protocol as follows. The verifier generates two commitments of two random strings, $\hat{s}_0$ and $\hat{s}_1$ in the first round and sends two openings in the third round. In parallel, the verifier provides a witness indistinguishable (WI) proof, Π_{comWI}, which guarantees that at least one of the two commitments is binding. In [30], the authors show how to obtain this protocol in a black-box-way. The prover instead uses a 3-round public-coin WI to prove that either the commitment Π_{wnmc} is well-formed or that it committed to $\hat{s}_b$, for some $b \in \{0,1\}$. Since the receiver discloses $\hat{s}_0, \hat{s}_1$ only in the last round, the sender has no way to commit (already in the second round), to either of these two values. As such, the (potentially corrupted) sender, can complete an accepting WI proof only by proving that the non-malleable commitment is well-formed. For more detail, we refer to the technical part of the paper.

3   Preliminaries

Notation. Here we recall some preliminaries that will be useful in the rest of the paper. Let λ denote the security parameter and $\mathsf{negl}(\lambda)$ any function which tends to zero faster than λ^{-c}, for any constant c. We write $[n]$ to denote the set $\{1, \ldots, n\}$. We use the abbreviation PPT to denote probabilistic polynomial-time.

Let $\mathcal{S}$ and $\mathcal{R}$ two interactive algorithms, we denote by $\langle \mathcal{S}(x), \mathcal{R}(y) \rangle(z)$ the distribution of $\mathcal{R}$'s output after an interaction with $\mathcal{S}$ on common input z and private inputs x and y. A *transcript* of $\langle \mathcal{S}(x), \mathcal{R}(y) \rangle(z)$ consists of all the messages exchanged during an interaction between $\mathcal{R}$ and $\mathcal{S}$.

3.1   Commitment Schemes

A commitment scheme $\Pi_{\mathsf{com}} = (\mathcal{S}, \mathcal{R})$ is a two-phase protocol between two PPT interactive algorithms, a sender $\mathcal{S}$ and a receiver $\mathcal{R}$. In the first phase, called *commit phase*, $\mathcal{S}$ on input a message m interacts with $\mathcal{R}$. Let com be the transcript of this interaction. In the second phase, called *decommitment phase*, the sender $\mathcal{S}$ reveals m' and $\mathcal{R}$ accepts the value committed to be m' if and only if S proves that $m = m'$. Typically, a commitment scheme satisfies two main properties: informally, the *binding* property ensures that S cannot open the commitment in two different ways; the *hiding* property guarantees that the commit phase does not reveal any information about the message m. We refer the reader to [18] for more details.

Ambiguous and Extractable Commitments. We formally introduce the notion of *ambiguous commitments*. Compared to regular commitment schemes, with standard commitment and opening algorithms (Com, Dec), ambiguous commitments have two additional algorithms $\mathsf{Com}^{\mathsf{eq}}$ and Eq, which allow the committer to equivocate, i.e., $\mathsf{Com}^{\mathsf{eq}}$ produces an "equivocable commitment" that Eq can open to any message $m \in \{0,1\}^{\ell}$. This type of commitment schemes are sometimes called *trapdoor* or *equivocal* commitments. We provide a formal definition and construction in the full version. In this work, we also use the notion of *extractable commitments* (we refer to the full version for the formal definition). Informally, a commitment scheme is said to be extractable if there exists an efficient extractor that, having black-box access to a malicious committer that successfully performs the commitment phase, is able to extract the committed message.

3.2 Non-malleable Commitments

Here we follow the same notation of Goyal et al. [24]. Let $\Pi = (S, \mathcal{R})$ be a statistically binding commitment scheme and let λ be the security parameter. Consider a man-in-the-middle (MiM) adversary $\mathcal{A}$ that is participating in two interactions called the left and the right interaction. In the left interaction $\mathcal{A}$ is the receiver and interacts with an honest committer S, whereas in the right interaction $\mathcal{A}$ is the committer and interacts with an honest receiver $\mathcal{R}$.

We compare between a MiM execution and a simulated execution. In the MiM execution the adversary $\mathcal{A}$, with auxiliary information z, is simultaneously participating in a left and right session. In the left sessions, the MiM adversary $\mathcal{A}$ interacts with S receiving commitments to values $m_i, i \in [\mathrm{poly}(\lambda)]$, using identities tg_i of its choice. In the right session, $\mathcal{A}$ interacts with $\mathcal{R}$ attempting to commit to related values $\tilde{m}_i$ again using identities of its choice $\widetilde{\mathsf{tg}}_i$. If any of the right commitments is invalid, or undefined, its value is set to $\perp$. For any i such that $\mathsf{tg}_i = \mathsf{tg}_j$, for some j, set $\tilde{m}_i = \perp$ (i.e., any commitment where the adversary uses the same identity of the honest sender is considered invalid). Let $\mathsf{mim}_{\Pi}^{\mathcal{A},m}(z)$ denote a random variable that describes the values $\tilde{m}_i$ and the view of $\mathcal{A}$, in the above experiment.

In the simulated execution, an efficient simulator Sim directly interacts with $\mathcal{R}$. Let $\mathsf{sim}_{\Pi}^{\mathsf{Sim}}(1^{\lambda}, z)$ denote the random variable describing the values $\tilde{m}_i$ committed by $\mathcal{A}$, and the output view of Sim; whenever the view contains in the right session the same identity of any of the identities of the left session, then m is set to $\perp$.

In all the paper we denote by $\tilde{\delta}$ a value associated with the right session (where the adversary $\mathcal{A}$ plays with a receiver) where δ is the corresponding value in the left session. For example, the sender commits to v in the left session while $\mathcal{A}$ commits to $\tilde{v}$ in the right session.

Definition 1 (Non-Malleable (NM) commitment scheme[24]). *A commitment scheme is* NM *with respect to commitment if, for every* PPT *MiM adversary* $\mathcal{A}$, *there exists a* PPT *simulator* Sim *such that for all* $m \in \{0,1\}^{\mathsf{poly}(\lambda)}$ *the following ensembles are computationally indistinguishable:*

$$\{\mathsf{mim}_{\Pi}^{\mathcal{A},m}(z)\}_{z\in\{0,1\}^*} \approx \{\mathsf{sim}_{\Pi}^{S}(1^\lambda,z)\}_{z\in\{0,1\}^*}.$$

In this work, we also consider a weaker class of MiM adversaries called *synchronizing adversaries*. A synchronizing adversary is one that sends its message for every round before obtaining the honest party's message for the next round.

3.3 Σ-Commitments

We introduce the notion of Σ-commitments, which is reminiscent of the notion of Σ-protocols.

Definition 2. *A* Σ-commitment $\Pi^{\Sigma} = ((\mathcal{S}^{\Sigma}, \mathcal{R}^{\Sigma}), \mathsf{Dec}^{\Sigma})$ *is a commitment scheme where: 1) The commitment phase consists of three rounds and it is public-coin, 2) The decommitment phase is non-interactive, and 3) It satisfies the following properties.*

- CORRECTNESS. *Let m be the message the sender $\mathcal{S}^{\Sigma}$ uses during the commitment phase. If both $\mathcal{S}^{\Sigma}$ and $\mathcal{R}^{\Sigma}$ follow the protocol, then the receiver always accepts the commitment as valid. Moreover, if the sender follows the protocol during the decommitment procedure Dec^{Σ} then the receiver accepts m as the committed message.*
- HONEST RECEIVER HIDING (HRH). *There exists a polynomial-time simulator* Sim *such that for any message $m \in \{0,1\}^{\ell}$ and on input a random c (sampled from the space of all the possible $\mathcal{R}^{\Sigma}$'s messages), outputs an accepting commitment transcript of the form (a, c, z) that is computationally indistinguishable from the transcript generated by the honest sender and receiver when the receiver uses m as its input (note that* Sim *needs to generate the transcript without knowing m).*
- t-SPECIAL BINDING. *From any set of t accepting transcripts $\{a, c_i, z_i\}_{i\in[t]}$, with $c_i \neq c_j$ for all $i, j \in [t]$, for the commitment phase it is possible to extract the message m in polynomial-time, where m is the only possible message that the (potentially corrupted) sender can decommit to.*

3.4 Adaptive-Input SHVZK

Definition 3 (Adaptive-input SHVZK). *A delayed-input 3-round protocol* $\Pi = (\mathcal{P}, \mathcal{V})$ *for relation* Rel *satisfies adaptive-input special honest-verifier zero-knowledge (AI-SHVZK) if there exists a* PPT *simulator* Sim $= (\mathsf{Sim}_0, \mathsf{Sim}_1)$ *such that for all* PPT *adversaries $\mathcal{A}$ and for all challenges π^2 there is a negligible function* negl *for which* $\left| \Pr[b' = b] - \frac{1}{2} \right| \leq \mathsf{negl}(\lambda)$ *in the following game.*

$\mathsf{ExpAISHVZK}_{\mathcal{A},\Pi}(1^\lambda, b, \pi^2)$:

1. *The challenger sends* π^1 *to* $\mathcal{A}$, *where:*
   - *If* $b = 0$, $(\pi^1, \mathsf{aux}) \leftarrow \mathcal{P}(1^\lambda, 1^m)$, *with* $m = |x|$
   - *Else, if* $b = 1$, $(\pi^1, \mathsf{aux}) \leftarrow \mathsf{Sim}_0(1^\lambda, 1^m, \pi^2)$
2. $\mathcal{A}$ *sends* (x, w) *to the challenger.*
   - *If* $(x, w) \in \mathsf{Rel}$, *the challenger sends* π^3 *to* $\mathcal{A}$, *where:*
     - *If* $b = 0$, $\pi^3 \leftarrow \mathcal{P}(x, w, \mathsf{aux}, \mathsf{aux}, \pi^2)$
     - *Else, if* $b = 1$, $\pi^3 \leftarrow \mathsf{Sim}_1(x, \mathsf{aux})$
   - *Else, the challenger sends* $\pi^3 = \bot$ *to* $\mathcal{A}$
3. *The adversary* $\mathcal{A}$ *outputs a bit* b'.

3.5 One-of-Two Binding Commitments

We propose a formal definition of the *one-of-two binding commitments* proposed by Khurana et al. in [30]. A one-of-two binding commitment is a three-round interactive protocol Π_{comWI} executed between a prover $\mathcal{P}_{\mathsf{comWI}}$ and a verifier $\mathcal{V}_{\mathsf{comWI}}$. Informally, in this, the prover generates two commitments in the first round, and sends their opening third round. In parallel, the prover performs a WI proof that guarantees that at least one of the two commitments is binding. Moreover, the prover can equivocate the non-binding commitment to any value he likes. In [30] the authors propose a one-of-two binding commitment scheme that makes black-box use of one-to-one OWFs. We propose a formal definition of the properties held by a one-of-two binding commitment scheme. We assume the prover and verifier algorithms are stateful in the following definitions.

Definition 4 (One-of-Two Binding Commitments). *A commitment is one-of-two binding if the following properties hold.*

Correctness:

- *The prover* $\mathcal{P}_{\mathsf{comWI}}$ *on input* 1^λ, *the message* $m_b \in \{0,1\}^\lambda$, *and a bit* b *returns* π_1^{comWI}
- *The verifier on input* 1^λ *and* π_1^{comWI} *samples a random* $\pi_2^{\mathsf{comWI}} \xleftarrow{\$} \{0,1\}^\lambda$ *and returns it.*
- *The prover on input* π_2^{comWI} *and a message* $m_{1-b} \in \{0,1\}^\lambda$ *computes* π_3^{comWI} *and returns* $(\pi_3^{\mathsf{comWI}}, m_0, m_1)$
- *The verifier on input* $(\pi_1^{\mathsf{comWI}}, \pi_2^{\mathsf{comWI}}, \pi_3^{\mathsf{comWI}}, m_0, m_1)$ *returns* $d \in \{0,1\}$, *where* $d = 1$ *denotes that the verifier accepts, and* 0 *that he rejects.*

Binding: *For any* PPT *adversary* $\mathcal{A}$, *we have that the following holds. Let* $\tau = (\pi_1^{\mathsf{comWI}}, \pi_2^{\mathsf{comWI}})$ *be the first two rounds generated during the execution of* Π_{comWI} *by an honest receiver* $\mathcal{V}_{\mathsf{comWI}}$ *and the stateful adversarial prover* $\mathcal{A}(1^\lambda)$. *We have that*

$$\Pr[(\pi_3^{\mathsf{comWI}}, m_0, m_1, \overline{\pi}_3^{\mathsf{comWI}}, \overline{m}_0, \overline{m}_1) \leftarrow \mathcal{A}(1^\lambda)| \, \mathcal{V}_{\mathsf{comWI}}(\tau, \pi_3^{\mathsf{comWI}}, m_0, m_1) = 1 \, \wedge$$
$$\mathcal{V}_{\mathsf{comWI}}(\tau, \overline{\pi}_3^{\mathsf{comWI}}, \overline{m}_0, \overline{m}_1) = 1 \, \wedge \, m_0 \neq \overline{m}_0 \, \wedge \, m_1 \neq \overline{m}_1] \leq \mathsf{negl}(\lambda)$$

Equivocability: *For any adversary $\mathcal{A}$ and any $m_0, m_1 \in \{0,1\}^\lambda$ we have that* $\left| \Pr[b' = b] - \frac{1}{2} \right| \leq \mathsf{negl}(\lambda)$ *in the following game.*
$\mathsf{ExpEq}_{\mathcal{A},\Pi}(1^\lambda, b, m_0, m_1)$:

1. *The challenger sends* $\pi_1^{\mathsf{comWI}} \leftarrow \mathcal{P}_{\mathsf{comWI}}(1^\lambda, m_b, b)$ *to* $\mathcal{A}$.
2. $\mathcal{A}$ *sends* π_2^{comWI} *to the challenger*
3. *The challenger sends* $\pi_3^{\mathsf{comWI}} \leftarrow \mathcal{P}_{\mathsf{comWI}}(\pi_2^{\mathsf{comWI}}, m_{1-b})$ *to* $\mathcal{A}$.
4. *The adversary* $\mathcal{A}$ *outputs a bit* b'.

3.6   MPC Definitions

In this work, we consider MPC protocols $\Pi = \Pi^{\mathsf{off,on}} = (\mathsf{P}_1, \ldots, \mathsf{P}_n)$, among n parties $\mathsf{P}_1, \ldots, \mathsf{P}_n$, that are composed of two sub-protocols $\Pi^{\mathsf{off}} = (\mathsf{P}_1, \ldots, \mathsf{P}_n)$ and $\Pi^{\mathsf{on}} = (\mathsf{P}_1, \ldots, \mathsf{P}_n)$, where the execution Π^{off} does not require parties' private inputs, namely Π^{off} is *input independent*. If each party P_i, for $i \in [n]$, runs Π honestly, then the execution of Π is called an *honest execution*. A view view_i of a party P_i is composed by its private input w_i, randomness r_i, and transcript τ_i, where τ_i is given by the set of messages received and sent by party P_i during the execution of the MPC protocol Π. We denote the view of the offline and of the online phase for a party P_i with $\mathsf{view}_i^{\mathsf{off}}$ and $\mathsf{view}_i^{\mathsf{on}}$ respectively.

In the rest of the paper, we consider MPC protocols where all parties share a public input x, and each party P_i additionally holds a local private input w_i and random tape r_i. We consider protocols $\Pi^{\mathsf{off,on}}$ which securely realize an n-party functionality f. The output $y = f(x, w_1, \ldots, w_n)$ can be computed from any $\mathsf{view}_i = (\mathsf{view}_i^{\mathsf{off}}, \mathsf{view}_i^{\mathsf{on}})$, i.e., $y = \Pi_f^{\mathsf{off,on}}(\mathsf{view}_i) = \mathsf{out}_i$, for each $i \in [n]$.

We assume familiarity with the standard definition of MPC (referring the reader to the full version for a formal discussion), and here we formally introduce a new special property for an MPC protocol $\Pi = \Pi^{\mathsf{off,on}} = (\mathsf{P}_1, \ldots, \mathsf{P}_n)$.

Looking ahead, in our delayed-input protocol the prover, while committed to $\mathsf{view}_1^{\mathsf{off}}, \ldots, \mathsf{view}_n^{\mathsf{off}}$, is allowed to generate the online views $\mathsf{view}_1^{\mathsf{on}}, \ldots, \mathsf{view}_n^{\mathsf{on}}$ only when it received (x, w), and after it is given any eventual random inputs and the set of k parties/views it will need to open. This means that a malicious prover $\mathcal{P}$ might arbitrarily create inconsistent views $\mathsf{view}_{i_1}^{\mathsf{on}}, \ldots, \mathsf{view}_{i_{n-k}}^{\mathsf{on}}$ that will not be opened, easily making all outputs to be incorrect without being caught. For this reason we need an underlying MPC protocol with strong security requirements and introduce the following definition of *robustness*.

Despite the name, this notion is different from the definition of robustness that was given in [28] to generalize the definition of correctness in case of malicious adversaries.

Roughly, an MPC protocol $\Pi = \Pi^{\mathsf{off,on}}$ is said to be robust if, given two subsets $A, H \subset [n]$, with $|H| = n - |A|$, and a correct execution of Π^{off}, the output out_j of some P_j, with $j \in A$, obtained by running the protocol on input $(x, (w_i)_{i \in A}, (w_i)_{i \in H})$ and using some arbitrary randomness r'_j, is not $\bot$ then $\mathsf{out}_j = y$, where $y = \Pi_f^{\mathsf{off,on}}(\mathsf{view}_i), \forall i \in H$. Note that our definition specifically assumes an MPC protocol $\Pi^{\mathsf{on,off}}$ in the pre-processing model with a correctly executed Π^{off} and requires that every unbounded adversary $\mathcal{A}$ cannot make the parties in A output a result inconsistent with the views of honest parties. The formal definition of robustness follows.

Definition 5 (Robustness). *Let* $\Pi^{\mathrm{off},\mathrm{on}} = (\mathrm{P}_1, \ldots, \mathrm{P}_n)$ *be as above. Let* $A \subset [n]$ *and* $H = [n] - A$. *Let us denote by* view *the view* $\{\mathrm{view}_i = (\mathrm{view}_i^{\mathrm{off}}, \mathrm{view}_i^{\mathrm{on}})\}_{i \in H}, \{\widetilde{\mathrm{view}}_i = (\widetilde{\mathrm{view}}_i^{\mathrm{off}}, \widetilde{\mathrm{view}}_i^{\mathrm{on}})\}_{i \in A}$, *such that:*

- $\widetilde{\mathrm{view}}_i^{\mathrm{off}}$ *and* $\widetilde{\mathrm{view}}_i^{\mathrm{on}}$ *are the views generated by running the code of* P_i *for* Π^{off} *and* Π^{on} *on input* (x, w_i), *respectively, with some arbitrary randomness* $r_i' \in \{0,1\}^\lambda$, *for each* $i \in A$;
- $\mathrm{view}_i^{\mathrm{off}}$ *is the view generated running the code of party* P_i *for* Π^{off} *with some arbitrary randomness* $r_i' \in \{0,1\}^\lambda$, *for each* $i \in H$;
- $\mathrm{view}_i^{\mathrm{on}} \in \{0,1\}^*$, *for each* $i \in H$.

We say that $\Pi^{\mathrm{off},\mathrm{on}}$ *realizes a deterministic n-party functionality* $f(x, w_1, \ldots, w_n)$ *with robustness if for any* A *and* H, *such that* $H = \{i_1, \ldots, i_{n-t}\}$ *and* $A = \{j_1, \ldots, j_t\}$, *the following holds: if, for each* $j_k \in A$, *party* P_{j_k}, *on input randomness* r_{j_k} *and* (x, w_{j_k}), *outputs* $\mathrm{out}_{j_k} = F \neq \bot$ *with respect to the view* view, *then* $F = f_A(x, w_{i_1}, \ldots, w_{i_{n-t}})$, *for some* $w_{i_1}, \ldots, w_{i_{n-t}}$ *with* $\{i_1, \ldots, i_{n-t}\} = H$, *where* f_A *is the function evaluated on* n *inputs where the inputs in positions* $A = \{j_1, \ldots, j_t\}$ *are* $w_{j_1}, \ldots, w_{j_t}$.

Intuitively, the above definition says that as long as Π^{off} is correct (concretely this can be achieved instantiating Π^{off} with a malicious secure protocol) and the online phase Π^{on} is a deterministic function of the offline phase, then Π is robust. Notice the definition of robustness is independent of the number of corruptions supported by Π and it can be achieved both with an honest and dishonest majority. In the full-version we show a concrete instantiation of a robust MPC protocol.

3.7 Verifiable Secret Sharing (VSS)

A verifiable secret sharing (VSS) scheme [6] is a two-phase protocol carried out among $n+1$ parties. In the first step, a special party, also referred to as the *dealer*, shares a secret among all the other n parties, referred to as *share-holders*, at most t of whom may be corrupt; in the second step, parties reconstruct the secret. While in standard secret-sharing schemes the dealer is assumed to be honest, in VSS schemes also the dealer can be corrupt. Loosely speaking, if the dealer is honest, then no information about the dealer's secret is revealed to the t corrupt parties by the end of the sharing phase; moreover, by the end of the sharing phase even a dishonest dealer is committed to some value that will be recovered by the honest parties in the reconstruction phase. Furthermore, if the dealer is honest then this committed value must be identical to the dealer's initial input.

Definition 6 (Verifiable Secret Sharing [5,6]). *An $(n+1, t)$-perfectly secure Verifiable Secret Sharing (VSS) scheme Π^σ consists of a pair of protocols (Share, Recon) that implement respectively the sharing and reconstruction phases as follows.*

- *Sharing Phase (Share). Party P_{n+1} (the dealer) runs on input a secret s and randomness r_{n+1}, while any other party P_i, $i \in [n]$, runs on input a randomness r_i. During this phase parties can send (both private and broadcast) messages in multiple rounds. We will indicate with view_i the view that P_i obtains at the end of sharing phase, and with $(\text{view}_1, \ldots, \text{view}_n) = \text{Share}(s, r_1, \ldots, r_n, r_{n+1})$ the process described above.*
- *Reconstruction Phase (Recon). Each shareholder sends its view view_i, $i \in [n]$, of the sharing phase to each other party, and on input the views of all parties (that might include corrupt or empty views) each party outputs a reconstruction of the secret s. All computations performed by honest parties are efficient.*

The following security properties hold.

Commitment. *If the dealer is dishonest then one of the following two cases happen: 1) during the sharing phase honest parties disqualify the dealer, therefore they output a special value $\perp$ and will refuse to run the reconstruction phase; 2) during the sharing phase honest parties do not disqualify the dealer, therefore such a phase determines a unique value s^*, that belongs to the set of possible legal values that does not include $\perp$, which will be reconstructed by the honest parties during the reconstruction phase.*

Secrecy. *The computationally unbounded adversary can corrupt up to t parties that can deviate from the above procedures. If the dealer is honest, then the adversary's view during the sharing phase reveals no information about s. More formally, the adversary's view is identically distributed under all different values of s.*

Perfect Correctness. *If the dealer is honest throughout the protocols then each honest party will output the shared secret s at the end of protocol Recon with probability 1.*

Assuming a broadcast channel, perfectly-secure $(n + 1, \lfloor n/4 \rfloor)$-VSS scheme are implemented in [17].

4 Non-malleable HVZK with Respect to Commitment

In this section, we introduce the new notion of non-malleable HVZK with respect to commitment (NMZKC). Let $\Pi = (\mathcal{P}, \mathcal{V})$ be a proof system, and Π_{com} be a (potentially interactive) commitment scheme. We consider a scenario where a man-in-the-middle adversary $\mathcal{A}$ interacts in the left session with the prover of Π (hence, $\mathcal{A}$ acts as the verifier for Π), and in the right session $\mathcal{A}$ acts as the sender for Π_{com} against an honest receiver. the formal definition of NMZKC follows, and we refer to the introductory section of the paper for an informal discussion about this definition. Let $(\mathsf{Sim}_0, \mathsf{Sim}_1)$ be the adaptive-input HVZK simulator for Π, we define the experiment $\mathsf{ExpZK}_{\mathcal{A},\Pi,\Pi_{\mathrm{com}}}(1^\lambda, b, c)$.

$\mathsf{ExpZK}_{\mathcal{A},\Pi,\Pi_{\mathrm{com}}}(1^\lambda, b, c)$: In the right session, interact with $\mathcal{A}$ as the receiver of Π_{com}. In the left session, act as follows.

1. Set $\pi_2 \leftarrow c$ and send π^1 to $\mathcal{A}$, where:
   - If $b = 0$, $(\pi^1, \mathsf{aux}) \xleftarrow{\$} \mathcal{P}(1^\lambda, 1^m)$, with $m = |x|$
   - If $b = 1$, $(\pi^1, \mathsf{aux}) \xleftarrow{\$} \mathsf{Sim}_0(1^\lambda, 1^m, \pi^2)$
2. Upon receiving (x, w) from $\mathcal{A}$ in the left session do the following
   - If $(x, w) \in \mathsf{Rel}$, the experiment sends π^3 to $\mathcal{A}$ in the left session where:
     - If $b = 0$, $\pi^3 \leftarrow \mathcal{P}(x, w, \mathsf{aux}, \pi^2)$
     - Else, if $b = 1$, $\pi^3 \xleftarrow{\$} \mathsf{Sim}_1(x, \mathsf{aux})$
   - Else, the experiment sets $\pi^3 \leftarrow \bot$
3. Set the output of the experiment as the output of $\mathcal{A}$ and its view.

Definition 7 (NMZKC). *Let Π_{com} be a commitment scheme. We say that an adaptive-input HVZK proof system Π, with challenge space $\mathcal{C}$, is a non-malleable HVZK with respect to commitment for Π_{com} if there exists a PPT simulator $\mathsf{Sim} = (\mathsf{Sim}_0, \mathsf{Sim}_1)$ such that, for all PPT adversary $\mathcal{A}$, the following two distributions are indistinghuishable:*

$$\{\mathsf{ExpZK}_{\mathcal{A},\Pi,\Pi_{\mathrm{com}}}(1^\lambda, 0, c), m_0\}_{\lambda \in \mathbb{N}, c \in \mathcal{C}}, \quad \{\mathsf{ExpZK}_{\mathcal{A},\Pi,\Pi_{\mathrm{com}}}(1^\lambda, 1, c), m_1\}_{\lambda \in \mathbb{N}, c \in \mathcal{C}}$$

where $\mathsf{ExpZK}_{\mathcal{A},\Pi,\Pi_{\mathrm{com}}}(1^\lambda, b, c)$ is the experiment described above and m_b, with $b \leftarrow \{0, 1\}$, is the message committed in the right session of $\mathsf{ExpZK}_{\mathcal{A},\Pi,\Pi_{\mathrm{com}}}(1^\lambda, b, c)$ by $\mathcal{A}$.

We note that non-malleable HVZK with respect to commitment property is parallel composable w.r.t. multiple left sessions. The proof would follow via standard hybrid arguments.

5   Our Delayed-Input MPC-in-the-Head Protocol Π_{AI}

Let L be an $\mathcal{NP}$-language and Rel be the corresponding $\mathcal{NP}$-relation. Let f be an $(n + 1)$-argument function, with $n > 2$, corresponding to Rel, i.e., $f(x, w_1, \ldots, w_n) = \mathsf{Rel}(x, w_1 \oplus \cdots \oplus w_n)$. Our protocol, $\Pi_{\mathsf{AI}} = (\mathcal{P}_{\mathsf{AI}}, \mathcal{V}_{\mathsf{AI}})$, for the $\mathcal{NP}$-relation Rel makes use of the following tools:

- A t_p-private MPC protocol $\Pi^{\mathsf{off},\mathsf{on}} = (\mathsf{P}_1, \ldots, \mathsf{P}_n)$ that realizes f with robustness (Definition 5).
- An ambiguous commitment scheme $\Pi_{\mathrm{com}} = (\mathsf{Com}, \mathsf{Dec}, \mathsf{Com}^{\mathsf{eq}}, \mathsf{Eq})$.

A complete description of $\Pi_{\mathsf{AI}} = (\mathcal{P}_{\mathsf{AI}}, \mathcal{V}_{\mathsf{AI}})$ for the $\mathcal{NP}$-relation Rel can be found in Fig. 1. At a high level, given an MPC protocol $\Pi^{\mathsf{off},\mathsf{on}}$, as specified above, $\mathcal{P}_{\mathsf{AI}}$ starts by emulating Π^{off} in its head. In particular, it generates n views

COMMON INPUTS: At the beginning of the third round both $\mathcal{P}_{AI}$ and $\mathcal{V}_{AI}$ gets x, while the parameters k, c, n (which are small constants) and $k < t_p$ are specified when the protocol starts.

PRIVATE INPUT: At the beginning of the third round $\mathcal{P}_{AI}$ gets a random n-out-of-n secret sharing of the witness $w = w_1 \oplus \cdots \oplus w_n$.

Round 1. $\mathcal{P}_{AI}$ computes the following steps.

1. Run Π^{off} "in its head" (by choosing uniform random coins r_i for each party) to generate the transcript of each party P_i. Let $\text{view}_i^{\text{off}}$ denote the view of P_i in the execution of Π^{off}.

2. For each $i \in [n]$, choose c random values $\{\text{view}_{(i,j)}^{\text{off}}\}_{j \in [c]}$ such that $\text{view}_i^{\text{off}} = \text{view}_{(i,1)}^{\text{off}} \oplus \text{view}_{(i,2)}^{\text{off}}, \ldots, \oplus \text{view}_{(i,c)}^{\text{off}}$.

3. For each $i \in [n]$, compute $\{(\text{com}_{(i,j)}, \text{dec}_{(i,j)}) \leftarrow \text{Com}(\text{view}_{(i,j)}^{\text{off}}; R_{(i,j)})\}_{j \in [c]}$.

4. Send $\{\text{com}_{(1,j)}, \ldots, \text{com}_{(n,j)}\}_{j \in [c]}$ to $\mathcal{V}_{AI}$.

Round 2. $\mathcal{V}_{AI}$ chooses a random a subset of distinct indices $I = \{i_1, \ldots, i_k\} \subset [n]$, with $|I| = k \leq t_p$; and for each index i_j it chooses a random value $q_{i_j} \in [c]$. $\mathcal{V}_{AI}$ sends $(I, q_{i_1}, \ldots, q_{i_k})$ to $\mathcal{P}_{AI}$.

Round 3. Upon receiving $(x, (w_1 \oplus \cdots \oplus w_n))$, where $w = w_1 \oplus \cdots \oplus w_n$ s.t. $\text{Rel}(x, w) = 1$, $\mathcal{P}_{AI}$ computes the following steps:

1. Simulate the behaviour of the party P_i while running Π^{on} on input r_i, x, w_i. For each $i_j \in I$, let view_{i_j} be the view of P_{i_j} in the execution of Π which is composed of $\text{view}_{i_j}^{\text{off}}$ and $\text{view}_{i_j}^{\text{on}}$.

2. Let $C_{i_j} = \{1, \ldots, c\} \setminus \{q_{i_j}\}$. For each $i_j \in I$, send to $\mathcal{V}_{AI}$ the following:
$$\left(\{(\text{view}_{(i_j,l)}^{\text{off}}, \text{dec}_{(i_j,l)})\}_{l \in C_{i_j}}, (\text{view}_{(i_j,q_{i_j})}^{\text{off}}), R_{(i_j,q_{i_j})}), \text{view}_{i_j}^{\text{on}} \right).$$

Verification step. $\mathcal{V}_{AI}$ outputs 1 if and only if all the following checks pass.

1. For $i_j \in I$ check that
   - $\text{Dec}(\text{com}_{(i_j,l)}, \text{view}_{(i_j,l)}^{\text{off}}, \text{dec}_{(i_j,l)}) = 1$, for all $l \in C_{i_j}$
   - $\text{Com}(\text{view}_{(i_j,q_{i_j})}^{\text{off}}; R_{(i_j,q_{i_j})}) = \text{com}_{(i_j,q_{i_j})}$.

2. The output of P_{i_j} is $\neq \perp$, for each $i_j \in I$.

3. The views $\text{view}_{i_1}, \ldots, \text{view}_{i_k}$ are consistent, where $\text{view}_{i_j}^{\text{off}} = \bigoplus_{l \in [c]} \text{view}_{(i_j,l)}^{\text{off}}$

Fig. 1. $\Pi_{AI} = (\mathcal{P}_{AI}, \mathcal{V}_{AI})$

$\text{view}_i^{\text{off}}, i \in [n]$, corresponding to the n virtual parties and separately commits to these views using an ambiguous commitment scheme Π_{com}. This is done by sampling c random values $\{\text{view}_{(i,j)}^{\text{off}}\}_{j \in [c]}$, for each $i \in [n]$, such that $\text{view}_i^{\text{off}} = \bigoplus_{j \in [c]} \text{view}_{i,j}^{\text{off}}$, and computing $\{(\text{com}_{(i,j)}, \text{dec}_{(i,j)}) \leftarrow \text{Com}(\text{view}_{(i,j)}^{\text{off}}; R_{(i,j)})\}_{j \in [c]}$. Notice here $c \geq 2$ is a small integer. This will allow the verifier to check that the commitments are correctly generated and Π^{off} is honestly executed; moreover, it will be crucial to prove adaptive-input SHVZK, as we will see later.

The prover sends the first message π^1, given by the concatenation of all the commitments, to $\mathcal{V}$ which replies with the challenge π^2, i.e., a set of random indices $I = \{i_1, \ldots, i_k\} \subset [n]$ with $k \leq t_p$, and one index $q_{i_j} \in [c]$ for each $i \in I$.

In the last round, both $\mathcal{P}$ and $\mathcal{V}$ receive the theorem x, while $\mathcal{P}$ also receives w. in the last round, $\mathcal{P}$ first completes the emulation of the MPC protocol, producing all the online views $\text{view}_i^{\text{on}}, i \in [n]$; secondly, it sends $\text{view}_i^{\text{on}}, i \in I$, and opens the corresponding commitments in π^1 as follows. The commitments corresponding to the indices q_{i_j} in π^2 are opened in a "binding way", by sending $\mathsf{view}^{\mathsf{off}}_{i_j,q_{i_j}}$ and $R_{i_j,q_{i_j}}$, $i_j \in I$, and the remaining $c-1$ commitments, for each $i_j \in I$, are opened by sending the opening information $\mathsf{dec}_{i_j,q}$, along with $\mathsf{view}^{\mathsf{off}}_{i_j,q}$, for each $q \in \{1,\ldots,c\} \setminus q_{i_j}$.

Finally, the verifier checks all the commitments. It verifies that all the parties in I output 1 and that their views are consistent with each other. To simplify the composition of our protocol with other primitives, we design the prover so that it expects to receive a (random) n-out-of-n secret sharing of the witness (instead of the witness itself). This is without loss of generality. We finally note that our protocol can be parameterized to work with any n-out-of-n secret sharing scheme. Moreover, it would remain black-box in the use of the underlying cryptographic primitives as long the reconstruction phase of the secret sharing scheme does make any calls to a cryptographic primitive. We prove the following result.

Theorem 1. *If $\Pi^{\mathsf{off},\mathsf{on}}$ is an MPC protocol that realizes f (which is described above) with t_p-privacy and robustness, and Π_{com} is an ambiguous commitment scheme, then $\Pi_{\mathsf{AI}} = (\mathcal{P}_{\mathsf{AI}}, \mathcal{V}_{\mathsf{AI}})$ (Fig. 1) for the $\mathcal{NP}$-relation Rel is a 3-round public-coin delayed-input protocol satisfying adaptive-input SHVZK adaptive-input soundness with constant soundness error.*

We establish adaptive correctness, adaptive-input soundness and adaptive-input SHVZK. Correctness follows by inspection.

ADAPTIVE-INPUT SOUNDNESS (Intuition). At a high level, we can see that soundness can be proved using the robustness property of the MPC protocol Π and the security properties of Π_{com}. If all the offline views are correctly generated, then robustness ensures that a malicious prover will always get caught. Hence a malicious prover can succeed either if incorrect offline views are generated, or if some of the commitments are not computed in *binding mode*. We can argue that the probability of the adversary being caught in either of the two cases is noticeable.

ADAPTIVE-INPUT SPECIAL HONEST-VERIFIER ZERO-KNOWLEDGE (Intuition). At a high level, the simulator $\mathsf{Sim} = (\mathsf{Sim}^0_{\mathsf{AI}}, \mathsf{Sim}^1_{\mathsf{AI}})$ works as follows. Let the challenge be $(I, q_{i_1}, \ldots, q_{i_k})$, and let $C_{i_j} = \{1,\ldots,c\} \setminus \{q_{i_j}\}$. For each $i_j \in I$, and each $l \in C_{i_j}$, $\mathsf{Sim}^0_{\mathsf{AI}}$ computes a random value $\mathsf{view}_{(i_j,l)}$. Then $\mathsf{Sim}^0_{\mathsf{AI}}$ generates the following commitments. For each $i_j \notin I$ and $q \in [c]$ set $\mathsf{com}_{(i_j,q)}$ as a commitment of the the all-zero string; for each $i_j \in I$ compute the commitment $\mathsf{com}_{(i_j,q_{i_j})}$ in binding mode, and for each $l \in C_{i_j}$ compute $\mathsf{com}_{(i_j,l)}$ in equivocal mode. These commitments constitute the simulated message π^1. In the second phase, when x is available, $\mathsf{Sim}^1_{\mathsf{AI}}$ uses the MPC simulator to obtain $(\mathsf{view}^{\mathsf{off}}_i, \mathsf{view}^{\mathsf{on}}_i)$, $i \in [n]$. For each $i_j \in I$ and for each $l \in C_{i_j}$ compute $\mathsf{view}^{\mathsf{off}}_{i_j,l}$, such that $\mathsf{view}^{\mathsf{off}}_{i_j,q_{i_j}} = \mathsf{view}^{\mathsf{off}}_{i_j} \bigoplus_{l \in C_{i_j}} \mathsf{view}^{\mathsf{off}}_{i_j,l}$. Finally, for each $i_j \in I$, $l \in C_{i_j}$ equivocate the commitment $\mathsf{com}_{i_j,l}$ to $\mathsf{view}^{\mathsf{off}}_{i_j,l}$, and sends the openings of all the commitments to complete the third round.

Lemma 1. *Let Π_{ComExt} be a 3-round extractable commitment scheme with a polynomial time extractor Ext, that extracts with non-negligible probability, then Π_{AI} is non-malleable HVZK with respect to commitment Π_{ComExt} against synchronizing adversaries.*

The proof of the lemma can be found in the full version.

We recall that the commitment scheme Π_{com} used in Π_{AI} can be instantiated with any NI statistically binding scheme, which can be constructed from any one-to-one OWF. In addition, following [28], when we say that our protocols make black-box use of $\Pi^{\mathsf{off,on}}$, it simply means that they are invoking the "next-message function" of each party. Therefore, when Π_{com} is implemented using a black-box reduction to one-way functions, the protocol Π_{AI} only makes black-box use of one-way functions. More formally,

Corollary 1. *Assuming the existence of one-to-one one-way functions, there exists a 3-round public-coin delayed-input protocol satisfying adaptive-input soundness (with constant soundness error), and adaptive-input SHVZK, which makes black-box use of 1-1 OWFs. Moreover, let Π_{ComExt} be a 3-round extractable commitment scheme with a polynomial time extractor, that extracts with non-negligible probability, then there exists a 3-round public-coin delayed-input protocol that is non-malleable HVZK with respect to commitment for Π_{ComExt} against synchronizing adversaries that makes black-box use of the 1-1 OWFs.*

6 The Building Blocks of the 4-Round Black-Box Non-malleable Commitment Scheme

In this section, we define the main building blocks necessary to define our 4-round non-malleable commitment scheme.

6.1 Commitment from Verifiable Secret Sharing

We start by recalling some of the techniques introduced by Goyal et al. [22]. We show that these techniques can be used to build a Σ-commitment (Definition 2) that we denote by $\Pi = ((\mathcal{S}^\Sigma, \mathcal{R}^\Sigma), \mathsf{Dec}^\Sigma)$ and formally describe it in Fig. 2. The protocol makes use of the following primitives:

- An $(n + 1, t)$-VSS protocol $\Pi^{\mathsf{vss}} = (\Pi_{\mathsf{Share}}, \Pi_{\mathsf{Recon}})$ as defined in Definition 6. Concretely, the protocol uses a VSS scheme with a deterministic reconstruction procedure, like the $(n + 1, \lfloor n/4 \rfloor)$-VSS scheme described by Gennaro et al. [17]
- A statistically binding commitment scheme $\Pi^{\mathsf{com}} = (\mathsf{Com}, \mathsf{Dec})$.

The protocol works as follows. To commit to a message w, the sender $\mathcal{S}^\Sigma$ runs "in its head" the protocol Π_{Share}, which implements the sharing phase of Π^{vss}, with input w. Then the sender commits to the views view_j (obtained by the execution of Π_{Share}) of each P_j separately using a statistical binding commitment

---

COMMON INPUTS: Both $\mathcal{S}^\Sigma$ and $\mathcal{R}^\Sigma$ get parameters t, n, k, where t, n are the parameters corresponding to the VSS $\Pi^{\text{vss}} = (\Pi_{\text{Share}}, \Pi_{\text{Recon}})$, and $k \leq t$.
PRIVATE INPUT: At the beginning $\mathcal{S}^\Sigma$ gets a private message w.

Commitment procedure: $(\mathcal{S}^\Sigma, \mathcal{R}^\Sigma)$

  Round 1. $\mathcal{S}^\Sigma$ proceeds as follows.
   1. Run the sharing phase of Π^{vss} "in its head" on input w to generate the views view_j^σ, for each $j \in [n]$.
   2. Compute $(\text{com}_j^\sigma, \text{dec}_j^\sigma) \leftarrow \text{Com}(\text{view}_j^\sigma)$ for $j \in [n]$.
   3. Set
      - $\text{dec}^\sigma = \{\text{dec}_j^\sigma, \text{view}_j^\sigma\}_{j \in [n]}$
      - $\pi_1^\sigma = (\text{com}_1^\sigma, \ldots, \text{com}_n^\sigma)$
   4. Send π_1^σ to $\mathcal{R}^\Sigma$.
  Round 2. $\mathcal{R}^\Sigma$ executes the following steps.
   1. Choose a random subset $I = \{i_1, \ldots, i_k\} \subset [n]$.
   2. Define and send $\pi_2^\sigma = (i_i, \ldots, i_k)$ to $\mathcal{S}^\Sigma$.
  Round 3. $\mathcal{S}^\Sigma$ computes the following steps:
   1. Define and send $\pi_3^\sigma = \{\text{view}_j^\sigma, \text{dec}_j^\sigma\}_{j \in I}$ to $\mathcal{R}^\Sigma$.
   2. Set $\text{com}_\sigma = (\pi_1^\sigma, \pi_2^\sigma, \pi_3^\sigma)$
  Verification step. $\mathcal{R}^\Sigma$ accepts the commitment if and only if:
   1. $\text{Dec}(\text{com}_j^\sigma, \text{view}_j^\sigma, \text{dec}_j^\sigma) = 1$ and the output of P_j in Π^{vss} is not $\perp$, for each $j \in I$.
   2. The views $\text{view}_{i_1}^\sigma, \ldots, \text{view}_{i_k}^\sigma$ are consistent.

Decommitment procedure: $\text{Dec}^\Sigma(\text{com}_\sigma, w, \text{dec}_\sigma)$
   1. Parse dec^σ as $\{\text{dec}_j^\sigma, \text{view}_j^\sigma, w_j\}_{j \in I}$.
   2. Use $\{\text{view}_j^\sigma\}_{j \in [n]}$ as the inputs of Π_{Recon} thus obtaining w.
   3. Check that for all $j \in [n]$ it holds that $\text{Dec}(\text{com}_j^\sigma, \text{view}_j^\sigma, \text{dec}_j^\sigma) = 1$.
  If the above conditions hold, $\mathcal{R}^\Sigma$ outputs w, else it returns $\perp$.

Fig. 2. $\Pi = ((\mathcal{S}^\Sigma, \mathcal{R}^\Sigma), \text{Dec}^\Sigma)$

scheme Π^{com}. The receiver, upon receiving these commitments, samples a random set $I \subset [n]$, with $|I| \leq t$, and sends it to the sender. Finally, the sender replies by decommitting the views corresponding to the challenge I. This concludes the commit phase.

In the full version, we prove the following theorem that we shall use in the next sections.

Theorem 2. *Let Π^{vss} be a $(n + 1, t)$-VSS protocol satisfying Definition 6, with $t = k$, $t < \frac{1}{4}n$, and let Π^{com} be a statistically binding commitment scheme, then $\Pi = ((\mathcal{S}^\Sigma, \mathcal{R}^\Sigma), \text{Dec}^\Sigma)$ (see Fig. 2) is a Σ-commitment.*

6.2   Commit-and-Prove

In this section we construct a 3-round public-coin commit-and-prove protocol $\Pi_{\text{CP}} = (\mathcal{P}_{\text{CP}}, \mathcal{V}_{\text{CP}})$ that allows proving the knowledge of a committed value w

such that $\mathsf{Rel}(x, w) = 1$, for some statement x. Our protocol makes black-box use of the underlying primitives.

The protocol $\Pi_{\mathsf{CP}} = (\mathcal{P}_{\mathsf{CP}}, \mathcal{V}_{\mathsf{CP}})$ is fully described in Fig. 3. It makes use of the following tools:

– The Σ-commitment $\Sigma = ((\mathcal{S}^\Sigma, \mathcal{R}^\Sigma), \mathsf{Dec}^\Sigma)$ defined in Fig. 2, Sect. 6.1.
– The adaptive-input SHVZK $\Pi_{\mathsf{AI}} = (\mathcal{P}_{\mathsf{AI}}, \mathcal{V}_{\mathsf{AI}})$ with adaptive-input soundness for the $\mathcal{NP}$-relation

$$\mathsf{Rel}_{\mathsf{AI}} = \{(x, a, \alpha, \{\mathsf{view}_{i_j}\}_{j \in [k]}), (r, \{\mathsf{view}_i\}_{j \in [n]}) : 1 \leq i_1 < \cdots < i_k < n \wedge$$
$$w = \mathsf{Recon}(\{\mathsf{view}_i\}_{j \in [n]}) \wedge \mathsf{Rel}(x, w) = 1 \wedge a = w + r\alpha\}.$$

where Recon is the reconstruction phase of an information-theoretic $(n + 1, t)$-VSS protocol Π^{vss}, with $k \leq t$. We recall that to run Π_{AI} the prover needs the statement and the witness only in the third round. Moreover, the prover expects to receive the witness in a secret shared form. We recall that Π_{AI} works for any type of secret sharing scheme, and in our case Π_{AI} is parametrized by the reconstruction algorithm of the verifiable secret sharing Π^{vss} (i.e., the prover expects to receive n views generated using the sharing algorithm of Π^{vss}). We note that given that Π^{vss} is information-theoretic, then Π_{AI} still makes black-box use of the underlying cryptographic primitives. We also need Π_{AI} with the same parameters n, k, t as Σ.

At a high-level $\mathcal{P}_{\mathsf{CP}}$ commits λ^2-times to the witness w running Σ (as described in Fig. 2) and proving, using $\mathcal{P}_{\mathsf{AI}}$, that each committed message w satisfies the relation Rel, and moreover that the views opened in the third round of Σ contain shares of the witness w. To make sure that the same message is committed in all the executions of Σ, we use a technique proposed by Khurana et al. in [30]. Namely, in each execution of Σ, instead of committing to w, we commit to $w\|r$, for some random value r, and use the protocol Π_{AI} to additionally prove that $a = w + r\alpha$, where α is chosen as part of the second round, and a is sent in the third round from the prover. As argued in [30], since r is global across all the executions, if $w \neq w'$ then $w + r\alpha \neq w' + r\alpha$ with overwhelming probability due to the Schwartz-Zippel lemma. Therefore, if the committed messages are different across the (multiple) executions, then the statement proven by Π_{AI} must be false, and the soundness of Π_{AI} guarantees that the verifier rejects.

More formally, we prove the following result.

Theorem 3. *Let $\Pi_{\mathsf{AI}} = (\mathcal{P}_{\mathsf{AI}}, \mathcal{V}_{\mathsf{AI}})$ be a 3-round public-coin, delayed-input complete, adaptive-input SHVZK with adaptive-input soundness for the $\mathcal{NP}$-relation $\mathsf{Rel}_{\mathsf{AI}}$, and $\Sigma = ((\mathcal{S}^\Sigma, \mathcal{R}^\Sigma), \mathsf{Dec}^\Sigma)$ (as defined in Fig. 2) be a Σ-commitment, then $\Pi_{\mathsf{CP}} = (\mathcal{P}_{\mathsf{CP}}, \mathcal{V}_{\mathsf{CP}})$ is a 3-round public-coin adaptive-input SHVZK commit-and-prove protocol for the $\mathcal{NP}$-relation Rel.*

We first give an intuition for the adaptive-SHVZK proof by describing how the simulator $(\mathsf{Sim}^0_{\mathsf{CP}}, \mathsf{Sim}^1_{\mathsf{CP}})$ works. For ease of exposition let us focus on the i-th transcript (out of λ^2) w.r.t. challenge $(\alpha, \pi_{2,i})$, where $\pi_{2,i}$ is composed by two sets of indices I, C. The simulator $\mathsf{Sim}^0_{\mathsf{CP}}$ on input challenge $\pi_{2,i}$ runs the

---

PUBLIC INPUT AND PARAMETERS: Parameters k, n, t of Σ, with $k = t$. $\mathcal{P}_{\mathsf{CP}}$ and $\mathcal{V}_{\mathsf{CP}}$ gets x in the third round.

PRIVATE INPUT: At the beginning $\mathcal{P}_{\mathsf{CP}}$ gets w.

Round 1 $\mathcal{P}_{\mathsf{CP}}$ executes the following steps:
   1. Sample $r \leftarrow \mathbb{F}$.
   2. For $i \in [\lambda^2]$, do the following:
      2.1. Execute $\mathcal{S}^\Sigma$ on input $(1^\lambda, w \| r)$, obtaining $\pi_{i,1}^\sigma = \{\mathsf{com}_{i,j}^\sigma\}_{j \in [n]}$, $\{\mathsf{dec}_{i,j}^\sigma\}_{j \in [n]}$ and $\{\mathsf{view}_{i,j}^\sigma\}_{j \in [n]}$.
      2.2. Run $\mathcal{P}_{\mathsf{AI}}$ on input 1^λ, obtaining $\pi_{i,1}$.
   3. Define and send $\pi_1 = \{\pi_{i,1}, \pi_{i,1}^\sigma\}_{i \in [\lambda^2]}$ to $\mathcal{V}_{\mathsf{CP}}$.
Round 2 $\mathcal{V}_{\mathsf{CP}}$ computes the following steps:
   1. For $i \in [\lambda^2]$, run $\mathcal{V}_{\mathsf{AI}}$ to choose challenge $\pi_{i,2}$.
   2. Sample $\alpha \leftarrow \mathbb{F}$.
   3. Set $\pi_2 = \{\pi_{i,2}\}_{i \in [\lambda^2]}$ and send (α, π_2) to $\mathcal{P}_{\mathsf{CP}}$.
Round 3 $\mathcal{P}_{\mathsf{CP}}$ performs the following steps:
   1. Compute $a = w + r\alpha$ and, for each $i \in [\lambda^2]$, do as follows.
      1.1. Parse $\pi_{i,2}$ as $(I, q_{i_1}, \ldots, q_{i_k})$.
      1.2. Compute the 3rd message $\pi_{i,3}^\sigma$ of Σ executing $\mathcal{S}^\Sigma$ on input I (note that $\pi_{i,3}^\sigma = \{\mathsf{dec}_{i,j}^\sigma, \mathsf{view}_{i,j}^\sigma\}_{j \in I}$).
      1.3. Run $\mathcal{P}_{\mathsf{AI}}$ on input the pair statement-witness[a] $((x, a, \alpha, \{\mathsf{view}_{i,j}^\sigma\}_{j \in I}), \{\mathsf{view}_{i,j}^\sigma\}_{j \in [n]})$ and $\pi_{i,2}$, thus obtaining the third round $\pi_{i,3}$.
      1.4. Set $\pi_3 = \{\pi_{i,3}^\sigma, \pi_{i,3}, a\}_{i \in [\lambda^2]}$ and send π_3 to $\mathcal{V}_{\mathsf{CP}}$.
Verification step. On input x outputs 1 if and only if, for each $i \in [\lambda^2]$, the following holds:
   1. $\mathcal{R}^\Sigma$ accepts the commitment $(\pi_{i,1}^\sigma, I, \pi_{i,3}^\sigma)$.
   2. $\mathcal{V}_{\mathsf{AI}}$ accepts the proof $(\pi_{i,1}, \pi_{i,2}, \pi_{i,3})$ for the statement $(x, a, \alpha, \{\mathsf{view}_{i,j}^\sigma\}_{j \in I})$.
   3. The j-th view $\mathsf{view}_{i,j}^\sigma$ that appears in $\pi_{i,3}^\sigma$ represents also the input share for the j-th view $\mathsf{view}_{i,j}$ that appears in $\pi_{i,3}$, for each $j \in I$.

Decommitment procedure: On input an accepting transcript of the protocol, and on input all the decommitment information for the λ^2 commitments generated via Σ, return m, if and only if the majority of the Σ-commitments are commitments of $(m \| \cdot)$.

---

[a] We recall that the protocol requires the witness to be secret shared.

Fig. 3. $\Pi_{\mathsf{CP}} = (\mathcal{P}_{\mathsf{CP}}, \mathcal{V}_{\mathsf{CP}})$

HRH simulator of Σ on input I obtaining $\pi_1^\sigma, \pi_3^\sigma$ and, consequently, the shares $\{\mathsf{view}_{i_j}^\sigma\}_{i_j \in I}$ which will be opened in the third round (denoted by π_3^σ). $\mathsf{Sim}_{\mathsf{CP}}^0$ then runs $\mathsf{Sim}_{\mathsf{AI}}^0$ on input $\pi_{2,i}$ thus obtaining $(\pi_{1,i}, \mathsf{aux})$. The simulator $\mathsf{Sim}_{\mathsf{CP}}^1$ on input theorem x samples a at random, sets $X = \{(x, a, \alpha, \{\mathsf{view}_{i_j}^\sigma\}_{i_j \in I})$ and runs $\mathsf{Sim}_{\mathsf{AI}}^1$ on input theorem (X, aux) thus obtaining $\pi_{3,i}$.

The full proof of Theorem 3 can be found in the full version. Similarly to previous protocols, we have the following result.

PUBLIC PARAMETERS: 1^λ, $\ell_{4\text{nmc}}$, tags $\text{tg}_1, \ldots, \text{tg}_{\ell_{4\text{nmc}}}$ and a large prime q s.t. $q > 2^{\text{tg}_i}$ for all i. A default second round message π_2^σ for Σ (i.e., $\pi_2^\sigma = \{1, 2, \ldots, k\}$).
PRIVATE INPUT: S_{wnmc} gets $m \in \mathbb{F}_q$.

Round 1 S_{wnmc} computes the following steps:
  1. Pick at random $r_1, \ldots, r_\ell$ and perform λ^2 executions of S^Σ on input $(1^\lambda, m\|r_1\|, \ldots, \|r_\ell)$, thus obtaining $\pi_1^\sigma = \{\pi_{1,i}^\sigma\}_{i \in [\lambda^2]}$ and $\text{dec}^\sigma = \{\text{dec}_i^\sigma\}_{i \in [\lambda^2]}$. Send π_σ^1 to R_{wnmc}.
Round 2 R_{wnmc} computes the following steps:
  1. Pick at random challenge vector $\vec{\alpha} = (\alpha_1, \ldots, \alpha_{\ell_{4\text{nmc}}})$, where $\alpha_i \in [2^{\text{tg}_i}] \subset \mathbb{F}_q$.
  2. Send $\vec{\alpha}, \pi_\sigma^2$ to S_{wnmc}.
Round 3 S_{wnmc} computes the following steps:
  1. Compute the third message π_3^σ of Σ executing S^Σ on input π_2^σ.
  2. For all $i \in [\ell_{4\text{nmc}}]$, compute $a_i \leftarrow r_i\alpha_i + m$, set $\vec{a} = (a_1, \ldots, a_{\ell_{4\text{nmc}}})$.
  3. Send $(\pi_3^\sigma, \vec{a})$ to R_{wnmc}.

Fig. 4. $\Pi_{\text{wnmc}} = (S_{\text{wnmc}}, R_{\text{wnmc}})$

Corollary 2. *Assuming the existence of one-to-one one-way functions, there exists a 3-round public-coin adaptive-input SHVZK commit-and-prove Π_{CP} for the $\mathcal{NP}$-relation* Rel *that makes black-box use of the 1-1 OWFs.*

Remark 1. To simplify the exposition of our non-malleable commitment scheme that internally uses the commit-and-prove protocol we have just described, we will consider the messages of Π_{CP} as divided into two parts: the messages related to the proof phase, and the messages related to the commitment phase. Hence, each round of Π_{CP} consists of two distinct components (e.g., the i-th round of Π_{CP} will be denoted by $\{\pi_i, \pi_i^\sigma\}$).

6.3   The 4-Round Non-malleable Commitment Scheme of [24]

The 4-round non-malleable commitment of Goyal et al. [24] is composed of two parts: the first one is a special public-coin Π_{wnmc} commitment scheme, that enjoys a weak form of non-malleability. Loosely speaking, Π_{wnmc} is non-malleable as long as the MiM, acting as a sender, is committing to a well-formed commitment. The second part is a zero-knowledge PoK that ensures that Π_{wnmc} is computed correctly. In Fig. 4, we recall the protocol Π_{wnmc}. This uses as an underlying building block a non-interactive commitment that is statistically binding. We replace this commitment with our interactive Σ-commitment Σ where the challenge is a default value (i.e., this trivially makes the Σ-commitment non-interactive). Finally, we prove that, after this modification, Π_{wnmc} remains hiding.

Lemma 2. *Let Σ be the Σ-commitment described in Fig. 2, then $\Pi_{\text{wnmc}} = (S_{\text{wnmc}}, R_{\text{wnmc}})$ described in Fig. 4 enjoys the hiding property.*

This follows from Theorem 2 and from the fact that $r_1, \ldots, r_{\ell_{4\text{nmc}}}$ and $a_1, \ldots, a_{\ell_{4\text{nmc}}}$ information theoretically hide the committed message.

7 Our 4-Round Black-Box Non-malleable Commitment Scheme

An informal overview of our 4-round NM commitment is given in the Introduction. Here we provide a formal description of the protocol Π_{nmc} presented in Fig. 5. We conclude this section with a sketch of the proof.

7.1 Formal Description of $\Pi_{\mathsf{nmc}} = ((\mathcal{S}_{\mathsf{nmc}}, \mathcal{R}_{\mathsf{nmc}}), \mathsf{Dec}_{\mathsf{nmc}})$

Our 4-round non-malleable commitment $\Pi_{\mathsf{nmc}} = ((\mathcal{S}_{\mathsf{nmc}}, \mathcal{R}_{\mathsf{nmc}}), \mathsf{Dec}_{\mathsf{nmc}})$ makes use of the following tools.

- A 3-round public-coin delayed-input adaptive-input SHVZK commit-and-prove protocol $\Pi_{\mathsf{tr}} = (\mathcal{P}_{\mathsf{tr}}, \mathcal{V}_{\mathsf{tr}})$ (as defined in Fig. 3) for the relation $\mathsf{Rel}_{\mathsf{tr}} = \{((m_0, m_1), w) : m_0 = w \vee m_1 = w\}$. We denote the adaptive-input SHVZK simulator with $\mathsf{Sim}_{\mathsf{tr}}$.
- A 3-round public-coin SHVZK, delayed-input complete commit-and-prove protocol $\Pi_{\mathsf{CP}} = (\mathcal{P}_{\mathsf{CP}}, \mathcal{V}_{\mathsf{CP}})$ (as defined in Fig. 3, but using λ^3 parallel repetitions) for the relation $\mathsf{Rel}_{\mathsf{CP}}$ defined as follows:

$$\mathsf{Rel}_{\mathsf{CP}} = \left\{ \begin{matrix} \mathbf{st} = \left(\{a_i, \alpha_i\}_{i \in [\ell_{\mathsf{nmc}}]}\right) \\ w = \left(m, \{r_i\}_{i \in [\ell_{\mathsf{nmc}}]}\right) \end{matrix} \middle| \ \forall \ i \ \in [\ell_{\mathsf{nmc}}] \ a_i = m + r_i \alpha_i \right\}.$$

- A one-of-two binding commitment scheme $\Pi_{\mathsf{comWI}} = (\mathcal{P}_{\mathsf{comWI}}, \mathcal{V}_{\mathsf{comWI}})$ (Definition 4).

The reason why we explicitly require Π_{tr} and Π_{CP} to be protocols constructed following the approach described in Sect. 6.2 is that in the security proof we will exploit the fact that Π_{tr} and Π_{CP} are based on non-malleable HVZK with respect to commitment protocols. We refer the reader to the full version for a thorough discussion on this and for the full proof.

Theorem 4. *Let* $\Pi_{\mathsf{tr}} = (\mathcal{P}_{\mathsf{tr}}, \mathcal{V}_{\mathsf{tr}})$ *be the 3-round public-coin adaptive-input SHVZK commit-and-prove for the relation* $\mathsf{Rel}_{\mathsf{tr}}$, *defined in Fig. 3, let* $\Pi_{\mathsf{CP}} = (\mathcal{P}_{\mathsf{CP}}, \mathcal{V}_{\mathsf{CP}})$ *be the 3-round public-coin SHVZK commit-and-prove for the relation* $\mathsf{Rel}_{\mathsf{CP}}$, *defined in Fig. 3, let* $\Pi_{\mathsf{comWI}} = (\mathcal{P}_{\mathsf{comWI}}, \mathcal{V}_{\mathsf{comWI}})$ *be the one-of-two binding commitment scheme, then* $\Pi_{\mathsf{nmc}} = ((\mathcal{S}_{\mathsf{nmc}}, \mathcal{R}_{\mathsf{nmc}}), \mathsf{Dec}_{\mathsf{nmc}})$, *described in Fig. 5 is a 4-round non-malleable commitment.*

The corollary given below immediately follows from the results shown in the previous sections and from the fact that Π_{comWI} can be instantiated in a black-box way from one-to-one one-way functions.

Corollary 3. *Assuming the existence of one-to-one one-way functions, there exists a 4-round non-malleable commitment that makes black-box use of the OWFs.*

COMMON INPUTS: 1^λ, parameters $k, n, t, \ell_{\mathsf{nmc}}$, tags $\mathsf{tg}_1, \ldots, \mathsf{tg}_\ell$ and a large prime q s.t. $q > 2^{\mathsf{tg}_i}$ for all i.

PRIVATE INPUT: At the beginning $\mathcal{S}_{\mathsf{nmc}}$ gets $m \in \mathbb{F}_q$.

Round 1. $\mathcal{R}_{\mathsf{nmc}}$ picks two random strings $\hat{s}_0, \hat{s}_1$ and runs $\mathcal{P}_{\mathsf{comWI}}$ on input $(1^\lambda, \hat{s}_0, 0)$ thus obtaining π_1^{comWI} and sends it to $\mathcal{S}_{\mathsf{nmc}}$.

Round 2. $\mathcal{S}_{\mathsf{nmc}}$ executes the following steps:

1. Compute the 1st round of Π_{wnmc}: Pick ℓ random strings $r_1, \ldots, r_{\ell_{\mathsf{nmc}}}$ and run $\mathcal{P}_{\mathsf{CP}}$ on input $(1^\lambda, m||r_1||, \ldots, ||r_{\ell_{\mathsf{nmc}}})$ thus obtaining $(\pi_1, \pi_1^{\mathsf{com}})$.

   1.1. Run the simulator for Π_{tr}: Pick a random β_0 from the space of all the possible challengers of Π_{tr}, set $\pi_2^{\mathsf{tr}} = \pi_1||\beta_0$.

   1.2. Run $\mathsf{Sim}_{\mathsf{tr}}$ on input π_2^{tr} thus obtaining $(\mathsf{aux}, \pi_1^{\mathsf{tr}})$.

   1.3. Compute the second round π_2^{comWI} of $\mathcal{V}_{\mathsf{comWI}}$.

2. Send $(\pi_1^{\mathsf{com}}, \pi_1^{\mathsf{tr}}, \pi_2^{\mathsf{comWI}})$ to $\mathcal{S}_{\mathsf{nmc}}$.

Round 3 $\mathcal{R}_{\mathsf{nmc}}$ executes the following steps:

1. Compute the 2nd round of Π_{wnmc}: Pick a random challenge vector $\vec{\alpha} = (\alpha_1, \ldots, \alpha_\ell)$, where $\alpha_i \in [2^{\mathsf{tg}_i}] \subset \mathbb{F}_q$.

2. Run the third round π_3^{comWI} of $\mathcal{P}_{\mathsf{comWI}}$ on input $(\pi_2^{\mathsf{comWI}}, \hat{s}_1)$.

3. Sample a random β_1 from the space of all the possible challenges of Π_{tr} and send $(\vec{\alpha}, \pi_3^{\mathsf{comWI}}, \hat{s}_0, \hat{s}_1, \beta_1)$ to $\mathcal{S}_{\mathsf{nmc}}$.

Round 4. $\mathcal{S}_{\mathsf{nmc}}$ computes the following steps:

1. If $\mathcal{V}_{\mathsf{comWI}}$ accepts the proof, $(\pi_1^{\mathsf{comWI}}, \pi_2^{\mathsf{comWI}}, \pi_3^{\mathsf{comWI}}, \hat{s}_0, \hat{s}_1)$ continue, else abort.

2. Compute the 3rd round of Π_{wnmc}: For all $i \in [\ell_{\mathsf{nmc}}]$, compute $a_i = r_i \alpha_i + m$.

3. Define $\mathsf{state} = \{a_i, \alpha_i\}_{i \in [\ell_{\mathsf{nmc}}]}$, and $w = (m, \{r_i\}_{i \in [\ell_{\mathsf{nmc}}]})$

4. Compute the third message of Π_{CP} by running $\mathcal{P}_{\mathsf{CP}}$ on input $(\mathsf{state}, w, \pi_2 = \beta_0 \oplus \beta_1)$, obtaining $(\pi_3, \pi_3^{\mathsf{com}})$.

5. Run the simulator for Π_{tr}: Run $\mathsf{Sim}_{\mathsf{tr}}$ on input $(\mathsf{aux}, \hat{s}_0, \hat{s}_1)$ thus obtaining π_3^{tr}

6. Send $\pi_2^{\mathsf{tr}} = (\pi_1||\beta_0), \pi_3^{\mathsf{tr}}, \pi_3, (a_i)_{i \in [\ell_{\mathsf{nmc}}]}$ to $\mathcal{R}_{\mathsf{nmc}}$.

Verification step. $\mathcal{R}_{\mathsf{nmc}}$ parses π_{tr}^2 as $(\pi_1||\beta_0)$, set $\pi_2 = \beta_0 \oplus \beta_1$ and accepts the commitment if and only if[a]:

1. $\mathcal{V}_{\mathsf{tr}}, \mathcal{V}_{\mathsf{CP}}$ accept, respectively, the proofs for $(\pi_1^{\mathsf{tr}}, \pi_2^{\mathsf{tr}}, \pi_3^{\mathsf{tr}})$ and $((\pi_1, \pi_1^{\mathsf{com}}), \pi_2, (\pi_3, \pi^{\mathsf{com}}))$

Decommitment procedure $\mathsf{Dec}_{\mathsf{nmc}}$: This proceeds as follows.

1. $\mathcal{S}_{\mathsf{nmc}}$ sends the decommitment information for Π_{CP} for $(m||r_1||, \ldots, ||r_{\ell_{\mathsf{nmc}}})$.

2. $\mathcal{R}_{\mathsf{nmc}}$ checks if the decommitment information for Π_{CP} are valid w.r.t. the message $(m||r_1||, \ldots, ||r_{\ell_{\mathsf{nmc}}})$, and accepts m as the decommitted message if $(m||r_1||, \ldots, ||r_\ell)$ is consistent with $\{a_i, \alpha_i\}_{i \in [\ell_{\mathsf{nmc}}]}$.

---

[a] We abuse of notation when using the $\oplus$ symbol because the challenge π_2 it is not a binary string, but a set of indices. In our case β_0 and β_1 are just a set of indexes, and π_2 is obtained by pairwise summing (with modular arithmetic) the indices in β_0 and β_1

Fig. 5. $\Pi_{\mathsf{nmc}} = ((\mathcal{S}_{\mathsf{nmc}}, \mathcal{R}_{\mathsf{nmc}}), \mathsf{Dec}_{\mathsf{nmc}})$

8   Comparison with Previous Non-black-box Approaches to Four-Round Non-malleable Commitments

As we argued, our main strategy to construct a non-malleable commitment scheme is to lift the security of the weak non-malleable commitment scheme of [25, Fig. 2] (that we also recall in Fig. 4), relying on a special notion of zero-knowledge that we call non-malleable HVZK with respect to commitment. This notion guarantees that a sender of a commitment scheme does not change the distribution of the committed messages depending on whether they receive an honestly generated zero-knowledge proof or a simulated one. We construct a NMZKC for a specific class of commitments, which includes the weak-non-malleable commitment scheme of [25, Fig. 2] that we mention above.

Although our approach is inspired by [25], where the authors also lift the security of a weak-non-malleable commitment scheme relying on zero-knowledge, concretely, our techniques significantly depart from those of [25]. In the next paragraphs, we highlight the main difference between the two approaches and explain why we could use as one of the main building block the simple weak-non-malleable commitment of [25, Fig. 2], instead of a modified version, as the authors of [25] do.

The main technical challenge in designing non-malleable commitments with low round complexity is due to arguing in the proof that the security of the primitives involved in the protocol is maintained despite performing rewinds to extract the message committed by the MiM (on the right session). One of the primitives involved in the scheme of Goyal et al. is a non-rewind secure witness-indistinguishable proof denoted by Π, and to cope with the rewinds performed by the extractor in the proof (while still relying on the WI property of Π), the prover prepares n first rounds for the non-rewind secure WI protocol (denoted with Π). Upon receiving one valid second round from the verifier, the prover picks one instance of Π at random (let us say the i-th) and completes the proof providing an accepting third round only with respect to the i-th instance. Let us denote the above protocol by Π_{rew}.

Despite this protocol being rewind secure, Goyal et al. cannot use just one execution of Π_{rew}, which proves that either the committer has behaved honestly in the algebraic part of the commitment or that the committer knows a trapdoor. The reason is that there is a simple adversarial strategy for which such a proof would not work in this case. Intuitively, consider a MiM that completes an execution on the right session only if it receives a proof for the j-th instance of Π, and aborts in any other case (note that this MiM is non-aborting with non-negligible probability). This MiM would make the reduction to the WI of Π fail. In particular, any rewind performed by the extractor on the right session would make the MiM ask different second rounds for the same execution of Π (or abort if on the left session a different instance of Π is completed). To solve this problem the authors of [25] compute a secret sharing of the message and perform one execution of Π_{rew} for each of the shares. Now, even if the MiM applies the same strategy to one run of Π_{rew}, it is safe to allow the MiM to perform this rewind since the only thing that will be leaked is a share of the message m (note that two accepting transcripts for the same execution of Π for two different second rounds might completely leak the witness). In the formal proof, Goyal et al. need to rely on the fact that the number of executions of Π that are not rewound (and consequently the number of shares not leaked) is sufficient to protect the secrecy of the message m. This modification also requires changing how the extractor works (e.g., by relying on the quadratic polynomials). Hence, to obtain their non-malleable commitment scheme, Goyal et al. rely on a more sophisticated version of the weak-non-malleable commitment described in their work. In our paper, we do not rely on any rewind secure primitive (which we replace with a proof system non-malleable with respect to commitments), so we do not need to split the message into shares and follow the strategy described above. We note that similarly to us, also [9] relies on the simpler sub-scheme of [25, Fig. 2] to obtain a 4-round concurrent non-malleable commitment scheme. To summarize, the main difference between ours and the approach of [25] (that relies on rewind secure primitive) is that our work is based on the observation that the rewinds are performed in the reductions or during the simulation, and as such, the adversary does not have clue that the rewinds are happening. Hence, relying on primitives that are rewind-secure (i.e., the adversary can consciously make rewinds and collect the transcripts generated during the rewinds) can be avoided for the application we consider in the paper.

Acknowledgements. We thank Carmit Hazay and Muthuramakrishnan Venkitasubramaniam for insightful discussions on the MPC-in-the-head approach. Emmanuela Orsini was supported by the Defense Advanced Research Projects Agency (DARPA) under contract No. HR001120C0085, and by CyberSecurity Research Flanders with reference number VR20192203. Any opinions, findings and conclusions or recommendations expressed in this material are those of the authors and do not necessarily reflect the views of the DARPA, the US Government or Cyber Security Research Flanders. The U.S. Government is authorized to reproduce and distribute reprints for governmental purposes notwithstanding any copyright annotation therein.

References

1. Badrinarayanan, S., Goyal, V., Jain, A., Kalai, Y.T., Khurana, D., Sahai, A.: Promise zero knowledge and its applications to round optimal MPC. In: Shacham, H., Boldyreva, A. (eds.) CRYPTO 2018. LNCS, vol. 10992, pp. 459–487. Springer, Cham (2018). https://doi.org/10.1007/978-3-319-96881-0_16
2. Barak, B.: Constant-round coin-tossing with a man in the middle or realizing the shared random string model. In: FOCS (2002)
3. Beaver, D., Micali, S., Rogaway, P.: The round complexity of secure protocols. In: 22nd Annual ACM Symposium on Theory of Computing, pp. 503–513. ACM Press, Baltimore, MD, USA (1990). https://doi.org/10.1145/100216.100287
4. Cao, Z., Visconti, I., Zhang, Z.: Constant-round concurrent non-malleable statistically binding commitments and decommitments. In: Nguyen, P.Q., Pointcheval, D. (eds.) PKC 2010. LNCS, vol. 6056, pp. 193–208. Springer, Heidelberg (2010). https://doi.org/10.1007/978-3-642-13013-7_12
5. Chatterjee, R., Liang, X., Pandey, O.: Improved black-box constructions of composable secure computation. In: Czumaj, A., Dawar, A., Merelli, E. (eds.) ICALP 2020: 47th International Colloquium on Automata, Languages and Programming. LIPIcs, vol. 168, pp. 28:1–28:20. Schloss Dagstuhl - Leibniz-Zentrum fuer Informatik, Saarbrücken, Germany (2020). https://doi.org/10.4230/LIPIcs.ICALP.2020.28

6. Chor, B., Goldwasser, S., Micali, S., Awerbuch, B.: Verifiable secret sharing and achieving simultaneity in the presence of faults. In: 26th Annual Symposium on Foundations of Computer Science, pp. 383–395. IEEE Computer Society Press, Portland, Oregon (1985). https://doi.org/10.1109/SFCS.1985.64

7. Rai Choudhuri, A., Ciampi, M., Goyal, V., Jain, A., Ostrovsky, R.: Round optimal secure multiparty computation from minimal assumptions. In: Pass, R., Pietrzak, K. (eds.) TCC 2020. LNCS, vol. 12551, pp. 291–319. Springer, Cham (2020). https://doi.org/10.1007/978-3-030-64378-2_11

8. Ciampi, M., Ostrovsky, R., Siniscalchi, L., Visconti, I.: Concurrent non-malleable commitments (and more) in 3 rounds. In: Robshaw, M., Katz, J. (eds.) CRYPTO 2016. LNCS, vol. 9816, pp. 270–299. Springer, Heidelberg (2016). https://doi.org/10.1007/978-3-662-53015-3_10

9. Ciampi, M., Ostrovsky, R., Siniscalchi, L., Visconti, I.: Four-round concurrent non-malleable commitments from one-way functions. In: Katz, J., Shacham, H. (eds.) CRYPTO 2017. LNCS, vol. 10402, pp. 127–157. Springer, Cham (2017). https://doi.org/10.1007/978-3-319-63715-0_5

10. Ciampi, M., Ostrovsky, R., Siniscalchi, L., Visconti, I.: Round-optimal secure two-party computation from trapdoor permutations. In: Kalai, Y., Reyzin, L. (eds.) TCC 2017. LNCS, vol. 10677, pp. 678–710. Springer, Cham (2017). https://doi.org/10.1007/978-3-319-70500-2_23

11. Ciampi, M., Parisella, R., Venturi, D.: On adaptive security of delayed-input sigma protocols and fiat-shamir nizks. In: Galdi, C., Kolesnikov, V. (eds.) SCN 2020. LNCS, vol. 12238, pp. 670–690. Springer, Cham (2020). https://doi.org/10.1007/978-3-030-57990-6_33

12. Ciampi, M., Persiano, G., Scafuro, A., Siniscalchi, L., Visconti, I.: Improved or-composition of sigma-protocols. In: Kushilevitz, E., Malkin, T. (eds.) TCC 2016. LNCS, vol. 9563, pp. 112–141. Springer, Heidelberg (2016). https://doi.org/10.1007/978-3-662-49099-0_5

13. Ciampi, M., Ravi, D., Siniscalchi, L., Waldner, H.: Round-optimal multi-party computation with identifiable abort. In: Dunkelman, O., Dziembowski, S. (eds.) EUROCRYPT 2022. LNCS, vol. 13275, pp. 335–364. Springer, Cham (2022). https://doi.org/10.1007/978-3-031-06944-4_12

14. Dachman-Soled, D., Malkin, T., Raykova, M., Venkitasubramaniam, M.: Adaptive and concurrent secure computation from new adaptive, non-malleable commitments. In: Sako, K., Sarkar, P. (eds.) ASIACRYPT 2013. LNCS, vol. 8269, pp. 316–336. Springer, Heidelberg (2013). https://doi.org/10.1007/978-3-642-42033-7_17

15. Dolev, D., Dwork, C., Naor, M.: Non-malleable cryptography. In: 23rd Annual ACM Symposium on Theory of Computing, pp. 542–552. ACM Press, New Orleans, LA, USA (1991). https://doi.org/10.1145/103418.103474

16. Feige, U., Lapidot, D., Shamir, A.: Multiple non-interactive zero knowledge proofs based on a single random string. In: 31st Annual Symposium on Foundations of Computer Science, pp. 308–317. IEEE Computer Society Press, St. Louis, MO, USA (1990). https://doi.org/10.1109/FSCS.1990.89549

17. Gennaro, R., Ishai, Y., Kushilevitz, E., Rabin, T.: The round complexity of verifiable secret sharing and secure multicast. In: 33rd Annual ACM Symposium on Theory of Computing, pp. 580–589. ACM Press, Crete, Greece (2001). https://doi.org/10.1145/380752.380853

18. Goldreich, O.: Foundations of Cryptography, vol. 1. Cambridge University Press, New York (2006)

19. Goldreich, O., Levin, L.A.: A hard-core predicate for all one-way functions. In: Proceedings of the 21st Annual ACM Symposium on Theory of Computing, 14–17 May 1989, Seattle, Washigton, USA, pp. 25–32 (1989)
20. Goyal, V.: Constant round non-malleable protocols using one way functions. In: STOC (2011)
21. Goyal, V., Khurana, D., Sahai, A.: Breaking the three round barrier for non-malleable commitments. In: 57th IEEE Annual Symposium on Foundations of Computer Science, FOCS 2016. IEEE (2016)
22. Goyal, V., Lee, C.K., Ostrovsky, R., Visconti, I.: Constructing non-malleable commitments: a black-box approach. In: 53rd Annual Symposium on Foundations of Computer Science, pp. 51–60. IEEE Computer Society Press, New Brunswick, NJ, USA (2012). https://doi.org/10.1109/FOCS.2012.47
23. Goyal, V., Richelson, S.: Non-malleable commitments using Goldreich-Levin list decoding. In: Zuckerman, D. (ed.) 60th Annual Symposium on Foundations of Computer Science, pp. 686–699. IEEE Computer Society Press, Baltimore, MD, USA (2019). https://doi.org/10.1109/FOCS.2019.00047
24. Goyal, V., Richelson, S., Rosen, A., Vald, M.: An algebraic approach to non-malleability. In: 55th Annual Symposium on Foundations of Computer Science, pp. 41–50. IEEE Computer Society Press, Philadelphia, PA, USA (2014). https://doi.org/10.1109/FOCS.2014.13
25. Goyal, V., Richelson, S., Rosen, A., Vald, M.: An algebraic approach to non-malleability. Cryptology ePrint Archive, Paper 2014/586 (2014). https://eprint.iacr.org/2014/586
26. Halevi, S., Hazay, C., Polychroniadou, A., Venkitasubramaniam, M.: Round-optimal secure multi-party computation. In: Shacham, H., Boldyreva, A. (eds.) CRYPTO 2018. LNCS, vol. 10992, pp. 488–520. Springer, Cham (2018). https://doi.org/10.1007/978-3-319-96881-0_17
27. Hazay, C., Venkitasubramaniam, M.: On the power of secure two-party computation. In: Robshaw, M., Katz, J. (eds.) CRYPTO 2016. LNCS, vol. 9815, pp. 397–429. Springer, Heidelberg (2016). https://doi.org/10.1007/978-3-662-53008-5_14
28. Ishai, Y., Kushilevitz, E., Ostrovsky, R., Sahai, A.: Zero-knowledge from secure multiparty computation. In: Johnson, D.S., Feige, U. (eds.) 39th Annual ACM Symposium on Theory of Computing, pp. 21–30. ACM Press, San Diego, CA, USA (2007). https://doi.org/10.1145/1250790.1250794
29. Khurana, D.: Round optimal concurrent non-malleability from polynomial hardness. In: Kalai, Y., Reyzin, L. (eds.) TCC 2017. LNCS, vol. 10678, pp. 139–171. Springer, Cham (2017). https://doi.org/10.1007/978-3-319-70503-3_5
30. Khurana, D., Ostrovsky, R., Srinivasan, A.: Round optimal black-box Commit-and-Prove. In: Beimel, A., Dziembowski, S. (eds.) TCC 2018. LNCS, vol. 11239, pp. 286–313. Springer, Cham (2018). https://doi.org/10.1007/978-3-030-03807-6_11
31. Lin, H., Pass, R.: Constant-round non-malleable commitments from any one-way function. In: Fortnow, L., Vadhan, S.P. (eds.) Proceedings of the 43rd ACM Symposium on Theory of Computing, STOC 2011, 6–8 June 2011, San Jose, CA, USA, pp. 705–714. ACM (2011)
32. Lin, H., Pass, R.: Constant-round nonmalleable commitments from any one-way function. J. ACM 62(1), 5:1-5:30 (2015)
33. Lin, H., Pass, R., Venkitasubramaniam, M.: Concurrent non-malleable commitments from any one-way function. In: Canetti, R. (ed.) TCC 2008. LNCS, vol. 4948, pp. 571–588. Springer, Heidelberg (2008). https://doi.org/10.1007/978-3-540-78524-8_31

34. Mahmoody, M., Pass, R.: The curious case of non-interactive commitments – on the power of black-box vs. non-black-box use of primitives. In: Safavi-Naini, R., Canetti, R. (eds.) CRYPTO 2012. LNCS, vol. 7417, pp. 701–718. Springer, Heidelberg (2012). https://doi.org/10.1007/978-3-642-32009-5_41

35. Ostrovsky, R., Persiano, G., Visconti, I.: Simulation-based concurrent non-malleable commitments and decommitments. In: Reingold, O. (ed.) TCC 2009. LNCS, vol. 5444, pp. 91–108. Springer, Heidelberg (2009). https://doi.org/10.1007/978-3-642-00457-5_7

36. Pass, R.: Unprovable security of perfect nizk and non-interactive non-malleable commitments. In: Sahai, A. (ed.) TCC 2013. LNCS, vol. 7785, pp. 334–354. Springer, Heidelberg (2013). https://doi.org/10.1007/978-3-642-36594-2_19

37. Pass, R., Rosen, A.: Bounded-concurrent secure two-party computation in a constant number of rounds. In: 44th Symposium on Foundations of Computer Science (FOCS 2003), 11–14 October 2003, Cambridge, MA, USA, Proceedings, pp. 404–413. IEEE Computer Society (2003)

38. Pass, R., Rosen, A.: Concurrent non-malleable commitments. In: Proceedings of the 46th Annual IEEE Symposium on Foundations of Computer Science (FOCS 2005), 23–25 October 2005, Pittsburgh, PA, USA, pp. 563–572 (2005)

39. Pass, R., Rosen, A.: New and improved constructions of non-malleable cryptographic protocols. In: STOC (2005)

40. Pass, R., Rosen, A.: Concurrent nonmalleable commitments. SIAM J. Comput. **37**(6), 1891–1925 (2008)

41. Pass, R., Rosen, A.: New and improved constructions of nonmalleable cryptographic protocols. SIAM J. Comput. **38**(2), 702–752 (2008)

42. Pass, R., Wee, H.: Constant-round non-malleable commitments from sub-exponential one-way functions. In: Gilbert, H. (ed.) EUROCRYPT 2010. LNCS, vol. 6110, pp. 638–655. Springer, Heidelberg (2010). https://doi.org/10.1007/978-3-642-13190-5_32

43. Wee, H.: Black-box, round-efficient secure computation via non-malleability amplification. In: 51th Annual IEEE Symposium on Foundations of Computer Science, FOCS 2010, 23–26 October 2010, Las Vegas, Nevada, USA, pp. 531–540. IEEE Computer Society (2010)

44. Yao, A.C.C.: Space-time tradeoff for answering range queries. In: 14th Annual ACM Symposium on Theory of Computing, pp. 128–136. ACM Press, San Francisco, CA, USA (1982). https://doi.org/10.1145/800070.802185

Theory I: Sampling and Friends

A Tight Computational Indistinguishability Bound for Product Distributions

Nathan Geier[✉][iD]

Tel Aviv University, Tel Aviv, Israel
nathangeier@mail.tau.ac.il

Abstract. Assume that distributions X_0, X_1 (respectively Y_0, Y_1) are d_X (respectively d_Y) indistinguishable for circuits of a given size. It is well known that the product distributions X_0Y_0, X_1Y_1 are $d_X + d_Y$ indistinguishable for slightly smaller circuits. However, in probability theory where unbounded adversaries are considered through statistical distance, it is folklore knowledge that in fact X_0Y_0 and X_1Y_1 are $d_X + d_Y - d_X \cdot d_Y$ indistinguishable, and also that this bound is tight.

We formulate and prove the computational analog of this tight bound. Our proof is entirely different from the proof in the statistical case, which is non-constructive. As a corollary, we show that if X and Y are d indistinguishable, then k independent copies of X and k independent copies of Y are almost $1 - (1 - d)^k$ indistinguishable for smaller circuits, as against $d \cdot k$ using the looser bound.

Our bounds are useful in settings where only weak (i.e. non-negligible) indistinguishability is guaranteed. We demonstrate this in the context of cryptography, showing that our bounds, coupled with the XOR Lemma, yield straightforward computational generalization to the analysis for information-theoretic amplification of weak oblivious transfer protocols.

1 Introduction

Computational indistinguishability is a fundamental concept in computational complexity and cryptography. One of the most basic bounds in this context, which is easy to see using a simple hybrid argument, is that for distributions X_0, X_1 of distance d_X, and Y_0, Y_1 of distance d_Y, with d_{XY} denoting the distance between X_0Y_0, X_1Y_1, we have that

$$d_{XY} \le d_X + d_Y,$$

which holds both statistically and in the computational setting holds for slightly smaller circuits. However, in probability theory where statistical distance, or

Supported by the European Research Council (ERC) under the European Union's Horizon Europe research and innovation programme (grant agreement No. 101042417, acronym SPP), by ISF grant 18/484, and by Len Blavatnik and the Blavatnik Family Foundation.

E. Kiltz and V. Vaikuntanathan (Eds.): TCC 2022, LNCS 13748, pp. 333–347, 2022.
https://doi.org/10.1007/978-3-031-22365-5_12

equivalently, indistinguishability against unbounded attackers is considered, it is folklore knowledge [9, Lemma 2.2] that a better, tight bound holds:

$$d_{XY} \leq d_X + d_Y - d_X \cdot d_Y.$$

It is tight in the sense that for every choice of d_X, d_Y, there exist distributions X_0, X_1 with distance d_X and distributions Y_0, Y_1 with distance d_Y, such that $d_{XY} = d_X + d_Y - d_X \cdot d_Y$. The proof of this bound uses coupling [7], and is thus inherently non-constructive and not easy to generalize to the computational setting. See Subsect. 1.1 for more information on dealing with coupling in the computational setting.

It is worth noting here that another very important and foundational bound that is easy to show statistically but was not easily generalized to the computational setting is the famous XOR Lemma, see [5] for a survey. Our bounds are related in spirit and some of the techniques and statement formulations presented in this paper were inspired by Levin's proof of the XOR Lemma [10], and its presentation in [5]. Further, in Sect. 5 we show how both bounds are needed and complement each other in order to achieve the computational generalization to the information-theoretic weak OT amplification.

We provide a direct constructive proof of the tight bound which also works in the computational setting, both uniform and non-uniform, with an additive loss of ε which can be made as small as we want, by paying in increasing the running time or circuit size with relation to $1/\varepsilon$. To be more specific, for the non-uniform case, we roughly show that.

Theorem 1 (Informal). *Let X_0, X_1 be d_X indistinguishable for size s_X circuits. (Respectively Y_0, Y_1, d_Y, s_Y.) Then, for every $k \in \mathbb{N}$, we have that (X_0, Y_0) and (X_1, Y_1) are $(d_X + d_Y - d_X \cdot d_Y + \varepsilon_k)$ indistinguishable for size s_k circuits, where*

$$\varepsilon_k \leq (d_Y)^k, \qquad s_k \approx \min\{s_Y, s_X/k\}.$$

Corollary 1 (Informal). *Let D, Q be distributions that are d indistinguishable for size s circuits. Then, for every $m \in \mathbb{N}$ and ε, we have that $D^{\otimes m}, Q^{\otimes m}$ are $(1 - (1 - d)^m + \varepsilon)$ indistinguishable for size $s_{m,\varepsilon}$ circuits, where*

$$s_{m,\varepsilon} \approx s(1 - d)^m / \log(1/\varepsilon).$$

And we also show similar results in the uniform setting, although with worse dependency on $1/\varepsilon$. The corollary essentially states that if the computational distance between X and Y is at most d, then the computational distance between the k-product of X and the k-product of Y is upper bounded by almost $1 - (1-d)^k$ for smaller circuits, as against $d \cdot k$ resulted by the looser well known bound, which in particular may be larger than 1. The proof of the corollary follows by (carefully) applying the bound of the isolated case again and again. It should be noted that the difference between the bounds is especially interesting when k is not very small compared to $1/d$. For example, if $d = 0.5$, $k = 3$, the tight bound is 0.875 while the looser bound of 1.5 ≥ 1 is trivial.

We also demonstrate how these bounds may be used in the computational setting for amplification of weak oblivious transfer protocols [2, 13], providing an alternative straightforward analysis to the fact that the information-theoretic amplification process also works computationally. In general, when considering cryptographic primitives with multiple security properties, it is common that amplifying one property may degrade another, inducing a trade-off. We expect these bounds may be used in order to achieve a larger range of parameters when amplifying a weakened version of such primitives.

Finally, an interesting observation regarding the above corollary is how the circuit size grows only logarithmically with respect to $1/\varepsilon$. We discuss it further in the context of the amplification beyond negligible problem.

1.1   Related Work

While the aforementioned coupling technique itself is non-constructive, Maurer and Tessaro [11] show how to derive a computational analog for it using Holenstein's tight version of the hardcore lemma [6]. This approach could also be used to derive the tight bound in a general way. However, we believe our direct and specific approach still holds some advantages:

- Better parameters in the non-uniform setting: In our direct approach, when building a distinguisher for D, Q from a distinguisher between $D^{\otimes m}, Q^{\otimes m}$, the circuit size is multiplied by roughly $\log(1/\varepsilon)/(1-d)^m$. In contrast, using the hardcore approach the circuit size is multiplied by roughly

$$(1/\varepsilon)^2 \, m^2 \left(\log |D| + \log |Q| \right).$$

Note that the latter must always be worse as $\varepsilon < (1-d)^m$ for the bound to be meaningful.
- Simplicity and explicitness: The distinguisher given by the hardcore lemma is somewhat more involved. In contrast, here the distinguisher is rather simple and easy to understand.

It should also be mentioned that the problem of tight direct product bounds has also been studied further in the statistical setting, when additional assumptions are made about the distributions. For example, see [4, 12].

1.2   Organization

We start by introducing basic definitions and notation in Sect. 2. We then continue to proving the non-uniform variants and their tightness in Sect. 3. We show how to generalize the non-uniform variants to the uniform setting in Sect. 4. We then demonstrate an application of these bounds in Sect. 5. Finally, in Sect. 6, we propose a conjecture aimed to capture the XOR analog to the observation made above regarding circuit size growth with relation to the slackness.

2 Definitions

For a distribution D, denote by $D^{\otimes k}$ the distribution of k independent copies of D. For distributions X_0, X_1 over Ω, a distinguisher is a boolean $A : \Omega \to \{0, 1\}$, and we let $\mathrm{adv}_A^+(X_0, X_1) := \mathbb{E}\left[A(X_1) - A(X_0)\right]$. (The expectation is also over A if it is not deterministic.) We say that distributions X_0, X_1 are d indistinguishable for size s circuits if for any such circuit C, we have that $\mathrm{adv}_C^+(X_0, X_1) \leq d$. For distributions X, Y we will denote by (X, Y) the product distribution, given by two independent samples from X and Y. We denote by $B(p)$ the Bernoulli distribution with parameter p, and more generally by $B^\ell(p)$ the distribution that is equal to 1^ℓ with probability p and otherwise 0^ℓ. For a string s, we denote by $s[i]$ the i'th bit of s. We will denote by $[m]$ the set $\{1, \ldots, m\}$. We denote by $X_{1/2}$ the distribution given by $b \leftarrow \{0, 1\}, x \leftarrow X_b$. An ensemble of distributions $X = \{X_n\}$ is efficiently samplable if there exists a uniform PPT sampler that given 1^n outputs a sample from X_n.

2.1 Notation

When the same distribution is used multiple times in a single expression, e.g. $(f(D), g(D))$ for D, it should be interpreted that a single value $d \leftarrow D$ is sampled and given to both f and g, rather than two independent samples.

3 The Non-uniform Bounds and Tightness

Let us start with the non-uniform version as it is more simple and clean. The uniform version is a generalization of the ideas presented below. Roughly speaking, we show that given a distinguisher C for $(X_0, Y_0), (X_1, Y_1)$, if $C(x, \cdot)$ is not a good enough distinguisher between Y_0, Y_1 for all values of x, then we can build an amplifier for X_0, X_1 distinguishers. We then use this amplifier to turn the trivial distinguisher that always outputs 1 into a good enough distinguisher.

Theorem 2. *Let X_0, X_1 be distributions over ℓ_X bits that are d_X indistinguishable for size s_X circuits. (Respectively $Y_0, Y_1, \ell_Y, d_Y, s_Y$.) Then, for every $k \in \mathbb{N}$, we have that (X_0, Y_0) and (X_1, Y_1) are $(d_X + d_Y - d_X \cdot d_Y + \varepsilon_k)$ indistinguishable for size s_k circuits, where*

$$\varepsilon_k := \frac{(d_Y)^k \cdot d_X (1 - d_Y)}{1 - (d_Y)^k} \leq (d_Y)^k, \qquad s_k := \min\left\{s_Y - \ell_X, \frac{s_X - 1}{k} - 5\ell_Y - 1\right\}.$$

Remark 1. We note that our starting point, $k = 1$, matches the simple hybrid argument bound of $d_X + d_Y$ since $\varepsilon_1 = d_X \cdot d_Y$, and as k grows larger our bound gets closer and closer to the tight bound of $d_X + d_Y - d_X \cdot d_Y$, while the circuits bound grows smaller. Also note that the bound is asymmetric with respect to the circuit size bounds. This asymmetry is important for preserving a similar circuit size when applying the isolated case over and over again. See a similar argument in [5, Section 3].

Proof. Assume toward contradiction that for some circuit C of size s_k, we have that

$$\mathrm{adv}_C^+\left((X_0, Y_0), (X_1, Y_1)\right) > (d_X + d_Y - d_X \cdot d_Y + \varepsilon_k).$$

For every fixed x, it must be that $C(x, \cdot)$ is able to distinguish between Y_0 and Y_1 by at most d_Y, otherwise we get a contradiction as the size of this circuit is $s_k + \ell_X \leq s_Y$. Then, for every candidate distinguisher A between X_0 and X_1, we have that

$$\mathrm{adv}_C^+\left((X_1, Y_{A(X_1)}), (X_1, Y_1)\right) \leq d_Y \cdot \Pr\left[A(X_1) = 0\right]$$
$$\mathrm{adv}_C^+\left((X_0, Y_0), (X_0, Y_{A(X_0)})\right) \leq d_Y \cdot \Pr\left[A(X_0) = 1\right]$$

where $x, y \leftarrow X_1, Y_{A(X_1)}$ is resulted by $x \leftarrow X_1$, $b \leftarrow A(x)$, $y \leftarrow Y_b$. This holds because

$$\mathrm{adv}_C^+\left((X_1, Y_{A(X_1)}), (X_1, Y_1)\right) = \mathbb{E}\left[C(X_1, Y_1) - C(X_1, Y_{A(X_1)})\right]$$
$$= \mathbb{E}\left[C(X_1, Y_1) - C(X_1, Y_0) | A(X_1) = 0\right] \cdot \Pr\left[A(X_1) = 0\right]$$
$$+ \mathbb{E}\left[C(X_1, Y_1) - C(X_1, Y_1) | A(X_1) = 1\right] \cdot \Pr\left[A(X_1) = 1\right]$$
$$= \mathbb{E}_{x \leftarrow X_1 | A(X_1) = 0}\left[C(x, Y_1) - C(x, Y_0)\right] \cdot \Pr\left[A(X_1) = 0\right]$$
$$= \mathbb{E}_{x \leftarrow X_1 | A(X_1) = 0}\left[\mathrm{adv}_{C(x, \cdot)}^+(Y_0, Y_1)\right] \cdot \Pr\left[A(X_1) = 0\right] \leq d_Y \cdot \Pr\left[A(X_1) = 0\right]$$

and using a symmetric argument for the second inequality. Using that (in general)

$$\sum_{i \in [n]} \mathrm{adv}_C^+(D_i, D_{i+1}) = \mathrm{adv}_C^+(D_1, D_{n+1})$$

we conclude that

$$\mathrm{adv}_C^+\left((X_0, Y_0), (X_1, Y_1)\right) = \mathrm{adv}_C^+\left((X_0, Y_0), (X_0, Y_{A(X_0)})\right)$$
$$+ \mathrm{adv}_C^+\left((X_0, Y_{A(X_0)}), (X_1, Y_{A(X_1)})\right) + \mathrm{adv}_C^+\left((X_1, Y_{A(X_1)}), (X_1, Y_1)\right)$$

and thus

$$\mathrm{adv}_C^+\left((X_0, Y_{A(X_0)}), (X_1, Y_{A(X_1)})\right) = \mathrm{adv}_C^+\left((X_0, Y_0), (X_1, Y_1)\right)$$
$$- \mathrm{adv}_C^+\left((X_1, Y_{A(X_1)}), (X_1, Y_1)\right) - \mathrm{adv}_C^+\left((X_0, Y_0), (X_0, Y_{A(X_0)})\right)$$
$$> (d_X + d_Y - d_X \cdot d_Y + \varepsilon_k) - (d_Y \cdot \Pr\left[A(X_1) = 0\right]) - (d_Y \cdot \Pr\left[A(X_0) = 1\right])$$
$$= (d_X - d_X \cdot d_Y + \varepsilon_k) + d_Y(1 - \Pr\left[A(X_1) = 0\right] - \Pr\left[A(X_0) = 1\right])$$
$$= (d_X - d_X \cdot d_Y + \varepsilon_k) + d_Y(\Pr\left[A(X_1) = 1\right] - \Pr\left[A(X_0) = 1\right])$$
$$= (d_X - d_X \cdot d_Y + \varepsilon_k) + d_Y(\mathbb{E}\left[A(X_1)\right] - \mathbb{E}\left[A(X_0)\right])$$
$$= (d_X - d_X \cdot d_Y + \varepsilon_k) + d_Y \cdot \mathrm{adv}_A^+(X_0, X_1).$$

In other words, we can build a new distinguisher A' for X_0, X_1 by applying A to our input x, sampling $y \leftarrow Y_{A(x)}$ and feeding (x, y) to C, and have that

$$\mathrm{adv}_{A'}^+(X_0, X_1) > (d_X - d_X \cdot d_Y + \varepsilon_k) + d_Y \cdot \mathrm{adv}_A^+(X_0, X_1).$$

If we start from A_0 being the trivial distinguisher that always outputs 1 and keep repeating this process for k steps, we get that

$$\text{adv}_{A_k}^+ (X_0, X_1) > (d_X - d_X \cdot d_Y + \varepsilon_k) + d_Y \cdot \text{adv}_{A_{k-1}}^+ (X_0, X_1)$$

$$> (d_X - d_X \cdot d_Y + \varepsilon_k) + d_Y \cdot (d_X - d_X \cdot d_Y + \varepsilon_k) + (d_Y)^2 \cdot \text{adv}_{A_{k-2}}^+ (X_0, X_1)$$

$$> \cdots > (d_X - d_X \cdot d_Y + \varepsilon_k) \sum_{i=0}^{k-1} (d_Y)^i + (d_Y)^k \cdot \text{adv}_{A_0}^+ (X_0, X_1)$$

$$= (d_X - d_X \cdot d_Y + \varepsilon_k) \sum_{i=0}^{k-1} (d_Y)^i = \frac{(d_X - d_X \cdot d_Y + \varepsilon_k) \left(1 - (d_Y)^k\right)}{1 - d_Y}$$

$$= \frac{\left(d_X (1 - d_Y) + \frac{(d_Y)^k \cdot d_X (1 - d_Y)}{1 - (d_Y)^k}\right) \left(1 - (d_Y)^k\right)}{1 - d_Y} = \left(d_X + \frac{(d_Y)^k \cdot d_X}{1 - (d_Y)^k}\right) \left(1 - (d_Y)^k\right)$$

$$= d_X \left(1 - (d_Y)^k\right) + (d_Y)^k \cdot d_X = d_X.$$

And so, we have concluded that A_k distinguishes X_0 from X_1 with advantage better than d_X. Next, for the circuit size, in order to implement A_k we start by applying A_{k-1}, sample $y_0 \leftarrow Y_0, y_1 \leftarrow Y_1$, use a multiplexer to choose $y \leftarrow y_b$ where b is the output gate of A_{k-1}, and finally use the circuit C. Instead of sampling y_0, y_1, we can simply use non-uniformity to hard-code the best samples, at the cost of $2\ell_Y$ gates. Implementing the multiplexer can be done using $3\ell_Y + 1$ gates, with one gate computing $\neg b$ and for every $i \in [\ell_Y]$ another 3 gates to compute $y[i] = (y_0[i] \wedge \neg b) \vee (y_1[i] \wedge b)$. Overall, we conclude that $\text{size}(A_k) = \text{size}(A_{k-1}) + 5\ell_Y + 1 + s_k$ and therefore

$$\text{size}(A_k) = \text{size}(A_0) + k \cdot (5\ell_Y + 1 + s_k) \leq 1 + k \cdot \left(5\ell_Y + 1 + \left(\frac{s_X - 1}{k} - 5\ell_Y - 1\right)\right) = s_X$$

which is a contradiction to our assumption that d_X is an upper bound on the advantage of size s_X circuits distinguishing X_0 from X_1.

3.1   The N-Fold Case

Corollary 2. *Let D, Q be distributions over ℓ bits that are d indistinguishable for size s circuits. Then, for every $m \in \mathbb{N}$ and ε, we have that $D^{\otimes m}, Q^{\otimes m}$ are $(1 - (1 - d)^m + \varepsilon)$ indistinguishable for size $s_{m,\varepsilon}$ circuits, where*

$$s_{m,\varepsilon} = \frac{s - 1}{k_{m,\varepsilon}} - 5m\ell - 1, \qquad k_{m,\varepsilon} = \left\lceil \frac{\log(d\varepsilon)}{\log(1 - (1 - d)^m + \varepsilon)} \right\rceil \leq \left\lceil \frac{\log(1/d\varepsilon)}{(1 - d)^m - \varepsilon} \right\rceil.$$

Proof. If $\varepsilon \geq (1 - d)^m$ the statement is trivially true. Otherwise, we start from D, Q and use Theorem 2 to repeatedly add copies of D, Q for $m - 1$ times, using $k_{m,\varepsilon}$ set at the statement, where each time the added copy of D, Q is treated as X_0, X_1 and $D^{\otimes i}, Q^{\otimes i}$ are treated as Y_0, Y_1. Let d_i denote the bound on the advantage of i copies, then we have that $d_1 = d$ and $d_i \leq d_{i-1} + d - d_{i-1} \cdot d + (d_{i-1})^{k_{m,\varepsilon}}$. We can see by induction that $d_i \leq 1 - (1 - d)^i + \varepsilon$ for $i \in [m]$ as

$$d_i \le d_{i-1} + d - d_{i-1} \cdot d + (d_{i-1})^{k_{m,\varepsilon}} = (1-d)d_{i-1} + d + (d_{i-1})^{k_{m,\varepsilon}}$$

$$\le (1-d)\left(1 - (1-d)^{i-1} + \varepsilon\right) + d + \left(1 - (1-d)^{i-1} + \varepsilon\right)^{k_{m,\varepsilon}}$$

$$= 1 - d - (1-d)^i + (1-d)\varepsilon + d + \left(1 - (1-d)^{i-1} + \varepsilon\right)^{k_{m,\varepsilon}}$$

$$= 1 - (1-d)^i + (1-d)\varepsilon + \left(1 - (1-d)^{i-1} + \varepsilon\right)^{k_{m,\varepsilon}}$$

$$\le 1 - (1-d)^i + (1-d)\varepsilon + \left(1 - (1-d)^m + \varepsilon\right)^{k_{m,\varepsilon}} \le 1 - (1-d)^i + \varepsilon$$

where in the last inequality we used the choice of $k_{m,\varepsilon}$. For the circuit size, we can easily see by induction on i that $s_{i,\varepsilon} \ge (s-1)/k_{m,\varepsilon} - 5i\ell - 1$, as we have that $s_{1,\varepsilon} = s$ and

$$s_{i,\varepsilon} \ge \min\left\{ s_{(i-1),\varepsilon} - \ell, \frac{s-1}{k_{m,\varepsilon}} - 5(i-1)\ell - 1 \right\}$$

$$\ge \min\left\{ \frac{s-1}{k_{m,\varepsilon}} - 5(i-1)\ell - 1 - \ell, \frac{s-1}{k_{m,\varepsilon}} - 5(i-1)\ell - 1 \right\} \ge \frac{s-1}{k_{m,\varepsilon}} - 5i\ell - 1.$$

3.2 Tightness

This is somewhat folklore knowledge, that we explicitly state for the sake of completeness. We show that for every choice of $d_X, d_Y, s_X, s_Y, \ell_X, \ell_Y$ there exist two pairs of distributions X_0, X_1 and Y_0, Y_1, such that X_0, X_1 are over ℓ_X bits and cannot be distinguished with advantage better than d_X by size s_X circuits (resp. for Y_0, Y_1 with ℓ_Y, d_Y, s_Y), yet (X_0, Y_0) and (X_1, X_1) can be distinguished with advantage $d_X + d_Y - d_X \cdot d_Y$ using a size 1 circuit. For the n-fold case, we show that for every choice of d, s, ℓ there exist distributions X, Y over ℓ bits with distance at most d against s-sized circuits, such that $X^{\otimes k}, Y^{\otimes k}$ can be distinguished with advantage $1 - (1-d)^k$ using a circuit of size $2k - 1$. We will use statistical distance in these examples, noting that the statistical distance between distributions is equal to the maximal advantage of unbounded adversaries distinguishing between them, and that the statistical distance from a constant variable is equal to the probability to differ from it.

For the isolated case, we let $X_0 \equiv 0^{\ell_X}$, $X_1 := B(d_X)^{\ell_X}$, $Y_0 \equiv 0^{\ell_Y}$, $Y_1 := B(d_Y)^{\ell_Y}$, where $B(p)^\ell$ denotes sampling from $B(p)$ and outputting ℓ copies of the result. We have that size s_X circuits can distinguish between X_0, X_1 with advantage at most d_X (resp. for Y_0, Y_1 with s_Y, d_Y) as this is the statistical distance between them. Also, it is easy to verify that the simple size 1 circuit which given (x, y) computes $x[1] \vee y[1]$ distinguishes between (X_0, Y_0) and (X_1, Y_1) with advantage $1 - (1 - d_X)(1 - d_Y) = d_X + d_Y - d_X \cdot d_Y$.

For the n-fold case, let $X \equiv 0^\ell$, $Y := B(d)^\ell$, then size s circuits can distinguish X from Y with advantage at most d. Yet, the circuit of size $2k - 1$ which given $(z_1, \ldots, z_k)$ computes $\vee_i z_i[1]$ (using a full binary tree of OR gates) distinguishes between $X^{\otimes k}$ and $Y^{\otimes k}$ with advantage $1 - (1 - d)^k$.

4   The Uniform Variant

We used non-uniformity two times in the proof of Theorem 2. The second time, which is easier to deal with, is in the circuit size analysis where we hard-coded the best samples of y_0, y_1 to each iteration of A_i. Instead, in the uniform version, we will use uniform samplers of Y_0, Y_1.

The first use of non-uniformity was when we assumed that $C(x, \cdot)$ is at most a d_Y-distinguisher between Y_0 and Y_1, for every fixed x, otherwise we can use non-uniformity to be done. More specifically, we used this assumption to get that

$$\mathrm{adv}_C^+\left((X_1, Y_{A(X_1)}), (X_1, Y_1)\right) \leq d_Y \cdot \Pr[A(X_1) = 0].$$

For the uniform case, we will relax this condition to x not being easy to hard-code, in the following sense:

$$\Pr_{x \leftarrow X_{1/2}}\left[\mathrm{adv}_{C(x, \cdot)}^+(Y_0, Y_1) > d_Y + \varepsilon_k\right] \leq \varepsilon_k$$

where $X_{1/2}$ is given by $b \leftarrow \{0, 1\}, x \leftarrow X_b$. If this condition does not hold then we can efficiently compute a good x, except for negligible probability, assuming that efficient uniform samplers for X_0, X_1, Y_0, Y_1 exist. Otherwise, we will see that

$$\mathrm{adv}_C^+\left((X_1, Y_{A(X_1)}), (X_1, Y_1)\right) \leq d_Y \cdot \Pr[A(X_1) = 0] + 3\varepsilon_k$$

and so almost the same argument from the non-uniform case works, except that now we lose another small additive term. Let us state and prove this more formally:

Lemma 1. *Let $X_0 = \{X_{0,n}\}, X_1 = \{X_{1,n}\}, Y_0 = \{Y_{0,n}\}, Y_1 = \{Y_{1,n}\}$ be ensembles of efficiently samplable distributions, and $d_X(n), d_Y(n)$ be efficiently computable functions between 0 and 1. Then, for every $k \in \mathbb{N}$ and time $t(n)$ Turing machine M distinguishing (X_0, Y_0) from (X_1, Y_1) infinitely often with advantage at least $(d_X + d_Y - d_X \cdot d_Y + 7\varepsilon_k)$ for*

$$\varepsilon_k := \frac{(d_Y)^k \cdot d_X(1 - d_Y)}{1 - (d_Y)^k} \leq (d_Y)^k,$$

we have that either M efficiently yields a distinguisher for Y_0, Y_1 through a hard-coding of x, in the sense that for infinitely many n's

$$\Pr_{x \leftarrow X_{1/2}}\left[\mathrm{adv}_{M(1^n, x, \cdot)}^+(Y_0, Y_1) > d_Y + \varepsilon_k\right] > \varepsilon_k,$$

or there exists a time $t \cdot \mathrm{poly}(nk)$ infinitely often distinguisher between X_0, X_1 with advantage at least d_X.

Proof. For the sake of notational ease, we will drop the asymptotic notation and replace $M(1^n)$ with C. Assume that for all but finitely many n's,

$$\Pr_{x \leftarrow X_{1/2}}\left[\mathrm{adv}_{C(x, \cdot)}^+(Y_0, Y_1) > d_Y + \varepsilon_k\right] \leq \varepsilon_k.$$

Then, for every candidate distinguisher A between X_0 and X_1, for all but finitely many n's, we have that

$$\text{adv}_C^+\left((X_1, Y_{A(X_1)}), (X_1, Y_1)\right) \leq d_Y \cdot \Pr[A(X_1) = 0] + 3\varepsilon_k$$
$$\text{adv}_C^+\left((X_0, Y_0), (X_0, Y_{A(X_0)})\right) \leq d_Y \cdot \Pr[A(X_0) = 1] + 3\varepsilon_k$$

where $x, y \leftarrow X_1, Y_{A(X_1)}$ is resulted by $x \leftarrow X_1$, $b \leftarrow A(x)$, $y \leftarrow Y_b$. To see this, we first note that

$$\varepsilon_k \geq \Pr_{x \leftarrow X_{1/2}} \left[\text{adv}_{C(x, \cdot)}^+ (Y_0, Y_1) > d_Y + \varepsilon_k\right]$$
$$\geq \frac{1}{2} \Pr[A(X_1) = 0] \Pr_{x \leftarrow X_1 | A(X_1) = 0} \left[\text{adv}_{C(x, \cdot)}^+ (Y_0, Y_1) > d_Y + \varepsilon_k\right]$$

which implies that

$$\mathbb{E}_{x \leftarrow X_1 | A(X_1) = 0} \left[\text{adv}_{C(x, \cdot)}^+ (Y_0, Y_1)\right] \leq d_Y + \varepsilon_k + \frac{2\varepsilon_k}{\Pr[A(X_1) = 0]} \leq d_Y + \frac{3\varepsilon_k}{\Pr[A(X_1) = 0]}.$$

Plugging it into the last inequality in the following, we get

$$\text{adv}_C^+ \left((X_1, Y_{A(X_1)}), (X_1, Y_1)\right) = \mathbb{E}\left[C(X_1, Y_1) - C(X_1, Y_{A(X_1)})\right]$$
$$= \mathbb{E}\left[C(X_1, Y_1) - C(X_1, Y_0) | A(X_1) = 0\right] \cdot \Pr[A(X_1) = 0]$$
$$+ \mathbb{E}\left[C(X_1, Y_1) - C(X_1, Y_1) | A(X_1) = 1\right] \cdot \Pr[A(X_1) = 1]$$
$$= \mathbb{E}_{x \leftarrow X_1 | A(X_1) = 0} \left[C(x, Y_1) - C(x, Y_0)\right] \cdot \Pr[A(X_1) = 0]$$
$$= \mathbb{E}_{x \leftarrow X_1 | A(X_1) = 0} \left[\text{adv}_{C(x, \cdot)}^+ (Y_0, Y_1)\right] \cdot \Pr[A(X_1) = 0] \leq d_Y \cdot \Pr[A(X_1) = 0] + 3\varepsilon_k$$

and use a symmetric argument for the second upper bound. Using that (in general)

$$\sum_{i \in [n]} \text{adv}_C^+(D_i, D_{i+1}) = \text{adv}_C^+(D_1, D_{n+1})$$

we conclude that

$$\text{adv}_C^+ \left((X_0, Y_0), (X_1, Y_1)\right) = \text{adv}_C^+ \left((X_0, Y_0), (X_0, Y_{A(X_0)})\right)$$
$$+ \text{adv}_C^+ \left((X_0, Y_{A(X_0)}), (X_1, Y_{A(X_1)})\right) + \text{adv}_C^+ \left((X_1, Y_{A(X_1)}), (X_1, Y_1)\right)$$

and thus

$$\text{adv}_C^+ \left((X_0, Y_{A(X_0)}), (X_1, Y_{A(X_1)})\right) = \text{adv}_C^+ \left((X_0, Y_0), (X_1, Y_1)\right)$$
$$- \text{adv}_C^+ \left((X_1, Y_{A(X_1)}), (X_1, Y_1)\right) - \text{adv}_C^+ \left((X_0, Y_0), (X_0, Y_{A(X_0)})\right)$$
$$> (d_X + d_Y - d_X \cdot d_Y + 7\varepsilon_k) - (d_Y \cdot \Pr[A(X_1) = 0] + 3\varepsilon_k) - (d_Y \cdot \Pr[A(X_0) = 1] + 3\varepsilon_k)$$
$$= (d_X - d_X \cdot d_Y + \varepsilon_k) + d_Y(1 - \Pr[A(X_1) = 0] - \Pr[A(X_0) = 1])$$
$$= (d_X - d_X \cdot d_Y + \varepsilon_k) + d_Y(\Pr[A(X_1) = 1] - \Pr[A(X_0) = 1])$$
$$= (d_X - d_X \cdot d_Y + \varepsilon_k) + d_Y(\mathbb{E}[A(X_1)] - \mathbb{E}[A(X_0)])$$
$$= (d_X - d_X \cdot d_Y + \varepsilon_k) + d_Y \cdot \text{adv}_A^+ (X_0, X_1).$$

In other words, we can build a new distinguisher A' for X_0, X_1 by applying A to our input x, sampling $y \leftarrow Y_{A(x)}$ and feeding (x, y) to C, and have that

$$\text{adv}_{A'}^+ (X_0, X_1) > (d_X - d_X \cdot d_Y + \varepsilon_k) + d_Y \cdot \text{adv}_A^+ (X_0, X_1).$$

If we start from A_0 being the trivial distinguisher that always outputs 1 and keep repeating this process for k steps, we get that

$$\text{adv}_{A_k}^+ (X_0, X_1) > (d_X - d_X \cdot d_Y + \varepsilon_k) + d_Y \cdot \text{adv}_{A_{k-1}}^+ (X_0, X_1)$$

$$> (d_X - d_X \cdot d_Y + \varepsilon_k) + d_Y \cdot (d_X - d_X \cdot d_Y + \varepsilon_k) + (d_Y)^2 \cdot \text{adv}_{A_{k-2}}^+ (X_0, X_1)$$

$$> \cdots > (d_X - d_X \cdot d_Y + \varepsilon_k) \sum_{i=0}^{k-1} (d_Y)^i + (d_Y)^k \cdot \text{adv}_{A_0}^+ (X_0, X_1)$$

$$= (d_X - d_X \cdot d_Y + \varepsilon_k) \sum_{i=0}^{k-1} (d_Y)^i = \frac{(d_X - d_X \cdot d_Y + \varepsilon_k)\left(1 - (d_Y)^k\right)}{1 - d_Y}$$

$$= \frac{\left(d_X (1 - d_Y) + \frac{(d_Y)^k \cdot d_X (1 - d_Y)}{1 - (d_Y)^k}\right)\left(1 - (d_Y)^k\right)}{1 - d_Y} = \left(d_X + \frac{(d_Y)^k \cdot d_X}{1 - (d_Y)^k}\right)\left(1 - (d_Y)^k\right)$$

$$= d_X \left(1 - (d_Y)^k\right) + (d_Y)^k \cdot d_X = d_X.$$

And so, we have concluded that A_k distinguishes X_0 from X_1 with advantage better than d_X. In order to implement A_k we need to run C, sample Y_0, Y_1 and use a multiplexer, for k times, so we conclude that $\text{time}(A_k) = t \cdot \text{poly}(n, k)$.

Remark 2. In particular, we can use this lemma to show that if X_0, X_1 are d_X ind. and Y_0, Y_1 are d_Y ind. then (X_0, Y_0) and (X_1, Y_1) are $d_X + d_Y - d_X \cdot d_Y + 7\varepsilon_k$ ind. for Turing machines with running time of

$$t = \min\{t_X/\text{poly}(n, k), t_Y/\text{poly}(n, 1/\varepsilon_k)\},$$

which may be good enough for a constant number of uses, but does not work well beyond that, as every use costs us a division of the time bound by a polynomial. This is why we cannot prove the n-fold case immediately by repeatedly applying Lemma 1. The key idea is that we do not need to keep resampling and testing over and over again, but instead, once we find a good enough x in the i'th coordinate, we fix it for the rest of the process, or if the hard-coding of the i'th coordinate does not succeed, the above lemma states we can distinguish there.

Theorem 3. *Let $X = \{X_n\}, Y = \{Y_n\}$ be ensembles of efficiently samplable distributions that are $d(n)$ indistinguishable for time $t(n)$ Turing machines. Then, for every $m = m(n)$, we have that $X^{\otimes m}$ and $Y^{\otimes m}$ are $(1 - (1-d)^m + 7m\varepsilon)$ indistinguishable for time $t_{m,\varepsilon}$ Turing machines, where*

$$t_{m,\varepsilon} = t/\text{poly}(n, m, k_{m,\varepsilon}, 1/\varepsilon), \quad k_{m,\varepsilon} = \left\lceil \frac{\log(\varepsilon)}{\log(1 - (1-d)^m + 7m\varepsilon)} \right\rceil \leq \left\lceil \frac{\log(1/\varepsilon)}{(1-d)^m - 7m\varepsilon} \right\rceil.$$

Proof. For $i = 0, 1, \ldots, m - 1$, we try to hard-code the $m - i$'th coordinate using $\text{poly}(n, 1/\varepsilon)$ samples, and getting a distinguisher for $X^{\otimes m-i}, Y^{\otimes m-i}$ with advantage of at least $1 - (1-d)^{m-i} + 7(m-i)\varepsilon$ except for negligible probability (the probability that the estimate was good but not truthful to the expectation) until for some i we fail to find a good value to hard-code (if we reached $i = m-1$ and succeeded then we are done). Once we fail, we apply the isolated case of Lemma 1, which essentially states that if the hard-coding of X, Y into such circuit failed, then one can build a distinguisher for them, and we are done.

Let us be more explicit about how we sample and hard-code the $m - i$'th coordinate: We are given (except for negligible probability) good samples for the coordinates in $m - i + 1, \ldots, m$ and hard-code them into A, getting a $1 - (1-d)^{m-i} + 7(m-i)\varepsilon$ distinguisher for $X^{\otimes m-i}, Y^{\otimes m-i}$, which we view as the product of $X^{\otimes m-i-1}, Y^{\otimes m-i-1}$ with X, Y. We first note that our choice of k guarantees that $\varepsilon_k \le \varepsilon$ for all $1 - (1-d)^{m-i} + 7(m-i)\varepsilon$. We start by trying to work under the "hard-coding" assumption that

$$\Pr_{z \leftarrow X/Y} \left[\mathrm{adv}^+_{A(z,\cdot)} \left(X^{\otimes m-i-1}, Y^{\otimes m-i-1} \right) > 1 - (1-d)^{m-i-1} + 7(m-i-1)\varepsilon + \varepsilon \right] > \varepsilon$$

and generate a distinguisher for $X^{\otimes m-i-1}, Y^{\otimes m-i-1}$ as follows: Keep sampling $z \leftarrow X/Y$ and estimating $\mathrm{adv}^+_{A(z,\cdot)} \left(X^{\otimes m-i-1}, Y^{\otimes m-i-1} \right)$ using r samples from $X^{\otimes m-i-1}/Y^{\otimes m-i-1}$, until we succeed in finding z with an estimate of at least $1 - (1-d)^{m-i-1} + 7(m-i-1)\varepsilon + 0.5\varepsilon$, then fix this good z in this coordinate and move forward, or stop after q tries if no such z has been found. Using Hoeffding's inequality, for every z, the probability that the estimate's error is greater than $\varepsilon/2$ is at most $2e^{-r\cdot(\varepsilon/2)^2/2}$. If all estimates were $\varepsilon/2$ accurate and a good z has been drawn, the process succeeds in finding a z with advantage of at least $1 - (1-d)^{m-i-1} + 7(m-i-1)\varepsilon$ and we can move on, so our probability to fail at that, under the above assumption, is at most

$$q \cdot 2e^{-r\cdot\varepsilon^2/32} + (1-\varepsilon)^q \le 2e^{\log(q/2)-r\cdot\varepsilon^2/32} + e^{-q\cdot\varepsilon} \le \mathrm{neg}(n)$$

by choosing, say,

$$q = n/\varepsilon = \mathrm{poly}(n, 1/\varepsilon), \quad r = 64n/\varepsilon^3 > (\log(q/2) + n) \cdot 32/\varepsilon^2 = \mathrm{poly}(n, 1/\varepsilon).$$

Hence paying with a time complexity of $t_{m,\varepsilon}$ poly$(n, 1/\varepsilon)$ for every coordinate.

If we could not find a good z, we use Lemma 1: If we can distinguish $X^{\otimes m-i}, Y^{\otimes m-i}$ with advantage

$$(1-d)\left(1 - (1-d)^{m-i-1} + 7(m-i-1)\varepsilon\right) + d + 7\varepsilon$$
$$= 1 - (1-d)^{m-i} + (1-d)7(m-i-1)\varepsilon + 7\varepsilon$$
$$\le 1 - (1-d)^{m-i} + 7(m-i)\varepsilon \le \mathrm{adv}^+_A \left(X^{\otimes m-i}, Y^{\otimes m-i} \right)$$

and the assumption about finding a good z to hard-code for $X^{\otimes m-i-1}, Y^{\otimes m-i-1}$ does not hold, then we can build a d-distinguisher for X, Y in time $t_{m,\varepsilon}$ · poly(n, k). The probability that at some point in the process we failed to hard-code a good z at the $m - i$'th coordinate even though the assumption held is $m(n) \cdot \mathrm{neg}(n) = \mathrm{neg}(n)$.

We remark this proof is easily generalized to the case where not all pairs in the product are identical, that is, for $\bigotimes X_i$ and $\bigotimes Y_i$, with a distance bound of $(1 - \prod_i(1 - d_i) + 7m\varepsilon)$.

5   Applications

As an application, we consider the amplification of weak oblivious transfer protocols. We briefly explain how our bounds, paired with Yao's XOR Lemma, yield a natural generalization in the computational setting to the amplification process presented in [2, Subsection 4.3]. We note that it was already shown, using The Hardcore Theorem [1,8], that the same amplification process also works computationally [13]. Yet we find our constructive and explicit approach more natural and straightforward.

For the sake of simplicity, let us consider the amplification of error-less (p,q)-weak semi-honest 1-2 OT: The receiver with bit c is trying to learn b_c, where (b_0, b_1) is the database of the sender. We say the protocol is (p,q) weak if the view of the sender when $c = 0$ is p-indistinguishable from its view when $c = 1$ (equivalently, c is at most p-correlated to the view of the sender), and the view of the receiver when $b_{\overline{c}} = 0$ is q-indistinguishable from its view when $b_{\overline{c}} = 1$.

In [2, Subsection 4.2], two fundamental operations that will be used as building blocks in the amplification process are presented. One is an operation called S-Reduce that amplifies indistinguishability against the sender but worsens indistinguishability against the receiver, and the other is an operation called R-Reduce that amplifies indistinguishability against the receiver but worsens indistinguishability against the sender. Both of them work using secret sharing over multiple applications of the underlying protocol, in the first the receiver's choice bit is secret shared and in the other, the sender's database. They receive a weak protocol $\mathcal{W}$ together with a parameter k and work as follows:

S-**Reduce**$(k, \mathcal{W})$

1: **Inputs:** c, (b_0, b_1)
2: The receiver splits c randomly into k shares $\{c_i\}_{i=1}^k$ conditioned on $\oplus_{i=1}^k c_i = c$.
3: The sender splits b_0 randomly into k shares $\{b_{0i}\}_{i=1}^k$ conditioned on $\oplus_{i=1}^k b_{0i} = b_0$, and sets $b_{1i} = b_{0i} \oplus b_0 \oplus b_1$.
4: **for** $i = 1$ **to** k **do**
5:     Run $\mathcal{W}$ with c_i, (b_{0i}, b_{1i}).
6: **end for**
7: The receiver outputs the XOR of all k received bits, that is, $\oplus_{i=1}^k b_{c_i, i}$.

R-**Reduce**$(k, \mathcal{W})$

1: **Inputs:** c, (b_0, b_1)
2: The receiver sets $c_i = c$ for $i \in [k]$.
3: The sender splits b_0 randomly into k shares $\{b_{0i}\}_{i=1}^k$ conditioned on $\oplus_{i=1}^k b_{0i} = b_0$, and also splits b_1 randomly into k shares $\{b_{1i}\}_{i=1}^k$ conditioned on $\oplus_{i=1}^k b_{1i} = b_1$.
4: **for** $i = 1$ **to** k **do**
5:    Run $\mathcal{W}$ with c_i, (b_{0i}, b_{1i}).
6: **end for**
7: The receiver outputs the XOR of all k received bits, that is, $\oplus_{i=1}^k b_{c_i, i}$.

Correctness of R-Reduce is straightforward. For S-Reduce, note that in the i'th call the receiver learns $b_{0i} \oplus c_i \cdot (b_0 \oplus b_1)$. When XORing them all together over $i \in [k]$, we get $b_0 \oplus c \cdot (b_0 \oplus b_1)$ which is exactly what we needed.

For receiver-security, if $\mathcal{W}$ has receiver-security of p, we can use the XOR Lemma to deduce that S-Reduce$(k, \mathcal{W})$ has receiver-security of $p^k + \varepsilon$, because the shares $\{c_i\}_{i=1}^k$ are random and independent (over a random choice of c) and for every fixing of the sender's randomness, the i'th transcript is independent of the rest and is at most p-correlated to c_i. We can also use our own product bound to deduce that R-Reduce$(k, \mathcal{W})$ has receiver-security of $1 - (1 - p)^k + \varepsilon$, because for every fixing of the sender's randomness, the transcripts are independent conditioned on c and each one is at most p-correlated to c. Using similar arguments, it can be shown that symmetrically, sender-security amplifies to $q^k + \varepsilon$ in R-Reduce$(k, \mathcal{W})$ and weakens to $1 - (1 - q)^k + \varepsilon$ in S-Reduce$(k, \mathcal{W})$. These are exactly the same bounds used in the information-theoretic OT amplification analysis, up to the additive ε paid for each use.

The goal is to use these two operations repeatedly one after the other in order to reduce both parameters. It is already shown in [2, Lemma 4] exactly how this is done, but for the sake of completeness let us summarize the process as follows: Assume without loss of generality that $p \leq q$ (other case is symmetric). If $p \geq 0.2$, by applying R-Reduce$(2, \cdot)$ followed by S-Reduce$(2, \cdot)$, the distance between the error sum $p + q$ and 1 is multiplied by at least 1.1. Otherwise, if $q > 0.4$, by applying R-Reduce$(2, \cdot)$ the distance between $p + q$ and 1 is multiplied by at least 1.2. Otherwise, if $p + q > 0.2$, we again apply R-Reduce$(2, \cdot)$ followed by S-Reduce$(2, \cdot)$, with the guarantee that the error sum $p + q$ multiplies by a factor of at most 0.8. Finally, in the case where $p + q \leq 0.2$, we apply R-Reduce$(4, \cdot)$ followed by S-Reduce$(4, \cdot)$, and the guarantee is that the error sum is at least squared, that is, $(p' + q') \leq (p + q)^2$, so the progress downwards is quick.

To conclude, the same analysis from the information-theoretic setting holds here, up to an additive ε accumulated at each use. Let $p(n)$ be a bound on the total number of calls to the original protocol in the information-theoretic transformation, then all advantages throughout the process are $1/p(n)$-bounded away from 1, otherwise we would not be able to reduce them to negligible. By setting $\varepsilon' = \varepsilon/p(n)$, for every advantage d through the process we have $d + \varepsilon' \leq \varepsilon + (1 - \varepsilon)d$, so we can imagine, for the sake of the analysis, as if every call to either S-Reduce or R-Reduce incurs a chance of ε at failing and revealing everything, and otherwise works exactly like the information-theoretic world. Since the number of calls is polynomial, the total probability of failing is at most $\text{poly}(n) \cdot \varepsilon$ and we can make it as (polynomially) small as we want.

There is one small issue, however - the running time. In the information-theoretic process we make $\log\log(n)$ calls to S-Reduce and R-Reduce (when p and q are constants), and each such call, when using Yao's XOR Lemma or the bounds in this paper, decreases the bound on the running time by a division in a polynomial. Therefore, we need the assumption that our weak OT is secure against $n^{O(\log\log n)}$ adversaries. We remark that this issue can be overcome by choosing an increasing series of errors instead of fixing ε throughout the process. If $1 - (p+q)$ is not lower bounded by a constant but by $1/\text{poly}(n)$, then we need security against $n^{O(\log n)}$ adversaries.

6 Open Questions

An issue that keeps appearing in security reductions where amplification is involved is the problem of amplification beyond negligible [3]. For example see [5, Lemma 3] and the discussion following it. Roughly speaking, in these types of reductions we can show security holds except for negligible probability but nothing concrete beyond that without increasing the running time of the reduction to be super-polynomial.

For a more specific example, let us consider Levin's proof of the XOR Lemma [10]. Informally, it is shown that if for X_0, X_1 we have that b is at most d-correlated to X_b by s-sized circuits, then $\bigoplus_{i=1}^{t} b_i$ is at most $d^t + \varepsilon$-correlated to $X_{b_1}, \ldots, X_{b_t}$ by $s \cdot \text{poly}(\varepsilon)$-sized circuits. Note the trade-off between the reduction accuracy and the circuit size bound. Another trade-off can also be seen in Theorem 2. If we only know that s is greater than any polynomial then we can push ε up to negligible but nothing concrete beyond that, otherwise the circuit size bound becomes meaningless.

As noted in [5], Rudich has observed that we cannot expect to overcome this issue in a black-box way. Further, in [3] an example is given, based on non-standard assumptions, of a weak OWF that cannot be amplified beyond negligible using the direct product transformation. That is, it may be that overcoming this issue is not just hard to prove, but can be altogether false. Nonetheless, what happens in general is still unclear, and there are still open directions of either strengthening the impossibilities by reducing assumptions, or of showing that some form of amplification beyond negligible is achievable.

Interestingly enough, when considering Corollary 2, we note how the circuit size growth is actually only logarithmic in $1/\varepsilon$, although linear in $1/(1 - d)^m$. Still, if d and m are constants, then we can reduce the error exponentially well while maintaining efficiency of the circuits. This brings us to the following conjecture, aiming to formulate the XOR equivalent of the above, stated with specific parameters for simplicity:

Conjecture 1 (Informal). If b is at most 0.5-correlated to X_b by s-sized circuits, then $b_1 \oplus b_2$ is at most $0.25 + 2^{-n}$-correlated to X_{b_1}, X_{b_2} by $s/\text{poly}(n)$-sized circuits.

In other words, as long as we are not trying to achieve correlation beyond negligible, we can get exponentially close efficiently. This could be seen as a first step towards a positive result.

References

1. Barak, B., Hardt, M., Kale, S.: The uniform hardcore lemma via approximate bregman projections. In: Mathieu, C. (ed.) Proceedings of the Twentieth Annual ACM-SIAM Symposium on Discrete Algorithms, SODA 2009, New York, NY, USA, 4–6 January 2009, pp. 1193–1200. SIAM (2009). http://dl.acm.org/citation.cfm?id=1496770.1496899
2. Damgård, I., Kilian, J., Salvail, L.: On the (im)possibility of basing oblivious transfer and bit commitment on weakened security assumptions. In: Stern, J. (ed.) EUROCRYPT 1999. LNCS, vol. 1592, pp. 56–73. Springer, Heidelberg (1999). https://doi.org/10.1007/3-540-48910-X_5
3. Dodis, Y., Jain, A., Moran, T., Wichs, D.: Counterexamples to hardness amplification beyond negligible. In: Cramer, R. (ed.) TCC 2012. LNCS, vol. 7194, pp. 476–493. Springer, Heidelberg (2012). https://doi.org/10.1007/978-3-642-28914-9_27
4. Fehr, S., Vaudenay, S.: Sublinear bounds on the distinguishing advantage for multiple samples. In: Aoki, K., Kanaoka, A. (eds.) IWSEC 2020. LNCS, vol. 12231, pp. 165–183. Springer, Cham (2020). https://doi.org/10.1007/978-3-030-58208-1_10
5. Goldreich, O., Nisan, N., Wigderson, A.: On Yao's XOR-lemma. Electron. Colloquium Comput. Complex 2(50) (1995). http://eccc.hpi-web.de/eccc-reports/1995/TR95-050/index.html
6. Holenstein, T.: Key agreement from weak bit agreement. In: Gabow, H.N., Fagin, R. (eds.) Proceedings of the 37th Annual ACM Symposium on Theory of Computing, Baltimore, MD, USA, 22–24 May 2005, pp. 664–673. ACM (2005). https://doi.org/10.1145/1060590.1060689
7. Hollander, F.: Probability theory: the coupling method (2012)
8. Impagliazzo, R.: Hard-core distributions for somewhat hard problems. In: 36th Annual Symposium on Foundations of Computer Science, Milwaukee, Wisconsin, USA, 23–25 October 1995, pp. 538–545. IEEE Computer Society (1995). https://doi.org/10.1109/SFCS.1995.492584
9. Kontorovich, A.: Obtaining measure concentration from Markov contraction. Markov Process. Related Fields 18(4), 613–638 (2012)
10. Levin, L.A.: One-way functions and pseudorandom generators. Combinatorica 7(4), 357–363 (1987). https://doi.org/10.1007/BF02579323
11. Maurer, U., Tessaro, S.: A hardcore lemma for computational indistinguishability: security amplification for arbitrarily weak PRGs with optimal stretch. In: Micciancio, D. (ed.) TCC 2010. LNCS, vol. 5978, pp. 237–254. Springer, Heidelberg (2010). https://doi.org/10.1007/978-3-642-11799-2_15
12. Renner, R.: On the variational distance of independently repeated experiments. CoRR abs/cs/0509013 (2005). http://arxiv.org/abs/cs/0509013
13. Wullschleger, J.: Oblivious-transfer amplification. In: Naor, M. (ed.) EUROCRYPT 2007. LNCS, vol. 4515, pp. 555–572. Springer, Heidelberg (2007). https://doi.org/10.1007/978-3-540-72540-4_32

Secure Sampling with Sublinear Communication

Seung Geol Choi[1]([✉])(iD), Dana Dachman-Soled[2](iD), S. Dov Gordon[3],
Linsheng Liu[4](iD), and Arkady Yerukhimovich[4](iD)

[1] United States Naval Academy, Annapolis, USA
choi@usna.edu
[2] University of Maryland, College Park, USA
danadach@ece.umd.edu
[3] George Mason University, Fairfax City, USA
gordon@gmu.edu
[4] George Washington University, Washington, USA
{lls,arkady}@gwu.edu

Abstract. Random sampling from specified distributions is an important tool with wide applications for analysis of large-scale data. In this paper we study how to randomly sample when the distribution is partitioned among two parties' private inputs. Of course, a trivial solution is to have one party send a (possibly encrypted) description of its weights to the other party who can then sample over the entire distribution (possibly using homomorphic encryption). However, this approach requires communication that is linear in the input size which is prohibitively expensive in many settings. In this paper, we investigate secure 2-party sampling with *sublinear communication* for many standard distributions. We develop protocols for L_1, and L_2 sampling. Additionally, we investigate the feasibility of sublinear product sampling, showing impossibility for the general problem and showing a protocol for a restricted case of the problem. We additionally show how such product sampling can be used to instantiate a sublinear communication 2-party exponential mechanism for differentially-private data release.

1 Introduction

Random sampling is an important tool when computing over massive data sets. It has wide application in generating small summaries of data, and serves as a key building block in the design of many algorithms and estimation procedures. In particular, L_p sampling has been used to develop important streaming algorithms such as the heavy hitters, L_p norm estimation, cascaded norm estimation, and finding duplicates in data streams [2,5,21,27].

In this work, we introduce and explore the problem of private two-party sampling. We consider a setting in which two parties would like to sample from a distribution whose probability mass function is distributed across the two parties. Specifically, we assume parties P_1 and P_2 each hold n-dimensional vectors $\mathbf{w}_1 = (w_{1,1}, \ldots, w_{1,n})$ and $\mathbf{w}_2 = (w_{2,1}, \ldots, w_{2,n})$ respectively where every $w_{b,j}$ is non-negative. These vectors each represent a (possibly non-normalized) probability

© The Author(s), under exclusive license to Springer Nature Switzerland 2022
E. Kiltz and V. Vaikuntanathan (Eds.): TCC 2022, LNCS 13748, pp. 348–377, 2022.
https://doi.org/10.1007/978-3-031-22365-5_13

mass function of a distribution. Specifically, for $b \in \{1,2\}$, $i \in [n]$, the non-negative value $\frac{w_{b,i}}{\|\mathbf{w}_b\|_1}$ represents the probability mass placed by distribution $\mathcal{D}_b$ on element i. We assume that the dimension n is very large, and our goal is to obtain secure sampling protocols with communication that is *sub-linear* in n.

We consider various ways of deriving the probability mass function $\mathcal{D}$ of the joint distribution from the two individual probability mass functions. Specifically, we consider:

- L_1 distribution: Sample item i with probability $\frac{w_{1,i}+w_{2,i}}{\|\mathbf{w}_1+\mathbf{w}_2\|_1} = \frac{w_{1,i}+w_{2,i}}{\sum_j (w_{1,j}+w_{2,j})}$.
- L_2 distribution: Sample item i with probability $\frac{(w_{1,i}+w_{2,i})^2}{\|\mathbf{w}_1+\mathbf{w}_2\|_2^2} = \frac{(w_{1,i}+w_{2,i})^2}{\sum_j (w_{1,j}+w_{2,j})^2}$.
- Product distribution: Sample item i with probability $\frac{w_{1,i} \cdot w_{2,i}}{\langle \mathbf{w}_1, \mathbf{w}_2 \rangle} = \frac{w_{1,i} \cdot w_{2,i}}{\sum_j (w_{1,j} \cdot w_{2,j})}$.[1]

Realizing these sampling functionalities securely is immediate via generic 2PC techniques, but the resulting protocols will require communication that is linear in the input length. With *sublinear* communication, however, it is unclear how to perform some of these tasks (or whether it is even possible to do so), even with an *insecure* protocol. We give a (partial) characterization of when such sublinear sampling is possible, and give secure protocols for realizing these functionalities where possible.

Product Sampling and the Exponential Mechanism. While L_1 and L_2 sampling are well-studied, to the best of our knowledge, we are the first to consider the notion of product sampling. We describe a concrete, independent application for this new notion: product sampling can be used to implement a distributed version of the well-known exponential mechanism for differentially-private data release [25].

1.1 Our Work

We explore the problems described above, providing multiple two-party protocols, all with sub-linear communication, in the semi-honest security model. We note that our protocol for product sampling has additional leakage, beyond what is revealed by the sampling functionality. We characterize exactly what this leakage is, and provide evidence that similar leakage is necessary to achieve sublinear communication. Specifically, we show the following.

L_1 **Sampling.** We begin by constructing a two-party protocol for L_1 sampling that relies on fully homomorphic encryption (FHE). The main idea behind the protocol is to obliviously sample from each of the two parties inputs independently, and then to securely choose one of the two samples using an appropriately biased coin toss. The results are described in Sect. 2.

---

[1] Of course, if $\langle \mathbf{w}_1, \mathbf{w}_2 \rangle = 0$, the probability space is not well-defined, and in this case, we require the protocol to simply output $\bot$.

L_2 **Sampling.** We also provide a protocol for secure L_2 sampling that relies on fully homomorphic encryption (see Sect. 3). In this case, however, achieving L_2 sampling is non-trivial. In fact, even relying on FHE, it is not immediately clear how to compute $\|\mathbf{w}_1 + \mathbf{w}_2\|_2^2$ with sublinear communication.

Surprisingly, our L_2 sampling protocol runs in constant rounds and with $\tilde{O}(1)$ communication[2]. Interestingly, it does not require us to compute $\|\mathbf{w}_1 + \mathbf{w}_2\|_2^2$. To achieve this, we developed a novel technique called "corrective sampling", which we overview in the next subsection. We note that our techniques straightforwardly extend to L_p sampling, for constant p.

Product Sampling. We then turn to product sampling. We assume, without loss of generality, that the vectors $\mathbf{w}_b$ are normalized (see Sect. 4 for justification).

We first begin with a communication lowerbound, demonstrating that product sampling with sublinear communication is impossible, even without privacy guarantees, if the two input distributions are insufficiently correlated (i.e., $\langle \mathbf{w}_1, \mathbf{w}_2 \rangle = o(\frac{1}{n^2})$). We show this through a reduction from the Set Disjointness problem.

Knowing this lowerbound, we consider the problem under a promise that the input vectors are sufficiently correlated. Assuming that $\langle \mathbf{w}_1, \mathbf{w}_2 \rangle = \omega(\frac{\log n}{n})$, we provide a two-party protocol for secure product sampling leaking (at most) the inner product of the two parties' inputs. We note that the promise itself leaks some information, so some leakage here is inevitable. Interestingly, we observe that the protocol can be modified to provide a trade-off between the communication cost and the leakage. We also discuss why this trade-off is inherent.

Constant Round Product Sampling. Our product sampling protocol has a round complexity that depends on the inner product. In Sect. 5, we show how to make our construction constant round while incurring small additional leakage. Importantly, we must do this *without computing the exact inner product* which itself requires $O(n)$ communication [3].

Two Party Exponential Mechanism. As mentioned previously, one important application of product sampling is the exponential mechanism for providing differential privacy [25]. Details are in Appendix F in the full version [7].

For this particular application we face an additional challenge: the leakage of $\langle \mathbf{w}_1, \mathbf{w}_2 \rangle$ that we relied on for achieving sub-linear communication in product sampling does not preserve differential privacy. To overcome this issue, we construct a new, differentially-private approximation for inner product, and show how to use this for building a sub-linear communication secure computation of the exponential mechanism.

---

[2] Throughout the paper, we will describe the round and communication complexities using the asymptotic notation only based on n. That is, all other parameters (e.g., security parameter) independent on n will be suppressed in the asymptotic expressions.

1.2   Technical Overview

In the following, we overload notation and let $\mathcal{D}$ denote a distribution as well as its probability mass function. As discussed previously, we consider the case where a probability mass function is distributed across two parties, and the parties would like to securely sample from the corresponding distribution. We consider several ways in which the probability mass function can be distributed across the two parties.

L_1 **Sampling of Convex Combinations.** In this case, party 1 (resp. party 2) holds a vector $\mathbf{w}_1$ (resp. $\mathbf{w}_2$), indexed from 1 to n. For $i \in [n]$, $w_{1,i}/\|\mathbf{w}_1\|_1$ (resp. $w_{2,i}/\|\mathbf{w}_2\|_1$) corresponds to the probability mass of i under distribution $\mathcal{D}_1$ (resp. $\mathcal{D}_2$). The goal of the parties is to sample from the distribution $\mathcal{D}$, defined as follows for $i \in [n]$:

$$
\begin{aligned}
\mathcal{D}[i] &:= \frac{\|\mathbf{w}_1\|_1}{\|\mathbf{w}_1\|_1 + \|\mathbf{w}_2\|_1} \cdot \frac{w_{1,i}}{\|\mathbf{w}_1\|_1} + \frac{\|\mathbf{w}_2\|_1}{\|\mathbf{w}_1\|_1 + \|\mathbf{w}_2\|_1} \cdot \frac{w_{2,i}}{\|\mathbf{w}_2\|_1} \\
&= \frac{\|\mathbf{w}_1\|_1}{\|\mathbf{w}_1\|_1 + \|\mathbf{w}_2\|_1} \cdot \mathcal{D}_1[i] + \frac{\|\mathbf{w}_2\|_1}{\|\mathbf{w}_1\|_1 + \|\mathbf{w}_2\|_1} \cdot \mathcal{D}_2[i]
\end{aligned}
$$

Note that the target distribution $\mathcal{D}$ is a convex combination of the distributions $\mathcal{D}_1$ and $\mathcal{D}_2$ held by the two parties.

A potentially straightforward sampling protocol is to therefore have party 1 locally draw a sample i_1 from $\mathcal{D}_1$, party 2 locally draw a sample i_2 from $\mathcal{D}_2$, and then run a secure two party computation that outputs i_1 with probability $\frac{\|\mathbf{w}_1\|_1}{\|\mathbf{w}_1\|_1 + \|\mathbf{w}_2\|_1}$ and i_2 with probability $\frac{\|\mathbf{w}_2\|_1}{\|\mathbf{w}_1\|_1 + \|\mathbf{w}_2\|_1}$.

This protocol clearly has sublinear communication, but it unfortunately does not securely realize the ideal functionality. The reason is as follows: conditioned on the ideal functionality outputting a certain index i^*, the probability that i^* was drawn by party 1 (resp. party 2) is $\frac{w_{1,i^*}}{w_{1,i^*} + w_{2,i^*}}$ (resp. $\frac{w_{2,i^*}}{w_{1,i^*} + w_{2,i^*}}$). Thus, if the simulator receives i^* from the ideal functionality and has to simulate the view of party 1, it needs to set $i_1 = i^*$ with probability $\frac{w_{1,i^*}}{w_{1,i^*} + w_{2,i^*}}$ and set $i_1 \neq i^*$ with probability $\frac{w_{2,i^*}}{w_{1,i^*} + w_{2,i^*}}$. However, the simulator is not able to simulate these probabilities correctly, since it does not know w_{2,i^*}.

To get around this issue we therefore have the parties sample i_1 and i_2 *obliviously*. To do this with sublinear communication, we can use fully homomorphic encryption (FHE). Specifically, to sample i_1, player 1 first encrypts his input $\mathbf{w}_1$ using an FHE scheme for which he does not know the secret key. The players then jointly choose a random value $r \in [0, \|\mathbf{w}_1\|_1)$. Player 1 then uses the homomorphic operations to find the value i_1 chosen by this r, and the parties use threshold decryption to recover a secret sharing of i_1. The parties reverse roles to sample i_2. Details of this construction are provided in Sect. 2.

Additionally, an alternative construction that uses sub-linear OT for the oblivious sampling is provided in Appendix D in the full version.

L_2 **Sampling of Component-wise Sum.** In this case, party 1 (resp. party 2) holds a vector $\mathbf{w}_1$ (resp. $\mathbf{w}_2$), indexed from 1 to n. For $i \in [n]$. The goal of the parties is to sample from the distribution $\mathcal{D}$ defined as follows for $i \in [n]$:

$$\mathcal{D}[i] := \frac{(w_{1,i} + w_{2,i})^2}{||\mathbf{w}_1 + \mathbf{w}_2||_2^2}.$$

We present a protocol that samples from this distribution with $\tilde{O}(1)$ communication. This protocol relies on a novel technique that we call "corrective sampling", which is an interesting type of rejection sampling. In what follows, we describe an insecure version of our protocol to give the intuition behind it. To make it secure, we carry out the corrective sampling under FHE as described in Protocol 4.

The main challenge that we face here, unlike in the case of L_1 sampling, is that it is impossible to compute $||\mathbf{w}_1 + \mathbf{w}_2||_2^2$ (and therefore impossible to compute $\mathcal{D}[i]$ for each i) with sublinear communication [3]. Instead, we sample index i from a different, related, distribution, which is easy to sample with sub-linear communication. We then show that we can efficiently correct this distribution by rejecting with the appropriate probability. Interestingly, we show that corrective rejection, which depends on the index i, doesn't require us to explicitly compute $||\mathbf{w}_1 + \mathbf{w}_2||_2^2$. In fact, the parties never learn the corrective term at all!

First, as in rejection sampling, corrective sampling proceeds in trials and in each trial, for every i, the probability that the protocol successfully samples index i is $\alpha \cdot \mathcal{D}[i]$ for some unknown constant $0 < \alpha < 1$. Since the same constant α is applied to every index i, by repeating the trials, the protocol samples index i correctly without skewing the distribution $\mathcal{D}$. The expected number of trials is $1/\alpha$. We therefore need to keep $1/\alpha \in O(1)$ to reach our target communication complexity.

As mentioned above, we observe that *the protocol never has to explicitly compute α*. Towards describing how this is done, first note that in $\mathcal{D}[i]$, the denominator, $||\mathbf{w}_1 + \mathbf{w}_2||_2^2$ – which we assume for purposes of this exposition is at least 1 – is the same for every i, so it can be pushed into α without impacting the discussion above: letting $\alpha' = \alpha/(||\mathbf{w}_1 + \mathbf{w}_2||_2^2)$, it suffices to implement rejection sampling with a protocol that samples index i with probability $\alpha' \cdot (w_{i,1} + w_{i,2})^2 = \alpha \cdot \mathcal{D}[i]$. This protocol would only need to explicitly compute $(w_{i,1} + w_{i,2})^2$ (which can be done efficiently given i), but not α'.

Unfortunately, this does not quite work. $||\mathbf{w}_1 + \mathbf{w}_2||_2^2$ can be very large, which would then make $1/\alpha'$ large. We therefore must combine the above with another idea to ensure that our corrective term introduces at most a $O(1)$ overhead.

We achieve this by having each trial of the protocol work as follows:

1. It samples index i from distribution $\mathcal{D}_{\text{ignore}}$, which is easy to sample. We note that the contribution of this distribution will be eventually canceled out through rejection. In particular, we choose the following distribution for $\mathcal{D}_{\text{ignore}}$:

$$\mathcal{D}_{\text{ignore}}[i] := \frac{w_{1,i}^2 + w_{2,i}^2}{\text{denom}},$$

where we set $\text{denom} = ||\mathbf{w}_1||_2^2 + ||\mathbf{w}_2||_2^2$ to make the distribution well-defined. Note that denom can be computed with $\tilde{O}(1)$ communication.

2. After sampling i from $\mathcal{D}_{\text{ignore}}$, the protocol computes a "corrective bias" for a coin flip that is dependent on $(w_{1,i} + w_{2,i})^2$. We stress that once i is determined, computing $(w_{1,i} + w_{2,i})^2$ is easy. In particular, a coin is flipped with the following bias:

$$\Pr[coin|i] := \frac{(w_{1,i} + w_{2,i})^2}{2 \cdot \mathcal{D}_{\text{ignore}}[i] \cdot \text{denom}}$$

Overall, this makes sure that the probability that each trial outputs index i is

$$\mathcal{D}_{\text{ignore}}[i] \cdot \Pr[coin|i] = \frac{(w_{1,i} + w_{2,i})^2}{2 \cdot \text{denom}} = \alpha \mathcal{D}[i],$$

where $\alpha = \frac{\|\mathbf{w_1} + \mathbf{w_2}\|_2^2}{2 \cdot \text{denom}}$.

To conclude that this is a valid and efficient sampling procedure, we need to show the following:

- α must be less than 1 for the procedure to be valid. This is implied by the fact that $\|\mathbf{w_1} + \mathbf{w_2}\|_2^2 \leq 2 \cdot \text{denom}$.
- $1/\alpha$ must be in $\tilde{O}(1)$ so that the procedure is efficient. We have $2 \cdot \text{denom} \leq 2\|\mathbf{w_1} + \mathbf{w_2}\|_2^2$, which implies that α is at least $1/2$. So, the expected number of trials is at most 2.

We extend our techniques to the setting of L_p sampling for constant p in Sect. 3.3.

Product Sampling. In this case, party 1 (resp. party 2) holds a normalized vector $\mathbf{w_1}$ (resp. $\mathbf{w_2}$), indexed from 1 to n. For $i \in [n]$, $w_{1,i}$ (resp. $w_{2,i}$) corresponds to the probability mass of i under distribution $\mathcal{D}_1$ (resp. $\mathcal{D}_2$).[3] The goal of the parties is to sample from the distribution $\mathcal{D}$ defined as follows for $i \in [n]$:

$$\mathcal{D}[i] := \frac{w_{1,i} \cdot w_{2,i}}{\langle \mathbf{w_1}, \mathbf{w_2} \rangle}.$$

We begin by noting (via a simple reduction from Set Disjointness) that it is impossible to achieve sublinear product sampling when no restrictions are placed on the inputs $\mathbf{w_1}, \mathbf{w_2}$. We further show (via a more complex reduction from Set Disjointness) that for every protocol Π (parametrized by dimension n) that correctly samples from $\mathcal{D}$, there are inputs $\mathbf{w_1} := \mathbf{w_1}(n), \mathbf{w_2} := \mathbf{w_2}(n)$, with $\langle \mathbf{w_1}, \mathbf{w_2} \rangle \in \Omega(1/n^2)$, that require linear communication complexity. See Sect. 4.1 for details.

This means that in order to achieve sublinear communication complexity, we would need–at the minimum–a promise on the inputs that guarantees that $\langle \mathbf{w_1}, \mathbf{w_2} \rangle \in \omega(1/n^2)$. We then present a protocol that has the following properties:

- When $\langle \mathbf{w_1}, \mathbf{w_2} \rangle \in \omega(\log n / n)$, the protocol achieves *expected* communication $\frac{\log n}{\langle \mathbf{w_1}, \mathbf{w_2} \rangle}$.

---

[3] Here the assumption that $\mathbf{w}$ are normalized is without loss of generality.

– The execution of the protocol leaks nothing more than the sampled output, and $\langle \mathbf{w}_1, \mathbf{w}_2 \rangle$. This is formalized via an Ideal/Real paradigm simulation, in which the simulator receives leakage of $\langle \mathbf{w}_1, \mathbf{w}_2 \rangle$ in the Ideal world.

The idea for the protocol is the following. The protocol proceeds in rounds: in round j, party 1 and 2 obliviously sample values i_1, i_2 from $\mathcal{D}_1, \mathcal{D}_2$, respectively (as described for L_1 sampling). Then the parties run a secure protocol that checks whether $i_1 = i_2$. If yes, they output i_1. Otherwise, the parties repeat the process in the next round.

The main technical portion of our security analysis is to show that the number of rounds (which is the only information leaked) is distributed as a geometric distribution with success probability $\langle \mathbf{w}_1, \mathbf{w}_2 \rangle$. This implies that the expected number of rounds is $1/\langle \mathbf{w}_1, \mathbf{w}_2 \rangle$, and furthermore, it implies that a simulator who knows $\langle \mathbf{w}_1, \mathbf{w}_2 \rangle$ can simulate the terminating round by making a draw from this geometric distribution. See Sect. 4.2 for more details. There, we also describe how we can pad the communication cost to the worst-case, which depends on the given promise, thereby removing the leakage of $\langle \mathbf{w}_1, \mathbf{w}_2 \rangle$.

Product Sampling in Constant Rounds. The protocol presented above for product sampling required a large number of rounds stemming from the iterative rejection sampling procedure. We now consider how to parallelize this process. To do so, we need to compute the inner product in order to determine, a priori, how many samples will suffice. However, computing this value requires $O(n)$ communication [3]!

The natural thing to do is therefore to use an approximation to the inner product that can be computed with sublinear communication. However, when replacing an exact computation of a function $f(\mathbf{w}_1, \mathbf{w}_2)$ with an approximation $\tilde{f}(\mathbf{w}_1, \mathbf{w}_2; r)$, one needs to be careful that *more* information is not leaked by the output. Specifically, Ishai et al. [14,15] introduced the notion of secure multiparty computation of approximations and, loosely speaking, their security definition says that the approximate computation is secure if its output can be simulated from the exactly correct output. While our result falls slightly short of that definition, we are still able to give a rigorous guarantee on the amount of additional information leaked by our approximate functionality. Specifically, we present an approximate functionality $\tilde{f}$ and prove that the output of $\tilde{f}(\mathbf{w}_1, \mathbf{w}_2; r)$ can be simulated given both the exactly correct output $f(\mathbf{w}_1, \mathbf{w}_2)$ (where f is the inner product), as well as the L_2 norms of the individual inputs.

To achieve this, we use a sublinear protocol from the Johnson-Lindenstrauss Transform (JLT) to approximate the dot product of the input vectors. This can be done with sublinear communication by having the parties jointly sample a $k \times n$ JLT matrix $\mathbf{M}$ for $k \ll n$ by choosing a short seed and expanding it under FHE. The rest of the computation is then done by communicating vectors $\mathbf{M}\mathbf{w}_b$, which are of length k rather than n. Based on this approximation, the parties can obliviously pre-sample a number of inputs that is sufficient with all but negligible probability, and then input them into a constant round secure computation protocol.

Our contribution here, is to show that this variant protocol only requires additional leakage of $||\mathbf{w}_1||_2^2$, $||\mathbf{w}_2||_2^2$, beyond what is already leaked by the original protocol (i.e., the inner product). Our analysis may be of independent interest, since it shows that given $\langle \mathbf{w}_1, \mathbf{w}_2 \rangle$, $||\mathbf{w}_1||_2^2$, $||\mathbf{w}_2||_2^2$, the values $\mathbf{M}\mathbf{w}_1$ and $\mathbf{M}\mathbf{w}_2$ can be efficiently sampled from exactly the correct distribution, when $\mathbf{M}$ is a JLT matrix, and is kept private from both parties. We prove this result by analyzing the underlying joint multivariate normal distributions corresponding to $\mathbf{M}\mathbf{w}_1$ and $\mathbf{M}\mathbf{w}_2$, and showing that the mean and covariance (which fully determine the distribution) depend *only* on the values $||\mathbf{w}_1||_2$, $||\mathbf{w}_2||_2$, and $\langle \mathbf{w}_1, \mathbf{w}_2 \rangle$ See Sect. 5 for more details.

Applications to Distributed Exponential Mechanism. We first briefly describe the connection between product sampling and the exponential mechanism. Ignoring many details, the joint exponential mechanism M outputs a value i on input $X = (x_1, \ldots, x_n)$ with probability proportional to

$$w_i = e^{c \cdot f(x_i)} = e^{c \cdot f(x_{1,i} + x_{2,i})},$$

where c is some constant, f is some scoring function, and the data values x_i are partitioned between the two parties (as $x_{1,i}, x_{2,i}$). If the scoring function f is linear, it holds that $f(x_{1,i} + x_{2,i}) = f(x_{1,i}) + f(x_{2,i})$, and, letting $w_{b,i} = e^{c \cdot f(x_{b,i})}$, we can rewrite w_i as follows:

$$w_i = w_{1,i} \cdot w_{2,i}.$$

Therefore, using product sampling, the parties can sample each item i with probability proportional to w_i.

Based on this connection, we present an application of our constant-round, product sampling protocol to realize a two-party exponential mechanism in Appendix F in the full version. However, to use our sampling protocol in this application, we must show that the leakage of our protocols preserves the differential privacy guarantee. We indeed prove that our constant-round JLT-based protocol can achieve differential privacy—even when the JLT matrix $\mathbf{M}$ is public—by adding correctly distributed noise to $\langle \mathbf{M}\mathbf{w}_1, \mathbf{M}\mathbf{w}_2 \rangle$. This allows parties to execute the exponential mechanism when the cost function is additively distributed across the two parties, with sublinear communication, in the case that $\langle \mathbf{w}_1, \mathbf{w}_2 \rangle \in \omega(\log n / n)$.

1.3   Related Work

Sampling from Streaming Data. Many prior papers (e.g. [10,16,22,27,35]) have studied the problem of sampling data from a data stream. In this setting the goal is to achieve L_p sampling for arbitrary p without having to process or store all the streaming data, thus requiring sublinear computation. These works generally operate in the one-party setting and do not consider privacy.

Secure Multiparty Sampling. A few prior works [31,32] have investigated the problem of two and multi-party private sampling in the information theoretic setting. These works focus on identifying the necessary setup to enable sampling from various distributions. We instead focus on the computational setting, and focus on reducing communication. Recently, Champion et al. [6] also considered the computational setting, but they focus on sampling from a publicly-known distribution whereas we sample from a private one.

Secure Multiparty Computation of Differentially Private Functionalities. Starting with the work of Dwork et al. [11] there has been a good amount of work (e.g. [1,9,13,17,29,30]) on using MPC to realize differentially private functionalities to protect the privacy of individual inputs given the output of the MPC. These works have focused on building efficient, private applications in machine learning and other fields, whereas we focus on reducing the communication necessary for the specific functionalities of sampling.

Secure Sketching. A long line of work [8,12,19,26,34] has investigated building secure sketches for securely estimating statistics of Tor usage, web traffic, and other applications. These works focus on building sublinear communication and computation protocols for computing specific statistics such as unique count, median, etc.

2   Two-Party L_1 Sampling

In this section, we describe a secure two-party L_1 sampling protocol. Given two n-dimensional vectors $\mathbf{w}_1 = (w_{1,1}, \ldots, w_{1,n})$ and $\mathbf{w}_2 = (w_{2,1}, \ldots, w_{2,n})$ as the private inputs from parties P_1 and P_2 respectively, the protocol samples from the L_1 distribution according to $\mathbf{w}_1 + \mathbf{w}_2$.

Notation: L_p norm. Let $\mathbf{w} = (w_1, \ldots, w_n) \in \mathbb{R}^n$ be a non-zero vector. *The L_p norm* $\|\mathbf{w}\|_p$ of $\mathbf{w}$ is defined as $\|\mathbf{w}\|_p := \left(\sum_j |w_j|^p \right)^{1/p}$. *When there is no subscript, it means L_2 norm; that is, $\|\mathbf{w}\| := \|\mathbf{w}\|_2$*

Assumptions. Throughout the paper, we assume that the values $w_{b,i}$ are represented by fixed-point precision numbers, and consider the cost of communicating such a number to be independent of n. We assume all weights in vectors $\mathbf{w}_1$ and $\mathbf{w}_2$ are non-negative.

Ideal Functionality. We first define an ideal functionality for the two-party L_1 sampling. Slightly abusing the notation, let $L_1(\mathbf{w}_1, \mathbf{w}_2)$ be a two-input sampling procedure based on the L_1 distribution of $\mathbf{w}_1 + \mathbf{w}_2$:

$$\Pr[L_1(\mathbf{w}_1, \mathbf{w}_2) \text{ samples } i] = \frac{w_{1,i} + w_{2,i}}{\|\mathbf{w}_1 + \mathbf{w}_2\|_1}.$$

We give a more formal description of the functionality $\mathcal{F}_{L_1}$ in the figure below. In Sect. 2.2, we present a protocol that securely realizes this functionality.

$\mathcal{F}_{L_1}$: Ideal functionality for two-party L_1 sampling

The functionality has the following parameter:

- $n \in \mathbb{N}$. The dimension of the input weight vectors $\mathbf{w}_1$ and $\mathbf{w}_2$.

The functionality proceeds as follows:

1. Receive inputs $\mathbf{w}_1$ and $\mathbf{w}_2$ from P_1 and P_2 respectively.
2. Sample $i \in [n]$ with probability $\frac{w_{1,i}+w_{2,i}}{\|\mathbf{w}_1+\mathbf{w}_2\|_1}$
3. Send i to P_1 and P_2.

2.1   A Toy Protocol Towards Securely Realizing $\mathcal{F}_{L_1}$

We describe our first attempt, which is insecure, but provides good intuition on how we construct a secure protocol. In fact, the attack on this broken protocol, as well as the fix presented in the next sub-section, remain relevant when we move to product sampling and L_2 sampling as well. Since we assume that all the weights are non-negative, we observe that letting $p = \frac{\|\mathbf{w}_1\|_1}{\|\mathbf{w}_1\|_1+\|\mathbf{w}_2\|_1}$, the above measure can be re-written as follows:

$$\Pr[L_1(\mathbf{w}_1,\mathbf{w}_2) \text{ samples } i] = \frac{w_{1,i}}{\|\mathbf{w}_1\|_1} \cdot p + \frac{w_{2,i}}{\|\mathbf{w}_2\|_1} \cdot (1-p). \tag{1}$$

Equation (1) leads us to the following natural approach.

1. Party P_1 samples i_1 from the L_1 distribution according to $\mathbf{w}_1$, such that $\Pr[P_1 \text{ samples } i_1] = \frac{w_{1,i_1}}{\|\mathbf{w}_1\|_1}$.
2. Party P_2 samples i_2 from the L_1 distribution according to $\mathbf{w}_2$, such that $\Pr[P_2 \text{ samples } i_2] = \frac{w_{2,i_2}}{\|\mathbf{w}_2\|_1}$.
3. Then, P_1 and P_2 execute a secure protocol for the following procedure:
   (a) Execute a coin toss protocol with bias p. Let b be the output of the coin-flip.
   (b) If $b = 0$ (resp., $b = 1$), output i_1 (resp., i_2).

The output of the protocol will achieve correct sampling.

Insecurity of the Protocol. However, this protocol has a subtle security issue. For example, let i be the eventual output index of the protocol. Then, we have the following:

- If the coin flip b is 0, which happens with probability p, it holds that i is always the same as i_1.
- On the other hand, if the coin flip b is 1, then i will be the same as i_1 if and only if $i_2 = i_1$, which happens with probability $\frac{w_{2,i_1}}{\|\mathbf{w}_2\|_1}$.

This implies that we have

$$\Pr[i = i_1 | i_1] = p + (1-p) \cdot \frac{w_{2,i_1}}{\|\mathbf{w}_2\|_1}$$

Now consider a distinguisher that corrupts P_1, chooses inputs $\mathbf{w}_1$ and $\mathbf{w}_2$, and checks the above conditional probability, which is possible *since the distinguisher can also see i_1 through the corrupted P_1*. To prove security, we should be able to construct a simulator for P_1 that fools this distinguisher. However, a simulator for P_1 doesn't know $\mathbf{w}_2$, which causes the above conditional probability to be unsimulatable.

In a sense, by having P_1 choose i_1, the protocol allows P_1 to measure the conditional probability $\Pr[i = i_1 | i_1]$, which depends on the value w_{2,i_1} thereby leaking information about P_2's input to P_1.

2.2 Secure L_1 Sampling Protocol

Oblivious Sampling. We address the insecurity of the toy protocol by having the parties sample *obliviously* from $\mathbf{w}_1, \mathbf{w}_2$. This way, each party would not know whether the final output index matches the sample taken from its own vector, or the sample taken from the other party's vector. Specifically, we will construct our protocol under the framework described below:

1. The parties obliviously sample i_1 according to L_1 distribution of $\mathbf{w}_1$. The output index i_1 is secret shared between the two parties. Let $\langle i_1 \rangle$ denote the secret share of i_1. Likewise, they obliviously sample $\langle i_2 \rangle$ from L_1 distribution of $\mathbf{w}_2$.
2. Execute a secure two-party protocol to compute the following:
   (a) Flip a coin b with bias p.
   (b) If $b = 0$, output the decryption of i_1; otherwise output the decryption of i_2.

Ideal Functionalities. Formally, we define an ideal functionality $\mathcal{F}_{\mathsf{osample}(\mathsf{L}_1)}$ as follows:

$\mathcal{F}_{\mathsf{osample}(\mathsf{L}_1)}$: Ideal functionality for oblivious L_1 sampling.

The functionality considers two participants, the sender and the receiver. The functionality is parameterized with a number n.

Inputs: The sender has an n-dimensional weight vector $\mathbf{w}$. The receiver has no input.

The functionality proceeds as follows:

1. Receive $\mathbf{w}$ from the sender.
2. Sample $i \in [n]$ with probability $\frac{w_i}{\|\mathbf{w}\|_1}$
3. Choose a random pad $\pi \in \{0,1\}^\ell$, where $\ell = \lceil \log_2 n \rceil$.
4. Send π to the sender and $i \oplus \pi$ to the receiver.

We also give an ideal functionality $\mathcal{F}_{\mathsf{biasCoin}}$ for the biased coin tossing.

$\mathcal{F}_{\text{biasCoin}}$: Ideal functionality for biased coin tossing.

The functionality considers two participants P_1 and P_2 and proceeds as follows:

1. Receive a number s_1 as input from P_1 and s_2 from P_2.
2. Flip a coin b with bias $p = \frac{s_1}{s_1+s_2}$.
3. Choose a random bit $r \in \{0,1\}$.
4. Send r to P_1 and $r \oplus b$ to the receiver.

L_1 **Sampling Protocol.** Based on the above functionalities, we describe a protocol securely realizing $\mathcal{F}_{L_1}$ in the $(\mathcal{F}_{\text{osample}(L_1)}, \mathcal{F}_{\text{biasCoin}})$-hybrid.

Protocol 1. Two-party L_1 sampling in the $(\mathcal{F}_{\text{osample}(L_1)}, \mathcal{F}_{\text{biasCoin}})$-hybrid.

Inputs: Party P_b has input $\mathbf{w}_b$.

1. Execute $\mathcal{F}_{\text{osample}(L_1)}$ with P_1 as a sender with input $\mathbf{w}_1$ and P_2 as a receiver. Let $\langle i_1 \rangle$ be the secret share of the output index.
2. Execute $\mathcal{F}_{\text{osample}(L_1)}$ with P_2 as a sender with input $\mathbf{w}_2$ and P_1 as a receiver. Let $\langle i_2 \rangle$ be the secret share of the output index.
3. Execute $\mathcal{F}_{\text{biasCoin}}$ where P_1 has input $\|\mathbf{w}_1\|_1$ and P_2 has input $\|\mathbf{w}_2\|_1$. Let $\langle b \rangle$ be the secret share of the output bit.
4. Execute $\mathcal{F}_{2PC}$ for the following circuit:
   (a) Input: $\langle i_1 \rangle, \langle i_2 \rangle, \langle b \rangle$.
   (b) Output: $i_1 \cdot (1 - b) + i_2 \cdot b$.

Theorem 1. *Protocol 1 securely realizes $\mathcal{F}_{L_1}$ with semi-honest security in the $(\mathcal{F}_{\text{osample}(L_1)}, \mathcal{F}_{\text{biasCoin}})$-hybrid.*

The proof is found in Appendix C.1 in the full version.

Securely Realizing $\mathcal{F}_{\text{osample}(L_1)}$ with threshold FHE. The main idea of the protocol is having the parties securely sample a random number r from $[s]$, where $s := \|\mathbf{w}\|_1$. Our construction is found in Protocol 2.

Theorem 2. *Assuming the existence of threshold FHE with IND-CPA security, Protocol 2 securely realizes $\mathcal{F}_{\text{osample}(L_1)}$ in the semi-honest security model.*

The proof is found in Appendix C.2 in the full version.

We note that we give another construction that relies on sub-linear 1-out-of-m oblivious transfer (OT), but requires computation that is exponential in the bit precision in Appendix D in the full version.

Securely Realizing $\mathcal{F}_{\text{biasCoin}}$. The secure construction for $\mathcal{F}_{\text{biasCoin}}$ is straightforward and can be found in Appendix B in the full version.

Protocol 2. Oblivious sampling from threshold FHE

Inputs: The sender has input $\mathbf{w} = (w_1, \ldots, w_n)$.

1. The sender computes $s := \|\mathbf{w}\|_1$.
2. The sender and the receiver execute $\mathcal{F}_{2PC}$ to uniformly sample r from the range $[0, s)$. This is possible, since s has a fixed point representation. Let r_1 and r_2 be the secret share of r given to P_1 and P_2 respectively.
3. The sender and the receiver set up a threshold FHE scheme. The plaintext space of the FHE is $GF(2)$, which allows homomorphic bitwise-xor and bitwise-AND operations. Let $[\![m]\!]$ denote an FHE encryption of plaintext m which can be a bit or bits depending on the context.
4. The receiver sends $[\![r_2]\!]$ so that the sender can compute $[\![r]\!] := [\![r_1]\!] \oplus [\![r_2]\!]$.
5. The sender homomorphically evaluates the following circuit:
   (a) Let $cnt_0 = 0$. For $j = 1, \ldots, n$, let $cnt_j = cnt_j + w_j$.
   (b) Output $i \in [1, n]$ such that $r \in [cnt_{i-1}, cnt_i]$.
   Let $[\![i]\!]$ be the output encryption from the above homomorphic evaluation.
6. The sender chooses a random pad π, and then it sends $[\![c]\!] = [\![i]\!] \oplus [\![\pi]\!]$ to the receiver.
7. The two parties perform threshold decryption so that c is decrypted to the receiver.
8. The sender outputs π and the receiver outputs the decryption of c.

---

3   Two Party L_2 Sampling

In this section we consider the two-party L_2 sampling functionality. Given input vectors $\mathbf{w}_1, \mathbf{w}_2$, this functionality samples from the distribution $D_{L_2}(\mathbf{w}_1, \mathbf{w}_2)$ with the following probability mass function:

$$\Pr[D_{L_2}(\mathbf{w}_1, \mathbf{w}_2) \text{ samples } i] = \frac{(w_{1,i} + w_{2,i})^2}{\sum_j (w_{1,j} + w_{2,j})^2} = \frac{(w_{1,i} + w_{2,i})^2}{\|\mathbf{w}_1 + \mathbf{w}_2\|_2^2}.$$

We begin by presenting a non-private protocol for two-party L_2 sampling with $\tilde{O}(1)$ communication in Sect. 3.1, the construction is found in Protocol 3. We then show how to implement the protocol securely in Sect. 3.2.

3.1   A Non-private L_2 Sampling Protocol with $\tilde{O}(1)$ Communication

We begin by defining and showing how to sample from a helper distribution D_{ignore}.

Definition 1. *For input vectors* $\mathbf{w}_1, \mathbf{w}_2$, *let* $D_{\text{ignore}}(\mathbf{w}_1, \mathbf{w}_2)$ *be the distribution that "ignores" the cross term in* $D_{L_2}(\mathbf{w}_1, \mathbf{w}_2)$. *I.e.* $D_{\text{ignore}}(\mathbf{w}_1, \mathbf{w}_2)$ *samples index* $i \in [n]$ *with probability* $\frac{w_{1,i}^2 + w_{2,i}^2}{\|\mathbf{w}_1\|_2^2 + \|\mathbf{w}_2\|_2^2}$.

Lemma 1. *There exists a protocol* Π_{ignore} *for sampling from* $D_{\text{ignore}}(\mathbf{w}_1, \mathbf{w}_2)$ *with* $\tilde{O}(1)$ *communication.*

Proof. Let $\mathbf{w}'_b = (w_{b,1}^2, \ldots, w_{b,n}^2)$. The lemma follows by observing the following:

$$D_{\text{ignore}}(\mathbf{w}_1, \mathbf{w}_2) = D_{L_1}(\mathbf{w}'_1, \mathbf{w}'_2).$$

$\square$

Definition 2. *For $i \in [n]$, let the corrective parameter function be defined as*

$$f_c(\mathbf{w}_1, \mathbf{w}_2, i) := \frac{w_{1,i}^2 + 2w_{1,i}w_{2,i} + w_{2,i}^2}{||\mathbf{w}_1||_2^2 + ||\mathbf{w}_2||_2^2}.$$

Definition 3. *The constant $c := c(\mathbf{w}_1, \mathbf{w}_2)$ is defined as*

$$c(\mathbf{w}_1, \mathbf{w}_2) := \frac{||\mathbf{w}_1 + \mathbf{w}_2||_2^2}{||\mathbf{w}_1||_2^2 + ||\mathbf{w}_2||_2^2}$$

This ensures that for every i, $f_c(\mathbf{w}_1, \mathbf{w}_2, i) = c \cdot \text{Pr}_{D_{L_2}(\mathbf{w}_1, \mathbf{w}_2)}[i]$.

The following lemma will be useful for arguing the validity of the final protocol.

Lemma 2. *For all $i \in \text{supp}(D_{L_2}(\mathbf{w}_1, \mathbf{w}_2))$, $\text{Pr}_{D_{L_2}(\mathbf{w}_1, \mathbf{w}_2)}[i] \leq 2/c \cdot \text{Pr}_{D_{\text{ignore}}(\mathbf{w}_1, \mathbf{w}_2)}[i]$.*

Proof.

$$\begin{aligned}
\Pr_{D_{L_2}(\mathbf{w}_1, \mathbf{w}_2)}[i] &= \frac{w_{1,i}^2 + 2w_{1,i}w_{2,i} + w_{2,i}^2}{||\mathbf{w}_1||_2^2 + 2\langle \mathbf{w}_1, \mathbf{w}_2 \rangle + ||\mathbf{w}_2||_2^2} \\
&= \frac{w_{1,i}^2 + 2w_{1,i}w_{2,i} + w_{2,i}^2}{c \cdot (||\mathbf{w}_1||_2^2 + ||\mathbf{w}_2||_2^2)} \\
&\leq \frac{2 \cdot (w_{1,i}^2 + w_{2,i}^2)}{c \cdot ||\mathbf{w}_1||_2^2 + ||\mathbf{w}_2||_2^2} \\
&= \frac{2}{c} \cdot \Pr_{D_{\text{ignore}}(\mathbf{w}_1, \mathbf{w}_2)}[i]
\end{aligned}$$

The inequality holds since

$$\begin{aligned}
2(w_{1,i}^2 + w_{2,i}^2) - (w_{1,i}^2 + 2w_{1,i}w_{2,i} + w_{2,i}^2) &= w_{1,i}^2 - 2w_{1,i}w_{2,i} + w_{2,i}^2 \\
&= (w_{1,i} - w_{2,i})^2 \\
&\geq 0.
\end{aligned}$$

$\square$

We now present the L_2 sampling protocol Π_{L_2}, which is described in Protocol 3. We show the correctness and efficiency of the protocol.

Lemma 3. *With all but negligible probability, on inputs $\mathbf{w}_1, \mathbf{w}_2$, Π_{L_2} samples exactly correctly from $D_{L_2}(\mathbf{w}_1, \mathbf{w}_2)$, and has communication $\tilde{O}(1)$.*

Protocol 3. Protocol for exact L_2 sampling (Π_{L_2})

Inputs: Parties P_1 and P_2 have inputs $\mathbf{w}_1$ and $\mathbf{w}_2$ respectively.

The protocol proceeds as follows:

1. Parties run Π_{ignore} with inputs $\mathbf{w}_1, \mathbf{w}_2$ that samples from $D_{\text{ignore}}(\mathbf{w}_1, \mathbf{w}_2)$ and obtain output i.
2. For $b \in \{1, 2\}$, P_b sends $w_{b,i}, \|\mathbf{w}_b\|_2^2$. Both parties compute

$$\Pr_{D_{\text{ignore}}(\mathbf{w}_1, \mathbf{w}_2)}[i] = \frac{w_{1,i}^2 + w_{2,i}^2}{\|\mathbf{w}_1\|_2^2 + \|\mathbf{w}_2\|_2^2} \quad \text{and} \quad f_c(\mathbf{w}_1, \mathbf{w}_2, i) = \frac{w_{1,i}^2 + 2w_{1,i}w_{2,i} + w_{2,i}^2}{\|\mathbf{w}_1\|_2^2 + \|\mathbf{w}_2\|_2^2}$$

3. Parties output i with probability

$$\frac{f_c(\mathbf{w}_1, \mathbf{w}_2, i)}{2 \cdot \Pr_{D_{\text{ignore}}(\mathbf{w}_1, \mathbf{w}_2)}[i]} = \frac{c \cdot \Pr_{D_{L_2}(\mathbf{w}_1, \mathbf{w}_2)}[i]}{2 \cdot \Pr_{D_{\text{ignore}}(\mathbf{w}_1, \mathbf{w}_2)}[i]}$$

$$= \frac{\Pr_{D_{L_2}(\mathbf{w}_1, \mathbf{w}_2)}[i]}{2/c \cdot \Pr_{D_{\text{ignore}}(\mathbf{w}_1, \mathbf{w}_2)}[i]}$$

and otherwise return to step 1.

Proof. Note that Π_{L_2} simply performs rejection sampling in a distributed setting where sampling from $D_{\text{ignore}}(\mathbf{w}_1, \mathbf{w}_2)$ and computing the probabilities is done in a distributed manner. It is therefore well-known that as long as for all $i \in [n]$,

$$\Pr_{D_{L_2}(\mathbf{w}_1, \mathbf{w}_2)}[i] \leq 2/c \cdot \Pr_{D_{\text{ignore}}(\mathbf{w}_1, \mathbf{w}_2)}[i], \tag{2}$$

then Π_{L_2} samples from the exact correct distribution, and the number of samples required from $D_{\text{ignore}}(\mathbf{w}_1, \mathbf{w}_2)$ in protocol Π_{L_2} follows a geometric distribution with probability $c/2$. Thus, if condition (2) is met, the protocol samples exactly correctly and completes in an expected $2/c$ (with $2/c \leq 2$, since $c \geq 1$) number of rounds. Further, it can be immediately noted that condition (2) is met due to Lemma 2. Finally, each round has $\tilde{O}(1)$ communication, since Π_{ignore} has communication $\tilde{O}(1)$ (by Lemma 1) and since, in addition to that, only a constant number of length $\tilde{O}(1)$ values are exchanged in each round. Combining the above, we have that Π_{L_2} has expected communication $\tilde{O}(1)$ and worst case (with all but negligible probability) communication $\tilde{O}(1)$. $\square$

Remark 1. Note that the protocol and analysis above did not require that vectors $\mathbf{w}_1, \mathbf{w}_2$ are normalized. I.e. we do not require that $\|\mathbf{w}_1\|_1$ or $\|\mathbf{w}_2\|_1$ are equal to 1 or to each other.

3.2   Secure L_2 Sampling from FHE

L_2 Sampling Protocol. We present our secure L_2 sampling protocol in Protocol 4. For two n-dimensional vectors $\mathbf{w}_1$ and $\mathbf{w}_2$, we denote by $\mathbf{w}_1 \odot \mathbf{w}_2$ the n-dimensional vector whose i-th entry is equal to $w_{1,i} \cdot w_{2,i}$.

Protocol 4. Two-party L_2 sampling in the $(\mathcal{F}_{L_1}, \mathcal{F}_{2PC})$-hybrid.

Inputs: Party P_b has input $\mathbf{w}_b$.

1. Let $B \in \tilde{O}(1)$. The parties perform the following steps for $j \in [B]$:
    (a) Sample from $D_{\text{ignore}}(\mathbf{w}_1, \mathbf{w}_2)$ by doing the following: Invoke ideal functionality $\mathcal{F}_{L_1}^{ss}$ with P_1's input set to $\mathbf{w}_1 \odot \mathbf{w}_1$ and P_2's input set to $\mathbf{w}_2 \odot \mathbf{w}_2$. Let $\langle i_j \rangle$ be the secret share of the output index.
    (b) Parties compute encryptions of w_{1,i_j}, w_{2,i_j} using a threshold FHE scheme as follows.
        - Parties compute an encryption of i_j by exchanging encryptions of their shares and adding them.
        - Party b encrypts $\mathbf{w}_b$ and uses FHE to locally compute an encryption of w_{b,i_j}.
        - The parties then send these ciphertexts to each other.
    (c) Rejection Sampling. Compute a threshold FHE ciphertext $\widehat{\text{bias}}_j$ that encrypts

$$\frac{f_c(\mathbf{w}_1, \mathbf{w}_2)_{i_j}}{2 \cdot \Pr_{D_{\text{ignore}}(\mathbf{w}_1, \mathbf{w}_2)}[i_j]} = \frac{w_{1,i_j}^2 + 2w_{1,i_j}w_{2,i_j} + w_{2,i_j}^2}{2(w_{1,i_j}^2 + w_{2,i_j}^2)}.$$

Invoke ideal functionality $\mathcal{F}_{2PC}$ that takes encrypted bias $\widehat{\text{bias}}_j$, the threshold decryption keys, index i_j, and random bits. The functionality executes a circuit that flips a coin with bias $\widehat{\text{bias}}_j$ and returns a ciphertext $\widehat{\text{out}}_j$, which is an encryption of i_j if the coin evaluates to 1 and an encryption of 0 otherwise.
2. Execute $\mathcal{F}_{2PC}$ for the following circuit:
    (a) Input: $(\widehat{\text{out}}_1, \ldots, \widehat{\text{out}}_B)$ and threshold decryption keys.
    (b) Output: i_j corresponding to the minimum j such that $\widehat{\text{out}}_j$ decrypts to $i_j \neq 0$. Or $\perp$ if no such $j \in [B]$ exists.

Our L_2 sampling protocol uses ideal functionality $\mathcal{F}_{L_1}^{ss}$, which works essentially the same as $\mathcal{F}_{L_1}$ except that the output index is secret shared among both parties. We can securely realize this functionality with semi-honest security through a trivial change in the protocol Π_{L_1}; for the sake of completeness, we provide the details in Appendix E in the full version.

Efficiency and Correctness. It is clear that the total communication complexity of the protocol is $\tilde{O}(1)$, since each step in the loop has complexity $\tilde{O}(1)$ and the loop iterates $B \in \tilde{O}(1)$ number of times. Correctness is also immediate, since the protocol simply implements the Π_{L_2} sampling procedure, which was proven in Sect. 3.1 to be correct, and to require at most $B \in \tilde{O}(1)$ samples, with all but negligible probability,

Security. Security of our protocol is stated through the following theorem.

Theorem 3. *Assuming the existence of threshold FHE with* IND-CPA *security, Protocol 4 securely realizes the L_2 sampling functionality in the $\{\mathcal{F}_{L_1}^{ss}, \mathcal{F}_{2PC}\}$-hybrid model with semi-honest security.*

We provide the proof in Appendix C.3 in the full version.

3.3   A Non-private L_p Sampling Protocol with $\tilde{O}(1)$ Communication

---

Protocol 5. Protocol for exact L_p sampling (Π_{L_p})

Inputs: Parties P_1 and P_2 have inputs $\mathbf{w}_1$ and $\mathbf{w}_2$ respectively.

The protocol proceeds as follows:

1. Parties run Π_{ignore} with inputs $\mathbf{w}_1, \mathbf{w}_2$ that samples from $D_{\text{ignore},p}(\mathbf{w}_1, \mathbf{w}_2)$ and obtain output i.
2. For $b \in \{1, 2\}$, P_b sends $w_{b,i}, ||\mathbf{w}_b||_p^p$. Both parties compute

$$\Pr_{D_{\text{ignore},p}(\mathbf{w}_1, \mathbf{w}_2)}[i] = \frac{w_{1,i}^p + w_{2,i}^p}{||\mathbf{w}_1||_p^p + ||\mathbf{w}_2||_p^p} \quad \text{and} \quad f_c(\mathbf{w}_1, \mathbf{w}_2, i) = \frac{(w_{1,i} + w_{2,i})^p}{||\mathbf{w}_1||_p^p + ||\mathbf{w}_2||_p^p}$$

3. Parties output i with probability

$$\frac{f_c(\mathbf{w}_1, \mathbf{w}_2, i)}{2^{p-1} \cdot \Pr_{D_{\text{ignore},p}(\mathbf{w}_1, \mathbf{w}_2)}[i]} = \frac{c \cdot \Pr_{D_{L_2}(\mathbf{w}_1, \mathbf{w}_2)}[i]}{2^{p-1} \cdot \Pr_{D_{\text{ignore},p}(\mathbf{w}_1, \mathbf{w}_2)}[i]}$$

$$= \frac{\Pr_{D_{L_2}(\mathbf{w}_1, \mathbf{w}_2)}[i]}{2^{p-1}/c \cdot \Pr_{D_{\text{ignore},p}(\mathbf{w}_1, \mathbf{w}_2)}[i]}$$

and otherwise return to step 1.

In this section we present a $\tilde{O}(1)$ sampling protocol for L_p sampling for constant p. We present only the insecure version, extending it to a secure sampling protocol can be done entirely analogously to the construction for L_2 sampling given in Sect. 3.2.

Given input vectors $\mathbf{w}_1, \mathbf{w}_2$, L_p sampling refers to sampling from the distribution $D_{L_p}(\mathbf{w}_1, \mathbf{w}_2)$ with the following probability mass function:

$$\Pr[D_{L_p}(\mathbf{w}_1, \mathbf{w}_2) \text{ samples } i] = \frac{(w_{1,i} + w_{2,i})^p}{\sum_j (w_{1,j} + w_{2,j})^p} = \frac{(w_{1,i} + w_{2,i})^p}{||\mathbf{w}_1 + \mathbf{w}_2||_p^p}.$$

We begin by defining and showing how to sample from a helper distribution $D_{\text{ignore},p}$.

Definition 4. *For input vectors $\mathbf{w}_1, \mathbf{w}_2$, let $D_{\text{ignore},p}(\mathbf{w}_1, \mathbf{w}_2)$ be the distribution that "ignores" the cross term in $D_{L_p}(\mathbf{w}_1, \mathbf{w}_2)$. I.e. $D_{\text{ignore},p}(\mathbf{w}_1, \mathbf{w}_2)$ samples index $i \in [n]$ with probability $\frac{w_{1,i}^p + w_{2,i}^p}{||\mathbf{w}_1||_p^p + ||\mathbf{w}_2||_p^p}$.*

Lemma 4. *There exists a protocol Π_{ignore} for sampling from $D_{\text{ignore},p}(\mathbf{w}_1, \mathbf{w}_2)$ with $\tilde{O}(1)$ communication.*

Proof. Let $\mathbf{w}'_b = (w_{b,1}^p, \ldots, w_{b,n}^p)$. The lemma follows by observing the following:

$$D_{\text{ignore}}(\mathbf{w}_1, \mathbf{w}_2) = D_{L_1}(\mathbf{w}'_1, \mathbf{w}'_2).$$

$\square$

Definition 5. *For $i \in [n]$, let the corrective parameter function be defined as*

$$f_c(\mathbf{w}_1, \mathbf{w}_2, i) := \frac{(w_{1,i} + w_{2,i})^p}{||\mathbf{w}_1||_p^p + ||\mathbf{w}_2||_p^p}.$$

Definition 6. *The constant $c := c(\mathbf{w}_1, \mathbf{w}_2)$ is defined as*

$$c(\mathbf{w}_1, \mathbf{w}_2) := \frac{||\mathbf{w}_1 + \mathbf{w}_2||_p^p}{||\mathbf{w}_1||_p^p + ||\mathbf{w}_2||_p^p}$$

This ensures that for every i, $f_c(\mathbf{w}_1, \mathbf{w}_2, i) = c \cdot \Pr_{D_{L_p}(\mathbf{w}_1, \mathbf{w}_2)}[i]$.

The following lemma will be useful for arguing the validity of the final protocol.

Lemma 5. *For all $i \in \mathsf{supp}(D_{L_p}(\mathbf{w}_1, \mathbf{w}_2))$,*

$$\Pr_{D_{L_p}(\mathbf{w}_1, \mathbf{w}_2)}[i] \leq 2^{p-1}/c \cdot \Pr_{D_{\mathsf{ignore}, p}(\mathbf{w}_1, \mathbf{w}_2)}[i].$$

The proof is found in Appendix C.4 in the full version.

We now present the L_p sampling protocol Π_{L_p} in Protocol 5. We show the correctness and efficiency of the protocol below.

Lemma 6. *With all but negligible probability, on inputs $\mathbf{w}_1$ and $\mathbf{w}_2$, protocol Π_{L_p} samples exactly correctly from $D_{L_p}(\mathbf{w}_1, \mathbf{w}_2)$. Further, for any constant p, the protocol has communication $\tilde{O}(1)$.*

The proof is found in Appendix C.5 in the full version. We note that this result strictly generalizes Lemma 3. In particular, setting $p = 2$ in the above protocol yields a protocol with exactly the same parameters as the L_2 sampling protocol.

4   Two-Party Product Sampling

We next consider the problem of two-party sampling from a product distribution. Specifically, given n-dimensional vectors $\mathbf{w}_1 = (w_{1,1}, \ldots, w_{1,n})$ and $\mathbf{w}_2 = (w_{2,1}, \ldots, w_{2,n})$ as the private inputs from P_1 and P_2 respectively, we wish to sample from the distribution D_{prod} defined by

$$\Pr[D_{\mathsf{prod}}(\mathbf{w}_1, \mathbf{w}_2) = i] = \frac{w_{1,i} \cdot w_{2,i}}{\sum_{j=1}^n w_{1,j} \cdot w_{2,j}} = \frac{w_{1,i} \cdot w_{2,i}}{\langle \mathbf{w}_1, \mathbf{w}_2 \rangle}$$

Of course, if $\langle \mathbf{w}_1, \mathbf{w}_2 \rangle = 0$, the probability space is not well-defined, and in this case, we require the protocol to simply output $\bot$.

As before, we assume that all weights in $\mathbf{w}_1$ and $\mathbf{w}_2$ are non-negative.

Ideal Functionality. We now define an ideal functionality $\mathcal{F}_{\mathsf{prod}}$ for two-party product sampling. This functionality is parametrized by a function f_{Leak} capturing the leakage that the functionality gives to the adversary.

$\mathcal{F}_{\mathsf{prod}}$: Ideal functionality for two-party product sampling

The functionality has the following parameters:

- $n \in \mathbb{N}$. The dimension of the input weight vectors $\mathbf{w}_1$ and $\mathbf{w}_2$.
- A function f_{Leak} describing the leakage.

The functionality proceeds as follows:

1. Receive inputs $\mathbf{w}_1$ and $\mathbf{w}_2$ from P_1 and P_2 respectively.
2. Compute $\mathsf{leak} = f_{\mathsf{Leak}}(\mathbf{w}_1, \mathbf{w}_2)$
3. If $\langle \mathbf{w}_1, \mathbf{w}_2 \rangle = 0$, send leak to the adversary and $\perp$ to P_1 and P_2.
4. Otherwise, sample i with probability $\frac{w_{1,i} \cdot w_{2,i}}{\langle \mathbf{w}_1, \mathbf{w}_2 \rangle}$, send leak to the adversary, and send i to P_1 and P_2.

4.1 Impossibility of Sublinear Product Sampling

Our goal is to find a protocol for two-party sampling with sublinear (in n) communication. However, unlike the case for L_1 sampling, we show that this goal is actually impossible. Roughly speaking, if parties are allowed to have arbitrary input vectors, then a sublinear communication solution to product sampling implies a sublinear communication solution to the disjointness problem, which is known to be impossible.

For our impossibility result, we first define the two-party disjointness problem.

Disjointness Problem. The disjointness problem checks if two input sets S and T are disjoint (i.e., $S \cap T = \emptyset$). Specifically, we consider a function DISJ^n : $\{0,1\}^n \times \{0,1\}^n \to \{0,1\}$ defined as:

$$\mathsf{DISJ}^n(v_S, v_T) = \begin{cases} 1 \text{ if } \langle v_S, v_T \rangle = 0 \\ 0 \text{ otherwise} \end{cases}$$

In the above, v_S and v_T are the characteristic vectors of S and T respectively. The communication complexity of the solution to the disjointness problem is known to have a linear lowerbound, as shown in the following Theorem:

Theorem 4 ([4,24,33]). *For any (even non-private) two-party protocol Π where each party holds v_S and v_T respectively, if Π computes $\mathsf{DISJ}^n(v_S, v_T)$ correctly with probability at least 2/3, the communication complexity of Π is $\Theta(n)$.*

Our Impossibility Result. We first observe that a simple reduction from Disjointness gives us that is impossible to achieve sublinear product sampling. Specifically, disjointness can be directly learned from whether the product sampling protocol outputs $\perp$ or not.

Our impossibility result is stronger. We show that it is impossible to achieve sublinear product sampling *even when the product sampling protocol is executed with input vectors* $\mathbf{w}_1$ *and* $\mathbf{w}_2$ *in which all coordinates are bounded away from* 0, which in particular guarantees that $\langle \mathbf{w}_1, \mathbf{w}_2 \rangle$ is bounded away from 0.

Before stating a formal theorem below, for $0 < \gamma < 1$, we first define γ-heaviness; we say that a vector $\mathbf{w}$ is *γ-heavy* when each coordinate of $\mathbf{w}$ is a number contained in $[\gamma, 1]$.

Theorem 5. *Let* $\mathbf{w}_1$ *and* $\mathbf{w}_2$ *be* γ-heavy vectors of length n, each respectively held by P_1 and P_2. Assume there exists a two-party protocol Π_{prod} for the product sampling from $\mathbf{w}_1$ and $\mathbf{w}_2$, with communication at most $C := C(n, \gamma)$.*

Then, for any $\gamma \leq 1/2n$, there exists a constant ρ and a probabilistic protocol computing DISJ^n correctly with probability at least 2/3 that has communication at most $\log(n) + 1 + \rho \cdot (C + 1)$.

Proof of Theorem 5. We construct a protocol computing DISJ^n by taking advantage of Π_{prod} as follows:

The Protocol for DISJ^n

Parties **A** and **B** each get as input a vector $\mathbf{a}, \tilde{\mathbf{b}} \in \{0, 1\}^n$. The goal is to output 1 if the vectors are "disjoint" and 0 otherwise.

Edge Case: If one of the parties' inputs has Hamming weight 0, then they output 1 and send 1 to the other party. From now on, we assume that the Hamming weight of each party's input is at least 1.

Preamble: We call the party with the lower Hamming weight input the *designated party*. To determine this, **A** sends to **B** the Hamming weight of its input vector $\tilde{\mathbf{a}}$. If **B**'s input has higher Hamming weight, it sends back the bit 1 to **A**; otherwise it sends 0.

Input Transformation: Let $g_\gamma : \{0, 1\} \to \mathbb{R}$ be a boosting function defined as $g_\gamma(0) = \gamma$ and $g_\gamma(1) = 1$. Each party **A**, **B** locally transforms their input vector $\tilde{\mathbf{a}}, \tilde{\mathbf{b}}$ to $\mathbf{a}, \mathbf{b}$ by applying the boosting function in order to ensure γ-heaviness. That is, for $i \in [n]$, set $a_i = g_\gamma(\tilde{a}_i)$ and $b_i = g_\gamma(\tilde{b}_i)$.

Sampling Protocol: The parties run the sampling protocol $\Pi_{\mathsf{prod}}(\mathbf{a}, \mathbf{b})$ and both receive some output i^*.

Output Computation: The *designated party* checks the i^*th bit of its input by which we denote x (i.e., $x = \tilde{a}_{i^*}$ or $x = \tilde{b}_{i^*}$ depending on which party is the designated party). It sends $1 - x$ to the other party. Both parties output $1 - x$.

The following lemmas give the completeness and soundness of the protocol.

Lemma 7. *If $\tilde{\mathbf{a}}, \tilde{\mathbf{b}}$ are disjoint, then the parties both output 1 with probability at least $\frac{1}{2 + n \cdot \gamma}$.*

Lemma 8. *If $\tilde{\mathbf{a}}, \tilde{\mathbf{b}}$ are not disjoint, then the parties both output 1 with probability at most $1 - \frac{1}{1 + n \cdot \gamma}$.*

Before we prove the lemmas, we briefly describe how we can use these lemmas to achieve a protocol that correctly computes DISJ with probability at least $2/3$. Note that we can get a gap by setting $\gamma = \frac{1}{2n}$. In other words, parties output 1 when disjoint with probability at least $\frac{2}{5}$. Parties output 1 when not disjoint with probability at most $\frac{1}{3}$. Since we have a constant gap between completeness and soundness, this can be amplified to $2/3$ and $1/3$ by running the protocol a constant number of times.

Remarks. We would like to characterize the sublinearity condition for product sampling protocols using the normalized input vectors. We can do this since without loss of generality we can assume that input vectors to the product sampling protocols are normalized; in particular, for any (non-normalized) vectors $\mathbf{w}_1$ and $\mathbf{w}_2$, we have

$$\Pr\left[D_{\text{prod}}\left(\frac{\mathbf{w}_1}{\|\mathbf{w}_1\|_1}, \frac{\mathbf{w}_2}{\|\mathbf{w}_2\|_1}\right) = i\right] = \frac{\frac{w_{1,i}}{\|\mathbf{w}_1\|_1} \cdot \frac{w_{2,i}}{\|\mathbf{w}_2\|_1}}{\left\langle \frac{\mathbf{w}_1}{\|\mathbf{w}_1\|_1}, \frac{\mathbf{w}_2}{\|\mathbf{w}_2\|_1}\right\rangle} = \Pr[D_{\text{prod}}(\mathbf{w}_1, \mathbf{w}_2) = i].$$

Specifically, we show below that the impossibility theorem implies that in order to achieve sublinear communication complexity for product sampling, we would need, at the minimum, a promise on the inputs that guarantees that

$$\langle \mathbf{w}_1, \mathbf{w}_2 \rangle \in \Omega(1/n^2),$$

when $\mathbf{w}_1, \mathbf{w}_2$ are normalized vectors.

To do this, first note that the theorem implies that sublinear communication product sampling needs to have $\gamma \in \Omega(1/n)$. Now, in the proof, any non-disjoint binary vectors $\tilde{\mathbf{a}}, \tilde{\mathbf{b}}$ to the DISJ problem has $\langle \tilde{\mathbf{a}}, \tilde{\mathbf{b}} \rangle \geq 1$, and these vectors are transformed to $g_\gamma(\tilde{\mathbf{a}})$ and $g_\gamma(\tilde{\mathbf{b}})$. Let $\mathbf{w}_1$ and $\mathbf{w}_2$ be the normalized vectors $g_\gamma(\tilde{\mathbf{a}})$ and $g_\gamma(\tilde{\mathbf{b}})$; that is, $\mathbf{w}_1 := g_\gamma(\tilde{\mathbf{a}})/\|g_\gamma(\tilde{\mathbf{a}})\|_1$ and $\mathbf{w}_2 = g_\gamma(\tilde{\mathbf{b}})/\|g_\gamma(\tilde{\mathbf{b}})\|_1$. Since each entry of $g_\gamma(\tilde{\mathbf{a}})$ and $g_\gamma(\tilde{\mathbf{a}})$ is at most 1, we have $\|g_\gamma(\tilde{\mathbf{a}})\|_1 \leq n$ and $\|g_\gamma(\tilde{\mathbf{b}})\|_1 \leq n$. Therefore, we have

$$\langle \mathbf{w}_1, \mathbf{w}_2 \rangle \geq \frac{\langle g_\gamma(\mathbf{a}), g_\gamma(\mathbf{b}) \rangle}{n \cdot n} \geq \frac{1}{n^2}.$$

Proof (Proof of Lemma 7). Assume that $\tilde{\mathbf{a}}, \tilde{\mathbf{b}}$ are disjoint, and moreover, assume WLOG that $\mathbf{A}$ is the designated party, and its input vector has Hamming weight w. Recall that $a_i = g_\gamma(\tilde{a}_i)$ and $b_i = g_\gamma(\tilde{b}_i)$. Let

$$W_{0,0} := \sum_{i:\tilde{a}_i=0,\tilde{b}_i=0} a_i \cdot b_i, \qquad W_{1,0} := \sum_{i:\tilde{a}_i=1,\tilde{b}_i=0} a_i \cdot b_i$$

$$W_{0,1} := \sum_{i:\tilde{a}_i=0,\tilde{b}_i=1} a_i \cdot b_i, \qquad W_{1,1} := \sum_{i:\tilde{a}_i=1,\tilde{b}_i=1} a_i \cdot b_i$$

Note that $W_{0,0} \leq n \cdot \gamma^2$. Further, $W_{1,1} = 0$, since the vectors are disjoint, and $W_{1,0} = w \cdot \gamma$ since the Hamming weight of $\tilde{\mathbf{a}}$ is exactly w. Additionally, note that $W_{0,1} \geq W_{1,0}$, since $\mathbf{A}$ is the designated party, so the Hamming weight of $\tilde{\mathbf{a}}$ is less than or equal to the Hamming weight of $\tilde{\mathbf{b}}$.

Note that when the designated party is $\mathbf{A}$, then the output of the protocol is $1 - a_{i^*}$. Using the above facts, the probability of outputting 1 is

$$
\frac{W_{0,0} + W_{0,1}}{W_{1,1} + W_{0,0} + W_{0,1} + W_{1,0}} \geq \frac{W_{0,1}}{W_{0,0} + W_{0,1} + W_{1,0}}
$$
$$
\geq \frac{W_{0,1}}{n\gamma^2 + 2W_{0,1}}
$$
$$
= \frac{w \cdot \gamma}{n\gamma^2 + 2w \cdot \gamma}
$$
$$
= \frac{w}{n\gamma + 2w}
$$
$$
\geq \frac{1}{n\gamma + 2},
$$

where the last inequality follows since $w \geq 1$, due to the Edge Case step of the protocol. □

Proof (Proof of Lemma 8). Assume that $\tilde{\mathbf{a}}, \tilde{\mathbf{b}}$ are not disjoint. As before, consider $W_{0,0}, W_{1,0}, W_{0,1}$, and $W_{1,1}$. Note that $W_{1,1} \geq 1$ since the inputs are not disjoint. We also have $W_{0,0} + W_{0,1} + W_{1,0} \leq n \cdot \gamma$, since a_i or b_i is γ in these cases.

Using the above facts, the probability of outputting 0 is

$$
\frac{W_{1,0} + W_{1,1}}{W_{1,1} + W_{0,0} + W_{0,1} + W_{1,0}} \geq \frac{W_{1,1}}{W_{1,1} + n \cdot \gamma}
$$
$$
\geq \frac{1}{1 + n \cdot \gamma}.
$$

□

4.2 Product Sampling While Leaking at Most the Inner Product

Assumptions. As before, we assume that all weights in $\mathbf{w}_1$ and $\mathbf{w}_2$ are non-negative. As discussed in the previous subsection, we also assume, without loss of generality, that

$$
\|\mathbf{w}_1\|_1 = \|\mathbf{w}_2\|_1 = 1.
$$

Overview. We now show that the impossibility result of Sect. 4.1 can be bypassed if we make some assumptions on the inputs. Specifically, if we restrict ourselves to the case when $\langle \mathbf{w}_1, \mathbf{w}_2 \rangle = \omega \left(\frac{\log n}{n} \right)$, then we can achieve a sublinear communication protocol for product sampling on inputs $\mathbf{w}_1, \mathbf{w}_2$[4]. Of course, by

---

[4] Regarding $\langle \mathbf{w}_1, \mathbf{w}_2 \rangle$, there is a gap between the lowerbound result (i.e., $\Omega(\frac{1}{n^2})$) and our construction (i.e., $\omega(\frac{\log n}{n})$). Resolving the gap is left as an interesting open problem.

observing that the protocol uses sub-linear communication, due to our lower-bound, both parties will learn that such a promise on the inputs is satisfied; the lower bound implies that some leakage about the inputs is necessary. In our protocol, we show that the information leaked is at most the inner product $\langle \mathbf{w}_1, \mathbf{w}_2 \rangle$. (Formally, we set $f_{\mathsf{Leak}}(\mathbf{w}_1, \mathbf{w}_2) = \langle \mathbf{w}_1, \mathbf{w}_2 \rangle$.) Interestingly, we show that this is the case even though our protocol does not, and cannot,[5] actually compute $\langle \mathbf{w}_1, \mathbf{w}_2 \rangle$.

Product Sampling Protocol. Roughly, the protocol works as follows. The protocol proceeds in rounds where in each round P_1 and P_2 use the oblivious L_1 sampling with a single input vector ($\mathcal{F}_{\mathsf{osample}(\mathsf{L}_1)}$) to produce two secret-shared sampled indices, one from P_1's input vector, and one from P_2's input vector. The parties then run a secure 2-PC protocol to securely compare these values, and if they are equal, output the sampled index. If the two sampled indices are not equal, the parties move to the next round.

We describe a private two-party protocol for product sampling leaking at most the inner product (see Protocol 6). This protocol is in the $\{\mathcal{F}_{\mathsf{osample}(\mathsf{L}_1)}, \mathcal{F}_{2PC}\}$-hybrid model.

Protocol 6. Product sampling (Π^{IP}_{prod}) in the $\{\mathcal{F}_{\mathsf{osample}(\mathsf{L}_1)}, \mathcal{F}_{2PC}\}$-hybrid.

Inputs: Party P_b has input $\mathbf{w}_b$ of length n.

1. Invoke the $\mathcal{F}_{\mathsf{osample}(\mathsf{L}_1)}$ ideal functionality with P_1 as the sender with input $\mathbf{w}_1$ and P_2 as the receiver. Let $i_{1,1}$ and $i_{1,2}$ be the output from the ideal functionality to P_1 and P_2 respectively.
2. Invoke the $\mathcal{F}_{\mathsf{osample}(\mathsf{L}_1)}$ ideal functionality with P_2 as the sender with input $\mathbf{w}_2$ and P_1 as the receiver. Let $i_{2,1}$ and $i_{2,2}$ be the output from the ideal functionality to P_1 and P_2 respectively.
3. Invoke the $\mathcal{F}_{2PC}$ ideal functionality with the following circuit:
   Input: $(i_{1,j}, i_{2,j})$ for $j = 1, 2$.
   (a) Let $i_1 = i_{1,1} \oplus i_{1,2}$, $i_2 = i_{2,1} \oplus i_{2,2}$.
   (b) If i_1 is equal to i_2, output i_1 to both P_1 and P_2. Otherwise, output $\perp$.
4. If the output from the ideal functionality is $\perp$, go back to Step 1. Otherwise, output whatever $\mathcal{F}_{2PC}$ outputs.

Output: Both parties output the sampled value i.

Security. We will prove the following theorem.

Theorem 6. *Protocol Π^{IP}_{prod} securely realizes $\mathcal{F}_{\mathsf{prod}}$ with leakage $f_{\mathsf{Leak}}(\mathbf{w}_1, \mathbf{w}_2) = \langle \mathbf{w}_1, \mathbf{w}_2 \rangle$ in the $\{\mathcal{F}_{\mathsf{osample}(\mathsf{L}_1)}, \mathcal{F}_{2PC}\}$-hybrid model with semi-honest security.*

---

[5] This can be shown by a simple modification of the lower bound proof from Sect. 4.1.

Proof. We describe the simulator Sim in the $\{\mathcal{F}_{\mathsf{osample}(\mathsf{L}_1)}, \mathcal{F}_{2PC}\}$-hybrid model for the case that Party 1 is corrupted. The simulator and proof of security are analogous in the case that Party 2 is corrupted.

Sim receives as input $\mathbf{w}_1$, the output i^*, and $\langle \mathbf{w}_1, \mathbf{w}_2 \rangle$. Sim samples r^* from a geometric distribution with success probability $p = \langle \mathbf{w}_1, \mathbf{w}_2 \rangle$.

Sim invokes Party 1 on input $\mathbf{w}_1$. For $i \in [r^* - 1]$, Party 1 sends its input to the first invocation of $\mathcal{F}_{\mathsf{osample}(\mathsf{L}_1)}$ and Sim returns to it a random value in $\mathbb{Z}_n$. Party 1 sends its input to the second invocation of $\mathcal{F}_{\mathsf{osample}(\mathsf{L}_1)}$ and Sim returns to it a random value in $\mathbb{Z}_n$. Party 1 sends its input to the $\mathcal{F}_{2PC}$ functionality and Sim returns to it $\perp$. For $i = r^*$, Party 1 sends its input to the first invocation of $\mathcal{F}_{\mathsf{osample}(\mathsf{L}_1)}$ and Sim returns to it a random value in $\mathbb{Z}_n$. Party 1 sends its input to the second invocation of $\mathcal{F}_{\mathsf{osample}(\mathsf{L}_1)}$ and Sim returns to it a random value in $\mathbb{Z}_n$. Party 1 sends its input to the $\mathcal{F}_{2PC}$ functionality and Sim returns to it i^*.

It is clear that the view of Party 1 is identical in the ideal and real world, assuming that Sim samples the first succeeding round, r^*, from the correct distribution. In the following, we argue that this is indeed the case.

First, note that on any given round, we have

$$p_c := \Pr[\text{collision}] = \sum_i \Pr[i_i - i \wedge i_2 = i] = \sum_i w_{1,i} \cdot w_{2,i} = \langle \mathbf{w}_1, \mathbf{w}_2 \rangle.$$

Let $\mathsf{FirstSuccess}(r)$ denote an event in which the protocol succeeds for the first time on the r-th round. Now, for $r \in \mathbb{N}$, we have

$\Pr[\mathsf{FirstSuccess}(r) \text{ AND the output is } i^*]$
$= \Pr[\text{no collision in first } r - 1 \text{ rounds}] \cdot \Pr[i_1 = i^* \wedge i_2 = i^* \text{ on the } r\text{th round}]$
$= (1 - p_c)^{r-1} \cdot \Pr[i_1 = i^* \wedge i_2 = i^*]$

Now, the probability that the protocol eventually outputs i^* is:

$\Pr[\text{protocol eventually outputs } i^* \text{ after some number of rounds}]$

$$= \sum_{j=1}^{\infty} \Pr[\mathsf{FirstSuccess}(j) \text{ AND the output is } i^*]$$

$$= \Pr[i_1 = i^* \wedge i_2 = i^*] \sum_{j=1}^{\infty} (1 - p_c)^{j-1} = \Pr[i_1 = i^* \wedge i_2 = i^*] \cdot \frac{1}{p_c}.$$

Thus, the probability of $\mathsf{FirstSuccess}(r)$ conditioned on the output being i^* is:

$\Pr[\mathsf{FirstSuccess}(r)| \text{ the output is } i^*]$
$$= \frac{\Pr[\mathsf{FirstSuccess}(r) \text{ AND the output is } i^*]}{\Pr[\text{protocol eventually outputs } i^* \text{ after some number of rounds}]}$$
$$= \frac{(\Pr[i_1 = i^* \wedge i_2 = i^*]) \cdot (1 - p_c)^{r-1}}{\Pr[i_1 = i^* \wedge i_2 = i^*] \cdot \frac{1}{p_c}}$$
$$= p_c \cdot (1 - p_c)^{r-1}.$$

The above is exactly the probability of the number of Bernoulli trials (with probability $p_c = \langle \mathbf{w}_1, \mathbf{w}_2 \rangle$) needed to get one success. Sampling the number of rounds is therefore equivalent to sampling the random variable corresponding to the number of rounds from a geometric distribution with success probability $p_c = \langle \mathbf{w}_1, \mathbf{w}_2 \rangle$, which is exactly what Sim does. □

Performance. As shown above, the number of rounds r needed by this protocol is distributed as the number of Bernoulli trials (with probability $p = \langle \mathbf{w}_1, \mathbf{w}_2 \rangle$) needed to get one success. Thus, the expected number of rounds is $r = \frac{1}{\langle \mathbf{w}_1, \mathbf{w}_2 \rangle}$. In each round, the communication consists of a secure 2-PC of equality on $O(\log n)$-bit inputs, which can be done in $O(\log n)$ communication and $O(1)$ rounds. Thus, in total, this protocol has expected communication $O(\frac{\log n}{\langle \mathbf{w}_1, \mathbf{w}_2 \rangle})$ and $O(\frac{1}{\langle \mathbf{w}_1, \mathbf{w}_2 \rangle})$ rounds. This communication is sublinear in n when $\langle \mathbf{w}_1, \mathbf{w}_2 \rangle = \omega \left(\frac{\log n}{n} \right)$.

Trading Efficiency for Privacy. In the proof above, the simulator requires the value of $\langle \mathbf{w}_1, \mathbf{w}_2 \rangle$, which is not revealed by the output. However, a slight modification to the protocol allows us to remove this leakage at the cost of additional, though still sub-linear, communication. Instead of terminating the protocol the first time there is a collision in the L_1 samples, we can pad the communication cost by making $O(\frac{n}{\log n})$ calls to $\mathcal{F}_{\mathsf{osample}(L_1)}$. Under the promise of $\langle \mathbf{w}_1, \mathbf{w}_2 \rangle = \omega(\frac{\log n}{n})$, this ensures a collision in the outputs (with all but negligible probability). The parties can then use $O(\frac{n}{\log n})$ communication to obliviously find and output the collision, without revealing the index, and avoiding the leakage of $\langle \mathbf{w}_1, \mathbf{w}_2 \rangle$.

Generalizing this idea, we arrive at a set of similar protocol modifications that support a continuous set of tradeoffs: instead of choosing between leaking $\langle \mathbf{w}_1, \mathbf{w}_2 \rangle$ to the simulator, or padding to the maximum communication, we can choose to leak some lower bound on $\langle \mathbf{w}_1, \mathbf{w}_2 \rangle$, and modify the protocol to make a proportionate number of calls to $\mathcal{F}_{\mathsf{osample}(L_1)}$, search (obliviously) for a collision, and repeat if necessary.

Without a full proof, we provide some intuition for the fact that this tradeoff between leakage and communication is inherent. We can do that by generalizing the statement of Theorem 5. We first modify the definition of γ-heavy defined previously: for any $t(n) = O(n)$, we say that a vector $\mathbf{w}$ of length n is $\gamma_{t,n}$-heavy if each of the $t := t(n)$ coordinates of $\mathbf{w}$ is a number contained in $[\gamma, 1]$. In particular, we now allow $t(n) = o(n)$. Then, with a small modification to the reduction, we can prove that if $\mathbf{w}_1$ and $\mathbf{w}_2$ are $\gamma_{t,n}$-heavy, and if there exists a protocol Π_{prod} for product sampling with communication at most $C := C(n, \gamma)$, then there exists a protocol for computing DISJ^t with communication $\log(n) + O(C)$. In the modified reduction, the parties simply increase the weights of the t input slots (as before), and append $n - t$ entries containing 0 at the end. Since we know that DISJ^t requires $O(t)$ communication, the implication is that we have increasingly weaker communication bounds as we are provided increasingly strong promises on the inner product. Conversely, for a certain set of input vectors, observing the communication of the sampling protocol gives you a bound on the inner product of the inputs. The less communication observed, the tighter that bound, and the greater the leakage.

5   Product Sampling in Constant Rounds

Achieving Constant Rounds through Parallel Repetition. In Sects. 4, we showed a sublinear communication protocol for product sampling when $\langle \mathbf{w}_1, \mathbf{w}_2 \rangle$ is sufficiently large. Moreover, this protocol provably leaked no more information than the inner product. However, this protocol required $O(1/\langle \mathbf{w}_1, \mathbf{w}_2 \rangle)$ rounds of communication. This raises the question of whether constant-round sublinear product sampling is possible under the same restrictions on the inputs.

Our protocol to achieve this takes a relatively standard approach. Suppose that we are given the value of $\langle \mathbf{w}_1, \mathbf{w}_2 \rangle$. Then, since the expected number of samples until a collision is a function of $\langle \mathbf{w}_1, \mathbf{w}_2 \rangle$, we can just run the inner loop of protocol $\varPi_{\mathsf{prod}}$ in parallel sufficiently many times to guarantee that the protocol would terminate with all but negligible probability.

How Many Times to Repeat? However, there is one catch. It is not actually possible to compute $\langle \mathbf{w}_1, \mathbf{w}_2 \rangle$ in sublinear communication! One simple solution is to use our promise on the input: we could run the inner loop enough times to guarantee termination for any inputs satisfying the promise (e.g. $\omega(\frac{n}{\log n})$ times). However, this forces us to adopt the worst-case communication cost, which might be undesirable. (Recall, it also offers the least leakage, which might be desirable.) Instead, we re-establish the trade-off between leakage and efficiency as follows. We begin by computing an approximation of the inner product in sublinear communication (see Sect. 5.1). Using this approximation, we can then realize our sublinear communication, constant round protocol for product sampling as follows in the next subsection.

5.1   Secure Approximation of the Inner Product

We achieve a protocol that securely approximates the inner product with sublinear communication. In particular, we take advantage of the well known Johnson-Lindenstrauss Transform (JLT) [18,20] sketch.

Additional Assumptions About $\mathbf{w}_1$ and $\mathbf{w}_2$. We assumed that $\mathbf{w}_1$ and $\mathbf{w}_2$ are normalized and correlated such that $\langle \mathbf{w}_1, \mathbf{w}_2 \rangle = \omega(\log n/n)$. In a similar vein, we assume that the cosine similarity of the two vectors $\mathbf{w}_1$ and $\mathbf{w}_2$ is not small, e.g., $\omega(1/\log n)$.

Recall the cosine similarity between the two vectors $\mathbf{w}_1$ and $\mathbf{w}_2$ is defined as $\cos(\mathbf{w}_1, \mathbf{w}_2) = \frac{\langle \mathbf{w}_1, \mathbf{w}_2 \rangle}{\|\mathbf{w}_1\|_2 \cdot \|\mathbf{w}_2\|_2}$. Since the L_1 norm of each vector is equal to 1, their L_2 norms will typically much smaller than 1, which implies that the cosine similarity is usually much larger than $\langle \mathbf{w}_1, \mathbf{w}_2 \rangle$.

Approximating the Inner Product Using JLT Sketches. The JLT sketch of $\mathbf{x}$ is equal to $\mathbf{Mx}$, where $\mathbf{M}$ is a random $k \times n$ matrix with $k \ll n$. More specifically, the inner product of the two vectors is approximated as follows:

approxIP($\mathbf{w}_1, \mathbf{w}_2$):   ▷ $\mathbf{w}_1$ and $\mathbf{w}_1$ are n dimensional vectors.

1. Choose $k \times n$ matrix $\mathbf{M}$ such that each entry $M_{i,j}$ is chosen from an independent Gaussian distribution of mean 0 and variance 1.
2. Output $\frac{1}{k} \cdot \langle \mathbf{M}\mathbf{w}_1, \mathbf{M}\mathbf{w}_2 \rangle$. (Here, we slightly abuse the notation and treat the vectors $\mathbf{w}_1$ and $\mathbf{w}_2$ as column vectors.)

Lemma 9. (cf. [23, Corollary 3.1]) *For all* $\mathbf{w}_1, \mathbf{w}_2$ *such that* $\cos(\mathbf{w}_1, \mathbf{w}_2) \geq t$, *the procedure* approxIP($\mathbf{w}_1, \mathbf{w}_2$) *approximates* $\langle \mathbf{w}_1, \mathbf{w}_2 \rangle$ *up to a* $1 \pm \epsilon$ *approximation factor with all but negligible probability (over the choice of the JLT matrix), using JLT dimension* $k = \omega \left(\frac{\log(n)}{t^2 \cdot \epsilon^2} \right)$.

Privacy of the Approximate Output. What is interesting is that the approximate inner product doesn't reveal anything more than the inner product itself. In this sense, it satisfies the notion of private approximation introduced in [15]. In particular, we prove the following:

Lemma 10. *The output of* approxIP($\mathbf{w}_1, \mathbf{w}_2$) *can be simulated perfectly given only* $\langle \mathbf{w}_1, \mathbf{w}_1 \rangle$, $\langle \mathbf{w}_2, \mathbf{w}_2 \rangle$, *and* $\langle \mathbf{w}_1, \mathbf{w}_2 \rangle$.

The proof is found in Appendix C.6 in the full version.

Private Protocol via JLT. Using the JLT sketch, we can design a private protocol approximating the inner product. See Protocol 7. The protocol uses threshold FHE (e.g., [28]).

Protocol 7. Private protocol for computing approximate inner product

---

Inputs: Parties P_1 and P_2 has inputs $\mathbf{w}_1$ and $\mathbf{w}_2$ respectively.

The protocol proceeds as follows:

1. Parties set up a threshold FHE scheme.
2. They securely sample $k \times n$ matrix $\mathbf{M}$ described in the above with in the threshold FHE. In particular, they jointly generate an encrypted random seed $[\![s]\!]$. Using this randomness, parties homomorphically evaluates $[\![PRG(s)]\!]$, where PRG is a pseudorandom generator, to obtain the JLT matrix $[\![\mathbf{M}]\!]$.
3. Each party P_b homomorphically evaluates $[\![\tilde{\mathbf{w}}_b]\!] = [\![\mathbf{M}\mathbf{w}_b]\!]$.
4. Party P_1 sends $[\![\tilde{\mathbf{w}}_1]\!]$ to P_2.
5. Party P_2 homomorphically evaluates $[\![\langle \tilde{\mathbf{w}}_1, \tilde{\mathbf{w}}_2 \rangle]\!]$ and sends it to P_1.
6. Parties execute threshold decryption to obtain and output $\frac{1}{k} \cdot \langle \tilde{\mathbf{w}}_1, \tilde{\mathbf{w}}_2 \rangle$.

Security. Since every protocol message is a ciphertext, based on semantic security of the threshold FHE, it is easy to see that the protocol securely realizes a functionality for computing approxIP. Based on Lemma 10, the leakage profile of the functionality is $\langle \mathbf{w}_1, \mathbf{w}_1 \rangle$, $\langle \mathbf{w}_2, \mathbf{w}_2 \rangle$, and $\langle \mathbf{w}_1, \mathbf{w}_2 \rangle$.

5.2 Constant-Round Protocol for Product Sampling

Note that the Protocol 6 has the following structure. In particular:

- The probability that Protocol 6 samples a good index and halts in a given trial is $p = \langle \mathbf{w}_1, \mathbf{w}_2 \rangle$.

We need to repeat r trials in parallel so that the probability that all r trials fail is negligible. In other words, we should have

$$(1 - p)^r \leq e^{-p \cdot r} \leq e^{-\omega(\log \lambda)}.$$

This means that we should have $r > \frac{\omega(\log \lambda)}{p}$.

Moreover, in the previous subsection, we discussed how to obtain a good estimate $\tilde{p} = (1 \pm \epsilon)p$. Therefore, we should have

$$r > \frac{(1 + \epsilon) \cdot \omega(\log \lambda)}{\tilde{p}} > \frac{\omega(\log \lambda)}{p}.$$

In summary, by running $\frac{(1+\epsilon) \cdot \omega(\log \lambda)}{\tilde{p}}$ instances in parallel, we achieve constant round protocols for product sampling with negligible failure probability. The final protocol should perform extra steps to hide from which trial the output comes from, and these changes can made in a straightforward way.

Acknowledgments. Seung Geol Choi is supported by NSF grant #CNS-1955319. Dana Dachman-Soled is supported in part by NSF grants #IIS-2147276, #CNS-1933033, #CNS-1453045 (CAREER), and by financial assistance awards 70NANB15H328 and 70NANB19H126 from the U.S. Department of Commerce, National Institute of Standards and Technology. Dov Gordon is supported by NSF grant #CNS-1955264. Arkady Yerukhimovich is supported by NSF grant #CNS-1955620.

References

1. Acar, A., Celik, Z.B., Aksu, H., Uluagac, A.S., McDaniel, P.: Achieving secure and differentially private computations in multiparty settings. In 2017 IEEE Symposium on Privacy-Aware Computing (PAC), pp. 49–59. IEEE (2017)
2. Andoni, A., Krauthgamer, R., Onak, K.: Streaming algorithms via precision sampling. In: Ostrovsky, R., IEEE 52nd Annual Symposium on Foundations of Computer Science, FOCS 2011, Palm Springs, CA, USA, 22–25 October 2011, pp. 363–372. IEEE Computer Society (2011)
3. Babai, L., Nisan, N., Szegedy, M.: Multiparty protocols and logspace-hard pseudorandom sequences (extended abstract). In: 21st ACM STOC, pp. 1–11. ACM Press (1989)
4. Bar-Yossef, Z., Jayram, T.S., Kumar, R., Sivakumar, D.: An information statistics approach to data stream and communication complexity. J. Comput. Syst. Sci. **68**(4), 702–732 (2004)
5. Braverman, V., Ostrovsky, R., Zaniolo, C.: Optimal sampling from sliding windows. J. Comput. Syst. Sci. **78**(1), 260–272 (2012)

6. Champion, J., Shelat, A., Ullman, J.: Securely sampling biased coins with applications to differential privacy. In: Cavallaro, L., Kinder, J., Wang, X., Katz, J., (eds.) ACM CCS 2019, pp. 603–614. ACM Press, (2019)

7. Choi, S.G., Dachman-Soled, D., Gordon, S.D., Liu, L., Yerukhimovich, A.: Secure sampling with sublinear communication. Cryptology ePrint Archive, Paper 2022/660 (2022). https://eprint.iacr.org/2022/660

8. Choi, S.G., Dachman-Soled, D., Kulkarni, M., Yerukhimovich, A.: Differentially-private multi-party sketching for large-scale statistics. PoPETs **2020**(3), 153–174 (2020)

9. Clifton, C., Anandan, B.: Challenges and opportunities for security with differential privacy. In: Bagchi, A., Ray, I. (eds.) ICISS 2013. LNCS, vol. 8303, pp. 1–13. Springer, Heidelberg (2013). https://doi.org/10.1007/978-3-642-45204-8_1

10. Cormode, G., Jowhari, H.: L p samplers and their applications: a survey. ACM Comput. Surv. (CSUR) **52**(1), 1–31 (2019)

11. Dwork, C., Kenthapadi, K., McSherry, F., Mironov, I., Naor, M.: Our data, ourselves: privacy via distributed noise generation. In: Vaudenay, S. (ed.) EUROCRYPT 2006. LNCS, vol. 4004, pp. 486–503. Springer, Heidelberg (2006). https://doi.org/10.1007/11761679_29

12. Elahi, T., Danezis, G., Goldberg, I.: PrivEx: private collection of traffic statistics for anonymous communication networks. In: Ahn, G.J., Yung, M., Li, N., (eds.) ACM CCS 2014, pp. 1068–1079. ACM Press (2014)

13. Eriguchi, R., Ichikawa, A., Kunihiro, N., Nuida, K.: Efficient noise generation to achieve differential privacy with applications to secure multiparty computation. In: Borisov, N., Diaz, C. (eds.) FC 2021. LNCS, vol. 12674, pp. 271–290. Springer, Heidelberg (2021). https://doi.org/10.1007/978-3-662-64322-8_13

14. Feigenbaum, J., Ishai, Y., Malkin, T., Nissim, K., Strauss, M., Wright, R.N.: Secure multiparty computation of approximations. In: Orejas, F., Spirakis, P.G., van Leeuwen, J. (eds.) ICALP 2001. LNCS, vol. 2076, pp. 927–938. Springer, Heidelberg (2001). https://doi.org/10.1007/3-540-48224-5_75

15. Feigenbaum, J., Ishai, Y., Malkin, T., Nissim, K., Strauss, M.J., Wright, R.N.: Secure multiparty computation of approximations. ACM Trans. Algorithms **2**(3), 435–472 (2006)

16. Ganguly, S.: Counting distinct items over update streams. Theoret. Comput. Sci. **378**(3), 211–222 (2007)

17. Goryczka, S., Xiong, L., Sunderam, V.: Secure multiparty aggregation with differential privacy: a comparative study. In: Proceedings of the Joint EDBT/ICDT 2013 Workshops, pp. 155–163 (2013)

18. Indyk, P., Motwani, R.: Approximate nearest neighbors: towards removing the curse of dimensionality. In: 30th ACM STOC, pp. 604–613. ACM Press (1998)

19. Jansen, R., Johnson, A.: Safely measuring tor. In: Weippl, E.R., Katzenbeisser, S., Kruegel, C., Myers, A.C., Halevi, S., (eds.) ACM CCS 2016, pp. 1553–1567. ACM Press (2016)

20. Johnson, W.B. Lindenstrauss, J.: Extensions of lipschitz mappings into a hilbert space (1984)

21. Jowhari, H., Saglam, M., Tardos, G.: Tight bounds for LP samplers, finding duplicates in streams, and related problems. In: Lenzerini, M., Schwentick, T., (eds.) Proceedings of the 30th ACM SIGMOD-SIGACT-SIGART Symposium on Principles of Database Systems, PODS 2011, 12–16 June 2011, Athens, Greece, pp. 49–58. ACM (2011)

22. Jowhari, H., Saglam, M., Tardos, G.: Tight bounds for LP samplers, finding duplicates in streams, and related problems. In: Proceedings of the Thirtieth ACM SIGMOD-SIGACT-SIGART Symposium on Principles of Database Systems, pp. 49–58 (2011)
23. Kabán, A.: Improved bounds on the dot product under random projection and random sign projection. In: Cao, L., Zhang, C., Joachims, T., Webb, G.I.B., Margineantu, D., Williams, G., (eds.) Proceedings of the 21th ACM SIGKDD International Conference on Knowledge Discovery and Data Mining, Sydney, NSW, Australia, 10–13 August 2015, pp. 487–496. ACM (2015)
24. Kalyanasundaram, B., Schnitger, G.: The probabilistic communication complexity of set intersection. SIAM J. Discret. Math. 5(4), 545–557 (1992)
25. McSherry, F., Talwar, K.: Mechanism design via differential privacy. In: 48th FOCS, pp. 94–103. IEEE Computer Society Press (2007)
26. Melis, L., Danezis, G., De Cristofaro, E.: Efficient private statistics with succinct sketches. In: NDSS 2016. The Internet Society (2016)
27. Monemizadeh, M., Woodruff, D.P.: 1-pass relative-error l_p-sampling with applications. In: Charikar, M., ed. Proceedings of the Twenty-First Annual ACM-SIAM Symposium on Discrete Algorithms, SODA 2010, Austin, Texas, USA, 17–19 January 2010, pp. 1143–1160. SIAM (2010)
28. Mouchet, C., Troncoso-Pastoriza, J., Bossuat, J.P., Hubaux, J.P.: Multiparty homomorphic encryption from ring-learning-with-errors. PoPETs 2021(4), 291–311 (2021)
29. Pathak, M., Rane, S., Raj, B.: Multiparty differential privacy via aggregation of locally trained classifiers. In: Advances in Neural Information Processing Systems, vol. 23 (2010)
30. Pentyala, S., et al.: Training differentially private models with secure multiparty computation. arXiv preprint arXiv:2202.02625 (2022)
31. Prabhakaran, M.M., Prabhakaran, V.M.: On secure multiparty sampling for more than two parties. In 2012 IEEE Information Theory Workshop, pp. 99–103. IEEE (2012)
32. Prabhakaran, V.M., Prabhakaran, M.M.: Assisted common information with an application to secure two-party sampling. IEEE Trans. Inf. Theor. 60(6), 3413–3434 (2014)
33. Razborov, A.A.: On the distributional complexity of disjointness. Theor. Comput. Sci. 106(2), 385–390 (1992)
34. Wails, R., Johnson, A., Starin, D., Yerukhimovich, A., Gordon, S.D.: Stormy: statistics in tor by measuring securely. In: Cavallaro, L., Kinder, J., Wang, X., Katz, J., (eds.) ACM CCS 2019, pp. 615–632. ACM Press (2019)
35. Woodruff, D.P., Zhong, P.: Distributed low rank approximation of implicit functions of a matrix. In: 2016 IEEE 32nd International Conference on Data Engineering (ICDE), pp. 847–858. IEEE (2016)

Secure Non-interactive Simulation from Arbitrary Joint Distributions

Hamidreza Amini Khorasgani, Hemanta K. Maji, and Hai H. Nguyen[✉]

Department of Computer Science, Purdue University, West Lafayette, USA
{haminikh,hmaji,nguye245}@purdue.edu

Abstract. *Secure non-interactive simulation* (SNIS), introduced in EUROCRYPT 2022, is the information-theoretic analog of *pseudo-correlation generators*. SNIS allows parties, starting with samples of a source correlated private randomness (correlation), to non-interactively and securely transform them into samples from a different correlation.

This work studies SNIS of *binary symmetric or erasure correlations* from any arbitrary source correlation. In this context, our work presents:
1. The characterization of all sources that facilitate such SNIS,
2. An upper and lower bound on their maximum achievable rate, and
3. Exemplar SNIS instances where non-linear reductions achieve optimal efficiency; however, any linear reduction is insecure.

These results collectively yield the fascinating instances of *computer-assisted search* for secure computation protocols that identify ingenious protocols that are more efficient than all known constructions.

Our work generalizes the algebraization of the simulation-based definition of SNIS as an approximate eigenvector problem. The following technical contributions are the underpinnings of the results above.
1. Characterization of Markov and adjoint Markov operators' effect on the Fourier spectrum of reduction functions.
2. A new concentration phenomenon in the Fourier spectrum of reduction functions.
3. A statistical-to-perfect lemma with broad consequences for feasibility and rate characterization of SNIS.

Our technical analysis relies on Fourier analysis over large alphabets with arbitrary measure, the orthogonal Efron-Stein decomposition, and junta theorems. Our technical approach motivates the new problem of "security-preserving dimension reduction" in harmonic analysis, which may be of independent interest.

The research effort is supported in part by an NSF CRII Award CNS–1566499, NSF SMALL Awards CNS–1618822 and CNS–2055605, the IARPA HECTOR project, MITRE Innovation Program Academic Cybersecurity Research Awards (2019–2020, 2020–2021), a Ross-Lynn Research Scholars Grant, a Purdue Research Foundation (PRF) Award, and The Center for Science of Information, an NSF Science and Technology Center, Cooperative Agreement CCF–0939370.
The full version is accessible at https://eprint.iacr.org/2021/190.

E. Kiltz and V. Vaikuntanathan (Eds.): TCC 2022, LNCS 13748, pp. 378–407, 2022.
https://doi.org/10.1007/978-3-031-22365-5_14

1   Introduction

Recently, Khorasgani, Maji, and Nguyen [32] introduced *secure non-interactive simulation* (SNIS) as an information-theoretic analog of *pseudo-correlation generator* [10,11]. In the two-party setting (refer to Fig. 1), Alice and Bob start with n independent samples of *correlated private randomness* (X, Y), the *source distribution*. Non-interactively, Alice and Bob compute $U = f_n(X^n)$ and $V = g_n(Y^n)$, where $f_n(\cdot)$ and $g_n(\cdot)$ are reduction functions,[1] and the joint distribution (U, V) is the *target distribution*. This construction is a SNIS of the target distribution (U, V) from the source distribution (X, Y) if it is *simulation-secure* [12–14]. Note that SNIS security against semi-honest or malicious adversaries is identical.

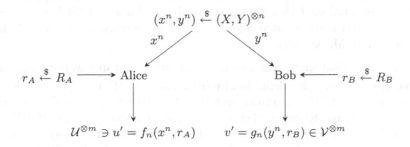

Fig. 1. System model for secure non-interactive simulation: SNIS.

Motivating Application for SNIS: Correlation generators [32]. Secure computation [26,52] protocols often offload most of their computationally and cryptographically expensive components to an offline procedure [8,17,39,45]. This offline procedure has high computation and communication costs, and it generates structured correlated private randomness like Beaver triples [5]. However, several inexpensive sources of correlated private randomness also facilitate secure computation, like correlated samples from noise sources [33]. Therefore, a natural solution is to *non-interactively* and *securely* convert these inexpensive correlations into ones used in secure computation protocols.

Boyle et al. [10,11] introduced *pseudorandom correlation generators* to achieve this objective against computationally bounded adversaries. Recently, Khorasgani et al. [32] introduced the information-theoretic analog of this primitive, modeled by the system in Fig. 1, to study the *feasibility* and *rate* of SNIS, which has straightforward consequences to the efficiency of secure computation.

---

[1]   The reduction functions $f_n(\cdot)$ and $g_n(\cdot)$ are randomized and use independent private randomness; however, for brevity, the randomness is being excluded from the formal representation. Strong *sample-preserving* derandomization results (i.e., the derandomized reductions use an identical number of source samples and produce an identical number of target samples) for SNIS [32] indicate the uselessness of independent private randomness.

Security & Rate Definition of SNIS [32]. Readers should follow the system in Fig. 1 for the discussion below. For feasibility considerations, substitute $m = 1$ in Fig. 1. Khorasgani et al. [32] said that a *SNIS of (U, V) from $(X, Y)^{\otimes n}$ using reduction functions f_n, g_n has insecurity $\nu(n)$* if the following three conditions are satisfied.

1. *Correctness.* The joint distribution of the output samples (u', v') is $\nu(n)$-close to the target distribution (U, V) in statistical (i.e., total variational) distance.
2. *Security against a corrupt Alice.* Fix any (u, v) in the support of the target distribution (U, V). The distribution of x^n conditioned on $u' = u$ and $v' = v$ is $\nu(n)$-close to being independent of v.[2] In other words, $X^n - U - V$ is an (approximate) Markov chain.
3. *Security against a corrupt Bob.* Likewise, for any (u, v) in the support of the target distribution (U, V), the conditional distribution $(Y^n | U' = u, V' = v)$ is $\nu(n)$-close to being independent of u. In other words, $Y^n - V - U$ is an approximate Markov chain.

[32] presented a simulation-based security definition that unifies these three conditions. We represent this definition by the notation: "$(U, V) \sqsubseteq_{f_n, g_n}^{\nu(n)} (X, Y)^{\otimes n}$".

Fix the source (X, Y) and the target (U, V). To discuss (the single-letter characterization of) rate, Khorasgani et al. [32] consider a SNIS *family* of $(U, V)^{\otimes m(n)}$ from $(X, Y)^{\otimes n}$ using reduction function f_n, g_n with insecurity $\nu(n)$, parameterized by $n \in \{1, 2, \dots\}$. The (production) *rate*, represented by $R(\ (U, V), (X, Y)\ )$, is the supremum of the maximum achievable $m(n)/n$ as $n \to \infty$ and $\nu(n) \to 0$ over all possible families of reductions.

This reduction-based investigation facilitates characterizing the efficiency limits of non-interactive secure computation irrespective of the origin of the source samples. For example, the source samples can originate from noisy physical processes, trusted hardware, or the output of a protocol relying on cryptographic hardness of computation assumptions.

Relation to Other Primitives and Additional Motivation. One-way secure computation [2, 22] uses one additional round of communication to transform the samples from source distributions into samples from a target distribution. *Non-interactive correlation distillation* [9, 16, 42, 43, 51] restricts SNIS to the target distribution (U, V) being the independent coin distribution. SNIS is the cryptographic extension of *non-interactive simulation of joint distribution* [18, 21, 24, 25, 30, 31, 48, 50] from information theory.

This non-cryptographic simulation problem (either non-interactive or with rate-limited communication) has diverse applications, for example, as discussed in [31], spanning from game-theoretic coordination in a network against an adversary to control a dynamical system over a distributed network. These applications naturally extend to the cryptographic context with adversarial agents, granting additional independent motivation to study SNIS.

---

[2] The conditional distribution $(A | B = b)$ is ν-close to being independent of b if there is a distribution A^* such that the statistical distance between A^* and the conditional distribution $(A | B = b)$ is at most ν for any $b \in \text{Supp}(B)$.

Studying the *cryptographic complexity* [6,7,36,38,44] also motivates the study of SNIS, as done in the independent work of [1].

Our Problem Statement. This work considers the simulation of two particular target distributions (U, V) (refer to Fig. 2).

1. *Noise from the binary symmetric channel.* Alice outputs uniformly random $u \in \{+1, -1\}$ and Bob outputs $v \in \{+1, -1\}$ such that, for each u, the probability of $u \neq v$ is $\varepsilon \in (0, 1/2)$. We represent this correlated private randomness by $\mathsf{BSS}(\rho)$, where $\rho = (1 - 2\varepsilon)$. For example, $\mathsf{BSS}(1/2)$ is a distribution where Alice and Bob samples disagree with a probability of $1/4$.
2. *Noise from the binary erasure channel.* Alice outputs uniformly random $u \in \{+1, -1\}$ and Bob outputs $v \in \{u, 0\}$ such that, for each u, the probability of $v = 0$ is $\varepsilon \in (0, 1)$. We represent this correlated private randomness by $\mathsf{BES}(\rho)$, where $\rho = \sqrt{1 - \varepsilon}$. So, $\mathsf{BES}(\sqrt{1/2})$ has erasure probability $1/2$.

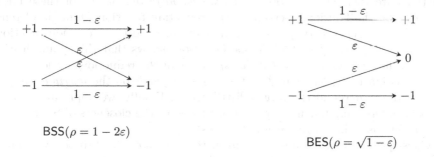

Fig. 2. Random correlated noise generated by the binary symmetric channel (BSS) and the binary erasure channel (BES) with maximal correlation ρ.

This work parameterizes the channels by their *maximal correlation* ρ for brevity in our technical presentation (see Sect. 3.2 for formal definition). [32] proved that a SNIS of $\mathsf{BSS}(\rho')$ from $\mathsf{BSS}(\rho)$ exists if and only if $\rho' = \rho^k$, for some $k \in \{1, 2, \ldots\}$. Furthermore, if this SNIS is feasible, it has a rate of $1/k$: each party outputs the product of k samples of their source – a linear reduction. Similarly, a SNIS of $\mathsf{BES}(\rho')$ from $\mathsf{BES}(\rho)$ exists if and only if $\rho' = \rho^k$, for some $k \in \{1, 2, \ldots\}$. This SNIS also has a rate of $1/k$, and linear reductions are rate-achieving.

Our work considers the problem of determining the *feasibility* and *rate* of SNIS generating BSS/BES*target noise* from *arbitrary source distributions* and identifying corresponding *maximum rate-achieving* secure constructions. The source distribution (X, Y) can be arbitrary; they may have arbitrary-size sample spaces, and their marginal distributions need not be uniform or identical.

Summary of Our Results. We present an exhaustive characterization of all source distributions that yield secure SNIS of BSS and BES target distributions. Furthermore, if the insecurity of a SNIS is sufficiently small, then one can slightly edit the reduction functions to convert them into perfectly secure SNIS. Next, we present (positive constant) lower and upper bounds on the production rate of such SNIS. Finally, we exhibit SNIS instances where non-linear reduction functions achieve optimal rate (also demonstrating the tightness of our rate estimates); however, every linear reduction is constant insecure. We efficiently searched the space of all reductions (guided by our technical results) to identify these fascinating non-linear reductions – even the authors were unaware of their existence.

These cryptographic consequences rely on several foundational and technical contributions of ours, which may be of independent and broader interest. We generalize the [32]'s framework for algebraizing SNIS from arbitrary source distributions using the source's Markov and the adjoint Markov operators (refer to Sect. 3.4 for definition). This algebraization translates SNIS into an *approximate eigenvector formulation* for appropriate linear operators, where the reduction functions are their eigenvectors. Next, we *quantify the impact* of these linear operators on the Fourier spectrum of the reduction functions. Our proof relies on a critical synergy between the linear operators and the reduction functions over the *orthogonal Efron-Stein basis*. Our work shows that this quantification entails a *concentration of the Fourier spectrum* of the reductions on low-degree terms. Fascinatingly, our bound on the degree depends on the *maximal correlations* of the source and the target distributions. Finally, we apply appropriate *junta theorems* (i.e., dimension reduction) to prove the closeness of SNIS reductions to juntas (a.k.a., *canonical reductions*).

Consequently, one obtains a technical tool: *the statistical to perfect lemma.* This lemma, for instance, implies the following non-trivial phenomena for any source and target pair.

1. One can error-correct any statistically-secure SNIS into a perfect SNIS.
2. The total number of canonical SNIS candidates is constant.
3. The rate of any feasible SNIS is a positive constant.

The presentation above is only a high-level overview of our proof strategy, highlighting its primary landmarks. There are several subtleties to address and technical challenges to overcome, which we further elaborate in Sect. 2.2.

Computer-Assisted Search for Optimal Secure Computation Protocols. Although computer-assisted constructions are common while constructing error-correcting codes and combinatorial designs [37], their role in secure protocols is novel. Our work presents fascinating instances of computer-assisted search for finding *optimal* secure computation protocols that are *more efficient than known protocols*. [32] discovered new alternative constructions that achieve already-known efficiency parameters. [15] also used computer assistance to recover known garbling constructions. Typically idealized information-theoretic models yield hardness of computation results; however, the SNIS model also yields non-trivial positive results. This research outcome indicates that one should be open to the possibility of relying on computer-assisted search to design new and more efficient secure computation protocols.

Overview of the Paper. Section 2 presents an informal overview of our results and technical approach. Section 3 introduces the preliminaries. Section 4 proves our results pertaining to determining the feasibility of SNIS. Section 5 presents our rate estimation results. Section 6 has results pertaining to 2×2 sources. Section 7 presents the remaining results.

2 Overview of Our Contributions

2.1 Overview of Our Results

This section presents an informal summary of our results and a technical overview of the proof. In the presentation below, without loss of generality, we assume that the SNIS reductions are deterministic [32].

Feasibility Characterization of SNIS from Arbitrary Sources. We present an efficient algorithm to determine whether a statistically secure SNIS of BSS/BES from the source (X, Y) is feasible or not (see Corollary 1). Theorem 1 states that if the simulation error of a SNIS of BSS/BES from the source (X, Y) is less than c/n, where c a suitable positive constant, one can edit the reduction functions into a perfect secure SNIS. Furthermore, these perfectly-secure reductions are canonical reductions that are *Boolean constant-juntas*. That is, they depend on a constant number of input variables, which entails that the total number of such canonical candidate reductions is only a constant. Therefore, one can exhaustively search for all such canonical reductions to determine if a SNIS of BSS/BES from (X, Y) is possible.

This technical result entails the following consequence for *cryptographic contexts*. Efficient secure constructions in cryptography insist on achieving $\mathsf{negl}(\lambda)$ insecurity, where λ is the security parameter, using $n = \mathsf{poly}(\lambda)$ source samples. Therefore, given a source and target, our result proves that either (a) there is a perfectly secure SNIS or (b) every SNIS construction is insecure (because we show that the insecurity is at least inverse-polynomial in the security parameter). In particular, our result rules out the possibility of negligibly-insecure SNIS existing where there is no perfectly secure SNIS.

Estimating Rate of SNIS from Arbitrary Sources. We prove that if a SNIS is feasible, it has a positive constant rate (see Corollary 2). Fix a BSS/BES target. To lower-bound the rate of such SNIS by a positive constant, observe that if a SNIS of BSS/BES from (X, Y) is feasible, there is a canonical SNIS, which is perfectly secure, and the reduction functions are constant-juntas. One can partition the samples of $(X, Y)^{\otimes n}$ into constant-size blocks, apply the canonical reduction to each block, and obtain one target sample from each block. This construction has a positive constant rate. Such results are rare in cryptography and challenging to prove for secure computation (cf., [28, 29, 32] for examples).

Theorem 5 upper-bounds the rate of SNIS of BSS/BES from any target distribution using the *maximal correlation* [3,4,27,47,48] of the target distribution (refer to Sect. 3.2 for the definition of maximal correlation) and the eigenvalue of the Markov operator $\mathsf{T}\overline{\mathsf{T}}$ (refer to Sect. 3.4) of the source distribution. We emphasize that this upper bound is *only for perfectly secure SNIS*. This restriction is unsurprising because, as demonstrated in [32], even estimating the rate of simulating BSS from BSS is known only for perfectly secure SNIS. [32] present evidence that overcoming this hurdle may require advances in harmonic analysis.

Our upper bounds for BSS and BES are tight as demonstrated by (1) the rate of self-simulation of BSS and BES [32], and (2) the reduction of BSS(1/2) and BES($\sqrt{1/2}$) from the ROLE correlation (defined below), whose maximal correlation is $\sqrt{1/2}$.

We clarify that this upper bound also extends to randomized perfectly-secure SNIS because the sample-preserving derandomization of [32] preserves perfect security.

Power of Non-linear Reductions and Computer-Assisted Search. The *random oblivious linear-function evaluation* [49] (ROLE) source samples uniformly and independently random $a, b, c \in \{0, 1\}$, provides Alice $x = (a, b)$, and provides Bob $y = (c, d)$, where $d = a \cdot c \oplus b$. The maximal correlation of ROLE is $\sqrt{1/2}$ (see the full version for the proof). Recall that BSS(1/2) is a random correlated sample from the binary symmetric channel where parties' samples are different with probability 1/4.

We show that there is an *optimal* rate-1/2 SNIS of BSS(1/2) from ROLE using non-linear reductions (refer to the protocol in Fig. 3 and the discussion in Sect. 7.3); however, any SNIS of BSS(1/2) from ROLE using linear reductions is constant-insecure (refer to Lemma 4).[3] The optimality of the rate follows from the upper bound of Theorem 5. In the optimal protocol each party's output indicates whether their source samples form a ROLE correlation or not.

The previous best construction (as far as the authors are aware) uses *three* ROLEs and *one round of communication* to implement a 1-out-of-4 bit-OT. Alice feeds a random permutation of $(u, u, u, 1 - u)$, where $u \xleftarrow{\$} \{0, 1\}$, into the 1-out-of-4 bit-OT. Bob chooses to receive the bit v at a random position $i \in \{1, 2, 3, 4\}$. In comparison, our construction uses one less ROLE sample and no communication, which significantly impacts the efficiency of this secure computation.[4]

---

[3] Observe that "linearity" of a reduction may depend on how the samples of the source are "named". We prove our impossibility result in a strong sense. For any renaming of the samples, we show that linear constructions are constant insecure.

[4] We identified *all* reductions realizing this SNIS at an optimal rate. All the reductions were essentially equivalent to each other. However, we chose this particular reduction because it admits an elegant intuitive formulation.

Source. Alice gets (a_1, b_1, a_2, b_2) and Bob gets (c_1, d_1, c_2, d_2) such that $a_1, b_1, c_1, a_2, b_2, c_2$ are chosen uniformly and independently at random from the set $\{0, 1\}$ and $d_1 = a_1 \cdot c_1 \oplus b_1$ and $d_2 = a_2 \cdot c_2 \oplus b_2$.

Reductions.
1. Alice outputs $u = +1$, if $b_2 = a_1 \cdot a_2 \oplus b_1$; otherwise, $u = -1$.
2. Bob outputs $v = +1$, if $d_2 = c_1 \cdot c_2 \oplus d_1$; otherwise, $v = -1$.

Source. (In multiplicative notation.) Alice gets (A_1, B_1, A_2, B_2) and Bob gets (C_1, D_2, C_2, D_2) such that $A_1, B_1, C_1, A_2, B_2, C_2$ are chosen uniformly and independently at random from the set $\{+1, -1\}$ and $D_1 = \frac{1}{2} \cdot (1 + A_1 + C_1 - A_1 \cdot C_1) \cdot B_1$ and $D_2 = \frac{1}{2} \cdot (1 + A_2 + C_2 - A_2 \cdot C_2) \cdot B_2$.

Reductions.
1. Alice outputs $U = \frac{1}{2} \cdot (1 + A_1 + A_2 - A_1 \cdot A_2) \cdot B_1 \cdot B_2$.
2. Bob outputs $V = \frac{1}{2} \cdot (1 + C_1 + C_2 - C_1 \cdot C_2) \cdot D_1 \cdot D_2$.

Fig. 3. SNIS of BSS(1/2) from ROLE achieving optimal production rate $1/2$. The top half of the figure presents the reduction using ROLE as defined for elements in $\{0, 1\}$. The bottom half presents the equivalent reduction using the multiplicative notation $0 \mapsto +1$ and $1 \mapsto -1$. In the multiplicative representation, the Fourier spectrum of each reduction function is explicit. One can verify that the (1) reduction functions are non-linear and (2) their Fourier weights are not concentrated on terms of identical degree.

Similarly, there is an *optimal* rate-1 SNIS of BES($\sqrt{1/2}$) from ROLE using non-linear reductions (refer to Sect. 7.3); however, any SNIS using linear reductions is constant-insecure (refer to Lemma 4). The optimality of this protocol follows from Theorem 5. Furthermore, the spectrums of these reduction functions are *not concentrated* on terms with an identical degree.

Additional Result: Explicit Characterization of SNIS of BSS from 2×2 Sources. Let the target distribution be BSS(ρ') and (X, Y) be an arbitrary source such that the support size of both its marginals is two. We prove in Theorem 6 that if the source $(X, Y) \neq$ BSS(ρ) or $(X, Y) =$ BSS(ρ) but $\rho' \neq \rho^k$, for all $k \in \{1, 2, \dots\}$, then any SNIS of BSS(ρ') from (X, Y) is constant insecure. If $(X, Y) =$ BSS(ρ), $\rho' = \rho^k$, for some $k \in \{1, 2, \dots\}$, and BSS(ρ') $\sqsubseteq_{f,g}^{\nu}$ BSS(ρ) for a sufficiently small ν, then one can slightly edit the reduction function to obtain new reduction functions f^*, g^* that are k-homogeneous[5] and BSS(ρ') $\sqsubseteq_{f^*,g^*}^{0}$ BSS(ρ) – a result already proved in [32]. The proof of Theorem 6 (additionally) depends on (1) Theorem 8: a statistical-to-perfect lemma for BSS target from arbitrary 2×2 source, and (2) Theorem 9: the characterization of sources facilitating perfect SNIS of BSS target.

Remark 1. For 2×2 sources, our definition of "sufficiently small simulation error" is slightly different from the arbitrary source case. In the 2×2 source case, "sufficiently small simulation error" is a (global) constant. For arbitrary

---

[5] A homogeneous function is a linear combination of terms with an identical degree.

sources, "sufficiently small simulation error" is c/n, where c is a global constant. This variation is a consequence of the different junta theorems our analysis uses. Typically in cryptography, the security requires that the simulation error falls faster than any inverse polynomial. Our results even work when considering inverse polynomial simulation error.

Additional Result: Explicit Characterization of SNIS of BESfrom 2×2 Sources. We show that any SNIS of BES from a 2×2 source is constant insecure (refer to Theorem 7). This generalizes the impossibility of SNIS of BES from BSS [32].

Additional Result: Necessary Condition for SNIS Feasibility. Theorem 11 presents easy-to-test necessary conditions for the feasibility of SNIS of BSS or BES from eigenvalues of the Markov operator of the source. Our "eigenvalue test" (derived independently) is identical to the test introduced in [1].

Additional Result: Incompleteness of String OT. Random samples from the string oblivious transfer functionality, parameterized by $\ell \in \{1, 2, \dots\}$, gives Alice two random ℓ-bit strings $(x_0, x_1) \in \{0, 1\}^{2\ell}$ and gives Bob $(b, x_b) \in \{0, 1\}^{\ell+1}$, where b is a uniformly random bit (see Definition 8). Lemma 5 states that this family (for $\ell \in \{1, 2, \dots\}$) of random samples from the string oblivious transfer is not complete for SNIS because all of them have maximal correlation $\sqrt{1/2}$. This family cannot yield a SNIS of any target with maximal correlation $> \sqrt{1/2}$, because of Imported Theorem 2, and Imported Theorem 1.

This family is complete for one-way secure computation [22]. [1] show that a single source cannot be complete for SNIS.

2.2 Overview of Our Technical Contributions

This section presents a high-level intuition of our technical contributions. It is instructive to read this section with SNIS for BSS target as a representative example.

Our Starting Point. For a source $(X, Y) \in \{BSS, BES\}$, Khorasgani et al. [32] algebraically captured the simulation-based security definition of SNIS using the Markov (T) and the adjoint-Markov ($\overline{T}$) operators associated with (X, Y). If a SNIS has a small simulation error, the reduction functions f and g are approximate eigenvectors of the linear operators $T\overline{T}$ and $\overline{T}T$, respectively. We generalize this result to an arbitrary source (X, Y) using a similar idea. Furthermore, algebraization of security in [32] is not scalable. We perform a normalization change (relying on maximal-correlation-based notation) to make it scalable. For example, compare Theorem 4 in our paper with Claim 10 in [32].

Characterization of Markov Operator's Effect on the Fourier Spectrum. It is essential to accurately characterize the impact on the Fourier spectrum when applying the $T\overline{T}$ linear operator on the reduction f and applying the $\overline{T}T$ linear operator on the reduction g. When the source is either BSS or BES as in [32], Fourier analysis over uniform measure suffices; both operators $\mathsf{T}\overline{\mathsf{T}}$ and $\overline{\mathsf{T}}\mathsf{T}$ are the well-behaved noise (Bonami-Beckner) operators. Therefore, the impact of Fourier spectrum is well understood. In contrast, if the source is an arbitrary joint distribution, the marginal distributions of the source need not be uniform or identical to each other and the two operators need not be the Bonami-Beckner operators, complicating this technical challenge even further. If the source is a 2-by-2 distribution, we present an accurate characterization of Markov's operator's effect on the Fourier spectrum (see Lemma 1) using biased Fourier analysis. This result is a generalization to correlated space of the Bonami-Beckner operator's effect on the Fourier spectrum.

When the source is an arbitrary joint distribution, straightforward control of the Markov operator's effect is not evident even when using Fourier analysis over arbitrary product measure. Instead, we take a detour and use the Efron-Stein orthogonal decomposition for this analysis step (see Sect. 3.5). Our linear operators synergize well with the reduction functions over this decomposition, and one bounds the effect of these operators on the reduction functions using the maximal correlation of the source (X, Y) (see Proposition 5 and Proposition 6). Finally, we return to the Fourier basis and translate the bounds on the Fourier spectrum using Proposition 7.

Fourier Concentration. The approximate eigenvector problem (a consequence of the SNIS definition) and the characterization of the Markov and adjoint-Markov operators' impact on the Fourier spectrum yields new Fourier concentration results. For 2×2 sources, we prove that the Fourier spectrum of the solutions of the approximate eigenvector problem (in particular, the reduction functions) are concentrated on terms of a fixed degree (see Theorem 10). [32] proved this concentration result for the particular cases of BSS and BES sources.

For arbitrary sources, we show that the Fourier spectrum is concentrated on low-degree terms (see Theorem 3). This relaxation in concentration is also necessary; i.e., we show perfectly secure reductions constructing BSS(1/2) and BES($\sqrt{1/2}$) from the ROLE source whose spectrums are *not concentrated on only one degree*. This Fourier concentration phenomenon is a manifestation of "security" and distinguishes our problems from those arising in non-interactive simulation (i.e., SNIS without security) [18, 21, 24, 25, 30, 31, 48, 50].

Statistical to Perfect Lemma. The set of all reductions with Fourier spectrum concentrated on low-degree multi-linear is still potentially huge.[6] Using appropriate junta theorems, Theorem 1 shows that Boolean functions satisfying such Fourier concentration properties are (close to) juntas. Since these juntas depend only on a constant number of inputs, the total number of such candidate juntas is also a constant. Therefore, this result implies that (1) SNIS is either perfectly secure or constant-insecure, (2) The size of the set of all canonical SNIS

---

[6] A function whose Fourier spectrum is concentrated on low-degree multi-linear terms may depend on all the variables. So, without using any additional properties of low-degree Boolean functions, one cannot prune down the set of candidate functions. Therefore, their number may be exponential in the number of variables.

of (U, V) from (X, Y) is a constant, and (3) Any feasible SNIS has a positive constant rate. Furthermore, these juntas yield perfectly-secure SNIS.

Consequently, for a particular number of source samples n and (sufficiently small constant) insecurity budget $\nu(n)$, our analysis determines whether such a SNIS exists or not. Furthermore, a constant-time algorithm can search for the witness reductions. For example, an *exhaustive search algorithm* discovered all SNIS of BSS(1/2) from ROLE, uncovering fascinating new reductions.

3   Preliminaries

3.1   Notation

We denote $[n]$ as the set $\{1, 2, \ldots, n\}$ and $\mathbb{N}_{<m} = \{0, 1, \ldots, m-1\}$. For two functions $f, g \colon \Omega \to \mathbb{R}$, the equation $f = g$ implies that $f(x) = g(x)$, for every $x \in \Omega$. We use Ω to denote the sample spaces, and π usually denotes a probability distribution. (Ω_x, Ω_y) is a joint probability space. For $x \in \Omega_x^n$, we represent $x_i \in \Omega_x$ as the i-th coordinate of x. A Boolean function is a $\{\pm 1\}$-valued function.

Correlated Spaces. We use (X, Y) to denote the joint distribution over (Ω_x, Ω_y) with probability mass function π, and π_x, π_y to denote the marginal probability distributions of X and Y, respectively. Sometimes we will use $(\Omega_x \times \Omega_y, \pi)$ to denote the joint distribution. We sometimes use notation $(X, Y)_\rho$ to emphasize that its maximal correlation (defined in Sect. 3.2) is ρ. We always use the following notation for the expectation of functions $f \in L^2(\Omega_x^n, \pi_x^{\otimes n}), g \in L^2(\Omega_y^n, \pi_y^{\otimes n})$ over correlated spaces.

$$\mathbb{E}[f] := \mathop{\mathbb{E}}_{x \sim \pi_x^{\otimes n}} [f(x)], \ \mathbb{E}[g] := \mathop{\mathbb{E}}_{y \sim \pi_y^{\otimes n}} [g(y)], \ \mathbb{E}[fg] := \mathop{\mathbb{E}}_{(x,y) \sim \pi^{\otimes n}} [f(x) \cdot g(y)]$$

Statistical Distance. The statistical distance (total variation distance) between two distributions P and Q over a finite sample space Ω is defined as $\mathrm{SD}\,(P, Q) = \frac{1}{2} \sum_{x \in \Omega} |P(x) - Q(x)|$.

3.2   Maximal Correlation

We define maximal correlation and its properties in this subsection.

Definition 1 (Maximal Correlation [3, 4, 23, 27, 47, 48]**).** *The Hirschfeld-Gebelein-Rényi maximal correlation of (X, Y) is defined as*

$$\rho(X; Y) := \max_{\substack{\mathbb{E}[f] = \mathbb{E}[g] = 0 \\ \mathbb{E}[f^2] = \mathbb{E}[g^2] = 1}} \mathbb{E}[f(X)g(Y)]$$

For example, the maximal correlation of BSS with flipping probability ε is $|1 - 2\varepsilon|$ for every $\varepsilon \in [0, 1]$, and the maximal correlation of BES with erasure probability ε is $\sqrt{1 - \varepsilon}$ [53]. Note that maximal correlation of any distribution is always between 0 and 1.

Imported Theorem 1 (Tensorization [48]**).** *If* $(X_1, Y_1)_{\rho_1}$ *and* $(X_2, Y_2)_{\rho_2}$ *are independent, then the maximal correlation of* $(X_1, X_2; Y_1, Y_2)$ *is equal to* $\max(\rho_1, \rho_2)$ *and so if* $(X_1, Y_1), (X_2, Y_2)$ *are i.i.d., then it is equal to* $\rho_1 = \rho_2$.

Imported Theorem 2 (Data Processing [48]**).** *Let* (X, Y) *be a joint distribution. Then, for any pair of (even randomized) functions, we* $\rho(f(X), g(Y)) \leqslant \rho(X, Y)$.

One can compute maximal correlation as follows.

Proposition 1 ([48])**.** *The maximal correlation of a finite joint distribution* (X, Y) *is the square root of the second largest eigenvalue of the Markov operator* $\mathsf{T}\overline{\mathsf{T}}$, *where* T *and* $\overline{T}$ *are Markov and adjoint Markov operator associated with* (X, Y).

3.3 Fourier Analysis Basics

We follow the notation of [46] to introduce some background in Fourier analysis over product measure.

Fourier Analysis over Higher Alphabet

Definition 2. *Let* (Ω, π) *be a finite probability space where* $|\Omega| \geqslant 2$ *and* π *denote a probability distribution over* Ω. *Let* $\pi^{\otimes n}$ *denote the product probability distribution on* Ω^n *such that* $\pi^{\otimes n}(x_1 x_2 \dots x_n) = \prod_{i=1}^{n} \pi(x_i)$. *For* $n \in \mathbb{N}$, *we write* $L^2(\Omega^n, \pi^{\otimes n})$ *to denote the real inner product space of functions* $f \colon \Omega^n \to \mathbb{R}$ *with inner product*

$$\langle f, g \rangle_{\pi^{\otimes n}} = \underset{x \sim \pi^{\otimes n}}{\mathbb{E}} [f(x)g(x)].$$

Moreover, the L_p-*norm of a function* $f \in L^2(\Omega^n, \pi^{\otimes n})$ *is defined as*

$$\|f\|_p := \underset{x \sim \pi^{\otimes n}}{\mathbb{E}} [|f(x)|^p]^{1/p}.$$

We define the distance between two functions $f, g \in L^2(\Omega, \mu)$ as $\|f - g\|_1$. Note that if f, g are bounded i.e. $|f(x)| \leqslant \alpha$ and $|g(x)| \leqslant \alpha$ for every $x \in \Omega$, then $\|f - g\|_2^2 \leqslant 2\alpha \|f - g\|_1$. In particular, for Boolean valued functions f, g, $\|f - g\|_2^2 \leqslant 2 \|f - g\|_1 = 4 \Pr_{x \sim \mu}[f(x) \neq g(x)]$. Therefore,

Claim 1. *Suppose* $f \in L^2(\Omega, \mu)$ *such that* $|f(x)| \leqslant \alpha$ *for every* $x \in \Omega$. *Then, we have* $\|f\|_2^2 \leqslant \alpha \cdot \|f\|_1$.

Definition 3. *A Fourier basis for an inner product space* $L^2(\Omega, \pi)$ *is an orthonormal basis* $\phi_0, \phi_1, \dots, \phi_{m-1}$ *with* $\phi_0 \equiv 1$, *where by orthonormal, we mean that for any* $i \neq j$, $\langle \phi_i, \phi_j \rangle = 0$ *and for any* i, $\langle \phi_i, \phi_i \rangle = 1$.

It can be shown that if $\phi_0, \phi_1, \dots, \phi_{m-1}$ is a Fourier basis for $L^2(\Omega, \pi)$, then the collection $(\phi)_{\alpha \in \mathbb{N}_{<m}^n}$ where $\phi_\alpha(x) := \prod_{i=1}^{n} \phi_{\alpha_i}(x_i)$ (each $\alpha_i \in \{0, 1, \dots, m-1\}$) is a Fourier basis for $L^2(\Omega^n, \pi^{\otimes n})$. Note that the size of the basis $(\phi)_{\alpha \in \mathbb{N}_{<m}^n}$ is m^n.

Definition 4. *Fix a Fourier basis* $\phi_0, \phi_1, \ldots, \phi_{m-1}$ *for* $L^2(\Omega, \pi)$, *then every* $f \in L^2(\Omega^n, \pi^{\otimes n})$ *can be uniquely written as* $f = \sum_{\alpha \in \mathbb{N}^n_{<m}} \widehat{f}(\alpha) \phi_\alpha$ *where* $\widehat{f}(\alpha) = \langle f, \phi_\alpha \rangle$. *The real number* $\widehat{f}(\alpha)$ *is called the Fourier coefficient of* f *at* α.

For $\alpha \in \mathbb{N}^n_{<m}$, we denote $|\alpha| := |\{i \in [n] \colon \alpha_i \neq 0\}|$. The *Fourier weight* of f at degree k is defined as $W^k[f] := \sum_{\alpha : |\alpha| = k} \widehat{f}(\alpha)^2$. The Fourier weight of f at degree strictly greater than k is defined as $W^{>k}[f] := \sum_{\alpha : |\alpha| > k} \widehat{f}(\alpha)^2$. We say that the *degree* of a function $f \in L^2(\Omega^n, \pi^{\otimes n})$, denoted by $\deg(f)$, is the largest value of $|\alpha|$ such that $\widehat{f}(\alpha) \neq 0$. For every coordinate $i \in [n]$, the *i-th influence* of f, denoted by $\mathsf{Inf}_i[f]$, is defined as $\mathsf{Inf}_i[f] := \sum_{\alpha : \alpha_i \neq 0} \widehat{f}(\alpha)^2$. And the *total influence* is defined as $\mathsf{Inf}(f) := \sum_{i=1}^n \mathsf{Inf}_i[f] = \sum_\alpha |\alpha| \widehat{f}(\alpha)^2 = \sum_{k=1}^n k \cdot W^k[f]$.

Biased Fourier Analysis over Boolean Cube. In the special case when $\Omega = \{\pm 1\}$, we define the product Fourier basis functions ϕ_S for $S \subseteq [n]$ as

$$\phi_S(x) = \prod_{i \in S} \phi(x_i) = \prod_{i \in S} \left(\frac{x_i - \mu}{\sigma} \right),$$

where $p = \pi(-1), \mu = 1 - 2p, \sigma = 2\sqrt{p}\sqrt{1-p}$.

Definition 5 (Junta Function). *A function* $f \colon \Omega^n \to \{\pm 1\}$ *is called a k-junta for* $k \in \mathbb{N}$ *if it depends on at most k of its inputs coordinates; in other words,* $f(x) = g(x_{i_1}, x_{i_2}, \ldots, x_{i_k})$, *where* $i_1, i_2, \ldots, i_k \in [n]$. *Informally, we say that f is a "junta" if it depends on only a constant number of coordinates. We also say that f is ε-close to a k-junta function h if* $\|f - h\|_1 \leqslant \varepsilon$.

3.4 Markov Operator

Definition 6 (Markov Operator [40]). *The Markov operator associated with joint distribution* (X, Y), *denoted by* T, *maps a function* $g \in L^p(\Omega_y, \pi_y)$ *to a function* $\mathsf{T}g \in L^p(\Omega_x, \pi_x)$ *by the following map:*

$$(\mathsf{T}g)(x) := \mathbb{E}[g(Y) \mid X = x],$$

where (X, Y) *is distributed according to* π.

Furthermore, we define the adjoint operator of T, denoted as $\overline{\mathsf{T}}$, maps a function $f \in L^p(\Omega_x, \pi_x)$ to a function $\overline{\mathsf{T}}f \in L^p(\Omega_y, \pi_y)$ by the following map:

$$(\overline{\mathsf{T}}f)(y) := \mathbb{E}[f(X) \mid Y = y].$$

Note that the two operators T and $\overline{\mathsf{T}}$ have the following property.

$$\langle \mathsf{T}g, f \rangle_{\pi_x} = \langle g, \overline{\mathsf{T}}f \rangle_{\pi_y} = \mathbb{E}[f(X^n)g(Y^n)].$$

Moreover, both Markov operators T and $\overline{\mathsf{T}}$ are linear operators. Both $\mathsf{T}\overline{\mathsf{T}}$ and $\overline{\mathsf{T}}\mathsf{T}$ are also Markov operators. We want to emphasize that the largest eigenvalue of any Markov operator is always 1.

Proposition 2. *Let* $\mathsf{T}, \overline{\mathsf{T}}$ *be respectively the Markov and adjoint operator associated with the 2-by-2 distribution* $(X,Y)_\rho^{\otimes n}$. *Let* $1 = \lambda_0 \geqslant \lambda_1 > 0$ *be the eigenvalues of* $\mathsf{T}\overline{\mathsf{T}}^{(1)}$ *(multiplication of Markov and adjoint operators for* $n = 1$*). Then, it holds that* $\rho = \sqrt{\lambda_1}$. *Moreover, the set of all eigenvalues of* $\mathsf{T}\overline{\mathsf{T}}$ *and* $\overline{\mathsf{T}}\mathsf{T}$ *is* $\{1, \rho^2, \rho^4, \ldots, \rho^{2n}\}$.

Proposition 3 [48]. *Suppose* (X,Y) *is a finite joint distribution over* (Ω_x, Ω_y). *Let* π *denote the probability mass function of* (X,Y) *and* T *and* $\overline{\mathsf{T}}$ *respectively denote the Markov operator and the adjoint Markov operator associated with* (X,Y). *Let* (X, X') *be the joint distribution over* $(\Omega_x \times \Omega_x, \mu)$ *such that the marginal distribution* μ_x *is the same as* π_x *and the associated Markov operator of* (X, X') *is* $\mathsf{T}\overline{\mathsf{T}}$. *Then, the marginal distributions of* (X, X') *are the same, in other words,* $\mu_x = \mu_{x'}$. *Furthermore, we have* $\rho(\Omega_x \times \Omega_x, \mu) = \rho^2$, *where* ρ *is the maximal correlation of* (X,Y).

This result shows that for $f \in L^2(\Omega_x, \pi_x)$, we have $(\mathsf{T}\overline{\mathsf{T}})f \in L^2(\Omega_x, \pi_x)$.

3.5 Efron-Stein Decomposition

We shall use the orthogonal Efron-Stein decomposition as one of the main technical tools.

Definition 7 (Chap. 8 of [46]). *Let* $\{(\Omega_i, \mu_i)\}_{i=1}^\ell$ *be discrete probability spaces and let* $(\Omega, \mu) = \prod_{i=1}^\ell (\Omega_i, \mu_i)$. *The Effron-Stein decomposition of* $f \colon \Omega \to \mathbb{R}$ *is defined as* $f = \sum_{S \subseteq [n]} f^{=S}$ *where the functions* $f^{=S}$ *satisfy (1)* $f^{=S}$ *depends only on* x_S, *and (2) for all* $S \nsubseteq S'$ *and all* $x_{S'}$, $\mathbb{E}[f^{=S}|X_{S'} = x_{S'}] = 0$.

Proposition 4 ([19]). *Efron-Stein decomposition exists and is unique.*

The following propositions give the relation between Markov operators and Efron-stein decompositions. The first proposition shows that the Efron-Stein decomposition commutes with Markov Operator.

Proposition 5 ([40,41] **Proposition 2.11**). *Let* (X^n, Y^n) *be a joint distribution over* $(\Omega_x^n \times \Omega_y^n, \pi^{\otimes n})$. *Let* $\mathsf{T}^{(i)}$ *be the Markov operator associated with* (X_i, Y_i). *Let* $\mathsf{T} = \otimes_{i=1}^n \mathsf{T}^{(i)}$, *and consider a function* $g \in L^2(\Omega_y^n, \pi_y^{\otimes n})$. *Then, the Efron-Stein decomposition of* g *satisfies* $(\mathsf{T}g)^{=S} = \mathsf{T}(g^{=S})$.

The next proposition shows that $\mathsf{T}g$ depends on the low degree expansion of g.

Proposition 6 ([41] **Proposition 2.12**). *Assuming the setting of Proposition 5 and let* ρ *be the maximal correlation of the distribution* (X,Y). *Then for all* $g \in L^2(\Omega_y^n, \pi_y^{\otimes n})$ *it holds that* $\|\mathsf{T}g^{=S}\|_2 \leqslant \rho^{|S|} \|g^{=S}\|_2$.

The next proposition shows the connection between Fourier decomposition and Efron-Stein decomposition.

Proposition 7 ([46] **Proposition 8.36**). *Let $f \in L^2(\Omega^n, \pi^{\otimes n})$ have the orthogonal decomposition $f = \sum_{S \subseteq [n]} f^{=S}$, and let $\{\phi_H\}_{H \in \Omega^n}$ be an orthonormal Fourier basis for $L^2(\Omega^n, \pi^{\otimes n})$. Then $f^{=S} = \sum_{\alpha:\ \mathrm{Supp}(\alpha)=S} \widehat{f}(\alpha)\phi_\alpha$. In particular, when $\Omega = \{\pm 1\}$ we have $f^{=S} = \widehat{f}(S)\phi_S$.*

This implies that $\left\| f^{=S} \right\|_2^2 = \sum_{\alpha:\ \mathrm{Supp}(\alpha)=S} \widehat{f}(\alpha)^2$. Therefore, it holds that $W^k[f] = \sum_{|S|=k} \left\| f^{=S} \right\|_2^2$, and $W^{>k}[f] = \sum_{|S|>k} \left\| f^{=S} \right\|_2^2$.

3.6   Imported Theorems

Imported Theorem 3 (Kindler-Safra Junta Theorem [34,35]). *Fix $d \geqslant 0$. There exists $\varepsilon_0 = \varepsilon_0(d)$ and constant C such that for every $\varepsilon < \varepsilon_0$, if $f: \{\pm 1\}^n \to \{\pm 1\}$ satisfies $W^{>d}[f] = \varepsilon$ then there exists a C^d-junta and degree d function $\tilde{f}: \{\pm 1\}^n \to \{\pm 1\}$ such that $\left\| f - \tilde{f} \right\|_2^2 \leqslant (\varepsilon + C^d \varepsilon^{5/4})$.*

Imported Theorem 4 (Friedgut's Junta Theorem [20,46]). *There exists a global constant M such that the following holds. Let (Ω, π) be a finite probability space such that every outcome has probability at least λ. If $f \in L^2(\Omega^n, \pi^n)$ has range $\{\pm 1\}$ and $0 < \varepsilon \leqslant 1$, then f is ε-close to a $(1/\lambda)^{M \cdot \mathrm{Inf}(f)/\varepsilon}$-junta $h: \Omega^n \to \{\pm 1\}$, i.e., $\mathrm{Pr}_{x \sim \pi^{\otimes n}}[f(x) \neq h(x)] \leqslant \varepsilon$.*

4   Characterization of SNIS from Arbitrary Sources

This section presents our feasibility characterization of SNIS from arbitrary joint distributions stated below.

Corollary 1 (Feasibility Characterization). *There is an algorithm that takes as input a constant $c > 0$, a source (X, Y), and a target $(U, V) \in \{\mathsf{BSS}(\rho'), \mathsf{BES}(\rho')\}$, and*

1. *outputs YES, if there is an infinite family of reduction functions $\{f_n, g_n\}$ satisfying $(U, V) \sqsubseteq_{f_n, g_n}^{\nu_n} (X, Y)^{\otimes n}$ and $\nu_n \leqslant c/n$, and*
2. *outputs NO, otherwise.*

In the YES instance, the algorithm additionally outputs a pair of reduction functions $f^*: \Omega_x^{n_0} \to \{\pm 1\}$ and $g^*: \Omega_y^{n_0} \to \{\pm 1\}$ that witness a perfect-SNIS construction for some $n_0 = n_0(c, \rho, \rho') \in \mathbb{N}$ where ρ represents the maximal correlation of source (X, Y). Furthermore, the algorithm's running time is bounded and computable.

This theorem says that there is an algorithm that can determine whether there is a statistically SNIS of BSS/BES from a given source. The algorithm also outputs a canonical (perfect) SNIS construction in the YES instance. Corollary 1 follows from the following statistical to perfect results.

Theorem 1 (Statistical-to-perfect). *Let (X, Y) be an arbitrary joint distribution and $(U, V) \in \{\mathsf{BSS}(\rho'), \mathsf{BES}(\rho')\}$. For any $c > 0$, there are positive constants n_0, d, D such that the following result holds. If $(U, V) \sqsubseteq_{f,g}^\nu (X, Y)^{\otimes n}$, for some $n \geqslant n_0$, and $\nu \leqslant c/n$, then f is ν^d-close to a D-junta reduction function f^*, and g is ν^d-close to a D-junta reduction function g^* such that $(U, V) \sqsubseteq_{f^*,g^*}^0 (X, Y)^{\otimes n}$.*

We remark that the constant D does not depend on n but might depend on the source, the target, the constant c, and the implicit constant in the Friedgut's junta theorem (Imported Theorem 4). Assuming this theorem, Fig. 4 gives an algorithm for Corollary 1. We provide the proof of Theorem 1 when $(U, V) = \mathsf{BSS}(\rho')$ in Sect. 4.1, and when $(U, V) = \mathsf{BES}(\rho')$ in Sect. 4.2. At a high level, our proof strategy for BES is similar to the strategy for BSS except one technical challenge due to Bob's reduction function, which is not a Boolean-valued function.

$\mathsf{SNISFeasChar}\,((X, Y), (U, V), c):$

1. Let $D = D(\rho', (X, Y), c)$ be the constant defined in Theorem 1.
2. Consider all functions $f: \Omega_x^D \to \{\pm 1\}$, and $g: \Omega_y^D \to \{\pm 1\}$
   - Return YES, if there exist f^*, g^* such that $\mathsf{BSS}(\rho') \sqsubseteq_{f^*,g^*}^0 (X, Y)^{\otimes D}$.
   - Return NO, otherwise.

Fig. 4. An algorithm to decide the feasibility of SNIS of $\mathsf{BSS}(\rho')$ from samples of (X, Y)

4.1 Statistical to Perfect: BSS Target

Consider a SNIS of $\mathsf{BSS}(\rho') \sqsubseteq_{f,g}^\nu (X, Y)_\rho^{\otimes n}$ where (X, Y) is an arbitrary joint distribution, $f \in L^2(\Omega_x^n, \pi_x^{\otimes n})$ and $g \in L^2(\Omega_y^n, \pi_y^{\otimes n})$.

Step 1: Algebraization of SNIS and approximate eigenvalue problem. Following a similar idea as in [32], we extend the algebraization of simulation-based SNIS to arbitrary source distribution as follows.

Theorem 2 (BSS   Algebraization of Security). *For any $\rho' \in (0, 1)$ and any joint distribution (X, Y), the following statements hold.*

1. *If $\mathsf{BSS}(\rho') \sqsubseteq_{f,g}^\nu (X, Y)^{\otimes n}$, then $\mathbb{E}[f] \leqslant \nu$, $\mathbb{E}[g] \leqslant \nu$, $\left\| \overline{\mathsf{T}} f - \rho' g \right\|_1 \leqslant 4\nu$, and $\left\| \mathsf{T} g - \rho' f \right\|_1 \leqslant 4\nu$.*
2. *If $\mathbb{E}[f] \leqslant \nu$, $\mathbb{E}[g] \leqslant \nu$, $\left\| \overline{\mathsf{T}} f - \rho' g \right\|_1 \leqslant \nu$, and $\left\| \mathsf{T} g - \rho' f \right\|_1 \leqslant \nu$, then $\mathsf{BSS}(\rho') \sqsubseteq_{f,g}^{2\nu} (X, Y)^{\otimes n}$.*

This theorem gives a qualitative equivalence of the simulation-based definition and the algebraized definition. Next, composing the two L_1-norm constraints yields $\left\| \mathsf{T}\overline{\mathsf{T}} f - \rho'^2 f \right\|_1 \leqslant 8\nu$ and $\left\| \overline{\mathsf{T}}\mathsf{T} g - \rho'^2 g \right\|_1 \leqslant 8\nu$. This implies that f and g are an approximate eigenvector of the two operators $\mathsf{T}\overline{\mathsf{T}}$ and $\overline{\mathsf{T}}\mathsf{T}$, respectively.

Claim 2 (Approximate Eigenvalue Constraint). *If* $\mathsf{BSS}(\rho') \sqsubseteq_{f,g}^{\nu}$ $(X,Y)^{\otimes n}$, *then* $\left\|\mathsf{T}\overline{\mathsf{T}}f - \rho'^2 f\right\|_1 \leqslant 8\nu$, *and* $\left\|\overline{\mathsf{T}}\mathsf{T}g - \rho'^2 g\right\|_1 \leqslant 8\nu$.[7]

Step 2: Effect of Markov operators on Fourier spectrum of reduction functions. Let $\{\phi_\alpha\}$ and $\{\psi_\alpha\}$ be some Fourier bases for $L^2(\Omega_x^n, \pi_x^{\otimes n})$ and $L^2(\Omega_y^n, \pi_y^{\otimes n})$, respectively. As common in Fourier analysis, it is natural to look at the effect of the Markov operators on the Fourier characters. However, we don't know how to control the behavior of $\mathsf{T}\overline{\mathsf{T}}\phi_\alpha$ and $\overline{\mathsf{T}}\mathsf{T}\psi_\alpha$. To circumvent this bottleneck, we take a detour and look at the effect of these operators on the orthogonal (Efron-Stein) decomposition. Let $f = \sum_{S \subseteq [n]} f^{=S}$ and $g = \sum_{S \subseteq [n]} g^{=S}$ be the orthogonal decomposition. [41] showed that the decomposition has two important properties: (1) it commutes with the Markov operators (Proposition 5) and (2) the higher order terms in the decomposition of $\mathsf{T}\overline{\mathsf{T}}f = \sum_{S \subseteq [n]} (\mathsf{T}\overline{\mathsf{T}}f)^{=S}$ have significantly smaller L_2 norm compared to the L_2 norm of the corresponding higher order terms in the decomposition of f (Proposition 6 and similarly for $\overline{\mathsf{T}}\mathsf{T}g$ and g). This help us first to rewrite

$$(\mathsf{T}\overline{\mathsf{T}}f)^{=S} = (\mathsf{T}\overline{\mathsf{T}})f^{=S} = \mathsf{T}\overline{\mathsf{T}}f^{=S}, \text{and } (\overline{\mathsf{T}}\mathsf{T}g)^{=S} = \overline{\mathsf{T}}\mathsf{T}g^{=S},$$

and then bound them as:

$$\left\|\mathsf{T}\overline{\mathsf{T}}f^{=S}\right\|_2 \leqslant \rho^{2|S|} \|f\|_2, \text{and } \left\|\overline{\mathsf{T}}\mathsf{T}g^{=S}\right\|_2 \leqslant \rho^{2|S|} \|g\|_2$$

Step 3: Fourier concentration, low total influence, and junta properties of reduction functions. Those inequalities above together with the connection between orthogonal decomposition and the Fourier decomposition (Proposition 7) yields that Fourier spectrum of f and g are concentrated on low-degree terms.

Theorem 3. *Suppose there exist reduction functions* $f\colon \Omega_x^n \to \{\pm 1\}$ *and* $g\colon \Omega_y^n \to \{\pm 1\}$ *such that* $\mathsf{BSS}(\rho') \sqsubseteq_{f,g}^{\delta} (X,Y)^{\otimes n}$ *for some* $\delta \geqslant 0$.[8] *Let* $k \in \mathbb{N}$ *such that* $\rho^k \geqslant \rho' > \rho^{k+1}$. *Then, the following bounds hold.*

$$\mathsf{W}^{>k}[f] := \sum_{\alpha:\, |\alpha|>k} \widehat{f}(\alpha)^2 \leqslant \frac{(1+\rho')^2}{(\rho^{2(k+1)} - \rho'^2)^2} \cdot \delta, \text{ and}$$

$$\mathsf{W}^{>k}[g] := \sum_{\alpha:\, |\alpha|>k} \widehat{g}(\alpha)^2 \leqslant \frac{(1+\rho')^2}{(\rho^{2(k+1)} - \rho'^2)^2} \cdot \delta,$$

Observe that if the Fourier weight of a function is mostly concentrated on low-degree terms, then the function has small total influence (Claim 3).

Claim 3 (Concentrated on Low Degree Implies Low Influence). *Let* f *be a Boolean-valued function in* $L^2(\Omega^n, \mu^{\otimes n})$. *If* $\mathsf{W}^{>k}[f] \leqslant \delta$, *then* $\mathsf{Inf}[f] \leqslant k + n\delta$.

---

[7] Note that in general the operator $\overline{\mathsf{T}}\mathsf{T}$ (or $\mathsf{T}\overline{\mathsf{T}}$) is not equal to the noise operator T_ρ.
[8] It is possible that δ depends on n.

In particular, when δ is sufficiently small, the total influence of reduction functions f, g are constant (not depend on n). This allows us to invoke the Friedgut's junta theorem (Imported Theorem 4) and conclude that reduction functions are close to some junta functions.

Step 4: Must be Perfect. Since junta functions $\tilde{f}$ and $\tilde{g}$ depend on a constant number of variables, so does $\overline{\mathsf{T}}\tilde{f}$ and $\mathsf{T}\tilde{g}$. Observe that two distinct bounded junta functions are always constant far (Claim 4).

Claim 4 (Distinct Bounded Junta are Far). *Suppose $h\colon \Omega_x^n \to \{\pm 1\}$ and $\ell\colon \Omega_y^n \to \{\pm 1\}$ are two D-junta Boolean functions in $L^2(\Omega_x^n, \pi_x)$ and $L^2(\Omega_y^n, \pi_y)$, respectively. If $\overline{\mathsf{T}}h \neq \rho'\ell$, then there exists a constant c that depends only on $\rho', D, (X, Y)$ such that $\left\| \overline{\mathsf{T}}h - \rho'\ell \right\|_2 \geqslant c$. Similarly, if $\mathsf{T}\ell \neq \rho'h$, then there exists a constant d that depends only on $\rho', D, (X, Y)$ such that $\left\| \mathsf{T}\ell - \rho'h \right\|_2 \geqslant d$.*

In particular, if $\overline{\mathsf{T}}\tilde{f} \neq \rho'\tilde{g}$, then they are constant far, which implies a constant insecurity; similarly, if $\mathsf{T}\tilde{g} \neq \rho'\tilde{f}$, then they are constant far, which also implies a constant insecurity. Thus, it must hold that $\overline{\mathsf{T}}\tilde{f} = \rho'\tilde{g}$ and $\mathsf{T}\tilde{g} = \rho'\tilde{f}$. The three facts that $\tilde{f}$ is a junta, $\tilde{f}$ and f are close, and $\mathbb{E}[f]$ is small imply that $\mathbb{E}[\tilde{f}] = 0$. Similarly, it holds that $\mathbb{E}[\tilde{g}] = 0$. Therefore, $\tilde{f}$ and $\tilde{g}$ witness a perfect construction.

Proof of Theorem 3. Observe that $\left| (\mathsf{T}\overline{\mathsf{T}}f - \rho'^2 f)(x) \right| \leqslant 2$, and $\left| (\overline{\mathsf{T}}\mathsf{T}g - \rho'^2 g)(x) \right| \leqslant 2$ for every x by the contraction property of Markov operator and boundedness of functions f and g. Observe that if a bounded function has small L_1 norm so does its L_2 norm square. Thus, we have

$$\left\| \mathsf{T}\overline{\mathsf{T}}f - \rho'^2 f \right\|_2^2 \leqslant 2\delta, \text{ and } \left\| \overline{\mathsf{T}}\mathsf{T}g - \rho'^2 g \right\|_2^2 \leqslant 2\delta. \tag{1}$$

Let $f = \sum_{S \subseteq [n]} f^{=S}$ be the orthogonal decomposition of f. Then, we have

$$\left\| \mathsf{T}\overline{\mathsf{T}}f - \rho'^2 f \right\|_2^2 = \sum_{S \subseteq [n]} \left\| \mathsf{T}\overline{\mathsf{T}}f^{=S} - \rho'^2 f^{=S} \right\|_2^2 \qquad \text{(Orthogonal property)}$$

$$\geqslant \sum_{S:\, |S| > k} \left\| \mathsf{T}\overline{\mathsf{T}}f^{=S} - \rho'^2 f^{=S} \right\|_2^2 \qquad \text{(Property of norms)}$$

$$\geqslant \sum_{S:\, |S| > k} \left| \left\| \mathsf{T}\overline{\mathsf{T}}f^{=S} \right\|_2 - \rho'^2 \left\| f^{=S} \right\|_2 \right|^2 \qquad \text{(Triangle inequality)}$$

By Proposition 6, we have $\left\| \mathsf{T}\overline{\mathsf{T}}f^{=S} \right\|_2 \leqslant \rho^{2|S|} \left\| f^{=S} \right\|_2$. This implies that, for every $S \subseteq [n]$ satisfying $|S| > k$,

$$\left\| \mathsf{T}\overline{\mathsf{T}}f^{=S} \right\|_2 - \rho'^2 \left\| f^{=S} \right\|_2 \leqslant (\rho^{2|S|} - \rho'^2) \left\| f^{=S} \right\|_2 \leqslant 0, \tag{2}$$

where the last inequality follows from $\rho^{2|S|} - \rho'^2 \leqslant \rho^{2(k+1)} - \rho'^2 \leqslant 0$ for every $|S| > k$, and $\left\| f^{=S} \right\|_2 \geqslant 0$. Thus, squaring both sides of inequality 2 for each $|S| > k$ yields

$$\left\| \mathsf{T}\overline{\mathsf{T}}f - \rho'^2 f \right\|_2^2 \geqslant \sum_{S:\, |S|>k} (\rho^{2|S|} - \rho'^2)^2 \left\| f^{=S} \right\|_2^2$$

$$\geqslant \min_{S:\, |S|>k} (\rho^{2|S|} - \rho'^2)^2 \sum_{S:\, |S|>k} \left\| f^{=S} \right\|_2^2$$

$$= (\rho^{2(k+1)} - \rho'^2)^2 \; \mathsf{W}^{>k}[f]$$

This together with the inequality (1) implies that $\mathsf{W}^{>k}[f] \leqslant \frac{(1+\rho')^2}{(\rho^{2(k+1)}-\rho'^2)^2} \cdot \delta$. Similarly, it also holds that $\mathsf{W}^{>k}[g] \leqslant \frac{(1+\rho')^2}{(\rho^{2(k+1)}-\rho'^2)^2} \cdot \delta$, as desired.

4.2 Statistical to Perfect: BES Target

Consider a SNIS of $\mathsf{BES}(\rho') \sqsubseteq_{f,g}^{\nu} (X,Y)_\rho^{\otimes n}$ where (X,Y) is an arbitrary joint distribution, $f \in L^2(\Omega_x^n, \pi_x^{\otimes n})$ and $g \in L^2(\Omega_y^n, \pi_y^{\otimes n})$. Step 2 and step 4 basically are the same as these steps in Sect. 4.1. So we shall discuss steps 1 and 3 only.

Step 1: Algebraization of SNIS and Approximate Eigenvalue Problem. We use a similar idea as in [32] to extend the algebraization to arbitrary source.

Theorem 4 (BES Target Algebraization of Security). *For any* $\rho' \in (0,1)$, *and any joint distribution* (X,Y), *the following statements hold.*

1. *If* $\mathsf{BES}(\rho') \sqsubseteq_{f,g}^{\nu} (X,Y)^{\otimes n}$, *then* $\mathbb{E}[f] \leqslant \nu$, $\mathbb{E}[g] \leqslant \nu$, $\left\| \overline{\mathsf{T}}f - g \right\|_1 \leqslant 4\nu$, *and* $\left\| \mathsf{T}g - \rho'^2 f \right\|_1 \leqslant 4\nu$.

2. *If* $\mathbb{E}[f] \leqslant \nu$, $\mathbb{E}[g] \leqslant \nu$, $\left\| \overline{\mathsf{T}}f - g \right\|_1 \leqslant \nu$, *and* $\left\| \mathsf{T}g - \rho'^2 f \right\|_1 \leqslant \nu$, *then it holds that* $\mathsf{BES}(\rho') \sqsubseteq_{f,g}^{2\nu} (X,Y)^{\otimes n}$.

Claim 5 (Approximate Eigenvalue Constraint). *If* $\mathsf{BES}(\rho') \sqsubseteq_{f,g}^{\nu} (X,Y)^{\otimes n}$, *then* $\left\| \mathsf{T}\overline{\mathsf{T}}f - \rho'^2 f \right\|_1 \leqslant 8\nu$, *and* $\left\| \overline{\mathsf{T}}\mathsf{T}g - \rho'^2 g \right\|_1 \leqslant 8\nu$.

Step 3: Fourier Concentration, Low Total Influence, and Junta Properties. When the target is a BSS both the ranges of reduction functions are Boolean, so the junta theorems can be applied for both functions. On the other hand, when the target is a BES, the existing junta theorem for functions with more than two values is not good enough for us. To overcome this barrier, we first use the same idea to show that Alice's reduction function f is close to a junta function $f^*: \Omega_x^n \to \{\pm 1\}$, and then prove that Bob's reduction function g is also close to a junta function using the security constraint $\left\| \overline{\mathsf{T}}f^* - g \right\|_1 \leqslant \nu$. More concretely, since f^* is a junta function, so is $\overline{\mathsf{T}}f^*$. This together with the security constraint imply that g is close to the junta function $\overline{\mathsf{T}}f^*$ whose range is not necessarily $\{\pm 1, 0\}$. However, we can round each value of $(\overline{\mathsf{T}}f^*)(y)$ to the closest value in $\{\pm 1, 0\}$. The rounded function is still a junta function and close to the original function $\overline{\mathsf{T}}f^*$. Therefore, g is close to the rounded junta function by triangle inequality. We formalize this step at follows.

Claim 6. *Suppose* $f^* \colon \Omega_x^n \to \{\pm 1\}$ *is a junta function and* $g \colon \Omega_y^n \to \{\pm 1, 0\}$ *is an arbitrary function such that* $\left\| \overline{\mathsf{T}}f^* - g \right\|_1 \leqslant \delta$ *for some* $\delta \geqslant 0$. *Then, there exists a junta function* $g^* \colon \Omega_y^n \to \{\pm 1, 0\}$ *such that* g *is* $\Theta(\sqrt{\delta})$-*close to* g^*.

5 Estimation of Rate from Arbitrary Sources

As a consequence of the statistical to perfect theorem (Theorem 1), we can lower bound the rate by a positive constant, if it is feasible.

Corollary 2 (Constant Rate Lower Bound). *Fix a constant* $c > 0$, *a source* (X, Y), *and a target* $(U, V) \in \{\mathsf{BSS}(\rho'), \mathsf{BES}(\rho')\}$ *for* $\rho' \in (0, 1)$. *If there exists an infinite family of reduction functions* $\{f_n, g_n\}$ *such that* $(U, V) \sqsubseteq_{f_n, g_n}^{\nu(n)} (X, Y)^{\otimes n}$, *and* $\nu(n) \leqslant c/n$, *then the production rate* $R(\ (U, V), (X, Y)\ ) \geqslant 1/D$ *for some constant* $D = D((X, Y), \rho', c)$.

We note that the constant D is the number of input variables that perfect reduction functions depend on. Next, we prove an upper bound the rate of perfect SNIS.

Theorem 5 (Perfect Security Rate). *Let* $(U, V) \in \{\mathsf{BSS}(\rho'), \mathsf{BES}(\rho')\}$ *for* $\rho' \in (0, 1)$. *If* $(U, V)^{\otimes m} \sqsubseteq_{f, g}^0 (X, Y)_\rho^{\otimes n}$ *for some* $m, n \in \mathbb{N}$, *then* $m/n \leqslant 1/\lfloor \log_\sigma \rho' \rfloor$, *where* σ^2 *is the smallest non-zero eigenvalue of the operator* $\mathsf{T}\overline{\mathsf{T}}$ *for the source* (X, Y).

Remark 2. For the SNIS self-reduction of BSS or BES, [32] showed that $\rho' = \rho^k$ for some $k \in \mathbb{N}$ and the rate $m/n \leqslant 1/k$ matching our bound here since $\sigma = \rho$, where ρ is the maximal correlation of the source (X, Y). The ROLE distribution has maximal correlation $\rho = 1/\sqrt{2}$ and $\sigma = 1/\sqrt{2}$. Thus, when $(X, Y) = \mathsf{ROLE}$, the rate is upper bounded by $1/2$. Our new construction realizes this bound, demonstrating its optimality.

Proof of Theorem 5. We shall prove for the case $(U, V) = \mathsf{BSS}$. The proof for the case $(U, V) = \mathsf{BES}$ is almost identical. Suppose $\mathsf{BSS}(\rho')^{\otimes m} \sqsubseteq_{f, g}^0 (X, Y)^{\otimes n}$ for some $m, n \in \mathbb{N}$ and (deterministic) reduction functions $f = (f_1, \cdots, f_m)$ and $g = (g_1, \cdots, g_m)$. For $\rho'' = \rho'^m$, there is a linear deterministic construction realizing $\mathsf{BSS}(\rho'') \sqsubseteq^0 \mathsf{BSS}(\rho')$. By sequential composition, it holds that $\mathsf{BSS}(\rho'') \sqsubseteq^0 (X, Y)^{\otimes n}$. Let $\mathsf{T}, \overline{\mathsf{T}}$ denote the Markov operator and the adjoint Markov operator associated with (X, Y). Note that $\mathsf{T}\overline{\mathsf{T}}$ is non-negative definite (see [48] for a proof). Let $1 = \lambda_1 \geqslant \lambda_2 \geqslant \ldots \geqslant \lambda_t = \sigma^2 > 0$ be all non-zero eigenvalues of $T\bar{T}$. Then, according to Theorem 1, we have $\rho''^2 = \prod_{i=2}^{t} \lambda_i^{k_i}$, where $k_i \in \mathbb{N}$ such that $\sum_{i=2}^{t} k_i \leqslant n$. This implies that

$$\rho''^2 = \rho'^{2m} = \prod_{i=2}^{t} \lambda_i^{k_i} \geqslant \lambda_t^{k_2 + \ldots + k_t} = \sigma^{2(k_2 + \ldots + k_t)} \geqslant \sigma^{2n}.$$

Taking the logarithm of base $\sigma < 1$ of both sides yields $2m \log_\sigma \rho' \leqslant 2n$ which implies that $m/n \leqslant 1/\log_\sigma \rho'$ as desired.

6 Characterization of **BSS** or **BES** from 2-by-2 Distributions

In this section, we present a succinct characterization of BSS/BES from a 2-by-2 source. The following theorem states that SNIS of $BSS(\rho')$ from $(X, Y)_\rho$ is possible if and only if the source is a $BSS(\rho)$ such that $\rho' = \rho^k$ for some $k \in \mathbb{N}$.

Theorem 6 (Characterization of BSS from 2-by-2). *Fix a 2-by-2 distribution $(X, Y)_\rho$, and also $BSS(\rho')$.*

1. *If $(X, Y)_\rho \neq BSS(\rho)$ or $\rho' \neq \rho^k$ for all $k \in \mathbb{N}$: There is a positive constant $c = c(\rho, \rho')$ such that $BSS(\rho') \sqsubseteq^\nu (X, Y)^{\otimes n}$, for any $n \in \mathbb{N}$, implies that $\nu \geqslant c$.*
2. *If $(X, Y)_\rho = BSS(\rho)$ and $\rho' = \rho^k$, for some $k \in \mathbb{N}$: There are positive constants $c = c(\rho, \rho')$ and $d = d(\rho, \rho')$ such that the following result holds. If $BSS(\rho') \sqsubseteq^\nu_{f,g} BSS(\rho)^{\otimes n}$, for any $n \in \mathbb{N}$, and $\nu \leqslant c$, then f is ν^d-close to a reduction function f^* and g is ν^d-close to a reduction function g^* such that $BSS(\rho') \sqsubseteq^0_{f^*, g^*} BSS(\rho)^{\otimes n}$. Furthermore, $f^* = g^*$ is a k-homogeneous[9] Boolean function.*

Remark 3. It is shown in [1] that $BES(\rho') \sqsubseteq^{\nu_n}_{f_n, g_n} (X, Y)^{\otimes n}$ (where $\nu_n = o(1)$) only if the spectrum[10] of (U, V) is contained in the spectrum of the $(X, Y)^{\otimes n}$ for some n. Note that Theorem 6 implies that the necessary condition mentioned in [1] is not sufficient since there exists a 2-by-2 distribution $(X, Y)_\rho \neq BSS(\rho)$ and $(U, V) = BSS(\rho')$ such that $\rho' = \rho^k$, the spectrum of (U, V) is contained in the spectrum of $(X, Y)^{\otimes n}$, but there is no SNIS of (U, V) from (X, Y).

Next, we show that SNIS of BES from a 2-by-2 source is impossible.

Theorem 7 (Characterization of BES from 2-by-2). *Fix a 2-by-2 distribution $(X, Y)_\rho$, and also $BES(\rho')$. There are positive constants $c = c(\rho, \rho')$ such that if $BES(\rho') \sqsubseteq^\nu_{f,g} (X, Y)^{\otimes n}$ for some $n \in \mathbb{N}$, then the simulation error ν is at least c.*

---

[9] A function $f: \{\pm 1\}^n \to \{\pm 1\}$ is k-homogeneous if all the terms in the multi-linear expansion of f have degree k.

[10] Spectrum of a distribution matrix M is defined in [1] as the multi-set of non-zero singular values of the matrix $\Delta_{M^T}^{-1/2} M \Delta_M^{-1/2}$ where Δ_M represents a diagonal matrix with the vector $\mathbf{1}^T M$ along its diagonal.

We shall first prove Theorem 6, and then we provide a proof of Theorem 7 in Sect. 6.3.

Proof Outline of Theorem 6. First, we show that if there is a statistical SNIS of $\mathsf{BSS}(\rho')$ from $(X,Y)^{\otimes n}$, then a perfect construction exists (Theorem 8). Next, we characterize for which 2-by-2 distribution (X,Y) there exists a perfect-SNIS of $\mathsf{BSS}(\rho')$ from $(X,Y)^{\otimes n}$. Theorem 9 says that (X,Y) must be a BSS. Finally we conclude the proof by using the characterization of SNIS between BSS distributions in [32].

Theorem 8 (Statistical-to-Perfect of BSS **from 2-by-2).** *Let $\rho' \in (0,1)$ and $(X,Y)_\rho$ be an arbitrary 2-by-2 joint distribution. There are positive constants $c = c((X,Y)_\rho, \rho')$, $d = d((X,Y)_\rho, \rho')$, and $D = D((X,Y)_\rho, \rho')$ such that the following result holds. If $\mathsf{BSS}(\rho') \sqsubseteq_{f,g}^\nu (X,Y)_\rho^{\otimes n}$, for any $n \in \mathbb{N}$, and $\nu \leqslant c$, then f is ν^d-close to a D-junta reduction function f^*, and g is ν^d-close to a D-junta reduction function g^* such that $\mathsf{BSS}(\varepsilon') \sqsubseteq_{f^*,g^*}^0 (X,Y)_\rho^{\otimes n}$. Furthermore, $\rho' = \rho^k$, and $\mathsf{W}^k[f^*] = \mathsf{W}^k[g^*] = 1$.*

Informally, there is a statistical SNIS of $\mathsf{BSS}(\varepsilon')$ from (X,Y) if and only if $(X,Y)_\rho = \mathsf{BSS}(\rho)$ for some ρ satisfying $\rho' = \rho^k$ for some $k \in \mathbb{N}$. Furthermore, any statistical reduction functions can be error-corrected to junta ones that witness a perfect construction.

Theorem 9 (Characterization of Perfect-SNIS of BSS **from 2-by-2).** *Suppose there exists $n \in \mathbb{N}$ and Boolean functions $f,g: \{\pm 1\}^n \to \{\pm 1\}$ such that $\mathsf{BSS}(\rho') \sqsubseteq_{f,g}^0 (X,Y)^{\otimes n}$. Then, the distribution (X,Y) must be a $\mathsf{BSS}(\rho)$ such that $\rho' = \rho^k$ for some positive integer $k \leqslant n$.*

As a consequence of Theorem 6, the rate for perfect SNIS of BSS from an arbitrary 2-by-2 distribution is completely settled, while the rate for statistical security (even if the source is BSS) is still open.

Corollary 3. *If $(X,Y) \neq \mathsf{BSS}(\rho)$ for all $\rho \in (0,1)$ or $\rho' \neq \rho^k$ for all $k \in \mathbb{N}$, then the rate of $\mathsf{BSS}(\rho')$ from (X,Y) is zero. Otherwise, it is shown in [32] that the maximum achievable rate is $1/k$ in perfect SNIS.*

6.1   Statistical to Perfect

This section presents the proof of the statistical to perfect (Theorem 8). The high-level idea is similar to the general case. The key different is that we are able to precisely characterize the effect of Markov operators on Fourier coefficients for 2-by-2 distribution. We remark that Fourier basis and the orthogonal Efron-Stein basis are the same in this case.

Proof Outline of Theorem 8. Consider a SNIS of $\mathsf{BSS}(\rho') \sqsubseteq_{f,g}^\nu (X,Y)_\rho^{\otimes n}$ where (X,Y) is a 2-by-2 distribution and $f,g: \{\pm 1\}^n \to \{\pm 1\}$.

Steps 1,3, and 4 are similar to these steps in Sect. 4.1 except that in step 3 (1) we prove that the Fourier spectrum of reduction functions are concentrated on a fixed degree (Theorem 10), and (2) we use the Kindler-Safra junta theorem [34,35] instead of the Friedgut's junta. So we shall discuss steps 2 only.

Step 2: Effect of Markov Operators on Fourier Spectrum of Reduction Functions.
If $\mathsf{T}\overline{\mathsf{T}}$ and/or $\overline{\mathsf{T}}\mathsf{T}$ is equal to the Bonami-Beckner operator T_γ for some appropriate γ, which happens when $(X, Y) = \mathsf{BSS}$, then the T_γ operator scales $\widehat{f}(S)$ proportional to $\gamma^{|S|}$, which, in turn, solves the approximate eigenvalue problem nicely as done in [32]. However, both $\mathsf{T}\overline{\mathsf{T}}$ and $\overline{\mathsf{T}}\mathsf{T}$ are not equal to T_ρ in general. We overcome this bottleneck by characterizing the effect of these Markov operators on the Fourier coefficients as follows.

Lemma 1. *Let $\{\phi_S\}_{S \subseteq [n]}$ be a biased Fourier basis for $L^2(\Omega_x^n, \pi_x^{\otimes n})$, and $\{\psi_S\}_{S \subseteq [n]}$ be a biased Fourier basis for $L^2(\Omega_y^n, \pi_y^{\otimes n})$. Then, for any $S \subseteq [n]$, it holds that*

$$\mathsf{T}\overline{\mathsf{T}}\phi_S = \rho^{2|S|}\phi_S, \text{ and } \overline{\mathsf{T}}\mathsf{T}\psi_S = \rho^{2|S|}\psi_S.$$

Consequently, for any real-valued functions $f \in L^2(\mathcal{X}^n, \pi_x^{\otimes n})$ and $g \in L^2(\Omega_y^n, \pi_y^{\otimes n})$, the Fourier expansion of $\mathsf{T}\overline{\mathsf{T}}f$ and $\overline{\mathsf{T}}\mathsf{T}g$ is given by

$$\mathsf{T}\overline{\mathsf{T}}f = \sum_{S \subseteq [n]} \rho^{2|S|}\widehat{f}(S)\phi_S, \text{ and } \overline{\mathsf{T}}\mathsf{T}g = \sum_{S \subseteq [n]} \rho^{2|S|}\widehat{g}(S)\psi_S.$$

One can view this lemma as an analog/extension of $\mathsf{T}_\rho\chi_S = \rho^{|S|}\chi_S$ and $\mathsf{T}_\rho f = \sum_S \rho^{|S|}\widehat{f}(S)\chi_S$ to correlated space. Intuitively, the $\mathsf{T}\overline{\mathsf{T}}$ and $\overline{\mathsf{T}}\mathsf{T}$ operator scales $\widehat{f}(S)$ and $\widehat{g}(S)$ proportional to $\rho^{2|S|}$, respectively. Lemma 1 is crucial to prove the concentration of Fourier spectrum of reduction functions.

Theorem 10 (Constant Insecurity or Close to Low Degree Junta).
Suppose that $\left\|\mathsf{T}\overline{\mathsf{T}}f - \rho'^2 f\right\|_1 = \delta_1$, $\left\|\overline{\mathsf{T}}\mathsf{T}g - \rho'^2 g\right\|_1 = \delta_2$. Then the following statements hold.

1. *If $\rho^{t+1} < \rho' < \rho^t$, then $\min(\delta_1, \delta_2) \geqslant \frac{1}{2}\min((\rho'^2 - \rho^{2t})^2, (\rho'^2 - \rho^{2(t+1)})^2)$.*
2. *If $\rho' = \rho^k$ for some $k \in [n]$, then there exists $D = D(k)$ such that*
   (a) *The functions f and g are $\frac{2\delta_1}{(1-\rho^2)^2\rho^{4k}}$, and $\frac{2\delta_2}{(1-\rho^2)^2\rho^{4k}}$ concentrated on degree k, respectively.*
   (b) *There exist Boolean degree-k D-junta functions $\tilde{f}, \tilde{g}: \{\pm1\}^n \to \{\pm1\}$ such that*
      $$\left\|f - \tilde{f}\right\|_2^2 \leqslant \sigma_1 + D\sigma_1^{5/4}, \text{ and } \|g - \tilde{g}\|_2^2 \leqslant \sigma_2 + D\sigma_2^{5/4}, \text{ where } \sigma_1 = \frac{2}{(1-\rho^2)^2\rho^{4k}} \cdot \delta_1 \text{ and } \sigma_2 = \frac{2}{(1-\rho^2)^2\rho^{4k}} \cdot \delta_2.$$

6.2   Perfect-SNIS Characterization

In this section, we prove Theorem 9. We need the following result for the proof.

Claim 7. *Suppose f is a Boolean function in $L^2(\{\pm1\}^n, \pi^{\otimes n})$ such that $\mathsf{W}^k[f] = 1$. Then, the distribution π must be the uniform distribution over $\{\pm1\}$.*

The following result is needed to prove Claim 7. First let us introduce some notation. Let $f\colon \{\pm 1\}^n \to \{\pm 1\}$ be a Boolean function. For each $p \in (0,1)$, we write a Boolean function f as $f^{(p)}$ when viewing f as an element of $L^2(\{\pm 1\}^n), \pi_p^{\otimes n})$, where π_p is a distribution over $\{\pm 1\}$ such that $\pi_p(-1) = p$ and $\pi_p(1) = 1 - p$. Observe that $\sigma = 2\sqrt{p}\sqrt{1-p}$ is the standard deviation of the distribution.

Claim 8. *If* $\mathsf{W}^{\leqslant k}[f^{(p)}] = 1$, *then* $\mathsf{W}^k[f^{(1/2)}] = \mathsf{W}^k[f^{(p)}]/\sigma^{2k}$ *where* $\sigma = 2\sqrt{p(1-p)}$.

Intuitively, this claim says that the Fourier weight measured over the p-biased distribution on a particular degree is equal to the product of the Fourier weight measured over the uniform distribution on the same degree and a power of the standard deviation the p-biased distribution.

Proof (Proof of Claim 7). Let $p := \pi(-1)$. It follows from Claim 8 that $\mathsf{W}^k[f^{(p)}] \leqslant \sigma^{2k}\mathsf{W}^k[f^{(1/2)}]$. Since f is Boolean it follows from Parseval identity that $\mathsf{W}^k[f^{(1/2)}] \leqslant 1$, and so $1 = \mathsf{W}^k[f^{(p)}] \leqslant \sigma^{2k}$ which implies that $\sigma = 1$ and so $p = 1/2$. Therefore, the distribution π is uniform.

Now we are ready to prove Theorem 9 as follow.

Proof (of Theorem 9). Suppose there exists $n \in \mathbb{N}$ and two Boolean functions $f, g\colon \{\pm 1\}^n \to \{\pm 1\}$ such that $\mathsf{BSS}(\rho') \sqsubseteq^0_{f,g} (X,Y)^{\otimes n}$. Then, applying Theorem 1 for insecurity bound $\nu = 0$ yields $\rho' = \rho^k$ for some $k \in \mathbb{N}$, and $\mathsf{W}^k[f] = \mathsf{W}^k[g] = 1$, where ρ is the maximal correlation of (X,Y). By Claim 7, both the marginal distributions π_x and π_y must be uniform distribution over $\{\pm 1\}$. This implies that the joint distribution (X,Y) is a $\mathsf{BSS}(\varepsilon)$ for some $\varepsilon \in (0,1/2)$. Using the fact that the the maximal correlation of $\mathsf{BSS}(\varepsilon) = \rho$ and the result from [32], one concludes that $\rho' = \rho^k$.

6.3   Proof Outline of Theorem 7

The proof of Theorem 7 is similar to the proof of Theorem 6 except that here we again use the same idea that we applied in BES from arbitrary to deal with the non-binary range of Bob's reduction function. Again, we have a statistical to perfect result. Similar to Theorem 9, we can show that the source must be a BSS. We conclude the proof by using the impossibility result of simulating BES from BSS even in the (non-secure) NIS due to reverse hypercontractivity.

7   Additional Results and Discussions

7.1   Necessary Condition on Eigenvalues

Theorem 11. *Let* (X,Y) *be an arbitrary joint distribution whose Markov operator and adjoint are respectively* $\mathsf{T}^{(1)}$ *and* $\overline{\mathsf{T}}^{(1)}$, *and let* $(U,V) \in \{\mathsf{BSS}(\rho'), \mathsf{BES}(\rho')\}$ *for* $\rho' \in (0,1)$. *For any* $c > 0$, *there are positive constants*

n_0 and $d = d((X,Y), \rho')$ such that the following result holds. If $(U,V) \sqsubseteq_{f,g}^{\nu}$ $(X,Y)^{\otimes n}$, for some $n \geqslant n_0$, and $\nu \leqslant c/n$, then $\rho'^2 = \prod_{i=1}^{t} \lambda_i^{k_i}$, where $1 = \lambda_1 \geqslant \lambda_2 \geqslant \ldots \geqslant \lambda_t$ are all eigenvalues of $(\mathsf{T}\overline{\mathsf{T}})^{(1)}$, and $k_i \in \mathbb{N}$ such that $\sum_{i=1}^{t} k_i = n$.

By the reduction of statistical to perfect (Theorem 1), without loss of generality, assume that $\mathsf{BSS}(\rho') \sqsubseteq_{f,g}^{0} (X,Y)^{\otimes n}$. Theorem 2 and Claim 2 imply that $\mathsf{T}\overline{\mathsf{T}} f = \rho'^2 f$. This means that ρ'^2 is an eigenvalue of the Markov operator $\mathsf{T}\overline{\mathsf{T}}$. Suppose $1 = \lambda_1 \geqslant \lambda_2 \geqslant \ldots \geqslant \lambda_t$ be all eigenvalues of $(\mathsf{T}\overline{\mathsf{T}})^{(1)}$, then it follows from tensorization property of eigenvalues that $\rho'^2 = \prod_{i=1}^{t} \lambda_i^{k_i}$ for some $k_i \in \mathbb{N}$ such that $k_1 + k_2 + \cdots + k_t = n$, as desired. As a consequence, we have the following result.

Corollary 4. *There is no complete joint distribution in SNIS.*

7.2 Decidability

Corollary 1 gives an algorithm to decide whether there is a statistical SNIS of $\mathsf{BSS}(\rho')$ from (X,Y) with insecurity bound $\nu(n) = \mathcal{O}(1/n)$. In (non-secure) NIS, [18,24,25] considered a different problem of decidability called gap decidability. Given a constant $\delta > 0$, a source (X,Y) and a target (U,V), the goal is to distinguish between (1) there exists a $n_0 \in \mathbb{N}$ such that (U,V) can be non-interactively simulated (not necessarily secure) from $(X,Y)^{\otimes n_0}$ with error at most δ and (2) for any $n \in \mathbb{N}$, any simulation of (U,V) from $(X,Y)^{\otimes n}$ has error at least $c\delta$, where c is some constant. The gap decidability of BSS from an arbitrary source in SNIS is still open. We formulate this problem as follows.

SNIS Gap Decidability Problem. Given any $c > 1, \delta > 0$, a source (X,Y), and a target $\mathsf{BSS}(\rho')$. Distinguish between the following 2 cases:

1. There exist $n_0 \in \mathbb{N}$ and functions $f\colon \Omega_x^{n_0} \to \{\pm 1\}$ and $g\colon \Omega_y^{n_0} \to \{\pm 1\}$ such that SNIS of $\mathsf{BSS}(\rho)$ from $(X,Y)^{\otimes n_0}$ has simulation error at most δ.
2. For any $n \in \mathbb{N}$ and $f\colon \Omega_x^n \to \{\pm 1\}$ and $g\colon \Omega_y^n \to \{\pm 1\}$, SNIS of $\mathsf{BSS}(\rho)$ from $(X,Y)^{\otimes n}$ has simulation error at least $c\delta$.

When the source is a 2-by-2 distribution, our characterization solves this problem and we know for sure it is a Yes instance when the threshold δ is less than the constant in our Theorem 8. We conjecture the following "junta theorem over correlated space"/"dimension reduction preserving security" that would help us solve the gap decidability problem for any $\delta > 0$. In the following, we abuse the notation and let $\mathsf{T}, \overline{\mathsf{T}}$ denote the Markov operator and adjoint Markov operator of both $(X,Y)^{\otimes n}$ and $(X,Y)^{\otimes n_0}$.

Conjecture 1. Given any $\delta \geqslant 0$, and $f\colon \Omega_x^n \to \{\pm 1\}$ and $g\colon \Omega_y^n \to \{\pm 1\}$ satisfying $\mathbb{E}[f] \leqslant \delta, \mathbb{E}[g] \leqslant \delta, \|\overline{\mathsf{T}}f - \rho'g\|_1 \leqslant \delta$ and $\|\mathsf{T}g - \rho'f\|_1 \leqslant \delta$, there exist

$n_0 = n_0((X,Y), \rho', \delta)$, functions $f^* \colon \Omega_x^{n_0} \to \{\pm 1\}$ and $g^* \colon \Omega_y^{n_0} \to \{\pm 1\}$ such that

$$(i) \ |\mathbb{E}[f^*] - \mathbb{E}[f]| \leqslant 2\delta, \quad (ii) \ |\mathbb{E}[g^*] - \mathbb{E}[g]| \leqslant 2\delta,$$
$$(iii) \ \left\| \overline{\mathsf{T}} f^* - \rho' g^* \right\|_1 \leqslant 2\delta, \text{ and } (iv) \ \left\| \mathsf{T} g^* - \rho' f^* \right\|_1 \leqslant 2\delta.$$

The conjecture holds true when the source is 2-by-2 and δ is a small enough constant due to our characterization theorem.

The requirement that both f^* and g^* remains Boolean-valued functions is unique to security constraint in SNIS. In contrast, the reduction functions in NIS setting [25] only need to be bounded functions since they only need to preserve the correlation (see Theorem 3.1 in [25]) not the security.

7.3   On Power of Non-linear Constructions

Lemma 2. *There are exactly 16 perfect non linear SNIS constructions of* BSS(1/2) *from two samples of* ROT.

By implementing our exhaustive search algorithm, we found 16 perfect constructions (see the full version for detailed constructions).

Lemma 3. *There is a perfect non linear SNIS construction of* BES($\sqrt{1/2}$) *from one sample of* ROT.

Next, we shall show that there is no SNIS construction of BSS(1/2) or BES($\sqrt{1/2}$) from n independent samples of ROT for any $n \in \mathbb{N}$.

Lemma 4. *For any naming of the samples from the* ROT *distribution, any* $n \in$ $\mathbb{N}$, *any SNIS of* BSS(1/2) *or* BES($\sqrt{1/2}$) *from* ROT$^{\otimes n}$ *with linear reductions has a constant simulation error.*

7.4   Incompleteness of String-ROT

Definition 8. *The ℓ-bit string random oblivious transfer source, represented as* ROT(ℓ), *samples uniformly and independently random* $x_1, x_2 \in \{0,1\}^\ell$ *and a bit* $b \in \{0,1\}^n$, *provides Alice* (x_1, x_2), *and provides Bob* (b, x_b).

In contrast to the completeness result in OWSC, we show that the family of string-ROT is not complete in SNIS.

Lemma 5. *The family of string-ROT is not complete for SNIS.*

This lemma follows from the fact that the maximal correlation of $ROT(\ell) = 1/\sqrt{2}$ for every $\ell \in \mathbb{N}$ and the data processing inequality (Imported Theorem 2).

References

1. Agarwal, P., Narayanan, V., Pathak, S., Prabhakaran, M., Prabhakaran, V.M., Rehan, M.A.: Secure Non-interactive reduction and spectral analysis of correlations. In: Dunkelman, O., Dziembowski, S. (eds.) EUROCRYPT 2022, Part III. LNCS, vol. 13277, pp. 797–827. Springer, Cham (2022). https://doi.org/10.1007/978-3-031-07082-2_28
2. Agrawal, S., et al.: Cryptography from one-way communication: on completeness of finite channels. In: Moriai, S., Wang, H. (eds.) ASIACRYPT 2020. LNCS, vol. 12493, pp. 653–685. Springer, Cham (2020). https://doi.org/10.1007/978-3-030-64840-4_22
3. Ahlswede, R., Gács, P.: Spreading of sets in product spaces and hypercontraction of the Markov operator. Ann. Probab. 925–939 (1976)
4. Anantharam, V., Gohari,A., Kamath, S., Nair, C.: On maximal correlation, hypercontractivity, and the data processing inequality studied by Erkip and Cover. arXiv preprint arXiv:1304.6133 (2013)
5. Beaver, D.: Efficient multiparty protocols using circuit randomization. In: Feigenbaum, J. (ed.) CRYPTO 1991. LNCS, vol. 576, pp. 420–432. Springer, Heidelberg (1992). https://doi.org/10.1007/3-540-46766-1_34
6. Beimel, A., Ishai, Y., Kumaresan, R., Kushilevitz, E.: On the cryptographic complexity of the worst functions. In: Lindell, Y. (ed.) TCC 2014. LNCS, vol. 8349, pp. 317–342. Springer, Heidelberg (2014). https://doi.org/10.1007/978-3-642-54242-8_14
7. Beimel, A., Malkin, T.: A quantitative approach to reductions in secure computation. In: Naor, M. (ed.) TCC 2004. LNCS, vol. 2951, pp. 238–257. Springer, Heidelberg (2004). https://doi.org/10.1007/978-3-540-24638-1_14
8. Ben-David, A., Nisan, N., Pinkas, B.: FairplayMP: a system for secure multi-party computation. In: Ning, P., Syverson, P.F., Jha, S. (eds.) ACM CCS 2008, pp. 257–266. ACM Press (2008). https://doi.org/10.1145/1455770.1455804
9. Bogdanov, A., Mossel, E.: On extracting common random bits from correlated sources. IEEE Trans. Inf. Theory 57(10), 6351–6355 (2011). https://doi.org/10.1109/TIT.2011.2134067
10. Boyle, E., Couteau, G., Gilboa, N., Ishai, Y., Kohl, L., Scholl, P.: Efficient pseudorandom correlation generators: silent OT extension and more. In: Boldyreva, A., Micciancio, D. (eds.) CRYPTO 2019, Part III. LNCS, vol. 11694, pp. 489–518. Springer, Cham (2019). https://doi.org/10.1007/978-3-030-26954-8_16
11. Boyle, E., Couteau, G., Gilboa, N., Ishai, Y., Kohl, L., Scholl, P.: Efficient pseudorandom correlation generators from ring-LPN. In: Micciancio, D., Ristenpart, T. (eds.) CRYPTO 2020, Part II. LNCS, vol. 12171, pp. 387–416. Springer, Cham (2020). https://doi.org/10.1007/978-3-030-56880-1_14
12. Canetti, R.: Security and composition of multiparty cryptographic protocols. J. Cryptol. 13(1), 143–202 (2000). https://doi.org/10.1007/s001459910006
13. Canetti, R.: Universally composable security: a new paradigm for cryptographic protocols. Cryptology ePrint Archive, Report 2000/067 (2000). https://eprint.iacr.org/2000/067
14. Canetti, R.: Universally composable security: a new paradigm for cryptographic protocols. In: 42nd FOCS, pp. 136–145. IEEE Computer Society Press (2001). https://doi.org/10.1109/SFCS.2001.959888
15. Carmer, B., Rosulek, M.: Linicrypt: a model for practical cryptography. In: Robshaw, M., Katz, J. (eds.) CRYPTO 2016, Part III. LNCS, vol. 9816, pp. 416–445. Springer, Heidelberg (2016). https://doi.org/10.1007/978-3-662-53015-3_15

16. Chan, S.O., Mossel, E., Neeman, J.: On extracting common random bits from correlated sources on large alphabets. IEEE Trans. Inf. Theory **60**(3), 1630–1637 (2014). https://doi.org/10.1109/TIT.2014.2301155
17. Damgård, I., Pastro, V., Smart, N., Zakarias, S.: Multiparty computation from somewhat homomorphic encryption. In: Safavi-Naini, R., Canetti, R. (eds.) CRYPTO 2012. LNCS, vol. 7417, pp. 643–662. Springer, Heidelberg (2012). https://doi.org/10.1007/978-3-642-32009-5_38
18. De, A., Mossel, E., Neeman, J.: Non interactive simulation of correlated distributions is decidable. In: Czumaj, A. (ed.) 29th SODA, pp. 2728–2746. ACM-SIAM (2018). https://doi.org/10.1137/1.9781611975031.174
19. Efron, B., Stein, C.: The jackknife estimate of variance. Ann. Stat. 586–596 (1981)
20. Friedgut, E.: Boolean functions with low average sensitivity depend on few coordinates. Combinatorica **18**(1), 27–35 (1998). https://doi.org/10.1007/PL00009809
21. Gács, P., Körner, J.: Common information is far less than mutual information. Probl. Control Inf. Theory **2**(2), 149–162 (1973)
22. Garg, S., Ishai, Y., Kushilevitz, E., Ostrovsky, R., Sahai, A.: Cryptography with one-way communication. In: Gennaro, R., Robshaw, M. (eds.) CRYPTO 2015, Part II. LNCS, vol. 9216, pp. 191–208. Springer, Heidelberg (2015). https://doi.org/10.1007/978-3-662-48000-7_10
23. Gebelein, H.: Das statistische problem der korrelation als variations-und eigenwertproblem und sein zusammenhang mit der ausgleichsrechnung. ZAMM-J. Appl. Math. Mech./Zeitschrift für Angewandte Mathematik und Mechanik **21**(6), 364–379 (1941)
24. Ghazi, B., Kamath, P., Raghavendra, P.: Dimension reduction for polynomials over gaussian space and applications. In: Servedio, R.A. (ed.) 33rd Computational Complexity Conference, CCC 2018, 22–24 June 2018, San Diego, CA, USA. LIPIcs, vol. 102 , pp. 28: 1–28: 37. Schloss Dagstuhl - Leibniz Center for u r Computer Science (2018). https://doi.org/10.4230/LIPIcs.CCC.2018.28
25. Ghazi, B., Kamath, P., Sudan, M.: Decidability of non-interactive simulation of joint distributions. In: Dinur, I. (ed.) 57th FOCS, pp. 545–554. IEEE Computer Society Press (2016). https://doi.org/10.1109/FOCS.2016.65
26. Goldreich, O., Micali, S., Wigderson, A.: How to play any mental game or a completeness theorem for protocols with honest majority. In: Aho, A. (ed.) 19th ACM STOC, pp. 218–229. ACM Press (1987). https://doi.org/10.1145/28395.28420
27. Hirschfeld, H.O.: A connection between correlation and contingency. In: Mathematical Proceedings of the Cambridge Philosophical Society, vol. 31, pp. 520–524. Cambridge University Press (1935). https://doi.org/10.1017/S0305004100013517
28. Ishai, Y., Kushilevitz, E., Ostrovsky, R., Prabhakaran, M., Sahai, A., Wullschleger, J.: Constant-rate oblivious transfer from noisy channels. In: Rogaway, P. (ed.) CRYPTO 2011. LNCS, vol. 6841, pp. 667–684. Springer, Heidelberg (2011). https://doi.org/10.1007/978-3-642-22792-9_38
29. Ishai, Y., Prabhakaran, M., Sahai, A.: Founding cryptography on oblivious transfer – efficiently. In: Wagner, D. (ed.) CRYPTO 2008. LNCS, vol. 5157, pp. 572–591. Springer, Heidelberg (2008). https://doi.org/10.1007/978-3-540-85174-5_32
30. Kamath, S., Anantharam, V.: Non-interactive simulation of joint distributions: the hirschfeld-gebelein-rényi maximal correlation and the hypercontractivity ribbon. In: 2012 50th Annual Allerton Conference on Communication, Control, and Computing (Allerton), pp. 1057–1064. IEEE (2012)
31. Kamath, S., Anantharam, V.: On non-interactive simulation of joint distributions. IEEE Trans. Inf. Theory **62**(6), 3419–3435 (2016)

32. Khorasgani, H.A., Maji, H.K., Nguyen, H.H.: Secure non-interactive simulation: feasibility and rate. In: Dunkelman, O., Dziembowski, S. (eds.) EUROCRYPT 2022, Part III. LNCS, vol. 13277, pp. 767–796. Springer, Heidelberg (2022). https://doi.org/10.1007/978-3-031-07082-2_27

33. Kilian, J.: More general completeness theorems for secure two-party computation. In: 32nd ACM STOC, pp. 316–324. ACM Press (2000). https://doi.org/10.1145/335305.335342

34. Kindler, G.: Property testing PCP. PhD thesis, Tel-Aviv University (2002)

35. Kindler, G., Safra, S.: Noise-resistant Boolean functions are juntas. Preprint (2002)

36. Kraschewski, D., Maji, H.K., Prabhakaran, M., Sahai, A.: A full characterization of completeness for two-party randomized function evaluation. In: Nguyen, P.Q., Oswald, E. (eds.) EUROCRYPT 2014. LNCS, vol. 8441, pp. 659–676. Springer, Heidelberg (2014). https://doi.org/10.1007/978-3-642-55220-5_36

37. MacWilliams, F.J., Sloane, N.J.A.: The Theory of Error Correcting Codes, vol. 16. Elsevier, Amsterdam (1977)

38. Maji, H.K., Prabhakaran, M., Rosulek, M.: Complexity of multi-party computation functionalities. In: Prabhakaran, M., Sahai, A. (eds.) Secure Multi-Party Computation. Cryptology and Information Security Series, vol. 10, pp. 249–283. IOS Press (2013). https://doi.org/10.3233/978-1-61499-169-4-249

39. Malkhi, D., Nisan, N., Pinkas, B., Sella, Y.: Fairplay - secure two-party computation system. In: Blaze, M. (ed.) USENIX Security 2004, pp. 287–302. USENIX Association (2004)

40. Mossel, E.: Gaussian bounds for noise correlation of functions and tight analysis of long codes. In: 49th FOCS, pp. 156–165. IEEE Computer Society Press (2008). https://doi.org/10.1109/FOCS.2008.44

41. Mossel, E.: Gaussian bounds for noise correlation of functions. Geom. Funct. Anal. **19**(6), 1713–1756 (2010)

42. Mossel, E., O'Donnell, R.: Coin flipping from a cosmic source: on error correction of truly random bits. Random Struct. Algorithms **26**(4), 418–436 (2005). https://doi.org/10.1002/rsa.20062

43. Mossel, E., O'Donnell, R., Regev, O., Steif, J.E., Sudakov, B.: Non-interactive correlation distillation, inhomogeneous Markov chains, and the reverse Bonami-Beckner inequality. Israel J. Math. **154**(1), 299–336 (2006)

44. Narayanan, V., Prabhakaran, M., Prabhakaran, V.M.: Zero-communication reductions. In: Pass, R., Pietrzak, K. (eds.) TCC 2020, Part III. LNCS, vol. 12552, pp. 274–304. Springer, Cham (2020). https://doi.org/10.1007/978-3-030-64381-2_10

45. Nielsen, J.B., Nordholt, P.S., Orlandi, C., Burra, S.S.: A new approach to practical active-secure two-party computation. In: Safavi-Naini, R., Canetti, R. (eds.) CRYPTO 2012. LNCS, vol. 7417, pp. 681–700. Springer, Heidelberg (2012). https://doi.org/10.1007/978-3-642-32009-5_40

46. O'Donnell, R.: Analysis of Boolean Functions. Cambridge University Press, Cambridge (2014)

47. Rényi, A.: On measures of dependence. Acta Math. Hung. **10**(3–4), 441–451 (1959). https://doi.org/10.1007/BF02024507

48. Witsenhausen, H.S.: On sequences of pairs of dependent random variables. SIAM J. Appl. Math. **28**(1), 100–113 (1975). https://doi.org/10.1137/0128010

49. Wolf, S., Wullschleger, J.: Oblivious transfer is symmetric. In: Vaudenay, S. (ed.) EUROCRYPT 2006. LNCS, vol. 4004, pp. 222–232. Springer, Heidelberg (2006). https://doi.org/10.1007/11761679_14

50. Wyner, A.: The common information of two dependent random variables. IEEE Trans. Inf. Theory **21**(2), 163–179 (1975). https://doi.org/10.1109/TIT.1975. 1055346
51. Yang, K.: On the (im)possibility of non-interactive correlation distillation. In: Farach-Colton, M. (ed.) LATIN 2004. LNCS, vol. 2976, pp. 222–231. Springer, Heidelberg (2004). https://doi.org/10.1007/978-3-540-24698-5_26
52. Yao, A.C.-C.: Protocols for secure computations (extended abstract). In: 23rd FOCS, pp. 160–164. IEEE Computer Society Press (1982). https://doi.org/10. 1109/SFCS.1982.38
53. Yin, Z., Park, Y.: Hypercontractivity, maximal correlation and non-interactive simulation (2014)

Secure Non-interactive Reducibility
is Decidable

Kaartik Bhushan[1(✉)], Ankit Kumar Misra[1], Varun Narayanan[2],
and Manoj Prabhakaran[1]

[1] Indian Institute of Technology Bombay, Mumbai, India
{kbhushan,ankitkmisra,mp}@cse.iitb.ac.in
[2] Technion, Haifa, Israel

Abstract. Secure Non-Interactive Reductions (SNIR) is a recently introduced, but fundamental cryptographic primitive. The basic question about SNIRs is how to determine if there is an SNIR from one 2-party correlation to another. While prior work provided answers for several pairs of correlations, the possibility that this is an undecidable problem in general was left open. In this work we show that the existence of an SNIR between *any pair of correlations* can be determined by an algorithm.

At a high-level, our proof follows the blueprint of a similar (but restricted) result by Khorasgani et al. But combining the spectral analysis of SNIRs by Agrawal et al. (Eurocrypt 2022) with a new variant of a "junta theorem" by Kindler and Safra, we obtain a complete resolution of the decidability question for SNIRs. The new junta theorem that we identify and prove may be of independent interest.

1 Introduction

The notion of Secure Non-Interactive Reductions (SNIR) has only recently been formally defined [1,2,18], but it is a fundamental cryptographic primitive that lies at the intersection of several major lines of research in information-theory and cryptography. On the one hand, it is a model of information-theoretically secure 2-party computation, using correlated randomness [13,14,16,19]. It is a minimal model *without any communication*, pushing the limits of minimalism in secure computation, as initiated by the influential work of Feige et al. [8]. Its non-secure counterpart, called *non-interactive simulation* commands a rich literature in both information-theory and computer science literature spanning half a century [3,7,10,11,17,26,27,29]. Another important motivation behind SNIR is also its relevance to *cryptographic complexity* [4,5,22–24] – namely, measuring the complexity of a function in terms of the number of samples of a correlation that need to be used in an (interactive) secure 2-party computation protocol for the function. As pointed out in [1], understanding the power of SNIR

Varun Narayanan—Supported by ERC Project NTSC (742754) and ISF Grants 1709/14 & 2774/20.

is an important part of understanding the interactive secure 2-party computation protocol for an inputless function: such a protocol consists of an interaction phase (with no security requirements of its own) followed by an SNIR used to securely sample the output from the correlated views at the end of the interaction.

Finally, and significantly, studying the minimalistic model of SNIR leads us to mathematical tools that are relatively unexploited in classical cryptography, including tools from spectral graph theory and harmonic analysis [1,2,18]. Conversely, as is the case in this work, studying SNIRs can lead to contributions back to the development of these tools and their applicability.

Decidability of SNIR. SNIR is a notion of reduction from a (2-output) *target* distribution D to a *source* distribution C. It is simply a statistically secure 2-party computation protocol for sampling from D, when the parties are given access to samples from C, with the restriction that the parties cannot communicate at all. (In this model, semi-honest security and UC security are equivalent.)

The most fundamental question about SNIRs is the decidability of the following problem:

SNIR Problem: *Given a pair of correlations (C, D), does there exist a statistical SNIR from D to C?*

In the works that defined SNIR, this question was tackled for specific pairs of correlations, using arguments specialized for them [1,2,18]. In [2,18], the authors insightfully observed that in certain cases, *a statistically secure SNIR implies a perfectly secure one*, which can in turn be used to design an algorithm to decide the existence of an SNIR. In this work too, we follow the same high-level approach. Further, [2,18] showed that Fourier analytic techniques can be used to prove the statistical-to-perfect security result. However, the decidability results in [2,18] were restricted to two specific target distributions, and did not cover weak notions of security (with only "vanishing" error).

In this work, starting from the spectral analysis of [1] (involving eigenvectors, or more precisely, the singular value decomposition of the "correlation operator"), we apply Fourier analytic techniques to SNIRs in an alternate fashion, to obtain a *full answer* to the fundamental decidability question.

Our Contributions. We summarize our contributions below:

- Our main technical result is a statistical-to-perfect security result for SNIRs, which shows that, for a pair of correlations D and C, a statistically secure SNIR (possibly with weak security) exists from D to C iff there is a perfectly secure SNIR from D to $C^{\otimes \ell}$ for some finite ℓ (that can be computed from D and C). The formal statement, in Theorem 1, involves certain technical restrictions on D and C, which are essential (but not a barrier to the decidability result).
  - In order to prove this, we formulate and prove a new "junta theorem" for "generalized Fourier transforms," that may be of independent interest. This is stated as Theorem 2 and proven in Sect. 5.

- Based on the above, we show that the SNIR problem is decidable.[1]
- We also illustrate how the statistical-to-perfect security result can be used to obtain new combinatorial necessary conditions for an SNIR to exist between a pair of correlations; these combinatorial conditions can in turn be used to rule out an SNIR from OT correlation to Rabin OT correlation, that was not covered by prior results.

We remark that our decidability result subsumes that of [18] in a couple of ways: it works for all pairs of correlations, and further works even for a very weak notion of security. That is, when our algorithm says "No" it rules out an SNIR with error that goes to 0 however slowly, and when we say "Yes" we obtain an SNIR with either perfect security (in the absence of common information) or negligible error. In contrast, the algorithm in [18] could not rule out an SNIR with error going to 0 slower than $1/n$ where n denotes the number copies of the source correlation used. More significantly, the algorithm of [18] is restricted to two special target correlations.

Related Work. As already mentioned, several lines of work in information-theoretically secure cryptography intersect with SNIR. Here we clarify the connection with some recent works.

SNIR was defined independently in two concurrent works [1,2], and was further developed in [18], which explicitly addressed the decidability of the SNIR problem. The approach of employing a statistical-to-perfect security result, and the general idea of using Fourier analysis to prove it, were both present in [18].

A similar sounding concept, called *Secure Zero Communication Reduction* (SZCR) was introduced in [24]. It is instructive to compare both SNIR and SZCR with the standard notion of (semi-honest) secure reduction (SR) to a correlation like OT (more familiarly known as 2-PC in the OT-hybrid model). Roughly put,

$$\text{SNIR} \Rightarrow \text{SR} \Rightarrow \text{SZCR}$$

indicating that SNIR is a "stronger" primitive than SR, which is in turn stronger than SZCR. While every function has an SR to the OT correlation (i.e., it is a complete correlation), that is not the case for SNIR: Indeed, there are no complete correlations for SNIR [1]. Both SNIR and SZCR are motivated by approaching the notoriously hard lower bound questions for SR, but they do it in different ways.

- Lower bounds (or impossibility results) for SNIR are an "easier" target than those for SR, and would provide a platform for nurturing new techniques; as and when we completely settle a question for SNIR (as we do here), we can approach SR by relaxing the model (e.g., allow one-directional communication).

---

[1] For simplicity, we assume a computational model in which real numbers can be represented, computed upon (w.r.t. addition, multiplication and division), and compared exactly. The results would extend to all reasonable models of computing with a subset of real numbers, that is closed under these operations.

- Lower bounds for SZCR are formally (but not necessarily conceptually) harder than those for SR. Here we seek to develop new techniques by asking simpler variants of the lower bound question: e.g., existential questions (a la the "invertible rank conjecture" of [24]) or lower bounds for randomized functions (as in [15])[2]. Also, the new perspective provided by SZCR may lead to fresh approaches to the original hard lower bound problems of SR.

2 Technical Overview

Recap of SNIR. We start with a brief recap of SNIR, as defined in [1], largely borrowing from the overview in that paper. As shown in [1], there are in fact multiple perspectives of SNIR, and we profit from switching among them as appropriate.

- An SNIR is simply a statistically secure 2-party computation protocol for an inputless functionality (namely, sampling from a 2-output *target* distribution D), in which the parties have access to a setup in the form of another inputless functionality (namely, sampling i.i.d. samples from a *source* distribution C), with the restriction that the parties cannot exchange messages.
- *Equivalently*, an SNIR can be specified as a pair of stochastic "protocol" matrices (A, B) representing Alice and Bob's actions (mapping a symbol from the source to a symbol in the target), and a pair of "simulation" matrices (U, V) such that – restricting here to the case of perfect security – they satisfy the following correctness and privacy conditions:

$$A^\mathsf{T} C B = D \qquad A^\mathsf{T} C = D V \qquad C B = U^\mathsf{T} D. \tag{1}$$

Here we have written C to denote $C^{\otimes n}$ where n is the number of i.i.d. samples from C that the protocol uses. In the general case of statistical security, there is a family of protocols indexed by the security parameter (n is allowed to increase with the security parameter), and the equalities above admit an additive (matrix) error term, whose (suitably defined) norms can be bounded by vanishing quantities.

- Finally, there is a *spectral perspective* of an SNIR. This is a set of *necessary* conditions on a pair of matrices $(\widehat{A}, \widehat{B})$ derived from an SNIR (A, B), and which satisfy a set of conditions analogous to the original security conditions as follows (restricting here to perfect security):

$$\widehat{A} = F_C A F_D^{-1} \qquad\qquad \widehat{B} = G_C B G_D^{-1}$$
$$\widehat{A}^\mathsf{T} \widehat{A} = I \qquad\qquad \widehat{B}^\mathsf{T} \widehat{B} = I \tag{2}$$
$$\widehat{A}^\mathsf{T} \Sigma_C \widehat{B} = \Sigma_D \qquad \widehat{A}^\mathsf{T} \Sigma_C = \Sigma_D \widehat{B}^\mathsf{T} \qquad \Sigma_C \widehat{B} = \widehat{A} \Sigma_D$$

---

[2] [15] is a concurrent submission to this conference and it also includes the above comparison between SNIR and SZCR.

where $(\boldsymbol{F_C}, \boldsymbol{\Sigma_C}, \boldsymbol{G_C})$ and $(\boldsymbol{F_D}, \boldsymbol{\Sigma_D}, \boldsymbol{G_D})$ are matrices associated with C and D, respectively, via singular value decomposition (with some careful scaling to account for the possibly non-uniform marginal distributions of C and D). This view uses notions from spectral graph theory to study correlations using their singular values.

In this work we shall exploit yet another perspective of an SNIR: namely, a Fourier analytic perspective. While closely related to the spectral perspective above, this perspective focuses on the case when the source distribution is of the form $C^{\otimes n}$, and treats the protocols as *functions* that take n-tuples as inputs. The Fourier analytic perspective is crucial in investigating if protocols can actually use an increasing number of copies of C. This perspective was already insighfully exploited in [2] for some specific correlations which could be related to the Fourier basis; however, starting from our spectral perspective above, we discover that any source correlation can be related to an appropriate *generalized* Fourier basis.

Statistical to Perfect Security. At a high level, the plan for decidability follows that of [2,18], namely, to show that a statistical reduction from D to C implies a deterministic, perfect reduction, using only a *constant number* of copies of C. (The number of copies of C needed should be effectively determinable from the correlations D and C.) Then, to see if there is a reduction, it is enough to search among a finite number of protocols. The outline of how we carry this out is as follows:

1. Our starting point is the *spectral protocol* characterization from [1] shown in (2). We focus on $\boldsymbol{F_C}$. We observe that multiplying by $\boldsymbol{F_C}$ corresponds to a "generalized Fourier transform." Hence we can interpret the columns of $\widehat{A}$ as a generalized Fourier transform applied to the columns of the matrix $\mathring{A} := A\boldsymbol{F_D^{-1}}$. ($\mathring{A}$ could be thought of as corresponding to a "half-way spectral protocol.")
   $\mathring{A}$ is a matrix with real entries, whose rows are indexed by symbols in $\mathcal{X}^n$, where $\mathcal{X}$ is the alphabet of the distribution C (on Alice's side). So each column of $\mathring{A}$ can be interpreted as a function $a : \mathcal{X}^n \to \mathbb{R}$. A generalized Fourier transform writes this function as a linear combination of basis functions of the form $\gamma : \mathcal{X}^n \to \mathbb{R}$. Nominally, each basis function takes n inputs from $\mathcal{X}$, but may depend on fewer of them (e.g., the basis contains the constant function which depends on 0 inputs); the number of inputs it actually depends on is called the *degree* of a basis function.

2. Then we use the spectral protocol conditions of [1] to obtain "approximate degree bounds" on the columns of $\mathring{A}$. That is, we show that under the generalized Fourier transform mentioned above, the contribution from higher degree basis functions has low "energy" (Lemma 7).
   There is a caveat: Each column of $\mathring{A}$ is associated with a singular value of (a normalized version of) D; the degree bound holds only for columns for which the singular value associated with them is non-zero. Below, we write $\check{A}$ to denote $\mathring{A}$ restricted to these columns with the degree bound.

3. Next, we appeal to a "junta theorem" to argue that each column of $\breve{A}$ (interpreted as a function, for which the approximate degree bound holds) can be well-approximated by a "junta"—i.e., a function which depends only on a constant number of its inputs. Here, the approximation guarantee given by the junta is in the sense that it matches the original function exactly on most inputs.

   - While there are several junta theorems available in the literature, the version we need (for generalized Fourier transforms) has not been previously stated or proved. As such, we adapt a proof of the Kindler-Safra junta theorem [21] by Filmus [9] for our purposes. Presenting this more general version of the junta theorem is a contribution of ours that may be of independent interest.

4. The next step is to translate the junta approximations of the columns of $\breve{A}$ to such an approximation of the protocol matrix A itself. For this step, we invoke an important insight which is evident from the cryptographic perspective: An SNIR exists from D to C iff there is one from D' to C, where D' is a "non-redundant" version of D, which merges output symbols which are "equivalent". This means that for the decidability question, we can w.l.o.g. restrict ourselves to the case when D is non-redundant. This insight was already crucially used in [1]. In our case, we further rely on it at this step: We show that if D is non-redundant, then each row of A is fully determined by the corresponding row of $\breve{A}$ (Lemma 5). This also relies on another assumption that [1] showed can be made w.l.o.g.—that A is deterministic—thanks to a determinization process that retains statistical security (with a polynomially bounded increase in error). Then, an approximation of $\breve{A}$ (in which most rows are correct) yields a similar approximation of A; further, since the approximations are juntas, so is each column of the approximation of A.

   The upshot of this step is that Alice's protocol matrix A can be replaced by one which consults only a constant number of the n copies of C that it is given access to, without increasing the error too much. This still yields a statistically secure protocol family.

5. The final step is to convert the protocol to one in which both Alice and Bob consult only a constant number of copies of C (Lemma 8).

   This is easiest to see from the cryptographic perspective: If we simply remove the copies of C that Alice ignores, and require Bob to locally sample his side of C for those copies from the marginal distribution, we obtain a protocol that is at least as secure as the original one. Note that this transformation results in a protocol that has only a constant number of copies of C, but does require Bob to be randomized. We can determinize this protocol again (increasing the error in a bounded manner) to obtain a statistically secure, deterministic protocol using only a constant number of copies of C.

   Finally, we note that there are only finitely many such protocols, and hence, to form a statistically secure protocol family (with error that approaches 0), at least one of those protocols should have perfect security.

A Counterexample. Before proceeding further, we point out an apparent contradiction to the above claim: Consider C to be a uniformly random bit (both Alice and Bob get the same bit) and D to be a bit that is 0 with probability, say, $1/3$. Now, there is a statistical SNIR from D to C, by sampling more and more uniform bits from C to sample from D with increasingly better accuracy. However, 3 not being a power of 2 prevents a perfectly secure protocol from existing.

The reason the statistical-to-perfect security argument above breaks down in this case is that the argument requires C to have *no common information*. Common information in a correlation refers to a value that Alice and Bob can always agree on, when each of them is given only a sample from their side of the correlation. The restriction that C has no common information comes at the very first step of the sequence of arguments above, where we interpreted $\boldsymbol{F_C}$ as a "generalized Fourier transform".

Nevertheless, using a result from [1], we can handle correlations with common information. Suppose C has common information – say, w.l.o.g., it is in the form of sampling an index $i \in [k]$ according to some fixed distribution, and then sampling from a correlation C_i, where $C_1, \cdots, C_k$ are correlations without common information, and over disjoint alphabets (called the *components* of C). Then, it is not hard to see (from the cryptographic perspective) that for the purposes of statistically secure SNIR, C is equivalent to a correlation C' which samples $(k+1)$-tuples $(x_0, \cdots, x_k)$ for Alice and $(y_0, \cdots, y_k)$ for Bob, where $x_0 = y_0$ is a single uniform random bit, and for $i > 0$, (x_i, y_i) is a sample from C_i. That is, $C' = C_{\text{coin}} \otimes C^{\|}$, where C_{coin} is the uniform common coin, and $C^{\|}$ is a correlation without any common information. Then, using a result from [1], it follows that a correlation D has an SNIR to C' iff each of the components of D has an SNIR to $C^{\|}$. Since $C^{\|}$ has no common information this can be tested using the statistical-to-perfect security argument, as discussed above.

With this we obtain an algorithm that can decide the existence of SNIR for any pair of source and target correlations. This is detailed in Sect. 4.2.

New Necessary Conditions and an Example of Interest. Despite its general and fundamental nature, our decidability result is practically unsatisfactory, as the underlying algorithm is hugely inefficient: it involves a brute-force search over a finite but large space of protocols. An important focus in prior work on SNIR has been to derive simpler necessary conditions for an SNIR to exist. In particular, in [1] it was shown that for there to be an SNIR from D to C, the *singular values of the correlation operator corresponding to D should all appear as singular values of that corresponding to $C^{\otimes \ell}$ for some ℓ*. Such a result can be used to "manually" infer impossibility results for examples of interest.

While the results from [1,2,18] covered several cryptographically interesting source-target pairs, they also left out some. For instance, it was not known whether one can reduce the correlation D corresponding to random $\binom{2}{1}$ bit-OT to the correlation C corresponding to Rabin OT – i.e., an erasure channel with erasure probability 0.5, for uniformly random input bit. The results in [1] did not cover this example, as the non-zero singular values of the correlation operator corresponding to D, namely 1 and $\frac{1}{\sqrt{2}}$ also happen to be those associated with C^3. The results in [2, 18] also do not cover the case of the target correlation being $\binom{2}{1}$-OT.

Our statistical-to-perfect security result for SNIR plugs this gap easily: It is easy to see that there is no perfectly secure SNIR from D to $C^{\otimes \ell}$ for any ℓ, and by our result, the impossibility extends to statistical security. Indeed, this readily generalizes to a broader class of target-source correlation pairs, as captured in Lemma 10.

Overview of the Proof of the Junta Theorem. In Sect. 5, we prove the version of the junta theorem mentioned above. We closely follow a recent proof of the Kindler-Safra junta theorem [20, 21] by Filmus [9], making several suitable generalizations based on results (and exercises) in [25]. Compared to the statement proven in [9], the main difference is that we do not restrict it to functions over the domain $\{0, 1\}^n$.

The theorem we seek to prove (roughly) states the following: Suppose $f : \Omega^n \to \mathcal{T} \subseteq \mathbb{R}$ is an approximately degree d function as mentioned above, with the higher degree components $f^{>d}$ having only ϵ energy (above we defined the degree of a function w.r.t. a generalized Fourier transform, but it is in fact a basis-invariant quantity; it however does depend on the distribution π over Ω w.r.t. which the fourier basis is defined). Then there is a degree d function $h : \Omega^n \to \mathcal{T}$ that is in fact a function of only $O(1)$ of its n inputs (the hidden constants depending on $\mathcal{T}, d$ and π, and not on f or n), and on all but $O(\epsilon)$ fraction of the domain Ω^n (as measured using the distribution $\pi^{\otimes n}$) h equals f.

Below we exposit the high-level structure of the proof.

* ⋆ For each coordinate i, we will show that its *influence* on $f^{\leq d}$ is either $O(\epsilon)$ or $\Omega(1)$ where the constants depend on $\mathcal{T}, d, \lambda$.
* • But the degree bound on $f^{\leq d}$ implies that the total influence can be at most $d\|f\|^2 = O(1)$. So at most $O(1)$ coordinates i can have $\Omega(1)$ influence on $f^{\leq d}$.
* ⋆ Outside of these $O(1)$ coordinates, the function is shown to have low *variance*.
* • Then averaging over those coordinates gives a function g that does not depend on those coordinates, and is a good approximation in the sense that the function $f - g$ has small energy.
* • This is not quite in the form of the approximation we desire, since we would like to ensure that $\Pr_{x \leftarrow \pi^{\otimes n}}[f(x) \neq g(x)]$ is small. This is ensured by considering a function h which rounds off g to use values in the set $\mathcal{T}$. Since the variance is small, this can be done in a way that keeps the energy of $f - h$ still small. Now, since $\mathcal{T}$ is a finite set, there is an $\Omega(1)$ lower bound on $|f(x) - h(x)|$ whenever $f(x) \neq h(x)$.

Above, apart from the starred items, the others rely on mostly elementary arguments. The first starred step relies on a *hypercontractivity* result. It

---

[3] There were additional interesting examples that the singular value condition did not cover, but were handled in [1] using another necessary condition – called the Mirroring Lemma. But the above example evaded those approaches as well.

is applied to the so-called Laplacians of the function w.r.t. each coordinate, to prove a dichotomy for each coordinate, between having very low influence and high influence. For the second starred step, a result called the *Invariance Principle* is invoked to translate the low influence of the variables to low variance. One of our technical contributions is to flesh out an appropriately generalized version of the invariance principle (Lemma 15), to complete this step.

3 Preliminaries

Notation. We extensively employ linear algebraic notation, carefully adapted to allow precise expression of Fourier analytic definitions in terms of matrix multiplications. Some of the following is borrowed from [1].

We write $[n]$ to denote $\{1, \cdots, n\}$ and $[\![n]\!]$ to denote the set $\{0, \ldots, n-1\}$. $\mathbb{R}$ stands for the set of real numbers. Throughout the paper, all sets defined are finite. We typically denote such sets as $\mathcal{X}, \mathcal{Y}$, and so on, and a member of $\mathcal{X}$ is denoted as x.

Vectors and matrices are indexed by elements of finite sets. For a set $\mathcal{X}$, we write $\boldsymbol{v} \in \mathbb{R}^{\mathcal{X}}$ to mean that $\boldsymbol{v}$ is a column vector with real numbers indexed by the elements of $\mathcal{X}$ as its entries (i.e., $\boldsymbol{v}$ is, essentially, a function $\boldsymbol{v} : \mathcal{X} \to \mathbb{R}$); we will often refer to $\boldsymbol{v}$ as an $\mathcal{X}$ dimensional vector. For an $\mathcal{X}$ dimensional vector $\boldsymbol{v}$, the entry at the position x is denoted by $(\boldsymbol{v})_x$. Similarly, for sets $\mathcal{X}$ and $\mathcal{Y}$, we write $H \in \mathbb{R}^{\mathcal{X} \times \mathcal{Y}}$ to mean that H is an $\mathcal{X} \times \mathcal{Y}$ dimensional matrix with real numbers as entries. The row of H indexed by x and the column indexed by y are denoted as $(H)_{(x,\cdot)}$ and $(H)_{(\cdot,y)}$, respectively, and the element indexed by (x, y) is denoted as $(H)_{(x,y)}$. The transpose is denoted by H^{T}. Finally, $|H|$ denotes the absolute value of H, i.e., $(|H|)_{(i,j)} = |(H)_{(i,j)}|$, for all $i \in [m]$ and $j \in [n]$. The parentheses are removed whenever there is no scope for confusion and the vector/matrix itself is subscripted; i.e., $(\boldsymbol{v})_x$, $(H)_{(\cdot,x)}$ and $(H)_{(x,y)}$ are simplified to $\boldsymbol{v}_x$, $H_{(\cdot,x)}$ and $H_{(x,y)}$, respectively.

A column vector over the set $\mathcal{X}$ with all elements being 1 (resp. 0) is denoted by $\mathbf{1}^{\mathcal{X}}$ (resp. $\mathbf{0}^{\mathcal{X}}$). For $x \in \mathcal{X}$, $\boldsymbol{\xi}_x^{\mathcal{X}}$ denotes the $\mathcal{X}$ dimensional unit vector along the 'direction x'; i.e., $\left(\boldsymbol{\xi}_x^{\mathcal{X}}\right)_x = 1$ and $\left(\boldsymbol{\xi}_x^{\mathcal{X}}\right)_{x'} = 0$ for all $x' \neq x$. The superscript is dropped when there is no scope for confusion regarding the dimension of these vectors.

We write $O_D(\epsilon)$ to denote an upper bound of the form $f(D) \cdot \epsilon$, for some fixed non-negative function f.

Probability. We only consider distributions over finite sets in this paper. A distribution over $\mathcal{X}$ is completely described by a *distribution vector* $\boldsymbol{\pi} \in \mathbb{R}_{\geq 0}^{\mathcal{X}}$ such that $\sum_{x \in \mathcal{X}} \boldsymbol{\pi}_x = 1$, and the probability of $x \in \mathcal{X}$ is $\boldsymbol{\pi}_x$. Sampling x according to the distribution $\boldsymbol{\pi}$ independent of all previously defined random variables is denoted by $x \sim \boldsymbol{\pi}$. The statistical distance or total variation distance between two distributions $\boldsymbol{\pi}$ and $\boldsymbol{\pi}'$ over the same set $\mathcal{X}$ is denoted by $\mathrm{SD}\,(\boldsymbol{\pi}, \boldsymbol{\pi}')$, and is computed as

$$\mathrm{SD}\,(\boldsymbol{\pi}, \boldsymbol{\pi}') = \frac{1}{2} \sum_{x \in \mathcal{X}} |\boldsymbol{\pi}_x - \boldsymbol{\pi}'_x|.$$

Throughout this paper, we are interested in correlations, which are joint distributions over the product of two finite sets. A correlation over $\mathcal{X} \times \mathcal{Y}$ is completely described by a joint distribution matrix $H \in \mathbb{R}_{\geq 0}^{\mathcal{X} \times \mathcal{Y}}$ such that

$$\sum_{x \in \mathcal{X}} \sum_{y \in \mathcal{Y}} H_{(x,y)} = 1.$$

In the sequel, we will always refer to a correlation by its joint distribution matrix. The left marginal of H or the marginal distribution of the first coordinate of the joint distribution is given by the distribution vector $H\mathbf{1}$; the right marginal of H is given by the row vector $\mathbf{1}^\mathsf{T} H$ or equivalently the column vector $H^\mathsf{T}\mathbf{1}$. We write $(X,Y) \sim H$ to imply that the random variables (X,Y) are distributed according to the distribution H; i.e., $\mathrm{P}_{X,Y}(x,y) = H_{(x,y)}$ for all $(x,y) \in \mathcal{X} \times \mathcal{Y}$.

When we say Alice and Bob receive a correlation (X,Y), we mean Alice and Bob receive random variables X and Y, respectively. The objective of non-interactive secure reductions is for Alice and Bob to *securely realize* a desired correlation among themselves using (potentially many copies) of the correlation at hand without communicating with each other.

Definition 1 (Norms). For an $\mathcal{X} \times \mathcal{Y}$ dimensional matrix H, 1-norm of the matrix, denoted by $\|H\|_{1,1}$, is the sum of the absolute values of all elements in H, *i.e.*,

$$\|H\|_{1,1} = \sum_{(x,y) \in \mathcal{X} \times \mathcal{Y}} |H_{(x,y)}| = (\mathbf{1}^{\mathcal{X}})^\mathsf{T} |H| \mathbf{1}^{\mathcal{Y}}.$$

The 2-norm of an n dimensional vector $\boldsymbol{v}$ is defined as $\|\boldsymbol{v}\|_2 = \left(\sum_{i \in [n]} \boldsymbol{v}_i^2 \right)^{\frac{1}{2}}$. ◁

Definition 2. A matrix $H \in \mathbb{R}_{\geq 0}^{\mathcal{X} \times \mathcal{Y}}$ with non-negative entries is said to be *stochastic* if $H\mathbf{1}^{\mathcal{Y}} = \mathbf{1}^{\mathcal{X}}$. A stochastic matrix in which every entry is either 0 or 1 is called a *deterministic* stochastic matrix or simply a deterministic matrix.

Definition 3. For a (row or column) vector $\boldsymbol{v} \in \mathbb{R}^{\mathcal{X}}$, we define $\mathrm{diag}(\boldsymbol{v}) \in \mathbb{R}^{\mathcal{X} \times \mathcal{X}}$ as the diagonal matrix given by

$$(\mathrm{diag}(\boldsymbol{v}))_{(x,x')} = \begin{cases} \boldsymbol{v}_x & \text{if } x = x', \\ 0 & \text{otherwise.} \end{cases}$$

For $H \in \mathbb{R}^{\mathcal{X} \times \mathcal{Y}}$, we define $\boldsymbol{\Delta}_H$ as the $\mathcal{Y} \times \mathcal{Y}$ dimensional diagonal matrix

$$\boldsymbol{\Delta}_H = \mathrm{diag}(\mathbf{1}^\mathsf{T} H). \qquad \qquad ◁$$

Tensor product. When $G \in \mathbb{R}^{\mathcal{X} \times \mathcal{Y}}$ and $H \in \mathbb{R}^{\mathcal{R} \times \mathcal{S}}$, tensor (Kronecker) product of G and H, denoted as $G \otimes H$, is an $(\mathcal{X} \times \mathcal{R}) \times (\mathcal{Y} \times \mathcal{S})$ dimensional matrix such that, for all $(x,r) \in \mathcal{X} \times \mathcal{R}$ and $(y,s) \in \mathcal{Y} \times \mathcal{S}$,

$$(G \otimes H)_{((x,r),(y,s))} = G_{(x,y)} \cdot H_{(r,s)}.$$

When G and H are joint distribution matrices, the distribution matrix of the product distribution– independent draws from distributions G and H–is $G \otimes H$. Hence, the distribution of $n \in \mathbb{N}$ i.i.d. samples drawn from a correlation with distribution matrix G is described by the joint distribution matrix $G^{\otimes n}$. We will use the following identity which follows from the definitions of matrix multiplication and tensor product.

Claim 1. *For matrices G, H, G', H', $(GH) \otimes (G'H') = (G \otimes G')(H \otimes H')$. In particular, for $t \in \mathbb{N}$, $(GH)^{\otimes t} = G^{\otimes t} H^{\otimes t}$.*

Definition 4. A correlation H over $\mathcal{X} \times \mathcal{Y}$ is said to be *redundant* if there exist distinct $x, x' \in \mathcal{X}$ and $c \in \mathbb{R}_{\geq 0}$ such that $H_{(x,\cdot)} = c \cdot H_{(x',\cdot)}$ or there exist $y, y' \in \mathcal{Y}$ and $c \in \mathbb{R}_{\geq 0}$ such that $H_{(\cdot,y)} = c \cdot H_{(\cdot,y')}$. ◁

By this definition, both the marginal distributions of a non-redundant distribution have full support since an all zero column (or row) is trivially a scalar multiple of any other column (or row). For a redundant correlation, we define its non-redundant *core* as the correlation obtained by collapsing redundant symbols (on both sides) to their equivalence classes.

A correlation is said to have non-zero common information if two parties can agree on a bit with non-trivial entropy using the correlation without communicating. We formally define this notion below:

Definition 5. Correlation H over $\mathcal{X} \times \mathcal{Y}$ has common-information if there exist functions $f : \mathcal{X} \rightarrow \{0,1\}$ and $g : \mathcal{Y} \rightarrow \{0,1\}$ such that, when $(X, Y) \sim H$,

$$P[f(X) = g(Y)] = 1 \text{ and } 0 < P[f(X) = 0] < 1.$$

H has non-zero common information if and only if there exist $\emptyset \subset \mathcal{X}_0 \subset \mathcal{X}$ and $\emptyset \subset \mathcal{Y}_0 \subset \mathcal{Y}$, joint distribution matrices H_0 and H_1 over $\mathcal{X}_0 \times \mathcal{Y}_0$ and $(\mathcal{X} \setminus \mathcal{X}_0) \times (\mathcal{Y} \setminus \mathcal{Y}_0)$, respectively, and $0 < \alpha < 1$ such that H can be written as

$$H = \begin{bmatrix} \alpha H_0 & \mathbf{0} \\ \mathbf{0} & (1-\alpha)H_1 \end{bmatrix}.$$

A correlation that does not admit such a decomposition is said to be common-information free. ◁

3.1 Generalized Fourier Transform

Let $\pi \in \mathbb{R}_{\geq 0}^{\Omega}$ be a distribution over a finite set Ω. We consider the normed vector space $L^2(\Omega, \pi)$. The elements of this space are $\boldsymbol{v} \in \mathbb{R}^{\Omega}$ – i.e., real-valued vectors indexed by Ω, or equivalently, functions $\boldsymbol{v} : \Omega \rightarrow \mathbb{R}$. The inner product between two such vectors $\boldsymbol{u}, \boldsymbol{v} \in \mathbb{R}^{\Omega}$, denoted by $\langle \boldsymbol{u}, \boldsymbol{v} \rangle_{\pi}$, is given by

$$\langle \boldsymbol{u}, \boldsymbol{v} \rangle_{\pi} = \sum_{\Omega \in \Omega} \pi_{\omega} \cdot \boldsymbol{u}_{\omega} \cdot \boldsymbol{v}_{\omega}.$$

A set of vectors $\{\boldsymbol{\gamma}_{\alpha} \in \mathbb{R}^{\Omega} : \alpha \in [\![|\Omega|]\!]\}$ constitute a *Fourier basis* of $L^2(\Omega, \pi)$ if

1. γ_0 is the constant function; i.e., $\gamma_0 = 1^{\Omega}$.
2. For all $\alpha \in [\![|\Omega|]\!]$, γ_α is unit norm; i.e., $\langle \gamma_\alpha, \gamma_\alpha \rangle_\pi = 1$.
3. For all distinct $\alpha, \alpha' \in [\![|\Omega|]\!]$, γ_α is orthogonal to $\gamma_{\alpha'}$; i.e., $\langle \gamma_\alpha, \gamma_{\alpha'} \rangle_\pi = 0$.

We shall identify the set Γ with a matrix $\Gamma \in \mathbb{R}^{\Omega \times [\![|\Omega|]\!]}$ with γ_α as its rows: i.e., $\Gamma_{(\alpha, \cdot)} = \gamma_\alpha^{\mathsf{T}}$.

Definition 6. The *generalized Fourier transform* w.r.t. a Fourier basis $\Gamma = \{\gamma_\alpha \in \mathbb{R}^\Omega : \alpha \in [\![|\Omega|]\!]\}$ of $L^2(\Omega, \boldsymbol{\pi})$ is a linear operation that maps a vector $v \in \mathbb{R}^\Omega$ to $\widehat{v} \in \mathbb{R}^{[\![|\Omega|]\!]}$ such that

$$\widehat{v}_\alpha = \langle \gamma_\alpha, v \rangle_\pi \text{ for all } \alpha \in [0, |\Omega|).$$

The linear operator F that effects this transformation – i.e., $F \in \mathbb{R}^{[\![|\Omega|]\!] \times \Omega}$ such that for all $v \in \mathbb{R}^\Omega$, $Fv = \widehat{v}$ – is called the *Fourier transform operator* for Γ in $L^2(\Omega, \boldsymbol{\pi})$.

Proposition 1. *Suppose* $\Gamma \in \mathbb{R}^{\Omega \times [\![|\Omega|]\!]}$ *and its rows* $\gamma_\alpha := \Gamma_{(\alpha, \cdot)}$ *form a Fourier basis of* $L^2(\Omega, \boldsymbol{\pi})$. *Then, the matrix* $F \in \mathbb{R}^{[\![|\Omega|]\!] \times \Omega}$ *defined as* $F = \Gamma \operatorname{diag}(\boldsymbol{\pi})$ *is the Fourier transform operator for* Γ.

Proof: For all $v \in L^2(\Omega, \boldsymbol{\pi})$ and $\alpha \in [\![|\Omega|]\!]$,

$$(Fv)_\alpha = F_{(\alpha, \cdot)} v = \gamma_\alpha^{\mathsf{T}} \operatorname{diag}(\boldsymbol{\pi}) v = \sum_{\omega \in \Omega} \pi_\omega \, (\gamma_\alpha)_\omega \, v_\omega = \langle \gamma_\alpha, v \rangle_\pi = \widehat{v}_\alpha.$$

Thus, $Fv = \widehat{v}$. $\square$

Energy and Degree. The energy of a vector $v \in L^2(\Omega, \boldsymbol{\pi})$ is defined as

$$\|v\|^2 = \langle v, v \rangle_\pi = \sum_{\omega \in \Omega} \pi_\omega \cdot v_\omega \cdot v_\omega.$$

Parseval's theorem refers to the following alternative for computing the energy of $v \in L^2(\Omega, \boldsymbol{\pi})$:

$$\|v\|^2 = \sum_{\alpha \in [\![|\Omega|]\!]} \widehat{v}_\alpha \cdot \widehat{v}_\alpha.$$

For any Fourier basis $\Gamma = \{\gamma_\alpha \mid \alpha \in [\![|\Omega|]\!]\}$ over $L^2(\Omega, \boldsymbol{\pi})$ and for any $n \in \mathbb{N}$, the following is a generalized Fourier basis over $L^2(\Omega^n, \boldsymbol{\pi}^{\otimes n})$:

$$\{\gamma_{\alpha_1} \otimes \gamma_{\alpha_2} \otimes \ldots \otimes \gamma_{\alpha_n} : \alpha_i \in [\![|\Omega|]\!] \text{ for all } i \in [n]\}.$$

For any $\boldsymbol{\alpha} = (\alpha_1, \ldots, \alpha_n) \in [\![|\Omega|]\!]^n$, degree of $\boldsymbol{\alpha}$ denoted by $\deg(\boldsymbol{\alpha})$ is given by

$$\deg(\boldsymbol{\alpha}) = |\{i \in [n] : \alpha_i \neq 0\}|.$$

We can project a vector to its low-degree and high-degree components. For a vector $v \in L^2(\Omega^n, \pi^{\otimes n})$ and $d \in [0, n]$,

$$v^{\leq d} = \sum_{\alpha \in [|\Omega|]^n : \deg(\alpha) \leq d} \widehat{v}_\alpha \cdot \gamma_\alpha$$

$$\text{and } v^{>d} = \sum_{\alpha \in [|\Omega|]^n : \deg(\alpha) > d} \widehat{v}_\alpha \cdot \gamma_\alpha$$

Even though we have written the low-degree component $v^{\leq d}$ in terms of the basis vectors, it should be noted that this is actually the same for all bases [25]. Furthermore, we say that a vector v *has degree* d when $v = v^{\leq d}$.

3.2   Secure Non-interactive Reduction

In this section, we formally define SNIR and import a set of statements established in [1] that we will need to prove our main result. The definitions and statement of theorem have been adapted to the current notations, but are otherwise imported verbatim from the older work.

Definition 7. Let C and D be correlations over $\mathcal{X} \times \mathcal{Y}$ and $\mathcal{R} \times \mathcal{S}$, respectively. For any $\epsilon \geq 0$, an ϵ-*secure non-interactive reduction* (ϵ-SNIR) from D to C is a pair of probabilistic algorithms $\mathfrak{A} : \mathcal{X} \to \mathcal{R}$ and $\mathfrak{B} : \mathcal{Y} \to \mathcal{S}$ such that, when $(X, Y) \sim C$ and $(R, S) \sim D$,

ϵ-**Correctness:**

$$\text{SD}\left((\mathfrak{A}(X), \mathfrak{B}(Y)), (R, S)\right) \leq \epsilon. \tag{3}$$

ϵ-**Security:** There exist a pair of probabilistic algorithms, $\text{Sim}_A : \mathcal{R} \to \mathcal{X}$ and $\text{Sim}_B : \mathcal{S} \to \mathcal{Y}$ such that,

$$\text{SD}\left((X, \mathfrak{B}(Y)), (\text{Sim}_A(R), S)\right) \leq \epsilon, \tag{4}$$

$$\text{SD}\left((\mathfrak{A}(X), Y), (R, \text{Sim}_B(S))\right) \leq \epsilon. \tag{5}$$

0-SNIR is alternatively called a perfect SNIR.   ◁

Definition 8. Let C and D be correlations over $\mathcal{X} \times \mathcal{Y}$ and $\mathcal{R} \times \mathcal{S}$, respectively. D is said to have a statistical SNIR to C if, for all $\epsilon > 0$, there exists a sufficiently large n for which, D has an ϵ-SNIR to $C^{\otimes n}$.   ◁

Suppose $(\mathfrak{A}, \mathfrak{B})$ is an SNIR from correlation D distributed over $\mathcal{U} \times \mathcal{V}$ to C distributed over $\mathcal{X} \times \mathcal{Y}$. The probabilistic algorithm $\mathfrak{A}$ employed by Alice can be equivalently thought of as a $\mathcal{X} \times \mathcal{Y}$ dimensional stochastic matrix A with $A_{(x,u)} = P_{\mathfrak{A}}(u|x)$ for each x, u. Similarly, probabilistic algorithm $\mathfrak{B}$ can be thought of as a $\mathcal{Y} \times \mathcal{U}$ dimensional stochastic matrix B. The simulators Sim_A and Sim_B can also be equivalently thought of as stochastic matrices U and V of dimensions $\mathcal{U} \times \mathcal{X}$ and $\mathcal{V} \times \mathcal{Y}$, respectively. The following proposition shows how the correctness and security conditions of SNIR translates to linear algebraic constraints in terms of these stochastic matrices.

Proposition 2 *([1, Theorem 2]). A correlation D over $\mathcal{U} \times \mathcal{V}$ has an ϵ-SNIR to a correlation C over $\mathcal{X} \times \mathcal{Y}$ if and only if there exist stochastic matrices A, B, U, and V of dimensions $\mathcal{X} \times \mathcal{U}$, $\mathcal{Y} \times \mathcal{V}$, $\mathcal{U} \times \mathcal{X}$, and $\mathcal{V} \times \mathcal{Y}$, respectively, such that*

$$\|A^\mathsf{T}CB - D\|_{1,1} \leq \epsilon \quad (6) \quad \|A^\mathsf{T}C - DV\|_{1,1} \leq \epsilon \quad (7) \quad \|CB - U^\mathsf{T}D\|_{1,1} \leq \epsilon. \quad (8)$$

Identifying the stochastic matrices with the probabilistic algorithms as discussed above, conditions (6), (7), and (8) can be seen to correspond to the correctness condition (3) and security conditions (4), and (5), respectively.

A (redundant) correlation has a perfect SNIR to its core and vice-versa (Lemma 5 of [1]). This leads to the following observation in [1]:

Proposition 3. *A redundant correlation D has a statistical SNIR to a correlation C iff the core of D has a statistical SNIR to C.*

Keeping this in mind, we focus on SNIR of non-redundant target correlations throughout this work.

Given a purported perfect SNIR (A, B) from D to C, one can verify it easily, thanks to the following result [1, Lemma 8]:

Proposition 4. *Let C and D be non-redundant correlations over $\mathcal{X} \times \mathcal{Y}$ and $\mathcal{U} \times \mathcal{V}$, respectively. If deterministic matrices A, B and stochastic matrices U and V satisfy (1); i.e., (A, B) is a perfect SNIR with U and V being the simulators for Alice and Bob, respectively, then*

$$V = \Delta_D^{-1}B^\mathsf{T}\Delta_C \qquad U = \Delta_{D^\mathsf{T}}^{-1}A^\mathsf{T}\Delta_{C^\mathsf{T}}. \qquad (9)$$

In [1], the authors observed that the algorithms employed by Alice and Bob in a perfect SNIR (to a non-redundant target) is determinsitic. Furthermore, given a probabilistic statistical SNIR, one can construct a deterministic SNIR with a slightly worse correctness and security error. This observation is crucially used in proving our main result.

Lemma 1 *([1, Lemma 7]). Let D be non-redundant correlation over $\mathcal{U} \times \mathcal{V}$ and C be a correlation over $\mathcal{X} \times \mathcal{Y}$. For any $\epsilon \geq 0$, if there exist stochastic matrices A, B, U and V such that*

$$\|A^\mathsf{T}CB - D\|_{1,1} \leq \epsilon \qquad \|A^\mathsf{T}C - DV\|_{1,1} \leq \epsilon \qquad \|CB - U^\mathsf{T}D\|_{1,1} \leq \epsilon$$

then there exist deterministic stochastic matrices $\bar{A}, \bar{B}$ such that,

$$\|\bar{A}^\mathsf{T}C\bar{B} - D\|_{1,1} \leq O_D(\sqrt{\epsilon}),$$
$$\|\bar{A}^\mathsf{T}C - DV\|_{1,1} \leq O_D(\sqrt{\epsilon}),$$
$$\|C\bar{B} - U^\mathsf{T}D\|_{1,1} \leq O_D(\sqrt{\epsilon}).$$

We recall the definitions coined in [1] relating to spectral protocols:

Definition 9 (Spectral decomposition of a correlation). For a correlation H distributed over $\mathcal{X} \times \mathcal{Y}$, its spectral decomposition $\widetilde{H}$ is a $\mathcal{X} \times \mathcal{Y}$ dimensional matrix

$$\widetilde{H} = \boldsymbol{\Delta}_{H^{\mathsf{T}}}^{-\frac{1}{2}} H \boldsymbol{\Delta}_{H}^{-\frac{1}{2}}.$$

Define $\boldsymbol{\Sigma}_H$, $\boldsymbol{\Psi}_H$ and $\boldsymbol{\Phi}_H$ to be given by a canonical singular value decomposition of $\widetilde{H}$, so that $\boldsymbol{\Sigma}_H$ is an $[\![|\mathcal{X}|]\!] \times [\![|\mathcal{Y}|]\!]$ dimensional non-negative diagonal matrix with the diagonal sorted in descending order, $\boldsymbol{\Psi}_H$ and $\boldsymbol{\Phi}_H$ are unitary matrices of dimensions $[\![|\mathcal{X}|]\!] \times \mathcal{X}$ and $[\![|\mathcal{Y}|]\!] \times \mathcal{Y}$, respectively, and

$$\widetilde{H} = \boldsymbol{\Psi}_H^{\mathsf{T}} \boldsymbol{\Sigma}_H \boldsymbol{\Phi}_H.$$

Finally, define $F_H = \boldsymbol{\Psi}_H \, \boldsymbol{\Delta}_{H^{\mathsf{T}}}^{1/2}$. ◁

The following properties of the spectral decomposition of a correlation were observed in [1].

Lemma 2 ([1, Lemma 9]). *Let $|\mathcal{X}| \leq |\mathcal{Y}|$ and H be a correlation over $\mathcal{X} \times \mathcal{Y}$. Then,*

(i) $1 = (\boldsymbol{\Sigma}_H)_{(0,0)} \geq (\boldsymbol{\Sigma}_H)_{(1,1)} \geq \ldots \geq (\boldsymbol{\Sigma}_H)_{(|\mathcal{X}|-1,|\mathcal{X}|-1)} \geq 0$. *Furthermore, if H is common information free, then $(\boldsymbol{\Sigma}_H)_{(1,1)} < 1$.*

(ii) *For all $\lambda \in (0,1)$, there exists $\delta > 0$ such that for all $n \in \mathbb{N}$ and for all $\alpha \in [\![|\mathcal{X}|]\!]$, either $\lambda = (\boldsymbol{\Sigma}_H)_{(\alpha,\alpha)}$ or $|\lambda - (\boldsymbol{\Sigma}_H)_{(\alpha,\alpha)}| > \delta$.*

Similar to the correlations, the SNIR protocol also allows a spectral decomposition, which we now define.

Definition 10 (Spectral Image of SNIR). Let D be a non-redundant correlation over $\mathcal{U} \times \mathcal{V}$, and C be a correlation over $\mathcal{X} \times \mathcal{Y}$. The *spectral image* of an SNIR (A, B) from D to C is $(\widehat{A}, \widehat{B})$, where $\widehat{A}$ and $\widehat{B}$ are matrices of dimensions $[\![|\mathcal{X}|]\!] \times [\![|\mathcal{U}|]\!]$ and $[\![|\mathcal{Y}|]\!] \times [\![|\mathcal{V}|]\!]$, respectively, defined as

$$\widehat{A} = F_C A F_D^{-1} \qquad\qquad \widehat{B} = G_C B G_D^{-1}. \qquad ◁$$

A crucial observation we make in this paper is that the columns of $\widehat{A}$ can be interpreted as a *generalized Fourier Transform* applied to the columns of a matrix derived from A. Loosely speaking, the following lemma in [1] shows that this Fourier spectrum is mostly concentrated on specific coefficients.

Lemma 3 ([1, Lemma 11]). *Suppose a non-redundant correlation D over $\mathcal{U} \times \mathcal{V}$ has a deterministic ϵ-SNIR (A, B) to C over $\mathcal{X} \times \mathcal{Y}$. Then, for all $\beta \in [\![|\mathcal{U}|]\!]$,*

$$\sum_{\substack{\alpha \in [\![|\mathcal{X}|]\!] \\ (\boldsymbol{\Sigma}_C)_{(\alpha,\alpha)} \neq (\boldsymbol{\Sigma}_D)_{(\beta,\beta)}}} \left((\boldsymbol{\Sigma}_C \boldsymbol{\Sigma}_C^{\mathsf{T}})_{(\alpha,\alpha)} - (\boldsymbol{\Sigma}_D \boldsymbol{\Sigma}_D^{\mathsf{T}})_{(\beta,\beta)} \right)^2 \left(\widehat{A}_{(\alpha,\beta)} \right)^2 = O_D(\epsilon).$$

Finally, we import a lemma that shows that presence of common randomness does not help in SNIR.

Lemma 4 ([1, Theorem 6]). *Let $C_w = \begin{bmatrix} 1/2 & 0 \\ 0 & 1/2 \end{bmatrix}$ be the 1-bit common randomness correlation. If a non-redundant common-information free correlation D has a statistical SNIR to $C_w \otimes C$ for a correlation C, then D also has a statistical SNIR to C.*

4   Decidability of SNIR

4.1   Statistical to Perfect Security

The crucial observation we make to show the decidability of SNIR is that a statistical reduction from D to C implies a deterministic perfect reduction from D to a constant number of copies of C. This is the main result of this section.

Theorem 1. *A non-redundant correlation D over $\mathcal{U} \times \mathcal{V}$ has a statistical SNIR to a common information free correlation C over $\mathcal{X} \times \mathcal{Y}$ if and only if, for a constant $\ell \in \mathbb{N}$ that depends only on D and C, D has a perfect SNIR to $C^{\otimes \ell}$.*

The proof of the theorem follows the outline presented in the technical overview. Without loss of generality, we assume that $|\mathcal{U}| \leq |\mathcal{V}|$ and focus on an ϵ-SNIR (for an arbitrary $\epsilon \geq 0$) implied by the assumption that D has a statistical SNIR to C. We make several observations about the spectral image of such an ϵ-SNIR (A, B) from D to (say) $C = C^{\otimes n}$ as defined in Definition 10. Since $|\mathcal{U}| \leq |\mathcal{V}|$, it is sufficient to focus on Alice's spectral protocol $\widehat{A} = F_C A F_D^{-1}$. In Lemma 6, we establish that F_C is a Fourier transform operator for the normed vector space $L^2(\mathcal{X}^n, \pi)$, where $\pi = C\mathbf{1}$ is the marginal of C at Alice. This makes $\widehat{A}$ the Fourier transform of the "half-way spectral protocol" AF_D^{-1} with respect to this operator. In Lemma 7, we use the properties of spectral protocols established in [1]–restated here as Lemma 3–to show that the columns of AF_D^{-1} associated with non-zero singular values of D concentrate most of their energy in the lower degree coefficients. We focus on this sub-matrix of AF_D^{-1} given by $A\check{F}_D$. Lemma 5 shows that each column of A is completely determined by the corresponding row of this sub-matrix. At this point, we appeal to a "generalized junta theorem" stated as Theorem 2 to argue that each column of $A\check{F}_D$ can be approximated by a junta–a vector in $\mathcal{X}^n$ that depends only on a constant number of coordinates of $\mathcal{X}^n$. Since A is determined by $A\check{F}_D$ which itself is close to a junta, A itself is close to a junta. Finally, in Lemma 8, we show that if Alice's protocol A 'almost entirely' depends only on a small subset of copies of the correlations in a sequence of SNIR protocols with progressively better security error, then there is a perfectly secure SNIR, concluding the proof.

We state the lemmas mentioned above which imply the theorem.

Lemma 5. *Let D be a non-degenerate correlation over $\mathcal{U} \times \mathcal{V}$, and let $(\Sigma_D)_{(\beta,\beta)} > 0$ if and only if $\beta < k \leq |\mathcal{U}|$. Define $\check{F}_D \in \mathbb{R}^{\mathcal{U} \times [\![k]\!]}$ such that*

$$(\check{F}_D)_{(\cdot,\beta)} = \left(F_D^{-1}\right)_{(\cdot,\beta)} \qquad\qquad \forall \beta \in [\![k]\!]. \tag{10}$$

There exists a function $\phi : \mathbb{R}^{[\![k]\!]} \to \{0,1\}^{\mathcal{U}}$ such that, for any $\mathcal{R}$ and $\mathcal{R} \times \mathcal{U}$ dimensional deterministic matrix A,

$$A_{(r,\cdot)} = \phi\left(A_{(r,\cdot)}\check{F}_D\right) \qquad\qquad \forall r \in \mathcal{R}. \tag{11}$$

Proof: For any $r \in \mathcal{R}$, the row $A_{(r,\cdot)}$ is a basis vector since A is a deterministic stochastic matrix. Fix $r \in \mathcal{R}$ and let $A_{(r,\cdot)} = \boldsymbol{\xi}_u^{\mathsf{T}}$ for some fixed u. Then, $A_{(r,\cdot)}\check{F}_D = \boldsymbol{\xi}_u^{\mathsf{T}}\check{F}_D = (\check{F}_D)_{(u,\cdot)}$. Suppose all the rows of $\check{F}_D$ are distinct, i.e., $(\check{F}_D)_{(u_1,\cdot)} \neq (\check{F}_D)_{(u_2,\cdot)}$ whenever $u_1 \neq u_2$. Consider the map $\phi : (\check{F}_D)_{(u,\cdot)} \mapsto \boldsymbol{\xi}_u$ for all u (and is otherwise defined arbitrarily). Then, $\phi\left(A_{(r,\cdot)}\check{F}_D\right) = A_{(r,\cdot)}$ for all r. Thus, there exists ϕ as required in the lemma whenever all the rows of $\check{F}_D$ are distinct.

The proof is completed by showing that D is degenerate if there exist $u_1, u_2 \in \mathcal{U}$ such that $(\check{F}_D)_{(u_1,\cdot)} = (\check{F}_D)_{(u_2,\cdot)}$.

$$\begin{aligned}
\Delta_{D^{\mathsf{T}}}^{-1}D &= \Delta_{D^{\mathsf{T}}}^{-1}\left(\Delta_{D^{\mathsf{T}}}^{1/2}\tilde{D}\Delta_{D^{\mathsf{T}}}^{1/2}\right) \\
&= \Delta_{D^{\mathsf{T}}}^{-1/2}\Psi_D^{\mathsf{T}}\Sigma_D\Phi_D\Delta_{D^{\mathsf{T}}}^{1/2} \\
&= \sum_{\beta:(\Sigma_D)_{(\beta,\beta)}>0} (\Sigma_D)_{(\beta,\beta)}\left(F_D^{-1}\right)_{(\cdot,\beta)} \cdot \left(\Phi_D\Delta_{D^{\mathsf{T}}}^{1/2}\right)_{(\beta,\cdot)}.
\end{aligned}$$

The last equality used the outer product expansion of $\Delta_{D^{\mathsf{T}}}^{-1/2}\Psi_D^{\mathsf{T}}\Sigma_D\Phi_D\Delta_{D^{\mathsf{T}}}^{1/2}$ with respect to the diagonal matrix Σ_D. Since $(\check{F}_D)_{(u_1,\cdot)} = (\check{F}_D)_{(u_2,\cdot)}$, substituting $\check{F}_D = F_D^{-1}$ in the above equation,

$$\begin{aligned}
\left(\Delta_{D^{\mathsf{T}}}^{-1}D\right)_{(u_1,\cdot)} &= \sum_{\beta:(\Sigma_D)_{(\beta,\beta)}>0} (\Sigma_D)_{(\beta,\beta)}\left(\check{F}_D\right)_{(u_1,\beta)} \cdot \left(\Phi_D\Delta_{D^{\mathsf{T}}}^{1/2}\right)_{(\beta,\cdot)} \\
&= \sum_{\beta:(\Sigma_D)_{(\beta,\beta)}>0} (\Sigma_D)_{(\beta,\beta)}\left(\check{F}_D\right)_{(u_2,\beta)} \cdot \left(\Phi_D\Delta_{D^{\mathsf{T}}}^{1/2}\right)_{(\beta,\cdot)} \\
&= \left(\Delta_{D^{\mathsf{T}}}^{-1}D\right)_{(u_2,\cdot)}.
\end{aligned}$$

But then,

$$D_{(u_1,\cdot)} = \frac{(\Delta_{D^{\mathsf{T}}})_{(u_1,u_1)}}{(\Delta_{D^{\mathsf{T}}})_{(u_2,u_2)}}D_{(u_2,\cdot)};$$

hence, D is degenerate. $\qquad\square$

Lemma 6. *Let C be the n-wise product of a correlation C over $\mathcal{X} \times \mathcal{Y}$ for some $n \in \mathbb{N}$; i.e., $C = C^{\otimes n}$. Rows of $\Gamma = \left(\Psi_C\Delta_{C^{\mathsf{T}}}^{-1/2}\right)$ form a generalized Fourier basis of the normed vector space $L^2(\mathcal{X}^n, \boldsymbol{\pi})$, where $\boldsymbol{\pi} = C\mathbf{1}$.*

Proof: For any $\alpha, \alpha' \in [\![|\mathcal{X}|]\!]^n$,

$$
\begin{aligned}
\left\langle \Gamma_{(\alpha,\cdot)}, \Gamma_{(\alpha',\cdot)} \right\rangle_\pi &= \sum_{x \in \mathcal{X}^n} \pi_x\, \Gamma_{(\alpha,x)}\, \Gamma_{(\alpha',x)} = \Gamma_{(\alpha,\cdot)}\, \Delta_{C^\intercal}\, (\Gamma^\intercal)_{(\cdot,\alpha')} \\
&= \left(\Psi_C \Delta_{C^\intercal}^{-1/2} \right)_{(\alpha,\cdot)} \Delta_{C^\intercal} \left(\Delta_{C^\intercal}^{-1/2} \Psi_C^\intercal \right)_{(\cdot,\alpha')} \\
&= \left(\left(\Psi_C \Delta_{C^\intercal}^{-1/2} \right) \Delta_{C^\intercal} \left(\Delta_{C^\intercal}^{-1/2} \Psi_C^\intercal \right) \right)_{(\alpha,\alpha')} \\
&= \begin{cases} 1 & \text{if } \alpha = \alpha', \\ 0 & \text{if } \alpha \neq \alpha'. \end{cases}
\end{aligned}
$$

We now show that $\Gamma_{(\mathbf{0},\cdot)} = \mathbf{1}^\intercal$. In the context of Lemma 1 in [1] and its proof, we observe that $\mathcal{L}(G_C)$ has an eigenvalue 0 corresponding to eigenvector $[(\mathbf{1}^\intercal \cdot C^\intercal)^{1/2}, (\mathbf{1}^\intercal \cdot C)^{1/2}]^\intercal$, and thus $((\mathbf{1}^\intercal \cdot C^\intercal)^{1/2})^\intercal = (C \cdot \mathbf{1})^{1/2}$ is a left singular vector of $\widetilde{C}$ corresponding to singular value 1. Assuming C has a single connected component, we get that the multiplicity of 1 in Λ_C is only one, and this is the maximum singular value as well, implying $(\Psi_C^\intercal)_{(\cdot,0)} = (C \cdot \mathbf{1})^{1/2}$, i.e., $(\Psi_C)_{(\mathbf{0},\cdot)} = (\mathbf{1}^\intercal \cdot C^\intercal)^{1/2}$. We then have

$$
\Gamma_{(\mathbf{0},\cdot)} = \left(\Psi_C \Delta_{C^\intercal}^{-1/2} \right)_{(\mathbf{0},\cdot)} = (\Psi_C)_{(\mathbf{0},\cdot)} \Delta_{C^\intercal}^{-1/2} = (\mathbf{1}^\intercal \cdot C^\intercal)^{1/2} \Delta_{C^\intercal}^{-1/2} = \mathbf{1}^\intercal.
$$

Thus, the rows of Γ form a generalized Fourier basis of $L^2(\mathcal{X}^n, \pi)$. Finally, by Proposition 1, $\Gamma \operatorname{diag}(\pi) = \left(\Psi_C \Delta_{C^\intercal}^{-1/2} \right) \Delta_{C^\intercal} = F_C$ is a Fourier transform operator for Γ in $L^2(\mathcal{X}^n, \pi)$. $\qquad\square$

Lemma 7. *Let D be a non-redundant correlation over $\mathcal{U} \times \mathcal{V}$ and $C = C^{\otimes n}$ be the n-wise product of a common information free correlation C over $\mathcal{X} \times \mathcal{Y}$. If (A, B) is a deterministic ϵ-SNIR from D to C, then there exists a number $d \in \mathbb{N}$ that depends only on C and D (and not on n) such that, for each β such that $(\Sigma_D)_{(\beta,\beta)} > 0$, the vector $a_\beta = \left(A F_D^{-1} \right)_{(\cdot,\beta)} \in L^2(\mathcal{X}^n, \pi)$, where $\pi = C\mathbf{1}$, satisfies $\|a_\beta^{>d}\|^2 \leq O_D(\sqrt{\epsilon})$.*

Proof: Consider the Fourier basis Γ of $L^2(\mathcal{X}^n, \pi)$ described in Lemma 6 and its Fourier transform operator $F_C = \Psi_C \Delta_{C^\intercal}^{1/2}$. By Definition 10, Fourier transform of a_β for any β w.r.t. Γ is given by

$$
\widehat{a_\beta} = F_C a_\beta = F_C \left(A F_D^{-1} \right)_{(\cdot,\beta)} = \widehat{A}_{(\cdot,\beta)}. \tag{12}
$$

By Lemma 3, for $\alpha \in [\![|\mathcal{X}|]\!]^n$,

$$
\sum_{\substack{\alpha \in [\![|\mathcal{X}|]\!]^n \\ (\Sigma_C)_{(\alpha,\alpha)} \neq (\Sigma_D)_{(\beta,\beta)}}} \left((\Sigma_C \Sigma_C^\intercal)_{(\alpha,\alpha)} - (\Sigma_D \Sigma_D^\intercal)_{(\beta,\beta)} \right)^2 \left(\widehat{A}_{(\alpha,\beta)} \right)^2 = O_D(\epsilon). \tag{13}
$$

By Lemma 2 (ii), $\exists \delta > 0$ such that, for any α, β, s.t. $(\Sigma_C)_{(\alpha,\alpha)} \neq (\Sigma_D)_{(\beta,\beta)}$ and $(\Sigma_D)_{(\beta,\beta)} > 0$,

$$(\Sigma_C)_{(\alpha,\alpha)} + (\Sigma_D)_{(\beta,\beta)} \geq \left| (\Sigma_C)_{(\alpha,\alpha)} - (\Sigma_D)_{(\beta,\beta)} \right| \geq \delta.$$

Using this in (13), for any β s.t. $(\Sigma_D)_{(\beta,\beta)} > 0$,

$$
O_D(\epsilon) = \sum_{\alpha : (\Sigma_C)_{(\alpha,\alpha)} \neq (\Sigma_D)_{(\beta,\beta)}} \left((\Sigma_C)^2_{(\alpha,\alpha)} - (\Sigma_D)^2_{(\beta,\beta)} \right)^2 \left(\widehat{A}_{(\alpha,\beta)} \right)^2
$$

$$
\geq \sum_{\alpha : (\Sigma_C)_{(\alpha,\alpha)} \neq (\Sigma_D)_{(\beta,\beta)}} \delta^2 \left(\widehat{A}_{(\alpha,\beta)} \right)^2.
$$

If there exists $d \in \mathbb{N}$ that depends only on C and D (and not on n) such that $(\Sigma_C)_{(\alpha,\alpha)} \neq (\Sigma_D)_{(\beta,\beta)}$ whenever $\deg(\alpha) > d$, by the above bound and (12),

$$
\sum_{\alpha : \deg(\alpha) > d} (\widehat{a_\beta})^2_\alpha = \frac{1}{\delta^2} \sum_{\alpha : \deg(\alpha) > d} \delta^2 \left(\widehat{A}_{(\alpha,\beta)} \right)^2 = O_D(\epsilon).
$$

Hence, it is sufficient to show that such a $d \in \mathbb{N}$ exists. By Lemma 2, when C is common-information free, there exists $\lambda < 1$ such that $(\Sigma_C)_{(\alpha,\alpha)} \leq \lambda$ for all $1 \leq \alpha < |\mathcal{X}|$. Hence, for $\alpha \in [\![|\mathcal{X}|]\!]^{[n]}$, (recalling $\Sigma_C = \Sigma_{C^{\otimes n}} = \Sigma_C^{\otimes n}$),

$$
(\Sigma_C)_{(\alpha,\alpha)} = \prod_{i \in [n]} (\Sigma_C)_{(\alpha_i,\alpha_i)} \leq \prod_{\substack{i \in [n] \\ \alpha_i \neq 0}} \lambda \leq \lambda^{\deg(\alpha)}.
$$

Choose d such that $(\Sigma_D)_{(\beta,\beta)} \geq \lambda^d$ for all β s.t. $(\Sigma_D)_{(\beta,\beta)} > 0$. Then, $(\Sigma_C)_{(\alpha,\alpha)} \neq (\Sigma_D)_{(\beta,\beta)}$ whenever $\deg(\alpha) > d$. This concludes the proof.   □

Theorem 2 (Generalized Junta Theorem). *Let (Ω, π) be a finite probability space, $|\Omega| = m \geq 2$, in which every outcome has probability at least λ. Let $\mathcal{T}$ be a finite set and let $d \geq 1$. If $f \in L^2(\Omega^n, \pi^{\otimes n})$ is a $\mathcal{T}$-valued function such that $\|f^{>d}\|^2 = \epsilon$, then there exists a $\mathcal{T}$-valued degree d function $h \in L^2(\Omega^n, \pi^{\otimes n})$, such that $\Pr[f \neq h] = O(\epsilon)$, and h depends on $O(1)$ coordinates.*

Lemma 8. *Let D be a non-redundant correlation over $\mathcal{U} \times \mathcal{V}$ and C be a correlation over $\mathcal{X} \times \mathcal{Y}$. Suppose, for each $i \in \mathbb{N}$, there is an ϵ_i-SNIR (A_i, B_i) from D to $C^{\otimes n_i}$ such that $\epsilon_i \to 0$ as $i \to \infty$. For each i, suppose there exists $\mathcal{S}_i \subset [n_i], |\mathcal{S}_i| = \ell$ and a deterministic matrix $\tilde{A}_i$ such that*

$$(\tilde{A}_i)_{(\boldsymbol{x},\cdot)} = (\tilde{A}_i)_{(\boldsymbol{x}',\cdot)} \text{ for all } \boldsymbol{x}, \boldsymbol{x}' \text{ s.t. } \boldsymbol{x}_j = \boldsymbol{x}'_j \text{ for all } j \in \mathcal{S}_i,$$

and, when $\pi_i = C^{\otimes n_i} \mathbf{1}$, it holds that

$$P_{\boldsymbol{x} \sim \pi_i} \left[(\tilde{A}_i)_{(\boldsymbol{x},\cdot)} \neq (A_i)_{(\boldsymbol{x},\cdot)} \right] \leq \epsilon_i. \tag{14}$$

Then, D has a perfect SNIR to $C^{\otimes \ell}$.

Proof: Fix $i \in \mathbb{N}$. By Proposition 2, there are stochastic matrices U_i and V_i such that

$$\|A_i^\mathsf{T} C^{\otimes n} - DV_i\|_{1,1} \le \epsilon_i \qquad\qquad \|C^{\otimes n} B_i - U_i^\mathsf{T} D\|_{1,1} \le \epsilon_i.$$

Since i is fixed, we will drop the subscript i and denote $n_i, \pi_i, A_i, \tilde{A}_i$ by $n, \pi, A, \tilde{A}$, and so on. Also, we will denote $C^{\otimes n}$ by C. We have,

$$\begin{aligned}
\|A^\mathsf{T} C - \tilde{A}^\mathsf{T} C\|_{1,1} &= \mathbf{1}^\mathsf{T} |(A - \tilde{A})^\mathsf{T} C| \mathbf{1} \\
&\le \mathbf{1}^\mathsf{T} |(A - \tilde{A})^\mathsf{T}| C \mathbf{1} = \mathbf{1}^\mathsf{T} |(A - \tilde{A})^\mathsf{T}| \pi.
\end{aligned}$$

The final equality used the definition $\pi_i = C^{\otimes n_i} \mathbf{1}$.

$$\begin{aligned}
\mathbf{1}^\mathsf{T} |(A - \tilde{A})^\mathsf{T}| \pi &= \sum_{x : A_{(x,\cdot)} \neq \tilde{A}_{(x,\cdot)}} \mathbf{1}^\mathsf{T} \left(|A - \tilde{A}|_{(x,\cdot)} \right)^\mathsf{T} \pi_x \\
&\overset{(a)}{\le} 2 \sum_{x : A_{(x,\cdot)} \neq \tilde{A}_{(x,\cdot)}} \pi_x \\
&= 2 \mathrm{P}_{x \sim \pi} \left[(\tilde{A}_i)_{(x,\cdot)} \neq (A_i)_{(x,\cdot)} \right] \overset{(b)}{\le} 2\epsilon_i.
\end{aligned}$$

Here, (a) used the fact $\mathbf{1}^\mathsf{T} \left(|A - \tilde{A}|_{(x,\cdot)} \right)^\mathsf{T} = 2$ whenever $A_{(x,\cdot)} \neq \tilde{A}_{(x,\cdot)}$ since A and $\tilde{A}$ are stochastic matrices; (b) used (14). Thus, we have argued that $\|A^\mathsf{T} C - \tilde{A}^\mathsf{T} C\|_{1,1} \le 2\epsilon_i$. Since $B\mathbf{1} = \mathbf{1}$, this further implies that $\|A^\mathsf{T} CB - \tilde{A}^\mathsf{T} CB\|_{1,1} \le 2\epsilon_i$. But then,

$$\begin{aligned}
\|\tilde{A}^\mathsf{T} CB - D\|_{1,1} &\le \|\tilde{A}^\mathsf{T} CB - A^\mathsf{T} CB\|_{1,1} + \|A^\mathsf{T} CB - D\|_{1,1} \le 3\epsilon_i, \\
\|\tilde{A}^\mathsf{T} C - DV\|_{1,1} &\le \|\tilde{A}^\mathsf{T} C - A^\mathsf{T} C\|_{1,1} + \|A^\mathsf{T} C - D\|_{1,1} \le 3\epsilon_i, \\
\|CB - U^\mathsf{T} D\|_{1,1} &\le \epsilon_i.
\end{aligned}$$

Thus, $(\tilde{A}, B)$ is a $3\epsilon_i$-SNIR from D to C.

From $(\tilde{A}, B)$, we derive an SNIR that uses only ℓ copies C but retains the same security guarantees as the original reduction. We argue this part from a cryptographic perspective: Consider the protocols $\tilde{\mathfrak{A}} : \mathcal{X}^n \to \mathcal{U}$ and $\mathfrak{B} : \mathcal{Y}^n \to \mathcal{V}$ corresponding to the stochastic matrices $\tilde{A}$ and B, respectively. If $x, x' \in \mathcal{X}^n$ are such that $x_i = x_i'$ for all $i \in \mathcal{S}$, then $\tilde{A}_{(x,\cdot)} = \tilde{A}_{(x',\cdot)}$. Equivalently, $\tilde{\mathfrak{A}}(x)$ and $\tilde{\mathfrak{A}}(x')$ are identically distributed for such x, x'. In other words, $\tilde{\mathfrak{A}}$ depends only on $\mathcal{X}^\mathcal{S}$. If we remove the copies of C that are ignored by $\mathfrak{A}$ and have $\mathfrak{B}$ sample its side of C for these copies from the marginal distribution, we obtain a protocol that depends only on $|\mathcal{S}| = \ell$ many copies of C and is at least as secure as the original SNIR. Let the deterministic protocol obtained by restricting $\tilde{\mathfrak{A}}$ to $\mathcal{X}^\mathcal{S}$ be called $\mathfrak{A}'$, and the stochastic (not necessarily deterministic) protocol obtained by restricting $\mathfrak{B}$ to $\mathcal{Y}^\mathcal{S}$ be called $\mathfrak{B}'$. Then, (A', B') is a $3\epsilon_i$-SNIR from D to $C^{\otimes \ell}$.

For each $i \in \mathbb{N}$, we constructed $3\epsilon_i$-SNIR (A'_i, B'_i) from D to $C^{\otimes \ell}$. But then, for each $i \in \mathbb{N}$, by Lemma 1, there exist deterministic matrices $\bar{A}_i \in \{0,1\}^{\mathcal{X}^\ell \times \mathcal{U}}$ and $\bar{B}_i \in \{0,1\}^{\mathcal{Y}^\ell \times \mathcal{V}}$ such that $(\bar{A}_i, \bar{B}_i)$ is a $O_D(\sqrt{\epsilon_i})$-SNIR from D to $C^{\otimes \ell}$. Since ℓ is a constant, there exist only a finite number of choices of $\bar{A}_i \in \{0,1\}^{\mathcal{X}^\ell \times \mathcal{U}}$ and $\bar{B}_i \in \{0,1\}^{\mathcal{Y}^\ell \times \mathcal{V}}$, and hence there exist deterministic matrices A^* and B^* such that (A^*, B^*) is a perfect SNIR from D to $C^{\otimes \ell}$. $\square$

Proof of Theorem 1. If D has a statistical SNIR to C, there is a sequence of protocols $(A_i, B_i)_{i \in \mathbb{N}}$ such that, for each $i \in \mathbb{N}$, (A_i, B_i) is an ϵ_i-SNIR from D to $C^{\otimes n_i}$ and $\epsilon_i \to 0$ as $i \to \infty$.

Fix $i \in \mathbb{N}$; we drop the subscript from $n_i, A_i, B_i, \epsilon_i$ and simply use n, A, B, ϵ instead. We denote $C^{\otimes n_i}$ by C and $C1$ by π. Consider the normed vector space $L^2(\mathcal{X}^n, \pi)$. Suppose $(\Sigma_D)_{(\beta,\beta)} > 0$ if and only if $\beta \in [\![k]\!] \subseteq [\![|\mathcal{U}|]\!]$. Define

$$\mathcal{T}_D = \left\{ \left(F_D^{-1}\right)_{(u,\beta)} : u \in \mathcal{U}, \beta \in [\![k]\!] \right\}.$$

For each $\beta \in [\![k]\!]$, define $\boldsymbol{a}_\beta \in \mathcal{T}_D^{\mathcal{X}^n}$ as

$$\boldsymbol{a}_\beta = \left(AF_D^{-1}\right)_{(\cdot, \beta)} \in L^2(\mathcal{X}^n, \pi).$$

By Lemma 7, there exists d that depends only on D and C (and not on n) such that $\|\boldsymbol{a}_u^{\geq d}\|_2 \leq O_D(\epsilon)$. By Theorem 2, for each $\beta \in [\![k]\!]$, there exists $\widetilde{\boldsymbol{a}_\beta} \in \mathcal{T}_D^{\mathcal{X}^n}$ and $\mathcal{S}_\beta \subset [n], |\mathcal{S}_\beta| = l$ where l depends only on d, C and $\mathcal{T}_D$ such that, $(\widetilde{\boldsymbol{a}_\beta})_{\boldsymbol{x}} = (\widetilde{\boldsymbol{a}_\beta})_{\boldsymbol{x}'}$, for all $\boldsymbol{x}, \boldsymbol{x}' \in \mathcal{X}^n$ such that $x_i = x'_i$ for all $i \in \mathcal{S}$, and

$$P_{\boldsymbol{x} \sim \pi} \left[(\boldsymbol{a}_\beta)_{\boldsymbol{x}} \neq (\widetilde{\boldsymbol{a}_\beta})_{\boldsymbol{x}} \right] = O_D(\epsilon). \tag{15}$$

Since D is non-redundant, by Lemma 5, there exists $\phi : \mathcal{T}_D^{[\![k]\!]} \to \mathbb{R}^\mathcal{U}$ such that for all $\boldsymbol{x} \in \mathcal{X}^n$,

$$A_{(\boldsymbol{x}, \cdot)} = \phi\left((\boldsymbol{a}_0)_{\boldsymbol{x}}, (\boldsymbol{a}_1)_{\boldsymbol{x}}, \ldots, (\boldsymbol{a}_k)_{\boldsymbol{x}}\right) \tag{16}$$

Hence,

$$\begin{aligned}
P_{\boldsymbol{x} \sim \pi} \left[A_{(\boldsymbol{x}, \cdot)} \neq \phi((\hat{\boldsymbol{a}_0})_{\boldsymbol{x}}, \ldots, (\hat{\boldsymbol{a}_k})_{\boldsymbol{x}}) \right] &\leq P_{\boldsymbol{x} \sim \pi} \left[\exists \beta : (\widetilde{\boldsymbol{a}_\beta})_{\boldsymbol{x}} \neq (\boldsymbol{a}_\beta)_{\boldsymbol{x}} \right] \\
&\leq \sum_{\beta \in [\![k]\!]} P_{\boldsymbol{x} \sim \pi} \left[(\widetilde{\boldsymbol{a}_\beta})_{\boldsymbol{x}} \neq (\boldsymbol{a}_\beta)_{\boldsymbol{x}} \right] \\
&\overset{(a)}{=} O_D(\epsilon),
\end{aligned}$$

where (a) follows from (15). Define the deterministic matrix $\tilde{A} \in \{0,1\}^{\mathcal{X}^n \times \mathcal{U}}$ such that, for an arbitrary $u^* \in \mathcal{U}$ and for all $\boldsymbol{x} \in \mathcal{X}^n$,

$$\tilde{A}_{(\boldsymbol{x}, \cdot)} = \begin{cases} \phi\left((\boldsymbol{a}_0)_{\boldsymbol{x}}, \ldots, (\boldsymbol{a}_k)_{\boldsymbol{x}}\right) & \text{if } \phi\left((\boldsymbol{a}_0)_{\boldsymbol{x}}, \ldots, (\boldsymbol{a}_k)_{\boldsymbol{x}}\right) \in \{\boldsymbol{\xi}_u : u \in \mathcal{U}\}, \\ \boldsymbol{\xi}_{u^*} & \text{otherwise.} \end{cases}$$

Since A is a deterministic matrix, i.e., each row of A belongs to $\{\boldsymbol{\xi}_u : u \in \mathcal{U}\}$,

$$\mathrm{P}_{\boldsymbol{x} \sim \pi}\left[A_{(\boldsymbol{x}, \cdot)} \neq \tilde{A}_{(\boldsymbol{x}, \cdot)}\right] \leq \mathrm{P}_{\boldsymbol{x} \sim \pi}\left[A_{(\boldsymbol{x}, \cdot)} \neq \phi((\hat{a}_0)_{\boldsymbol{x}}, \ldots, (\hat{a}_k)_{\boldsymbol{x}})\right] = O_D(\epsilon).$$

Finally, since $\widehat{a}_\beta$ depends only on $\mathcal{X}^{\mathcal{S}_\beta}$ for each $\beta \in [\![k]\!]$, $\tilde{A}$ depends only on $\mathcal{X}^{\cup_{\beta \in [\![k]\!]} \mathcal{S}_\beta}$.

We have shown that, for each $i \in \mathbb{N}$, there exists a deterministic matrix $\tilde{A}_i \in \mathbb{R}^{\mathcal{X}^{n_i} \times \mathcal{U}}$ such that

$$(\tilde{A}_i)_{(\boldsymbol{x}, \cdot)} = (\tilde{A}_i)_{(\boldsymbol{x}', \cdot)} \, \forall \boldsymbol{x}, \boldsymbol{x}' \in \mathcal{X}^n \text{ s.t. } \boldsymbol{x}_j = \boldsymbol{x}'_j \text{ for all } j \in \bigcup_{\beta \in [\![k]\!]} \mathcal{S}_{i,\beta},$$

$$\text{and } \mathrm{P}_{\boldsymbol{x} \sim \pi_i}\left[(\tilde{A}_i)_{(\boldsymbol{x}, \cdot)} \neq (A_i)_{(\boldsymbol{x}, \cdot)}\right] \leq \epsilon_i,$$

where $\mathcal{S}_{i,\beta}$ corresponds to $\mathcal{S}_\beta$ considered for a fixed i in the above discussion. Since $\cup_{\beta \in [\![k]\!]} \mathcal{S}_{i,\beta} \leq (k+1)l = \ell$ for all $i \in \mathbb{N}$, the statement of the theorem follows from Lemma 8. $\qquad\qquad\qquad\qquad\qquad\qquad\qquad\qquad\qquad\quad$ □

4.2 An Algorithm for the SNIR Problem

In this section, we show that the SNIR problem is decidable. Theorem 1 showed that existence of a statistical SNIR implies that of a perfect SNIR when the source correlation is common information free and the target correlation is non-redundant. As previously observed, it is sufficient to study SNIR between non-redundant correlations. Next, we tackle source correlations with non-zero common information.

Dealing with Common Information. An early work [28] on *non-secure* non-interactive reduction by Witsenhausen characterized correlations with non-zero common information to be the *complete correlations*—correlations that can be used to derive any desired target correlation—for non-secure reductions. However, as intuition suggests, common information does not help when security is required. This was formally established in [1] and restated in this paper as Lemma 4. Using this result, we will show that decidability of SNIR between general correlations reduces to SNIR between common information free correlations.

Definition 11. For positive numbers $0 < \alpha_1 \leq \ldots \leq \alpha_k < 1$ that add up to 1, and common information free correlations $H_1, \ldots, H_k$, consider the correlation

$$H = \begin{bmatrix} \alpha_1 H_1 & 0 & \cdots & 0 \\ 0 & \alpha_2 H_2 & \cdots & 0 \\ \vdots & & \ddots & \vdots \\ 0 & 0 & \cdots & \alpha_k H_k \end{bmatrix}.$$

The *parallelization* of H, denoted by $H^{\|}$ is defined as

$$H^{\|} = H_1 \otimes H_2 \otimes \ldots \otimes H_k.$$

◁

$H^{\|}$ is a common information free correlation, and when H is non-redundant, $H^{\|}$ is also non-redundant.

Lemma 9. *Let C be a correlation with non-zero common information. A non-redundant correlation D (with or without common information) has a statistical SNIR to C if and only if $D^{\|}$ has a statistical SNIR to $C^{\|}$.*

Proof: Let $C_{\text{coin}} = \begin{bmatrix} 1/2 & 0 \\ 0 & 1/2 \end{bmatrix}$ be the 1-bit common randomness correlation. We will later show that, since C has non-zero common information, C has a statistical SNIR to $C_{\text{coin}} \otimes C^{\|}$ and vice-versa. By the composability of SNIR protocols, this implies that D has a statistical SNIR to C if and only if it has a statistical SNIR to $C_{\text{coin}} \otimes C^{\|}$. If D is common information free, then $D^{\|} = D$, and if D has non-zero common information, then D has a statistical SNIR to $C_{\text{coin}} \otimes D^{\|}$ and vice-versa, as in the case of C. Since common randomness can be (securely) sampled using common randomness, $C_{\text{coin}} \otimes D^{\|}$ has a statistical SNIR to $C_{\text{coin}} \otimes C^{\|}$ if and only if $D^{\|}$ has a statistical SNIR to $C_{\text{coin}} \otimes C^{\|}$. But, by Lemma 4, $D^{\|}$ has a statistical SNIR to $C_{\text{coin}} \otimes C^{\|}$ only if $D^{\|}$ has a statistical SNIR to $C^{\|}$. Since the other direction is trivially true, we have established the statement of the lemma.

It remains to show that C has a statistical SNIR to $C_{\text{coin}} \otimes C^{\|}$ and vice-versa. Observe that Alice and Bob can agree on the distribution π over $[k]$ such that $(\pi)_i = \alpha_i$ for all i with arbitrarily small error using sufficiently many copies of C_{coin}. But then, by sampling i according to π and then sampling according to C_i, Alice and Bob have essentially sampled according to C.

To sample $C_{\text{coin}} \otimes C$ using C, Alice and Bob approximate (with arbitrarily small error) the 1-bit common randomness correlation C_{coin} using the sufficiently many copies of π distribution that they (implicitly) share. Furthermore, with probability $\prod_{i=1}^{k} \alpha_i$, the distribution $C^{\otimes l}$ is distributed according to $C_1 \otimes \ldots \otimes C_k$. Hence, Alice and Bob can approximately sample (with arbitrarily small error) from $C_{\text{coin}} \otimes C$ using sufficiently many copies of C. It is easily verified that both the above mentioned sampling schemes are secure, concluding the proof. □

Putting Things Together. Now we can put together our results so far into an algorithm for the SNIR problem.

1. Given a pair of correlations (C, D) as input, proceed as follows.
2. First replace D by its core and proceed (see Proposition 3). In the following we assume D is non-redundant.
3. If C has non-zero common information, then replace C by $C^{\|}$ and D by $D^{\|}$ (see Lemma 9). (Else retain both C and D unchanged.) In the following we assume C has no common information.
4. Compute $\ell \in \mathbb{N}$ associated with C and D, as stated in Theorem 1. Let $C = C^{\otimes \ell}$.
5. For every pair of (deterministic) matrices $A \in \{0,1\}^{\mathcal{X}^\ell \times \mathcal{U}}$ and $B \in \{0,1\}^{\mathcal{Y}^\ell \times \mathcal{V}}$, check if (A, B) is a perfect SNIR from D to C, using Proposition 4. That is,

compute $V = \Delta_D^{-1} B^\mathsf{T} \Delta_C$ and $U = \Delta_{D^\mathsf{T}}^{-1} A^\mathsf{T} \Delta_{C^\mathsf{T}}$, and check if A, B, U, and V satisfy the conditions in (1). If any pair is a perfect SNIR, accept the input and halt.
6. Else, reject the input and halt.

Steps 2 and 3 are justified by Proposition 3 and Lemma 9 respectively. Then, at the end of Step 3, given a non-redundant D and C with no common information, and the rest of the algorithm is justified by Theorem 1. This leads us to the main result of this paper:

Theorem 3. *The SNIR problem is decidable.*

4.3 More Necessary Conditions

As mentioned in Sect. 2, even given an algorithm for the SNIR problem, there is value in simple necessary conditions for an SNIR to exist. Here we present a new condition, exploiting Theorem 1.

A Concrete Example. The motivation for our new condition is the question of whether there is a statistical SNIR of the OT correlation (or more generally, any Oblivious Linear-Function Evaluation (OLE) correlation) to the (string) erasure correlation. We formally define these correlations before formally stating our resolution of the above question (in the negative).

(String) Erasure Correlation. An n-bit string erasure correlation with erasure probability $p \in (0, 1)$, denoted by SEC_l^p, is a correlation over $\{0,1\}^l \times (\{0,1\}^l \cup \{\bot\})$ such that, for all $x \in \{0,1\}^l$,

$$(\mathsf{SEC}_l^p)_{(x,y)} = \begin{cases} \frac{1-p}{2^l} & \text{if } y = x, \\ \frac{p}{2^l} & \text{if } y = \bot. \end{cases}$$

OLE Correlation. The OLE correlation (or Oblivious Linear-Function Evaluation) over a finite field or ring $\mathbb{F}$ is the correlation $\mathsf{OLE}_\mathbb{F}$ over the domain $\mathbb{F}^2 \times \mathbb{F}^2$ such that, for all $a, b, x, y \in \mathbb{F}$,

$$(\mathsf{OLE}_\mathbb{F})_{((a,b),(x,y))} = \begin{cases} \frac{1}{|\mathbb{F}|^3} & \text{if } a \cdot b = x + y, \\ 0 & \text{otherwise .} \end{cases}$$

A New Impossibility Criterion. We state the following combinatorial criterion to rule out a SNIR.

Lemma 10. *Let C be a correlation over $\mathcal{X} \times \mathcal{Y}$ such that, for some x, $C_{(x,y)} > 0$ for all y. Let D be a non-redundant correlation over $\mathcal{U} \times \mathcal{V}$ such that, for each u, there exists v such that $D_{(u,v)} = 0$. Then, D does not have a statistical SNIR to C.*

Proof: By Theorem 1, D has a statistical SNIR to C only if there is a perfect SNIR $(\mathfrak{A}, \mathfrak{B})$ from D to $C^{\otimes \ell}$ for some $\ell \in \mathbb{N}$. By our assumption, there exists $x \in \mathcal{X}^\ell$ such that $\left(C^{\otimes \ell}\right)_{(x,y)} > 0$ for all $y \in C^{\otimes \ell}$. Consider any u such that $P[\mathfrak{A}(x) = u] > 0$ (indeed $\mathfrak{A}$ is a deterministic protocol, but we do not need this property). It is easy to see that, for all v in the image of $\mathfrak{B}$,

$$P_{(X,Y) \sim C^{\otimes \ell}}[\mathfrak{A}(X) = u, \mathfrak{B}(Y) = v] > 0.$$

This contradicts our assumption about D.   □

The above lemma implies that statistical SNIR of $\mathsf{OLE}_{\mathbb{F}}$ to SEC_l^p is impossible for all $p \in (0,1)$, $l \in \mathbb{N}$ and ring $\mathbb{F}$. This follows from the fact that, when (X,Y) is distributed according to the n-bit string erasure correlation, $P_{(X,Y)}[x, \bot] > 0$ for all $x \in \{0,1\}^n$. Whereas, when (U,V) is distributed according to SEC_l^p, for any (a,b) such that $a \cdot b \neq x + y$, $P_{(U,V)}[U = (a,b), V = (x,y)] = 0$.

5   Generalized Junta Theorem

Kindler and Safra showed that if the energy of a function above degree d is small, then it is close to a junta that only depends on $O(d)$ many variables [20,21]. We need a generalized version of this result, Theorem 2, which we will prove in this section. The generalization is in terms of using a *generalized* Fourier transform to define degree and energy for functions over a domain Ω^n rather than $\{0,1\}^n$ (see Sect. 3). Our statement and proof closely follow the treatment by Filmus [9], which itself gives a generalization of the original result in [20,21] (which was restricted to functions with boolean *outputs* as well as inputs). The proofs of the lemmas are provided in the full version of the paper [6].

5.1   Tools: Influence, Hypercontractivity and Invariance Principle

We will first present some definitions that will be used later in this section. Let (Ω, π) be a finite probability space, $|\Omega| = m \geq 2$, in which every outcome has probability at least λ.

Definition 12. For a function $f \in L^2(\Omega^n, \pi^{\otimes n})$, and a position $i \in [n]$, we define the following:

$$\mathbb{E}[f] = \operatorname*{\mathbb{E}}_{x \sim \pi^{\otimes n}}[f(x)], \qquad \mathsf{Var}[f] = \|f - \mathbb{E}[f]\|^2,$$

$$\mathsf{E}_i f = \operatorname*{\mathbb{E}}_{x' \sim \pi}[f(x_{[n] \setminus i}||x')] \qquad \mathsf{L}_i f = f - \mathsf{E}_i f,$$

$$\mathsf{Inf}_i[f] = \|\mathsf{L}_i f\|^2 \qquad \mathsf{TotInf}[f] = \sum_{i=1}^n \mathsf{Inf}_i[f]$$

where $x_{[n] \setminus i}||x'$ denotes replacing x_i by x' in x.   ◁

Note that $L_i f$ is a function associated with f, called its *Laplacian*, and it captures the contribution of a particular coordinate i for each point in the domain of f. Its energy $\mathsf{Inf}_i[f]$, called the *influence* of a position i, is a quantity that measures this contribution. The total influence $\mathsf{TotInf}[ff]$ simply sums up the influence from all coordinates. We also note that the expectation $\mathbb{E}$ (and variance Var) for a function f w.r.t. a distribution over its domain are defined as the expectation (and variance) of the random variable corresponding to the output of f when evaluated on an input drawn from the given distribution; these definitions extend to continuous domains as well.

Hypercontractivity. We will need a generalization of the Bonami Lemma in the hypercontractivity type of results. The following version is obtained by substituting $q = 4$ in Theorem 10.21 in [25]. Here we state this lemma restricted to the case when all the variables are coming from the same domain Ω and are distributed identically according to π.

Lemma 11 (Hypercontractivity [25]). *Let (Ω, π) be a finite probability space, $|\Omega| = m \geq 2$, in which every outcome has probability at least λ. Let $f \in L^2(\Omega^n, \pi^{\otimes n})$ be a function of degree at most d, then*

$$\|f^2\|^2 \leq (9/\lambda)^d \|f\|^4.$$

We will use the above lemma to prove a result that is a dichotomy (given below), which will be used as a tool in the main proof. This has been taken verbatim from [9], the only difference being that now we use the generalized version of the Bonami lemma given above. Also, the expectations and probability calculations will now be with respect to the probability distribution given by $\pi^{\otimes n}$ instead of the uniform distribution.

Lemma 12. *Let S be a finite set and let $d \geq 1$. If $f \in L^2(\Omega^n, \pi^{\otimes n})$ is a S-valued function satisfying $\|f^{>d}\|^2 = \epsilon$ then either $\|f\|^2 = O(\epsilon)$ or $\|f^{\leq d}\|^2 = \Omega(1)$.*

Invariance Principle. Given a function in $f \in L^2(\Omega^n, \pi^{\otimes n})$, we define a *polynomial* $\mathsf{P}f$ with $n(|\Omega|-1)$ variables, obtained by replacing the generalized Fourier basis with a polynomial basis. More precisely, the polynomial $\mathsf{P}f$ with formal variables $\{X_{i,\alpha}\}_{i\in[n], \alpha\in[|\Omega|-1]}$ is defined as

$$\mathsf{P}f(X_{1,1}, \ldots, X_{n,|\Omega|-1}) = \sum_{\alpha\in[\![|\Omega|]\!]^n} \widehat{f_\alpha} \prod_{i\in[n]:\alpha_i\neq 0} X_{i,\alpha_i}.$$

We will be using the following variant of the invariance principle to complete our proof of the generalized junta theorem, that is implicit in [25] (obtained from Exercise 11.49(b) followed by an application of the technique used in the proof of Corollary 11.67):

Lemma 13 (Invariance Principle [25]). *Let (Ω, π) be a finite probability space, $|\Omega| = m \geq 2$, in which every outcome has probability at least λ. Suppose $f \in$*

$L^2(\Omega^n, \pi^{\otimes n})$ has degree at most d, with $\mathsf{Var}[f] = 1$,[4] and $\mathsf{Inf}_t[f] \leq \epsilon$, for every $t \in [n]$. Then for any $\psi : \mathbb{R} \to \mathbb{R}$ that has a continuous third derivative and satisfies $\|\psi'''\|_\infty \leq c$, we have

$$\left| \mathbb{E}[\psi \circ f] - \underset{w \sim N(0,1)^{(m-1)n}}{\mathbb{E}} [\psi(Pf(w))] \right| \leq \frac{2c}{3}(2\sqrt{2/\lambda})^d d\sqrt{\epsilon}.$$

Following [25], we will use the above lemma along with Proposition 5 below to get the desired version of the invariance principle, that compares probabilities of the functions taking values less than some threshold.

Proposition 5 (Carbery-Wright Theorem.). *Let* $p : \mathbb{R}^{(m-1)n} \to \mathbb{R}$ *be a poly-nomial of degree at most* d, *let* $w \sim N(0,1)^{(m-1)n}$, *and assume* $\mathbb{E}[p(w)^2] = 1$. *Then, for all* $\epsilon > 0$,

$$\Pr[|p(w)| \leq \epsilon] \leq O(d\epsilon^{1/d}),$$

where the $O(\cdot)$ *hides a universal constant.*

The lemma given below will also be used in our proof of the invariance prin-cipal. Its proof has been completed after following exercises 11.40 and 11.41(b) from [25].

Lemma 14. *Fix* $u \in \mathbb{R}$, *let* $\psi(s) = 1_{s \leq u}$, *and* $0 < \eta < 1/2$. *Then there exists a smooth approximation* $\widetilde{\psi}_\eta$ *of* ψ *that satisfies the following properties:*

- $\widetilde{\psi}_\eta$ *is a non-increasing function which agrees with the indicator function* $\psi(s) = 1_{s \leq u}$ *on the intervals* $(-\infty, u - \eta]$ *and* $[u + \eta, \infty)$.
- $\widetilde{\psi}_\eta$ *is smooth and satisfies* $\|\widetilde{\psi}_\eta^{(k)}\|_\infty \leq c_k/\eta^k$ *for each* $k \in \mathbb{N}$, *where* c_k *only depends on* k.

We prove the below lemma by following a line of reasoning in [25], similar to the way this version is proved for the Berry-Esseen theorem (which consid-ers sums of random variables instead of multilinear polynomials). The smooth approximation function $\widetilde{\psi}_\eta$ for the desired indicator function $\psi(s) = 1_{s \leq u}$ has been taken from Lemma 14. We first apply the basic invariance principle Lemma 13 to this approximation and then use its properties to derive some basic inequal-ities, concluding in the desired result.

Lemma 15. *Let* (Ω, π) *be a finite probability space,* $|\Omega| = m \geq 2$, *in which every outcome has probability at least* λ. *Suppose* $f \in L^2(\Omega^n, \pi^{\otimes n})$ *has degree at most* d, *with* $\mathsf{Var}[f] = 1$, *and* $\mathsf{Inf}_t[f] \leq \epsilon$, *for every* $t \in [n]$. *Then, for all* $u \in \mathbb{R}$,

$$\left| \underset{x \sim \pi^{\otimes n}}{\Pr}[f(x) \leq u] - \underset{w \sim N(0,1)^{(m-1)n}}{\Pr}[Pf(w) \leq u] \right| \leq O(d\epsilon^{\frac{1}{3d+1}}\lambda^{\frac{-1}{3}}).$$

---

[4] Actually, this lemma holds even when $\mathsf{Var}[f] \leq 1$, but the unit variance case is sufficient for us to be able to apply the Carbery-Wright theorem later.

5.2   Main Proof

In this section, we give our proof for the junta theorem. Lemma 16 states that for every function whose high-degree energy is small, there is a set J of small number of co-ordinates s.t. all other positions have low influence on the function f_z obtained by fixing these co-ordinates to the value $z \in \Omega^J$. The remaining lemmas then basically try to show that low influence implies low variance. To this end, the invariance principle is used inside Lemma 18 to claim that the function f_z has low probability on every value in the domain. Lemma 19 then shows that if we consider a restriction of the function f to J and average out the rest, we get a good approximation g for f. From there, one only needs to round g to the nearest values in the set T to get the final approximation h. Most of the following description has been taken verbatim from [9], with the expectations and probabilities now being calculated w.r.t. the general distribution given by products of π instead of a uniform distribution. Whenever not mentioned, the variable α is coming from $[\![|\Omega|]\!]^n$.

There are some updates to the proof of the following lemma in the generalized setting as compared to [9]. First, the Laplacian functions $L_i f$, for $i \in [n]$, have a different range defined with respect to π, whereas it is a much simpler description in the uniform setting. Secondly, the constant $2^{|J|}$ in an inequality comparing the conditional expectation of $(L_i f)^2$ when the input at positions J has been set to z and the normal expectation of $(L_i f)^2$, must be replaced by $(1/\lambda)^{|J|}$.

Lemma 16. *Let T be a finite set and let $d \geq 1$. If $f \in L^2(\Omega^n, \pi^{\otimes n})$ is a T-valued function such that $\|f^{>d}\|^2 = \epsilon$ then we can find a set J of $O(1)$ coordinates such that for each $z \in \Omega^J$, the function $[f_z]$ on $\Omega^{\bar{J}}$ obtained by substituting $x|_J = z$ satisfies*

$$\mathsf{Inf}_i[f_z] = O(\epsilon) \text{ for every } i \in \bar{J}.$$

There is a similar difference to the following lemma from the version in [9], that the constant in an inequality comparing norms of f_z and f must be replaced from $2^{|J|}$ to $(1/\lambda)^{|J|}$.

Lemma 17. *Assuming the setting of Lemma 16, then for every $z \in \Omega^J$, either $\mathsf{Var}[f_z] = O(\epsilon)$ or $\mathsf{Var}[f_z] = \Omega(1)$.*

The following lemma finally concludes that variance of f_z is small, for every $z \in \Omega^J$. The key ingredient used here is our variant of the generalized invariance principle (Lemma 15) that we have proved earlier. This is used to first show that the difference in the (appropriately-defined) probabilities that the functions g and Pg take values in the set $(u-\gamma, u]$ (for any u) is small, where $g = f_z / \mathsf{Var}[f_z]$. Since the variable obtained by substituting a Gaussian distribution to Pg is continuous, this probability goes to 0 as we take the limit γ going to 0.

Lemma 18. *Assuming the setting of Lemma 16, for every $z \in \Omega^J$, we have $\mathsf{Var}[f_z] = O(\epsilon)$.*

Lemma 19. *Assuming the setting of Lemma 16, there is a function $g \in L^2(\Omega^n, \pi^{\otimes n})$, depending only on the co-ordinates in J, such that $\|f-g\|^2 = O(\epsilon)$.*

We will now finish the proof of the generalized junta theorem.

Proof of Theorem 2: Lemma 19 gives a function g, depending on $O(1)$ co-ordinates, such that $\|f - g\|^2 = O(\epsilon)$. Let $h(x)$ be obtained by rounding $g(x)$ to the closest element of $\mathcal{T}$. For every x we have $|h(x) - g(x)| \leq |f(x) - g(x)|$ and so $|h(x) - f(x)| \leq |h(x) - g(x)| + |g(x) - f(x)| \leq 2|f(x) - g(x)|$. Consequently, $\|h - f\|^2 \leq 4\|g - f\|^2 = O(\epsilon)$.

Since f and h are both $\mathcal{T}$-valued, for all x either $f(x) = h(x)$ or $|h(x) - f(x)| = \Omega(1)$. Consequently, $\mathbb{E}_{x \sim \pi^{\otimes n}}[(h - f)^2] = \Omega(\Pr[h \neq f])$, and so $\Pr[h \neq f] = O(\|h - f\|^2) = O(\epsilon)$.

Finally, suppose that h does not have degree d. Then $\widehat{h}_\alpha \neq 0$ for some $|\alpha| > d$. Since h depends on $M = O(1)$ coordinates, $\widehat{h}_\alpha = \mathbb{E}[h \cdot \gamma_\alpha]$ is a non-zero value which is the average of m^M elements, and consequently $(\widehat{h}_\alpha)^2 = \Omega(1)$, implying that $\|h^{>d}\|^2 = \Omega(1)$. On the other hand,

$$\|h^{>d}\|^2 \leq 2\|f^{>d}\|^2 + 2\|h^{>d} - f^{>d}\|^2 = 2\epsilon + 2\|(h-f)^{>d}\|^2 \leq 2\epsilon + \|h - f\|^2 = O(\epsilon).$$

This shows that $\epsilon = \Omega(1)$. In such a setting, we can just ignore all the above analysis and pick some constant function h as the approximation. This function has degree 0, it depends on no co-ordinates, while the probability that it differs from f is still less than 1, and hence $O(\epsilon)$. $\square$

References

1. Agarwal, P., et al.: Secure non-interactive reduction and spectral analysis of correlations. In: Dunkelman, O., Dziembowski, S. (eds) Advances in Cryptology EUROCRYPT 2022. Lecture Notes in Computer Science, vol. 13277, pp. 797–827. Springer, Cham (2022). https://doi.org/10.1007/978-3-031-07082-2_28
2. Amini Khorasgani, H., Maji, H.K., Nguyen, H.H.: Secure non-interactive simulation: feasibility and rate. In: Dunkelman, O., Dziembowski, S. (eds) Advances in Cryptology - EUROCRYPT 2022. EUROCRYPT 2022. Lecture Notes in Computer Science, vol. 13277, pp 767–796. Springer, Cham (2022). https://doi.org/10.1007/978-3-031-07082-2_27
3. Anantharam, V., Gohari, A., Kamath, S., Nair, C.: On maximal correlation, hypercontractivity, and the data processing inequality studied by Erkip and cover. CoRR, abs/1304.6133 (2013)
4. Beimel, A., Ishai, Y., Kumaresan, R., Kushilevitz, E.: On the cryptographic complexity of the worst functions. In: Lindell, Y. (ed.) TCC 2014. LNCS, vol. 8349, pp. 317–342. Springer, Heidelberg (2014). https://doi.org/10.1007/978-3-642-54242-8_14
5. Beimel, A., Malkin, T.: A quantitative approach to reductions in secure computation. In: Naor, M. (ed.) TCC 2004. LNCS, vol. 2951, pp. 238–257. Springer, Heidelberg (2004). https://doi.org/10.1007/978-3-540-24638-1_14
6. Bhushan, K., Misra, A.K., Narayanan, V., Prabhakaran, M.: Secure non-interactive reducibility is decidable. Cryptol. ePrint Arch. (2022)
7. De, A., Mossel, E., Neeman, J.: Non interactive simulation of correlated distributions is decidable. In: Proceedings of the Twenty-Ninth Annual ACM-SIAM Symposium on Discrete Algorithms, SODA 2018, USA, pp. 2728–2746. Society for Industrial and Applied Mathematics (2018)

8. Feige, U., Kilian, J., Naor, M.: A minimal model for secure computation (extended abstract). In: STOC, pp. 554–563 (1994)
9. Filmus, Y.: A simple proof of the Kindler-Safra theorem. https://yuvalfilmus.cs.technion.ac.il/Manuscripts/KindlerSafra.pdf (2022)
10. Gács, P., Körner, J.: Common information is far less than mutual information. Prob. Control Inf. Theory **2**(2), 149–162 (1973)
11. Ghazi, B., Kamath, P., Sudan, M.: Decidability of non-interactive simulation of joint distributions. In: FOCS, pp. 545–554. IEEE (2016)
12. Goldreich, O.: Foundations of Cryptography: Basic Applications. Cambridge University Press, Cambridge (2004)
13. Micali, S., Goldreich, O., Wigderson, A.: How to play any mental game. In: STOC, pp. 218–229 (1987). See [12, Chap. 7] for more details
14. Goldreich, O., Vainish, R.: How to solve any protocol problem - an efficiency improvement (extended abstract). In: Pomerance, C. (ed.) CRYPTO 1987. LNCS, vol. 293, pp. 73–86. Springer, Heidelberg (1988). https://doi.org/10.1007/3-540-48184-2_6
15. Goyal, S., Narayanan, V., Prabhakaran, M.: Oblivious-transfer complexity of noisy coin-toss via secure zero communication reductions. In: these proceedings (2022)
16. Ishai, Y., Prabhakaran, M., Sahai, A.: Founding cryptography on oblivious transfer – efficiently. In: Wagner, D. (ed.) CRYPTO 2008. LNCS, vol. 5157, pp. 572–591. Springer, Heidelberg (2008). https://doi.org/10.1007/978-3-540-85174-5_32
17. Kamath, S., Anantharam, V.: On non-interactive simulation of joint distributions. IEEE Trans. Inf. Theory **62**(6), 3419–3435 (2016)
18. Khorasgani, H.A., Maji, H.K., Nguyen, H.H.: Decidability of secure non-interactive simulation of doubly symmetric binary source. Cryptology ePrint Archive, Report 2021/190 (2021). https://eprint.iacr.org/2021/190
19. Kilian, J.: Founding cryptography on oblivious transfer. In: STOC, pp. 20–31 (1988)
20. Kindler, G.: Property Testing, PCP, and juntas. PhD thesis, Tel Aviv University (2002)
21. Kindler, G., Safra, S.: Noise-resistant Boolean functions are juntas. Manuscript available from http://www.math.tau.ac.il/~safra/PapersAndTalks/nibfj.ps (2002)
22. Kraschewski, D., Maji, H.K., Prabhakaran, M., Sahai, A.: A full characterization of completeness for two-party randomized function evaluation. In: Nguyen, P.Q., Oswald, E. (eds.) EUROCRYPT 2014. LNCS, vol. 8441, pp. 659–676. Springer, Heidelberg (2014). https://doi.org/10.1007/978-3-642-55220-5_36
23. Maji, H.K., Prabhakaran, M., Rosulek, M.: Complexity of multi-party computation functionalities. In: Cryptology and Information Security Series, vol. 10, pp. 249–283. IOS Press, Amsterdam (2013)
24. Narayanan, V., Prabhakaran, M., Prabhakaran, V.M.: Zero-communication reductions. In: Pass, R., Pietrzak, K. (eds.) TCC 2020. LNCS, vol. 12552, pp. 274–304. Springer, Cham (2020). https://doi.org/10.1007/978-3-030-64381-2_10
25. O'Donnell, R.: Analysis of Boolean Functions. CoRR, abs/2105.10386 (2021)
26. Sudan, M., Tyagi, H., Watanabe, S.: Communication for generating correlation: a unifying survey. IEEE Trans. Inf. Theory **66**(1), 5–37 (2020)
27. Witsenhausen, H.S.: On sequences of pairs of dependent random variables. SIAM J. Appl. Math. **28**(1), 100–113 (1975)
28. Witsenhausen, H.: The zero-error side information problem and chromatic numbers (corresp.). IEEE Trans. Inf. Theory **22**(5), 592–593 (1976)
29. Wyner, A.D.: The common information of two dependent random variables. IEEE Trans. Inf. Theory **21**(2), 163–179 (1975)

Multi-party Computation II

Round-Optimal Black-Box Secure Computation from Two-Round Malicious OT

Yuval Ishai[1], Dakshita Khurana[2], Amit Sahai[3],
and Akshayaram Srinivasan[4(✉)]

[1] Technion, Haifa, Israel
yuvali@cs.technion.il
[2] UIUC, Champaign, USA
dakshita@illinois.edu
[3] UCLA, Los Angeles, USA
sahai@cs.ucla.edu
[4] Tata Institute of Fundamental Research, Mumbai, India
akshayaram.srinivasan@tifr.res.in

Abstract. We give round-optimal *black-box* constructions of two-party and multiparty protocols in the common random/reference string (CRS) model, with security against malicious adversaries, based on any two-round oblivious transfer (OT) protocol in the same model. Specifically, we obtain two types of results.

1. **Two-party protocol.** We give a (two-round) *two-sided NISC* protocol that makes black-box use of two-round (malicious-secure) OT in the CRS model. In contrast to the standard setting of non-interactive secure computation (NISC), two-sided NISC allows communication from both parties in each round and delivers the output to both parties at the end of the protocol. Prior black-box constructions of two-sided NISC relied on idealized setup assumptions such as OT correlations, or were proven secure in the random oracle model.

2. **Multiparty protocol.** We give a three-round secure multiparty computation protocol for an arbitrary number of parties making black-box use of a two-round OT in the CRS model. The round optimality of this construction follows from a black-box impossibility proof of Applebaum et al. (ITCS 2020). Prior constructions either required the use of random oracles, or were based on two-round malicious-secure OT protocols that satisfied additional security properties.

1 Introduction

The *round complexity* of secure multiparty computation (MPC) has been the subject of intensive research. In this work, we continue this study, focusing on the case of computationally secure MPC protocols without an honest majority. We start with some relevant background.

© The Author(s), under exclusive license to Springer Nature Switzerland 2022
E. Kiltz and V. Vaikuntanathan (Eds.): TCC 2022, LNCS 13748, pp. 441–469, 2022.
https://doi.org/10.1007/978-3-031-22365-5_16

The Semi-honest Model. Consider first the simpler setting of *semi-honest* adversaries, who may passively corrupt an arbitrary subset of the parties. In the two-party case, Yao's protocol [Yao86] is a two-round protocol that can rely on any *two-round oblivious transfer* (OT) protocol. The latter primitive is not only simple and minimal (as a special case of the general result), but also one that pragmatically serves as a useful basis for protocol design. Indeed, two-round OT can be implemented at a low amortized cost with interactive preprocessing [Bea95,IKNP03] and even from scratch [BCG+19]. The question of generalizing Yao's two-round protocol to the *multiparty* setting remained open for many years. This question was settled by Garg and Srinivasan [GS18] and Benhamouda and Lin [BL18], who showed that two-round OT indeed suffices also for two-round MPC with an arbitrary number of parties.

Black-Box vs. Non-black-box Constructions. A major distinction between Yao's two-party protocol and the recent MPC protocols from [GS18,BL18] is the way in which the OT primitive is used. While the former makes a *black-box*[1] use of OT, in the sense that the construction uses the next-message function of the OT protocol as an oracle, the latter MPC protocols cannot use the OT protocol as an oracle and need to depend on its implementation. This qualitative difference results in a big efficiency gap between the two types of protocols, raising a question about the possibility of a black-box alternative for the multiparty case. Unfortunately, Applebaum et al. [ABG+20] obtained a negative answer: for any $n \geq 3$, general two-round n-party MPC protocols *cannot* make a black-box use of two-round OT. More recently, Patra and Srinivasan [PS21] closed the remaining gap, presenting a black-box construction of *three-round* MPC protocols from two-round OT (improving over a previous four-round protocol from [ACJ17]). This gives us a full understanding of the round complexity of black-box *semi-honest* MPC based on two-round OT.

From Semi-honest to Malicious. The case of security against malicious adversaries is far less understood. Targeting the goal of matching the round complexity of semi-honest protocols, one needs to rely on a setup assumption. (See Sect. 1.2 for discussion of results in the plain model.) A minimal form of setup, originating from non-interactive zero knowledge (NIZK) proofs [BFM88], assumes the availability of a *common random string* or, more generally, a (structured) *common reference string*. Our results will apply to both kinds of setup, to which we collectively refer as a *CRS setup*. Given a CRS setup, NIZK can serve as a general round-preserving tool for enforcing an honest behavior by malicious parties. However, general NIZK-based protocols are inherently non-black-box. This raises the following natural question about the round complexity of black-box MPC in the CRS model:

---

[1] A bit more precisely, we refer here to the usual notion of a *fully* black-box reduction [IR90,RTV04], where not only the construction makes a black-box use of OT but also the security reduction makes a black-box use of the adversary.

Can we make a black-box use of two-round OT to obtain two-round (resp., three-round) two-party (resp., multiparty) MPC protocols with security against malicious adversaries?

To make this question more precise, we need to specify which kind of two-round OT we consider. Ideally, one would have liked to use *semi-honest* two-round OT as a basis for round-optimal malicious-secure MPC. However, even if we restrict our attention to realizing the OT functionality, it is not known how to construct two-round malicious-secure OT in the CRS model from two-round semi-honest OT, let alone in a black-box way.[2] Indeed, while semi-honest two-round OT protocols are quite easy to construct from essentially every concrete assumption known to imply public-key encryption, obtaining similar protocols with malicious security required ingenious new ideas [PVW08, DGH+20, BF22]. Given this state of affairs, we use *malicious-secure* two-round OT in the CRS model as our basic building block.

Known Results. In the case of two-party "sender-receiver" functionalities, which take inputs from both parties but only deliver the output to the designated receiver, the above question was answered in the affirmative in [IKO+11]. Such two-party protocols, known as *non-interactive secure computation* (NISC) protocols, provide a black-box extension of Yao's protocol that offers security against malicious parties while still requiring only two rounds. However, for general two-party functionalities that deliver outputs to both parties, no analogous result is known. Note that such a "two-sided NISC" protocol cannot be obtained by simply running two instances of standard (one-sided) NISC in parallel, since there is nothing preventing a malicious party from using different inputs in the two executions. The question is similarly open for three-round MPC with $n \geq 3$ parties. Partial progress was made in [PS21], where black-box protocols were constructed from a stronger variant of two-round OT that required some form of adaptive security. However, this extra requirement not only makes the OT primitive qualitatively stronger, but also excludes some existing protocols from the literature (such as CDH- and LPN-based protocols from [DGH+20]). A different kind of progress was recently made in [IKSS21, IKSS22], where positive answers were given using two distinct kinds of idealized setups: either the random oracle model or a random OT correlations setup. To conclude, without strong idealized setups and without strengthening the OT primitive, the above question remained open in both the two-party and the multiparty case.

1.1 Our Contribution

We settle the above question by presenting the first round-optimal black-box constructions of MPC protocols from two-round (malicious-secure) OT in the CRS model. In the two-party case, we obtain the first extension of the black-box NISC protocol from [IKO+11] to general functionalities that deliver outputs to both parties.

---

[2] The same is true even for the plain-model variant of OT with unbounded receiver simulation [NP01, AIR01]. Here we only consider OT and MPC with efficient simulation in the CRS model.

Informal Theorem 1. *There is a (two-round, malicious-secure) two-sided NISC protocol in the CRS model that makes a black-box use of two-round malicious-secure OT in the CRS model.*

See Theorem 1 for a formal version. From a concrete efficiency perspective, this compiler may be better than the recent random-oracle based compiler from [IKSS22] in that it replaces a computational security parameter by a statistical one.[3] We also obtain an arithmetic variant of this result that makes a black-box use of the underlying field as well as a two-round malicious-secure OLE protocol over the same field [CDI+19, BDM22]. (See Theorem 2 for a formal statement.) This variant leverages another advantage of black-box constructions, namely respecting the arithmetic nature of an underlying semi-honest protocol.

Informal Theorem 2. *There is a three-round malicious-secure MPC protocol in the CRS model that makes a black-box use of two-round malicious-secure OT in the CRS model.*

See Theorem 3 for a formal statement. The optimality of three rounds follows from the proof of the black-box separation in [ABG+20]. While the main theorem statement of [ABG+20] only refers to a separation between two-round MPC and two-round *semi-honest* OT, the oracle used for the separation actually implies malicious-secure two-round OT.

Open Questions. Our results leave several avenues for future work.

- Is two-round *semi-honest* OT sufficient? As discussed above, the non-triviality of realizing malicious-secure two-round OT from concrete assumptions suggests that even a non-black-box round-preserving compiler from semi-honest to malicious OT would be difficult to obtain. Moreover, the existence of black-box constructions in the random oracle model [MR19, IKSS22] makes a potential black-box separation more challenging.
- Does *three-round* OT suffice in the multiparty case? We conjecture that the black-box separation from [ABG+20] can be extended to rule out this possibility, and leave formalizing this to future work.
- Can similar results be obtained in the *OT-hybrid model*, namely using calls to an ideal OT oracle rather an OT protocol? For standard (one-side) NISC, this is achieved by the construction from [IKO+11]. In the multiparty case, this question is open even in the semi-honest model, where evidence for the difficulty of settling it in the negative is given in [ABG+20]. Our protocols, similarly to the ones from [PS21], inherently make use of the messages generated by the OT protocol, and thus cannot replace the protocol by an oracle.

---

[3] Jumping ahead, both compilers use a virtual honest-majority MPC protocol in which the number of parties serves as a security parameter. The use of the Fiat-Shamir paradigm in [IKSS22] requires the use of a computational security parameter instead of a statistical one.

1.2   Related Work

A long line of work [KOS03, KO04, Wee10, Goy11, ORS15, GMPP16, ACJ17, BHP17, BGJ+18, HHPV18, CCG+20] studied the question of minimizing the round complexity of MPC with security against any number of malicious parties in the *plain model.* In this setting, one cannot hope to match the round complexity of our protocols in the CRS model regardless of the underlying assumptions. Indeed, protocols with black-box simulators must use at least four rounds [KO04, GMPP16]. Even if one allows a non-black-box (polynomial-time) simulation, two-round two-party protocols are unlikely to exist even for the special case of zero knowledge functionalities [BLV03]. We note that there is an interesting line of work [GGJS12, KMO14, GKP17, BGJ+17, BGI+17, ABG+21, FJK21, AMR21] that aims to get around this lower bound by considering a weaker notion of security, namely, security with super-polynomial time simulation (SPS) security.

The quest for minimizing the round complexity of MPC in the plain model, with a standard notion of simulation-based security, culminated in the work of Choudhuri et al. [CCG+20], who obtained a four-round protocol making a *non-black-box* use of four-round malicious-secure OT. The round complexity of this protocol is optimal for protocols with black-box simulation. Additionally requiring the *construction* to be black-box, as in this work, a five-round protocol in the plain model making use of strong flavors of two-round semi-honest OT was given in [IKSS21]. See [CCG+20, IKSS21] and references therein for a more comprehensive survey of this line of work.

2   Technical Overview

In this section, we describe the key technical ideas behind our construction of black-box two-sided NISC (in Sect. 2.1) and our black-box three-round secure multiparty computation protocol (in Sect. 2.2).

2.1   Black-Box Two-Sided NISC

Challenges. The main challenge in constructing a two-sided NISC protocol is to design a "black-box" mechanism wherein the adversarial party is somehow forced to use the same input when it plays the role of the sender and the receiver respectively. This is the reason why a natural attempt of constructing a two-sided NISC by running two versions of one-sided NISC in opposite directions fails. The prior works of Ishai et al. [IKSS21, IKSS22] constructed such a "black-box" mechanism by making use of the IPS compiler [IPS08]. However, both these works resorted to idealized setups such as OT correlations, or made use of random oracles in order to implement the watchlist mechanism, one of the key building blocks in this compiler. As we explain later, we encounter significant barriers while trying to remove these idealized setups from the above works. To circumvent these barriers, we develop new techniques to implement this mechanism and prove the security of the protocols based only on a two-message malicious OT. In the rest of the subsection, we elaborate on this in much more detail. As our work also builds on the IPS compiler, we recall the main ideas behind this compiler below.

IPS Compiler. At a high level, the IPS compiler constructs a malicious-secure MPC in the dishonest majority setting via a combination of: (1) a malicious-secure honest-majority client-server MPC (called the outer protocol)[4], and (2) a semi-honest secure protocol in the dishonest majority setting (called the inner protocol). In more detail, each party in the compiled protocol plays the role of a client in the outer protocol. The parties then invoke the inner protocol to emulate the computation done by the servers. Since the outer protocol can be information-theoretic, the computations done by the servers avoid any cryptographic operations. This feature enables the compiled protocol to be black-box. However, as such, this compilation results in an insecure protocol. This is because an adversary can cheat in all the executions of the inner protocol and break their security (as they are only secure against semi-honest adversaries). Since the outer protocol is only guaranteed to be secure as long as a constant ($< 1/2$) fraction of the servers are corrupted, by corrupting all the servers, the adversary has effectively broken the security of the outer protocol and could extract non-trivial information about the honest party inputs. To prevent such an attack, the IPS compiler uses a novel cut-and-choose mechanism referred to as the *watchlist protocol*. In this protocol, each party chooses a random subset of the servers as part of its private "watchlist". The watchlist protocol provides the input and the randomness used by every other party for those server executions that are being watched by this party. The input and randomness of the other server executions are hidden. Every party then checks if the server executions in its watchlist are emulated correctly and aborts if it detects any inconsistency. This guarantees that if the adversary cheats in many server executions, then all the honest parties will detect this and abort, preventing the adversary from learning any useful information about the inputs of the honest parties. On the other hand, if the adversary only cheats in a small number of server executions, then we can rely on the security of the outer MPC protocol to show that the adversary only learns the output of the functionality.

Prior Works. For two-sided NISC, recent black-box protocols from [IKSS21, IKSS22] used the watchlist mechanism to catch a cheating adversary that is *using different inputs* while playing the role of the sender and the receiver respectively. Specifically, if the adversary is using inconsistent inputs in many server executions, then the honest party detects this via the watchlist mechanism and aborts the execution. On the other hand, if the adversary is using inconsistent inputs in a small number of executions, then the servers that are emulated by these executions can be considered as corrupted in the outer protocol. Since the outer protocol is secure as long as a constant fraction of the servers are corrupted, this

---

[4] By an honest-majority client-server MPC, we mean a setting where a malicious adversary can corrupt any subset of the clients and a constant fraction of the servers.

prevents the adversary from breaking the privacy of the honest party's inputs. This was the main intuition behind both works. However, these works differed in their choice of the outer protocol, the inner protocol, and the implementation of the watchlist mechanism. We tabulate these choices in Table 1. A common limitation of these two works is their reliance on idealized setups, such as OT correlations [IKSS21] or a random oracle [IKSS22] to implement the watchlist mechanism. We now explain the challenges in trying to remove the idealized setups from these works.

Table 1. Choice of outer protocol, inner protocol, and idealized model for watchlist implementation in prior works.

Citation	Outer protocol	Inner protocol	Watchlist implementation
[IKSS21]	2-round client-server MPC with selective abort	Two-round semi-malicious protocol with first-message equivocality	1-out-of-2 OT correlations model
[IKSS22]	2-round pairwise verifiable MPC	Two-round semi-honest protocol	Random Oracle Model

Need for Idealized Models. The key reason why the prior works needed to resort to idealized models is due to a subtle technical difficulty in implementing the IPS compiler. Specifically, the simulator in the IPS compiler needs to know the set of executions that are watched by the corrupted party before it sends its first-round message on behalf of the honest party. Note that in the real world, the honest party's input and randomness corresponding to the adversarial watched executions pass the consistency check and hence, we need to make sure that these checks pass even in the ideal world. Hence, the simulator needs to produce a consistent input and randomness that explains the inner protocol messages in all the executions that are watched by the corrupted party. This is further complicated in the rushing adversarial model where the adversary expects to see the first-round message from the honest party before it sends its own first-round message. Hence, if the set of watched executions are known to the simulator only after it sends the first-round message, then the simulator needs produce randomness that consistently explains the "simulated" first-round inner protocol message w.r.t. some input. In other words, the simulator needs to equivocate the first-round message of the inner protocol. This requires stronger assumptions. However, if we use idealized setups, then the simulator can learn the watched executions of the corrupted party before it sends the first-round message. In particular, this is done by allowing the simulator to implement the dealer while setting up the OT correlations in [IKSS21], or program the output of the random oracle in [IKSS22]. The above issue also precludes a natural attempt of trying to implement the watchlist functionality using a two-round k-out-of-m OT protocol. Indeed, the first-round message that encodes the set of watched executions is sent by the adversary only after it receives the first-round message from the honest party and hence, this approach too requires the first-round message of the inner protocol to be equivocal.

Our Solution. To overcome this difficulty, we need a watchlist protocol implementation where the simulator *can bias the watched executions* of the corrupted parties whereas the corrupted parties cannot bias the watched executions of the honest parties. These two conflicting features are obtained simultaneously via a *coin-tossing protocol.* Specifically, the watched executions of each party is sampled randomly where the randomness is contributed by both the parties and not just by the receiver party. This ensures that the simulator can set the randomness on behalf of the honest party in such a way that the corrupted party receives a randomly sampled set of executions that was chosen prior to sending the first-round message. At the same time, since the receiver party also provides a part of the randomness, this ensures that the corrupted party cannot bias the set of watched executions of the honest party. This helps in overcoming the above mentioned technical difficulty in implementing the IPS compiler. The next question is can we construct such a watchlist protocol? Indeed, the work of Ishai et al. [IKO+11] provides an instantiation that makes black-box use of a two-round malicious-secure OT. However, such a watchlist protocol alone does not solve all the issues and we elaborate more on this below.

Need for Watchlist Output at the End of the First Round. While the above watchlist protocol ensures that the simulator has the power to bias the watched executions of the corrupted parties, it leads to new incompatibility issues with the prior techniques. Specifically, the prior works crucially relied on the output of the watchlist protocol to be delivered to the honest parties at the end of the first round. This is indeed possible if we rely on idealized setups. However, in the above described approach, the honest party learns the output of the watchlist protocol only after the corrupted party sends its second-round message. Hence, it can only perform all the watchlist checks after it has sent its final round message in the protocol (since we are dealing with rushing adversaries). This leads to new problems and let us explain them in a bit more detail.

Firstly, the work of Ishai et al. [IKSS21] considered a two-round semi-honest inner protocol where the first-round message could be equivocated (see Table 1). However, a malicious party can also equivocate its first-round message and thereby, break the security of the inner protocol. This was not a problem in their setting since the output of the watchlist protocol is made available to the honest parties at the end of the first round (this is possible in the OT correlations model). Hence, the honest party can detect if the first-round message is equivocated in many inner protocol executions and abort if it is the case. However, in our watchlist protocol, the output is delivered to the honest party only at the end of the second round. By this time, the honest party would have sent the second-round message in the inner protocol and the adversary could potentially recover the entire input of the uncorrupted party.

In a more recent work, Ishai et al. [IKSS22] removed the need for an inner protocol with first message equivocality by considering a "stronger" outer protocol. This outer protocol which they termed as pairwise verifiable MPC protocol is a two-round client-server MPC protocol that additionally satisfies a special error correction property. Specifically, for any choice of second-round message from the corrupted servers, the error correction property requires that the output of the honest client remains the same. Unfortunately, obtaining such a protocol against standard malicious adversaries is hard due to the known barriers [GIKR02]. To overcome this, Ishai et al. considered security against weaker adversaries called pairwise verifiable adversaries. Roughly speaking, pairwise verifiable adversarial clients are restricted to send a first-round message such that the messages received by all the honest servers pass some consistency check. However, this restriction of only considering pairwise verifiable adversaries also seems incompatible with our watchlist protocol. Specifically, before we send the second-round message, we need to make sure that the first-round message in the outer protocol pass the pairwise consistency check and we must proceed only if these checks pass. In the work of Ishai et al. [IKSS22], this was made possible by making use of a random oracle. But in our setting, since the output of the watchlist functionality is only delivered after the honest party sends the second-round message, we cannot perform this check before sending the final message. Thus, an adversarial party can use first-round messages in the outer protocol that do not pass the pairwise consistency check and completely break the privacy of the honest party's inputs.

Our Approach. We note that the above mentioned incompatibility issue could be alleviated if we use a two-round malicious secure oblivious transfer protocol that has equivocal first-round message [GS18,PS21]. Specifically, such an OT protocol forces a corrupt receiver to send a valid first-round message but enables the simulator to equivocate the first-round message to both bits 0 and 1. Indeed, a malicious party is forced to send a valid first-round message whereas the simulator could equivocate the first-round message as in [IKSS21]. However, we do not know of a black-box construction of this primitive from any two-round malicious secure OT protocol.[5] Moreover, recent protocols from the literature (such as ones based on CDH and LPN [DGH+20]) do not satisfy this property. Our goal here is to overcome this issue by only making black-box use of a two-round malicious secure OT.

Instead of relying on a pairwise verifiable MPC protocol, our solution to this problem is to rely on a standard outer protocol satisfying security with abort, say for instance, the one given by Ishai, Kushilevitz, and Paskin [IKP10, Pas12]. To make this outer protocol compatible with the IPS compiler, Ishai et al. [IKSS21] observed that the inner protocol needed to additionally satisfy first-round equivocality (see Table 1). The key insight behind our solution is that first-round equivocality of the inner protocol is actually on overkill and we could instead use a far weaker security property. We now explain this in detail.

Recall that the watchlist mechanism is guaranteed to catch a malicious party that cheats in a large number of inner protocol executions. However, a malicious party can cheat in a small number of executions such that it goes undetected by the watchlist of the honest party with some non-negligible probability. In this case, we should be able to rely on the security of the outer protocol as the

---

[5] We note that [GS18] gave a non-black-box construction.

number of malicious server corruptions is "small". However, in order to invoke this security property, we need to compute the inner protocol output received by the honest party in each of the executions where the adversary has cheated. This corresponds to the second-round message sent by the corrupted servers to the honest client and we need to provide this information to the simulator of the outer protocol. [IKSS21] argued that if the inner protocol satisfies first-round equivocality then it is possible for the simulator to compute this output. In particular, the simulator can equivocate the first-round message as per the honest party's input and then use the corresponding randomness to compute the output of this inner protocol execution. In this work, we observe that this property can be weakened, specifically, to what we call as *output equivocality*. This property requires that if the adversary cheated in generating the second-round message, then the simulator (that is additionally provided the input of the honest party) must produce an output that is computationally indistinguishable from the honest party's output in the real execution. Specifically, instead of requiring the entire first-round message to be equivocable, we only need the output computation to be equivocable. This property is implied by first message equivocality and could be potentially be realized under weaker assumptions. Further, since the output of our watchlist protocol is only delivered after we send the second-round message, we need our inner protocol to also be secure against malicious receivers. Hence, it is sufficient to construct an inner protocol that is secure against malicious receivers and also satisfies output equivocality.

Somewhat surprisingly, both of these properties can be obtained simultaneously if we simply replace the two-round semi-honest OT in the Yao's protocol with a two-round malicious secure OT. Specifically, the security against malicious receivers follows from the folklore observation about Yao's protocol when instantiated with a two-round malicious secure OT protocol. The output equivocality property is argued using the security of the oblivious transfer against malicious senders. In particular, the simulator could use the extractor for the OT protocol and extract the set of both labels for each input wire of the garbled circuit that was generated. Now, given the honest party's input, the output equivocal simulator can just evaluate the received garbled circuit on the chosen set of labels according to the honest receiver's input and output the result of the evaluation. From the sender security of the OT protocol, we infer that the output of this evaluation is computationally indistinguishable from the honest evaluation. This allows us to construct an inner protocol with the desired properties and thereby instantiate the IPS compiler.

The full description of the inner protocol along with the security properties it needs to satisfy is given in Sect. 3. The construction and the security analysis of our two-sided black-box NISC protocol can be found in Sect. 4.

Further Remarks. We observe that there is no need to rely on a special inner protocol that was constructed based on Yao's garbled circuits. Instead, we can start with any one-sided OT-based NISC protocol. This follows from the fact that security against malicious receivers comes for free, and the output equivocality follows from security of the one-sided NISC against malicious senders. Thus, our work can be viewed as a black-box construction of two-sided NISC from any one-sided NISC. This allows us to directly transfer any efficiency improvements in the one-sided NISC setting to the more challenging two-sided NISC. Furthermore, this allows us to upgrade known one-sided NISC protocols in the arithmetic setting [CDI+19, DIO21] (making a black-box use of the underlying field) to similar two-sided NISC protocols.

2.2 Black-Box Three-Round MPC

To construct a black-box three-round MPC protocol, we again rely on the IPS compiler. Specifically, we start with an outer protocol that supports an arbitrary number of clients and satisfying security with selective abort (such a protocol was constructed in [IKP10, Pas12]). As in the black-box two-sided NISC case, we implement the watchlist protocol via a coin-tossing based approach. This enables the simulator to bias the watched executions of the corrupted parties before it sends its first-round message on behalf of the honest parties. The only difference from the two-sided NISC case is that we need to rely on an inner protocol that runs in three rounds (due to the black-box impossiblity of [ABG+20]). To make the inner protocol compatible with the above outer protocol, we need it to satisfy the following two additional properties:

- **Robustness:** Even if the adversary cheats in generating the messages in the first two rounds of the protocol, it cannot break the privacy of the honest party inputs. This is needed since the output of the watchlist is delivered only at the end of the second round and any cheating in the first two rounds should not enable the corrupted party to break the privacy of the honest parties.

- **Last Round Equivocality:** If the adversary has cheated in the first two rounds, then the simulator when provided with the inputs of all the honest parties must produce a last round message which is computationally indistinguishable from the real execution. This is needed to generate the last round message in the inner protocol executions where the adversary has cheated in the first two rounds.

We note that robustness and last round equivocality was also needed in the inner protocol used in [IKSS21]. However, their inner protocols could either run in two rounds (in the presence of OT correlations), or four rounds in the plain model. Here, our focus is on constructing such an inner protocol in three rounds in the CRS model.

Constructing Multiparty Inner Protocol. Our first observation is that to construct such an inner protocol for computing arbitrary functionalities, it is sufficient to construct an inner protocol that computes the 3MULTPlus functionality. 3MULTPlus is a special multiparty functionality that takes (x_1, y_1) from the first party, (x_2, y_2) from the second party, and (x_3, y_3) from the third party where x_i, y_i are bits and delivers $x_1 \cdot x_2 \cdot x_3 + y_1 + y_2 + y_3$ to all the parties. Indeed, the standard bootstrapping results from 3MULTPlus to general functions [BGI+18, GIS18, ABG+20] for the case of semi-honest adversaries also extends to the above security definition. Thus, it is sufficient to construct an inner protocol for 3MULTPlus functionality that satisfies both robustness and last round equivocality.

The starting point of our construction of such a protocol is the work of Patra and Srinivasan [PS21] who gave a construction in the semi-honest setting based on any two-round semi-honest OT protocol. The main result that we prove is that if we replace the two-round semi-honest OT protocol in their construction with a two-round malicious-secure version, then the resultant protocol is robust. However, proving this is not straightforward and requires a careful security analysis (this appears in Proposition 2). To prove last round equivocality, we observe that the last round message sent by each party in the protocol of [PS21] is obtained by decrypting some sender OT message. As in the case of two-sided NISC setting, we show that this message can be equivocated if the two-round OT protocol is secure against malicious senders. This allows us to construct a three-round inner protocol that satisfies robustness and equivocality by making black-box use of a two-round malicious-secure OT.

The formal description of the security properties along with the construction and the proof of security of the multiparty inner protocol appears in Sect. 5.

Putting Things Together. As mentioned before, our three-round black-box multiparty protocol is obtained by combining the two-round coin-tossing based watchlist protocol along with a three-round inner protocol satisfying both robustness and last round equivocality. At the end of the second round, the output of the watchlist protocol is delivered to all the parties. If the adversary cheats in many inner protocol executions, then this is detected by the honest parties who abort before sending the final round message. In this case, we rely on the robustness property of the inner protocol to show that the adversary learns no information about the private inputs of the honest parties. On the other hand, if the adversary only cheats in a small number of executions, then we corrupt the corresponding servers in the outer protocol. We use the last round equivocality to generate the final message in the inner protocol for these executions. We finally rely on the security of the outer protocol to argue that only the output of the functionality is leaked to the adversary since the number of server corruptions is "small".

The construction of the three-round black-box MPC protocol and the proof of security can be found in Sect. 6.

2.3   Another Perspective

A different way to view our techniques is as follows. Let us start with the simplest, round-optimal semi-honest protocols for 2PC and MPC that make black-box use of two-round semi-honest OT. For the case of two parties, we consider Yao's protocol and for the case of multiple parties, we consider the protocol from the work of Patra and Srinivasan [PS21]. In both these protocols, we replace the underlying semi-honest OT protocol with a malicious secure OT protocol and ask what security properties are satisfied by this modification. In this work, we show that the properties satisfied correspond to that of the inner protocols. Later, we use the IPS compiler to bootstrap this "weaker" security notion to the standard malicious security. However, this runs into several technical hurdles (as explained earlier) and we develop new techniques to overcome them.

Organization. We assume basic familiarity with the definitions of the standard building blocks used in our construction. We provide the formal definitions in the full version. We give the description of the two-party inner protocol in Sect. 3. In Sect. 4, we give our construction of black-box two-sided NISC protocol. We give the construction of our multiparty inner protocol in Sect. 5. In Sect. 6, we give our construction of black-box multiparty protocol that runs in three rounds.

3   Two-Party Inner Protocol

In this section, we give a definition of a two-party protocol that satisfies some special properties (known as two-party inner protocol). We give a construction of such a two-party inner protocol making black-box use of a two-round malicious-secure OT. In the next section, we use this protocol to construct a two-sided NISC.

3.1   Definition

A two-round two-party protocol for computing a two-party function f is given by a tuple of PPT algorithms $(\mathsf{Setup}, \Pi_1, \Pi_2, \mathsf{out}_\Pi)$. Setup algorithm takes in the security parameter 1^λ (encoded in unary) and outputs the common reference string crs. Π_1 is run by the receiver and takes in crs and the receiver input x_0 and outputs π_1. Π_2 is run by the sender and takes in crs, π_1, the sender input x_1 and outputs π_2. out_Π takes in crs, π_2, x_0 and the random tape of Π_1 and outputs $f(x_0, x_1)$.

Definition 1. *A two-party protocol* $(\mathsf{Setup}, \Pi_1, \Pi_2, \mathsf{out}_\Pi)$ *for computing a functionality f that delivers the output to the receiver is said to be a two-party inner protocol if there exists a (stateful) PPT simulator-extractor pair* $(\mathsf{Sim}_\Pi, \mathsf{Ext}_\Pi)$ *such that the following properties hold:*

- *Security Against Malicious Receivers: For any (stateful) non-uniform PPT adversary $\mathcal{A}$ corrupting the receiver and for any sender input x_1, we have:*

$$\mathsf{Real}_R(1^\lambda, \mathcal{A}, x_1) \approx_c \mathsf{Ideal}_R(1^\lambda, \mathcal{A}, x_1, (\mathsf{Sim}_\Pi, \mathsf{Ext}_\Pi))$$

  where Real_R and Ideal_R are described in Fig. 1.
- *Correctness of Extraction. For any non-uniform PPT adversary $\mathcal{A}$ corrupting the receiver, we have*

$$\Pr\Big[\mathsf{Ext}_\Pi(R, \mathsf{td}, \Pi_1(\mathsf{crs}, x_0; r_0)) \neq x_0\Big|$$
$$(\mathsf{crs}, \mathsf{td}) \leftarrow \mathsf{Sim}_\Pi(1^\lambda, R), (x_0, r_0) \leftarrow \mathcal{A}(\mathsf{crs})\Big] \leq \mathsf{negl}(\lambda)$$

– **Robust Security Against Semi-Malicious Senders (a.k.a., output equivocality):** *Informally, this property requires that if a malicious sender sends a second round message that is not explainable (by providing a valid (input, randomness) pair), then we require an equivocal simulator that when given the private input of the honest receiver computes an output such that the joint distribution of the view of $\mathcal{A}$ and the output of the honest receiver in the real execution is indistinguishable to the ideal execution using this special simulator. Formally, for any (stateful) non-uniform PPT adversary $\mathcal{A}$ corrupting the sender and for any receiver input x_0, we have:*

$$\mathsf{Real}_S(1^\lambda, \mathcal{A}, x_1) \approx_c \mathsf{Ideal}_S(1^\lambda, \mathcal{A}, x_0, (\mathsf{Sim}_\Pi, \mathsf{Ext}_\Pi))$$

where Real_S *and* Ideal_S *are described in Fig. 2.*

$\mathsf{Real}_R(1^\lambda, \mathcal{A}, x_1)$	$\mathsf{Ideal}_R(1^\lambda, \mathcal{A}, x_1, (\mathsf{Sim}_\Pi, \mathsf{Ext}_\Pi))$
1. $\mathsf{crs} \leftarrow \mathsf{Setup}(1^\lambda)$.	1. $(\mathsf{crs}, \mathsf{td}) \leftarrow \mathsf{Sim}_\Pi(1^\lambda, R)$.
2. $\pi_1 \leftarrow \mathcal{A}(\mathsf{crs})$.	2. $\pi_1 \leftarrow \mathcal{A}(\mathsf{crs})$.
3. $\pi_2 \leftarrow \Pi_2(\mathsf{crs}, \pi_1, x_1)$.	3. $x_0 \leftarrow \mathsf{Ext}_\Pi(R, \mathsf{td}, \pi_1)$.
4. Output $\mathcal{A}(\pi_2)$.	4. $\pi_2 \leftarrow \mathsf{Sim}(\mathsf{crs}, x_0, f(x_0, x_1))$.
	5. Output $\mathcal{A}(\pi_2)$.

Fig. 1. Descriptions of Real_R and Ideal_R experiments.

Remark 1. We note that correctness of extraction is implicitly implied by security against malicious receivers. However, for the ease of usage in the next section, we state it as a separate property.

We defer the proof of the following proposition to the full version.

$\mathsf{Real}_S(1^\lambda, \mathcal{A}, x_0)$	$\mathsf{Ideal}_S(1^\lambda, \mathcal{A}, x_0, (\mathsf{Sim}_\Pi, \mathsf{Ext}_\Pi))$
1. $\mathsf{crs} \leftarrow \mathsf{Setup}(1^\lambda)$.	1. $(\mathsf{crs}, \mathsf{td}, \pi_1) \leftarrow \mathsf{Sim}_\Pi(1^\lambda, S)$.
2. $\pi_1 \leftarrow \Pi_1(\mathsf{crs}, x_0; r_0)$ where $r_0 \leftarrow \{0, 1\}^\lambda$.	2. $(\pi_2, (x_1, r_1)) \leftarrow \mathcal{A}(\mathsf{crs}, \pi_1)$.
	3. $\mathsf{st} \leftarrow \mathsf{Ext}_\Pi(S, \mathsf{td}, \pi_2)$.
3. $(\pi_2, (x_1, r_1)) \leftarrow \mathcal{A}(\mathsf{crs}, \pi_1)$.	4. If $\pi_2 = \Pi_2(\mathsf{crs}, \pi_1, x_1; r_1)$ then:
4. Output	(a) Output $(\mathsf{crs}, \pi_1, f(x_0, x_1))$.
$(\mathsf{crs}, \pi_1, \mathsf{out}_\Pi(\mathsf{crs}, \pi_2, (x_0, r_0)))$.	5. If $\pi_2 \neq \Pi_2(\mathsf{crs}, \pi_1, x_1; r_1)$ then:
	(a) Output
	$(\mathsf{crs}, \pi_1, \mathsf{Sim}_\Pi(\mathsf{st}, \pi_2, x_0))$.

Fig. 2. Descriptions of Real_S and Ideal_S experiments.

Proposition 1. *Assume black-box access to a two-round oblivious transfer protocol secure against malicious adversaries in the common random/reference string model. There exists a two-party inner protocol for computing any two-party functionality f satisfying Definition 1. The computational and communication complexity of the protocol is* $\mathsf{poly}(\lambda, |f|)$ *where* $|f|$ *denotes the circuit-size of* f.

3.2 Construction from One-Sided NISC

We note that any one-sided NISC protocol gives rise to a two-party protocol satisfying Definition 1. This is because security against malicious receivers is implied by the security of one-sided NISC against malicious receivers. Robust security against semi-malicious senders is implied by security of one-sided NISC against malicious senders. Thus, we get the following corollary.

Corollary 1. *Let* f *be an arbitrary two-party functionality. Assume black-box access to an one-sided NISC protocol that securely computes* f. *Then, there exists a two-party inner protocol for computing* f *satisfying Definition 1. The computational and communication complexity of the protocol are the same as that of the NISC protocol.*

4 Two-Sided Black-Box NISC

In this section, we give our construction of black-box two-sided NISC protocol. We prove the following theorems.

Theorem 1 (Black-box two-sided NISC). *Assume black-box access to a two-round oblivious transfer protocol secure against malicious adversaries in the common random/reference string model. Then, there exists a two-round protocol for securely computing any two-party functionality f against malicious adversaries in the common random/reference string model where both parties get the output of f at the end of the protocol. The computational and communication complexity of the protocol is* $\mathsf{poly}(\lambda, |f|)$ *where* $|f|$ *denotes the circuit-size of* f.

Theorem 2 (Black-box arithmetic two-sided NISC). *Let* $\mathbb{F}$ *be a finite field and let* f *be a two-party functionality that is computable by an arithmetic branching program over* $\mathbb{F}$. *Assume black-box access to a two-round oblivious linear evaluation (OLE) protocol over* $\mathbb{F}$ *and an oblivious transfer protocol that is secure against malicious adversaries in the common random/reference string model. Then, there exists a two-round protocol for securely computing f against malicious adversaries in the common random/reference string model where both parties get the output of f at the end of the protocol. The computational and communication complexity of the protocol is* $\mathsf{poly}(\lambda, |f|)$ *where* $|f|$ *denotes the size of the branching program computing f and the protocol makes black-box use of* $\mathbb{F}$.

4.1   Building Blocks

The construction makes use of the following building blocks:

1. A two-round, two client, m server outer MPC protocol $\Psi = (\mathsf{Share}, \mathsf{Eval}, \mathsf{Dec})$ for computing the function f that satisfies security with abort against t server corruptions. We set $t = 2\lambda$ and $m = 3t + 1$. Based on [IKP10, Pas12], we give a construction of such a protocol making black-box use of a PRG in the full version where Eval does not involve cryptographic operations.
2. A two-round, two-party inner protocol (see Definition 1) $(\mathsf{Setup}_{\Pi_j}, \Pi_{j,1}, \Pi_{j,2},$ $\mathsf{out}_{\Pi_j})$ that delivers output to the receiver and computes $\mathsf{Eval}(j, \cdot)$ for each $j \in [m]$. From Proposition 1 and Corollary 1, such a protocol can be constructed making black-box use of a two-round malicious secure OT protocol or an one-sided NISC protocol.
3. A two-round malicious-secure two-party computation protocol $(\mathsf{CRSGen}, \Phi_1,$ $\Phi_2, \mathsf{out}_\Phi)$ for computing the $\mathsf{Sel}_{\lambda,m}$ functionality. The $\mathsf{Sel}_{\lambda,m}$ functionality takes in a string ρ_1 from the receiver, $(\rho_2, (s_1, \ldots, s_m))$ from the sender. It computes $\rho_1 \oplus \rho_2$ and uses it as random tape to select a random multiset (with replacement) K of $[m]$ of size λ. It then outputs $(K, \{s_i\}_{i \in K})$ to the receiver. [IKO+11] gave a two-round black-box protocol for computing $\mathsf{Sel}_{\lambda,m}$ based on two-round malicious-secure OT protocol.

The key lemma that we will prove in this section is the following.

Lemma 1. *Assume black-box access to a PRG and the protocols* $\{\Pi_j\}_{j \in [m]}$ *and* Φ *as described above. Then, there exists a two-round protocol for securely computing any two-party functionality* f *against malicious adversaries where both parties get the output of* f *at the end of the protocol.*

Theorem 1 is obtained by instantiating $\{\Pi_j\}_{j \in [m]}$ from Proposition 1. To obtain Theorem 2, we observe that in the protocols of [IKP10, Pas12], if f is computable by an arithmetic branching program then $\mathsf{Eval}(j, \cdot)$ is computable by a log-depth arithmetic circuit and does not involve any cryptographic operations. Thus, we can instantiate Π_j for each $j \in [m]$ using the one-sided NISC protocol for computing log-depth arithmetic circuits based on two-round malicious secure OLE [IKO+11, CDI+19, DIO21] using Corollary 1.

We give the construction of the protocol in Sect. 4.2 and the proof of security in Sect. 4.3

4.2   Construction

Let P_0 and P_1 be the two parties with private inputs x_0 and x_1 respectively. The parties additionally have as a common input the description of the function f. We give the formal description of the construction in Fig. 3.

4.3   Proof of Security

We give the description of the simulator below and show that the real and the ideal executions are computationally indistinguishable. Since the protocol is symmetric w.r.t. both P_0 and P_1, we assume without loss of generality that P_1 is corrupted by $\mathcal{A}$.

Description of Sim.

- CRSGen(1^λ): Sim does the following:
    1. It chooses $(\mathsf{crs}^0, \mathsf{td}^0, \phi_1^0) \leftarrow \mathsf{Sim}_\Phi(1^\lambda, S)$ and $(\mathsf{crs}^1, \mathsf{td}^1) \leftarrow \mathsf{Sim}_\Phi(1^\lambda, R)$.
    2. It samples a uniform multiset K^1 of $[m]$ of size λ.
    3. For each $j \in K^1$, it samples $\mathsf{crs}_j^0, \mathsf{crs}_j^1 \leftarrow \mathsf{Setup}_{\Pi_j}(1^\lambda)$.
    4. For each $j \notin K^1$, it samples $(\mathsf{crs}_j^0, \mathsf{td}_j^0, \pi_{j,1}^0) \leftarrow \mathsf{Sim}_{\Pi_j}(1^\lambda, S)$ and $(\mathsf{crs}_j^1, \mathsf{td}_j^1) \leftarrow \mathsf{Sim}_{\Pi_j}(1^\lambda, R)$.
    5. It outputs $(\{\mathsf{crs}_j^0, \mathsf{crs}_j^1\}_{j \in [m]}, \mathsf{crs}^0, \mathsf{crs}^1)$ as the CRS of the overall protocol.
- **Round-1:** To generate the first round message, Sim does the following:
    1. It runs the simulator Sim_Ψ for the outer protocol by corrupting the client P_1 and the set of servers given by K^1. Sim_Ψ provides with $\{x_j^0\}_{j \in K^1}$.
    2. For each $j \in K^1$, it computes $\pi_{j,1} \leftarrow \Pi_{j,1}(\mathsf{crs}_j^0, x_j^0; r_j^0)$ for uniformly chosen r_j^0.
    3. It sends ϕ_1^0 and $\{\pi_{j,1}^0\}_{j \in [m]}$ to $\mathcal{A}$.
    4. It receives the first round message from $\mathcal{A}$. For each $j \notin K^1$, it computes $x_j^1 \leftarrow \mathsf{Ext}_{\pi_j}(\mathsf{td}_j^1, \pi_{j,1}^1)$. It computes $\rho_1^1 \leftarrow \mathsf{Ext}_\Phi(R, \phi_1^1, \mathsf{td}^1)$.
- **Round-2:** To generate the second round message, Sim does the following:
    1. It sends $\{x_j^1\}_{j \notin K^1}$ to Sim_Ψ as the first round message from the corrupted client to the honest servers. Sim_Ψ queries the ideal functionality on input x_1 and Sim forwards this query to its own ideal functionality. It forwards the response from the ideal functionality back to Sim_Ψ. Sim_Ψ sends $\{z_j^1\}_{j \notin K^1}$ as the second round message from the honest servers to the corrupted client.
    2. For each $j \notin K^1$, it generates $\pi_{j,2}^1 \leftarrow \mathsf{Sim}_{\Pi_j}(R, \mathsf{crs}_j^1, z_j^1, x_j^1)$. For each $j \in K^1$, it generates $\pi_{j,2}^1$ as $\Pi_{j,1}(\mathsf{crs}_j^1, \pi_{j,1}^1, x_j^0; t_j^1)$ for uniformly chosen t_j^1.
    3. It generates $\phi_2^1 \leftarrow \mathsf{Sim}_\Phi(R, \{K^1, \{x_j^0, r_j^0, t_j^1\}_{j \in K^1}\})$.
    4. It sends ϕ_2^1 and $\{\pi_{j,2}^1\}_{j \in [m]}$ to $\mathcal{A}$.
    5. It receives the second round message from $\mathcal{A}$. For each $j \notin K^1$, it computes $\mathsf{st}_j \leftarrow \mathsf{Ext}_{\Pi_j}(S, \mathsf{td}_j^0, \pi_{j,2}^0)$.
    6. It also computes $(\rho_2^0, s_1^1, \ldots, s_m^1) \leftarrow \mathsf{Ext}_\Phi(S, \phi_2^0, \mathsf{td}^0)$.
- **Output Computation:** To compute the output, Sim does the following:
    1. It chooses a uniform multiset K^0 of $[m]$ size λ and uses it to perform the same checks as done by honest P_0 using $\{s_j^1\}_{j \in K^0}$. If any of the checks fail, it instructs the ideal functionality to deliver $\perp$ to P_0.
    2. Otherwise, it initializes an empty set C_1.
    3. For each $j \notin K^1$,
        (a) It parses s_j^1 as $(\overline{x}_j^1, r_j^1, t_j^0)$.

- **CRS Generation:** To generate the CRS,
  1. Sample $\mathsf{crs}_j^0, \mathsf{crs}_j^1 \leftarrow \mathsf{Setup}_{\Pi_j}(1^\lambda)$ for each $j \in [m]$.
  2. Sample $\mathsf{crs}^0, \mathsf{crs}^1 \leftarrow \mathsf{CRSGen}(1^\lambda)$.
  3. Output $(\{\mathsf{crs}_j^0, \mathsf{crs}_j^1\}_{j \in [m]}, \mathsf{crs}^0, \mathsf{crs}^1)$.
- **Round-1:** In the first round, each party P_i for $i \in \{0, 1\}$ does the following:
  1. It computes $(x_1^i, \ldots, x_m^i) \leftarrow \mathsf{Share}(1^\lambda, i, x_i; r_i)$ for uniformly chosen $r_i \leftarrow \{0, 1\}^\lambda$.
  2. For each $j \in [m]$, it samples a uniform random string r_j^i and computes $\pi_{j,1}^i \leftarrow \Pi_{j,1}(\mathsf{crs}_j^i, i, x_j^i; r_j^i)$.
  3. It samples a uniform random string $\rho_1^i \leftarrow \{0, 1\}^*$ and computes $\phi_1^i \leftarrow \Phi_1(\mathsf{crs}^i, i, \rho_1^i)$.
  4. It sends $\{\pi_{j,1}^i\}_{j \in [m]}$ and ϕ_1^i to the other party.
- **Round-2:** In the second round, each party P_i for $i \in \{0, 1\}$ does the following:
  1. For each $j \in [m]$, it samples a uniform random string t_j^{1-i} and computes $\pi_{j,2}^{1-i} \leftarrow \Pi_{j,2}(\mathsf{crs}_j^{1-i}, i, \pi_{j,1}^{1-i}, x_j^i; t_j^{1-i})$.
  2. For each $j \in [m]$, it sets $s_j^i = (x_j^i, r_j^i, t_j^{1-i})$.
  3. It samples a uniform random string $\rho_2^{1-i} \leftarrow \{0, 1\}^*$ and computes $\phi_2^{1-i} \leftarrow \Phi_2(\mathsf{crs}^{1-i}, i, \phi_1^{1-i}, (\rho_2^{1-i}, (s_1^i, \ldots, s_m^i)))$.
  4. It sends $\{\pi_{j,2}^{1-i}\}_{j \in [m]}$ and ϕ_2^{1-i} to the other party.
- **Output Computation:** To compute the output P_i for $i \in \{0, 1\}$ does the following:
  1. It computes $(K^i, \{s_j^{1-i}\}_{j \in K^i})$ using out_Φ on crs^i, ϕ_2^i and the random tape used to generate ϕ_1^i.
  2. For each $j \in K^i$, it:
     (a) Parses s_j^{1-i} as $(x_j^{1-i}, r_j^{1-i}, t_j^i)$.
     (b) Checks if (x_j^{1-i}, r_j^{1-i}) is a consistent input, randomness pair that explains the message $\pi_{j,1}^{1-i}$ and if (x_j^{1-i}, t_j^i) is a consistent input, randomness pair that explains the message $\pi_{j,2}^i$.
  3. If any of the above checks fail, then P_i aborts and outputs $\bot$.
  4. Else, for each $j \in [m]$, it computes $z_j^i := \mathsf{out}_{\Pi_j}(\mathsf{crs}_j^i, \pi_{j,2}^i, (x_j^i, r_j^i))$.
  5. It outputs $\mathsf{Dec}(z_1^i, \ldots, z_m^i, r_i)$.

Fig. 3. Black-Box Two-Sided NISC Protocol

(b) If either $(\overline{x}_j^1, r_j^1)$ is not a consistent input, randomness pair that explains the message $\pi_{j,1}^1$ or if $(\overline{x}_j^1, t_j^0)$ is not a consistent input, randomness pair that explains the message $\pi_{j,2}^1$, then we add j to C_1.

4. If $|C_1| \geq \lambda$, then it instructs the ideal functionality to output $\bot$ to P_1. Otherwise, it instructs Sim_Ψ to adaptively corrupt the set of servers indexed by C_1 and obtains $\{x_j^0\}_{j \in C_1}$.

5. For each $j \in C_1$, it computes z_j^0 as $\mathsf{Sim}_{\Pi_j}(S, \mathsf{st}_j, \pi_{j,2}^0, x_j^0)$. For each $j \in K^1$, it computes z_j^0 as $\mathsf{out}_{\Pi_j}(\mathsf{crs}_j^0, \pi_{j,2}^0, (x_j^0, r_j^0))$.

6. It sends $\{z_j^0\}_{j \in C_1 \cup K^1}$ to Sim_Ψ as the second round message from the corrupted servers to the honest client. If Sim_Ψ instructs the P_0 to abort,

then Sim instructs the ideal functionality to deliver $\perp$ to P_0. Otherwise, it instructs it to deliver the output of f to P_0.

Proof of Indistinguishability.

- $\underline{\mathsf{Hyb}_1}$: This corresponds to the output of the real experiment which comprises of the view of $\mathcal{A}$ corrupting P_1 and the output of honest P_0.
- $\underline{\mathsf{Hyb}_2}$: In this hybrid, we make the following changes:
    1. Sample $(\mathsf{crs}^0, \mathsf{td}^0, \phi_1^0) \leftarrow \mathsf{Sim}_\Phi(1^\lambda, S)$.
    2. Obtain ϕ_2^0 from $\mathcal{A}$.
    3. Compute $(\rho_2^0, (s_1^1, \ldots, s_m^1)) \leftarrow \mathsf{Ext}_\Phi(S, \phi_2^0, \mathsf{td}^0)$.
    4. Sample ρ_1^0 uniformly from $\{0,1\}^*$ and sample a multiset K^0 of size λ from $[m]$ using $\rho_1^0 \oplus \rho_2^0$ as the random tape.
    5. Use $(K^0, \{s_j^1\}_{j \in K^0})$ to perform the same checks described in output computation.

  In Lemma 2, we show from the simulation security of Φ against corrupted senders that $\mathsf{Hyb}_1 \approx_c \mathsf{Hyb}_2$.
- $\underline{\mathsf{Hyb}_3}$: In this hybrid, we make the following changes:
    1. Sample $(\mathsf{crs}^1, \mathsf{td}^1) \leftarrow \mathsf{Sim}_\Phi(1^\lambda, R)$.
    2. Obtain ϕ_1^1 from $\mathcal{A}$.
    3. Compute $\rho_1^1 \leftarrow \mathsf{Ext}_\Phi(R, \phi_1^1, \mathsf{td}^1)$.
    4. Sample a multiset K^1 of size λ from $[m]$ using a random tape ρ^1.
    5. Generate $\phi_2^1 \leftarrow \mathsf{Sim}_\Phi(R, \{K^1, \{s_j^0\}_{j \in K^1}\})$.
    6. Use ϕ_2^1 to generate the final round message in the protocol.

  In Lemma 3, we use the simulation security of Φ against corrupted receivers to show that $\mathsf{Hyb}_2 \approx_c \mathsf{Hyb}_3$.
- $\underline{\mathsf{Hyb}_4}$: In this hybrid, we make the following changes:
    1. For each $j \in [m]$, we parse s_j^1 as $(\overline{x}_j^1, r_j^1, t_j^0)$.
    2. We initialize an empty set C_1.
    3. For each $j \notin K^1$,
        (a) If either $(\overline{x}_j^1, r_j^1)$ is not a consistent input, randomness pair that explains the message $\pi_{j,1}^1$, or if $(\overline{x}_j^1, t_j^0)$ is not a consistent input, randomness pair that explains the message $\pi_{j,2}^1$, then we add j to C_1.
    4. If $|C_1| \geq \lambda$, then we abort and use $\perp$ as the output of honest P_0.

  In Lemma 4, we show that $\mathsf{Hyb}_3 \approx_s \mathsf{Hyb}_4$.
- $\underline{\mathsf{Hyb}_5}$: In this hybrid, we make the following changes:
    1. Before generating the CRS, we sample a uniform multiset K^1 of $[m]$ with size λ.
    2. We sample $(\mathsf{crs}_j^0, \mathsf{td}_j^0, \pi_{j,1}^0) \leftarrow \mathsf{Sim}_{\Pi_j}(1^\lambda, S)$ for each $j \notin K^1$. We use $\{\mathsf{crs}_j^0\}_{j \notin K^1}$ as part of the CRS and use $\{\pi_{j,1}^0\}_{j \notin K^1}$ to generate the first round message from P_0.
    3. We receive the second round message from $\mathcal{A}$ (that includes $\pi_{j,2}^0$ for each $j \in [m]$) and extract $\{(\overline{x}_j^1, r_j^1, t_j^0)\}_{j \in [m]}$ as before.
    4. For each $j \notin K^1$, we compute $\mathsf{st}_j \leftarrow \mathsf{Ext}_{\Pi_j}(S, \mathsf{td}_j^0, \pi_{j,2}^0)$.
    5. We compute the set C_1 as before.

6. For each $j \in C_1$, we set $z_j^0 = \mathsf{Sim}_{\Pi_j}(S, \mathsf{st}_j, \pi_{j,2}^0, x_j^0)$.
7. For each $j \in K^1$, we compute z_j^0 as before.
8. For each $j \notin C_1 \cup K^1$, we set $z_j^0 = \mathsf{Eval}(j, x_j^0, \overline{x}_j^1)$.

In Lemma 5, we rely on the robust security of Π_j against semi-malicious senders to show that $\mathsf{Hyb}_4 \approx_c \mathsf{Hyb}_5$.

- Hyb_6 : In this hybrid, we make the following changes:
  1. We generate $(\mathsf{crs}_j^1, \mathsf{td}_j^1) \leftarrow \mathsf{Sim}_{\Pi_j}(1^\lambda, R)$ for each $j \notin K^1$.
  2. On receiving $\{\pi_{j,1}^1\}_{j \in [m]}$ from $\mathcal{A}$, we run $\mathsf{Ext}_{\Pi_j}(\mathsf{td}_j^1, \pi_{j,1}^1)$ to obtain x_j^1 for each $j \notin K^1$.
  3. For each $j \notin K^1$, we generate $\pi_{j,2}^1 \leftarrow \mathsf{Sim}_{\Pi_j}(R, \mathsf{crs}_j^1, z_j^1 = \mathsf{Eval}(j, x_j^0, x_j^1), x_j^1)$. We use this to generate the second round message from P_0.

In Lemma 6, we use the security of Π_j against malicious senders for each $j \in [m]$ to show that $\mathsf{Hyb}_5 \approx_c \mathsf{Hyb}_6$.

- Hyb_7 : In this hybrid, for each $j \notin K^1 \cup C_1$, we use z_j^1 instead of z_j^0 to compute the output of honest P_0. It follows from the correctness of extraction property of $\{\Pi_j\}_{j \notin K^1 \cup C_1}$ that $z_j^0 = z_j^1$ for each $j \notin K^1 \cup C_1$ except with negligible probability and hence, $\mathsf{Hyb}_6 \approx_s \mathsf{Hyb}_7$.

- Hyb_8 : In this hybrid, we make the following changes:
  1. We start running the simulator Sim_Ψ by corrupting the client P_1 and the set of servers indexed by K^1. We receive $\{x_j^1\}_{j \in K^1}$ from the simulator and use this to generate the first round message from P_0.
  2. On receiving $\{\pi_{j,1}^1\}_{j \in [m]}$ from $\mathcal{A}$, we run $\mathsf{Ext}_{\Pi_j}(\mathsf{td}_j^1, \pi_{j,1}^1)$ to obtain x_j^1 for each $j \notin K^1$. We send $\{x_j^1\}_{j \notin K^1}$ to Sim_Ψ as the first round message from the adversarial client P_1 to the honest servers.
  3. Sim_Ψ queries its ideal functionality on an input x_1 and we forward this to our ideal functionality and respond with $f(x_0, x_1)$.
  4. Sim_Ψ provides $\{z_j^1\}_{j \notin K^1}$. We use this to generate $\pi_{j,2}^1 \leftarrow \mathsf{Sim}_{\Pi_j}(z_j^1, x_j^1)$ for each $j \notin K^1$.
  5. We receive the second round message from $\mathcal{A}$ and use this to extract $\{s_j^1\}_{j \in [m]}$ as before. We compute the set C_1 and abort if $|C_1| \geq \lambda$.
  6. For each $j \notin K^1$, we compute $\mathsf{st}_j \leftarrow \mathsf{Ext}_{\Pi_j}(S, \mathsf{td}_j^0, \pi_{j,2}^0)$.
  7. We now instruct Sim_Ψ to adaptively corrupt the set of servers corresponding to C_1 and obtain $\{x_j^0\}_{j \in C_1}$. We then compute $z_j^0 = \mathsf{Sim}_{\Pi_j}(\mathsf{st}_j, \pi_{j,2}^0, x_j^0)$ for each $j \in C_1$. We compute z_j^0 for each $j \in K^1$ as before.
  8. We send $\{z_j^0\}_{j \in C_1 \cup K^1}$ as the second round message from the corrupted servers to the honest client to Sim_Ψ. If Sim_Ψ instructs the client to abort, we instruct P_0 to do the same. Otherwise, we instruct P_0 to output $f(x_0, x_1)$.

In Lemma 7, we use the security of the outer protocol to argue that $\mathsf{Hyb}_7 \approx_c \mathsf{Hyb}_8$. Notice that Hyb_8 is identically distributed to the ideal world using Sim.

Lemma 2. *Assuming the simulation security of the protocol Φ against corrupted senders, we have $\mathsf{Hyb}_1 \approx_c \mathsf{Hyb}_2$.*

Proof. Assume for the sake of contradiction that Hyb_1 and Hyb_2 are computationally distinguishable with non-negligible advantage. We show that this contradicts the simulation security of the protocol Φ against corrupted senders.

We start interacting with the external challenger and provide a uniformly chosen random string ρ_1^0 as the challenge receiver input. The challenger responds with crs^0. We use this to generate the CRS in the overall protocol. The challenger also sends ϕ_1^0. We use this to generate the first round message in the protocol by sampling the other components of the first round message as in Hyb_1. We generate the second round message as before and obtain the second round message from $\mathcal{A}$. We forward ϕ_2^0 from the second round message received from $\mathcal{A}$ to the external challenger. The external challenger provides with $K^0, \{s_j^1\}_{j \in K^0}$ as the output of the honest P_0. We use this to perform the same checks as described in the output computation. We finally output the view of $\mathcal{A}$ and the output of P_0.

If the messages in the protocol Φ and the CRS and the output of honest P_0 are generated as in the real experiment, then the output of the above reduction is identically distributed to Hyb_1. Else, it is identically distributed to Hyb_2. Thus, if Hyb_2 and Hyb_1 are computationally distinguishable with non-negligible advantage then this breaks the simulation security of Φ against corrupted senders and this is a contradiction.

Lemma 3. *Assuming the simulation security of* Sim_Φ *against corrupted senders, we have* $\mathsf{Hyb}_2 \approx_c \mathsf{Hyb}_3$.

Proof. Assume for the sake of contradiction that Hyb_2 and Hyb_3 are computationally distinguishable with non-negligible advantage. We show that this contradicts the simulation security of Φ against corrupted receivers.

We interact with the external challenger and provide a uniformly chosen ρ_2^1 and $(s_1^0, \ldots, s_m^0)$ as the challenge sender input. The external challenger provides with crs^1 and we use this to generate the CRS of the overall protocol. We start interacting with the adversary and obtain the first round message ϕ_1^1 from it. We forward this to the external challenger. The external challenger provides with the second round message ϕ_2^1 and we use this to generate the second round message in the overall protocol. We compute the output of honest P_0 as before and finally output the view of $\mathcal{A}$ and the output of the honest P_0.

Note that if the messages in the protocol Φ and the CRS are generated by the external challenger as in the real experiment then the output of the above reduction is distributed identically to Hyb_2. Else, it is distributed identically to Hyb_3. Thus, if Hyb_3 and Hyb_2 are computationally distinguishable with non-negligible advantage then this breaks the simulation security of Φ against corrupted receivers and this is a contradiction.

Lemma 4. $\mathsf{Hyb}_3 \approx_s \mathsf{Hyb}_4$.

Proof. Note that the only difference between Hyb_3 and Hyb_4 is that in Hyb_4 we abort if $|C_1| \geq \lambda$ To show that Hyb_3 and Hyb_4 are statistically close, we prove that if the above condition holds, then in Hyb_3, the checks done by the honest P_0 fails with overwhelming probability.

Note that K^0 is distributed as a random multiset of $[m]$ of size λ. If $C_1 \cap K^0 \neq \emptyset$, then the the honest P_0 in Hyb_3 also aborts. We show that this event happens with overwhelming probability.

$$\Pr[|K^0 \cap C_1| = 0] = (1 - \frac{|C_1|}{m})^\lambda$$
$$\leq e^{-|C_1|\lambda/m}$$
$$\leq e^{-\lambda^2/m}$$
$$\leq e^{-O(\lambda)}$$

where the last inequality follows since $m = O(\lambda)$. This completes the proof of the lemma.

Lemma 5. *Assuming the robust security of Π_j against semi-malicious senders for each $j \in [m]$, we have $\mathsf{Hyb}_4 \approx_c \mathsf{Hyb}_5$.*

Proof. Assume for the sake of contradiction that Hyb_4 and Hyb_5 are distinguishable with non-negligible advantage. We sample a uniform multiset K^1 of $[m]$ of size λ. We now show that if Hyb_4 and Hyb_5 are computationally distinguishable then this contradicts the robust security of Π_j against semi-malicious senders for some $j \notin K^1$.

Let $\prec$ be a total order on the set $[m] \setminus K^1$. If Hyb_4 and Hyb_5 are distinguishable with non-negligible advantage, then by a standard averaging argument there exists $\mathsf{Hyb}_{4,j}$ and $\mathsf{Hyb}'_{4,j}$ (described below) that are distinguishable with non-negligible advantage. In both the hybrids, for each $j^* \prec j$, $(\mathsf{crs}^0_{j^*}, \pi^0_{j^*,1})$ is generated as in Hyb_5 whereas for each $j \prec j^*$, $(\mathsf{crs}^0_{j^*}, \pi^0_{j^*,1})$ is generated as in Hyb_4. The only difference is that in $\mathsf{Hyb}_{4,j}$, $(\mathsf{crs}^0_j, \pi^0_{j,1})$ is generated as in Hyb_5 whereas it is generated as in Hyb_4 in $\mathsf{Hyb}'_{4,j}$. We use this to construct an attacker that breaks the robust security of Π_j against semi-malicious senders.

We interact with the external challenger and provide x^0_j as the challenge receiver message. The challenger provides $(\mathsf{crs}^0_j, \pi^0_{j,1})$. We use this to generate the CRS and the first round message of the overall protocol. We receive the second round message from the adversary and use it to extract $\{(\overline{x}^1_j, r^1_j, t^0_j)\}_{j \in [m]}$. We compute the set C_1 as before and abort if $|C_1| \geq \lambda$. For each $j \in C_1$, we send $\overline{x}^1_j$ and an arbitrary t^0_j (that does not explain the messages correctly) along with $\pi^0_{j,2}$ to the external challenger. If $j \notin C_1 \cup K^1$, we send $(\overline{x}^1_j, t^0_j)$ along with $\pi^0_{j,2}$ to the external challenger. We receive the output z^0_j and use this to compute the output of the overall protocol as before.

We note that if $(\mathsf{crs}^0_j, \pi^0_{j,1}, z^0_j)$ was generated by the external challenger as in the Real_S experiment then the output of the above reduction is identically distributed to $\mathsf{Hyb}'_{4,j}$. Else, it is distributed identically to $\mathsf{Hyb}_{4,j}$. Thus, if $\mathsf{Hyb}_{4,j}$ and $\mathsf{Hyb}'_{4,j}$ are distinguishable with non-negligible advantage, then the above reduction breaks the robust security of Π_j against semi-malicious senders with non-negligible advantage and this is a contradiction.

Lemma 6. *Assuming the security of Π_j against malicious receivers for each $j \in [m]$, we have $\mathsf{Hyb}_6 \approx_c \mathsf{Hyb}_5$.*

Proof. Assume for the sake of contradiction that Hyb_5 and Hyb_6 are distinguishable with non-negligible advantage. We sample a uniform multiset K^1 of $[m]$ of size λ. We now show that this contradicts the security of Π_j against malicious receiver for some $j \notin K^1$.

Let $\prec$ be a total order on the set $[m] \setminus K^1$. If Hyb_5 and Hyb_6 are distinguishable with non-negligible advantage then by a standard averaging argument, there exists $\mathsf{Hyb}_{5,j}$ and $\mathsf{Hyb}'_{5,j}$ (described below) that are distinguishable with non-negligible advantage. In both the hybrids, for each $j^* \prec j$, $(\pi^1_{j^*,2}, \mathsf{crs}^1_{j^*})$ is generated as in Hyb_6 whereas for each $j \prec j^*$, $(\pi^1_{j,2}, \mathsf{crs}^1_{j^*})$ is generated as in Hyb_5. The only difference is that in $\mathsf{Hyb}_{5,j}$, $(\mathsf{crs}^1_j, \pi^1_{j,2})$ is generated as in Hyb_6 whereas it is generated as in Hyb_5 in $\mathsf{Hyb}'_{5,j}$. We use this to construct an attacker that breaks the security of Π_j against malicious receivers.

We interact with the external challenger and provide x_j^0 as the challenge sender input. We obtain crs^1_j from the external challenger. We receive $\pi^1_{j,1}$ from the adversary and forward this to the challenger. The challenger responds with $\pi^1_{j,2}$ and we use these to generate the view of the adversary $\mathcal{A}$ and compute the output of P_0 as in $\mathsf{Hyb}'_{5,j}$.

We note that if $(\pi^1_{j,2}, \mathsf{crs}^1_j)$ was generated by the external challenger as in Real_R then the output of the above reduction is identically distributed to $\mathsf{Hyb}'_{5,j}$. Else, it is distributed identically to $\mathsf{Hyb}_{5,j}$. Thus, if $\mathsf{Hyb}_{5,j}$ and $\mathsf{Hyb}'_{5,j}$ are distinguishable with non-negligible advantage, then the above reduction breaks the security of Π_j against malicious receivers with non-negligible advantage and this is a contradiction.

Lemma 7. *Assuming the security of the outer MPC protocol $\Psi = (\mathsf{Share}, \mathsf{Eval}, \mathsf{Dec})$, we have that $\mathsf{Hyb}_7 \approx_c \mathsf{Hyb}_8$.*

Proof. Assume for the sake of contradiction that Hyb_7 and Hyb_8 are computationally distinguishable with non-negligible advantage. We show that this contradicts the security of outer protocol Ψ.

We start interacting with the outer protocol challenger and provide x_0 as the honest client input. We instruct the challenger to corrupt P_1 and the set of servers indexed by K^1. The challenger provides $\{x_j^0\}_{j \in K^1}$ as the first round message from the honest client to the corrupted servers and we use this to generate the first round message in the protocol. On receiving the first round message from $\mathcal{A}$, we obtain $x_j^1 \leftarrow \mathsf{Ext}_{\Pi_j}(\mathsf{td}^1_j, \pi^1_{j,1})$ for each $j \notin K^1$ and send $\{x_j^1\}_{j \notin K^1}$ as the first round message from the adversarial client to the honest servers. The challenger replies with $\{z_j^1\}_{j \notin K^1}$. We use this to generate $\pi^1_{j,2} \leftarrow \mathsf{Sim}_{\Pi_j}(z_j^1, x_j^1)$ for each $j \notin K^1$ and compute the second round message of the overall protocol. We receive the second round message from the adversary. We use this to extract $\{s_j^1\}_{j \in [m]}$ as before. We compute the set C_1 and abort if $|C_1| \geq \lambda$. Additionally, for each $j \in C_1$, we compute $\mathsf{st}_j \leftarrow \mathsf{Ext}_{\Pi_j}(S, \mathsf{td}^0_j, \pi^0_{j,2})$. We now instruct the challenger to adaptively corrupt the set of servers corresponding to C_1 and obtain $\{x_j^0\}_{j \in C_1}$.

We then compute $z_j^0 = \mathsf{Sim}_{\Pi_j}(\mathsf{st}_j, \pi_{j,2}^0, x_j^0)$ for each $j \in C_1$. We compute z_j^0 for each $j \in K^1$ as before. We send $\{z_j^0\}_{j \in C_1 \cup K^1}$ as the second round message from the corrupted servers to the honest client to the challenger. If the challenger instructs the client to abort, we instruct P_0 to do the same. Otherwise, we instruct P_0 to output whatever is provided by the challenger as the output. We output the view of $\mathcal{A}$ and the output of P_0.

Note that if the messages received from the challenger are computed as in the real execution of the protocol Ψ, then the output of the above reduction is identically to Hyb_7. Else, it is distributed identically to Hyb_8. Hence, if Hyb_7 and Hyb_8 are distinguishable with non-negligible advantage, then the above reduction breaks the security of the outer protocol Ψ with non-negligible advantage and this is a contradiction.

5   Multiparty Inner Protocol

In this section, we give the definition of a three-round multiparty protocol that satisfies some special properties (known as multiparty inner protocol) and give a construction based on two-round malicious secure oblivious transfer. In the next section, we will use this multiparty inner protocol as the key ingredient to construct a three-round malicious secure protocol for general functionalities.

5.1   Definition

A three-round n-party protocol for computing a function f is given by a tuple of PPT algorithms $(\mathsf{Setup}, \Pi_1, \Pi_2, \Pi_3, \mathsf{out}_\Pi)$ and has the following syntax. Setup algorithm takes in the security parameter 1^λ (encoded in unary) and outputs the common reference string crs. For each $r \in [3]$, Π_r is the r-th round message function that takes in crs, index i of the party, the transcript seen so far (denoted by $\pi(r-1)$), the i-th party's private input x_i, its random tape r_i and outputs π_r^i. out_Π is the public decoder (see [ABG+20] for the definition of a publicly decodable MPC) that takes in the transcript of the three rounds $\pi(3)$ and outputs $f(x_1, \ldots, x_n)$.

Definition 2. *A three-round n-party protocol* $(\mathsf{Setup}, \Pi_1, \Pi_2, \Pi_3, \mathsf{out}_\Pi)$ *for computing a function f is said to be a multiparty inner protocol with publicly decodable transcript if it satisfies:*

- **Correctness:** *For any choice of inputs $x_1, \ldots, x_n$, we have:*

$$\Pr[\mathsf{out}_\Pi(\pi(3)) = f(x_1, \ldots, x_n)] = 1$$

  where $\pi(3)$ is the transcript generated in the first three rounds of the protocol.
- **Security:** *For any subset $M \subset [n]$ of the parties, there exists a (stateful) PPT simulator Sim_Π such that for any (stateful) non-uniform PPT adversary $\mathcal{A}$*

corrupting the set of parties given by M and for any set $\{x_i\}_{i \in [n] \setminus M}$ of the honest party inputs, we have:

$$\Big| \Pr[\mathsf{Real}(1^\lambda, M, \mathcal{A}, \{x_i\}_{i \in [n] \setminus M}) = 1]$$

$$- \Pr[\mathsf{Ideal}(1^\lambda, M, \mathcal{A}, \{x_i\}_{i \in [n] \setminus M}, \mathsf{Sim}_\Pi) = 1] \Big| \leq \mathsf{negl}(n)$$

where Real and Ideal experiments are described in Fig. 4.

In this section, we state the following proposition and defer the proof to the full version.

Proposition 2. *Assume black-box access to a two-round oblivious transfer protocol that is secure against malicious adversaries in the common random/reference string model. Then, there exists a three-round inner protocol for computing any n-party functionality f satisfying Definition 2. The computational and communication complexity of this protocol is $\mathsf{poly}(\lambda, n, |f|)$ where $|f|$ is the circuit-size of f.*

6 Round-Optimal Black-Box MPC

In this section, we give a construction of a three-round MPC protocol that makes black-box use of two-round malicious secure oblivious transfer. The round-

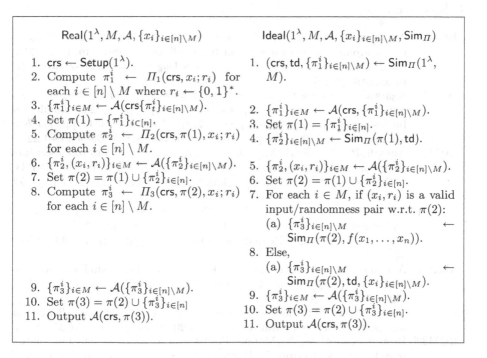

Fig. 4. Descriptions of Real and Ideal experiments.

optimality of this construction follows from [ABG+20]. We prove the following theorem.

Theorem 3 (Black-box three-round MPC). *Assume black-box access to a two-round oblivious transfer protocol that is secure against malicious adversaries in the common random/reference string model. Then, there exists a three-round protocol for computing any n-party functionality f in the common random/reference string model that satisfies security with unanimous abort against malicious adversaries corrupting an arbitrary subset of the parties. The protocol works over broadcast channels and its computational and communication complexity is* $\mathsf{poly}(\lambda, n, |f|)$ *where* $|f|$ *is the circuit-size of f.*

The proof of this theorem is deferred to the full version of the paper.

Acknowledgments. Y. Ishai was supported in part by ERC Project NTSC (742754), BSF grant 2018393, and ISF grant 2774/20. D. Khurana was supported in part by DARPA SIEVE award, a gift from Visa Research, and a C3AI DTI award. A. Sahai was supported in part from a Simons Investigator Award, DARPA SIEVE award, NTT Research, NSF Frontier Award 1413955, BSF grant 2012378, a Xerox Faculty Research Award, a Google Faculty Research Award, and an Okawa Foundation Research Grant. This material is based upon work supported by the Defense Advanced Research Projects Agency through Award HR00112020024. A. Srinivasan was supported in part by a SERB startup grant.

References

[ABG+20] Applebaum, B., Brakerski, Z., Garg, S., Ishai, Y., Srinivasan, A.: Separating two-round secure computation from oblivious transfer. In: ITCS 2020, vol. 151 of LIPIcs, pp. 71:1–71:18. Schloss Dagstuhl - Leibniz-Zentrum für Informatik (2020)

[ABG+21] Agarwal, A., Bartusek, J., Goyal, V., Khurana, D., Malavolta, G.: Two-round maliciously secure computation with super-polynomial simulation. In: Nissim, K., Waters, B. (eds.) TCC 2021. LNCS, vol. 13042, pp. 654–685. Springer, Cham (2021). https://doi.org/10.1007/978-3-030-90459-3_22

[ACJ17] Ananth, P., Choudhuri, A.R., Jain, A.: A new approach to round-optimal secure multiparty computation. In: Katz, J., Shacham, H. (eds.) CRYPTO 2017. LNCS, vol. 10401, pp. 468–499. Springer, Cham (2017). https://doi.org/10.1007/978-3-319-63688-7_16

[AIR01] Aiello, B., Ishai, Y., Reingold, O.: Priced oblivious transfer: how to sell digital goods. In: Pfitzmann, B. (ed.) EUROCRYPT 2001. LNCS, vol. 2045, pp. 119–135. Springer, Heidelberg (2001). https://doi.org/10.1007/3-540-44987-6_8

[AMR21] Abdolmaleki, B., Malavolta, G., Rahimi, A.: Two-round concurrently secure two-party computation. IACR Cryptol. ePrint Arch., pp. 1357 (2021)

[BCG+19] Boyle, E., et al.: Efficient two-round OT extension and silent non-interactive secure computation. In: CCS 2019, pp. 291–308. ACM (2019)

[BDM22] Branco, P., Döttling, N., Mateus, P.: Two-round oblivious linear evaluation from learning with errors. In: Hanaoka, G., Shikata, J., Watanabe, Y. (eds.) PKC 2022. LNCS, vol. 13177, pp. 379–408. Springer, Cham (2022). https://doi.org/10.1007/978-3-030-97121-2_14

[Bea95] Beaver, D.: Precomputing oblivious transfer. In: Coppersmith, D. (ed.) CRYPTO 1995. LNCS, vol. 963, pp. 97–109. Springer, Heidelberg (1995). https://doi.org/10.1007/3-540-44750-4_8

[BF22] Bitansky, N., Freizeit, S.: Statistically sender-private OT from LPN and derandomization. In: Crypto 2022 (2022)

[BFM88] Blum, M., Feldman, P., Micali, S.: Non-interactive zero-knowledge and its applications. In: STOC, vol. 1988, pp. 103–112 (1988)

[BGI+17] Badrinarayanan, S., Garg, S., Ishai, Y., Sahai, A., Wadia, A.: Two-message witness indistinguishability and secure computation in the plain model from new assumptions. In: Takagi, T., Peyrin, T. (eds.) ASIACRYPT 2017. LNCS, vol. 10626, pp. 275–303. Springer, Cham (2017). https://doi.org/10.1007/978-3-319-70700-6_10

[BGI+18] Boyle, E., Gilboa, N., Ishai, Y., Lin, H., Tessaro, S.: Foundations of homomorphic secret sharing. In: ITCS 2018, pp. 21:1–21:21 (2018)

[BGJ+17] Badrinarayanan, S., Goyal, V., Jain, A., Khurana, D., Sahai, A.: Round optimal concurrent MPC via strong simulation. In: Kalai, Y., Reyzin, L. (eds.) TCC 2017. LNCS, vol. 10677, pp. 743–775. Springer, Cham (2017). https://doi.org/10.1007/978-3-319-70500-2_25

[BGJ+18] Badrinarayanan, S., Goyal, V., Jain, A., Kalai, Y.T., Khurana, D., Sahai, A.: Promise zero knowledge and its applications to round optimal MPC. In: Shacham, H., Boldyreva, A. (eds.) CRYPTO 2018. LNCS, vol. 10992, pp. 459–487. Springer, Cham (2018). https://doi.org/10.1007/978-3-319-96881-0_16

[BHP17] Brakerski, Z., Halevi, S., Polychroniadou, A.: Four round secure computation without setup. In: Kalai, Y., Reyzin, L. (eds.) TCC 2017. LNCS, vol. 10677, pp. 645–677. Springer, Cham (2017). https://doi.org/10.1007/978-3-319-70500-2_22

[BL18] Fabrice Benhamouda and Huijia Lin. k-round MPC from k-round OT via garbled interactive circuits. EUROCRYPT, 2018

[BLV03] Barak, B., Lindell, Y., Vadhan, S.P.: Lower bounds for non-black-box zero knowledge. In: FOCS, vol. 2003, pp. 384–393 (2003)

[CCG+20] Rai Choudhuri, A., Ciampi, M., Goyal, V., Jain, A., Ostrovsky, R.: Round optimal secure multiparty computation from minimal assumptions. In: Pass, R., Pietrzak, K. (eds.) TCC 2020. LNCS, vol. 12551, pp. 291–319. Springer, Cham (2020). https://doi.org/10.1007/978-3-030-64378-2_11

[CDI+19] Chase, M., Dodis, Y., Ishai, Y., Kraschewski, D., Liu, T., Ostrovsky, R., Vaikuntanathan, V.: Reusable non-interactive secure computation. In: Boldyreva, A., Micciancio, D. (eds.) CRYPTO 2019. LNCS, vol. 11694, pp. 462–488. Springer, Cham (2019). https://doi.org/10.1007/978-3-030-26954-8_15

[DGH+20] Döttling, N., Garg, S., Hajiabadi, M., Masny, D., Wichs, D.: Two-round oblivious transfer from CDH or LPN. In: Canteaut, A., Ishai, Y. (eds.) EUROCRYPT 2020. LNCS, vol. 12106, pp. 768–797. Springer, Cham (2020). https://doi.org/10.1007/978-3-030-45724-2_26

[DIO21] Dittmer, S., Ishai, Y., Ostrovsky, R.: Line-point zero knowledge and its applications. In: ITC 2021, pp. 5:1–5:24 (2021)

[FJK21] Fernando, R., Jain, A., Komargodski, I.: Maliciously-secure mrnisc in the plain model. In: IACR Cryptol. ePrint Arch., pp. 1319 (2021)

[GGJS12] Garg, S., Goyal, V., Jain, A., Sahai, A.: Concurrently secure computation in constant rounds. In: Pointcheval, D., Johansson, T. (eds.) EUROCRYPT 2012. LNCS, vol. 7237, pp. 99–116. Springer, Heidelberg (2012). https://doi.org/10.1007/978-3-642-29011-4_8

[GIKR02] Gennaro, R., Ishai, Y., Kushilevitz, E., Rabin, T.: On 2-round secure multiparty computation. In: Yung, M. (ed.) CRYPTO 2002. LNCS, vol. 2442, pp. 178–193. Springer, Heidelberg (2002). https://doi.org/10.1007/3-540-45708-9_12

[GIS18] Garg, S., Ishai, Y., Srinivasan, A.: Two-round MPC: information-theoretic and black-box. In: Beimel, A., Dziembowski, S. (eds.) TCC 2018. LNCS, vol. 11239, pp. 123–151. Springer, Cham (2018). https://doi.org/10.1007/978-3-030-03807-6_5

[GKP17] Garg, S., Kiyoshima, S., Pandey, O.: On the exact round complexity of self-composable two-party computation. In: Coron, J.-S., Nielsen, J.B. (eds.) EUROCRYPT 2017. LNCS, vol. 10211, pp. 194–224. Springer, Cham (2017). https://doi.org/10.1007/978-3-319-56614-6_7

[GMPP16] Garg, S., Mukherjee, P., Pandey, O., Polychroniadou, A.: The exact round complexity of secure computation. In: Fischlin, M., Coron, J.-S. (eds.) EUROCRYPT 2016. LNCS, vol. 9666, pp. 448–476. Springer, Heidelberg (2016). https://doi.org/10.1007/978-3-662-49896-5_16

[Goy11] Goyal, V.: Constant round non-malleable protocols using one way functions. In: Fortnow, L., Vadhan, S.P. (eds) 43rd ACM STOC, pp. 695–704, San Jose, CA, USA, 6–8 June 2011. ACM Press

[GS18] Garg, S., Srinivasan, A.: Two-round multiparty secure computation from minimal assumptions. In: Nielsen, J.B., Rijmen, V. (eds.) EUROCRYPT 2018. LNCS, vol. 10821, pp. 468–499. Springer, Cham (2018). https://doi.org/10.1007/978-3-319-78375-8_16

[HHPV18] Halevi, S., Hazay, C., Polychroniadou, A., Venkitasubramaniam, M.: Round-optimal secure multi-party computation. Journal of Cryptology 34(3), 1–63 (2021). https://doi.org/10.1007/s00145-021-09382-3

[IKNP03] Ishai, Y., Kilian, J., Nissim, K., Petrank, E.: Extending oblivious transfers efficiently. In: Boneh, D. (ed.) CRYPTO 2003. LNCS, vol. 2729, pp. 145–161. Springer, Heidelberg (2003). https://doi.org/10.1007/978-3-540-45146-4_9

[IKO+11] Ishai, Y., Kushilevitz, E., Ostrovsky, R., Prabhakaran, M., Sahai, A.: Efficient non-interactive secure computation. In: Paterson, K.G. (ed.) EUROCRYPT 2011. LNCS, vol. 6632, pp. 406–425. Springer, Heidelberg (2011). https://doi.org/10.1007/978-3-642-20465-4_23

[IKP10] Ishai, Y., Kushilevitz, E., Paskin, A.: Secure multiparty computation with minimal interaction. In: Rabin, T. (ed.) CRYPTO 2010. LNCS, vol. 6223, pp. 577–594. Springer, Heidelberg (2010). https://doi.org/10.1007/978-3-642-14623-7_31

[IKSS21] Ishai, Y., Khurana, D., Sahai, A., Srinivasan, A.: On the round complexity of black-box secure MPC. In: Malkin, T., Peikert, C. (eds.) CRYPTO 2021. LNCS, vol. 12826, pp. 214–243. Springer, Cham (2021). https://doi.org/10.1007/978-3-030-84245-1_8

[IKSS22] Ishai, Y., Khurana, D., Sahai, A., Srinivasan, A.: Round-optimal black-box protocol compilers. In: Dunkelman, O., Dziembowski, S. (eds.) EUROCRYPT 2022. LNCS, vol. 13275, pp. 210–240. Springer, Cham (2022). https://doi.org/10.1007/978-3-031-06944-4_8

[IPS08] Ishai, Y., Prabhakaran, M., Sahai, A.: Founding cryptography on oblivious transfer – efficiently. In: Wagner, D. (ed.) CRYPTO 2008. LNCS, vol. 5157, pp. 572–591. Springer, Heidelberg (2008). https://doi.org/10.1007/978-3-540-85174-5_32

[IR90] Impagliazzo, R., Rudich, S.: Limits on the provable consequences of one-way permutations. In: Goldwasser, S. (ed.) CRYPTO 1988. LNCS, vol. 403, pp. 8–26. Springer, New York (1990). https://doi.org/10.1007/0-387-34799-2_2

[KMO14] Kiyoshima, S., Manabe, Y., Okamoto, T.: Constant-round black-box construction of composable multi-party computation protocol. In: Lindell, Y. (ed.) TCC 2014. LNCS, vol. 8349, pp. 343–367. Springer, Heidelberg (2014). https://doi.org/10.1007/978-3-642-54242-8_15

[KO04] Katz, J., Ostrovsky, R.: Round-optimal secure two-party computation. In: Franklin, M. (ed.) CRYPTO 2004. LNCS, vol. 3152, pp. 335–354. Springer, Heidelberg (2004). https://doi.org/10.1007/978-3-540-28628-8_21

[KOS03] Katz, J., Ostrovsky, R., Smith, A.: Round efficiency of multi-party computation with a dishonest majority. In: Biham, E. (ed.) EUROCRYPT 2003. LNCS, vol. 2656, pp. 578–595. Springer, Heidelberg (2003). https://doi.org/10.1007/3-540-39200-9_36

[MR19] Masny, D., Rindal, P.: Endemic oblivious transfer. In: CCS 2019, pp. 309–326. ACM (2019)

[NP01] Naor, M., Pinkas, B.: Efficient oblivious transfer protocols. In Rao Kosaraju, S. (ed.), Proceedings of the Twelfth Annual Symposium on Discrete Algorithms, 7–9 January 2001, Washington, DC, USA., pp. 448–457. ACM/SIAM (2001)

[ORS15] Ostrovsky, R., Richelson, S., Scafuro, A.: Round-optimal black-box two-party computation. In: Gennaro, R., Robshaw, M. (eds.) CRYPTO 2015. LNCS, vol. 9216, pp. 339–358. Springer, Heidelberg (2015). https://doi.org/10.1007/978-3-662-48000-7_17

[Pas12] Paskin-Cherniavsky, A.: Secure Computation with minimal interaction. Ph.D. thesis, Technion (2012). http://www.cs.technion.ac.il/users/wwwb/cgi-bin/tr-get.cgi/2012/PHD/PIID-2012-16.pdf

[PS21] Patra, A., Srinivasan, A.: Three-round secure multiparty computation from black-box two-round oblivious transfer. In: Malkin, T., Peikert, C. (eds.) CRYPTO 2021. LNCS, vol. 12826, pp. 185–213. Springer, Cham (2021). https://doi.org/10.1007/978-3-030-84245-1_7

[PVW08] Peikert, C., Vaikuntanathan, V., Waters, B.: A framework for efficient and composable oblivious transfer. In: Wagner, D. (ed.) CRYPTO 2008. LNCS, vol. 5157, pp. 554–571. Springer, Heidelberg (2008). https://doi.org/10.1007/978-3-540-85174-5_31

[RTV04] Reingold, O., Trevisan, L., Vadhan, S.: Notions of reducibility between cryptographic primitives. In: Naor, M. (ed.) TCC 2004. LNCS, vol. 2951, pp. 1–20. Springer, Heidelberg (2004). https://doi.org/10.1007/978-3-540-24638-1_1

[Wee10] Wee, H.: Black-box, round-efficient secure computation via non-malleability amplification. In: 51st FOCS, pp. 531–540, Las Vegas, NV, USA, 23–26 October 2010. IEEE Computer Society Press

[Yao86] Yao, A.C.C.: How to generate and exchange secrets. In: 27th Annual Symposium on Foundations of Computer Science, Toronto, Canada, October 27–29 1986, pp. 162–167. IEEE Computer Society (1986)

Fully-Secure MPC with Minimal Trust

Yuval Ishai[1], Arpita Patra[2], Sikhar Patranabis[3], Divya Ravi[4(✉)],
and Akshayaram Srinivasan[5]

[1] Technion, Haifa, Israel
yuvali@cs.technion.ac.il
[2] Indian Institute of Science, Bangalore, India
arpita@iisc.ac.in
[3] IBM Research India, Bangalore, India
sikhar.patranabis@ibm.com
[4] Aarhus University, Aarhus, Denmark
divya@cs.au.dk
[5] Tata Institute of Fundamental Research, Mumbai, India
akshayaram.srinivasan@tifr.res.in

Abstract. The task of achieving *full security* (with guaranteed output delivery) in secure multiparty computation (MPC) is a long-studied problem. Known impossibility results (Cleve, STOC 86) rule out general solutions in the dishonest majority setting. In this work, we consider solutions that use an *external trusted party* (TP) to bypass the impossibility results, and study the *minimal* requirements needed from this trusted party. In particular, we restrict ourselves to the extreme setting where the size of the TP is *independent* of the size of the functionality to be computed (called "small" TP) and this TP is invoked *only once* during the protocol execution. We present several positive and negative results for fully-secure MPC in this setting.

- For a natural class of protocols, specifically, those with a *universal output decoder*, we show that the size of the TP must necessarily be exponential in the number of parties. This result holds irrespective of the computational assumptions used in the protocol. The class of protocols to which our lower bound applies is broad enough to capture prior results in the area, implying that the prior techniques necessitate the use of an exponential-sized TP. We additionally rule out the possibility of achieving information-theoretic full security (without the restriction of using a universal output decoder) using a "small" TP in the plain model (i.e., without any setup).

- In order to get around the above negative result, we consider protocols without a universal output decoder. The main positive result in our work is a construction of such a fully-secure MPC protocol assuming the existence of a succinct Functional Encryption scheme. We also give evidence that such an assumption is likely to be necessary for fully-secure MPC in certain restricted settings.

S. Patranabis—Most of the work was done while the author was affiliated with ETH Zürich, Switzerland and Visa Research USA.

– Finally, we explore the possibility of achieving full-security with a semi-honest TP that could collude with other malicious parties (which form a dishonest majority). In this setting, we show that even fairness is impossible to achieve regardless of the "small TP" requirement.

1   Introduction

Secure Multiparty Computation (MPC) allows a set of mutually distrusting parties to compute a joint function of their private inputs such that only the output of the function is revealed. Security of MPC protocols is required to hold even if the participating parties are controlled by a centralized *malicious* adversary, who may instruct them to deviate from the protocol specification.

Two desired properties for MPC protocols are *fairness* and *full security* (a.k.a guaranteed output delivery). Fairness requires that if the adversary learns the output of the functionality, then all the honest parties also learn this output. Full security strengthens fairness by requiring that the adversary cannot prevent the honest parties from learning the output of the functionality. Unfortunately, a classical impossibility result of Cleve [Cle86] shows that many functions cannot be fairly computed in the presence of an adversary corrupting a majority of the parties. Two ways to bypass this impossibility result are to restrict the adversary to corrupt only a minority of the parties, or to make use of some external help. In this work, we focus on the second approach, referring to the external help as a *trusted party* (TP).[1] A trusted party can be realized via different standard mechanisms, such as trusted execution environments, hardware tokens, blockchain based approaches, or cloud service providers.

Size of the TP. TPs are useful in circumventing the above impossibility result as they can be used as an ideal functionality that takes inputs from the parties and provides them outputs. A simple way to obtain protocols that satisfy full security in the TP model is for the TP to perform the entire computation on the private inputs of the parties and provide them outputs. However, this approach is less desirable as the size of the TP grows with the size of the function to be computed. Fitzi et al. [FGMO01] showed how to make the TP in the above solution *universal*, in the sense that it is independent of the function being computed. They also showed that to achieve full security, it is necessary to use TPs that take inputs from all the parties. However, this negative result does not rule out a TP which is independent of circuit size of the functionality. Thus, an interesting line of inquiry is to construct protocols where the size of the TP is independent of the circuit size of the functionality to be computed.

Apart from being a theoretically interesting question, it is also motivated by the practical goal of minimizing the use of trustworthy resources. For instance, if a trusted party service is implemented by a cloud service provider who charges

---

[1] This notion differs from the line of work on token-based cryptography initiated by Katz [Kat07], where the tamper-proof tokens are generated locally, and the main challenge is to guarantee security even when tokens can be maliciously generated.

fees for the use of its computational resources, it is obviously desirable (for the clients) to minimize the fees. The same holds if the TP is emulated via the use of a large-scale honest-majority MPC protocol. We refer to a setting of a trusted party whose size is independent of the circuit size of the function as the *small-TP* model. This problem is not new to our work and has already been considered in the works of Gordon et al. [GIM+10] and Ishai et al. [IOS12] for the case of fairness and full security respectively. The state of the art result from [IOS12] gave a protocol that achieves guaranteed output delivery with statistical security (in the OT-hybrid model) with a small TP, where the parties make n sequential calls to this TP. In the same work, the authors gave a protocol where the parties make a single call to the TP but where the size of the TP grows exponentially in the number of parties (and is otherwise independent of the size of the function to be computed).

Number of Calls to TP. In this work, in addition to considering a small-TP model, we are interested in designing *fully-secure* protocols that make a single call to the TP. Theoretically, one call is the minimal requirement to circumvent the impossibility of [Cle86] for fair and fully-secure MPC. It further opens up the possibility of protocols in a minimal model, reminiscent of private simultaneous message (PSM) [FKN94] model, where given a common randomness, the parties communicate one-shot message to the TP and compute the output on receiving the reply from the TP. One call as opposed to many calls is also likely to generate more practical solution in the real world settings where, for instance, the TP is replaced with a cloud service provider, or a blockchain based approach.

The question which is the main focus to our work is:

Can we construct efficient protocols that make a single call to a "small" TP and achieve full security?

1.1   Our Results

We obtain both positive and negative results on the existence of fully-secure MPC protocols using a small TP. We first discuss the negative results below.

Impossibility with a Universal Output Decoder. We give evidence that the prior approaches to this problem necessarily require a TP whose size is exponential in the number of parties. To show this, we abstract out the key features of prior protocols and show that any protocol having these features requires an exponential-sized TP (irrespective of the computational assumptions used in the protocol). More concretely, we consider the class of protocols where the parties could interact with each other (in an arbitrary number of rounds), then they make a single call to the trusted party, get a reply from TP, and then apply a *universal decoder* on this reply and their state to compute the output. By universal decoder, we mean that the size of the decoder is independent of the size of the functionality to be computed (considering single bit output functionalities). This model is interesting because it is quite natural and, more importantly, it captures prior approaches of realizing TP-aided MPC protocols

[IOS12]. We show that for such protocols, the size of the TP necessarily grows exponentially with the number of parties. Our result holds irrespective of the computational assumptions used by the protocol. Additionally, our result holds even if the size of the TP is allowed to grow with the size of the function output.

Theorem 1 (Informal). *For any fully-secure MPC protocol with a universal output decoder, the size of the TP must necessarily be exponential in the number of parties.*

Necessity of Setup or Computational Assumptions. The above result naturally leads to the question of whether we can have small TP-aided fully secure MPC protocols once the restriction of using a universal decoder is relaxed. In this regard, we prove that any statistically secure protocol (without any trusted setup or correlated randomness) that makes a single call to a small TP cannot be even *semi-honest* secure. This impossibility holds even against protocols that may not have a universal output decoder. This shows that to achieve full security it is necessary to resort to computational assumptions, or assume some sort of setup (such a correlated randomness).

Theorem 2 (Informal). *There exists no MPC protocol that achieves information-theoretic security against semi-honest adversaries in the plain model with a TP whose size is a fixed polynomial in the input size of the functionality.*

Positive Results. We now focus on the problem of achieving fully-secure MPC protocols using a small TP based on computational assumptions. Our main positive result is captured by the following theorem:

Theorem 3 (Informal). *Assuming a single-key succinct Functional Encryption (FE) scheme, there exists a fully secure efficient MPC protocol that makes a single call to the small TP.*

A single-key succinct Functional Encryption is an FE scheme [SW05,O'N10, BSW11] where the size of the encryption algorithm does not grow with size of the function for which a secret key is released. Using known instantiations of these primitives from various assumptions, we get the following corollary (building on [GKP+13, GGSW13, Wat15]).

Corollary 1 (Informal). *There exists a fully secure efficient MPC protocol that makes a single call to a TP, assuming:*

1. *Learning with Errors (with sub-exponential modulus-to-noise ratio) [GKP+13] if the size of the TP is allowed to only grow with the depth and the output length of the functionality.*
2. *Witness Encryption scheme [GGSW13] and FHE if the size of the TP is allowed to only grow with the output length of the functionality.*
3. *Indistinguishability Obfuscation (iO) [BGI+01, GGH+13, JLS21] and one-way functions, where the size of the TP is independent of the depth and the output length.*

We also give evidence that this assumption might be necessary in certain restricted settings. Specifically, consider a restricted model of computation where the parties do not interact with each other, but make a single-call to the TP and could compute the output of the functionality based on the reply from the TP. This model is reminiscent of the Private Simulataneous Messages setting [FKN94]. It is not too hard to see that this restricted model is equivalent to an MPC protocol with a succinct online phase. Specifically, the computation done by the parties before the TP call can be thought of as the pre-processing phase and this could grow with the circuit-size of the functionality. The messages sent to the TP and the computation performed by the TP correspond to the online phase of the protocol. Since we restrict the size of the TP to be small, it follows that the computation and the communication cost of the online phase is independent of the size of the functionality (i.e., the protocol has succinct online phase). The post-processing phase could grow with the size of the functionality to be computed (this is in fact necessary considering our impossibility with a universal output decoder).

Currently, the only known constructions of an MPC protocol with a succinct online phase are based on Laconic Functional Evaluation [QWW18] (LFE), which is known to imply succinct FE. This suggests that such assumptions are *likely* to be necessary in the restricted setting outlined above. In fact, an MPC protocol with a succinct online phase implies a weaker flavor of LFE with the following property: unlike standard LFE where the size of the encryption algorithm only grows with the input size, the encryption algorithm in this weaker notion of LFE has two components: (i) a pre-processing algorithm which takes the input and the size of the functionality and produces a hint that only grows with the input size, and (ii) a second algorithm that takes the input and the hint and outputs a ciphertext (the size of the second algorithm only grows with the input size). Finally, in this restricted model, we give a positive result by constructing a fully-secure MPC protocol with a single call to a small TP based on LFE.

(Im)Possibility of Reducing the Trust in TP. Finally, we explore the possibility of weakening the security requirements from the TP. Interestingly, our above solutions maintain privacy against the TP, which is an additional desirable feature. More specifically, our constructions are secure if the adversary corrupts the TP in a semi-honest manner (but does not corrupt any of the parties). This led us to explore what happens if we allow the semi-honest TP to collude with the other malicious parties. We showed that irrespective of the size of the TP, such a model would not be enough to circumvent Cleve's impossibility of fairness. This impossibility holds even if we restrict the malicious parties to be fail-stop.[2]

Our results are summarized in Table 1.

---

[2] The notion of fail-stop corruption lies between semi-honest and malicious corruption, where eavesdropping like semi-honest corruption is allowed and the only possible malicious corruption is stopping the execution of the protocol.

Table 1. Results on fully-secure MPC in dishonest majority using *small* TP under different kinds of setup (plain model i.e. no setup/C.R. i.e. correlated randomness setup/CRS i.e. common random string), security guarantees (statistical/computational) and different TP computation models (with/without the restrictions on pre-TP call interaction and universal output decoder).

Security	No. of calls	Setup	Pre-TP call interaction	Universal Output Decoder	Possible?	Reference
Statistical	1	Plain	Yes	No	No	Theorem 7
Computational	1	C.R	Yes	Yes	No	Theorem 6
Computational	1	CRS	No	No	Yes (based on LFE)	Theorem 4
Computational	1	Plain	Yes	No	Yes (based on succinct FE)	Theorem 5
Statistical	n	C.R	Yes	Yes	Yes	[IOS12]
Computational	n	Plain	Yes	Yes	Yes (based on OT)	[IOS12]
Statistical	1	C.R	Yes	No	**Open**	

1.2 Open Directions

Our work opens up several interesting research directions. We highlight some of them below.

- **Showing Necessity of Succinct FE.** In this work, we argued that any protocol in the restricted model (where the parties do not communicate with each other before and after the TP invocation) is equivalent to an MPC protocol with a succinct online phase. However, we are unable to extend this to the setting where the parties could potentially communicate with each other before making the TP call. Can we show that such a weaker model also implies some weakening of an MPC protocol with a succinct online phase? This would justify the necessity of a succinct FE assumption.
- **Making more than a Single Call to TP.** As our goal was to minimize the requirements from the TP as much as possible, we considered the extreme setting where a single call is made to the TP. A fascinating direction is to explore the possibility of constructing fully-secure MPC protocols from weaker assumptions which could make more than one call but less than n calls. The key challenge here is to design protocols using a stateless TP. If we allow the TP to be stateful, we can realize a construction based on FHE that makes two calls to a stateful TP.
- **Characterization of Fair Computation in the Colluding TP model.** As mentioned previously, in this work we show that it is impossible to achieve fairness in the colluding TP model (where the adversary can corrupt the TP in a semi-honest manner, in addition to corrupting majority of the parties maliciously) for general functions. However, it is still possible to achieve fairness for restricted classes of (non-trivial) functions such as coin-tossing (by

using the TP to directly compute the desired function). It is an interesting open question to give a complete characterization of which function classes can be fairly computed in the colluding TP model.

1.3   Technical Highlights and Discussion

In this section, we present a high-level technical overview of our results.

1.3.1   Positive Results

We present two protocols based on LFE [QWW18] and single-key succinct FE [SW05, BSW11] respectively utilizing a *single* call to a stateless "small" TP. We start off with their trade-offs below.

LFE-Based Construction. LFE's 2-round minimal communication pattern leads to an MPC in a minimal communication setting that is reminiscent of PSM-style [FKN94] communication. Here, the parties start off with a common randomness. Based on the respective inputs and this randomness, the parties communicate a single message to the TP, which performs certain computation and returns a message to each party. In the end, each party recovers the output receiving the message from the TP. Further, the encryption algorithm of LFE enjoys computation that is only dependent on the depth and the output length (and not size) of the function to be computed. This allows our TP to be "small". Here with the best known realizations of LFE, we can achieve a TP of size $\texttt{poly}(n, \kappa, d, m)$, where d denotes depth of the circuit and m denotes input and output size of the circuit, n denotes the number of parties and κ denotes the security parameter. Removing m from the complexity of the TP seems hard, intuitively because the parties never communicate with each other and they communicate only once via the TP. Achieving depth and input-size independence in this minimal communication setting is left as an interesting open question which can possibly contribute back to the LFE regime. In particular, a solution in our setting where TP is of size $\texttt{poly}(n, \kappa, m)$ will lead to a LFE where the encryption scheme and size of the ciphertext are completely independent of the depth of the function under consideration.

FE-Based Construction. Unlike the LFE-based construction, our FE-based construction requires communication amongst the parties before making the TP call. While it loses on this front, there are two positive features that it brings to the table: (a) possibly weaker assumption (b) the TP's computation can be independent of d, m. Elaborating further, LFE is seemingly a stronger assumption than FE, since it is known to imply FE, while the other way is not known [QWW18]. Based on the realization of FE under various assumptions, we achieve multiple variants of the protocol where the TP's computation ranges from being completely independent of input, output and function to linearly dependent on output size (yet independent of the function) to linearly dependent on the output size and the depth of the function. To be specific, under iO and OWFs, our FE based construction leads to a TP of size $\texttt{poly}(n, \kappa)$, completely independent of the function to be computed.

Construction Overview. Our constructions follow a three-phase structure as follows: (a) phase 1: here the parties, on holding a common randomness and respective inputs, prepare a (message, state) pair, where the message is sent to the TP and the state is saved; (b) phase 2: the TP, on receiving messages from the parties, performs some computation and returns a message to every party; and (c) phase 3: the parties, on receiving the message from the TP, uses its state to recover the output. Phase 1 involves communication amongst the parties in the FE-based construction. We provide an informal overview behind the idea for each construction below.

Overview of LFE-Based Solution. We present here a simplified version of our LFE-based construction of fully-secure MPC for ease of exposition. The actual construction, detailed in Sect. 3.3, is significantly more nuanced and uses several techniques to achieve full security against malicious corruptions of parties. In the simplified treatment presented here, we focus on the case of semi-honest corruption, with the aim of highlighting how we manage to keep the TP size small (i.e., independent of the function size). Note that throughout this paper, we assume that each party communicates with the TP via a separate secure channel, and hence an adversary (corrupting a subset of the parties) cannot eavesdrop on the communication between the TP and any honest party.

Given this model, a simplified version of our LFE-based protocol works as follows. Each party first uses a common randomness to (locally) derive a CRS for the LFE scheme and a digest corresponding to the function f. Each party then sends the LFE CRS and the function digest to the TP, along with its own input. The TP uses the CRS and the digest to compute an LFE ciphertext encapsulating the inputs of all of the parties, and sends this ciphertext back to the parties. Finally, each party uses the LFE CRS and its local randomness of digest generation to recover the function output. Observe that the size of the messages to the TP and the computation done by the TP are independent of the size of the function f; this follows immediately from the succinctness properties of the underlying LFE scheme. Finally, we can invoke the privacy guarantees of LFE to argue that the parties learn no more information than the output of the MPC protocol, as desired.

As mentioned earlier, our actual LFE-based protocol uses additional techniques to guarantee full security in the presence of malicious corruptions. This includes techniques that enable the TP to "partition" the parties into various sets depending on their messages to the TP, and to substitute default input values for (malicious) parties not in the partition when preparing partition-specific LFE ciphertexts. Further, we augment the construction to achieve privacy against the TP. We refer to Sect. 3.3 for the detailed description and analysis of our construction.

Overview of FE-Based Solution. We now present a simplified version of our FE-based construction of fully-secure MPC. Once again, our actual protocol, detailed in Sect. 3.3 uses additional techniques to achieve full security against malicious corruptions of parties; we avoid detailing all of these in the simplified treatment for ease of exposition and focus on the setting of semi-honest corruptions. As in the LFE-base solution, we again assume that each party communicates with the TP via a separate secure channel, and hence an adversary (corrupting a subset of the parties) cannot eavesdrop on the communication between the TP and any honest party.

Given this model, the simplified version of our FE-based protocol works as follows. The parties initially engage in an MPC protocol (with identifiable abort security) to decide on a common set of public parameters and a common master public key for the FE scheme. The MPC protocol additionally outputs to each party a functional secret key for the function f to be evaluated. Each party then simply sends the master public key and its own input to the TP. The TP uses the master public key to compute an FE ciphertext encapsulating the inputs of all of the parties, and sends this ciphertext back to the parties. Finally, each party uses the functional secret key to recover the function output. Observe that the size of the messages to the TP and the computation done by the TP are independent of the size of the function f as long as the FE scheme is succinct. Finally, we can invoke the privacy guarantees of FE to argue that the parties learn no more information than the output of the MPC protocol, as desired.

Note that in the above simplified exposition, the TP incurs an overhead that grows with the size of the inputs and output of the function f to be evaluated. In our actual protocol, we use additional techniques to get rid of this dependence. In particular, we use a carefully designed indirection mechanism that allows the TP to simply partition the set of parties (depending on their messages to the TP) and encapsulate this partition information into the FE ciphertext, while delegating all computation dependent on the input/function size entirely to the parties. These techniques serve two purposes: (a) making the TP size independent of the function input/output size (and thereby asymptotically smaller than the TP size for our LFE-based solution) and (b) achieving full security against malicious corruptions of parties. Interestingly, this solution also achieves privacy against the TP. We refer to Sect. 3.4 for the detailed description and analysis of our construction.

1.3.2   Negative Results

We present two impossibility results for fully-secure MPC that utilizes a small TP. Our two results are as follows: (1) First, we show that it is impossible to achieve a fully secure TP-aided MPC utilizing a single call to a small TP, for a class of protocols that have an universal output decoder. This result holds irrespective of computational assumptions used in the protocol. The universal output decoder is independent of the function to be computed and only performs $\text{poly}(n, \kappa)$ computation. (2) Second, we show an impossibility in the plain model, for any statistically-secure MPC even in the semi-honest setting. This result does not assume that the protocol uses an universal output decoder. We present the high-level intuition of both the impossibility arguments.

Impossibility of Fully-Secure MPC Protocols with Universal Output Decoder in the Correlated Randomness Model. We now present a simplified argument of our impossibility result and refer to Sect. 4.1 for the details. Consider an execution of an MPC protocol with full security, where the adversary behaves honestly until the TP call. During the TP call, he can choose to make any subset of corrupt parties, say S, abort; where the number of such subsets is exponential in the number of parties. Since the protocol achieves full security, it must be the case that the TP is able to enable output computation by the parties, no matter which subset S the adversary chooses. Further, the output must be such that it is computed on the default input of the corrupt parties in S and the honest inputs of others (i.e. the input used until and including the TP call). Intuitively, this means that the information given to the TP is such that it can be used to recover 2^n output values (one for each possible subset). Since the TP is small, this information must be 'short' and can therefore be perceived as a 'compression' of the 2^n output values. Building on the above intuition, we show that a fully secure protocol with universal output decoder would imply an (encoding, decoding) scheme which can produce an encoding that is smaller than the size of the message domain of the encoding scheme. This breaches the known incompressibility argument. Precisely, we use a result of De et al. [DTT10], which formalizes the notion that it is impossible to compress every element in a set X to a string less than $\log |X|$ bits long.

Impossibility of Statistical MPC in the Plain Model. At a high-level, we show this impossibility by demonstrating that such a protocol would imply a semi-honest information-theoretic oblivious transfer (OT) extension, which is known to be impossible [Bea96]. Here, OT extension refers to a protocol that allows a sender and a receiver to extend a relatively small number of base OTs (say k) to a larger number of OTs (say $k+1$) using only symmetric-key primitives.

The main idea of the proof is to construct an OT extension protocol using the semi-honest statistically-secure protocol, say Π, as follows. We choose the functionality computed by Π as computing $(k+1)$ oblivious transfer instances. Since the TP is small, its size must be strictly less than the circuit computing $(k+1)$ oblivious transfer instances. Roughly speaking, Π can thus be viewed as a protocol that enables the parties to generate $(k+1)$ OTs, by having access to the TP whose functionality can be realized by strictly less than $(k+1)$ OTs (say k OTs). We build on this idea to construct an information-theoretic semi-honest OT extension protocol where the parties begin with k base OTs and use Π to generate $(k+1)$ OTs.

1.3.3 Impossibility of Fair MPC with Colluding TP

Our results show that small TP is sufficient for positive results in the computational security regime. But what happens when the TP is no longer a stand-alone entity, but behaves as another party that can not only eavesdrop but also collude with the corrupt parties (while remaining semi-honest by itself)? This is a model where the adversary controls a majority of the parties maliciously (or even fail-stop fashion) and *simultaneously* corrupts the TP semi-honestly. For this model, we ask the questions: *Can such a TP circumvent Cleve's* [Cle86] *impossibility result?*

We show a negative result for the above question even for fail-stop adversaries (i.e., the malicious parties still follow the protocol specification but may choose to stop arbitrarily). At a high level, we take the following route. Note that the colluding adversarial model can be viewed more generally, in terms of the general mixed adversarial model that has been studied in works such as [HMZ08, FHM99, BFH+08]. We then use the characterization proposed in [HMZ08] for fair and fully-secure MPC tolerating mixed adversaries to rule out a fair protocol in the colluding model even when malicious corruption is replaced with fail-stop corruption. In particular, we define an adversarial structure complying with the colluding security model and show that this structure is ruled out by the characterization provided in [HMZ08].

In light of this generic negative result, we also explore whether a TP can be used in the colluding model to realize fair MPC protocols for certain *specific* classes of non-trivial functions such as randomized functions without inputs (e.g. coin-tossing). A naïve solution uses the TP to directly compute the desired function; however, such a TP can no longer be small. We give evidence that a better solution using a small TP is unlikely to exist.

1.4   Related Work

There are several fascinating works in the MPC literature that attempt to bypass fundamental feasibility results using external aid. Impossibility of fair MPC in dishonest majority [Cle86] is one such classic impossibility result that has received noteworthy attention. We focus on three broad categories of related works. First is the most closely related line of work to ours which studies the 'minimal help' required to compute all functions fairly, where the helper is characterized as a 'complete' primitive. Second, we outline the line of works that circumvent the impossibility of [Cle86] by considering non-standard notions of fairness. Lastly, we outline the works that circumvent yet another classical impossibility, namely, impossibility of secure computation of general functionalities within the universal composability (UC) framework in presence of dishonest majority in the plain model [CF01] by using hardware tokens and physically unclonable functions (PUFs).

The work of [FGMO01] initiated the study of minimal complete primitives for secure computation, focusing on the minimal cardinality of complete primitives for various thresholds. In particular, they showed that cardinality n is necessary for any complete primitive in dishonest majority and proposed Universal Black Box (UBB) as one such primitive. Subsequently, the work of [GIM+10] proposed a simpler complete primitive for fairness in dishonest majority, namely 'fair reconstruction'. While [GIM+10] focused on the computational setting, [IOS12] presented the first unconditional construction of a complete primitive for full security, whose complexity does not grow with the complexity of the function being evaluated (in contrast to the UBB solution of [FGMO01]). However, this unconditional construction of [IOS12] utilizes number of calls that scales with the circuit size. To improve the number of calls, [IOS12] also proposes another construction where the number of calls depends only on the number of parties

(n) and the output size of the circuit but settles for computational security in the plain model. Finally, they also have a variant where the number of calls is reduced to 1 at the price of increasing the complexity of the computation done by the complete primitive exponentially in n.

As mentioned earlier, an interesting feature that our constructions satisfy is to maintain privacy against the TP. We note that the unconditional variant of [IOS12] (that utilizes number of calls scaling with circuit size) leaks the inputs of the parties to the TP. With respect to the computational variants in [IOS12] that only leak the output of the computation to the TP, we note that it can be tweaked to maintain privacy of the output by adopting the technique of [GIM+10].

Other works related to breaking barriers imposed by the impossibility of [Cle86] include the works of [GK09, GHKL11, ABMO15] that achieve fairness in dishonest majority for restricted functionalities. Some other works explore non-standard notions of fairness such as [GK12, BOO15, BLOO20] that considers partial fairness, [BK14, KB14, ADMM14] that enforce fairness by imposing penalties, [CGJ+17] that use bulletin boards and [EGL85, GMPY11, PST17] that explore resource-fairness.

The sequence of works of [Kat07, CKS+14, DMRV13, CGS08, CCOV19, HPV16] study UC-security with tamper-proof hardware token, both in the stateful and stateless variants. Another interesting utility of hardware tokens is reflected in designing Non-Interactive Secure Computation (NISC) protocols using minimal assumptions. The work of [BJOV18] proposes a UC-secure NISC protocol based on the minimal assumption of one-way functions using hardware token. Lastly, the works of [BFSK11, OSVW13, BKOV17] explore UC-secure computation assuming access to PUFs.

Paper Outline. We formally define TP-aided MPC protocols in Sect. 2. Our positive results appear in Sect. 3. Our negative results for TP-aided MPC appear in Sect. 4. Our negative result for fair MPC in the colluding TP model is briefly summarized in Sect. 5. Due to lack of space, we defer certain proof details and extensions of the above results to the full version of our paper.

2   Security Model

In this section, we present our definitions in the UC-framework [Can01]. We denote by $[p]$ the set $\{1, \ldots, p\}$, for a positive integer p.

The Real World. An n-party protocol Π with n parties $\mathcal{P} = (P_1, \ldots, P_n)$ is an n-tuple of probabilistic polynomial-time (PPT) interactive Turing machines (ITMs), where each party P_i is initialized with input $x_i \in \{0, 1\}^*$ and random coins $r_i \in \{0, 1\}^*$. These parties interact in synchronous rounds. In every round parties can communicate either over a broadcast channel or a fully connected point-to-point (P2P) network, where we additionally assume all communication to be private and ideally authenticated. Further, we assume that there exists a special party P^* called a "trusted party" (abbreviated henceforth as TP) such that each party P_i can interact with P^* via private and authenticated point-to-point channels. The TP P^* does not typically hold any inputs, and also does not obtain any output at the end of the protocol. Further, the TP is *stateless* in the sense that it does not keep any state between calls.

We let $\mathcal{A}$ denote a special ITM that represents the adversary. $\mathcal{A}$ is coordinated by another special non-uniform ITM environment $\mathcal{Z} = \mathcal{Z}_\kappa$. At setup, $\mathcal{Z}$ gives input $(1^\kappa, x_i)$ to each party P_i. At the same time, $\mathcal{Z}$ provides to $\mathcal{A}$ the tuple $(\mathcal{C}, \{x_i\}_{i \in \mathcal{C}}, \mathsf{aux})$, where $\mathcal{C} \subset [n] \cup \{P^*\}$ denotes the set of all corrupt parties, and aux denotes some auxiliary input.

During the execution of the protocol, the maliciously corrupt parties (sometimes referred to as 'active') receive arbitrary instructions from the adversary $\mathcal{A}$, while the honest parties and the semi-honestly corrupt (sometimes referred to as 'passive') parties faithfully follow the instructions of the protocol. We consider the adversary $\mathcal{A}$ to be rushing, i.e., during every round the adversary can see the messages the honest parties sent before producing messages from corrupt parties.

At the conclusion of the protocol, $\mathcal{A}$ gives to the environment $\mathcal{Z}$ an output which is an arbitrary function of $\mathcal{A}$'s view throughout the protocol. $\mathcal{Z}$ is additionally given the outputs of the honest parties. Finally, $\mathcal{Z}$ outputs a bit. We let $\mathsf{real}_{\pi, \mathcal{A}, \mathcal{Z}}(\kappa)$ be a random variable denoting the value of this bit.

Definition 1 (Real-world execution). *Let Π be an n-party protocol amongst $(P_1, \ldots, P_n)$ computing an n-party function $f : (\{0,1\}^*)^n \rightarrow (\{0,1\}^*)^n$ and let $\mathcal{C} \subseteq [n] \cup \{P^*\}$ denote the set of indices of the corrupted parties. The execution of Π under $(\mathcal{Z}, \mathcal{S}, \mathcal{C})$ in the real world, on input vector $\vec{x} = (x_1, \ldots, x_n)$, auxiliary input aux and security parameter κ, denoted $\mathsf{real}_{\Pi, \mathcal{C}, \mathcal{A}(\mathsf{aux})}(\vec{x}, \kappa)$, is defined as the output of $\mathcal{Z}$ resulting from the protocol interaction.*

The Ideal World. We describe ideal world executions with unanimous abort (un-abort), identifiable abort (id-abort), fairness (fairness) and full security aka. guaranteed output delivery (full).

Definition 2 (Ideal Computation). *Consider* type $\in$ {un-abort, id-abort, fairness, full}. *Let* $f : (\{0,1\}^*)^n \rightarrow (\{0,1\}^*)^n$ *be an n-party function. Once again, we have a non-uniform environment $\mathcal{Z} = \mathcal{Z}_\kappa$ that gives (at setup) input $(1^\kappa, x_i)$ to each party P_i, while also providing to the simulator $\mathcal{S}$ the tuple $(\mathcal{C}, \{x_i\}_{i \in \mathcal{C}}, \mathsf{aux})$, where $\mathcal{C} \subset [n] \cup \{P^*\}$ denotes the set of all corrupt parties, and aux denote some auxiliary input. Then, the ideal execution of f under $(\mathcal{Z}, \mathcal{S}, \mathcal{C})$ on input vector $\vec{x} = (x_1, \ldots, x_n)$, auxiliary input aux to $\mathcal{S}$ and security parameter κ, denoted $\mathsf{ideal}_{f, \mathcal{C}, \mathcal{S}, (\mathsf{aux})}^{\mathsf{type}}(\vec{x}, \kappa)$, is defined as the output bit of $\mathcal{Z}$ resulting from the following ideal process.*

1. Parties send inputs to trusted party: *An honest party P_i sends its input x_i to the trusted party. The simulator $\mathcal{S}$ may send to the trusted party arbitrary inputs for the corrupt parties. Let x_i' be the value actually sent as the input of party x_i.*

2. Trusted party speaks to simulator: *The trusted party computes $(y_1, \ldots, y_n) = f(x_1', \ldots, x_n')$. If there are no corrupt parties or* type = full, *proceed to step 4.*
   (a) If type $\in$ {un-abort, id-abort}: *The trusted party sends $\{y_i\}_{i \in \mathcal{C}}$ to $\mathcal{S}$.*

(b) If type = fairness: *The trusted party sends* ready *to* S.
3. Simulator S responds to trusted party:
   (a) If type $\in$ {un-abort, fairness}: *The simulator can send* abort *to the trusted party.*
   (b) If type = id-abort: *If it chooses to abort, the simulator* S *can select a corrupt party* $i^* \in C$ *who will be blamed, and send* (abort, i^*) *to the trusted party.*
4. Trusted party answers parties:
   (a) If the trusted party got abort *from the simulator* S,
      i. It sets the abort message abortmsg, *as follows:*
         – *if* type $\in$ {un-abort, fairness}, *we let* abortmsg = $\perp$.
         – *if* type = id-abort, *we let* abortmsg = $(\perp, i^*)$.
      ii. The trusted party then sends abortmsg *to every party* P_j, $j \in [n] \setminus C$. *Note that, if* type = full, *we will never be in this setting, since* S *was not allowed to ask for an abort.*
   (b) Otherwise, it sends y_j to every P_j, $j \in [n]$.
5. Outputs: *Honest parties always output the message received from the trusted party while the corrupt parties output nothing. At the conclusion of the above execution, S provides Z with an output which is an arbitrary function of S's view throughout the protocol. Z is additionally given the outputs of the honest parties. Finally, Z outputs a bit. We let* $\mathsf{ideal}^{\mathsf{type}}_{f,S,Z}(\kappa)$ *be a random variable denoting the value of this bit.*

Security Definitions. We now define the security notions used in this paper.

Definition 3 (Colluding and Non-colluding Security). *Consider* type $\in$ {un-abort, id-abort, fairness, full}. *Let* $f : (\{0,1\}^*)^n \rightarrow (\{0,1\}^*)^n$ *be an n-party function. A protocol Π securely computes the function f in the* colluding *model with* type *security if for any adversary A, there exists a simulator S such that for any security parameter κ and any circuit family $Z = \{Z_\kappa\}$ corrupting any $C \subset [n]$ maliciously and the TP P^* semi-honestly simultaneously, we have*

$$\left\{\mathsf{real}_{\Pi,C,A(\mathsf{aux})}(\vec{x}, \kappa)\right\}_{\vec{x} \in (\{0,1\}^*)^n, \kappa \in \mathbb{N}} \equiv \left\{\mathsf{ideal}^{\mathsf{type}}_{f,C,S(\mathsf{aux})}(\vec{x}, \kappa)\right\}_{\vec{x} \in (\{0,1\}^*)^n, \kappa \in \mathbb{N}}.$$

When the corruption is non-simultaneous *i.e. either any subset of $[n]$ are maliciously corrupt or the TP P^* is semi-honestly corrupt, we denote the security by* non-colluding. *Therefore we need the above indistinguishability to hold in two corruption cases: (a) $C \subset [n]$ malicious corruption (b) $C = P^*$ semi-honest corruption.*

A protocol achieves computational security, if the above distributions are computationally close in the presence of the parties, A, S, Z that are PPT. A protocol achieves statistical (resp. perfect) security if the distributions are statistically close (resp. identical).

3 Fully-Secure MPC with Single Call to Small TP

Here, we present TP-aided MPC protocols that make a single call to a small TP and achieve full security in the non-colluding setting against malicious corruption

of majority of parties and semi-honest corruption of the TP. We present two flavors of protocols– one based on laconic function evaluation (LFE) [QWW18] and
the other based on succinct single-key functional encryption (FE) [GKP+13]. We
begin by recalling the definitions for these primitives.

3.1   Laconic Function Evaluation (LFE)

We recall the definition of LFE – a primitive introduced in [QWW18].

Definition 4 (Laconic Function Evaluation). *An* LFE *scheme for a class
of circuits* $\mathcal{H} = \{\mathcal{H}_m\}_{m\in\mathbb{N}}$ *(represented as Boolean circuits with m-bit inputs) is
a tuple* (LFE.Setup, LFE.Compress, LFE.Enc, LFE.Dec) *defined below.*

- LFE.Setup(1^κ) $\rightarrow$ LFE.crs: *On input the security parameter 1^κ, the generation
  algorithm returns a common random string* LFE.crs.
- LFE.Compress(LFE.crs, h) $\rightarrow$ (digest, r): *On input* LFE.crs *and a circuit h, the
  compression algorithm returns a digest* digest *and a decoding information r.*
- LFE.Enc(LFE.crs, digest, x) $\rightarrow$ ct: *On input* LFE.crs, *a digest* digest, *and a
  message x, the encryption algorithm returns a ciphertext* ct.
- LFE.Dec(LFE.crs, ct, r) $\rightarrow$ y: *On input* LFE.crs, *a ciphertext* ct, *and a decoding
  string r, the decoding algorithms returns a message y.*

In this work, we use LFE schemes that satisfy correctness, simulation-security
and function-hiding security, as defined formally below.

Definition 5 (Correctness). *Let* LFE = (LFE.Setup, LFE.Compress, LFE.Enc,
LFE.Dec) *be an LFE scheme for a class of functions* $\mathcal{H} = \{\mathcal{H}_m\}_{m\in\mathbb{N}}$. *We say
that* LFE *is a correct LFE scheme if for any $m = \texttt{poly}(\kappa)$, for all $h \in \mathcal{H}_m$, and
for all $x \in \{0,1\}^m$, letting* LFE.crs $\leftarrow$ LFE.Setup(1^κ), *and letting*

$$(\text{digest}, r) \leftarrow \text{LFE.Compress}(\text{LFE.crs}, h), \quad \text{ct} \leftarrow \text{LFE.Enc}(\text{LFE.crs}, \text{digest}, x),$$

the following holds:

$$\Pr[\text{LFE.Dec}(\text{LFE.crs}, \text{ct}, r) = h(x)] = 1 - \texttt{negl}(\kappa),$$

where the probability is taken over the random coins of LFE.Setup, LFE.Compress,
and LFE.Enc.

Definition 6 (Simulation-Security). *Let* LFE = (LFE.Setup, LFE.Compress,
LFE.Enc, LFE.Dec) *be an LFE scheme for a class of functions* $\mathcal{H} = \{\mathcal{H}_m\}_{m\in\mathbb{N}}$.
For every non-uniform PPT adversary $\mathcal{A} = (\mathcal{A}_1, \mathcal{A}_2)$ *and every PPT simulator
$\mathcal{S}$, consider the following two experiments (κ being the security parameter):*

Experiment $\mathsf{Expt}_{\mathsf{LFE},\mathcal{A}}^{\mathsf{real}}(1^\kappa)$:

    LFE.crs ← LFE.Setup(1^κ)
    $(x, h, s, \mathsf{st}_\mathcal{A}) \leftarrow \mathcal{A}_1(1^\kappa, \mathsf{LFE.crs})$
    (digest, r) ← LFE.Compress(LFE.crs, h; s)
    ct ← LFE.Enc(LFE.crs, digest, x)
    Output $b \leftarrow \mathcal{A}_2(\mathsf{st}_\mathcal{A}, \mathsf{ct})$

Experiment $\mathsf{Expt}_{\mathsf{LFE},\mathcal{A},\mathcal{S}}^{\mathsf{ideal}}(1^\kappa)$:

    LFE.crs ← LFE.Setup(1^κ)
    $(x, h, s, \mathsf{st}_\mathcal{A}) \leftarrow \mathcal{A}_1(1^\kappa, \mathsf{LFE.crs})$
    (digest, r) ← LFE.Compress(LFE.crs, h; s)
    $\widetilde{\mathsf{ct}} \leftarrow \mathcal{S}(\mathsf{LFE.crs}, \mathsf{digest}, h, h(x))$
    Output $b \leftarrow \mathcal{A}_2(\mathsf{st}_\mathcal{A}, \widetilde{\mathsf{ct}})$

The LFE scheme LFE is said to satisfy (semi-malicious)-simulation-security if for any security parameter $\kappa \in \mathbb{N}$, there exists a PPT simulator $\mathcal{S}$ such that for every non-uniform PPT adversary $\mathcal{A} = (\mathcal{A}_1, \mathcal{A}_2)$, the outcomes of the real and ideal experiments are computationally indistinguishable, i.e., we have

$$\left| \Pr[\mathsf{Expt}_{\mathsf{LFE},\mathcal{A}}^{\mathsf{real}}(1^\kappa) = 1] - \Pr[\mathsf{Expt}_{\mathsf{LFE},\mathcal{A},\mathcal{S}}^{\mathsf{ideal}}(1^\kappa) = 1] \right| \leq \mathsf{negl}(\kappa),$$

where $\mathcal{A}$ is admissible if $h \in \mathcal{H}_m$ for some $m = \mathsf{poly}(\kappa)$, and the probability is taken over the random coins of LFE.Setup, LFE.Compress, LFE.Enc, $\mathcal{A}_1$, and $\mathcal{S}$.

Definition 7 (Function-Hiding Security). *Let* LFE $=$ (LFE.Setup, LFE.Compress, LFE.Enc, LFE.Dec) *be an LFE scheme for a class of functions* $\mathcal{H} = \{\mathcal{H}_m\}_{m \in \mathbb{N}}$. *For every non-uniform PPT adversary* $\mathcal{A} = (\mathcal{A}_1, \mathcal{A}_2)$ *and every PPT simulator* $\mathcal{S}$, *consider the following two experiments (κ being the security parameter):*

Experiment $\mathsf{Expt}_{\mathsf{LFE},\mathcal{A}}^{\mathsf{real,FH}}(1^\kappa)$:

    LFE.crs ← LFE.Setup(1^κ)
    $(h, \mathsf{st}_\mathcal{A}) \leftarrow \mathcal{A}_1(1^\kappa, \mathsf{mpk})$
    (digest, r) ← LFE.Compress(LFE.crs, h)
    Output $b \leftarrow \mathcal{A}_2(\mathsf{st}_\mathcal{A}, \mathsf{digest})$

Experiment $\mathsf{Expt}_{\mathsf{LFE},\mathcal{A},\mathcal{S}}^{\mathsf{ideal,FH}}(1^\kappa)$:

    LFE.crs ← LFE.Setup(1^κ)
    $(h\mathsf{st}_\mathcal{A}) \leftarrow \mathcal{A}_1(1^\kappa, \mathsf{LFE.crs})$
    digest ← $\mathcal{S}(\mathsf{LFE.crs}, \mathcal{F})$
    Output $b \leftarrow \mathcal{A}_2(\mathsf{st}_\mathcal{A}, \widetilde{\mathsf{digest}})$

The LFE scheme LFE is said to satisfy function-hiding simulation-security if for any security parameter $\kappa \in \mathbb{N}$, there exists a PPT simulator $\mathcal{S}$ such that for every non-uniform PPT adversary $\mathcal{A} = (\mathcal{A}_1, \mathcal{A}_2)$, the outcomes of the real and ideal experiments are computationally indistinguishable, i.e., we have

$$\left| \Pr[\mathsf{Expt}_{\mathsf{LFE},\mathcal{A}}^{\mathsf{real,FH}}(1^\kappa) = 1] - \Pr[\mathsf{Expt}_{\mathsf{LFE},\mathcal{A},\mathcal{S}}^{\mathsf{ideal,FH}}(1^\kappa) = 1] \right| \leq \mathsf{negl}(\kappa),$$

where $\mathcal{A}$ is admissible if $h \in \mathcal{H}_m$ for some $m = \mathsf{poly}(\kappa)$, and the probability is taken over the random coins of LFE.Setup, LFE.Compress, $\mathcal{A}_1$, and $\mathcal{S}$.

3.2   Succinct Single-Key Functional Encryption

We now recall the definition of succinct single-key functional encryption (FE).

Definition 8 (Functional Encryption). *A functional encryption scheme* FE *for a class of functions* $\mathcal{H} = \{\mathcal{H}_m\}_{m \in \mathbb{N}}$ *(represented as Boolean circuits with m-bit inputs), is a tuple of four PPT algorithms* (FE.Setup, FE.KeyGen, FE.Enc, FE.Dec) *such that:*

- FE.Setup$(1^\kappa) \rightarrow$ (mpk, msk)*: On input the security parameter* κ*, the setup algorithm outputs a master public key* mpk *and a master secret key* msk.
- FE.KeyGen(msk, h) $\rightarrow$ sk$_h$*: On input the master secret key* msk *and a function* $h \in \mathcal{H}$*, the key generation algorithm outputs a key* sk$_h$.
- FE.Enc(mpk, x) $\rightarrow$ ct*: On input the master public key* mpk *and an input* $x \in \{0,1\}^m$ *for some* $m = \text{poly}(\kappa)$*, the encryption algorithm outputs a ciphertext* ct.
- FE.Dec(sk$_h$, ct) $\rightarrow y$*: On input a key* sk$_h$ *and a ciphertext* ct*, the decryption algorithm outputs a value* y.

In this work, we use single-key FE schemes that satisfy correctness, single-key full-simulation-security and succinctness, as defined formally below.

Definition 9 (Correctness). *Let* FE = (FE.Setup, FE.KeyGen, FE.Enc, FE.Dec) *be a single-key FE scheme for a class of functions* $\mathcal{H} = \{\mathcal{H}_m\}_{m \in \mathbb{N}}$*. We say that* FE *is a correct single-key FE scheme if for any* $m = \text{poly}(\kappa)$*, for all* $h \in \mathcal{H}_m$*, and for all* $x \in \{0,1\}^m$*, letting*

$$(\text{mpk}, \text{msk}) \leftarrow \text{FE.Setup}(1^\kappa), \quad \text{sk}_h \leftarrow \text{FE.KeyGen}(\text{msk}, h), \quad \text{ct} \leftarrow \text{FE.Enc}(\text{mpk}, x),$$

the following holds:

$$\Pr[\text{FE.Dec}(\text{sk}_h, \text{ct}) = h(x)] = 1 - \text{negl}(\kappa),$$

where the probability is taken over the random coins of FE.Setup, FE.KeyGen, *and* FE.Enc.

Definition 10 (Full-Simulation Security). *Let* FE = (FE.Setup, FE.KeyGen, FE.Enc, FE.Dec) *be a single-key FE scheme for a class of functions* $\mathcal{H} = \{\mathcal{H}_m\}_{m \in \mathbb{N}}$*. For every non-uniform PPT adversary* $\mathcal{A} = (\mathcal{A}_1, \mathcal{A}_2)$ *and every PPT simulator* $\mathcal{S}$*, consider the following two experiments (*κ *being the security parameter):*

Experiment $\text{Expt}_{\text{FE},\mathcal{A}}^{\text{real}}(1^\kappa)$:	**Experiment** $\text{Expt}_{\text{FE},\mathcal{A},\mathcal{S}}^{\text{ideal}}(1^\kappa)$:
(mpk, msk) $\leftarrow$ FE.Setup(1^κ)	(mpk, msk) $\leftarrow$ FE.Setup(1^κ)
$(h, \text{st}_\mathcal{A}) \leftarrow \mathcal{A}_1(1^\kappa, \text{mpk})$	$(h, \text{st}_\mathcal{A}) \leftarrow \mathcal{A}_1(1^\kappa, \text{mpk})$
sk$_h$ $\leftarrow$ FE.KeyGen(msk, h)	sk$_h$ $\leftarrow$ FE.KeyGen(msk, h).
$(x, \text{st}'_\mathcal{A}) \leftarrow \mathcal{A}_2(\text{st}_\mathcal{A}, \text{sk}_h)$	$(x, \text{st}'_\mathcal{A}) \leftarrow \mathcal{A}_2(\text{st}_\mathcal{A}, \text{sk}_h)$
ct $\leftarrow$ FE.Enc(mpk, x)	$\widetilde{\text{ct}} \leftarrow \mathcal{S}(\text{mpk}, \text{sk}_h, h(x), 1^{|x|})$
Output $(\text{st}'_\mathcal{A}, \text{ct})$	Output $(\text{st}'_\mathcal{A}, \widetilde{\text{ct}})$

The FE scheme FE is said to satisfy (single-key) full-simulation-security if for any security parameter $\kappa \in \mathbb{N}$, there exists a PPT simulator $\mathcal{S}$ such that for every non-uniform PPT adversary $\mathcal{A} = (\mathcal{A}_1, \mathcal{A}_2)$, the outcomes of the real and ideal experiments are computationally indistinguishable, i.e., we have

$$\mathsf{Expt}^{\mathsf{real}}_{\mathsf{FE}, \mathcal{A}}(1^\kappa) \approx_c \mathsf{Expt}^{\mathsf{ideal}}_{\mathsf{FE}, \mathcal{A}, \mathcal{S}}(1^\kappa).$$

Definition 11 (Succinctness). *Let* FE $=$ (FE.Setup, FE.KeyGen, FE.Enc, FE.Dec) *be a single-key FE scheme for a class of functions* $\mathcal{H} = \{\mathcal{H}_m\}_{m \in \mathbb{N}}$. *We say that* FE *is succinct if for any* $m = \mathtt{poly}(\kappa)$, *for all* $h \in \mathcal{H}_m$, *and for all* $x \in \{0,1\}^m$, *letting*

$$(\mathsf{mpk}, \mathsf{msk}) \leftarrow \mathsf{FE.Setup}(1^\kappa), \quad \mathsf{ct} \leftarrow \mathsf{FE.Enc}(\mathsf{mpk}, x),$$

the size of the ciphertext ct *(i.e.,* $|\mathsf{ct}|$*) does not grow with the size of the circuit for* h, *but only with its depth.*

3.3   Fully-secure MPC from Laconic Cryptography

In this subsection, we present our construction of TP-aided MPC from LFE.

Construction Overview. The high-level description of the construct, following the three-phase structure (as discussed in Sect. 1.3), is presented in two steps. In the first step, we assume an honest TP and allow the parties to hand out the inputs to the TP in the clear. In the second step, input privacy against the TP is put in place via *function-hiding* LFE. Throughout, we assume an LFE with a common *random* string (CRS), as is the case for the construction of LFE in [QWW18].

In the first phase, every party uses the common randomness to derive a CRS for the LFE and subsequently computes a digest of f (the function to be computed) using the CRS. It sends the CRS, the digest and its input to the TP. The TP needs to compute an encryption of the collective inputs under the correct digest and CRS. However, a malicious party may send a incorrect digest, say for a function that leaks an honest party's input. The TP can verify the correctness of the digest, since the compress function of the LFE scheme is deterministic. But this amounts to a computation that is dependent on the circuit size, breaking the promise of small TP. To tackle this issue without recomputing the function digest, the TP partitions the set of parties based on the CRS and digest. For every set that sends the same copy of both, gets an encryption under the digest, of the message that consists of the real inputs received from that set and default inputs for those outside that set. This trick ensures that a corrupt party does not get encryption of the inputs of the honest parties under its ill-formed digest. Lastly, on receiving the encryption from the TP, a party simply uses the CRS to learn the function output.

To additionally ensure input privacy against the TP, the function f for LFE is replaced with a related function g that hard-codes n random masks and takes as input n masked inputs of the parties. It first unmasks the masked inputs and then performs the f-computation. The masks are derived from common randomness and thus are known to all. We can use one-time pad for masking. This implies every party has the knowledge of g and can generate a digest that is supposed to be the same. Now, every party uses its respective mask to mask its input before sending to the TP. The TP performs the same computation as before, but now on the received masked inputs, digest for g and CRS. To hide the random masks that are hard-coded inside g from the TP who will learn the digest, we switch to *function-hiding* LFE. This makes sure the TP learns neither about the inputs, not about the output. The LFE security ensures the parties learn nothing but the output of g. The detailed construction is as described below.

Protocol Π_{LFE}

Inputs: Each party P_i has input x_i. All parties share a common randomness of the form $r\|r'$.

Output: $f(x_1, \ldots x_n)$

Primitive: The following building blocks are used
- An LFE scheme $\mathsf{LFE} = (\mathsf{LFE.Setup}, \mathsf{LFE.Compress}, \mathsf{LFE.Enc}, \mathsf{LFE.Dec})$.

Phase 1 (Pre-TP Call): Each party P_i does the following:
- Set $\mathsf{LFE.crs} := r$, where r is obtained from the common randomness $r\|r'$.
- Derive n random pads $\{r_j\}_{j \in [n]}$, where $|r_j| = |x_j|$, using r' obtained from the common randomness $r\|r'$.
- Compute $(\mathsf{digest}^g, r^g) \leftarrow \mathsf{LFE.Compress}\Big(g, \mathsf{LFE.crs}\Big)$, where function g is as follows and send $(\mathsf{LFE.crs}, \mathsf{digest}^g, z_i = x_i \oplus r_i)$ to the TP.
  - g hard-codes the n pads $\{r_j\}_{j \in [n]}$
  - it takes n inputs $z_1, \ldots, z_n$
  - it computes f on input $\{z_j \oplus r_j\}_{j \in [n]}$.
  We note that $(\mathsf{LFE.crs}, \mathsf{digest}^g, r^g)$ is supposed to be the same for all parties, since they use the common randomness r and f.

Phase 2(TP Call): The TP carries out the following computation:
- Initialize the set $\mathcal{Z} = \varnothing$. Add P_j to $\mathcal{Z}$ if nothing (or syntactically incorrect message) is received from P_j.
- Partition the set $\mathcal{P} \setminus \mathcal{Z}$ into subsets $S_1, S_2 \ldots S_\ell$ according to the values of ($\mathsf{LFE.crs}, \mathsf{digest}^g$) received from the parties i.e. all parties in a subset have sent the same $(\mathsf{LFE.crs}, \mathsf{digest}^g)$.
- For each S_α for $\alpha \in \{1, \ldots, \ell\}$
  - Let $\mathsf{LFE.crs}_\alpha, \mathsf{digest}^g_\alpha$ denote the common values submitted by parties in S_α.
  - For each $j \in \{1, \ldots, n\}$, set $\bar{z}_j = z_j$ if $j \in S_\alpha$, and $\bar{z}_j = z'_j$ otherwise, where z_j is received from P_j and $\{z'_j\}_{j \in \{1, \ldots, n\}}$ are the default (masked) inputs sampled randomly by the TP.
  - Send $\mathsf{ct}_\alpha, S_\alpha$ to every party in S_α, where $\mathsf{ct}_\alpha \leftarrow \mathsf{LFE.Enc}\Big(\mathsf{digest}^g_\alpha, \big(\bar{z}_1, \ldots, \bar{z}_n\big)\Big)$.

Phase 3 (Post-TP Call): A party P_i, on receiving ct, computes output y as

$$y \leftarrow \mathsf{LFE.Dec}\Big(\mathsf{LFE.crs}, \mathsf{ct}, r^g\Big),$$

using $\mathsf{LFE.crs}, r^g$ from Phase 1.

Fig. 1. Fully-secure MPC with single TP call based on LFE

Our result can be summarized via the following theorem.

Theorem 4 (TP-Aided MPC from LFE). *Assuming the existence of a laconic function evaluation (LFE) scheme that satisfies correctness, simulation-security and function-hiding security, there exists a TP-aided MPC protocol Π_{LFE} for any functionality f that:*

- *utilizes a single call to a stateless TP of size $\mathsf{poly}(n, \kappa, m, \alpha, \beta)$ (where n is the number of parties, κ is the security parameter, m is the size of each party's input to f, and α and β denote the sizes of a single digest and a single ciphertext, respectively, in the LFE scheme), and*
- *achieves full security against malicious corruption of up to $(n-1)$ parties and semi-honest corruption of the TP in the non-colluding model (see Definition 3).*

We defer the formal proof of this theorem to the full version of our paper.

3.4 Fully-Secure MPC from Single-Key Succinct FE

In this subsection, we show how to construct TP-aided MPC from single-key succinct FE.

Construction Overview. The high-level description of the construct, following the three-phase structure (as discussed in Sect. 1.3), is presented in two steps. In the first step, we assume an honest TP and allow the parties to hand out the inputs to the TP. In the second step, input privacy is put in place via a SKE.

For our construction, in the first phase, the parties execute an MPC protocol with identifiable abort[3] amongst the n parties that establishes the setup of the FE and gives the parties sk_f (corresponding to the function f desired to be computed) to aid in output computation. Since this execution may result in abort (where only corrupt parties may get the output), we cannot allow the MPC to output the FE ciphertext corresponding to the parties' inputs directly. Instead, the ciphertext is computed by the TP to whom the parties submit their inputs when Phase 1 is successful (which may need repeated run of the MPC with identifiable abort). To enable the TP to do so, the parties additionally submit mpk (obtained in Phase 1) to the TP. In order to ensure that privacy of honest parties' inputs is maintained against a corrupt party who sends mpk distinct

---

[3] Some of the protocols in the literature realizing this functionality for general functions are [GS18].

from the one obtained in Phase 1, the TP does the following: partition the set of parties based on the value of mpk they submitted. For each partition, the TP returns ciphertext based on actual inputs of parties within the partition and default otherwise. This ensures that a corrupt party who submits an incorrect mpk (say mpk' which is distinct from the one obtained from Phase 1) never get access to a ciphertext computed using mpk' that involves an honest party's input. Lastly, the parties use the ciphertext obtained from the TP and sk_f to obtain the output.

Note that the above protocol is not secure in the non-colluding model as it does not achieve input privacy against a semi-honest TP. Further, the computation done by the TP grows with the size of the parties' inputs. In order to achieve security against a semi-honest TP and make the computation of the TP independent of the size of the parties' inputs, we make the following modifications. First, the input of each party is hidden in a ciphertext of a SKE. The MPC with identifiable abort now takes as input the inputs of the parties, computes distinct ciphertexts for the inputs, each under a distinct secret key, and delivers only the ith secret key to P_i. Instead of the inputs, these keys are sent to the TP, who performs similar computation as before, but with respect to these keys. To make the both ends meet, the function to be computed by FE is changed to a related function g (instead of the function to be computed f) that hard-codes the ciphertexts of the inputs and takes the n keys as inputs. The function g first decrypts the ciphertexts and then compute f on the decrypted messages. The MPC with identifiable abort now prepares and gives out the secret key of FE corresponding to g. To prevent the parties from tampering the secret keys for SKE while sending to the TP, we use a signature scheme. The MPC samples a (public, secret) key pair for a digital signature scheme and delivers signed messages meant for TP (SKE key and mpk in this case) and the public key for verification to a party. The parties forward this to the TP, who now discards the parties whose verification fails, partitions the parties based on the verification key and proceeds as before. The detailed construction is as described below.

Protocol Π_{FE}

Inputs: Each P_i participates with input x_i.

Output: $f(x_1, \ldots x_n)$

Primitive: The following building blocks are used
- An MPC protocol Π_{idua} that achieves security with identifiable abort.
- A succinct single-key simulation-secure FE scheme $\text{FE} = (\text{FE.Setup}, \text{FE.KeyGen}, \text{FE.Enc}, \text{FE.Dec})$.
- An IND-CPA secure symmetric-key encryption scheme $\text{SKE} = (\text{SKE.Gen}, \text{SKE.Enc}, \text{SKE.Dec})$.
- A digital signature scheme $(\text{Sign}, \text{Vrfy})$.

Phase 1 (Pre-TP Call): Each P_i invokes an instance of Π_{idua} with input x_i to compute a function that does the following:
- Generate a default input x_i' for every P_i.
- Generate a secret key $k_i \leftarrow \text{SKE.Gen}(1^\kappa)$ for every party P_i.
- Generate $(\text{msk}, \text{mpk}) \leftarrow \text{FE.Setup}(1^\kappa)$.
- Generate $e_i \leftarrow \text{SKE.Enc}(k_i, x_i)$ for every P_i.
- Generate $\text{sk}_g = \text{FE.KeyGen}(\text{msk}, g)$, where g is a function defined as follows:
  - g embeds the ciphertexts $\{e_j\}_{j \in [n]}$ and default inputs $\{x_j'\}_{j \in [n]}$.
  - g takes as input a set of keys $\{k_j\}_{j \in [n]}$ and an n-length bit vector $\{b_j\}_{j \in [n]}$.
  - g outputs $f(\bar{x}_1, \ldots, \bar{x}_n)$ where for each $j \in [n]$, $\bar{x}_j = \text{SKE.Dec}(k_i, e_j)$ if $b_i = 1$ and $\bar{x}_j = x_j'$ otherwise.
- Generate (sk, vk) for the digital signature scheme.
- For each $i \in [n]$, output $(\text{vk}, \text{mpk}, k_i, \sigma_i, \text{sk}_g)$ to P_i where $\sigma_i = \text{Sign}(\text{sk}, (i, \text{mpk}, k_i))$.

If Π_{idua} outputs $(\bot, \mathcal{C})$, re-run **Phase 1** among the set of parties $\mathcal{P} \setminus \mathcal{C}$ (the inputs of parties in $\mathcal{C}$ are substituted using default inputs). Else, continue to the next phase. Each P_i invokes the TP with $\text{in}_i = (\text{vk}, \text{mpk}, k_i, \sigma_i)$.

Phase 2 (TP Call): The TP carries out the following computation:
- Initialize $\mathcal{Z} = \varnothing$. Add P_j to $\mathcal{Z}$ if nothing is received or $\text{Vrfy}(\text{vk}, (j, \text{mpk}, k_j, \sigma_j)) = 0$, for a tuple $(\text{vk}, \text{mpk}, k_j, \sigma_j)$ received from P_j.
- Partition the set $\mathcal{P} \setminus \mathcal{Z}$ into subsets $S_1, S_2 \ldots S_\ell$ according to the values of vk received from the parties i.e. all parties in a subset have sent the same vk.
- For each S_α for $\alpha \in \{1, \ldots, \ell\}$
  - Let mpk_α denote the common mpk submitted by parties in S_α.
  - For each $j \in [n]$, set $k_{\alpha,j} = k_j$ and $b_{\alpha,j} = 1$ if $j \in S_\alpha$, and $k_{\alpha,j} = \bot$ and $b_{\alpha,j} = 0$ otherwise.
  - Compute and return ct_α to every party in S_α, where

$$\text{ct}_\alpha \leftarrow \text{FE.Enc}\Big(\text{mpk}_\alpha, \big(\{k_{\alpha,j}\}_{j \in [n]}, \{b_{\alpha,j}\}_{j \in [n]}\big)\Big).$$

Phase 3 (Post-TP Call): A party computes output $y = \text{FE.Dec}\Big(\text{sk}_g, \text{ct}_\alpha\Big)$ using sk_g obtained from Phase 1 and ct_α obtained from Phase 2.

Fig. 2. Fully-secure MPC with single TP call based on Succinct Single-Key FE

Our result can be summarized via the following theorem:

Theorem 5 (TP-Aided MPC from Single-Key Succinct FE). *Assuming the existence of an FE scheme that satisfies correctness, (single-key) simulation-security and succinctness, there exists a TP-aided MPC protocol Π_{FE} for any functionality f that:*

- *utilizes a single call to a stateless TP of size* $\mathsf{poly}(n, \kappa, \beta)$ *(where n is the number of parties, κ is the security parameter, and β denotes the size of a single ciphertext in the FE scheme), and*
- *achieves full security against malicious corruption of up to $(n-1)$ parties and semi-honest corruption of the TP in the non-colluding model (see Definition 3).*

We defer the formal proof of this theorem to the full version of our paper.

4   Impossibilities in the Non-colluding Model

In this section, we present our negative results for small-TP aided MPC.

4.1   Impossibility in the Correlated Randomness Model for Protocols with Universal Output Decoder

Here, we make following assumptions– (a) small TP: the TP performs $\mathsf{poly}(n, \kappa)$ computation, (b) small output decoder: the parties, on receiving the message from the TP, perform $\mathsf{poly}(n, \kappa)$ computation to compute the output. We show that in this model, it is impossible to design a fully secure MPC, even if parties have access to correlated randomness and irrespective of computational assumptions used in the protocol. This holds even if the parties are corrupted in fail-stop fashion in the non-colluding model. Before we begin, we formalize the class of protocols for which the impossibility holds.

Notation. A fully-secure n-party protocol Π in the correlated randomness model that utilizes a single call to a small stateless TP comprises of the following phases.

- **Correlated Randomness Setup.** The setup computes correlated randomness $(\mathsf{cr}_1, \mathsf{cr}_2, \dots, \mathsf{cr}_n)$ and outputs cr_i to P_i $(i \in [n])$.
- **Pre-TP Computation.** In this phase, the parties may interact with each other (before the TP call), where each P_i participates with input x_i and randomness r_i. Let st_i denotes the state of P_i at the end of this phase, where st_i comprises of its input x_i, randomness r_i, correlated randomness cr_i (received as part of the setup) and in addition, the messages sent/received during this phase, if this phase was interactive. Lastly, each P_i computes algorithm $(\mathsf{in}_i, \mathsf{st}_i') \leftarrow \mathsf{preTP}_i(\mathsf{st}_i)$ and invokes TP with in_i.

- **TP Computation.** For each $i \in [n]$, the TP computes its response as $\mathsf{out}_i \leftarrow \mathsf{TP}_i(\mathsf{in}_1, \ldots, \mathsf{in}_n; r_{\mathsf{TP}})$, where r_{TP} denotes the internal randomness of the TP and TP_i denotes the algorithm used by the TP to compute its response to P_i.
- **Post-TP Computation.** Each P_i ($i \in [n]$) computes its output as $y \leftarrow \mathsf{postTP}_i(\mathsf{st}'_i, \mathsf{out}_i)$, where postTP_i denotes the algorithm used by P_i to compute its output. We refer to this algorithm as output decoder occasionally.[4]

In our model, (a) each TP_i for $i \in [n]$ is $\mathsf{poly}(n, \kappa)$-time (b) each postTP_i for $i \in [n]$ is $\mathsf{poly}(n, \kappa)$-time.

To show the impossibility, we show that a fully secure protocol would imply a statistically-correct (encoding, decoding) scheme which can produce an encoding that is smaller than the size of the message domain of the encoding scheme. This breaches the known incompressibility argument. Precisely, we use the following proposition of De et al. [DTT10], which formalizes the notion that it is impossible to compress every element in a set X to a string less than $\log|X|$ bits long.

Proposition 1. *[Incompressibility Argument [DTT10]] Let $E : X \times \{0,1\}^\rho \to \{0,1\}^m$ and $D : \{0,1\}^m \times \{0,1\}^\rho \to X$ be randomized encoding and decoding procedures such that, for every $x \in X$, $Pr_{r \in \{0,1\}^\rho}[D(E(x,r),r) = x] \geq \delta$. Then $m \geq \log(|X|) - \log(1/\delta)$.*

Theorem 6. *A general fully secure MPC protocol is impossible in the non-colluding model (see Definition 3), where the parties have access to arbitrary correlated randomness, a single call to a TP of size $\mathsf{poly}(n, \kappa)$, and are allowed to use an output decoder of size $\mathsf{poly}(n, \kappa)$, even when malicious corruption of parties in $\mathcal{P}$ is restricted to fail-stop corruption.*

Proof. Towards a contradiction, assume such a protocol Π computing an arbitrary function f exists (f is defined later) that achieves full security in the correlated randomness model, satisfying correctness with overwhelming probability. Without loss of generality, Π comprises of the phases (Correlated randomness setup, pre-TP computation, TP computation, post-TP computation) described previously.

Below, we show that Π leads to a statistically-correct randomized (encoding, decoding) scheme (E, D) (as defined in Proposition 1).

---

[4] We believe that a non-interactive post-TP computation phase is essentially without loss of generality. In other words, any fully secure MPC protocol (having access to one TP call) with interaction amongst the parties can be transformed to one where the parties do not communicate at all amongst themselves after receiving TP's response. We give a proof in the full version of our paper.

Algorithm(E, D)

$E : \{0,1\}^{2^{n-1}} \times \{0,1\}^{\rho} \to \{0,1\}^m$: This algorithm takes as input 2^{n-1} bits, say $(b_1, b_2, \ldots, b_{2^{n-1}})$, an randomness $r \in \{0,1\}^{\rho}$ and computes its encoding as follows:

1. For each $i \in [n]$, choose a pair of inputs (x_i, x_i^*) using r.
2. Consider a set S containing tuples of the form $(x_1, x_2', \ldots, x_n')$ where $x_i' \in \{x_i, x_i^*\}$ for $i \in \{2, \ldots, n\}$. Note that x_1 is fixed in all the tuples and $|S| = 2^{n-1}$.
3. Consider a lexicographic ordering of the elements in S generated as follows. For each $i \in [n]$, map x_i to bit 0 and x_i^* to bit 1. Now each tuple in S can be viewed as an n bit string and the elements in S can be lexicographically ordered. Let us denote the jth element as S_j. Let M be a mapping between S and $(b_1, b_2, \ldots, b_{2^{n-1}})$, where S_j is mapped to b_j for $j \in [2^{n-1}]$.
4. Construct an n-input function $f(X_1, \ldots, X_n)$ that outputs $M(X_1, \ldots, X_n)$, when $(X_1, \ldots, X_n) \in S$ and $\perp$ otherwise.
5. Suppose Π computes f on input X_i from P_i. Consider an execution of Π where parties $\{P_1, \ldots, P_n\}$ participate using inputs $\{x_i\}_{i \in [n]}$, randomness $\{r_i\}_{i \in [n]}$ and correlated randomness $\{\mathsf{cr}_i\}_{i \in [n]}$ (the latter two picked using r). Further, Π uses x_i^* as the default input of P_i ($i \in [n]$). Emulate the steps of this execution until the pre-TP computation to obtain $\{\mathsf{st}_i', \mathsf{in}_i\}_{i \in [n]}$. Let $\bar{\mathsf{st}}_1'$ denote the subset of st_1' used in postTP$_1$; with size restricted to $\mathsf{poly}(n, \kappa)$, as dictated by Π (recall that postTP function is allowed to do only $\mathsf{poly}(n, \kappa)$ computation).
6. The encoding of input $(b_1, b_2, \ldots, b_{2^{n-1}})$ is defined as $\{\bar{\mathsf{st}}_1', \mathsf{in}_1, \ldots, \mathsf{in}_n\}$, TP$_1$ (the algorithm used by the TP to compute its response to P_1) and postTP$_1$ (the output computation algorithm of P_1).

$D : \{0,1\}^m \times \{0,1\}^{\rho} \to \{0,1\}^{2^{n-1}}$: It takes as input the encoding $\{\bar{\mathsf{st}}_1', \mathsf{in}_1, \ldots, \mathsf{in}_n\}$ and the $r \in \{0,1\}^{\rho}$ used by E. For each subset $S' \subseteq \{2, \ldots, n\}$ in lexicographic order (starting from $S' = \varnothing$ to $S' = \{2, \ldots, n\}$), do the following (below we abuse the notation and use S' to denote the decimal value corresponding to the binary representation):

1. Compute $\mathsf{out}_1^{(S')} \leftarrow \mathsf{TP}_1(\mathsf{in}_1', \mathsf{in}_2', \ldots, \mathsf{in}_n'; r_{\mathsf{TP}})$, where $\mathsf{in}_i' = \mathsf{in}_i$ for $i \notin S'$ [a] and $\mathsf{in}_i' = \perp$ for $i \in S'$. Here, r_{TP} is derived from r as per the distribution corresponding to the internal randomness of the TP in Π.
2. Compute $b_{(S')} \leftarrow \mathsf{postTP}_1(\bar{\mathsf{st}}_1', \mathsf{out}_1^{(S')})$.

Output $(b_1, b_2, \ldots, b_{2^{n-1}})$.

---

[a] Note $\mathsf{in}_1' = \mathsf{in}_1$ is always satisfied as S' is defined as subsets of $\{2, \ldots, n\}$.

Fig. 3. A randomized encoding and decoding scheme

Lemma 1. (E, D) *is a statistically-correct encoding and decoding scheme.*

Proof. We now claim that the above pair (E, D) is statistically correct. That is the following holds good: for every $(b_1, \ldots, b_{2^{n-1}}) \in \{0,1\}^{2^{n-1}}$, $Pr_{r \in \{0,1\}^{\rho}}[D(E((b_1, \ldots, b_{2^{n-1}}), r), r) = (b_1, \ldots, b_{2^{n-1}})] \geq \delta$. This is because Π computes f that, for every input in S, as defined in E, maps to one distinct bit in the sequence $(b_1, \ldots, b_{2^{n-1}})$ (recall that the jth element of S, S_j is mapped to b_j). Further, Π computes f and achieves full security (guaranteed output delivery) and satisfies correctness with overwhelming probability. Specifically, if a subset of parties P_i such that $i \in S'$ do not invoke the TP during Π, then the TP receives $\{in_i\}$ only from the other parties P_i where $i \notin S'$ and sets $in_i = \bot$ for parties in S'. The output computed by the TP is on the default input x_i^* for each party P_i with $i \in S'$ and x_i for each party P_i with $i \notin S'$.

Since S' is defined as subsets of $\{2, \ldots, n\}$ and never includes the index 1, the above captures executions of Π where P_1 is honest, participated honestly with input x_1 and invoked the TP with $in_1' = in_1$. This allows us to rely on the correctness of the output computed by postTP_1. We can thus infer that the 2^{n-1} bits computed during decoding indeed correspond to the set of outputs of f for each subset S', namely $(b_1, b_2, \ldots, b_{2^{n-1}})$.

Notice that the above argument holds good even if Π satisfies full security tolerating fail-stop corruption where the parties do not send their message to the TP. Furthermore, Π satisfying fairness is not enough to claim that (E, D) is (statistically) correct, because D may fail to recover $(b_1, \ldots, b_{2^{n-1}})$ always.

By the incompressibility argument of [DTT10] (which is formally stated above), it must hold that $|\bar{st}_1'| + |in_1| + \ldots |in_n| + |out_1| + |\mathsf{postTP}_1| \geq 2^{n-1}$. We can thus infer that at least one of the terms $\geq \frac{2^{n-1}}{n+3}$. Recall that by our assumption on small output decoder, the terms $|\bar{st}_1'|$ and $|\mathsf{postTP}_1|$ are bounded by size $\mathsf{poly}(n, \kappa)$. Therefore, it must be the case that one of the terms $in_1, \ldots, in_n, out_1$ must be of size $\geq \frac{2^{n-1}}{n+3}$. However, this contradicts our assumption that the TP has size $\mathsf{poly}(n, \kappa)$ as $in_1, \ldots, in_n$ comprises of the input to the TP and out_1 is the algorithm run by the TP to compute its response to P_1. We have thus arrived at a contradiction; completing the proof.

4.2   Impossibility in the Plain Model

In this section, we show that in the plain model (without correlated randomness), it is impossible to design statistically secure MPC with the non-colluding security, even when the parties are only semi-honestly corrupt. That is, we prove that a protocol is impossible when the adversary in the non-colluding TP model can either (a) corrupt majority of the parties $\{P_1, \ldots, P_n\}$ semi-honestly or (b) control the TP semi-honestly). We state the formal theorem below.

Theorem 7. *A general statistically-secure MPC protocol is impossible in the plain and the non-colluding TP model (see Definition 3), where the parties have access to a single call to a small TP of size $\mathsf{poly}(n, \kappa)$, even when malicious corruption of parties in $\mathcal{P}$ is restricted to semi-honest corruption.*

Proof. Towards a contradiction, assume that there exists a statistically-secure 2-party protocol Π securely computing f against a semi-honest adversary in the non-colluding TP model. Let f be defined as the functionality computing $(k+1)$ oblivious transfer (OT) instances i.e.

$$f\left(x_1 = (m_i^0, m_i^1)_{i \in [k+1]}, x_2 = (b_1, \ldots, b_k, b_{k+1})\right) = (m_1^{b_1}, m_2^{b_2} \ldots, m_{k+1}^{b_{k+1}})$$

Here, the input of P_1 (who acts as the sender) consists of $(k+1)$ pairs of bits and the input of P_2 (who acts as the receiver) consists of $(k+1)$ bits.

Suppose C_{TP} denotes the circuit describing the function $\{\mathsf{TP}\}_{i \in [n]}$ computed by the TP during Π. Based on our assumption that the TP is 'small', it must hold that $|C_{\mathsf{TP}}| \leq \texttt{poly}(n, \kappa)$ which is independent of the function f being computed. Specifically, this means that the computation done by the TP must be strictly less than computing $(k+1)$ OTs.

We claim that Π computing f can be used to build a semi-honest OT extension protocol Π'. Assume a semi-honest setting where the parties are given k OT correlations generated as the base OTs of the OT extension protocol Π'. Π' proceeds as follows:

1. The parties execute the steps of Π in the pre-TP computation phase.
2. Next, the parties emulate the TP computation phase of Π by executing the perfectly-secure semi-honest GMW protocol [GMW87] to compute the function described by C_{TP}. For this, the parties use the k OT correlations (given as base OTs). Note that these OT correlations must suffice as computing C_{TP} must involve computing fewer than $(k+1)$ OTs (based on our assumption).
3. Finally, the parties use the output of the execution of the GMW protocol (which computes the TP response of Π) to carry out the steps of output computation as per Π. This will result in the parties obtaining the output of f.

We note that Π' does not involve any calls to the stateless TP. Since Π' computes $(k+1)$ OTs starting with k base OTs and involves execution of steps in Π and the GMW protocol, which are both information-theoretically secure; we can conclude that Π' is indeed a semi-honest information-theoretic OT extension protocol. However, this is a contradiction as information-theoretically secure OT extension does not exist in the plain model [Bea96]. This completes the proof.

5   Impossibility of Fair MPC in the Colluding Model

In this section, we briefly summarize our negative results for fair MPC in the colluding security model (see Definition 3). Recall that, in this model, we assume that the adversary controls a majority of the parties among $\{P_1, \ldots, P_n\}$ maliciously and simultaneously corrupt the TP semi-honestly. Our impossibility holds good even when malicious corruption is weakened to fail-stop corruption and the requirement of full security is relaxed to fairness. Our result is summarized by the following theorem.

Theorem 8. *There exists a function f such that it is impossible to design a fair MPC protocol securely computing f in the computational colluding model (see Definition 3) even when malicious corruption of parties in $\mathcal{P}$ is restricted to fail-stop corruption.*

We defer the detailed proof of this theorem to the full version of our paper. At a high level, we follow the following route. We note that the colluding adversarial model can be viewed more generally, in terms of the general mixed adversarial model that has been studied in works such as [HMZ08, FHM99, BFH+08]. Recall that a general mixed adversary is characterized by an adversary structure $\mathbb{Z} = \{(A_1, E_1, F_1), \ldots, (A_m, E_m, F_m)\}$ (for some m), which is a monotone set of triples of party sets. At the beginning of the protocol, the adversary chooses one of these triples $\mathbb{Z}^* = (A^*, E^*, F^*) \in \mathbb{Z}$ and actively corrupts parties in A^*, semi-honestly corrupts the parties in E^* and fail-corrupts the parties in F^*.

Viewing the TP as an additional party P_{n+1} (who can be semi-honestly corrupted) and the party set $\mathcal{P} = \{P_1, \ldots, P_n, P_{n+1}\}$, the adversarial structure for the colluding TP model can be expressed as: $\mathbb{Z} = \{\{\mathbb{Z}_1, \ldots, \mathbb{Z}_n\}$, where for each $i \in [n]$, we have

$$\mathbb{Z}_i = \left(A_i = \mathcal{P} \setminus \{P_i, P_{n+1}\}, E_i = \mathcal{P} \setminus \{P_i\}, F_i = \mathcal{P} \setminus \{P_i, P_{n+1}\} \right).$$

Specifically, the above denotes the maximal class of the adversarial structure of the colluding TP model, since these subsume all other possible corruption scenarios indicated by subsets of the triples in each $\mathbb{Z}_i$, i.e. the adversary can choose to corrupt (A^*, E^*, F^*), such that there exists $(\bar{A}, \bar{E}, \bar{F}) \in \mathbb{Z} : A^* \subseteq \bar{A}, E^* \subseteq \bar{E}, F^* \subseteq \bar{F}$. Now restricting the malicious adversaries to behave in a fail-stop manner, we refine the maximal adversarial structure as $\mathbb{Z}' = \{\mathbb{Z}'_1, \ldots, \mathbb{Z}'_n\}$, where for each $i \in [n]$,

$$\mathbb{Z}'_i = \left(A_i = \emptyset, E_i = \mathcal{P} \setminus \{P_i\}, F_i = \mathcal{P} \setminus \{P_i, P_{n+1}\} \right).$$

Given this adversarial structure, we show that our desired impossibility result is implied by the impossibility of fair (non-reactive) MPC shown in [HMZ08]. The proof requires a careful mapping between the maximal adversarial structures between our model of TP-aided MPC and the general mixed adversarial model considered in [HMZ08] (see the full version of our paper for details). Note that in above analysis, we consider the TP to be just another party that can communicate freely with the other parties while maintaining states across the communication. This implies that our impossibility holds even for stateful TPs.

Acknowledgments. We thank the anonymous reviewers of TCC 2022 for their helpful comments and suggestions. Y. Ishai was supported in part by ERC Project NTSC (742754), BSF grant 2018393, and ISF grant 2774/20. A. Patra would like to acknowledge financial support from DST National Mission on Interdisciplinary Cyber-Physical Systems (NM-ICPS) 2020–2025. D. Ravi was funded by the European Research Council (ERC) under the European Unions's Horizon 2020 research and innovation programme under grant agreement No 803096 (SPEC). A. Srinivasan was supported in part by a SERB startup grant.

References

[ABMO15] Asharov, G., Beimel, A., Makriyannis, N., Omri, E.: Complete characterization of fairness in secure two-party computation of boolean functions. In: Dodis, Y., Nielsen, J.B. (eds.) TCC 2015. LNCS, vol. 9014, pp. 199–228. Springer, Heidelberg (2015). https://doi.org/10.1007/978-3-662-46494-6_10

[ADMM14] Andrychowicz, M., Dziembowski, S., Malinowski, D., Mazurek, L.: Secure multiparty computations on bitcoin. In: IEEE SP 2014, pp. 443–458. IEEE Computer Society (2014)

[Bea96] Beaver, D.: Correlated pseudorandomness and the complexity of private computations. In: ACM STOC 1996, pp. 479–488. ACM (1996)

[BFH+08] Beerliová-Trubíniová, Z., Fitzi, M., Hirt, M., Maurer, U., Zikas, V.: MPC vs. SFE: perfect security in a unified corruption model. In: Canetti, R. (ed.) TCC 2008. LNCS, vol. 4948, pp. 231–250. Springer, Heidelberg (2008). https://doi.org/10.1007/978-3-540-78524-8_14

[BFSK11] Brzuska, C., Fischlin, M., Schröder, H., Katzenbeisser, S.: Physically uncloneable functions in the universal composition framework. In: Rogaway, P. (ed.) CRYPTO 2011. LNCS, vol. 6841, pp. 51–70. Springer, Heidelberg (2011). https://doi.org/10.1007/978-3-642-22792-9_4

[BGI+01] Barak, B., Goldreich, O., Impagliazzo, R., Rudich, S., Sahai, A., Vadhan, S., Yang, K.: On the (Im)possibility of obfuscating programs. In: Kilian, J. (ed.) CRYPTO 2001. LNCS, vol. 2139, pp. 1–18. Springer, Heidelberg (2001). https://doi.org/10.1007/3-540-44647-8_1

[BJOV18] Badrinarayanan, S., Jain, A., Ostrovsky, R., Visconti, I.: Non-interactive secure computation from one-way functions. In: Peyrin, T., Galbraith, S. (eds.) ASIACRYPT 2018. LNCS, vol. 11274, pp. 118–138. Springer, Cham (2018). https://doi.org/10.1007/978-3-030-03332-3_5

[BK14] Bentov, I., Kumaresan, R.: How to use bitcoin to design fair protocols. In: Garay, J.A., Gennaro, R. (eds.) CRYPTO 2014. LNCS, vol. 8617, pp. 421–439. Springer, Heidelberg (2014). https://doi.org/10.1007/978-3-662-44381-1_24

[BKOV17] Badrinarayanan, S., Khurana, D., Ostrovsky, R., Visconti, I.: Unconditional UC-secure computation with (stronger-malicious) PUFs. In: Coron, J.-S., Nielsen, J.B. (eds.) EUROCRYPT 2017. LNCS, vol. 10210, pp. 382–411. Springer, Cham (2017). https://doi.org/10.1007/978-3-319-56620-7_14

[BLOO20] Beimel, A., Lindell, Y., Omri, E., Orlov, I.: 1/p-secure multiparty computation without an honest majority and the best of both worlds. J. Cryptol. **33**(4), 1659–1731 (2020)

[BOO15] Beimel, A., Omri, E., Orlov, I.: Protocols for multiparty coin toss with a dishonest majority. J. Cryptol. **28**(3), 551–600 (2015)

[BSW11] Boneh, D., Sahai, A., Waters, B.: Functional encryption: definitions and challenges. In: Ishai, Y. (ed.) TCC 2011. LNCS, vol. 6597, pp. 253–273. Springer, Heidelberg (2011). https://doi.org/10.1007/978-3-642-19571-6_16

[Can01] Canetti, R.: Universally composable security: a new paradigm for cryptographic protocols. In: FOCS (2001)

[CCOV19] Chandran, N., Chongchitmate, W., Ostrovsky, R., Visconti, I.: Universally composable secure computation with corrupted tokens. In: Boldyreva, A., Micciancio, D. (eds.) CRYPTO 2019. LNCS, vol. 11694, pp. 432–461. Springer, Cham (2019). https://doi.org/10.1007/978-3-030-26954-8_14

[CF01] Canetti, R., Fischlin, M.: Universally composable commitments. In: Kilian, J. (ed.) CRYPTO 2001. LNCS, vol. 2139, pp. 19–40. Springer, Heidelberg (2001). https://doi.org/10.1007/3-540-44647-8_2

[CGJ+17] Choudhuri, A.R., Green, M., Jain, A., Kaptchuk, G., Miers, I.: Fairness in an unfair world: fair multiparty computation from public bulletin boards. In: ACM CCS 2017, pp. 719–728. ACM (2017)

[CGS08] Chandran, N., Goyal, V., Sahai, A.: New constructions for UC secure computation using tamper-proof hardware. In: Smart, N. (ed.) EUROCRYPT 2008. LNCS, vol. 4965, pp. 545–562. Springer, Heidelberg (2008). https://doi.org/10.1007/978-3-540-78967-3_31

[CKS+14] Choi, S.G., Katz, J., Schröder, D., Yerukhimovich, A., Zhou, H.-S.: (Efficient) universally composable oblivious transfer using a minimal number of stateless tokens. In: TCC 2014, pp. 638–662 (2014)

[Cle86] Cleve, R.: Limits on the security of coin flips when half the processors are faulty (extended abstract). In: ACM STOC (1986)

[DMRV13] Dachman-Soled, D., Malkin, T., Raykova, M., Venkitasubramaniam, M.: Adaptive and concurrent secure computation from new adaptive, non-malleable commitments. In: Sako, K., Sarkar, P. (eds.) ASIACRYPT 2013. LNCS, vol. 8269, pp. 316–336. Springer, Heidelberg (2013). https://doi.org/10.1007/978-3-642-42033-7_17

[DTT10] De, A., Trevisan, L., Tulsiani, M.: Time space tradeoffs for attacks against one-way functions and PRGs. In: Rabin, T. (ed.) CRYPTO 2010. LNCS, vol. 6223, pp. 649–665. Springer, Heidelberg (2010). https://doi.org/10.1007/978-3-642-14623-7_35

[EGL85] Even, S., Goldreich, O., Lempel, A.: A randomized protocol for signing contracts. Commun. ACM 28(6), 637–647 (1985)

[FGMO01] Fitzi, M., Garay, J.A., Maurer, U., Ostrovsky, R.: Minimal complete primitives for secure multi-party computation. In: Kilian, J. (ed.) CRYPTO 2001. LNCS, vol. 2139, pp. 80–100. Springer, Heidelberg (2001). https://doi.org/10.1007/3-540-44647-8_5

[FHM99] Fitzi, M., Hirt, M., Maurer, U.: General Adversaries in Unconditional Multi-party Computation. In: Lam, K.-Y., Okamoto, E., Xing, C. (eds.) ASIACRYPT 1999. LNCS, vol. 1716, pp. 232–246. Springer, Heidelberg (1999). https://doi.org/10.1007/978-3-540-48000-6_19

[FKN94] Feige, U., Kilian, J., Naor, M.: A minimal model for secure computation (extended abstract). In: ACM STOC 1994, pp. 554–563 (1994)

[GGH+13] Garg, S., Gentry, C., Halevi, S., Raykova, M., Sahai, A., Waters, B.: Candidate indistinguishability obfuscation and functional encryption for all circuits. In: IEEE FOCS 2013, pp. 40–49. IEEE Computer Society (2013)

[GGSW13] Garg, S., Gentry, C., Sahai, A., Waters, B.: Witness encryption and its applications. In: ACM STOC 2013, pp. 467–476. ACM (2013)

[GHKL11] Dov Gordon, S., Hazay, C., Katz, J., Lindell, Y.: Complete fairness in secure two-party computation. J. ACM 58(6), 24:1–24:37 (2011)

[GIM+10] Dov Gordon, S., Ishai, Y., Moran, T., Ostrovsky, R., Sahai, A.: On complete primitives for fairness. In: TCC 2010, pp. 91–108 (2010)

[GK09]   Gordon, S.D., Katz, J.: Complete fairness in multi-party computation without an honest majority. In: Reingold, O. (ed.) TCC 2009. LNCS, vol. 5444, pp. 19–35. Springer, Heidelberg (2009). https://doi.org/10.1007/978-3-642-00457-5_2

[GK12]   Dov Gordon, S., Katz, J.: Partial fairness in secure two-party computation. J. Cryptol. **25**(1), 14–40 (2012)

[GKP+13] Goldwasser, S., Kalai, Y.T., Popa, R.A., Vaikuntanathan, V., Zeldovich, N.: Reusable garbled circuits and succinct functional encryption. In: STOC 2013, pp. 555–564 (2013)

[GMPY11] Garay, J.A., MacKenzie, P.D., Prabhakaran, M., Yang, K.: Resource fairness and composability of cryptographic protocols. J. Cryptol. **24**(4), 615–658 (2011)

[GMW87]   Goldreich, O., Micali, S., Wigderson, A.: How to play any mental game or A completeness theorem for protocols with honest majority. In: ACM STOC (1987)

[GS18]   Garg, S., Srinivasan, A.: Two-round multiparty secure computation from minimal assumptions. In: Nielsen, J.B., Rijmen, V. (eds.) EUROCRYPT 2018. LNCS, vol. 10821, pp. 468–499. Springer, Cham (2018). https://doi.org/10.1007/978-3-319-78375-8_16

[HMZ08]   Hirt, M., Maurer, U., Zikas, V.: MPC vs. SFE: unconditional and computational security. In: Pieprzyk, J. (ed.) ASIACRYPT 2008. LNCS, vol. 5350, pp. 1–18. Springer, Heidelberg (2008). https://doi.org/10.1007/978-3-540-89255-7_1

[HPV16]   Hazay, C., Polychroniadou, A., Venkitasubramaniam, M.: Composable security in the tamper-proof hardware model under minimal complexity. In: Hirt, M., Smith, A. (eds.) TCC 2016. LNCS, vol. 9985, pp. 367–399. Springer, Heidelberg (2016). https://doi.org/10.1007/978-3-662-53641-4_15

[IOS12]   Ishai, Y., Ostrovsky, R., Seyalioglu, H.: Identifying cheaters without an honest majority. In: Cramer, R. (ed.) TCC 2012. LNCS, vol. 7194, pp. 21–38. Springer, Heidelberg (2012). https://doi.org/10.1007/978-3-642-28914-9_2

[JLS21]   Jain, A., Lin, H., Sahai, A.: Indistinguishability obfuscation from well-founded assumptions. In: STOC 2021, pp. 60–73 (2021)

[Kat07]   Katz, J.: Universally composable multi-party computation using tamper-proof hardware. In: Naor, M. (ed.) EUROCRYPT 2007. LNCS, vol. 4515, pp. 115–128. Springer, Heidelberg (2007). https://doi.org/10.1007/978-3-540-72540-4_7

[KB14]   Kumaresan, R., Bentov, I.: How to use bitcoin to incentivize correct computations. In: Ahn, G.-J., Yung, M., Li, N. (eds.) ACM CCS 2014, pp. 30–41. ACM (2014)

[O'N10]   O'Neill, A.: Definitional issues in functional encryption. IACR Cryptol. ePrint Arch., p. 556 (2010)

[OSVW13] Ostrovsky, R., Scafuro, A., Visconti, I., Wadia, A.: Universally composable secure computation with (malicious) physically uncloneable functions. In: Johansson, T., Nguyen, P.Q. (eds.) EUROCRYPT 2013. LNCS, vol. 7881, pp. 702–718. Springer, Heidelberg (2013). https://doi.org/10.1007/978-3-642-38348-9_41

[PST17] Pass, R., Shi, E., Tramèr, F.: Formal abstractions for attested execution secure processors. In: Coron, J.-S., Nielsen, J.B. (eds.) EUROCRYPT 2017. LNCS, vol. 10210, pp. 260–289. Springer, Cham (2017). https://doi.org/10.1007/978-3-319-56620-7_10

[QWW18] Quach, W., Wee, H., Wichs, D.: Laconic function evaluation and applications. In: Thorup, M. (ed.) IEEE FOCS 2018, pp. 859–870. IEEE Computer Society (2018)

[SW05] Sahai, A., Waters, B.: Fuzzy identity-based encryption. In: Cramer, R. (ed.) EUROCRYPT 2005. LNCS, vol. 3494, pp. 457–473. Springer, Heidelberg (2005). https://doi.org/10.1007/11426639_27

[Wat15] Waters, B.: A punctured programming approach to adaptively secure functional encryption. In: Gennaro, R., Robshaw, M. (eds.) CRYPTO 2015. LNCS, vol. 9216, pp. 678–697. Springer, Heidelberg (2015). https://doi.org/10.1007/978-3-662-48000-7_33

SCALES
MPC with Small Clients and Larger Ephemeral Servers

Anasuya Acharya[1]([✉])(iD), Carmit Hazay[1](iD), Vladimir Kolesnikov[2](iD),
and Manoj Prabhakaran[3]

[1] Bar-Ilan University, Ramat Gan, Israel
{acharya,carmit.hazay}@biu.ac.il
[2] Georgia Institute of Technology, Atlanta, USA
kolesnikov@gatech.edu
[3] Indian Institute of Technology Bombay, Mumbai, India
mp@cse.iitb.ac.in

Abstract. The recently proposed YOSO model is a groundbreaking approach to MPC, executable on a public blockchain, circumventing adaptive player corruption by hiding the corruption targets until they are worthless. Players are selected unpredictably from a large pool to perform MPC subtasks, in which each selected player sends a single message (and reveals their identity). While YOSO MPC has attractive asymptotic complexity, unfortunately, it is concretely prohibitively expensive due to the cost of its building blocks.

We propose a modification to the YOSO model that preserves resilience to adaptive server corruption, but allows for much more efficient protocols. In *SCALES (Small Clients And Larger Ephemeral Servers)* only the servers facilitating the MPC computation are ephemeral (unpredictably selected and "speak once"). Input providers (clients) publish problem instance and collect the output, but do not otherwise participate in computation SCALES offers attractive features, and improves over YOSO in outsourcing MPC to a large pool of servers under adaptive corruption.

We build SCALES from Rerandomizable Garbling Schemes (RGS). RGS is a contribution of independent interest with additional applications.

1   Introduction

A recent line of research, motivated by platforms such as blockchains, studies multi-party computation (MPC) with specialized communication and computation patterns [BGG+20, GHK+21, CGG+21, GMPS21]. While the specifics differ, these models leverage a dynamic pool of workers, unavailable throughout the protocol. Most excitingly, [BGG+20, GHK+21] show it is possible to only depend on *ephemeral* workers, who carry out some local computation, publish a *single* message on a bulletin board, and then vanish from the system. This is pithily captured in the name YOSO (You Only Speak Once) [GHK+21]. An attractive model for leveraging short-term workers, crucially, YOSO eliminates or drastically reduces the window for *adaptive corruption* of these workers. In particular,

E. Kiltz and V. Vaikuntanathan (Eds.): TCC 2022, LNCS 13748, pp. 502–531, 2022.
https://doi.org/10.1007/978-3-031-22365-5_18

this for the first time enables efficient massive-scale MPC with adaptive corruption, achieved simply by delegating the computation to a small unpredictably selected YOSO subcommittee.

Even as the YOSO results [BGG+20, GHK+21] are powerful, they do leave room for improvement: they rely on strong honest-majority assumptions and expensive target-anonymous channels. Similarly, non-YOSO work requires honest majority [CGG+21] or complex setups, such as Conditional Storage and Retrieval in [GMPS21].

We propose an alternate model, where *light-weight input parties* participate in the initial and final stages of the protocol and do retain some state in between; but the bulk of the computation is carried out by *ephemeral servers* that are capable of performing computationally demanding tasks. Here, by 'light-weight', we mean that the complexity of each input does not depend on the function's complexity or inputs of other parties, but only on the size of its own inputs, and the number of participating ephemeral servers. There is no setup other than a bulletin board, and the corruption model allows all-but-one server participating in the computation to be corrupt, allowing for even very small numbers of servers. Moreover, by requiring the input parties to send a second message, we let them *control when the computation finishes*—arguably a desirable feature, especially when the number of servers used can be dynamic. Crucially, our ephemeral servers send a single message each, maintaining YOSO-like resilience to adaptive corruptions.

Note that a bulletin board is much simpler than target-anonymous channels in many ways. In particular, in a semi-honest setting, a bulletin board can be implemented by a *single* party, without requiring any honest majority assumptions, as there are no secrets to hide. But a target-anonymous channel would need more than a single honest party, and further if an efficient implementation involving a small committee is resorted to and the adversary can corrupt parties adaptively, a large honest majority is needed: $> 50\%$ [GHM+21] or $> 71\%$ [BGG+20].

We seek a protocol without complex setup and based only on standard cryptographic assumptions. Our solution builds on *rerandomizable* Garbled Circuits, formalized as Rerandomizable Garbling Schemes (RGS). In this work we shall focus on security against passive corruption.

1.1 Summary of Our Contributions

Before going further, we summarize the contributions in this work:

- *MPC with Small Clients and Larger Ephemeral Servers (SCALES).* Our main high-level contribution is the introduction of an attractive setting for MPC with ephemeral servers and limited interaction in Sect. 3. SCALES preserves YOSO-like resilience to adaptive server corruptions, and hence also allows outsourcing secure computation to blockchain (Sect. 1.2). We construct an efficient semi-honest SCALES protocol, where each server does work proportional to the circuit size, and each client proportional to its input size (Sect. 6).

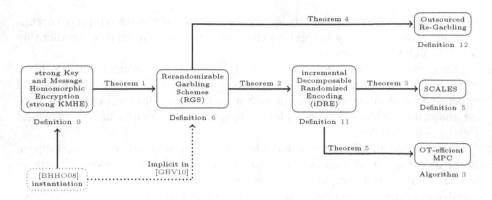

Fig. 1. Our contributions

- *Defining basic cryptographic primitives.* We formalize the following notions used in constructing a SCALES protocol, which we believe to be of independent interest, and investigate their relationship: 1) *Rerandomizable Garbling Scheme* (RGS) (Sect. 4), a generalization of Garbling Schemes (GS) to the setting of multiple garblers, each is *sequentially* involved in garbling, 2) *Strong Key-and-Message Homomorphic Encryption* (strong KMHE), and 3) A new multi-party notion of a randomized encoding, *incremental Decomposable Randomized Encoding* (iDRE) (Sect. 5).
- *Corresponding constructions.* We show that a construction of Boneh et al. [BHHO08], following the analysis in [NS09,GHV10], yields strong KMHE for a useful class of key and message transformations. Next, we show that such a strong KMHE scheme, when used as the encryption scheme in a version of garbled circuit (GC) yields an RGS. We then combine this RGS with a (weak) KMHE scheme, to obtain an iDRE scheme, which can be directly used for SCALES.
- *Further Applications.* Beyond being building blocks for protocols in the SCALES setting, RGS and iDRE are highly useful for other MPC settings as well.
  - **Outsourced Regarbling.** We show that an RGS directly yields an "Outsourced Regarbling" scheme. In a secure 2-party computation (2PC) setting, when Alice's (secret) function is to be securely evaluated on many inputs held by Bob, an outsourced re-garbling scheme allows Alice to outsource much of her work to a semi-honest server.
  - **Efficient MPC with optimal OT complexity.** An iDRE can be used to implement general n-party MPC protocols secure against a semi-honest corruption of $(n-1)$ parties. For an input size m, such a protocol takes $O(n \times m)$ string-OT calls, meeting the lower bound on OT complexity for this setting, as proven in [HIK07]. While [HIK07] also presents a protocol that meets this bound, their protocol requires OT strings to be of the size of the truth-table of the function being computed. In contrast, an iDRE-based protocol (Sect. 7.2) runs OT of constant-size strings. Unlike [HIK07] which is in the information-theoretic OT-hybrid model, we do allow a

single *black-box* invocation of iDRE. However, we note that invoking iDRE with each party carrying out at most one (re-)encoding step does not trivialize OTs: thanks to the sequential communication pattern, such an invocation of iDRE by itself would not provide a means to implement MPC without OTs or further computational assumptions.

- *Closing an analysis gap in previous work.* Rerandomizing GCs has previously been explored in the context of multi-hop homomorphic encryption by Gentry et al. [GHV10]. They define *rerandomizable SFE* (Secure Function Evaluation) and instantiate it using the encryption scheme of [BHHO08], though the specific security guarantees of strong KMHE were not identified there. Although their construction does satisfy their definition of rerandomizable SFE, their proof has a gap, which we point out. We also clarify that although [GHV10] uses similar building blocks, its multi-hop homomorphic encryption setting is inherently different from SCALES.

1.2   Our Main Contribution: SCALES MPC

The motivation for SCALES follows that of the recently proposed YOSO MPC. The YOSO (You Only Speak Once) property and model of MPC, introduced by Gentry et al. [GHK+21], requires that protocol participants each send a single message during the execution. Combined with known techniques for players to self-select at random for a task (cf. Bitcoin miners who self-select for proposing a block by finding a hash preimage of a special form), YOSO finally *offers hope* for efficient large-scale MPC in the setting with adaptive player corruption. Indeed, standard adaptively secure n-party MPC protocols have costs quadratic in n. In large-scale MPC, electing a small committee who will then evaluate the function on behalf of all n players is far more efficient, asymptotically and practically. Unfortunately, with adaptive corruptions, this breaks down, as adaptive adversary will simply corrupt all members of the committee (its corruption budget is a fraction of n, which is greater than the committee size). This is where YOSO saves the day: committee members are unidentifiable since they are self-selected and are removed from the committee as soon as they post a message, or "speak". Thus, an adaptive adversary does not know whom to corrupt until it is too late, and the committee executing the YOSO MPC is secure against adaptive corruptions. A particular application of interest of YOSO MPC is MPC over a blockchain, where blockchain nodes form the pool of MPC players, and inputs may come from participants such as accounts or wallets. Quite surprisingly, YOSO is achievable [GHK+21], despite numerous technical obstacles, such as the need for players executing i-th MPC round to send encrypted messages (e.g. containing internal state) to unidentified future round-$(i+1)$ committee members. Unfortunately, however, this protocol's costs are prohibitive for practice.

SCALES MPC Motivation. Motivated by *practically efficient* YOSO-style large-scale MPC, and with a particular eye on outsourced MPC and blockchain MPC, we introduce our SCALES (Small Clients And Larger Ephemeral Servers) MPC model. We keep the crucial YOSO property that servers speak once (and hence committee is protected against full dynamic corruption). Our clients (input providers) speak twice, to publish a problem instance and to collect the answer. This weakening of the model allows us to have a much more efficient instantiation than YOSO. We compare the two models in more detail in Sect. 1.4.

Syntactically, this is more permissive than YOSO; this is consistent with the goals of blockchain and outsourced MPC, and YOSO. Indeed, dynamic corruption of individual clients only threatens their security, and not of the computation and other clients. Essentially, YOSO's main advantage over SCALES is the ability to hide client identities, a less appealing feature that can still be added to SCALES by clients sending their state to future decoding players using expensive YOSO technique *once*. In return, we get a much higher performance as discussed in Sects. 1.3 and 1.4 and several additional features. Note, we do not reduce computation *per server*, but rather total servers' work.

SCALES Model. A set of *lightweight* input providers wish to securely compute a function of all their inputs. The bulk of the computation itself is *outsourced* to a pool of servers. We assume broadcast through a public bulletin board and that every message to be sent is posted onto it. In the computation, the set of input providers first post encoding of their inputs. Next, one by one, a server from the pool, upon turning online, reads the state of the bulletin board, performs specified computation, erases its state, posts its outcome, and goes offline. Once sufficiently many servers have been involved in the computation, the input providers post a second message based on the state of the bulletin board, and the decoding procedure can take place publicly using all the information posted[1].

SCALES Features.

1. As in YOSO, the servers are speak-once and dynamically *self-selected*. Their identities are unknown until they have completed their part of the computation and erased their internal state. Hence they are not vulnerable to dynamic corruption.
2. The number of participating servers need not be fixed ahead of time. For instance, it can be based on a function of the (unpredictable) server identities.
3. The input parties need not interact with, or even be aware of, each other. Their complexity is independent of the number of other input players.
4. A SCALES protocol is also useful in settings with very few – say, two – non-colluding servers. We remark that while similar non-interactive outsourcing using GC has been considered [MRZ15], without rerandomization they require that the GC evaluator does not collude with *either* of the two servers.
5. An input provider could ensure that it is happy with the set of servers who have taken part in the protocol, before allowing the final decoding to proceed (by holding off from posting its second message).
6. In the case that more than one server posts a message in the same round, creating a fork in the computation, the input providers can choose which

---

[1] The final output of the protocol can easily be made private - known only to the clients. This is done by computing a function that gives an encryption of the desired output under the client's key.

chain of server computations they want to recognize (by posting a second message only for that set of servers).

Further, one could add a requirement that the first message from the input parties be "reusable," in the spirit of recent two-round MPC protocols [BJKL21, BGSZ21]. We omit this from our definition for simplicity. However, this is satisfied by our construction that is based on a 2-round OT protocol with a reusable first message.

1.3 Other Contributions in More Detail

Rerandomizable Garbling Schemes. We formalize RGS as a powerful generalization of Garbling Schemes (GS) to the setting of multiple garblers. This deviates from the multi-party garbling of [BMR90] where all garblers symmetrically contribute to the final garbling. An RGS retains the standard garbling procedure Gb, and supplements it with an additional function Rerand. Given a garbling (without its input encoding function), Rerand rerandomizes it, producing a new garbling that is indistinguishable from a fresh garbling. Rerand also supplies a transformation that, when applied to the encoding function of the original garbling, will yield the encoding function of the regarbling.

The RGS approach allows the garblers to be ephemeral. Further, the number of garblers can be dynamically selected, if desired. The computation and communication complexity of garblers remain *constant* with the number of garblers, vs *quadratic* in the traditional approach.

Constructing a Rerandomizable Garbling Scheme. We provide an RGS construction based on GC [Yao86] that we endow with a secure regarbling procedure. To rerandomize GC, we follow [GHV10], where each output label is additively secret-shared into two shares, and each share is encrypted (with strong KMHE) under a single input label as key. This garbling variant is rerandomization-friendlier than the double-key encryption schemes used in standard versions of garbled circuits (e.g., [LP09]).

Our strong KMHE abstraction supports both key and message homomorphism, a property that is crucial for achieving private garbling rerandomization. In essence, rerandomization follows by transforming every garbled row into a fresh ciphertext, encrypting a new label share. To maintain consistency across garbled gates, we apply a corresponding transformation to wire labels.

RGS security requires that a fresh garbling is indistinguishable from a rerandomized one, even given randomness used in the initial GC. Somewhat informally, this property boils down to indistinguishability between a ciphertext that is either encrypted under a transformed key or a fresh independent key, even given the original key. This is the property needed to close the gap in the [GHV10] proof. We further prove that the scheme of [BHHO08] meets our security definition.

A SCALES Scheme. In a SCALES scheme, all servers must garble jointly to prevent a successful server-evaluator collusion. Our model requires that this is done in a sequential manner. We build SCALES protocol from RGS by letting the ephemeral servers play the role of the (re-)garblers, and output is obtained by evaluating the resulting GC. We must also securely apply the input encoding transformations generated by RGS. Regarblers can do this because we use KMHE as our encryption scheme. Finally, active input keys are obtained by clients by running OT with each of the garblers. This can be done to fit with our communication pattern. Our resulting protocol is secure against all-but-one corruption of the ephemeral garblers and, given an OT that is secure against adaptive corruption of receivers, our protocol also withstands adaptive corruption of a subset of the clients.

Performance. As SCALES approximates YOSO both in motivation and formalization, we focus on the YOSO comparison (simplified to the semi-honest setting, without considering their use of NIZKs). In SCALES, per client's input bit, his work to generate the first message (of total two) is constant; to generate the second message, client's work is proportional to the number of ephemeral servers. Unlike all previous YOSO work, the number of ephemeral servers required for SCALES, is arbitrary (as long as at least one of them is honest), and is independent of the computed functionality, allowing small client, as well as small total server cost. Further, unlike YOSO protocols, we do not require the use of expensive target-anonymous channels or even a PKI.

Our message and round complexity is significantly lower than in prior YOSO work. This is *crucial* for performance in the blockchain setting, as blockchain latency dominates the overall turn around time. We have a small number of messages posted, grouped into a smaller number of rounds (the clients post in parallel, and the number of servers can be as low as 2, depending on the trust assumptions – each server posting one message), while other works (YOSO and non-YOSO such as fluid MPC, [RS21], and others) are based on GMW/Beaver triples and have a number of rounds linear in the circuit depth, each one with a committee (whose size depends on the trust assumptions).

1.4   Related Work

Alternate MPC Models. Several recent works, many inspired by a blockchain-like setting, have considered MPC with specialized communication patterns. These models are generally incomparable with each other, and with SCALES. However, they do share some of the motivations and features of SCALES, and we briefly discuss them below. Table 1 summarizes some of the features discussed below.

You Only Speak Once (YOSO). As discussed in Sect. 1.2, our work is motivated by the YOSO model of MPC [BGG+20,GHK+21], which aims to eliminate the threat of adaptive corruptions by ensuring that the adversary does not know who the committee members are among *many* possible players, and hence cannot take advantage of its adaptive corruption power.

We consider a complementary MPC model that admits potentially more efficient solutions. We eliminate the need for expensive target-anonymous channels by requiring that each server accesses a bulletin board and sends a *single* message to it. Further, we permit a corrupted majority over *all participating servers*, whereas YOSO requires minority of corruptions *in each committee*, with threshold close to $t = 1/4$. At the same time, we keep the main attraction of YOSO: ephemeral servers that may securely self-select, and thus facilitate, MPC service in the presence of an adaptive adversary.

Table 1. Related MPC committee-based protocols and a summary of their features.

Construction	Adversary type	Corruption threshold	Adaptive corruption	Ephemeral-servers	Setup
YOSO [BGG+20] [GHK+21]	Malicious	Minority	Yes	Yes	Target-Anonymous Channels
Fluid MPC [CGG+21]	Unbounded malicious	Minority in each committee	No	No	Broadcast, private channels
Le Mans [RS21]	Malicious	All-but-one in each committee	No	No	Broadcast, private channels
MPC on the Blockchain [GMPS21]	Malicious	As in the underlying protocol	No	No	CSaR
SCALES Definition 5	Semi-honest	All-but one server	Yes	Yes	Bulletin board

As a trade off for better efficiency and larger corruption threshold, SCALES relies on a less constrained communication model than YOSO's: our input players speak twice. However, corrupting input player only results in compromise of that player's input. We believe this does not significantly weaken the applicability of the model: in practice, MPC input providers may be known to the adversary anyway. We outline conceptual performance improvements over prior YOSO protocols in Sect. 1.3.

We remark that while in this work we have limited ourselves to semi-honest SCALES, full security can be readily achieved using generic NIZK proofs, matching YOSO in this aspect. However, given the specific nature of our protocol using RGS, it is plausible that cheaper cut-and-choose techniques can be used instead of generic NIZK. We leave this for future work.

Blockchain-Enabled Non-Interactive MPC. Goyal et al. [GMPS21] explores blockchain-assisted MPC. Here input providers enjoy least-possible participation: they deposit input and garblings of an MPC protocol's next-message function into so-called conditional storage and retrieval systems (CSaRs). CSaRs' correct and secure operation is delegated to the blockchain. Then the blockchain executes the MPC protocol at its leisure by processing the garbled next-message functions. In contrast, our motivating application is MPC computation on the blockchain performed by a committee of servers, which the adversary is unable to adaptively corrupt. While our communication model is more constrained, our solution is far more practical and only requires a bulletin board; [GMPS21] should be viewed as a fundamental feasibility result.

Fluid-MPC. Fluid MPC [CGG+21] allows parties to dynamically join and leave the computation. These parties are designated by a computing committee, whose membership itself evolves. It keeps and evolves the state of an MPC instance, eventually obtaining the output. Fluid MPC is a practical protocol, which relies on a strong corruption assumption: the adversary can corrupt only a minority of the servers in each committee. In contrast, in our motivating application, we aim to frustrate adaptive corruption of committee members by ensuring they only speak once.

A recent work [RS21] extends Fluid MPC to the dishonest majority setting. Crucially, [RS21] still does not meet the YOSO speak-once requirement. We note other costs of [RS21] (e.g., the number of epochs proportional to the size of the function) that we avoid.

Distributed Garbling Schemes. The RGS-based protocol for SCALES can be viewed as distributed garbling with crucial special properties needed for our application: (1) each garbler posts one message, and (2) unidirectional communication among garblers. We achieve this without preprocessing or correlated randomness. Previous distributed garbling protocols do not offer these properties, even given correlated randomness, e.g., authenticated triples.

Two-Round MPC. It is also instructive to compare SCALES with 2-round MPC [GGHR14, GS18, BL18, BJKL21, BGSZ21]. The latter also involves input parties posting two rounds of messages to a bulletin board, based on which the output can be publicly computed. However, there the input parties incur communication and computation costs proportional to the entire circuit size of the function (in fact, the circuit size of an MPC protocol for the function). SCALES could be thought of as allowing ephemeral servers to process the bulletin board between the two rounds, so that the computational costs of the input parties becomes only proportional to the size of their own inputs.

Further, while not part of our formal definition, the SCALES setting can be extended to require the first message from the input players to be "reusable," a feature explored in the recent works on 2-round MPC [BJKL21, BGSZ21]. Our RGS-based construction already meets this additional requirement, at no additional cost.

Where efficiency of our protocols is concerned, note that we require security in the dishonest majority setting and so the concrete efficiency of our SCALES protocol is incomparable to that of previous work in the honest majority setting (YOSO, Fluid-MPC, etc.). Additionaly, note that although the servers sequentially perform computation only after the previous server has posted a message, the local actions of each server during rerandomizing are highly parallelizable:

the server chooses a homomorphic function for each circuit wire independently, and each garbled gate can be rerandomized independently.

Randomized Encodings. The abstraction of randomized encodings was introduced in [IK00], and has found a host of applications. A garbled circuit (GC) is a randomized encoding with desirable properties that were exploited in works such as [BMR90]. We mention the following constructions that are somewhat similar to iDRE introduced in this work.

- **Multi-party randomized encodings.** A notion of randomized encoding generated by multiple parties has been considered in the literature: [ABT18] proposed *Multi-Party Randomized Encoding* (MPRE). As in the case of iDRE, MPRE considers a distributed encoding of $f(x_1, \ldots, x_n)$. It uses many random strings, with the property that revealing a subset of these random strings will keep the other inputs hidden. A crucial distinction between iDRE and MPRE is that there is a protected part of the randomness in MPRE that must not be revealed at all. This is adequate for honest majority MPC, the main application in [ABT18], as this protected randomness remains secret-shared. In iDRE, there is no protected randomness, and all-but-one party could be corrupt. The two primitives also differ in several other ways, as their goals are quite different (reducing rounds in honest majority-MPC, in the case of MPRE, versus reducing the number of OTs in MPC with unrestricted collusion, in the case of iDRE).
- **Multi-hop homomorphic encryption.** Gentry et al. in [GHV10] introduced *multi-hop homomorphic encryption*. Setting aside the formulation as an encryption (which requires a rerandomizable 2-round OT protocol to be interpreted as an encryption process), their construction involved a set of servers jointly creating a garbled circuit. A crucial difference from the MPC setting is that an adversary who corrupts a subset of the players including the final evaluator would be able to learn much more about the individual inputs than just the final output. Nevertheless, a key tool used in this work – rerandomizable garbled circuits – turns out to be useful in our work. Though the specific manner in which garbled circuit rerandomization is defined and used by [GHV10] is not adequate for our purposes, we follow their approach of using a key-and-message-homomorphic encryption to implement it.

1.5 Technical Overview

We define and realize a new notion of randomized encodings [IK00] (Definition 3), the iDRE. This is the key construction underlying our SCALES protocol. For concreteness and simplicity, we first discuss our approach in the terminology of garbling schemes [BHR12], before casting it in terms of randomized encodings.

To be cast as a SCALES protocol, informally, our goal is minimally interactive multi-party circuit garbling. Therefore, we do not follow the constant-round BMR approach [BMR90], but instead explore *GC rerandomization*. This is a mechanism where an initial garbler generates a GC and each subsequent re-garbler re-randomizes the previous circuit and the labels. Breaking the connection between the labels of the garbled circuit and its regarbling, will allow for security in the presence of all-but-one corruption: indeed, even a single honest rerandomization will (if done right - we pay careful attention to precisely defining security requirements here) result in a GC where none of the generators knows the secrets completely (we get GC correctness "for free" in the semi-honest model).

Informally, a re-randomized garbled circuit $\hat{C}$ should allow the evaluation of a circuit C, where neither the garbler nor regarbler individually knows the correspondence between the labels and the actual wire values; the wire labels of the resulting garbled circuit $\hat{C}$ are effectively secret shared between them. To evaluate $\hat{C}$, each party $\mathcal{P}$ with an input bit (aka, an input party) picks up the shares of its input wire labels from the garblers (e.g., via OT), reconstructs them, and uses them for the evaluation. To violate input privacy, the evaluator would need to collude with *all* the garblers.

Rerandomizable Garbled Circuits from Strong KMHE. Our main technical challenge was to design a garbling scheme that supports garbling rerandomization. We demonstrate how this can be achieved based on a strong key-and-message-homomorphic encryption (strong KMHE) scheme. We formalize a strong KMHE scheme as an encryption scheme [2] that permits transforming the key and/or the message in a ciphertext to obtain fresh-looking ciphertexts. Even a party who knows the original ciphertext's key should not be able to distinguish the result of randomly transforming the key from a fresh ciphertext using a fresh key. This is required to hold, even when given some leakage on the key transformation, in the form of a different input-output pair of the transformation. For our purposes, the message and key spaces would be the same, and the space of transformations supported for the two will be the same as well; these transformations will be linear. The specific instantiation of a strong KMHE scheme we use was constructed by Boneh et al. for a different purpose [BHHO08], and was shown to be leakage resilient by Naor and Segev [NS09]; further this scheme was used in [GHV10] for constructing a somewhat related task, rerandomizable secure function evaluation (or SFE), but without abstracting out the security properties we need.

We briefly sketch our construction of rerandomizable garbling schemes given a strong KMHE scheme. We view a garbled circuit as a collection of garbled gates where each gate consists of four ciphertexts, each requires a pair of keys to decrypt. However, instead of implementing a double-encryption scheme, as in standard garbling schemes, we additively share the plaintexts and encrypt each share using a single key. Therefore, each garbled row contains a *pair* of ciphertexts, encrypted under a single input key. (see Sect. 4).

To rerandomize a gate, the re-garbler R homomorphically alters each ciphertext, such that the result is a (new share of the) new output label encrypted

---

[2] We define this notion as a symmetric key primitive which suffices for our purposes. Nevertheless, the instantiation we give uses a public key encryption scheme [BHHO08].

under a new input key label. At a high level, we achieve this as follows. For each wire w_i, R first chooses a transformation σ_i that maps the space of the wire labels to itself. R's goal is to re-randomize each gate to enable correct evaluation. We do this by applying a sequence of homomorphic operations to (each element of) each garbled row, encrypted using strong KMHE: (1) update the plaintext using a transformation σ_g for the output wire of gate g and (2) update the key using a transformation σ_i for the input wire w_i. Furthermore, the homomorphic operations we use are linear. This ensures that applying the above to the ciphertexts encrypting secret shares of the output label will allow for the reconstruction of the new rerandomized label: σ_g applied to the old output label. To prevent a colluding G and E learning extra information, we require that the rerandomized garbled circuit $\hat{C}$ together with active input wire labels reveals no additional information. As a final step for rerandomization, the new 4-tuple of garbled rows is permuted.

Depending on how strong KMHE is instantiated, there are different tweaks that let the evaluator know which row of the garbled gate, when decrypted, gives a correct label. One such way would be to append a known prefix to the message labels that are encrypted. Care should be taken that during rerandomizing, the message domain operations do not affect this message prefix. The [BHHO08] instantiation for strong KMHE, explained next, supports such operations.

Strong KMHE Instantiation. The encryption scheme of [BHHO08] can be used to instantiate strong KMHE in the computational setting under the Decisional Diffie-Hellman (DDH) hardness assumption. It allows homomorphic operations in both the key and plaintext domains and has the property that a transformed ciphertext is indistinguishable from a freshly encrypted ciphertext. For our purposes, and similarly in [GHV10], the key and plaintext domains are identical and amount to the set of balanced binary strings. Similarly, the key and plaintext domains are identical and correspond to the set of permutations. In order to differentiate a correct decryption during evaluation, this construction allows padding the plaintext label shares with an all-zero string. During rerandomizing, this prefix is always mapped onto itself. During evaluation, each garbled row is decrypted and the row yielding plaintexts padded with all-zero strings indicates the correct output label shares. We point the reader to the full version [AHKP22] for more details.

Casting as a Randomized Encoding. For generality, we use this approach to describe a variant of a randomized encoding (Sect. 5). W.l.o.g., consider parties providing a single input bit each. We separate the role of parties $\mathcal{P} = (P_1, \cdots, P_m)$ providing input bits $x_1, \cdots, x_m$ from the role of *encoders* $\mathcal{E} = (E_1, \cdots, E_d)$ creating the randomized encoding. A garbled circuit presented above can be cast as a decomposable randomized encoding (DRE) $\hat{f}(x, r) = (\hat{f}_0(r), \hat{f}_1(x_1, r), \cdots, \hat{f}_m(x_m, r))$, where part of the encoding $\hat{f}_0(r)$ is independent of the input (and corresponds to the garbled circuit itself), and each $\hat{f}_i(x_i, r)$ depends on a bit x_i of the input (corresponding to the input labels).

Let $r = (r_1, \cdots, r_d)$ be the total randomness where encoder E_j possesses r_j. Each E_j creates values that act as shares of $\hat{f}_i(x_i, r)$ for both possible values of each $x_i \in \{0, 1\}$. Then each input party $P_i \in \mathcal{P}$ upon concluding an OT with each encoder, receives all these shares of $\hat{f}_i(x_i, r)$. E_1 uses r_1 to initiate the creation of $\hat{f}_0(r)$ similarly to G above. E_1 also incorporates encodings of the shares of each $\hat{f}_i(x_i, r)$ that it created, hence initiating the creation of a *final share* s_i. E_1 passes its initial $\hat{f}_0(r)$ and all such s_i to E_2. In turn, E_2 uses $r_2 \in r$ to rerandomize the initial $\hat{f}_0(r)$ it received, augments each s_i, and passes it on. This incremental process continues and the last encoder E_d hands the completed $\hat{f}_0(r)$ to the decoder D. Each value s_i is given to the corresponding input party $P_i \in \mathcal{P}$. These final shares are such that s_i, when combined with all the initial shares from the OT phase, gives $\hat{f}_i(x_i, r)$. This is reconstructed and sent to D. D decodes the complete DRE and receives the output. We denote our abstracted object by *incremental Decomposable Randomized Encoding* to highlight the incremental nature in which the DRE is created. A construction for this object directly implies a SCALES protocol.

2 Preliminaries

Circuit Notation. For a function $f : \{0, 1\}^m \to \{0, 1\}^l$, a boolean circuit that computes it is denoted by $C = (\mathcal{W}, I, O, \mathcal{G})$. $\mathcal{W}$ is the set of all wires and $I \subset \mathcal{W}$ and $O \subset \mathcal{W}$ are the set of input and output wires respectively. Within $\mathcal{W}$, $I = (w_1, \cdots, w_m)$ are the m input wires, $w_{m+1}, \cdots, w_{m+p}$ are the p internal wires, and $O = (w_{m+p+1}, \cdots, w_{m+p+l})$ are the l output wires. These make $v = m+p+l$ total wires. $\mathcal{G} = (g_{m+1}, ..., g_{m+q})$ is the set of gates. Each $g_i = (w_\ell, w_r, w_i, op)$ is a binary gate where w_ℓ and w_r are the left and right input wires respectively, w_i is the output wire (uniquely defined by the gate index), and op represents the gate functionality (AND, XOR, etc.).

2.1 Garbled Circuits

Garbling Schemes. We recall the notion of a garbling scheme abstracted in [BHR12] and simplify it for our use. That is, a garbling scheme is a tuple of algorithms $\mathsf{GS} = (\mathsf{Gb}, \mathsf{En}, \mathsf{Ev})$ where the probabilistic garbling algorithm Gb takes the function description f and outputs a garbled representation F and an input encoding function e. The deterministic input encoding algorithm En gets e and the function input x; and returns a garbled input representation X. Finally, the deterministic evaluation algorithm Ev takes F and X and outputs $f(x)$ by evaluating the garbling.

For simplicity, we limit the security properties of a garbling scheme to just *correctness* and *privacy* (and correspondingly, omit the separation between evaluation and "decoding" in [BHR12]). More formally,

Definition 1. *A **Garbling Scheme** for a function family $\mathcal{F}$ with input domain $\mathcal{X}$, and a leakage function $\phi : \mathcal{F} \to \{0, 1\}^*$, is a tuple $\mathsf{GS} = (\mathsf{Gb}, \mathsf{En}, \mathsf{Ev})$ of PPT algorithms, satisfying the following properties:*

– **Correctness:** *For every* $f \in \mathcal{F}$ *and input* $x \in \mathcal{X}$,

$$\Pr[y = f(x) : (F, e) \leftarrow \mathsf{Gb}(f), \ X = \mathsf{En}(e, x), \ y = \mathsf{Ev}(F, X)] = 1$$

– **Privacy:** *For all functions* $f_0, f_1 \in \mathcal{F}$ *such that* $\phi(f_0) = \phi(f_1)$, *and every* $x_0, x_1 \in \mathcal{X}$ *such that* $f_0(x_0) = f_1(x_1)$,

$$\{F_0, X_0\}_{(F_0, e_0) \leftarrow \mathsf{Gb}(f_0), X_0 = \mathsf{En}(e_0, x_0)} \overset{c}{\approx} \{F_1, X_1\}_{(F_1, e_1) \leftarrow \mathsf{Gb}(f_1), X_1 = \mathsf{En}(e_1, x_1)}$$

The above distribution ensembles are indexed by a security parameter κ that is an implicit input to Gb. When we need to make the randomness used by Gb explicit, we write it as an additional input, namely as $\mathsf{Gb}(f; r)$.

A special case of the above, a *projective garbling scheme* [BHR12] is a variant of garbling schemes whose input encoding function En is *projective*.

Definition 2. *A **Projective Garbling Scheme** for a function family $\mathcal{F}$ with input domain $\{0, 1\}^m$, is a tuple $\mathsf{GS} = (\mathsf{Gb}, \mathsf{En}, \mathsf{Ev})$ of PPT algorithms, such that GS is a garbling scheme (Definition 1) for $\mathcal{F}$ and the encoding function $\mathsf{En} : \{0, 1\}^m \times \mathcal{E} \to \mathcal{Z}^m$ is such that $\forall x, x' \in \{0, 1\}^m$ and $\forall e \in \mathcal{E}$, $\mathsf{En}(x, e) = (L_1, \cdots, L_m)$ and $\mathsf{En}(x', e) = (L_1', \cdots, L_m')$ such that $\forall i \in [m]$, if $x_i = x_i'$ then $L_i = L_i'$.*

Our construction employs *projective* garbling schemes. Looking ahead, we extend Definition 1 to a Rerandomizable Garbling Scheme (RGS) and instantiate it with rerandomizable GCs.

2.2 Randomized Encodings

A *Randomized Encoding*, defined in [IK00], is as follows:

Definition 3. *Let $X, Y, \hat{Y}, R$ be finite sets and let $f : X \to Y$. A function $\hat{f} : X \times R \to \hat{Y}$ is a **Randomized Encoding** of f, if it satisfies:*

– **Correctness:** *There exists a function Dec, a decoder, $\forall x \in X, r \in R$,*

$$\mathsf{Dec}(\hat{f}(x; r)) = f(x)$$

– **Privacy:** *There exists a randomized function Sim, a simulator, $\forall x \in X$,*

$$\{\mathsf{Sim}(f(x))\} \overset{c}{\approx} \{\hat{f}(x; r)\}_{r \in R}$$

We require that $\hat{f}$ is efficiently derivable from f using the function Enc, and that Dec and Sim are PPT. A variant of the above, a *Decomposable Randomized Encoding* (DRE), is defined as follows:

Definition 4. *For $f : X_1 \times \cdots \times X_m \to Y$, where $\forall i \in [m], X_i = \{0, 1\}$, a **Decomposable Randomized Encoding** is a Randomized Encoding (Definition 3) of f with the form:*

$$\hat{f}((x_1, \cdots, x_m); r) = (\hat{f}_0(r), \hat{f}_1(x_1; r), \cdots, \hat{f}_m(x_m; r))$$

In a decomposable randomized encoding, each part of the encoding can depend on at most one input bit. It is well known that a projective garbling scheme (Definition 2) is a DRE. Looking ahead, we extend Definition 4 to an incremental Decomposable Randomized Encoding (iDRE) and instantiate it using a projective RGS.

2.3   Oblivious Transfer

Oblivious Transfer (OT) is a two party functionality between a sender S and a receiver R defined by $(e_b, \perp) \leftarrow \mathsf{OT}(b, (e_0, e_1))$. Our protocol in the SCALES model (Sect. 6), requires a 2-round OT protocol (with semi-honest, adaptive-receiver security). We denote this by the set of algorithms $\Pi^{\mathsf{OT}} = (\mathsf{OT}_1, \mathsf{OT}_2, \mathsf{OT}_{out})$. The protocol starts by R computing $(m_1, \mathsf{Aux}) \leftarrow \mathsf{OT}_1(b)$ and sending the first OT message m_1 to S. Next, S computes the second OT message $m_2 \leftarrow \mathsf{OT}_2(m_1, (e_0, e_1))$ that is sent to R. Finally, R computes its output via $e_b \leftarrow \mathsf{OT}_{out}(\mathsf{Aux}, m_2)$. We require that Π^{OT} be secure in the presence of a semi-honest adversary that statically corrupts S and adaptively corrupts R. A more detailed discussion can be found in the full version [AHKP22].

3   MPC with Small Clients and Larger Ephemeral Servers

We define a model, MPC with Small Clients and Larger Ephemeral Servers (SCALES), that is inspired by considerations that also underlie recent models like YOSO [BGG+20, GHK+21] and MPC on a blockchain [GMPS21]. Our goal is to achieve secure MPC in a setting where a set of light-weight input providers take the help of a dynamic set of stateless workers or *ephemeral servers*. The entire process involves communication only over a public bulletin board, and takes this form:

1. Initially, each input player posts a message on the bulletin board.
2. For as many iterations as desired, an ephemeral server is dynamically activated, which reads the bulletin board, carries out some local computation, erases its state, and posts a message back on the bulletin board. This computation may be proportional to size of the computed functionality.
3. Each input player reads the bulletin board (in parallel), and posts back another message on the bulletin board. These light weight parties' work is proportional to their input size times the number of ephemeral servers.
4. The output can be computed publicly based on the information in the bulletin board, implemented by another ephemeral server.

We shall require that the amount of computation and communication by each input player is proportional to its number of input bits, *independent of the size of the overall computation, or even the size of the overall input*. The communication constraints apart, we require the above to meet a standard security definition for MPC, against an adversary who can corrupt any subset of input players (possibly adaptively) and *all but one server*. As each server posts a single message before being erased, we shall consider only security against static corruption of servers (since a server's state is erased before it has started posting its message on the bulletin board). In this work, we focus on security against semi-honest corruption.

Definition 5. *A scheme for **MPC with Small Clients and Larger Ephemeral Servers** (SCALES) for a function family $\mathcal{F}$ over $\{0,1\}^m$ is a tuple of PPT algorithms* (InpEnc, FEnc, Aggregate, Decode) *such that the following random variables are defined as a function of $f \in \mathcal{F}$ and $x \in \{0,1\}^m$ (where R and T denote random-tape spaces for* FEnc *and* InpEnc *respectively):*

$$r_j \leftarrow R, t_i \leftarrow T \qquad\qquad\qquad \forall j \in [d], i \in [m]$$
$$(z_i, w_i) \leftarrow \mathsf{InpEnc}(x_i; t_i) \qquad\qquad\qquad \forall i \in [m]$$
$$\mathcal{B}_j \leftarrow \begin{cases} (f, \{z_i\}_{i \in m}) & \text{for } j = 1 \\ (\mathcal{B}_{j-1}, \mathsf{FEnc}(\mathcal{B}_{j-1}; r_j)) & \text{for } 1 < j \le d \end{cases}$$
$$y_i \leftarrow \mathsf{Aggregate}(\mathcal{B}_d, w_i) \qquad\qquad\qquad \forall i \in [m].$$

Then the following properties hold:

– **Correctness:** $\forall x = (x_1, \cdots, x_m) \in \{0,1\}^m$ and $d \in \mathbb{N}$,

$$\Pr[\mathsf{Decode}(\mathcal{B}_d, \{y_i\}_{i \in [m]}) = f(x)] = 1$$

where $\forall j \in [d], \mathcal{B}_j = (\{z_i\}_{i \in [m]}, \{\alpha_k\}_{k \in [j]})$.

– **Privacy:** *There exists a 2-stage PPT simulator* Sim $= (\mathsf{Sim}_1, \mathsf{Sim}_2)$ *such that,* $\forall f \in \mathcal{F}, x \in \{0,1\}^m, j^* \in [d]$, *and* $\mathcal{A}_1, \mathcal{A}_2 \subseteq [m]$,

$$(\alpha, \mathsf{Aux}) \leftarrow \mathsf{Sim}_1(f, f(x), j^*, \{x_i\}_{i \in \mathcal{A}_1})$$
$$\beta \leftarrow \mathsf{Sim}_2(\mathsf{Aux}, \{x_i\}_{i \in \mathcal{A}_2}).$$

It holds that,

$$\{\alpha\} \stackrel{c}{\approx} \{\mathcal{B}_d, \{y_i\}_{i \in [m]}, \{r_j\}_{j \in [d] \setminus \{j^*\}}, \{t_i\}_{i \in \mathcal{A}_1}\}$$
$$\{\alpha, \beta\} \stackrel{c}{\approx} \{\mathcal{B}_d, \{y_i\}_{i \in [m]}, \{r_j\}_{j \in [d] \setminus \{j^*\}}, \{t_i\}_{i \in \mathcal{A}_1}, \{t_i\}_{i \in \mathcal{A}_2}\}$$

Complexity. For simplicity, we have stated the definition without including any complexity requirements. To formalize the complexity requirement, we consider the functions in $\mathcal{F}$ as parameterized by a size parameter k, as $f_k : \{0,1\}^{m(k)} \to \{0,1\}^{q(k)}$, so that f_k has a circuit of size polynomial in k. Then, the algorithms InpEnc and Aggregate are required to be independent of k (but may depend on the security parameter κ)[3]. This requirement on the complexity of InpEnc and Aggregate is an important aspect of a SCALES protocol.

---

[3] Note that $\mathcal{B}_d$ has been specified as an input to Aggregate, but Aggregate is required to only use a part of $\mathcal{B}_d$ which is independent of k.

In a SCALES protocol, first, each input player runs the algorithm InpEnc and posts z_i on the bulletin board $\mathcal{B}$ (Step 1). Next, for each round j, each ephemeral server (as in Step 2) runs FEnc in the present state of the bulletin board $\mathcal{B}_{j-1}$ and posts a message α_j on the board. After enough number of such iterations, each input player run Aggregate (Step 3) and post a message y_i. Finally, the function output is publicly derived using Decode (Step 4). The *privacy* guarantee requires that an adversary can corrupt all but the server indexed $j^* \in [d]$. It may corrupt an initial subset $\mathcal{A}_1 \in [m]$ of clients and between the first and the second time the clients speak, it can adaptively corrupt an additional set of $\mathcal{A}_2 \in [m]$ clients. Even in such a scenario, the view of the adversary needs to be simulatable. Building towards a protocol in the SCALES setting, we now define and construct our key building blocks.

4   Rerandomizable Garbling Schemes

In this section we define *Rerandomizable Garbling Schemes* (RGS) and construct such a scheme (Sect. 4.3) using a strong Key and Message Homomorphic Encryption scheme (strong KMHE - Sect. 4.1). Loosely speaking, a rerandomizable garbling scheme allows us to take a garbled representation F of a function and transform it into another garbled representation F' for the same function. This is done in such a way that it is impossible for a PPT distinguisher, given all the randomness used for garbling F, to distinguish F' from a fresh garbling of the function.

Formally, an RGS is a GS with an additional PPT algorithm $(F', \pi_{En}) \leftarrow$ Rerand(F) that outputs a rerandomized garbling F' and a transformation π_{En} to be applied on e such that the new encoding X', derived from applying En to $\pi_{En}(e)$, when used with F', decodes correctly to $f(x)$. The security of RGS is captured by an additional property denoted by Rerand *-privacy* that is formalized as follows:

Definition 6. *A **Rerandomizable Garbling Scheme** for a function family $\mathcal{F}$ is a tuple of PPT algorithms* GS$' = ($Gb, Rerand, En, Ev$)$ *where,* $($Gb, En, Ev$)$ *is a garbling scheme (Definition 1) for $\mathcal{F}$, and* Rerand *is a PPT algorithm such that the following is satisfied:*

- Rerand -*Privacy: For every $f \in \mathcal{F}$, $x \in \mathcal{X}$,*

$$\{r, F_0, X_0\}_{\substack{r \leftarrow R,\ (F,e) \leftarrow \text{Gb}(f;r), \\ (F_0, \pi_{En}) \leftarrow \text{Rerand}(F),\ X_0 = \text{En}(\pi_{En}(e), x)}} \overset{c}{\approx} \{r, F_1, X_1\}_{\substack{r \leftarrow R, (F_1, e_1) \leftarrow \text{Gb}(f), \\ X_1 = \text{En}(e_1, x)}}$$

where R is the space of random tapes for Gb. *(Note that (F_1, e_1) is generated using fresh randomness independent of r.)*

Note that Rerand-privacy and *correctness* of garbling schemes together imply that the rerandomized garbling F_0 produced by Rerand is correct – i.e., for any input x, and (F, e) produced by Gb(f), for $(F_0, \pi_{En}) \leftarrow$ Rerand(F), it must be the case that Ev$(F_0, \text{En}(\pi_{En}(e), x)) = f(x)$ (except possibly with negligible probability). Indeed, otherwise it would be easy to distinguish this from a fresh garbling based on the outputs of garbled evaluation. Note also that Rerand does not get f as input. Therefore, it cannot operate by ignoring the prior garbling F and simply generating a fresh garbling as F'.

Definition 6 can be applied to a projective encoding as well by simply requiring that the input encoding $X' = (L'_1, \cdots, L'_m) = \mathsf{En}(\pi_{\mathsf{En}}(e), x)$ is projective. Formally,

Definition 7. *A **Projective Rerandomizable Garbling Scheme** is a tuple* $\mathsf{GS}' = (\mathsf{Gb}, \mathsf{Rerand}, \mathsf{En}, \mathsf{Ev})$ *where,* $(\mathsf{Gb}, \mathsf{En}, \mathsf{Ev})$ *is a projective garbling scheme (Definition 2) for a family $\mathcal{F}$ of functions with input domain $\{0,1\}^m$, and* Rerand *is a PPT algorithm as in Definition 6 that satisfies the following:*

π_{En} *produced by* Rerand *is in the form of encoding transformations* $\{\sigma_i\}_{i \in [m]}$ *such that* $\forall x \in \{0,1\}^m$, $\forall e \in \mathcal{E}$, $\mathsf{En}(e, x) = (L_1, \cdots, L_m)$ *and* $\mathsf{En}(\pi_{\mathsf{En}}(e), x) = (L'_1, \cdots, L'_m)$, *such that* $\sigma_i(L_i) = L'_i$.

Looking ahead, we point out that for the construction of the SCALES protocol, a slightly relaxed notion of projective RGS suffices. In this relaxed version we allow for encoding transformations of the form $\{\sigma_i^b\}_{i \in [m], b \in \{0,1\}}$ where a different transformation may be applied to the labels L_i^0 and L_i^1 to obtain their rerandomized counterparts. But we omit this for the sake of simplicity.

4.1   Strong Key and Message Homomorphic Encryption

Homomorphic encryption schemes allow the execution of mathematical operations over the plaintexts within the encrypted domain. In this work we are interested in schemes that support transformations on both the secret key and the plaintext domains within a ciphertext, resulting in a ciphertext that looks "fresh". We refer to such a scheme as a Key-and-Message Homomorphic Encryption scheme (KMHE). We abstract KMHE as a private key encryption primitive (Gen, Enc, Dec),[4] that is amplified with an additional Eval algorithm. This algorithm applies two homomorphic (potentially distinct and private) transformations on a ciphertext, one on the secret key and one on the plaintext.

Definition 8. *A **key-and-message homomorphic encryption scheme** is a set of PPT algorithms* $\mathsf{KMH} = (\mathsf{Gen}, \mathsf{Enc}, \mathsf{Dec}, \mathsf{Eval})$ *defined on domains of (private) keys, messages and ciphertexts* $\mathcal{K}, \mathcal{M}, \mathcal{C}$, *a key transformation family* $\mathcal{F}_{key}$, *and a message transformation family* $\mathcal{F}_{msg}$ *(all indexed by an implicit security parameter κ) such that the following conditions hold:*

– *Correctness:* $\forall m \in \mathcal{M}, k \in \mathcal{K}$,

$$\Pr[k \leftarrow \mathsf{Gen}(1^\kappa); \mathsf{Dec}(k, \mathsf{Enc}(k, m)) = m] = 1$$

---

[4] For simplicity we define KMHE as a private key primitive (where encryption is carried out using the secret key). Nevertheless, the definition can be naturally extended to a public key setting as well.

- **KMH Correctness:** $\forall m \in \mathcal{M}, k \in \mathcal{K}, f \in \mathcal{F}_{key}, g \in \mathcal{F}_{msg}, r_1, r_2 \in R$, $\exists r' \in R$,

$$\mathsf{Eval}(\mathsf{Enc}(k, m; r_1), f, g; r_2) = \mathsf{Enc}(f(k), g(m); r')$$

where R is the space of random tapes for Enc and Eval.

- **CPA Security:** $\forall$ PPT adversary $\mathcal{A}$, the advantage $\Pr[b' = b] \leq \frac{1}{2} + \nu(\kappa)$ for a negligible function ν in the following experiment (κ being an implicit input to C and $\mathcal{A}$):
  1. C samples a uniform random bit $b \leftarrow \{0, 1\}$.
  2. For as many times as $\mathcal{A}$ wants:
     - $\mathcal{A}$ produces arbitrary $m_0, m_1 \in \mathcal{M}$ and sends them to C.
     - C samples a key $k \leftarrow \mathsf{Gen}(1^\kappa)$ and sends $c_b = \mathsf{Enc}(k, m_b)$ to $\mathcal{A}$.
  3. $\mathcal{A}$ outputs b'.
- **Key Privacy:** $\forall k, k' \leftarrow \mathsf{Gen}(1^\kappa), f \in \mathcal{F}_{key}$,

$$\{k, f(k)\} \overset{s}{\approx} \{k, k'\}$$

Looking ahead, we use KMHE as a primitive along with RGS in the construction for *incremental Decomposable Randomized Encodings* in Sect. 5.

Next, we define a new object, a *strong* Key-and-Message Homomorphic Encryption scheme (strong KMHE), that has an additional security property, KMH privacy, that is required for rerandomizable garbling. We use strong KMHE as a building block in our construction for rerandomizable garbled circuits (Sect. 4.3).

Definition 9. *A **strong key-and-message homomorphic encryption** scheme (strong KMHE) is the set of PPT algorithms* $\mathsf{KMH} = (\mathsf{Gen}, \mathsf{Enc}, \mathsf{Dec}, \mathsf{Eval})$ *defined on domains of (private) keys, messages and ciphertexts* $\mathcal{K}, \mathcal{M}, \mathcal{C}$, *a key transformation family* $\mathcal{F}_{key}$, *and a message transformation family* $\mathcal{F}_{msg}$ *(all indexed by an implicit security parameter* κ*) such that* KMH *is a KMHE scheme as in Definition 8 and the following additional condition holds:*

- **KMH Privacy:** $\forall$ PPT adversary $\mathcal{A}$, the advantage $\Pr[b' = b] \leq \frac{1}{2} + \nu(\kappa)$ for a negligible function ν in the following experiment (κ being an implicit input to C and $\mathcal{A}$):
  1. C samples a uniform random bit $b \leftarrow \{0, 1\}$, keys $k_0, k_1, k' \leftarrow \mathsf{Gen}(1^\kappa)$, and $f \leftarrow \mathcal{F}_{key}$. It sends $(k_0, k_1, f(k_1))$ to $\mathcal{A}$.
  2. For as many times as $\mathcal{A}$ wants:
     - $\mathcal{A}$ produces arbitrary $m, m' \in \mathcal{M}$ and $g \in \mathcal{F}_{msg}$, and computes $c \leftarrow \mathsf{Enc}(k_0, m)$. It sends (c, g, m') to C.
     - C sends c_b to $\mathcal{A}$, where $c_0 \leftarrow \mathsf{Eval}(c, f, g)$ and $c_1 \leftarrow \mathsf{Enc}(k', m')$.
  3. $\mathcal{A}$ outputs b'.

We would like to stress here that we do not require the scheme to be *fully* homomorphic, but only homomorphic with respect to certain (affine) function families. We prove that the [BHHO08] scheme satisfies strong KMHE. The details can be found in the full version [AHKP22]. The [BHHO08] encryption scheme is based on the DDH hardness assumption. We follow the construction in [GHV10] and restrict the key space $\mathcal{K}$ to all binary strings of length κ with $\frac{\kappa}{2}$ 0's and the rest 1's. In order to use this scheme for garbling, we require that $\mathcal{M} = \mathcal{K}$, and so we restrict the message space accordingly as well. The function family $\mathcal{F}_{key}$ for key domain transformations contains all permutations over κ-bit positions: $\sigma : \{0,1\}^\kappa \rightarrow \{0,1\}^\kappa$ over the sub-domain of balanced strings. Therefore, *key privacy* is maintained since $\forall k, k' \leftarrow \mathsf{Gen}(1^\kappa)$, $f \in \mathcal{F}_{key}$, the distributions $\{k, f(k)\}$ and $\{k, k'\}$ are exactly identical. [BHHO08] also supports homomorphic operations on the key and message domains in a way that *KMH privacy* is preserved.

Since a scheme satisfying Definition 9 also satisfies Definition 8, to avoid overloaded notations, we instantiate both strong KMHE and KMHE in the same way.

4.2   A Gap in the Proof of [GHV10]

Strong KMHE is implicit in the rerandomizable SFE protocol of [GHV10]. We outline a gap in the proof (but not the protocol!) of [GHV10] in the full version [AHKP22].

Informally, secure rerandomizing requires that any PPT distinguisher, given all the randomness used for a *prior* garbling M, cannot distinguish between a garbling that is rerandomized from M and a freshly created garbling M'. [GHV10] instantiated rerandomizable garbled circuits using the encryption scheme from [BHHO08] and argues that it is rerandomizable by reductions to the semantic security and key leakage resilience properties of this scheme (the latter property has been proven in [NS09]). This latter property allows semantic security even when the distinguisher is given some information about the secret key. (This is required for showing that privacy is preserved in a rerandomized GC even given *leakage* in the form of the two labels (k_0, k_1) of the *prior* GC and a transformed active label $f(k_b)$ of the RGC.)

However, such a security argument applies only to indistinguishability of two ciphertexts both encrypted under the same (transformed) key. In particular, it does not rule out adversary's ability to identify if a ciphertext was encrypted using a key obtained by transforming a known key, or from a fresh key. This allows distinguishing between a freshly garbled and a rerandomized GC.

We handle this security gap by strengthening the security definition of the underlying encryption scheme. Specifically, in our abstraction of strong KMHE, a *KMH privacy* property explicitly requires that a ciphertext computed under a fresh key be indistinguishable from a ciphertext acquired after homomorphic transformations that corresponds to a transformed key. Another security property, denoted by *key privacy*, requires that the distribution of transformed keys in the clear is indistinguishable from that of freshly sampled keys.

4.3   Constructing Rerandomizable Garbled Circuits

In this section we present a construction for rerandomizable garbled circuits. By GC rerandomization we mean a procedure that takes only the GC for a circuit C and generates another GC for the same circuit, so that the latter is indistinguishable from a freshly garbled circuit, even given input labels for one set of inputs, and all the randomness used to generate the original GC that the rerandomized GC was derived from.

We describe a GC rerandomization procedure that is implicit in the construction of [GHV10] with the difference that the underlying encryption scheme is a strong KMHE scheme KMH = (Gen, Enc, Dec, Eval), as specified in Definition 9. We consider a special case of KMH with an additional structural property:

Definition 10. *A **sharable key-and-message homomorphic encryption scheme** is a set of PPT algorithms* (Gen, Enc, Dec, Eval, Share, Recon) *where* KMH = (Gen, Enc, Dec, Eval) *is a strong KMHE scheme as in Definition 9 for domains of (private) keys, messages and ciphertexts* $\mathcal{K}, \mathcal{M}, \mathcal{C}$, *a key transformation family* $\mathcal{F}_{key}$, *and a message transformation family* $\mathcal{F}_{msg}$ *with the additional property that* $\mathcal{K} = \mathcal{M}$ *and* $\mathcal{F}_{key} = \mathcal{F}_{msg}$.

The scheme has two additional functions (1) $([k]_0, [k]_1) \leftarrow$ Share(k) *that outputs two random shares of a key* $k \in \mathcal{K}$. *(2)* $k \leftarrow$ Recon$([k]_0, [k]_1)$ *that reconstructs the label* k *from its shares. These functions are such that the following property holds* $\forall \sigma \in \mathcal{F}_{key}$ *and* $\forall k \in \mathcal{K}$,

$$\mathsf{Share}(\sigma(k)) \equiv \{(\sigma([k]_0), \sigma([k]_1)\}_{([k]_0, [k]_1) \leftarrow \mathsf{Share}(k)}$$

We denote by GS = (Gb$_{\mathsf{KMH}}$, En$_{\mathsf{KMH}}$, Ev$_{\mathsf{KMH}}$, Rerand$_{\mathsf{KMH}}$) a rerandomized garbling scheme where all the garbling scheme algorithms are instantiated with a sharable KMHE scheme KMH as the underlying encryption scheme. We next provide an overview of this garbling scheme:

The garbling algorithm Gb$_{\mathsf{KMH}}(C, 1^\kappa)$ works as follows:

- For every wire $w_i \in \mathcal{W} - O$, sample labels $L^0_{w_i}, L^1_{w_i} \leftarrow$ Gen(1^κ).
- For every output wire $w_i \in O$, use the same labels $\mathsf{L}_0, \mathsf{L}_1 \in \mathcal{K}$ across all output wires. These are publicly known.
- For every gate $g_i = (w_\ell, w_r, w_i, op) \in \mathcal{G}$, let $([L^b_{w_i}]_0, [L^b_{w_i}]_1)$ be the shares of g_i's output labels for $b \in \{0, 1\}$ and π be a permutation on four positions. Then the garbling of gate g_i can be defined as:

$$G_i = \begin{cases} (\mathsf{Enc}(L^0_{w_\ell}, [L^{op(0,0)}_{w_i}]_0), \mathsf{Enc}(L^0_{w_r}, [L^{op(0,0)}_{w_i}]_1)) \\ (\mathsf{Enc}(L^0_{w_\ell}, [L^{op(0,1)}_{w_i}]_0), \mathsf{Enc}(L^1_{w_r}, [L^{op(0,1)}_{w_i}]_1)) \\ (\mathsf{Enc}(L^1_{w_\ell}, [L^{op(1,0)}_{w_i}]_0), \mathsf{Enc}(L^0_{w_r}, [L^{op(1,0)}_{w_i}]_1)) \\ (\mathsf{Enc}(L^1_{w_\ell}, [L^{op(1,1)}_{w_i}]_0), \mathsf{Enc}(L^1_{w_r}, [L^{op(1,1)}_{w_i}]_1)) \end{cases}$$

these four rows are then permuted according to π.
- Output $\hat{C} = ((G_1, \cdots, G_q), (\mathsf{L}_0, \mathsf{L}_1))$ and $\mathcal{L} = \{L^0_{w_i}, L^1_{w_i}\}_{w_i \in I}$.

An encoding algorithm En$_{\mathsf{KMH}}(\mathcal{L}, x)$ gets a set of input labels $\mathcal{L}$ and the function input $x = (x_1, \cdots, x_m)$ and outputs $\mathcal{I} = \{L^{x_i}_{w_i}\}_{w_i \in I}$.

The evaluation algorithm Ev$_{\mathsf{KMH}}(\hat{C}, \mathcal{I})$ works gate by gate, by decrypting each row in the garbled gate.[5] The resulting plaintexts are combined to the output

---

[5] We assume that the evaluator identifies the valid output label by adding a fixed suffix to the plaintext as suggested originally in [LP09].

label using Recon. Evaluating a gate lets us derive one label for a wire in the circuit. Following the terminology of [LP09], this label is termed the *active label* of that wire. Such a label is also derived for each output wire of the circuit and this belongs in the set (L_0, L_1) and can be mapped to output values 0 or 1. This set of labels yields the function's output $f(x)$.

The rerandomizing algorithm $(\hat{C}', \Pi) \leftarrow \mathsf{Rerand}_{\mathsf{KMH}}(\hat{C})$ works as follows:

- For all wires $w_i \in \mathcal{W} - O$, sample $\sigma_i \in \mathcal{F}_{key}$.
- For all output wires $w_i \in O$, let σ_i be the identity function.
- For all gates $g_i \in \mathcal{G}$, let $(\sigma_\ell, \sigma_r, \sigma_i)$ correspond to the wires (w_ℓ, w_r, w_i). Let π_i be a permutation on four elements. In order to rerandomize G_i into G_i', the following is carried out:

$$
G_i' = \begin{cases} (\mathsf{Eval}(c_{0,0}, \sigma_\ell, \sigma_i), \mathsf{Eval}(c_{0,1}, \sigma_r, \sigma_i)) \\ (\mathsf{Eval}(c_{1,0}, \sigma_\ell, \sigma_i), \mathsf{Eval}(c_{1,1}, \sigma_r, \sigma_i)) \\ (\mathsf{Eval}(c_{2,0}, \sigma_\ell, \sigma_i), \mathsf{Eval}(c_{2,1}, \sigma_r, \sigma_i)) \\ (\mathsf{Eval}(c_{3,0}, \sigma_\ell, \sigma_i), \mathsf{Eval}(c_{3,1}, \sigma_r, \sigma_i)) \end{cases} \quad \text{where } G_i = \begin{cases} (c_{0,0}, c_{0,1}) \\ (c_{1,0}, c_{1,1}) \\ (c_{2,0}, c_{2,1}) \\ (c_{3,0}, c_{3,1}) \end{cases}
$$

the rows in G_i' are permuted using π_i.
- Output $\hat{C}' = ((G_1', \cdots, G_q'), (L_0, L_1))$ and $\Pi = \{\sigma_i\}_{w_i \in I}$.

The function $\mathsf{Rerand}(\cdot)$ has computational complexity $O(|C|)$ and the size of its output is $O(|C| \cdot \kappa)$ where κ is a security parameter.

Theorem 1. *Let* KMH *be a sharable KMHE scheme (Definition 10). Then* GS = $(\mathsf{Gb}_{\mathsf{KMH}}, \mathsf{Rerand}_{\mathsf{KMH}}, \mathsf{En}_{\mathsf{KMH}}, \mathsf{Ev}_{\mathsf{KMH}})$ *is an RGS with projective encoding (Definition 7).*

The detailed proof for this can be found in the full version [AHKP22].

5   Incremental Decomposable Randomized Encodings

In this section, we introduce a variant of Decomposable Randomized Encodings (DRE - Definition 4): an *incremental Decomposable Randomized Encoding* (iDRE). We also present a construction for an iDRE scheme based on an RGS, and a KMHE scheme (Definition 8). An iDRE is a key ingredient in realizing a secure protocol in the SCALES setting.

The goal of iDRE is to allow multiple encoders to collaborate in an encoding process while using minimal interaction. Specifically, our abstraction allows a chain of encoders to *incrementally* carry out the encoding, with each one receiving the output of the previous one. Informally, for a function f with m-bit inputs x, a chain of d encoders first each locally prepare $\{e_{ij}^0, e_{ij}^1\}_{i \in [m]}$ during an initial encoding phase (which prepares the labels and may work offline). Then, in the incremental encoding phase, the first encoder runs En to prepare an initial encoding B_1. Each subsequent encoder runs En* which prepares B_j from B_{j-1}. Next, each input bit x_i is encoded as $Z_i = \mathsf{Combine}(\{e_{ij}^{x_i}\}_{j \in [d]}, B_d)$. The final encoding for $f(x)$ consists of $(Y, \{Z_i\}_{i\in[m]})$ where $Y \in B_d$. The formal definition below separates the encoding into PreEn and En* to allow for better efficiency and flexibility; also Combine does not take all of B_d as input, but only a part of it, s_i. A basic privacy condition would require that only $f(x)$ is revealed by the final encoding; but as detailed below, we shall require a stronger privacy condition corresponding to when a subset of the encoders and input parties (combiners) are passively corrupt, privacy continues to hold.

Definition 11. *An **incremental Decomposable Randomized Encoding** (iDRE) scheme defined for a function family $\mathcal{F}$, where each $f \in \mathcal{F}$ has domain $\{0,1\}^m$, is a tuple of polynomial time algorithms* iDRE $=$ (PreEn, En, En*, Combine, Dec) *for ℓ polynomial in m. Defining the following random variables as a function of $x \in \{0,1\}^m$:*

$$r_j \leftarrow \{0,1\}^\ell \qquad\qquad \forall j \in [d],$$
$$\{e_{ij}^0, e_{ij}^1\}_{i\in[m]} \leftarrow \mathsf{PreEn}(j; r_j) \qquad\qquad \forall j \in [d],$$
$$B_j \leftarrow \begin{cases} \mathsf{En}(f; r_1) & \text{for } j = 1 \\ \mathsf{En}^*(B_{j-1}; r_j) & \text{for } 1 < j \le d \end{cases}$$
$$(Y, \{s_i\}_{i\in[m]}) \leftarrow B_d$$
$$Z_i \leftarrow \mathsf{Combine}(\{e_{ij}^{x_i}\}_{j\in[d]}, s_i) \qquad\qquad \forall i \in [m]$$

Then the following properties need to be satisfied:

- **Correctness:** $\forall x \in \{0,1\}^m$, *with probability 1 (over the choice of $\{r_j\}_{j\in[d]}$),*

$$\mathsf{Dec}(Y, \{Z_i\}_{i\in[m]}) = f(x).$$

- **Privacy:** *There exists a simulator* Sim *such that $\forall x \in \{0,1\}^m$, $j^* \in [d]$ and $\mathcal{A} \subseteq [m]$,*

$$\left\{ \mathsf{Sim}(f, f(x), j^*, \{x_i\}_{i\in\mathcal{A}}) \right\} \overset{c}{\approx} \left\{ \{r_j\}_{j\neq j^*}, B_{j^*}, \{e_{ij^*}^{x_i}\}_{i\in\mathcal{A}}, \{Z_i\}_{i\notin\mathcal{A}} \right\}$$

The privacy condition above corresponds to a semi-honest adversary who corrupts all encoders other than the one with index j^* – i.e., it learns r_j for all $j \neq j^*$, as well as the output B_{j^*}; further, for a set $\mathcal{A} \subseteq [m]$ it learns the input bits x_i as well as the label $e_{ij^*}^{x_i}$, for each $i \in \mathcal{A}$. Note that this provides the adversary with enough information to decode $f(x)$. We require that such an adversary learns nothing more about the input bits $\{x_i\}_{i\notin\mathcal{A}}$ beyond what $f(x)$ and $\{x_i\}_{i\in\mathcal{A}}$ reveals.

5.1   Realizing iDRE Using RGS

In this section we outline our construction of iDRE based on a projective RGS (Definition 6) and KMHE scheme (Definition 8) which has the following design:

En generates a projective garbling as well as a set of *encrypted labels*. The latter is a set of ciphertexts encrypting both labels for every input bit position within the garbling. Next, each instance of En* takes both a garbling and its encrypted labels as inputs, and outputs a rerandomized garbling and a matching set of encrypted labels. This is achieved by modifying the encrypted plaintexts to match the labels of the new garbling by applying consistent transformations to the encrypted labels by exploiting the homomorphic properties.

Additionally, the keys under which the labels are encrypted are homomorphically refreshed by each encoder using new randomness.[6] This set of transformations is generated by the different instances of algorithm PreEn. At last, the Combine algorithm takes the final encrypted label for each input bit and all the randomness used to create the encryption key, and creates the final key that is used to decrypt the label. This label corresponds to an input label for the last GS, all given as inputs to the decoding algorithm Dec.

Notation. Let the input to the function f be $x = \{x_i\}_{i \in [m]}$. Moreover, let F_1 be the GS created by En and F_j be the rerandomized GS output by the jth instance of En*. We denote by $\mathcal{L}^j$ the set containing all the labels (corresponding to both the 0 and 1 value) for all input bit positions of F_j. Namely, $\mathcal{L}^j = \{L_{ij}^b\}_{i \in [m], b \in \{0,1\}}$, where $L_{ij}^b \in \{0,1\}^\kappa$ denotes the label used in F_j for the ith input bit whose vale is $b \in \{0,1\}$. Finally, we denote the subset of *active labels* within F_j by $X^j = \{L_{ij}^{x_i}\}_{i \in [m]}$ for the input $x = \{x_i\}_{i \in [m]} \in \{0,1\}^m$.

The encrypted labels set that corresponds to F_j is denoted by $\mathcal{EL}^j$ where $\mathcal{EL}^j = \{\mathsf{Enc}(K_{ij}^b, L_{ij}^b)\}_{i \in [m], b \in \{0,1\}}$. Starting with F_1, each label $L_{i1}^b \in \mathcal{L}^1$ is encrypted using a key K_{i1}^b that is chosen from a KMHE scheme. We represent by $\Pi\mathcal{K}^1 = \{K_{i1}^b\}_{i \in [m], b \in \{0,1\}}$ the set of these keys. Each subsequent $\mathcal{EL}^j$ is created from $\mathcal{EL}^{j-1}$. Namely, let $\rho_{ij}^b \in \mathcal{F}_{key}$ denote a transformation chosen to randomize the key ρ_{ij-1}^b, yielding a new transformed key ρ_{ij}^b in the key domain. Then $\Pi\mathcal{K}^j = \{\rho_{ij}^b\}_{i \in [m], b \in \{0,1\}}$ denote this set of transformations for all $j > 1$.

Another set of transformations denoted by $\pi_{\mathsf{En}} = \{\sigma_i \in \mathcal{F}_{key}\}_{i \in [m]}$ plays a different role in our construction. Namely, these transformations are applied on the plaintexts within $\mathcal{EL}^{j-1}$ with the aim of rerandomizing the input labels to match the garbling F_j. Figure 2 contains the details of the algorithms for this instantiation using a KMHE and a projective RGS. The circuit C that represents the function f is publicly available to all involved parties.

Theorem 2. *Let* KMH $=$ (Gen, Enc, Dec, Eval) *be a KMHE scheme (Definition 8) and let* GS $=$ (Gb, Rerand, En, Ev) *be a projective RGS (Definition 7), then Fig. 2 is an iDRE (Definition 11).*

The detailed proof for this theorem can be found in the full version [AHKP22].

---

[6] As different transformations are applied to the keys used for encrypting the different input labels, and only on the key domain, it suffices to use KMHE.

---

iDRE construction using projective RGS

Building blocks:
Projective RGS: $GS = (Gb, Rerand, En, Ev)$
KMHE: $KMH = (Gen, Enc, Dec, Eval)$ such that the set of encoding transformations of GS is a subset of the message transformation family $\mathcal{F}_{msg}$ of KMH

Function $f : \{0,1\}^m \rightarrow \{0,1\}^l$
Function input $x = (x_1, \cdots, x_m)$

function $\mathsf{PreEn}(j; r_j)$
  parse $r_j = (r'_j, r^0_{1j}, \cdots, r^0_{mj}, r^1_{1j}, \cdots, r^1_{mj})$
  if $j = 1$ **then**
    $e^b_{i1} = K^b_{i1} \leftarrow \mathsf{KMH.Gen}(1^\kappa; r^b_{ij})$ $\forall i \in [m], b \in \{0,1\}$
  else
    $e^b_{ij} = \rho^b_{ij} \leftarrow \mathcal{F}_{key}$ using r^b_{ij} $\forall i \in [m], b \in \{0,1\}$
  return $\{e^0_{ij}, e^1_{ij}\}_{i \in [m]}$

function $\mathsf{En}(f; r_1)$
  parse $r_1 = (r'_1, r^0_{11}, \cdots, r^0_{m1}, r^1_{11}, \cdots, r^1_{m1})$
  $\{K^b_{i1}\}_{i \in [m], b \in \{0,1\}} \leftarrow \mathsf{PreEn}(1; r_1)$
  $(F_1, e_1) \leftarrow \mathsf{GS.Gb}(f; r'_1)$
  $(L^b_{11}, \cdots, L^b_{m1}) \leftarrow \mathsf{GS.En}(b^m, e_1)$ $\forall b \in \{0,1\}$
  $\alpha^b_{i1} \leftarrow \mathsf{KMH.Enc}(K^b_{i1}, L^b_{i1})$ $\forall i \in [m], b \in \{0,1\}$
  return $(F_1, \{\alpha^b_{i1}\}_{i \in [m], b \in \{0,1\}})$

function $\mathsf{En}^*(B_{j-1}; r_j)$
  parse $B_{j-1} = (F_{j-1}, \{\alpha^b_{ij-1}\}_{i \in [m], b \in \{0,1\}})$
  parse $r_j = (r'_j, r^0_{1j}, \cdots, r^0_{mj}, r^1_{1j}, \cdots, r^1_{mj})$
  $\{\rho^b_{ij}\}_{i \in [m], b \in \{0,1\}} \leftarrow \mathsf{PreEn}(j; r_j)$
  $(F_j, \{\sigma_i\}_{i \in [m]}) \leftarrow \mathsf{GS.Rerand}(F_{j-1}; r'_j)$
  $\alpha^b_{ij} \leftarrow \mathsf{KMH.Eval}(\alpha^b_{ij-1}, \rho^b_{ij}, \sigma_i)$ $\forall i \in [m], b \in \{0,1\}$
  return $B_j = (F_j, \{\alpha^b_{ij}\}_{i \in [m], b \in \{0,1\}})$

function $\mathsf{Combine}(\{e^{x_i}_{ij}\}_{j \in [d]}, s_i)$
  parse $\{e^{x_i}_{ij}\}_{j \in [d]} = (K^{x_i}_{i1}, \rho^{x_i}_{i2}, \cdots, \rho^{x_i}_{id})$
  parse $s_i = (\alpha^0_{id}, \alpha^1_{id})$
  $K^{x_i}_{id} \leftarrow \rho^{x_i}_{id} \circ \cdots \circ \rho^{x_i}_{i2}(K^{x_i}_{i1})$
  return $\mathsf{KMH.Dec}(K^{x_i}_{id}, \alpha^{x_i}_i)$

function $\mathsf{Dec}(Y, \{Z_i\}_{i \in [m]})$
  return $\mathsf{GS.Ev}(Y, \{Z_i\}_{i \in [m]})$

Fig. 2. Instantiating an iDRE using a projective RGS and KMHE

6   Realizing SCALES

In Construction 1, we show how one can obtain a SCALES scheme from an iDRE scheme, combined with a 2-message OT protocol (with semi-honest, adaptive-receiver security), $\Pi^{\mathsf{OT}} = (\mathsf{OT}_1, \mathsf{OT}_2, \mathsf{OT}_{out})$ (corresponding to computing the receiver's message and state, the sender's message, and the receiver computing its output) as described in Sect. 2.3. The construction is quite simple: Each P_i encodes x_i as $(z_i, w_i) = \mathsf{OT}_1(x_i)$ and posts z_i. The ephemeral servers play the role of the encoders in iDRE: E_j will post the encoding B_j and also, for each input party P_i, it will post $\mathsf{OT}_2(z_i, e_{ij}^0, e_{ij}^1)$ on the bulletin board. Afterwards, each input party P_i reads the OT messages posted by each E_j, and using w_i, recovers $e_{ij}^{x_i}$; then it runs Combine and posts the result back on the bulletin board. The final output computation is done using iDRE's Dec algorithm.

Construction 1. *Let f be the function for input $x = (x_1, \cdots, x_m)$ where x_i is P_i's private input. Let* iDRE $=$ (PreEn, En, En*, Combine) *be the iDRE (Definition 11) for f and $\Pi^{\mathsf{OT}} = (\mathsf{OT}_1, \mathsf{OT}_2, \mathsf{OT}_{out})$ be the OT protocol as above. Then the algorithms in SCALES are instantiated as:*

- $\forall i \in [m], (z_i, w_i) \leftarrow \mathsf{InpEnc}(i, x_i; t_i)$ -
    - *output* $(z_i, w_i) \leftarrow \mathsf{OT}_1(x_i; t_i)$ *where z_i is the OT first message*
- $\forall j \in [d], \alpha_j \leftarrow \mathsf{FEnc}(\mathcal{B}_{j-1}; r_j)$ -
    - *if $j = 1$, compute $B_1 = \mathsf{iDRE.En}(f; r_1)$*
    - *if $j \neq 1$, compute $B_j = \mathsf{iDRE.En}^*(j, B_{j-1}; r_j)$ using $B_{j-1} \in \mathcal{B}_{j-1}$*
    - *compute $\{e_{ij}^0, e_{ij}^1\}_{i \in [m]} = \mathsf{iDRE.PreEn}(j; r_j)$*
    - *compute $\forall i \in [m], m_2^{i,j} \leftarrow \mathsf{OT}_2(z_i, (e_{ij}^0, e_{ij}^1))$*
    - *output $\alpha_j = \{B_j, \{m_2^{i,j}\}_{i \in [m]}\}$*
- $\forall i \in [m], y_i \leftarrow \mathsf{Aggregate}(\mathcal{B}_d, w_i)$ -
    - *compute $\forall j \in [d], e_{ij}^{x_i} \leftarrow \mathsf{OT}_{out}(w_i, m_2^{i,j})$ using $m_2^{i,j} \in \mathcal{B}_d$*
    - *output $y_i = \mathsf{iDRE.Combine}(\{e_{ij}^{x_i}\}_{j \in [n]}, s_i)$ using $s_i \in \mathcal{B}_d$*
- $y \leftarrow \mathsf{Decode}(\mathcal{B}_d, \{y_i\}_{i \in [m]})$ -
    - *output $f(x) = \mathsf{iDRE.Dec}(\hat{f}_0(r), \{y_i\}_{i \in [m]})$ using $\hat{f}_0(r) \in \mathcal{B}_d$*

Complexity. We note that in this construction, each ephemeral server carries out one execution of PreEn and En* (or En) and m executions of OT_2 (reading their inputs from the bulletin board, and posting the outputs back there); when instantiated using our iDRE construction, this translates to $O(\kappa|f|)$ computational and communication complexity for each server. More importantly, note that each input party carries out a single execution of OT_1, d instances of OT_{out}, and a single instance of Combine, all of which are independent of the complexity of f.

Theorem 3. *Let* iDRE $=$ (PreEn, En, En*, Combine) *be an iDRE (Definition 11) for the function family $\mathcal{F}$ where each $f \in \mathcal{F}$ has domain $\{0,1\}^m$ and let $\Pi^{\mathsf{OT}} = (\mathsf{OT}_1, \mathsf{OT}_2, \mathsf{OT}_{out})$ be a 2-message OT protocol (Sect. 2.3) that semi-honest securely computes the 2-party OT functionality OT in the presence of a static-corrupted sender and an adaptively corrupted receiver. Then the protocol described in Construction 1 is a secure SCALES scheme (Definition 5).*

The detailed proof for this can be found in the full version [AHKP22].

7 Applications of RGS and iDRE

We outline certain other applications for the cryptographic objects we define.

7.1   RGS for Outsourced Re-Garbling

Consider a setting where a party P_{fun} holding a private function f would like to let a client P_{eval} securely evaluate $f(x)$ on various inputs x of its choice, using a GC-based protocol. Because of the one-time nature of GCs, this requires P_{fun} to carry out garbling once for each evaluation. This motivates the problem of *outsourced re-garbling* – i.e., out-sourcing the task of creating many copies of a garbled circuit for a private function to a semi-honest server (say, a cloud service).

Outsourced Re-Garbling presents an immediate application of RGS. The following definition of the Outsourced Re-Garbling task captures the security requirement that the parties P_{fun} and P_{eval} learn nothing more than in the original two-party setting, while a regarbling server S_{gb} that P_{fun} interacts with (before P_{eval} arrives) would learn nothing about the function f (except a permitted leakage $\phi(f)$). The security guarantees below assume that the server S_{gb} does not collude with P_{eval}.

Definition 12. *An **Outsourced Re-Garbling** scheme for a function family $\mathcal{F}$ with input domain $\mathcal{X}$ and a leakage function $\phi : \mathcal{F} \to \{0,1\}^*$, is a tuple of PPT algorithms* $(\mathsf{InitGb}, \mathsf{ReGb}, \mathsf{En}, \mathsf{Ev})$ *that satisfy the following properties:*

- **Correctness:** $\forall f \in \mathcal{F}, \forall x \in \mathcal{X}$,

$$\Pr[\mathsf{Ev}(F, X) = f(x) \ : (F_0, e) \leftarrow \mathsf{InitGb}(f),$$
$$(F, \pi) \leftarrow \mathsf{ReGb}(F_0), X \leftarrow \mathsf{En}(x, \pi(e))] = 1$$

- **Privacy against** S_{gb}: $\forall f \in \mathcal{F}$, *there exists a PPT simulator* $\mathsf{Sim}_{\mathsf{gb}}$ *such that*

$$\{\mathsf{Sim}_{\mathsf{gb}}(\phi(f))\} \overset{c}{\approx} \{F_0\}_{(F_0, e) \leftarrow \mathsf{InitGb}(f)}$$

- **Privacy against** P_{eval}: $\forall f \in \mathcal{F}, \forall n \in \mathbb{N}, \forall i \in [n]$ *and* $\forall x_i \in \mathcal{X}$, *there exists a PPT simulator* $\mathsf{Sim}_{\mathsf{eval}}$ *such that*

$$\{\mathsf{Sim}_{\mathsf{eval}}(\{f(x_i), x_i\}_{i \in [n]}, \phi(f))\} \overset{c}{\approx} \{\{F_i, X_i\}_{i \in [n]}\} \begin{smallmatrix} (F_0, e) \leftarrow \mathsf{InitGb}(f), \\ \{(F_i, \pi_i) \leftarrow \mathsf{ReGb}(F_0), \\ X_i \leftarrow \mathsf{En}(x_i, \pi_i(e))\}_{i \in [n]} \end{smallmatrix}$$

These algorithms can be employed by the parties P_{fun}, P_{eval} and S_{gb} as follows. P_{fun} first executes $(F_0, e) \leftarrow \mathsf{InitGb}(f)$ and sends F_0 to S_{gb}. Then S_{gb} runs multiple instances of $(F_i, \pi_i) \leftarrow \mathsf{ReGb}(F_0)$ and sends all π_i back to P_{fun}. When P_{eval} comes online with an input x_i to f, it first gets F_i directly from S_{gb} (so P_{fun} does not incur the corresponding communication overhead). It then participates in a protocol with P_{fun} to obtain $X_i \leftarrow \mathsf{En}(x_i, \pi_i(e))$; this can be implemented directly using parallel OTs. Following that, P_{eval} computes $f(x_i) \leftarrow \mathsf{Ev}(F_i, X_i)$.

Note that the computational and communication complexity of P_{fun} involves a single instance of InitGb, followed by n instances of computing $\pi_i(e)$ and n instances of carrying out En. There is an implicit efficiency requirement that the latter two steps (which are repeated n times each) depend linearly on the *input* size m and are independent of its *circuit size* $|f|$, reducing the computational complexity of P_{fun} from $O(|f|n)$ to $O(|f| + mn)$ (ignoring factors involving the security parameter). This is a significant saving when $|f|$ and n are both large (e.g., evaluating a large machine learning model on inputs from the user-base of a popular app).

Theorem 4. *An RGS* $\mathsf{GS} = (\mathsf{Gb}, \mathsf{Rerand}, \mathsf{En}, \mathsf{Ev})$ *(Definition 6) is an Outsourced Re-Garbling scheme* $(\mathsf{InitGb}, \mathsf{ReGb}, \mathsf{En}, \mathsf{Ev})$ *(Definition 12).*

The detailed proof for this can be found in the full version [AHKP22].

7.2   iDRE for MPC

An iDRE can be used to implement a general n-party protocol under static semi-honest corruption of up to $n - 1$ parties. Let $P_1, \cdots, P_n$ be the parties, f be the public function and $x \in \{0, 1\}^m$ be its input out of which each P_i possesses $x^i \subset x$. The iDRE-based protocol can compute $f(x)$ using $O(n \times m)$ string-OT

---

n party protocol for t=n-1 corruption

$f : \{0, 1\}^m \to \{0, 1\}^l$ is a public function to be computed
$(\mathsf{PreEn}, \mathsf{En}, \mathsf{En}^*, \mathsf{Combine}, \mathsf{Dec})$ is the iDRE for f
for input $x \in \{0, 1\}^m$, the subset of bits $x^{i'} \subset x, |x^{i'}| = m_{i'}$ is $\mathcal{P}_{i'}$'s private input

for $\mathcal{P}_j \in \{\mathcal{P}_1, \cdots, \mathcal{P}_n\}$ **do**
  $\mathcal{P}_j$ executes $\mathsf{PreEn}(r_j; j) \to \{e_{ij}^0, e_{ij}^1\}_{i \in [m]}$

for $\mathcal{P}_{i'} \in \{\mathcal{P}_1, \cdots, \mathcal{P}_n\}$ **do**
  for $x_i \in x^{i'}$ **do**
    for $\mathcal{P}_j \in \{\mathcal{P}_1, \cdots, \mathcal{P}_n\} - \{\mathcal{P}_{i'}\}$ **do**   ▷ get shares
    $\mathcal{P}_{i'}$ performs OT with $\mathcal{P}_j$:
      Receiver $\mathcal{P}_{i'}$'s input choice bit is x_i
      Sender $\mathcal{P}_j$'s input strings are e_{ij}^0, e_{ij}^1
      $\mathcal{P}_{i'}$ receives $e_{ij}^{x_i}$

$\mathcal{P}_1$ executes $\mathsf{En}(r_1) \to B_1$
for $\mathcal{P}_j \in (\mathcal{P}_2, \cdots, \mathcal{P}_n)$ **do**   ▷ actions for each party $\mathcal{P}_j$
  $\mathcal{P}_j$ gets B_{j-1} from $\mathcal{P}_{j-1}$
  $\mathcal{P}_j$ executes $\mathsf{En}^*(r_j; j, B_{j-1}) \to B_j$

for $\mathcal{P}_{i'} \in \{\mathcal{P}_1, \cdots, \mathcal{P}_n\}$ **do**
  for $x_i \in x^{i'}$ **do**
    get $s_i \in B_n$ from $\mathcal{P}_n$
    execute $\mathsf{Combine}(\{e_{ij}^{x_i}\}_{j \in [n]}, s_i) \to Z_i$
  send $Z_{i'}' = \{Z_i\}_{x_i \in x^{i'}}$ to $\mathcal{P}_n$

$\mathcal{P}_n$ gets $Z_1', \cdots, Z_{n-1}'$ ▷ actions for $\mathcal{P}_n$
$\mathcal{P}_n$ has Z_n', B_n
$\mathcal{P}_n$ executes $\mathsf{Dec}(\hat{f}_0(r), \{Z_i\}_{i \in [m]}) \to f(x)$

Fig. 3. Semi-honest MPC protocol based on iDRE

calls, meeting the lower bound on OT complexity for this setting, as proven in [HIK07]. This is achieved by letting each P_i act as one of the encoders in the sequential process along with playing the role of an input party. All the parties first employ PreEn and then every pair of parties engages in an OT for every input bit. Next, starting from P_1, the incremental chain of encoding follows with each P_i creating B_i and passing it on to P_{i+1}. Finally, P_n passes $\{s_i\}_{i \in [m]}$ to all other parties. Each party runs Combine for each of their input bits. These results are passed back to P_n that decodes and broadcasts the output.

Theorem 5. *Let* (PreEn, En, En*, Combine, Dec) *be an iDRE (Definition 11) for the function family $\mathcal{F}$ where $f \in \mathcal{F}$ has domain $\{0,1\}^m$. Figure 3 is an n-party semi-honest protocol computing f in the (string) OT-hybrid under $(n-1)$-corruption using $((n-1) \times m)$ OT calls and the iDRE in a black-box way.*

The proof for this theorem can be found in the full version [AHKP22]. The communication complexity for this protocol is $O(n\kappa|f| + \kappa n^2)$. While there exist other MPC protocols with better communication complexity, our protocol meets the lower-bound in the number of required OT calls (see discussion in Sect. 1.1). Further, our protocol is black-box in its use of the iDRE.

Acknowledgments. We thank Shai Halevi for discussions including feedback regarding the gap in [GHV10]. Anasuya Acharya and Carmit Hazay are supported by the BIU Center for Research in Applied Cryptography and Cyber Security in conjunction with the Israel National Cyber Bureau in the Prime Minister's Office, and by ISF grant No. 1316/18. Vladimir Kolesnikov was supported in part by NSF award #1909769, by a Facebook research award, a Cisco research award, and by Georgia TechâĂŹs IISP cybersecurity seed funding (CSF) award. Manoj Prabhakaran is supported by a Ramanujan Fellowship of the Department of Science and Technology, India. Carmit Hazay and Manoj Prabhakaran are also supported by the Algorand Centres of Excellence programme managed by Algorand Foundation. Any opinions, findings, and conclusions or recommendations expressed in this material are those of the author(s) and do not necessarily reflect the views of Algorand Foundation.

References

[ABT18]   Applebaum, B., Brakerski, Z., Tsabary, R.: Perfect secure computation in two rounds. In: TCC, pp. 152–174 (2018)

[AHKP22] Acharya, A., Hazay, C., Kolesnikov, V., Prabhakaran, M.: Scales: Mpc with small clients and larger ephemeral servers. IACR Cryptol. ePrint Arch., p. 751 (2022)

[BGG+20] Benhamouda, F., et al.: Can a public blockchain keep a secret? In: TCC, pp. 260–290 (2020)

[BGSZ21] Bartusek, J., Garg, S., Srinivasan, A., Zhang, Y.: Reusable two-round MPC from LPN. IACR Cryptol. ePrint Arch., p. 316 (2021)

[BHHO08] Boneh, D., Halevi, S., Hamburg, M., Ostrovsky, R.: Circular-secure encryption from decision diffie-hellman. In: CRYPTO, pp. 108–125 (2008)

[BHR12]   Bellare, M., Hoang, V.T., Rogaway, P.: Foundations of garbled circuits. In: CCS, pp. 784–796 (2012)

[BJKL21] Benhamouda, F., Jain, A., Komargodski, I., Lin, H.: Multiparty reusable non-interactive secure computation from LWE. In: Canteaut, A., Standaert, F.-X. (eds.) EUROCRYPT 2021. LNCS, vol. 12697, pp. 724–753. Springer, Cham (2021). https://doi.org/10.1007/978-3-030-77886-6_25

[BL18] Benhamouda, F., Lin, H.: k-round multiparty computation from k-round oblivious transfer via garbled interactive circuits. In: Nielsen, J.B., Rijmen, V. (eds.) EUROCRYPT 2018. LNCS, vol. 10821, pp. 500–532. Springer, Cham (2018). https://doi.org/10.1007/978-3-319-78375-8_17

[BMR90] Beaver, D., Micali, S., Rogaway, P.: The round complexity of secure protocols (extended abstract). In: STOC, pp. 503–513 (1990)

[CGG+21] Choudhuri, A.R., Goel, A., Green, M., Jain, A., Kaptchuk, G.: Fluid MPC: secure multiparty computation with dynamic participants. In: CRYPTO, pp. 94–123 (2021)

[GGHR14] Garg, S., Gentry, C., Halevi, S., Raykova, M.: Two-round secure MPC from indistinguishability obfuscation. In: TCC, pp. 74–94 (2014)

[GHK+21] Gentry, C., Halevi, S., Krawczyk, H., Magri, B., Nielsen, J.B., Rabin, T., Yakoubov, S.: YOSO: You Only Speak Once. In: Malkin, T., Peikert, C. (eds.) CRYPTO 2021. LNCS, vol. 12826, pp. 64–93. Springer, Cham (2021). https://doi.org/10.1007/978-3-030-84245-1_3

[GHM+21] Gentry, C., Halevi, S., Magri, B., Nielsen, J.B., Yakoubov, S.: Random-index PIR and applications. In: TCC, pp. 32–61 (2021)

[GHV10] Gentry, C., Halevi, S., Vaikuntanathan, V.: i-Hop homomorphic encryption and rerandomizable yao circuits. In: Rabin, T. (ed.) CRYPTO 2010. LNCS, vol. 6223, pp. 155–172. Springer, Heidelberg (2010). https://doi.org/10.1007/978-3-642-14623-7_9

[GMPS21] Goyal, V., Masserova, E., Parno, B., Song, Y.: Blockchains enable non-interactive MPC. IACR Cryptol. ePrint Arch., pp. 1233 (2021)

[GS18] Garg, S., Srinivasan, A.: Two-round multiparty secure computation from minimal assumptions. In: Nielsen, J.B., Rijmen, V. (eds.) EUROCRYPT 2018. LNCS, vol. 10821, pp. 468–499. Springer, Cham (2018). https://doi.org/10.1007/978-3-319-78375-8_16

[HIK07] Harnik, D., Ishai, Y., Kushilevitz, E.: How many oblivious transfers are needed for secure multiparty computation? In: Menezes, A. (ed.) CRYPTO 2007. LNCS, vol. 4622, pp. 284–302. Springer, Heidelberg (2007). https://doi.org/10.1007/978-3-540-74143-5_16

[IK00] Ishai, Y., Kushilevitz, E.: Randomizing polynomials: A new representation with applications to round-efficient secure computation. In: FPCS, pp. 294–304 (2000)

[LP09] Lindell, Y., Pinkas, B.: A proof of security of Yao's protocol for two-party computation. J. Cryptol. **22**(2), 161–188 (2009)

[MRZ15] Mohassel, P., Rosulek, M., Zhang, Y.: Fast and secure three-party computation: The garbled circuit approach. In: SIGSAC, pp. 591–602 (2015)

[NS09] Naor, M., Segev, G.: Public-key cryptosystems resilient to key leakage. In: Halevi, S. (ed.) CRYPTO 2009. LNCS, vol. 5677, pp. 18–35. Springer, Heidelberg (2009). https://doi.org/10.1007/978-3-642-03356-8_2

[RS21] Rachuri, R., Scholl, P.: Le mans: Dynamic and fluid MPC for dishonest majority. IACR Cryptol. ePrint Arch., p. 1579 (2021)

[Yao86] Yao, A.C.-C.: How to generate and exchange secrets (extended abstract). In: FOCS, pp. 162–167 (1986)

On Perfectly Secure Two-Party Computation for Symmetric Functionalities with Correlated Randomness

Bar Alon[1]([✉]), Olga Nissenbaum[1], Eran Omri[1], Anat Paskin-Cherniavsky[1], and Arpita Patra[2]

[1] Department of Computer Science, Ariel University, Ariel Cyber Innovation Center (ACIC), Ari'el, Israel
alonbar08@gmail.com,olga@nissenbaum.ru,omrier@gmail.com,anps83@gmail.com
[2] Indian Institute of Science, Bangalore, India
arpita@iisc.ac.in

Abstract. A multiparty computation protocol is *perfectly secure* for some function f if it perfectly emulates an ideal computation of f. Thus, perfect security is the strongest and most desirable notion of security, as it guarantees security in the face of any adversary and eliminates the dependency on any security parameter. Ben-Or et al. [2] [STOC '88] and Chaum et al. [5] [STOC '88] showed that any function can be computed with perfect security if strictly less than one-third of the parties can be corrupted. For two-party sender-receiver functionalities (where only one party receives an output), Ishai et al. [9] [TCC '13] showed that any function can be computed with perfect security in the correlated randomness model. Unfortunately, they also showed that perfect security cannot be achieved in general for two-party functions that give outputs to both parties (even in the correlated randomness model).

We study the feasibility of obtaining perfect security for deterministic symmetric two-party functionalities (i.e., where both parties obtain the same output) in the face of malicious adversaries. We explore both the plain model as well as the correlated randomness model. We provide positive results in the plain model, and negative results in the correlated randomness model. As a corollary, we obtain the following results.

1. We provide a characterization of symmetric functionalities with (up to) four possible outputs that can be computed with perfect security. The characterization is further refined when restricted to three possible outputs and to Boolean functions. All characterizations are the same for both the plain model and the correlated randomness model.
2. We show that if a functionality contains an embedded XOR or an embedded AND, then it cannot be computed with perfect security (even in the correlated randomness model).

Keywords: Perfect security · Two-party computation · Correlated randomness

E. Kiltz and V. Vaikuntanathan (Eds.): TCC 2022, LNCS 13748, pp. 532–561, 2022.
https://doi.org/10.1007/978-3-031-22365-5_19

1   Introduction

Secure Multiparty Computation (MPC) protocols allow a set of mutually distrusting parties to compute a joint function of their private inputs. The two
main security properties that are desirable for protocols are correctness of the
computation and privacy (i.e., the adversary should not learn anything about
the inputs or outputs of the honest parties except what is leaked from the output
of the function). There are two main types of adversaries that are considered.
These are semi-honest (passive) adversaries and malicious (active) adversaries.
A semi-honest adversary always follows the prescribed protocol, but may try to
infer additional information from the joint view of the corrupted parties in the
protocol. A malicious adversary may instruct the corrupted parties to deviate
from the prescribed protocol in any manner it chooses.

A general paradigm for defining the desired security of protocols is known
as the ideal vs real paradigm. This paradigm avoids the need to specify a list of
desired properties. Rather, security is defined by describing an ideal functionality,
where parties interact via a trusted party to compute the task at hand. A real-
world protocol is then deemed secure, if no adversary can do more harm than
an adversary in the ideal-world. In a bit more detail, the definition requires
that the view of the adversary in a real-world execution, can be simulated by an
adversary (corrupting the same parties) in the ideal-world. There are three types
of measurements for the strength of security that may be considered. These are
called computational, statistical, and perfect security. Computational security
requires that the distribution of the view in the real-world is indistinguishable
from the distribution of the view in the ideal-world to a computationally bounded
machine. Statistical security requires these distributions to be statistically close
(indistinguishable even for unbounded machines). Finally, perfect security means
that the views in both worlds are identically distributed.

In this paper we consider perfect security for two-party computation (i.e.,
with no honest majority), in the face of malicious adversaries (when considering perfect security, we naturally assume the adversary to be computationally
unbounded). Apart from being a natural research goal, perfect security provides
important and useful security advantages over protocols that offer computational
security and even over those that have a negligible probability of failure (i.e.,
offer statistical security). Because of the stringent requirement, perfectly secure
constructions tend to have a simple structure. More importantly, perfect security
completely eliminates the need for a security parameter, making protocols that
are perfectly secure highly scalable.

Perfect Security in the Plain Model

In the basic setting of secure computation, parties communicate with each other
over some communication network. It is generally assumed that the channels are
secure, but no other setup assumption is made. In this setting, Ben-Or et al. [2],
Chaum et al. [5] showed the feasibility of computing any function with perfect

security in the face of malicious adversaries that can corrupt strictly less than one-third of the parties.[1]

In the two party setting, Kushilevitz [10] characterized the set of functions that can be computed with perfect security in the face of semi-honest adversaries. Cleve [7] showed that full-security (where honest parties always receive an output) is impossible in general, even for computationally bounded malicious adversaries. For the setting of two-party plain-model protocols with perfect security in the face of malicious adversaries, very little was known prior to our work.

Perfect Security with Correlated Randomness

It is natural to ask whether the impossibilities of obtaining prefect security can be circumvented by making some reasonable assumption. This brings to the table the correlated-randomness model that is both theoretically and practically motivated. In this model, parties are given strings sampled from some fixed joint distribution at the onset of the protocol. These strings are independent of their inputs, and are then used alongside the inputs of the parties to run a secure computation protocol. Interestingly, Cleve's [7] impossibility result does not apply to this setting.

In the correlated randomness setting, Ishai et al. [9] showed that it is possible to construct perfectly and maliciously secure protocols in the sender-receiver model, i.e., where both parties have an input, but only one receives an output. On the negative side, [9] showed that, in general, perfect security is impossible to achieve for two-party functionalities that deliver outputs to both the parties. In particular, they show that it is impossible to compute the XOR function in this setting. In fact, the negative implication carries forward even to security with abort, where the adversary may itself get the output, but can deprive the honest parties from the output. Other than this result, very little was known prior to our work regarding perfect security in the correlated randomness setting where both parties receive an output.

In light of the above, the main question studied in this paper is.

Characterize the set of two-party functionalities that can be computed with perfect (full) security in the face of malicious adversaries.

We make substantial progress in this direction and leave open several challenging followup questions. We summarize our results below.

1.1   Our Contribution

In this work, we consider the model of two-party computation of deterministic symmetric functionalities (i.e., where both parties have the same output in the computation). We are interested in perfect security and consider computation both in the plain model and in the correlated randomness model. We provide

---

[1] For semi-honest adversaries, they showed that an honest majority is sufficient.

both positive results in the plain model, and negative results in the correlated randomness model. In particular, our results form a full characterization for four-output functionalities, showing that there are only two families of functionalities that can be computed with perfect security.

Before giving the results in more details, let us first define the two families of functionalities mentioned above. In the following, for any symmetric deterministic functionality $f : \mathcal{X} \times \mathcal{Y} \mapsto \mathcal{Z}$, we associate with it a matrix $\mathbf{M}_f \in \mathcal{Z}^{|\mathcal{X}| \times |\mathcal{Y}|}$ defined as $\mathbf{M}_f(x, y) = f(x, y)$, for all $x \in \mathcal{X}$ and $y \in \mathcal{Y}$.

Definition 1 (Spiral functionality, informal). *A symmetric deterministic functionality $f : \mathcal{X} \times \mathcal{Y} \mapsto \mathcal{Z}$ is called* spiral, *if $\mathbf{M}_f$ is either constant, or, up to permuting the rows and columns, and transposing the matrix, is of the form $(\mathbf{M} \| \mathbf{M}')$ where $\mathbf{M}$ is constant-column, $\mathbf{M}'$ is spiral, and where the set of entries in the two matrices are disjoint.*

As an example, consider the following spiral matrix.

$$\begin{pmatrix} 7 & 7 & 7 & 7 & 7 \\ 6 & 6 & 6 & 6 & 6 \\ 5 & 4 & 4 & \boxed{1} & 2 \\ 5 & 4 & 4 & \boxed{0} & 2 \\ 5 & 4 & 4 & \boxed{3} & 3 \end{pmatrix}$$

Definition 2 (Transparent transfer functionality, informal). *A symmetric deterministic functionality $f : \mathcal{X} \times \mathcal{Y} \mapsto \{0, 1, 2, 3\}$ is called* transparent transfer *if, up to permuting and duplicating the rows and columns, and transposing the matrix, $\mathbf{M}_f$ is of the form*

$$\begin{pmatrix} a & c \\ a & d \\ b & c \\ b & d \end{pmatrix} \tag{1}$$

where $\{a, b, c, d\} = \{0, 1, 2, 3\}$.

We refer the reader to Remark 2 for the reasoning behind the name. We are now ready to state our main result, providing a full characterization for the four-output functionalities that can be computed with perfect security.

Theorem 1 (Characterization of four-output functionalities, informal). *Let $f : \mathcal{X} \times \mathcal{Y} \mapsto \{0, 1, 2, 3\}$ be a symmetric deterministic four-output two-party functionality. If f can be computed with perfect security in the correlated randomness model, then f is either spiral or transparent transfer. Conversely, any spiral and transparent transfer functionality can be computed with perfect security in the plain model.*

A few notes are in place. First, observe that, in particular, we obtain a characterization for symmetric ternary-output and Boolean functionalities. Specifically, since transparent transfer functionalities require four outputs, for the ternary-output case, it follows that the only functionalities that can be computed with perfect security are spiral. Thus, we have the following.

Corollary 1. *Let $f : \mathcal{X} \times \mathcal{Y} \mapsto \{0, 1, 2\}$ be a symmetric deterministic ternary-output two-party functionality. If f can be computed with perfect security in the correlated randomness model, then f is spiral. Conversely, any spiral functionality can be computed with perfect security in the plain model.*

As for the Boolean case, observe that a Boolean functionality is spiral if and only if it is independent of one of its inputs, which we refer to as trivial functionalities. Therefore, we obtain the following result.

Corollary 2. *Let $f : \mathcal{X} \times \mathcal{Y} \mapsto \{0, 1\}$ be a Boolean symmetric deterministic two-party functionality. If f can be computed with perfect security in the correlated randomness model, then f is trivial. Conversely, any trivial functionality can be computed with perfect security in the plain model.*

Second, although our main results consider only four-output functionalities, we stress that both our positive and negative results can be extended to the more general case. However, it is currently unknown if these results provide a characterization for even five-output functionalities.

Third, observe that Theorem 1 implies that for four-output functionalities, the plain model and the correlated randomness model are equivalent.

Finally, our techniques for the negative direction provide an impossibility result for a larger class of functionalities, including those with more than four outputs. An interesting corollary of this general result, is that if a functionality has an embedded XOR or an embedded AND,[2] then the functionality cannot be computed with perfect securit.

1.2   Our Techniques

We now turn to describe our techniques. To warm-up for our techniques, we first briefly explain the impossibility result for the symmetric XOR functionality $\mathsf{XOR}(x, y) = x \oplus y$ due to Ishai et al. [9]. We then show where it falls short even for the AND functionality $\mathsf{AND}(x, y) = x \wedge y$. Then, we show how to overcome this shortcoming and prove a general impossibility result. Finally, we show how to compute spiral and transparent transfer functionalities with perfect security.

---

[2] A functionality f is said to have an embedded XOR if there exists $x_1, x_2 \in \mathcal{X}$ and $y_1, y_2 \in \mathcal{Y}$ such that $f(x_1, y_1) = f(x_2, y_2) \neq f(x_1, y_2) = f(x_2, y_1)$. The functionality is said to have an embedded AND if $f(x_2, y_2) \neq f(x_1, y_1) = f(x_1, y_2) = f(x_2, y_1)$.

Impossibility of XOR. Let us start with recalling the proof that $\mathsf{XOR}(x, y) = x \oplus y$ cannot be computed with perfect security, even when the parties are given correlated randomness. Assume towards contradiction that there is a protocol $\varPi$ for computing f with perfect security in the correlated randomness model.

Consider an execution of $\varPi$ on inputs $(x, y) \leftarrow \{0, 1\}^2$ chosen uniformly at random. Since the protocol is perfectly correct, there exists a round where the output of party A is fixed (e.g., the last round). That is, regardless of the correlated randomness generated for the parties, any continuation of the protocol results in A outputting $x \oplus y$. Let i be the first such round. Similarly, let j be the first round, where the output of B is fixed to $x \oplus y$. Since the parties send message one after the other, it holds that $i \neq j$. Assume without loss of generality that $i < j$. Then at round i, party A "knows" the output, while party B does not. In more details, there exists correlated randomness (r_1, r_2) for which at round i, there exists messages that A can send causing party B to output $1 \oplus x \oplus yy$ (Table 1).

Table 1. The table below shows the functionalities that can be computed with perfect security with correlated randomness (for presentation, we do not include constant functions). As stated in Theorem 1, up to transposing the matrix, re-encoding the output, and permuting and duplicating the rows and columns, these are the *only* functionalities that can be computed with perfect security.

Functionality	Trivial	Spiral			Transparent transfer
Boolean	$\begin{pmatrix} 0 & 1 \\ 0 & 1 \end{pmatrix}$	–			–
Ternary	$\begin{pmatrix} 0 & 1 & 2 \\ 0 & 1 & 2 \end{pmatrix}$	$\begin{pmatrix} 0 & 1 \\ 0 & 2 \end{pmatrix}$			
Four-output	$\begin{pmatrix} 0 & 1 & 2 & 3 \\ 0 & 1 & 2 & 3 \end{pmatrix}$	$\begin{pmatrix} 0 & 1 & 2 \\ 0 & 1 & 3 \end{pmatrix};$	$\begin{pmatrix} 0 & 1 & 1 \\ 0 & 3 & 2 \end{pmatrix};$	$\begin{pmatrix} 0 & 0 & 0 \\ 1 & 2 & 3 \end{pmatrix}$	$\begin{pmatrix} 0 & 0 & 1 & 1 \\ 2 & 3 & 2 & 3 \end{pmatrix}$

Consider the following adversary $\mathcal{A}$ corrupting A, that aims to "bias" the output of B towards 0. It instructs A to behave honestly until round i. At this point, $\mathcal{A}$ can locally compute the output $z = x \oplus y$. If $z = 0$, then it instructs A to continue honestly until the termination of the protocol. Otherwise, it sends random messages sampled independently and uniformly random.

Observe that the probability the adversary sees $z = 0$ is $1/2$, where the probability is taken over the sampling of the inputs and the correlated randomness. In this case, by the definition of $\mathcal{A}$, the honest party will output 0. On the other hand, if $z = 1$, then as the output of B is not fixed, there is a non-zero probability that both the correlated randomness is (r_1, r_2), and A sends the "correct messages" to B, causing it to output 0. Overall, it follows that the probability that B outputs 0 is *strictly greater* than $1/2$. On the other hand, in the ideal world, the output of B is 0 with probability exactly $1/2$ regardless of the input of corrupted A to the trusted party, since B's input y is chosen uniformly at random.

Impossibility of AND. Before generalizing the impossibility result of [9] let us first explain where their argument fails even for the AND functionality $\text{AND}(x, y) = x \wedge y$. Consider the adversary $\mathcal{A}$ defined previously, that aims to bias the output of B towards 0. Note that if $y = 1$, then a simulator can simulate the attack by sending $x = 0$ with the "correct" probability (i.e., the probability that the correlated randomness and the messages that $\mathcal{A}$ sends cause B to output 0). On the other hand, if $y = 0$, then regardless of what $\mathcal{A}$ does in the real world, B already "knows" that the output is 0, thus $\mathcal{A}$ cannot introduce any bias. A similar argument shows that biasing towards 1 might also be simulatable.

To overcome this issue, instead of just biasing the output of the honest party towards a certain value, we let the adversary also guess uniformly at random the input of the honest party. To see why it works, let us first analyze the probability that $\mathcal{A}$ biases the output of B towards 0 and guesses its input correctly. Let Succ be the event where the adversary succeeds. First, consider the case where $x = 0$. Here, $\mathcal{A}$ will guess y correctly with probability $1/2$, and always cause B to output 0. Therefore, $\Pr[\text{Succ} \mid x = 0] = 1/2$. Next, consider the case where $x = 1$. In this case, $\mathcal{A}$ always learns y from the output. Additionally, if $y = 0$ then B will always output 0. If $y = 1$, then $\mathcal{A}$ will send random messages starting at round i, hence with non-zero probability, B will output 0. Therefore,

$$\begin{aligned}
\Pr[\text{Succ} \mid x = 1] &= \Pr[y = 0] \cdot \Pr[\text{Succ} \mid x = 1 \wedge y = 0] \\
&\quad + \Pr[y = 1] \cdot \Pr[\text{Succ} \mid x = 1 \wedge y = 1] \\
&= \frac{1}{2} + \frac{1}{2} \cdot \Pr[\text{Succ} \mid x = 1 \wedge y = 1] \\
&> \frac{1}{2}.
\end{aligned}$$

Overall, we conclude that the adversary succeeds with probability $\Pr[\text{Succ}] > 1/2$.

To see why no simulator exists for $\mathcal{A}$, observe that if a simulator sends $x = 0$ to the trusted party, then it does not obtain any information on y, and if it sends $x = 1$, then B will output 0 only if $y = 0$, which occurs with probability $1/2$. Overall, the simulator can succeed with probability at most $1/2$, hence no simulator can perfectly simulate $\mathcal{A}$.

Generalizing the Impossibility Result. We now explain how to generalize the above argument to a more general, possibly non-Boolean, class of functionalities. Our argument applies for a class of functionalities that are not captured by Theorem 1. We next describe this set of functionalities, and claim they cannot be computed with perfect security with correlated randomness.

Lemma 1 (Informal). *Let $f : \mathcal{X} \times \mathcal{Y} \mapsto \mathcal{Z}$ be symmetric deterministic two-party functionality. Suppose there exists $\mathcal{X}' \subseteq \mathcal{X}$, $\mathcal{Y}' \subseteq \mathcal{Y}$, and $\mathcal{Z}' \subset \mathcal{Z}$ such that the submatrix $\mathbf{M}'$ of matrix $\mathbf{M}_f$ induced by $\mathcal{X}'$ and $\mathcal{Y}'$ satisfies the following.*

1. $\mathbf{M}'$ contains an element from $\mathcal{Z} \backslash \mathcal{Z}'$.
2. There is a natural $h \geq 1$, such that every row in $\mathbf{M}'$ contains exactly h distinct elements from $\mathcal{Z}'$, and every other row in the matrix $\mathbf{M}_f$ associated with f contains at most h distinct elements from $\mathcal{Z}'$, within the columns of $\mathcal{Y}'$.
3. There is a natural $h' \geq 1$, such that every column in $\mathbf{M}'$ contains exactly h' distinct elements from $\mathcal{Z}'$, and every other column in the matrix $\mathbf{M}_f$ contains at most h' distinct elements from $\mathcal{Z}'$, within the rows of $\mathcal{X}'$.

Then f cannot be computed with perfect security in the correlated randomness model.

The negative direction of Theorem 1 follows from Lemma 1 via a combinatorial argument, showing that if such a submatrix does not exist, then f is either spiral or transparent transfer. The proof is somewhat technical and is therefore omitted from the introduction. We refer the reader to Sect. 5 for the proof.

Let us first describe the attacker. Roughly speaking, the attack follows similar ideas to the attacker for AND, however, instead of biasing towards a specific value, $\mathcal{A}$ will bias the output of the honest party towards the set $\mathcal{Z}' \subset \mathcal{Z}$. In more details, if $\mathcal{A}$ sees that the output z is inside $\mathcal{Z}'$ then it will continue honestly. Otherwise, it will send random messages. Additionally, $\mathcal{A}$ outputs a guess for y that is consistent with the output it saw, i.e., it outputs a uniform y^* conditioned on $f(x, y^*) = z$.

We next show that $\mathcal{A}$ cannot be simulated for $x \leftarrow \mathcal{X}'$ and $y \leftarrow \mathcal{Y}'$. We first analyze the success probability of the adversary in the real world. Let Succ denote the event that $\mathcal{A}$ both guesses y correctly, and causes B to output a value from $\mathcal{Z}'$. We denote by z_B the output of B. First, observe that for any fixed $x \in \mathcal{X}'$ it holds that

$$\Pr[z_\mathsf{B} \in \mathcal{Z}' \wedge y^* = y] = \sum_{z \in \mathcal{Z}'} \Pr[z_\mathsf{B} = z] \cdot \Pr[y^* = y \mid z_\mathsf{B} = z]$$

$$= \sum_{z \in \mathcal{Z}'} \frac{|\{y' \in \mathcal{Y}' : f(x, y') = z\}|}{|\mathcal{Y}'|} \cdot \frac{1}{|\{y' \in \mathcal{Y}' : f(x, y') = z\}|}$$

$$= \frac{h}{|\mathcal{Y}'|},$$

where the last equality follows from Item 2, asserting there are exactly h distinct element from $\mathcal{Z}'$ in the xth row of $\mathbf{M}'$. Therefore

$$\Pr[\mathsf{Succ}] = \frac{h}{|\mathcal{Y}'|} + \Pr[z \notin \mathcal{Z}'] \cdot \Pr[\mathsf{Succ} \mid z \notin \mathcal{Z}']$$

for every fixed $x \in \mathcal{X}'$. Now, since we assume that $\mathbf{M}'$ contains an element outside of $\mathcal{Z}'$, it follows that there exists a choice of x, for which $\Pr[z \notin \mathcal{Z}'] > 0$. Furthermore, since the output of B is not fixed, there is a non-zero chance that the random messages that $\mathcal{A}$ sends to it will cause it to output a value from $\mathcal{Z}'$. Therefore $\Pr[\mathsf{Succ} \mid z \notin \mathcal{Z}'] > 0$. We conclude that $\Pr[\mathsf{Succ}] > h/|\mathcal{Y}'|$.

To show that $\mathcal{A}$ cannot be simulated, we prove that any simulator can both guess y correctly and cause B to output a value from $\mathcal{Z}'$, with probability at most $h/|\mathcal{Y}'|$. We show that this is true for any input x the simulator sends to the trusted party. Indeed, the probability that B outputs a fixed value $z \in \mathcal{Z}'$ is exactly $\frac{|\{y' \in \mathcal{Y}' : f(x,y')=z\}|}{|\mathcal{Y}'|}$. Given this output z, the simulator can guess y with probability $\frac{1}{|\{y' \in \mathcal{Y}' : f(x,y')=z\}|}$. However, among all the appearances of values from $\mathcal{Z}'$, at most h of them are distinct. Thus, the simulator successfully guesses y correctly and force B to output a value from $\mathcal{Z}'$, with probability at most $h/|\mathcal{Y}'|$.

Impossibility of Embedded XOR or Embedded AND. To show the usefulness of Lemma 1, we next show that if f contains an embedded XOR or an embedded AND, then f cannot be computed with perfect security in the correlated randomness model. In fact, we show that if there exists inputs $x_1, x_2 \in \mathcal{X}$ and $y_1, y_2 \in \mathcal{Y}$, and there exists $a \neq b \in \mathcal{Z}$ such that the 2×2 submatrix $\mathbf{M}$ induced by those inputs is of the form $\left(\begin{smallmatrix} a & b \\ b & * \end{smallmatrix}\right)$ or $\left(\begin{smallmatrix} b & a \\ * & b \end{smallmatrix}\right)$, where $*$ is any element from $\mathcal{Z}$, then f cannot be computed with perfect security in the correlated randomness model. We show that the constraints from Lemma 1 hold for $\mathcal{X}' = \{x_1, x_2\}$, $\mathcal{Y}' = \{y_1, y_2\}$, and $\mathcal{Z}' = \{b\}$. Indeed, $\mathbf{M}$ contains the element $a \notin \mathcal{Z}'$, and every row and column in $\mathbf{M}$ contains exactly one (distinct) element from $\mathcal{Z}'$. Finally, any other row or column in the matrix $\mathbf{M}_f$ associated with f, will contain at most one (distinct) element from $\mathcal{Z}'$.

The Positive Direction. We now turn to prove our positive results. Let us start with describing a protocol for (non-constant) spiral functionalities. Recall that f is said to be spiral, if its associated matrix $\mathbf{M}_f$ or its transpose is, up to permuting the rows and columns, of the form $(\mathbf{M}||\mathbf{M}')$ where the entries of $\mathbf{M}$ and $\mathbf{M}'$ are disjoint, $\mathbf{M}$ is constant, and $\mathbf{M}'$ is spiral. Assume without loss of generality that $\mathbf{M}_f$ is of the form $(\mathbf{M}||\mathbf{M}')$. The idea is to let party B (which is associated with the columns) to send to A the output in case the input y belongs to the columns of $\mathbf{M}$. Otherwise, it sends $\perp$ and the parties inductively compute $\mathbf{M}'$. The security of the protocol stems from the fact that the entries of $\mathbf{M}$ and $\mathbf{M}'$ are disjoint. Thus, the output reveals to A whether y belongs to the columns of $\mathbf{M}$.

We next show that any transparent transfer functionality f can be computed with perfect security. We assume without loss of generality that the associated matrix is

$$\mathbf{M}_f = \begin{pmatrix} 0 & 2 \\ 0 & 3 \\ 1 & 2 \\ 1 & 3 \end{pmatrix}.$$

Consider the protocol, where B sends its input y to A, and then A sends $f(x,y)$ back to B. Clearly the protocol is correct and secure against any corrupt B. We argue that the protocol is secure against any adversary $\mathcal{A}$ corrupting A as well. First, as we are concerned with perfect security if there is no simulator for $\mathcal{A}$, then there exists a fixed choice of the randomness of $\mathcal{A}$ for which no simulator exists. Therefore, we may assume without loss of generality that $\mathcal{A}$ is deterministic.

Let $\mathcal{Y} = \{y_1, y_2\}$ be the domain of B. The idea is to let the simulator query $\mathcal{A}$ on both possible inputs y_1 and y_2, rewinding it each time. This provides the simulator with two outputs $z_1 \in \{0, 1\}$ and $z_2 \in \{2, 3\}$. Since $\mathbf{M}_f$ contains all possible rows from $\{0, 1\} \times \{2, 3\}$, the simulator can find an input x^* whose corresponding row is (z_1, z_2). Finally, the simulator sends x^* to the trusted party, and outputs as the view y_1 if the output it received is from $\{0, 1\}$, and outputs y_2 otherwise.

1.3 Additional Related Work

In the semi-honest setting, [2] showed that AND is impossible to compute with statistical security, let alone perfect security in the dishonest-majority setting. The work of [6] characterizes the Boolean functionalities that can be computed with dishonest majority.

One of the commonly-known correlated randomness is that of oblivious transfer (OT) which is a pair-wise correlation. In this, the first party gets a pair of inputs (x_0, x_1) and the second party gets (b, x_b). Brassard et al. [3] showed that given sufficiently many invocations of the above OT correlation, the 1-out-of-n string OT functionality can be computed with perfect security against malicious adversaries. Wolf and Wullschleger [11] showed how to compute 1-out-of-2 bit TO perfectly, which is the same as OT where the roles of the parties are reversed. Finally, [1] showed that given access to sufficiently many parallel ideal computations of OT, most sender-receiver functionalities, where the sender's domain size is strictly larger than the receiver's domain size, can be computed with perfect security.

1.4 Organization

The preliminaries and definition of the model of computation appear in Sect. 2. The statements of our main results are provided in Sect. 3. The negative direction is proved in Sects. 4 and 5. Specifically, in Sect. 4 we prove the more general impossibility result, and in Sect. 5 we deduce the result for four-output functionalities. Finally, we prove the positive direction in Sect. 6.

2 Preliminaries

2.1 Notations

For $n \in \mathbb{N}$ we let $[n] = \{1, 2 \ldots n\}$. For a set $\mathcal{S}$ we write $s \leftarrow \mathcal{S}$ to indicate that s is selected uniformly at random from $\mathcal{S}$. Given a random variable (or a distribution) X, we write $x \leftarrow X$ to indicate that x is selected according to X.

Given a matrix $\mathbf{M}$ whose rows and columns are indexed by $\mathcal{X}$ and $\mathcal{Y}$, respectively, we let $\mathbf{M}(x, \cdot) = (\mathbf{M}(x, y))_{y \in \mathcal{Y}}$ be the xth row, where $x \in \mathcal{X}$. Similarly, we let $\mathbf{M}(\cdot, y) = (\mathbf{M}(x, y))_{x \in \mathcal{X}}$ be the yth column, where $y \in \mathcal{Y}$. We call a matrix $\mathbf{M}$ *constant-row* if for all $x \in \mathcal{X}$ it holds that $\mathbf{M}(x, \cdot)$ is a constant vector. Similarly, we call $\mathbf{M}$ *constant-column* if $\mathbf{M}(\cdot, y)$ is constant for all $y \in \mathcal{Y}$. Given two matrices $\mathbf{M}_1$ and $\mathbf{M}_2$ with the same number of rows, we let $(\mathbf{M}_1\|\mathbf{M}_2)$ denote the matrix obtained from concatenating $\mathbf{M}_1$ and $\mathbf{M}_2$.

The following notion captures when two matrices are the same up to permuting the rows and columns, and transposing either of the matrices.

Definition 3. *Let $\mathbf{M}_1 \in \mathcal{Z}^{n_1 \times m_1}$ and $\mathbf{M}_2 \in \mathcal{Z}^{n_2 \times m_2}$ be two matrices. We say that $\mathbf{M}_1 \sim \mathbf{M}_2$ if one of the following holds.*

- $n_1 = n_2$, $m_1 = m_2$, *and there exists a permutation π over the rows of $\mathbf{M}_1$ and a permutation σ over the columns of $\mathbf{M}_1$, such that*

$$\mathbf{M}_1(\pi(x), \sigma(y)) = \mathbf{M}_2(x, y)$$

  for all x and y.
- $n_1 = m_2$, $m_1 = n_2$, *and there exists a permutation π over the rows of $\mathbf{M}_1$ and a permutation σ of $\mathbf{M}_1$ over the columns, such that*

$$\mathbf{M}_1(\pi(x), \sigma(y)) = \mathbf{M}_2^T(y, x)$$

  for all x and y.

We next define the reduced form of matrix, which removes all duplicated rows and columns.

Definition 4 (Reduced form of a matrix). *For a matrix $\mathbf{M}$, its reduced form, denoted $\mathrm{red}(\mathbf{M})$, is the matrix obtained by repeatedly removing all duplicated rows and columns from $\mathbf{M}$ (note that this is well-defined).*

The next definition associates a matrix with any 2-ary function f.

Definition 5 (The matrix associated with a function). *Let $f : \mathcal{X} \times \mathcal{Y} \mapsto \mathcal{Z}$ be a 2-ary function. The matrix associated with f, denoted $\mathbf{M}_f \in \mathcal{Z}^{|\mathcal{X}| \times |\mathcal{Y}|}$, is defined as $\mathbf{M}_f(x, y) = f(x, y)$ for all $x \in \mathcal{X}$ and $y \in \mathcal{Y}$.*

We next define a combinatorial rectangle.

Definition 6 (Combinatorial rectangles). *Given two sets $\mathcal{X}$ and $\mathcal{Y}$, a combinatorial rectangle (in short, a rectangle) over $\mathcal{X} \times \mathcal{Y}$, is a subset $\mathbf{R} = \mathcal{X}_\mathbf{R} \times \mathcal{Y}_\mathbf{R}$, where $\mathcal{X}_\mathbf{R} \subseteq \mathcal{X}$ and $\mathcal{Y}_\mathbf{R} \subseteq \mathcal{Y}$.*

Given a matrix and combinatorial rectangle over its rows and columns, we can define the submatrix induced by the rectangle.

Definition 7 (The submatrix induced by a rectangle). *Let $\mathcal{X}$, $\mathcal{Y}$, and $\mathcal{Z}$ be three sets, and let $\mathbf{M} \in \mathcal{Z}^{|\mathcal{X}| \times |\mathcal{Y}|}$ be a matrix, whose rows and columns are indexed with elements from $\mathcal{X}$ and $\mathcal{Y}$, respectively. For a combinatorial rectangle $\mathbf{R} = \mathcal{X}_\mathbf{R} \times \mathcal{Y}_\mathbf{R}$ over $\mathcal{X} \times \mathcal{Y}$, we denote by $\mathbf{M}^\mathbf{R} \in \mathcal{Z}^{|\mathcal{X}_\mathbf{R}| \times |\mathcal{Y}_\mathbf{R}|}$ the submatrix of $\mathbf{M}$ induced by $\mathbf{R}$, i.e., $\mathbf{M}^\mathbf{R}(x, y) = \mathbf{M}(x, y)$ for all $x \in \mathcal{X}_\mathbf{R}$ and $y \in \mathcal{Y}_\mathbf{R}$.*

2.2 Security Model

We provide the basic definitions for secure multiparty computation according to the real/ideal paradigm, for further details see [8]. Intuitively, a protocol is considered secure if whatever an adversary can do in the real execution of the protocol, can be done also in an ideal computation, in which an uncorrupted trusted party assists the computation. For concreteness, we present the model and the security definition of perfect two-party computation with an adversary corrupting a single party, as this is the main focus of this work. We refer to [8] for the general definition.

In this paper we focus on deterministic symmetric two-party functionalities $f : \mathcal{X} \times \mathcal{Y} \mapsto \mathcal{Z}$, i.e., both parties receive the same output.[3]

The Real Model

A two-party protocol Π is defined by a set of two interactive Turing machines A and B. Each Turing machine (party) holds at the beginning of the execution a private input, and random coins. The *adversary* $\mathcal{A}$ is an interactive Turing machine describing the behavior of a corrupted party $\mathsf{P} \in \{\mathsf{A}, \mathsf{B}\}$. It starts the execution with input that contains the identity of the corrupted party and its input. We assume the protocol proceeds in round, where every odd round party A sends a message, and every even round party B sends a message.

Throughout the execution of the protocol, all the honest parties follow the instructions of the prescribed protocol, whereas the corrupted party receive its instructions from the adversary. The adversary is considered to be *malicious*, meaning that it can instruct the corrupted party to deviate from the protocol in any arbitrary way. Additionally, the adversary has full-access to the view of the corrupted party, which consists of its input, its random coins, and the messages it sees throughout this execution. At the conclusion of the execution, the honest parties output their prescribed output from the protocol, the corrupted party outputs nothing, and the adversary outputs a function of its view (containing the views of the corrupted party).

We denote by $\text{REAL}_{\Pi, \mathcal{A}}(x, y)$ the joint output of the adversary $\mathcal{A}$ (that may corrupt one of the parties) and of the honest parties in a random execution of Π, on input $x \in \mathcal{X}$ for A and input $y \in \mathcal{Y}$ for B.

Remark 1 (On the absence of a security parameter). Typically, the parties are also given a security parameter 1^κ, which is also used to bound the computational complexity of the parties. However, we are concerned with perfect security and functionalities of constant domain, thus having a security parameter is redundant.

---

[3] The typical convention in secure computation is to let $f : \{0, 1\}^* \times \{0, 1\}^* \mapsto \{0, 1\}^*$. However, we consider only functionalities with a constant domain, which is why we introduce this notation.

Additionally, the adversary is usually said to be non-uniform, and holds an auxiliary input. However, as there is no security parameter in our setting, the auxiliary input does not provide $\mathcal{A}$ any additional power.

The Correlated Randomness Hybrid Model. For some of our result, we consider an augmentation of the real world where the parties are provided with a trusted setup for generating correlated randomness. Formally, we let CR denote the randomized functionality that receives no input, and outputs random values r_1 and r_2 to A and B, respectively. Here, $(r_1, r_2) \leftarrow D$ where D is a fixed distribution known in advance. At the start of the protocol (before the parties receive their inputs), the parties call the functionality CR exactly once to obtain r_1 and r_2. The parties then continue in a real execution as described previously. We call this model the CR-hybrid world.

We denote by $\text{REAL}_{\Pi,\mathcal{A}}^{\text{CR}}(x, y)$ the joint output of the adversary $\mathcal{A}$ (that may corrupt one of the parties) and of the honest parties in a random execution of Π in the CR-hybrid world, on input $x \in \mathcal{X}$ for A and input $y \in \mathcal{Y}$ for B.

The Ideal Model

We consider an ideal computation with *guaranteed output delivery* (also referred to as *full security*), where a trusted party performs the computation on behalf of the parties, and the ideal-world adversary *cannot* abort the computation. An ideal computation of a deterministic symmetric two-party functionality $f : \mathcal{X} \times \mathcal{Y} \to \mathcal{Z}$, on inputs $x \in \mathcal{X}$ and $y \in \mathcal{Y}$, with an ideal-world adversary $\mathcal{A}$ corrupting a single party $\mathsf{P} \in \{\mathsf{A}, \mathsf{B}\}$ proceeds as follows:

Parties send inputs to the trusted party: Each honest party sends its input to the trusted party. The adversary $\mathcal{A}$ sends a value w from the corrupted party's domain as the input for the corrupted party. Let (x', y') denote the inputs received by the trusted party.

The trusted party performs computation: The trusted party computes $z = f(x', y')$ and sends z to both A and B.

Outputs: Each honest party outputs whatever output it received from the trusted party, and the corrupted party outputs nothing. The adversary $\mathcal{A}$ outputs some function of its view (i.e., the input and output of the corrupted party).

We denote by $\text{IDEAL}_{f,\mathcal{A}}(x, y)$ the joint output of the adversary $\mathcal{A}$ (that may corrupt one of the parties) and the honest parties in a random execution of the ideal-world computation of f on input x for A and input y for B.

The Security Definition

Having defined the real and ideal models, we can now define security of protocols according to the real/ideal paradigm.

Definition 8 (Security). *Let $f : \mathcal{X} \times \mathcal{Y} \to \mathcal{Z}$ be a deterministic symmetric two-party functionality, and let Π be a two-party protocol. We say that Π computes f with perfect security, if for every adversary $\mathcal{A}$, controlling at most one party in the real world, there exists an adversary Sim, controlling the same party (if there is any) in the ideal world such that for every $x \in \mathcal{X}$ and every $y \in \mathcal{Y}$ it holds that*

$$\text{IDEAL}_{f,\text{Sim}}(x, y) \equiv \text{REAL}_{\Pi,\mathcal{A}}(x, y).$$

To remove possible confusion, we will explicitly write that Π computes f with perfect security in the plain model.

We say that Π computes f with perfect security in the CR-hybrid model if

$$\text{IDEAL}_{f,\text{Sim}}(x, y) \equiv \text{REAL}_{\Pi,\mathcal{A}}^{\text{CR}}(x, y)$$

for all $x \in \mathcal{X}$ and $y \in \mathcal{Y}$.

The Hybrid Model

The *hybrid model* is a model that extends the real model with a trusted party that provides ideal computation for specific functionalities. The parties communicate with this trusted party in exactly the same way as in the ideal model described above.

Let f be a functionality. Then, an execution of a protocol Π computing a functionality g in the f-hybrid model involves the parties sending normal messages to each other (as in the real model) and, in addition, having access to a trusted party computing f. It is essential that the invocations of f are done sequentially, meaning that before an invocation of f begins, the preceding invocation of f must finish. In particular, there is at most a single call to f per round, and no other messages are sent during any round in which f is called. Note that the CR-hybrid is a special case, where the parties call CR once at the onset of the protocol.

Let $\mathcal{A}$ be an adversary controlling a single party $\mathsf{P} \in \{\mathsf{A}, \mathsf{B}\}$. We denote by $\text{HYBRID}_{\Pi,\mathcal{A}}^{f}(x, y)$ the random variable consisting of the output of the adversary and the output of the honest parties, following an execution of Π with ideal calls to a trusted party computing f, on input x given to A and input y given to B.

Similarly to Definition 8, we say that Π computes g with perfect security in the f-hybrid model if for any adversary $\mathcal{A}$ there exists a simulator Sim such that $\text{HYBRID}_{\pi,\mathcal{A}}^{f}(x, y)$ and $\text{IDEAL}_{g,\text{Sim}}(x, y)$ are identically distributed.

The sequential composition theorem of Canetti [4] states the following. Let ρ be a protocol that computes f with perfect security. Then, if a protocol Π computes g in the f-hybrid model, then the protocol Π^{ρ}, that is obtained from Π by replacing all ideal calls to the trusted party computing f with the protocol ρ, computes g in the real model with perfect security.

Theorem 2 ([4]). *Let f be a two-party functionality, let ρ be a protocol that computes f with perfect security, and let Π be a protocol that computes g with perfect security in the f-hybrid model. Then, protocol Π^{ρ} computes g with perfect security in the real model.*

3 Analyzing Symmetric Functionalities

In this section, we state our results. Our main results is a characterization of the symmetric deterministic two-party functionalities with four-outputs that can be computed with perfect security. Furthermore, the impossibility result can be extended to functionalities with more than four outputs. Interestingly, although the impossibility result holds in the CR-hybrid world, for any choice of CR, the positive results are stated in the *plain model*, where the parties do not receive correlated randomness.

Before stating our results, we first describe three families of symmetric deterministic two-party functionalities. We then assert that among the four-output functionalities, these are the *only* ones that can be computed with perfect security in the CR-hybrid world.

We first define trivial functionalities, for which the output depends on only one of the inputs.

Definition 9 (Trivial functionalities). *Let $f : \mathcal{X} \times \mathcal{Y} \mapsto \mathcal{Z}$ be a deterministic symmetric two-party functionality. We say that f is* trivial *if it is independent of one of its inputs, i.e., either $f(x, y) = g(x)$ or $f(x, y) = g(y)$ for some function g.*

Note that for the matrix $\mathbf{M}_f$ of a trivial functionality f, either all rows are constant or all columns are constant.

We next define the family of spiral functionalities, which is an extension of the family of trivial functionalities. The definition is recursive. Roughly, a functionality f is spiral, if it's trivial or if by removing constant columns or constant rows (containing a single value α) from the associated matrix $\mathbf{M}_f$, results in a matrix associated with a spiral functionality, and contains no α values.

Definition 10 (The spiral functionality and matrix). *We call a matrix $\mathbf{M}$ a spiral matrix if one of the following holds.*

- $\mathbf{M}$ *is a constant matrix.*
- *There exist a constant-column matrix $\mathbf{M}_1 \in \mathcal{Z}_1^{n_1 \times m_1}$, and there a spiral matrix $\mathbf{M}_2 \in \mathcal{Z}_2^{n_2 \times m_2}$, where $\mathcal{Z}_1 \cap \mathcal{Z}_2 = \emptyset$, such that $\mathbf{M} \sim (\mathbf{M}_1 \| \mathbf{M}_2)$, i.e., equality holds up to permutation of the rows and columns and transposing the matrix.*

We call a deterministic symmetric two-party functionality f a spiral functionality, if its associated matrix $\mathbf{M}_f$ is a spiral matrix.

Definition 11. *Let $f : \mathcal{X} \times \mathcal{Y} \mapsto \{0, 1, 2, 3\}$ be a deterministic symmetric two-party functionality. We call it a transparent transfer if the reduced form of its associated matrix satisfies*

$$\operatorname{red}(\mathbf{M}_f) \sim \begin{pmatrix} a & c \\ a & d \\ b & c \\ b & d \end{pmatrix}$$

where $\{a, b, c, d\} = \{0, 1, 2, 3\}$.

Remark 2 (On the naming of the function). Let us provide the reasoning behind the naming of transparent transfer functions. Consider the symmetric functionality $f' : \{0,1\}^2 \times \{0,1\} \mapsto \{0,1\}^2$ defined as $f'((x_0, x_1), i) = (x_i, i)$. Observe that, up to the encoding of the output, it is the same as the transparent transfer functionality defined in Definition 11. Indeed, mapping the output $(x_i, i) \mapsto x_i + 2i$ results in a matrix of the form

$$\begin{pmatrix} 0 & 2 \\ 0 & 3 \\ 1 & 2 \\ 1 & 3 \end{pmatrix}.$$

Since the mapping is bijective, we conclude the functions to be the equivalent.

3.1 Characterization of Four-Output Functionalities

We are now ready to state our main result, providing a characterization of the symmetric deterministic four-output two-party functionalities that can be computed with perfect security in the CR-hybrid model.

Theorem 3 (Characterization of four-output functionalities). *Let $f :$ $\mathcal{X} \times \mathcal{Y} \mapsto \{0,1,2,3\}$ be a deterministic symmetric two-party four-output functionality. Then, f can be computed with perfect security in the CR-hybrid model if and only if it is either a spiral function or a transparent transfer function.*

The proof of Theorem 3 follows from the combination of the following two lemmas. For the negative direction, we prove the following.

Lemma 2 (Lower bound for four-output functionalities). *Let $f : \mathcal{X} \times \mathcal{Y} \mapsto \{0,1,2,3\}$ be a deterministic symmetric two-party four-output functionality. Assume that f can be computed with perfect security in the CR-hybrid model. Then, f is either a spiral function or a transparent transfer function.*

Lemma 2 is proved in Sect. 5. Towards proving it, in Sect. 4, we prove a more general impossibility result, Lemma 4, which holds for functionalities that are not necessarily four-output. When restricting the discussion to four-output functionalities, our general impossibility result yields the lower bound for four-output functionalities, see Sect. 5 for the full details.

For the positive direction of Theorem 3, we prove the following lemma stating that every spiral functionality, and that the transparent transfer functionality can be computed with perfect security. Furthermore, this can be done using deterministic protocols in the plain model, and it holds regardless of the number of outputs.

Lemma 3 (Upper bound for four-output functionalities). *Let $f : \mathcal{X} \times \mathcal{Y} \mapsto \mathcal{Z}$ be a deterministic symmetric two-party functionality. If f is a spiral or a transparent transfer functionality, then f can be computed with perfect security in the plain model.*

Lemma 3 is proved in Sect. 6.

3.2   Characterization of Boolean and Ternary-Output Functionalities

When restricting the discussion to functions with range of size two and of size three, Theorem 3 yields more refined characterizations. First, note that Definition 11 requires at least four distinct output values. It hence follows that a ternary-output functionality can be computed with perfect security if and only if the functionality is a spiral.

Corollary 3 (Characterization of ternary-output functionalities). *Let* $f : \mathcal{X} \times \mathcal{Y} \mapsto \{0, 1, 2\}$ *be a deterministic symmetric two-party ternary functionality. Then* f *can be computed with perfect security in the* CR-*hybrid model if and only if it is spiral.*

Second, observe that any spiral Boolean functionality must be trivial. Thus, we obtain the following characterization for Boolean functionalities.

Corollary 4 (Characterization of Boolean functionalities). *Let* $f : \mathcal{X} \times \mathcal{Y} \mapsto \{0, 1\}$ *be a deterministic symmetric two-party Boolean functionality. Then,* f *can be computed with perfect security in the* CR-*hybrid model if and only if it is trivial.*

3.3   Impossibility of Embedded XOR and Embedded AND

In this section we show that any functionality that contains an embedded XOR or an embedded AND cannot be computed with perfect security in the CR-hybrid model. Recall that a functionality f is said to have an embedded XOR, if there exists $x_1, x_2 \in \mathcal{X}$ and $y_1, y_2 \in \mathcal{Y}$ such that $f(x_1, y_1) = f(x_2, y_2) \neq f(x_1, y_2) = f(x_2, y_1)$. The functionality is said to have an embedded AND if $f(x_2, y_2) \neq f(x_1, y_1) = f(x_1, y_2) = f(x_2, y_1)$. In fact, we are able to prove a stronger result. To formalize this, we first define the notion of a forbidden submatrix.

Definition 12 (Forbidden 2×2 submatrices and rectangles). *Let* $\mathbf{M}$ *be a matrix with entries from some set* $\mathcal{Z}$*. We call a* 2×2 *rectangle* $\mathbf{R}$ *forbidden if its induced submatrix* $\mathbf{M}^{\mathbf{R}}$ *satisfies*

$$\mathbf{M}^{\mathbf{R}} \sim \begin{pmatrix} a & b \\ b & * \end{pmatrix} \tag{2}$$

where a *and* b *denote distinct elements of* $\mathcal{Z}$*, and* $*$ *denotes an arbitrary element of* $\mathcal{Z}$*. We also say that* $\mathbf{M}$ *is forbidden if it contains a forbidden combinatorial rectangle.*

Theorem 4. *Let* $f : \mathcal{X} \times \mathcal{Y} \mapsto \mathcal{Z}$ *be a deterministic symmetric two-party functionality. Assume there exists a* 2×2 *rectangle* $\mathbf{R}$ *such that its corresponding induced submatrix is forbidden. Then* f *cannot be computed with perfect security in the* CR-*hybrid model.*

The proof is given in Sect. 5 and is derived from the general impossibility result proven in Sect. 4. We get the following corollary.

Corollary 5. *Let $f : \mathcal{X} \times \mathcal{Y} \mapsto \mathcal{Z}$ be a deterministic symmetric two-party functionality. Assume that $\mathbf{M}_f$ contains an embedded* XOR *or an embedded* AND. *Then f cannot be computed with perfect security in the* CR*-hybrid model.*

4   A General Impossibility Result for Perfect Security

In this section, we prove a general impossibility result for perfectly secure two-party protocols for a large class of functionalities. Roughly speaking, we identify several properties that cannot coincide for any sub-matrix, and show that if the matrix associated with the functionality f contains a sub-matrix that has all these properties, then f cannot be computed with perfect security in the CR-hybrid model.

Lemma 4. *Let $f : \mathcal{X} \times \mathcal{Y} \mapsto \mathcal{Z}$ be a deterministic symmetric two-party functionality. Assume there exists a combinatorial rectangle $\mathbf{R} = \mathcal{X}_\mathbf{R} \times \mathcal{Y}_\mathbf{R}$, where $\mathcal{X}_\mathbf{R} \subseteq \mathcal{X}$ and where $\mathcal{Y}_\mathbf{R} \subseteq \mathcal{Y}$, and assume there exists a strict subset of the outputs $\mathcal{Z}_\mathbf{R} \subset \mathcal{Z}$ such that the following hold.*

1. *At least one entry of $\mathbf{M}_f^\mathbf{R}$ (recall that $\mathbf{M}_f^\mathbf{R}$ is the sub-matrix induced by $\mathbf{R}$) contains an element from $\mathcal{Z} \backslash \mathcal{Z}_\mathbf{R}$.*
2. *There exists $h \in \mathbb{N}^+$ such that for all $x \in \mathcal{X}_\mathbf{R}$ it holds that*

$$\left| \{ \mathbf{M}_f^\mathbf{R}(x, y) : y \in \mathcal{Y}_\mathbf{R} \} \cap \mathcal{Z}_\mathbf{R} \right| = h.$$

In other words, every row in $\mathbf{M}_f^\mathbf{R}$ contains exactly h distinct elements from $\mathcal{Z}_\mathbf{R}$.
Additionally, for all $x \in \mathcal{X} \backslash \mathcal{X}_\mathbf{R}$ it holds that

$$\left| \{ \mathbf{M}_f(x, y) : y \in \mathcal{Y}_\mathbf{R} \} \cap \mathcal{Z}_\mathbf{R} \right| \leq h,$$

namely, every row $x \notin \mathcal{X}_\mathbf{R}$ of $\mathbf{M}_f$ contains at most h elements from $\mathcal{Z}_\mathbf{R}$, within the columns of $\mathcal{Y}_\mathbf{R}$.
3. *There exists $h' \in \mathbb{N}^+$ such that for all $y \in \mathcal{Y}_\mathbf{R}$ it holds*

$$\left| \{ \mathbf{M}_f^\mathbf{R}(x, y) : x \in \mathcal{X}_\mathbf{R} \} \cap \mathcal{Z}_\mathbf{R} \right| = h'.$$

Additionally, for all $y \in \mathcal{Y} \backslash \mathcal{Y}_\mathbf{R}$ it holds that

$$\left| \{ \mathbf{M}_f(x, y) : x \in \mathcal{X}_\mathbf{R} \} \cap \mathcal{Z}_\mathbf{R} \right| \leq h'.$$

Then f cannot be computed in CR*-hybrid model with perfect security.*

Example 1. To illustrate the requirements of Lemma 4, consider the ternary-output functionality f whose associated matrix is defined as

$$\mathbf{M}_f = \begin{pmatrix} 0\,1\,2\,2 \\ 2\,1\,0\,2 \\ 0\,1\,2\,1 \end{pmatrix}.$$

For $\mathbf{R} = \{x_1, x_2\} \times \{y_1, y_2, y_3\}$, $\mathcal{Z}_\mathbf{R} = \{0, 1\}$ the condition is satisfied with $h = 2, h' = 1$. Thus, the precondition of Lemma 4 is satisfied, hence f cannot be computed with perfect security in the CR-hybrid model. It also, for example, satisfies the precondition with $\mathbf{R} = \{x_1, x_2\} \times \{y_1, y_3\}$, $\mathcal{Z}_\mathbf{R} = \{0\}$, and $h = h' = 1$ (indeed, there is no uniqueness requirement on $\mathbf{R}$).

Before formally proving Lemma 4, let us provide some intuition. First, similarly to the impossibility of XOR due to Ishai et al. [9], we use the fact that any protocol for computing f has a first round i in which (in any honest execution of the protocol) one of the parties, say A, "fully knows" the output, while the other does not. That is, any continuation from round i would result in A outputting the correct output. Conversely, there exists a continuation (and a choice of correlated randomness) forcing B to output a different value.

Recall that the attack of [9] used the existence of such a round to present an attacker that "biases" the output of the honest party. We extend this attack strategy to one, where the adversary, corrupting A, tries to both bias the output of the honest B towards the subset of outputs $\mathcal{Z}_\mathbf{R}$, and at the same time, guess the input of the honest party. Additionally, we are more lenient with the knowledge of the adversary, requiring it only to "wait" until it knows whether the output is in $\mathcal{Z}_\mathbf{R}$ or not. We show that if the inputs of the parties are chosen independently and uniformly at random from the rectangle $\mathbf{R}$, then the attacker can both guess the input of the honest party correctly, and force it to output a value from $\mathcal{Z}_\mathbf{R}$, with probability higher than what any simulator can do in the ideal world. We now provide the formal argument.

Proof (of Lemma 4). Assume towards contradiction that there exists a protocol Π in the CR-hybrid model computing f with perfect security. Consider an honest execution of Π, where the inputs of A and B are $\tilde{x} \leftarrow \mathcal{X}_\mathbf{R}$ and $\tilde{y} \leftarrow \mathcal{Y}_\mathbf{R}$, respectively, and are sampled independently. The next claim asserts the existence of a round, in which one of the parties always "knows" if the output is in $\mathcal{Z}_\mathbf{R}$ or not, regardless of the choice of the correlated randomness, while the other party does not necessarily "know" this.

Claim 5. *There exists a round $i > 0$, and a party $\mathsf{P} \in \{\mathsf{A}, \mathsf{B}\}$, such that the following hold.*

1. *For all inputs $x \in \mathcal{X}_\mathbf{R}$ and $y \in \mathcal{Y}_\mathbf{R}$, and for every possible correlated randomness $(r_1, r_2) \in \mathrm{Supp}(D)$, there exists a set $\mathcal{Z}' \in \{\mathcal{Z}_\mathbf{R}, \mathcal{Z} \setminus \mathcal{Z}_\mathbf{R}\}$, such that the following holds. In any execution of Π, where up to (and including) round i, party A acts honestly (according to x, r_1) and party B acts honestly (according to y, r_2), the output of an honest P must be a value from $\mathcal{Z}'$, regardless of the messages it receives in the following rounds (i.e., regardless of the behavior of the other party).*

2. *There exist inputs* $x \in \mathcal{X}_\mathbf{R}$ *and* $y \in \mathcal{Y}_\mathbf{R}$, *with* $f(x, y) \in \mathcal{Z} \backslash \mathcal{Z}_\mathbf{R}$, *and there exists correlated randomness* $(r_1, r_2) \in \mathrm{Supp}(D)$, *such that the following holds. Consider an execution of* Π, *where up to (and including) round* i, *party* A *acts honestly (according to* x, r_1) *and party* B *acts honestly (according to* y, r_2). *Then, there exists a continuation of* Π, *in which the remaining party* $\mathsf{P}' \neq \mathsf{P}$ *continues to behave honestly, such that, the output of* P' *is a value from* $\mathcal{Z}_\mathbf{R}$. *Specifically, there exists a sequence of messages that* P *can send in the following rounds to cause this effect.*

The proof of the claim is given below. We first use it to conclude the proof of Lemma 4. We fix the round i as given by Claim 5, and assume without loss of generality that $\mathsf{P} = \mathsf{A}$. The case where $\mathsf{P} = \mathsf{B}$ is handled analogously. We next construct an attacker corrupting A and show that it cannot be simulated in the ideal world.

Define the adversary $\mathcal{A}$ that corrupts A as follows.

1. Given the input $\tilde{x}$ of party A and the randomness r_1 it obtains from CR, the adversary $\mathcal{A}$ emulates A honestly up to and including round i.
2. Consider the lexicographically first honest continuation of the protocol, and let z' denote the resulting output of A in such an execution.
3. If $z' \in \mathcal{Z}_\mathbf{R}$, then $\mathcal{A}$ continues to emulate A honestly until the termination of the protocol.
4. Otherwise, if $z' \notin \mathcal{Z}_\mathbf{R}$, then in the remaining rounds $\mathcal{A}$ sends (on behalf of A) random messages chosen independently and uniformly at random.
5. The adversary outputs a guess for the input of B (one that is consistent with the output). That is, $\mathcal{A}$ samples

$$y^* \leftarrow \{y \in \mathcal{Y}_\mathbf{R} : f(\tilde{x}, y) = z'\},$$

and outputs y^*.

We next prove that $\mathcal{A}$ cannot be simulated, and hence the protocol is not secure. It follows that f cannot be realized with perfect security. We analyze the probability that $\mathcal{A}$ successfully, both guesses the input $\tilde{y}$ of B, and causes B to output a value from $\mathcal{Z}_\mathbf{R}$. We then compare this to an arbitrary simulator in the ideal world, showing that no simulator can do the same with exactly the same probability. Formally, we prove the following two claims. In the following, let $\mathsf{Succ}_{\mathrm{REAL}}$ denote the event in the real-world that the output of the adversary is $y^* = \tilde{y}$ and B outputs an element from $\mathcal{Z}_\mathbf{R}$. Similarly, let $\mathsf{Succ}_{\mathrm{IDEAL}}$ denote the event in the ideal-world that the output of the simulator implies $y^* = \tilde{y}$ and B outputs an element from $\mathcal{Z}_\mathbf{R}$.

The proof (of Lemma 4) is concluded from the following two Claims (6 and 7) that show that $\Pr[\mathsf{Succ}_{\mathrm{REAL}}] > \Pr[\mathsf{Succ}_{\mathrm{IDEAL}}]$, and hence, that $\mathcal{A}$ cannot be simulated for random $(\tilde{x}, \tilde{y}) \leftarrow \mathbf{R}$. Thus, there exists inputs $x \in \mathcal{X}_\mathbf{R}$ and $y \in \mathcal{Y}_\mathbf{R}$ for which $\mathcal{A}$ cannot be simulated. Therefore, f cannot be computed with perfect security in the CR-hybrid model.

We introduce some notations that will be useful for the following two claims. For every $x \in \mathcal{X}$ and for every $z \in \mathcal{Z}_{\mathbf{R}}$ let

$$w_x(z) := |\{y \in \mathcal{Y}_{\mathbf{R}} : f(x,y) = z\}|$$

denote the number of appearances of z in the xth row of $\mathbf{M}_f$ and the columns corresponding to $\mathcal{Y}_{\mathbf{R}}$. Finally, let

$$W_x := \sum_{z \in \mathcal{Z}_{\mathbf{R}}} w_x(z) = |\{y \in \mathcal{Y}_{\mathbf{R}} : f(x,y) \in \mathcal{Z}_{\mathbf{R}}\}|$$

denote the number of entries from $\mathcal{Z}_{\mathbf{R}}$ in the xth row of $\mathbf{M}_f$ and the columns corresponding to $\mathcal{Y}_{\mathbf{R}}$.

Claim 6. *In the real world, it holds that*

$$\Pr\left[\mathsf{Succ}_{\mathrm{REAL}}\right] > \frac{h}{|\mathcal{Y}_{\mathbf{R}}|}.$$

Proof. We next analyze the probability that $\mathsf{Succ}_{\mathrm{REAL}}$ occurs in the real world. Recall that $\tilde{x}$ denotes the input given to A, that z' denotes the prescribed output before the attack, and that y^* is the adversary's guess for the input $\tilde{y}$ held by B. Observe that

$$\Pr[\mathsf{Succ}_{\mathrm{REAL}}] = \sum_{x \in \mathcal{X}_{\mathbf{R}}} \Pr\left[\tilde{x} = x\right] \cdot \Pr\left[\mathsf{Succ}_{\mathrm{REAL}} \mid \tilde{x} = x\right]$$

$$= \sum_{x \in \mathcal{X}_{\mathbf{R}}} \Pr\left[\tilde{x} = x\right] \cdot \Pr\left[z' \in \mathcal{Z}_{\mathbf{R}} \mid \tilde{x} = x\right] \cdot \Pr\left[\mathsf{Succ}_{\mathrm{REAL}} \mid z' \in \mathcal{Z}_{\mathbf{R}} \wedge \tilde{x} = x\right]$$

$$+ \sum_{\substack{x \in \mathcal{X}_{\mathbf{R}}: \\ W_x < |\mathcal{Y}_{\mathbf{R}}|}} \Pr\left[\tilde{x} = x\right] \cdot \Pr\left[z' \notin \mathcal{Z}_{\mathbf{R}} \mid \tilde{x} = x\right] \cdot \Pr\left[\mathsf{Succ}_{\mathrm{REAL}} \mid z' \notin \mathcal{Z}_{\mathbf{R}} \wedge \tilde{x} = x\right]$$

$$= \frac{1}{|\mathcal{X}_{\mathbf{R}}|} \cdot \sum_{x \in \mathcal{X}_{\mathbf{R}}} \Pr\left[z' \in \mathcal{Z}_{\mathbf{R}} \mid \tilde{x} = x\right] \cdot \Pr\left[y^* = y \mid z' \in \mathcal{Z}_{\mathbf{R}} \wedge \tilde{x} = x\right]$$

$$+ \frac{1}{|\mathcal{X}_{\mathbf{R}}|} \cdot \sum_{\substack{x \in \mathcal{X}_{\mathbf{R}}: \\ W_x < |\mathcal{Y}_{\mathbf{R}}|}} \Pr\left[z' \notin \mathcal{Z}_{\mathbf{R}} \mid \tilde{x} = x\right] \cdot \Pr\left[\mathsf{Succ}_{\mathrm{REAL}} \mid z' \notin \mathcal{Z}_{\mathbf{R}} \wedge \tilde{x} = x\right], \quad (3)$$

where the probabilities are taken over the sampling of the inputs $\tilde{x}$ and $\tilde{y}$, the sampling of the correlated randomness, and the sampling of y^*. The second equality follows from fact that if $W_x < |\mathcal{Y}_{\mathbf{R}}|$, then there exists $y \in \mathcal{Y}_{\mathbf{R}}$ such that $f(x,y) \notin \mathcal{Z}_{\mathbf{R}}$. We now analyze each term in the summation. Observe that for every $x \in \mathcal{X}_{\mathbf{R}}$ it holds that

$$\Pr\left[z' \in \mathcal{Z}_{\mathbf{R}} \mid \tilde{x} = x\right] = \Pr\left[f(\tilde{x},\tilde{y}) \in \mathcal{Z}_{\mathbf{R}} \mid \tilde{x} = x\right] = \frac{W_x}{|\mathcal{Y}_{\mathbf{R}}|}.$$

Additionally, for every $x \in \mathcal{X}_{\mathbf{R}}$ it holds that

$$
\begin{aligned}
\Pr\left[y^* = \tilde{y} \mid z' \in \mathcal{Z}_{\mathbf{R}} \wedge \tilde{x} = x\right] &= \sum_{\substack{z \in \mathcal{Z}_{\mathbf{R}}: \\ w_x(z) > 0}} \Pr\left[z' = z \mid z' \in \mathcal{Z}_{\mathbf{R}} \wedge \tilde{x} = x\right] \\
&\qquad \cdot \Pr\left[y^* = \tilde{y} \mid z' = z \wedge \tilde{x} = x\right] \\
&= \sum_{\substack{z \in \mathcal{Z}_{\mathbf{R}}: \\ w_x(z) > 0}} \frac{w_x(z)}{W_x} \cdot \frac{1}{w_x(z)} \\
&= \frac{h}{W_x}.
\end{aligned}
$$

Substituting this into the first summation in Eq. (3) for $\frac{W_x}{|\mathcal{Y}_{\mathbf{R}}|} \cdot \frac{h}{W_x}$, we obtain

$$
\Pr[\textsc{Succ}_{\text{REAL}}] = \frac{h}{|\mathcal{Y}_{\mathbf{R}}|} + \frac{1}{|\mathcal{X}_{\mathbf{R}}|} \cdot \sum_{\substack{x \in \mathcal{X}_{\mathbf{R}}: \\ W_x < |\mathcal{Y}_{\mathbf{R}}|}} \Pr\left[z' \notin \mathcal{Z}_{\mathbf{R}} \mid \tilde{x} = x\right] \tag{4}
$$
$$
\cdot \Pr\left[\textsc{Succ}_{\text{REAL}} \mid z' \notin \mathcal{Z}_{\mathbf{R}} \wedge \tilde{x} = x\right].
$$

To conclude the proof, it suffices to show that there exists $x \in \mathcal{X}_{\mathbf{R}}$ where $W_x < |\mathcal{Y}_{\mathbf{R}}|$, such that

$$
\Pr\left[z' \notin \mathcal{Z}_{\mathbf{R}} \mid \tilde{x} = x\right] \cdot \Pr\left[\textsc{Succ}_{\text{REAL}} \mid z' \notin \mathcal{Z}_{\mathbf{R}} \wedge \tilde{x} = x\right] \neq 0.
$$

Now, for every $x \in \mathcal{X}_{\mathbf{R}}$ where $W_x < |\mathcal{Y}_{\mathbf{R}}|$, let

$$
\varepsilon_x := \Pr\left[\textsc{Succ}_{\text{REAL}} \mid z' \notin \mathcal{Z}_{\mathbf{R}} \wedge \tilde{x} = x\right],
$$

where the probability is taken over the sampling of the input $\tilde{y}$, the guess y^* of the adversary, and the sampling of the correlated randomness. Then

$$
\Pr\left[z' \notin \mathcal{Z}_{\mathbf{R}} \mid \tilde{x} = x\right] \cdot \Pr\left[\textsc{Succ}_{\text{REAL}} \mid z' \notin \mathcal{Z}_{\mathbf{R}} \wedge \tilde{x} = x\right] = \left(1 - \frac{W_x}{|\mathcal{Y}_{\mathbf{R}}|}\right) \cdot \varepsilon_x.
$$

We now show that there exists $x \in \mathcal{X}_{\mathbf{R}}$ such that $\varepsilon_x > 0$ and that $W_x < |\mathcal{Y}_{\mathbf{R}}|$. By Claim 5, there exists inputs $x \in \mathcal{X}_{\mathbf{R}}$ and $y \in \mathcal{Y}_{\mathbf{R}}$, and correlated randomness $(r_1, r_2) \in \text{Supp}(D)$, such that $f(x, y) \in \mathcal{Z} \backslash \mathcal{Z}_{\mathbf{R}}$, and for which there is a continuation of Π after round i causing B to output a value from $\mathcal{Z}_{\mathbf{R}}$. Observe that since $f(x, y) \in \mathcal{Z} \backslash \mathcal{Z}_{\mathbf{R}}$, the adversary $\mathcal{A}$ sends messages sampled uniformly at random and independently starting from round i. Therefore, conditioned on $\tilde{x} = x$, the probability it causes B to output a value from $\mathcal{Z}_{\mathbf{R}}$, is the probability that $\tilde{y} = y$, the correlated randomness is (r_1, r_2), and $\mathcal{A}$ sampled the correct messages and guessed $y^* = \tilde{y}$ correctly. By Claim 5, this event occurs with non-zero probability, i.e., $\varepsilon_x > 0$.

Claim 7. *For any simulator* $\text{Sim}_{\mathcal{A}}$ *in the ideal world, it holds that*

$$
\Pr[\textsc{Succ}_{\text{IDEAL}}] \leq \frac{h}{|\mathcal{Y}_{\mathbf{R}}|}.
$$

Intuitively, by Item 2, regardless of the input the simulator sends to the trusted party, any distinct output $z \in \mathcal{Z}_{\mathbf{R}}$ contributes $1/|\mathcal{Y}_{\mathbf{R}}|$ to the probability the simulator both guesses the input of the honest party, and forces the honest party to output z. Due to lack of space, the proof is given in the full-version.

It is left to prove Claim 5, roughly asserting that there exists a round where the output of one party is fixed, while the output of the other is not.

Proof (of Claim 5). For any certain inputs $(x, y) \in \mathbf{R}$ and correlated randomness $(r_1, r_2) \in \mathrm{Supp}(D)$, denote as $i_{\mathsf{A}}(x, y, r_1, r_2)$ the first round for which given an honest execution of Π up to and including round $i_{\mathsf{A}}(x, y, r_1, r_2)$, the following holds. There exists a set $\mathcal{Z}' \in \{\mathcal{Z}_{\mathbf{R}}, \mathcal{Z} \backslash \mathcal{Z}_{\mathbf{R}}\}$ such that any continuation of Π when A continues to behave honestly results in A outputting a value from $\mathcal{Z}'$ (regardless of the behavior of B). Note that such a round exists, since perfect correctness implies that at the end of the protocol, if both parties behave honestly, then for any fixed (x, y, r_1, r_2) party A outputs $f(x, y)$.

Similarly, denote by $i_{\mathsf{B}}(x, y, r_1, r_2)$ the first round for which given an honest execution of Π up to and including round $i_{\mathsf{B}}(x, y, r_1, r_2)$, any continuation of Π when B continues to behave honestly results in it outputting a value from $\mathcal{Z}'' \in \{\mathcal{Z}_{\mathbf{R}}, \mathcal{Z} \backslash \mathcal{Z}_{\mathbf{R}}\}$ (regardless of the behavior of A).

Next, we let i_{A} be the first round, for which for all inputs $(x, y) \in \mathbf{R}$ and for all possible correlated randomness $(r_1, r_2) \in \mathrm{Supp}(D)$, the output of A is defined to be either in $\mathcal{Z}_{\mathbf{R}}$ or in $\mathcal{Z} \backslash \mathcal{Z}_{\mathbf{R}}$. In the same way, we define i_{B} for B. Formally,

$$i_{\mathsf{A}} := \max_{\substack{(x,y) \in \mathbf{R} \\ (r_1, r_2) \in \mathrm{Supp}(D)}} i_{\mathsf{A}}(x, y, r_1, r_2), \qquad i_{\mathsf{B}} := \max_{\substack{(x,y) \in \mathbf{R} \\ (r_1, r_2) \in \mathrm{Supp}(D)}} i_{\mathsf{B}}(x, y, r_1, r_2).$$

Observe that there exists a row $x \in \mathcal{X}_{\mathbf{R}}$ and a column $y \in \mathcal{Y}_{\mathbf{R}}$, such that $\mathbf{M}_f^{\mathbf{R}}(x, \cdot)$ and $\mathbf{M}_f^{\mathbf{R}}(\cdot, y)$ contain both values from $\mathcal{Z}_{\mathbf{R}}$ and from $\mathcal{Z} \backslash \mathcal{Z}_{\mathbf{R}}$. Indeed, by Item 1 (in the statement of Lemma 4), there exists a cell $(x, y) \in \mathbf{R}$ where $\mathbf{M}_f^{\mathbf{R}}(x, y) \in \mathcal{Z} \backslash \mathcal{Z}_{\mathbf{R}}$. By Item 2 and Item 3 it follows that $\mathbf{M}_f^{\mathbf{R}}(x, \cdot)$ and $\mathbf{M}_f^{\mathbf{R}}(\cdot, y)$ contain at least one element from $\mathcal{Z}_{\mathbf{R}}$ each. This implies that $i_{\mathsf{A}}, i_{\mathsf{B}} > 0$, because there exist $(x, y) \in \mathbf{R}$ where the possible output for both parties before the first round can be from $\mathcal{Z}_{\mathbf{R}}$ and from $\mathcal{Z} \backslash \mathcal{Z}_{\mathbf{R}}$. Furthermore, as the parties send messages one after another, it follows that $i_{\mathsf{A}} \neq i_{\mathsf{B}}$. If $i_{\mathsf{A}} < i_{\mathsf{B}}$ then assign $\mathsf{P} := \mathsf{A}$ and $i := i_{\mathsf{A}}$, else we set $\mathsf{P} := \mathsf{B}$ and $i := i_{\mathsf{B}}$.

The claim follows from the definition of i_{A} and i_{B}. Indeed, assume that $i_{\mathsf{A}} < i_{\mathsf{B}}$, then for all inputs $(x, y) \in \mathbf{R}$ and correlated randomness $(r_1, r_2) \in \mathrm{Supp}(D)$, given an honest execution of Π up to and including round i_{A}, there exists a set $\mathcal{Z}' \in \{\mathcal{Z}_{\mathbf{R}}, \mathcal{Z} \backslash \mathcal{Z}_{\mathbf{R}}\}$ such that any continuation of i_{A} when A behaves honestly, results in A outputting a value from $\mathcal{Z}'$. On the other hand, as $i_{\mathsf{B}} > i_{\mathsf{A}}$, by the definition of i_{B}, there exist inputs $(x, y) \in \mathbf{R}$ and correlated randomness $(r_1, r_2) \in \mathrm{Supp}(D)$ such that $i_{\mathsf{B}}(x, y, r_1, r_2) > i_{\mathsf{A}}$. Hence, for such (x, y, r_1, r_2) there are possible continuations of Π resulting in honest B outputting a value from $\mathcal{Z}_{\mathbf{R}}$, and continuations resulting in honest B outputting a value from $\mathcal{Z} \backslash \mathcal{Z}_{\mathbf{R}}$. Furthermore, there exists such $(x, y) \in \mathbf{R}$ satisfying $f(x, y) \in \mathcal{Z} \backslash \mathcal{Z}_{\mathbf{R}}$ as well. Indeed, observe that since there exists a malicious continuation making B output a value from $\mathcal{Z}\backslash\mathcal{Z}_{\mathbf{R}}$ (regardless of the value of the real output $f(x, y)$), then there must exist an input $x' \in \mathcal{X}_{\mathbf{R}}$ and randomness r_1' for A that are consistent with the transcript up to round i_A, and that cause B to output a value from $\mathcal{Z}\backslash\mathcal{Z}_{\mathbf{R}}$. Notice that it must be the case that $f(x', y) \in \mathcal{Z}\backslash\mathcal{Z}_{\mathbf{R}}$ (in addition to $i_B(x', y, r_1', r_2) > i_A$), thus $(x', y) \in \mathbf{R}$ is the desired pair of inputs. The case where $i_A > i_B$ follows an analogous argument.

Remark 3 (On proving impossibility of security-with-abort). Similarly to [9], we can prove that the class of functionality captured by Lemma 4 cannot be computed with perfect security-with-abort. To see this, observe that the real world adversary still has a non-zero chance of increasing the probability that the honest party outputs a value from $\mathcal{Z}_{\mathbf{R}}$, while in the ideal world, giving the simulator the ability to cause the honest party to output $\perp$ will not increase its success probability.

5   An Impossibility Result for Perfect Security for Four-Output Functionalities

In this section, we prove Lemma 2. Our starting point is the general impossibility result stated in Lemma 4, which appears in Sect. 4. Let us first restate the lemma.

Lemma 5 (Restatement of Lemma 2). *Let $f : \mathcal{X} \times \mathcal{Y} \mapsto \{0, 1, 2, 3\}$ be a deterministic symmetric two-party four-output functionality. Assume that f can be computed with perfect security in the CR-hybrid model. Then, f is either a spiral function or a transparent transfer function.*

Towards proving the lemma, we first derive Theorem 4 as a corollary from Lemma 4.

Corollary 6 (Restatement of Theorem 4). *Let $f : \mathcal{X} \times \mathcal{Y} \mapsto \mathcal{Z}$ be a deterministic symmetric two-party functionality. Assume there exists a 2×2 rectangle $\mathbf{R}$ such that its corresponding submatrix $\mathbf{M}_f^{\mathbf{R}}$ is forbidden (see Definition 12). Then f cannot be computed with perfect security in the CR-hybrid model.*

Proof. We show that for $\mathcal{Z}_{\mathbf{R}} = \{b\}$ and $h = h' = 1$, the constraints from Lemma 4 hold. Indeed, since $\mathbf{M}_f^{\mathbf{R}}$ contains the element $a \neq b$, Item 1 holds. As for Items 2 and 3, note that $|\mathcal{Z}_{\mathbf{R}}| = h = h' = 1$, and each row and column in $\mathbf{M}_f$ cannot contain more than one distinct elements from $\mathcal{Z}_{\mathbf{R}}$.

As a corollary, any 2×2 rectangle of a functionality that can be computed with perfect security in the CR-hybrid model, must be one of the remaining forms. That is, we have the following result.

Corollary 7. *Let $f : \mathcal{X} \times \mathcal{Y} \mapsto \mathcal{Z}$ be a deterministic symmetric two-party functionality. Suppose that f can be computed with perfect security in the CR-hybrid* *model. Then any* 2×2 *rectangle* $\mathbf{R} \subseteq \mathcal{X} \times \mathcal{Y}$ *induces one of the following sub-matrices:*

$$\mathbf{M}_f^{\mathbf{R}} \sim \begin{pmatrix} a & a \\ a & a \end{pmatrix}; \quad \mathbf{M}_f^{\mathbf{R}} \sim \begin{pmatrix} a & a \\ b & b \end{pmatrix}; \quad \mathbf{M}_f^{\mathbf{R}} \sim \begin{pmatrix} a & a \\ b & c \end{pmatrix}; \quad \mathbf{M}_f^{\mathbf{R}} \sim \begin{pmatrix} a & b \\ c & d \end{pmatrix}, \tag{5}$$

where a, b, c *and* d *denote distinct elements of* $\mathcal{Z}$.

We are now ready to prove Lemma 2, which gives necessary conditions for a two-party four-output symmetric deterministic functionality $f : \mathcal{X} \times \mathcal{Y} \mapsto \{a, b, c, d\}$, to be computable with perfect security in the CR-hybrid model. Recall that Lemma 2 asserts that for such functionalities to be computable with perfect security, they must be one of two types: either a spiral or a transparent transfer functionality. The proof follows from the following two claims, that give the conditions for when a four-output functionalities is a spiral, and when it is a transparent transfer.

Claim 8. *Let* $f : \mathcal{X} \times \mathcal{Y} \mapsto \{0, 1, 2, 3\}$ *be a deterministic symmetric four-output two-party functionality. Assume that* f *can be computed with perfect security in the* CR-*hybrid model. Further, assume that* $\mathbf{M}_f$ *contains a* 2×2 *submatrix of the form*

$$\begin{pmatrix} a & b \\ c & d \end{pmatrix},$$

where $\{a, b, c, d\} = \{0, 1, 2, 3\}$. *Then* f *is a transparent transfer functionality.*

Claim 9. *Let* $f : \mathcal{X} \times \mathcal{Y} \mapsto \{0, 1, 2, 3\}$ *be a deterministic symmetric four-output two-party functionality. Assume that in* $\mathbf{M}_f$ *there is no forbidden* 2×2 *submatrix and no* 2×2 *submatrix of the form*

$$\begin{pmatrix} a & b \\ c & d \end{pmatrix},$$

where $\{a, b, c, d\} = \{0, 1, 2, 3\}$. *Then* f *is a spiral functionality.*

Claim 8 is proven below. Due to lack of space, we defer the proof of Claim 9 to the full version. We next use the above two claims to prove Lemma 2.

Proof (of Lemma 2). Fix a symmetric deterministic functionality $f : \mathcal{X} \times \mathcal{Y} \mapsto \{0, 1, 2, 3\}$, and assume it can be computed with perfect security in the CR-hybrid model. By Corollary 7, every 2×2 submatrix of $\mathbf{M}_f$ is of one of the following forms (up to permuting the rows and columns, and transposing the matrix).

$$\begin{pmatrix} a & a \\ a & a \end{pmatrix}; \quad \begin{pmatrix} a & a \\ b & b \end{pmatrix}; \quad \begin{pmatrix} a & a \\ b & c \end{pmatrix}; \quad \text{or} \quad \begin{pmatrix} a & b \\ c & d \end{pmatrix}.$$

If $\mathbf{M}_f$ contains the last submatrix, then by Claim 8 the functionality f is the transparent transfer functionality. Otherwise, by Claim 9 it is spiral.

It is left to prove Claim 8.

Proof (of Claim 8). Suppose there exists a 2×2 rectangle $\mathbf{R} = \{x_1, x_2\} \times \{y_1, y_2\}$ such that

$$\mathbf{M}_f^{\mathbf{R}} = \begin{pmatrix} a & b \\ c & d \end{pmatrix}.$$

Using the notation of Lemma 4, consider taking $\mathcal{Z}_{\mathbf{R}} = \{a, d\}$. As each row and each column in $\mathbf{M}_f^{\mathbf{R}}$ contains exactly 1 element from $\mathcal{Z}_{\mathbf{R}}$, and the submatrix contains an element from $\mathcal{Z} \backslash \mathcal{Z}_{\mathbf{R}}$, Item 1 from Lemma 4 holds. As we assume that f can be computed with perfect security in the CR-hybrid model, by Lemma 4, at least one of the following must hold.

- There exists a row $x_3 \in \mathcal{X} \backslash \{x_1, x_2\}$ such that

$$\{\mathbf{M}_f(x_3, y_1), \mathbf{M}_f(x_3, y_2)\} = \{a, d\}.$$

Observe that if $\mathbf{M}_f(x_3, y_1) = d$ and $\mathbf{M}_f(x_3, y_2) = a$, then the submatrix induced by $\{x_1, x_3\} \times \{y_1, y_2\}$ is $\left(\begin{smallmatrix} a & b \\ d & a \end{smallmatrix}\right)$. As this is a forbidden submatrix, by Corollary 6 this contradicts the assumption that f can be computed with perfect security in the CR-hybrid model. Thus,

$$(\mathbf{M}_f(x_3, y_1), \mathbf{M}_f(x_3, y_2)) = (a, d).$$

- There exists a column $y_3 \in \mathcal{Y} \backslash \{y_1, y_2\}$ such that

$$\{\mathbf{M}_f(x_1, y_3), \mathbf{M}_f(x_2, y_3)\} = \{a, d\}.$$

Similarly to the previous case, it must be the case where

$$(\mathbf{M}_f(x_1, y_3), \mathbf{M}_f(x_2, y_3)) = (a, d).$$

Taking $\mathcal{Z}_{\mathbf{R}} = \{b, c\}$ and using an analogous argument, it follows that at least one of the following holds.

- There exists a row $x_4 \in \mathcal{X} \backslash \{x_1, x_2\}$ such that

$$(\mathbf{M}_f(x_4, y_1), \mathbf{M}_f(x_4, y_2)) = (c, b).$$

- There exists a column $y_3 \in \mathcal{Y} \backslash \{y_1, y_2\}$ such that

$$(\mathbf{M}_f(x_1, y_4), \mathbf{M}_f(x_2, y_4)) = (b, c).$$

We conclude that one of the following must be a submatrix of $\mathbf{M}_f$.

$$\begin{pmatrix} a & b \\ c & d \\ a & d \\ c & b \end{pmatrix} \; ; \quad \left(\begin{array}{cc|cc} a & b & a & b \\ c & d & d & c \end{array} \right) ; \quad \left(\begin{array}{cc|c} a & b & b \\ c & d & c \\ \hline a & d & * \end{array} \right) ; \quad \left(\begin{array}{cc|c} a & b & a \\ c & d & d \\ \hline c & b & * \end{array} \right), \tag{6}$$

where $*$ is an arbitrary element of $\{a, b, c, d\}$. Next, observe that the latter two cases are impossible. This is true since for any assignment for value of $*$ (out of the four possible values), yields a 2×2 forbidden submatrix (in particular, an embedded AND). Hence, by Corollary 6 these two submatrices are forbidden. We assume without loss of generality that the first submatrix from Equation (6) appears in $\mathbf{M}_f$. It is left to show that any other row and column in $\mathbf{M}_f$ is a duplication.

Consider $x_5 \in \mathcal{X} \backslash \{x_1, x_2, x_3, x_4\}$ (assuming such exists). Observe that $\mathbf{M}_f(x_5, y_1) \neq b$ as otherwise, the submatrix induced by $\{x_1, x_5\} \times \{y_1, y_2\}$ is the forbidden submatrix $\left(\begin{smallmatrix} a & b \\ b & * \end{smallmatrix} \right)$ where $*$ is an arbitrary value. By Corollary 6, this contradicts the assumption that f can be computed with perfect security in the CR-hybrid model. Similarly, it holds that $\mathbf{M}_f(x_5, y_1) \neq d$ and $\mathbf{M}_f(x_5, y_2) \notin \{a, c\}$, as otherwise this induces a forbidden submatrix. Therefore, $\mathbf{M}_f(x_5, y_1) \in \{a, c\}$ and $\mathbf{M}_f(x_5, y_2) \in \{b, d\}$. All possible rows satisfying those conditions are $\mathbf{M}_f(x_1, \cdot)$, $\mathbf{M}_f(x_2, \cdot)$, $\mathbf{M}_f(x_3, \cdot)$, and $\mathbf{M}_f(x_4, \cdot)$. Therefore, any possible row $\mathbf{M}_f(x_5, \cdot)$ must be a duplication.

Next, consider a column $y_3 \in \mathcal{X} \backslash \{y_1, y_2\}$. Observe that $\mathbf{M}_f(x_1, y_3) \neq c$, as otherwise the submatrix induced by the rectangle $\{x_1, x_2\} \times \{y_1, y_3\}$ is the forbidden submatrix $\left(\begin{smallmatrix} a & c \\ c & * \end{smallmatrix} \right)$. Similarly, it holds that $\mathbf{M}_f(x_1, y_3) \neq d$. We next consider two cases.

We assume that $\mathbf{M}_f(x_1, y_3) = a$, as the case where $\mathbf{M}_f(x_1, y_3) = b$ can be handled using an analogous argument. Then $\mathbf{M}_f(x_3, y_3) = a$, as otherwise the submatrix induced by a rectangle $\{x_1, x_3\} \times \{y_1, y_3\}$ is forbidden. Similarly, note that if $\mathbf{M}_f(x_2, y_3) \neq c$ then $\mathbf{M}_f$ contains an induced forbidden submatrix. Finally, $\mathbf{M}_f(x_4, y_3) = c$, as otherwise the submatrix induced by a rectangle $\{x_2, x_4\} \times \{y_1, y_3\}$ is forbidden. Thus,

$$(\mathbf{M}_f(x_1, y_3), \mathbf{M}_f(x_2, y_3), \mathbf{M}_f(x_3, y_3), \mathbf{M}_f(x_4, y_3)) = (a, c, a, c),$$

which is a duplication of the first column.

6   Positive Results for Perfect Security

In this section, we prove Lemma 3, serving as the positive direction of Theroem 3. Specifically, we prove that every spiral functionality and the transparent transfer functionality can be computed with perfect security. In fact, we show that these functionalities can be computed by deterministic protocols in the plain model, i.e., where the parties do not receive correlated randomness. We first restate the lemma.

Lemma 6 (Restatement of Lemma 3) *Let* $f : \mathcal{X} \times \mathcal{Y} \mapsto \mathcal{Z}$ *be a deterministic symmetric two-party functionality. If* f *is a spiral or a transparent transfer functionality, then* f *can be computed with perfect security in the plain model.*

We prove that spiral functionalities can be computed with perfect security in Sect. 6.1. We handle transparent transfer functionalities in Sect. 6.2.

6.1   Computing Spiral Functionalities

In this section, we prove that any spiral functionality can be computed with perfect security. This result follows from the following two propositions, asserting the status of a functionality that is obtained from another by adding certain new rows or columns to the associated matrix.

The first proposition states an intuitive observation that for a symmetric functionality f, duplicating rows and columns in $\mathbf{M}_f$ does not affect the existence of a perfectly secure protocol.

Proposition 1. *Let* $f : \mathcal{X} \times \mathcal{Y} \mapsto \mathcal{Z}$ *be a deterministic symmetric two-party functionality, and let* $f' : \mathcal{X}' \times \mathcal{Y} \mapsto \mathcal{Z}$ *be such that* $\mathrm{red}(\mathbf{M}_f) \sim \mathrm{red}(\mathbf{M}_{f'})$. *Then* f' *can be computed with perfect security in the* f-*hybrid model (and vice versa). Similarly, for* $f'' : \mathcal{X} \times \mathcal{Y}'' \mapsto \mathcal{Z}$ *such that* $\mathrm{red}(\mathbf{M}_f) \sim \mathrm{red}(\mathbf{M}_{f''})$, *it holds that* f'' *can be computed with perfect security in the* f-*hybrid model (and vice versa).*

Due to lack of space, the proof of Proposition 2 is given in the full version. We next state the second proposition, which asserts that given a functionality f that can be computed with perfect security, adding a constant row or column to $\mathbf{M}_f$ with new values, results in a functionality that can still be computed with perfect security.

Proposition 2. *Let* $f : \mathcal{X} \times \mathcal{Y} \mapsto \mathcal{Z}$ *be a deterministic symmetric two-party functionality, and let* $x_+ \notin \mathcal{X}$ *and* $z_+ \notin \mathcal{Z}$. *Consider the functionality* $f_+ :$ $(\mathcal{X} \cup \{x_+\}) \times \mathcal{Y} \mapsto \mathcal{Z} \cup \{z_+\}$ *defined as*

$$f_+(x,y) = \begin{cases} f(x,y) & \textit{if } x \in \mathcal{X} \\ z_+ & \textit{otherwise} \end{cases}$$

Then f_+ *can be computed with perfect security in the* f-*hybrid model.*

Due to lack of space, the proof of Proposition 2 is given in the full version. We first observe that, combined with the composition theorem and the fact that any constant functionality can be computed with perfect security in the plain model, it follows that any spiral functionality can also be computed with perfect security in the plain model.

Corollary 8. *Let* $f : \mathcal{X} \times \mathcal{Y} \mapsto \mathcal{Z}$ *be a deterministic symmetric two-party functionality. Assume that* f *is spiral. Then* f *can be computed with perfect security in the plain model.*

6.2   Computing Transparent Transfer Functionalities

In this section we show that the transparent transfer functionality defined in Definition 11 can be computed with perfect security (in the plain model). In fact, we show a family of functionalities, extending the transparent transfer functionality and show that they can be computed with perfect security. Let us first define this family.

Definition 13 (Generalized transparent transfer functionality) *Let* $k, n \in \mathbb{N}$ *and let* $\Sigma = \{0, \ldots, k-1\}$. *We define the symmetric* (k, n)-*transparent transfer functionality* $\mathsf{TT}_{k,n} : \Sigma^n \times [n] \mapsto \Sigma \times [n]$ *as*

$$\mathsf{TT}_{k,n}\left((x_1, \ldots, x_n), i\right) = (x_i, i).$$

Note that $\mathsf{TT}_{2,2}$ *is equivalent to the transparent transfer functionality from Definition 11 (i.e., by applying the mapping* $(x_i, i) \mapsto (x_i + (i-1) \cdot k)$ *to the output).*

We next show that any (k, n)-transparent transfer functionality can be computed with perfect security in the plain model.

Claim 10. *For every* $k, n \in \mathbb{N}$ *the* (k, n)-*transparent transfer functionality* $\mathsf{TT}_{k,n}$ *can be computed with perfect security in the plain model.*

Proof. We define a protocol Π for $\mathsf{TT}_{k,n}$ as follows:

Protocol 11
Inputs: *Party* A *holds input* $(x_1, \ldots, x_n) \in \Sigma^n$ *and party* B *holds input* $i \in [n]$.

1. B *sends its input* i *to* A.
2. A *sends* x_i *to* B, *and outputs* (x_i, i).
3. *If* B *received a value* $x_i \notin \Sigma$, *then it outputs* $(0, i)$.

Clearly, the protocol admits perfect correctness. We next show that it is secure. Consider an adversary $\mathcal{A}$ corrupting A. We may assume without loss of generality that A is deterministic (by an averaging argument). We define its simulator $\mathsf{Sim}_{\mathcal{A}}$ as follows.

1. Query $\mathcal{A}$ on every possible $j \in [n]$ (rewinding each time). Let $(x_1^*, \ldots, x_n^*)$ be the corresponding messages sent by $\mathcal{A}$ to B for every such j. For any $j \in [n]$, if $x_j^* \notin \Sigma$ then change it to 0. Let $(x_1', \ldots, x_n')$ be the resulting vector.
2. Send $(x_1', \ldots, x_n')$ to the trusted party T, and let (x_i', i) denote the output it sends.
3. Rewind $\mathcal{A}$ to the beginning, send it i, output whatever it outputs, and halt.

We now analyze the simulator. Since $\mathcal{A}$ is deterministic, the input x_i^* it sends upon receiving i, is the same after rewinding. Thus, the simulator will send the same input to the trusted party (changing to 0 in case $x_i^* \notin \Sigma$).

We now consider the case where B is corrupted by an adversary $\mathcal{B}$. Its simulator $\mathsf{Sim}_{\mathcal{B}}$ proceeds as follows.

1. Query $\mathcal{B}$ to obtain the message i it sends to A in the first round.
2. Send i to the trusted party T, and obtain a value x.
3. Send x to $\mathcal{B}$, output whatever $\mathcal{B}$ outputs, and halt.

Clearly, the output of A is i in both worlds, and the view of $\mathcal{B}$ is x_i. Therefore, the real and ideal worlds are identical.

Acknowledgements. The work of B. Alon, O. Nissenbaum, E. Omri, and A. Paskin-Cherniavsky was supported in part by the Ariel Cyber Innovation Center in conjunction with the Israel National Cyber directorate in the Prime Minister's Office. The work of B. Alon, O. Nissenbaum, and E. Omri was also supported in part by grants from the Israel Science Foundation (no.152/17). This work was done while E. Omri was visiting Georgetown University, supported by the Robert L. McDevitt, K.S.G., K.C.H.S. and Catherine H. McDevitt L.C.H.S. endowment at Georgetown University. The work of A. Patra was supported by DST National Mission on Interdisciplinary Cyber-Physical Systems (NM-ICPS) 2020–2025 and SERB MATRICS (Theoretical Sciences) Grant 2020–2023.

References

1. Alon, B., Paskin-Cherniavsky, A.: On perfectly secure 2PC in the OT-hybrid model. In: Hofheinz, D., Rosen, A. (eds.) TCC 2019. LNCS, vol. 11891, pp. 561–595. Springer, Cham (2019). https://doi.org/10.1007/978-3-030-36030-6_22

2. Ben-Or, M., Goldwasser, S., Wigderson, A.: Completeness theorems for non-cryptographic fault-tolerant distributed computing. In: Proceedings of the 20th STOC, pp. 1–10 (1988). https://doi.org/10.1145/3335741.3335756

3. Brassard, G., Crépeau, C., Santha, M.: Oblivious transfers and intersecting codes. IACR Cryptology ePrint Archive, vol. 1996, p. 10 (1996). http://eprint.iacr.org/1996/010

4. Canetti, R.: Security and composition of multiparty cryptographic protocols. J. Cryptol. **13**(1), 143–202 (2000). https://doi.org/10.1007/s001459910006

5. Chaum, D., Crépeau, C., Damgard, I.: Multiparty unconditionally secure protocols. In: Proceedings of the Twentieth Annual ACM Symposium on Theory of Computing, pp. 11–19 (1988). https://doi.org/10.1145/62212.62214

6. Chor, B., Kushilevitz, E.: A zero-one law for Boolean privacy. SIAM J. Discret. Math. **4**(1), 36–47 (1991)

7. Cleve, R.: Limits on the security of coin flips when half the processors are faulty. In: Proceedings of the Eighteenth Annual ACM Symposium on Theory of Computing, pp. 364–369 (1986)

8. Goldreich, O.: Foundations of Cryptography - VOLUME 2: Basic Applications. Cambridge University Press, Cambridge (2004)

9. Ishai, Y., Kushilevitz, E., Meldgaard, S., Orlandi, C., Paskin-Cherniavsky, A.: On the power of correlated randomness in secure computation. In: Sahai, A. (ed.) TCC 2013. LNCS, vol. 7785, pp. 600–620. Springer, Heidelberg (2013). https://doi.org/10.1007/978-3-642-36594-2_34

10. Kushilevitz, E.: Privacy and communication complexity. SIAM J. Discret. Math. **5**(2), 273–284 (1992)

11. Wolf, S., Wullschleger, J.: Oblivious transfer is symmetric. In: Vaudenay, S. (ed.) EUROCRYPT 2006. LNCS, vol. 4004, pp. 222–232. Springer, Heidelberg (2006). https://doi.org/10.1007/11761679_14

Lattices

Public-Key Encryption from Homogeneous CLWE

Andrej Bogdanov[1], Miguel Cueto Noval[2]([envelope]), Charlotte Hoffmann[2],
and Alon Rosen[3,4]

[1] Chinese University of Hong Kong, Hong Kong, China
andrejb@cse.cuhk.edu.hk
[2] Institute of Science and Technology Austria, Klosterneuburg, Austria
{miguel.cuetonoval,charlotte.hoffmann}@ist.ac.at
[3] Bocconi University, Milan, Italy
alon.rosen@unibocconi.it
[4] Reichman University, Herzliya, Israel

Abstract. The homogeneous continuous LWE (hCLWE) problem is to
distinguish samples of a specific high-dimensional Gaussian mixture from
standard normal samples. It was shown to be at least as hard as Learning
with Errors, but no reduction in the other direction is currently known.

We present four new public-key encryption schemes based on the hardness of hCLWE, with varying tradeoffs between decryption and security errors, and different discretization techniques. Our schemes yield a
polynomial-time algorithm for solving hCLWE using a Statistical Zero-
Knowledge oracle.

Keywords: Public-key encryption · Continuous Learning with
Errors · Statistical Zero-Knowledge · Hypercontractivity ·
Statistical-computational gaps · Discrete Gaussian Sampling

1 Introduction

Existing public-key encryption schemes are based on relatively few hard computational problems, all from the domains of number theory [RSA78, Rab79,
EG85], coding theory [McE78], lattices [AD97, Reg05], and noisy linear algebra [Ale03, ABW10]. Each of these domains yields to different tradeoffs between
functionality, security, and efficiency.

In this work we explore public-key encryption based on a new type of assumption: computational hardness in statistical inference. The input of a statistical
inference problem is a sequence of independent samples coming from some distribution with unknown parameters. The search (or estimation) task is to identify
the parameters; the easier distinguishing (or hypothesis testing) task is to distinguish the samples from ones coming from a fixed null distribution.

Our statistical inference problem of interest is one that has attracted much
algorithmic attention: learning Gaussian mixtures in high dimension. A mixture is a convex combination of k Gaussians with different means and possibly different covariance matrices. When k is constant polynomial-time learning

E. Kiltz and V. Vaikuntanathan (Eds.): TCC 2022, LNCS 13748, pp. 565–592, 2022.
https://doi.org/10.1007/978-3-031-22365-5_20

algorithms are known [HP15, BS15] assuming sufficiently many samples are available. Diakonikolas et al. [DKS17] showed that in general the learning problem is intractable for statistical query algorithms. Bruna et al. [BRST21] proved that even the task of distinguishing mixtures of Gaussians from standard normal samples is intractable assuming the hardness of short vectors and short bases in lattices (the GapSVP and GapSIVP problems). Gupte et al. [GVV22] recently showed the stronger claim that the hardness can be based on the Learning with Errors (LWE) problem.

The hard Gaussian mixture of [BRST21, GVV22], called the homogeneous Continuous Learning with Errors (hCLWE) distribution, consists of samples in $\mathbb{R}^n$ that have a standard normal distribution in every direction perpendicular to a secret direction $\mathbf{w} \in \mathbb{R}^n$. The distribution in direction $\mathbf{w}$ is a noisy discrete Gaussian, i.e. a mixture of "Gaussian pancakes" of standard deviation $\beta/\sqrt{\beta^2 + \gamma^2} \approx \beta/\gamma$ and spacing $\gamma/(\beta^2 + \gamma^2) \approx 1/\gamma$ (Fig. 1.a). The (decision) hCLWE problem is to distinguish hCLWE samples from purely normal ones.

The full version of this paper [BNHR22] contains all the missing proofs.

1.1   Our Contributions

In this work we construct public-key encryption that is at least as hard to break as hCLWE. The hCLWE problem not only inherits advantages of LWE (such as reduction to worst-case hardness and resistance to known quantum attacks), but is potentially more secure: hCLWE is certainly no easier than LWE and can be potentially harder.

Our constructions imply limits on the hardness of hCLWE: just as LWE, hCLWE is tractable in Statistical Zero-Knowledge. It follows that hCLWE is unlikely to be helpful for constructing encryption as secure as NP (unless NP is contained in coAM).

Four Public-Key Encryption Schemes: We present four public-key encryption schemes that offer varying tradeoffs between decryption and security errors, and use different techniques when discretizing continuous values.

The third cryptosystem of Ajtai and Dwork [AD97] already contains essentially all the ingredients needed to obtain hCLWE-based public-key encryption. Our most efficient scheme—discretized encryption—is largely based on it. We believe that our other schemes are simpler to describe, more intuitive to analyze, and offer the potential of wider applicability to other Gaussian mixtures.

Some of our schemes are based on a variant of hCLWE called $(0, 1/2)$-hCLWE. In the $1/2$-hCLWE distribution, the mode in the hidden direction $\mathbf{w}$ is shifted by a relative phase of $1/2$ (Fig. 1.b). The hidden direction in $(0, 1/2)$-hCLWE is a labeled mixture of hCLWE and $1/2$-hCLWE (Fig. 1.c). Technically, $(0, 1/2)$-hCLWE is at least as hard as LWE and no harder than hCLWE.

Our first scheme ("pancake") is based on hCLWE. It has inverse polynomial decryption and constant security errors. These parameters, along with the specifics of the scheme, already suffice to prove that hCLWE can be solved in

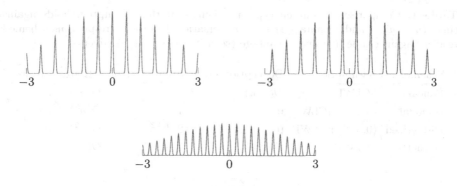

Fig. 1. Probability density function of the hidden direction in the (a) hCLWE, (b) 1/2-hCLWE, and (c) $(0, 1/2)$-hCLWE distributions with parameters $\beta = 0.05$ and $\gamma = 2$

Statistical Zero-Knowledge (SZK), and therefore is in coAM.[1] The discretization step in the scheme can be performed during encryption, and so the public key is continuous. Arguing security then necessitates proving an analog of the leftover hash lemma for Gaussian matrices, which may be of independent interest.

One could in principle rely on standard techniques to reduce decryption and security errors in the first scheme [HR05] , albeit at the price of a significant loss in efficiency. Instead, we present three different ideas to reduce the errors directly.

In the second scheme ("bimodal"), we achieve perfect decryption error by publishing $(0, 1/2)$-hCLWE samples as the public key. To encrypt a 0, Bob uses samples with $z = 0$ and to encrypt a 1, he uses samples with $z = 1/2$. This eliminates the probability that a random normal ciphertext of 1 is of the form of an hCLWE sample and thus makes decryption perfect.

The third scheme ("discretized") achieves negligible security error by mapping the samples into a parallelpiped spanned by hCLWE samples; a technique due to Ajtai and Dwork [AD97]. Here the discretization step takes place already in public-key generation, allowing for the use of the standard leftover hash lemma and yielding favorable security error in comparison with the other schemes.

In the fourth scheme ("baguette") we achieve negligible decryption error assuming only hCLWE. Instead of publishing samples that have a "pancake" distribution in one direction, we sample vectors that have a pancake distribution in ℓ hidden directions. In [BRST21] the authors give a reduction from hCLWE to this hCLWE(ℓ) distribution.

The parallelepiped technique can also be applied to the fourth scheme, yielding an hCLWE-based scheme with negligible decryption and security error. We omit a formal analysis of this step as it is similar to the discretized scheme (Table 1 and Fig. 2).

---

[1] A distinguishing problem is in class $\mathcal{C}$ if there is an algorithm in $\mathcal{C}$ that accepts at least 2/3 of the yes instances and rejects at least 2/3 of the no instances.

Table 1. Comparison of our encryption schemes. If the assumption holds against time $t(n) + n^{O(1)}$ and advantage $\Omega(\epsilon(n))$ adversaries then the corresponding scheme is resilient against time $t(n)$ and advantage (security error $+ \epsilon(n)$) adversaries.

Scheme	Assumption	Decryption error	Security error	PK size	SK size
Pancake	hCLWE	$O(1/n)$	$1/4$	$\tilde{O}(n^3)$	n
Bimodal	$(0, 1/2)$-hCLWE	0	$1/2$	$\tilde{O}(n^3)$	n
Discretized	$(0, 1/2)$-hCLWE	0	2^{-n+2}	$\tilde{O}(n^2)$	n
Baguette	hCLWE(ℓ)	$O(1/n^\ell)$	$1/4$	$\tilde{O}(n^3)$	$n\ell$

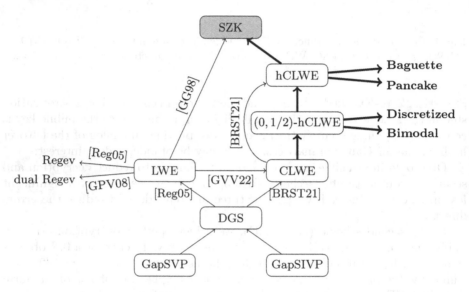

Fig. 2. Reductions between problems and encryption schemes (new results are in bold).

1.2 Related Work

Bruna et al. [BRST21] show a worst-case to average-case reduction from Discrete Gaussian Sampling (DGS) to hCLWE. Their reduction factors through an intermediate problem called Continuous LWE (CLWE).

A sample from the CLWE distribution [BRST21] is of the form $(\mathbf{a}, z)$, where $\mathbf{a} \in \mathbb{R}^n$ is a vector with individual entries sampled independently from the standard normal distribution $\mathcal{N}(0, 1)$, and $z := \gamma\langle\mathbf{a}, \mathbf{w}\rangle + e \mod 1$. Here e is the noise drawn from a Gaussian distribution with mean 0 and variance β^2 for some $\beta > 0$, $\gamma > 0$ is a fixed parameter and $\mathbf{w} \in \mathbb{R}^n$ is a secret unit vector. CLWE is the problem of distinguishing multiple CLWE samples from an equal number of samples of the form $(\mathbf{a}, u)$, where u is uniform over $[0, 1)$ and independent of $\mathbf{a}$.

An hCLWE sample is a CLWE sample conditioned on $z = 0$; Bruna et al.'s reduction from CLWE to hCLWE is based on this property. We obtain an analogous reduction from CLWE to $(0, 1/2)$-hCLWE by modifying the condition on z. It is not known if there is a reduction in the opposite direction.

The CLWE problem can be viewed as a continuous analog of Regev's LWE problem [Reg05] and is at least as (quantumly) hard as the same worst-case lattice problems underlying LWE [BRST21]. Gupte et al. [GVV22] recently showed a reduction from LWE to CLWE. They in fact showed that LWE is equivalent in hardness to a variant of CLWE with a different distribution over the secrets that is supported on a discrete subset of the unit sphere. CLWE is at least as hard as this variant.

1.3 CLWE, SZK, and Statistical-Computational Gaps

Several works [BR13,HWX15,BB20] uncover that hypothesis testing tasks in statistical inference tend to exhibit *statistical-computational gaps*: There is a range of sample complexities $m \in [m_{stat}, m_{comp}]$ for which hypothesis testing is possible, but no efficient (in terms of the length of a single sample) algorithm is known.

A striking feature of the hCLWE problem is that it is potentially intractable even when the sample complexity is unbounded, i.e., m_{comp} is infinite. Our Theorem 9.2 shows that when $m \geq \tilde{O}(n^2)$ samples are available hCLWE becomes solvable in SZK. Thus, in a world in which SZK = BPP, the computational threshold m_{comp} for hCLWE is at most $\tilde{O}(n^2)$.

In contrast, the statistical threshold for CLWE is $m_{stat} = O(n)$. It is an intriguing open question whether a statistical-computational gap for hCLWE exists assuming SZK = BPP. One approach for ruling out this possibility is to design a more efficient hCLWE-based PKE scheme.

Applying the reduction from CLWE to hCLWE of Bruna et al., our result also implies that CLWE is in SZK. As their reduction does not preserve sample complexity, the resulting SZK algorithm for CLWE requires a larger number of samples.

2 Technical Overview

The messages in our encryption schemes are single bits. The distributions of encryptions of zero and one, respectively, are efficiently distinguishable with the secret key but not without it. The public keys are independent samples of the hCLWE or $(0, 1/2)$-hCLWE distributions and the secret key is the hidden direction $\mathbf{w}$ of the corresponding yes instances.

As can be seen in Fig. 1, the hCLWE samples used to generate the public-key have a periodic discrete structure along the secret direction $\mathbf{w}$. Encryption is designed to retain this discrete structure in the ciphertext even though the sender is oblivious to it. Decryption calculates the correlation between the secret key $\mathbf{w}$ and the ciphertext. This correlation is close to an integer multiple of the period for encryptions of zero and (typically) far from it for encryptions of one.

2.1 "Pancake" Encryption

The first scheme (Sect. 4) is based on the hCLWE problem. The secret key is a random unit vector $\mathbf{w}$ and the public key is an $n \times m$ matrix $\mathbf{A}$ that consists of m hCLWE samples conditioned on the secret direction $\mathbf{w}$. To encrypt a 0, sample a uniform vector $\mathbf{t} \leftarrow \{1/\sqrt{m}, -1/\sqrt{m}\}^m$ and compute $\mathbf{At}$. To encrypt a 1, sample a standard normal vector. The ciphertext $\mathbf{c}$ is a discretization of the resulting vector using a rounding function that divides the real line into intervals ("buckets") of equal Gaussian measure.[2] To decrypt a ciphertext $\mathbf{c}$, compute $\gamma\sqrt{m}\langle \mathbf{w}, \mathbf{c} \rangle$ and output 0 if the result is close to an integer. Otherwise output 1.

The scheme has inverse polynomial decryption error since the probability of $\gamma\sqrt{m}\langle \mathbf{w}, \mathbf{c} \rangle$ being close to an integer is inverse polynomial for a random choice of $\mathbf{c}$. The main technical contribution in this scheme is the security proof, in particular Proposition 4.3. This result is an analog of the leftover hash lemma for the multiplication of Gaussian matrices with vectors with uniform vectors $\mathbf{t} \leftarrow \{1/\sqrt{m}, -1/\sqrt{m}\}^m$ which shows that the security error is $1/2$ for our choice of parameters.

2.2 "Bimodal" Encryption

In the second scheme (Sect. 6) we introduce the following changes: We base the scheme on the $(0, 1/2)$-hCLWE problem and publish two matrices $(\mathbf{A}_0, \mathbf{A}_1)$ as the public key. The matrix $\mathbf{A}_0$ consists of hCLWE samples conditioned on $\mathbf{w}$ and $\mathbf{A}_1$ consists of $1/2$-hCLWE samples conditioned on $\mathbf{w}$. To encrypt a 0, do the same as in the pancake scheme with the matrix $\mathbf{A}_0$. To encrypt a 1, do exactly the same with $\mathbf{A}_1$. To decrypt, check if $\gamma\sqrt{m}\langle \mathbf{w}, \mathbf{c} \rangle \mod 1$ is closer to 0 or to $1/2$. Replacing one hCLWE matrix by two $(0, 1/2)$-hCLWE matrices yields perfect decryption error for all but negligibly many choices of the public key. The security error however remains constant.

2.3 "Discretized" Encryption

The third scheme (Sect. 7) has perfect decryption for all but an inverse polynomial fraction of public keys and negligible security error. To achieve this we make use of the parallelepiped technique due to Ataj and Dwork [AD97] to obtain uniform matrices from $(0, 1/2)$-hCLWE samples.

We change the secret key to $\mathbf{B}^T \mathbf{w}$, where $\mathbf{B}$ is a square matrix whose columns are hCLWE samples. The public key $(\mathbf{A}_0, \mathbf{A}_1)$ again consists of 2 matrices: A matrix $\mathbf{A}_0$ that is obtained by mapping hCLWE samples into the parallelepiped $\mathcal{P}(\mathbf{B})$ spanned by the columns of $\mathbf{B}$, and a matrix $\mathbf{A}_1$ that is obtained in the same way but with $1/2$-hCLWE samples mapped to $\mathcal{P}(\mathbf{B})$. This mapping into the

---

[2] In the body of the paper we use the notation $1/\gamma' = \gamma/(\beta^2 + \gamma^2)$ for the period of the hCLWE hidden direction. As the difference between $1/\gamma'$ and $1/\gamma$ is small we make no distinction between the two in this overview.

parallelepiped transforms Gaussian vectors in $\mathbb{R}$ into uniform vectors in $\mathcal{P}(\mathbf{B})$, while preserving the pancakes in the secret direction. An additional rounding step discretizes the matrices $\mathbf{A}_0, \mathbf{A}_1$.

To encrypt a bit b, sample a vector $\mathbf{t}$ with uniform entries in $\{-1, 1\}$ and set $\mathbf{c} := \mathbf{A}_b \mathbf{t} \mod q$. To decrypt, check if $\gamma \langle \mathbf{B}^T w, \mathbf{c}/q \rangle \mod 1$ is closer to 0 or to $1/2$. For all but an inverse polynomial fraction of choices of the matrix $\mathbf{B}$ this scheme has perfect correctness. Security follows from the classical leftover hash lemma [IZ89] since the matrices $\mathbf{A}_0$ and $\mathbf{A}_1$ are uniform and discrete.

2.4 "Baguette" Encryption

The fourth scheme (Sect. 8) is based on the hCLWE(ℓ) problem, which is potentially harder than $(0, 1/2)$-hCLWE. We achieve negligible decryption error by modifying our first scheme as follows: Instead of publishing samples that have a pancake distribution in only one hidden direction, we publish a matrix $\mathbf{A}$ of samples that have a pancake distribution in $\log n$ many hidden directions, i.e. we replace the Gaussian pancakes with "Gaussian Baguettes". To encrypt 0, sample a uniform $\mathbf{t} \leftarrow \{1/\sqrt{m}, -1/\sqrt{m}\}^m$ and compute $\mathbf{At}$, and to encrypt 1, sample a standard normal vector. Discretization is identical to the first scheme.

To decrypt, multiply the ciphertext with a matrix that consists of all hidden directions. If all of the entries in the resulting vectors are close to an integer, output 0, otherwise output 1. While the probability that the inner product of the ciphertext of 1 with one secret direction is close to an integer is polynomial, the probability that this happens for all of the $\log n$ directions is negligible. The security error of this scheme remains constant but could be amplified either by a standard approach or by the above parallelepiped method.

2.5 SZK Membership

Our SZK membership proof of hCLWE is established by reduction to the complete problem statistical distance: hCLWE samples are mapped to a distribution that is far from uniform over some discrete set, while standard normal samples are mapped to a distribution that is close to uniform. The two distributions are obtained by pancake encrypting a zero under an actual public key and a random placebo. Completeness and soundness then follow from the functionality and security of pancake encryption.[3]

We find it instructive to directly describe the distributions resulting from this reduction. Our Proposition 4.3 can be interpreted as saying that random $\pm 1/\sqrt{m}$ linear combinations of $m = \tilde{\Theta}(n^2)$ standard Gaussian samples fill up space evenly: For every set of sufficiently large Gaussian measure, the fraction of linear combinations that lands in the set is approximately equal to its measure. Thus if $\mathbb{R}^n$ is partitioned into suitably many regions of equal Gaussian measure,

---

[3] By relying on discretized encryption instead we can prove the stronger claim of coNISZK membership [GSV99] and improve the sample complexity. Details will be spelled out in the final version.

the induced distribution on the regions is close to uniform. In contrast, if there are periodic gaps in some (unknown) direction like in the hCLWE distribution, the linear combinations of samples are concentrated on few regions and the induced distribution is far from uniform.

An intriguing question left open by our work is if SZK membership also holds for aperiodic mixtures of Gaussians such as the ones underlying the statistical query lower bound of Diakonikolas et al. [DKS17].

3   The (homogeneous) CLWE Distribution

Definition 3.1 (CLWE Distribution). *Given a dimension n and parameters $\beta, \gamma > 0$, and a unit vector $\mathbf{w} \in \mathbb{R}^n$, samples $(\mathbf{y}, z) \in \mathbb{R}^n \times [0, 1)$ from the CLWE distribution $\mathcal{A}_{\mathbf{w},\beta,\gamma,n}$ are generated as follows:*

1. *Sample $\mathbf{y} \leftarrow \mathcal{N}_n(0, 1)$.*
2. *Sample $e \leftarrow \mathcal{N}(0, \beta^2)$.*
3. *Output $(\mathbf{y}, \gamma \langle \mathbf{w}, \mathbf{y} \rangle + e \mod 1)$.*

Definition 3.2 (CLWE Distinguishing Problem). *For real numbers $\beta, \gamma > 0$ and $n \in \mathbb{N}$, the (average-case) distinguishing problem $\mathrm{CLWE}_{\beta,\gamma,n}$ asks to distinguish between $\mathcal{A}_{\mathbf{w},\beta,\gamma,n}$ for a uniform vector $\mathbf{w} \in \mathbb{R}^n$ and $\mathcal{N}_n(0,1) \times \mathcal{U}$, where $\mathcal{U}$ is the uniform distribution on $[0, 1)$.*

Definition 3.3 (hCLWE Distribution). *Given a dimension n, parameters $\beta, \gamma > 0$, and a unit vector $\mathbf{w} \in \mathbb{R}^n$, samples $\mathbf{y} \in \mathbb{R}^n$ from the hCLWE distribution $\mathcal{H}_{\mathbf{w},\beta,\gamma,n}$ are generated as follows:*

1. *The pancake: Sample $k \in \mathbb{Z}$ with probability proportional to $\exp(-k^2/(2\gamma^2 + 2\beta^2))$.*
2. *The noise: Sample e from $\mathcal{N}(0, \beta'^2)$, where $\beta'^2 = \beta^2/(\gamma^2 + \beta^2)$.*
3. *The rest: Sample $\mathbf{w}^\perp$ as $\mathcal{N}_{n-1}(0,1)$ on the subspace orthogonal to $\mathbf{w}$.*
4. *Output $\mathbf{w}^\perp + (k/\gamma' + e)\mathbf{w}$, where $1/\gamma' = \gamma/(\gamma^2 + \beta^2)$.*

Definition 3.4 (hCLWE Distinguishing Problem). *For real numbers $\beta, \gamma > 0$ and $n \in \mathbb{N}$, the (average-case) distinguishing problem $\mathrm{hCLWE}_{\beta,\gamma,n}$ asks to distinguish between $\mathcal{H}_{\mathbf{w},\beta,\gamma,n}$ for a uniform vector $\mathbf{w} \in \mathbb{R}^n$ and $\mathcal{N}_n(0,1)$.*

The (s, ε) homogeneous CLWE (hCLWE(s, ε)) assumption [BRST21] postulates that for a random $\mathbf{w}$, a hCLWE oracle cannot be distinguished in size s from an oracle that outputs $\mathcal{N}(0,1)$ samples on $\mathbb{R}^n$ with advantage ε. As evidence Bruna, Regev, Song, and Tang show a polynomial-time quantum reduction from the problem of sampling a discrete gaussian of width $O(\sqrt{n}/\beta)$ times the smoothing parameter assuming $\gamma \geq 2\sqrt{n}$. Specifically, if γ and β are polynomial in n then it is plausible that hCLWE holds with s and $1/\varepsilon$ exponential in n. Note that they define the standard normal distribution as $\mathcal{N}(0, 1/(2\pi))$ instead of $\mathcal{N}(0,1)$.

It can be shown that all hCLWE versions with different variances are equivalent by rescaling the samples and the problem parameters γ and β. In particular hCLWE with normal distribution $\mathcal{N}(0, 1/(2\pi))$ and problem parameters γ and β is equivalent to hCLWE with normal distribution $\mathcal{N}(0, 1)$ and problem parameters $\gamma/\sqrt{2\pi}$ and $\beta/\sqrt{2\pi}$. We will always work with the $\mathcal{N}(0, 1)$ distribution for which $\gamma \geq \sqrt{n}$ is sufficient.

4   Scheme 1: Pancake Encryption

The first encryption scheme relies on the hCLWE assumption and has polynomial decryption- and constant security error. It is the basis for all of the following encryption schemes that achieve better error bounds but either rely on an assumption that is potentially easier to break and/or incur a blow-up in the key size. Furthermore, this scheme enables us to prove that hCLWE is in the complexity class SZK. Before presenting the scheme, we define a rounding function that we will need to discretize the ciphertexts of the scheme.

4.1   Rounding into Buckets of Equal Measure

We use of the following Gaussian rounding function $\text{round}_r\colon \mathbb{R} \to \{1, \ldots, r\}$ given by
$$\text{round}_r(x) = \lceil r \cdot \mu((-\infty, x)) \rceil,$$
where μ is the standard Gaussian measure on the line. In words, partition $\mathbb{R}$ into r intervals ("buckets") $J_1, J_2, \ldots, J_r$ of equal Gaussian measure, and set $\text{round}_r(x)$ to be the unique i such that $x \in J_i$. We extend the definition over $\mathbb{R}^n$ coordinate-wise, i.e. $\text{round}_r(x_1, \ldots, x_n) = (\text{round}_r(x_1), \ldots, \text{round}_r(x_n))$.

Some of the buckets are very wide (at least two of them are infinite!) so the rounding will cause encryption errors with some probability. We will argue that this is an unlikely event using the following regularity property of round_r. The *width* of an interval $J = (a, b)$ is $b - a$.

Proposition 4.1. *For every $0 < \alpha < 1$ and all r such that $r^{1-\alpha} \geq 19$, the number of i for which the width of $J_i = \text{round}_r^{-1}(i)$ exceeds $r^{-\alpha}$ is at most $2r^\alpha/\sqrt{\ln r^{1-\alpha}} + 2$.*

The k widest intervals capture a k/r fraction of the probability mass μ at the tails of the normal distribution. If t is chosen so that $\mu((-\infty, t) \cup (t, \infty)) = k/r$ then the next widest interval is of the form (t', t) and t' is uniquely determined by the constraint $\mu((t', t)) = 1/r$. Using suitable analytic approximations for the normal CDF the maximum width $t - t'$ of all remaining intervals can be bounded by $r^{-\alpha}$ when $k = \lfloor 2r^\alpha/\sqrt{\ln r^{1-\alpha}} + 2 \rfloor$.

4.2   The Encryption Scheme

The scheme is parametrized by $\gamma > 0$; $\beta > 0$; $r > 0$ and $n, m \in \mathbb{Z}$.

- The secret key is a uniformly random unit vector $\mathbf{w} \in \mathbb{R}^n$.

- The public key is a matrix $\mathbf{A} \in \mathbb{R}^{n \times m}$ whose columns are independent hCLWE samples from $\mathcal{H}_{\mathbf{w}, \beta, \gamma, n}$.
- To encrypt a 0, sample a vector $\mathbf{t} \in \{-1/\sqrt{m}, +1/\sqrt{m}\}^m$ uniformly at random and output $\mathbf{c} := \text{round}_r(\mathbf{At})$.
- To encrypt a 1, sample $\mathbf{c} \leftarrow \{1, 2, \ldots, r\}^n$ at random and output $\mathbf{c}$.
- To decrypt a ciphertext $\mathbf{c}$, take any $\mathbf{z}$ such that $\text{round}_r(\mathbf{z}) = \mathbf{c}$, compute $\gamma' \sqrt{m} \langle \mathbf{w}, \mathbf{z} \rangle \mod 1$ and check if it is in the interval $(-1/2n, 1/2n)$. If yes, output 0, else output 1.

Theorem 4.2. *Let* $\gamma = \sqrt{n}, \beta = (40000n^{3/2} \log(n))^{-1}, r = (40000n^3 \log(n))^{5/3}$ *and* $m = 10^8 \log(n)^2 n^2$. *Assuming* hCLWE(s, ε), *the scheme has decryption error* $O(1/n) + \varepsilon$ *and security error at most* $1/4 + 2\varepsilon$.

We prove correctness and security of the scheme separately. We will assume that $\mathbf{w}$ and $\mathbf{A}$ have infinite precision. In Sect. 4.5 we argue that $O(\log n)$ bits of precision are sufficient.

4.3 Correctness

There are two sources of error in this encryption scheme: key generation error and encryption error. While the key generation error is negligible, the encryption error may be noticeable.

We will call a public key $\mathbf{A}$ *good* if in all its column samples the noise e has magnitude at most $\sqrt{n}\beta$. By hCLWE(s, ε) and a union bound, a public key is good except with probability $m/e^n + \varepsilon$.

The following two claims show that the scheme is correct.

Claim. Assuming hCLWE(s, ε) where s is the complexity of rounding, the probability that $\text{Dec}(\mathbf{w}, \text{Enc}(\mathbf{A}, 0)) \neq 0$ is at most $1/2n + \varepsilon$ for all but a fraction of $m/e^n + \varepsilon$ choices of $\mathbf{A}$.

Claim. The probability that $\text{Dec}(\mathbf{w}, \text{Enc}(\mathbf{A}, 1)) \neq 1$ is at most $3/2n$.

4.4 Security

We show that the above scheme has constant security error by the following argument:

1. Under the hCLWE(s, ε) assumption, $(\mathbf{A}, \text{Enc}(\mathbf{A}, b))$ is ε-indistinguishable from $(\mathbf{N}, \text{Enc}(\mathbf{N}, b))$ for both $b = 0$ and $b = 1$, where $\mathbf{N}$ is a $n \times m$ matrix with i.i.d. entries sampled from $\mathcal{N}(0, 1)$.
2. The distributions $(\mathbf{N}, \text{Enc}(\mathbf{N}, 0))$ and $(\mathbf{N}, \text{Enc}(\mathbf{N}, 1))$ are $1/4$-statistically close.
3. It follows that the distributions $(\mathbf{A}, \text{Enc}(\mathbf{A}, 0))$ and $(\mathbf{A}, \text{Enc}(\mathbf{A}, 1))$ are at most $(1/4 + 2\varepsilon)$-indistinguishable.

The first claim follows directly from the hCLWE assumption using the fact that the encryption is an efficiently computable function of the public-key. To prove the second claim (Proposition 4.5) we will argue that for each possible set (bucket) S that is the of the form $\mathrm{round}_r^{-1}(\mathbf{c})$, the random variable $\Pr[\mathbf{Nt} \in S|\mathbf{N}]$ is unlikely to deviate from its mean $\mathbb{E}[\Pr[\mathbf{Nt} \in S|\mathbf{N}]] = \Pr[\mathbf{g} \in S]$ by much, where $\mathbf{g}$ is a standard normal vector. Then by a union bound over all the buckets we can say that with high probability over the choice of $\mathbf{N}$ the statistical distance between the two distributions is small (given $\mathbf{N}$). Recall that $\mu(S) = \Pr[\mathbf{g} \in S]$ is the standard Gaussian measure over $\mathbb{R}^n$.

Proposition 4.3. *Let $\mathbf{N}$ be an $n \times m$ matrix of independent $\mathcal{N}(0,1)$ random variables, $\mathbf{t}$ a random m-dimensional $\{-1/\sqrt{m}, +1/\sqrt{m}\}$ vector, and S be any event in $\mathbb{R}^n$. Assuming $\mu(S) \geq \exp(-\sqrt{m}/4e)$, we have*

$$\mathrm{Var}[\Pr[\mathbf{Nt} \in S|\mathbf{N}]] \leq 4e\mu(S)^2 \ln(1/\mu(S))/\sqrt{m}.$$

Proof. Using the definition $\mathrm{Var}[Z] = \mathbb{E}[Z^2] - \mathbb{E}[Z]^2$ for any random variable Z we get:

$$\mathrm{Var}[\Pr[\mathbf{Nt} \in S|\mathbf{N}]] = \Pr[\mathbf{Nt} \in S \text{ and } \mathbf{Nt'} \in S] - \Pr[\mathbf{Nt} \in S]\Pr[\mathbf{Nt'} \in S], \quad (1)$$

where $\mathbf{t}, \mathbf{t'}$ are two independent copies of a random $\pm 1/\sqrt{m}$-valued m-dimensional vector. Let $X = (X_1, \ldots, X_n) = \mathbf{Nt}$ and $X = (X_1', \ldots, X_n') = \mathbf{Nt'}$. Conditioned on $\mathbf{t}$ and $\mathbf{t'}$, each pair (X_i, X_i') is a correlated Gaussian pair (independent of the others) with covariance matrix $\mathbb{E}[X_i^2] = \mathbb{E}[X_i'^2] = 1$, $\mathbb{E}[X_i X_i'] = \rho$, where $\rho = \langle \mathbf{t}, \mathbf{t'} \rangle$ is the inner product of the vectors $\mathbf{t}$ and $\mathbf{t'}$. By contractivity we get

$$\Pr[\mathbf{Nt} \in S \text{ and } \mathbf{Nt'} \in S] \leq \Pr[\mathbf{Nt} \in S]^{1/(1+|\rho|)} \Pr[\mathbf{Nt'} \in S]^{1/(1+|\rho|)}$$

for fixed choices of $\mathbf{t}$ and $\mathbf{t'}$. The quantities $\Pr[\mathbf{Nt} \in S]$ and $\Pr[\mathbf{Nt'} \in S]$ are simply the Gaussian measure $\mu(S)$ of the bucket S, so (1) gives

$$\mathrm{Var}[\Pr[\mathbf{Nt} \in S|\mathbf{N}]] \leq \mathbb{E}[\mu(S)^{2/(1+|\rho|)} - \mu(S)^2] = \mathbb{E}[\mu(S)^{-2|\rho|/(1+|\rho|)} - 1]\mu(S)^2.$$
$$(2)$$

The expectation here is taken over the choice of $\rho = \langle \mathbf{t}, \mathbf{t'} \rangle = (Z_1 + \cdots + Z_m)/m$, where Z_i are i.i.d. ± 1. If we further use $\mu(S) \leq 1$ and $|\rho| \geq 0$, we get that

$$\mathbb{E}[\mu(S)^{-2|\rho|/(1+|\rho|)} - 1] \leq \mathbb{E}[\mu(S)^{-2|\rho|}] - 1.$$

We further bound this expression by using the following claim:

Claim. $\mathbb{E}[\mu^{-2|\rho|}] \leq \sum_{k=0}^{\infty}(es)^k$, where $s = (2\ln 1/\mu)/\sqrt{m}$.

By our assumption $\mu(S) \geq \exp(-\sqrt{m}/4e)$, we have $0 \leq es \leq 1/2$ so we get $\sum_k (es)^k = 1/(1 - es) \leq 1 + 2es$. Plugging into (2) we get the proposition.

Using Proposition 4.3 we can now bound the statistical distance between $(\mathbf{N}, \mathrm{round}_r(\mathbf{Nt}))$ and $(\mathbf{N}, \mathrm{round}_r(\mathbf{g}))$ which are basically encryptions of 0 and 1 with a standard normal matrix instead of a public key. Security of the scheme then follows from the fact that under the hCLWE assumption $\mathbf{N}$ is indistinguishable from a public key.

Corollary 4.4. *Let* round *be any discrete-valued function on* $\mathbb{R}^n$ *such that the value* $\mu(\text{round}^{-1}(\mathbf{c})) \geq \alpha$ *for all* $\mathbf{c}$ *in the range of* round*. Then the statistical distance between* $(\mathbf{N}, \text{round}(\mathbf{Nt}))$ *and* $(\mathbf{N}, \text{round}(\mathbf{g}))$ *is at most* $\sqrt{4e\ln(1/\alpha)}/\sqrt{m}$.

Proof. We will assume $\alpha \geq \exp(-\sqrt{m}/4e)$ for otherwise $\sqrt{4e\ln(1/\alpha)}/\sqrt{m} \geq 1$ and the claim is true. Fix $\mathbf{c}$ and let $S = \text{round}^{-1}(\mathbf{c})$. Applying the Cauchy-Schwarz inequality to Proposition 4.3 we have

$$\mathbb{E}\left|\Pr[\mathbf{Nt} \in S|\mathbf{N}] - \mu(S)\right| \leq \sqrt{\frac{4e\ln(1/\mu(S))}{\sqrt{m}}} \cdot \mu(S).$$

In particular, if $\mu(\text{round}^{-1}(\mathbf{c})) \geq \alpha \geq \exp(-\sqrt{m}/4e)$ for every $\mathbf{c}$, then

$$\Delta((\mathbf{N}, \text{round}(\mathbf{Nt})); (\mathbf{N}, \text{round}(\mathbf{g})))$$

$$= \frac{1}{2}\mathbb{E}\left[\sum_{\mathbf{c}}|\Pr[\text{round}(\mathbf{Nt}) = \mathbf{c}|\mathbf{N}] - \Pr[\text{round}(\mathbf{g}) = \mathbf{c}|\mathbf{N}]|\right]$$

$$\leq \frac{1}{2}\sum_{\mathbf{c}}\sqrt{\frac{4e\ln(1/\mu(\text{round}^{-1}(\mathbf{c})))}{\sqrt{m}}} \cdot \mu(\text{round}^{-1}(\mathbf{c}))$$

$$\leq \sqrt{\frac{e\ln(1/\alpha)}{\sqrt{m}}}\sum_{\mathbf{c}}\mu(\text{round}^{-1}(\mathbf{c})),$$

which is at most the desired expression as the summation equals $\mu(\mathbb{R}^n) = 1$.

Proposition 4.5. *The distributions* $(\mathbf{N}, \text{Enc}(\mathbf{N}, 0))$ *and* $(\mathbf{N}, \text{Enc}(\mathbf{N}, 1))$ *are* $1/4$-*statistically close for a matrix* $\mathbf{N}$ *of independent standard Gaussians.*

Proof. By construction, $\mu(\text{round}_r^{-1}(b)) = r^{-n}$ for all b. By Corollary 4.4 the statistical distance between encryptions is then at most $\sqrt{4e\ln r^n}/\sqrt{m}$ which is at most $1/4$ by our choice of parameters.

Corollary 4.6. *Assuming* hCLWE(s, ε), $(\mathbf{A}, \text{Enc}(\mathbf{A}, 0))$ *and* $(\mathbf{A}, \text{Enc}(\mathbf{A}, 1))$ *are* $(s - \text{poly}(n), 1/4 + 2\varepsilon)$-*indistinguishable where* $\mathbf{A}$ *is the public key matrix.*

Proof. Let $\mathbf{N}$ be a random normal matrix. By hCLWE(s, ε), $(\mathbf{A}, \text{Enc}(\mathbf{A}, b))$ and $(\mathbf{N}, \text{Enc}(\mathbf{N}, b))$ are $(s - \text{poly}(n), \varepsilon)$-indistinguishable for both $b = 0$ and $b = 1$. By Proposition 4.5, $(\mathbf{N}, \text{Enc}(\mathbf{N}, 0))$ and $(\mathbf{N}, \text{Enc}(\mathbf{N}, 1))$ are $(\infty, 1/4)$-indistinguishable. The corollary follows from the triangle inequality.

4.5   Precision

As we are working with real numbers it is also necessary to discuss how precision can affect the scheme. We denote by ρ the positive integer that determines the precision and for $\rho = \omega(\log n)$ the distance between the real value and the one obtained as a result of the approximation errors is negligible. This guarantees that decryption is not affected (up to a negligible fraction).

5   The s-hCLWE and $(0, 1/2)$-hCLWE Distributions

In this section we introduce two distributions that are indistinguishable from $\mathcal{N}_n(0,1)$ (i.e. n-dimensional vectors with i.i.d. entries from $\mathcal{N}(0,1)$) by the CLWE assumption: the s-hCLWE and the $(0,1/2)$-hCLWE distributions. Samples from the s-hCLWE distribution are CLWE samples $(\mathbf{y}_i, z_i)$ with $z_i = s$. Note that by definition the 0-hCLWE distribution is just the hCLWE distribution. Samples from the $(0,1/2)$-hCLWE distribution are CLWE samples $(\mathbf{y}_i, z_i)$ with $z_i \in \{0, 1/2\}$. We obtain them by flipping a coin and, depending on the outcome, generating either an hCLWE sample or a $1/2$-hCLWE sample. In the next two encryption schemes ("bimodal" in Sect. 6 and "discretized" in Sect. 7) we use samples from the $(0,1/2)$-hCLWE distribution to construct the public key.

To argue that these two distributions are indistinguishable from $\mathcal{N}_n(0,1)$, we give a reduction from CLWE to both distributions. We also give a reduction from $1/2$-hCLWE to hCLWE for completeness even though it is not needed in the rest of the paper.

5.1   The s-hCLWE Distribution

We begin by formally defining the distribution and then we show that there exists a reduction from CLWE.

Definition 5.1 (s-hCLWE Distribution). *For a unit vector $\mathbf{w} \in \mathbb{R}^n$, real numbers $\beta, \gamma > 0$, $n \in \mathbb{N}$ and $s \in [0,1]$, samples $\mathbf{y} \in \mathbb{R}^n$ for the s-hCLWE distribution $\mathcal{H}^s_{\mathbf{w},\beta,\gamma,n}$ are generated as follows:*

1. *Sample $k \in \mathbb{Z} + s$ with probability proportional to $\exp(-k^2/(2\gamma^2 + 2\beta^2))$.*
2. *Sample $e \leftarrow \mathcal{N}(0, \beta'^2)$, where $\beta'^2 := \beta^2/(\gamma^2 + \beta^2)$.*
3. *Sample $\mathbf{v}$ as $\mathcal{N}_{n-1}(0,1)$ from the subspace orthogonal to $\mathbf{w}$.*
4. *Output $\mathbf{y} := \mathbf{v} + (k/\gamma' + e)\mathbf{w}$, where $\gamma' := (\gamma^2 + \beta^2)/\gamma$.*

It follows from the definition that hCLWE corresponds to the case $s = 0$. When $s = 0$, we write $\mathcal{H}_{\mathbf{w},\beta,\gamma,n}$ instead of $\mathcal{H}^0_{\mathbf{w},\beta,\gamma,n}$. The s-hCLWE distinguishing problem is to distinguish between s-hCLWE samples and standard normal ones.

Definition 5.2 (s-hCLWE Distinguishing Problem). *For real numbers $\beta, \gamma > 0$, $n \in \mathbb{N}$ and $s \in [0,1]$, the (average-case) distinguishing problem s-hCLWE$_{\beta,\gamma,n}$ asks to distinguish between $\mathcal{H}^s_{\mathbf{w},\beta,\gamma,n}$ for a uniform unit vector $\mathbf{w} \in \mathbb{R}^n$ and $\mathcal{N}_n(0,1)$.*

We do not consider the worst-case formulation of this problem as it is equivalent to the average-case one. The proof is analogous to [BRST21, Claim 2.22] for hCLWE and CLWE.

We now proceed to compare s-hCLWE to hCLWE and CLWE. First of all, using rejection sampling it is possible to obtain s-hCLWE samples from CLWE samples. This result follows from [BRST21, Lemma 4.1], which shows this for the case $s = 0$. Let $\mathcal{A}_{\mathbf{w},\beta,\gamma,n}$ denote the distribution of CLWE samples.

Lemma 5.3. *For a unit vector* $\mathbf{w} \in \mathbb{R}^n$, *real numbers* $\beta, \gamma > 0$, $n \in \mathbb{N}$ *and* $s \in [0, 1]$, *there exists a probabilistic algorithm that runs in time* $\mathrm{poly}(n, 1/\delta)$ *and that on input* $\delta \in (0, 1)$ *and samples from* $\mathcal{A}_{\mathbf{w}, \beta, \gamma, n}$, *outputs samples from* $\mathcal{H}^s_{\mathbf{w}, \sqrt{\beta^2 + \delta^2}, \gamma, n}$.

Proof. The same proof as the one of Lemma 4.1 in [BRST21] with $g_0(z) := \sum_{k \in \mathbb{Z}} \rho_\delta(z + s + k)$.

If we take $\delta = \beta/\sqrt{2}$, we obtain as a corollary the following reduction:

Proposition 5.4. *For* $s \in [0, 1]$, $n \in \mathbb{N}$ *and real numbers* $\beta = \beta(n), \gamma = \gamma(n) > 0$ *such that* β *is the inverse of a polynomial in* n, *there exists a polynomial-time reduction from* $\mathrm{CLWE}_{\beta/\sqrt{2}, \gamma, n}$ *to* $s\text{-hCLWE}_{\beta, \gamma, n}$.

Now that we have given a reduction from CLWE to s-hCLWE it is a natural question to ask whether there is a reduction from s-hCLWE to CLWE. However, we do not know if this is possible for any value of s.

5.2   The $(0, 1/2)$-hCLWE Distribution

We now define the $(0, 1/2)$-hCLWE distribution, which is the distribution on which the following two encryptions schemes are based. Afterwards we show that there is a reduction from CLWE to $(0, 1/2)$-hCLWE.

Definition 5.5 ($(0, 1/2)$**-hCLWE Distribution**). *For a unit vector* $\mathbf{w} \in \mathbb{R}^n$ *and real numbers* $\beta, \gamma > 0$, $n \in \mathbb{N}$, *samples* $(\mathbf{y}, z) \in \mathbb{R}^n \times \{0, 1/2\}$ *for the* $(0, 1/2)vhCLWE$ *distribution* $\mathcal{H}^{(0, 1/2)}_{\mathbf{w}, \beta, \gamma, n}$ *are generated as follows:*

1. *Sample* $z \leftarrow \{0, 1/2\}$.
2. *Sample* $\mathbf{y} \leftarrow \mathcal{H}^z_{\mathbf{w}, \beta, \gamma, n}$.
3. *Output* $(\mathbf{y}, z)$.

Definition 5.6 ($(0, 1/2)$**-hCLWE Distinguishing Problem**). *For real numbers* $\beta, \gamma > 0$ *and* $n \in \mathbb{N}$, *the (average-case) problem* $(0, 1/2)\text{-hCLWE}_{\beta, \gamma, n}$ *asks to distinguish between* $\mathcal{H}^{(0, 1/2)}_{\mathbf{w}, \beta, \gamma, n}$ *for a uniform unit vector* $\mathbf{w} \in \mathbb{R}^n$ *and* $\mathcal{N}_n(0, 1) \times \mathcal{U}(\{0, 1/2\})$.

Lemma 5.7. *For a unit vector* $\mathbf{w} \in \mathbb{R}^n$, $n \in \mathbb{N}$ *and real numbers* $\beta, \gamma > 0$, *there exists a probabilistic algorithm that runs in time* $\mathrm{poly}(n, 1/\delta)$ *and that on input* $\delta \in (0, 1)$ *and samples from* $\mathcal{A}_{\mathbf{w}, \beta, \gamma, n}$, *outputs samples from* $\mathcal{H}^{(0, 1/2)}_{\mathbf{w}, \sqrt{\beta^2 + \delta^2}, \gamma, n}$.

Proof. We first sample $z \leftarrow \{0, 1/2\}$ uniformly at random. By Lemma 5.3 we can obtain a sample $\mathbf{y}$ from $\mathcal{H}^z_{\mathbf{w}, \sqrt{\beta^2 + \delta^2}, \gamma, n}$ using samples from $\mathcal{A}_{\mathbf{w}, \beta, \gamma, n}$ in time $\mathrm{poly}(n, 1/\delta)$ and $(\mathbf{y}, z)$ is a sample from $\mathcal{H}^{(0, 1/2)}_{\mathbf{w}, \sqrt{\beta^2 + \delta^2}, \gamma, n}$.

If we take $\delta = \beta/\sqrt{2}$, we obtain as a corollary the following result:

Proposition 5.8. *For* $n \in \mathbb{N}$ *and real numbers* $\beta = \beta(n), \gamma = \gamma(n) > 0$ *such that* β *is the inverse of a polynomial in* n, *there exists a polynomial-time reduction from* $\mathrm{CLWE}_{\beta/\sqrt{2}, \gamma, n}$ *to* $(0, 1/2)\text{-hCLWE}_{\beta, \gamma, n}$.

5.3   A Reduction from 1/2-hCLWE to hCLWE

Finally, we show that there exists a reduction from 1/2-hCLWE to hCLWE (with slightly different parameters) to get a finer understanding of the relative hardness of these phased hCLWE problems. We obtain the reduction by constructing samples from $\mathcal{H}_{\mathbf{w},\sqrt{2}\beta,\sqrt{2}\gamma,n}$ using samples from $\mathcal{H}^{1/2}_{\mathbf{w},\beta,\gamma,n}$.

Lemma 5.9. *For a unit vector* $\mathbf{w} \in \mathbb{R}^n$, $n \in \mathbb{N}$, *real numbers* $\beta, \gamma > 0$ *such that* $\gamma > \sqrt{n}$, *and independent random variables* Y_1, Y_2 *with distribution* $\mathcal{H}^{1/2}_{\mathbf{w},\beta,\gamma,n}$, *the distribution of* $(Y_1 - Y_2)/\sqrt{2}$ *is* e^{1-n}-*statistically close to* $\mathcal{H}_{\mathbf{w},\sqrt{2}\beta,\sqrt{2}\gamma,n}$.

This gives the following result:

Proposition 5.10. *For* $n \in \mathbb{N}$ *and real numbers* $\beta = \beta(n), \gamma = \gamma(n) > 0$, *there exists a polynomial-time reduction from* 1/2-hCLWE$_{\beta/\sqrt{2},\gamma/\sqrt{2},n}$ *to* hCLWE$_{\beta,\gamma,n}$.

6   Scheme 2: Bimodal Encryption

In this section we modify the "pancake" scheme from Sect. 4 to achieve perfect correctness. Note that the decryption error in this scheme can be at least polynomial since the pancakes have polynomial width in the secret direction. This is due to the fact that the hCLWE assumption can be broken whenever the error distribution has exponentially small width as was shown in [BRST21]. A random normal vector therefore "hits" a pancake with probability $1/\mathrm{poly}(n)$. If we encrypt a 1 with such a vector, decryption fails. A standard approach to amplify the decryption error is sending multiple independent ciphertexts of the same message [DNR04]. This amplification increases the size of the ciphertext and the security error since a potential adversary only needs to be successful in decrypting one of the ciphertexts. Instead, we modify the encryption process of the bit 1. We introduce the following two changes:

- The public key consists of two matrices. A matrix $\mathbf{A}_0$ whose columns are independent hCLWE samples and a matrix $\mathbf{A}_1$ whose columns are independent 1/2-hCLWE samples. The samples from both matrices are obtained from the same secret direction $\mathbf{w}$.
- To encrypt a 0, take the matrix $\mathbf{A}_0$ and perform the same encryption as in the first scheme. To encrypt a 1, do exactly the same but with the matrix $\mathbf{A}_1$.

In Sect. 4 we have already seen that the decryption of Enc(0) is $1/\mathrm{poly}(n)$-close to 0 mod 1. We show that in our modified scheme the decryption of Enc(1) is $1/\mathrm{poly}(n)$ to 1/2 so the scheme has perfect correctness. Security of the scheme follows by Proposition 4.5 and the triangle inequality.

6.1   The Encryption Scheme

The scheme is parametrized by $\gamma > 0$, $\beta > 0$, $n \in \mathbb{Z}, r > 0$ and $m \in \mathbb{Z} \setminus 2\mathbb{Z}$ an odd integer.

- The secret key is a uniformly random unit vector $\mathbf{w} \in \mathbb{R}^n$.
- The public key is a pair of matrices $(\mathbf{A}_0, \mathbf{A}_1) \in \mathbb{R}^{n \times m} \times \mathbb{R}^{n \times m}$. The columns of $\mathbf{A}_0$ are independent hCLWE samples and the columns of $\mathbf{A}_1$ are independent 1/2-hCLWE samples.
- To encrypt a bit $b \in \{0, 1\}$, compute $\mathbf{c} := \mathrm{round}_r(\mathbf{A}_b \mathbf{t})$, where $\mathbf{t} \leftarrow \{-1/\sqrt{m}, 1/\sqrt{m}\}^m$ is sampled uniformly at random. Check if all of the entries of $\mathbf{c}$ correspond to a bucket of width less than $1/(5\sqrt{nm}\gamma')$. If yes, output $\mathbf{c}$. If no, output b.
- To decrypt a ciphertext $\mathbf{c}$, take any $\mathbf{z}$ such that $\mathrm{round}_r(\mathbf{z}) = \mathbf{c}$, compute $\gamma'\sqrt{m} \cdot \langle \mathbf{w}, \mathbf{z} \rangle \bmod 1$ and check if it is closer to 0 or closer to 1/2. In the former case output 0 in the latter case output 1.

The continuous quantities $\mathbf{w}, \mathbf{A}_0, \mathbf{A}_1$ are represented with $O(\log n)$ bits of precision. As the precision analysis is analogous to the one for pancake encryption we omit it.

Theorem 6.1. *Let* $\gamma = \sqrt{n}$, $\beta = (40000n^{5/2}\log(n)^2)^{-1}$, $r = (40000n^3 \log(n))^{5/3}$ *and* $m = 10^8 n^2 \log(n)^2$. *Assuming* $(0, 1/2)$-hCLWE(s, ε) *we have that for all but a fraction of* $2^{-\Omega(n)}$ *choices of the public key the scheme has perfect correctness and security error at most* $1/2 + 1/n^2 + 3\varepsilon$.

We prove correctness and security of the scheme separately.

6.2   Correctness

We call a public key good if the norm of the noise vector is less than $m\beta'$ in both matrices. This holds except with probability $2^{-\Omega(n)}$. During the construction of the public key it can be efficiently tested if a public key is good by checking if the absolute value of the generated noise value is small enough.

Claim. If the public key is good, the scheme has perfect correctness.

6.3   Security

There are two sources of security error in this scheme:

1. If at least one of the entries of the ciphertext corresponds to a bucket of width larger than $1/(5\sqrt{nm}\gamma')$, the encryption algorithm outputs the plaintext in the clear.
2. If the above event does not happen, the ciphertexts of 0 and of 1 are $1/2 + 2\varepsilon$-indistinguishable.

Claim. Let $\mathbf{A}_b \in \mathbb{R}^{n \times m}$ be a matrix whose columns consist either of independent hCLWE-samples or of independent 1/2-hCLWE samples. Let $\mathbf{t} \leftarrow \{-1/\sqrt{m}, 1/\sqrt{m}\}^m$ be sampled uniformly at random. Assuming hCLWE(s, ε) and 1/2-hCLWE(s, ε), where s is the complexity of rounding, the probability that any entry of the vector $\mathbf{c} := \text{round}_r(\mathbf{A}_b \mathbf{t})$ corresponds to a bucket of width larger than $1/(5\sqrt{m}\gamma')$ is at most $1/n^2 + \varepsilon$.

Proof. First consider a matrix $\mathbf{A}$ with i.i.d. entries from $\mathcal{N}(0, 1)$. Since $\|\mathbf{t}\| = 1$ we get that $\mathbf{At}$ is a vector with i.i.d. entries in $\mathcal{N}(0, 1)$. By Proposition 4.1 we know that the number of intervals of length larger than $1/(5\sqrt{nm}\gamma')$ is at most $10\sqrt{nm}\gamma'/\sqrt{\ln(r/(5\sqrt{nm}\gamma'))} + 2$, so the probability that any entry lands in such a bucket is at most

$$\frac{10n\sqrt{nm}\gamma'}{r\sqrt{\ln(r/(5\sqrt{nm}\gamma'))}} + \frac{2n}{r} \leq \frac{\gamma'n\sqrt{nm} + 2n}{r} \leq \frac{1}{n^2}.$$

The claim follows from the fact that the matrices $\mathbf{A}_0$ and $\mathbf{A}_1$ are ε-indistinguishable from $\mathbf{A}$ and the rounding function being efficiently computable.

Remark 6.2. Note that we can avoid the above event by rejection sampling the public key. Since $\mathbf{t}$ is a unit vector, the absolute value of the inner product of any vector $\mathbf{a}$ with $\mathbf{t}$ is bounded by the norm of $\mathbf{a}$. This means that we can avoid the event that an entry of the ciphertext $\mathbf{c}$ corresponds to a wide bucket by rejection sampling the matrices $\mathbf{A}_0, \mathbf{A}_1$: As long as the rows of these matrices have small enough norm, the entries of the vector $\mathbf{A}_b \mathbf{t}$ will not land in a wide bucket for both $b \in \{0, 1\}$. We omit a formal analysis of this optimization because the main security issue is not the rounding error but the probability of distinguishing ciphertexts of 0 and 1 as is shown by the next claim.

Claim. The distributions $(\mathbf{N}_0, \mathbf{N}_1, \text{Enc}(\mathbf{N}_0, 0))$ and $(\mathbf{N}_0, \mathbf{N}_1, \text{Enc}(\mathbf{N}_1, 1))$ are 1/2-statistically close for matrices $\mathbf{N}_0, \mathbf{N}_1$ of independent standard Gaussians.

Proof. By Proposition 4.5 we have

$$\Delta((\mathbf{N}_0, \mathbf{N}_1, \text{Enc}(\mathbf{N}_b, b)), (\mathbf{N}_0, \mathbf{N}_1, \mathbf{g})) \leq 1/4,$$

where $\mathbf{g}$ is a vector with i.i.d. entries sampled uniformly from $\{1, 2, \ldots, r\}$ and $b \in \{0, 1\}$. By the triangle inequality we follow that

$$\Delta((\mathbf{N}_0, \mathbf{N}_1, \text{Enc}(\mathbf{N}_0, 0)), (\mathbf{N}_0, \mathbf{N}_1, \text{Enc}(\mathbf{N}_1, 1))) \leq 1/2.$$

Corollary 6.3. *Assuming* $(0, 1/2)$-hCLWE(s, ε), *the distributions* $(\mathbf{A}_0, \mathbf{A}_1,$ Enc$(\mathbf{A}_0, 0))$ *and* $(\mathbf{A}_0, \mathbf{A}_1, \text{Enc}(\mathbf{A}_1, 1))$ *are* $(s - \text{poly}(n), 1/2 + 2\varepsilon)$-*indistinguishable where* $\mathbf{A}_0, \mathbf{A}_1$ *are the public key matrices.*

Proof. Let $\mathbf{N}_0, \mathbf{N}_1$ be standard normal matrices. By $(0, 1/2)$-hCLWE(s, ε), the distributions $(\mathbf{A}_0, \mathbf{A}_1 \text{Enc}(\mathbf{A}_b, b))$ and $(\mathbf{N}_0, \mathbf{N}_1, \text{Enc}(\mathbf{N}_b, b))$ are $(s - \text{poly}(n), \varepsilon)$-indistinguishable for both $b = 0$ and $b = 1$. By Claim 6.3, $(\mathbf{N}_0, \mathbf{N}_1, \text{Enc}(\mathbf{N}_0, 0))$ and $(\mathbf{N}_0, \mathbf{N}_1, \text{Enc}(\mathbf{N}_1, 1))$ are $(\infty, 1/2)$-indistinguishable. The corollary follows from the triangle inequality.

7   Scheme 3: Discretized Encryption

In this section we describe an encryption scheme based on CLWE that has negligible soundness error and perfect correctness for all but a fraction of $1/\mathrm{poly}(n)$ many public keys. The scheme is inspired by the encryption scheme in [AD97] which also achieves negligible soundness error but only polynomial decryption error. We reduce this decryption error by applying their techniques to the bimodal encryption scheme from Sect. 6 which is based on $(0, 1/2)$-hCLWE. Alternatively, it could be applied to the baguette encryption scheme presented in Sect. 8 which would yield a scheme based on hCLWE. An important concept from [AD97] is the parallelepiped technique which enables us to transform continuous Gaussian samples into uniform ones. We first describe the technique before we present the encryption scheme and prove its correctness and security.

7.1   The Parallelepiped Technique and $\mathbb{Z}_q$

We will make use of the parallelepiped technique introduced by Ataj and Dwork in [AD97]. Let $\mathbf{B} = (\mathbf{b}_1, \ldots, \mathbf{b}_n) \in \mathbb{R}^{n \times n}$ be an arbitrary matrix of rank n. We denote by $\mathcal{P}(\mathbf{B})$ the n-dimensional parallelepiped that is defined by the columns of $\mathbf{B}$, i.e.

$$\mathcal{P}(\mathbf{B}) := \left\{ \sum_{i \in [n]} \lambda_i \mathbf{b}_i : 0 \le \lambda_i < 1 \text{ for all } i \in [n] \right\}.$$

We denote by $\mathcal{P}_q(\mathbf{B})$ the set we obtain by partitioning $\mathcal{P}(\mathbf{B})$ into q^n smaller parallelpipeds of equal volume, labelling them by vectors with entries from 0 to $q - 1$ and then identifying each vector with the corresponding label, i.e.

$$\mathcal{P}_q(\mathbf{B}) := \left\{ \lfloor q\mathbf{B}^{-1}\mathbf{c} \rfloor : \mathbf{c} \in \mathcal{P}(\mathbf{B}) \right\}.$$

We will later need the following fact:

Fact 7.1. Let $\mathbf{B} = (\mathbf{b}_1, \ldots, \mathbf{b}_n) \in \mathbb{R}^{n \times n}$ be an arbitrary matrix of rank n. Then $(\mathcal{P}_q(\mathbf{B}), +)$ is a group isomorphic to $\mathbb{Z}_q^n$.

This can be seen by the following argument: We obtain $\mathcal{P}_q(\mathbf{B})$ by partitioning each vector $\mathbf{b}_i$ into q equal parts. Labelling the parts by $\{0, 1, 2, \ldots, q - 1\}$ in the natural way gives an isomorphism between the q parts of $\mathbf{b}_i$ and $\mathbb{Z}_q$ for any $i \in [n]$. Fact 7.1 follows by taking the direct product of the labellings of the $\mathbf{b}_i$.

In the construction of our public key we essentially map continuous Gaussian vectors into $\mathcal{P}(\mathbf{B})$. We will need the next lemma to show that this mapping transforms them into uniformly random vectors. We denote by $\eta_\varepsilon(\mathbf{B})$ the smoothing parameter of the lattice with basis $\mathbf{B}$.

Lemma 7.1 ([MR07, Lemma 4.1]). *Let $\mathbf{B} \in \mathbb{R}^{n \times n}$ be a square matrix of rank n. For any $\varepsilon > 0$ and any $s > \eta_\varepsilon(\mathbf{B})$ the statistical distance between $\mathcal{N}_n(0, s^2)$ mod $\mathbf{B}$ and the uniform distribution over $\mathcal{P}(\mathbf{B})$ is at most $\varepsilon/2$.*

The following lemma is a special case of [MR07, Lemma 3.2].

Lemma 7.2. *For any n-dimensional lattice L with basis $B = \{b_1, b_2, \ldots, b_n\}$ we have $\eta_{2^{-n}}(B) \leq \sqrt{n} \max_i \|b_i\|$.*

7.2   The Encryption Scheme

The scheme is parametrized by $\gamma > 0$; $\beta > 0$; $n, m, q \in \mathbb{Z} \setminus 2\mathbb{Z}$ odd integers. We set n to be an odd integer only to clarify the description and the analysis, m and q however are always required to be odd.

- The secret key is a vector $\mathbf{B}^T \mathbf{w}$, where $\mathbf{w} \in \mathbb{R}^n$ is a uniformly random unit vector and $\mathbf{B}$ is a matrix whose columns consist of hCLWE samples, such that the smallest singular value of $\mathbf{B}$ is larger than $1/m$.
- The public key is a pair of matrices $(\mathbf{A}_0, \mathbf{A}_1) \in \mathbb{Z}_q^{n \times m} \times \mathbb{Z}_q^{n \times m}$. The columns of $\mathbf{A}_0$ and $\mathbf{A}_1$ are of the form

$$B\text{-round}(n\mathbf{a}_i \quad \mathrm{mod}\ \mathbf{B}),$$

where $B\text{-round} = B\text{-round}_q : \mathbb{R}^n \to \mathbb{Z}_q^n$ is defined as $B\text{-round}_q(a) = \lfloor q\mathbf{B}^{-1}a \rceil$. In the case of $\mathbf{A}_0$ the vectors $\mathbf{a}_i$ are samples from the hCLWE distribution $\mathcal{H}_{\mathbf{w},\beta,\gamma,n}$ and in the case of $\mathbf{A}_1$ they are $1/2$-hCLWE samples from $\mathcal{H}_{\mathbf{w},\beta,\gamma,n}^{1/2}$.
- To encrypt a bit $b \in \{0, 1\}$, compute

$$\mathbf{c} := \mathbf{A}_b \mathbf{t} \quad \mathrm{mod}\ q,$$

where $\mathbf{t} \leftarrow \{-1, 1\}^m$ is sampled uniformly at random.
- To decrypt a ciphertext $\mathbf{c}$, compute

$$\gamma' \langle \mathbf{B}^T \mathbf{w}, \mathbf{c}/q \rangle \quad \mathrm{mod}\ 1$$

and check if it is closer to 0 or closer to $1/2$. In the former case output 0 in the latter case output 1.

Remark 7.3. In the next section we will see that we require n to be an odd integer only because we need that the inner product of $\mathbf{w}$ with $1/2$-hCLWE samples scaled by a factor n is approximately $1/2 \bmod 1$ and not 0. One can slightly change the scheme for even values of n: Scale the samples by a factor $n+1$ instead of n. In the rest of the section we will assume that n is odd without loss of generality.

Theorem 7.4. *Set the parameters of the scheme to $\gamma = \sqrt{n}, m = 8n\log(n), \beta = 1/n^{10}, q = n^7$. Assuming $(0, 1/2)$-hCLWE(s, ε) we get that for all but a fraction of $1/(8n^{1/2}\log(n)) + O(\varepsilon)$ choices of the public key the scheme has perfect correctness and negligible soundness error.*

We prove correctness and soundness of the scheme separately in the next two subsections.

7.3   Correctness

We show that for all but a fraction of at most $1/(8n^{1/2}\log(n)) + \varepsilon$ choices of the key pair decryption is always correct. We denote by $\{\mathbf{b}_1, \ldots, \mathbf{b}_n\}$ the columns of $\mathbf{B}$, by $\{\mathbf{a}_1^0, \ldots, \mathbf{a}_m^0\}$ the hCLWE samples used to construct $\mathbf{A}_0$ and by $\{\mathbf{a}_1^1, \ldots, \mathbf{a}_m^1\}$ the $1/2$-hCLWE samples used to construct $\mathbf{A}_1$. We define $\mathbf{e} := \gamma' \mathbf{w}^T \mathbf{B} \mod 1$ which is the noise vector of the hCLWE samples $\mathbf{b}_i$. For $b \in \{0,1\}$ we define

$$\mathbf{e}_b^T := \gamma' \mathbf{w}^T \left(n\mathbf{a}_1^b, n\mathbf{a}_2^b, \ldots, n\mathbf{a}_m^b\right) - b \cdot (1/2, 1/2, \ldots, 1/2) \mod 1.$$

If $b = 0$ this is the vector where each entry is the noise value corresponding to the hCLWE sample scaled by n during the construction of $\mathbf{A}_0$. If $b = 1$ this is the noise vector we get during the construction of $\mathbf{A}_1$. We call a key pair $(\mathbf{B}^T\mathbf{w}, (\mathbf{A}_0, \mathbf{A}_1))$ *good* if the following holds:

1. $\|\mathbf{e}_0\|, \|\mathbf{e}_1\| \leq mn\beta'$;
2. $\|\mathbf{e}\| \leq n\beta'$;
3. For all $i \in [m]$ the entries of $\mathbf{a}_i^0, \mathbf{a}_i^1$ lie in the interval $[-n^{3/2}, n^{3/2}]$;
4. For all $i \in [n]$ the entries of $\mathbf{b}_i$ lie in the interval $[-n, n]$;
5. the smallest singular value of $\mathbf{B}$ is larger than $1/m$.

Note that all of these conditions can be efficiently tested during the key generation.

Claim.
If the $(0, 1/2)$-hCLWE(s, ε) assumption holds, a key pair $(\mathbf{B}^T\mathbf{w}, (\mathbf{A}_0, \mathbf{A}_1))$ is good except with probability $1/(8n^{1/2}\log(n)) + O(\varepsilon)$.

For a proof of this result see the full version.

Claim. If the key-pair $(\mathbf{B}^T\mathbf{w}, (\mathbf{A}_0, \mathbf{A}_1))$ is good, decryption is correct with probability 1.

For a proof of this result see the full version.

7.4   Security

We show that encryptions of 0 and 1 are indistinguishable under the $(0, 1/2)$-hCLWE assumption by showing that the following distributions are indistinguishable for $b \in \{0,1\}$:

1. Real$_b$: $(\mathbf{A}_0, \mathbf{A}_1, \mathbf{A}_b\mathbf{t} \mod q)$ is a public key of the encryption scheme together with an encryption of b.
2. Hybrid$_b$: $(\mathbf{A}_0, \mathbf{A}_1, \mathbf{A}_b\mathbf{t} \mod q)$ is a tuple where the columns of $\mathbf{A}_0$ and $\mathbf{A}_1$ are uniformly random vectors in $\mathbb{Z}_q^{n \times m}$.
3. Ideal: $(\mathbf{A}_0, \mathbf{A}_1, \mathbf{r})$ is the same as above but with $\mathbf{r}$ a uniformly random vector in $\mathbb{Z}_q^n$.

Real_b and Hybrid_b are computationally indistinguishable under the $(0, 1/2)$-hCLWE assumption. Hybrid_b and Ideal are statistically indistinguishable by the leftover hash lemma. In the rest of the section we formally prove the above statements. We start by showing the first claim.

Claim. Under the $(0, 1/2)$-hCLWE(s, ε) assumption the distributions Real_b and Hybrid_b are $(s - \text{poly}(n), 2^{-n+1} + \varepsilon)$-indistinguishable.

Proof. Assume that there is a distinguisher D that decides if $(\mathbf{A}_0, \mathbf{A}_1, \mathbf{A}_b \mathbf{t} \mod q)$ is from Real_b or from Hybrid_b with probability δ. We construct an algorithm D' that distinguishes between $(0, 1/2)$-hCLWE samples and random samples with probability $\delta - 2^{-n+1}$ as follows:

1. Given poly(n) many $(0, 1/2)$-hCLWE samples $\{(\mathbf{y}_i, z_i)\}_{i \in [\text{poly}(n)]}$, define a matrix $\mathbf{B}$ by choosing n samples with $z_i = 0$ such that the corresponding vectors $\mathbf{y}_i$ are linearly independent. These vectors are the columns of $\mathbf{B}$.
2. Choose m samples of the form $\{(\hat{\mathbf{y}}_i, 0)\}_{i \in [m]}$ and compute

$$\mathbf{y}_i^0 = B\text{-round}\,(n\hat{\mathbf{y}}_i \mod \mathbf{B})$$

   and choose m samples of the form $\{(\tilde{\mathbf{y}}_i, 1/2)\}_{i \in [m]}$ and compute

$$\mathbf{y}_i^1 = B\text{-round}\,(n\tilde{\mathbf{y}}_i \mod \mathbf{B}),$$

   where $B\text{-round} = B\text{-round}_q : \mathbb{R}^n \to \mathbb{Z}_q^n$ is defined as $\text{-round}_q(\mathbf{a}) = \mathbf{B}\lfloor q\mathbf{B}^{-1}\mathbf{a}\rfloor$.
3. Let $\mathbf{A}_0$ be the matrix with columns $\mathbf{y}_i^0$ and $\mathbf{A}_1$ be the matrix with columns $\mathbf{y}_i^1$. Give $(\mathbf{A}_0, \mathbf{A}_1, \mathbf{A}_b \mathbf{t} \mod q)$ to the distinguisher D.

Note that in the case where the samples $\{(\mathbf{y}_i, z_i)\}_{i \in [\text{poly}(n)]}$ are $(0, 1/2)$-hCLWE samples, $(\mathbf{A}_0, \mathbf{A}_1)$ is a public key of our scheme. It remains to prove that given samples $\{(\mathbf{y}_i, z_i)\}_{i \in [\text{poly}(n)]}$, where the $\mathbf{y}_i$ are normal random vectors and the z_i are uniform in $\{0, 1/2\}$, the resulting matrices $\mathbf{A}_0, \mathbf{A}_1$ are statistically close to uniform matrices in $\mathbf{Z}_q^{n \times m}$. Lemma 7.1 says that if we sample a vector from a Gaussian distribution with standard deviation larger than $\eta_{2^{-n}}(\mathbf{B})$ and map it into $\mathcal{P}_q(\mathbf{B})$, the resulting vector is statistically close to uniform in $\mathcal{P}_q(\mathbf{B})$ and hence in $\mathbb{Z}_q^n$.

Now we only need an upper bound on the smoothing parameter in order to prove that the columns of $\mathbf{A}_0$ and $\mathbf{A}_1$ are sampled from a Gaussian with sufficiently large variance. The length of a vector with entries independently sampled from $\mathcal{N}(0, 1)$ is at most n except with probability $\sqrt{n}e^{-n}$. Hence, the smoothing parameter of $\mathbf{B}$ is at most $n^{3/2}$ by Lemma 7.2 except with probability $\sqrt{n}e^{-n}$. The entries of $\mathbf{A}_0$ and $\mathbf{A}_1$ are sampled from $\mathcal{N}(0, n^2)$. Since $n^2 > n^{3/2}$ we follow from Lemma 7.1 that $\mathbf{A}_0$ and $\mathbf{A}_1$ are 2^{-n+1}-statistically close to uniformly random matrices in $\mathbf{Z}_q^{n \times m}$.

Next we show that Hybrid_b is statistically close to Ideal, which completes the proof of soundness. This can be done using the classical leftover hash lemma [IZ89]. To this end we need to show that multiplication of a $\{-1, 1\}^m$ vector by a uniform matrix $\mathbf{H} \in \mathbb{Z}_q^{m \times n}$ is a universal family of hash functions, i.e.:

Claim. For q odd, $\mathbf{x}, \mathbf{y} \in \{-1, 1\}^m$ such that $\mathbf{x} \neq \mathbf{y}$ we have

$$\Pr_{\mathbf{H} \leftarrow \mathbb{Z}_q^{m \times n}} [\mathbf{Hx} = \mathbf{Hy} \mod q] = q^{-n}.$$

See the full version for a proof. The following is a special case of the leftover hash lemma [IZ89, Reg05]:

Lemma 7.5. *Let q be an odd integer. Let $\mathbf{H} \in \mathbb{Z}_q^{n \times m}$ be with columns chosen uniformly at random from $\mathbb{Z}_q^n$ and $\mathbf{t} \leftarrow \{-1, 1\}^m$ a uniformly random vector. Then the statistical distance of the uniform distribution on $\mathbb{Z}_q^n$ and the distribution given by multiplying $\mathbf{H}$ with $\mathbf{t}$ is at most $(q^n/2^m)^{1/4}$ w.p. $1 - (q^n/2^m)^{1/4}$.*

By our choice of parameters we have $m = 8n \log(n)$ and $q = n^7$. We follow that the statistical distance of Hybrid_0 and Hybrid_1 to Ideal is $(n^{7n}/2^{n^2})^{1/4} \leq 2^{-n}$ for large enough values of n. Hence, Hybrid_0 is at least 2^{-n+1}-close to Hybrid_1. Together with Claim 7.4 this yields that an encryption of 0 is $2^{-n+2} + 2\varepsilon$-indistinguishable from an encryption of 1.

7.5   Precision

A precision value of $\rho = O(\log n)$ guarantees that decryption is unaffected as a result of the approximations. The matrix entries of the public key are integer values.

Correctness of decryption remains unaffected and the proof is analogous to the one given for the pancake scheme in Sect. 4.5.

8   Scheme 4: Baguette Encryption

We now present a second approach that reduces the decryption error of the pancake scheme. The security error remains constant but could be reduced by the parallelepiped technique presented in Sect. 7. Instead of publishing samples that have a pancake distribution in only one secret direction, we publish samples that have a pancake distribution in multiple secret directions, i.e. samples from the hCLWE(ℓ) distribution. This is a distribution defined in [BRST21] to which the authors give a reduction from hCLWE. To decrypt we take the inner products of the ciphertext with all secret directions. If the ciphertext is an encryption of 0 all of the results are polynomially close to an integer. If the ciphertext is an encryption of 1, at least one of the results is not close to an integer with high probability since taken modulo 1 they are uniformly random values in $[0, 1)$. Before presenting the encryption scheme we formally define the hCLWE(ℓ) distribution.

8.1   The hCLWE(ℓ) Distribution

Both the hCLWE(ℓ), distribution and the corresponding decision problem were introduced in [BRST21]. This problem is the extension of hCLWE to the case of ℓ hidden orthogonal directions.

Definition 8.1 (hCLWE(ℓ) Distribution). *For a matrix $\mathbf{W} = (\mathbf{w}_1|\dots|\mathbf{w}_\ell) \in \mathbb{R}^{n \times \ell}$ such that $\mathbf{W}^T\mathbf{W} = \mathbf{I}_\ell$, real numbers $\beta, \gamma > 0$, $n \in \mathbb{N}$ and $\ell \in \mathbb{N}$ with $0 \le \ell \le n$, samples $\mathbf{y} \in \mathbb{R}^n$ for the hCLWE(ℓ) distribution $\mathcal{H}_{\mathbf{W},\beta,\gamma,n,\ell}$ are generated as follows:*

1. *Sample $k_1, \dots, k_\ell \in \mathbb{Z}$ independently with distribution $\mathcal{D}_{\mathbb{Z},\gamma^2+\beta^2}$.*
2. *Sample $e_1, \dots, e_\ell \leftarrow \mathcal{N}(0, \beta'^2)$ independently where $\beta'^2 := \beta^2/(\gamma^2 + \beta^2)$.*
3. *Sample $\mathbf{v}$ as $\mathcal{N}_{n-\ell}(0,1)$ from the subspace orthogonal to $\mathbf{W}$.*
4. *Output $\mathbf{y} := \mathbf{v} + \sum_{i=1}^{\ell}(k_i/\gamma' + e_i)\mathbf{w}_i$ where $\gamma' := (\gamma^2 + \beta^2)/\gamma$.*

For $\ell = 0$ we get the normal distribution with covariance matrix $\mathbf{I}_n$ and for $\ell = 1$ we recover the hCLWE distribution. We refer to the columns of $\mathbf{W}$ as the hidden directions. Note that they are orthonormal vectors.

Definition 8.2 (hCLWE(ℓ) Distinguishing Problem). *For real numbers $\beta, \gamma > 0$, $n \in \mathbb{N}$ and $\ell \in \mathbb{N}$ with $0 \le \ell \le n$, the (average-case) distinguishing problem $\text{hCLWE}_{\beta,\gamma,n}(\ell)$ asks to distinguish between $\mathcal{H}_{\mathbf{W},\beta,\gamma,n,\ell}$ for a uniform matrix $\mathbf{W} \in \mathbb{R}^{n \times \ell}$ such that $\mathbf{W}^T\mathbf{W} = \mathbf{I}_\ell$, and $\mathcal{N}_n(0,1)$.*

The hCLWE(ℓ)(s,ϵ) assumption postulates that the hCLWE(ℓ) distinguishing problem cannot be solved in size s with advantage ϵ. As shown in [BRST21] (Lemma 9.3.), if $n - \ell = \Omega(n^k)$ for some constant $k > 0$, there is an efficient reduction from $\text{hCLWE}_{\beta,\gamma,n-\ell+1}$ to $\text{hCLWE}_{\beta,\gamma,n}(\ell)$.

8.2 Encryption Scheme

We now give an encryption scheme that builds on the pancake scheme from Sect. 4. It achieves negligible decryption error using more hidden directions instead of the $(0, 1/2)$-hCLWE distribution.

The scheme is parametrized by $\gamma > 0$; $\beta > 0$; $r > 0$, $n, \ell, m \in \mathbb{N}$ and a parameter $a > 0$ for which we will only consider two possible values, namely, $a = n$ and $a = 100$.

- The secret key is a uniformly random matrix $\mathbf{W} \in \mathbb{R}^{n \times \ell}$ such that $\mathbf{W}^T\mathbf{W} = \mathbf{I}_\ell$.
- The public key is a matrix $\mathbf{A} \in \mathbb{R}^{n \times m}$ whose columns are independently sampled from $\mathcal{H}_{\mathbf{W},\beta,\gamma,n,\ell}$.
- To encrypt 0, choose a vector $\mathbf{t} \in \{-1/\sqrt{m}, +1/\sqrt{m}\}^m$ uniformly at random and output

$$\mathbf{c} := \text{round}_r(\mathbf{At}).$$

Check if all entries of $\mathbf{c}$ correspond to buckets of width less than $1/(4a\sqrt{n}\sqrt{m}\gamma')$. If yes, output $\mathbf{c}$. Otherwise, output 0.
- To encrypt 1, choose a vector $\mathbf{c} \leftarrow \{1, 2, \dots, r\}^n$ uniformly at random. Check if all entries of $\mathbf{c}$ correspond to buckets of width less than $1/(4a\sqrt{n}\sqrt{m}\gamma')$. If yes, output $\mathbf{c}$. Otherwise, output 1.

- To decrypt a ciphertext $\mathbf{c}$, take any $\mathbf{z}$ such that $\operatorname{round}_r(\mathbf{z}) = \mathbf{c}$, compute

$$\gamma'\sqrt{m}\mathbf{W}^T\mathbf{z} \mod 1$$

and check if all ℓ entries are in $(-1/2a, 1/2a)$. If yes, output 0, else output 1.

The real matrices and vectors $\mathbf{W}, \mathbf{A}, \mathbf{t}$ are represented with $O(\log n)$ bits of precision. The precision analysis is analogous to the one done in Sect. 4.5 for pancake encryption, so we omit it.

Theorem 8.3. *Set the parameters of the scheme to* $\gamma = \sqrt{n}$, $\beta = (16 \cdot 10^4 n^3 \log(n))^{-1}$, $\ell = \log n$, $m = 10^8 n^2 \log(n)^2$, $r = (40001 n^3 \log(n))^{5/3}$ *and* $a = n$. *Assuming* hCLWE(s, ε), *the scheme has negligible decryption error and security error at most* $1/4 + 4\varepsilon$.

We prove correctness and security of the scheme separately in the next two subsections.

We are also interested in using this scheme to prove that hCLWE and hCLWE(ℓ) are in SZK (statistical zero knowledge), what is shown in Sect. 9 for the following choice of parameters:

$$a = 100$$
$$\beta'\gamma' \ln \gamma' < 1/(4 \cdot 10^4 \, Kn \log n)$$
$$\gamma' > 1 \tag{3}$$
$$m = (Kn \log n \ln \gamma')^2$$
$$r = m^{10}(\gamma')^{5/3}$$

where $K = 4 \cdot 9 \cdot 10 \cdot e \cdot 2 \cdot 5$.

8.3   Correctness

The following two claims assert that the scheme is correct.

Claim. The probability that $\operatorname{Dec}(\mathbf{W}, \operatorname{Enc}(\mathbf{A}, 0)) = 0$ over the joint choice of the public key and encryption randomness is at least

$$1 - \ell\sqrt{\frac{2\beta'^2\gamma'^2 m}{\pi}} \frac{e^{-\frac{(1/4a)^2}{2\beta'^2\gamma'^2 m}}}{1/4a}.$$

In particular,

- for the choice of parameters made in Theorem 8.3, it is at least $1 - e^{-n}$, i.e., the error is a negligible function.
- for the choice of parameters suggested in Eq. 3, the probability is at least $1 - e^{-5000}$.

Claim. If $n \geq 4$, the probability that $\operatorname{Dec}(\mathbf{w}, \operatorname{Enc}(\mathbf{A}, 1)) = 1$ is at least $1 - (3/2a)^\ell - \exp(-\gamma'^2 m)$. In particular,

- for the choice of parameters made in Theorem 8.3, the probability is at least $1 - (3/2n)^{\log n} - \exp(-n^3)$, i.e., the error is negligible.
- for the choice of parameters suggested in Eq. 3, the probability is at least $1 - (3/200)^\ell - \exp(-n^2)$.

8.4   Security

In order to analyze the security of the scheme we have to take into account the possibility that at least one of the entries of the ciphertext corresponds to a bucket of width larger than $1/(4a\sqrt{n}\sqrt{m}\gamma')$ as the encryption algorithm outputs the plaintext in the clear in that case.

Claim. Let r be such that the following inequalities are satisfied

$$r^{-3/5} \leq \frac{1}{4a\sqrt{n}\sqrt{m}\gamma'} \tag{4}$$

$$\frac{2nr^{-2/5}}{\sqrt{\ln r^{2/5}}} + \frac{2n}{r} \leq \delta(n). \tag{5}$$

Let $\mathbf{A} \in \mathbb{R}^{n \times m}$ be a matrix whose columns consist of independent hCLWE(ℓ) samples and assume hCLWE(ℓ)(s, ε) where s is the complexity of rounding and ε is a function of n. Let $\mathbf{t} \leftarrow \{-1/\sqrt{m}, 1/\sqrt{m}\}^m$ be sampled uniformly at random. The probability that any entry of the vector $\mathbf{c} := \text{round}_r(\mathbf{At})$ corresponds to a bucket of width larger than $1/(4a\sqrt{n}\sqrt{m}\gamma')$ is at most $\delta(n) + \varepsilon$. For the choice of parameters made in Theorem 8.3 and in Eq. 3 both conditions are satisfied for $\delta(n) = \frac{1}{24}$.

The next claim follows directly from Proposition 4.5.

Claim. If the ciphertexts are not the messages, the distributions $(\mathbf{N}, \text{Enc}(\mathbf{N}, 0))$ and $(\mathbf{N}, \text{Enc}(\mathbf{N}, 1))$ are $\sqrt{4e \ln r^n}/\sqrt{m}$-statistically close for a matrix $\mathbf{N}$ of independent standard Gaussians. In particular,

- for the choice of parameters made in Theorem 8.3, the distance is at most $1/\sqrt{50} < 1/4$.
- for the choice of parameters suggested in Eq. 3, the distance is at most $1/3$.

Corollary 8.4. *If* hCLWE(ℓ)(s, ε) *holds, then the distributions* $(\mathbf{A}, \text{Enc}(\mathbf{A}, 0))$ *and* $(\mathbf{A}, \text{Enc}(\mathbf{A}, 1))$ *are* $(s - \text{poly}(n), \sqrt{4e \ln r^n}/\sqrt{m} + 4\varepsilon)$-*indistinguishable where* $\mathbf{A}$ *is the public key matrix. In particular,*

- *for the choice of parameters made in Theorem 8.3, and* $\varepsilon = 1/24$, *we get* $1/4 + 4/24 < 1/2$.
- *for the choice of parameters suggested in Eq. 3 and* $\varepsilon = 1/24$, *we get* $1/3 + 4/24 = 1/2$.

9   hCLWE and hCLWE(ℓ) are in SZK

In this section we prove that hCLWE and hCLWE(ℓ) are in SZK, which is the class of decision problems that admit a statistical zero-knowledge proof [GMR89]. Zero-knowledge is defined with respect to honest verifiers.

We say that a sampling problem is in SZK if there is a polynomial-time honest-verifier statistical zero-knowledge protocol that accepts at least 2/3 of the YES instances and rejects at least 2/3 of the NO instances. The choice of threshold 2/3 is operational.

Our proof consists in a reduction from hCLWE to the statistical difference problem (SD). Sahai and Vadhan proved in [SV03] that SD is complete for SZK.

Definition 9.1 (SD **Problem**). *The YES instances of the Statistical Difference (SD) problem are pairs of circuits (C_0, C_1) such that $\Delta(C_0, C_1) > 2/3$ and the NO instances are pairs of circuits (C_0, C_1) such that $\Delta(C_0, C_1) < 1/3$.*

Here Δ is the statistical (total variation) distance between the output distributions sampled by the circuits when instantiated with a uniformly random seed. That is, if the output space of C_0 and C_1 is some finite set Ω,

$$\Delta(C_0, C_1) = \sup_{A \subseteq \Omega} |\Pr[C_0 \in A] - \Pr[C_1 \in A]| = \frac{1}{2} \sum_{\omega \in \Omega} |\Pr[C_0 = \omega] - \Pr[C_1 = \omega]|$$

Since SD is a complete problem for the SZK class and SZK is a class closed under reductions (see [SV03]), we can study the SZK class by considering reductions to SD instead of interactive proof systems. This approach also removes any reference to zero-knowledge.

In order to show that hCLWE is in SZK, it suffices to define two circuits that satisfy the conditions of Definition 9.1.

Theorem 9.2. *Let K, K' be sufficiently large constants. If $\gamma' > 1$, $\beta'\gamma' \ln \gamma' < 1/(K'n \log n)$ and γ' is polynomially bounded, the $\mathrm{hCLWE}_{\beta,\gamma,n}$ problem with $m = (Kn \log n \ln \gamma')^2$ samples is in SZK.*

Proof. Take K and r as in Eq. 3, that is, $K = 4 \cdot 9 \cdot 10 \cdot e \cdot 2 \cdot 5$ and $r = m^{10}(\gamma')^{5/3}$. Let $K' = 4 \cdot 10^4 K$. Let $\mathbf{X}$ be either a valid public key $\mathbf{A} \in \mathbb{R}^{n \times m}$ or a matrix $\mathbf{N} \in \mathbb{R}^{n \times m}$ with i.i.d. entries sampled from $\mathcal{N}(0, 1)$. We define two circuits C_0, C_1 that take as input the pair $(\mathbf{t}, \mathbf{u})$ where $\mathbf{t} \in \{-1/\sqrt{m}, 1/\sqrt{m}\}^m$ and $\mathbf{u} \in \{1, 2, \ldots, r\}^n$. C_0 outputs $\mathrm{round}_r(\mathbf{Xt})$, i.e., an encryption of 0 using randomness t, while C_1 outputs $\mathbf{u}$, i.e., an encryption of 1 with randomness $\mathbf{u}$.

If $\mathbf{X} = \mathbf{A}$, by Claim 8.3 and Claim 8.3 and Claim 8.4 for $\epsilon(n) = 1/24 = \delta(n)$, the decryption error is at most $e^{-5000} + 3/200 + \exp(-n^2) + 1/24 + 1/24$. It follows that $\Delta(C_0, C_1) > 2/3$.

If $\mathbf{X} = \mathbf{N}$, then the statistical distance between C_0 and C_1 is at most $1/3$ by Proposition 4.5. $\square$

We also have an analogous statement for hCLWE(ℓ).

Theorem 9.3. *Let K, K' be sufficiently large constants. If $\gamma' > 1$, $\beta'\gamma' \ln \gamma' < 1/(K'n \log n)$, γ' is polynomially bounded and $1 \leq \ell \leq n$, $\mathrm{hCLWE}_{\beta,\gamma,n}(\ell)$ with $m = (Kn \log n \ln \gamma')^2$ samples is in SZK.*

Acknowledgements. We are grateful to Devika Sharma and Luca Trevisan for their insight and advice and to an anonymous reviewer for helpful comments.

This work was supported by the European Research Council (ERC) under the European Union's Horizon 2020 research and innovation programme (Grant agreement No. 101019547). The first author was additionally supported by RGC GRF CUHK14209920 and the fourth author was additionally supported by ISF grant No. 1399/17, project PROMETHEUS (Grant 780701), and Cariplo CRYPTONOMEX grant.

References

[ABW10] Applebaum, B., Barak, B., Wigderson, A.: Public-key cryptography from different assumptions. In: Proceedings of the Forty-Second ACM Symposium on Theory of Computing, STOC 2010, pp. 171–180. Association for Computing Machinery, New York (2010)

[AD97] Ajtai, M., Dwork, C.: A public-key cryptosystem with worst-case/average-case equivalence. In: Proceedings of the Twenty-Ninth Annual ACM Symposium on Theory of Computing, STOC 1997, pp. 284–293. Association for Computing Machinery, New York (1997)

[Ale03] Alekhnovich, M.: More on average case vs approximation complexity. In: 44th Annual IEEE Symposium on Foundations of Computer Science, Proceedings, pp. 298–307 (2003)

[BB20] Brennan, M.S., Bresler, G.: Reducibility and statistical-computational gaps from secret leakage. In: Abernethy, J.D., Agarwal, S. (eds.) Conference on Learning Theory, COLT 2020, 9–12 July 2020, Virtual Event [Graz, Austria], Proceedings of Machine Learning Research, , vol. 125, pp. 648–847. PMLR (2020)

[BNHR22] Bogdanov, A., Noval, M.C., Hoffmann, C., Rosen, A.: Public-key encryption from continuous LWE. Cryptology ePrint Archive, Paper 2022/093 (2022). https://eprint.iacr.org/2022/093

[BR13] Berthet, Q., Rigollet, P.: Complexity theoretic lower bounds for sparse principal component detection. In: Shalev-Shwartz, S., Steinwart, I. (eds.) Proceedings of the 26th Annual Conference on Learning Theory, Proceedings of Machine Learning Research, vol. 30, pp. 1046–1066. PMLR, Princeton, 12–14 June 2013

[BRST21] Bruna, J., Regev, O., Song, M.J., Tang, Y.: Continuous LWE. In: Proceedings of the 53rd Annual ACM SIGACT Symposium on Theory of Computing, STOC 2021, pp. 694–707. Association for Computing Machinery, New York (2021)

[BS15] Belkin, M., Sinha, K.: Polynomial learning of distribution families. SIAM J. Comput. 44(4), 889–911 (2015)

[DKS17] Diakonikolas, I., Kane, D.M., Stewart, A.: Statistical query lower bounds for robust estimation of high-dimensional gaussians and gaussian mixtures. In: 2017 IEEE 58th Annual Symposium on Foundations of Computer Science (FOCS), pp. 73–84 (2017)

[DNR04] Dwork, C., Naor, M., Reingold, O.: Immunizing encryption schemes from decryption errors. In: Cachin, C., Camenisch, J.L. (eds.) EUROCRYPT 2004. LNCS, vol. 3027, pp. 342–360. Springer, Heidelberg (2004). https://doi.org/10.1007/978-3-540-24676-3_21

[EG85] ElGamal, T.: A public key cryptosystem and a signature scheme based on discrete logarithms. In: Blakley, G.R., Chaum, D. (eds.) CRYPTO 1984. LNCS, vol. 196, pp. 10–18. Springer, Heidelberg (1985). https://doi.org/10.1007/3-540-39568-7_2

[GG98]   Goldreich, O., Goldwasser, S.: On the limits of non-approximability of lattice problems. In: Proceedings of the Thirtieth Annual ACM Symposium on Theory of Computing, STOC 1998, pp. 1–9. Association for Computing Machinery, New York (1998)

[GMR89] Goldwasser, S., Micali, S., Rackoff, C.: The knowledge complexity of interactive proof systems. SIAM J. Comput. **18**(1), 186–208 (1989)

[GPV08] Gentry, C., Peikert, C., Vaikuntanathan, V.: Trapdoors for hard lattices and new cryptographic constructions. In: Dwork, C. (ed.) Proceedings of the 40th Annual ACM Symposium on Theory of Computing, Victoria, British Columbia, Canada, 17–20 May 2008, pp. 197–206. ACM (2008)

[GSV99] Goldreich, O., Sahai, A., Vadhan, S.: Can statistical zero knowledge be made non-interactive? or on the relationship of SZK and *NISZK*. In: Wiener, M. (ed.) CRYPTO 1999. LNCS, vol. 1666, pp. 467–484. Springer, Heidelberg (1999). https://doi.org/10.1007/3-540-48405-1_30

[GVV22] Gupte, A., Vafa, N., Vaikuntanathan, V.: Continuous LWE is as hard as LWE & applications to learning gaussian mixtures. Cryptology ePrint Archive, Report 2022/437 (2022). https://ia.cr/2022/437

[HP15]   Hardt, M., Price, E.: Tight bounds for learning a mixture of two gaussians. In: Proceedings of the Forty-Seventh Annual ACM on Symposium on Theory of Computing, STOC 2015, Portland, OR, USA, 14–17 June 2015, pp. 753–760 (2015)

[HR05]   Holenstein, T., Renner, R.: One-way secret-key agreement and applications to circuit polarization and immunization of public-key encryption. In: Shoup, V. (ed.) CRYPTO 2005. LNCS, vol. 3621, pp. 478–493. Springer, Heidelberg (2005). https://doi.org/10.1007/11535218_29

[HWX15] Hajek, B., Wu, Y., Xu, J.: Computational lower bounds for community detection on random graphs. In: Proceedings of The 28th Conference on Learning Theory, Proceedings of Machine Learning Research, vol. 40, pp. 899–928. PMLR, Paris, 03–06 Jul 2015

[IZ89]   Impagliazzo, R., Zuckerman, D.: How to recycle random bits,pp. 248–253. IEEE (1989)

[McE78] McEliece, R.J.: A public-key cryptosystem based on algebraic coding theory. Deep Space Netw. Progr. Rep. **44**, 114–116 (1978)

[MR07]   Micciancio, D., Regev, O.: Worst-case to average-case reductions based on gaussian measures. SIAM J. Comput. **37**, 267–302 (2007)

[Rab79] Rabin, M.O.: Digitalized signatures and public-key functions as intractable as factorization. MIT Laboratory for Computer Science (1979)

[Reg05] Regev, O.: On lattices, learning with errors, random linear codes, and cryptography. In: STOC, pp. 84–93 (2005). Full version in [Reg09]

[Reg09] Regev, O.: On lattices, learning with errors, random linear codes, and cryptography. J. ACM **56**(6) (2009)

[RSA78] Rivest, R.L., Shamir, A., Adleman, L.: A method for obtaining digital signatures and public-key cryptosystems. Commun. ACM **21**(2), 120–126 (1978)

[SV03]   Sahai, A., Vadhan, S.: A complete problem for statistical zero knowledge. J. ACM **50**(2), 196–249 (2003)

PPAD is as Hard as LWE and Iterated Squaring

Nir Bitansky[1]([✉]), Arka Rai Choudhuri[2], Justin Holmgren[3], Chethan Kamath[1],
Alex Lombardi[4], Omer Paneth[1], and Ron D. Rothblum[5]

[1] Tel Aviv University, Tel Aviv, Israel
nirbitan@tau.ac.il, ckamath@protonmail.com, omerpa@tauex.tau.ac.il
[2] UC Berkeley, Berkeley, USA
arkarc@berkeley.edu
[3] NTT Research, Palo Alto, USA
justin.holmgren@ntt-research.com
[4] MIT, Cambridge, USA
alexlombardi@alum.mit.edu
[5] Technion, Haifa, Israel
rothblum@cs.technion.ac.il

Abstract. One of the most fundamental results in game theory is that
every finite strategic game has a Nash equilibrium, an assignment of
(randomized) strategies to players with the stability property that no
individual player can benefit from deviating from the assigned strategy.
It is not known how to efficiently *compute* such a Nash equilibrium—
the computational complexity of this task is characterized by the class
PPAD, but the relation of **PPAD** to other problems and well-known
complexity classes is not precisely understood. In recent years there has
been mounting evidence, based on cryptographic tools and techniques,
showing the hardness of **PPAD**.

We continue this line of research by showing that **PPAD** is as hard
as *learning with errors* (LWE) and the *iterated squaring* (IS) problem,
two standard problems in cryptography. Our work improves over prior
hardness results that relied either on (1) sub-exponential assumptions,
or (2) relied on "obfustopia," which can currently be based on a particular combination of three assumptions. Our work additionally establishes *public-coin* hardness for **PPAD** (computational hardness for a
publicly sampleable distribution of instances) that seems out of reach of
the obfustopia approach.

Following the work of Choudhuri et al. (STOC 2019) and subsequent
works, our hardness result is obtained by constructing an *unambiguous
and incrementally-updateable* succinct non-interactive argument for IS,
whose soundness relies on polynomial hardness of LWE. The result also
implies a verifiable delay function *with unique proofs*, which may be of
independent interest.

1 Introduction

The concept of a Nash equilibrium is fundamental to the modern understanding of *games*: given a description of payoffs as a function of k player strategies

© The Author(s), under exclusive license to Springer Nature Switzerland 2022
E. Kiltz and V. Vaikuntanathan (Eds.): TCC 2022, LNCS 13748, pp. 593–622, 2022.
https://doi.org/10.1007/978-3-031-22365-5_21

(which take value in a finite domain), what are a collection of strategy *distribu-tions* that cannot be locally improved? It is not a priori clear that such mixed strategies should exist, but the seminal work of Nash [46] shows that they do. In the language of modern computational complexity, this implies that Nash equi-librium is a *total search problem*, a search problem such that every instance of the problem is guaranteed to have a solution. It turns out that computing (arbi-trarily good approximate) solutions to this problem is in fact in the complexity class **TFNP** [45], the class of total search problems with *efficient verification*. In fact, it is *complete* for its subclass called **PPAD** [14,21,48], for which the existence of solution is guaranteed via "polynomial parity argument on directed graphs". Thus, understanding the computational complexity of **PPAD** exactly corresponds to understanding the complexity of computing a Nash equilibrium.

Despite many decades of attention, we do not currently have polynomial-time algorithms for Nash (or any **PPAD**-complete problem); indeed, it is widely believed that **PPAD** is computationally intractable. Understanding to what extent this is the case, and why, has been a major line of research at the inter-section of game theory, computational complexity, and (perhaps surprisingly) *cryptography*. In our work, we further explore this connection to cryptography and prove new hardness results for **PPAD** under cryptographic assumptions.

Prior Work. Before describing our results, we summarize the state of affairs prior to our work. The goal of this line of work is to prove theorems of the form "if **PPAD** can be solved in polynomial-time, then standard cryptography is broken." The usual notion of "cryptography is broken" is that there is a probabilistic polynomial-time (PPT) algorithm solving a problem fundamental to cryptography with non-negligible advantage or success probability. As we will see, prior work, which fall into the two categories described below, falls somewhat short of achieving this ideal.

- **Specialized Proof Systems**: Starting from [15], there has been a sequence of works obtaining hardness in **PPAD** by building *unambiguous, incremental, succinct non-interactive arguments* [15,16,23,39,41,43], which in turn implies the hardness of **PPAD**. These works build such proof systems (and thereby establish hardness of **PPAD**) based on (1) the hardness of breaking the Fiat-Shamir heuristic [15,16,23], (2) the subexponential hardness of both iterated squaring (IS) and learning with errors (LWE) [43], (3) the subexponential hardness only of LWE [39], or (4) the superpolynomial hardness of a problem about bilinear groups [41] along with the exponential-time hypothesis (ETH). Unfortunately, none of these results achieve what we required above: a polynomial-time reduction from breaking cryptography (in polynomial time) to **PPAD**. In particular, these results leave open the possibility that there is a polynomial-time algorithm for **PPAD** and yet *all* of these problems are hard in the standard cryptographic sense.
- **Obfustopia**: Another sequence of works [4,29,34] show that **PPAD** is hard in "obfustopia", which is a world where indistinguishability obfuscation [3,28] and functional encryption [7,47] exist. Unlike the previous approach, this

line of work *is* capable of relying on polynomial hardness: in particular, [29] showed that if **PPAD** is easy, then functional encryption cannot exist. Combined with the groundbreaking results of [36,37], this in turn would imply that one of three seemingly hard problems[1] in cryptography must be easy. While the results of [36,37] are based on well-founded assumptions, they have received less scrutiny than other cryptographic assumptions. Even more fundamentally, we do not want to base the hardness of such a central complexity class such as **PPAD** only on the conjunction of three specific hardness assumptions.

In our work, we ask whether it is possible for the *first* line of work – basing **PPAD**-hardness on unambiguous proof systems – to rely on standard, polynomial-time hardness assumptions.

1.1   Our Results

Our first result shows that (average-case) **PPAD** hardness follows from the polynomial-time hardness of iterated squaring in RSA groups and LWE. In fact, as showed in [34], the same techniques imply hardness in the sub-class **CLS** $\subseteq$ **PPAD** introduced in [22]. We further strengthen these hardness results to the subclass **UEOPL** $\subseteq$ **CLS**, which is one of the lowest known sub-classes of **TFNP** [24].

Theorem 1 (Following Theorem 3 and Corollary 3, informally stated).
*If there exists a PPT algorithm that solves **PPAD** with non-negligible probability, then there exists a PPT algorithm that breaks either IS in RSA groups or LWE with non-negligible probability.*

Slightly more formally, for a complete problem P in **PPAD**, we construct a distribution $\mathcal{D}$ on instances of P with the following property: if there is a polynomial-time algorithm A such that A(x) is a solution to $P(x)$ with non-negligible probability when sampling $x \leftarrow \mathcal{D}$, then there is a polynomial-time algorithm B that solves IS or solves LWE with non-negligible probability.

Public-Coin **PPAD** *Hardness.* Our hardness result is actually slightly stronger than what is achieved by the obfustopia reductions. We show *public-coin* hardness of P: there is a sampling algorithm for $\mathcal{D}$ such that the existence of such a B is guaranteed *even if* A is given the random coins used in sampling x. To our knowledge, this is the first hardness result for publicly sampleable distributions in **PPAD**. Moreover, previous hardness results that were based on polynomially falsifiable assumptions [4,29,34] seem inherently limited to secret-coin hardness because their instance distributions contain obfuscated circuits (or functional encryption ciphertexts that simulate the functionality of an obfuscated circuit). We remark that our public-coin hardness result may be somewhat surprising because the IS problem in an RSA modulus does not itself have a public-coin sampler.

---

[1] The problems, roughly, are to break an SXDH assumption, to break a large-field LPN assumption, and to break a low-depth PRG.

Unique VDFs from Standard Assumptions. Our techniques also yield new results for verifiable delay functions (VDFs) [6]. We construct VDFs with *unique* proofs, which we call unique VDFs, based on the standard LWE assumption and the standard sequential hardness assumption regarding IS.

Theorem 2 (informally stated). *If IS in RSA group is sequentially-hard and LWE is polynomially-hard, then there exists a unique VDF.*

Ours is the first construction of unique VDFs that is based on a polynomial hardness assumption. Recently, Freitag, Pass and Sirkin [27], constructed VDFs from polynomial hardness of LWE and *any* sequentially-hard function, but it does not satisfy uniqueness. We view it as an interesting question whether such VDFs have applications in cryptography.

The Building Block. Along the way (as in previous work) we construct an unambiguous, incremental, succinct non-interactive argument system for IS. This serves as the building block for all our results stated above. The soundness of our argument system is based on LWE, and is established by instantiating the Fiat-Shamir heuristic applied to a variant of Pietrzak's interactive proof system for IS. We also formulate an abstract protocol template (that we call "outline-and-batch" protocols) that generically implies **PPAD**-hardness and captures essentially all existing results as well as our new protocol.

1.2   Technical Overview

Toward the construction of hard **PPAD** instances, we resort to a common paradigm in the literature, that of constructing *mergeable and unambiguous proofs* [15,16,23,39,41,43]. In this paradigm, we consider some underlying computation:

$$x_1 \rightarrow x_2 \rightarrow \cdots \rightarrow x_T ,$$

where each step $x_t \rightarrow x_{t+1}$, $1 \le t < T$, is computable in fixed polynomial time, but computing the last state x_T cannot be done efficiently for large (super-polynomial) T. For concreteness, the reader may think of iterated squaring over the RSA group $\mathbb{Z}_N^\times$ where, for a (randomly sampled) $g \in \mathbb{Z}_N^\times$, $x_t := g^{2^t} \bmod N$; note that computing $x_t \rightarrow x_{t+1}$ can be carried out by one modular squaring, but computing x_T for a large T is believed to be infeasible [53]. For $1 \le t < t' \le T$, the corresponding proof system should allow computing (non-interactive) proofs $\pi_{t \rightarrow t'}$ for statements of the form $x_t \rightarrow x_{t'}$ (i.e., the state $x_{t'}$ is reachable from state x_t) and should satisfy the following requirements:

1. **Soundness:** it should be computationally hard to prove false statements.
2. **Unambiguity:** for any (true) statement $x_t \rightarrow x_{t'}$, it should be computationally hard to find any accepting proof $\pi_{t \rightarrow t'}^*$ other than the "prescribed" proof $\pi_{t \rightarrow t'}$ computed by the efficient merging process.
3. **Recursive proof-merging:** given d proofs $\pi_{1 \rightarrow t}, \pi_{t \rightarrow 2t}, \ldots, \pi_{(d-1)t \rightarrow dt}$, for statements

$$x_1 \rightarrow x_t, x_t \rightarrow x_{2t}, \ldots, x_{(d-1)t} \rightarrow x_{dt},$$

computing a proof $\pi_{1 \to dt}$ for the statement $x_1 \to x_{dt}$, where $d \in \mathbb{N}$ is some fixed merging parameter, can be efficiently reduced to computing a single proof $\pi'_{1 \to t}$ for some related statement $x'_1 \to x'_t$. In other words, the d proofs for statements of "size" t can be merged into a proof for a statement of "size" dt via a recursive call to compute an additional (related) proof of size t. In the concrete example of iterated squaring, the "size" of the statement corresponds to the number of modular squaring operations required to go from $x_t := g^{2^t}$ to $x_{t'} := g^{2^{t'}}$.

Mergeable, Unambigous Proofs from Iterated Squaring and Fiat-Shamir. As mentioned, the mergeable unambiguous proofs paradigm has by now several instantiations in the literature. Focusing on obtaining a polynomial reduction, we consider one particular instantiation, based on Pietrzak's protocol for the iterated squaring (IS) problem [51]. The protocol is a public-coin interactive proof for statements of the form "g^{2^T} equals h modulo N", where N is a public modulus whose factorization is known to neither the prover nor the verifier — we denote such a statement by $g \xrightarrow{T} h$. At the heart of Pietrzak's protocol is a technique for reducing a statement $g \xrightarrow{T} h$ to a related, new statement $g' \xrightarrow{T/2} h'$ that is half the size.[2] This is done by having the (honest) prover specify an integer μ such that the intermediate statements $g \xrightarrow{T/2} \mu$ and $\mu \xrightarrow{T/2} h$ hold (i.e., μ is the "midpoint"), and then having the verifier *reduce* these two statements into one, using its random challenge r as follows:

$$g' := g^r \mu \bmod N \text{ and } h' := \mu^r h \bmod N.$$

The above, "halving sub-protocol" is repeated for $\log(T)$ rounds, at the end of which the verifier ends up with a statement of the form $g'' \xrightarrow{2} h''$, which it can, itself, check by modular squaring. To make this proof system non-interactive, previous works turn to the Fiat-Shamir paradigm [25] of applying an appropriate hash function to the statement to derive the verifier's challenge.

Instantiating Fiat-Shamir. Since Pietrzak's protocol has statistical soundness, the above approach already yields hard **PPAD** instances in the random oracle model [16,23]. Our focus is of course on obtaining a construction without random oracles. Indeed, a recent surge of results has successfully instantiated Fiat-Shamir without random oracles in various scenarios [8,11,12,17–20,32,33,35,38,39,42, 43,50]. This has, in fact, also yielded hard **PPAD** instances, but so far none based on polynomial hardness assumptions. Especially relevant to us is the work of Lombardi and Vaikuntanathan [43] who instantiate the Fiat-Shamir transform for Pietrzak's protocol, based on *sub-exponential* hardness of LWE. At a high level, the sub-exponential loss in [43] comes from the difficulty of computing (or successfully guessing) the so called *bad verifier challenges* in the protocol—the

---

[2] Throughout this section, we assume for simplicity that the time parameter T is a power of 2.

precise quantitative complexity of this task turns out to crucially affect Fiat-Shamir instantiability. For the particular case of Pietrzak's protocol, a verifier challenge is bad if either of the intermediate statements $g \xrightarrow{T/2} \mu$ or $\mu \xrightarrow{T/2} h$ is false, but the new randomized statement $g' \xrightarrow{T/2} h'$ happens to be true. As a part of the soundness argument, it was demonstrated in [51] that the set of bad verifier challenges consists of at most a few elements, but it turns out that computing them (even given the factorization of N) requires solving an intractable discrete-log problem (see, e.g., [43] for a discussion).

Reduced Challenge Space and Soundness Amplification. A first observation toward eliminating the subexponential loss is that bad challenges in Pietrzak's protocol are *efficiently verifiable* given the factorization of N. In particular, there is a straight-forward modification of Pietrzak's protocol that uses a poly-nomial size challenge space, which makes it trivial to find the bad challenges by enumerating and testing every possibility (which can be done efficiently given the above observation). However, this modification causes the protocol to have inverse polynomial soundness error, so the resulting protocol cannot be made interactive via Fiat-Shamir.

A natural attempt to resolve this is to repeat the small-challenge protocol many times in parallel to reduce the soundness error. Indeed parallel repetition reduces the soundness error and importantly, using a recent work of Holmgren, Lombardi and Rothblum [33], we can even instantiate Fiat-Shamir for such a protocol based on (polynomially secure) LWE.[3] Their instantiation essentially works for any parallel-repeated three-message proof, as long as the bad challenges in each individual copy of the protocol are efficiently verifiable. (It also works for protocols with more rounds provided a certain round-by-round soundness requirement that is satisfied by Pietrzak's protocol, further discussed below). It turns out, however, that this approach falls short of our goal. The issue is that *the resulting proofs are not unambiguous.* As noted in [52], while parallel repetition amplifies soundness, it *does not* amplify unambiguity. The reason is that a cheating prover that breaks unambiguity in a *single* copy of the base protocol (out of many), can in particular obtain two accepting proofs for the same statement, breaking the unambiguity of the whole protocol.

Amplifying Unambiguity. As described above, while parallel repetition has the desired effect on soundness, unambiguity suffers from a *single point of failure*: that is, it suffices to cheat in a single copy of the base protocol without affecting the other copies. Instead we would like to start with a protocol that morally still works with many copies (as in parallel repetition) but mixes these together so that any deviations propagate across the entire protocol. Indeed such a protocol was constructed by Block et al. [5], who construct an interactive proof system

---

[3] In fact, this yields a (non-unique) VDF based on the standard hardness of IS and LWE. However, this is subsumed by the result from [27] mentioned in Sect. 1.1. In Sect. 1.2, we will construct *unique* VDF from same assumptions.

for IS for a completely different purpose than considered here.[4] Specifically, for an arbitrary group $\mathbb{G}$, they consider λ (possibly-identical) statements

$$\left(g_1 \xrightarrow{T} h_1, \cdots, g_\lambda \xrightarrow{T} h_\lambda \right), \tag{1}$$

where (in the honest case) $h_i = g_i^{2^T}$ over $\mathbb{G}$ for all $i \in [1, \lambda]$. As in Pietrzak's protocol, the prover sends over a tuple of midpoints $(\mu_1, \cdots, \mu_\lambda)$, for claimed values $\mu_i = g_i^{2^{T/2}}$. This results in 2λ intermediate statements of the form

$$\left(g_1 \xrightarrow{T/2} \mu_1, \mu_1 \xrightarrow{T/2} h_1, \cdots, g_\lambda \xrightarrow{T/2} \mu_\lambda, \mu_\lambda \xrightarrow{T/2} h_\lambda \right),$$

which we rewrite as

$$\left(\widetilde{g}_1 \xrightarrow{T/2} \widetilde{h}_1, \cdots, \widetilde{g}_{2\lambda} \xrightarrow{T/2} \widetilde{h}_{2\lambda} \right). \tag{2}$$

To recurse, λ new statements are derived by a 2λ-to-λ (batch) reduction, where the i-th new statement $g_i' \xrightarrow{T/2} h_i'$ is constructed by choosing a random subset S_i of the 2λ statements as follows:

$$g_i' = \prod_{j \in S_i} \widetilde{g}_j \text{ and } h_i' = \prod_{j \in S_i} \widetilde{h}_j. \tag{3}$$

Even if a single original statement in Eq. (1) is false, it was shown in [5] that each new statement in Eq. (3) is true with probability at most $1/2$ (over the choice of S_i): intuitively, in the (worst) case that the j^*-th statement is the only false statement in Eq. (1), then it is included in Eq. (4) with probability $1/2$, rendering the new statement false. Since there are λ new statements, constructed using *independent* random subsets, the soundness of the resulting protocol is $1/2^\lambda$. Unambiguity amplifies in an identical manner: a cheating prover deviating from the prescribed honest prover strategy affects each new statement with probability roughly $1/2$, "propagating" false statements and, as a result, circumventing the issue of a single point of failure we had previously discussed. By recursing, as above, $\log(T)$ times, the statement reduces to a statement which can be efficiently checked by the verifier.

Applying [33]. Now that we have solved the issues with unambiguity in the interactive protocol, we would like to make it non-interactive in the common reference string (CRS) model by applying the Fiat-Shamir transform. Briefly, the Fiat-Shamir transform for any *public-coin* interactive proof is defined with respect to some hash function family $\mathcal{H}$, where a single hash function H sampled from this family is set to be the CRS. The round-collapse is due to the fact that the verifier's message for each round is simply computed to be the output of H

---

[4] The goal in [5] (also see [30]) was to construct a statistically-sound protocol that works for IS in *arbitrary* groups. In comparison, Pietrzak's protocol is statistically-sound only in groups that are guaranteed to have no low-order elements, e.g., in the group of *signed quadratic residues* [26,31].

applied to the transcript of the protocol up to that point. The security of the instantiated transform relies on correlation intractability of hash functions for *bad challenges* [13]. This is, in particular, true for random oracles when the bad challenges are "sparse".

As already stated, the Fiat-Shamir transform has been successfully instantiated based on standard assumptions for several protocols. Of particular interest to our work is a recent work of Holmgren, Lombardi and Rothblum [33]. We illustrate their idea directly for the [5] protocol. Consider the 2λ intermediate statements from Eq. (2) and let $j^* \in [1, 2\lambda]$ be an index such that $\widetilde{g}_{j^*}^{2^{T/2}} \neq \widetilde{h}_{j^*}$. This can occur either due to the fact that one of the initial λ statements was incorrect, or a cheating prover deviated from the prescribed prover strategy. Then, the i-th new statement $g_i' \xrightarrow{T/2} h_i'$ is true if and only if

$$\prod_{j \in S_i} (\widetilde{g}_j)^{2^{T/2}} = \prod_{j \in S_i} \widetilde{h}_j. \tag{4}$$

Recall that the above only happens with probability at most $1/2$ and, consequently, the probability that at least one of the λ new statements is false is $1 - 1/2^\lambda$. We can now define the set of bad challenges, i.e., the *bad set* $\mathcal{B}$, that results in *all* λ new statements to be true. To be precise,

$$\mathcal{B} = \mathcal{B}_{(\widetilde{g}_1, \cdots, \widetilde{g}_{2\lambda}), (\widetilde{h}_1, \cdots, \widetilde{h}_{2\lambda}), T/2} := \Big\{ S_1, \cdots, S_\lambda \subseteq [1, 2\lambda]$$
$$\Big| \prod_{j \in S_i} (\widetilde{g}_j)^{2^{T/2}} = \prod_{j \in S_i} \widetilde{h}_j \text{ for all } i \in [1, \lambda] \Big\}.$$

Note that $\mathcal{B}^5$ can be represented as the product of λ sets, i.e.

$$\mathcal{B} = \mathcal{B}_1 \times \cdots \times \mathcal{B}_\lambda, \tag{5}$$

where each

$$\mathcal{B}_i := \{ S_i \subseteq [1, 2\lambda] \mid \prod_{j \in S_i} (\widetilde{g}_j)^{2^{T/2}} = \prod_{j \in S_i} \widetilde{h}_j \}. \tag{6}$$

This *product structure* of $\mathcal{B}$ shown in Eq. (5) is crucial for us to invoke [33] who show, assuming polynomial hardness of LWE, that there exists a hash function family $\mathcal{H}$ such that the Fiat-Shamir transform is sound whenever $\mathcal{B}$ is a product set such that each $\mathcal{B}_i$ is *efficiently verifiable*.[6] Here the set $\mathcal{B}_i$ is said to be efficiently verifiable if there is a polynomial-sized circuit C that on input $((\widetilde{g}_1, \cdots, \widetilde{g}_{2\lambda}), (\widetilde{h}_1, \cdots, \widetilde{h}_{2\lambda}), i, S_i)$ that decides whether $S_i \in \mathcal{B}_i$. In our setting, C needs to check whether Eq. (4) holds, which can be done efficiently if C could compute the product $\prod_{j \in S_i} (\widetilde{g}_j)^{2^{T/2}}$ in Eq. (6), even for super-polynomial T. This is possible, for instance, in any group of the form $\mathbb{Z}_N^\times$ (including RSA groups) if C has a *trapdoor*, viz., the factorization of the modulus N, hardcoded in its

---

[5] We drop the subscript for the $\mathcal{B}$ set for clarity when the subscript is clear from the context.

[6] We refer the reader to the technical section for full details on invoking [33].

description: C can first compute the intermediate value $e := 2^{T/2} \mod \phi(N)$ using the trapdoor and then compute $g^e \mod N$ by a single modular exponentiation. Thus, as long as we work in groups where one can efficiently verify each $\mathcal{B}_i$ (with the help of a trapdoor), the Fiat-Shamir transform applied to the [5] protocol is a secure non-interactive argument in the CRS model.

Additionally, in order for the resulting non-interactive argument to preserve properties of the multi-round unambiguous interactive proof, the protocol needs to satisfy the stronger property [10,43] of *unambiguous round-by-round soundness*. In the technical section, we show that the soundness and unambiguity discussion of [5] earlier easily extend to satisfy this property.

Application to Unique VDFs. Having constructed an unambiguous (succinct) non-interactive argument system for IS, we essentially immediately obtain a VDF family with *unique* proofs based on (1) the polynomial hardness of LWE, and (2) the assumption that IS is an inherently sequential function. The only detail that needs to be verified is that the computational complexity of the prover is $T \cdot (1 + o(1))$ for T sequential squarings. This can be proved following an analogous argument in [51]: after applying $T + 1$ sequential squaring operations

$$g_0 = g, g_1 = g^2, \ldots, g_T = g^{2^T},$$

it is possible to compute all prover messages with $\mathsf{poly}(\lambda) \cdot \sqrt{T}$ additional group operations as follows.

- Compute all prover messages from round $\frac{1}{2} \log(T)$ onwards with the naive prover algorithm, incurring an additive computational overhead of $\mathsf{poly}(\lambda) \cdot \sqrt{T}$, and
- Compute all prover messages in the first $\frac{1}{2} \log(T)$ rounds by storing $\sqrt{T}$ of the computed g_is, where each prover message is computed a product-combinations of a (pre-determined) subset of these stored values. This incurs a *total* additive overhead of $\mathsf{poly}(\lambda) \cdot \sqrt{T}$.

Remark 1 (Comparison to the [43] VDF). The [43] VDF uses complexity leveraging in a way so that the honest prover is only efficient (relative to the squaring computation) when the squaring parameter T is subexponentially large in the description of the RSA modulus. Relatedly, the protocol then only achieves a slightly superpolynomial gap between the complexity of the honest prover and the complexity of the cheating provers ruled out by soundness. In contrast, our construction does not require complexity leveraging, resulting in a VDF with far more standard efficiency parameters.

Applications to PPAD-Hardness. For establishing hardness of **PPAD**, we have to show that the non-interactive argument obtained above satisfies the third requirement, i.e., recursive proof-merging. The two sets of intermediate statements from Eq. (2) can be succinctly denoted as

$$(g_1, \cdots, g_\lambda) \xrightarrow{T/2} (\mu_1, \cdots, \mu_\lambda) \text{ and } (\mu_1, \cdots, \mu_\lambda) \xrightarrow{T/2} (h_1, \cdots, h_\lambda) \quad (7)$$

with corresponding [5] proofs

$$\pi((g_1, \cdots, g_\lambda) \xrightarrow{T/2} (\mu_1, \cdots, \mu_\lambda)) \text{ and } \pi((\mu_1, \cdots, \mu_\lambda) \xrightarrow{T/2} (h_1, \cdots, h_\lambda)).$$

The proof for $(g_1, \cdots, g_\lambda) \xrightarrow{T} (h_1, \cdots, h_\lambda)$ can be computed as

$$\pi((g_1, \cdots, g_\lambda) \xrightarrow{T} (h_1, \cdots, h_\lambda)) := \left((\mu_1, \cdots, \mu_\lambda), \pi((g'_1, \cdots, g'_\lambda) \xrightarrow{T/2} (h'_1, \cdots, h'_\lambda)) \right)$$

where $(g'_1, \cdots, g'_\lambda) \xrightarrow{T/2} (h'_1, \cdots, h'_\lambda)$ is derived via the 2λ-to-λ (batch) reduction from the statements in Eq. (7). Furthermore, the proof

$$\pi((g'_1, \cdots, g'_\lambda) \xrightarrow{T/2} (h'_1, \cdots, h'_\lambda))$$

is generated by recursing on the statement $(g'_1, \cdots, g'_\lambda) \xrightarrow{T/2} (h'_1, \cdots, h'_\lambda)$ to compute its proof. Since the reduction is efficient, the non-interactive argument satisfies recursive proof merging as desired. As shown in [15], this actually implies hardness of the sub-class **CLS** $\subseteq$ **PPAD**. We strengthen this result further to show hardness in **UEOPL** $\subseteq$ **CLS**, one of the lowest-lying sub-classes of **TFNP** [24].

Remark 2 (Abstract protocol). While we have limited our discussion specifically to the case of IS, in the technical sections (Sects. 3 and 5) we describe an abstract protocol template that we call "outline and batch." We show that any problem family admitting a *downward self-reduction* and a *(randomized) batching reduction* (reducing k' instances of the problem to sufficiently fewer $k < k'$ instances) admits an unambiguous and incremental non-interactive argument system that suffices for our hardness results. We refer the reader to the technical sections for details.

Obtaining Public-Coin Hardness in PPAD. Finally, we discuss how to obtain hard distributions of **PPAD** instances that are *publicly samplable* under the same computational assumptions as before: the polynomial hardness of LWE and IS over RSA group. It is a priori unclear why one should expect to obtain public-coin hardness under these assumptions, since we don't know a public-coin algorithm for sampling an RSA modulus! Nevertheless, we obtain the result via the following two ideas.

First, we observe that our Fiat-Shamir hash function $\mathcal{H}$ can be sampled from a public-coin distribution. In [33], the hash functions have a *computationally pseudorandom* (and private-coin) description, but they can be switched to uniformly random because even the adaptive unambiguous soundness of the protocol considered in our work is an efficiently verifiable property (given the group order as a trapdoor). Put another way, the adaptive soundness of the protocol follows from an efficiently falsifiable form of correlation intractability, which is thus preserved under computational indistinguishability.

The more serious issue is how to handle the *group* (and group element) description. We handle this by working over $\mathbb{Z}_N^\times$ for a *different* value of N (rather than an RSA modulus). A naive idea would be to work over a *uniformly random modulus* N; unfortunately, the squaring problem mod a uniformly random N is not hard, because N will be prime with inverse polynomial probability (by the prime number theorem), in which case the group order $\phi(N) = N-1$ is efficiently computable. Our actual solution is as follows: consider $N = N_1 \cdot \ldots \cdot N_{\mathsf{poly}(\lambda)}$ for a sufficiently large $\mathsf{poly}(\lambda)$, where all integers N_i are public and uniformly random in the range $[1, 2^\lambda]$. First of all, we note that our techniques for constructing hard **PPAD** instances from iterated squaring apply to this choice of modulus as well: all that is required is that there is a way to efficiently sample (necessarily using *secret coins*) the squaring problem description along with a trapdoor containing the group order $|\mathbb{Z}_N^\times| = \phi(N)$ (this is captured by our generic construction). This is possible using efficient algorithms for generating random factored integers [2,40].

This tells us that public-coin hardness in **PPAD** follows from the hardness of LWE along with the polynomial hardness of IS modulo N (given the coins for sampling the IS instance). To complete the proof, we show that this follows from the polynomial hardness of (secret-coin) IS in an RSA modulus. We prove this by a direct reduction that embeds an RSA modulus IS problem instance into a public-coin instance of this new IS problem; crucially, we use the fact that with all but negligible probability over $N_1, \ldots, N_{\mathsf{poly}(\lambda)}$, at least one N_i is an RSA modulus.

1.3   Organisation

We state definitions and provide background relevant to the paper in Sect. 2. In Sect. 3, we describe the abstract 'outline-and-batch' protocol, prove its unambiguous soundness and explain how existing protocols fit this abstraction. In Sect. 4, we describe the unambiguous non-interactive argument for IS that forms the basis of the results in this work. Hardness of the class **PPAD** is shown in Sect. 5 by constructing hard instances of RSVL using the results from Sect. 4. Due to a lack of space, we defer some details to the full version of the paper.

2   Preliminaries

Notation. First, we list the notation that will be used throughout this paper.

1. For $a, b \in \mathbb{N}$, $a < b$, by $[a, b]$ we denote the sequence of integers $\{a, a+1, \cdots, b\}$.
2. For an alphabet Σ and $n \in \mathbb{N}$, we write Σ^n, $\Sigma^{<n}$ and $\Sigma^{\leq n}$ to denote, respectively, strings over Σ with length equal to, less than, and less than or equal to n. We use ε to denote the empty string. For strings a and b we use ab to denote string concatenation.
3. Vectors and tuples are in bold face. We parse a vector or a tuple $\boldsymbol{x} \in \mathcal{X}^k$ as $\boldsymbol{x} =: (x_0, \cdots, x_{k-1})$; $\boldsymbol{x}$ is said to be a k-vector. A subscripted vector $\boldsymbol{x}_v \in \mathcal{X}^k$ is parsed as $\boldsymbol{x}_v =: (x_{v,0}, \cdots, x_{v,k-1})$.

4. For $x \in \mathcal{X}$, $y \in \mathcal{Y}$ and a function $f : \mathcal{X} \to \mathcal{Y}$, we write $x \xrightarrow{f} y$ to denote the (true or false) *statement* "y equals $f(x)$". Sometimes, when the context is clear, we will simplify the notation: e.g., for $h := g^{2^T} \bmod N$, we simply write $g \xrightarrow{T} h$ to denote

$$g \xrightarrow{(\cdot)^{2^T} \bmod N} h.$$

We extend this notation to vectors: for $\boldsymbol{x} \in \mathcal{X}^k$ and $\boldsymbol{y} \in \mathcal{Y}^k$, we define $\boldsymbol{f} = f^k : \mathcal{X}^k \to \mathcal{Y}^k$ as $(f(x_0)1 = , \cdots 1 = , f(x_{k-1}))$ and therefore $\boldsymbol{x} \xrightarrow{f} \boldsymbol{y}$ denotes statement that $x_i \xrightarrow{f} y_i$ for all $i \in [0, k-1]$.

5. For a statement x, we denote $\pi(x)$ to denote a non-interactive proof for x. For example, for x, y and f as in Item 4, we write $\pi(x \xrightarrow{f} y)$ to denote a non-interactive proof for the statement $x \xrightarrow{f} y$.

6. For $x \in \mathcal{X}$ and $y \in \mathcal{Y}$, we write $y := \mathsf{A}(x)$ (resp., $y \leftarrow \mathsf{A}(x)$) to denote the execution of a deterministic (resp., randomised) algorithm A on input x to output y. For $k \in \mathbb{N}$, vectors $\boldsymbol{x} \in \mathcal{X}^k$ and $\boldsymbol{y} \in \mathcal{Y}^k$, we denote repeated *parallel* execution of A by $\boldsymbol{y} := \mathsf{A}(\boldsymbol{x})$, i.e., $y_i := \mathsf{A}(x_i)$ for all $i \in [0, k-1]$.

2.1   Search Problems, TFNP, and Reductions

We define below search problems, and the relevant complexity classes needed for our work. We start by defining search problems.

Definition 1 (Search Problems [1]). *A* search problem *is a relation* $\mathcal{R} \subseteq \{0,1\}^* \times \{0,1\}^*$. *Let* $\mathcal{R}(x)$ *denote* $\{y : (x,y) \in \mathcal{R}\}$. *A function* $f : \{0,1\}^* \to \{0,1\}^* \cup \{\bot\}$ *is said to* solve $\mathcal{R}$ *if for every* $x \in \{0,1\}^*$ *satisfying* $\mathcal{R}(x) \neq \emptyset$, *it holds that* $f(x) \in \mathcal{R}(x)$; *and for all other* x, $f(x) = \bot$.

Definition 2 (Total Relations). *A relation* $\mathcal{R}$ *is said to be* total *if for all* $x \in \{0,1\}^*$, *there exists* y *such that* $(x, y) \in \mathcal{R}$.

Definition 3 (Polynomially Balanced). *A relation* $\mathcal{R}$ *is said to be* polynomially balanced *if there is a polynomial* p *such that for any strings* $x, y \in \{0,1\}^*$, *if* $(x, y) \in \mathcal{R}$ *then* $|y| \leq p(|x|)$.

Definition 4 (FNP). *The complexity class* **FNP** *consists of all polynomially balanced search problems* $\mathcal{R}$ *for which there is a polynomial-time algorithm that on input* (x, y) *outputs whether or not* $(x, y) \in \mathcal{R}$.

Definition 5 (TFNP). *The complexity class* **TFNP** *consists of all total search problems in* **FNP**.

For further discussion of relevant sub-classes of **TFNP**, we refer the reader to the full version of this work.

Definition 6 (Reductions). *If P and Q are search problems, a* randomized Karp reduction *from P to Q with error $\epsilon(\cdot)$ is a pair of p.p.t. machines* (M, N) *such* *that if f is a function that solves Q, then for any $x \in \{0,1\}^n$ with $P(x) \neq \emptyset$, we have*

$$\Pr\left[(x,y) \in P\right] \geq 1 - \epsilon(n)$$

when sampling $x' \leftarrow \mathsf{M}(x)$, $y \leftarrow \mathsf{N}\left(f(x')\right)$.

Next, we consider the search problem RELAXEDSINKOFVERIFIABLELINE (RSVL), which is relevant to the main result of this paper. We point out that RSVL *not* a total problem since, looking ahead, there is no way to syntactically guarantee that the successor and verifier circuits are well-behaved (see Remark 3).

Definition 7 [15]. RELAXEDSINKOFVERIFIABLELINE *(RSVL)*

- Instance.
    1. *Boolean circuit* $\mathsf{S} : \{0,1\}^m \rightarrow \{0,1\}^m$
    2. *Boolean circuit* $\mathsf{V} : \{0,1\}^m \times [0, 2^m - 1] \rightarrow \{\mathsf{accept}, \mathsf{reject}\}$
    3. *Integer* $L \in [0, 2^m - 1]$
    4. *String* $v_0 \in \{0,1\}^m$
- Promise. *For every* $v \in \{0,1\}^m$ *and* $i \in [0, 2^m - 1]$, $\mathsf{V}(v, i) = 1$ *if* $i \leq L$ *and* $v = \mathsf{S}^i(v_0)$.
- Solution. *One of the following:*
    1. **The sink:** *a vertex* $v \in \{0,1\}^m$ *such that* $\mathsf{V}(v, L) = 1$; *or*
    2. **False positive:** *a pair* $(v, i) \in \{0,1\}^m \times [0, 2^m - 1]$ *such that* $v \neq \mathsf{S}^i(v_0)$ *and* $\mathsf{V}(v, i) = 1$.

Remark 3. It seems likely that RSVL is not in **FNP**, let alone in **PPAD**. Specifically, checking that a pair (v, i) constitutes a false positive is difficult because i may be super-polynomial in the instance size.

Nevertheless, [15] constructed a (randomized) reduction from RSVL to EOML (which is a search problem complete for **CLS** $\subseteq$ **PPAD**) with error that is inversely polynomially bounded away from 1. This error is somewhat large, and allows for the possibility EOML is "slightly" easier than RSVL.

Still, the reduction suffices for establishing the standard cryptographic hardness of EOML (i.e. that no polynomially bounded algorithm can succeed with *any* non-negligible probability) based on analogous hardness for RSVL. In turn, we establish the latter hardness based on LWE (Assumption 4) and the iterated squaring assumption (Assumption 9).

Theorem 3 [15]. *There is a randomized Karp reduction from RSVL to EOML with error probability* $\epsilon(n) = 1 - n^{-O(1)}$.

2.2 Learning with Errors

The following standard preliminaries about the Learning with Errors (LWE) problem are based on [43,49].

Definition 8 (LWE Distribution). *For any* $\mathbf{s} \in \mathbb{Z}_q^n$ *and any distribution* $\chi \subseteq \mathbb{Z}_q$, *the* LWE *distribution* $A_{\mathbf{s},\chi} \in \mathbb{Z}_q^n \times \mathbb{Z}_q$ *is sampled by choosing* $\mathbf{a} \in \mathbb{Z}_q^n$ *uniformly at random, sampling* $e \leftarrow \chi$, *and outputting* $(\mathbf{a}, b = \langle \mathbf{s}, \mathbf{a} \rangle + e)$.

Assumption 4 (Decision LWE). *Let* $m = m(n) \geq 1$, $q = q(n) \geq 2$ *be integers, and let* $\chi(n)$ *be a probability distribution on* $\mathbb{Z}_{q(n)}$. *The* LWE$_{n,m,q,\chi}$ *problem, parameterized by* n, *is to distinguish whether* $m(n)$ *independent samples are drawn from* $A_{\mathbf{s},\chi}$ *(for* $\mathbf{s}$ *that is sampled uniformly at random) or are drawn from the uniform distribution. The hardness assumption is that is hard for* poly(n)-*sized adversaries to decide the* LWE$_{n,m,q,\chi}$ *problem.*

2.3 Correlation-Intractable Hash Families

The following preliminaries are partially taken from [33,43].

Definition 9 (Hash family). *For a pair of efficiently-computable functions* $(n(\cdot), m(\cdot))$, *a* hash family *with input length* n *and output length* m *is a collection* $\mathcal{H} = \{H_\lambda : \{0,1\}^{s(\lambda)} \times \{0,1\}^{n(\lambda)} \to \{0,1\}^{m(\lambda)}\}_{\lambda \in \mathbb{N}}$ *of keyed hash functions, along with a pair of p.p.t. algorithms:*

- $\mathcal{H}$.Gen(1^λ) *outputs a hash key* $k \in \{0,1\}^{s(\lambda)}$.
- $\mathcal{H}$.Hash(k,x) *computes the function* $H_\lambda(k,x)$. *We may use the notation* $H(k,x)$ *to denote hash evaluation when the hash family is clear from context.*

As in prior works [11,50] we consider the security notion of correlation intractability [13] for single-input relations and its restriction to (single-input) functions.

Definition 10 (Correlation Intractability). *For a given relation ensemble* $\mathcal{R} = \{\mathcal{R}_\lambda \subseteq \{0,1\}^{n(\lambda)} \times \{0,1\}^{m(\lambda)}\}$, *a hash family* $\mathcal{H} = \{H_\lambda : \{0,1\}^{s(\lambda)} \times \{0,1\}^{n(\lambda)} \to \{0,1\}^{m(\lambda)}\}$ *is said to be* $\mathcal{R}$-correlation intractable with security (s,δ) *if for every* s-*size* $\mathsf{A} = \{\mathsf{A}_\lambda\}$,

$$\Pr_{\substack{k \leftarrow \mathcal{H}.\mathsf{Gen}(1^\lambda) \\ x \leftarrow \mathsf{A}(k)}} \left[(x, H(k,x)) \in \mathcal{R} \right] = O(\delta(\lambda)).$$

We say that $\mathcal{H}$ *is* $\mathcal{R}$-correlation intractable with security δ *if it is* (λ^c, δ)-*correlation intractable for all* $c > 1$. *Finally, we say that* $\mathcal{H}$ *is* $\mathcal{R}$-correlation intractable *if it is* $(\lambda^c, 1/\lambda^c)$-*correlation intractable for all* $c > 1$.

We will use the recent result of [33] on correlation intractability for *product relations*.

Definition 11 (Product Relation). *We say that* $\mathcal{R} \subseteq \mathcal{X} \times \mathcal{Y}^t$ *is a* product relation *if for every* $x \in \mathcal{X}$, *the set* $\mathcal{R}(x) = \{y : (x,y) \in \mathcal{R}\} \subseteq \mathcal{Y}^t$ *has a decomposition*

$$\mathcal{R}(x) := \mathcal{B}_1(x) \times \mathcal{B}_2(x) \times \ldots \mathcal{B}_t(x)$$

(where each $\mathcal{B}_i(x)$ is a subset of $\mathcal{Y}$). We say that such an $\mathcal{R}$ is efficiently product
verifiable *if for some such choice of $\mathcal{B}_i$, there is a poly-size circuit $\mathsf{C}(\mathsf{x}, \mathsf{i}, \mathsf{y_i})$ that
decides whether $y_i \in \mathcal{B}_i(x)$.*

Theorem 5 ([33]). *Assume the hardness of* LWE. *Then, for every size bound
$S(\lambda) = \mathsf{poly}(\lambda)$, input length $n(\lambda)$, and output length $m(\lambda) \cdot t(\lambda)$ such that $t(\lambda) \geq
\lambda^{\Omega(1)}$, there exists a correlation intractable hash family $\mathcal{H}$ for product relations $\mathcal{R}$
that are (1) product verifiable by size $S(\lambda)$ circuits, and (2) sparse in the sense
that for every x, i, we have that $|\mathcal{B}_i(x)| \leq \frac{1}{2} \cdot 2^{m(\lambda)}$.*

Remark 4. In [33], hash function keys have a computationally pseudorandom
distribution. However, for the purposes of Theorem 5, hash function keys may
be taken to be uniformly random strings (by invoking the pseudorandomness
property), because the security property in Theorem 5 is efficiently falsifiable.

2.4   Interactive Proofs and the Fiat-Shamir Heuristic

The following preliminaries are partially taken from [33,43]. We begin by recalling the definitions of interactive proofs and arguments.

Definition 12 (Interactive proof and argument system). *An* interactive
proof *(resp.,* interactive argument*) for a promise problem $\mathcal{L} = (\mathcal{L}_{\mathrm{YES}}, \mathcal{L}_{\mathrm{NO}})$ is a
pair* (P, V) *of interactive algorithms satisfying:*

- **Completeness.** *For any $x \in \mathcal{L}_{\mathrm{YES}}$, when P and V interact on common input
  x, the verifier V outputs 1 with probability 1.*
- **Soundness.** *For any $x \in \mathcal{L}_{\mathrm{NO}} \cap \{0,1\}^n$ and any* unbounded *(resp.,
  polynomial-time) interactive P^*, when P^* and $\mathsf{V}(x)$ interact, the probability
  that V outputs 1 is a negligible function of n.*

The protocol is public-coin *if each of V's messages is an independent uniformly
random string of some length (and the verifier's decision to accept or reject does
not use any secret state). In this setting, we will denote prover messages by
$(\alpha_1, \ldots, \alpha_\ell)$ and verifier messages by $(\beta_1, \ldots, \beta_{\ell-1})$ in a $2\ell - 1$-round protocol.*

Definition 13 (Non-interactive argument system). *A* non-interactive
argument scheme *(in the CRS model) for a promise problem $\mathcal{L} = (\mathcal{L}_{\mathrm{YES}}, \mathcal{L}_{\mathrm{NO}})$ is
a triple* $(\mathsf{Setup}, \mathsf{P}, \mathsf{V})$ *of non-interactive algorithms with the following properties:*

- $\mathsf{Setup}(1^n)$ *outputs a common reference string* CRS.
- $\mathsf{P}(\mathsf{CRS}, x)$ *outputs a proof π.*
- $\mathsf{V}(\mathsf{CRS}, x, \pi)$ *outputs a bit $b \in \{0, 1\}$*

*It satisfies the notions of completeness and (computational) soundness as
above.*

We next define the notion of *unambiguous soundness* [52]. For non-interactive
arguments, the soundness notion we consider is *adaptive* in that we allow the
prover P^* to adaptively choose the statement x after seeing the CRS.

Definition 14. (Unambiguous Soundness [15,52]). *A public-coin interactive proof system Π is* unambiguously sound *if (1) it is sound, and (2) for every $x \in \mathcal{L}$ and every (complete) collection of verifier messages $(\beta_1, \ldots, \beta_{\ell-1})$, there exists a distinguished proof $\pi^*(x, \beta_1, \ldots, \beta_{\ell-1})$ such that the following soundness condition holds: For all $x \in \mathcal{L}$ and all cheating provers P^*, the probability that the transcript $\langle \mathsf{P}^*(x), \mathsf{V}(x) \rangle$ contains a proof π such that $\mathsf{V}(x, \pi) = 1$ and $\pi \neq \pi^*(x, \beta_1, \ldots, \beta_{\ell-1})$ is negligible.*

Definition 15 (Adaptive Unambiguous Soundness). *A non-interactive argument system $\Pi = (\mathsf{Setup}, \mathsf{P}, \mathsf{V})$ is* adaptively unambiguously sound *against (uniform or non-uniform) time T adversaries if for all instances $x \in \mathcal{L}$ and all common reference strings CRS, there exists a "distinguished proof" $\pi^*(\mathsf{CRS}, x)$ such that the following soundness condition holds: For all time T cheating provers P^*, the probability that $\mathsf{P}^*(\mathsf{CRS}) = (x, \pi)$ where $\mathsf{V}(x, \pi) = 1$ and either $x \notin \mathcal{L}$ or $\pi \neq \pi^*(\mathsf{CRS}, x)$ is negligible.*

Our results proceed by constructing (unambiguously sound) interactive proof systems and compiling them into non-interactive argument systems using the Fiat-Shamir transform, which we describe next.

Definition 16 (Fiat-Shamir Transform). *Let Π denote a public coin interactive proof (or argument) system Π that has ℓ prover messages and $\ell-1$ verifier messages of length $m = m(\lambda)$. Then, for a hash family*

$$\mathcal{H} = \left\{ \left\{ H_k : \{0,1\}^* \to \{0,1\}^{m(\lambda)} \right\}_{k \in \{0,1\}^\lambda} \right\}_\lambda,$$

we define the Fiat-Shamir non-interactive protocol $\Pi_{\mathrm{FS}, \mathcal{H}} = (\mathsf{Setup}, \mathsf{P}_{\mathrm{FS}}, \mathsf{V}_{\mathrm{FS}})$ as follows:

- $\mathsf{Setup}(1^\lambda)$: *sample a hash key $k \leftarrow \mathcal{H}.\mathsf{Gen}(1^\lambda)$.*
- $\mathsf{P}_{\mathrm{FS}}(x)$: *for $i \in \{1, \ldots, \ell\}$, recursively compute the following pairs (α_i, β_i):*
  - *Compute $\alpha_i = \mathsf{P}(\tau_i)$ for $\tau_i = (x, \alpha_1, \beta_1, \ldots, \alpha_{i-1}, \beta_{i-1})$.*
  - *Compute $\beta_i = H_k(\tau_{i-1}, \alpha_i)$.*
  Then, $\mathsf{P}_{\mathrm{FS}}(x)$ outputs $\pi = (\alpha_1, \beta_1, \ldots, \alpha_\ell)$.
- $\mathsf{V}_{\mathrm{FS}}(\mathsf{CRS}, x, \pi)$ *parses $\pi = (\alpha_1, \beta_1, \ldots, \alpha_\ell)$ and verifies that:*
  - $\beta_i = H_k(\tau_{i-1}, \alpha_i)$ *for all $1 \leq i \leq \ell - 1$, and*
  - $\mathsf{V}(x, \pi) = 1$.

We note the following facts about $\Pi_{\mathrm{FS}, \mathcal{H}}$

1. *The honest prover complexity of $\Pi_{\mathrm{FS}, \mathcal{H}}$ is equal to the honest prover complexity of Π with an additive overhead of computing $\ell - 1$ hash values.*
2. *The verifier complexity of $\Pi_{\mathrm{FS}, \mathcal{H}}$ is equal to the verifier complexity of Π with the same hashing additive overhead.*
3. *The protocol $\Pi_{\mathrm{FS}, \mathcal{H}}$ is not necessarily sound, even if Π is sound and $\mathcal{H}$ is a "strong cryptographic hash function". As we will discuss later, soundness is guaranteed when Π satisfies what is called "round-by-round soundness", defined next.*

Round-by-Round (Unambiguous) Soundness and Fiat-Shamir. Following [10, 11,15,43], we consider the notion of round-by-round (unambiguous) soundness to capture a particular kind of soundness analysis for super-constant round interactive proofs. For these proof systems, it has been shown that correlation intractability for an appropriate relation suffices for a hash family to instantiate the Fiat-Shamir heuristic for unambiguously round-by-round sound interactive proofs.

Definition 17 (Unambiguous Round-by-Round Soundness [10, 15, 43]).
Let $\Pi = (\mathsf{P}, \mathsf{V})$ be a $2\ell - 1$-message public coin interactive proof system for a language $\mathcal{L}$.

We say that Π has unambiguous round-by-round soundness error $\epsilon(\cdot)$ *if there exist functions* (State, NextMsg) *with the following syntax.*

- State *is a deterministic (not necessarily efficiently computable) function that takes as input an instance x and a transcript prefix τ and outputs either* accept *or* reject.
- NextMsg *is a deterministic (not necessarily efficiently computable) function that takes as input an instance x and a transcript prefix τ and outputs a (possibly aborting) prover message $\alpha \in \{0,1\}^* \cup \{\bot\}$.*

We additionally require that the following properties hold.

1. *If $x \notin \mathcal{L}$, then $\mathsf{State}(x, \emptyset) = $ reject, where $\emptyset$ denotes the empty transcript.*
2. *If $\mathsf{State}(x, \tau) = $ reject for a transcript prefix τ, then $\mathsf{NextMsg}(x, \tau) = \bot$. That is, $\mathsf{NextMsg}(x, \tau)$ is only defined on accepting states.*
3. *For every input x and partial transcript $\tau = \tau_i$, then for every potential prover message $\alpha_{i+1} \neq \mathsf{NextMsg}(x, \tau)$, it holds that*

$$\Pr_{\beta_{i+1}} \left[\mathsf{State}\big(x, \tau | \alpha_{i+1} | \beta_{i+1}\big) = \mathsf{accept} \right] \leq \epsilon(n)$$

4. *For any full[7] transcript τ, if $\mathsf{State}(x, \tau) = $ reject then $\mathsf{V}(\mathsf{x}, \tau) = 0$.*

We say that Π is unambiguously round-by-round sound *if it has unambiguous round-by-round soundness error ϵ for some $\epsilon(n) = \mathsf{negl}(n)$.*

Next, we restate the result that specific forms of correlation intractability suffice to instantiate the Fiat-Shamir transform for protocols satisfying unambiguous round-by-round soundness.

Theorem 6 [10,43]. *Suppose that $\Pi = (\mathsf{P}, \mathsf{V})$ is a $2\ell - 1$-message public-coin interactive proof for a language $\mathcal{L}$ with perfect completeness and unambiguous round-by-round soundness with corresponding functions* (State, NextMsg). *Let $\mathcal{X}_n$ denote the set of partial transcripts (including the input and all messages sent) and let $\mathcal{Y}_n$ denote the set of verifier messages when Π is executed on an input of length n.*

---

[7] By a full transcript, we mean a transcript for which the verifier halts.

Finally, define the relation ensemble $\mathcal{R} = \mathcal{R}_{\text{State,NextMsg}}$ *as follows:*

$$\mathcal{R}^{(n)}_{\text{State,NextMsg}} := \left\{ \left((x, \tau | \alpha), \beta \right) : \begin{array}{c} x \in \{0,1\}^n, \\ \alpha \neq \text{NextMsg}(x, \tau) \\ and \\ \text{State}(x, \tau | \alpha | \beta) = \text{accept} \end{array} \right\}.$$

If a hash family $\mathcal{H} = \{\mathcal{H}_n : \mathcal{X}_n \to \mathcal{Y}_n\}$ *is correlation intractable for* $\mathcal{R}$, *then the round-reduced protocol* $\Pi_{\text{FS},\mathcal{H}}$ *is an adaptively unambiguously sound argument system for* $\mathcal{L}$.

3   The Outline-and-Batch Protocol

For $\mathcal{X}, \mathcal{Y} \subseteq \{0,1\}^*$, let $f : \mathcal{X} \to \mathcal{Y}$ be a function and $\| \cdot \| : \mathcal{X} \to \mathbb{N}$ denote a "size measure" for inputs to f. Let $\mathcal{X}_n$ denote $\{x \in \mathcal{X} : \|x\| = n\}$, and let $f_n : \mathcal{X}_n \to \mathcal{Y}$ denote the restriction of f to $\mathcal{X}_n$. Recall from Sect. 2 that $f_n^k : \mathcal{X}_n^k \to \mathcal{Y}^k$ denotes the function mapping $(x_1, \ldots, x_k)$ to $(f_n(x_1), \ldots, f_n(x_k))$.

Definition 18 (Downwards self-reduction). *A downwards self-reduction for* f *is a deterministic oracle algorithm* D *such that for any* n *and* $x \in \mathcal{X}_n$, $\mathsf{D}^{f_{n-1}}(x) = f(x)$. *If on input* x, D *queries* $q_1, \ldots, q_d$, *then we say that* D *is a* d-query *downwards self-reduction and we refer to* $((q_1, f(q_1)), \ldots, (q_k, f(q_k)))$ *as an* outline *of the evaluation of* f *on* x.

Definition 19 (Batching reduction). *A* k'-to-k *batching reduction for* f *with* soundness error ϵ *is a probabilistic algorithm* B *that on input* $\{(x_i', y_i') \in \mathcal{X}_n \times \mathcal{Y}\}_{i \in [1,k']}$ *outputs* $\{(x_i, y_i) \in \mathcal{X}_n \times \mathcal{Y}\}_{i \in [1,k]}$ *such that:*

- *(Completeness) If* $y_i' = f(x_i')$ *for all* $i \in [1, k']$, *then with probability 1,* $y_i = f(x_i)$ *for all* $i \in [1, k]$.
- *(Soundness) If* $y_i' \neq f(x_i')$ *for some* $i \in [1, k']$, *then with all but* ϵ *probability over the randomness of* B, $y_i \neq f(x_i)$ *for some* $i \in [1, k]$.

We remark that it may be useful to consider batching reductions that are interactive, but for our purposes, non-interactive batching reductions suffice for our instantiations. We leave discussion of abstract interactive batching reductions to future work.

Theorem 7. *If* f *has a* d-query *downwards self reduction* D *and a* dk-to-k-*batching reduction* B *with error* ϵ, *then there is a public-coin interactive proof for the language*

$$\mathcal{L}_{f_n}^k := \{((x_1, \cdots, x_n), (y_1,, \cdots, y_n)) \in \mathcal{X}^k \times \mathcal{Y}^k : f_n(x_i) = y_i \text{ for all } i \in [1, k]\}$$

with $n-1$ *rounds of interaction and with unambiguous round-by-round soundness error* ϵ.

Remark 5. We remark that the hypotheses of Theorem 7 can be relaxed to only require completeness and soundness for B when applied to inputs that correspond to the queries of an evaluation of D. This relaxation captures the classical sumcheck protocol [44] as a special case.

Proof of Theorem 7. The prover P and verifier V both take as input a statement $((x_1, \ldots, x_k), (y_1, \ldots, y_k)) \in \mathcal{X}_n^k \times \mathcal{Y}_n^k$, and the protocol is defined recursively.

Base Case: If $n = 1$, then no messages are sent (P does nothing), and V accepts only if $f_1(x_i) = y_i$ for all $i \in [1, k]$.

Recursive Case: If $n > 1$, then:

1. P computes $\mathsf{D}^{f_{n-1}}(\mathsf{x_i})$ for each $i \in [1, k]$, recording the queries made by D and answering queries according to f_{n-1}. Then P sends all k corresponding d-tuples of query-answer pairs to V. Let $((\tilde{x}_1', \tilde{y}_1'), \ldots, (\tilde{x}_{dk}', \tilde{y}_{dk}'))$ denote the concatenation of all k d-tuples of query-answer pairs received by V.
2. When V receives k d-tuples of query-answer pairs, V checks for each i that the i-th tuple is consistent with an execution of D^8 on input x_i (if not, then V rejects). V then samples randomness r for B and sends it to P.
3. Let $((\tilde{x}_1'', \tilde{y}_1''), \ldots, (\tilde{x}_k'', \tilde{y}_k''))$ denote B $((\tilde{x}_1', \tilde{y}_1'), \ldots, (\tilde{x}_{dk}', \tilde{y}_{dk}'); r)$. P and V recursively invoke the interactive proof for f^k on $((\tilde{x}_1', \ldots, \tilde{x}_k'), (\tilde{y}_1', \ldots, \tilde{y}_k'))$.

We next describe how to give Π the structure of an unambiguous round-by-round sound protocol.

- At any step in the recursion, we have "current inputs" $x_1, \ldots, x_k$ as well as outputs $y_1, \ldots, y_k$ claimed in the previous recursive step. At this execution point, we define State to be accept if and only if $f(x_i) = y_i$ for all i.
- After Step 1 in a recursive call, we define State to be accept iff $\mathcal{V}$ has not rejected and $f(\tilde{x}') = \tilde{y}'$ for every pair $(\tilde{x}', \tilde{y}')$ in the lists sent by the prover.

We define NextMsg(τ) to be the output of the honest prover algorithm in the description of the recursion above, which means to:

- Compute B on its previous message and the verifier's challenge r, and
- Compute the downwards self-reduction on the resulting tuple of inputs.

Given this description of (State, NextMsg), unambiguous round-by-round soundness follows from the correctness of the downwards self-reduction and the soundness of the batching reduction. $\square$

Finally, we discuss instantiating the Fiat-Shamir transform for the protocol Π in Theorem 7 by appealing to Theorem 6. Since the round-by-round State function is fairly simple for our protocol Π (in that it does not depend on the entire protocol history), we can rely on correlation intractability for relations with a fairly simple description. By invoking Theorem 6, we obtain the following corollary.

---

[8] That is, V emulates an execution of D on each x_i, checking that for every j, the jth oracle call in the sequence of k executions is to $\tilde{x}_j'$; it then uses $\tilde{y}_j'$ as the oracle's output in its emulation.

Corollary 1. *Under the hypotheses of Theorem 7 and additionally assuming the existence of a hash family $\mathcal{H}$ that is correlation intractable for the following relation $\mathcal{R}$:*

$$\mathcal{R}^{(n)}_{\text{State,NextMsg}} := \left\{ \left(\alpha = (n, \tilde{x}'_1, \tilde{y}'_1, \ldots, \tilde{x}'_{dk}, \tilde{y}'_{dk}), r \right) : \begin{array}{c} \tilde{y}'_j \neq f_{n-1}(\tilde{x}'_j) \text{ for some } j \\ \text{and} \\ \tilde{y}''_i = f_{n-1}(\tilde{x}''_i) \text{ for all } i \end{array} \right\},$$

where $\{(\tilde{x}''_i, \tilde{y}''_i)\}_{i \in [1,k]}$ is the output of B on input $\{(\tilde{x}'_j, \tilde{y}'_j)\}_{j \in [1,dk]}$ and random coins r, there is a non-interactive argument system for $\mathcal{L}^k_{f_n}$ with adaptive unambiguous soundness.

3.1   Instantiations of Outline-and-Batch

Appropriate instantiations of our outline-and-batch protocol (Theorem 7, Corollary 1) can recover the interactive proof systems or non-interactive argument systems constructed in the following works:

1. *The [44] interactive proof system for #SAT and its Fiat-Shamir instantiations* [15,39]. The sumcheck protocol can be viewed as a composition of
   (a) a $(d+1)$-query downward self-reduction that reduces a statement about the sum $\sum_{x_1,\ldots,x_n \in \{0,1\}} p(x_1, \ldots, x_n)$ of a d-degree, n-variate polynomial p (over some finite field) to $d+1$ statements of the form $\sum_{x_2,\ldots,x_n} p(\alpha, x_2, \ldots, x_n)$ (for hard-coded values of α); and
   (b) a $(d+1)$-to-1 batching reduction reducing these $(d+1)$ statements to a single statement about $\sum_{x_2,\ldots,x_n} p(r, x_2, \ldots, x_n)$ for a *uniformly random* r.
2. *The [16,51] interactive proof system for IS over the* signed quadratic residue group $\mathbb{QR}^+_N$ *and its Fiat-Shamir instantiation in the standard model* [43]. Let $x \xrightarrow{T} y$ (now) denote the statement "x^{2^T} equals y over $\mathbb{QR}^+_N$". These protocols consist of a 2-query downward self-reduction from a statement $x \xrightarrow{T} y$ to two statements of the form $x_i \xrightarrow{T/2} y_i$ and a 2-to-1 batching reduction that combines these two statements to a single such statement using a random linear combination.
3. *The [23] continuous VDF adapted to $\mathbb{QR}^+_N$.* This protocol consists of a d-query downward self-reduction from a statement $x \xrightarrow{T} y$ to d statements of the form $x_i \xrightarrow{T/d} y_i$ and a d-to-1 batching reduction from these d statements to a single such statement using, again, a random linear combination. The parameter d is set in their construction to $O(\lambda)$, for the security parameter λ.
4. *The [5] interactive proof system for IS.* In Sect. 4.3, we describe how this protocol fits the "outline-and-batch" framework and then show how to instantiate Fiat-Shamir for this protocol in the standard model.

4 Non-interactive Argument for Iterated Squaring in a Trapdoor Group of Unknown Order

We first recall the iterated squaring (IS) problem modulo an integer N and discuss the hardness of IS. This includes a new hardness reduction showing that certain *public-coin* variants of IS are as hard as the "traditional" IS problem in the RSA group. Next, we consider a general IS problem over an arbitrary group of unknown order and construct our unambiguous "outline-and-batch" argument system in this setting.

4.1 Iterated Squaring Modulo N

We first define IS and then recall the assumption of [53] on its sequential hardness that our VDF is based on. Our hardness assumption on IS required for **PPAD** hardness is a relaxation of this assumption.

Definition 20 ([9,53]). ITERATEDSQUARING *(IS)*

- Instance.
  1. *Integers $N, T \in \mathbb{N}$*
  2. *Group element $g \in \mathbb{Z}_N^*$*
- Solution. $f(N, g, T) := g^{2^T} \bmod N$

Assumption 8 (Sequential hardness of IS [53]). For a security parameter $\lambda \in \mathbb{N}$, let $\lambda_{RSA} \in \lambda^{O(1)}$ denote the size of RSA modulus that corresponds to λ bits of security. Sample $N = pq$ as the product of two random $\lambda_{RSA}/2$-bit primes and $g \leftarrow \mathbb{Z}_N^*$. Consider any time parameter $T = 2^{o(\lambda)}$. Any A that uses $2^{o(\lambda)}$ amount of parallelism and computes $f(N, g, T)$ with a probability that is non-negligible in λ requires *sequential time* $T(1 - o(1))$ group operations.

Assumption 9 (Standard hardness of IS [16]). For a security parameter $\lambda \in \mathbb{N}$, let N and g be sampled as in Assumption 8. There exists an efficiently computable function $T(1^\lambda)$, such that no $\lambda^{O(1)}$-time algorithm can compute $f(N, g, T)$ with a non-negligible probability.

Remark 6 (Assumption 9 vs. assumption in [16,51]). The hardness assumption in [16,51] is slightly different from Assumption 9. Firstly, the modulus N in [16, 51] is sampled a product of two random $\lambda_{RSA}/2$-bit *safe primes* – the statistical soundness of Pietrzak's proof-of-exponentiation (PoE) is guaranteed only in such moduli. Secondly, to attain unambiguity, [16,51] switch to the algebraic setting of *signed quadratic residues* [26,31]. In comparison, our assumption is made on the conventional RSA modulus and this suffices since we rely the PoE from [5] which achieves statistical soundness and (as we show) unambiguity for arbitrary groups.

4.2   Trapdoor Groups with Unknown Order

Definition 21 (Group of unknown order) *A group sampler for a group of unknown order consists of the following two functionalities:*

- *A setup algorithm* Setup(1^λ) *that samples the description of a group* $\mathbb{G}_\lambda$ *of order at most* 2^λ. *For our purposes, a group description consists of a distinguished identity element* $\mathsf{id}_\mathbb{G}$ *and efficient membership testing algorithm that takes as input an arbitrary string and decides whether the string is a valid element of* $\mathbb{G}_\lambda$.
- *Efficient* poly(λ)*-time algorithms, given a description of* $\mathbb{G}_\lambda$, *for:*
  - *Sampling a uniformly random group element,*
  - *Computing the group law* $(g, h) \mapsto gh \in \mathbb{G}_\lambda$, *and*
  - *Computing the inverse map* $g \mapsto g^{-1} \in \mathbb{G}_\lambda$.

These efficient group operations generically imply that one can compute exponentiations $g \mapsto g^x$ in time poly$(\lambda) \cdot \log(x)$ by repeated squaring. For example, this implies that $g \mapsto g^{2^T}$ can be computed in time $T \cdot$ poly(λ) (or T group operations).

Note that if the order of $\mathbb{G}_\lambda$ is known, then the map g^{2^T} can actually be computed in time poly$(\lambda, \log T)$ by first reducing 2^T modulo the order of the group. However, when the order of the group is unknown, it is plausible that this map requires time roughly T group operations, as originally proposed by [53]. We formulate two flavors of this assumption, matching Assumptions 8 and 9 in the case of RSA groups.

Assumption 10 $((T, p)$-Sequential Hardness$)$. Given the description of $\mathbb{G}_\lambda$ and a random group element g, any algorithm running in sequential time $T(1 - o(1))$ with $p(\lambda)$ parallelism outputs g^{2^T} with only negligible probability.

Assumption 11 (Polynomial Hardness of Iterated Squaring). There exists an efficiently computable function $T(1^\lambda)$ such that, given the description of $\mathbb{G}_\lambda$ and a random group element g, no algorithm running in time $\lambda^{O(1)}$ can output g^{2^T} with non-negligible probability.

In order to prove the unambiguous soundness of our non-interactive argument system for IS, we will make use of groups satisfying Assumption 11 that have *trapdoors* allowing for efficient iterated squaring. We formalize this by requiring that the group distribution $\mathbb{G}_\lambda$ could be sampled along with its order (using secret coins).

Definition 22 (Trapdoor group with unknown order) *A trapdoor group with unknown order is a group with unknown order (Definition 21) equipped with an additional setup algorithm* TrapSetup(1^λ) *that outputs the description of a group* $\mathbb{G}_\lambda$ *along with its order* M. *We require that the distribution of groups output by* Setup(1^λ) *is statistically indistinguishable from the distribution of groups output by* TrapSetup(1^λ) *(where the order information is dropped).*

RSA groups $\mathbb{Z}_{pq}^\times$ are naturally equipped with the required trapdoor structure, because if $N = pq$ is sampled as the product of two known primes, then the order of $\mathbb{Z}_N^\times$ is equal to $\phi(pq) = (p-1)(q-1)$.

4.3   Interactive Iterated Squaring Protocol

In this section, we recall the interactive proof system Π of [5] for IS and analyze the Fiat-Shamir heuristic applied to Π using an appropriate correlation-
intractable hash family. Since the groups output by $\mathsf{Setup}(1^\lambda)$ and $\mathsf{TrapSetup}(1^\lambda)$
are statistically indistinguishable, we assume that $\mathsf{TrapSetup}(1^\lambda)$ is used for the
purposes of both the construction and its analysis.

Let $\mathbb{G}_\lambda \leftarrow \mathsf{Setup}(1^\lambda)$ denote a group (distribution) with unknown order and
associated generator g. For simplicity, we only consider T of the form $T = 2^t$.[9]
For T of this form, we construct an interactive proof system for IS by having
the prover invoke the "outline and batch" protocol (Theorem 7) on λ *identical*
computations of g^{2^T}, i.e., $((g, \cdots, g), (g^{2^T}, \cdots, g^{2^T}))$. By Theorem 7, it suffices
to show that the function $f : g \mapsto g^{2^T}$ has a 2-query downwards self reduction
(Definition 18) and a 2λ-to-λ batching reduction (Definition 19).

- **2-Downwards Self-Reduction**: Given an instance of the T-IS problem
  $f(g, T)$, we can query $f(g, T/2)$ to obtain an intermediate group element
  μ, and then call $f(\mu, T/2)$ to obtain $\mu^{2^{T/2}} = g^{2^T}$.
- **2λ-to-λ Batching Reduction**: Given 2λ instances $g_1, \ldots, g_{2\lambda}$ for $f(\cdot, T)$
  and 2λ candidate outputs $h_1, \ldots, h_{2\lambda}$, the batching reduction samples λ i.i.d.
  vectors $r_1, \ldots, r_\lambda \leftarrow \{0, 1\}^{2\lambda}$. The reduction then outputs λ statements about
  $f(\cdot, T)$:

$$\left(\prod_{j=1}^{2\lambda} g_j^{r_{1,j}} \xrightarrow{T} \prod_{j=1}^{2\lambda} h_j^{r_{1,j}}, \ldots, \prod_{j=1}^{2\lambda} g_j^{r_{\lambda,j}} \xrightarrow{T} \prod_{j=1}^{2\lambda} h_j^{r_{\lambda,j}} \right).$$

Completeness of the batching reduction is immediate by group axioms. For
soundness, suppose that $g_j^{2^T} \neq h_j$ for some j. The i-th statement output by
the reduction is true if and only if

$$\prod_{j=1}^{2\lambda} (g_j^{2^T})^{r_{i,j}} = \prod_{j=1}^{2\lambda} h_j^{r_{i,j}},$$

which is equivalent to the equation

$$\prod_{j=1}^{2\lambda} (g_j^{2^T} h_j^{-1})^{r_{i,j}} = \mathsf{id}_{\mathbb{G}_\lambda}.$$

For $r_i \leftarrow \{0, 1\}^{2\lambda}$, $i \in [1, \lambda]$, this event occurs with probability at most
$1/2$ (see [5, Fact 8.1]). Thus, at least one of the λ resulting statements is
false except with probability $2^{-\lambda}$. In fact, this analysis gives a product set
description for the "bad challenges" of the batching reduction. For a fixed

---

[9] A protocol for general T can be obtained by dividing T by computing a binary
decomposition of the resulting integer, and sequentially composing squaring protocols for integers of the form 2^t.

$\alpha = ((g_1, h_1), \ldots, (g_{2\lambda}, h_{2\lambda}))$, the bad set $\mathcal{R}_\alpha = \mathcal{B}_\alpha^{(1)} \times \ldots \times \mathcal{B}_\alpha^{(\lambda)} \subset (\{0,1\}^{2\lambda})^\lambda$, where

$$\mathcal{B}_\alpha^{(i)} = \left\{ \mathbf{r} \in \{0,1\}^{2\lambda} : \prod_{j=1}^{2\lambda} (g_j^{2^T})^{r_j} = \prod_{j=1}^{2\lambda} h_j^{r_j} \right\}$$

(in fact, we have that each $\mathcal{B}_\alpha^{(i)} = \mathcal{B}_\alpha$ for a fixed set $\mathcal{B}_\alpha$). As mentioned above, we have that $|\mathcal{B}_\alpha^{(i)}| \leq 2^{2\lambda}/2$ for every j and every false α. Thus, the bad-challenge relation $\mathcal{R}$ is a product relation with the appropriate sparsity, where $\mathcal{R}$ is defined as the set of pairs $(\alpha, \beta = (\mathbf{r}_1, \ldots, \mathbf{r}_\lambda))$ for which at least one of the 2λ statements defined by α is false but all of the λ statements output by the reduction are true.

Finally, we observe that for $(\mathbb{G}_\lambda, M) \leftarrow \mathsf{TrapSetup}(1^\lambda)$, the relation $\mathcal{R}$ is also *efficiently product verifiable*: to verify that $v \in \mathcal{B}_\alpha^{(i)}$, it suffices to check the equation

$$\prod_{j=1}^{2\lambda} (g_j^{2^T})^{r_j} = \prod_{j=1}^{2\lambda} h_j^{r_j}.$$

This can be checked in time $\mathsf{poly}(\lambda, \log T)$ given the order M of $\mathbb{G}_\lambda$, by first computing 2^T modulo M and then checking the equation above using the group law and repeated squaring.

Thus, by Theorem 7 we conclude that there is a $t = \log(T)$-round unambiguous interactive proof system for the T-IS problem with $\mathsf{poly}(\lambda)$ communication. Moreover, by Corollary 1 this protocol can be round-collapsed to a computationally unambiguous non-interactive argument system using a hash function family that is correlation-intractable for the relation R above (where we consider T as part of the input to the relation). Finally, by Theorem 5, such hash functions can be built under the learning with errors assumption. This is captured by the following corollary.

Corollary 2. *For a security parameter $\lambda \in \mathbb{N}$, let $\mathbb{G}_\lambda$ be a trapdoor group of unknown defined in Definition 22. Assuming polynomial hardness of* LWE *(Assumption 4), $\Pi_{\mathsf{FS},\mathcal{H}}$ is an adaptively unambiguously-sound non-interactive argument for the language*

$$\mathcal{L}_{\mathbb{G}_\lambda}^\lambda := \{((g_1, \cdots, g_\lambda), (h_1, \cdots, h_\lambda), T) \in \mathbb{G}_\lambda^\lambda \times \mathbb{G}_\lambda^\lambda \times \mathbb{N} : h_i = g^{2^T} \text{ for all } i \in [1, \lambda]\}.$$

5   PPAD Hardness

In this section, we construct a hard distribution of RSVL from any hard f that is downward self-reducible and batch-reducible, additionally assuming the unambiguous soundness of $\Pi_{\mathsf{FS},\mathcal{H}}$, the non-interactive "outline-and-batch" argument system for $\mathcal{L}_{f_n}^k$ (Corollary 1). By Theorem 3, this implies hardness of EOML, which is complete for **CLS**; since **CLS** $\subseteq$ **PPAD**, **PPAD**-hardness follows.

Our construction follow the blueprint from [15,16]. Further, since our construction works with *any* f that is downward self-reducible and batch-reducible, it generalises the constructions of RSVL instance in [15,16] and the continuous VDF in [23]. Indeed, as we saw in Sect. 3, both iterated squaring and the sumcheck problem satisfy downward self-reducibility and batch-reducibility. Due to a lack of space, we only state below the relevant theorems and refer the reader to the full version of the paper for the details.

Assumption 12 (Hardness of f). *Let* $f : \mathcal{X} \to \mathcal{Y}$ *be a function as defined in Sect. 3 and let* X *denote a sampler for* $\mathcal{X}$. *The function* f *is* $(s(\lambda), \epsilon(\lambda))$-*hard with respect to* X *if for every* $s(\lambda)$-*sized adversary* $A = \{A_\lambda\}_{\lambda \in \mathbb{N}}$

$$\Pr_{\substack{x \leftarrow X(1^\lambda) \\ y \leftarrow A(x)}} [y = f(x)] = O(\epsilon(\lambda)).$$

Theorem 13 (Hardness of RSVL from f and $\Pi_{\mathrm{FS},\mathcal{H}}$). *Let* $k, d \in \mathbb{N}$ *be parameters and* $\lambda \in \mathbb{N}$ *be a security parameter. Let*

- $f : \mathcal{X} \to \mathcal{Y}$ *be a d-query downwards self-reducible and dk-to-k batch-reducible function with sampler* X; *and*
- $\Pi_{\mathrm{FS},\mathcal{H}} = (\mathsf{Setup}, \mathsf{P}, \mathsf{V})$ *denote the non-interactive outline-and-batch protocol for* $\mathcal{L}_{f_n}^k$ *from Corollary 1.*

Furthermore, for $H \leftarrow \Pi_{\mathrm{FS},\mathcal{H}}.\mathsf{Setup}(1^\lambda)$ *and* $x \leftarrow X(1^\lambda)$, *with* $n := |x|$, *define*

$$m = m(d, k, |x|) \in \mathsf{poly}(d, k, |x|) \text{ and } L = L(d, k) := (d + 1)^n, \qquad (8)$$

there exists

$$\mathsf{S} : \{0, 1\}^m \to \{0, 1\}^m \text{ and } \mathsf{V} : \{0, 1\}^m \times [0, 2^m - 1] \to \{\mathsf{accept}, \mathsf{reject}\}, \qquad (9)$$

hardwired with $(f, H, \mathsf{D}, \widetilde{\mathsf{B}}, x, \Pi_{\mathrm{FS},\mathcal{H}}.\mathsf{V})$. *Such that if* f *is hard with respect to* X *and* $\Pi_{\mathrm{FS},\mathcal{H}}$ *is (adaptively) unambiguously sound argument, then* RSVL $:= (\mathsf{S}, \mathsf{V}, L, s_{0^n})$ *constitutes a hard distribution of* RSVL.

On instantiating f with IS as sampled in Assumption 9 and $\Pi_{\mathrm{FS},\mathcal{H}}$ with non-interactive argument from Corollary 2, we get the following corollary to Theorem 13.

Corollary 3 (Hardness of RSVL from ISand LWE). *For a security parameter* $\lambda \in \mathbb{N}$, *let* $(\mathbb{G}_\lambda, g, T)$ *be sampled as in Assumption 11, which defines* $f_n(g, T) := g^{2^T}$ *for* $n := \log(T)$. *Also, let* $\Pi_{\mathrm{FS},\mathcal{H}} = (\mathsf{Setup}, \mathsf{P}, \mathsf{V})$ *denote the non-interactive protocol for* $\mathcal{L}_{\mathbb{G}_\lambda}^k$ *from Corollary 2, which implies* $k \in \lambda^{O(1)}$ *and* $d = 2$. *Furthermore, for* $H \leftarrow \Pi_{\mathrm{FS},\mathcal{H}}.\mathsf{Setup}(1^\lambda)$, *define*

$$m = m(n, k, \lambda) := n^2 k \cdot \mathsf{poly}(\lambda) \text{ and } L = L(n) = 3^n, \qquad (10)$$

there exists

$$\mathsf{S} : \{0, 1\}^m \to \{0, 1\}^m \text{ and } \mathsf{V} : \{0, 1\}^m \times [0, 2^m - 1] \to \{\mathsf{accept}, \mathsf{reject}\}, \qquad (11)$$

hardwired with $((\mathbb{G}_\lambda, g, T), H, \mathsf{D}, \widetilde{\mathsf{B}}, \Pi_{\mathrm{FS},\mathcal{H}}.\mathsf{V})$. *Such that if Assumption 11 and Assumption 4 hold then* RSVL $:= (\mathsf{S}, \mathsf{V}, L, s_{0^n})$ *constitutes a hard distribution of* RSVL.

6 Conclusion and Open Problems

In this work, we demonstrated hardness in the class **PPAD** assuming the polynomial hardness of iterated squaring and LWE. Moreover, in the full version of this paper, we (1) strengthened this result to show hardness in **UEOPL** ⊆ **PPAD** (which is first cryptographic hardness shown for that class) and (2) constructed a unique VDF based on similar assumptions.

We briefly mention two interesting open questions that are closely related to this work:

- Can the iterated squaring hardness assumption be replaced by a weaker assumption such as the hardness of factoring? This seems plausible since to achieve **PPAD** hardness, it suffices for iterated squaring to be polynomially hard for *some* efficiently computable iteration parameter. This question was also posed in [16].
- Can we show **PPAD**-hardness solely from polynomial hardness of LWE, and thus establish a (polynomially) tight hardness result for quantum algorithms? Currently, only [39] demonstrates post-quantum hardness of **PPAD** (under sub-exponential LWE).

Acknowledgements. Nir Bitansky is a member of the checkpoint institute of information security and is supported by the European Research Council (ERC) under the European Union's Horizon Europe research and innovation programme (grant agreement No. 101042417, acronym SPP), and by Len Blavatnik and the Blavatnik Family Foundation.

Arka Rai Choudhuri is supported in part by DARPA under Agreement No. HR00112020026, AFOSR Award FA9550-19-1-0200, NSF CNS Award 1936826, and research grants by the Sloan Foundation, and Visa Inc. Any opinions, findings and conclusions or recommendations expressed in this material are those of the author(s) and do not necessarily reflect the views of the United States Government or DARPA.

Chethan Kamath is supported by Azrieli International Postdoctoral Fellowship and ISF grants 484/18 and 1789/19. He thanks Alexandros Hollender and Ninad Rajagopal for discussions on the class **UEOPL** and Krzysztof Pietrzak for clarifications about unique VDFs.

Alex Lombardi is supported in part by DARPA under Agreement No. HR00112020023, a grant from MIT-IBM Watson AI, a grant from Analog Devices, a Microsoft Trustworthy AI grant, the Thornton Family Faculty Research Innovation Fellowship and a Charles M. Vest fellowship. Any opinions, findings and conclusions or recommendations expressed in this material are those of the author(s) and do not necessarily reflect the views of the United States Government or DARPA.

Omer Paneth is a member of the checkpoint institute of information security and is supported by an Azrieli Faculty Fellowship, Len Blavatnik and the Blavatnik Foundation, the Blavatnik Interdisciplinary Cyber Research Center at Tel Aviv University, and ISF grant 1789/19.

Ron Rothblum was funded by the European Union. Views and opinions expressed are however those of the author(s) only and do not necessarily reflect those of the European Union or the European Research Council. Neither the European Union nor the granting authority can be held responsible for them.

References

1. Arora, S., Barak, B.: Computational Complexity - A Modern Approach. Cambridge University Press, Cambridge (2009)
2. Bach, E.: How to generate factored random numbers. SIAM J. Comput. **17**(2), 179–193 (1988)
3. Barak, B., et al.: On the (im)possibility of obfuscating programs. In: Kilian, J. (ed.) CRYPTO 2001. LNCS, vol. 2139, pp. 1–18. Springer, Heidelberg (2001). https://doi.org/10.1007/3-540-44647-8_1
4. Bitansky, N., Paneth, O., Rosen, A.: On the cryptographic hardness of finding a Nash equilibrium. In: Guruswami, V. (ed.) 56th FOCS, pp. 1480–1498. IEEE Computer Society Press, October 2015. https://doi.org/10.1109/FOCS.2015.94
5. Block, A.R., Holmgren, J., Rosen, A., Rothblum, R.D., Soni, P.: Time- and space-efficient arguments from groups of unknown order. In: Malkin, T., Peikert, C. (eds.) CRYPTO 2021. LNCS, vol. 12828, pp. 123–152. Springer, Cham (2021). https://doi.org/10.1007/978-3-030-84259-8_5
6. Boneh, D., Bonneau, J., Bünz, B., Fisch, B.: Verifiable delay functions. In: Shacham, H., Boldyreva, A. (eds.) CRYPTO 2018. LNCS, vol. 10991, pp. 757–788. Springer, Cham (2018). https://doi.org/10.1007/978-3-319-96884-1_25
7. Boneh, D., Sahai, A., Waters, B.: Functional encryption: definitions and challenges. In: Ishai, Y. (ed.) TCC 2011. LNCS, vol. 6597, pp. 253–273. Springer, Heidelberg (2011). https://doi.org/10.1007/978-3-642-19571-6_16
8. Brakerski, Z., Koppula, V., Mour, T.: NIZK from LPN and trapdoor hash via correlation intractability for approximable relations. In: Micciancio, D., Ristenpart, T. (eds.) CRYPTO 2020. LNCS, vol. 12172, pp. 738–767. Springer, Cham (2020). https://doi.org/10.1007/978-3-030-56877-1_26
9. Cai, J.Y., Lipton, R.J., Sedgewick, R., Yao, A.C.: Towards uncheatable benchmarks. In: [1993] Proceedings of the Eighth Annual Structure in Complexity Theory Conference, pp. 2–11, May 1993. https://doi.org/10.1109/SCT.1993.336546
10. Canetti, R., Chen, Y., Holmgren, J., Lombardi, A., Rothblum, G.N., Rothblum, R.D.: Fiat-Shamir from simpler assumptions. Cryptology ePrint Archive, Report 2018/1004 (2018). https://eprint.iacr.org/2018/1004
11. Canetti, R., et al.: Fiat-Shamir: from practice to theory. In: Charikar, M., Cohen, E. (eds.) 51st ACM STOC, pp. 1082–1090. ACM Press, June 2019. https://doi.org/10.1145/3313276.3316380
12. Canetti, R., Chen, Y., Reyzin, L., Rothblum, R.D.: Fiat-Shamir and correlation intractability from strong KDM-secure encryption. In: Nielsen, J.B., Rijmen, V. (eds.) EUROCRYPT 2018. LNCS, vol. 10820, pp. 91–122. Springer, Cham (2018). https://doi.org/10.1007/978-3-319-78381-9_4
13. Canetti, R., Goldreich, O., Halevi, S.: The random oracle methodology, revisited (preliminary version). In: 30th ACM STOC, pp. 209–218. ACM Press, May 1998. https://doi.org/10.1145/276698.276741
14. Chen, X., Deng, X., Teng, S.H.: Settling the complexity of computing two-player Nash equilibria. J. ACM (JACM) **56**(3), 1–57 (2009)
15. Choudhuri, A.R., Hubácek, P., Kamath, C., Pietrzak, K., Rosen, A., Rothblum, G.N.: Finding a Nash equilibrium is no easier than breaking Fiat-Shamir. In: Charikar, M., Cohen, E. (eds.) 51st ACM STOC, pp. 1103–1114. ACM Press, June 2019. https://doi.org/10.1145/3313276.3316400
16. Choudhuri, A.R., Hubacek, P., Kamath, C., Pietrzak, K., Rosen, A., Rothblum, G.N.: PPAD-hardness via iterated squaring modulo a composite. Cryptology ePrint Archive, Report 2019/667 (2019). https://eprint.iacr.org/2019/667

17. Choudhuri, A.R., Jain, A., Jin, Z.: Non-interactive batch arguments for NP from standard assumptions. In: Malkin, T., Peikert, C. (eds.) CRYPTO 2021. LNCS, vol. 12828, pp. 394–423. Springer, Cham (2021). https://doi.org/10.1007/978-3-030-84259-8_14

18. Choudhuri, A.R., Jain, A., Jin, Z.: SNARGs for P from LWE. In: FOCS, pp. 68–79. IEEE (2021)

19. Ciampi, M., Parisella, R., Venturi, D.: On adaptive security of delayed-input sigma protocols and Fiat-Shamir NIZKs. In: Galdi, C., Kolesnikov, V. (eds.) SCN 2020. LNCS, vol. 12238, pp. 670–690. Springer, Cham (2020). https://doi.org/10.1007/978-3-030-57990-6_33

20. Couteau, G., Katsumata, S., Ursu, B.: Non-interactive zero-knowledge in pairing-free groups from weaker assumptions. In: Canteaut, A., Ishai, Y. (eds.) EUROCRYPT 2020. LNCS, vol. 12107, pp. 442–471. Springer, Cham (2020). https://doi.org/10.1007/978-3-030-45727-3_15

21. Daskalakis, C., Goldberg, P.W., Papadimitriou, C.H.: The complexity of computing a Nash equilibrium. SIAM J. Comput. **39**(1), 195–259 (2009)

22. Daskalakis, C., Papadimitriou, C.H.: Continuous local search. In: Randall, D. (ed.) 22nd SODA, pp. 790–804. ACM-SIAM, January 2011. https://doi.org/10.1137/1.9781611973082.62

23. Ephraim, N., Freitag, C., Komargodski, I., Pass, R.: Continuous Verifiable Delay Functions. In: Canteaut, A., Ishai, Y. (eds.) EUROCRYPT 2020. LNCS, vol. 12107, pp. 125–154. Springer, Cham (2020). https://doi.org/10.1007/978-3-030-45727-3_5

24. Fearnley, J., Gordon, S., Mehta, R., Savani, R.: Unique end of potential line. In: Baier, C., Chatzigiannakis, I., Flocchini, P., Leonardi, S. (eds.) ICALP 2019. LIPIcs, vol. 132, pp. 56:1–56:15. Schloss Dagstuhl, July 2019. https://doi.org/10.4230/LIPIcs.ICALP.2019.56

25. Fiat, A., Shamir, A.: How To prove yourself: practical solutions to identification and signature problems. In: Odlyzko, A.M. (ed.) CRYPTO 1986. LNCS, vol. 263, pp. 186–194. Springer, Heidelberg (1987). https://doi.org/10.1007/3-540-47721-7_12

26. Fischlin, R., Schnorr, C.P.: Stronger security proofs for RSA and Rabin bits. J. Cryptol. **13**(2), 221–244 (2000). https://doi.org/10.1007/s001459910008

27. Freitag, C., Pass, R., Sirkin, N.: Parallelizable delegation from LWE. Cryptology ePrint Archive, Report 2022/1025 (2022). https://eprint.iacr.org/2022/1025

28. Garg, S., Gentry, C., Halevi, S., Raykova, M., Sahai, A., Waters, B.: Candidate indistinguishability obfuscation and functional encryption for all circuits. In: 54th FOCS, pp. 40–49. IEEE Computer Society Press, October 2013. https://doi.org/10.1109/FOCS.2013.13

29. Garg, S., Pandey, O., Srinivasan, A.: Revisiting the cryptographic hardness of finding a Nash equilibrium. In: Robshaw, M., Katz, J. (eds.) CRYPTO 2016. LNCS, vol. 9815, pp. 579–604. Springer, Heidelberg (2016). https://doi.org/10.1007/978-3-662-53008-5_20

30. Hoffmann, C., Hubáček, P., Kamath, C., Klein, K., Pietrzak, K.: Practical statistically-sound proofs of exponentiation in any group. Cryptology ePrint Archive, Report 2022/1021 (2022). https://eprint.iacr.org/2022/1021

31. Hofheinz, D., Kiltz, E.: The group of signed quadratic residues and applications. In: Halevi, S. (ed.) CRYPTO 2009. LNCS, vol. 5677, pp. 637–653. Springer, Heidelberg (2009). https://doi.org/10.1007/978-3-642-03356-8_37

32. Holmgren, J., Lombardi, A.: Cryptographic hashing from strong one-way functions (or: one-way product functions and their applications). In: Thorup, M. (ed.) 59th

FOCS, pp. 850–858. IEEE Computer Society Press, October 2018. https://doi. org/10.1109/FOCS.2018.00085

33. Holmgren, J., Lombardi, A., Rothblum, R.D.: Fiat-Shamir via list-recoverable codes (or: parallel repetition of GMW is not zero-knowledge). In: STOC, pp. 750–760. ACM (2021)

34. Hubáček, P., Yogev, E.: Hardness of continuous local search: query complexity and cryptographic lower bounds. In: Klein, P.N. (ed.) 28th SODA, pp. 1352–1371. ACM-SIAM, January 2017. https://doi.org/10.1137/1.9781611974782.88

35. Hulett, J., Jawale, R., Khurana, D., Srinivasan, A.: SNARGs for P from sub-exponential DDH and QR. In: Dunkelman, O., Dziembowski, S. (eds.) EURO-CRYPT 2022, Part II. LNCS, vol. 13276. pp. 520–549. Springer, Heidelberg (2022). https://doi.org/10.1007/978-3-031-07085-3_18

36. Jain, A., Lin, H., Sahai, A.: Indistinguishability obfuscation from LPN over F_p, DLIN, and PRGs in NC^0. Cryptology ePrint Archive, Report 2021/1334 (2021). https://eprint.iacr.org/2021/1334

37. Jain, A., Lin, H., Sahai, A.: Indistinguishability obfuscation from well-founded assumptions. In: Proceedings of the 53rd Annual ACM SIGACT Symposium on Theory of Computing, pp. 60–73 (2021)

38. Jain, A., Jin, Z.: Non-interactive zero knowledge from sub-exponential DDH. In: Canteaut, A., Standaert, F.-X. (eds.) EUROCRYPT 2021. LNCS, vol. 12696, pp. 3–32. Springer, Cham (2021). https://doi.org/10.1007/978-3-030-77870-5_1

39. Jawale, R., Kalai, Y.T., Khurana, D., Zhang, R.Y.: Snargs for bounded depth computations and PPAD hardness from sub-exponential LWE. In: STOC, pp. 708–721. ACM (2021)

40. Kalai, A.: Generating random factored numbers, easily. J. Cryptol. **16**(4), 287–289 (2003). https://doi.org/10.1007/s00145-003-0051-5

41. Kalai, Y.T., Paneth, O., Yang, L.: Delegation with updatable unambiguous proofs and PPAD-hardness. In: Micciancio, D., Ristenpart, T. (eds.) CRYPTO 2020, Part III. LNCS, vol. 12172, pp. 652–673. Springer, Cham (2020). https://doi.org/10. 1007/978-3-030-56877-1_23

42. Kalai, Y.T., Rothblum, G.N., Rothblum, R.D.: From obfuscation to the security of Fiat-Shamir for proofs. In: Katz, J., Shacham, H. (eds.) CRYPTO 2017. LNCS, vol. 10402, pp. 224–251. Springer, Cham (2017). https://doi.org/10.1007/978-3-319-63715-0_8

43. Lombardi, A., Vaikuntanathan, V.: Fiat-Shamir for repeated squaring with applications to PPAD-hardness and VDFs. In: Micciancio, D., Ristenpart, T. (eds.) CRYPTO 2020. LNCS, vol. 12172, pp. 632–651. Springer, Cham (2020). https://doi.org/10.1007/978-3-030-56877-1_22

44. Lund, C., Fortnow, L., Karloff, H.J., Nisan, N.: Algebraic methods for interactive proof systems. In: 31st FOCS, pp. 2–10. IEEE Computer Society Press, October 1990. https://doi.org/10.1109/FSCS.1990.89518

45. Megiddo, N., Papadimitriou, C.H.: On total functions, existence theorems and computational complexity. Theoret. Comput. Sci. **81**(2), 317–324 (1991)

46. Nash, J.: Non-cooperative games. Ann. Math. 286–295 (1951)

47. O'Neill, A.: Definitional issues in functional encryption. Cryptology ePrint Archive, Report 2010/556 (2010). https://eprint.iacr.org/2010/556

48. Papadimitriou, C.H.: On the complexity of the parity argument and other ineffi-cient proofs of existence. J. Comput. Syst. Sci. **48**(3), 498–532 (1994)

49. Peikert, C.: A decade of lattice cryptography. Found. Trends® Theor. Comput. Science **10**(4), 283–424 (2016)

50. Peikert, C., Shiehian, S.: Noninteractive zero knowledge for NP from (plain) learning with errors. In: Boldyreva, A., Micciancio, D. (eds.) CRYPTO 2019. LNCS, vol. 11692, pp. 89–114. Springer, Cham (2019). https://doi.org/10.1007/978-3-030-26948-7_4

51. Pietrzak, K.: Simple verifiable delay functions. In: Blum, A. (ed.) ITCS 2019, vol. 124, pp. 60:1–60:15. LIPIcs, Janurary 2019. https://doi.org/10.4230/LIPIcs.ITCS.2019.60

52. Reingold, O., Rothblum, G.N., Rothblum, R.D.: Constant-round interactive proofs for delegating computation. In: Wichs, D., Mansour, Y. (eds.) 48th ACM STOC, pp. 49–62. ACM Press, June 2016. https://doi.org/10.1145/2897518.2897652

53. Rivest, R.L., Shamir, A., Wagner, D.A.: Time-lock puzzles and timed-release crypto. Technical report, Cambridge, MA, USA (1996)

Parallelizable Delegation from LWE

Cody Freitag[1]([⊠]) [ID], Rafael Pass[1,2], and Naomi Sirkin[1] [ID]

[1] Cornell Tech, New York, NY 10044, USA
{cfreitag,rafael,nephraim}@cs.cornell.edu
[2] Tel Aviv University, Tel Aviv, Israel

Abstract. We present the first non-interactive delegation scheme for P with *time-tight parallel prover efficiency* based on standard hardness assumptions. More precisely, in a time-tight delegation scheme—which we refer to as a SPARG (succinct parallelizable argument)—the prover's parallel running time is $t + \text{polylog}(t)$, while using only $\text{polylog}(t)$ processors and where t is the length of the computation. (In other words, the proof is computed essentially in parallel with the computation, with only some minimal additive overhead in terms of time).

Our main results show the existence of a publicly-verifiable, non-interactive, SPARG for P assuming polynomial hardness of LWE. Our SPARG construction relies on the elegant recent delegation construction of Choudhuri, Jain, and Jin (FOCS'21) and combines it with techniques from Ephraim et al. (EuroCrypt'20).

We next demonstrate how to make our SPARG *time-independent*—where the prover and verifier do not need to known the running-time t in advance; as far as we know, this yields the first construction of a time-tight delegation scheme with time-independence based on any hardness assumption.

We finally present applications of SPARGs to the constructions of VDFs (Boneh et al., Crypto'18), resulting in the first VDF construction from standard polynomial hardness assumptions (namely LWE and the minimal assumption of a sequentially hard function).

1 Introduction

In an interactive proof system, a prover interacts with a verifier in order to prove the validity of a computational statement, with the guarantee that the verifier will be convinced if and only if the statement is true. Since their introduction by Goldwasser, Micali, and Rackoff [34], proof systems have become one of the most fundamental concepts in cryptography and more generally in theoretical computer science.

In this work, we focus on the application of proof systems to computational delegation, where a weak verifier outsources a potentially expensive computation to a powerful yet untrusted prover, who performs the computation and returns the output as well as a proof certifying its validity. We focus on delegating deterministic polynomial-time computation with the non-trivial requirement that the

© The Author(s), under exclusive license to Springer Nature Switzerland 2022
E. Kiltz and V. Vaikuntanathan (Eds.): TCC 2022, LNCS 13748, pp. 623–652, 2022.
https://doi.org/10.1007/978-3-031-22365-5_22

proof system is *succinct* [40,42], meaning that the verifier's running time and the length of the communication between the prover and verifier is essentially independent of the running time of the delegated computation.

Interest in succinct delegation has exploded in recent years due to its many applications in internet-scale, distributed protocols like blockchains and cryptocurrencies. Two key features for enabling these applications are non-interactivity and public verifiability. Non-interactivity stipulates that a proof consists of just a single message to the verifier, and public verifiability means that any third party can trust the validity of the proof. Such delegation schemes are known as publicly-verifiable SNARGs (succinct, non-interactive, arguments), and have seen immense effort in recent years from both the applied and theoretical communities in cryptography (see, e.g., [8,10,15,22,43]).

On the theory side, constructing publicly verifiable SNARGs from standard assumptions was previously elusive for many years, partially because of inherent bottlenecks for constructing SNARGs for all of NP from falsifiable assumptions [32]. However, the beautiful recent works of Kalai, Paneth, and Yang [38] and Choudhuri, Jain, Jin [22] have shown that when restricting to languages in P, SNARGs can be constructed from falsifiable assumptions, including most recently from the polynomial hardness of LWE [22].

On Parallel Prover Efficiency. Aside from improving the underlying assumptions, a major bottleneck for the adoption of SNARGs has been prover efficiency. There have been many works (e.g., [16–18,23,35,48] to name a few) focused on improving the asymptotic efficiency of the prover as much as possible under various assumptions. In the setting of delegation, this means that the running time of the prover should ideally be as close as possible to the time t of the delegated computation, which is inherent for the prover to even compute the output itself. To date, the best asymptotic constructions achieve quasi-linear overhead by the prover, with running time $t \cdot \mathrm{poly}(\lambda, \log t)$ where λ is the security parameter.

Recently, the work of Ephraim, Freitag, Komargodski, and Pass [29] showed how to construct parallelizable delegation schemes (which they call SPARKs) where the prover has *parallel* running time $t + \mathrm{poly}(\lambda, \log t)$ (i.e., with only *additive overhead* and no multiplicative overhead) using only a modest number, $\mathrm{poly}(\lambda, \log t)$, of processors. Their protocols even work for NP, but at the cost of either assuming SNARKs (succinct non-interactive arguments of knowledge) for NP—that are only known to exist from non-standard and non-falsifiable assumptions—or only achieving an *interactive* protocol (assuming just standard collision-resistant hash functions). Thus, the state-of-the art leaves open the question of whether we can get a *non-interactive* delegation scheme, even just for P, with tight prover efficiency from standard (falsifiable) assumptions:

Can we construct publicly verifiable, succinct, parallelizable delegation schemes for P from standard, falsifiable, assumptions?

We refer to such publicly verifiable, succinct, parallelizable delegation schemes as SPARGs (succinct parallelizable arguments) for P, following the notation of SPARKs from [29].

In this work, we resolve the above-mentioned problem, constructing the first non-interactive delegation schemes where the prover has $t + \text{poly}(\lambda, \log t)$ parallel running time using $\text{poly}(\lambda, \log t)$ processors based on standard assumptions. More precisely, our construction only relies on the polynomial hardness of the LWE assumption.

Theorem 1.1 (SPARGs for P from LWE; Informal (see Corollary 2)). *Assuming hardness of LWE, there exists a non-interactive SPARG for* P.

We additionally present strengthenings of the above theorem—including a SPARG for computations that are themselves parallelized, and obtaining so-called *time-independent* SPARGs, where the prover and verifier need not know the length t of the computation in advance—and present corollaries of these results, including the first construction of a Verifiable Delay Function (VDF) [19] from standard (polynomial) hardness assumptions.

1.1   Our Results in More Detail

Let us present our results in more detail. As a starting point for our work, we observe that SPARGs for P can be constructed based on the notion of RAM delegation, following the framework of the SPARK construction due to [29], so long as the RAM delegation scheme satisfies *quasi-linear prover efficiency*. RAM delegation is known under various assumptions, and most recently was shown secure under LWE [22]. Unfortunately, known RAM delegation schemes do not satisfy the quasi-linear prover efficiency that we desire. Therefore, our main result is to show how to adapt existing schemes to satisfy a notion of efficiency that will suffice for our construction.

Updatable RAM Delegation. We start by defining the notion of an *updatable* RAM delegation scheme with quasi-linear efficiency. From an efficiency perspective, this is weaker than a (non-updatable) RAM delegation scheme satisfying quasi-linear efficiency. Nevertheless, we show that it suffices for our purposes, and can be constructed by relying on the RAM delegation scheme of [22].

At a high level, an updatable RAM delegation scheme is a delegation scheme for RAM computations that allows for incremental updates and proofs for intermediate pieces of the overall computation. Specifically, a prover can perform part of a computation and obtain the resulting state as well as some additional auxiliary information aux corresponding to this section of the computation. Given aux, it can then continue to update the computation to a new state, producing a new piece of auxiliary information aux′. The auxiliary information aux for any sub-computation can be used as a "witness" to *efficiently* compute a proof for the corresponding piece of the computation. (We note that the proof is for a deterministic computation, but the auxiliary input/ witness is provided for efficiency purposes.) This enables a large computation to be updated and proved in different pieces, and in particular allows for taking advantage of the prover's knowledge of aux, from running the computation, in order to generate a proof with significantly less overhead.

In more detail, we require an updatable delegation scheme with the following efficiency properties:

- **Efficiency of computing aux:** Given a RAM configuration cf, auxiliary information aux_{cf}, and time t, the new configuration cf' and its associated auxiliary information $aux_{cf'}$ that results after t steps of computation starting from cf can be computed in time $t + poly(\lambda)$ using $poly(\lambda)$ parallel processors.
- **Efficiency of generating proofs given aux:** Given auxiliary information aux corresponding to a t step transition from initial configuration cf to final configuration cf', a proof of correctness for this transition can be generated in time $t \cdot poly(\lambda, \log t)$. For an updatable scheme, we refer to this as *quasi-linear prover efficiency*. (Note that this is a stronger efficiency requirement than the one used in [22], where the prover running-time would grow with $|cf|$.)

Let us highlight that any RAM delegation scheme is also an updatable one (by simply letting aux be empty), but does not necessarily satisfy quasi-linear overhead when generating proofs given aux. Using the auxiliary information, aux, is helpful for us in achieving this prover efficiency. In particular, we show how to combine the ideas behind the SNARG construction of [22] with the updatable hash tree from [29] to get an updatable RAM delegation from LWE with the desired efficiency.

Theorem 1.2 (Efficient Updatable RAM Delegation; Informal (see Theorem 4.2)). *Assuming hardness of LWE, there exists a succinct, publicly verifiable, updatable RAM delegation scheme with quasi-linear prover efficiency.*

SPARGs from Updatable RAM Delegation. Next, we show how to adapt the SPARK construction of [29] to rely on any updatable RAM delegation scheme with quasi-linear prover efficiency, rather than relying on SNARKs with quasi-linear prover efficiency. We highlight that the construction in [29] relied on the proof of knowledge property of the underlying delegation scheme (i.e., the SNARK in use) and it is not known how to replace it with just a SNARG. This is why we resort to using the more complicated object of an updatable RAM delegation scheme with quasi-linear prover efficiency.

Theorem 1.3 (SPARGs from Updatable RAM Delegation; Informal (see Theorem 5.1)). *Assume the existence of a succinct, publicly verifiable, updatable RAM delegation scheme with quasi-linear efficiency. Then there exists a non-interactive SPARG for* P.

Theorem 1.1 then follows as a direct corollary of Theorems 1.2 and 1.3.

We also extend this result to the setting of *parallel* computations. Specifically, given a computation that can be done in time t with p processors, we show a SPARG that preserves depth by running in time $t + poly(\lambda, \log(t \cdot p))$, while only using $p \cdot \text{poly}(\lambda, \log(t \cdot p))$ processors. This is in contrast to the naive approach of using the above SPARG for sequential computations, which would naively result in parallel time that depends on the total work $t \cdot p$ rather than the depth t. We obtain this result by extending the updatable RAM delegation scheme above to be depth-preserving for parallel computations—that is, *both* the parallel time and processors used by the delegation scheme scale quasi-linearly with that of the computation.

Theorem 1.4 (SPARGs for Parallel Computations; Informal). *Assume the existence of a succinct, publicly verifiable, updatable RAM delegation scheme for parallel computations that is depth-preserving. Then there exists a non-interactive SPARG for polynomial-time, parallel computations.*

Time-Independent SPARGs. SPARKs [29] were initially defined such that in order to prove a t-time computation, the prover was provided the time bound t as input. It is perhaps natural to assume that this might be necessary in order to "fit the computation of the proof" in during the computation itself. However, in many scenarios, the time bound t may not be a priori known. To circumvent this issue, we define the notion of a *time-independent* SPARG, which satisfies the same properties as a SPARG except that the prover and verifier no longer get t as input. We additionally show how to extend the above construction to achieve a time-independent SPARG from LWE:

Theorem 1.5 (Time-independent SPARGs from LWE; Informal). *Assuming hardness of LWE, there exists a non-interactive, time-independent SPARG for* P.

As far as we know, this yields the first construction of a SPARG with time-independence based on any hardness assumption (that is, a similar result was not known from the stronger notion of SPARKs).

To prove Theorem 1.5, we define the notion of a *time-tight*, updatable RAM delegation. Essentially, this is a RAM delegation as above, but with the prover efficiency properties of a SPARG, where the final configuration is not known at the start of proof generation. We emphasize that the prover for such a scheme is given the time bound t as input in order to compute the proof in time $t + \text{poly}(\lambda, \log(t))$. We then give a generic transformation that starts with any time-tight, updatable RAM delegation scheme (that is given the time bound t as input) and constructs a non-interactive, time-independent SPARG.

Theorem 1.6 (Time-independent SPARG transformation; Informal). *Given any time-tight, updatable RAM delegation scheme, there exists a non-interactive, time-independent SPARG for* P.

Furthermore, a minor adaptation of our construction of a SPARG for P from LWE (Theorem 1.1 above) satisfies the notion of a time-tight, updatable RAM delegation scheme, which gives Theorem 1.5 above.

Applications: Verifiable Delay Functions from Standard Assumptions.
Finally, we observe that one of the main applications of non-interactive SPARKs
for P from [29] was to constructing verifiable delay functions [19]. Roughly
speaking, a VDF is *publicly-verifiable* function that can be computed in time
t, but cannot be noticeably sped up with $\text{poly}(t)$ processors. VDFs have important applications in generating trusted randomness in distributed applications
(see [19,21,30] for more details).

[29] showed that any function f can be made verifiable essentially "for free"",
by computing the output of the f and a proof certifying its correctness using a
SPARK for f, and that a VDF can be obtained by simply computing any *sequential function*—that is, a function that can be computed in time t, but cannot be
noticeably sped up with $\text{poly}(t)$ processors—with a SPARK. But given that non-
interactive SPARKs are only known based on non-falsifiable assumptions, this
only gave new VDF constructions assuming non-falsifiable assumptions (namely,
the existence of SNARKs for NP).

We note, however, that the transformation in [29] actually does not rely on
the argument of knowledge property of the underlying SPARK and a SPARG for
parallel P computations suffices. Consequently, we can achieve the same results
but replacing the SNARK assumptions from [29] with just polynomial hardness
of LWE.

**Theorem 1.7 (VDFs from LWE and any sequential function; Infor-
mal (see Corollary *3*)).** *Assuming the (polynomial) hardness of LWE and the
existence of a sequential function, there exists a verifiable delay function.*

Let us highlight that the assumption that sequential functions exist is *necessary*
for the construction of a VDF—any VDF trivially is a sequential function. On
top of this minimal assumption, our construction only assume the hardness of
LWE. As far as we know, before our work, it was not known how to get VDF
(in the plain model, without random oracles) based on any standard polynomial
hardness + the assumption that sequential functions exist. In particular, previously, VDFs were known based on either (a) *iteratively-sequential functions*[1]
and SNARGs [19], (b) sequential functions and SNARKs for NP [29], or (c)
sub-exponential LWE assumption and the sequentiality of repeated squaring in
a group of unknown order [41], or various construction in the random oracle
model [28,44,47]. We emphasize that in terms of practical efficiency, our construction does not compete with constructions in the ROM (such as [44,47]),
but our goal here is simply to show that VDFs as a primitive can be based on
standard hardness assumptions.

As pointed out in [29], since a SPARG makes any deterministic computation
verifiable, our transformation applies to sequential functions that may satisfy
other properties like memory-hardness. We note that memory-hardness is useful for ASIC-resistance in VDFs, making so attackers cannot easily invest in

---

[1] An iteratively sequential function f has the property that the t-wise composition
$f^{(t)}$ of f cannot be computed faster than computing f sequentially t times, even
with $\text{poly}(t)$ processors.

special-purpose hardware and gain an advantage in computing the VDF quicker. Informally, a *memory-hard sequential function* is a sequential function that additionally requires a large memory footprint throughout the computation (for a more formal treatment, see, e.g., [1–4, 25–27] for examples of different definitions and constructions of candidate memory-hard functions). It follows that our techniques can be used to achieve a memory-hard VDF based on the hardness of LWE and the existence of any memory-hard sequential function (and our result is not tailored to any specific definition of memory-hardness). Previously, the only known construction of a memory-hard VDF was the construction in [29] which relied on the existence of a memory-hard sequential function and SNARKs for NP.

1.2 Related Work

We first focus on the computational assumptions needed for SNARGs and RAM delegation. In the setting of information-theoretic security, the celebrated protocols of Goldwasser, Kalai, and Rothblum [33] and Reingold, Rothblum, and Rothblum [45] first showed how to construct *interactive* delegation protocols for bounded depth and bounded space computations, respectively. Shifting our attention to simple 2-round protocols or non-interactive protocols in the CRS model with only computational security, Kalai, Raz, and Rothblum [39] construct *privately verifiable* delegation for any time and space Turing machines based on the quasi-polynomial hardness of LWE. Kalai and Paneth [37] extend this to the setting of privately verifiable RAM delegation, and it was shown how to implement this approach based on polynomial-hardness assumptions by Brakerski, Holmgren, and Kalai [20]. Holmgren and Rothblum [35] show how to implement the approach of [39] for RAM delegation with a specific no-signaling MIP with quasi-linear overhead in both time and space, based on the subexponential hardness of LWE. Kalai, Paneth, and Yang [38] achieved the first *publicly verifiable* RAM delegation scheme based on a new falsifiable decisional assumption on groups with bilinear maps. Jawale, Kalai, Khurana, and Zhang [36] show how to achieve publicly verifiable delegation for bounded depth computation from subexponential hardness of LWE. Finally, Choudhuri, Jain, and Jin [22] construct publicly verifiable RAM delegation from polynomial hardness of LWE.

We note that implicit in the works of [20,22,37,38], building off the techniques of [39], is the notion of a quasi-argument for a class of restricted NP statements. This is an argument system that has a special "no-signaling" extractor for certain NP languages that is used to prove soundness of RAM delegation statements relative to an associated hash tree.

Efficient PCPs. We note that many SNARGs and delegation protocols are based on probabilistically checkable proofs (PCPs) building off the protocols of Kilian [40] (in the interactive setting) and Micali [42] (in the random oracle model using the Fiat-Shamir heuristic [31]). Originally PCP constructions required polynomial length and prover running time [5,6]. Ben-Sasson and Sudan [14] gave the first construction of a PCP with quasi-linear overhead, meaning that a PCP for a t-time (possibly non-deterministic) computation had overall size $t \cdot \mathrm{polylog}(t)$. Subsequent work by [11] give a highly parallelizable PCP that can be computed in parallel time $\mathrm{polylog}(t)$ with t processors, *after computing the computation tableau.* Interactive oracle proofs (IOPs) are a multi-round generalization of PCPs, introduced in [45] and [13], that are also useful for delegation protocols. There is a fruitful line of work [9,12,46] resulting in linear-size IOPs useful for delegation, although the prover still runs in at least quasi-linear time.

Parallelism in Proofs. The works of [19] and [24] first introduced the technique of computing a proof in parallel to a computation in order to improve the prover's parallel efficiency. They first applied this technique to iteratively sequential functions, which necessarily have low space, in the context of verifiable delay functions. The work of [29] shows how to apply this technique generically to any, not necessarily space bounded, computation. However, their generic transformation requires interaction or relies on SNARKs in the non-interactive setting.

1.3   Organization

In Sect. 2, we give an overview of our SPARG constructions. Then, in Sect. 3, we give preliminaries. Next, in Sect. 4, we give our construction of updatable RAM delegation with quasilinear overhead from LWE. Then, in Sect. 5, we give our construction of SPARGs from updatable delegation. Our VDF construction is given in Sect. 6. Our construction of time-tight SPARGs, and that of SPARGs for parallel computations, are deferred to the full version.

2   Techniques

In this section, we give an overview of our SPARG constructions. Our constructions will be for RAM computations, so we start with a brief overview of our model. Recall that a RAM machine M is an algorithm with random access to a (possibly long) string D in memory, and keeps a small local state state. At each step of computation, M reads or writes to a location in memory and updates its local state. We say that $M(x)$ outputs y in t steps if, when the initial memory of M contains x, after t steps the local state has a special halting symbol and y is written to memory. The *configuration* cf of a RAM machine at any step of the computation consists of its memory and local state, and hence fully describes the computation at that point.

2.1   SPARGs from LWE

In this section, we overview our construction of SPARGs for P. Our starting point is the non-interactive SPARK construction for NP due to [29]. Recall that to construct SPARGs, we are only concerned with proving *soundness* for deterministic, polynomial-time computations, whereas the SPARK construction is an argument of knowledge, which is a stronger notion that in turn relies on assumptions that are too strong for our setting. We start by giving an overview of the SPARK construction, and then discuss how we modify it to achieve SPARGs from weaker assumptions.

SPARK Construction. We start by overviewing the SPARK construction of [29], henceforth the EFKP construction, which relies on a SNARK for NP. To prove that a $M(x) = y$ in t steps, recall that the goal is for the SPARK prover to run in time at most $t + \text{polylog}\, t$. The high-level approach of EFKP is to split the computation into sub-computations, and give a SNARK proof for each sub-computation in parallel to computing and proving subsequent steps of the computation.

To illustrate this, suppose that the underlying SNARK requires time $2k$ to prove k steps of RAM computation. Then, the largest portion of computation that can be computed and proven by time t is $k = t/3$, as one can spend time $t/3$ computing these steps of the computation, and then spend time $2t/3$ proving that it was done correctly, thus obtaining a proof π_1 of the first $t/3$ steps by time t. The observation of EFKP (following prior works [19,24]) is that this idea can be applied recursively. Specifically, while π_1 is being proven, they continue by computing and proving $1/3$ of the remaining computation *in parallel to proving* π_1. Overall, they show that this results in roughly $O(\log t)$ "threads", where each thread computes $1/3$ of the remaining computation, and then begins a SNARK proof while the next parallel thread starts computing. Thus, the full SPARK proof consists of $O(\log t)$ SNARK proofs, all completing by time t. More generally, if the underlying SNARK could prove k steps of computation in time $\alpha^\star \cdot k$, then this would result in having roughly $\alpha^\star \cdot \log t$ proofs (and parallel processors).

While this approach seems promising, it only gives a SPARK for computations with bounded memory size. In particular, it requires giving proofs about intermediate states of the RAM computation. Since the intermediate state of a RAM computation is its configuration cf, the above approach requires using the SNARK to prove statements of the form $(M, \mathsf{cf}, \mathsf{cf}', k)$ stating the M transitions from configuration cf to configuration cf′ in time k. However, the size of each configuration scales with the memory size of M, and thus giving SNARK proofs for these statements will depend on the memory size as well.

To remedy this, rather than proving that M transitions from cf to cf′ in k steps, EFKP show that the prover can maintain an updatable digest rt to the configuration at any given time step, and prove that there exists a sequence of k updates to rt, according to M, that result in rt′. At a high level, the digest corresponds to a Merkle tree of the memory at each time step based on a collision-resistant hash function, and each time M reads or writes to memory, the corresponding update is done to the Merkle tree. At the end of the computation, the prover can simply open the bits of the output y with respect to the final digest, which the verifier can then check efficiently.

Crucially, each update to the digest can be certified with a very short proof (corresponding to its authentication path in the Merkle tree). Therefore, they rely on a SNARK for the NP language $\mathcal{L}_{upd}$ that where an instance $(M, \mathsf{rt}, \mathsf{rt}', k)$ has a witness consisting of the k updates to the Merkle tree. The relation for this language has complexity roughly $k \cdot \mathrm{poly}(\lambda)$, as it only requires running M for k steps and checking that each update was done correctly. It is therefore feasible to have a SNARK where the prover overhead for proving $\mathcal{L}_{upd}$ statements is independent of t. Specifically, EFKP instantiate this framework with a SNARK with *quasilinear overhead*, where an instance corresponding to k updates can be proven in time roughly $k \cdot \mathrm{poly}(\lambda, \log k)$.

Relaxing SPARKs to SPARGs. Given that the EFKP construction relies on an underlying argument of knowledge, a natural approach to constructing a SPARG is to replace the underlying SNARK with a SNARG, and try to prove soundness for computations in P.

Consider the following straightforward attempt to prove soundness with this approach. Suppose for contradiction that there exists an adversary $\mathcal{A}$ who succeeds at convincing the verifier of a false statement (M, x, t, y) where $M(x) \neq y$. Following the EFKP construction, this means that $\mathcal{A}$ outputs sub-proofs $\pi_1, \ldots, \pi_m$, where the ith sub-proof certifies that M transitions from digest rt_{i-1} to digest rt_i in some number of steps. Ideally, we would like to say that if the statement itself is false, then there must be a sub-proof corresponding to a false statement, hence breaking soundness of the underlying SNARG. However, we cannot claim that this is the case—all the sub-proofs could correspond to true statements if one of them contains a collision in the hash function.

Specifically, it could be the case that for some i, the sequence of updates used by $\mathcal{A}$ to prove that rt_{i-1} transitions to rt_i corresponds to a "divergent" path of computation, and in reality M makes a different sequence of updates after the step corresponding to rt_{i-1}.

The proof of [29] relied on the extractability of the SNARK to show that if all sub-statements were true, then $\mathcal{A}$ must be able to produce a hash collision at the point where the computation diverged, in contradiction. However, if we are only relying on a SNARG, we have no way to extract the collision and reach a contradiction.

Nevertheless, we have one advantage over the EFKP approach which we have not yet used—we are only trying to prove soundness for deterministic computations, whereas their proof had to hold even for non-deterministic ones. In particular, this means that given M, x, we can actually compute the true sequence of updates in polynomial time, and thus determine exactly in which sub-proof the computation diverged.

This does not quite solve the problem, because we still have no way to extract a collision between rt_{i-1} and rt_i. However, it does capture an important soundness property, which will turn out to be the key component of our construction. Observe that the above proof of soundness would succeed if the underlying SNARG satisfied the following:

No PPT adversary $\mathcal{A}$ can produce a proof π, a transcript of the computation of M as well as digests rt, rt' and some number of steps k such that (a) the verifier accepts π as a proof for $(M, \text{rt}, \text{rt}', k)$, (b) rt is the correct digest at the beginning of the computation, but (c) rt' is not the correct resulting digest after k steps.

This definition morally captures the fact that $\mathcal{A}$ should not be able to find a collision in the hash function, but does not require extractability to actually produce that collision. In particular, it can be viewed as a notion of soundness relative to a CRH, where the verifier only sees a digest of the statement, yet cannot be convinced on digests of false statements.

From RAM Delegation to SPARGs. We observe that this property stated above is in fact the notion of soundness for RAM delegation schemes. In particular, prior work (such as [22,37,38]) adopted this as a meaningful notion of soundness for RAM delegation to capture the setting where a weak verifier, who may have pre-computed a digest of a large database, delegates a computation on that database and can verify the updated digest after the computation to enable future outsourcing on the updated database.

Putting everything together, to prove soundness of the EFKP construction for deterministic computations, it suffices to rely on a RAM delegation scheme with the above soundness notion, rather than a SNARK. By relying on the recent RAM delegation scheme due to [22], we obtain a sound scheme based only on LWE.

Updatable Delegation. There is one remaining caveat to the construction, which is that by replacing the SNARK with a delegation scheme, we have to ensure that each sub-proof computed using the delegation scheme can be done with low prover overhead so that the resulting construction satisfies the tight efficiency requirements of a SPARG.

Looking at the delegation scheme due to [22], in order to delegate the computation of M starting at configuration cf, the scheme first computes a Merkle tree of cf (analogously to the Merkle tree approach in [29]), and then proceeds to compute the updates to the Merkle, and prove their correctness using underlying building blocks. We observe that other than computing this initial Merkle tree, the delegation prover has quasilinear overhead. Specifically, we show that when delegating a statement corresponding to k steps of computation, everything other than computing the initial Merkle tree can be done in time $k \cdot \text{poly}(\lambda, \log k)$.

To put this into context in our scheme, recall that we will be breaking up the computation of M into sub-computations, indexed by configurations $\text{cf}_0, \text{cf}_1, \ldots, \text{cf}_m$, for which we will then use the delegation scheme to prove that cf_{i-1} transitions to cf_i for each sub-computation i. However, if the delegation prover then hashes down each cf_i at the beginning of each sub-proof, the running time of our SPARG will then rely on the memory size, which as mentioned above, does not suffices for us.

We resolve this by using another piece of the EFKP construction, specifically their Merkle tree instantiation. Recall that they gave a construction, termed a *concurrently updatable hash function*, which enabled updating the Merkle tree in parallel to the computation with very little overhead. We observe that if the Merkle tree in the RAM delegation scheme is instantiated with a concurrently updatable hash function, then when computing each configuration cf_i, we can compute in parallel the Merkle tree digest of cf_i, and give this to the delegation prover as auxiliary input.

At a high level, this captures a notion which we call *updatability* for RAM delegation schemes, since while running the computation from computing a proof that cf_{i-1} transitions to cf_i, the Merkle tree for cf_i computed during the proof can be given to the next prover.

We show that the [22] scheme satisfies this notion of upatability when instantiated with the hash tree due to [29], and that this notion of updatability suffices to achieve the required prover efficiency from the delegation scheme in order to instantiate the EFKP framework and obtain a SPARG for P.

2.2 SPARGs for Parallel Computations

The above framework gives a SPARG for *sequential* computations—namely, a proof system that runs in time $t + \text{poly}(\lambda, \log t)$ for t-time computations. However, it is very natural to consider the setting where the computation itself can be parallelized. In this setting, we show that our SPARG construction can be extended to prove parallel computations while preserving the depth of the computation. Specifically, for computations that take time t with p processors, our SPARG will run in time $t + \text{poly}(\lambda, \log(t \cdot p))$ with $p \cdot \text{poly}(\lambda, \log(t \cdot p))$ processors.

To achieve this, recall that the prover in our SPARG construction above splits the computation into many sub-computations. For each sub-computation, the prover runs the computation in parallel to updating a hash tree to its memory. It then uses an updatable RAM delegation scheme to prove correctness of this sub-computation. Efficiency of the resulting construction relies on the fact that (1) computing $M(x)$ and updating the hash tree can be done in parallel in time essentially t, and (2) the delegation scheme has quasi-linear overhead, so proving any sequence of k steps takes time $k \cdot \text{poly}(\lambda, \log k)$.

To extend this to the setting of parallel computations, we observe that the prover can run the computation in time t with p processors. Moreover, the hash tree due to [29] allows for concurrent updates, and so the updates can be done in parallel to the computation. However, a challenge arises when using the updatable RAM delegation scheme in this setting, as we have to prove correctness of *concurrent* updates. Specifically, for a sub-computation corresponding to k steps, the concurrent updates to the hash tree result in k updates each to p locations in memory (as opposed to a single location each, as in the sequential case). The efficiency of our updatable RAM delegation scheme depends, in particular, polynomially on the time to verify a single update, which is $\text{poly}(p)$ when considering concurrent updates. Therefore, this would not result in a delegation scheme with quasilinear prover efficiency—instead, the prover time would depend polynomially on p, which is undesirable when p is large.

The dependence on the time to verify a single update is inherent to our updatable RAM delegation construction, and in particular stems from the underlying building blocks used in [22]. Therefore, it is not immediately clear how to move forward—in order to avoid any delays with running the main computation, we have to perform concurrent updates, but the delegation scheme is incompatible with these updates.

To solve this, we observe that we can transform *concurrent* updates to *sequential* ones—namely, k concurrent updates on p locations each can be turned into $k \cdot p$ updates, each to a single location. We call a hash tree with this property *sequentializable*. At a high level, we do so by taking advantage of the Merkle tree structure, and the fact that an authentication path for an individual location ℓ can be derived from the updates to a set of locations containing ℓ. We form the authentication paths corresponding to the sequential updates level by level, resulting in time $\text{poly}(\lambda, \log p)$ to sequentialize a concurrent update when using p processors. Therefore, for a sub-computation with k steps, we can sequentialize the updates in parallel time $k \cdot \text{poly}(\lambda, \log p)$. Crucially, sequentializing the updates does not delay the main computation of $M(x)$—instead, the sequentialization can be seen as part of the "proof" phase, before calling the RAM delegation prover.

After sequentializing the updates, a k-time sub-computation results in $k \cdot p$ individual updates. We are not quite done, because applying our updatable RAM delegation scheme to prove correctness of these updates would result in time quasilinear in the total work $k \cdot p$, rather than simply k. As the final step in our construction, we observe that the computation of the RAM delegation proof can be parallelized as well. Specifically, recall that our RAM delegation scheme is given the updates as a witness to the computation, and is only required to compute the proof. When given $T = t \cdot p$ sequentialized updates, it runs in quasilinear time $T \cdot \text{poly}(\lambda, \log T)$. As a final observation, we show that for any number of processors p, the RAM delegation prover can be made to run in time $T/p \cdot \text{poly}(\lambda, \log T)$ with p processors, when given these updates. At a high level, this follows due to the fact that the underlying updatable delegation scheme treats the T updates as a batch of T individual statements for which it proves correctness. In particular, we show that the proofs of these statements (and the information tying them together) can be computed in parallel, thus giving the desired efficiency.

Putting everything together, the combination of sequentializing the updates and running the parallelized delegation prover gives the desired quasilinear efficiency for our RAM delegation scheme, which in turn suffices to get a SPARG for parallel computations.

2.3   Time-Independent SPARGs

We consider the application of SPARGs to *time-tight* RAM delegation, where by time-tight we mean a delegation protocol that satisfies the same efficiency properties as a SPARG. So far, we have assumed that the time bound t for the computation is provided as input. This seems like the a natural requirement as we have to compute the proof of the computation *completely during* the computation itself. We show that this is actually not necessary, at least in the case of non-interactive delegation. In particular, we show how to construct a non-interactive SPARG for any t-time computation $M(x)$ where t does not need to be provided as input—we refer to this as a *time-independent* SPARG—given a non-interactive SPARG that does take as input the time bound t. (In fact, we actually use a time-tight RAM delegation scheme in order to break up the computation into different parts, which we will discuss more below.)

As a first attempt, what if the prover computed a SPARG for all possible time bounds T? The prover could run the computation on the side, see when it halts, and use the proof corresponding to the actual time bound t, ignoring all other proofs. If we compute all the SPARG proofs in parallel, then the prover will compute a proof in the desired parallel time, but this requires using more than t processors! Even worse, we don't necessarily know a priori a bound on what the running time will be, so we would even need to use potentially super-polynomially many processors to handle all polynomial-time computations. Instead, we want to compute the time-independent SPARG using only a modest, say fixed polynomial $\text{poly}(\lambda)$ in the security parameter, overhead in the number of processors required.

In an effort to reduce the number of processors used, the prover could instead compute proofs only for the time bounds $T = 2^0, 2^1, 2^2, 2^4, \ldots, 2^\lambda$, assuming that the polynomial time bound t is at most 2^λ for large enough security parameters λ. Now we only have a $\lambda + 1$ overhead in the number of processors required. However, if in computing $M(x)$ we find out that the true time bound t is not close to a power of 2, then we may have a factor of 2 over head in the time to compute the next largest proof that encapsulates the full computation. Even a small multiplicative overhead is not allowed for SPARGs, so this approach unfortunately does not achieve what we want.

In order to maintain optimal parallel time with only a small overhead in the number of processors used, we leverage the techniques described in Sect. 2.1 to break down the proof of the entire computation into proofs of various subcomputations while still guaranteeing soundness. This is why we actually need to start with RAM delegation for our underlying scheme so that breaking the proofs into many parts does not scale with the space of the underlying computation (Fig. 1).

The idea of the full construction is to compute proofs for the time bounds $T = 2^0, 2^1, \ldots, 2^\lambda$, but after each proof of size 2^i finishes, to continue to compute proofs in regular intervals of size 2^i that continue that computation (using the same associated memory). So, for every size 2^i and every $j \geq 1$, we will have a proof corresponding to the interval of the computation between steps $(j - 1) \cdot 2^i$ and $j \cdot 2^i$. For any such starting point a and ending point b, we let $\pi_{(a,b)}$ denote the associated proof. Ignoring efficiency for now, this means that after the machine $M(x)$ halts at time t, we can simply collect m proofs $\pi_{(0,a_1)}, \pi_{(a_1,a_2)}, \ldots, \pi_{(a_{m-1},t)}$ that cover the entire interval from 0 to t via intervals of powers of 2. These intervals will then simply correspond to the binary representation of t, so there will be $m \leq \lambda$ proofs in total.

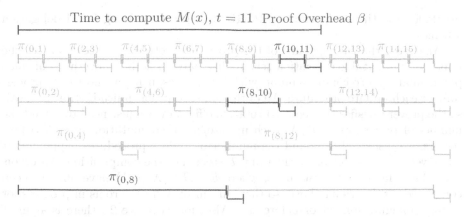

Fig. 1. An example of the time-independent SPARG prover for a computation $M(x)$ that takes $t = 11$ steps. A proof $\pi_{(a,b)}$ corresponds to a RAM delegation proof that M on input x starts at configuration cf_a and ends at configuration cf_b. The horizontal axis represents parallel time, and the prover is computing all proofs along a given vertical slice in parallel. Each separate thread corresponds to a memory block that is being updated and outputting proofs for the corresponding intervals at the same time. The additive overhead per interval is indicated in red, but can be computed separately while the subsequent update continues. The final proof output by the prover consists of the sub-proofs corresponding to the 1's in the binary representation of the actual time t. For $t = 11$ shown in the picture, this corresponds to the 8, 2, and 1 digits, so the prover eventually outputs the proofs $\pi_{(0,8)}$, $\pi_{(8,10)}$, and $\pi_{(10,11)}$. All other proofs are discarded, and are thus greyed out in the picture above.

In order to make this approach work, we need a specific, extremely efficient, underlying RAM delegation scheme. Concretely, we need it to be the case that we can have a thread of computation that computes proofs for all size 1 intervals $(0, 1)$, $(1, 2)$, $(2, 3)$, $\ldots$, $(t - 1, t)$ without blowing up the complexity of the protocol. Fortunately, our main SPARG construction actually gives us an updatable delegation scheme that is also *time-tight*. Essentially, this is an updatable delegation scheme where an update of any sequence of k steps also outputs a proof of correctness for those k steps. Furthermore, these updates and proofs can be pipelined together efficiently, ensuring that computing a proof for all size 1 intervals in a row as above does not blow up the overall complexity nor delay the output of later proofs in the sequence (namely the proof for the interval $(i, i+1)$ still finishes at time $i + 1 + \mathrm{poly}(\lambda)$, where the delay is independent of i or t).

We finish by arguing why the protocol is succinct and satisfies the optimal parallel time requirement of a SPARG while using only a fixed $\mathrm{poly}(\lambda)$ number of processors. For succinctness, recall the number of proofs that the prover needs to output is simply the number of 1s in the binary representation of the actual time bound t. Assuming $t < 2^\lambda$, this implies that the number of delegation proofs m that need to be sent at most λ, so there is at most a λ overhead in the size of the proofs for the time-independent SPARG over the underlying RAM delegation scheme.

Analyzing the running time of the prover, we note that by assumption, the underlying updatable delegation scheme has only an additive overhead of some polynomial $\beta(\lambda)$ to compute proofs with its updates, using at most $\beta(\lambda)$ processors for each update procedure. All of the required proofs finish by time $t + \beta(\lambda)$, so the prover satisfies the required runtime efficiency, we just need to bound the number of processors used. As each update/proof computation uses $\beta(\lambda)$ processors, we just need to bound the number of update procedures happening at any given time. To do so, consider any T steps into the computation. All proofs $\pi_{(a,b)}$ for a final configuration cf_b where $b < T - \lambda \cdot \beta(\lambda)$ have already been completed, as described above, so there are most $\lambda \cdot \beta(\lambda)$ proofs in progress for ending configurations at or before cf_T. Also, for each size 2^i, there is at most one proof of size 2^i that could have been started and ends after cf_T. This implies that are at most $\lambda + \lambda \cdot \beta(\lambda)$ updates computed at any given time, so the prover requires only a $\mathrm{poly}(\lambda)$ number of processors in total.

We emphasize that this transformation fundamentally relies on the fact that the underlying delegation scheme is "time-tight" like a SPARG. Otherwise the overlap among all of the proofs would be too great, and the protocol would require too many processors.

3   Preliminaries

In this section, we include the relevant preliminaries. Additional preliminaries, including definitions of verifiable delay functions, concurrently updatable hash functions, and succinct arguments for parallel computations are deferred to the full version.

3.1   RAM Model

RAM computation consists of a machine M which keeps some local state state and has read/write access to memory $D \in (\{0,1\}^\lambda)^*$ (equivalent to the tape of a Turing machine). Here, λ is the security parameter and length of a word, and we let $n \leq 2^\lambda$ be the number of words in memory required to run M (see below). When we write $M(x)$ to denote running M on input x, this means that M expects its initial memory D to consist of x followed by zeros. The computation of $M(x)$ is defined in steps, where at each step the machine either reads or writes to a location in memory and updates its local state. We assume that when M writes to a memory location ℓ, it receives the word previously at ℓ. Without loss of generality, we assume that the state can hold $O(\log n)$ bits, or a constant number of words, and that the local state at each time step includes the word read in the previous step. We also assume that n words in memory can be allocated and initialized to zeros for free.

The computation halts when the local state consists of a special halting value with the output y of $M(x)$ written at the start of the memory. We define the running time of a RAM machine M as the number of accesses it makes to its working memory, which corresponds to the number of steps.

We define the *configuration* cf at any step of the computation to include the local state and full memory at that step. This representation allows us to refer to RAM machines that transition from a configuration cf to configuration cf' in some number of steps, as the configuration has all information required to perform a step.

In order to measure the complexity of RAM computation, we note that on a fixed CPU architecture, RAM computation can be modeled where the program M and input x are both given in memory and executed using a fixed machine U. We therefore fix any universal RAM machine U and define the complexity of running $M(x)$ to be the number of steps required to run $U(M, x)$. As all of our RAM computation will be in this model, for simplicity we say that $M(x)$ requires access to n words of memory if $U(M, x)$ uses a total of n words in memory to write M, x, and all the memory used by the computation. Henceforth, we say that $M(x)$ halts in time t if running U on memory $M||x||0^{n-|M,x|}$ for t steps results in a halting state.

3.2 Universal Languages

In this section we define a universal language for deterministic RAM computation with long output, following the universal relation introduced by [7].

Definition 1. *The universal language $\mathcal{L}^{\mathcal{U}}$ is the set of instances (M, x, y, L, t) where M is a deterministic RAM machine such that $M(x)$ outputs y within t steps, and additionally $|y| \leq L$.*

Additionally, we will be considering intermediate portions of RAM computation, where the universal RAM machine U (see Sect. 3.1) transitions from configuration cf to cf' in t steps.

Definition 2. *The universal RAM delegation language $\mathcal{L}^{\mathsf{del}}$ is the set of instances $(\mathsf{cf}, \mathsf{cf}', t)$ such that the universal RAM machine U transitions from configuration cf to configuration cf' in t steps.*

3.3 RAM Delegation

In this section, we define RAM delegation, which will be the main building block for our SPARG construction. Following [20,22,37,38], we define RAM delegation to capture the following scenario: A verifier wishes to delegate a RAM computation M with some initial configuration cf, such that running M for t steps starting with cf results in configuration cf'. As M may potentially use a large amount of memory, these configurations could be very long, and thus the approach in recent works has been to consider a verifier that only receives digests rt, rt' of the configurations cf, cf'.

Recently, [22,38] showed delegation schemes for RAM where soundness holds when the verifier only receives these digests, and moreover suffice to delegate general computation with Turing machines. We adopt this notion for this work.

As discussed in Sect. 3.1, we will assume that the machine M is already part of the memory in cf and thus give a definition for a fixed universal RAM computation with the universal machine U.

Definition 3 (RAM Delegation). *A publicly verifiable, succinct RAM delegation scheme for $\mathcal{L}^{\mathsf{del}}$ is a tuple of probabilistic algorithms* (Del.S, Del.D, Del.P, Del.V) *with the following syntax:*

- (crs, dk) $\leftarrow$ Del.S(1^λ): *A PPT algorithm that on input a security parameter λ outputs a common reference string* crs *and a digest key* dk. *We assume without loss of generality that* crs *contains* dk.
- rt $=$ Del.D(dk, cf): *A deterministic algorithm that on input a digest key* dk *and a RAM configuration* cf *outputs a digest* rt.
- $\pi \leftarrow$ Del.P(crs, (cf, cf′, t)): *A probabilistic algorithm that on input a common reference string* crs, *and a statement* (cf, cf′, t), *outputs a proof* π.
- $b \leftarrow$ Del.V(crs, (rt, rt′, t), π): *A PPT algorithm that on input a a common reference string* crs, *common reference string* crs, *statement* (rt, rt′, t), *and a proof* π, *outputs a bit b indicating whether to accept or reject.*

We require the following properties:

- **Completeness:** *For every $\lambda \in \mathbb{N}$ and* (cf, cf′, t) $\in \mathcal{L}^{\mathsf{del}}$ *with $t, n \leq 2^\lambda$ where n is the memory size of the configurations, it holds*

$$\Pr\left[\begin{array}{l}(\mathsf{crs}, \mathsf{dk}) \leftarrow \mathsf{Del.S}(1^\lambda) \\ \mathsf{rt} = \mathsf{Del.D}(\mathsf{dk}, \mathsf{cf}) \\ \mathsf{rt}' = \mathsf{Del.D}(\mathsf{dk}, \mathsf{cf}') \\ \pi \leftarrow \mathsf{Del.P}(\mathsf{crs}, (\mathsf{cf}, \mathsf{cf}', t))\end{array} : \mathcal{V}(\mathsf{crs}, (\mathsf{rt}, \mathsf{rt}', t), \pi) = 1\right] = 1.$$

- **Soundness:** *For any non-uniform polynomial-time algorithm $\mathcal{A} = \{\mathcal{A}_\lambda\}_{\lambda \in \mathbb{N}}$, polynomial-time computable function T, and polynomial $\overline{T}$ such that $T(\lambda) \leq \overline{T}(\lambda)$ for all $\lambda \in \mathbb{N}$, there exists a negligible function negl such that for every $\lambda \in \mathbb{N}$, it holds that*

$$\Pr\left[\begin{array}{l}(\mathsf{crs}, \mathsf{dk}) \leftarrow \mathsf{Del.S}(1^\lambda) \\ (\mathsf{cf}, \mathsf{cf}', \mathsf{rt}, \mathsf{rt}', \pi) \leftarrow \mathcal{A}_\lambda(\mathsf{crs}, \mathsf{dk})\end{array} : \begin{array}{l}\mathcal{V}(\mathsf{crs}, (\mathsf{rt}, \mathsf{rt}', t), \pi) = 1 \\ \wedge\ (\mathsf{cf}, \mathsf{cf}', t) \in \mathcal{L}^{\mathsf{del}} \\ \wedge\ \mathsf{rt} = \mathsf{Del.D}(\mathsf{dk}, \mathsf{cf}) \\ \wedge\ \mathsf{rt}' \neq \mathsf{Del.D}(\mathsf{dk}, \mathsf{cf}')\end{array}\right] \leq \mathsf{negl}(\lambda),$$

where $t = T(\lambda)$.

- **Collision resistance:** *For any non-uniform polynomial-time algorithm $\mathcal{A} = \{\mathcal{A}_\lambda\}_{\lambda \in \mathbb{N}}$, there exists a negligible function negl such that for every $\lambda \in \mathbb{N}$, it holds that*

$$\Pr\left[\begin{array}{l}(\mathsf{crs}, \mathsf{dk}) \leftarrow \mathsf{Del.S}(1^\lambda) \\ (\mathsf{cf}, \mathsf{cf}') \leftarrow \mathcal{A}_\lambda(\mathsf{crs}, \mathsf{dk})\end{array} : \begin{array}{l}\mathsf{cf} \neq \mathsf{cf}' \\ \wedge\ \mathsf{Del.D}(\mathsf{dk}, \mathsf{cf}) = \mathsf{Del.D}(\mathsf{dk}, \mathsf{cf}')\end{array}\right] \leq \mathsf{negl}(\lambda).$$

- **Succinctness:** *There exist polynomials q_1, q_2, q_3 such that for any $\lambda \in \mathbb{N}$, (crs, dk) in the support of* Del.S(1^λ), (cf, cf′, t) $\in \mathcal{L}^{\mathsf{del}}$, *and proof π in the support of $\mathcal{P}(\mathsf{crs}, (\mathsf{cf}, \mathsf{cf}', t))$, it holds that*

- $|\mathsf{Del.V}(\mathsf{crs}, (\mathsf{rt}, \mathsf{rt}', t), \pi)| \leq q_1(\lambda, \log t)$ and
- $|\pi| \leq q_2(\lambda, \log t)$.
- $\mathsf{Del.D}(\mathsf{dk}, \mathsf{cf})$ is computable in time $|\mathsf{cf}| \cdot q_3(\lambda)$ and has output length λ.

3.4 SPARGs

In this section, we define SPARGs for P based on the notion of SPARKs introduced in [29]. We note that while they do not restrict to computations with $t \leq 2^\lambda$ steps, we require this as it is standard in related notions (e.g., RAM delegation) and required for our construction.

Definition 4 (Non-interactive SPARGs for P). *A Non-interactive Succinct Parallelizable Argument for a language* $\mathcal{L} \subseteq \mathcal{L}^{\mathcal{U}}$ *is a tuple of probabilistic algorithms* $(\mathcal{G}, \mathcal{P}, \mathcal{V})$ *with the following syntax:*

- $\mathsf{crs} \leftarrow \mathcal{G}(1^\lambda)$: *A PPT algorithm that on input a security parameter* λ *outputs a common reference string* crs.
- $(y, \pi) \leftarrow \mathcal{P}(\mathsf{crs}, (M, x, L, t))$: *A probabilistic algorithm that on input a common reference string* crs, *and a statement* (M, x, L, t), *outputs a value* y *and a proof* π.
- $b \leftarrow \mathcal{V}(\mathsf{crs}, (M, x, y, L, t), \pi)$: *A PPT algorithm that on input a common reference string* crs, *a statement* (M, x, y, L, t), *and a proof* π, *outputs a bit* b *indicating whether to accept or reject.*

We require the following properties:

- **Completeness:** *For every* $\lambda \in \mathbb{N}$ *and* $(M, x, y, L, t) \in \mathcal{L}$ *where* M *has access to* $n \leq 2^\lambda$ *words in memory and* $t \leq 2^\lambda$,

$$\Pr \begin{bmatrix} \mathsf{crs} \leftarrow \mathcal{G}(1^\lambda) \\ (y, \pi) \leftarrow \mathcal{P}(\mathsf{crs}, (M, x, L, t)) & : b = 1 \\ b \leftarrow \mathcal{V}(\mathsf{crs}, (M, x, y, L, t), \pi) \end{bmatrix} = 1.$$

- **Soundness for P:** *For all non-uniform polynomial-time provers* $\mathcal{P}^* = \{\mathcal{P}^*_\lambda\}_{\lambda \in \mathbb{N}}$ *and every polynomial* T, *there is a negligible function* negl *such that for every* $\lambda \in \mathbb{N}$, *it holds that*

$$\Pr \begin{bmatrix} \mathsf{crs} \leftarrow \mathcal{G}(1^\lambda) & \mathcal{V}(\mathsf{crs}, (M, x, y, L, t), \pi) = 1 \\ ((M, x, y, L), \pi) \leftarrow \mathcal{P}^*_\lambda(\mathsf{crs}) & : \wedge (M, x, y, L, t) \notin \mathcal{L} \end{bmatrix} \leq \mathsf{negl}(\lambda),$$

where $t = T(\lambda)$.
- **Succinctness:** *There exist polynomials* q_1, q_2 *such that for any* $\lambda \in \mathbb{N}$, crs *in the support of* $\mathcal{G}(1^\lambda)$, $(M, x, L, t) \in \mathcal{L}$ *where* M *uses* $n \leq 2^\lambda$ *words in memory,* $t \leq 2^\lambda$, *and* (y, π) *in the support of* $\mathcal{P}(\mathsf{crs}, (M, x, L, t))$, *it holds that*
  - $\mathsf{work}_\mathcal{V}(\mathsf{crs}, (M, x, y, L, t), \pi) \leq q_1(\lambda, |(M, x)|, L, \log t)$,
  - $|y| \leq L$, *and*
  - $|\pi| \leq q_2(\lambda, L, \log t)$.

- **Optimal prover depth:** *There exists polynomials q_1 and q_2 such that for all $\lambda \in \mathbb{N}$ and $(M, x, t, L, y) \in \mathcal{L}$ where M has access to $n \leq 2^\lambda$ words in memory and $t \leq 2^\lambda$, it holds that*

$$\mathsf{depth}_{\mathcal{P}}(\mathsf{crs}, (M, x, L, t)) = t + q_1(\lambda, |(M, x)|, L, \log t)$$

and the total number of processors used by $\mathcal{P}$ is in $q_2(\lambda, \log t)$.

If the above holds for $\mathcal{L} = \mathcal{L}^{\mathcal{U}}$, we say that $(\mathcal{G}, \mathcal{P}, \mathcal{V})$ is a non-interactive SPARG for polynomial-time RAM computation.

4   Updatable RAM Delegation

In this section, we discuss the main building block for our construction—updatable RAM delegation with quasilinear overhead and local opening.

4.1   The CJJ Delegation Scheme

Our starting point will be the recent delegation scheme due to Choudhuri, Jain, and Jin [22], henceforth referred to as the CJJ construction. We start by giving an overview. We note that they present their construction for a specific RAM machine M, but we simply treat this as the universal RAM machine U.

The CJJ construction relies on the following building blocks:

- A hash tree that supports local reads and writes. This can be instantiated from collision-resistant hash functions.
- A no-signalling somewhere-extractable commitment scheme, with a locality parameter ℓ corresponding to the size of extracted sets, which in particular determines the efficiency of the commitment.
- A non-interactive batch argument (BARG) for NP. This is an argument where k instances of a language can certified with a proof that only depends sublinearly on k.

At a high level, their construction follows an approach in recent works (see, e.g., [29,37,38]) which uses a locally updatable hash tree (based on Merkle trees) to succinctly prove that each step of RAM computation was done correctly. Specifically, to prove that a RAM machine transitions from configuration cf to configuration cf' in t steps, they run the computation while simultaneously maintaining a hash tree of the memory at each step. Each step can then be verified succinctly (in particular in time independent of $|\mathsf{cf}|$) by verifying succinct local openings to the hash tree. To turn this approach into a full-fledged delegation scheme, previous works have employed a combination of succinct proof systems with various extractability properties to show soundness.

In the CJJ construction, they follow this framework. After running the computation along with computing a short opening to the hash tree at each step, they give a no-signalling commitment c to the sequence of t updates to the hash tree. They then prove, using a BARG, that each step of the computation was done correctly and consistently. Specifically, the BARG is for the relation computed by the circuit C_{step} that on input an index i and openings to c corresponding to the ith step of computation, checks that (1) these openings are consistent with c, (2) correspond to a valid step of computation, and (3) are valid openings to the hash tree. To show that this construction is sound, they rely on a combination of BARG soundness, the no-signalling extraction of the commitment scheme, and collision resistance. They show that this results in a scheme for (deterministic) RAM delegation which can be based solely on LWE.

In the full version, we discuss the differences between the notion of RAM delegation satisfied by this construction, and Definition 3, and show that the CJJ scheme satisfies our notion of RAM delegation. As their scheme is based on LWE, the following holds.

Theorem 4.1 [22]. *Assuming the hardness of LWE, there exists a publicly verifiable, succinct RAM delegation scheme for $\mathcal{L}^{del}$.*

4.2 Updatable Delegation with Quasilinear Overhead

For our SPARG construction, we will be concerned with delegation schemes with tight prover efficiency. In this section, we analyze the prover efficiency of the CJJ construction, and then show that it can be made quasilinear in t when the prover is additionally given a *witness* for the RAM computation. Along the way, we introduce the notion of Updatable Delegation, which enables the desired prover efficiency and may be of independent interest.

We start by looking at the efficiency of each building block in the CJJ scheme individually.

– Hash tree: The hash tree used in [22] is effectively a Merkle tree based on a collision resistant hash function. Computing the hash tree of a given configuration cf can be done in time $|cf| \cdot \text{poly}(\lambda)$, but when given the hash tree already in memory, updating a word in the tree can be done in time logarithmic in the size of the memory of the RAM program, and so can be done in time $\text{poly}(\lambda)$.
– BARG: Recall that the BARG enables proving k instances of an NP relation computable by a circuit C. At a high level, the BARG prover in the construction due to [22] does the following:
  1. For each $i \in [k]$, it first computes a PCP π_i for the i'th statement. This takes time $k \cdot \text{poly}(\lambda, |C|)$. Let $L \in \text{poly}(\lambda, |C|)$ denote the length of a single PCP.
  2. It then commits columnwise to the PCPs. Creating L commitments to k bits each takes time $L \cdot k \cdot \text{poly}(\lambda)$ (similar to below, the commitment is a variation on a Merkle tree, where committing can be done in time linear in the committed message).
  3. It then applies a correlation-intractable hash to the circuit C and commitment. As shown in [22], the hash can be evaluated in time $\text{poly}(\lambda, \log k, |C|)$.

4. Next, it samples PCP queries for a single PCP using randomness derived from the correlation-intractable hash. They use a PCP requiring $\mathrm{poly}(\lambda, \log |C|)$ queries that can be sampled in time $\mathrm{poly}(\lambda, |C|)$.

5. For each PCP, it then opens the query locations in the commitments. For each PCP, this corresponds to opening a bit in $\mathrm{poly}(\lambda, \log |C|)$ commitments. As each value can be opened in time $\mathrm{poly}(\lambda, \log k)$ due to the Merkle-tree structure of the commitment, putting everything together this takes time $k \cdot \mathrm{poly}(\lambda, \log k, \log |C|)$.

6. Finally, it recurses by running a BARG for $k/2$ instances, where they show that the circuit for the smaller BARG has size $\mathrm{poly}(\lambda, \log k, \log |C|)$. Overall, there are $\log k$ recursions.

Putting everything together, the BARG prover runs in time $k \cdot \mathrm{poly}(\lambda, |C|, \log k)$.

– No-signalling somewhere-extractable commitment: The no-signalling commitment construction is parameterized by an integer ℓ, which determines the number of bits extractable from the commitment scheme. For a fixed parameter ℓ, the construction consists of ℓ independent Merkle trees. Each Merkle tree consists of an FHE encryption of the committed message at the leaves, and uses FHE evaluation to compute the value of each node based on the values of its child nodes. Thus, computing the commitment to a message of length N can be done in time $\ell \cdot N \cdot \mathrm{poly}(\lambda)$, because it requires computing ℓ Merkle trees, which each require encrypting N bits and performing N FHE evaluations. Moreover, local openings to a single bit in this commitment can be computed and verified in time $\ell \cdot \mathrm{poly}(\lambda, \log N)$, as openings consist of an authentication path in each of the ℓ Merkle trees.

Putting everything together, to delegate a t-time computation using the CJJ scheme, the prover (a) creates a hash tree of the starting configuration, (b) runs the computation while simultaneously updating the hash tree, (c) commits to the sequence of updates to the hash tree, where each update additionally contains some efficiently computable auxiliary information, (d) creates local openings in the commitment as a witness to each step of computation, and (e) proves that the computation is correct using a BARG for the circuit C_{step}. From the above analysis, (a) takes the time to run $\mathsf{Del.D}(\mathsf{dk}, \mathsf{cf})$ when cf is the starting configuration, (b) takes time $t \cdot \mathrm{poly}(\lambda)$, (c) takes time $\ell \cdot N \cdot \mathrm{poly}(\lambda)$ where ℓ is the length of a single update and N is the length of the committed message, (d) takes time $(t \cdot \ell) \cdot \ell \cdot \mathrm{poly}(\lambda, \log N)$ to open ℓ bits for each of the t steps, and (e) takes time $t \cdot \mathrm{poly}(\lambda, |C_{\mathsf{step}}|, \log t)$. It remains to discuss the specific values $|C_{\mathsf{step}}|$, ℓ, and N used in the protocol. The parameter ℓ corresponds to the length of the values needed verify a single step of computation, by computing that step and verifying the openings in the hash tree, and so $\ell \in \mathrm{poly}(\lambda)$ (for a fixed polynomial that depends on the size of the universal RAM machine U). The committed message consists of these values for each of the t steps, and thus $N = t \cdot \ell$. Finally, the circuit C_{step} consists of computing a single step of the RAM program and verifying the openings to the hash tree and commitment, which together takes time $\ell \cdot \text{poly}(\lambda, \log N) \in \text{poly}(\lambda, \log t)$. All together, this shows that the prover runs in time

$\text{Time}\left(\text{Del.P}(1^\lambda, (\text{cf}, \text{cf}', t))\right)$

$\leq \text{Time}\left(\text{Del.D}(\text{dk}, \text{cf})\right) + t \cdot \text{poly}(\lambda) + \ell \cdot N \cdot \text{poly}(\lambda) + t \cdot \ell^2 \cdot \text{poly}(\lambda, \log N)$
$\quad + t \cdot \text{poly}(\lambda, |C_{\text{step}}|, \log t)$

$\leq |\text{cf}| \cdot \text{poly}(\lambda) + t \cdot \text{poly}(\lambda) + t \cdot \text{poly}(\lambda) + t \cdot \text{poly}(\lambda, \log t) + t \cdot \text{poly}(\lambda, \log t)$

$\in |\text{cf}| \cdot \text{poly}(\lambda) + t \cdot \text{poly}(\lambda, \log t).$

Achieving Quasilinear Efficiency. For our SPARG construction, it will be crucial that the running time of the delegation prover Del.P does not depend on n, the memory size of the RAM program. Therefore, the CJJ prover efficiency does not suffice for us, since the running time of the prover on $(\text{cf}, \text{cf}', t)$ depends linearly on $|\text{cf}|$.

We observe that this dependence on $|\text{cf}|$ is due to the fact that the prover is given an arbitrary starting configuration cf, and must compute a Merkle tree on the memory given in cf. For our SPARG construction, we are not concerned with RAM computation from an arbitrary starting point cf. Instead, we will start from an initial (short) configuration cf_0, for which we can afford to run in time proportional to $|\text{cf}_0|$ to generating the initial hash tree.

However, this does not entirely solve the problem, because rather than proving that cf_0 results in the final configuration cf' after t steps of computation, we will instead determine "midpoints"—namely, configurations $\text{cf}_1, \ldots, \text{cf}_m$, where $\text{cf}_m = \text{cf}'$. We will then rely on the delegation scheme to prove statements of the form $(\text{cf}_0, \text{cf}_1, k_1), (\text{cf}_1, \text{cf}_2, k_2), \ldots, (\text{cf}_{m-1}, \text{cf}_m, k_m)$, that is, that starting at cf_{i-1} and running for some number of steps k_i results in configuration cf_i. The main idea below is that when we prove each statement $(\text{cf}_{i-1}, \text{cf}_i, k_i)$, we will already have information about cf_{i-1} from proving the previous statement. In particular, we will show that we can already have the Merkle tree for cf_{i-1} in memory when we start the ith statement, rather than creating it from scratch.

This exact setting was addressed in [29], where they showed that the hash tree can be instantiated with collision-resistant hash functions to achieve the following guarantees:

1. Computing the hash tree for the initial configuration can be done in time $|\text{cf}_0| \cdot \text{poly}(\lambda)$.
2. Given a hash tree in memory corresponding to *any* configuration cf, it holds that the computation can be run for any number of steps k while updating the hash tree with only $\text{poly}(\lambda)$ additive overhead. This implies that if cf results in cf' after k steps of computation, and we have already computed a hash tree for cf, then we can compute the hash tree for cf' in time $k + \text{poly}(\lambda)$.

The requirements for the hash tree of [22] (which is based on [37]) are satisfied by that of [29] (see [29] for a more in-depth discussion and comparison between various definitions). Therefore, we observe that the CJJ construction satisfies the following notion.

Definition 5. *Consider a RAM delegation scheme* (Del.S, Del.D, Del.P, Del.V) *with the following syntax modifications and additional algorithm* Del.Update*:*

- (rt, tree) = Del.D(dk, cf)*: The digest algorithm additionally outputs a value* tree*.*
- (rt′, tree′, w) = Del.Update(dk, t, tree)*: The update algorithm takes as input a digest key* dk, *integer* t, *and a value* tree, *and outputs a digest* rt′, *a value* tree′ *and a witness* w*.*
- π ← Del.P(crs, (cf, cf′, t), w)*: The prover additionally takes as input a witness* w*. We require that completeness is preserved when* Del.P *receives the witness* w *computed by* Del.Update*.*

We note that tree *and* w *can be communicated as pointers to memory. In particular, this implies that* Del.D(dk, cf) *still runs in time* |cf| · poly(λ).

We say that the scheme is β*-updatable if for any* λ ∈ ℕ, *statement* (cf, cf′, t) ∈ 𝓛^{del}, *keys* (crs, dk) *in the support of* Del.S(1^λ), (rt, tree) = Del.D(dk, cf), *and* (rt′, tree′, w) = Del.Update(dk, t, tree),

$$(rt', tree') = Del.D(dk, cf')$$

and Del.Update *runs in* t + β(λ) *steps with* β(λ) *processors. Furthermore, for any two consecutive updates of length* t_1 *and* t_2 *starting at initial state* (rt$_0$, tree$_0$), *let* (rt$_1$, tree$_1$, w_1) = Del.Update(dk, t_1, tree$_0$) *and* (rt$_2$, tree$_2$, w_2) = Del.Update(dk, t_2, tree$_1$). *Then, the output* (rt$_2$, tree$_2$, w_2) *can be computed in time* $t_1 + t_2 + β(λ)$. *When* β(λ) ∈ poly(λ), *we say the scheme is updatable.*

We emphasize that Del.P no longer has access to the hash tree in memory, as this would create memory conflicts between Del.P and Del.Update. Instead, we can view Del.Update as the algorithm that runs the computation on the hash tree, and collects all of the information needed to prove correctness—namely, the hash tree updates, which make up the witness w. The prover Del.P can then use this witness to form the proof. In the following definition, we quantify the prover efficiency in an updatable delegation scheme.

Definition 6. *An updatable RAM delegation scheme satisfies* α*-prover efficiency if for all* λ ∈ ℕ, (crs, dk) *in the support of* Del.S(1^λ), *statement* (cf, cf′, t) ∈ 𝓛^{del} *using* n ≤ 2^λ *memory with* t ≤ 2^λ, (rt, tree) = Del.D(dk, cf), *and* (rt′, tree′, w) = Del.Update(dk, t, tree), *it holds that*

$$\text{Time}\left(Del.P(crs, (cf, cf', t), w)\right) = α(λ, t).$$

Based on the above discussion, the CJJ scheme can be made to satisfy updatability and quasi-linear prover efficiency. Specifically, we will instantiate the hash tree in the CJJ construction with that of [29], and modify the delegation scheme as follows:

- Del.D(1^λ, cf) will output rt as before, as the root of the hash tree, and set tree to be the full hash tree.

- Del.Update(dk, t, tree) will start with the hash tree in tree, run the computation for t steps while updating the hash tree, and then output (rt′, tree′, w) where rt′ is the resulting root, tree′ is the updated tree, and w is the list of all authentication paths for the t updates.
- Del.P(crs, (cf, cf′, t), w) will use the updates in w to run the prover algorithm, rather than computing them from scratch.

By combining the above discussion with Theorem 4.1, we get the following.

Theorem 4.2. *Assuming the hardness of LWE, there exists a publicly verifiable, succinct, and updatable RAM delegation scheme* (Del.S, Del.D, Del.P, Del.V, Del.Update) *for* $\mathcal{L}^{\mathsf{del}}$ *with α-prover efficiency for* $\alpha(\lambda, t) \leq t \cdot \mathrm{poly}(\lambda, \log t)$.

The proof of Theorem 4.2 is deferred to the full version.

4.3 Local Opening

Given a RAM delegation scheme in which the verifier receives *digests* of the full configuration, we will also require a scheme with a very natural *local opening* property: a set of locations can be locally opened with respect to a digest, providing a short proof of the opening. As most RAM delegation schemes employ an underlying Merkle tree, these are amenable to efficient local openings whenever the Merkle tree is already in memory. In this full version, we formally define the local opening property by giving additional algorithms (Del.Open, Del.VerOpen) to the updatable delegation scheme to capture this notion. We also show that our updatable RAM delegation scheme satisfies local opening (by relying on the local opening property of the [29] hash tree), and therefore get the following corollary to Theorem 4.2.

Corollary 1. *Assuming the hardness of LWE, there exists a publicly verifiable, succinct, and updatable RAM delegation scheme for* $\mathcal{L}^{\mathsf{del}}$ *with local opening and α-updatable prover efficiency for* $\alpha(\lambda, t) \leq t \cdot \mathrm{poly}(\lambda, \log t)$.

5 SPARGs for P

In this section, we give our construction of SPARGs for (sequential) RAM computations. Our construction relies on a β-updatable RAM delegation scheme Del = (Del.S, Del.D, Del.P, Del.V, Del.Update, Del.Open, Del.VerOpen) for $\mathcal{L}^{\mathsf{del}}$ with local opening and α-prover efficiency (see Sect. 3.3). We use the following parameters when proving a statement (M, x, L, t).

- $n \leq 2^\lambda$ is the memory used by M.
- α is the function denoting the prover efficiency of Del. We let $\alpha^\star \triangleq \alpha(\lambda, t)/t$ be the multiplicative overhead, with respect to t, of running Del.P.
- β is the function denoting the efficiency of Del.Update.
- $\gamma \triangleq \alpha^\star + 1$ is the fraction of remaining steps done in each chunk of the computation.

SPARG $(\mathcal{G}, \mathcal{P}, \mathcal{V})$ for $\mathcal{L}^{\mathcal{U}}$ given an updatable delegation scheme with local opening (Del.S, Del.D, Del.P, Del.V, Del.Update, Del.Open, Del.VerOpen):

- $\mathcal{G}(1^\lambda)$:
    1. $(\mathsf{crs}, \mathsf{dk}) \leftarrow \mathsf{Del.S}(1^\lambda)$.
    2. Output $\mathsf{pp} = (\mathsf{crs}, \mathsf{dk})$.
- $\mathcal{P}(1^\lambda, \mathsf{pp}, (M, x, L, t))$:
    1. Let cf_0 be the initial configuration for $M(x)$, which includes the (empty) local state and M, x. Let $(\mathsf{rt}_0, \mathsf{tree}_0) = \mathsf{Del.D}(\mathsf{dk}, \mathsf{cf}_0)$.

    2. Compute γ as in the parameters paragraph. Initialize $T := t$ to be the number of steps remaining in the computation.

    3. For $i = 1, 2, \ldots$, repeat the following until $T = 0$:
        (a) Calculate the number of steps k_i to compute in this iteration. If $T > \gamma \log T$, set $k_i = \lfloor T/\gamma \rfloor$, and otherwise set $k_i = T$.

        (b) Compute k_i steps of M starting with configuration cf_{i-1}. Let cf_i be the resulting configuration.

        (c) In parallel to Step 3b, compute $(\mathsf{rt}_i, \mathsf{tree}_i, w_i) \leftarrow \mathsf{Del.Update}(\mathsf{dk}, k_i, \mathsf{tree}_{i-1})$.

        (d) Without waiting for Step 3c to halt (but after Step 3b), spawn a process that continues to the next iteration with $T = T - k_i$.

        (e) After Steps 3b and 3c complete, spawn a parallel thread to compute $\tau_i \leftarrow \mathsf{Del.P}(\mathsf{crs}, (M, \mathsf{cf}_{i-1}, \mathsf{cf}_i, k_i), w_i)$.

    4. Let $(y, \mathsf{st}, \pi_y) = \mathsf{Del.Open}(\mathsf{dk}, [L], \mathsf{tree}_m)$, where m is the number of iterations of the loop above.

    5. Let $\vec{\mathsf{rt}} = (\mathsf{rt}_1, \ldots, \mathsf{rt}_m)$, $\vec{\tau} = (\tau_1, \ldots, \tau_m)$, and $\vec{k} = (k_1, \ldots, k_m)$. Output (y, π) where $\pi = (\vec{\mathsf{rt}}, \vec{\tau}, \vec{k}, \mathsf{st}, \pi_y)$.
- $\mathcal{V}(1^\lambda, \mathsf{pp}, (M, x, y, L, t), \pi)$:
    1. Parse $\pi = (\vec{\mathsf{rt}}, \vec{\tau}, \vec{k}, \mathsf{st}, \pi_y)$.

    2. Let cf_0 be the initial configuration of $M(x)$ and compute rt_0 as $\mathsf{Del.D}(\mathsf{dk}, \mathsf{cf}_0)$.

    3. Output 1 if and only if the following hold, and 0 otherwise:
        (a) $\mathsf{Del.V}(\mathsf{crs}, (\mathsf{rt}_{i-1}, \mathsf{rt}_i, k_i), \tau_i)$ accepts for all $i \in [m]$.

        (b) k_i is as defined above for each $i \in [m]$, and $t \le 2^\lambda$.

        (c) $\mathsf{Del.VerOpen}(\mathsf{dk}, \mathsf{rt}_m, [L], y, \mathsf{st}, \pi_y) = 1$.

        (d) st is a halting state, and $|y| \le L$.

Fig. 2. SPARG for $\mathcal{L}^{\mathcal{U}}$.

Theorem 5.1. *Let* Del *be a publicly verifiable, succinct, and updatable delegation scheme for* $\mathcal{L}^{\mathsf{del}}$ *with local opening and* α-*prover efficiency. Then,* $(\mathcal{G}, \mathcal{P}, \mathcal{V})$, *given in Fig. 2, is a SPARG for* $\mathcal{L}^{\mathcal{U}}$. *Specifically, for all* $\lambda \in \mathbb{N}$ *and* $(M, x, y, L, t) \in \mathcal{L}^{\mathcal{U}}$ *where* M *has access to* $n \le 2^\lambda$ *words in memory and* $t \le 2^\lambda$, *the following hold. Let* α^* *be the multiplicative overhead of* Del.P *with respect to the number of steps of computation. Then:*

- *The depth of the prover is bounded by* $t + L + (\alpha^\star)^2 \cdot \mathrm{poly}(\lambda, |M, x|, \log t)$ *when using* $\mathrm{poly}(\lambda) + \alpha^\star \log t$ *processors.*
- *The proof size is bounded by* $\alpha^\star \cdot \mathrm{poly}(\lambda, \log t)$.
- *The work of the verifier is bounded by* $\alpha^\star \cdot L \cdot \mathrm{poly}(\lambda, |M, x|, \log t)$.

By Corollary 1, it holds that there exists an updatable RAM delegation scheme with local opening based on LWE where $\alpha^\star \in \mathrm{poly}(\lambda, \log t)$. Therefore, by combining Theorem 5.1 with Corollary 1, we get the following corollary.

Corollary 2. *Assuming the hardness of LWE, there exists a SPARG for* $\mathcal{L}^{\mathcal{U}}$.

The proof of Theorem 5.1 is deferred to the full version.

6   Application to Verifiable Delay Functions

In this section, we show that SPARGs for P and any sequential function imply a VDF. We note that a sequential function is a minimal assumption as VDFs directly imply sequential functions. We use the following building blocks and parameters.

- A sequential function $\mathsf{SF} = (\mathsf{SF.Gen}, \mathsf{SF.Sample}, \mathsf{SF.Eval})$. Let $p_{\mathsf{SF}}, q_{\mathsf{SF}}$ be the polynomials from the honest evaluation property of SF such that $\mathsf{SF.Eval}(1^\lambda, \cdot, \cdot, t)$ runs in time $t + p_{\mathsf{SF}}(\lambda, \log t)$ with $q_{\mathsf{SF}}(\lambda, \log t)$ processors. Let ℓ_{SF} be the polynomial such that the output length is bounded by $\ell_{\mathsf{SF}}(\lambda, \log t)$.
- A SPARG $(\mathcal{G}, \mathcal{P}, \mathcal{V})$ for any $\mathcal{L} \in \mathcal{L}^{\mathcal{U}}_{\mathsf{par}}$ containing $\mathsf{SF.Eval}$.

Construction. Our VDF construction $\mathsf{VDF} = (\mathsf{VDF.Gen}, \mathsf{VDF.Sample}, \mathsf{VDF.Eval}, \mathsf{VDF.Verify})$ is as follows.

- $\mathsf{pp} \leftarrow \mathsf{VDF.Gen}(1^\lambda)$:
  1. Sample $\mathsf{crs} \leftarrow \mathcal{G}(1^\lambda)$ and $k \leftarrow \mathsf{SF.Gen}(1^\lambda)$.
  2. Output $\mathsf{pp} = (\mathsf{crs}, k)$.
- $x \leftarrow \mathsf{VDF.Sample}(1^\lambda, \mathsf{pp})$:
  1. Sample and output $x \leftarrow \mathsf{SF.Sample}(1^\lambda, k)$.
- $(y, \pi) \leftarrow \mathsf{VDF.Eval}(1^\lambda, \mathsf{pp}, x, t)$:
  1. Recall that $p_{\mathsf{SF}}, q_{\mathsf{SF}}, \ell_{\mathsf{SF}}$ are the polynomials denoting the efficiency of $\mathsf{VDF.Eval}$. Let statement $= (\mathsf{SF.Eval}, (1^\lambda, k, x, t), \ell_{\mathsf{SF}}(\lambda, \log t), t + p_{\mathsf{SF}}(\lambda, \log t), q_{\mathsf{SF}}(\lambda, \log t))$.
  2. Compute and output $(y, \pi) \leftarrow \mathcal{P}(1^\lambda, \mathsf{crs}, \mathsf{statement})$.
- $b \leftarrow \mathsf{VDF.Verify}(1^\lambda, \mathsf{pp}, x, t, (y, \pi))$:
  1. Let statement$' = (\mathsf{SF.Eval}, (1^\lambda, k, x, t), y, \ell_{\mathsf{SF}}(\lambda, \log t), t + p_{\mathsf{SF}}(\lambda, \log t), q_{\mathsf{SF}}(\lambda, \log t))$ (note that statement$'$ differs from statement used by $\mathsf{VDF.Eval}$ as it contains the output y).
  2. Output $b \leftarrow \mathcal{V}(1^\lambda, \mathsf{crs}, \mathsf{statement}', \pi)$.

Theorem 6.1. *Assuming the existence of a SPARG for* $\mathcal{L}^{\mathcal{U}}_{\mathsf{par}}$ *and a sequential function, there exists a VDF.*

Here, $\mathcal{L}^{\mathcal{U}}_{\mathsf{par}}$ is the notion of $\mathcal{L}^{\mathcal{U}}$ extended to parallel computations (this is defined formally in the full version). In the full version, we show that a SPARG for $\mathcal{L}^{\mathcal{U}}_{\mathsf{par}}$ can be based on LWE, which gives the following.

Corollary 3. *Assuming the hardness of LWE and a sequential function, there exists a VDF.*

The proof of Theorem 6.1 is deferred to the full version.

Acknowledgements. This work was supported in part by NSF CNS-2149305, CNS-2128519, NSF Award SATC-1704788, NSF Award RI-1703846, AFOSR Award FA9550-18-1-0267, DARPA Award HR00110C0086, and a JP Morgan Faculty Award. Rafael Pass's work was done partially while visiting Tel-Aviv University. Cody Freitag's work was done partially during an internship at NTT Research, and he is also supported in part by the National Science Foundation Graduate Research Fellowship under Grant No. DGE-2139899. Naomi Sirkin was also supported in part by a JP Morgan AI Research PhD Fellowship. The views and conclusions contained herein are those of the authors and should not be interpreted as necessarily representing the official policies, either expressed or implied, of NSF, DARPA or the U.S. Government. The U.S. Government is authorized to reproduce and distribute reprints for governmental purposes notwithstanding any copyright annotation therein.

References

1. Alwen, J., Blocki, J., Pietrzak, K.: Depth-robust graphs and their cumulative memory complexity. In: Coron, J.-S., Nielsen, J.B. (eds.) EUROCRYPT 2017. LNCS, vol. 10212, pp. 3–32. Springer, Cham (2017). https://doi.org/10.1007/978-3-319-56617-7_1
2. Alwen, J., Blocki, J., Pietrzak, K.: Sustained space complexity. In: Nielsen, J.B., Rijmen, V. (eds.) EUROCRYPT 2018. LNCS, vol. 10821, pp. 99–130. Springer, Cham (2018). https://doi.org/10.1007/978-3-319-78375-8_4
3. Alwen, J., Chen, B., Kamath, C., Kolmogorov, V., Pietrzak, K., Tessaro, S.: On the complexity of scrypt and proofs of space in the parallel random oracle model. In: Fischlin, M., Coron, J.-S. (eds.) EUROCRYPT 2016. LNCS, vol. 9666, pp. 358–387. Springer, Heidelberg (2016). https://doi.org/10.1007/978-3-662-49896-5_13
4. Alwen, J., Serbinenko, V.: High parallel complexity graphs and memory-hard functions. In: STOC, pp. 595–603. ACM (2015)
5. Arora, S., Lund, C., Motwani, R., Sudan, M., Szegedy, M.: Proof verification and the hardness of approximation problems. J. ACM **45**(3), 501–555 (1998)
6. Babai, L., Fortnow, L., Levin, L.A., Szegedy, M.: Checking computations in polylogarithmic time. In: STOC, pp. 21–31. ACM (1991)
7. Barak, B., Goldreich, O.: Universal arguments and their applications. SIAM J. Comput. **38**(5), 1661–1694 (2008)
8. Ben-Sasson, E., Bentov, I., Horesh, Y., Riabzev, M.: Scalable zero knowledge with no trusted setup. In: Boldyreva, A., Micciancio, D. (eds.) CRYPTO 2019. LNCS, vol. 11694, pp. 701–732. Springer, Cham (2019). https://doi.org/10.1007/978-3-030-26954-8_23
9. Ben-Sasson, E., Chiesa, A., Gabizon, A., Riabzev, M., Spooner, N.: Interactive oracle proofs with constant rate and query complexity. In: ICALP. LIPIcs, vol. 80, pp. 40:1–40:15. Schloss Dagstuhl - Leibniz-Zentrum für Informatik (2017)
10. Ben-Sasson, E., et al.: Zerocash: decentralized anonymous payments from bitcoin. In: IEEE Symposium on Security and Privacy, pp. 459–474. IEEE Computer Society (2014)

11. Ben-Sasson, E., Chiesa, A., Genkin, D., Tromer, E.: On the concrete efficiency of probabilistically-checkable proofs. In: STOC, pp. 585–594. ACM (2013)
12. Ben-Sasson, E., Chiesa, A., Goldberg, L., Gur, T., Riabzev, M., Spooner, N.: Linear-size constant-query IOPs for delegating computation. In: Hofheinz, D., Rosen, A. (eds.) TCC 2019. LNCS, vol. 11892, pp. 494–521. Springer, Cham (2019). https://doi.org/10.1007/978-3-030-36033-7_19
13. Ben-Sasson, E., Chiesa, A., Spooner, N.: Interactive oracle proofs. In: Hirt, M., Smith, A. (eds.) TCC 2016. LNCS, vol. 9986, pp. 31–60. Springer, Heidelberg (2016). https://doi.org/10.1007/978-3-662-53644-5_2
14. Ben-Sasson, E., Sudan, M.: Short PCPS with polylog query complexity. SIAM J. Comput. 38(2), 551–607 (2008)
15. Bitansky, N., et al.: The hunting of the SNARK. J. Cryptol. 30(4), 989–1066 (2017)
16. Bitansky, N., Chiesa, A.: Succinct arguments from multi-prover interactive proofs and their efficiency benefits. In: Safavi-Naini, R., Canetti, R. (eds.) CRYPTO 2012. LNCS, vol. 7417, pp. 255–272. Springer, Heidelberg (2012). https://doi.org/10.1007/978-3-642-32009-5_16
17. Block, A.R., Holmgren, J., Rosen, A., Rothblum, R.D., Soni, P.: Public-coin zero-knowledge arguments with (almost) minimal time and space overheads. In: Pass, R., Pietrzak, K. (eds.) TCC 2020. LNCS, vol. 12551, pp. 168–197. Springer, Cham (2020). https://doi.org/10.1007/978-3-030-64378-2_7
18. Block, A.R., Holmgren, J., Rosen, A., Rothblum, R.D., Soni, P.: Time- and space-efficient arguments from groups of unknown order. In: Malkin, T., Peikert, C. (eds.) CRYPTO 2021. LNCS, vol. 12828, pp. 123–152. Springer, Cham (2021). https://doi.org/10.1007/978-3-030-84259-8_5
19. Boneh, D., Bonneau, J., Bünz, B., Fisch, B.: Verifiable delay functions. In: Shacham, H., Boldyreva, A. (eds.) CRYPTO 2018. LNCS, vol. 10991, pp. 757–788. Springer, Cham (2018). https://doi.org/10.1007/978-3-319-96884-1_25
20. Brakerski, Z., Holmgren, J., Kalai, Y.T.: Non-interactive delegation and batch NP verification from standard computational assumptions. In: STOC, pp. 474–482. ACM (2017)
21. Chia network. https://chia.net/. Accessed 17 May 2019
22. Choudhuri, A.R., Jain, A., Jin, Z.: Snargs for $\mathcal{P}$ from LWE. In: FOCS, pp. 68–79. IEEE (2021)
23. Costello, C., et al.: Geppetto: versatile verifiable computation. In: IEEE Symposium on Security and Privacy, pp. 253–270. IEEE Computer Society (2015)
24. Döttling, N., Garg, S., Malavolta, G., Vasudevan, P.N.: Tight verifiable delay functions. In: Galdi, C., Kolesnikov, V. (eds.) SCN 2020. LNCS, vol. 12238, pp. 65–84. Springer, Cham (2020). https://doi.org/10.1007/978-3-030-57990-6_4
25. Dryja, T., Liu, Q.C., Park, S.: Static-memory-hard functions, and modeling the cost of space vs. time. In: Beimel, A., Dziembowski, S. (eds.) TCC 2018. LNCS, vol. 11239, pp. 33–66. Springer, Cham (2018). https://doi.org/10.1007/978-3-030-03807-6_2
26. Dwork, C., Goldberg, A., Naor, M.: On memory-bound functions for fighting spam. In: Boneh, D. (ed.) CRYPTO 2003. LNCS, vol. 2729, pp. 426–444. Springer, Heidelberg (2003). https://doi.org/10.1007/978-3-540-45146-4_25
27. Dwork, C., Naor, M., Wee, H.: Pebbling and proofs of work. In: Shoup, V. (ed.) CRYPTO 2005. LNCS, vol. 3621, pp. 37–54. Springer, Heidelberg (2005). https://doi.org/10.1007/11535218_3
28. Ephraim, N., Freitag, C., Komargodski, I., Pass, R.: Continuous verifiable delay functions. In: Canteaut, A., Ishai, Y. (eds.) EUROCRYPT 2020. LNCS, vol. 12107, pp. 125–154. Springer, Cham (2020). https://doi.org/10.1007/978-3-030-45727-3_5

29. Ephraim, N., Freitag, C., Komargodski, I., Pass, R.: SPARKs: succinct parallelizable arguments of knowledge. In: Canteaut, A., Ishai, Y. (eds.) EUROCRYPT 2020. LNCS, vol. 12105, pp. 707–737. Springer, Cham (2020). https://doi.org/10.1007/978-3-030-45721-1_25

30. Ethereum foundation. https://www.ethereum.org/. Accessed 17 May 2019

31. Fiat, A., Shamir, A.: How to prove yourself: practical solutions to identification and signature problems. In: Odlyzko, A.M. (ed.) CRYPTO 1986. LNCS, vol. 263, pp. 186–194. Springer, Heidelberg (1987). https://doi.org/10.1007/3-540-47721-7_12

32. Gentry, C., Wichs, D.: Separating succinct non-interactive arguments from all falsifiable assumptions. In: STOC, pp. 99–108. ACM (2011)

33. Goldwasser, S., Kalai, Y.T., Rothblum, G.N.: Delegating computation: interactive proofs for muggles. J. ACM **62**(4), 27:1–27:64 (2015)

34. Goldwasser, S., Micali, S., Rackoff, C.: The knowledge complexity of interactive proof systems. SIAM J. Comput. **18**(1), 186–208 (1989)

35. Holmgren, J., Rothblum, R.: Delegating computations with (almost) minimal time and space overhead. In: FOCS, pp. 124–135. IEEE Computer Society (2018)

36. Jawale, R., Kalai, Y.T., Khurana, D., Zhang, R.: Snargs for bounded depth computations and PPAD hardness from sub-exponential LWE. In: STOC, pp. 708–721. ACM (2021)

37. Kalai, Y., Paneth, O.: Delegating RAM computations. In: Hirt, M., Smith, A. (eds.) TCC 2016. LNCS, vol. 9986, pp. 91–118. Springer, Heidelberg (2016). https://doi.org/10.1007/978-3-662-53644-5_4

38. Kalai, Y.T., Paneth, O., Yang, L.: How to delegate computations publicly. In: STOC, pp. 1115–1124. ACM (2019)

39. Kalai, Y.T., Raz, R., Rothblum, R.D.: How to delegate computations: the power of no-signaling proofs. In: STOC, pp. 485–494. ACM (2014)

40. Kilian, J.: A note on efficient zero-knowledge proofs and arguments (extended abstract). In: STOC, pp. 723–732. ACM (1992)

41. Lombardi, A., Vaikuntanathan, V.: Fiat-Shamir for repeated squaring with applications to PPAD-hardness and VDFs. In: Micciancio, D., Ristenpart, T. (eds.) CRYPTO 2020. LNCS, vol. 12172, pp. 632–651. Springer, Cham (2020). https://doi.org/10.1007/978-3-030-56877-1_22

42. Micali, S.: Computationally sound proofs. SIAM J. Comput. **30**(4), 1253–1298 (2000)

43. Parno, B., Howell, J., Gentry, C., Raykova, M.: Pinocchio: nearly practical verifiable computation. In: IEEE Symposium on Security and Privacy, pp. 238–252. IEEE Computer Society (2013)

44. Pietrzak, K.: Simple verifiable delay functions. In: ITCS. LIPIcs, vol. 124, pp. 60:1–60:15. Schloss Dagstuhl - Leibniz-Zentrum für Informatik (2019)

45. Reingold, O., Rothblum, G.N., Rothblum, R.D.: Constant-round interactive proofs for delegating computation. SIAM J. Comput. **50**(3) (2021)

46. Ron-Zewi, N., Rothblum, R.D.: Local proofs approaching the witness length [extended abstract]. In: FOCS, pp. 846–857. IEEE (2020)

47. Wesolowski, B.: Efficient verifiable delay functions. In: Ishai, Y., Rijmen, V. (eds.) EUROCRYPT 2019. LNCS, vol. 11478, pp. 379–407. Springer, Cham (2019). https://doi.org/10.1007/978-3-030-17659-4_13

48. Wu, H., Zheng, W., Chiesa, A., Popa, R.A., Stoica, I.: DIZK: a distributed zero knowledge proof system. In: USENIX Security Symposium, pp. 675–692. USENIX Association (2018)

How to Sample a Discrete Gaussian (and more) from a Random Oracle

George Lu[1(✉)] and Brent Waters[1,2]

[1] University of Texas at Austin, Austin, USA
{gclu,bwaters}@cs.utexas.edu
[2] NTT Research, Austin, USA

Abstract. The random oracle methodology is central to the design of many practical cryptosystems. A common challenge faced in several systems is the need to have a random oracle that outputs from a structured distribution $\mathcal{D}$, even though most heuristic implementations such as SHA-3 are best suited for outputting bitstrings.

Our work explores the problem of sampling from discrete Gaussian (and related) distributions in a manner that they can be programmed into random oracles. We make the following contributions:

- We provide a definitional framework for our results. We say that a sampling algorithm Sample for a distribution is explainable if there exists an algorithm Explain which, when given an x in the support of $\mathcal{D}$, outputs an $r \in \{0,1\}^n$ such that $\mathsf{Sample}(r) = x$. Moreover, if x is sampled from $\mathcal{D}$ the explained distribution is statistically close to choosing r uniformly at random. We consider a variant of this definition that allows the statistical closeness to be a "precision parameter" given to the Explain algorithm. We show that sampling algorithms which satisfy our 'explainability' property can be programmed as a random oracle.
- We provide a simple algorithm for explaining *any* sampling algorithm that works over distributions with polynomial sized ranges. This includes discrete Gaussians with small standard deviations.
- We show how to transform a (not necessarily explainable) sampling algorithm Sample for a distribution into a new Sample' that is explainable. The requirements for doing this is that (1) the probability density function is efficiently computable (2) it is possible to efficiently uniformly sample from all elements that have a probability density above a given threshold p, showing the equivalence of random oracles to these distributions and random oracles to uniform bitstrings. This includes a large class of distributions, including all discrete Gaussians.
- A potential drawback of the previous approach is that the transformation requires an additional computation of the density function. We provide a more customized approach that shows the Miccancio-Walter discrete Gaussian sampler is explainable as is. This suggests that other discrete Gaussian samplers in a similar vein might also be explainable as is.

B. Waters—Supported by NSF CNS-1908611, CNS-1414082, Packard Foundation Fellowship, and Simons Investigator Award.

E. Kiltz and V. Vaikuntanathan (Eds.): TCC 2022, LNCS 13748, pp. 653–682, 2022.
https://doi.org/10.1007/978-3-031-22365-5_23

1   Introduction

The random oracle methodology proposed by Bellare and Rogaway [5] allows one to develop a cryptosystem under the premise that all users have access to an oracle that outputs a random string for each queried input. In practice, when deploying said systems, the calls to the oracle are heuristically replaced with calls to an appropriate hash function, such as SHA-3. While the use of such a heuristic comes with some controversy [13], the methodology has been leveraged for a broad spectrum of problems such as chosen-ciphertext security [17] and non-interactive zero knowledge proofs [16], to name just a few. In addition, it has been key to the development of many practical and deployed cryptosystems.

Although the heuristic of replacing a random oracle with a hash function such as SHA-3 is naturally aligned with oracles that output random bitstrings, there are many examples of cryptosystems that require random oracles to output from other distributions. For instance, the seminal identity-based encryption (IBE) scheme of Boneh-Franklin [7] uses a random oracle that outputs a bilinear group element, as does the Boneh-Lynn-Shacham signature scheme [8] and the multi-authority Attribute-Based Encryption (ABE) systems of [26]. Other examples include the GPV IBE scheme [19], which needs a random oracle to output a vector over $\mathbb{Z}_p$ for some prime p as well as RSA-based full domain hash signatures [6], which need an element over $\mathbb{Z}_N$ for a composite N. Other works explored constructing random oracles which hash into elliptic curves [20,23].

If one delves deeper into the deployment of such cryptosystems, we can see that there is no specialized hash function for each of these different domains. Instead, to create a random oracle scheme for a certain distribution $\mathcal{D}$ (e.g. random elements over a particular bilinear group), one will utilize a sampling function Sample. The function Sample will take in a string r and outputs something in the desired domain. The distribution of calling Sample on a random string should be statistically close to that of a given distribution $\mathcal{D}$.

While achieving statistical (or computational) closeness to a given distribution is a necessary property of a sampling function, it is not sufficient, as the sampling function may not allow for the "programmability" of a random oracle necessary in a security proof. For example, suppose we ran the BLS signature scheme over a bilinear group $\mathbb{G}$ of prime order p with generator g, public key g^a and secret key $a \in \mathbb{Z}_p$. In the scheme, a signature on a message m is created as $H(m)^a$ where $H(\cdot)$ is an oracle function that outputs a bilinear group element. Suppose we implement H by employing a random oracle H' that outputs bitstrings alongside a Sample algorithm that computes g^r (interpreting r as an integer) so that $H(m) = g^{H'(m)}$. Such an instantiation will indeed output elements statistically close to random bilinear group elements so long as r is sufficiently long. However, this results in a completely broken cryptosystem. To see this, observe that if an attacker can obtain a signature σ on message m, the attacker can then create a signature $\tilde{\sigma}$ on any other message $\tilde{m}$ by computing $\tilde{\sigma} = \sigma^{H'(\tilde{m})/H'(m)}$. Similar counterexamples exist for the other cryptosystems mentioned.

The more general goal of defining sufficient conditions of replacing crypto-graphic functionalities with each other has been explored in the line of work on indifferentiability initiated in [29], and further expanded on in papers such as [32]. Indeed, the application of the indifferentiability framework with regard to sampling from particular elliptic curve groups was explored in [11].

We define an important property for any sampler to also have a property we call explainability. This can be viewed as a relaxation of indifferentiability spe-cific to sampling functionalities. Roughly, given an element x in the domain, it should be possible to efficiently "reverse sample" an r such that $\mathsf{Sample}(r) = x$. Moreover, the distribution of receiving an x from $\mathcal{D}$ and then outputting r from reverse sampling should be close to just choosing r uniformly at random. Prior works dealt with this issue with various levels of formality. For many of the afore-mentioned works, 'ad-hoc' workarounds often invoking specific cryptographic assumptions are used to obtain a proof from the plain random oracle model. In bilinear groups, one often calls this a "hash-to-point" function which is present for many bilinear groups, but not necessarily guaranteed. In general there can exist distributions where sampling cannot be explained; consider if the function Sample were a one way function.

Sampling and Explaining Discrete Gaussian Distributions
In this work we explore the problem of sampling and explaining discrete Gaus-sian distributions. And consequentially, the problem of programming discrete Gaussian distributions into random oracles. Discrete Gaussian distributions are heavily utilized in the design and analysis of lattice-based cryptosystems, a flourishing area of research over the last several years. The problem of sam-pling discrete Gaussians has been well studied. While it is possible to sam-ple such distributions using a very basic form of rejection sampling [19], fur-ther works have both improved on the efficiency of the rejection sampling method [10,12,25], as well as explore other techniques to sample from discrete Gaussians [2,4,15,18,22,24,30,31,33,34] such as computing the cumulative den-sity function, or taking convolutions of smaller standard deviation discrete Gaus-sians. The goal of most of these works focus on making these samplers more secure and usable, allowing for features such as being constant time, providing better memory-time tradeoffs, or supporting a greater deal of offline precompu-tation.

To the best of our knowledge, however, the problem of explaining and pro-gramming random oracles with discrete Gaussian distributions has received lit-tle attention to date, with a few exceptions. One exception is the universal sampler work of Hofheinz et al. [21] that implicitly shows how indistinguisha-bility obfuscation can be used to obtain a computational form of explainability for any efficiently sampleable distribution from a random oracle. However, all current indistinguishability obfuscation candidates are highly impractical and at best invoke further computational assumptions that go beyond those typ-ically used in lattice-based cryptosytems. Our solutions will be both statisti-cal and significantly more efficient. In a more recent work [1], Agrawal, Wichs and Yamada sketch how the rejection sampling algorithm of Gentry-Peikert and Vaikuntanathan [19] is explainable.

Interestingly, the problem of explaining such distributions has come up in multiple contexts. Brakerski, Cash, Tsabary, and Wee [9] gave a homomorphic ABE scheme provably secure from the LWE assumption in the random oracle model. At one point, their construction required a random oracle that outputs a discrete Gaussian. Since no such solution were available, the authors worked around this by using a specialized sampler due to Lyubashevsky and Wichs [28] which is a blend of a standard discrete Gaussian and a binary string. Another example is in a recent multi-authority scheme of Datta, Komargodski and Waters [14] where the need for a random oracle that outputs discrete Gaussians arises. In this case the authors compensate by using a random oracle that outputs an integer over a subexponentially large integer range that can hide a smaller discrete Gaussian by smudging [3]. In this case the workaround resulted in a subexponentially large modulus. (It should be noted that smudging was used elsewhere in their analysis as well).

Finally, we want to emphasize that the need to explainably sample distributions also arises outside of the random oracle model. An interesting example comes up in the aforementioned work of [1], which requires public parameters that can generate discrete Gaussians, but should look like uniform bitstrings. To prove security the authors require the distribution to be explainable.

We advocate for this importance of studying the problem of explaining and programming discrete Gaussian distributions. Ideally, such solutions will match the performance of the prior works on discrete Gaussian sampling (e.g. [2,4,15, 18,22,24,30,31,33,34]) that were focused on performance, but not explainability. Pursuing this goal is a natural and fundamental property given the important role of discrete Gaussians in lattice-based cryptography.

1.1   Our Contributions

Our work consists of the following contributions.

Definitional

We begin by providing a definitional framework for describing our results. We define an explainable sampling system for distribution $\{\mathcal{D}_\lambda\}_\lambda$ to have two efficiently computable algorithms. The first is a $\mathsf{Sample}(1^\lambda; r)$ algorithm which is parameterized by a security parameter and takes in random coins r. This algorithm should output a distribution statistically close (in λ) to $\mathcal{D}_\lambda$ when r is chosen randomly. The second algorithm is a randomized algorithm $\mathsf{Explain}(1^\lambda, 1^\kappa, x)$ that takes as input the security parameter, a "precision" parameters κ and an element $x \in \mathcal{D}_\lambda$. Its job is to output an r such that $\mathsf{Sample}(1^\lambda; r) = x$. In addition, calling $\mathsf{Explain}$ on an x sampled from $\mathcal{D}$ should have a statistically close distribution to that of simply choosing r at random.

A particular feature of our definition is the use of a tunable precision parameter κ where we only require a statistical distance of $\frac{1}{\kappa}$, as opposed to requiring the statistical distance (or computational advantage) to be negligibly close like in indifferentiability. We show that this is sufficient to allow for proofs to go through in programming a random oracle. Intuitively, the parameter κ will in a reduction will be tuned to an attacker's advantage. We note that the parameter

κ is only used in the Explain algorithm and is not a priori set in the Sample algorithm used in a construction. Thus it can be adjusted to fit a particular attacker with a particular advantage in a reduction. This relaxation allows us to prove explainability, and hence show equivalence of random oracles, to a broader range of distributions than otherwise.

We note that our use of a tunable precision parameter is the main definitional difference between our framework and other works that explored reverse sampling.

Sampling over Small Ranges

We next show a simple algorithm for explainable sampling over small ranges. Suppose that $\mathbb{R}_\lambda$ is the range of distribution $\mathcal{D}_\lambda$ where $|\mathbb{R}_\lambda|$ grows polynomially in λ. We show that *any* sampling algorithm Sample for $\{\mathcal{D}_\lambda\}_\lambda$ is explainable. One simply calls Sample repeatedly until it outputs a desired x or until $|\mathbb{R}_\lambda| \cdot \kappa$ attempts occur without success. This simple process illustrates the flexibility given by the precision parameter in our framework.

A basic corollary extends this lemma to any distribution which is statistically close to a distribution with polynomial support. This implies sampling for discrete Gaussians with poly-sized standard deviations.

Generic Sampling over Conforming Distributions

A drawback of the previous approach is that it is only applicable when the distribution range is small, and thus cannot be used to explain, say, a discrete Gaussian with a super-polynomial sized standard deviation. We show an approach to generically sample from a broad class of distributions that includes discrete Gaussians with large standard deviations. Unlike the prior solution we will not be able to use a Sample algorithm as is and explain it. Instead we will transform it into a new Sample' algorithm that is explainable. For our transformation we will require a distribution with:

1. A (not necessarily explainable) Sample algorithm for the distribution.
2. A probability density function PDens where $\text{PDens}(1^\lambda, x)$ returns a value proportional to the probability x occurs for distribution $\mathcal{D}_\lambda$.
3. A "heavy element sampler" SampleUniform where $\text{SampleUniform}(1^\lambda, p; r)$ is an explainable sampling algorithm that samples uniformly from all elements in the range of $\mathcal{D}_\lambda$ that have a probability density above p.

Given these we can build an explainable Sample' algorithm that operates by first sampling x' from Sample. Then computing the probability density p' of x'. Next, it randomly "scales" p' by choosing a random $s_0 \in [0,1]$ and letting $p = s_0 p'$. Finally, it outputs $x \leftarrow \text{SampleUniform}(1^\lambda, p; r)$. We go on to show that this distribution is explainable.

We additionally give an explicit heavy element sampler for the case of discrete Gaussians, and in general observe that this primitive can be computed from the probability density function for many natural distributions. This gives us an explainable sampler for all discrete Gaussians with exponentially bounded centers and standard deviations.

Finally, we show that something akin to the heavy element sampler is needed for a truly generic transformation. We describe oracles which describe a distribution which has the first two properties above, but not the third and show that it is impossible to create an explainable sampler.

Explaining the Miccancio-Walter '17 [30] Sampling Algorithm
While the previous technique can create a sampler for discrete Gaussians with large standard deviations, it requires creating a new sampler rather than using one as is. If such a sampler is in a critical path, the additional introduced overhead of a high precision computation of the probability distribution function may be undesirable.

As our final contribution, we provide a tailored explain algorithm to the MW sampler. With any sampler, proving its explainability is vital to enabling its use in random oracle based applications, and allows us to securely instantiate such cryptosystems while carrying over the performance benefits of the sampler in question. While we focus on the MW sampler in particular, we believe that the ideas we demonstrate can extend to similar works [31] and provide techniques for showing explainability of other classes of discrete Gaussian samplers.

2   Preliminaries

We say a function $\mathsf{negl}(x)$ is negligible if for all polynomials $p(x)$, there exists some N such that $\forall x > N, \mathsf{negl}(x) < \frac{1}{p(x)}$. A function is noticeable if it is not negligible. The notation $\mathsf{poly}(x)$ will be used to refer to a polynomial function in x, and $\mathsf{EXP}(x)$ will refer to a function $\leq 2^{\mathsf{poly}(x)}$. We will indicate sampling an element from a probability distribution $\mathcal{D}$ as $x \xleftarrow{R} \mathcal{D}$. Similarly, we will use $x \xleftarrow{R} S$ to indicate sampling over the uniform distribution on a set S. We will use $[a, b]$ and (a, b) to denote the closed and open interval from a to b respectively on $\mathbb{R}$. We will subscript the brackets with $\mathbb{Z}$ to denote the same interval on $\mathbb{Z}$. We will use $\mathrm{range}(\mathcal{D})$ to refer to the set of elements in $\mathcal{D}$ which occur with probability > 0.

We will use log as logarithms base 2 if no base is explicitly specified. We use $\lfloor x \rfloor$, $\lceil x \rceil$ to refer to the usual floor and ceiling rounding operations to the integers, and $\lfloor x \rceil$ to mean a randomized rounding to $\lceil x \rceil$ with probability $x \mod 1$ and otherwise $\lfloor x \rfloor$. We subscript rounding operations (e.g. $\lfloor x \rfloor_k$) to round to $\mathbb{Z}/2^k$ instead of $\mathbb{Z}$.

We use statistical distance between two probability distributions $\mathcal{D}_1$ and $\mathcal{D}_2$ to refer to

$$\max_{A \subseteq \mathrm{range}(\mathcal{D}_1)\,\cup\,\mathrm{range}(\mathcal{D}_2)} \left| \Pr[x_1 \xleftarrow{R} \mathcal{D}_1, x_1 \in A] - \Pr[x_2 \xleftarrow{R} \mathcal{D}_2, x_2 \in A] \right|$$

We will denote a family of distributions indexed by λ as $\{\mathcal{D}_\lambda\}_\lambda$. We say two distribution families $\{\mathcal{D}_\lambda^1\}_\lambda$, $\{\mathcal{D}_\lambda^2\}_\lambda$ are statistically close if exists some negligible function $\mathsf{negl}(\lambda)$ such that the statistical distance between $\mathcal{D}_\lambda^1$ and $\mathcal{D}_\lambda^2$ is $< \mathsf{negl}(\lambda)$.

We notate a randomized function f which takes as input x and randomness r by $f(x; r)$. For brevity, the function may be written as $f(x)$ when fresh randomness r is used but does not need to be referenced.

Definition 1. *We say a function* $\mathsf{PDens}(1^\lambda, x)$ *with domain* $x \in D_\lambda$ *computes the probability density of a distribution family* $\{\mathcal{D}_\lambda\}_\lambda$ *if it runs in* $\mathsf{poly}(\lambda)$ *time, returns a nonnegative integer, and the distribution where element* x' *is selected with probability*

$$\frac{\mathsf{PDens}(1^\lambda, x')}{\sum_{x \in D_\lambda} \mathsf{PDens}(1^\lambda, x)}$$

is statistically close to $\mathcal{D}_\lambda{}^1$.

Since PDens *runs in* $\mathsf{poly}(\lambda)$, *it's output length is at most polynomial, so we can bound the maximum value with some* $\mathsf{PDF}_{\max} = \mathsf{PDF}_{\max}(\lambda) \le \mathsf{EXP}(\lambda)$.[2]

The discrete Gaussian distribution on a set $S \subseteq \mathbb{R}$ with center c and standard deviation σ is defined as the distribution where an element $i \in S$ is picked with probability

$$\frac{e^{-\frac{(i-c)^2}{2\sigma^2}}}{\sum_{x \in S} e^{-\frac{(x-c)^2}{2\sigma^2}}}$$

When the set S is not specified, assume $S = \mathbb{Z}$. This distribution is of particular interest to cryptography due to its presence in the learning with errors assumption and other lattice-based cryptosystems. For simplicity, we will mostly consider univariate discrete gaussians, as, much like their continuous counterparts, discrete gaussians over arbitrary multivariate lattices can be generated via a linear transformation on a set of independent univariate discrete gaussians, where the linear transformation is derived from the covariance of the target discrete gaussian.

3   Explainable Sampling

In this section we define our notion of explainable sampling. Intuitively a distribution $\{\mathcal{D}_\lambda\}_\lambda$ can be sampled by a function $\mathsf{Sample}(1^\lambda; r)$ if $\mathsf{Sample}(1^\lambda; r)$ gives a distribution that is statistically close (in λ) to $\{\mathcal{D}_\lambda\}_\lambda$ for when the string r is chosen uniformly at random. We will further say that such a sampling algorithm is explainable if given an element x in the domain of the distribution there is a function $\mathsf{Explain}(1^\lambda, x) \to r'$ that will output an r' such that $\mathsf{Sample}(1^\lambda; r') \to x$. Moreover, the process of picking random coins to sample an element compared to

---

[1] While this definition is not the most general for probability distributions over infinite sets, it will suffice for the cases we consider.

[2] Note that we only require the probability density to be proportional to the probability of an element being sampled, rather than equal to. As such, any PDens function which outputs fixed precision reals can be converted to one which outputs integers as above by simply multiplying a sufficiently large constant. We choose to define our output to be integers to give a convenient fixed granularity.

first sampling a random element and then calculating the coins should be statistically close. This final property is what allows one to program in a random oracle.

Below we give our formal definitions of a distribution being sampleable and a Sample algorithm being explainable. Then we sketch how a pair of algorithms meeting this criteria can be used in a cryptographic game to sample from a random oracle.

Definition 2. *We say an algorithm* Sample$(1^\lambda; r \in \{0,1\}^n)$ *is a sampler for probability distribution family* $\{\mathcal{D}_\lambda\}_\lambda$ *if* Sample *runs in* poly(λ) *time and the output of* Sample$(1^\lambda; r)$ *is statistically close to* $\{\mathcal{D}_\lambda\}_\lambda$.

Definition 3. *We say a* Sample *algorithm using* $n = n(\lambda)$ *bits of randomness is explainable if there exists a (likely randomized) algorithm* Explain$(1^\lambda, 1^\kappa, x)$ *such that* Explain *runs in* poly(λ, κ) *time, and there exists a negligible function* negl(λ) *such that the statistical distance between the following two distributions is at most* $\frac{1}{\kappa} +$ negl(λ)[3].

Distribution A	Distribution B
- $r \xleftarrow{R} \{0,1\}^n$.	- $r' \xleftarrow{R} \{0,1\}^n$
- $x \leftarrow$ Sample$(1^\lambda; r)$.	- $x \leftarrow$ Sample$(1^\lambda; r')$.
- Return r, x.	- $r \leftarrow$ Explain$(1^\lambda, 1^\kappa, x)$.
	- Return r, x.

We make a few brief remarks on our definition. First, notice that a call to Explain$(1^\lambda, 1^\kappa, x)$ algorithm is not explicitly required to even return an r such that Sample$(1^\lambda; r) = x$. However, the definition implies that if it does not do so with sufficiently high probability, it will not meet our requirements.

Next, our Explain definition takes in a "fidelity" parameter κ in unary. Here we only require that the explain algorithm is within $1/\kappa$ statistical difference in the above game. While also requiring the explain algorithm to run in time polynomial in κ and λ.

Our motivation is to allow for greater flexibility in the case where it might be difficult to design a polytime explain algorithm where the statistical difference is negligibly close, but that there is a natural running time versus precision tradeoff in the explain algorithm. As we will see below, the latter is sufficient for proving security in a game which uses said sampler to programs a random oracle. Suppose there exists an attacker that wins with non-negligible probability ϵ in a cryptographic game that samples using a random oracle. In proving security we will "tune" κ, so we can switch from sampling from the random oracle to 'reverse sampling' using explain such that the statistical distance between these two games is still some nonnegligible fraction (say $\epsilon/2$). We again remark that

---

[3] One could consider a computational analogue of this definition.

this relaxation to a tunable precision parameter is the main definitional difference between our framework and other works that explored reverse sampling.

Finally, we note that it will often be convenient to interpret the randomness r as being drawn from the uniform distribution on an interval of $\mathbb{Z}$ or an exponentially precise element of $\mathbb{R}$ rather than over uniformly random bits. It is easy to see we can interpret a bitstring as a binary representation either of the aforementioned domains of values, and so we will directly show that r is uniform on said domain rather than on the underlying bit representation.

3.1 Explainability in Cryptographic Games

We will use $\mathsf{Game}^{\mathsf{R}(\cdot)}(1^\lambda, \mathcal{A})$ to refer to a series of cryptographic game parameterized by λ where parties are permitted oracle access to some $\mathsf{R}(\cdot)$ against an adversary $\mathcal{A}$ consisting of one or more algorithms (also with access to $\mathsf{R}(\cdot)$). We say $\mathsf{Game}^{\mathsf{R}(\cdot)}(1^\lambda, \cdot)$ is secure, if for all adversaries $\mathcal{A}$ which run in $\mathsf{poly}(\lambda)$ time, $\Pr[\mathsf{Game}^{\mathsf{R}(\cdot)}(1^\lambda, \mathcal{A}) = 1] = \mathsf{negl}(\lambda)$. We will refer to the event of Game returning 1 as 'winning'.

Theorem 1. *Suppose* Sample *is an explainable sampler for* $\{\mathcal{D}_\lambda\}_\lambda$ *with corresponding* $\mathsf{Explain}$ *algorithm. Let* $\mathsf{R}(\cdot)$ *be a random oracle to distribution* $\{\mathcal{D}_\lambda\}_\lambda$, *and* $\mathsf{R}'(\cdot)$ *be a random oracle to* (r, x) *where* $r \xleftarrow{R} \{0,1\}^n$ *and* $x = \mathsf{Sample}(1^\lambda; r)$. *Then if* $\mathsf{Game}^{\mathsf{R}}(1^\lambda, \cdot)$ *is secure, then so is* $\mathsf{Game}^{\mathsf{R}'}(1^\lambda, \cdot)$.

Proof.

Lemma 1. *Suppose* Sample *is an explainable sampler for* $\{\mathcal{D}_\lambda\}_\lambda$ *with corresponding* $\mathsf{Explain}$ *algorithm. Let* $\mathsf{R}(\cdot)$ *be a random oracle to distribution* $\{\mathcal{D}_\lambda\}_\lambda$, *and* $\mathsf{R}_\kappa(\cdot)$ *be a random oracle to* (r, x) *where* $x \xleftarrow{R} \{\mathcal{D}_\lambda\}_\lambda$ *and* $r \leftarrow \mathsf{Explain}(1^\lambda, 1^\kappa, x)$. *Then if* $\mathsf{Game}^{\mathsf{R}}(1^\lambda, \cdot)$ *is secure, then* $\mathsf{Game}^{\mathsf{R}_\kappa}(1^\lambda, \cdot)$ *is secure for all* $\kappa \in \mathsf{poly}(\lambda)$.

Proof. Assume there is some PPT adversary $\mathcal{A}^{\mathsf{R}_\kappa}$ for which there exists $\kappa'(\lambda)$ such that $\mathcal{A}$ wins $\mathsf{Game}^{\mathsf{R}_\kappa}(1^\lambda, \cdot)$ with noticeable probability. Then define $\mathcal{A}'$ to be an adversary for $\mathsf{Game}^{\mathsf{R}}(1^\lambda, \cdot)$ which runs $\mathcal{A}^{\mathsf{R}_\kappa}$ and simulates oracle calls to R_κ by taking calling oracle R and running $\mathsf{Explain}(1^\lambda, 1^\kappa, \cdot)$ on the output. Since this is exactly the same game, we conclude $\mathcal{A}'$ has a noticeable probability of winning $\mathsf{Game}^{\mathsf{R}}(1^\lambda, \cdot)$. Since $\kappa \in \mathsf{poly}(\lambda)$, this is efficient.   □

Lemma 2. *Let* $\mathsf{R}_\kappa(\cdot)$ *be a random oracle to* (r, x) *where* $x \xleftarrow{R} \{\mathcal{D}_\lambda\}_\lambda$ *and* $r \leftarrow \mathsf{Explain}(1^\lambda, 1^\kappa, x)$. *and* $\mathsf{R}'(\cdot)$ *be a random oracle to* (r, x) *where* $r \xleftarrow{R} \{0,1\}^n$ *and* $x = \mathsf{Sample}(1^\lambda; r)$. *Suppose* $\mathsf{Game}^{\mathsf{R}_\kappa}(1^\lambda, \cdot)$ *is secure for all* $\kappa \in \mathsf{poly}(\lambda)$, *then* $\mathsf{Game}^{\mathsf{R}'(\cdot)}(1^\lambda, \cdot)$ *is secure.*

Proof. Again, assume for sake of contradiction there is some adversary PPT $\mathcal{A}^{\mathsf{R}'}$ which wins $\mathsf{Game}^{\mathsf{R}'}(1^\lambda, \cdot)$ with noticeable probability. Specifically, since it is poly time, let's suppose there exists constants a, b such that $\mathcal{A}^{\mathsf{R}'}$ wins $\mathsf{Game}^{\mathsf{R}'}(1^\lambda, \cdot)$ makes at most λ^a queries and wins with probability $> \lambda^{-b}$ infinitely often.

However, notice that by Definition 3, the statistical distance between queries to a query to R' and a query to R_κ is $\frac{1}{\kappa}$. Thus, if we set $\kappa = 2\lambda^{a+b}$, we can union bound the total statistical difference of *all* queries with $\frac{1}{2\lambda^b} + \mathsf{negl}(\lambda)$. Observe that this means we can bound

$$\left| \Pr[\mathsf{Game}^{R'}(1^\lambda, \mathcal{A}) = 1] - \Pr[\mathsf{Game}^{R_{2\lambda^{a+b}}}(1^\lambda, \mathcal{A}) = 1] \right| \leq \frac{1}{2\lambda^b} + \mathsf{negl}(\lambda)$$

However, Since $\mathcal{A}$ wins $\mathsf{Game}^{R_{2\lambda^{a+b}}}(1^\lambda, \mathcal{A})$ with probability $\frac{1}{\lambda^b}$ infinitely often, that means it wins $\mathsf{Game}^{R_{2\lambda^{a+b}}}(1^\lambda, \mathcal{A})$ with probability $\geq \frac{1}{2\lambda^b}$ infinitely often, contradicting the assumption that $\mathsf{Game}^{R_\kappa}(1^\lambda, \cdot)$ is secure for all $\kappa \in \mathsf{poly}(\lambda)$. $\square$

Taking Lemma 1 and Lemma 2 together gives us the theorem statement.

$\square$

4   Explaining Sampling over Small Ranges with Respect to Discrete Gaussian Samplers

We begin by showing that *any* efficient Sample algorithm over a polynomial sized range, $\{R_\lambda\}_\lambda$, is explainable. The core idea is rather simple. A call to $\mathsf{Explain}(1^\lambda, 1^\kappa, x)$ will simply call the Sample algorithm up to $\kappa \cdot |R_\lambda|$ times until x is output.

We show an immediate corollary to the theorem where if a distribution family has a super-polynomial size range $\{R_\lambda\}_\lambda$, but there exists subsets of the range $\{S_\lambda\}_\lambda$ where $S_\lambda \subseteq R_\lambda$ and $\{S_\lambda\}_\lambda$ are polynomially sized, then our sampling algorithm also works for these distribution. In particular, this covers a discrete Gaussian where the standard deviation σ grows polynomially with λ. We will see that this simple procedure can serve for explaining the "base case" for the Micciancio-Walter algorithm. Below we formally give our theorem and proof.

Theorem 2. *Let* Sample *be an sampler for some distribution family* $\{\mathcal{D}_\lambda\}_\lambda$ *on range* $\{R_\lambda\}_\lambda$. *If* $|R_\lambda| \leq \mathsf{poly}(\lambda)$, *then* Sample *is explainable.*

Proof. The idea here is to simply brute force the sampler output to find a valid randomness to a given element x. We use the fact that the range is polynomial to bound the amount of probability mass which can be contained by 'infrequent' elements. Consider the algorithm below:

$\mathsf{Explain}(1^\lambda, 1^\kappa, x)$
  – Repeat $\kappa \cdot |R_\lambda|$ times
    • Select fresh randomness r
    • $x' \leftarrow \mathsf{Sample}(1^\lambda; r)$
    • If $x' = x$, stop and return r.
  – Return $\perp$

Claim 3. $\mathsf{Explain}$ *runs in* $\mathsf{poly}(\lambda, \kappa)$ *time*

Proof. First, by the efficiency requirement of Definition 2 $\kappa \cdot |R_\lambda|$, $\mathsf{Sample}(1^\lambda; r)$ has runtime $\mathsf{poly}(\lambda)$. Explain simply calls $\mathsf{Sample}(1^\lambda; r)$ up to $\kappa \cdot |R_\lambda|$ many times (along with some other minor efficient computation). Thus, we can bound the runtime with $\kappa \cdot |R_\lambda| \cdot \mathsf{poly}(\lambda)$. Since $|R_\lambda| \le \mathsf{poly}(\lambda)$ by assumption, this bounds the runtime with $\kappa \cdot \mathsf{poly}(\lambda) \in \mathsf{poly}(\lambda, \kappa)$. □

Claim 4. Explain *returns* $\bot$ *in Game B with probability* $\le \frac{1}{\kappa}$

Proof. Observe that over the course of Game B, Sample is called on independent randomness up to $\kappa \cdot |R_\lambda| + 1$ times (once directly from the Game and $\kappa \cdot |R_\lambda|$ times in the execution of Game B). Let us call these outputs x_0 and $x_1, x_2, \ldots, x_{\kappa \cdot |R_\lambda|}$ respectively. Let the set $\mathcal{X} = \{x_i : \forall j \ne i \; x_j \ne x_i\}$ By pigeonhole, we know that $|\mathcal{X}| \le |R_\lambda| - 1$. Thus, since the calls are independent, the probability that the single call directly from Game B (x_0) is in this set $\mathcal{X}$ is $\frac{|\mathcal{X}|}{\kappa |R_\lambda| + 1} \le \frac{|R_\lambda| - 1}{\kappa |R_\lambda| + 1} < \frac{1}{\kappa}$. On the other hand, if this call is not unique, we can see $\mathsf{Explain}$ finds $j > 0$: $x_j = x_0$ and so does not return $\bot$. □

Claim 5. *The statistical distance of Game A and Game B in Definition 3 using* $\mathsf{Explain}$ *is* $\le \frac{1}{\kappa}$

Proof. We first note that if $\mathsf{Explain}(1^\lambda, 1^\kappa, x)$ returned $r \ne \bot$, then $x = x' = \mathsf{Sample}(1^\lambda; r)$. Thus, since x is the same function of r in both games, it suffices to show that r in Game B has statistical distance $\le \frac{1}{\kappa}$ to uniform.

Consider an alternate $\mathsf{Explain}'$ which, rather than sampling x' at most $\kappa \cdot |R_\lambda|$ times, samples x' until it finds an appropriate r. Here, we can compute the probability that any particular r is chosen as the probability the x chosen for $\mathsf{Explain}$ is equal to $\mathsf{Sample}(1^\lambda; r)$ multiplied by the probability that r is chosen conditional on $x' \leftarrow \mathsf{Sample}(1^\lambda; r)$. This is equal to

$$\Pr[\mathsf{Sample}(1^\lambda) = x] \cdot \frac{2^{-n}}{\Pr[\mathsf{Sample}(1^\lambda) = x']} = 2^{-n}$$

so r is uniform on $\{0, 1\}^n$. Now note that $\mathsf{Explain}'$ only differs from $\mathsf{Explain}$ when $\mathsf{Explain}$ returns $\bot$ before finding such an r. By Claim 4, this happens with probability $< \frac{1}{\kappa}$, bounding the statistical distance. □

Corollary 6. *Let* Sample *be a sampler for some distribution family* $\{\mathcal{D}_\lambda\}_\lambda$ *with range* $\{R_\lambda\}_\lambda$. *If there exists sets* $\{S_\lambda\}_\lambda$ *where* $S_\lambda \subseteq R_\lambda$, $|S_\lambda| \le \mathsf{poly}(\lambda)$, *and*

$$\Pr\left[\begin{matrix} x \xleftarrow{R} \mathcal{D}_\lambda \\ x \notin S_\lambda \end{matrix}\right] < \mathsf{negl}(\lambda),$$

then Sample *is explainable.*

Proof. Let $\{\mathcal{D}'_\lambda\}_\lambda$ be the distribution $\{\mathcal{D}_\lambda\}_\lambda$ conditional on the output being $\in \{S_\lambda\}_\lambda$. It is easy to see that $\{\mathcal{D}'_\lambda\}_\lambda$ satisfies the conditions for Theorem 2, and so any sampler for $\{\mathcal{D}'_\lambda\}_\lambda$ is explainable. Since $\{\mathcal{D}'_\lambda\}_\lambda$ is statistically close to $\{\mathcal{D}_\lambda\}_\lambda$, any sampler for $\{\mathcal{D}_\lambda\}_\lambda$ is a sampler for $\{\mathcal{D}'_\lambda\}_\lambda$, and so is explainable. □

5   Sampling and Explaining Conforming Distributions

The previous section showed how one could explain arbitrary sampler so long as the corresponding distributions grew polynomially in the security parameter. In this section we explore a class of distributions for which we can build explainable samplers. This includes distributions with superpolynomial sized ranges. To perform this we require the distribution family to have:

1. A Sample algorithm for the distribution. (It is not necessarily explainable).
2. A probability density function PDens where $\mathsf{PDens}(1^\lambda, x)$ returns the probability density function of x for distribution $\mathcal{D}_\lambda$.
3. An "heavy element sampler" algorithm SampleUniform which explainably samples from the uniform distribution over elements in the support of $\mathcal{D}_\lambda$ that have probability density above p.

We show that if a distribution has all three elements, then there exists another pair of algorithms Sample′, Explain′ that comprise an explainable sampler for the family $\{\mathcal{D}_\lambda\}_\lambda$.

We argue for the utility of this transformation by observing that many natural distributions, including the discrete Gaussian, have an easily computable heavy element sampler. If we consider the discrete Gaussian in particular, then a heavy element sampler simply needs to calculate the values x_0, x_1 such that $\mathsf{PDens}(1^\lambda, x_0) = \mathsf{PDens}(1^\lambda, x_1) = p$, which can be done by explicitly solving for p using the probability density function of $e^{-\frac{(x-c)^2}{2\sigma^2}} = p$. We can then choose integers uniformly at random in the interval $[x_0, x_1]$.

In fact, in general for monotonic distributions (or distributions which can be partitioned into a polynomial number of monotone segments) on ordered sets, we can easily compute an explainable heavy element sampler by binary searching for the endpoints of the ranges of heavy element with only polynomially many calls to the probability density function, then uniformly sampling on the interval found. As long as the underlying domain has an explainable representation (such as $\mathbb{Z}$ or $\mathbb{R}$), this sampler too is explainable. This condition alone encompasses almost all frequently seen distributions such as (discrete) Gaussians, binomial, geometric, Poisson, etc.

We conclude by arguing that having such a heavy element sampler is necessary for a generic transformation. To do this we provide a distribution for which oracle access to the first two properties is not sufficient to construct an explainable sampler to said distribution.

5.1   Explainable Sampling Through Heavy Element Samplers

Definition 4. *We say a function* $\mathsf{SampleUniform}(1^\lambda, p; r)$ *is a heavy element sampler for a distribution family* $\{\mathcal{D}_\lambda\}_\lambda$ *with probability density function* PDens *if it runs in* $\mathsf{poly}(\lambda)$ *time, and for all* $p \in [0, \mathsf{PDF}_{\max})$, $S_p(1^\lambda; r) = \mathsf{SampleUniform}(1^\lambda, p; r)$ *is a sampler for the uniform distribution on elements* $x \in R_\lambda$ *with* $\mathsf{PDens}(1^\lambda, x) \geq p$ *(we will notate said set as* R_λ^p. *We say a* *heavy element sampler is explainable if there exists a* $\mathsf{poly}(1^\lambda, 1^\kappa)$ *algorithm* $\mathsf{ExplainUniform}(1^\lambda, 1^\kappa, p, x)$ *such that for all* $p = p(\lambda) \in \mathsf{EXP}(\lambda)$, $E_p(1^\lambda, 1^\kappa, x) = \mathsf{ExplainUniform}(1^\lambda, 1^\kappa, p, x)$ *is an explainer for* S_p.

Theorem 7. *Let* Sample, PDens, $\mathsf{SampleUniform}$ *be a sampler, probability density function, and explainable heavy element sampler for the probability distribution family* $\{\mathcal{D}_\lambda\}_\lambda$ *on range* $\{R_\lambda\}_\lambda$. *Then there exists a* Sample' *which is an explainable sampler for* $\{\mathcal{D}_\lambda\}_\lambda$.

Proof. The underlying idea of the construction of this $\mathsf{Sample}', \mathsf{Explain}'$ is very similar to the generic $\mathsf{Explain}$ algorithm in Theorem 2 - we can use a brute force approach to polynomially approximate $\{\mathcal{D}_\lambda\}_\lambda$. However, because the domain can now be superpolynomial, we can no longer hope polynomially approximate the exact elements of $\{\mathcal{D}_\lambda\}_\lambda$ itself. Instead, we categorize elements into 'buckets' of similar approximate probability density. However, ordinarily, finding an element of a similar probability density would not suffice to satisfy the 'correctness' of an $\mathsf{Explain}$ algorithm. Here, we modify our sampler Sample' so that it uses Sample to produce an initial sample in the range, but this is then 'smudged' to an element of the range with similar probability density which is the actual output of Sample'.

By increasing the precision parameter κ, we decrease the size of each bucket, decreasing the statistical distance of $\mathsf{Explain}'$ but simultaneously increasing the expected number of tries to find an element in the same bucket.

Let Sample' be as follows:

$\mathsf{Sample}'(1^\lambda; r = r_0 \in \{0,1\}^n, s_0 \in [0,1], t_0 \in \{0,1\}^n)$
- $x' \leftarrow \mathsf{Sample}(1^\lambda; r_0)$
- $p' \leftarrow \mathsf{PDens}(1^\lambda, x')$
- $p \leftarrow p' \cdot s_0$
- $x \leftarrow \mathsf{SampleUniform}(1^\lambda, p; t_0)$
- Return x

As noted in Sect. 3, we can interpret a uniform bitstring as the binary expansion of a real number $\in [0, 1]$. Since randomness s_0 is only used to compute the probability density on $\mathsf{SampleUniform}$, which is integral, it suffices to use only $\log(\mathsf{PDF}_{\max}) \in \log(\mathsf{EXP}(\lambda)) = \mathsf{poly}(\lambda)$ bits of randomness.

Proof of Sampleability. We first prove that Sample' is a good sampler per Definition 2.

Definition 5. *We define the distribution* $\{\mathsf{PDF}(\mathcal{D}_\lambda)\}_\lambda$ *be defined as the joint distribution on two variables* (a, b) *such that the distribution of* a *is* $\mathcal{D}_\lambda$ *and* b *is uniform from* $[0, \mathsf{PDens}(1^\lambda, a))$ *where* PDens *is a probability density function of* $\mathcal{D}_\lambda$.

Lemma 3. *The following distributions are statistically close*

Distribution $1 = \mathcal{D}_1$

- $(a, b) \xleftarrow{R} \mathsf{PDF}(\mathcal{D}_\lambda)$
- Output (a, b)

Distribution $2 = \mathcal{D}_2$

- $(a', b) \xleftarrow{R} \mathsf{PDF}(\mathcal{D}_\lambda)$
- $a \xleftarrow{R} \mathsf{SampleUniform}(1^\lambda, b)$
- Output (a, b)

Proof. Consider some fixed (a^*, b^*) in the support of $\mathsf{PDF}(\mathcal{D}_\lambda)$. We can compute the explicit probability this element is picked in distribution 1 as the probability a^* is picked - which is $\frac{\mathsf{PDens}(a^*)}{\sum_{a \in R_\lambda} \mathsf{PDens}(a)}$, multiplied by the probability that b^* is picked given that a^* - which is $\frac{1}{\mathsf{PDens}(a^*)}$, as this is a uniform distribution of size $\mathsf{PDens}(a^*)$. Together, we get

$$\Pr[(a^*, b^*) \leftarrow \mathcal{D}_1] = \frac{\mathsf{PDens}(a^*)}{\sum_{a \in R_\lambda} \mathsf{PDens}(a)} \cdot \frac{1}{\mathsf{PDens}(a^*)} = \frac{1}{\sum_{a \in R_\lambda} \mathsf{PDens}(a)}$$

In distribution 2, we can write the probability (a^*, b^*) occurs as

$$\Pr[(\_, b^*) \leftarrow \mathsf{PDF}(\mathcal{D}_\lambda)] \cdot \Pr[a^* = \mathsf{SampleUniform}(1^\lambda, b^*) | (\_, b^*) \leftarrow \mathsf{PDF}(\mathcal{D}_\lambda)]$$

Note that since $\mathsf{SampleUniform}$ and $\mathsf{PDF}(\mathcal{D}_\lambda)$ are invoked independently, we can ignore the conditional. Using our analysis from distribution 1, we can compute the first probability as

$$\Pr[(\_, b^*) \leftarrow \mathsf{PDF}(\mathcal{D}_\lambda)] = \sum_{a : \mathsf{PDens}(a) > b^*} \Pr[(a, b^*) \leftarrow \mathsf{PDF}(\mathcal{D}_\lambda)]$$

$$= \sum_{a : \mathsf{PDens}(a) > b^*} \frac{1}{\sum_{a \in R_\lambda} \mathsf{PDens}(a)}$$

Meanwhile, since by definition $\mathsf{SampleUniform}$ outputs a uniform element of sufficiently high probability density, we have that

$$\Pr[\mathsf{SampleUniform}(1^\lambda, b^*) = a^*] = \frac{1}{|\{a : \mathsf{PDens}(a) > b^*\}|}$$

Which brings the total probability of $(a^*, b^*) \leftarrow \mathcal{D}_2$ as

$$\sum_{a : \mathsf{PDens}(a) > b^*} \frac{1}{\sum_{a \in R_\lambda} \mathsf{PDens}(a)} \cdot \frac{1}{|\{a : \mathsf{PDens}(a) > b^*\}|} = \frac{1}{\sum_{a \in R_\lambda} \mathsf{PDens}(a)}$$

the same as in $\mathcal{D}_1$ □

Lemma 4. *Sample$'$ is an sampler for $\{\mathcal{D}_\lambda\}_\lambda$.*

Proof.

Claim 8. Sample$'$ *produces a distribution statistically close to* $\{\mathcal{D}_\lambda\}_\lambda$.

Proof. Since Sample is a sampler to $\{\mathcal{D}_\lambda\}_\lambda$, the distribution of (x', p) as defined in Sample' is statistically close to $\{\mathrm{PDF}(\mathcal{D}_\lambda)\}_\lambda$. By Lemma 3, the distribution of (x, p) must also be statistically close to $\{\mathrm{PDF}(\mathcal{D}_\lambda)\}_\lambda$. By Definition 5, the distribution of x must be statistically close to $\{\mathcal{D}_\lambda\}_\lambda$. $\qquad\square$

Claim 9. Sample' *runs in* $\mathrm{poly}(\lambda)$ *time.*

Proof. Sample' makes a single call to each of Sample, PDens, SampleUniform, which, by assumption, are $\mathrm{poly}(\lambda)$ time algorithms along with a single multiplication, and so is also $\mathrm{poly}(\lambda)$ time. $\qquad\square$

By Claim 8 and Claim 9, Sample' fulfills the definition of a sampler for $\{\mathcal{D}_\lambda\}_\lambda$ $\qquad\square$

Proof of Explainability. We next prove that Sample' is explainable per Definition 3. The general idea here is that because x is chosen randomly using the value p generated by PDens rather than directly from Sample, elements x' with similar PDens values are similarly likely to be explanation for x. We can then use our precision parameter κ to define intervals of $\mathrm{PDens}(1^\lambda, x')$ and sample an interval of 'acceptable' p values relative to the correct conditional density. By restricting the number and size of such intervals, we can guarantee that a polynomial number of calls to Sample finds an x' in the chosen interval while still ensuring the p is approximated fairly closely.

Lemma 5. Sample' *is explainable.*

Proof. Consider the following Explain' algorithm for Sample'.

$\mathsf{PIdx}(x, \rho)$
- Let $b = 1 + \frac{1}{\rho}$
- If $\mathrm{PDens}(x) = 0$,
  return $\bot$
- Return
  $\lfloor \log_b(\mathrm{PDens}(x)) \rfloor$

$\mathsf{Explain}'(1^\lambda, 1^\kappa, x)$
- $p \xleftarrow{R} [0, \mathrm{PDens}(x)]$
- $x_0 \leftarrow \mathsf{SampleUniform}(1^\lambda, p)$
- Run $9 \ln(\mathrm{PDF}_{\max}) \cdot \kappa^2 \cdot \lambda$ times:
  - Generate fresh randomness r'.
  - $x' \leftarrow \mathsf{Sample}(1^\lambda; r')$.
  - If $\mathsf{PIdx}(x_0, 3\kappa) = \mathsf{PIdx}(x', 3\kappa)$.
    * Set $r_0 = r'$
    * Set $s_0 = \frac{p}{\mathrm{PDens}(x')}$
    * Set $t_0 = \mathsf{ExplainUniform}(1^\lambda, 1^{3\kappa}, p, x)$
    * Return $r = (r_0, s_0, t_0)$
- Return $\bot$.

Claim 10. Explain' *runs in* $\mathrm{poly}(\lambda, \kappa)$ *time.*

Proof. Explain' utilizes some efficient (polynomial time) subprocedures in Sample, SampleUniform, PDens, and PIdx. Moreover, since $\mathrm{PDF}_{\max} \in \mathrm{EXP}(\lambda)$, $\log(\mathrm{PDF}_{\max}) \in \mathrm{poly}(\lambda)$, so the algorithm loops only a $\mathrm{poly}(\lambda, \kappa)$ amount of times. $\qquad\square$

Claim 11. *The statistical distance of Game A and Game B in Definition 3 using* Explain' *is* $< \frac{1}{\kappa} + \mathsf{negl}(\lambda)$

Proof. We will proceed with a sequence of games argument, where Game 0 is an execution of Game A using Sample' and Game 11 is an execution of Game B using Sample', Explain'.

Game 0

- $r = (r_0, s_0, t_0) \xleftarrow{R} \{0,1\}^n \times \{0,1\} \times \{0,1\}^n$
- $x \leftarrow \mathsf{Sample}'(x; r)$
- Return r, x.

Game 0 (Sample' Expanded)

- $r_0 \xleftarrow{R} \{0,1\}^n$, $s_0 \xleftarrow{R} [0,1]$, $t_0 \xleftarrow{R} \{0,1\}^n$
- $x' \leftarrow \mathsf{Sample}(1^\lambda; r_0)$
- $p' \leftarrow \mathsf{PDens}(1^\lambda, x')$
- $p = p' \cdot s_0$
- $x \leftarrow \mathsf{SampleUniform}(1^\lambda, p; t_0)$
- Return r_0, s_0, t_0, x.

Game 1

- $r_0 \xleftarrow{R} \{0,1\}^n$, $s_0 \xleftarrow{R} [0,1]$, $t_0 \xleftarrow{R} \{0,1\}^n$
- $x'' \xleftarrow{R} \mathcal{D}_\lambda$
- Run until break[4]
  - Generate fresh randomness r'
  - $x' \leftarrow \mathsf{Sample}(1^\lambda, r')$
  - If $x' = x''$
    * Set $r_0 = r'$ and break
- $p' \leftarrow \mathsf{PDens}(1^\lambda, x'')$
- $p = p' \cdot s_0$
- $x \leftarrow \mathsf{SampleUniform}(1^\lambda, p; t_0)$
- Return r_0, s_0, t_0, x.

Game 2

- $s_0 \xleftarrow{R} [0,1]$, $t_0 \xleftarrow{R} \{0,1\}^n$
- $x'' \xleftarrow{R} \mathcal{D}_\lambda$
- Run until break
  - Generate fresh randomness r'
  - $x' \leftarrow \mathsf{Sample}(1^\lambda, r')$
  - If $x'' = x'$
    * Set $r_0 = r'$ and break
- $p'' \xleftarrow{R} [0, \mathsf{PDens}(1^\lambda, x'')]$
- Set $s_0 = \frac{p''}{\mathsf{PDens}(1^\lambda, x'')}$
- $x \leftarrow \mathsf{SampleUniform}(1^\lambda, p''; t_0)$
- Return r_0, s_0, t_0, x.

---

[4] This process could potentially take unbounded time, but simply act as 'bridging' steps to make the change in distribution easier to see. The final game will be efficient.

Game 3

- $t_0 \xleftarrow{R} \{0,1\}^n$
- $(x'', p'') \xleftarrow{R} \mathsf{PDF}(\mathcal{D}_\lambda)$
- Run until break
    - Generate fresh randomness r'
    - $x' \leftarrow \mathsf{Sample}(1^\lambda, r')$
    - If $x' = x''$
        * Set $r_0 = r'$ and break
- Set $s_0 = \frac{p''}{\mathsf{PDens}(1^\lambda, x_0)}$
- $x \leftarrow \mathsf{SampleUniform}(1^\lambda, p''; t_0)$
- Return r_0, s_0, t_0, x.

Game 4

- $\cancel{t_0 \xleftarrow{R} \{0,1\}^n}$
- $(x'', p'') \xleftarrow{R} \mathsf{PDF}(\mathcal{D}_\lambda)$
- Run until break
    - Generate fresh randomness r'
    - $x' \leftarrow \mathsf{Sample}(1^\lambda, r')$
    - If $x' = x''$
        * Set $r_0 = r'$ and break
- Set $s_0 = \frac{p''}{\mathsf{PDens}(1^\lambda, x'')}$
- $x \leftarrow \mathsf{SampleUniform}(1^\lambda, p'')$
- Set $t_0 = \mathsf{ExplainUniform}(1^\lambda, 1^{3\kappa}, p'', x)$
- Return r_0, s_0, t_0, x.

Game 5

- $(x'', p'') \xleftarrow{R} \mathsf{PDF}(\mathcal{D}_\lambda)$
- $x \leftarrow \mathsf{SampleUniform}(1^\lambda, p'')$
- Run until break
    - Generate fresh randomness r'
    - $x' \leftarrow \mathsf{Sample}(1^\lambda, r')$
    - If $x' = x''$
        * Set $r_0 = r'$
        * Set $s_0 = \frac{p''}{\mathsf{PDens}(1^\lambda, x')}$
        * Set $t_0 = \mathsf{ExplainUniform}(1^\lambda, 1^{3\kappa}, p'', x)$
        * Break
- Return r_0, s_0, t_0, x.

Game 6

- $(x'', p'') \xleftarrow{R} \mathsf{PDF}(\mathcal{D}_\lambda)$
- Set $x_0 = x''$
- $p \xleftarrow{R} [0, \mathsf{PDens}(1^\lambda, x_0)]$
- $x \leftarrow \mathsf{SampleUniform}(1^\lambda, p)$

– Run until break
  • Generate fresh randomness r'
  • $x' \leftarrow \mathsf{Sample}(1^\lambda, r')$
  • If $x' = x''$
    * Set $r_0 = r'$
    * Set $s_0 = \frac{p}{\mathsf{PDens}(1^\lambda, x')}$
    * Set $t_0 = \mathsf{ExplainUniform}(1^\lambda, 1^{3\kappa}, p, x)$
    * Break
– Return r_0, s_0, t_0, x.

Game 7

– $(x'', p'') \xleftarrow{R} \mathsf{PDF}(\mathcal{D}_\lambda)$
– Sample $x_0 \xleftarrow{R} \mathcal{D}_\lambda$ conditional on $\mathsf{PIdx}(x_0, 3\kappa) = \mathsf{PIdx}(x'', 3\kappa)$
– $p \xleftarrow{R} [0, \mathsf{PDens}(1^\lambda, x_0)]$
– $x \leftarrow \mathsf{SampleUniform}(1^\lambda, p)$
– Run until break
  • Generate fresh randomness r'
  • $x' \leftarrow \mathsf{Sample}(1^\lambda, r')$
  • If $x' = x''$
    * Set $r_0 = r'$
    * Set $s_0 = \frac{p}{\mathsf{PDens}(1^\lambda, x')}$
    * Set $t_0 = \mathsf{ExplainUniform}(1^\lambda, 1^{3\kappa}, p, x)$
    * Break
– Return r_0, s_0, t_0, x.

Game 8

– $(x_0, p) \xleftarrow{R} \mathsf{PDF}(\mathcal{D}_\lambda)$
– Sample $x'' \xleftarrow{R} \mathcal{D}_\lambda$ conditional on $\mathsf{PIdx}(x_0, 3\kappa) = \mathsf{PIdx}(x'', 3\kappa)$
– $x \leftarrow \mathsf{SampleUniform}(1^\lambda, p)$
– Run until break
  • Generate fresh randomness r'
  • $x' \leftarrow \mathsf{Sample}(1^\lambda, r')$
  • If $x' = x''$
    * Set $r_0 = r'$
    * Set $s_0 = \frac{p}{\mathsf{PDens}(1^\lambda, x')}$
    * Set $t_0 = \mathsf{ExplainUniform}(1^\lambda, 1^{3\kappa}, p, x)$
    * Break
– Return r_0, s_0, t_0, x.

Game 9

– $(x_0, p) \xleftarrow{R} \mathsf{PDF}(\mathcal{D}_\lambda)$
– $x \leftarrow \mathsf{SampleUniform}(1^\lambda, p)$
– Run $9 \ln(\mathsf{PDF}_{\max}) \cdot \kappa^2 \cdot \lambda$ times
  • Generate fresh randomness r'

- $x' \leftarrow \mathsf{Sample}(1^\lambda, r')$
- If $\mathsf{PIdx}(x_0, 3\kappa) = \mathsf{PIdx}(x', 3\kappa)$
    * Set $r_0 = r'$
    * Set $s_0 = \frac{p}{\mathsf{PDens}(1^\lambda, x')}$
    * Set $t_0 = \mathsf{ExplainUniform}(1^\lambda, 1^{3\kappa}, p, x)$
    * Break
- Return r_0, s_0, t_0, x.

Game 10

- $(x, p) \xleftarrow{R} \mathsf{PDF}(\mathcal{D}_\lambda)$
- $x_0 \leftarrow \mathsf{SampleUniform}(1^\lambda, p)$
- Run $9 \ln(\mathsf{PDF}_{\max}) \cdot \kappa^2 \cdot \lambda$ times
    - Generate fresh randomness r'
    - $x' \leftarrow \mathsf{Sample}(1^\lambda, r')$
    - If $\mathsf{PIdx}(x_0, 3\kappa) = \mathsf{PIdx}(x', 3\kappa)$
        * Set $r_0 = r'$
        * Set $s_0 = \frac{p}{\mathsf{PDens}(1^\lambda, x')}$
        * Set $t_0 = \mathsf{ExplainUniform}(1^\lambda, 1^{3\kappa}, p, x)$
        * Break
- Return r_0, s_0, t_0, x.

Game 11

- $x \leftarrow \mathsf{Sample'}(1^\lambda)$
- $p \xleftarrow{R} [0, \mathsf{PDens}(x)]$
- $x_0 \leftarrow \mathsf{SampleUniform}(1^\lambda, p)$
- Run $9 \ln(\mathsf{PDF}_{\max}) \cdot \kappa^2 \cdot \lambda$ times
    - Generate fresh randomness r'
    - $x' \leftarrow \mathsf{Sample}(1^\lambda, r')$
    - If $\mathsf{PIdx}(x_0, 3\kappa) = \mathsf{PIdx}(x', 3\kappa)$
        * Set $r_0 = r'$
        * Set $s_0 = \frac{p}{\mathsf{PDens}(1^\lambda, x')}$
        * Set $t_0 = \mathsf{ExplainUniform}(1^\lambda, 1^{3\kappa}, p, x)$
        * Break
- Return r_0, s_0, t_0, x.

Game 11 (Shortened)

- $x \leftarrow \mathsf{Sample'}(1^\lambda)$
- $r = (r_0, s_0, t_0) \leftarrow \mathsf{Explain}(1^\lambda, 1^\kappa, x)$
- Return r, x.

Claim 12. *The distributions output by Game 0 and Game 1 have statistical distance* $\mathsf{negl}(\lambda)$.

Proof. By Definition 2, the distribution of x' in Game 0 (from Sample) and Game 1 (from $\mathcal{D}_\lambda$) are statistically close. Now since r_0 is uniform, the conditional probability of r_0 on any fixed x' is still uniform on all r_0 such that $\mathsf{Sample}(1^\lambda; r_0) = x'$ in both games. The only other changes are notational between x' and x'', which are equal in this game.   □

Claim 13. *The distributions output by Game 1 and Game 2 have statistical distance 0.*

Proof. This game only changes the way s_0 is generated. In Game 1, the distribution of s_0 is uniform on $[0, 1]$. In Game 2, it is the quotient of p'' which is uniform on $[0, \mathsf{PDens}(1^\lambda, x'')]$ and $\mathsf{PDens}(1^\lambda, x'')$, which is simply uniform on $[0, 1]$.   □

Claim 14. *The distributions output by Game 2 and Game 3 have statistical distance 0.*

Proof. By definition, $(x'', p'') \xleftarrow{R} \mathsf{PDF}(\mathcal{D}_\lambda)$ is defined to be $x'' \xleftarrow{R} \mathcal{D}_\lambda$ and $p'' \xleftarrow{R} [0, \mathsf{PDens}(1^\lambda, x'')]$, which is exactly how it is generated in Game 3.   □

Claim 15. *The distributions output by Game 3 and Game 4 have statistical distance $\frac{1}{3\kappa} + \mathsf{negl}(\lambda)$.*

Proof. By Definition 3, the distributions

Game A	Game B
– $t_0 \xleftarrow{R} \{0, 1\}^n$.	– $x \leftarrow \mathsf{SampleUniform}(1^\lambda, p)$.
– $x \leftarrow \mathsf{SampleUniform}(1^\lambda, p; t_0)$.	– $r \leftarrow \mathsf{ExplainUniform}(1^\lambda, 1^{3\kappa}, p, x)$.
– Return t_0, x.	– Return t_0, x.

---

have statistical distance $\frac{1}{3\kappa} + \mathsf{negl}(\lambda)$. Note this corresponds exactly to how t_0, x are generated in Games 3 and 4 respectively.   □

Claim 16. *The distributions output by Game 4 and Game 5 have statistical distance 0.*

Proof. The changes in Game 5 only change the order some variables are generated, but not the way they are generated.   □

Claim 17. *The distributions output by Game 5 and Game 6 have statistical distance 0.*

Proof. In this game, we substitute all uses of p'' with p. By Definition 1, $x'' \xleftarrow{R} \mathcal{D}_\lambda$, so (x'', p) is distributed according to $\mathsf{PDF}(\mathcal{D}_\lambda)$, so are statistically identical. $\qquad\qquad\square$

Claim 18. *The distributions output by Game 6 and Game 7 have statistical distance $\frac{1}{3\kappa}$.*

Proof. In this game, rather than setting $x_0 = x''$, we set x_0 to be an element with the same PIdx as x''. Observe that x_0 is only used to sample p, and by definition of PIdx, $\frac{|\mathsf{PDens}(1^\lambda, x_0) - \mathsf{PDens}(1^\lambda, x'')|}{\mathsf{PDens}(1^\lambda, x'')}$ is at most $\frac{1}{3\kappa}$, and so we can conclude that the uniform distribution on $[0, \mathsf{PDens}(1^\lambda, x_0)]$ and $[0, \mathsf{PDens}(1^\lambda, x'')]$ have statistical distance at most $\frac{1}{3\kappa}$. $\qquad\qquad\square$

Claim 19. *The distributions output by Game 7 and Game 8 have statistical distance 0.*

Proof. By this game, note that p'' is unused, so we can examine the difference in how the joint distribution on x_0, x'', p is generated. Let $x_0{}^*, x'''^*, p^*$ be some set of values taken by x_0, x'', p. We can see the probability density of this is in Game 7 proportional to

$$\Pr_{x'' \xleftarrow{R} \mathcal{D}_\lambda}[x'''^* = x''] \cdot \Pr_{x_0 \xleftarrow{R} \mathcal{D}_\lambda}[x_0{}^* = x_0 | \mathsf{PIdx}(x'''^*, 3\kappa) = \mathsf{PIdx}(x_0, 3\kappa)] \cdot \frac{1}{\mathsf{PDens}(1^\lambda, x_0)}$$

$$= \Pr_{x'' \xleftarrow{R} \mathcal{D}_\lambda}[x'''^* = x''] \cdot \frac{\Pr_{x_0 \xleftarrow{R} \mathcal{D}_\lambda}[x_0{}^* = x_0]}{\Pr_{x_0 \xleftarrow{R} \mathcal{D}_\lambda}[\mathsf{PIdx}(x'''^*, 3\kappa) = \mathsf{PIdx}(x_0, 3\kappa)]} \cdot \frac{1}{\mathsf{PDens}(1^\lambda, x_0)}$$

by definition of conditional probability

$$= \frac{\Pr_{x'' \xleftarrow{R} \mathcal{D}_\lambda}[x'''^* = x'']}{\Pr_{x_0 \xleftarrow{R} \mathcal{D}_\lambda}[\mathsf{PIdx}(x'''^*, 3\kappa) = \mathsf{PIdx}(x_0, 3\kappa)]} \cdot \Pr_{x_0 \xleftarrow{R} \mathcal{D}_\lambda}[x_0{}^* = x_0] \cdot \frac{1}{\mathsf{PDens}(1^\lambda, x_0)}$$

via simple algebraic manipulation

$$= \frac{\Pr_{x'' \xleftarrow{R} \mathcal{D}_\lambda}[x'''^* = x'']}{\Pr_{x'' \xleftarrow{R} \mathcal{D}_\lambda}[\mathsf{PIdx}(x'''^*, 3\kappa) = \mathsf{PIdx}(x'', 3\kappa)]} \cdot \Pr_{x_0 \xleftarrow{R} \mathcal{D}_\lambda}[x_0{}^* = x_0] \cdot \frac{1}{\mathsf{PDens}(1^\lambda, x_0)}$$

by simply renaming x_0 to x''

$$= \Pr_{x'' \xleftarrow{R} \mathcal{D}_\lambda}[x'''^* = x'' | \mathsf{PIdx}(x'''^*, 3\kappa) = \mathsf{PIdx}(x'', 3\kappa)] \cdot \Pr_{x_0 \xleftarrow{R} \mathcal{D}_\lambda}[x_0{}^* = x_0] \cdot \frac{1}{\mathsf{PDens}(1^\lambda, x_0)}$$

again by definition of conditional probability. We can see the final line is the probability density of $x_0{}^*, x'''^*, p^*$ in Game 8. $\qquad\qquad\square$

Claim 20. *The distributions output by Game 8 and Game 9 have statistical distance $\frac{1}{3\kappa} + \mathsf{negl}(\lambda)$.*

Proof. Game 9 contains 2 changes. One is purely notational, where x'' is eliminated and we directly test if $\mathsf{PIdx}(x_0, 3\kappa) = \mathsf{PIdx}(x', 3\kappa)$. Since x'' was drawn from $\mathcal{D}_\lambda$ and x' is drawn from $\mathsf{Sample}(1^\lambda)$, the distribution of x' is statistically close from this change. The other change made here is that we restrict the loop to $9\ln(\mathsf{PDF}_{\max}) \cdot \kappa^2 \cdot \lambda$ iterations rather than an unbounded number. Note that the loop terminating is entirely dependent on sampling x' such that $\mathsf{PIdx}(x_0, 3\kappa) = \mathsf{PIdx}(x', 3\kappa)$. So we will show that in Game 8, such an x' is found in the first $9\ln(\mathsf{PDF}_{\max}) \cdot \kappa^2 \cdot \lambda$ iterations with probability $\leq \frac{1}{3\kappa} + \mathsf{negl}(\lambda)$.

To see this, we first want to observe that the total number of possible values of PIdx is bounded by

$$\log_{1+\frac{1}{3\kappa}}(\mathsf{PDF}_{\max}) = \ln(\mathsf{PDF}_{\max}) / \ln(((1 + \frac{1}{3\kappa})^{3\kappa \cdot \frac{1}{3\kappa}}))$$

$$= \ln(\mathsf{PDF}_{\max}) \cdot 3\kappa / \ln((1 + \frac{1}{3\kappa})^{3\kappa}) \approx 3\ln(\mathsf{PDF}_{\max}) \cdot \kappa$$

as the PDens function is nonnegative and integral, so PIdx returns $\perp$ or an integer in the range $[0, \ln(\mathsf{PDF}_{\max}) \cdot \kappa)]$. Let the set $A = \{a_1, a_2, \ldots a_q\}$ denote the range of values PIdx can take.

We partition A into sets A_0 and A_1 such that

$$a \in A_0 \Leftrightarrow \Pr \begin{bmatrix} x_0 \leftarrow \mathcal{D}_\lambda \\ \mathsf{PIdx}(x_0, 3\kappa) = a \end{bmatrix} \leq \frac{1}{9\ln(\mathsf{PDF}_{\max}) \cdot \kappa^2}$$

and similarly

$$a \in A_1 \Leftrightarrow \Pr \begin{bmatrix} x_0 \leftarrow \mathsf{Sample}(1^\lambda) \\ \mathsf{PIdx}(x_0, 3\kappa) = a \end{bmatrix} > \frac{1}{9\ln(\mathsf{PDF}_{\max}) \cdot \kappa^2}$$

Since A has $3\ln(\mathsf{PDF}_{\max}) \cdot \kappa$ elements, we can bound

$$\Pr \left[x_0 \leftarrow \mathcal{D}_\lambda \mathsf{PIdx}(x_0, 3\kappa) \in A_0 \right] \leq \frac{3\ln(\mathsf{PDF}_{\max}) \cdot \kappa}{9\ln(\mathsf{PDF}_{\max}) \cdot \kappa^2} = \frac{1}{3\kappa}$$

If we suppose $\mathsf{PIdx}(x_0, 3\kappa) \in A_1$, then we can see the probability that $9\ln(\mathsf{PDF}_{\max}) \cdot \kappa^2 \cdot \lambda$ fail to find an x' is lower bounded by

$$\left(1 - \frac{1}{9\ln(\mathsf{PDF}_{\max}) \cdot \kappa^2} \right)^{9\ln(\mathsf{PDF}_{\max}) \cdot \kappa^2 \cdot \lambda} \approx e^{-\lambda} \in \mathsf{negl}(\lambda)$$

Since we know $\mathsf{PIdx}(x_0, 3\kappa) \in A_1$ with probability at least $1 - \frac{1}{3\kappa}$, we can lower bound the probability that this loop terminates within $9\ln(\mathsf{PDF}_{\max}) \cdot \kappa^2 \cdot \lambda$ iterations as $1 - \frac{1}{3\kappa} - \mathsf{negl}(\lambda)$, which bounds the statistical distance between Games 8 and 9 with $\frac{1}{3\kappa} + \mathsf{negl}(\lambda)$. $\square$

Claim 21. *The distributions output by Game 9 and Game 10 have statistical distance* $\mathsf{negl}(\lambda)$.

Proof. In Game 10, we alter the way which we generate the variables x, p, x_0. From Lemma 3, the distributions of x_0, p below are statistically close

$$(x_0, p) \xleftarrow{R} \mathsf{PDF}(\mathcal{D}_\lambda) \qquad\qquad (\_, p) \xleftarrow{R} \mathsf{PDF}(\mathcal{D}_\lambda)$$
$$x_0 \leftarrow \mathsf{SampleUniform}(1^\lambda, p)$$

Using this, we can see that the following distributions of x_0, x, p are statistically close as well (note that the lefthand side is the distribution generated by Game 9)

$$(x_0, p) \xleftarrow{R} \mathsf{PDF}(\mathcal{D}_\lambda) \qquad\qquad (\_, p) \xleftarrow{R} \mathsf{PDF}(\mathcal{D}_\lambda)$$
$$x \leftarrow \mathsf{SampleUniform}(1^\lambda, p) \qquad\qquad x_0 \leftarrow \mathsf{SampleUniform}(1^\lambda, p)$$
$$x \leftarrow \mathsf{SampleUniform}(1^\lambda, p)$$

However, note in the latter distribution, x_0 and x are generated independently, so this is the same as the left side distribution below

$$(\_, p) \xleftarrow{R} \mathsf{PDF}(\mathcal{D}_\lambda) \qquad\qquad (x, p) \xleftarrow{R} \mathsf{PDF}(\mathcal{D}_\lambda)$$
$$x \leftarrow \mathsf{SampleUniform}(1^\lambda, p) \qquad\qquad x_0 \leftarrow \mathsf{SampleUniform}(1^\lambda, p).$$
$$x_0 \leftarrow \mathsf{SampleUniform}(1^\lambda, p).$$

Applying Lemma 3 again, we can see the above 2 distributions are statistically close. We can see the final distribution above is the distribution of x_0, x, p in Game 10. □

Claim 22. *The distributions output by Game 10 and Game 11 have statistical distance* $\mathsf{negl}(\lambda)$.

$\mathcal{D}_1$	$\mathcal{D}_2$	$\mathcal{D}_3$
$(x, p) \xleftarrow{R} \mathsf{PDF}(\mathcal{D}_\lambda)$	$x \xleftarrow{R} \mathcal{D}_\lambda$	$x \leftarrow \mathsf{Sample}'(1^\lambda)$
	$p \xleftarrow{R} [0, \mathsf{PDens}(1^\lambda, x)].$	$p \xleftarrow{R} [0, \mathsf{PDens}(1^\lambda, x)].$

Proof. By Definition 5, the distribution of (x, p) in $\mathcal{D}_1$ and $\mathcal{D}_2$ are identical. From Lemma 4, $\mathcal{D}_2$ is statistically close to $\mathcal{D}_3$. Note $\mathcal{D}_1$ is the distribution of (x, p) in Game 10 and $\mathcal{D}_3$ is the distribution of (x, p) in Game 11. □

Combining Claim 12 through Claim 22, we get the total statistical distance of Game 0 and 11 is $\leq \frac{1}{\kappa} + \mathsf{negl}(\lambda)$

$\square$

Combining Claim 11 and Claim 10, we get the explainability of Sample$'$.

$\square$

Combining Lemma 4 and Lemma 5, we get that Sample$'$ is an explainable sampler for $\{\mathcal{D}_\lambda\}_\lambda$.

$\square$

5.2   Instantiation on Discrete Gaussians

As an example, we can observe that the above gives us an explainable sampler for discrete Gaussians centered at $c(\lambda)$ with standard deviation $\sigma(\lambda)$. For the Sample algorithm, we can use any of the discrete Gaussian samplers present in literature. We can use $\mathsf{PDens}(1^\lambda, x) = e^{-\frac{(x-c)^2}{2\sigma^2}}$, which is efficienty computable, and we can let $\mathsf{SampleUniform}(1^\lambda, p)$ simply sample uniformly from integers on the interval $\left[\left\lceil c - \sigma\sqrt{-2\ln(p)}\right\rceil, \left\lfloor c + \sigma\sqrt{-2\ln(p)}\right\rfloor\right]$. Since the only randomness here is sampling uniform integers on a fixed interval, this is easily explainable.

5.3   Impossibility of Generic Sampling Without Heavy Element Samplers

We give some evidence on the tightness of the above result by showing an impossibility of a black box construction of an explainable sampler from only a sampler and probability density function to some distribution. This also highlights the inherent need of non-black-box techniques such as indistinguishability obfuscation used to construct universal samplers in [21].

Theorem 23. *There exists a distribution family $\{\mathcal{D}_\lambda\}_\lambda$ such that there does not exist an efficient explainable sampler for $\{\mathcal{D}_\lambda\}_\lambda$ given oracle access to a sampler* Sample *and probability density function* PDens.

We defer the proof of this theorem to the full version of the paper [27].

6   Explaining Discrete Gaussian Samplers

In this section we show an explanation algorithm for the Miccancio-Walter [30] Gaussian Sampling algorithm. This algorithm follows a series of works improving the practicality of discrete Gaussian sampling [2,4,10,12,15,22,24,25,31,33,34]. This usually comes in the form of some combination of decreased runtime (in either an offline or online phase), decreased memory usage, and decreased entropy usage. While we could simply apply our transformation of Sect. 5 to the MW sampler to get explainability, this may not in general preserve special properties of many samplers that could be leveraged, and would add an additional overhead for computing the probability density function. In this section we will show a tailored approach to make it explainable as is.

We begin by giving an adapted definition for explainable discrete Gaussian samplers that explicitly allows for the standard deviation and center of the distribution to be given as parameters. The syntax from the previous sections restricts these to be functions of the security parameter λ. We then describe the explainability algorithm for the Miccancio-Walter discrete Gaussian sampler.

Discrete Gaussians

To talk specifically about discrete Gaussians, we will modify need to expand the definition of distribution samplers to accomodate parameterization. The theorems and their proofs shown in the previous sections translate analogously to the definitions here. For completeness, the proofs will be available in the appendices.

Definition 6. *We say an algorithm* $\mathsf{SampleDG}(1^\lambda, c, \sigma; r)$ *is an* $f_\sigma(\lambda)$-*discrete Gaussian sampler for a discrete Gaussians if for all* $c \in [0,1]$ *and* $\sigma \leq f_\sigma(\lambda)$, *Sample runs in* $\mathsf{poly}(\lambda)$ *time and the output of* $\mathsf{SampleDG}(1^\lambda, c, \sigma; r)$ *is statistically close to the discrete Gaussian on* $\mathbb{Z}+c$ *centered at* 0 *with standard deviation* σ. *Note that this is equivalent to producing discrete Gaussians samples on* $\mathbb{Z}$ *centered at any* $c' \in \exp(\lambda)$, *as we can simply generate a sample on* $\mathbb{Z} + (-c \mod 1)$ *centered at* 0 *and add* c.

Definition 7. *Analogously, we say a* $\mathsf{SampleDG}$ *algorithm is explainable if there exists a (possibly randomized) algorithm* $\mathsf{ExplainDG}(1^\lambda, 1^\kappa, x, c, \sigma)$ *such that* $\mathsf{ExplainDG}$ *runs in* $\mathsf{poly}(\lambda, \kappa)$ *time, and there exists a negligible function* $\mathsf{negl}(\lambda)$ *such that for all* $c \in [0,1]$, $\sigma \leq f_\sigma(\lambda)$, *the statistical distance between the following 2 distributions is at most* $\frac{1}{\kappa} + \mathsf{negl}(\lambda)$.

Game A	Game B
$-\ r \xleftarrow{R} \{0,1\}^n$.	$-\ x \leftarrow \mathsf{SampleDG}(1^\lambda, c, \sigma)$.
$-\ x \leftarrow \mathsf{SampleDG}(1^\lambda, c, \sigma; r)$.	$-\ r \leftarrow \mathsf{ExplainDG}(1^\lambda, 1^\kappa, x, c, \sigma)$.
$-$ Return r, x.	$-$ Return r, x.

While Theorem 7 does imply the existence of an explainable discrete Gaussian sampler, oftentimes, it may be of interest whether existing implementations using particular sampling algorithms are explainable. We'll use this MW17 as an example of a practical discrete Gaussian sampler and prove its explainability, along the way hopefully demonstrating some techniques useful for proving explainability of other sampling algorithms.

6.1   Miccancio-Walter '17

Here, we look at a fairly recent method of sampling discrete Gaussians presented in [30]. Informally, this is done by taking a sampler SampleBase to discrete

Gaussians with small standard deviation, for which there are easier and more efficient to compute, then taking particular linear combinations to create discrete Gaussian samples with large standard deviation in SampleI, before employing a randomized rounding technique in SampleC to sample from a specific coset of $\mathbb{Z}$.

In comparison to previous works, this has the advantage of better performance, as well as taking time independent of the sample value. In addition, much of the computation can be done offline, without knowing the standard deviation or center an algorithm which calls the sampler may request.

SampleI($1^\lambda, i$)
   – If $i = 0$
      • $x \leftarrow$ SampleBase($1^\lambda, 0, s_0$)
      • Return x
   – $x_1 \leftarrow$ SampleI($1^\lambda, i - 1$)
   – $x_2 \leftarrow$ SampleI($1^\lambda, i - 1$)
   – $y = z_i x_1 + \max(1, z_i - 1)x_2$
   – Return y

SampleC($1^\lambda, c, k$)
   – If $k = 0$
      • Return 0.
   – $g \leftarrow 2^{-k+1} \cdot$ SampleBase($1^\lambda, 2^{k-1}c, s_0$)
   – Return $g +$ SampleC($1^\lambda, c - g, k - 1$)

SampleDG($1^\lambda, c, s$)[a]
   – $x \leftarrow$ SampleI(m)
   – $K \leftarrow \sqrt{s^2 - \bar{s}_k^2}/s_m$
   – $c' \leftarrow \lfloor c + Kx \rceil_k$
   – $y \leftarrow$ SampleC($1^\lambda, c', k$)
   – Return y

---

[a]This was referred to as SampleZ in [30]

We remark that the notation of the above algorithms has been slightly altered to better fit with our definition of a discrete Gaussian sampler. To align with our definition of statistical closeness, we consider $k \in \Theta(\lambda)$. As in the original construction, we let s_i denote the exact standard deviation of SampleI, z_i denote the multipliers used in SampleI, and $\bar{s}_k$ to be the standard deviation 'added' by SampleC, whose explicit values are determined recursively by the equations below. The exact formula is given as a function of the smoothing parameter $\eta_\epsilon(\mathbb{Z})$ of the discrete Gaussian, which, for our purposes, we will only bound as a value $\in O(\log(\lambda))$. Similarly, $m = m(\lambda)$ is a parameter controlling the precision controlling the maximum standard deviation SampleDG can generate, which we can think of as a value bounded by $\log(\lambda) + O(1)$. Readers of [30] may notice the lack of a base parameter b which controls the 'base' for (e.g. binary, decimal) which randomized rounding occurs. This has been fixed to 2 for simplicity.

$$s_0 = \sqrt{2}\eta_\epsilon(\mathbb{Z}), \quad z_i = \left\lfloor \frac{s_{i-1}}{\sqrt{2}\eta_\epsilon(\mathbb{Z})} \right\rfloor$$

$$s_i^2 = \left(z_i^2 + \max((z_i - 1)^2, 1)\right) s_{i-1}^2, \quad \bar{s}_k = s_0 \cdot \left(\sqrt{\sum_{i=0}^{k-1} 2^{-2i}}\right)$$

Theorem 24. *Suppose* $\mathsf{SampleBase}(1^\lambda, c)$ *is an* $O(\log(\lambda))$*-discrete Gaussian sampler. Then* $\mathsf{SampleDG}(1^\lambda, c, s; r)$ *is an explainable* $\exp(\lambda)$*-discrete Gaussian sampler for the family of discrete Gaussians centered at* c *with standard deviation* s.

Proof.
Lemma 6. *Suppose* $\mathsf{SampleBase}(1^\lambda, c)$ *is an* $O(\log(\lambda))$*-discrete Gaussian sampler. Then for* $i \leq \log(\lambda) + O(1)$, $\mathsf{SampleI}(1^\lambda, i)$ *is a sampler for the family of discrete Gaussians centered at* 0 *with standard deviation* $\omega(2^{2^i})$.

See [30] for proof.

Lemma 7. *Suppose* $\mathsf{SampleBase}(1^\lambda, c)$ *is an* $O(\log(\lambda))$*-discrete Gaussian sampler. Then* $y = \mathsf{SampleC}(1^\lambda, c, k)$ *is a sampler for the distribution of discrete Gaussians on* $c + \mathbb{Z}$ *with standard deviation* $\bar{s}_k$.

See [30] for proof.

Corollary 25. *Suppose* $\mathsf{SampleBase}(1^\lambda, c)$ *is an* $O(\log(\lambda))$*-discrete Gaussian sampler. Let* c' *be a sample from a discrete Gaussians on* $\mathbb{Z}/2^k$ *with standard deviation* $\sqrt{\sigma^2 - \bar{s}_k^2}$ *and center* c. *Then for* $k \in \Theta(\lambda)$, *in* $\mathsf{SampleC}(1^\lambda, c', k)$, *the output to the recursive call to* $\mathsf{SampleC}(1^\lambda, c'', i)$ *is statistically close to the discrete Gaussian on* $\mathbb{Z} + c''$ *with standard deviation* $\sqrt{\sigma^2 - \bar{s}_i^2}$.

Proof. This follows from a straightforward induction argument on i. $\square$

Lemma 8. *Suppose* $\mathsf{SampleBase}(1^\lambda, c)$ *is an* $O(\log(\lambda))$*-discrete Gaussian sampler. Then* $\mathsf{SampleDG}(1^\lambda, c, \sigma)$ *is a* $\exp(\lambda)$*-discrete Gaussian sampler.*

See [30] for proof.

Lemma 9. *Any* $O(\log(\lambda))$*-discrete Gaussian sampler is explainable.*

Proof. Note that we can bound the probability a sample is outside $\log(\lambda)$ standard deviations with $2 \cdot \sum_{i=\log(\lambda)\sigma}^{\infty} e^{-\frac{i^2}{2\sigma}}$ Since this decays exponentially, this is $\leq O(e^{-\log(\lambda)^2}) \in O(\lambda^{-\log(\lambda)})$. Thus, we can take the set S_λ to be the set of elements within $\log(\lambda)$ standard deviations of the center. By Corollary 6 from Sect. 4, this is explainable. $\square$

Lemma 10. *Suppose* $\mathsf{SampleBase}(1^\lambda, c)$ *is an* $O(\log(\lambda))$*-discrete Gaussian sampler. Then* $\mathsf{SampleI}(1^\lambda, i)$ *is an* **explainable** *sampler for the family of discrete Gaussians centered at* 0 *with standard deviation* $\omega(2^{2^i})$.

We defer the proof of this lemma to the full version of the paper [27].

Lemma 11. *Suppose* $\mathsf{SampleBase}(1^\lambda, c)$ *is an* $O(\log(\lambda))$*-discrete Gaussian sampler. Let* $\mathsf{SampleDG}_{2^k}(1^\lambda, c, \sigma)$ *be an explainable sampler for discrete Gaussians on* $\mathbb{Z}/2^k$ *with standard deviation* σ *and center* c. *Then for* $k \in O(\lambda)$, $\mathsf{SampleC}'(1^\lambda, c, \sigma) = \mathsf{SampleC}(1^\lambda, \mathsf{SampleDG}_{2^k}(1^\lambda, c, \sqrt{\sigma^2 - \bar{s}_k^2}), k)$ *is an explainable discrete Gaussian sampler.*

We defer the proof of this lemma to the full version of the paper [27].

Using Lemma 10, we know the Sample1 algorithm is an explainable sampler for discrete Gaussians centered at 0 with standard deviation s_m. We know from this that c' is a sample from a discrete Gaussian on $\mathbb{Z}/2^k$ centered at c with standard deviation $\sqrt{s^2 - \bar{s}_k^2}$. Moreover, this is explainable (the only non-reversible step is the rounding to the nearest 2^{-k}, but since $k \in \Theta(\lambda)$, we can pick a uniform preimage to the rounding and still be statistically close). Thus, using Lemma 11, taking SampleDG to be the first 3 lines of SampleDG, we can conclude SampleDG is explainable. Combined with Lemma 8, this gives us the statement of Theorem 24. □

References

1. Agrawal, S., Wichs, D., Yamada, S.: Optimal broadcast encryption from LWE and pairings in the standard model. In: Pass, R., Pietrzak, K. (eds.) TCC 2020. LNCS, vol. 12550, pp. 149–178. Springer, Cham (2020). https://doi.org/10.1007/978-3-030-64375-1_6

2. Aguilar-Melchor, C., Albrecht, M.R., Ricosset, T.: Sampling from arbitrary centered discrete Gaussians for lattice-based cryptography. In: Gollmann, D., Miyaji, A., Kikuchi, H. (eds.) ACNS 2017. LNCS, vol. 10355, pp. 3–19. Springer, Cham (2017). https://doi.org/10.1007/978-3-319-61204-1_1

3. Asharov, G., Jain, A., López-Alt, A., Tromer, E., Vaikuntanathan, V., Wichs, D.: Multiparty computation with low communication, computation and interaction via threshold FHE. In: Pointcheval, D., Johansson, T. (eds.) EUROCRYPT 2012. LNCS, vol. 7237, pp. 483–501. Springer, Heidelberg (2012). https://doi.org/10.1007/978-3-642-29011-4_29

4. Barthe, G., Belaïd, S., Espitau, T., Fouque, P.-A., Rossi, M., Tibouchi, M.: GALACTICS: Gaussian sampling for lattice-based constant-time implementation of cryptographic signatures, revisited, pp. 2147–2164, November 2019

5. Bellare, M., Rogaway, P.: Random oracles are practical: a paradigm for designing efficient protocols. In: Denning, D.E., Pyle, R., Ganesan, R., Sandhu, R.S., Ashby, V. (eds.) CCS 1993: Proceedings of the 1st ACM Conference on Computer and Communications Security, Fairfax, Virginia, USA, 3–5 November 1993, pp. 62–73. ACM (1993)

6. Bellare, M., Rogaway, P.: The exact security of digital signatures-how to sign with RSA and Rabin. In: Maurer, U. (ed.) EUROCRYPT 1996. LNCS, vol. 1070, pp. 399–416. Springer, Heidelberg (1996). https://doi.org/10.1007/3-540-68339-9_34

7. Boneh, D., Franklin, M.: Identity-based encryption from the Weil pairing. In: Kilian, J. (ed.) CRYPTO 2001. LNCS, vol. 2139, pp. 213–229. Springer, Heidelberg (2001). https://doi.org/10.1007/3-540-44647-8_13

8. Boneh, D., Lynn, B., Shacham, H.: Short signatures from the Weil pairing. In: Boyd, C. (ed.) ASIACRYPT 2001. LNCS, vol. 2248, pp. 514–532. Springer, Heidelberg (2001). https://doi.org/10.1007/3-540-45682-1_30

9. Brakerski, Z., Cash, D., Tsabary, R., Wee, H.: Targeted homomorphic attribute-based encryption. In: Hirt, M., Smith, A. (eds.) TCC 2016. LNCS, vol. 9986, pp. 330–360. Springer, Heidelberg (2016). https://doi.org/10.1007/978-3-662-53644-5_13

10. Brakerski, Z., Langlois, A., Peikert, C., Regev, O., Stehlé, D.: Classical hardness of learning with errors. In: Proceedings of the Forty-Fifth Annual ACM Symposium on Theory of Computing, STOC 2013, pp. 575–584. Association for Computing Machinery, New York (2013)

11. Brier, E., Coron, J.-S., Icart, T., Madore, D., Randriam, H., Tibouchi, M.: Efficient indifferentiable hashing into ordinary elliptic curves. In: Rabin, T. (ed.) CRYPTO 2010. LNCS, vol. 6223, pp. 237–254. Springer, Heidelberg (2010). https://doi.org/10.1007/978-3-642-14623-7_13

12. Buchmann, J., Cabarcas, D., Göpfert, F., Hülsing, A., Weiden, P.: Discrete Ziggurat: a time-memory trade-off for sampling from a Gaussian distribution over the integers. In: Lange, T., Lauter, K., Lisoněk, P. (eds.) SAC 2013. LNCS, vol. 8282, pp. 402–417. Springer, Heidelberg (2014). https://doi.org/10.1007/978-3-662-43414-7_20

13. Canetti, R., Goldreich, O., Halevi, S.: The random oracle methodology, revisited (preliminary version). In: Vitter, J.S. (ed.) Proceedings of the Thirtieth Annual ACM Symposium on the Theory of Computing, Dallas, Texas, USA, 23–26 May 1998, pp. 209–218. ACM (1998)

14. Datta, P., Komargodski, I., Waters, B.: Decentralized multi-authority ABE for DNFs from LWE. In: Canteaut, A., Standaert, F.-X. (eds.) EUROCRYPT 2021. LNCS, vol. 12696, pp. 177–209. Springer, Cham (2021). https://doi.org/10.1007/978-3-030-77870-5_7

15. Dwarakanath, N.C., Galbraith, S.D.: Sampling from discrete Gaussians for lattice-based cryptography on a constrained device. Appl. Algebra Eng. Commun. Comput. 25(3), 159–180 (2014). https://doi.org/10.1007/s00200-014-0218-3

16. Fiat, A., Shamir, A.: How to prove yourself: practical solutions to identification and signature problems. In: Odlyzko, A.M. (ed.) CRYPTO 1986. LNCS, vol. 263, pp. 186–194. Springer, Heidelberg (1987). https://doi.org/10.1007/3-540-47721-7_12

17. Fujisaki, E., Okamoto, T.: Secure integration of asymmetric and symmetric encryption schemes. In: Wiener, M. (ed.) CRYPTO 1999. LNCS, vol. 1666, pp. 537–554. Springer, Heidelberg (1999). https://doi.org/10.1007/3-540-48405-1_34

18. Genise, N., Micciancio, D.: Faster Gaussian sampling for trapdoor lattices with arbitrary modulus. In: Nielsen, J.B., Rijmen, V. (eds.) EUROCRYPT 2018. LNCS, vol. 10820, pp. 174–203. Springer, Cham (2018). https://doi.org/10.1007/978-3-319-78381-9_7

19. Gentry, C., Peikert, C., Vaikuntanathan, V.: Trapdoors for hard lattices and new cryptographic constructions. In: Proceedings of the Fortieth Annual ACM Symposium on Theory of Computing, pp. 197–206 (2008)

20. Goh, E.-J., Jarecki, S., Katz, J., Wang, N.: Efficient signature schemes with tight reductions to the Diffie-Hellman problems. J. Cryptol. 20(4), 493–514 (2007). https://doi.org/10.1007/s00145-007-0549-3

21. Hofheinz, D., Jager, T., Khurana, D., Sahai, A., Waters, B., Zhandry, M.: How to generate and use universal samplers. In: Cheon, J.H., Takagi, T. (eds.) ASIACRYPT 2016. LNCS, vol. 10032, pp. 715–744. Springer, Heidelberg (2016). https://doi.org/10.1007/978-3-662-53890-6_24

22. Howe, J., Prest, T., Ricosset, T., Rossi, M.: Isochronous Gaussian sampling: from inception to implementation. In: Ding, J., Tillich, J.-P. (eds.) PQCrypto 2020. LNCS, vol. 12100, pp. 53–71. Springer, Cham (2020). https://doi.org/10.1007/978-3-030-44223-1_4

23. Icart, T.: How to hash into elliptic curves. In: Halevi, S. (ed.) CRYPTO 2009. LNCS, vol. 5677, pp. 303–316. Springer, Heidelberg (2009). https://doi.org/10.1007/978-3-642-03356-8_18

24. Karmakar, A., Roy, S.S., Reparaz, O., Vercauteren, F., Verbauwhede, I.: Constant-time discrete Gaussian sampling. IEEE Trans. Comput. **67**(11), 1561–1571 (2018)
25. Karney, C.F.F.: Sampling exactly from the normal distribution. ACM Trans. Math. Softw. **42**(1), 1–14 (2016)
26. Lewko, A., Waters, B.: Decentralizing attribute-based encryption. In: Paterson, K.G. (ed.) EUROCRYPT 2011. LNCS, vol. 6632, pp. 568–588. Springer, Heidelberg (2011). https://doi.org/10.1007/978-3-642-20465-4_31
27. Lu, G., Waters, B.: How to sample a discrete Gaussian (and more) from a random oracle. Cryptology ePrint Archive, Paper 2022/1227 (2022). https://eprint.iacr.org/2022/1227
28. Lyubashevsky, V., Wichs, D.: Simple lattice trapdoor sampling from a broad class of distributions. In: Katz, J. (ed.) PKC 2015. LNCS, vol. 9020, pp. 716–730. Springer, Heidelberg (2015). https://doi.org/10.1007/978-3-662-46447-2_32
29. Maurer, U., Renner, R., Holenstein, C.: Indifferentiability, impossibility results on reductions, and applications to the random oracle methodology. In: Naor, M. (ed.) TCC 2004. LNCS, vol. 2951, pp. 21–39. Springer, Heidelberg (2004). https://doi.org/10.1007/978-3-540-24638-1_2
30. Micciancio, D., Walter, M.: Gaussian sampling over the integers: efficient, generic, constant-time. In: Katz, J., Shacham, H. (eds.) CRYPTO 2017. LNCS, vol. 10402, pp. 455–485. Springer, Cham (2017). https://doi.org/10.1007/978-3-319-63715-0_16
31. Pöppelmann, T., Ducas, L., Güneysu, T.: Enhanced lattice-based signatures on reconfigurable hardware. In: Batina, L., Robshaw, M. (eds.) CHES 2014. LNCS, vol. 8731, pp. 353–370. Springer, Heidelberg (2014). https://doi.org/10.1007/978-3-662-44709-3_20
32. Ristenpart, T., Shacham, H., Shrimpton, T.: Careful with composition: limitations of the indifferentiability framework. In: Paterson, K.G. (ed.) EUROCRYPT 2011. LNCS, vol. 6632, pp. 487–506. Springer, Heidelberg (2011). https://doi.org/10.1007/978-3-642-20465-4_27
33. Zhao, R.K., Steinfeld, R., Sakzad, A.: COSAC: compact and scalable arbitrary-centered discrete Gaussian sampling over integers. In: Ding, J., Tillich, J.-P. (eds.) PQCrypto 2020. LNCS, vol. 12100, pp. 284–303. Springer, Cham (2020). https://doi.org/10.1007/978-3-030-44223-1_16
34. Zhao, R.K., Steinfeld, R., Sakzad, A.: FACCT: fast, compact, and constant-time discrete Gaussian sampler over integers. IEEE Trans. Comput. **69**(1), 126–137 (2020)

Anonymity, Verifiability and Robustness

Anonymous Whistleblowing
over Authenticated Channels

Thomas Agrikola[2](✉), Geoffroy Couteau[1], and Sven Maier[2]

[1] CNRS, IRIF, Université de Paris, Paris, France
geoffroy.couteau@irif.fr
[2] Karlsruhe Institute of Technology, Karlsruhe, Germany
{thomas.agrikola,sven.maier}@kit.edu

Abstract. The goal of *anonymous whistleblowing* is to publicly disclose a message while at the same time hiding the identity of the sender in a way that even if suspected of being the sender, this cannot be proven. While many solutions to this problem have been proposed over the years, they all require some form of interaction with trusted or non-colluding parties. In this work, we ask whether this is fundamentally inherent. We put forth the notion of *anonymous transfer* as a primitive allowing to solve this problem *without* relying on any participating trusted parties.

We initiate the theoretical study of this question, and derive negative and positive results on the existence of such a protocol. We refute the feasibility of *asymptotically* secure anonymous transfer, where the message will be received with overwhelming probability while at the same time the identity of the sender remains hidden with overwhelming probability. On the other hand, resorting to *fine-grained* cryptography, we provide a heuristic instantiation (assuming ideal obfuscation) which guarantees that the message will be correctly received with overwhelming probability and the identity of the sender leaks with vanishing probability. Our results provide strong foundations for the study of the possibility of anonymous communications through authenticated channels, an intriguing goal which we believe to be of fundamental interest.

1 Introduction

The term whistleblowing denotes "the disclosure by a person, usually an employee in a government agency or private enterprise, to the public or to those in authority, of mismanagement, corruption, illegality, or some other wrongdoing" [Whi]. Consider the following scenario. You are happily employed by some government agency. However, one day, you learn that your employer violates human rights. You strongly disagree with this breach of trust and law but you are bound by law to keep internal information secret. Consequently, you are faced with a dilemma: either you ignore the human rights violation, or you

---

T. Agrikola and S. Maier—Supported by funding from the topic Engineering Secure Systems of the Helmholtz Association (HGF) and by KASTEL Security Research Labs.
G. Couteau—Supported by ANR SCENE.

E. Kiltz and V. Vaikuntanathan (Eds.): TCC 2022, LNCS 13748, pp. 685–714, 2022.
https://doi.org/10.1007/978-3-031-22365-5_24

face dishonorable discharge or even jail. In fact, whistleblowers often take an immense personal risk, and face sentences ranging from exile [BEA14] to incarceration [Phi18] or worse. Whistleblowing is crucial for democracy to educate the public of misdeeds and to call those in power to account. Therefore, it is desirable to cryptographically protect the identity of the whistleblower to allow a low-risk disclosure of wrongdoing.

The importance of this question is well recognized in cryptography and security. It has been the subject of several influential works (e.g. DC-nets [Cha88], Riposte [CBM15] or Blinder [APY20]). Concrete solutions include the use of secure messaging apps [CGCDGS20, Ber16], mix-nets [Cha03], onion routing systems such as the Tor network [DMS04], or solutions built on top of DC-nets and secure computation techniques [CBM15, APY20] (see also [ECZB21, NSSD21]).

Yet, all current approaches to anonymous whistleblowing rely on trusted parties (or non-colluding partially trusted servers), which either receive privately the communication, or implement a distributed protocol to emulate an anonymous network. Therefore, however ingenious and scalable some of these solutions are, whistleblowers must ultimately trust that they will interact with parties or servers which will (at least for some of them) remain honest and refuse to collude throughout the transmission.

In this work, we ask whether this is fundamentally inherent, or whether anonymous whistleblowing is possible in theory without having to privately communicate with trusted parties. In its most basic form, the question we ask is the following:

*Is it possible for a whistleblower (who is communicating solely through authenticated point-to-point or broadcast channels)
to publicly reveal some message m while remaining anonymous
without assuming trusted participating parties?*

We do allow a Common Reference String (CRS) for technical reasons, and stress that while it is technically also a trust assumption, it is much weaker; instead of trusting a set of parties *every time* to follow the exact protocol and to not cheat in any way, we *only* require a CRS to be set up *once*: A CRS that was successfully sampled just once can be used for all future interactions.

The above is, of course, trivially impossible if the whistleblower is the only communicating party. However, it becomes meaningful in a multiparty setting, where a number of parties (unaware of the intent of the whistleblower) exchange innocent-looking messages (think of a group of people having a conversation, or using some public messaging service like Twitter or Facebook to broadcast information). In this context, the question translates as follows: could the whistleblower somehow disguise its communication as an innocent-looking conversation with the other parties, such that the message m can be publicly extracted (by anyone) from the *entire conversation*, yet the identity of which party was indeed the whistleblower remains hidden? To our knowledge, this intriguing question has never been studied in the past. Our main contributions are threefold:

1. **A definitional framework.** We put forth a formal definition for a cryptographic primitive that realizes the above goal, which we call an *Anonymous Transfer*. We study the relation between variants of the notion.
2. **Impossibility results.** We prove a strong impossibility result: we show that Anonymous Transfer with overwhelming correctness and anonymity cannot be realized in any polynomial number of rounds, by exhibiting a general attack against any such protocol. This non-trivial result demonstrates that anonymously communicating over authenticated channels is impossible with standard cryptographic security levels, even assuming strong cryptographic primitives such as ideal obfuscation.
3. **Feasibility result.** We complement our impossibility result by an intriguing *feasibility* result: we show that *fine-grained* Anonymous Transfer is possible assuming ideal obfuscation. The term fine-grained refers to cryptographic constructions which are only guaranteed secure against adversaries whose computational power is a fixed polynomial in the computing power of the honest parties (in our case, the gap is quadratic). Our instantiation is a plausible heuristic candidate when instantiating the ideal obfuscation by candidate indistinguishability obfuscation schemes.

Both our negative and positive results are highly non-trivial and require a very careful analysis. We view our work as addressing a fundamental question regarding the a priori possibility of secure whistleblowing without interacting with trusted parties, through the lens of anonymous communications over authenticated channels. Nevertheless, our study is of a purely theoretical nature, and does not have immediate practical relevance. In particular, we do not compare our results to the practical real-world methods which whistleblowers can employ.

Anonymous Transfer and Plausible Deniability. The fundamental goal of an Anonymous Transfer protocol is to achieve plausible deniability: the whistleblower should be able to hide its identity among a group of parties, such that even if it is strongly *suspected* that he is the whistleblower, this cannot be *proven* – any party could equally be the whistleblower. Importantly, the involved parties are never required to be aware that a message is being transmitted: their consent or collaboration is not needed for the Anonymous Transfer to take place, and they themselves have no advantage in finding out who the whistleblower was.

1.1 Undetectable Secure Computation

Secure Multiparty Computation (MPC) allows a set of parties to jointly evaluate a function on their inputs without revealing these inputs. In certain scenarios, however, the standard guarantees of MPC become insufficient: the mere fact that a party is participating to a certain protocol already reveals information about that party. Consider for example the following scenario: your company was hacked, but you do not have enough forensic data to trace the attackers. If several companies fell victim to the same hacker, a joint effort may yield enough information to successfully trace the hacker. However, the very fact that you are *initiating* such a protocol reveals that your company has been hacked.

The notion of Covert Multiparty Computation (CMPC) [vHL05,CGOS07] was introduced to cope with situations in which even revealing one's participation to the protocol is undesirable. CMPC allows a set of parties to securely compute a protocol among n parties with the following two guarantees: (1) If all parties are actually willing to participate in the protocol (and are not simply having innocent conversations), and if the output of the protocol was *acceptable* (which is specified by some function g of the joint input), then everyone learns the result of the protocol. (2) Otherwise (if at least *one* party was not participating, or the output was not acceptable), no one learns anything about who were the participating parties (or even whether there was any).

CMPC is a powerful strengthening of secure computation. However, it still has two important downsides: a single non-participating party is sufficient to make the entire protocol fail (no one gets any output), and when all parties participate, they all learn that they participated (hence, no one can deny anymore having participated in the protocol). One of the primary motivations behind the study of Anonymous Transfer, which we put forth in this work, is to open the avenue to the study of a significantly more powerful form of secure computation that provides the strongest deniability guarantees one can hope for: a secure computation protocol where, even after the successful protocol execution, no one learns *who the participants were*. Specifically, we consider the following setting: N individuals are interacting. Among them, k players are willing to jointly compute a public function f on their private inputs $(x_1, \ldots, x_k)$, while the remaining $(N - k)$ are not interested in taking part to the protocol (nor are even aware of the fact that a secure computation might be taking place). At the end of the protocol, the k participants should all receive the output, but no party should be able to find out which of the parties were actually participating. We call this strengthening of secure computation *undetectable secure computation*.

Since undetectable secure computation is stronger than Anonymous Transfer (which it implies), our impossibility results for Anonymous Transfer also translate to impossibility results for undetectable secure computation[1]. Furthermore, building on our positive result, we show how to construct *anonymous oblivious transfer* (in the fine-grained security setting), a core building block for constructing undetectable secure computation for more general functionalities.

1.2   Defining Anonymous Transfer

An Anonymous Transfer (AT) protocol describes the interaction between a sender, a receiver and a non-participant. We assume all parties to interact in the synchronous model over a public broadcast channel, i.e., in each round each

---

[1] This follows directly from the fact that given undetectable secure computation for *any* function f, we can directly construct AT by computing a function that lets two potential senders insert either a bitstring for transfer or $\bot$ and outputs one of them (*i.e.* the one input that is not $\bot$) to the receiver.

participant broadcasts a message which only depends on messages from previous rounds. The non-participant is not aware that a protocol takes place, and is only having an innocent conversation (we call them the "dummy player", or the "dummy friend"). We follow [vHL05, CGOS07] and model non-participating parties as parties that only broadcast uniform randomness in each round, since any ordinary communication pattern can be viewed as an embedding of the uniform distribution due to standard techniques [vHL05, HLv02, vH04]. The sender aims to transmit a message to the receiver in a way that does not leak its identity (the notion easily generalizes to more non-participating parties). We say that an AT protocol is ε-correct if the probability that the receiver successfully receives the message is at least ε. Further, we say that an AT protocol is δ-anonymous if no adversary is able to determine the identity of the sender (given the transcript and the receiver's random tape) with advantage more than $(1 - \delta)/2$ over guessing. These are the core properties which shape an AT protocol. If the protocol allows the receiver to remain silent throughout the protocol execution, sending a message corresponds to publicly revealing the message (i.e., whistleblowing). Eventually, we call *fine-grained* AT an Anonymous Transfer, where anonymity is only required to hold against adversaries from a restricted complexity class (typically, adversaries whose runtime is bounded by a fixed polynomial in the runtime of the honest parties).

1.3 Impossibility Result

Our first main result shows that AT is impossible in a strong sense.

Theorem 1 (Impossibility of AT, informal). *There is no Anonymous Transfer protocol with overwhelming correctness and anonymity, with any polynomial number of rounds and any number $n \geq 1$ of non-participating parties, even for transmitting a single bit message.*

Our proof proceeds in several steps. First, we show that any Anonymous Transfer for transmitting a single bit with n non-participants, with overwhelming correctness and anonymity implies (in a black-box way) a *silent-receiver* Anonymous Transfer (where the receiver never speaks) for transmitting κ bits (where κ is some security parameter) with a single non-participating party. This reduction uses a relatively standard indistinguishability-based hybrid argument.

Then, the core of the proof rules out the existence of κ-bit silent-receiver 1-non-participant Anonymous Transfer with overwhelming correctness and anonymity. The key intuition is the following: let P_0, P_1 be the two parties interacting with the receiver, where P_b is the sender, and P_{1-b} is the non-participant. Let Π_{AT}^{κ} be the protocol which these two parties execute, and assume that it satisfies ε-correctness and δ-anonymity. Suppose that during their interaction, the parties produce a transcript π. We consider an adversary $\mathcal{A}$ which replaces the last message of P_0 by a random value, before running the receiver algorithm to reconstruct the transmitted message. Then if $b = 1$, the adversary just replaced the last (random) message of the non-participating party by another random message, and the transcript is still a perfectly valid transcript for Π_{AT}^κ, hence the reconstruction algorithm must still output the right string Σ with overall probability ε. On the other hand, if $b = 0$, then the transcript is a valid transcript for a "round-reduced" version of Π_{AT}^κ, where the last round is replaced by two random messages. By the δ-anonymity, $\mathcal{A}$ should not distinguish between the two situations with advantage better than $(1 - \delta)/2$. This implies that the correctness of the round-reduced protocol cannot be much lower than ε, hence that we constructed a δ-anonymous $(c - 1)$-round protocol with non-trivial correctness guarantees. Then, $\mathcal{A}$ keeps repeating this procedure until we reach a 0-round protocol, which cannot possibly have any non-trivial correctness guarantee.

While the above provides an intuition of the approach, the real strategy is much more involved. In particular, using $\mathcal{A}$ to distinguish between a random transcript of Π_{AT}^κ and a random round-reduced transcript does not suffice to rule out arbitrary polynomial-round protocols (more precisely, it would only rule out logarithmic-round protocols, since the correctness guarantees would decrease roughly by a factor two at each step of round reduction). Instead, $\mathcal{A}$ will replace independently the last message of each party by a random value, getting two distinct transcripts (π_0, π_1). Then, $\mathcal{A}$ attempts to distinguish whether π_0 is a transcript of Π_{AT}^κ and π_1 is a round-reduced transcript, or the other way around. While this is the proper way to attack the protocol, the analysis is more involved, since now π_0, π_1 are not independent random variables anymore, as they share a common prefix (the transcript of the first $c-1$ rounds). Nevertheless, a more careful analysis shows that this dependency cannot significantly lower the distinguishing probability of $\mathcal{A}$.

In the full version [ACM21] we further prove that no AT protocol for $N > 3$ parties with overwhelming correctness and anonymity can exist unless a $N = 3$-party protocol exists with overwhelming correctness and anonymity—which cannot exist. It suffices to prove that any N-party Silent Receiver AT for $N > 3$ implies a (N)-party "normal" (*i.e.* with an actively participating receiver) AT, without losing the overwhelming correctness and anonymity in the process.

Intuitively, the receiver does not broadcast any messages in the N-party protocol; all communication comes from the $(N-1)$ potential senders. We construct an $(N-1)$-party protocol by letting the receiver play one non-participant, with the one difference being that this party is known not to be the sender (since it is the receiver); the sender can only be one of the $(N - 2)$ other parties. While the correctness remains unaffected, the anonymity decreases due to the fact that *guessing* with one party less yields better results; yet we show that the anonymity still remains overwhelming in the security parameter. We then transform any N-party AT to an N-party SR-AT as described above and that to a $(N-1)$-party AT, until we have a 3-party AT that, assuming that the N-party AT has overwhelming anonymity and correctness, maintains these properties.

On a high level, this process lets the actual participants *simulate* non-participants behavior in their head; one-by-one their random tape is moved to the CRS until only three parties are left: a sender, a receiver, and a non-participant.

Our negative result applies to a weak model. In particular, non-participants are modeled to be semi-honest. Hence, our negative result does not leave much room for positive results.

1.4 A Candidate Fine-Grained Anonymous Transfer

To circumvent the above impossibility result, we need to give up asymptotic security and resort to the fine-grained setting: We only require anonymity against adversaries which require polynomially— quadratically, in our case— more resources than an honest protocol execution.

That is, our second main result shows that (perhaps surprisingly) non-trivial AT is indeed possible in a weaker setting:

Theorem 2 (Feasibility of AT, informal). *Let $N = 3$ be the number of individuals. Assuming ideal obfuscation, for any anonymity δ, there is a c-round Anonymous Transfer protocol Π^1_{AT} (for ℓ bit messages) that has overwhelming correctness, where anonymity δ holds against any adversary $\mathcal{A}$ with runtime $\ll c^2$.*

That is, for our second main contribution we propose a protocol which— assuming ideal obfuscation—allows to reduce the problem of de-anonymizing the sender to a distribution testing problem. More precisely, we show that determining the real sender in a c-round protocol given only a transcript of the AT protocol is as hard as differentiating between two *Bernoulli* oracles, where one returns 1 with probability p and the other returns 1 with $p + 1/(2c)$. For this distribution testing problem, strong lower bounds on the number of required samples and thus the adversarial runtime are known.

The protocol proceeds in rounds, where each honest message from the sender gradually increases the probability that the transmitted bit is correctly received. The sender first encrypts a verification key that is to-be-used be the obfuscated circuit, and in each successive round the sender encrypts the bit and a signature on both messages from the previous round to limit the ability of the adversary to manipulate the transcript when attacking anonymity. The non-participant only broadcasts random bits in each round. The Common Reference String contains an obfuscated program with hard-coded keys for the pseudorandom encryption scheme. The circuit checks the validity of the signatures of each round. Each consecutive valid round increases the confidence in the transmitted bit. Finally, the circuit outputs random bit according to the confidence gained. If all rounds are valid, the correct bit will be output with probability 1, if no round is valid, the correct bit will be output with probability 0.5.

While the high level intuition of the protocol is relatively clear, its exact instantiation is particularly delicate – any small variant in the design seems to open the avenue to devastating attacks. Furthermore, its analysis relies on long and complex hybrid arguments that progressively reduce the advantage of the adversary to contradictions with respect to known distribution testing bounds with a limited number of samples. The majority of our proof can be found in our full version [ACM21].

Our proof can be split in two parts. The first part exploits properties of the encryption schemes, the signature scheme, and ideal obfuscation to prove indistinguishability (against even PPT adversaries) between the actual protocol and a hybrid, where all reported messages are truly random and independent from the sender and the transferred bit, and the obfuscated circuit only *counts* how many input messages are identical to those from the challenge transcript.

This game still contains information on the sending party as it treats those messages differently. To remove this dependency, we resort to *distribution testing* and view the obfuscated circuit as a *Bernoulli oracle* which follows one of two (known) distributions, and where the goal is to determine which one.

1.5 Discussions and Implications

In this section, we further discuss some implications and relations of our results to the literature.

'Philosophical Implications:' Between Obfustopia and Impossibilitopia. There is a small remaining gap between our negative and positive results: the possibility of building anonymous transfer secure against arbitrary polytime adversaries, but with non-negligible (e.g. inverse polynomial) anonymity error remains open. Closing this gap would have an intriguing philosophical consequence: stretching the terminology of Impagliazzo on the "worlds" of cryptography, it would establish the existence of a cryptographic primitive that plausibly exists in obfustopia (the world where indistinguishability obfuscation is possible) in the fine-grained setting, yet does not exist ("reside in impossibilitopia") with standard hardness gaps. Interestingly, there are several known examples where fine-grained constructions of a "higher world" primitive reside in a lower world; for example, (exponentially secure) one-way functions (a Minicrypt assumption) imply fine-grained public-key encryption (a Cryptomania assumption). Our work seems to provide a new example of this behavior, at the highest possible level of the hierarchy, showing that impossible primitives might end up existing if we weaken their security to the fine-grained setting.

Relation to the Anonymous Whistleblowing Literature. We clarify how our (positive and negative) results relate to the literature on anonymous broadcast and secure whistleblowing. In general, a whistleblower willing to reveal something anonymously has two alternative choices: (1) the whistleblower has access to an anonymous communication channel, for example by putting their message (say, encrypted with the receiver public key) on some public website that somehow cannot be traced to them. However, access to an anonymous channel is typically a 'physical' assumption, and one which is *very* hard to guarantee. This issue is developed in great detail in the literature: see for example the discussion in Spectrum [NSSD21] about how metadata have been used by federal judges to trace and prosecute people who leaked data through secure messaging apps, or the discussion in Riposte [CBM15] and Express [ECZB21] on how traffic analysis can be used to trace whistleblowers on the Tor network or the SecureDrop service. Hence, most of the literature focuses on scenario (2): the individuals interact over a communication network, and we do not assume that this network guarantees anonymity in itself. In this case, what we want is to *emulate* this anonymity, by developing a strategy to help the whistleblower transmit a message anonymously to the receiver.

The literature on this subject is incredibly vast, but this emulated anonymity is *always* achieved using the same template in all solutions we are aware of (including Spectrum, Blinder, Riposte, Express, Talek, P3, Pung, Riffle, Atom, XRD, Vuvuzela, Alpenhorn, Stadium (or any other Mixnet-based solution), Karaoke, Dissent, Verdict, and many more): when the whistleblower wants to anonymously transmit a message, either to everyone (anonymous broadcast) or to a target receiver, other users generate 'honest' traffic in which communications can be hidden. To do so, the users interact with a set of *non-colluding* servers (sometimes two servers, sometimes more, some with honest majority, some without). This is never even discussed or remarked: it is taken as an obvious fact that this is *the* structure of an anonymous broadcast (or messaging) protocol. And indeed, the need to generate honest traffic feels clear – if the whistleblower is the sole sender, observing traffic directly leaks their identity. That the use of non-colluding servers was never challenged or even discussed probably means that it also *feels* clear – but this assumption is precisely what we challenge in our work: we do assume that some users generate honest traffic, but we ask whether the assumption of non-colluding participating servers is avoidable. Of course, any scientific treatment of a broad question ('are non-colluding helpful participants required for anonymous broadcast?') is bound to move from the broad question to a formal model, in which (feasibility or impossibility) results can be achieved. Nevertheless, we believe that our impossibility result demonstrates that the use of non-colluding servers in all previous works was indeed unavoidable, at least insofar as their aim was to achieve anonymity against arbitrary polynomial-time adversaries.

Non-participating Parties Versus Malicious Parties. Our choice of formalism, with the notion of anonymous transfer, allows to study whether the assumption of honest, non-colluding, participating servers can be replaced by a considerably weaker trust assumption: that of non-participating parties, not trying to take part to the protocol in any way (and not even required to be *aware* of the execution of the protocol) beyond generating traffic. As we show, this weaker assumption does not suffice against arbitrary polynomial-time adversaries, but possibly suffices against bounded polynomial-time adversaries (where the bound is sub-quadratic). As a natural next step, one could push the question even further and ask: what if some of the non-participating parties were in fact planted by a malicious adversary, and now play *maliciously* during the protocol? It seems plausible, that our general strategy can be extended to deal with malicious non-participants. However, we expect the analysis to require different techniques than the ones we used. We leave a formal proof of this to future work.

1.6 Further Results and Open Questions

In the full version [ACM21] we extend our fine-grained AT such that it transfers ℓ-bit messages directly, which achieves the same level of security as the single-bit AT but requires twice as many rounds. We instantiate asymptotically secure AT in the designated-sender setting with non-trivial (but not useful) parameters for ε and δ. We define an extension of AT called *Strong AT* which we require for Undetectable Computation. We define undetectable versions of both OT (called *Undetectable Oblivious Transfer (UOT)*) and MPC (called Undetectable Multiparty Computation (UMPC)), where k parties hide the respective execution in a group of N individuals. We provide an instantiation of UOT based on strong AT and use that to instantiate UMPC for $k = 3$.

Our work leaves open two exciting questions:

(1) *Can our impossibility result for asymptotically secure AT with overwhelming correctness and anonymity be extended to rule out asymptotically secure AT with anonymity $1 - 1/\mathsf{poly}(\kappa)$?*

(2) *Is it possible to instantiate AT in the fine-grained setting from "Obfustopia" standard assumptions achieving similar parameter as our instantiation?*

Given that both our open questions can be answered affirmatively, this would separate the realm of asymptotic security from the realm of fine-grained security.

2 Preliminaries

2.1 Notations

For any party P we denote by T_{P} the random tape of P.

For events (A, B), $\bar{A}$ denotes the complementary even of A, $\Pr[A \mid B]$ denotes the probability of A happening conditioned on B happening. For values (a, b), the notation $[\![a = b]\!]$ denote the bit value of the corresponding predicate. We let κ be a security parameter; we write $\mathsf{negl}(\kappa)$ to denote any function negligible in κ and $\mathsf{owhl}(\kappa)$ to denote a function overwhelming in κ (that is, $1 - \mathsf{owhl}(\kappa) = \mathsf{negl}(\kappa)$). For any probability distribution D, we denote by R(D) the support of D, and by $x \xleftarrow{\$} \mathsf{D}$ we denote that x is uniformly sampled from D.

For probability distributions p and q we write $p^{\otimes t}$ as the distribution arising from taking t sample from p, and $p \circ q$ as the distribution obtained by sampling one time from p and one time from q. We write $\|p\|_1$ to denote the L_1 norm of p.

For two bitstrings $A, B \in \{0, 1\}^m$, $A \oplus B$ denotes the bitwise XOR of A and B. We write by $[n]$ for $n \in \mathbb{N}$ the set of numbers $\{1, \dots, n\}$.

2.2   Distribution Testing

In this section, we introduce preliminaries for probability testing. We start by describing the *Total Variational Distance* between two distributions.

Definition 1 (Total Variational Distance). *Let p and q be two probability distributions over the countable set of possible outcomes Ω. The* total variational distance *between p and q is defined as:*

$$d_{TV}(p,q) := \frac{1}{2} \sum_{\omega \in \Omega} |p(\omega) - q(\omega)| = \frac{1}{2}\|p - q\|_1 \tag{1}$$

An important property of the total variational distance is that it acts *sublinear* when taking many samples. When taking t samples from a Bernoulli distribution the corresponding distribution can be described by taking a single sample from a t-bit *Binomial* distribution. The sub-additivity then bounds the total variational distance of the corresponding binomial distribution:

Lemma 1 (Total variational distance of a t-fold probability distribution, folklore). *Let p and q be two Bernoulli distributions with total variational distance $d_{TV}(p,q)$. Then it holds for the binomial distributions $p^{\otimes t}$ and $q^{\otimes t}$ that result from sampling t times from the respective distributions:*

$$d_{TV}(p^{\otimes t}, q^{\otimes t}) \leq t \cdot d_{TV}(p,q) \tag{2}$$

Thus we can bound the distinguishing advantage of *any* distinguisher who has taken t samples form the same oracle using the total variational distance of the respective distributions directly.

A similar rule also holds for two *different* distributions, where the distinguisher has to distinguish whether two samples originate from $p \otimes r$ or from $q \otimes s$ for known values of p, q, r and s. In this case the rule states that:

Lemma 2 (Sub-Additivity of the Total Variational Distance for Product Distributions, folklore). *Let p and q be a probability distribution over $\{0,1\}^m$ with total variational distance $d_{TV}(p,q)$. Let r and s be two Bernoulli distributions with total variational distance $d_{TV}(r,s)$. Then it holds for the distribution derived from sampling from each distribution once and concatenating the outputs (which yields a sample from $\{0,1\}^{m+1}$ originating either from $p \circ r$ or $q \circ s$) that*

$$d_{TV}(p \circ r, q \circ s) \leq d_{TV}(p,q) + d_{TV}(r,s)$$

The following lemma limits the distinguishing advantage of any distinguisher that tries to distinguish two distributions p and q based on a single sample.

Lemma 3 (Distinguishing distributions based on the Total Variational Distance). *Let p and q be two distributions with total variational distance $d_{TV}(p,q)$. If $d_{TV}(p,q) < \frac{1}{3}$, then no algorithm can exist that distinguishes p and q with probability $\geq \frac{2}{3}$ based on a single sample.*

Using Lemmas 1 and 3 we can provide lower bounds on the sampling complexity of distinguishing two distributions p and q with advantage $\alpha/2$.

Corollary 1 (Distinguishing two Bernoulli-Distributions with t samples). *Any distinguisher $\mathcal{D}$ that distinguishes between p and q with probability $\geq \frac{1}{2} + \frac{\alpha}{2}$ requires $t \in \Omega\left(\frac{\alpha}{d_{\mathsf{TV}}(p,q)}\right)$ samples.*

We refer the reader to [ACM21] for proofs of Lemma 3 and Corollary 1.

3   Anonymous Transfer

We consider the following situation: some secret agent P_b is willing to transfer a message Σ to a receiver R, while hiding his identity b among two individuals. We call Anonymous Transfer (AT) an interactive protocol that achieves this goal.

3.1   Network Model and Non-participating Parties

The goal of an anonymous transfer protocol is to hide the transferred message among innocent conversations by individuals, which are not taking part in the protocol. By a well-established folklore result in steganography, this task can be reduced to the simpler task of hiding the transferred message among *uniformly random beacons*, broadcast by the other individuals: the uniform channel, where all protocol messages look uniformly random, can be compiled into any other ordinary communication pattern [vHL05, HLv02, vH04]. Therefore, as in previous works (see von Ahn, Hopper, and Langford [vHL05] and Chandran, Goyal, Ostrovsky, and Sahai [CGOS07]), we consider a set of k parties who interact with each other via broadcast channels and focus, without loss of generality, on protocols for the uniform channel. Consequently, we will model the non-participating parties as "dummy parties" that only broadcast uniformly random messages of a fixed length at each round.

3.2   The Model

Let $b \in \{1, \cdots, N-1\}$ denote the index of the sender and let $\Sigma \in \{0,1\}^{\ell}$ be the message that P_b wants to transfer to the receiver. We consider an interactive protocol in the Common Reference String (CRS) model between N players $(\mathsf{P}_1, \cdots, \mathsf{P}_{N-1}, \mathsf{R})$, where R and P_b participate in the protocol, and P_i for $i \neq b$ are non-participating but present players that only broadcast random strings. The receiver R gets the CRS as input and the sender P_b gets the CRS and the message Σ as input. For any player P, let T_{P} denote the random tape from which P draws his random coins. The players interact through authenticated broadcast channels in the synchronous model: the protocol proceeds in rounds, and each player broadcasts a message at each round. We denote by $\langle \mathsf{R}, \mathsf{P}_1, \cdots, \mathsf{P}_{N-1} \rangle (crs, b, \Sigma)$ the distribution of the possible transcripts of the protocol in this setting (*i.e.*, the sequence of all messages broadcasted by the players during an execution of the protocol), where the probabilities are taken over the random coins T_{P} of the players $\mathsf{P} \in \{\mathsf{R}, \mathsf{P}_1, \cdots, \mathsf{P}_{N-1}\}$ and the random choice of the CRS crs.

Definition 2 ($(\varepsilon, \delta, c, \ell)$-Anonymous Transfer). *An N-party $(\varepsilon, \delta, c, \ell)$-Anonymous Transfer (AT) for $\varepsilon, \delta \in \mathbb{R}_{[0,1]}$ and $N, c, \ell \in \mathbb{N}$ (all possibly functions in κ) is a tuple containing three PPT algorithms (Setup, Transfer, Reconstruct). The number of rounds in the Transfer protocol is given as c and the bitlength ℓ defines the length of the transferred message Σ. The algorithms are defined as follows:*

Setup(1^κ) *takes as input the security parameter 1^κ in unary encoding and outputs a Common Reference String crs.*

Transfer(*crs*, *b*, Σ) *defines a c-round protocol[2] that takes as input the Common Reference String crs, an index $b \leq N - 1$ specifying the sender, and the message $\Sigma \in \{0,1\}^\ell$ from the sender and outputs a transcript π. The non-sender sends independent uniformly distributed noise in each round. All protocol messages sent by the receiver, the sender and the non-participating parties at each round are bitstrings of length $m = m(\kappa)$, where m is implicitly specified by the Transfer protocol.*

Reconstruct(*crs*, π, T_R) *is a local algorithm executed by the receiver that takes as input the CRS crs, the protocol transcript π and the receiver's random tape T_R and outputs a message Σ'.*

The algorithms additionally satisfy the ε-correctness and the δ-anonymity properties defined in Definitions 3 and 4.

Definition 3 (ε-Correctness). *For any sufficiently large security parameter κ, for any number of individuals $N \in \text{poly}(\kappa)$, for any participant $b \in [N - 1]$, for any message length $\ell \in \text{poly}(\kappa)$, for any message $\Sigma \in \{0,1\}^\ell$, and for any CRS crs $\leftarrow$ Setup(1^κ), an Anonymous Transfer protocol Π_{AT}^ℓ between players $(P_1, \ldots, P_{N-1}, R)$ is ε-correct if the following holds:*

$$\Pr\left[\begin{array}{l} \pi \xleftarrow{\$} \text{Transfer}_{\langle R, P_1, \ldots, P_{N-1}\rangle}(crs, b, \Sigma) \\ \Sigma' \leftarrow \text{Reconstruct}(crs, \pi, T_R) \end{array} : \Sigma = \Sigma'\right] > \varepsilon \qquad (3)$$

Note that ε can take on any value between 0 and 1. The naive algorithm that lets the receiver sample a uniformly random ℓ-bit string has $\varepsilon = 1/2^\ell$.

Definition 4 (δ-Anonymity). *For any PPT algorithm $A = (A_0, A_1)$, for all sufficiently large security parameters κ, for any number of individuals $N \in \text{poly}(\kappa)$, and for any message length $\ell \in \text{poly}(\kappa)$, an Anonymous Transfer protocol Π_{AT}^ℓ between players $(P_1, \ldots, P_{N-1}, R)$ is δ-anonymous if it holds that*

$$\left| \Pr_{b \xleftarrow{\$} [N-1]}\left[Exp_{\Pi_{AT}^\ell, A, b}^{anon}(\kappa) = b \right] - \frac{1}{N-1} \right| \leq (1 - \delta) \cdot \frac{N-2}{N-1} \qquad (4)$$

where $Exp_{\Pi_{AT}^\ell, A, b}^{anon}(\kappa)$ is defined in Fig. 1.

---

[2] A c-round protocol corresponds to a synchronous model, where each message is broadcasted and the messages in each round only depend on messages from previous rounds, see [ACM21] for a formal definition.

$$\frac{\mathrm{Exp}^{\mathrm{anon}}_{\Pi^{\ell}_{AT},\mathsf{A},N,b}(\kappa)}{}$$

$crs \xleftarrow{\$} \mathsf{Setup}(1^{\kappa})$

$T_{\mathsf{R}} \xleftarrow{\$} \{0,1\}^{\mathsf{poly}(\kappa)}$

$(\Sigma, st) \leftarrow \mathsf{A}_0(crs, T_{\mathsf{R}})$

$\pi \xleftarrow{\$} \mathsf{Transfer}_{(\mathsf{R},\mathsf{P}_1,\ldots,\mathsf{P}_{N-1})}(crs, b, \Sigma; T_{\mathsf{R}}, \cdot, \cdot)$

return $\mathsf{A}_1(\pi, T_{\mathsf{R}}, st)$

Fig. 1. Definition of the game $\mathrm{Exp}^{\mathrm{anon}}_{\Pi^{\ell}_{AT},\mathsf{A},b}(\kappa)$.

The value δ can take any value between 0 and 1. The higher δ the stronger the provided anonymity guarantees. If a protocol is $\delta = 1$-anonymous, the advantage over guessing at random equals 0, and if a protocol is $\delta = 0$-anonymous, the advantage over guessing at random equals 1. The right-hand-side of Definition 4 contains a scaling factor of $(N-1)/(N-2)$. This is due to the fact that even under perfect anonymity ($\delta = 1$), the receiver can still *guess* the sender. Knowing that one of the N parties—namely itself—is *not* the sender, there are $(N-1)$ potential senders, of which $(N-2)$ are just dummy friends. Thus, the probability of *guessing wrong* is given by the aforementioned factor.

Note that we require anonymity to hold, in particular, against the receiver. Therefore, the adversary in the anonymity game may know the receiver's random tape T_{R} from the beginning.

The guessing algorithm is split between A_0 who is given the CRS and the random tape T_{R} the receiver is going to use during the protocol, and outputs the target message Σ that should be transferred and a state st. In the second phase, the algorithm A_1 which is given the inputs π and the state.

Unless stated otherwise, we consider the case $N = 3$, i.e., one non-participant.

3.3   Fine-Grained Anonymous Transfer

Fine-grained cryptographic primitives are only secure against adversaries with an a-priori bounded runtime which is greater than the runtime of the honest algorithms, [Mer78, DVV16]. We use the notion of [DVV16]. In the following, $\mathfrak{C}_1$ and $\mathfrak{C}_2$ are function classes.

Definition 5 ($\mathfrak{C}_1$-fine-grained $(\varepsilon, \delta, c, \ell)$-Anonymous Transfer against $\mathfrak{C}_2$). *The tuple* (Setup, Transfer, Reconstruct) *(as defined in Definition 2) is a $\mathfrak{C}_1$-fine-grained $(\varepsilon, \delta, c, \ell)$-Anonymous Transfer for $\varepsilon, \delta \in \mathbb{R}_{[0,1]}$ and $c, \ell \in \mathbb{N}$ against $\mathfrak{C}_2$ if the following two conditions hold:*

Efficiency. *The algorithms* (Setup, Transfer, Reconstruct) *are in $\mathfrak{C}_1$.*

Security. *Anonymity (Definition 4) is only required to hold against adversaries in $\mathfrak{C}_2$.*

The definition of correctness remains as in Definition 3.

Example 1 (Merkle-Puzzles). Merkle-Puzzles [Mer78] are a fine-grained protocol to exchange a shared key from symmetric encryptions where successful encryptions can be efficiently distinguished from false ones. The sender S creates n_{mer} many ciphertexts, each under a different (relatively short) key, containing a unique identifier and a symmetric key. The receiver R then randomly picks one of the ciphertexts and runs a brute-force attack (which we assume to cost m_{mer} many steps) to recover the key and to send the identifier back to the sender.

Here $\mathfrak{C}_1 := \mathcal{O}(n_{\mathrm{mer}} + m_{\mathrm{mer}})$ as the sender has to create n_{mer} puzzles and the receiver must use m_{mer} steps to break one of them, and $\mathfrak{C}_2 := \mathcal{O}(n_{\mathrm{mer}} \cdot m_{\mathrm{mer}})$ as an adversary has to break at worst all the n_{mer} ciphertexts to recover the key.

3.4   Trivial Anonymous Transfers

For simplicity, we focus on 3-party anonymous transfer in the following discussions, with two players P_0, P_1 and a receiver R.

Remark 1 (Perfect correctness.). A perfectly correct (*i.e.* $\varepsilon = 1$) protocol is impossible. Given a player P_b with input Σ, there is always a probability that the non-participating player P_{1-b} behaves exactly as a participating player with input $\Sigma' \neq \Sigma$, in which case R cannot obtain the correct output for sure.

Therefore, the best one can hope for is a correctness statistically close to 1. In the following, we demonstrate ATs with trivial parameters.

Example 2 (Trivial single-bit AT). Consider the following trivial single-round AT to transfer a single bit σ: P_b broadcasts his input σ (and P_{1-b} broadcasts a random bit). Upon receiving (σ_0, σ_1) from P_0 and P_1, if $\sigma_0 = \sigma_1$, R outputs σ_0; otherwise, R outputs a uniformly random bit. As P_{1-b} broadcasts a random bit, it holds that $\sigma_0 = \sigma_1$ with probability $1/2$, in which case R obtains the correct output $\sigma = \sigma_b$; else, R obtains the correct output with probability $1/2$. Overall, R obtains the correct output with probability $3/4$. The protocol is $1/2$-anonymous since the adversary knows the message to be transmitted and can hence determine the sender whenever the transmitted bits are distinct and guess with probability $1/2$ otherwise. Hence, the above protocol is a $(3/4, 1/2, 1, 1)$-AT.

Example 3 (Trivial ℓ-bit AT). One can also construct a trivial ℓ-bit AT. To transmit a message $\Sigma \in \{0,1\}^\ell$: P_b simply sends Σ repeated κ times. Clearly, (not only) R finds out both Σ and b with overwhelming probability. Hence, the above protocol is a $(1 - \mathsf{negl}(\kappa), \mathsf{negl}(\kappa), \kappa \cdot \ell, \ell)$-AT.

In this work, we study whether ATs with non-trivial parameters can exist.

3.5   Reductions Among AT Protocols

In this section, we show that several simplified variants of anonymous transfer are equivalent to the original definition.

AT Implies Silent-Receiver AT. We say that an anonymous transfer has *silent receiver* if the receiver never sends messages during the Transfer protocol, and Reconstruct is a deterministic function of the CRS and the transcript π. Any AT directly implies a silent-receiver AT with the same parameters for correctness and anonymity, but at the cost of secrecy: Any (non-)participant is able to reconstruct the message given only the transcript of broadcasted messages, not just the receiving party of the protocol, which might be undesirable for practical applications. Let Π_{AT}^{ℓ} be a $(\varepsilon, \delta, c, \ell)$-Anonymous Transfer. Define the silent-receiver AT Π_{SR}^{ℓ} as follows:

Π_{SR}^{ℓ}.Setup(1^{κ}) runs $crs \leftarrow \Pi_{AT}^{\ell}$.Setup($1^{\kappa}$) and samples a uniform random tape T_{R} for R. It outputs (crs, T_{R}).

Π_{SR}^{ℓ}.Transfer(crs, b, Σ) proceeds exactly as Π_{AT}^{ℓ}.Transfer(crs, b, Σ), except that the receiver R does not broadcast any message. At each round $\chi = 1$ to $\chi = c$, the sender P_{b} locally appends the χ-th receiver message x_{χ} in Π_{AT}^{ℓ}.Transfer($crs, b, \Sigma; T_{R}, \cdot, \cdot$) to the current transcript $\pi[\chi]$ (note that x_{χ} can be computed deterministically from $\pi[\chi]$ and T_{R}), and compute its next message as in Π_{AT}^{ℓ}.Transfer using the transcript $\pi[\chi] \| x_{\chi}$.

Π_{SR}^{ℓ}.Reconstruct(crs, π, T_{R}) is defined exactly as Π_{AT}^{ℓ}.Reconstruct(crs, π, T_{R}), except that it first expands the transcript π by recomputing (deterministically) the messages of R in Π_{AT}^{ℓ}.Transfer($crs, b, \Sigma; T_{R}, \cdot, \cdot$) and appending them to π at each round.

The notion of silent receiver AT captures the notion of an anonymous transfer whose aim is to *publicly reveal* a message (*i.e.*, whistleblowing) rather than sending it to a single receiver. An other way to look at it is to consider that the silent receiver transformation can be seen as *passive to active security transformation* for the receiver: If there is a secure AT protocol against a *passive* receiver, then there is a secure silent receiver AT against an *active* receiver, simply because the receiver has no option to cheat as no messages are sent.

Lemma 4. Π_{SR}^{ℓ} *is an* $(\varepsilon, \delta, c, \ell)$-*Anonymous Transfer.*

Proof (sketch). Correctness and number of rounds follow directly from the description of Π_{SR}^{ℓ}, which simply mimics Π_{AT}^{ℓ}, except that the random tape of the receiver is made public, and its messages are computed on the fly locally by the sender and during the reconstruction. Anonymity follows also immediately by observing that T_{R} is given to the adversary in the anonymity game, hence making it public cannot harm anonymity.   □

Since the converse direction is straightforward, AT and silent receiver AT are therefore equivalent.

Single-bit AT Implies Many-bit AT. In this section, we analyze how a single-bit AT can be generically transformed into an AT which allows to transmit bitstrings. We construct an ℓ-bit AT by executing the single-bit AT ℓ times (sequentially) to transmit the message bit-by-bit. Let Π_{AT}^1 be a $\mathfrak{C}_1$-fine-grained-$(\varepsilon, \delta, c, 1)$-Anonymous Transfer against $\mathfrak{C}_2$. Further, let Π_{AT}^ℓ be the protocol which uses ℓ instances of Π_{AT}^1 to transmit ℓ-bit messages bit-by-bit.

We analyze Π_{AT}^ℓ using the fine-grained definition. The results directly apply using asymptotic security.

Lemma 5. *Let Π_{AT}^1 be a $\mathfrak{C}_1$-fine-grained $(\varepsilon, \delta, c, 1)$-Anonymous Transfer against $\mathfrak{C}_2$. Then, the protocol Π_{AT}^ℓ is a $\mathfrak{C}_1' := \mathfrak{C}_1 \cdot \ell$-fine-grained $(\varepsilon', \delta', c \cdot \ell, \ell)$-AT against $\mathfrak{C}_2' := \mathfrak{C}_2 - \ell \cdot \mathfrak{C}_1$, where $\varepsilon' = \varepsilon^\ell$ and $\delta' = (\delta\ell - \ell - \delta + 2)$.*[3]

Proof. For $\Sigma \in \{0,1\}^\ell$, we have $\varepsilon' = \Pr_{crs,\pi,\Sigma'}[\Sigma = \Sigma'] = \varepsilon^\ell$.

For the purpose of avoiding notational overhead, we prove anonymity for $N = 3$ parties, i.e., for one non-participant. The general case follows by generalizing notation. Let A be an adversary against the anonymity of Π_{AT}^ℓ. We define a sequence of hybrid games $H_1, \ldots, H_\ell$ between $\mathrm{Exp}_{\Pi_{AT}^\ell, A, 0}^{\mathrm{anon}}(\kappa)$ and $\mathrm{Exp}_{\Pi_{AT}^\ell, A, 1}^{\mathrm{anon}}(\kappa)$ in Fig. 2. H_1 is identical to $\mathrm{Exp}_{\Pi_{AT}^\ell, A, 1}^{\mathrm{anon}}(\kappa)$ and H_ℓ is identical to $\mathrm{Exp}_{\Pi_{AT}^\ell, A, 0}^{\mathrm{anon}}(\kappa)$.

We construct an adversary B against the anonymity of Π_{AT}^1 in Fig. 2. If B plays $\mathrm{Exp}_{\Pi_{AT}^1, B, 0}^{\mathrm{anon}}(\kappa)$, then B simulates H_{i+1} for A. Otherwise, if B plays $\mathrm{Exp}_{\Pi_{AT}^1, B, 1}^{\mathrm{anon}}(\kappa)$, then B simulates H_i for A.

H_i	$B_0(crs, T_R)$	$B_1(\pi, st)$
for $j \in [\ell]$ **do**	$i \leftarrow \{1, \ldots, \ell-1\}$	parse $st =: (\Sigma, i, st_A)$
$\quad crs_j \leftarrow \mathsf{Setup}(1^\kappa)$	**for** $j \in [\ell] \setminus \{i\}$ **do**	**for** $j \in \{1, \ldots, i-1\}$ **do**
$crs' := (crs_1, \ldots, crs_\ell)$	$\quad crs_j \leftarrow \mathsf{Setup}(1^\kappa)$	$\quad \pi_j \leftarrow \mathsf{Transfer}(crs, 0, \Sigma[j]; T_{R,j}, \cdot, \cdot)$
$T_R' := (T_{R,1}, \ldots, T_{R,\ell}) \leftarrow (\{0,1\}^{\mathrm{poly}(\kappa)})^\ell$	$\quad T_{R,j} \leftarrow \{0,1\}^{\mathrm{poly}(\kappa)}$	**for** $j \in \{i+1, \ldots, \ell\}$ **do**
$(\Sigma, st_A) \leftarrow A_0(crs', T_R')$	$crs_i := crs, T_{R,i} := T_R$	$\quad \pi_j \leftarrow \mathsf{Transfer}(crs, 1, \Sigma[j]; T_{R,j}, \cdot, \cdot)$
for $j \in \{1, \ldots, i-1\}$ **do**	$crs' := (crs_1, \ldots, crs_\ell)$	$\pi_i := \pi$
$\quad \pi_j \leftarrow \mathsf{Transfer}(crs, 0, \Sigma[j]; T_{R,i}, \cdot, \cdot)$	$T_R' := (T_{R,1}, \ldots, T_{R,\ell})$	**return** $A_1((\pi_1, \ldots, \pi_\ell), st_A)$
for $j \in \{i, \ldots, \ell\}$ **do**	$(\Sigma, st_A) \leftarrow A_0(crs', T_R')$	
$\quad \pi_j \leftarrow \mathsf{Transfer}(crs, 1, \Sigma[j]; T_{R,i}, \cdot, \cdot)$	$st := (\Sigma, i, st_A)$	
return $A_1((\pi_1, \ldots, \pi_\ell), st_A)$	**return** $(\Sigma[i], st)$	

Fig. 2. Hybrid games for the expansion of single-bit AT to multi-bit AT (left) and the adversary (middle and right).

Provided that B is in $\mathfrak{C}_2$, we have

$$1 - \delta \geq |\Pr[\mathrm{Exp}_{\Pi_{AT}^\ell, B, 0}^{\mathrm{anon}}(\kappa)] - \Pr[\mathrm{Exp}_{\Pi_{AT}^\ell, B, 1}^{\mathrm{anon}}(\kappa)]|$$

$$= \frac{1}{\ell - 1}(\Pr[H_\ell] - \Pr[H_1]) = \frac{1}{\ell - 1}\left(\Pr[\mathrm{Exp}_{\Pi_{AT}^\ell, A, 0}^{\mathrm{anon}}(\kappa)] - \Pr[\mathrm{Exp}_{\Pi_{AT}^\ell, A, 1}^{\mathrm{anon}}(\kappa)]\right)$$

We have that $\mathfrak{T}(B) = \mathfrak{T}(A) + (\ell - 1) \cdot \mathfrak{C}_1 = \mathfrak{T}(A) + \ell \cdot \mathfrak{C}_1$. Hence, given that $\mathfrak{T}(A) = \mathfrak{T}(B) - \mathfrak{C}_1 \in \mathfrak{C}_2 - \ell \cdot \mathfrak{C}_1$, the anonymity advantage of A is $(1 - \delta)(\ell - 1)/2$, yielding anonymity of $\delta' = \delta\ell - \ell - \delta + 2$. $\qquad\square$

---

[3] We slightly abuse notation but we believe the meaning to be clear.

4   Impossibility of Anonymous Transfer

In this section, we prove that no anonymous transfer protocol, with an arbitrary polynomial number of rounds, can simultaneously enjoy overwhelming correctness ($\varepsilon = 1 - \mathsf{negl}(\kappa)$) and overwhelming anonymity ($\delta = 1 - \mathsf{negl}(\kappa)$), even for transmitting single bit messages.

Theorem 3 (Impossibility of AT). *Let $\mu : \mathbb{N} \mapsto \mathbb{R}$ be any negligible function and p be any polynomial. There is no $(1 - \mu(\kappa), 1 - \mu(\kappa), p(\kappa), 1)$-Anonymous Transfer, for any number of parties.*

Theorem 3 will follow as a corollary from a more general result bounding the relation between ε and δ in any c-round protocol. Throughout this section we will focus on $N = 3$, that is, the case with one dummy player. This is without loss of generality as we will show in the full version [ACM21] that any N-party anonymous transfer with $N > 3$ implies in particular a 3-party anonymous transfer, for which we will show here that it can not exist.

4.1   The Attacker

From now on, we focus on building a generic attack against 3-party *silent-receiver* anonymous transfer for κ-bit messages. The theorem will follow from the reductions from 1-bit anonymous transfer to multibit silent-receiver anonymous transfer described in Sect. 3.5.

Let Π_{AT}^{κ} be a silent-receiver $(\varepsilon, \delta, c, \kappa)$-Anonymous Transfer. Let $m = m(\kappa)$ be the bitlength of the message from the non-participating party. Let Rand denote the following procedure: on input a transcript π of Π_{AT}^{κ}, $\mathsf{Rand}(\pi)$ truncates π to $c - 1$ rounds of the AT protocol, and replaces the messages of the last round by two uniformly random length-m bitstrings[4]. It outputs the new rerandomized transcript π'. For every $\Sigma \in \{0,1\}^{\kappa}$ and $b \in \{0,1\}$, we let $\mathcal{D}_{b,\Sigma}, \mathcal{D}'_{b,\Sigma}, \mathcal{DR}$ denote the following distribution:

$$\mathcal{D}_{b,\Sigma} = \{\Sigma' : crs \leftarrow \mathsf{Setup}(1^{\kappa}), \pi \leftarrow \mathsf{Transfer}(b, \Sigma), \Sigma' \leftarrow \mathsf{Reconstruct}(crs, \pi)\}$$

$$\mathcal{D}'_{b,\Sigma} = \qquad\qquad\qquad\qquad\qquad \mathcal{DR} =$$

$$\left\{ \Sigma' : \begin{array}{l} crs \leftarrow \mathsf{Setup}(1^{\kappa}), \\ \pi' \leftarrow \mathsf{Rand}(\mathsf{Transfer}(b, \Sigma)), \\ \Sigma' \leftarrow \mathsf{Reconstruct}(crs, \pi') \end{array} \right\}, \quad \left\{ \Sigma' : \begin{array}{l} crs \leftarrow \mathsf{Setup}(1^{\kappa}), \\ \pi' \xleftarrow{\$} (\{0,1\}^m \times \{0,1\}^m)^c, \\ \Sigma' \leftarrow \mathsf{Reconstruct}(crs, \pi') \end{array} \right\}$$

Fix an arbitrary polynomial t. We define an attacker $\mathcal{A}^t = (\mathsf{A}_0^t, \mathsf{A}_1^t)$ against the anonymity of Π_{AT}^{κ}, parameterized by the polynomial t, on Fig. 3. In the following, we will not use $\mathcal{A}^t$ directly to attack the full c-round protocol: rather, we will use $\mathcal{A}^t$ as a distinguisher between the c-round protocol Π_{AT}^{κ}, and the

---

[4] Since the protocol is silent-receiver, there is no message from the receiver; furthermore, assuming that the sender message is m-bit is without loss of generality, since otherwise the protocol is trivially not anonymous.

Attacker $\mathcal{A}^t = (\mathsf{A}_0^t, \mathsf{A}_1^t)$

Algorithm A_0^t

- On input crs, sample $(\Sigma_1, \cdots, \Sigma_t) \xleftarrow{\$} \mathcal{DR}$, and set Σ^t to be an arbitrary element of $\{0,1\}^\kappa \setminus \{\Sigma_1, \cdots, \Sigma_t\}$ (which exists since $t \ll 2^\kappa$).
- Output $(\Sigma^t, st = (crs, \Sigma^t))$.

Algorithm A_1^t

- On input Σ, st, parse st as (crs, Σ^t) and π as a triple $(\pi[c-1], x_0, x_1)$, where $\pi[c-1]$ is a transcript for the first $c-1$ rounds (if $c = 1$, it is the empty string), and $(x_0, x_1) \in \{0,1\}^m \times \{0,1\}^m$ are the last-round messages from P_0 and P_1 respectively.
- Pick $(x_0', x_1') \xleftarrow{\$} \{0,1\}^m \times \{0,1\}^m$, set $\pi_0 \leftarrow (\pi[c-1], x_0, x_1')$, $\pi_1 \leftarrow (\pi[c-1], x_0', x_1)$, and compute $\Sigma_{b^*}' \leftarrow \mathsf{Reconstruct}(crs, \pi_{b^*})$ for $b^* = 0, 1$.
- Return the following:
  - if $\Sigma_0' = \Sigma^t$, output 0;
  - else, if $\Sigma_1' = \Sigma^t$, output 1;
  - else, return a uniformly random bit $b' \xleftarrow{\$} \{0,1\}$.

Fig. 3. Attacker $\mathcal{A}^t$ against the δ-anonymity of the silent-receiver κ-bit AT protocol Π_{AT}^κ, parameterized by a polynomial $t = t(\kappa)$.

$(c-1)$-round protocol obtained by running Π_{AT}^κ for $(c-1)$ rounds, and replacing the messages of the last round by uniformly random m-bit strings. From there, the proof of impossibility will proceed by induction; we refer the reader to the introduction for a high-level intuition of our proof.

Base Case: Advantage of $\mathcal{A}^t$ when $c = 1$. We start the induction by bounding the advantage of $\mathcal{A}^t$ in the anonymity game when Π_{AT}^κ is non-interactive (i.e., Transfer consists of a single message from each of $\mathsf{P}_0, \mathsf{P}_1$ to the receiver). Before proceeding, we make two key observations:

(1) When $c = 1$, $\mathcal{D}_{b,\Sigma}' = \mathcal{DR}$ for any (b, Σ). In particular, this means that $\mathcal{D}_{b,\Sigma}'$ is independent of (b, Σ).

(2) When $c = 1$ and $b = 0$, the distribution of the values (Σ_0', Σ_1') constructed by A_1^t given as input a random transcript $\pi \leftarrow \mathsf{Transfer}(0, \Sigma^t)$ is exactly the distribution $\mathcal{D}_{0,\Sigma^t} \times \mathcal{DR}$. This is because x_0 is a random message from the sender with input $b = 0$ and value Σ^t, and (x_1, x_0', x_1') are three uniformly random elements of $\{0,1\}^m$, hence (x_0, x_1') is exactly a random transcript of Π_{AT}^κ with (b, Σ^t), while (x_0', x_1) is just a pair of random messages. Similarly, if $b = 1$, the distribution of the values (Σ_0', Σ_1') constructed by A_1^t given as input a random transcript $\pi \leftarrow \mathsf{Transfer}(1, \Sigma^t)$ is exactly the distribution $\mathcal{DR} \times \mathcal{D}_{1,\Sigma^t}$.

Both observations follow directly from the definitions of $\mathcal{D}_{b,\Sigma}, \mathcal{D}_{b,\Sigma}', \mathcal{DR}$ and of A_1^t. Building on the above observations, we show that for an appropriate choice of t, the advantage of $\mathcal{A}^t$ in the anonymity game can be made arbitrarily close to $(\varepsilon - 1)/2$:

Claim. For any polynomial n, there is a polynomial t such that

$$\left| \Pr_{b \xleftarrow{\$} \{0,1\}} \left[\mathsf{Exp}^{\mathsf{anon}}_{\Pi^\kappa_{AT}, \mathcal{A}^t, b}(\kappa) = b \right] - 1/2 \right| \geq \frac{\varepsilon}{2} - \frac{1}{n}, \tag{5}$$

which implies that any silent-receiver $(\varepsilon, \delta, 1, \kappa)$-Anonymous Transfer must satisfy $\delta \leq 1 - \varepsilon + 2/n$ for any polynomial n; equivalently, $\delta \leq 1 - \varepsilon + \mathsf{negl}(\kappa)$. In particular, this means that if the AT has overwhelming correctness ($\varepsilon = 1 - \mathsf{negl}(\kappa)$), then δ must be negligible.

The proof for this claim can be found in the full version [ACM21].

4.2   Putting the Pieces Together

With the above analysis, we showed that for any silent-receiver $(\varepsilon, \delta, c, \kappa)$-Anonymous Transfer, it must necessarily hold that $(1 - \delta)/2 \geq \varepsilon/2c - \mathsf{negl}(\kappa)$. Since any $(\varepsilon, \delta, c, \kappa)$-Anonymous Transfer implies a silent-receiver $(\varepsilon, \delta, c, \kappa)$-Anonymous Transfer (with the exact same parameters, see Sect. 3.5), we obtain:

Corollary 2. *Any $(\varepsilon, \delta, c, \kappa)$-Anonymous Transfer must satisfy*

$$\frac{1 - \delta}{2} \geq \frac{\varepsilon}{2c} - \mathsf{negl}(\kappa).$$

In particular, this implies that there exists no κ-bit AT with overwhelming correctness and anonymity, for any polynomial number of rounds.

Furthermore, as shown in Sect. 3.5, any *single-bit* c-round AT with correctness $\varepsilon = 1 - \mathsf{negl}(\kappa)$ and anonymity $\delta = 1 - \mathsf{negl}(\kappa)$ implies a κ-bit AT with correctness $\varepsilon' = \varepsilon^\kappa = (1 - \mathsf{negl}(\kappa))^\kappa = 1 - \mathsf{negl}(\kappa)$, and anonymity $\delta' = (\delta - 1) \cdot \kappa - \delta + 2 = 1 - \mathsf{negl}(\kappa)$. Combining this reduction with Corollary 2 concludes the proof of Theorem 3.

4.3   Extensions and Limitations

The adversary in our impossibility result makes a black-box use of an arbitrary 3-party silent receiver multibit anonymous transfer; the reduction to N-party single-bit anonymous transfer is black-box as well. In particular, this means that our impossibility result relativizes: it remains true relative to any oracle, where access to the oracle is granted to all participants and all algorithms (including the adversary).

In the next section, we will provide a heuristic construction of *fine-grained* anonymous transfer. The aim of this construction is to complement our impossibility result, and to draw an interesting and surprising picture: anonymous transfer appears to be impossible to realize with the standard superpolynomial cryptographic hardness gaps, but becomes feasible if one settles for a small polynomial hardness gap. Our fine-grained construction is described and formally proven secure using an ideal obfuscation scheme; instantiating the scheme with candidate indistinguishability obfuscation schemes gives a plausible heuristic construction (the same way that instantiating the random oracle model with standard hash functions gives plausible heuristic constructions of various cryptographic primitives, when the construction is not pathological). Because our impossibility result relativizes, in contrast, standard anonymous transfer remains provably impossible relative to an ideal obfuscation oracle (while fine-grained anonymous transfer, as we will see, provably exist relative to such an oracle).

Impossibility of Fine-Grained Multibit AT with Overwhelming Correctness and Anonymity. In the multibit setting, where the sender wants to transmit $\omega(\log \kappa)$ bits to the receiver, our result further demonstrates that there exists no *fine-grained* anonymous transfer with overwhelming correctness and anonymity $1 - \mathsf{negl}(\kappa)$, even with an *arbitrary small polynomial gap* between the runtime of the honest parties and that of the adversary. Indeed, let $r = \mathcal{O}(c \cdot m)$ be a lower bound on the runtime of the honest parties (r is the total number of bits sent by the sender, hence it is a clear lower bound on its running time), and consider an adversary $\mathcal{A}^t$ with $t = \kappa \cdot c^g$, where $g > 0$ is an arbitrarily small constant. Then by construction, the runtime of $\mathcal{A}^t$ is $\mathcal{O}(\kappa \cdot r \cdot c^g) \leq \mathcal{O}(\kappa \cdot r^{1+g})$ (as it is dominated by the cost of sampling t random transcripts for A_0^t). Then this adversary satisfies

$$\frac{1-\delta}{2} \geq \left| \Pr[\mathsf{Exp}_{\Pi_{AT}^\kappa, \mathcal{A}^t, b}^{\mathsf{anon}}(\kappa) = b] - \frac{1}{2} \right| \geq \frac{1}{c} \cdot \left(\frac{\varepsilon}{2} - \frac{1}{c^g} \right), \qquad (6)$$

which implies that δ and ε cannot be simultaneously equal to $1 - \mathsf{negl}(\kappa)$ (since $1/(2c) - 1/c^{1+g}$ cannot be a negligible function for any polynomial c and any constant $g > 0$).

Limitations of the Impossibility Result. Even putting aside the heuristic security guarantee of our fine-grained construction (or its security in an idealized model), a gap remains between our impossibility result and our construction: our impossibility result does not rule out the possibility of having, say, a $(1 - \mathsf{negl}(\kappa), 1 - 1/c, c, \kappa)$-Anonymous Transfer – that is, an anonymous transfer with overwhelming correctness, and vanishing anonymity error $1/c$ in c rounds, with standard (superpolynomial) security. In contrast, our heuristic construction only achieves overwhelming correctness and anonymity arbitrarily close to $1/c$ against *fine-grained* adversaries. It is an interesting open question to close this gap. We conjecture that the true answer is negative:

Conjecture 1. There exists no $(1 - \mathsf{negl}(\kappa), 1 - 1/c, c, \kappa)$-Anonymous Transfer.

What follows assumes that the reader is familiar with standard philosophical considerations on the worlds of Impagliazzo. Proving the above conjecture would have a very interesting (theoretical) consequence: it would demonstrate

---

Fine-grained Protocol Π^1_{AT}.

Upon activation, R draws $OTP \overset{\$}{\leftarrow} \{0,1\}$ and computes $(k_R, vk_R) \leftarrow \text{SIG.KeyGen}(1^\kappa)$.
Then R sets $x_R^{(0)} \leftarrow \text{PKE.Enc}(pk_P, (OTP, vk_R))$ and broadcasts $x_R^{(0)}$.
On input (b, σ), P_b computes a signature key pair $(vk_b, k_b) \leftarrow \text{SIG.KeyGen}(1^\kappa)$ and a
symmetric key $sk_b \leftarrow \text{SKE.KeyGen}(1^\kappa)$.
Then, P_b computes a signature $\mu \leftarrow \text{SIG.Sig}(k_b, x_R^{(0)})$ and broadcasts $x_b^{(0)} \leftarrow$
$\text{PKE.Enc}(pk_P, (sk_b, vk_b)) \| \text{SKE.Enc}(sk_b, (\sigma, \mu))$.
Upon activation , P_{1-b} sets uniformly random $x_{1-b}^{(0)}$.
For each round χ **from** 1 **to** c :
  P_b computes $\mu \leftarrow \text{SIG.Sig}(k_b, (x_0^{(\chi-1)}, x_1^{(\chi-1)}))$ and sets $x_b^{(\chi)} \leftarrow$
  $\text{SKE.Enc}(sk_b, (\sigma, \mu))$.
  P_{1-b}: Broadcast $x_{1-b}^{(\chi)} \overset{\$}{\leftarrow} \{0,1\}^m$.
R: computes $\mu \leftarrow \text{SIG.Sig}(k_R, (x_R^{(0)}, (x_0^{(0)}, x_1^{(0)}), \dots, (x_0^{(c)}, x_1^{(c)})))$, compute $\sigma' :=$
$P_{AT}(x_R^{(0)}, (x_0^{(0)}, x_1^{(0)}), \dots, (x_0^{(c)}, x_1^{(c)}), \mu)$ and output $OTP \oplus \sigma'$.

Fig. 4. The protocol Π^1_{AT} for fine-grained Anonymous Transfer. The circuit P_{AT} is defined in Fig. 5.

the existence of a natural cryptographic primitive that plausibly exists within the realm of fine-grained cryptography, yet is impossible with standard hardness gap. It is known that fine-grained constructions sometimes allow building "high-end" cryptographic primitives in "low-end" cryptographic realms. For example, Merkle puzzles, which can be instantiated under exponentially strong one-way functions [BGI08], provide a fine-grained key exchange; borrowing Impagliazzo's terminology [Imp95], this places "fine-grained Cryptomania" inside (a strong form of) Minicrypt. Proving the conjecture would induce a comparable result, but at the highest level of the hierarchy: it would, in a sense, place fine-grained Impossibilitopia (a world of cryptographic primitives so powerful that they simply cannot exist) inside Obfustopia.

5 Fine-Grained AT from Ideal Obfuscation

In this section, we focus on realizing Anonymous Transfer with fine-grained security according to Definition 5. More precisely, we construct a c-round protocol which achieves anonymity δ, where the honest parties have runtime in $\mathfrak{C}_1 := \mathcal{O}(c)$ against adversaries in $\mathfrak{C}_2 := o(c^2(1 - \delta))$, where $c = c(\kappa)$ is a polynomial in κ. For the sake of simplicity we introduce the protocol with $N = 3$, implying a single dummy friend. However, expanding this protocol to an arbitrary $N \in \mathbb{N}$ is straightforward as the behavior of all dummy friends is the same by definition and instead of two messages, each round now contains $N - 1$ messages.

We exploit the limited runtime of the adversary and provide a protocol in Fig. 4 with c rounds. In each new round (or with each valid sender message) the probability that the correct bit is eventually returned increases, *i.e.*, each valid round increases the receiver's confidence in the message. Each round lets the

$$P_{AT}[\mathsf{pk}_P, c]\left(x_R^{(0)}, \left(x_0^{(0)}, x_1^{(0)}\right), \left(x_0^{(1)}, x_1^{(1)}\right) \ldots, \left(x_0^{(c)}, x_1^{(c)}\right)\right)$$

$(OTP, \mathsf{vk}_R) := \mathsf{PKE.Dec}^*(\mathsf{sk}_P, x_R^{(0)}),$

$(\mathsf{sk}_0, \mathsf{vk}_0) := \mathsf{PKE.Dec}^*(\mathsf{sk}_P, x_0^{(0)}[1:m]), \quad (\sigma_0, \mu_0) := \mathsf{SKE.Dec}^*(\mathsf{sk}_0, x_0^{(0)}[m+1:2m]),$

$(\mathsf{sk}_1, \mathsf{vk}_1) := \mathsf{PKE.Dec}^*(\mathsf{sk}_P, x_1^{(0)}[1:m]), \quad (\sigma_1, \mu_1) := \mathsf{SKE.Dec}^*(\mathsf{sk}_1, x_1^{(0)}[m+1:2m]),$

if $\neg\mathsf{SIG.Vfy}(\mathsf{vk}_R, (x_R^{(0)}, (x_0^{(0)}, x_1^{(0)}), \ldots, (x_0^{(c)}, x_1^{(c)})))$ **then**:

    return $\mathsf{CointossS}_{(0.5)}^{(\pi)}(0,1)$

$\chi_0 := [\![\mathsf{SIG.Vfy}(\mu_0, \mathsf{vk}_0, x_R^{(0)})]\!] \cdot (c+1), \quad \chi_1 := [\![\mathsf{SIG.Vfy}(\mu_1, \mathsf{vk}_1, x_R^{(1)})]\!] \cdot (c+1),$

foreach $\chi \in \{1, \ldots, c\}$ **do**:

    foreach $b \in \{b' | b' \in \{0,1\}, \chi_b = (c+1)\}$ **do**: // Take on the role of each potential sender.

        $X_b := \mathsf{SKE.Dec}^*(\mathsf{sk}_b, x_b^{(\chi)}), \qquad \sigma_b' := X_b[0], \qquad \mu_b := X_b[1:|X_b|]$

        if $\neg\mathsf{SIG.Vfy}(\mu_b, \mathsf{vk}_b, \pi[\chi - 1]) \lor \sigma_b \neq \sigma_b'$ **then**:

            $\chi_b := \chi$ // Remember first bad round.

$b' := \mathbf{argmax}_b(\chi_b)$

return $OTP \oplus \mathsf{CointossS}_{(1/2 \cdot (1 + \chi_{b'}/c))}^{(\pi)}(\sigma_{b'}, (1 - \sigma_{b'}))$

Fig. 5. Obfuscated program P_{AT} for the fine-grained setting with c rounds.

sender compute a signature μ using a sEUF-CMA secure signature scheme[5] for the transcript of the previous round. The transferred bit σ and the signature μ are then sent. The verification key for the signature scheme is transmitted by the sender in the first round. In order to make the sent messages look random the message is not sent directly. Instead, the sender encrypts the message using an IND\$-CCA secure encryption scheme (See footnote 5), [Rog04]. Since not every length m bitstring is a valid ciphertext, we use a special function Dec^* instead of the normal function Dec, which is defined as follows: If Dec on input ct returns $\perp$ then Dec^* returns $F(ct)$, otherwise Dec^* returns $\mathsf{Dec}(ct)$. Hence, every possible input allows an interpretation as a cleartext. We use those for both the asymmetric and symmetric schemes.

In order to make the output unusable for any other party, the receiver draws a One-Time-Pad as first message which eventually masks the final output, and a verification key of a signature scheme. The latter is used to ensure that the receiver *approves* with the transcript; after the two potential senders provided all messages, the receiver *signs* the entire transcript and only if this signature verifies the entire previous transcript, the circuit continues. The first message of the receiver is broadcast, while the signature is only used locally.

The receiver obtains its output by computing the signature as described above and feeding the final transcript alongside the signature into an obfuscated circuit which is supplied in a common reference string. The circuit is obfuscated using ideal obfuscation(See footnote 5). It hides a PRF key and a secret decryption key sk_P for the IND\$-CCA secure PKE. The corresponding encryption key pk_P is also part of the CRS and, hence, known to all parties. This

---

[5] See [ACM21] for a definition of sEUF-CMA, IND\$-CCA and ideal obfuscation.

encryption scheme is used by the sender and the receiver to hide their respective *first* message. This uniquely determines the symmetric key used to decrypt the remaining messages of each potential sender. The message also contains a verification key used to sign the previous messages in future rounds, the bit that the sender wants to transfer, and the initial signature on the receivers message. The remaining rounds of the sender are encrypted using a *symmetric* scheme, namely the IND\$-CCA secure SKE scheme, using the key transferred to the circuit in the first round.

The circuit is shown in Fig. 5. It starts by extracting the verification keys and symmetric encryption keys (one per potential sender) alongside the bits that the respective party wants to transfer and the initial signatures on the first receiver messages from the respective initial messages of both parties, and the receivers OTP and verification key from the receiver message. Then the circuit starts by verifying the signature of the receiver on the entire transcript, and if that does not match, returns a uniformly random bit[6]. Otherwise, if the receiver's signature is valid, the circuit searches for the first *faulty* round of each potential sender. That is, the first round of each potential sender where the signature on the previous round fails to verify or where the encoded bit differs from the bit extracted from the initial message. The party who sent the most consecutive valid rounds is selected as the sending party. The circuit outputs the bit transmitted by that party with probability depending on the ratio between valid sender messages and the total number of rounds, which ranges between $1/2$ (*i.e.*, a uniformly random bit) if no round was valid for any party and 1 (*i.e.*, deterministically returning the correct bit) if all rounds were correct. However, as stated before, the circuit does not output that bit directly, but instead *masks* it using the OTP extracted from the receiver's first message. This ensures secrecy[7], as other parties only get a masked output which information-theoretically hides the actual bit.

5.1   Security Analysis

Theorem 4 (Correctness). *If the protocol from Fig. 4 is instantiated with an Ideally Obfuscated version of the circuit from Fig. 5 the protocol is ε-correct with* $\varepsilon = (1 - \mathsf{negl}(\kappa))$.

At the end of an honest protocol execution, the maximum round in which a valid signature has been provided equals the number of rounds c. With overwhelming probability, the sending parties' input is the only one that contains c many valid rounds. Hence, the correctly masked bit is returned. Since the mask

---

[6] This is denoted in the figure by the $\mathsf{CointossS}^{(\pi)}_{(p)}(\sigma, \overline{\sigma})$ function, which returns σ, *i.e.* the first argument, with probability p, and $\overline{\sigma}$, *i.e.* the second argument, with the complementary probability $(1 - p)$, where the randomness for p is extracted from the argument provided by π.

[7] Secrecy is an additional property we require for *Strong AT*. Secrecy means that no third party can extract the transferred bit from the transcript (see the full version [ACM21] for the formal definition). This property will be relevant for applications that use AT as a building block.

is input by the receiver and later applied to the output, the receiver obtains the correctly masked bit. We refer the reader to [ACM21] for a formal proof.

Theorem 5 (Anonymity). *Let* PKE *be an IND\$-CCA secure asymmetric encryption scheme, let* SKE *be a tightly secure multi-challenge IND\$-CCA secure symmetric encryption scheme, let* SIG *be an sEUF-CMA secure signature scheme, let* $\mathbb{O}$ *be an ideal obfuscator, let* F *be a secure PRF, and let* κ *be the security parameter. Then the c-round protocol* Π_{AT}^1 *for* $N = 3$ *satisfies* δ-*anonymity for all adversaries in* $\mathfrak{C}_2 := o(c^2(1 - \delta))$.

Proof (sketch). An outline of the entire proof is given in the full version [ACM21]. On a high level, the proof is structured into two parts. In the first part, we successively modify the anonymity game $\mathrm{Exp}_{\Pi_{AT}^1, \mathcal{A}, b}^{\mathrm{anon}}(\kappa)$ and the obfuscated circuit oracle P_{AT} to remove as much computationally hidden information about b as possible. More precisely, we exploit the non-malleability of PKE and sEUF-CMA security of Sig to unnoticeably alter the oracle to determine the number of valid rounds by counting how many rounds of the input transcript are identical to the challenge transcript provided by $\mathrm{Exp}_{\Pi_{AT}^1, \mathcal{A}, b}^{\mathrm{anon}}(\kappa)$. The first round which is not entirely identical to the challenge transcript (i.e. either the sender message or the non-sender message differ) increases the valid rounds count only if the input sender message is identical to the challenge sender message or if the input sender message decrypts to the same content as the challenge sender message. The following round will be counted as invalid since the signature verification will fail. After this step, the decryption keys of SKE and PKE are not necessary for chosen-ciphertext simulation anymore. Then, we first replace the sender messages which are encrypted using SKE and then the first round sender message which is encrypted using PKE with uniform randomness exploiting the IND\$-CCA security of both encryption schemes.

The only information about the bit b that is left in the present game is due to the oracle which counts valid sender messages by comparing the input sender message with the challenge sender message. Clearly, the final modification of the game must be the removal of this dependency on b. However, this removal will noticeably alter the output distribution of the oracle. Hence, an adversary with arbitrary polynomial runtime will be able to distinguish this hop with constant probability [CDVV14]. However, if we can limit the runtime of the adversary to be sub-quadratic in the runtime of the honest protocol execution, we are able to apply results from distribution testing to achieve a good bound for this distinguishing advantage. We will elaborate on this final game hop in more detail below and will refer to the second last game as $\mathrm{Game}_7^\sigma(\kappa)$ and to the last game (i.e. the game, where no information about b remains) as $\mathrm{Game}_8^\sigma(\kappa)$. For detailed descriptions of all game hops, we refer the reader to the full version [ACM21].

For the sake of reducing complexity of the problem of proving indistinguishability between $\mathrm{Game}_7^\sigma(\kappa)$ and $\mathrm{Game}_8^\sigma(\kappa)$ we describe an intermediate game in Fig. 6 that is provably as hard to solve as distinguishing the two games.

The key idea is the following: The challenger $\mathcal{C}$ creates c oracles where the probability to return 1 is equally distributed between $1/2$ and 1 in c steps.

Oracle O_i^β	$\mathcal{C}(c)$	$\mathcal{A}(1^\kappa)$
if $\beta = 0$ then	$\beta \xleftarrow{\$} \{0,1\}$	for $j = 1 \ldots t$ do
$\quad p_i := \dfrac{i+c-1}{2c}$	return $\mathcal{A}^{O_1^\beta,\ldots,O_c^\beta}(1^\kappa)$	$\quad i_j \leftarrow Computations$
else		$\quad x_j \xleftarrow{\$} O_{i_j}$
$\quad p_i := \dfrac{i+c}{2c}$		$\beta' \leftarrow Computations((i_j, x_j)_{j=1}^t)$
return $\mathrm{Ber}(p_i)$		return β'

Fig. 6. Game to distinguish whether Bernoulli oracles follow a given distribution p or $q = p - 1/2c$.

On $\beta = 0$ the oracles are distributed equally between $[1/2, 1)$. On $\beta = 1$ the oracles are distributed equally between $(1/2, 1]$. That is, on $\beta = 0$ the oracle χ returns 1 with probability $(c + \chi - 1)/(2c)$ and on $\beta = 1$ it returns 1 with probability $(c + \chi)/(2c)$.

We now stress that this game is *as hard* as the problem of distinguishing the two games from $\mathrm{Game}_7^\sigma(\kappa)$ and $\mathrm{Game}_8^\sigma(\kappa)$: $\qquad\qquad\qquad$ □

Lemma 6. *Let $\mathcal{D}$ be a distinguisher distinguishing $\mathrm{Game}_7^\sigma(\kappa)$ and $\mathrm{Game}_8^\sigma(\kappa)$ with advantage α over guessing. Let t be the number of queries that $\mathcal{D}$ sends to the obfuscated circuit. There is a reduction adversary $\mathcal{A}$ that uses $\mathcal{D}$ which has advantage α over guessing in winning Fig. 6.*

Proof (sketch). To create the transcript, the adversary samples bits σ and b for the transferred bit and the sending party, respectively. It then creates π_C by sampling $2c$ random bitstrings of length m and assigns them to the two parties.

The oracle is simulated by letting $\mathcal{A}$ follow the behavor of the oracle: If the input is the challenge transcript, output the bit directly; if it is a completely new transcript, follow the honest protocol; otherwise, if the first-round messages of both parties are the same, $\mathcal{A}$ searches χ^* as the first round where the input differs from the challenge transcript.

If the message from the sending party in round $(\chi^* + 1)$ is from the challenge trascript, then $\mathcal{A}$ sends χ^* to the oracle O_{χ^*} provided by the challenger and obtains a bit σ^*, and returns $\sigma^* \oplus \bar{\sigma}$ (*i.e.* the return gets flipped if it should go towards 0). Otherwise, $\mathcal{A}$ returns σ with probability proportional to χ^*/c.

It follows (we elaborate on that in [ACM21]) that the result can be translated; if the distinguisher guesses $\mathrm{Game}_8^\sigma(\kappa)$ then $\mathcal{A}$ reports that the χ-th oracle returns 1 with probability $(\chi + c - 1)/2c$. Otherwise, if the distinguisher guesses $\mathrm{Game}_7^\sigma(\kappa)$, $\mathcal{A}$ reports that the probabilities were given as $(\chi + c)/2$.

The simulation is such that the challenge oracles are only queried if the input transcript contains the first χ^* messages of the challenge transcript from both parties and then in round $\chi^* + 1$ only the message of the sending party. In that case, the difference induced by the game hop states that in $\mathrm{Game}_7^\sigma(\kappa)$ the sending parties message still increases the probability by $1/(2c)$, whereas in $\mathrm{Game}_8^\sigma(\kappa)$ the message is ignored; which correspond exactly to the case we have

to distinguish in our challenge. The full proof can be found in the full version
[ACM21]. □

Proving indistinguishability has thus been reduced to showing that no fine-
grained adversary can win the game from Fig. 6 with non-negligible advantage.
The interface of an adversary in this game is given as a set of $2c$ oracles. Each
oracle follows a *Bernoulli* distribution that returns the correct bit σ_C with probability p. For each round $\chi < c$ any distinguisher $\mathcal{D}$ is given access to two oracles.
Each oracle can be queried by copying the first χ messages of *both* parties, but
then using (exactly) one new message for round $(\chi + 1)$—which replaces either
the sending parties message or that of the dummy friend. Any upper bound on
winning the game from Fig. 6 translates to the underlying problem of distinguishing the final two games.

Analyzing the game from Fig. 6 comes down to probability theory. Recall
from Corollary 1 that in order to distinguish two Bernoulli distributions p and
q with advantage $\alpha/2$ we require $\Omega(\alpha/\mathsf{d}_{\mathsf{TV}}(p,q))$ many samples. Applying this
corollary to Fig. 6 implies that we have c instances where the χ-th instance is
to distinguish $p = \frac{\chi+c}{2c}$ from $q = \frac{\chi+c-1}{2c}$. This implies the following L_1-norm
between p and q in round χ:

$$
\begin{aligned}
\mathsf{d}_{\mathsf{TV}}(p,q) &= \frac{1}{2}(|\Pr[p=1] - \Pr[q=1]| + |\Pr[p=0] - \Pr[q=0]|) \\
&= \frac{1}{2}\left(\left|\frac{c+\chi}{2c} - \frac{c+\chi-1}{2c}\right| + \left|\frac{c-\chi}{2c} - \frac{c-\chi+1}{2c}\right|\right) = \frac{1}{2c}
\end{aligned}
\tag{7}
$$

Note here that the total variational distance in round χ is *independent* from
the round χ and the same for all c oracles. Combining this information with
Lemma 2 means that *any* distribution p and q resulting from sampling t times
from *arbitrary* oracles results in a total variational distance $\leq t\frac{1}{2c}$.[8]

We now merge this insight with the result of Eq. (7) and the bound of Corollary 1. This leads a lower bound of:

$$
t \in \Omega\left(\frac{\alpha}{\mathsf{d}_{\mathsf{TV}}(p,q)}\right) = \Omega(\alpha c)
\tag{8}
$$

We thus have:

Corollary 3. *Let $\mathcal{D}$ be a distinguisher in Fig. 6 that uses t samples and has
runtime in $\mathfrak{C}_2 := \mathrm{o}(c^2/\alpha)$. Let the cost of acquiring a single sample be $\mathcal{O}(c)$.
Then the distinguisher $\mathcal{D}$ is correct with probability at most $1/2 + \alpha/2$.*

Proof. The bound from Eq. (8) covers any adversary trying to win Fig. 6 regardless of how the t samples are distributed between the c oracles. This follows from

---

[8] This is in contrast to the Hellinger-distance H which yields tighter bounds but
where the amount of information from a single query really depends on the oracle O_χ
which is queried. This makes it harder to provide meaningful bounds for adversaries
querying different oracles with their t samples.

the subadditional property of the total variational distance shown in Lemma 2 and the computation in Eq. (7) showing that the total variational distance is the same between all oracles; thus the bound from Lemma 1 still is valid and the total variational distance between any pair of t-fold distributions is at most $t \cdot \frac{1}{2c}$.

Thus Lemma 3 maintains its validity. Hence the lower bound of Eq. (8) matches our setting. The bound is linear in c with the linear cost of querying a single sample (as the adversary has to evaluate the entire circuit for each sample, which requires $\mathcal{O}(c)$ runtime) this limits the distinguisher in such a way that only strictly less samples can be drawn than required according to Eq. (8).   □

Putting everything together, we have that for all PPT distinguishers D, $|\Pr[\text{out}_{0,D} = 1] - \Pr[\text{out}_{8,D} = 1]|$ is negligible in κ. In particular, $|\Pr[\text{out}_{0,D} = 1] - \Pr[\text{out}_{8,D} = 1]|$ is negligible for distinguishers D in $\mathfrak{C}_2$. Additionally, the employed reductions are in $\mathfrak{C}_1 = \mathcal{O}(c)$. Furthermore, for all adversaries $\mathcal{A}$, $|\Pr[\text{out}_{8,\mathcal{A}} = 1 | b = 0] - \Pr[\text{out}_{8,\mathcal{A}} = 1 | b = 1]| \leq \alpha$, where the runtime of the game also is in $\mathfrak{C}_1$. Hence, we may conclude that for all adversaries $\mathcal{A}$ in $\mathfrak{C}_2$, $|\Pr_{b \xleftarrow{\$} \{0,1\}}[\text{Exp}^{\text{anon}}_{\Pi^1_{AT}, \mathcal{A}, b}(\kappa) = b] - 1/2| \leq \alpha/2$.

On the Need for Stronger Obfuscation. Due to [CLTV15], indistinguishability obfuscation (or more precisely, its probabilistic variant) can only guarantee indistinguishability if the distance between the output distributions of two circuits is statistically close to zero. This is not the case in our final game hop. Therefore, we crucially require a stronger form of obfuscation such as virtual black-box obfuscation or ideal obfuscation. Due to [JLLW22], employing ideal obfuscation yields a heuristic candidate proven secure in an idealized model. Hence, our result constitutes a first step towards instantiating anonymous transfer.

Stronger Anonymity Notions. Our positive result demonstrates that despite our strong negative result, *some* non-trivial anonymity is achievable. Note, however, that our positive result is still weak in many regards. Strengthening the achieved notion to, for instance, achieve anonymity against malicious non-participants, seems highly non-trivial. In particular, malicious non-participants may easily nullify any correctness guarantee by behaving exactly like a sender. Straightforward attempts to address this problem, e.g. letting the obfuscated circuit output all messages with equal confidence, open the gates for new attacks. For instance, in the above setup, replacing the last message of half of all possible senders causes the circuit to output either both the sender message and the injected message or only the injected message, depending on whether the real sender is part of the parties whose messages are replaced. This strategy allows to de-anonymize the sender in runtime $\mathcal{O}(c \log c)$.

5.2 Final Result

Let $c = c(\kappa)$ be a polynomial in κ. Let $\mathfrak{C}_1 := \mathcal{O}(c)$ and let $\mathfrak{C}_2 := o(c^2(1 - \delta))$ for some $\delta \in \mathbb{R}_{[0,1]}$. Putting Theorems 4 and 5 together, we have:

Corollary 4. *The protocol Π_{AT}^1 is a strong $\mathfrak{C}_1$-fine-grained $(1 - \mathsf{negl}(\kappa), \delta, c, 1)$-AT against $\mathfrak{C}_2$.*

Applying Lemma 5 to transform our single-bit AT into an ℓ-bit AT yields:

Corollary 5. *The protocol Π_{AT}^ℓ is a strong $\mathfrak{C}_1'$-fine-grained $(1 - \mathsf{negl}(\kappa), (\delta\ell - \ell - \delta + 2), c \cdot \ell, \ell)$-AT against $\mathfrak{C}_2'$, where $\mathfrak{C}_1' = \ell \cdot \mathfrak{C}_1$ and $\mathfrak{C}_2' = \mathfrak{C}_2 - \ell \cdot \mathfrak{C}_1$.*

Using $\delta = 1 - \frac{1}{\sqrt{c}}$ and $c = \Omega(\ell^2)$ for the single-bit AT Π_{AT}^1 we get that $\delta' := 1 - \frac{\ell-1}{c}$ and $\mathfrak{C}_1' = \mathcal{O}(\ell \cdot c)$ and $\mathfrak{C}_2' = \mathsf{o}(c^2(1-\delta) - \ell \cdot c) = \mathsf{o}(c^2(1-\delta)) = \mathsf{o}(c^{1.5})$. A non-black-box change to the protocol Π_{AT}^1 from Figs. 4 and 5 leads to better overall parameters. We introduce the necessary changes to the protocol alongside a security analysis in the full version [ACM21].

Acknowledgements. We thank Rafael Pass for insightful comments and contributions to early stages of this work.

References

[ACM21] Agrikola, T., Couteau, G., Maier, S.: Anonymous whistleblowing over authenticated channels. Cryptology ePrint Archive, Report 2021/1341 (2021). https://eprint.iacr.org/2021/1341

[APY20] Abraham, I., Pinkas, B., Yanai, A.: Blinder - scalable, robust anonymous committed broadcast. In: Ligatti, J., Ou, X., Katz, J., Vigna, G., (eds.) ACM CCS 2020, pp. 1233–1252. ACM Press, Nov 2020

[BEA14] Burrough, B., Ellison, E., Andrews, S.: The snowden saga: a shadowland of secrets and light. Vanity Fair **23** (2014)

[Ber16] Berret, C.: Guide to securedrop (2016)

[BGI08] Biham, E., Goren, Y.J., Ishai, Y.: Basing weak public-key cryptography on strong one-way functions. In: Canetti, R. (ed.) TCC 2008. LNCS, vol. 4948, pp. 55–72. Springer, Heidelberg (2008)

[CBM15] Corrigan-Gibbs, H., Boneh, D., Mazières, D.: Riposte: an anonymous messaging system handling millions of users. In: 2015 IEEE Symposium on Security and Privacy, pp. 321–338. IEEE Computer Society Press, May 2015

[CDVV14] Chan, S., Diakonikolas, I., Valiant, P., Valiant, G.: Optimal algorithms for testing closeness of discrete distributions. In: 25th SODA, pp. 1193–1203 (2014)

[CGCDGS20] Cohn-Gordon, K., Cremers, C., Dowling, B., Garratt, L., Stebila, D.: A formal security analysis of the signal messaging protocol. J. Cryptol. **33**(4), 1914–1983 (2020)

[CGOS07] Chandran, N., Goyal, V., Ostrovsky, R., Sahai, A.: Covert multi-party computation. In: 48th FOCS, pp. 238–248. IEEE Computer Society Press, Oct 2007

[Cha03] Chaum, D.: Untraceable electronic mail, return addresses and digital pseudonyms. In: Gritzalis, D., (ed.) Secure Electronic Voting, vol. 7. Advances in Information Security, pp. 211–219. Springer, (2003). https://doi.org/10.1007/978-1-4615-0239-5_14

[Cha88] Chaum, D.: The dining cryptographers problem: Unconditional sender and recipient untraceability. J. Cryptol. **1**(1), 65–75 (1988)

[CLTV15] Canetti, R., Lin, H., Tessaro, S., Vaikuntanathan, V.: Obfuscation of probabilistic circuits and applications. In: Dodis, Y., Nielsen, J.B. (eds.) TCC 2015.
Part II, volume 9015 of LNCS, pp. 468–497. Springer, Heidelberg (2015)

[DMS04] Dingledine, R., Mathewson, N., Syverson, P.F.: Tor: the second-generation
onion router. In: Blaze, M., (ed.) USENIX Security 2004, pp. 303–320.
USENIX Association, Aug 2004

[DVV16] Degwekar, A., Vaikuntanathan, V., Vasudevan, P.N.: Finegrained cryptography. In: Robshaw, M., Katz, J. (eds.) CRYPTO 2016. Part III, volume 9816
of LNCS, pp. 533–562. Springer, Heidelberg (2016)

[ECZB21] Eskandarian, S., Corrigan-Gibbs, H., Zaharia, M., Boneh, D.: Express: low-
ering the cost of metadata-hiding communication with cryptographic privacy.
In Bailey, M., Greenstadt, R., (eds.) USENIX Security 2021, pp. 1775–1792.
USENIX Association, Aug 2021

[HLv02] Hopper, N.J., Langford, J., von Ahn, L.: Provably secure steganography.
In: Yung, M. (ed.) CRYPTO 2002. LNCS, vol. 2442, pp. 77–92. Springer,
Heidelberg (2002)

[Imp95] Impagliazzo, R.: A personal view of average-case complexity. In: . Tenth
Annual IEEE Conference on Proceedings of Structure in Complexity Theory,
pp. 134–147. IEEE (1995)

[JLLW22] Jain, A., Lin, H., Luo, J., Wichs, D.: The pseudorandom oracle model
and ideal obfuscation. Cryptology ePrint Archive, Report 2022/1204 (2022).
https://eprint.iacr.org/2022/1204

[Mer78] Merkle, R.C.: Secure communications over insecure channels. Commun.
ACM **21**(4), 294–299 (1978)

[NSSD21] Newman, Z., Servan-Schreiber, S., Devadas, S.: Spectrum: high-bandwidth
anonymous broadcast with malicious security. Cryptology ePrint Archive,
Report 2021/325 (2021). https://eprint.iacr.org/2021/325

[Phi18] Philipps, D.: Reality winner, former nsa translator, gets more than 5 years
in leak of russian hacking report. New York Times, 23 (2018)

[Rog04] Rogaway, P.: Nonce-based symmetric encryption. In: Roy, B.K., Meier, W.
(eds.) FSE 2004. LNCS, vol. 3017, pp. 348–359. Springer, Heidelberg (2004)

[vH04] von Ahn, L., Hopper, N.J.: Public-key steganography. In: Cachin, C.,
Camenisch, J. (eds.) EUROCRYPT 2004. LNCS, vol. 3027, pp. 323–341.
Springer, Heidelberg (2004)

[vHL05] von Ahn, L., Hopper, N.J., Langford, J.: Covert two-party computation. In
Gabow, H.N., Fagin, R., (eds.) 37th ACM STOC, pp. 513–522. ACM Press,
May 2005

[Whi] Whistleblowing   (2008).   https://legal-dictionary.thefreedictionary.com/
Whistleblowing. Accessed: 2021-09-29 from West's Encyclopedia of Ameri-
can Law, edition 2

Poly Onions: Achieving Anonymity in the Presence of Churn

Megumi Ando[1], Miranda Christ[2(✉)], Anna Lysyanskaya[3], and Tal Malkin[2]

[1] MITRE, Massachusetts, USA
[2] Columbia University, New York, USA
mchrist@cs.columbia.edu
[3] Brown University, Providence, USA

Abstract. Onion routing is a popular approach towards anonymous communication. Practical implementations are widely used (for example, Tor has millions of users daily), but are vulnerable to various traffic correlation attacks, and the theoretical foundations, despite recent progress, still lag behind. In particular, all works that model onion routing protocols and prove their security only address a single run, where each party sends and receives a single message of fixed length, once. Moreover, they all assume a static network setting, where the parties are stable throughout the lifetime of the protocol. In contrast, real networks have a high rate of churn (nodes joining and exiting the network), real users want to send multiple messages, and realistic adversaries may observe multiple runs of the protocol.

We initiate a formal treatment of onion routing in a setting with multiple runs over a dynamic network with churn. We provide definitions of both security and anonymity in this setting, and constructions that satisfy them. In particular, we define a new cryptographic primitive called *Poly Onions* and show that it can be used to realize our definitions.

1 Introduction

Anonymous Communication. Privacy is a fundamental human right, and it is increasingly under threat. We need to be able to connect to our desired websites and communicate with each other privately without being subject to scrutiny and interference, and, in some cases – such as when dissidents are trying to help each other in an oppressive regime – physical threats. While encryption provides confidentiality of message content, much information can still be gleaned from observed traffic patterns in a network, revealing such information as who is communicating with whom, when, and for how long.

Our goal is to implement anonymous channels over a point-to-point network, such as the Internet. Specifically, we want every user to be able to send a message to another user so that an adversary monitoring the network and controlling (passively or actively) a fraction of its nodes, possibly including the recipient of the message, should not be able to tell who is communicating with whom. That is, the scenario in which Alice sends a message to Bob should be indistinguishable from the one in which she sends one to Carol, instead.

E. Kiltz and V. Vaikuntanathan (Eds.): TCC 2022, LNCS 13748, pp. 715–746, 2022.
https://doi.org/10.1007/978-3-031-22365-5_25

How can we achieve such anonymous communication? A trivial solution is to use a secure computation protocol among all parties, where each party inputs their message and destination, and the functionality delivers the messages (where the output of each party is the set of all messages sent to that party, in lexicographic order). This solution is clearly not adequate: it is extremely inefficient and involves massive communication among the parties, all of whom should be available and interact back and forth throughout the protocol run. A few other approaches towards achieving anonymity have been proposed, but the gap between what is needed and the existing solutions remains large. In this paper, we focus on bridging this gap, working within the onion routing framework.

Onion Routing. Onion routing [10, 15, 19] is a popular approach towards achieving anonymity. The basic idea is that when Alice wants to send a message to Bob, she chooses random intermediate nodes constituting a path from her to Bob. She then prepares a cryptographic object called an "onion," which consists of layered ciphertexts, with one layer per node on the path. Alice then sends the onion through the path, with each intermediate party "peeling" a layer of the onion to discover the next node on the path until the onion reaches its destination. When several onions are peeled by the same honest intermediary in the same round, the adversary cannot correlate the incoming onions with the outgoing ones; we refer to this as "mixing." Thanks to mixing, it is possible to expect anonymity with onion routing. Tor ("The onion router") is the most widely used anonymity network, consisting of thousands of routers and used by millions of users daily [19]. While clearly practical, it is also vulnerable to traffic correlation attacks [27, 29, 31].

Starting with [9], in recent years there have been several works attempting to put onion routing on a solid theoretical foundation. For example, we know that sufficiently shuffling the onions provides anonymity from the passive adversary [3] and that a polylog (in the security parameter) number of rounds is both necessary (e.g., [12, 17, 18]) and sufficient (e.g., [3, 28]) for this. Providing anonymity from the active adversary is significantly more challenging than shuffling. Surprisingly, a polylog number of rounds is still sufficient for achieving anonymity in the active adversary setting with fault tolerance [3]. Exciting recent work considers a relaxed notion of anonymity called differential obliviousness, shows that it is useful in the shuffle model of differential privacy, and constructs an efficient differentially oblivious onion routing protocol [21]. Several other works address only onion construction without analyzing the onion routing protocol (e.g., [2, 23]).

However, the theoretical modeling, while solving important challenges, is still quite far from what we need in practice. Perhaps the most glaring issue is the fact that all the works that model and analyze onion routing protocols only address a *single* instance of message routing for a restricted set of communication patterns. Specifically, each party is instructed to send a (fixed length) message to another party such that everyone sends a message and everyone receives a message, and the protocol for communicating all messages only occurs once. This is in contrast to real-world scenarios where parties send messages of varying lengths and many times without coordinating with other parties. An additional challenge for a system that supports ongoing traffic is *network churn*: the nodes on the network may go offline or join back. Realistic networks have high rates of churn, but this has not been addressed by the above works. Other recent protocols addressing anonymity [25,32,33] also operate only in the static network setting (without any nodes joining or exiting the network).

Network Churn. Onion routing schemes rely on communication through intermediate nodes, which should be known at the time the onion is created. However, practical networks are dynamic, allowing for significant node churn. For example, measurement studies of real-world P2P networks [20,30] show that the churn rate is quite high: nearly 50% of peers in real-world networks can be replaced within an hour.

Churn poses significant challenges for anonymous routing, even at the definitional level. One obvious issue is that in standard onion routing, the entire route of an onion is chosen in advance when the onion is created. Thus, if only just one of the parties on the route churns out and goes offline, the onion is lost. We note that this is a problem not only with correctness and reliability, but also with security/anonymity. Indeed, if an adversary observes an onion originating with Alice and going to an offline node (hence dropped), and then sees that Bob ended up receiving fewer onions than other parties, the adversary may conclude that the dropped onion from Alice was likely intended for Bob.

Our Contributions. In this work we initiate the formal treatment of onion routing in a setting with multiple runs over a dynamic network with churn.

A natural idea towards overcoming churn is to construct an onion in a way that allows for more than one option for each hop on the route. This way the onion will not be dropped if one intermediate node is offline, and can instead be routed to a backup intermediary. This idea was put forward by Iwanik, Klonowski, and Kutyłowski [22], who suggested "duo onion" encryption as a way to improve onion delivery rates when there is network churn. A duo onion has two candidate intermediary servers for each onion layer. If the first candidate is offline, the onion can be sent to the second candidate. While Iwanik et al. proposed a duo onion construction and did a back-of-the-envelope analysis of its efficiency, they did not formalize duo onion routing nor prove the security of this scheme. In fact, as we show in Sect. 6.1, duo onions are less secure than regular onion routing because the adversary corrupting at least one candidate in each hop (which is more likely with more candidates) can trace the onion through the network.

Poly Onion Encryption Definition. Our first contribution (Definitions 1 and 2) is a formal definition of *poly onion encryption*. Poly onion encryption is inspired by duo onion encryption described above, but it does not suffer from the same security flaw.

Our definition introduces auxiliary parties, called *helpers*, for each hop in the routing path. The helpers can ensure that an onion is routed to its backup intermediary for the next hop only if the preferred one is offline. This fixes the flaw in duo onions: a corrupted backup party must enlist the help of the committee in order to peel an onion, so an adversary corrupting only one candidate can no longer necessarily peel the onion to trace its next hop. It also makes onion encryption more complicated: processing a poly onion is an interactive proto-col involving the current intermediate node, the candidates for where to send it next, and the helpers. However, this complication seems necessary; we show in Sect. 6.1 that natural simpler solutions are insufficient.

In part because of this interactivity, defining correctness and security for a poly onion requires some care. Intuitively, correctness (Definition 1) captures the requirement that the onion will reach its intended destination, and the intended message will be recovered, as long as some condition holds (for standard onion routing, the condition is that every intermediate party on the path behaves hon-estly). Security (Definition 2) captures the requirement that the adversary will not be able to correlate an input onion with one of several output onions coming out of a processing party, as long as some condition holds (for standard onion routing, the condition is that the processing party is honest). These conditions can be complex, since they depend on who is online, and each hop involves many potential parties (candidates and helpers). We capture these conditions through correctness and security predicates. (Note that different poly onion encryption schemes may be correct/secure with respect to different predicates.)

Poly Onion Encryption Construction. Our second contribution is a construction of poly onions from standard cryptographic primitives: CCA secure public-key encryption with tags [13,14], PRP, MAC, and secret sharing. Our construction, Poly Onion Encryption (Sect. 4), is parameterized in terms of the number of candidates κ, the size ν of the helper committee, and the secret sharing recon-struction threshold α.

In our construction, the committee members are responsible for ensuring that a processing party indeed sends its onion to the first online candidate in its list. At a high level, an onion is valid only if it comes with a key header used for processing it. An onion typically comes with a key header encrypted for the first candidate in its next hop. If the first candidate is offline, the processing party must enlist the help of the committee to construct this key header for an alternate candidate. For this purpose, each onion comes with inputs for the onion processing protocol. The processing party distributes these inputs to the committee members, who check that the first candidate is indeed offline and select the next online candidate in the list. The committee members return secret shares; given at least $\alpha \cdot \nu$ shares the processing party reconstructs the header for the alternate candidate.

We prove that our construction is correct and secure against an active adver-sary, with respect to corresponding predicates that we define. The correctness predicate for each step roughly requires that the processing party is honest and online, and that at most $\alpha \cdot \nu$ members of the committee are corrupted. The security predicate roughly requires that there are no corrupted parties appear-ing before the first honest and online party in the list of next candidates, and that fewer than $\alpha \cdot \nu$ members of the committee are corrupted. This is analogous to the condition for standard onions (where the processing party is required to be honest), so our predicate is only minimally stronger than that of standard onion encryption. As long as enough parties overall are honest, and committees are chosen randomly, we can increase the committee size to boost the probability that fewer than $\alpha \cdot \nu$ committee members are corrupted. These parameters can be instantiated so that the predicates are satisfied with high enough probability to achieve anonymity in the overall onion routing protocol, discussed below.

Anonymity Definitions. Let us revisit why achieving anonymity in the presence of churn is difficult. As an illustrative example, consider the simple onion routing protocol Π_p [3]. In Π_p, each sender routes an onion randomly through a network of server nodes such that the onion mixes with a polylog number of onions, a polylog number of times. It was shown that Π_p is anonymous from the passive adversary who corrupts up to a constant fraction of the servers (in the static setting) just by shuffling the onions in this way. However, it is not necessarily anonymous when we add churn to the equation: if the adversary observes that Alice's onion churns out before it gets a chance to mix with too many onions, then she may be able to infer who Alice's recipient is by observing who doesn't receive an onion at the end of the protocol. Intuitively, Iwanik et al.'s duo onion idea [22] is a partial solution to this problem; it is more difficult for Alice's onion to churn out if, at each hop, it can route to an alternative random server if the preferred one is offline. However, duo onions (without helper parties) don't necessarily mix at honest servers. This is, in part, because an adversarial intermediary P_i may behave honestly and route Alice's onion to the honest preferred next server P_{i+1}^{+} but still learn what the peeled onion looks like if the alternative next server P_{i+1}^{-} is adversarial: in this case, P_i knows what the alternative onion O_{i+1}^{-} for P_{i+1}^{-} looks like, and P_{i+1}^{-} knows how to peel it. A similar, slightly more complicated attack works even for the passive adversary and is described in Sect. 6.1. Naive solutions, such as adding more candidates, somewhat mitigate the risk but have drawbacks, as we show in Sect. 6.1. However, helper parties, which we introduce in poly onions, do prevent this attack. Thus, a natural question is: can we make Π_p anonymous in the setting with churn by using poly onions?

Before we could answer this question, it was necessary to first define what it means for an onion routing protocol to be anonymous in the presence of churn. Prior definitions of anonymity are defined only for a single protocol run in the static setting, whereas most applications operate over multiple runs over a long period of time, and so we should model them as operating (concurrently with other runs) in a dynamic setting. For our third contribution, we present a definition of anonymity for the multi-run setting with churn.

Our definition of anonymity (Definition 3) is roughly as follows. An onion routing protocol is *anonymous* if the adversary cannot tell whether it is interacting with the challenger over L runs on input vectors $\sigma_1^0, \ldots, \sigma_L^0$ or on input vectors $\sigma_1^1, \ldots, \sigma_L^1$. It is *strongly* anonymous if the adversary can query the challenger to peel onions before and after the L challenge runs. It is *adaptively* anonymous if the adversary chooses the inputs and who is online/offline for the ith run based on the prior $i - 1$ runs. The strongest definition that is most helpful in an operational setting is the strong multi-run adaptive version of the definition, and that's the one we aim to achieve.

From Single-run to Multi-run Anonymity. Our fourth contribution is to show (Theorem 2) that for a large class of onion routing protocols, which we call simulatable, multi-run (strong, adaptive) anonymity is equivalent to single-run (strong, adaptive) anonymity. This holds both for the static setting (no churn) and dynamic setting (with churn), whether the adversary is passive or active. Informally, a *simulatable* onion routing protocol (Definition 4) is one where the adversary cannot tell whether it is interacting in the real setting in which the challenger runs the protocol on behalf of honest parties using the honest parties' secret keys, or in the ideal setting in which the challenger fakes the run without knowledge of the honest parties' secret keys. Since most onion routing protocols are simulatable, including Π_p, an immediate consequence is that practical onion routing protocols that satisfy multi-run anonymity exist – albeit in the static setting without churn.

Achieving Anonymity in the Presence of Churn. Armed with a definition of anonymity for the dynamic setting and Theorem 2, we answer our question about Π_p in the affirmative. For our final contribution, we present a new onion routing protocol, Poly Π_p, that uses Poly Onion Encryption instead of standard onion encryption and prove that it satisfies (strong,adaptive) multi-run anonymity when fewer than half of the parties can be offline or passively corrupted.

Open Problems. Our work makes significant progress towards bridging the gap between theoretical foundations of onion routing, and required anonymity in realistic settings. Still, some important problems remain open.

First, can we achieve anonymous routing with churn against active adversaries? Note that Poly Π_p already provides protection against some types of active malicious behavior: poly onion encryption is secure against active adversaries, and Poly Π_p is also secure against an adversary that decides the churn schedule. However, anonymity breaks when an active adversary can selectively drop onions in a more "adaptive" way, namely in the middle of a run. We also note that in the static setting, the protocol $\Pi_{\bowtie}$ of Ando, Lysyanskaya and Upfal [4] achieves anonymity even against active adversaries. However, simply replacing their onions with our poly onions would still not yield a scheme that is anonymous in the setting with churn, because used as is, their protocol would equate churn with malicious activity and simply not work; an added complication is that $\Pi_{\bowtie}$ is not simulatable.

A second open problem is to address more general communication patterns. As in prior work [3,4,32,33], a single run of our protocol is also restricted to the so called "Simple I/O" setting, where each party sends and receives exactly one message of a fixed length. The fact that we address the multi-run case partially mitigates the issue, as it provides a way to handle longer messages, by breaking them to several runs. Nonetheless, the assumption that the communication pattern in each run is a permutation is still limiting. Defining what anonymity should mean for more general communication patterns, which patterns can be efficiently supported anonymously, and how to construct such protocols, is a challenging and interesting topic for future work.

Related Work. To the best of our knowledge, all existing onion routing works either (i) do not have any theoretical modeling or provable security, or deviate from standard notions of indistinguishability [6–8,11,16,22,23]; (ii) address only onion construction, without discussing or analyzing the routing algorithm [2,9, 22–24]; (iii) consider routing only in the single run static network setting [3,4, 25,28,32,33]; or (iv) focus on lower bounds [4,12,17,18].

2   Modeling the problem

Here, we introduce the setting used for our formal definitions in Sect. 3 and Sect. 5. Because our setting involves network churn, our model is more involved than previous models used for analogous definitions in the static setting. We base our treatment of churn on practical onion routing, namely Tor [19], which consists of thousands of routers and is used by millions of users. Tor relies on five to ten semi-trusted directory authorities to maintain up-to-date information on relay nodes and their availabilities and capabilities including network capacity. In the latest version (version 3) of Tor, routers periodically upload "router descriptors" that list their keys, capabilities, etc. to the directory authorities [1]. From these descriptors, the directory authorities update their view of the routers every 12 to 18 hours. Tor users and routers download "diffs" of the updated views from multiple directory authorities; these contain information on the currently available routers. The bulletins in our model are loosely modeled on this; like in Tor, at the start of every run, the parties obtain a global view of who's currently online. During a run, some parties may churn out; we allow the adversary to control who these parties are and when the churn happens since this corresponds to the most pessimistic scenario. Within a run, a party can P_j check whether a party P'_j is currently online by sending a message and waiting for a response. An actively corrupted P'_j may pretend to be offline.

Let λ be the security parameter and N be the number of parties.

Notation. For a natural number n, $[n]$ is the set $\{1, \ldots, n\}$. For a set Set, we denote the cardinality of Set by $|\text{Set}|$, and item $\leftarrow_s$ Set is an item from Set chosen uniformly at random. If Dist is a probability distribution over Set, item $\leftarrow$ Dist is an item sampled from Set according to Dist. For an algorithm Algo, output $\leftarrow$ Algo(input) is the (possibly probabilistic) output from running Algo on input. A function $f(\lambda)$ of the security parameter λ is said to be *negligible* if it decays faster than any inverse polynomial in λ. An event occurs *with overwhelming probability* if its complement occurs with negligible probability.

Time. We assume the synchronous setting and model time as passing in *rounds*, with some fixed number of rounds making up each larger *run*. Let $R_1, \ldots, R_L$ be a series of runs. Assume that L is bounded above by a polynomial in λ.

Parties. Let $P_1, \ldots, P_N$ be the N parties in our universe. Assume that N is bounded above by a polynomial in λ. We assume that each party has a public key accessible to all. Let $\mathsf{Bad} \subseteq \{P_1, ..., P_N\}$ be the set of corrupted parties. Corrupted parties are those that can be observed or controlled by the adversary, depending on the adversary's abilities, which we define later.

Churn Bulletins. Let $B_1, ..., B_L$ be the *bulletins*, which accurately indicate which parties are online at the beginning of each run. More precisely, $B_i \subseteq \{P_1, ..., P_N\}$, and party P_j is online at the beginning of run R_i if and only if $P_j \in B_i$.

Churn Schedule. Let $C_1, ..., C_L$ be the *churn schedule* for the runs. For each i, C_i is a set of party-round pairs: $C_i = \{(P_{i_1}, r_1), (P_{i_2}, r_2), ...\}$, where a pair (P_{i_j}, r_j) indicates that in run R_i, party P_{i_j} goes offline at the beginning of round r_j of that run. All parties in the list C_i must be online at the start of the run according to B_i. As a simplification, we allow parties to come online at the start of a run but not during a run. Thus the churn schedule specifies only which parties go offline and when. Since parties come online only at the start of a run, this will be specified in the bulletins rather than in the churn schedule.

Churn Limit. Let $c(N)$, a function of N (e.g., $\frac{N}{2}$), be the *churn limit* [5]; that is, at most $c(N)$ parties can be offline at any point in time. We require that the number of offline parties specified by the bulletins and churn schedule does not exceed the churn limit $c(N)$. More precisely, for every i, $N - |B_i| + |C_i| \leq c(N)$ since $N - |B_i|$ parties are offline at the start of run R_i, and $|C_i|$ additional parties go offline during R_i.

Inputs. We represent an input for a run R_i as a vector $\sigma_i = (\sigma_{i,1}, \sigma_{i,2}, ..., \sigma_{i,N})$ where $\sigma_{i,j}$ is the input for party P_j. Each party's input is either a recipient-message pair (P_k, m) specifying that that party sends message m to party P_k, or it is $\perp$. An input of $\perp$ indicates that that party sends no information in that run (although that party can still send dummy messages in a protocol).

For run i, we say an input vector σ_i is *valid* if there exists some permutation $f : [B_i] \rightarrow [B_i]$ such that for each party $P_j \in B_i$, the input to P_j is $(f(P_j), m_j)$ for some message m_j. Furthermore, the input for each party $P_j \notin B_i$ is $\perp$. Our allowed inputs here are analogous to the "Simple I/O" setting in prior work (e.g., [3, 4, 32, 33]), adapted for churn.

For defining anonymity using a game-based approach, we allow the adversary to choose a pair of inputs for an onion routing protocol, and its goal is to determine, by running the protocol, which of these inputs the challenger chose. If the adversary can choose any two inputs without any constraints on its choices, then it can trivially win, for example, by choosing two inputs that differ on a corrupted party's input. Thus, the adversary is constrained to choose the two inputs from the same equivalence class [4]. We say two input vectors $\sigma = (\sigma_1, ..., \sigma_N)$ and $\sigma' = (\sigma'_1, ..., \sigma'_N)$ are *equivalent* w.r.t. the set of corrupted parties Bad if for all $P_j \in \mathsf{Bad}$, $\sigma_j = \sigma'_j$, and the content of the honest messages for which P_j is the recipient is the same in σ and σ'. We denote this equivalence $\sigma \equiv_{\mathsf{Bad}} \sigma'$.

We note that that the input specifies the messages that the parties would like to send. However, a protocol might result in some parties receiving additional dummy messages, or some parties receiving no messages (perhaps due to churn).

Adversary Model. The adversary can control the churn, observe the network traffic, and choose which parties to corrupt (if any). We assume authenticated communication, and we assume that the adversary can only drop messages sent by corrupted parties or offline parties. In particular, the adversary cannot interfere with communication between two honest and online parties. We define three classes of adversaries of varying capabilities: the network adversary, the passive adversary, and the active adversary. An adversary in any of these classes can observe all of the network traffic. In particular, it can observe the traffic on all communication links. The *network adversary* can control the churn, make these observations, and no more. The *passive adversary* can additionally corrupt a constant fraction of the parties and observe the computations and states of these parties. It cannot control these parties to deviate from the protocol. The *active adversary* can do all of the above and can also control the corrupted parties to do anything, including deviating from the protocol.

3   Onion Encryption for Churn

In this section, we formalize a generalization of duo onion encryption [22], where each onion has two candidate intermediary servers for each layer. As mentioned by Iwanik et al. [22] if the processing party can choose which candidate to send to next, then whenever possible, a corrupted party processing an onion can send to a corrupted candidate. If a fraction c of the parties are corrupted, the probability that at least one of a given list of k candidates is corrupted is $1 - (1 - c)^k$.

As discussed in the introduction, we address this issue by introducing auxiliary parties, called *helpers*. The helpers for an onion O in a hop i are parties that are involved in some way in sending the peeled onion of O to its next intermediary server. This prevents a corrupted party from choosing any candidate it wishes for the next hop.

3.1   I/O syntax

Poly onion encryption is parameterized by the security parameter λ, the number of candidates κ, and the number of helpers ν and consists of algorithms (KeyGen, FormOnion) and protocol ProcOnion, as follows:

- KeyGen takes as input the security parameter 1^λ, and a party name P_i. It outputs the public key pk_{P_i} and the secret key sk_{P_i} for P_i.
- FormOnion takes as input a message m; a run number R (recall that a run consists of a number of rounds; see Sect. 2); two ordered lists,
  $P_1, \ldots, \mathcal{P}_\ell, \mathcal{P}_{\ell+1}$ and $\mathcal{Q}_1, \ldots, \mathcal{Q}_\ell$ such that for all i, $|\mathcal{P}_i| = \kappa$ and $|\mathcal{Q}_i| = \nu$,
  and the public keys for all the parties on these lists. $\mathcal{P}_i$ is the ordered list of parties who are candidates for intermediaries for hop i. $\mathcal{Q}_i$ is the list of parties who will serve as helpers for hop i. The first party $P_{\ell+1,1}$ in $\mathcal{P}_{\ell+1}$ is the recipient.
  The output is the list of lists of onions $\mathcal{O}_1, \ldots, \mathcal{O}_{\ell+1}$. Each $\mathcal{O}_i$ corresponds to the ith layer of this onion; each $\mathcal{O}_i$ consists of κ onions $O_{i,1}, \ldots O_{i,\kappa}$. An onion $O_{i,j}$ corresponds to the representation of the ith layer of the onion that is suitable for processing by candidate $P_{i,j}$.

- ProcOnion is a protocol that $P_{i,j} \in \mathcal{P}_i$ can initiate on input $O_{i,j}$ and its secret key; the other participants in the protocol (if any) is the set of helpers $\mathcal{Q}_i$, each helper takes its own secret key as input. As a result of the protocol, $P_{i,j}$ obtains output $O_{i+1,j'} \in \mathcal{O}_{i+1}$ and its intended recipient $P_{i+1,j'} \in \mathcal{P}_{i+1}$; the helpers receive no output.

Remark 1. We fix κ and ν for convenience; while in practice they may vary, fixing them does not lose much generality.

Remark 2. The list $\mathcal{P}_i = (P_{i,1}, \ldots, P_{i,\kappa})$ is ordered. For $j > 1$, $P_{i,j}$ is not supposed to serve as the intermediary for processing the onion unless for all $u < j$, $P_{i,u}$ is unavailable.

Remark 3. The candidate list $\mathcal{P}_{\ell+1}$ may seem superfluous: only the recipient $P_{\ell+1,1}$ is important. As we will see, requiring it as part of the input is helpful for preventing adversarial helpers from learning whether the onion to be processed has reached the end of the routing path, or not.

Remark 4. The recipient $P_{\ell+1,1}$ of the onion, upon receiving the onion $O_{\ell+1,1}$ should be able to process it, infer that he is the recipient, and obtain the original message m. An alternate candidate $P_{\ell+1,j}$, upon receiving the onion $O_{\ell+1,j}$ should be able to process it, infer that he is not the recipient, and output $\bot$. Correctness, defined in the next section, will ensure that this is the case.

3.2   Correctness

A standard onion encryption [2,9,23] is correct if having each intermediary peel it using the algorithm ProcOnion will get it to its destination and yield the original message. In poly onions, we have a set of candidates for each layer rather than a specific intermediary, and a set of helpers with which an intermediary can run ProcOnion in order to peel the onion; that alone makes correctness somewhat harder to pin down since now it is a protocol rather than an algorithm.

What makes it really complicated, however, is churn. A processing party may change its behavior based on whether the candidates for the next hop are online. In other words, processing an onion correctly depends on factors that cannot be accounted for at the time that the onion was formed.

We introduce a correctness predicate $\phi_{B,C}$ that corresponds to the bulletin B and churn schedule C. It takes as input the onion's candidate lists $\mathcal{P}$, the helper lists $\mathcal{Q}$, the pair of indices (i, j) where i is a hop in the routing path and j is the index of the jth party $P_{i,j}$ in $\mathcal{P}_i$, a round r, and a number of rounds Δ. Δ should be an upper bound on the number of rounds required to process an onion. The correctness predicate $\phi_{B,C}(\mathcal{P}, \mathcal{Q}, (i, j), r, \Delta)$ accepts if $P_{i,j}$ and (a sufficient number of) helpers in $\mathcal{Q}_i$ are online at round r according to B and C. The definition of correctness is given with respect to this predicate (which, in turn, dictates how many helpers are sufficient).

In poly onion encryption, there is a set of onions rather than a single onion corresponding to each hop in the evolution. The path the onion will take through the network (i.e. which candidate will be picked for each hop) depends on which parties are online and which are corrupted. Recalling that $\mathcal{P}_{i+1}$ is a list of candidates in order of preference, O_i should not peel to an onion $O_{i+1,j}$ for party $P_{i+1,j} \in \mathcal{P}_{i+1}$ if there is an honest and online party $P_{i+1,k} \in \mathcal{P}_{i+1}$ where $k < j$. Note that if $P_{i+1,k}$ is online but corrupted, it may pretend to be offline, in which case we can allow O_i to peel to $O_{i+1,j}$. More formally:

Definition 1 (Correctness with respect to predicate ϕ). *Let $\Sigma =$ (KeyGen, FormOnion, ProcOnion) be a poly onion encryption scheme, with ProcOnion taking at most Δ rounds to run. Let Bad be the set of corrupted parties. Let B be any bulletin. Let C be any churn schedule. Let m be any message. Let R be the current run number. Let $\mathcal{P} = (\mathcal{P}_1, \ldots, \mathcal{P}_{\ell+1}) = ((P_{1,1}, \ldots, P_{1,\kappa}), \ldots, (P_{\ell+1,1}, \ldots, P_{\ell+1,\kappa}))$ be any list of $\ell + 1$ lists of κ candidates. Let $\mathcal{Q} = (\mathcal{Q}_1, \ldots, \mathcal{Q}_\ell) = ((Q_{1,1}, \ldots, Q_{1,\nu}), \ldots, (Q_{\ell,1}, \ldots, Q_{\ell,\nu}))$ be any list of ℓ lists of ν helpers. Let $\mathsf{pk}_{\mathcal{P}\cup\mathcal{Q}}$ denote the public keys of the parties in $\mathcal{P} \cup \mathcal{Q}$.*

Let $\mathcal{O} = ((O_{1,1}, \ldots, O_{1,\kappa}), \ldots, (O_{\ell+1,1}, \ldots, O_{\ell+1,\kappa})) \leftarrow$ FormOnion$(m, R, \mathcal{P}, \mathcal{Q}, \mathsf{pk}_{\mathcal{P}\cup\mathcal{Q}})$ be an evolution of onions obtained from running FormOnion on the above parameters.

Σ is correct w.r.t. the predicate $\phi_{B,C}$ if for any candidate location (i, j), round r, and number of rounds Δ such that $\phi_{B,C}(\mathcal{P}, \mathcal{Q}, (i, j), r, \Delta) = 1$, the following items are satisfied:

i. *Let $\mathcal{S} \subseteq \mathcal{P}_{i+1}$ be the following set of parties. If $\mathcal{P}_{i+1}$ contains an honest party that is online in rounds r through $r + \Delta$, $\mathcal{S}$ includes the first honest and online party P' in $\mathcal{P}_{i+1}$, along with any corrupted parties preceding P' in $\mathcal{P}_{i+1}$.*

ii. *When ProcOnion is initiated by an intermediary party $P_{i,j} \in \mathcal{P}_i$ in round r, and $P_{i,j}$ follows the protocol (i.e., if it is adversarial, then it can only be honest-but-curious), $P_{i,j}$'s output is $(P_{\mathsf{next}}, O_{\mathsf{next}})$ where $P_{\mathsf{next}} \in \mathcal{S} \cup \{\perp\}$. (The presence of $\perp$ on this list of parties means that it is possible that after the participants have processed the ith layer of the onion, the adversary can drop this onion.)*

iii. *$O_{\mathsf{next}} = \perp$ if $P_{\mathsf{next}} = \perp$. Otherwise, $O_{\mathsf{next}} = O_{i+1,k}$ is the onion layer for party $P_{\mathsf{next}} = P_{i+1,k}$ output by FormOnion.*

iv. *When ProcOnion is initiated by $P_{\ell+1,1}$ on input $O_{\ell+1,1}$, the output is $(m, \perp)$. When ProcOnion is initiated by $P_{\ell+1,j}$ on input $O_{\ell+1,j}$, $j > 1$, the output is $(\perp, \perp)$.*

Remark 5. The evolution of an onion includes a representation of every layer of the onion, which is explicitly output by FormOnion. Implicitly, it also includes the innermost layer, i.e., the message that will ultimately be output by the recipient. Thus, we will sometimes think of an onion evolution with ℓ intermediaries as consisting of $\ell + 2$ onion layers. For $1 \leq i \leq \ell$, an honest intermediary $P_{i,j}$ receives a representation $O_{i,j}$ of the ith layer of $\mathcal{O}$ and, upon processing it, sends $O_{i+1,j'}$ to $P_{i+1,j'}$. If the recipient $P_{\ell+1,1}$ is online, it will receive the onion $O_{\ell+1,1}$ and, upon processing it, will output $(m, \perp)$. Sometimes, by $O_{\ell+2,j}$ we will denote $(m, \perp)$.

3.3 Security

On a high level, an onion scheme is secure if an adversary cannot correlate an honest participant's incoming onions with its outgoing onions. For poly onions, this is captured via a security game, POSecurityGame described below.

One reason that this game is more complicated than the security game for regular onions is that the adversary controlling the helpers obtains additional information; what the adversary may learn also depends on the network churn. We introduce a security predicate ψ to capture whether or not a particular set of circumstances — who is processing an onion, at what round, with what helpers — dictates whether the adversary should not be able to determine a correlation.

More precisely, the security predicate $\psi_{B,C}$ is parameterized by a bulletin B and churn schedule C. Let $\mathcal{P} = (\mathcal{P}_1, \ldots, \mathcal{P}_{\ell+1}) = ((P_{1,1}, \ldots, P_{1,\kappa}), \ldots, (P_{\ell+1,1}, \ldots, P_{\ell+1,\kappa}))$ be any list of $\ell + 1$ lists of κ candidates. Let $\mathcal{Q} = (\mathcal{Q}_1, \ldots, \mathcal{Q}_\ell) = ((Q_{1,1}, \ldots, Q_{1,\kappa}), \ldots, (Q_{\ell,1}, \ldots, Q_{\ell,\kappa}))$ be any list of ℓ lists of ν helpers. $\psi_{B,C}$ takes as input $\mathcal{P}$, $\mathcal{Q}$, a hop number h, a round r, and a number of rounds Δ.

For example, for regular onion routing, we would define ψ to be 1 if and only if the (only) candidate in hop h, P_h, is honest. Here, we don't need to refer to the bulletin or churn, since with regular onion routing, the adversary should not be able to peel an onion for honest P_h, regardless of whether or not P_h is online.

Consider another example, the original duo onion encryption [22] without helpers. Here, a processing party P_{h-1} in hop $h-1$ can choose which destination in $\mathcal{P}_h$ to send the onion to; there are no helpers verifying that this destination is the first candidate on the list $\mathcal{P}_h$ that is online. Here, we can define ψ to be 1 if and only if all parties in $\mathcal{P}_h$ are honest. If all parties in $\mathcal{P}_h$ are honest, the adversary should not be able to peel the onion since it does not know these honest parties' secret keys. On the other hand, if any party in $\mathcal{P}_h$ is corrupted, a corrupted P_{h-1} can choose to send to the corrupted party in $\mathcal{P}_h$, allowing the adversary to peel the onion in the following hop h. So the hop number h corresponds to the onion layer that shouldn't be "peelable" by the adversary.

POSecurityGame. The following game is between an adversary $\mathcal{A}$ and a challenger. It is parameterized by a security predicate $\psi_{B,C}(\mathcal{P}, \mathcal{Q}, h, r, \Delta)$, where B is a bulletin, C is a churn schedule, $\mathcal{P} = (\mathcal{P}_1, \ldots, \mathcal{P}_{\ell+1})$ is a list of $\ell + 1$ lists of candidates, $\mathcal{Q} = (\mathcal{Q}_1, \ldots, \mathcal{Q}_\ell)$ is a list of ℓ lists of helpers, h is an index of a hop in the path, r is a round, and Δ is an upper bound on the number of rounds that ProcOnion takes to complete.

  i. $\mathcal{A}$ receives the public keys for all parties.
  ii. $\mathcal{A}$ chooses the set of corrupted parties Bad, the bulletin B, the churn schedule C restricted to the honest parties, and the public keys for Bad. $\mathcal{A}$ sends all of these to the challenger.
  iii. $\mathcal{A}$ can invoke the protocol ProcOnion in two ways, as follows.

Honestly initiated $\mathcal{A}$ sends to the challenger an onion O to be processed, an honest processing party P, and a round r_O in which the processing of O should begin. Next, the challenger acts on behalf of P as well as the honest helpers in the protocol ProcOnion initiated by P on input O, while $\mathcal{A}$ acts on behalf of the participants in Bad. Upon completing ProcOnion, the challenger reveals P's output (O', P') (if any) to $\mathcal{A}$.

Adversarially initiated $\mathcal{A}$ initiates ProcOnion on behalf of a participant $P \in$ Bad. Next, the challenger acts on behalf of the honest helpers in the protocol ProcOnion initiated by P on input O, while $\mathcal{A}$ acts on behalf of the participants in Bad (including P).

iv. $\mathcal{A}$ chooses the parameters for the challenge onion. It chooses a routing path length ℓ, a message m, a routing position $1 \leq h \leq \ell + 1$, a round r, a series of helper parties for each hop $(\mathcal{Q}_1, \ldots, \mathcal{Q}_\ell)$, and a path consisting of a series of alternate destinations for each hop $(\mathcal{P}_1, \ldots, \mathcal{P}_{\ell+1})$. For the adversary's choices, it must hold that $\psi_{B,C}(\mathcal{P}, \mathcal{Q}, h, r, \Delta) = 1$.

v. The challenger samples a bit $b \leftarrow_{\$} \{0,1\}$. If $b = 0$, the challenger uses FormOnion to create an onion $\mathcal{O}^0$ exactly as specified by the routing path and helper parties. Let $\mathcal{O}_1^0$ be the list of outermost onion layers of this onion. If $b = 1$, the challenger creates two lists of lists of onions. The challenger creates the first list of lists of onions $\mathcal{O}^1 = (\mathcal{O}_1^1, \ldots, \mathcal{O}_{h+1}^1)$ by running FormOnion with message $\perp$, candidates $(\mathcal{P}_1, \ldots, \mathcal{P}_{h+1})$, helpers $(\mathcal{Q}_1, \ldots, \mathcal{Q}_h)$, and those parties' public keys. The challenger creates the second list of lists of onions $\mathcal{O}' = (\mathcal{O}_{h+1}', \ldots, \mathcal{O}_{\ell+2}')$ by running FormOnion with message m, candidates $(\mathcal{P}_{h+1}, \ldots, \mathcal{P}_{\ell+1})$, helpers $(\mathcal{Q}_{h+1}, \ldots, \mathcal{Q}_\ell)$, and those parties' public keys. Let $\mathcal{O}_1^1 = \mathcal{O}_1$ as formed above. (Recall that $\mathcal{O}_{\ell+2}^1$ consists of entries $O_{\ell+2,j} = (m, \perp)$ as explained in Remark 5.) The challenger sends $\mathcal{O}_1^b$ to $\mathcal{A}$.

vi. $\mathcal{A}$ can again invoke the ProcOnion in two ways, with a slight modification if honestly initiated.

Honestly initiated $\mathcal{A}$ can direct honest participants to invoke ProcOnion as described in step 3.3 but with the following modification: onions $O_j \in \mathcal{O}_h^b$ can only be queried in round r. If $b = 0$ was chosen, the challenger follows the protocol ProcOnion.

If $b = 1$, and $\mathcal{A}$ directed $P_j \in \mathcal{P}_h$ to invoke ProcOnion on input $O_j \in \mathcal{O}_h^1$, the challenger begins by faithfully following the protocol on behalf of honest helpers and the honest P_j. Suppose that doing so produces output $O_{h+1,j'} \in \mathcal{O}_{h+1}^1$ and candidate $P_{h+1,j'} \in \mathcal{P}_{h+1}$. If $h \leq \ell$ (i.e., $P_j = P_{h+1,j}$ is an intermediary) or $(h, j) = (\ell + 1, 1)$ (i.e., $P_j = P_{h,j}$ is the onion's recipient), then instead of returning these to $\mathcal{A}$, the challenger switches the onion and returns $O_{h+1,j'} \in \mathcal{O}_{h+1}'$, $P_{h+1,j'}$ to $\mathcal{A}$.

Adversarially initiated Behavior is the same as defined in step 3.3

vii. $\mathcal{A}$ submits a guess b' of b. See Fig. 1 for a schematic of the poly onion security game.

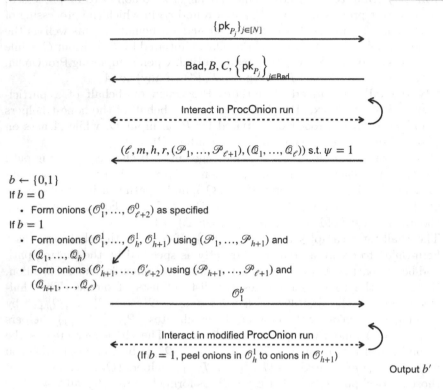

Fig. 1. Schematic of the poly onion security game.

We say $\mathcal{A}$ wins POSecurityGame if $b' = b$. A poly onion encryption scheme is secure if no efficient adversary can win POSecurityGame with non-negligible advantage; more formally:

Definition 2 (Poly Onion Security with respect to predicate ψ).
We say a poly onion encryption scheme Σ is poly onion secure with respect to ψ against the class of adversaries $\mathbb{A}$ if for every adversary $\mathcal{A} \in \mathbb{A}$,
$\left| \Pr[\mathcal{A} \text{ wins } \mathsf{POSecurityGame}(\mathcal{A}, \Sigma, \lambda, \kappa, \nu, \psi_{.,.})] - \frac{1}{2} \right| = \mathsf{negl}(\lambda).$

Remark 6. During the ProcOnion protocol, the adversary may see additional information other than the oracle's output, depending on the adversary's capabilities. For example, the network, passive, and active adversaries can see the traffic across all links during the protocol.

4   Our Poly Onion Encryption Scheme

In this section, we construct an instance of poly onion encryption, define its correctness and security predicates, and prove its correctness and security.

Our construction, Poly Onion Encryption, has parameters κ (the number of candidates per hop), ν (the number of helpers per hop), α (the fraction of helpers needed to process an onion), and d (for bounding the length of the routing path). We construct Poly Onion Encryption using the following cryptographic primitives: CCA secure public-key encryption with tags [13,14], pseudorandom permutations (or block ciphers), a message authentication code (MAC) (Gen, Tag, Ver), and a $(\alpha \cdot \nu, \nu)$ Secret Sharing scheme (Share, Recon). We denote public-key encryption and decryption as $\mathsf{Enc}_{\mathsf{pk}}(\cdot)$ and $\mathsf{Dec}_{\mathsf{sk}}(\cdot)$ where pk and sk are the public key and secret key, respectively. Following the work by Camenisch and Lysyanskaya [9] and Ando and Lysyanskaya [2], we will continue the tradition of using "$\{\cdot\}_k$" to denote evaluating a PRP in the forward direction under the symmetric key k, and "$\} \cdot \{_k$" to denote evaluating a PRP in the backward direction.

Throughout this section, we describe our construction for $\kappa = 2$ candidates per hop for ease of readability, although our construction generalizes to any $\kappa \in \mathbb{N}$. We explain how it generalizes in the full version of this paper.

For every hop of the routing path, let P_i^+ denote the *preferred* candidate for the ith hop (this is the sender's first choice), and let P_i^- denote the *alternate* candidate for the ith hop (the second choice). The idea is that (at the ith hop) the onion should be routed to P_i^+, unless P_i^+ is offline, in which case the onion can be routed to P_i^- instead. We sometimes refer to the party P_i for the ith hop without specifying whether it is the preferred candidate or the alternate.

Forming an onion on input the message m, the candidate parties $\mathcal{P} = ((P_i^+, P_i^-))_{i \in [d]}$, the helpers (committee members) $\mathcal{Q} = (\mathcal{Q}_i)_{i \in [d]}$, and the public keys $\mathsf{pk}_{\mathcal{P} \cup \mathcal{Q}}$ of the candidates and helpers, produces a list of lists of onions, $((O_1^+, O_1^-), \ldots, (O_d^+, O_d^-)) \leftarrow \mathsf{FormOnion}(m, \mathcal{P}, \mathcal{Q}, \mathsf{pk}_{\mathcal{P} \cup \mathcal{Q}})$, where each O_i^+ is the onion to be processed by party P_i^+, and each O_i^- is the onion to be processed by P_i^-. If it is possible for the processing party P_i of an onion O_i to send an onion to the preferred next candidate P_{i+1}^+, P_i will produce an onion O_{i+1}^+ and send it to P_{i+1}^+; otherwise, P_i enlists the help of the committee members $\mathcal{Q}_i$ to produce the alternate onion O_{i+1}^- to send to the alternate candidate P_{i+1}^- instead. The point of this committee is to ensure that P_{i+1}^- can only process the onion if the preferred candidate P_{i+1}^+ is truly offline. Otherwise, a corrupted P_i could always choose to send to the corrupted party among P_{i+1}^+ and P_{i+1}^- if such a party exists, thereby significantly increasing the effective corruption rate.

4.1 Overview of Poly Onion Encryption

Anatomy of an Onion. We describe at a high level the pertinent information contained in each onion $O_i = (K_i, H_i, U_i)$, where the index i denotes the hop number in which this onion is processed. O_i contains many blocks containing information for each hop in the routing path; we use the variable j to index the blocks. A detailed description of how O_i is constructed is given in the full version of this paper.

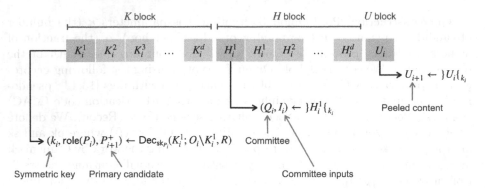

Fig. 2. The structure of an onion O_i received by a processing party P_i.

- K_i contains d blocks, including a block for each hop j in the routing path. The first block K_i^1 is a ciphertext under the processing party's public key. It contains a key k_i, which will be used to decrypt the rest of the onion. K_i^1 also contains the role of the party (whether it is an intermediary or a recipient), and the identity P_{i+1}^+ of the preferred candidate for the next hop. The rest of the onion O_i (denoted $O_i \setminus K_i^1$), as well as the run/round number R, serves as the tag for this ciphertext; in other words, the ciphertext K_i^1 will not decrypt correctly unless the decryption occurs within the context of the correct onion O_i in run/round R:

$$(k_i, \mathrm{role}(P_i), P_{i+1}^+) \leftarrow \mathsf{Dec}_{\mathsf{sk}_{P_i}}(K_i^1; O_i \setminus K_i^1, R).$$

- H_i contains d blocks, including a block for each hop j in the routing path. Each H_i^j is encrypted using a block cipher with key k_i. The first block H_i^1 contains the identities of the committee $\mathcal{Q}_i$ and the set of inputs $I_i = \{I_{i,j}\}_{j \in [\nu]}$ for the committee to run the protocol.

$$(\mathcal{Q}_i, I_i) \leftarrow \} H_i^1 \{_{k_i}.$$

- The input $I_{i,j}$ for the jth committee member $Q_{i,j} \in \mathcal{Q}_i$ is $\mathsf{Enc}_{\mathsf{pk}_{Q_{i,j}}}(P_{i+1}^+, P_{i+1}^-, \sigma_{i,j}, T_{i,j}, R)$, where P_{i+1}^+ is the preferred candidate for the next hop, P_{i+1}^- is the alternate candidate for the next hop, $\sigma_{i,j}$ is $Q_{i,j}$'s share for reconstructing the alternate candidate's version of the onion, $T_{i,j}$ is the authentication tag for $\sigma_{i,j}$, and R is the run/round number when the ProcOnion protocol should take place. $\sigma_{i,j}$ verifies under the MAC with the tag $T_{i,j}$ and key k_i; that is, $\mathsf{Ver}_{k_i}(\sigma_{i,j}, T_{i,j}) = $ "accept."
- U_i contains the contents of the onion and is similar to the content in regular onion encryption. U_i is encrypted using a block cipher with key k_i.

Overview of Processing an Onion. Let P_i be the processing party for onion $O_i = (K_i, H_i, U_i)$. Note that P_i can decrypt K_i^1 only if the onion wasn't modified en route; this is the purpose of using encryption with tags. P_i first decrypts K_i^1 with its secret key sk_{P_i}, to obtain the symmetric key k_i, learn its role $\mathrm{role}(P_i)$

(whether it is an intermediary for the onion or the recipient), and learn the identity of the preferred next destination P_{i+1}^+. The symmetric key k_i will allow P_i to decrypt the rest of the onion.

If the preferred next candidate P_{i+1}^+ is online, then P_i forms the "peeled" onion O_{i+1}^+ by decrypting the remaining blocks $K_i^2, \ldots, K_i^d, H_i^1, \ldots, H_i^d, U_i$ with k_i. P_i then shifts these blocks down so that, for example, $K_{i+1}^1 = \}K_i^2\{_{k_i}$. The last blocks of K_{i+1} and H_{i+1} are $K_{i+1}^d = \}11\ldots1\{_{k_{i+1}}$ and $H_{i+1}^d = \}00\ldots0\{_{k_{i+1}}$. This shifted, decrypted onion is $O_{i+1}^+ = (K_{i+1}^+, H_{i+1}, U_{i+1})$, the onion for P_{i+1}^+.

If the preferred next candidate P_{i+1}^+ is offline, P_i enlists the help of the committee $\mathcal{Q}_i$ to help peel the onion. It first decrypts H_i^1 with k_i to obtain $\mathcal{Q}_i$ (the set of committee members) and I_i (the set of inputs for $\mathcal{Q}_i$). P_i initiates the protocol by sending each share $I_{i,j}$ to its corresponding committee member $Q_{i,j}$ in $\mathcal{Q}_i$. Each committee member $Q_{i,j}$ decrypts its input $I_{i,j}$ to obtain P_{i+1}^+, P_{i+1}^-, $\sigma_{i,j}$ (a sharing of the key block necessary to construct O_{i+1}^-), $T_{i,j}$ (the authentication tag for $\sigma_{i,j}$), and R (a run/round number). If R is not the current run/round, $Q_{i,j}$ aborts and outputs $\bot$. If $Q_{i,j}$ determines that P_{i+1}^+ is offline and P_{i+1}^- is online, it sends $\mathsf{Enc}_{\mathsf{pk}_{P_i}}(P_{i+1}^-, \sigma_{i,j}, T_{i,j})$ to P_i. Thus, if at least α fraction of the committee members are honest and online, and P_{i+1}^+ is offline and P_{i+1}^- is online, P_i will receive from the committee members, the identity of P_{i+1}^- and at least $\alpha|\mathcal{Q}_i|$ shares that verify using the set of tags T_i and the key k_i. P_i uses these shares to reconstruct the alternate first key block $(K_{i+1}^1)^-$. P_i now processes the rest of the onion as in the case where P_{i+1}^+ is online, decrypting the other blocks with k_i and shifting them down, then again forming K_{i+1}^d and H_{i+1}^d as encryptions of $00\ldots0$ and $11\ldots1$ respectively. It then replaces the first key block $(K_{i+1}^1)^+$ of K_{i+1}^+ with the reconstructed key block $(K_{i+1}^1)^-$ to obtain K_{i+1}^-. The resulting peeled onion is the alternate onion $O_{i+1}^- = (K_{i+1}^-, H_{i+1}, U_{i+1})$. We give a more detailed description of processing an onion in the full version of this paper.

4.2   Analysis of Poly Onion Encrypion

Here, we analyze Poly Onion Encryption for $\kappa = 2$.

Correctness. We define the predicate function $\phi_{B,C,\alpha}^{\mathsf{poly}}(\mathcal{P}, \mathcal{Q}, (i,j), r, \Delta)$ to be 1 when $P_{i,j}$ is honest and online in rounds r through $r + \Delta$, and fewer than $\alpha \cdot \nu$ of the parties in $\mathcal{Q}_i$ are corrupted.

Poly Onion Encryption is correct with respect to $\phi_{B,C,\alpha}^{\mathsf{poly}}(\mathcal{P}, \mathcal{Q}, (i,j), r, \Delta)$. Suppose $P_{i,j}$ is honest and initiates the ProcOnion protocol on an onion $O_{i,j}$ in round r. We break the scenario into the following cases and show that they satisfy Definition 1:

P_{i+1}^+ **honest and online.** $P_{i,j}$ does not need the committee to process $O_{i,j}$.
   Since $P_{i,j}$ is honest, it will output (P_{i+1}^+, O_{i+1}^+) as prescribed by correctness.

P_{i+1}^+ **honest and offline.** $P_{i,j}$ will see that P_{i+1}^+ is offline and will enlist the
   help of the committee. The committee protocol returns either $\bot$ or the key
   block for O_{i+1}^-. Thus, $P_{i,j}$ will either output (P_{i+1}^-, O_{i+1}^-) or $\bot$.

P_{i+1}^+ **corrupted.** Depending on whether P_{i+1}^+ behaves as if it is online, $P_{i,j}$ may output $(P_{i+1}^+, O_{i+1}^+), (P_{i+1}^-, O_{i+1}^-)$, or $\perp$.

Security. Let $\psi_{B,C,\alpha}^{\text{poly}}(\mathcal{P}, \mathcal{Q}, h, r, \Delta)$ be the predicate function that returns 1 if and only if the following both hold: (i) no corrupted party precedes the first honest party in $\mathcal{P}_h$ that is online in all rounds r through $r + \Delta$; and (ii) fewer than $\alpha \cdot \nu$ parties in $\mathcal{Q}_{h-1}$ are corrupted.

Recall that ν is the committee size and α is the number of committee members' shares required to reconstruct the onion for the alternate candidate. By the above definition of $\psi_{B,C,\alpha}^{\text{poly}}$, if the first candidate in $\mathcal{P}_{h+1}$ is honest and online, and fewer than $\alpha \cdot \nu$ members in $\mathcal{Q}_h$ are corrupted, the adversary cannot win the security game with non-negligible advantage, i.e., the onion mixes in hop $h + 1$. As long as enough parties in our universe are honest, and committees are chosen randomly, we can increase the committee size to boost the probability that fewer than $\alpha \cdot \nu$ members in $\mathcal{Q}_h$ are corrupted; we discuss this further in Sect. 6. Given that fewer than $\alpha \cdot \nu$ members of $\mathcal{Q}_h$ are corrupted, the onion mixes in hop $h + 1$ if the first party in $\mathcal{P}_{h+1}$ is honest and online. We show later in Sect. 6 that $\psi_{B,C,\alpha}^{\text{poly}}$ is indeed satisfied with high enough probability to provide anonymity.

Theorem 1 (Security of construction). *Poly Onion Encryption is poly onion secure with respect to the security predicate $\psi_{B,C,\alpha}^{\text{poly}}$ for $0 < \alpha \leq 1$ and $\nu \geq \frac{1}{\alpha}$ assuming that all of the underlying standard primitives exist.*

We prove that the scheme is secure using a hybrid argument that is similar to the security proof of shallot encryption by Ando and Lysyanskaya [2]. We give a proof sketch below and provide thee full proof in the full version of this paper.

Proof sketch. Let Experiment^0 be the same as running the security game with $b = 0$; this is when the challenger creates the challenge onion as usual. Let Experiment^1 be the same as running the security game with $b = 1$; this is when the challenger creates two unrelated sets of onion layers $\mathcal{O}$ and $\mathcal{O}'$, and the onion $O \in \mathcal{O}$ peels to $O' \in \mathcal{O}'$ at the chosen server.

We construct the following hybrids that act as stepping stones from Experiment^0 to Experiment^1. Let $i = h - 1$. The hybrids involve changing the onion layers $\mathcal{O}_{i+1}$. In all of the hybrids, the ProcOnion oracle behaves as if $b = 1$ in POSecurityGame. That is, when an onion $O_j \in \mathcal{O}_{i+1}$ is queried, it returns the onion in $\mathcal{O}_{i+2}$ corresponding to the appropriate candidate. This behavior is consistent with $b = 0$ in POSecurityGame for Experiment^0 and with $b = 1$ in POSecurityGame for Experiment^1:

Experiment^0: security game with $b = 0$.
    $\updownarrow$ These are identically distributed.
Hybrid^1: since onions are layered encryption objects, we form challenge onion by first forming O_{i+2}^+ and then "wrapping" it in more layers of encryption to get $\mathcal{O}_1$. We formally define wrapping in the full version of this paper.

$\updownarrow$ Indistinguishable by security of public key encryption.

Hybrid^2: same as Hybrid^1, except change the oracle so that in step 6 of POSecurityGame, if it is queried with $(O_{i+1}^-)'$ to be processed by P_{i+1}^-, it instead runs ProcOnion with O_{i+1}^-.

$\updownarrow$ Indistinguishable by security of secret sharing/public key encryption.

Hybrid^3: same as Hybrid^2, except in block H_i^1 of $\mathcal{O}_i$, change the share of every member of committee $\mathcal{Q}_i$ to a share of $\mathsf{Enc}_{\mathsf{pk}_{P_{i+1}^-}}(00\ldots0)$ instead of $\mathsf{Enc}_{\mathsf{pk}_{P_{i+1}^-}}(k_{i+1}, \mathrm{role}(P_{i+1}^-), P_{i+2}^+)$.

$\updownarrow$ Indistinguishable by security of public key encryption.

Hybrid^4: same as Hybrid^3, except in the key block K_{i+1}^1 of $\mathcal{O}_{i+1}$, change k_{i+1} to $00\ldots0$.

$\updownarrow$ Indistinguishable by security of the block cipher.

Hybrid^5: same as Hybrid^4, except change $\mathcal{O}_{i+1}$ from a wrapping of O_{i+2}^+ to the output for hop $(i+1)$ of FormOnion on the first segment of the routing path, up to P_{i+1}.

$\updownarrow$ Indistinguishable by security of public key encryption.

Hybrid^6: same as Hybrid^5, except in the key block K_{i+1}^1 of $\mathcal{O}_{i+1}$, change the key back from $00\ldots0$ to k_{i+1}, and change the role of P_{i+1} from intermediary to recipient.

$\updownarrow$ Indistinguishable by security of secret sharing/public key encryption.

Hybrid^7: same as Hybrid^6, except in block H_i^1 of $\mathcal{O}_i$, change all committee members' shares back from shares of $\mathsf{Enc}_{\mathsf{pk}_{P_{i+1}^-}}(00\ldots0)$ to shares of $\mathsf{Enc}_{\mathsf{pk}_{P_{i+1}^-}}(k_{i+1}, \mathrm{role}(P_{i+1}^-), P_{i+2}^+)$

$\updownarrow$ Indistinguishable by security of public key encryption.

Hybrid^8: same as Hybrid^7, except change the oracle so that it no longer treats $(O_{i+1}^-)'$ specially.

$\updownarrow$ These are identically distributed.

$\mathsf{Experiment}^1$: security game with $b = 1$. $\square$

Remark 7. We remark that this construction can be generalized for any number of candidates κ. That is, every onion has κ candidate processing parties per hop. We can do so by modifying the committee members' inputs so that each input $I_{i,j}$ contains the full list of candidates rather than just P_{i+1}^+ and P_{i+1}^-. We also include $\kappa - 1$ shares $\sigma_{i,j}^2, \ldots, \sigma_{i,j}^\kappa$ in $I_{i,j}$ instead of just $\sigma_{i,j}$. Each share $\sigma_{i,j}^c$ is used to construct the version of the onion for candidate $P_{i+1,c} \in \mathcal{P}_{i+1}$. The processing party knows from the committee members' responses which candidate each committee member votes for. If enough committee members vote for one of the candidates, the processing party can reconstruct that candidate's version of the onion. Correctness and security still hold with respect to the same predicates $\phi_{B,C,\alpha}^{\mathsf{poly}}$ and $\psi_{B,C,\alpha}^{\mathsf{poly}}$ defined in Sect. 4.2. The proofs of correctness and security are given in the full version of this paper.

5   Anonymity in the Setting with Churn

So far we have explored new onion encryption techniques for handling network churn, defining poly onion encryption, and constructing a scheme that satisfies poly onion security. In this section, we turn our attention to the problem of how to route onions such as those constructed using Poly Onion Encryption through a dynamic network to achieve anonymity. To begin with, we must first formally define what it means for an onion routing protocol to be anonymous in a setting with network churn. Our new definitions of anonymity, including multi-run anonymity, are provided in Sect. 5.1.

To establish that our proposed multi-run anonymity definition is a usable notion, we must also show that it is achievable. In Sect. 5.3, we prove a general theorem (Theorem 2) that states that for a class of onion routing protocols, which we call "simulatable" protocols, single-run anonymity is equivalent to multi-run anonymity. An implication of this is that all previously known simulatable protocols that are single-run anonymous are also multi-run anonymous. These include Π_p [3]. However, these new multi-run results are for the static setting, without network churn. In Sect. 6, we prove (again relying on Theorem 2) that Π_p can achieve multi-run anonymity in the presence of churn. Our formal definition of the class of simulatable onion routing protocols is provided in Sect. 5.2.

5.1   Definitions of Anonymity

Here, we define what it means for an onion routing protocol to achieve multi-run anonymity. First, we define an anonymity game, StrongAnonGame, which we then use in the formal definition of multi-run anonymity (Definition 3).

StrongAnonGame$(\mathcal{A}, \Pi, L, \lambda)$ is parameterized by the adversary $\mathcal{A}$, the onion routing protocol Π, the number of runs L, and the security parameter λ. The game proceeds in three phases: (i) the setup phase where $\mathcal{A}$ has access to the oracle for responding to queries for processing onions on behalf of honest parties, (ii) the challenge phase where $\mathcal{A}$ and the challenger run the protocol Π, and (iii) the final phase where $\mathcal{A}$ again has access to the oracle.

During *setup*, the adversary $\mathcal{A}$ first picks the set of corrupted parties Bad and sends Bad to the challenger. The challenger generates the keys for the honest parties according to Π and sends only the public portion of these keys to $\mathcal{A}$. $\mathcal{A}$ sends the corrupt parties' public keys to the challenger. $\mathcal{A}$ can now submit ProcOnion queries to the the challenger. For each ProcOnion query, $\mathcal{A}$ submits a bulletin B and a churn schedule C such that the number of parties ever offline is bounded above by the churn limit $c(N)$, an onion O, an honest processing party P for peeling O, and a round number r. The challenger receives only the restriction of C to the honest parties. The challenger interacts with $\mathcal{A}$ to run the ProcOnion protocol on O starting in round r, with the challenger acting on behalf of the honest parties following the protocol and $\mathcal{A}$ controlling the behavior of the corrupted parties.

In the *challenge phase*, $\mathcal{A}$ and the challenger run the protocol L times. To begin with, the challenger picks the challenge bit $b \in \{0, 1\}$. For each of the

L runs, $\mathcal{A}$ and the challenger repeat the same procedure. In run i, $\mathcal{A}$ picks a bulletin B_i and a churn schedule C_i with at most $c(N)$ parties offline during that run. $\mathcal{A}$ also picks input vectors σ_0^i and σ_1^i that are both valid with respect to B_i, i.e., $\sigma_0^i \equiv_{\mathsf{Bad}} \sigma_1^i$. $\mathcal{A}$ sends B_i, the restriction of C_i to the honest parties, σ_0^i, and σ_1^i to the challenger. $\mathcal{A}$ and the challenger interact in a protocol run of σ_b^i with online parties specified by bulletin B_i and churn schedule C_i, and with the challenger acting as the honest parties, and $\mathcal{A}$ acting as the corrupt parties.

After the challenge phase, in the *final phase*, $\mathcal{A}$ can again interact with the challenger by submitting ProcOnion queries, with the additional restriction that $\mathcal{A}$ cannot ask about onions formed by honest parties during the challenge phase. That is, $\mathcal{A}$ picks a bulletin B and churn schedule C (such that the number of offline parties is at most $c(N)$), an onion O (not observed during the challenge phase), and a processing party P. $\mathcal{A}$ again sends C restricted to the honest parties. Finally, $\mathcal{A}$ outputs a guess b' of the challenge bit b. We say $\mathcal{A}$ wins StrongAnonGame($\mathcal{A}, \Pi, L, \lambda$) if its guess b' is equal to b. See Fig. 3 for a schematic of the strong anonymity game.

We now define several variants of strong anonymity using StrongAnonGame.

Definition 3 (Strong Anonymity). *An onion routing protocol Π with security parameter λ is L-strongly anonymous against the class of adversaries $\mathbb{A}$ if for every adversary $\mathcal{A} \in \mathbb{A}$, $\left|\Pr[\mathcal{A} \text{ wins StrongAnonGame}(\mathcal{A}, \Pi, L, \lambda)] - \frac{1}{2}\right| = \mathsf{negl}(\lambda)$.*

Note that when $c(N) = 0$, this is the static setting; when $c(N) > 0$, this is the dynamic setting with network churn.

Multi-run vs. Single-run. We say a protocol Π is multi-run anonymous if it is anonymous for polynomially bounded $L > 1$ in the above definition. A protocol Π is single-run anonymous if it is anonymous for $L = 1$.

Strong vs. Weak. We say a protocol Π is weakly anonymous if it satisfies the analogous definition for a modified anonymity game, where the adversary does not have oracle access to the ProcOnion queries. We say a protocol Π is strongly anonymous if it satisfies the definition using StrongAnonGame.

Adaptive vs. Non-Adaptive. In StrongAnonGame, the adversary is adaptive in that it can choose the bulletin, the schedule, and the inputs before each run based on prior history. We also define a weaker non-adaptive anonymity definition, in which the adversary must choose all inputs, churn schedules, and bulletins before observing any protocol runs. Using our terminology above, the standard anonymity definition in prior papers (e.g., [2,3,25,32,33]) is weak single-run non-adaptive anonymity in our new terms.

5.2   Simulatable Onion Routing Protocols

Here, we formally define the class of simulatable onion routing protocols. As we will show in Sect. 5.3, simulatability is a property that can reduce multi-run anonymity to single-run anonymity. The idea is that if a simulatable onion

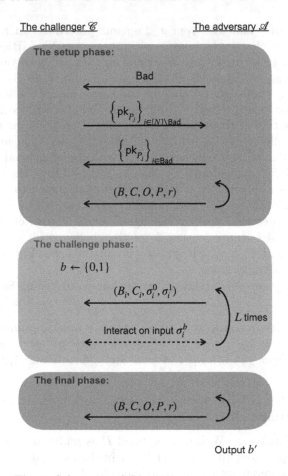

Fig. 3. Schematic of the strong anonymity game.

routing protocol is single-run anonymous, then we can prove that it is also multi-run anonymous via a sequence of reductions that "simulate" extraneous runs for an adversary that expects to interact in multiple runs. (See our proof of Theorem 2 in Sect. 5.3.)

Thus, what we mean by "simulatable" is that the reduction should be able to recreate what the honest parties do in a run, using only information that it has access to – namely, the public keys of all the parties, the bulletin, the churn schedule, the run number, and the inputs for the honest parties. Consider the following two settings: (i) the real setting, in which the challenger interacts with the adversary by following the protocol and (ii) the ideal setting, in which the challenger interacts with the adversary by using the algorithm GenOnions that generates (from just the public parameters and the honest parties' inputs) all possible onions that the honest parties might send out during the run and the algorithm ScheduleProcOnions that determines (from just the honest parties' message buffers) if/when these onions are processed. An onion routing protocol is simulatable if no (efficient) adversary can tell whether it is interacting in the real setting or the ideal one except with negligible advantage. We define these concepts more concretely below.

The Real Setting. RealGame($\mathcal{A}, \Pi, \lambda$) is parametrized by the adversary $\mathcal{A}$, the onion routing protocol Π with onion encryption scheme (KeyGen, FormOnion, ProcOnion), and the security parameter λ.

The game proceeds as follows. First, the adversary $\mathcal{A}$ chooses the adversarial parties Bad, the bulletin B, the churn schedule C, the run number R, and the keys for the parties in Bad. The public portions of these keys are relayed to the challenger. The challenger generates the keys for the honest parties by running KeyGen and relays the public portion of these keys to $\mathcal{A}$. $\mathcal{A}$ picks the input vector σ, and the inputs for the honest parties are relayed to the challenger.

The challenger and $\mathcal{A}$ interact in a run of Π on input σ, with the challenger running Π on behalf of the honest parties, and $\mathcal{A}$ controlling the adversarial parties. At the end of the run, $\mathcal{A}$ outputs a bit b.

The Ideal Setting. This setting is defined with respect to two algorithms:

- An onion generation algorithm GenOnions takes as input the security parameter 1^λ, the public keys $\{pk_{P_j}\}_{j=1}^N$ of all the parties, the bulletin B, the churn schedule C, the run number R, the identity P_i of an honest party, and the input σ_i for P_i; and outputs a set $\mathcal{O}_i^{(1)}$ of onions for P_i, i.e.,
$$\mathcal{O}_i^{(1)} \leftarrow \text{GenOnions}(1^\lambda, \{pk_{P_j}\}_{j=1}^N, B, C, R, P_i, \sigma_i).$$
- A scheduling algorithm ScheduleProcOnions takes as input the security parameter 1^λ, the round number r, the identity P_i of an honest party, and the state OnionBuffer$_i^{(r)}$ of P_i at round r; and outputs a set $\mathcal{O}_i^{(r)}$ of onions to be processed starting at round r and an updated state OnionBuffer$_i^{(r+1)}$, i.e.,
$$(\mathcal{O}_i^{(r)}, \text{OnionBuffer}_i^{(r+1)}) \leftarrow \text{ScheduleProcOnions}(1^\lambda, r, P_i, \text{OnionBuffer}_i^{(r)}).$$

IdealGame($\mathcal{A}$, GenOnions, ScheduleProcOnions, λ) is parametrized by the adversary $\mathcal{A}$, the onion generation algorithm GenOnions, the scheduling algorithm ScheduleProcOnions, and the security parameter λ.

The game proceeds as follows. Like in the real setting, the adversary first picks Bad, B, C, R, and the keys $\{pk_{P_j}\}_{j\in\text{Bad}}$ for the adversarial parties, while the challenger runs KeyGen to generate the keys $\{pk_{P_j}\}_{j\in[N]\setminus\text{Bad}}$ for honest parties; and $\mathcal{A}$ determines the input vector $\sigma = (\sigma_1, \ldots, \sigma_N)$ for the run.

The challenger and $\mathcal{A}$ interact in a run of Π on input σ, with the challenger acting as the honest parties, and $\mathcal{A}$ controlling the rest. In contrast to the real setting, the challenger doesn't run the protocol Π.

Instead, in the first round, for each honest party P_i, the challenger runs GenOnions($1^\lambda, \{pk_{P_j}\}_{j=1}^N, B, C, R, P_i, \sigma_i$) and sets P_i's initial state OnionBuffer$_i^{(1)}$ to the output $\mathcal{O}_i^{(1)} \leftarrow$ GenOnions($1^\lambda, \{pk_{P_j}\}_{j=1}^N, B, C, R, P_i, \sigma_i$). Then, still within the first round, for each honest party P_i, the challenger runs ScheduleProcOnions($1^\lambda, 1, P_i, \text{OnionBuffer}_i^{(1)}$) to obtain a set $\mathcal{O}_i^{(1)} \subseteq$ OnionBuffer$_i^{(1)}$ of onions to be processed and an updated state OnionBuffer$_i^{(2)}$.

The challenger updates P_i's state to $\mathsf{OnionBuffer}_i^{(2)}$. For each onion $O \in \mathcal{O}_i^{(1)}$, the challenger initiates ProcOnion with P_i as the processing party and O as the onion to be processed and sends out the peeled onion $O_{1,i \rightarrow j}$ to its next destination $P_{1,i \rightarrow j}$ (whenever ProcOnion terminates).

In each subsequent round r, and for each honest party P_i, the challenger first adds the onions that P_i received in the previous round to $\mathsf{OnionBuffer}_i^{(r)}$. Then, the challenger runs $\mathsf{ScheduleProcOnions}(1^\lambda, r, P_i, \mathsf{OnionBuffer}_i^{(r)})$ to obtain $\mathcal{O}_i^{(r)}$ and $\mathsf{OnionBuffer}_i^{(r+1)}$. The challenger updates P_i's state to $\mathsf{OnionBuffer}_i^{(r+1)}$. For each $O \in \mathcal{O}_i^{(r)}$, the challenger initiates ProcOnion with P_i as the processing party and O as the onion to be processed and sends out the peeled onion $O_{r,i \rightarrow j}$ to its next destination $P_{r,i \rightarrow j}$ (whenever ProcOnion terminates).

At the end of the run, $\mathcal{A}$ outputs a bit b.

Definition 4 (Simulatablity).   *An onion routing protocol Π is simulatable if for every p.p.t. adversary $\mathcal{A}$ there exist p.p.t. algorithms* (GenOnions, ScheduleProcOnions) *such that $\mathcal{A}$ can distinguish between* RealGame *and* IdealGame *with only negligible advantage, i.e.,*

$$| \Pr\left[1 \leftarrow \mathsf{RealGame}(\mathcal{A}, \Pi, \lambda)\right]$$
$$- \Pr\left[1 \leftarrow \mathsf{IdealGame}(\mathcal{A}, \Pi, \mathsf{GenOnions}, \mathsf{ScheduleProcOnions}, \lambda)\right]| = \mathsf{negl}(\lambda).$$

5.3   From Single-Run to Multi-run Anonymity

Theorem 2. *Let Π be a simulatable onion routing protocol with security parameter λ. For any $L = \mathsf{poly}(\lambda)$, Π is L-strongly anonymous from the active (resp. passive) adversary $\mathbb{A}$ with churn limit $c(N)$ if and only if it is single-run strongly anonymous from $\mathbb{A}$.*

Proof. It is evident that multi-run anonymity implies single-run anonymity since the former holds for any (polynomially bounded) number of runs, including one. Thus, to prove the theorem, it suffices to show that single-run anonymity implies multi-run anonymity. We do this using a hybrid argument.

Let Π be an onion routing protocol with security parameter λ that is single-run strongly anonymous against the active (resp. passive) adversary. Let $\mathcal{A}$ be any p.p.t. adversary from the class of active (resp. passive) adversaries.

Let $\mathsf{Experiment}_0$ be the anonymity game $\mathsf{StrongAnonGame}(\mathcal{A}, \Pi, L, \lambda)$ conditioned on the challenge bit b equaling zero, i.e., $b = 0$. Let $\sigma_0 = (\sigma_0^1, \ldots, \sigma_0^L)$ denote the sequence of input vectors that $\mathcal{A}$ chooses for the L runs in $\mathsf{Experiment}_0$; that is, σ_0^i is the input vector for the ith run.

Likewise, let $\mathsf{Experiment}_1$ be $\mathsf{StrongAnonGame}(\mathcal{A}, \Pi, L, \lambda)$ when $b = 1$. Let $\sigma_1 = (\sigma_1^1, \ldots, \sigma_1^L)$ be the L input vectors in $\mathsf{Experiment}_1$.

We define a sequence of hybrids as follows. For all $1 \leq i \leq L + 1$, let Hybrid_i be the experiment where the input vector for run j is σ_0^j if $j < i$, and otherwise, it is σ_1^j. Clearly, $\mathsf{Experiment}_0$ is the same as Hybrid_{L+1}, and $\mathsf{Experiment}_1$ is the same as Hybrid_1.

To complete the hybrid argument that Π is multi-run anonymous, we show that any two consecutive hybrids are distinguishable. To do so, we define another anonymity game, FlipAnonGame($\mathcal{A}, \Pi, \lambda, L, i$), that we use only in this proof. This game is essentially the same as StrongAnonGame with the same parameters, except the challenger runs Π on σ_0 up to (but not necessarily including) run i and runs Π on σ_1 for the remaining runs when $b = 1$. The index i specifies where this switch from σ_0 to σ_1 happens. The challenger chooses $b \in \{0, 1\}$ uniformly at random. If $b = 0$, the first run with input σ_0 is run i. If $b = 1$, the first run with input σ_0 is run $i + 1$. The adversary $\mathcal{A}$ makes a guess b' of whether the challenger switched in run i or in run $i + 1$ and wins if $b' = b$.

To prove that consecutive hybrids are indistinguishable, we prove that $\mathcal{A}$ wins FlipAnonGame($\mathcal{A}, \Pi, \lambda, L, i$) with only negligible advantage. Suppose there exists an index i such that $\mathcal{A}$ wins FlipAnonGame($\mathcal{A}, \Pi, \lambda, L, i$) with non-negligible advantage. Then, we can construct a reduction $\mathcal{B}$ that uses $\mathcal{A}$ to "break" single-run strong anonymity. $\mathcal{B}$ goes between $\mathcal{A}$ and the challenger $\mathcal{C}$ in StrongAnonGame($\mathcal{B}, \Pi, \lambda, 1$). We describe the interactions between $\mathcal{A}, \mathcal{B}$, and $\mathcal{C}$ in terms of the phases in StrongAnonGame.

The Setup Phase. During setup, the reduction $\mathcal{B}$ serves as a channel between the adversary $\mathcal{A}$ (of FlipAnonGame) and the challenger (of the single-run anonymity game). $\mathcal{A}$ sends the set of adversarial parties to the reduction $\mathcal{B}$; $\mathcal{B}$ relays this to $\mathcal{C}$. $\mathcal{C}$ sends the honest parties' public keys to $\mathcal{B}$; $\mathcal{B}$ relays them to $\mathcal{A}$. $\mathcal{A}$ sends the adversarial parties' public keys to $\mathcal{B}$; $\mathcal{B}$ relays them to $\mathcal{C}$. During the first query phase, $\mathcal{A}$ can send ProcOnion queries to $\mathcal{B}$. Whenever $\mathcal{A}$ sends a ProcOnion query with a bulletin B and a churn schedule C (such that the number of offline parties is at most $c(N)$), an onion O, a processing party P, and a round number r, $\mathcal{B}$ relays the query to $\mathcal{C}$ and replies to $\mathcal{A}$ with $\mathcal{C}$'s response.

The Challenge Phase. Since (from the hypothesis) Π is simulatable, it follows that there exist efficient algorithms (GenOnions, ScheduleProcOnions) such that no efficient algorithm can tell whether $\mathcal{B}$ is running the protocol Π, or simulating the run by running GenOnions and ScheduleProcOnions and submitting ProcOnion queries to the challenger, instead.

For each run j of the challenge phase, $\mathcal{A}$ sends the run parameters $(B_j, C_j, \sigma_0^j, \sigma_1^j)$ to $\mathcal{B}$. If $j < i$, $\mathcal{B}$ simulates a run of Π with parameters B_j, C_j, and σ_0. If $j > i$, $\mathcal{B}$ simulates the run with parameters B_j, C_j, and σ_1 instead. The ith run is the challenge run in FlipAnonGame. In this run, $\mathcal{B}$ uses these parameters in its challenge run, relaying them all to $\mathcal{C}$ and serving as a channel between $\mathcal{A}$ and $\mathcal{C}$ in running Π on either $\sigma_0^{j=i}$ or $\sigma_1^{j=i}$, depending on the challenge bit b chosen by $\mathcal{C}$.

The Final Phase. During the second query phase, $\mathcal{A}$ is again allowed to submit ProcOnion queries. Whenever $\mathcal{A}$ sends a ProcOnion query with a bulletin B and a churn schedule C (such that the number of offline parties is at most $c(N)$), an onion O (where O was not produced by an honest party during the challenge phase), a processing party P, and a round number r, $\mathcal{B}$ relays the query to $\mathcal{C}$ and replies to $\mathcal{A}$ with $\mathcal{C}$'s response. Finally, $\mathcal{A}$ makes its guess b' for FlipAnonGame and passes b' to $\mathcal{B}$. If $\mathcal{A}$ guesses $b' = 0$, this means that $\mathcal{A}$ suspects that the first run with input σ_1 is run i. Thus if $\mathcal{A}$'s guess is correct, the input in the challenge run i for StrongAnonGame was likely σ_1, and $\mathcal{B}$ should output 1. Thus, $\mathcal{B}$ outputs the opposite of b' (i.e., 1 if $b' = 0$ and 0 if $b' = 1$).

Since $\mathcal{B}$ essentially wins whenever $\mathcal{A}$ wins, we conclude that no efficient adversary can win FlipAnonGame with non-negligible advantage.

Corollary 1. *If Π is a simulatable onion routing protocol, then, in the static setting (i.e. for $c(N) = 0$), Π is multi-run strongly anonymous from the active (resp. passive) adversary iff it is single-run strongly anonymous from the active (resp. passive) adversary.*

6   Multi-run Strongly Anonymous Onion Routing with Churn

Note that we can turn any weakly anonymous onion routing protocol strongly anonymous by using a sufficiently secure onion encryption scheme (e.g., any scheme that realizes Camenisch and Lysyanskaya's onion ideal functionality [9]). Thus from Corollary 1, in the static setting, any simulatable onion routing protocol shown to be single-run anonymous is also anonymous over multiple runs. For example, Ando, et al. [3] proved that their protocol Π_p is anonymous from the passive adversary in the static setting; we show that Π_p is simulatable (Lemma 2), implying that running Π_p multiple times is still anonymous.

However, as we show below, Π_p does not work in the dynamic setting; e.g., when the churn limit is linear in the number of participants, Π_p either fails to deliver any messages or is not anonymous (Theorem 3). Furthermore, Duo Onion Encryption and naive modifications of it fail in the same way. In this section, after demonstrating these problems with previous solutions, we show that we can make Π_p multi-run anonymous from the passive adversary with a linear churn limit (a minority of churned or corrupted parties) if we use poly onion encryption instead of regular onion encryption (Theorem 4).

The Protocol Π_p. Ando, Lysyanskaya, and Upfal [3] showed that the simple protocol Π_p is weakly anonymous from the passive adversary in the (simple I/O) static setting. For this protocol, there are N users that send and receive messages: $\mathcal{P} = P_1, \ldots, P_N$; and $n < N$ mix-servers that serve as intermediaries on routing paths: $\mathcal{S} = S_1, \ldots, S_n$. During the onion-forming phase of a protocol execution, each user P_i forms an onion to carry the message $m_{i \to j}$ to his recipient P_j. Specifically, P_i first picks a random sample $T_1, \ldots, T_\ell$ from the set $\mathcal{S}$ of mix-servers (with replacement), i.e., $T_1, \ldots, T_\ell \leftarrow_{\$} \mathcal{S}$, then generates an onion using the message $m_{i \to j}$, the path $(T_1, \ldots, T_\ell, P_j)$, and the public keys for all the parties on the path. During the first round of the execution phase, the users send the generated onions to their first locations (i.e., first parties on the paths). During all subsequent rounds, each party peels the onions from the previous round and sends the peeled onions to their next locations or outputs the received messages for the final round.

Ando et al. [3] proved that Π_p is anonymous from the passive adversary that corrupts up to a constant $0 \leq \beta_1 < 1$ fraction of the servers when both the server load (the average number of onions per server per round) $\frac{N}{n}$ and the number ℓ of rounds are at least polylog in the security parameter λ. This result holds in the static setting without any churn.

6.1 Insufficiencies of Previous Solutions

We show both that Π_p fails in terms of either delivery rate or anonymity, and duo onion encryption or natural modifications thereof do little to help. For all the results below, let λ denote the security parameter and let $\mathsf{polylog}(\lambda)$ denote any polylog function in λ. Additionally, we say a server is *online* when it is online throughout the entire protocol run; otherwise, the server is *offline*.

Theorem 3. *When the churn limit is $c(N) = \beta_2 N$ where $0 < \beta_2 \leq 1$ is any positive constant, a single run of Π_p either fails to deliver any message with overwhelming probability, or else it is not (single-run weakly) anonymous.*

Proof. Case 1: when the length of the routing path $\ell \geq \mathsf{polylog}(\lambda)$. Let P_i be any sender. Let E_i be the event that the onion generated by P_i makes it to the recipient of P_i. This is the event that all of the intermediaries $T_1, \ldots, T_\ell$ that P_i picks are online. Since each T_j is online with probability $(1 - \beta_2)$, $\Pr[E_i] = (1 - \beta_2)^\ell \leq (1 - \beta_2)^{\mathsf{polylog}(\lambda)}$. In other words, E_i occurs with negligible probability. By a union bound, the probability that *any* of the $\ell = \mathsf{poly}(\lambda)$ messages gets through is also negligibly small. Thus, in this case, Π_p fails to route any message.

Case 2: when the length of the routing path $\ell < \mathsf{polylog}(\lambda)$. We know from previous work [12,17,18] that with a passive adversary corrupting a constant fraction of the parties, no onion routing protocol with fewer than polylog rounds of mixing is anonymous.

We just demonstrated that the protocol Π_p, using standard onion encryption, doesn't work when the churn limit is linear in the number of participants. Before using Poly Onion Encryption, with its more complicated committee protocol, one might hope to replace standard onion encryption with Duo Onion Encryption instead. However, Duo Onion Encryption with two candidates yields only a small improvement in effective churn rate: the probability that an onion is dropped in a given round is now β_2^2, which is still a positive constant, and Theorem 3 still holds. The same is true for any constant number of candidates.

At the other extreme, when the number of candidates is "large," with $\mathsf{polylog}(\lambda)$ candidates, the probability that an onion is dropped in a given hop becomes $\beta_2^{\mathsf{polylog}(\lambda)}$, which is negligible if β_2 is a constant. However, anonymity becomes an issue here. Consider the following attack, where the adversary traces an onion O back to its honest sender P_i.

Suppose that the passive adversary manages to corrupt some candidate in every hop in the routing path of O. In Duo Onion Encryption, like in Poly Onion Encryption, each onion layer O_i is encrypted with a symmetric key k_i. Unlike

Poly Onion Encryption, which requires running the committee protocol to obtain k_i in the event that the first candidate is offline, Duo Onion Encryption includes in O_i an encryption of k_i under each candidate's public key. This allows the adversary $\mathcal{A}$ to trace O through the network as follows. $\mathcal{A}$ observes P_i send O_1 to its first intermediary P_1. O_1 contains $\mathsf{Enc}_{\mathsf{pk}_{P_1'}}(k_1)$ for some corrupted party P_1', since some candidate in every hop is corrupted. $\mathcal{A}$ silently decrypts this to obtain k_1, which it uses to peel the onion to get O_2. $\mathcal{A}$ then sees the outgoing traffic from P_1, which includes P_1 sending O_2 to what $\mathcal{A}$ now knows is the next intermediary P_2. In this way, $\mathcal{A}$ continues peeling O in parallel with the network, observing the network traffic and knowing in each round exactly where O is. $\mathcal{A}$ does this until O reaches its recipient, allowing $\mathcal{A}$ to discover who P_i is communicating with. Thus, mixing only occurs in a hop where all candidates are honest.

If a constant fraction β_1 of the parties are corrupted and chosen uniformly at random, the probability that all candidates are honest in a given hop is at most $(1 - \beta_1)^{\mathsf{polylog}(\lambda)}$, which is negligible. By a union bound, given ℓ hops, the probability that any of them has all honest candidates is at most $\ell \cdot \mathsf{negl}(\lambda)$. That is, with overwhelming probability, every hop has at least one corrupted candidate. Thus, for any polynomial length routing path, this shadow routing attack succeeds with non-negligible probability, and the protocol is not anonymous.

While it may be possible to set κ between the two extremes and balance the effective delivery and corruption rates, doing so is nontrivial. Furthermore, even if such a value exists, previous proofs of anonymity such as that of Π_p no longer necessarily hold. We can instead achieve anonymous message delivery even with a constant churn limit by modifying Π_p so that it uses Poly Onion Encryption.

6.2   Poly Π_p is Multi-run Anonymous in the Presence of Churn

Π_p *with Poly Onion Encryption.* To generate a poly onion, each sender P_i first randomly chooses κ candidates $\mathcal{P}_h = (P_{h,1}, \ldots, P_{h,\kappa})$ for each intermediary hop h of the path and $\kappa - 1$ candidates $(P_{\ell+1,2}, \ldots, P_{\ell+1,\kappa})$ for the final $(\ell+1)^{st}$ hop. P_i then randomly chooses ν helpers $\mathcal{Q}_h = (Q_{h,1}, \ldots, Q_{h,\nu})$ for each hop h of the path, i.e., $P_{1,1}, \ldots, P_{1,\kappa}, \ldots, P_{\ell+1,2}, \ldots, P_{\ell+1,\kappa}, Q_{1,1}, \ldots, Q_{1,\nu}, \ldots, Q_{\ell,1}, \ldots, Q_{\ell,\nu} \leftarrow_{\$} \mathcal{S}$. P_i then forms an onion using the message m to her recipient $P_{\ell+1,1}$, the candidates $(\mathcal{P}_1, \ldots, \mathcal{P}_\ell, (P_{\ell+1,1}, P_{\ell+1,2}, \ldots, P_{\ell+1,\kappa}))$, the helpers $(\mathcal{Q}_1, \ldots, \mathcal{Q}_\ell)$, and all the required public keys.

For the analysis below, we will make the simplifying assumption that ProcOnion runs within a single round since making this assumption doesn't change the results. We use the committee threshold parameter $\alpha = \frac{1}{2}$. By the security of Poly Onion Encryption (Theorem 1), onions formed by honest parties "mix" in hop h when the first online candidate in $\mathcal{P}_h$ is honest (event E_3 in the proof), and fewer than $\frac{1}{2}$ of the members of $\mathcal{Q}_{h-1}$ are corrupted (event E_4 in the proof). Note that these conditions are stronger than what is required for security to hold.

For all the results below, let *Poly* Π_p be the protocol Π_p modified to use Poly Onion Encryption instead of regular onion encryption with the following parameter settings: security parameter λ, length of the routing path $\ell \geq \mathsf{polylog}(\lambda)$, and number of candidates per hop $\kappa \geq \mathsf{polylog}(\lambda)$, and number of helpers per hop $\nu \geq \mathsf{polylog}(\lambda)$.

Towards showing that Poly Π_p is multi-run anonymous when the churn limit is linear in the number of mix-servers, we now prove that Poly Π_p is both single-run anonymous in the setting with churn (Definition 3) and simulatable (Definition 4).

Lemma 1. *Poly Π_p is single-run (strongly) anonymous from the passive adversary who corrupts up to a constant $0 \leq \beta_1 < 1$ fraction of the mix-servers, when the churn limit is $c(N) = \beta_2 N$ and $0 \leq \beta_1 + \beta_2 < \frac{1}{2}$ is a constant. Moreover, it delivers all messages with overwhelming probability.*

Proof. An onion is dropped at an intermediary $P_{h,j} \in \mathcal{P}_h$ due to churn only if all of the candidates $\mathcal{P}_h$ are offline (event E_1), or at least $\frac{\nu}{2}$ of the helpers $\mathcal{Q}_{h-1}$ are offline (event E_2). The probability of E_1 is negligibly small since the probability that each randomly chosen candidate is offline is bounded above by $\frac{1}{2}$. We can show that the probability of E_2 is also negligibly small by using a Chernoff bound for Poisson trials [26, Corollary 4.6]; with overwhelming probability, the fraction of offline parties in the committee is arbitrarily close to the expected value, which is strictly less than $\frac{\nu}{2}$. Since E_1 and E_2 occur with only negligible probabilities, this onion (layer) at $P_{i,j}$ is not dropped. Since the total number of onion layers is polynomially bounded in the security parameter, by a union bound, it follows that with overwhelming probability, no onion is dropped.

Since no onions are dropped, we can apply the proof of weak anonymity of Π_p from Ando et al. [3], with a slight modification. In that proof, mixing occurs at an intermediary server as long as that server is honest. This happens with constant probability in Ando et al.'s construction. With Poly Onion Encryption, mixing occurs when the first online candidate in $\mathcal{P}_h$ is honest (event E_3), and fewer than $\frac{1}{2}$ of the members of $\mathcal{Q}_{h-1}$ are corrupted (event E_4). The probability that any random party is both honest and online is at least $1 - \beta_1 - \beta_2 > \frac{1}{2}$ since, in the most pessimistic scenario, the adversary chooses the set of corrupted servers to be disjoint from the set of offline servers. Thus, E_3 happens with probability at least $\frac{1}{2}$. Similar to the analysis of $\bar{E}_2$, from a Chernoff bound, E_4 also occurs with overwhelming probability. Thus, the proof of weak anonymity of Π_p still holds for Poly Π_p, and all onions will be untraceable to their senders by the time they reach their last intermediaries. An onion may be dropped in its final relay to its recipient with non-negligible probability; however, it is already untraceable to its sender at this point. This proves that Poly Π_p is single-run weakly anonymous. The protocol is also single-run *strongly* anonymous since it is constructed with a sufficiently strong encryption scheme that is poly-onion secure.

Lemma 2. *Poly Π_p is simulatable.*

Proof. We describe algorithms GenOnions and ScheduleProcOnions for which Poly Π_p is simulatable.

Defining GenOnions. Recall that GenOnions takes as input the security parameter 1^λ, the public keys $\{\mathsf{pk}_{P_k}\}_{k=1}^N$ of all the parties, the bulletin B, the churn schedule C, the run number R, the identity P_i of an honest party, and the input σ_i for P_i; and outputs a set $\mathcal{O}_i^{(1)}$ of onions for P_i, i.e., $\mathcal{O}_i^{(1)} \leftarrow$ GenOnions$(1^\lambda, \{\text{pk}_{P_k}\}_{k=1}^N, B, C, R, P_i, \sigma_i)$. Let P_j denote the recipient and let m denote the message for that recipient included in σ_i. GenOnions first generates a list of candidate lists $\mathcal{P}_1, \ldots, \mathcal{P}_\ell, \mathcal{P}_{\ell+1}$, where $P_{\ell,1} = P_j$, and all other candidates is chosen independently and uniformly at random. GenOnions then generates a list of committees $\mathcal{Q}_1, \ldots, \mathcal{Q}_\ell$, where each party in each list is chosen independently and uniformly at random. Let $\{\text{pk}_{P_k}\}_{k \in \mathcal{P} \cup \mathcal{Q}}$ denote the set of public keys of all parties in some candidate list $\mathcal{P}_j$ or some committee $\mathcal{Q}_j$. Each candidate list has length κ, and each committee has size ν, where κ and ν are our chosen Poly Onion Encryption parameters. GenOnions then runs FormOnion to obtain $((\mathcal{O}_{1,1}, \ldots, \mathcal{O}_{1,\kappa}), \ldots, (\mathcal{O}_{\ell,1}, \ldots, \mathcal{O}_{\ell,\kappa}) \leftarrow$ FormOnion$(m, R, (\mathcal{P}_1, \ldots, \mathcal{P}_{\ell+1}), (\mathcal{Q}_1, \ldots, \mathcal{Q}_{\ell+1}), \{\text{pk}_{P_k}\}_{k \in \mathcal{P} \cup \mathcal{Q}})$.

The output $\mathcal{O}_i^{(1)}$ of GenOnions should be the singleton containing an onion O_0 such that processing it right away has the same effect as the sender P_i sending the first onion $O_{1,u}$ to the first available candidate $P_{1,u} \in \mathcal{P}_1$ for the first hop. We can construct O_0 from the onion $O_{1,1}$ for the preferred candidate $P_{1,1}$ by "wrapping" it with an extra layer of encryption using as parameters, the candidate lists $\mathcal{P}_0 = (P_i, \ldots, P_i)$ and $\mathcal{P}_1$ and the helper list $\mathcal{Q}_0 = \mathcal{P}_0 = (P_i, \ldots, P_i)$.

Defining ScheduleProcOnions. Recall that ScheduleProcOnions takes as input the security parameter 1^λ, the round number r, the identity P_i of an honest party, and the state OnionBuffer$_i^{(r)}$ of P_i at round r; and outputs a set of onions $\mathcal{O}_i^{(r)}$ to be processed and sent out during round r and an updated state OnionBuffer$_i^{(r+1)}$. We define ScheduleProcOnions for Π_p to return all onions on OnionBuffer$_i^{(r)}$ to be processed immediately, and to return an empty buffer OnionBuffer$_i^{(r+1)}$ for the next round.

Simulatability. Π_p is simulatable using GenOnions and ScheduleProcOnions as defined here because they are defined identically to the honest parties' behavior in the actual protocol. In Π_p, each party sends its onion on the first round, processes onions immediately when it receives them, and forwards onions immediately when processed. Thus, RealGame is identical to IdealGame.

We just proved that Poly Π_p is single-run (strongly) anonymous (Lemma 1) and simulatable (Lemma 2). Thus, from Theorem 2, it follows that:

Theorem 4. *Poly Π_p is multi-run (strongly) anonymous from the passive adversary who corrupts up to a constant $0 \le \beta_1 < 1$ fraction of the mix-servers, when the churn limit is $c(N) = \beta_2 N$ and $0 \le \beta_1 + \beta_2 < \frac{1}{2}$ is a constant. Moreover, it delivers all messages with overwhelming probability.*

Acknowledgments. We thank Eli Upfal for helpful discussions. This research was supported in part by NSF grants CCF-2107187 and CNS-2154170, the U.S.DOE award DE-SC-0001234, the Columbia-IBM center for Blockchain and Data Transparency, JPMorgan Chase & Co., LexisNexis, and Meta. Any views or opinions expressed herein are solely those of the authors listed.

References

1. Tor directory protocol, version 3. http://gittweb.torproject.org/torspec.git/plain/dir-spec.txt
2. Ando, M., Lysyanskaya, A.: Cryptographic shallots: A formal treatment of repliable onion encryption. In: TCC (2021)
3. Ando, M., Lysyanskaya, A., Upfal, E.: Practical and provably secure onion routing. In: ICALP (2018)
4. Ando, M., Lysyanskaya, A., Upfal, E.: On the complexity of anonymous communication through public networks. In: ITC (2021)
5. Augustine, J., Pandurangan, G., Robinson, P., Roche, S.T., Upfal, E.: Enabling robust and efficient distributed computation in dynamic peer-to-peer networks. In: 56th FOCS
6. Backes, M., Goldberg, I., Kate, A., Mohammadi, E.: Provably secure and practical onion routing. In: 2012 IEEE 25th Computer Security Foundations Symposium
7. Backes, M., Kate, A., Manoharan, P., Meiser, S., Mohammadi, E.: Anoa: A framework for analyzing anonymous communication protocols. In: 2013 IEEE 26th Computer Security Foundations Symposium
8. Blaze, M., Ioannidis, J., Angelos, D., Keromytis, T.M., Rubin, A.D.: Anonymity in wireless broadcast networks, IJ Network Security (2009)
9. Camenisch, J., Lysyanskaya, A.: A formal treatment of onion routing. In: Shoup, V. (ed.) CRYPTO 2005. LNCS, vol. 3621, pp. 169–187. Springer, Heidelberg (2005). https://doi.org/10.1007/11535218_11
10. Chaum, D.L.: Untraceable electronic mail, return addresses, and digital pseudonyms. In: Communications of the ACM (1981)
11. Chen, C., Asoni, D.E., Barrera, D., Danezis, G., Perrig, A.: High-speed onion routing at the network layer. In: ACM CCS, HORNET (2015)
12. Christ, M.: New lower bounds on the complexity of provably anonymous onion routing. Undergraduate honors thesis, Brown University (2020)
13. Cramer, R., Shoup, V.: A practical public key cryptosystem provably secure against adaptive chosen ciphertext attack. In: Krawczyk, H. (ed.) CRYPTO 1998. LNCS, vol. 1462, pp. 13–25. Springer, Heidelberg (1998). https://doi.org/10.1007/BFb0055717
14. Cramer, R., Shoup, V.: Universal hash proofs and a paradigm for adaptive chosen ciphertext secure public-key encryption. In: Knudsen, L.R. (ed.) EUROCRYPT 2002. LNCS, vol. 2332, pp. 45–64. Springer, Heidelberg (2002). https://doi.org/10.1007/3-540-46035-7_4
15. Danezis, G., Dingledine, R., Mathewson, N.: Mixminion: Design of a type III anonymous remailer protocol. In: 2003 IEEE Symposium on Security and Privacy
16. Danezis, G., Goldberg, I.: Sphinx: A compact and provably secure mix format. In: 2009 IEEE Symposium on Security and Privacy
17. Das, D., Meiser, S., Mohammadi, E., Kate, A.: Anonymity trilemma: Strong anonymity, low bandwidth overhead, low latency-choose two. In: 2018 IEEE Symposium on Security and Privacy
18. Das, D., Meiser, S., Mohammadi, E., Kate, A.: Comprehensive anonymity trilemma: User coordination is not enough. In: Proceedings on Privacy Enhancing Technologies (2020)
19. Dingledine, R., Mathewson, N., Syverson, P.F.: Tor: the second-generation onion router. In: USENIX Security Symposium (2004)

20. Falkner, J., Piatek, M., John, J.P., Krishnamurthy, A., Anderson, T.: Profiling a million user dht. In: IMC 2007
21. Dov Gordon, S., Katz, J., Liang, M., Xu, J.: Spreading the privacy blanket: - differentially oblivious shuffling for differential privacy. In: ACNS 2022
22. Iwanik, J., Klonowski, M., Kutyłowski, M.: Duo-onions and hydra-onions-failure and adversary resistant onion protocols. In: Communications and Multimedia Security 2005
23. Kuhn, C., Beck, M., Strufe, T.: Breaking and (partially) fixing provably secure onion routing. In: 2020 IEEE Symposium on Security and Privacy
24. Kuhn, C., Hofheinz, D., Rupp, A., Strufe, T.: Onion routing with replies. In: ASISACRYPT 2021
25. Kwon, A., Corrigan-Gibbs, H., Devadas, S., Ford, B.: Atom: Horizontally scaling strong anonymity. In: 26th ACM SOSP
26. Mitzenmacher, M., Upfal, E.: Probability and computing: Randomized algorithms and probabilistic analysis. Cambridge University Press
27. Murdoch, S.J., Danezis, G.: Low-cost traffic analysis of tor. In: 2005 IEEE Symposium on Security and Privacy
28. Rackoff, C., Simon, D.R.: Cryptographic defense against traffic analysis. In: 25th ACM STOC
29. Ropek, L.: Someone is running hundreds of malicious servers on the Tor network and might be de-anonymizing users. https://tinyurl.com/2p999e8e
30. Stutzbach, D., Rejaie, R.: Understanding churn in peer-to-peer networks. In: IMC 2006
31. Sun, Y., et al.: Routing Attacks on Privacy in Tor. In: USENIX Security Symposium, RAPTOR (2015)
32. Tyagi, N., Gilad, Y., Leung, D., Zaharia, M., Zeldovich, N.: A distributed metadata-private messaging system. In: Symposium on Operating Systems Principles, Stadium (2017)
33. van den Hooff, J., Lazar, D., Zaharia, M., Zeldovich, N.: Vuvuzela: Scalable private messaging resistant to traffic analysis. In: Proceedings of the 25th Symposium on Operating Systems Principles 2015

The Price of Verifiability: Lower Bounds for Verifiable Random Functions

Nicholas Brandt[✉][iD], Dennis Hofheinz, Julia Kastner[iD], and Akin Ünal[iD]

Department of Computer Science, ETH Zurich, Zurich, Switzerland
{nicholas.brandt,hofheinz,julia.kastner,akin.uenal}@inf.ethz.ch

Abstract. Verifiable random functions (VRFs) are a useful extension of pseudorandom functions for which it is possible to generate a *proof* that a certain image is indeed the correct function value (relative to a public verification key). Due to their strong soundness requirements on such proofs, VRFs are notoriously hard to construct, and existing constructions suffer either from complex proofs (for function images), or rely on complex and non-standard assumptions.

In this work, we attempt to explain this phenomenon. We first propose a framework that captures a large class of pairing-based VRFs. We proceed to show that in our framework, it is not possible to obtain short proofs *and* a reduction to a simple assumption simultaneously. Since the class of "consecutively verifiable" VRFs we consider contains in particular the VRF of Lysyanskaya and that of Dodis-Yampolskiy, our results explain the large proof size, resp. the complex assumption of these VRFs.

1   Introduction

Verifiable Random Functions. Pseudorandomness, and in particular pseudorandom generators [6,47] and pseudorandom functions (PRFs, [21]) have proven to be immensely useful and universal cryptographic building blocks. A PRF takes as input a short seed (or key) sk, and an input x, and outputs a function value $\mathbf{y} = \mathsf{prf}_{\mathsf{sk}}(x)$. The distinguishing feature of a PRF is that for a fixed but random sk, oracle access to $\mathsf{prf}_{\mathsf{sk}}(\cdot)$ cannot be distinguished from oracle access to a truly random function. This allows to use prf as a compact drop-in replacement for a truly random function.

In this work, we focus on a special class of PRFs whose image can be *proven* to be correct (relative to a public key vk that fixes prf's behavior). Indeed, a verifiable random function (VRF [38]) vrf is a PRF for which it is possible to generate proofs π (from a given sk and x) that show that a given $\mathbf{y}$ really satisfies $\mathbf{y} = \mathsf{vrf}_{\mathsf{sk}}(x)$. We want such proofs to be sound in a very strong sense: We require that for *any* vk and x, no two $\mathbf{y} \neq \mathbf{y}'$ can both be proven to be $\mathsf{vrf}_{\mathsf{sk}}(x)$. This property, dubbed "unique provability", is crucial for most applications of VRFs, and is the main reason why constructing VRFs is difficult. For instance, unique provability cannot be achieved by using non-interactive zero-knowledge

A. Ünal—Work done while all authors were supported by ERC Project PREP-CRYPTO 724307.

proofs on a given PRF. (This would require a trusted common reference string, which we cannot assume in the VRF setting.) We do note, however, that (non-straightforward) solutions with non-interactive witness-indistinguishable (NIWI) proofs are possible [5, 23].

VRFs have a number of interesting applications. These include signatures with very strong verifiability guarantees [22], resettable zero-knowledge proofs [36], lottery systems [37], transaction escrow schemes [27], updatable zero-knowledge databases [33], and e-cash systems [2, 4].

Existing Constructions of VRFs. There are a variety of constructions of VRFs already [1, 5, 9, 15, 16, 23–26, 30–32, 34, 38, 41, 43, 46]. These constructions are diverse in the used techniques and the resulting features: For instance, some constructions (such as Lysyanskaya's VRF [34] and its variants [9, 24–26, 43]) are based on the specific algebraic properties of the Naor-Reingold PRF [39], while others (such as [5, 23]) are based on more generic primitives such as NIWI proofs. However, none of the above VRF constructions achieves all of the following useful features simultaneously:

- its input space is large (i.e., exponential in the security parameter),
- its proofs π are short (i.e., comprise a constant number of group elements),
- its security proof is based on a "simple" (i.e., non-interactive and compact[1]) assumption.

We do note that some of the constructions come close: e.g., Kohl's VRF [30] achieves all of the above properties, except that proofs π comprise $\omega(1)$ group elements. Conversely, the VRF of Dodis and Yampolskiy [16] enjoys very compact proofs, but relies on a complex hardness assumption (with challenges as large as the input space). While there exists work on the difficulty of achieving VRFs (e.g., from trapdoor one-way functions [17], cf. [11], or in a tightly secure way [41]), the proof size and necessary assumptions for VRFs are generally not well-understood.

Our Contribution. In this work, we are concerned with the reason *why* it is difficult, even after a plethora of different approaches and 20 years of research, to construct useful and compact VRFs from standard assumptions. In order to give a meaningful answer, we put forward a framework of VRF restrictions that however covers many existing constructions. We proceed to show lower bounds within this framework.

Specifically, we restrict ourselves to VRFs vrf in the standard model (i.e., that do not use random oracles or generic groups) that are algebraic over a group, such that secret keys sk are comprised of exponents, and public keys vk,

---

[1] With a non-interactive and compact assumption, we mean one in which the adversary gets a constant number of group elements as challenge and is then supposed to output a solution (e.g., a decision bit).

images $\mathbf{y}$, and proofs π are all comprised of group elements. We do allow pairings, however, such that in particular images may be elements of a target group.

Furthermore, we require that verification (of a proof π for an image $\mathbf{y}$) operates in a specific and "consecutive" way. We give more details on the conditions on verification below in the technical overview. We stress, however, that we believe that this way to verify is natural, and in fact many existing VRFs support consecutive verification, including Lysyanskaya's VRF [34], the VRF of Dodis and Yampolskiy [16], and many more (see Fig. 1). A convenient consequence of this type of consecutive verification is that the function image $\mathbf{y}$ has a specific form: We can deduce that $\mathbf{y} = \mathsf{vrf}_{\mathsf{sk}}(x)$ is of the form $\mathbf{g}^{\sigma_x(\vec{v})/\rho_x(\vec{v})}$, where

- $\mathbf{g}$ is a fixed group generator,
- σ_x and ρ_x are multivariate polynomials (that depend in any efficiently computable way on the preimage), and
- $\vec{v}$ is the vector of discrete logarithms of the verification key vk.

We finally assume a large (i.e., superpolynomial in the security parameter) input space. Again, while this of course severely restricts the VRFs we consider, many previous constructions fall into this class.[2]

For such algebraic VRFs with consecutive verification, we show necessary relations between the size of proofs π and the "size" of the underlying assumption (i.e., the size of the challenge in group elements in a non-interactive hardness assumption). To develop and express these relations, it is useful to consider what we call the *evaluation degree* of the VRF. Formally, this degree is simply the maximum of the degrees of the (multivariate) polynomials σ_x and ρ_x from the image $\mathbf{y} = \mathbf{g}^{\sigma_x(\vec{v})/\rho_x(\vec{v})}$ above (and for this exposition, we assume that these degrees do not depend on x).

We show that for any VRF vrf that matches all of our formal requirements,

(a) if the size of π (in group elements) is small, then so is the degree of vrf,
(b) if vrf's degree is small, then vrf cannot be proven secure with a generic reduction to a constant-size non-interactive hardness assumption. (We note that almost all existing cryptographic reductions are generic.)

As an example, our results show that the VRF of Dodis and Yampolskiy cannot be proven secure (at least not generically) from more traditional hardness assumptions. Our results also show that the (comparatively large) proofs in Lysyanskaya's VRF are inherent, at least when relying on standard hardness assumptions. Figure 1 lists more VRFs that fulfill our requirements (and whose proof sizes and/or assumptions can hence be justified with our results).

---

[2] A prominent verifiable *unpredictable* function (VUF, a weaker form of VRF) that does not fall into this class is the one by Brakerski *et al.* [11]. This VUF takes group elements *as input*, and hence does not quite fit our framework. We will discuss this particular construction in Sect. 2.1, and argue that this approach is unlikely to yield purely group-based *VRFs*.

While our result (a) is a direct consequence of our requirement on consecutive verifiability, we in fact give two versions of statement (b) that differ in exact requirements and formalization. For instance, one version of (b) even excludes *algebraic* reductions (i.e., is formalized within the algebraic group model [19]) from non-interactive assumptions of any polynomial size, but only applies to VRFs whose verification keys depend on a single variable or from non-interactive computational assumptions that depend on a single variable. This allows to model Dodis and Yampolskiy's VRF, but not Lysyanskaya's. The other version of (b) allows more general verification keys, but only excludes *generic* reductions (i.e., is formalized within the generic group model [35, 40, 45]). In the next section, we give a more technical overview over our results.

Discussion. While the formal requirements for our lower bounds seem restrictive, their preconditions are met by most existing VRFs (see Fig. 1). In that sense, they justify the limitations of existing constructions, resp. proofs. An obvious question is thus: How can one circumvent our lower bounds (in order to construct VRFs with short proofs from standard assumptions)?

First of all, one could of course circumvent our results by not (or at least not completely) working over cyclic groups. However, while there are a few more generic VRF constructions (e.g., [5, 23]) that do not rely on groups, it seems that generic VRF constructions are less well-investigated than constructions based on cyclic groups.

Second, one could try to circumvent the more specific requirements of our lower bounds. In particular, our "consecutive verifiability" requirement seems like a very specific requirement. An "interesting" (as opposed to a purely mechanical) way to circumvent consecutive verifiability would be the following. Recall that consecutive verifiability implies that VRF images consist of rational functions, i.e., are of the form $\mathbf{y} = \mathbf{g}^{\sigma_x(\vec{v})/\rho_x(\vec{v})}$. Jumping ahead, we will be interested in small-degree polynomials σ_x, ρ_x. The following VRF candidate does not have this property:

$$\mathsf{vk} = e(\mathbf{g}, \mathbf{g})^s, \qquad \mathbf{y} = \mathbf{g}^{\sqrt[3]{s+x}} \qquad \pi = \mathbf{g}^{(\sqrt[3]{s+x})^2}.$$

Verification checks that $e(\mathbf{y}, \mathbf{y}) = e(\mathbf{g}, \pi)$ and $e(\pi, \mathbf{y}) = \mathsf{vk} \cdot e(\mathbf{g}, \mathbf{g})^x$. The security of this VRF candidate seems unclear, but observe that we require $3 \nmid (\mathrm{ord}(\mathbf{g}) - 1)$ both for uniqueness, and to be able to compute $\sqrt[3]{s+x} \bmod \mathrm{ord}(\mathbf{g})$.

More generally, our results do not exclude VRFs in which the image is an active ingredient in intermediate verification computations, and not only considered in a final verification step (that involves previously computed and/or verified proof elements). Of course, for constructions that use, e.g., roots of exponents (like the above candidate), it may be challenging to prove their security from Diffie-Hellman-like assumptions.

1.1   High-Level Technical Overview

The Evaluation Degree of a VRF. Our technical results rely on the "evaluation degree" of a VRF vrf as a helpful technical notion that connects vrf's proof sizes

Reference	CV	degree	|vk|	|π|	assumption	remark
MRV99 [38]	x	—	large	large	RSA	tree-based
Lys02 [34]	✓	λ	2λ	λ	q-type	
Dod03 [15]	✓	$O(\lambda)$	$O(\lambda)$	$O(\lambda)$	ad-hoc	
DY05 [16]	✓	1	2	1	q-type	small inputs
ACF09 [1]	✓	$\lambda + 2$	$2\lambda + 2$	$\lambda + 1$	q-type	
BCKL09 [4]	x	1	3	$O(1)$	q-type	small inputs
BGRV09 [11]	x	—	1	1	gap-CDH	weak security
BMR10 [9]	✓	$\lambda + 1$	$(\lambda + 2)$	λ	q-type	small inputs
HW10 [25]	✓	$\lambda + 1$	$\lambda + 3$	$\lambda + 1$	q-type	
Jag15 [26]	✓	$O(\lambda)$	$O(\lambda)$	$O(\lambda)$	q-type	
LLC15 [32]	✓	$\lambda + 1$	$2\lambda + 1$	1	q-type	multilinear maps
HJ16 [24]	✓	$O(\lambda)$	$O(\lambda)$	$O(\lambda)$	DLIN	
Bit17 [5]	x	—	depends	large	depends	generic/NIWI-based
GHKW17 [23]	x	—	depends	large	depends	generic/NIWI-based
Kat17 [28]	✓	$\omega(\log(\lambda)^2)$	$\omega(\sqrt{\lambda}\log(\lambda))$	$\omega(\sqrt{\lambda})$	q-type	
Yam17 [46]	✓	$O(\log(\lambda)^2)$	$O(\lambda\log(\lambda)^2)$	$O(\log(\lambda)^2)$	q-type	
Ros18 [43]	✓	$O(\lambda)$	$O(\lambda)$	$O(\lambda)$	DLIN	smaller π than [24]
Koh19 [30]	✓	κ	poly(λ)	κ	DLIN	$\kappa \in \omega(1)$ parameter
Nie21 [41]	✓	$O(\lambda)$	$\omega(\log(\lambda))$	$O(\lambda)$	q-type	

Fig. 1. Existing VRF constructions. The "CV" column indicates whether the construction is consecutively verifiable in our sense. "Degree" denotes its evaluation degree (where applicable), and \|vk\| and \|π\| denote its verification key size, resp. proof size in group elements. When possible, we have chosen parameters such that the input size is $\{0,1\}^\lambda$. For comparability, we classify assumptions with polynomially many challenge elements as "q-type", and other nonstandard assumptions as "ad-hoc". "Small inputs" (as a remark) means that the VRF only supports polynomially-small input spaces. Theorem 1 applies to [11,16], Theorem 2 applies to [16], Theorem 3 applies to [9,11,16] in the sense that these VUF/VRFs cannot have constant size proofs based on standard assumptions.

and vrf's underlying hardness assumption. Hence, let us first take a closer look at this notion of degree.

First, we recall one of our restrictions on the VRFs we consider. We assume that vk and π consist of group elements, and that verification operates in a "consecutive" way, in the following sense: Assume that verification wants to verify a proof π (which consists of, say, κ group elements $\pi_1, \ldots, \pi_\kappa$) for an alleged image $\pi_{\kappa+1} := \mathbf{y}$ (which is a single group element). Then, we require that verification proceeds in $\kappa + 1$ steps, and in the i-th step checks an a priori fixed system of pairing product equations in variables $\pi_1, \ldots, \pi_i$ and vk. We also require that in the equations for the check for π_i, this element only occurs linearly (but not quadratically, i.e., in both arguments of a pairing).

Verification succeeds if all these systems of equations hold. In other words, proof elements (and eventually image $\mathbf{y}$) are verified one at a time, each time checking a quadratic equation in the corresponding exponents of this and all previous elements and vk.

This notion of consecutive verification sounds natural in a pairing setting, and indeed many existing vrf constructions (including the ones from [16, 34]) have a consecutive verification procedure in the above sense. Intuitively, consecutive verification requires that "higher-degree" exponents in proof elements or image must be verified using intermediate group elements with intermediate degrees. Fortunately, as already outlined, consecutive verification also implies that images **y** are of the form

$$\mathsf{vrf}_{\mathsf{sk}}(x) = \mathbf{y} = \mathbf{g}^{\sigma_x(\vec{v})/\rho_x(\vec{v})}$$

for multivariate polynomials σ_x and ρ_x (which both are efficiently computable from x), and the component-wise discrete logarithm $\vec{v}$ of vk. Now we say that the *evaluation degree* of vrf (or **y**) is simply the maximum of the polynomial degrees of σ_x and ρ_x. The evaluation degree of the VRF is then simply the maximal degree over all inputs x.

First Result: Proof Size Bounds Degree for VRFs with Consecutive Verification. Our first result ((a) above, described in more detail in Sect. 2.1, and in full detail in Sect. 4) shows that for VRFs vrf with consecutive verification (as above), the size of proofs π imposes a limit on the vrf's evaluation degree. Concretely, we show that the evaluation degree of vrf is at most exponential in the proof size κ. Hence, if its proof size is constant, then so is the evaluation degree of vrf.

This result is not too surprising, since intuitively, each additional proof element only raises the degree of computed exponents (as algebraic fractions in $\vec{v}$) by a factor of 2. In fact, our proof largely consists in keeping track of expressions of all intermediate proof elements (and finally of **y**) as expressions in $\vec{v}$. The main technical work consists in maintaining a suitable canonical form of these (rational) expressions at all times.

Interlude: The Case of Trivial Denominators. If function images are of the form $\mathbf{y} = \mathbf{g}^{\sigma_x(\vec{v})}$ for a constant-degree (but multivariate) polynomial σ_x, already a very simple linear algebra attack breaks the pseudorandomness of the given VRF. In fact, for sufficiently many preimages x_i, the polynomials σ_{x_i} must eventually become linearly dependent (because the set of their monomials is polynomially small). Hence, it is possible to linearly combine sufficiently many given images to form the image of a fresh preimage. This breaks pseudorandomness, and we detail this attack in the full version [12] for completeness. The case of rational function images $\mathbf{y} = \mathbf{g}^{\sigma_x(\vec{v})/\rho_x(\vec{v})}$ (with $\deg(\rho_x) \geq 1$) is hence not only more general (and covers, e.g., the Dodis-Yampolskiy VRF), but also technically much more interesting.

Second Result: Security of Polynomial-Degree VRFs Requires Complex Assumptions (for Univariate Verification Keys and in the Algebraic Group Model). Our second result (first variant of (b) above, described in Sect. 2.2 more extensively, and in Sect. 5 in full detail) shows that for any polynomial-degree VRF vrf, we can rule out the existence of an "algebraic black-box" reduction to a class of non-interactive group-based computational assumptions. Here, an "algebraic black-box" reduction $\mathcal{B}$ fulfills the following requirements:

- It is algebraic (in the sense of [19]): That means that whenever $\mathcal{B}$ outputs a group element $\mathbf{g}^*$, it also outputs (on a special channel) an explanation as to how $\mathbf{g}^*$ is computed from previously seen group elements.
- It uses the VRF adversary $\mathcal{A}$ only in a black-box way (i.e., it gets oracle access to polynomially many instances of $\mathcal{A}$).

Most existing reductions (in particular for VRFs) are simple in the above sense.

A non-interactive (group-based) computational assumption (NICA) states that it is hard for any efficient adversary $\mathcal{B}$ to win the following game: $\mathcal{B}$ gets a challenge (that is a vector of s group elements), and is then supposed to output a solution to that challenge (which is an exponent related to s). The size of such a NICA is simply the length (i.e., number of entries) of s.

We are now ready to state our result a bit more formally: Assume we are given a polynomial-degree VRF vrf with verification key $\mathsf{vk} = \mathbf{g}^v$. Furthermore, assume that vrf enjoys a simple reduction $\mathcal{B}$ to a NICA. Then, we construct a meta-reduction [13] that wins the NICA game without any external help. Our meta-reduction $\mathcal{M}$ interacts with $\mathcal{B}$ (which gets a NICA challenge), and then attempts to take the role of a successful VRF adversary $\mathcal{A}$. In order to do this, $\mathcal{M}$ can query many VRF images $\mathbf{y}_i$, and use the algebraicity of $\mathcal{B}$ to obtain representations of these $\mathbf{y}_i$ in terms of the NICA challenge elements. Hence, eventually $\mathcal{B}$ will find linear dependencies between the queried VRF images by making sufficiently (but still polynomially) many queries. These linear dependencies can then be used to compute the verification key's exponent v. Using v, the meta-reduction can predict any challenge image as $\mathbf{g}^{\sigma_x(v)/\rho_x(v)}$. This allows $\mathcal{A}$ to win the VRF security game, and hence $\mathcal{M}$ can use $\mathcal{B}$ to solve the NICA.

This intuition neglects a number of technical obstacles: For instance, the linear dependencies among the algebraic representations of VRF images linearly connect the algebraic fractions $\sigma_{x_i}(v)/\rho_{x_i}(v)$ of the corresponding images. To construct a new image $\mathbf{g}^{\sigma_{x^*}(v)/\rho_{x^*}(v)}$ from these, we need to distinguish the cases when the polynomial fraction $\sigma_{x^*}(X)/\rho_{x^*}(X)$ of the challenge can be expressed as a linear combination of the polynomial fractions $\sigma_{x_i}(X)/\rho_{x_i}(X)$ of the queries, and when this is not the case. In the first case, the corresponding linear dependence immediately allows to compute $\mathbf{g}^{\sigma_{x^*}(v)/\rho_{x^*}(v)}$. Note that this is also possible for an adversary that does not get to see the algebraic representations because the linear dependence holds for the fractions, not only for the representations.

In the second case, we have to develop a linear dependence among the algebraic representations (in the NICA challenge elements) of the $\sigma_{x_i}(v)/\rho_{x_i}(v)$. In this case, in fact the linear *independence* of the fractions $\sigma_{x_i}(X)/\rho_{x_i}(X)$ guarantees that these linearly dependent algebraic representations allow to extract the secret v.

In these observations, we crucially use that we deal with univariate polynomials σ_{x_i} and ρ_{x_i} of small degree (which can be represented by short coefficient vectors). In a separate result, we generalize this approach to multivariate σ_{x_i} and ρ_{x_i} where the underlying assumption only depends on a single variable with polynomial degree.

Third Result: Security of Low-Degree VRFs Requires Complex Assumptions (in the Generic Group Model). Our last result (second variant of (b) above, explained more extensively in Sect. 2.3, and in full detail in the full version [12] is similar in spirit to our second result, but features different requirements on the considered VRFs and reductions. Specifically, we prove that no generic reduction (i.e., that treats the underlying group as generic in the sense of [45]) that is algebraic black-box (as outlined above) is able to show security of a constant-degree VRF based on any "Uber-assumption" [8,10] of arbitrary polynomial degree but constant challenge size.

An "Uber-assumption" is a special class of a NICA in which an adversary $\mathcal{B}$ is given a number of group elements $\mathbf{g}^{f_i(\vec{z})}$, where the f_i are multivariate polynomials specific to the concrete assumption, and $\vec{z}$ is a vector of secret (and uniformly randomly chosen) exponents. Typically, the task of $\mathcal{B}$ is then to compute a group element not in the linear span of the given group elements (or to distinguish such an element from random). Here, we restrict ourselves to Uber-assumptions in which the degree of the f_i is at most polynomial in the security parameter.

We again give a meta-reduction $\mathcal{M}$ that shows the following: Any simple generic reduction $\mathcal{B}$ that shows the security of a constant-degree VRF under such an Uber-assumption can be transformed into a successful Uber-solver. Again, $\mathcal{M}$ takes the role of a VRF adversary that interacts with $\mathcal{B}$. In the following, we outline our technique for the specific case of the Dodis-Yampolskiy VRF, in which $\mathsf{vk} = (\mathsf{vk}_1, \mathsf{vk}_2) = (\mathbf{h}, \mathbf{h}^s)$, $\mathbf{y} = e(\mathbf{h}, \mathbf{h})^{1/(s+x)}$ (for a pairing e), and $\pi = \mathbf{h}^{1/(s+x)}$.

Our meta-reduction $\mathcal{M}$, when interacting with a reduction $\mathcal{B}$ in the role of a VRF adversary $\mathcal{A}$, first of all gets to see vk and an algebraic representation of vk in terms of the NICA challenge. (In this work, we call an algorithm generic iff it is generic in the sense of Shoup's GGM *and* algebraic, cf. Definition 5.) This representation of $\mathsf{vk} = (\mathsf{vk}_1, \mathsf{vk}_2)$ allows $\mathcal{M}$ to write $\mathsf{vk}_i = \mathbf{g}^{g_i(\vec{z})}$ for polynomials g_i in the Uber-assumption secrets $\vec{z}$.

Now we distinguish two cases: First, if the polynomial g_2 is a scalar multiple of g_1, (i.e., if $g_2 = s' \cdot g_1$ for a scalar s'), then we have found the VRF secret key $s = s'$. This s can directly be used to break VRF security and allows $\mathcal{M}$ to imitate a successful adversary for $\mathcal{B}$ (which in turn breaks the underlying Uber-assumption). But in case g_2 is not a scalar multiple of g_1, such a simple extraction of s is not possible.

The main technical work in our proof consists in showing that this second case cannot, in fact, occur with non-negligible probability. Essentially, we do so by observing that the representations of VRF proofs $\pi_i = \mathbf{h}^{1/(s+x_i)}$ (i.e., of $(s+x_i)$-th roots of $\mathbf{h} = \mathsf{vk}_1$) imply polynomial factors of g_1. We prove that if g_2 is not a scalar multiple of g_1, then these factors are coprime for different x_i. Hence, querying sufficiently many VRF proofs (for different x_i) yields many non-trivial coprime factors of g_1. Since we assumed that the degree of g_1 is polynomial (since the Uber-assumption polynomials f_i are of polynomial degree), this eventually yields a contradiction. Hence, g_2 must be a scalar multiple of g_1, and our meta-reduction $\mathcal{M}$ can proceed as described above.

In the full version [12], we also show how to generalize this argument to a broader class of constant-degree VRFs which we call *parameterized rational*.

Omitted Details. All the above explanations have omitted or simplified a few details. For instance, we did not discuss the role of *group parameters* (that fix the concrete group and pairing setting). For VRFs, such group parameters should be *certified* [24] (i.e., reliably defining an actual group), and they can be an additional part of vk or any public parameters. Since generic groups can be viewed as "implicitly trusted", we omit this certification in the generic group model.

Furthermore, we have treated the VRF image always as a target group element. However, since we are in a pairing setting, this image can also (and in fact without loss of generality) be an element of the *source group* of the pairing. (This does not change any of the arguments above.) Finally, we mostly consider verifiable *unpredictable* functions (VUFs), a relaxation of verifiable *random* functions. Since we present lower bounds, this only makes our results stronger.

2 Detailed Technical Overview

2.1 First Result: Connecting the Proof Size with the Evaluation Degree

Consecutively Verifiable VUFs/VRFs. To make the connection between the number of group elements in the proof and the evaluation degree, we first define a class of VUFs/VRFs that have a very straightforward verification algorithm. We assume that the VUFs/VRFs in question operate over a symmetric[3] pairing group with pairing $e\colon \mathbb{G} \times \mathbb{G} \to \mathbb{G}_T$:

- The verification key vk consists of group elements $\mathbf{v}_1, \ldots, \mathbf{v}_n \in \mathbb{G} \cup \mathbb{G}_T$
- For each input x, the proof consist of group elements $\pi_1, \ldots, \pi_\kappa \in \mathbb{G} \cup \mathbb{G}_T$
- For each input x, the evaluation value is a group element $\mathbf{y} \in \mathbb{G}_T$

Each possible input element x of the VUF/VRF defines a set of pairing equations E_x that can be efficiently derived[4] from the input x. By pairing equations we mean a set of polynomial equations of degree 2 in the input variables. We make the additional restriction that variables that represent elements from the target group may appear only in monomials of degree 1. We require that the pairing equations can be verified *consecutively*, that is, there is an ordering of the group elements in the proof and subsets $E_{i,x}$ of the sets of pairing equations such that the following hold:

---

[3] We note that our results can easily be transferred to asymmetric pairings, but for simplicity we restrict ourselves to symmetric pairings.

[4] We note that the weak VRF by Brakerski *et al.* [11] does not have this efficiency property, as the inputs are group elements and the pairing equations can only be derived from the discrete logarithm of the inputs.

- in the pairing equation set $E_{i,x}$ for the i-th proof element, only the verification key elements and proof elements up to the i-th occur, i.e., $E_{i,x} \subset \mathbb{Z}_p[V_1, \ldots, V_n, P_1, \ldots P_i]$
- in the pairing equation set $E_{i,x}$ for the i-th proof element, there is at least one equation where the i-th proof element occurs only linearly, i.e., there exist polynomials $a_i \in \mathbb{Z}_p[V_1, \ldots, V_n, P_1, \ldots, P_{i-1}], b_i \in \mathbb{Z}_p[V_1, \ldots, V_n, P_1, \ldots P_i]$ such that $a_i \cdot P_i + b_i = 0$ is an equation that occurs in $E_{i,x}$.

We further make a more technical requirement that the coefficient a_i of the i-th proof element in the equation where it occurs linearly cannot become zero. Let the proof have κ many elements, then we consider the evaluation value to be the $\kappa + 1$st proof element, i.e., it is the last group element to be "verified" in this way.

This consecutive verification property on the one hand yields an efficient pairing-based verification algorithm (for input x, first efficiently derive the pairing equation sets $E_{i,x}$, then consecutively check them). On the other hand, the linearity requirement actually implies that given the verification key and the previous proof elements, each proof element is uniquely defined. As the evaluation value is the last element to be verified, i.e., the $\kappa + 1$st "proof element", it is therefore also uniquely provable.

We note that this consecutive verification property applies to many known VRFs, see Fig. 1 for a detailed overview.

We briefly sketch how the pairing equations look for the VRF of Dodis & Yampolskiy [16]: Recall that the evaluation key is $\mathsf{sk} = s \in \mathbb{Z}_p$ and the verification key is $\mathsf{vk} = \mathbf{h}^s$ for a publicly known group generator $\mathbf{h}$ of $\mathbb{G}$. Evaluation at value x computes $\mathbf{y} = e(\mathbf{h}, \mathbf{h})^{\frac{1}{s+x}}$ as well as the proof $\pi = \mathbf{h}^{\frac{1}{s+x}}$. We can consecutively verify this as follows: First verify the proof via $E_{1,x} = \{(V + x) \cdot P = 1\}$ where V represents the verification key, and P represents the group element. That is, the verification algorithm checks $e(\mathsf{vk} \cdot \mathbf{h}^x, \pi) = e(\mathbf{h}, \mathbf{h})$. Then, we verify $E_{2,x} = \{P \cdot 1 = Y\}$ where P is as before and Y represents the evaluation value, that is the verification algorithm checks $e(\pi, \mathbf{h}) = \mathbf{y}$.

Remark 1 (Consecutive Verifiability of the VUF of Brakerski et al. [11]). As we pointed out above, the weak VUF of Brakerski *et al.* [11], where evaluation works by $\mathsf{Eval}_{\mathsf{vuf}}(\mathsf{sk}, \mathbf{h}) = \mathbf{h}^{\mathsf{sk}}$ for $\mathsf{sk} \in \mathbb{Z}_p$ and $\mathsf{vk} = \mathbf{g}^{\mathsf{sk}}$ and an input $\mathbf{h} \in \mathbb{G}$, and verification accepts if $e(\mathbf{h}, \mathsf{vk}) = e(\mathbf{y}, \mathbf{g})$, is not consecutively verifiable in the sense of this work. In fact, we would need to know the discrete logarithm of the input $\mathbf{h}$ to efficiently compute a pairing equation for it. Therefore, the results of this paper are not applicable to this VUF.

However, while this might seem to limit the class of VUFs we consider in this work, we claim that weak VUFs that have group elements as inputs are – for the pursuit of strong VRFs – not relevant, anyway. In fact, images of the weak VUF of Brakerski *et al.* [11] can easily be predicted for adversarially chosen inputs. This observation can be extended to other weak VRF/VUF candidates that operate in a similar algebraic manner, i.e., that take group elements as inputs and interpret them *as group elements* only and use the group operations and pairing operations on them to compute the output. We show in the full version [12] that these VRFs/VUFs become insecure by as their evaluation degree is at most 2 in the inputs if the discrete logarithms of the input group elements are known to the adversary.

Rational VUFs/VRFs. We want to show that the formerly mentioned class of consecutively verifiable VUFs/VRFs has a particularly straightforward way to describe their evaluation algorithm. To this end, we define rational VUFs. These are VUFs whose evaluation value consists of a (publicly known) group generator raised to a rational function evaluated on the exponents of the verification key. More formally, for each input value x, there are polynomials ρ_x and σ_x such that the output $\mathbf{y}$ evaluated at x is

$$\mathbf{y} = \mathbf{g_T}^{\frac{\sigma_x(v_1,\ldots,v_n)}{\rho_x(v_1,\ldots,v_n)}}$$

where $v_1,\ldots,v_n$ are the exponents of the group elements in the verification key vk. We say that the total degree of the polynomials σ_x and ρ_x is the *evaluation degree* of the VUF/VRF.

From Consecutive Verifiability to Rationality with Bounded Degree. We show, using an inductive argument, that (a) consecutively verifiable pairing based VUFs/VRFs are also rational VUFs/VRFs, and (b) that the evaluation degree is at most exponential in the proof size – this implies that the proof size needs to be at least logarithmic in the evaluation degree for consecutively verifiable VUFs/VRFs. The proof uses induction to show that in fact all proof elements can be expressed through rational functions in the exponent, i.e., there exist σ_{x,π_i} and ρ_{x,π_i}, and that the degree of the i-th proof element is at most 4^i. The base case is easy to see: To obtain σ_{x,π_1} and ρ_{x,π_1} from the first set of pairing equations, we use the pairing equation that contains P_1 as a linear factor. This equation can be expressed as $a \cdot P_1 + b = 0$ where a, b are polynomials (a has degree at most 1 and b degree at most 2). We can therefore express $P_1 = b/-a$.

For the inductive step it is again crucial that the i-th proof element occurs only linearly in at least one pairing equation, as it can then be viewed as a zero of a linear equation and expressed as a rational function of the previous proof elements and the verification key. We replace the previous proof element P_{i-1} by its rational expression $\frac{\sigma_{x,\pi_{i-1}}}{\rho_{x,\pi_{i-1}}}$ in the pairing equation set $E_{i,x}$ to obtain $P_i \cdot a_i' + b_i' = 0$ where the a_i' and b_i' are rational functions in the verification key elements. We then derive the rational expression for $P_i = b_i'/-a_i' = \sigma_{x,\pi_i}/\rho_{x,\pi_i}$ where σ_{x,π_i} and ρ_{x,π_i} are polynomials. It remains to show that the resulting polynomials have the degrees required by our statement which can be done using some simple arguments.

Inductively replacing all proof elements by such rational expressions in the verification key elements yields the result for the last element to be verified – the evaluation value.

2.2   Second Result: Security of Univariate Polynomial-Degree VRFs Requires Complex Assumptions

In current pairing-based constructions of VRFs there seems to be a tradeoff between the size/complexity of the underlying assumption and the size of the proofs. Some constructions, like [16], achieve constant-sized proofs but require a q-type assumption, while others [30] achieve proofs of any superconstant size under a constant-sized assumption. Here, we consider VRF constructions based on non-interactive (group-based) computational assumptions (NICA), i.e., search problems as opposed to a decisional assumptions. These NICAs state that any "efficient" algorithm only has a negligible probability of solving the corresponding computational problem, e.g. finding some "secret" exponent. In particular, we consider NICAs where the challenge elements' exponents only depend on a single variable with polynomial degree. These include for example the q-DLog-assumption and the q-DHI-assumption. There the challenge is $\mathbf{g}, \mathbf{g}^\alpha, \mathbf{g}^{\alpha^2}, \ldots, \mathbf{g}^{\alpha^q}$ and the secret exponent is α. We give two meta-reductions [14] (for slightly different settings) that break the resp. underlying assumption if there is an algebraic reduction from the assumption to the unpredictability (resp. pseudorandomness) of the VUF (resp. VRF).

Theorem 1 (Informal Lower Bound for Univariate VUFs). *Let* vuf *be a rational VUF whose verification key exponents depend — with polynomial degree— on a single common variable. Let* NICA *be any NICA of polynomial size. If there exists an algebraic reduction that transforms an adversary for the weak selective unpredictability of* vuf *into a solver for* NICA, *then* NICA *can be solved in polynomial time with some noticable advantage.*

Theorem 2 (Informal Lower Bound for Univariate NICAs). *Let* vrf *be a rational VRF. Let* NICA *be any NICA of polynomial size whose exponents depend— with polynomial degree— on a single common variable (e.g. q-DLog or q-DHI). If there exists an algebraic reduction that transforms an adversary for the weak selective pseudorandomness into a solver for* NICA, *then* NICA *can be solved in polynomial time with some noticable advantage.*

Remark 2 (Separation between Decisional and Computational Assumptions). As a theoretical sidenote, we observe that on the one hand non-interactive *decisional* assumptions, like q-DDH, suffice for constructing VRFs [46], while on the other hand (univariate) non-interactive *computational* assumptions, like the q-DLog or q-DHI assumption, do not suffice via algebraic reductions. This yields in particular an algebraic separation between the q-DDH and the q-DLog assumption.

Remark 3 (No Algebraic GL Construction). One can transform a VUF (e.g. the VUF of Dodis & Yampolskiy [16] based on the q-DHI assumption) into a VRF via the construction of Goldreich & Levin [20]. While this seems like a contradiction (because it gives a VRF based on the q-DHI assumption), it is actually consistent with our results because the GL hardcore bit is not an algebraic technique[5],

---

[5] The GL construction uses the bits of the representation of the group elements.

hence the reduction from the q-DHI assumption to the pseudorandomness of the resulting VRF is not an algebraic reduction. By contraposition, our results show that there cannot be an algebraic analogue of the GL construction.

Our Technique. Both meta-reductions share the same core idea. In a nutshell, the meta-reduction— when simulating an adversary towards the reduction— uses the representation vectors[6] of the received group elements to either (a) predict the challenge image, e.g. as a linear combination of received representations, or (b) construct a polynomial function over the exponent field $\mathbb{Z}_p$ which has the NICA's secret exponent as a zero. Thus, in case (a) the meta-reduction could successfully answer the reduction's challenge while in case (b) the meta-reduction can leverage the fact that polynomials over some finite field can be efficiently factorized and solve its own challenge directly using the NICA's secret exponent. In both cases the meta-reduction relies on the facts that the VUF (resp. VRF) has correctness and unique provability, and that the VUF (resp. VRF) is of *rational* form, i.e., $\mathsf{vrf}_{\mathsf{sk}}(x) => ^{\sigma_x(\overrightarrow{v})/\rho_x(\overrightarrow{v})}$ where σ_x, ρ_x are of polynomial degree and $\overrightarrow{v}$ is the vector of verification key exponents. Because the reduction is algebraic, whenever it outputs a group element $\mathbf{y} \in \mathbb{G}_T$ it must also provide a representation $\overrightarrow{z} \in \mathbb{Z}_p^L$ w.r.t. the NICA challenge elements s.t.

$$\mathbf{g_T}^{\sigma_x(\overrightarrow{v})/\rho_x(\overrightarrow{v})} = \mathbf{y} = \mathbf{g_T}^{f_1(s)z_1 + \ldots + f_L(s)z_L} \tag{1}$$

$$\Longleftrightarrow \sigma_x(\overrightarrow{v}) - (f_1(s)z_1 + \ldots + f_L(s)z_L)\rho_x(\overrightarrow{v}) = 0 \tag{2}$$

where $\mathbf{g}^{(f_1(s),\ldots,f_L(s))} \in \mathbb{G}^L$ is the NICA challenge and $s \xleftarrow{\$} \mathbb{Z}_p$ is the secret exponent. Equation (2) is the basis for both meta-reductions. For Theorem 1 the meta-reduction queries many preimages $x_1, \ldots, x_Q$ and challenge x_0 uniformly at random. We consider two cases (for simple exposition we assume that the verification key only has one group element $\mathbf{g}^v$):

In the first case (a) the rational functions $\sigma_{x_i}(V)/\rho_{x_i}(V)$ are linearly dependent. With this linear dependence the meta-reduction can predict the challenge image by combining the representations of the queried images.[7]

In the second case (b) although the rational functions $\sigma_{x_i}(V)/\rho_{x_i}(V)$ are linearly independent, by a counting argument there must exist a linear dependence $\alpha \in \mathbb{Z}_p^Q$ among the representations of the queried preimages. The meta-reduction computes the polynomial $\psi(V) := \rho_{x_1}(V) \cdots \rho_{x_Q}(V) \cdot \sum_{\ell=1}^{Q} \alpha_\ell \sigma_\ell(V)/\rho_\ell(V)$. Because $\sigma_{x_i}(V)/\rho_{x_i}(V)$ are linearly independent, the polynomial is non-zero yet it contains the vk's exponent v as a zero (due to $\sum_{\ell=1}^{Q} \alpha_\ell \sigma_\ell(v)/\rho_\ell(v) = 0$). Thus the meta-reduction can factor the polynomial ψ to obtain the secret exponent and predict the challenge image as $> ^{\sigma_{x_0}(v)/\rho_{x_0}(v)}$.

For Theorem 2 we consider pseudorandomness, hence the meta-reduction obtains a representation for each verification key element and a representation

---

[6] Recall that we consider algebraic reductions here, so they have to output a vector of representations with each group element.

[7] If all $\sigma_{x_i}(V)/\rho_{x_i}(V)$ are linearly dependent, then with noticable probability the challenge's function $\sigma_{x_0}(V)/\rho_{x_0}(V)$ will be linearly dependent on the other rational functions because all x_i are independent and identitically distributed.

$\overrightarrow{z}^*$ for the challenge image $\mathbf{y}^*$. That is, the meta-reduction knows a function[8] $\xi : \mathbb{Z}_p \to \mathbb{Z}_p^L$ that maps the NICA challenge's secret key to the verification key exponents $\overrightarrow{v} = \xi(s)$. Plugging ξ into Eq. (2) gives

$$\sigma_x(\xi(s)) - (f_1(s)z_1 + \ldots + f_L(s)z_L)\rho_x(\xi(s)) = 0 . \tag{3}$$

Now, for any representation $\overrightarrow{z}$ of the real challenge image the univariate polynomial $\psi_{\overrightarrow{z}}(S) := \sigma_x(\xi(S)) - (f_1(S)z_1 + \ldots + f_L(S)z_L)\rho_x(\xi(S))$ must vanish on the secret exponent s due to Eq. (3).

If $\psi_{\overrightarrow{z}}(S) \not\equiv 0$ is non-zero for all $\overrightarrow{z}$, then the meta-reduction can factorize $\psi_{\overrightarrow{z}^*}(S)$ and find a list of polynomially many candidates for the NICA's secret exponent. If no candidate matches the NICA's secret exponent, then the challenge image $\mathbf{y}^*$ must be random, otherwise the meta-reduction has trivially found the NICA's secret exponent.

On the other hand, if $\psi_{\overrightarrow{z}}(S) \equiv 0$ is zero for some $\overrightarrow{z}$, then the meta-reduction can efficiently find such a representation $\overrightarrow{z}$. Due to Eq. (3) such a $\overrightarrow{z}$ must correspond to the correct challenge image, hence the meta-reduction can distinguish the given element from random.

2.3 Third Result: Security of Low-Degree VRFs Requires Complex Assumptions

As explained before, Theorem 1 states that there is no algebraic reduction that transforms an adversary for the unpredictability of a rational VUF with polynomial evaluation degree to a solver for a hard polynomial size assumption. However, this result has the caveat that the VUF in question needs to have univariate verification keys, i.e., the verification key needs to be fully determined by one secret variable.

In the remaining part of this work, we will circumvent this problem and show lower bounds for another class of VUFs – the class of *rational parametrized VUFs* (see the full version [12]) – which imposes no restrictions on the verification keys of its VUFs. This class contains the candidates of Dodis & Yampolskiy [16] and of Belenkiy et al. [4] and all other DY-inspired candidates.

However, this result comes at a cost: It only shows the impossibility of *generic* reductions that transform adversaries for the unpredictability of parametrized VUFs into solvers of *extremely small* – yet superconstant – Uber-assumptions.

Informally, our result states the following:

Theorem 3 (Informal Lower Bound for Rational Parametrized VUFs). *Let* vuf *be a parametrized rational VUF of constant evaluation degree, i.e., it is rational and the numerators and denominators for evaluation depend polynomially on the input* $x \in \mathbb{Z}_p$. *Let* NICA *be an Uber-assumption of size* $\sqrt{\log\log \text{poly}(\lambda)}$.

Then, there is no generic reduction that transforms an adversary for the weak selective unpredictability of vuf *to a* NICA *solver.*

---

[8] For simplicity assume that all f_i and hence ξ are polynomials.

We want to emphasize the significance of Theorem 3 for the pursuit of pairing-based VRFs with proofs of constant size. Theorem 3 shows that the security of each VUF in the style of [16] with constant proofs cannot be generically based on a constant-size Uber-assumption.

Now, we want to explain some details that appear in the statement of Theorem 3 before we jump to a proof:

Uber-Assumptions. We demand that NICA is an Uber-assumption [10], i.e., its challenges consist of group elements $\mathbf{g}, \mathbf{g}^{f_1(\overrightarrow{z})}, \ldots, \mathbf{g}^{f_{q_1}(\overrightarrow{z})}, \mathbf{g_T}^{g_1(\overrightarrow{z})}, \ldots, \mathbf{g_T}^{g_{q_2}(\overrightarrow{z})}$ where $\overrightarrow{z} \xleftarrow{\$} \mathbb{Z}_p^t$ has been sampled secretly and uniformly at random by the challenger and $f_1, \ldots, f_{q_1}, g_1, \ldots, g_{q_2} \in \mathbb{Z}_p[Z_1, \ldots, Z_t]$ are publicly known polynomials.

Parametrized Rational VUFs. It is required that vuf is parametrized rational of constant evaluation degree. Formally, this means there are constant-degree polynomials $\sigma, \rho \in \mathbb{Z}_p[V_1, \ldots, V_n, X]$ s.t. we have for each input $x \in \mathbb{Z}_p$ and each verification key vk and corresponding secret key sk

$$\mathsf{Eval}_{\mathsf{vuf}}(\mathsf{sk}, x) = \mathbf{g_T}^{\frac{\sigma(x, \overrightarrow{v})}{\rho(x, \overrightarrow{v})}}$$

where $\overrightarrow{v}$ denotes the vector of exponents of the group elements of vk.

We are now able to sketch a proof for Theorem 3:

Sketch of Proof, Part 1. Assume that Theorem 3 is false for some parametrized VUF vuf and let $\mathcal{R}$ be a reduction that solves instances of some Uber-assumption NICA when given access to an adversary for the unpredictability of vuf. To show a contradiction we construct a meta-reduction $\mathcal{M}$ that takes the role of a successful adversary in the weak selective unpredictability game with $\mathcal{R}$.

$\mathcal{R}$ is given a challenge $\mathbf{g}, \mathbf{g}^{f_1(\overrightarrow{z})}, \ldots, \mathbf{g}^{f_{q_1}(\overrightarrow{z})}, \mathbf{g_T}^{g_1(\overrightarrow{z})}, \ldots, \mathbf{g_T}^{g_{q_2}(\overrightarrow{z})}$ by the NICA challenger and has to compute some solution from this tuple of group elements while having oracle access to $\mathcal{M}$. Since $\mathcal{R}$ is a generic algorithm, we can apply a hybrid step and change the groups $\mathbb{G}, \mathbb{G}_T$ which encode elements of $\mathbb{Z}_p$ to groups $\mathbb{G}^Z, \mathbb{G}_T^Z$ that encode polynomials of $\mathbb{Z}_p[Z_1, \ldots, Z_t]$ without $\mathcal{R}$ noticing the internal change of groups. Additionally, the NICA challenger will now give the group elements $\mathbf{g}, \mathbf{g}^{f_1(\overrightarrow{Z})}, \ldots, \mathbf{g}^{f_{q_1}(\overrightarrow{Z})}, \mathbf{g_T}^{g_1(\overrightarrow{Z})}, \ldots, \mathbf{g_T}^{g_{q_2}(\overrightarrow{Z})}$ as challenge to $\mathcal{R}$. Further, because of the genericness of $\mathcal{R}$, the exponent of each target group element it outputs must be a polynomial of the form

$$\alpha + \sum_{i=1}^{q_1} \beta_i \cdot f_i(\overrightarrow{Z}) + \sum_{i,j=1}^{} \gamma_{i,j} \cdot f_i(\overrightarrow{Z}) \cdot f_j(\overrightarrow{Z}) + \sum_{i=1}^{q_2} \delta_i \cdot g_i(\overrightarrow{Z}) \qquad (4)$$

for scalars $\alpha, \beta_i, \gamma_{i,j}, \delta_i \in \mathbb{Z}_p$. Let W denote the vector space of all polynomials that can be expressed in the above way, i.e., $W = \mathrm{span}_{\mathbb{Z}_p}\{1, (f_i)_i, (f_i \cdot f_j)_{i,j}, (g_i)_i\} \subset \mathbb{Z}_p[Z]$. The space W contains the exponents of all target group elements that can be constructed by generic group operations and pairings from the elements of the NICA challenge. In particular, the exponent of each group element outputted by $\mathcal{R}$ must lie in W.

Now, when $\mathcal{R}$ accesses $\mathcal{M}$ it sends a verification key vk, random inputs $x_0, \ldots, x_Q$, image values $\mathbf{y}_1, \ldots, \mathbf{y}_Q$ and proofs $\pi_1, \ldots, \pi_Q$ to $\mathcal{M}$. To win the unpredictability game, $\mathcal{M}$ needs to return the evaluation $\mathbf{y}_0$ of vuf at x_0 to $\mathcal{R}$. As stated above, the exponents of each group element of vk and of the image values $\mathbf{y}_1, \ldots, \mathbf{y}_Q$ must lie in W. Let $v_1(\overrightarrow{Z}), \ldots, v_n(\overrightarrow{Z}), y_1(\overrightarrow{Z}), \ldots, y_Q(\overrightarrow{Z}) \in W$ be exponents of these group elements. Since $\mathcal{R}$ is generic, $\mathcal{M}$ can extract those polynomials from $\mathcal{R}$ while playing the unpredictability game with $\mathcal{R}$ (we assume in this work that genericness always implies algebraicity, cf. Definition 5). With the help of $\pi_1, \ldots, \pi_Q$ the meta-reduction $\mathcal{M}$ can ensure that for each $i \in [Q]$ the equation

$$\frac{\sigma(x_i, v_1(\overrightarrow{Z}), \ldots, v_n(\overrightarrow{Z}))}{\rho(x_i, v_1(\overrightarrow{Z}), \ldots, v_n(\overrightarrow{Z}))} = y_i(\overrightarrow{Z}) \tag{5}$$

holds.

Sketch of Proof, Part 2. In the first part of the proof, we showed that the fractions $\frac{\sigma(x_i, \overrightarrow{v}(\overrightarrow{Z}))}{\rho(x_i, \overrightarrow{v}(\overrightarrow{Z}))}$, $i \in [Q]$, are not only polynomials, but additionally lie in W. This is the point where we can spring our mathematical trap: we can show if all fractions $\frac{\sigma(x_1, \overrightarrow{v}(\overrightarrow{Z}))}{\rho(x_1, \overrightarrow{v}(\overrightarrow{Z}))}, \ldots, \frac{\sigma(x_Q, \overrightarrow{v}(\overrightarrow{Z}))}{\rho(x_Q, \overrightarrow{v}(\overrightarrow{Z}))}$ lie in W for a large enough number Q then, in fact, the fraction $\frac{\sigma(x, \overrightarrow{v}(\overrightarrow{Z}))}{\rho(x, \overrightarrow{v}(\overrightarrow{Z}))}$ must be an element of W for *each* $x \in \mathbb{Z}_p$. In particular, the exponent $\frac{\sigma(x_0, \overrightarrow{v}(\overrightarrow{Z}))}{\rho(x_0, \overrightarrow{v}(\overrightarrow{Z}))}$ of $\mathbf{y}_0$ must be of this form and therefore $\mathcal{M}$ can compute the element $\mathbf{y}_0 => \frac{\sigma(x_0, \overrightarrow{v}(\overrightarrow{Z}))}{\rho(x_0, \overrightarrow{v}(\overrightarrow{Z}))}$ from the group elements of the NICA challenge on its own. Ergo, $\mathcal{M}$ can successfully answer the queries of $\mathcal{R}$ for a large enough number of queries Q which gives rise to a generic PPT NICA solver. A contradiction to the hardness of NICA!

2.4 Organization of This Work

In Sect. 3, we introduce notations and preliminaries. In Sect. 4, we define consecutive verifiable and rational VUFs and show our first result: a consecutive verifiable VUF is rational and its evaluation degree is exponentially bounded by the size of its proofs. In Sect. 5, we show our second result: Theorem 1 and Theorem 2, which state that the security of rational VUFs cannot be based by an algebraic reduction on the hardness of a NICA, if either the verification key of the VUF or the NICA is univariate. Finally, in Sect. 6, we introduce the notion of parametrized rational VUFs and Uber-assumptions, state the formal version of Theorem 3 and give a very high-level idea of its proof.

3 Preliminaries

3.1 Notation

We denote the security parameter by λ. We denote vectors by $\vec{x}$ and group elements by $\mathbf{g}$. For a matrix M we denote by $m_{i,j}$ the entry in the i-th row and the j-th column. For a finite set X we denote by $x \xleftarrow{\$} X$ that x is sampled uniformly at random from X.

For a probabilistic algorithm Alg we denote by $y \xleftarrow{\$} \mathsf{Alg}(x)$ that y is computed by Alg on input x with a uniform random tape. Set further $\mathsf{poly}(\lambda) := \{f : \mathbb{N} \to \mathbb{N} \mid \exists a, b \in \mathbb{N}, \forall n \in \mathbb{N} : f(n) \leq a + n^b\}$ and $\mathsf{negl}(\lambda) := \{\varepsilon : \mathbb{N} \to \mathbb{R} \mid \forall c \in \mathbb{N} : \lim_{n\to\infty} n^c \cdot \varepsilon(n) = 0\}$. For any $n \in \mathbb{N}$ we set $[n] := \{1, \ldots, n\}$. We call an algorithm PPT iff it is probabilistic, and its time complexity lies in $\mathsf{poly}(\lambda)$.

3.2 Mathematical Foundations

Definition 1 (Rational Functions). *For a prime p we define the field of* **rational functions** *over $\mathbb{Z}_p$ in variables $X_1, \ldots, X_n$ by*

$$\mathbb{Z}_p(X_1, \ldots, X_n) := \left\{ \frac{\sigma(X_1, \ldots, X_n)}{\rho(X_1, \ldots, X_n)} \middle| \sigma, \rho \in \mathbb{Z}_p[X_1, \ldots, X_n], \ \rho \neq 0 \right\}.$$

Given a rational function $f \in \mathbb{Z}_p(X_1, \ldots, X_n)$, the **degree** *of f is defined as*

$$\deg(f) := \min\{\max(\deg(\sigma), \deg(\rho)) \mid \sigma, \rho \in \mathbb{Z}_p[X_1, \ldots, X_n], \rho \neq 0, \rho \cdot f = \sigma\}$$

where $\deg(\sigma), \deg(\rho)$ denote the total degrees of the polynomials σ, ρ.

We recall the following helpful lemma:

Lemma 1 (Schwartz-Zippel-Lemma, [44]). *Let $f \in \mathbb{Z}_p[X_1, \ldots, X_n]$ be a non-zero polynomial over $\mathbb{Z}_p$. Denote by $\deg(f)$ the total degree of f. Then*

$$\Pr_{r_1, \ldots, r_n \xleftarrow{\$} \mathbb{Z}_p} [f(r_1, \ldots, r_n) = 0] \leq \frac{\deg(f)}{p}.$$

3.3 Cryptographic Groups

Definition 2 (Bilinear Group Generator, [24]). *A* **bilinear group generator** *is a probabilistic polynomial-time algorithm GrpGen that takes as input a security parameter λ (in unary) and outputs $\Pi = (p, \mathsf{pp}_{\mathbb{G}}, \mathsf{pp}_{\mathbb{G}_T}, \circ, \circ_{\mathsf{T}}, e, \phi(1)) \xleftarrow{\$} \mathsf{GrpGen}(1^\lambda)$ such that the following requirements are satisfied.*

1. *The parameter p is prime and $\log(p) \in \Omega(\lambda)$.*
2. *$\mathbb{G}$ and $\mathbb{G}_T$ as described by $\mathsf{pp}_{\mathbb{G}}$ and $\mathsf{pp}_{\mathbb{G}_T}$ are subsets of $\{0, 1\}^*$, defined by algorithmic descriptions of maps $\phi : \mathbb{Z}_p \to \mathbb{G}$ and $\phi_{\mathsf{T}} : \mathbb{Z}_p \to \mathbb{G}_T$.*
3. *$\circ$ and $\circ_{\mathsf{T}}$ are algorithmic descriptions of efficiently computable (in λ) maps $\circ : \mathbb{G} \times \mathbb{G} \to \mathbb{G}$ and $\circ_{\mathsf{T}} : \mathbb{G}_T \times \mathbb{G}_T \to \mathbb{G}_T$, such that*

(a) $(\mathbb{G}, \circ)$ *and* $(\mathbb{G}_T, \circ_T)$ *form abstract groups and*

(b) ϕ *is a group isomorphism from* $(\mathbb{Z}_p, +)$ *to* $(\mathbb{G}, \circ)$ *and*

(c) ϕ_T *is a group isomorphism from* $(\mathbb{Z}_p, +)$ *to* $(\mathbb{G}_T, \circ_T)$.

4. *e is an algorithmic description of an efficiently computable (in* λ*) bilinear map* $e : \mathbb{G} \times \mathbb{G} \to \mathbb{G}_T$. *We require that e is non-degenerate, i.e.,* $x \neq 0 \implies e(\phi(x), \phi(x)) \neq \phi_T(0)$.

Remark 4. For simplicity, we only consider symmetric pairings. However, while our upcoming formulation of "consecutive verifiability" is easier to state with symmetric pairings, our results do not depend on symmetry of the pairing.

Definition 3 (Certified Generator, [24]). *We say a bilinear group generator* GrpGen *is **certified**, if there exists a deterministic polynomial-time algorithm* GrpVfy *with the following properties:*

Parameter Validation. *Given a string* Π *(which may not necessarily be generated by* GrpGen*), algorithm* GrpVfy(Π) *outputs 1 if and only if* Π *has the form* $\Pi = (p, \mathsf{pp}_{\mathbb{G}}, \mathsf{pp}_{\mathbb{G}_T}, \circ, \circ_T, e, \phi(1))$ *and all requirements from Definition 2 are satisfied.*

Recognition and Unique Representation of Elements of $\mathbb{G}$ ($\mathbb{G}_T$). *Furthermore, we require that each element in* $\mathbb{G}$ ($\mathbb{G}_T$) *has a unique representation, which can be efficiently recognized. That is, on input two strings* Π *and* s, GrpVfy(Π, s) *outputs 1 if and only if* GrpVfy(Π) $= 1$ *and it holds that* $s = \phi(x)$ ($s = \phi_T(x)$) *for some* $x \in \mathbb{Z}_p$. *Here* $\phi : \mathbb{Z}_p \to \mathbb{G}$ ($\phi_T : \mathbb{Z}_p \to \mathbb{G}_T$) *denotes the fixed group isomorphism contained in* Π *to specify the representation of elements of* $\mathbb{G}$ *(of* $\mathbb{G}_T$*) (see Definition 2).*

We recall the definition of algebraic algorithms which was first used by [7,42] in the context of meta-reductions. Our definition of algebraic algorithms is closer to that of [3,19].

Definition 4 (Algebraic Algorithms [3,19]). *Let* $\mathsf{pp}_{\mathbb{G}} = (p, \mathsf{pp}_{\mathbb{G}}, \mathsf{pp}_{\mathbb{G}_T}, \circ_{\mathbb{G}}, \circ_{\mathbb{G}_T}, e, \phi_{\mathbb{G}}, \phi_{\mathbb{G}_T})$ *be as in Definition 2. Let* $\mathcal{A}$ *be an algorithm that receives as input source group elements* $\mathbf{g}_1, \ldots, \mathbf{g}_s \in \mathbb{G}$, *target group elements* $\mathbf{h}_1, \ldots, \mathbf{h}_t \in \mathbb{G}_T$ *and some non-group-element input* x.

We say that $\mathcal{A}$ *is **algebraic** if, whenever* $\mathcal{A}$ *outputs a group element* $\mathbf{y}$, *it also outputs one of the following representations: If* $\mathbf{y} \in \mathbb{G}$, *a vector*

$$\vec{z} \in \mathbb{Z}_p^s \quad s.t. \quad \mathbf{y} = \prod_{i=1}^{s} \mathbf{g}_i^{z_i}$$

and if $\mathbf{y} \in \mathbb{G}_T$, *a vector and a matrix*

$$\vec{z} \in \mathbb{Z}_p^t, M = (m_{ij})_{i,j=1}^{s} \in \mathbb{Z}_p^{s \times s} \quad s.t. \quad \mathbf{y} = \prod_{i=1}^{t} \mathbf{h}_i^{z_i} \cdot \left(\prod_{i,j=1}^{s} e(\mathbf{g}_i, \mathbf{g}_j)^{m_{ij}} \right)$$

Definition 5 (The Generic Group Model [40,45]). *An algorithm interacting with a group (or pairing group) is called **generic** if it is algebraic in the sense of Definition 4 and it suffices that the algorithm accesses the group only through an oracle. More concretely, all group elements $\mathbf{g}_i$ that the algorithm receives as input are represented by random strings $\sigma(\mathbf{g}_i)$, called **handles**, and whenever the algorithm wants to compute the product $\mathbf{g}_i \cdot \mathbf{g}_j$ resp. the exponentiation $\mathbf{g}^x$, it passes $(\sigma(\mathbf{g}_i), \sigma(\mathbf{g}_j))$ resp. $(\sigma(\mathbf{g}_i), x)$ to the corresponding group operation oracle, and the oracle returns $\sigma(\mathbf{g}_i \cdot \mathbf{g}_j)$ resp. $\sigma(\mathbf{g}_i^x)$. In a pairing setting the algorithm is given access to a second such group oracle for the target group, as well as a pairing oracle that takes as input two handles $\sigma(\mathbf{g}_i), \sigma(\mathbf{g}_j)$ and outputs $\sigma(e(\mathbf{g}_i, \mathbf{g}_j))$ if both elements $\mathbf{g}_i, \mathbf{g}_j$ are elements of the source group.*

Remark 5. It has been shown recently – despite popular belief – that an algorithm that only interacts with a group by oracles in Shoup's GGM does not need to be algebraic [29,48]. To circumvent this problem, we require in the definition of generic algorithms explicitly that a generic algorithm is algebraic.

Remark 6. It is not clear how to adapt the notion of a certified group generator (Definition 3) to generic groups. Indeed, in the generic group model, there are no group descriptions as in Definition 2, and instead all algorithms have access to a group via group operation oracles. However, these oracles can be viewed as "implicitly trusted", in the sense that the properties from Definition 2 are always guaranteed. Hence, we will not consider certified (bilinear) group generators in the context of generic groups.

Definition 6 (Non-interactive Computational Assumptions, NICAs) [18]). *A **non-interactive computational assumption** NICA is defined by the following two oracles available to the adversary:*

Setup. *Generates a challenge $c \xleftarrow{\$} \mathcal{D}(1^\lambda)$ from a challenge distribution $\mathcal{D}(1^\lambda)$ parameterized over the security parameter λ. Saves an internal state st.*

Finalize. *On input of a candidate solution s and the internal state st, outputs either 1 (indicating that s is a correct solution) or 0 (indicating that s is not a correct solution).*

*We say that an adversary $\mathcal{A}$ (t, ϵ)-**breaks** the assumption if the adversary outputs a correct solution with probability at least $\epsilon(\lambda)$ in time at most $t(\lambda)$. We further say the assumption is (t, ϵ)-**hard** if there exists no adversary $\mathcal{A}$ that (t, ϵ)-breaks the assumption. If NICA is $(t, \frac{1}{r})$-hard for all $t, r \in \mathsf{poly}(\lambda)$, $r > 0$, we call NICA **hard**.*

*For a NICA in a group where the challenge consists of m group elements, we call m the **size** of the NICA. If m is linear in a parameter q, we call NICA a q-**type assumption**. If m is constant we call NICA a **constant-size assumption**.*

Definition 7 (Univariate Polynomial-Degree Assumptions). *Let $p = p(\lambda)$ be a superpolynomial group order. Let $l_1, l_2, d_{\mathsf{NICA}} \in \mathsf{poly}(\lambda)$, let $r_1, \ldots, r_{l_1}$, $t_1, \ldots, t_{l_2} \in \mathbb{Z}_p[S]$ be non-zero polynomials of degree at most d_{NICA}. We say*

NICA *is a univariate polynomial-degree assumption, iff it is an $(l_1 + l_2)$-type NICA according to Definition 6 and if its challenge distribution[9] is $\mathcal{D}(1^\lambda) \rightarrow c = (\Pi, \mathbf{g}^{r_1(s)}, \ldots, \mathbf{g}^{r_{l_1}(s)}, \mathbf{g}^{1/t_1(s)}, \ldots, \mathbf{g}^{1/t_{l_2}(s)})$ where $s \overset{\$}{\leftarrow} \mathbb{Z}_p$ is the secret exponent and $\Pi = (p, \mathsf{pp}_\mathbb{G}, \mathsf{pp}_{\mathbb{G}_T}, \circ, \circ_T, e, \phi(1)) \overset{\$}{\leftarrow} \mathsf{GrpGen}(1^\lambda)$ is a certified group description.*

Definition 8 (DLog-Hard Assumptions). *Let $l_1, l_2, d_\mathsf{NICA} \in \mathsf{poly}(\lambda)$, let $r_1, \ldots, r_{l_1}, t_1, \ldots, t_{l_2} \in \mathbb{Z}_p[S]$ be non-zero polynomials of degree at most d_NICA. We say* NICA *is a DLog-hard assumption, iff it is an $(l_1 + l_2)$-type assumption according to Definition 7 and if no polynomial-time algorithm has noticable probability of solving the corresponding DLog problem, i.e., outputting the secret exponent $s \in \mathbb{Z}_p$.*

Remark 7. In particular the *computational q-DHI* assumption (Diffie-Hellman inversion assumption) is a univariate polynomial-degree assumption for $q \in \mathsf{poly}(\lambda)$. The decisional variant is *not* univariate because of the last challenge element.

3.4 Verifiable Unpredictable Functions

Definition 9 (Verifiable Unpredictable Functions, VUFs [38]). *Let* $\mathsf{vuf} = (\mathsf{Gen}_\mathsf{vuf}, \mathsf{Eval}_\mathsf{vuf}, \mathsf{Verify}_\mathsf{vuf})$ *be a tuple of algorithms of the following form:*

- $\mathsf{Gen}_\mathsf{vuf}(1^\lambda)$ *outputs a secret key* sk *and a verification key* vk.
- $\mathsf{Eval}_\mathsf{vuf}(\mathsf{sk}, x)$ *on input a secret key* sk *and* $x \in \mathcal{X} = (\mathcal{X}_\lambda)_\lambda$ *outputs an image* $y \in \mathcal{Y} = (\mathcal{Y}_\lambda)_\lambda$ *and a proof* π. *We assume that the input space* $\mathcal{X}_\lambda$ *has a superpolynomial cardinality in the security parameter* λ.
- $\mathsf{Verify}_\mathsf{vuf}(\mathsf{vk}, x, y, \pi)$ *on input a verification key* vk, *a preimage* x, *an image* y *and a proof* π *outputs a bit* $b \in \{0, 1\}$.

We say that vuf *is a (t, Q, ϵ)-**verifiable unpredictable function** (VUF) if the following holds:*

Statistical Correctness. *There exists a negligible function $\mu \in \mathsf{negl}(\lambda)$ s.t. for all $\lambda \in \mathbb{N}$ and for all inputs $x \in \mathcal{X}_\lambda$ it holds that*

$$\Pr_{(\mathsf{sk},\mathsf{vk}) \overset{\$}{\leftarrow} \mathsf{Gen}_\mathsf{vuf}(1^\lambda)} [\mathsf{Verify}_\mathsf{vuf}(\mathsf{vk}, x, y, \pi) = 1 \mid (y, \pi) \leftarrow \mathsf{Eval}_\mathsf{vuf}(\mathsf{sk}, x)] \geq 1 - \mu(\lambda) .$$

Unique Provability. *For all $\lambda \in \mathbb{N}$ and all possible vk (not necessarily generated by $\mathsf{Gen}_\mathsf{vuf}$), all $x \in \mathcal{X}_\lambda$, all $y_1, y_2 \in \mathcal{Y}_\lambda$ and all possible proofs π_1, π_2 it holds that*

$$\mathsf{Verify}_\mathsf{vuf}(\mathsf{vk}, x, y_1, \pi_1) = 1 \wedge \mathsf{Verify}_\mathsf{vuf}(\mathsf{vk}, x, y_2, \pi_2) = 1 \implies y_1 = y_2$$

---

[9] For exposition, we assume all group element to be in the source group. Our technique applies as well for assumptions with target group elements.

Weak Q-Selective Unpredictability [11]. *For any adversary $\mathcal{A}$ running in time at most $t(\lambda)$, we have*

$$\left| \Pr\left[\mathcal{A}(\mathsf{vk}, \overrightarrow{x}, \overrightarrow{y}, \overrightarrow{\pi}) = \mathsf{y}_0 \;\middle|\; \begin{array}{l} \overrightarrow{x} = (x_0, \ldots, x_Q) \xleftarrow{\$} \mathcal{X}_\lambda^{Q+1} \\ (\mathsf{sk}, \mathsf{vk}) \xleftarrow{\$} \mathsf{Gen}_{\mathsf{vrf}}(1^\lambda) \\ (\mathsf{y}_i, \pi_i) \leftarrow \mathsf{Eval}_{\mathsf{vrf}}(\mathsf{sk}, x_i) \\ \overrightarrow{y} = (\mathsf{y}_1, \ldots, \mathsf{y}_Q) \\ \overrightarrow{\pi} = (\pi_1, \ldots, \pi_Q) \end{array} \right] - \frac{1}{|\mathcal{Y}_\lambda|} \right| \le \epsilon(\lambda) .$$

Remark 8. Our notion of weak selective unpredicability is even weaker than the eponymous notion used by Niehues [41] with a loss of $1/Q$ by guessing the adversary's challenge index and reordering the preimages. However, our notion has the advantage that it is a non-interactive game, in particular, no state has to be transmitted between parts of the adversary ($\mathcal{A}_1, \mathcal{A}_2$) as in [41].

Remark 9. We note that we do not require *perfect* correctness as for some of the VUFs we consider in this work this property does not hold perfectly (e.g. in the case where $\mathsf{Eval}_{\mathsf{vuf}}(\mathsf{sk}, x)$ is undefined for a small number of $x \in \mathcal{X}$ for some secret key sk).

Remark 10. We consider pairing-based VUFs where $y \in (\mathbb{G} \cup \mathbb{G}_T)$ and $\pi \in (\mathbb{G} \cup \mathbb{G}_T)^*$. W.l.o.g. we assume that a VUF's image is an element of the target group, i.e., $\mathcal{Y} = \mathbb{G}_T$. Otherwise, we can modify the VUF by appending the original (source group) image $\mathsf{y}_\mathsf{S} \in \mathbb{G}$ to the proof elements, and set the new image as $\mathsf{y}_\mathsf{T} := e(\mathsf{g}_\mathsf{S}, \mathsf{y}_\mathsf{S})$ where g_S is a designated generator of the source group in the verification key. Obviously, the unpredictability of the former VUF can be reduced to the unpredictability of latter, without any loss.

Definition 10 (Verifiable Random Functions, VRFs [38]). *Let* $\mathsf{vrf} = (\mathsf{Gen}_{\mathsf{vrf}}, \mathsf{Eval}_{\mathsf{vrf}}, \mathsf{Verify}_{\mathsf{vrf}})$ *be a VUF according to Definition 9. We say that* vrf *is a* (t, ϵ)-*verifiable random function (VRF) if the following*[10] *holds:*

Weak Q-Selective Pseudorandomness. *For any adversary $\mathcal{A}$ running in time at most $t(\lambda)$, we have*

$$\left| \Pr\left[\mathcal{A}(\mathsf{vk}, \overrightarrow{x}, \overrightarrow{y}^b, \overrightarrow{\pi}) = b \;\middle|\; \begin{array}{l} \overrightarrow{x} = (x_0, \ldots, x_Q) \xleftarrow{\$} \mathcal{X}_\lambda^{Q+1} \\ (\mathsf{sk}, \mathsf{vk}) \xleftarrow{\$} \mathsf{Gen}_{\mathsf{vrf}}(1^\lambda) \\ (\mathsf{y}_i, \pi_i) \leftarrow \mathsf{Eval}_{\mathsf{vrf}}(\mathsf{sk}, x_i) \\ \mathsf{y}_0' \leftarrow \mathbb{G}_T \\ \overrightarrow{y}^0 = (\mathsf{y}_0, \mathsf{y}_1, \ldots, \mathsf{y}_Q) \\ \overrightarrow{y}^1 = (\mathsf{y}_0', \mathsf{y}_1, \ldots, \mathsf{y}_Q) \\ \overrightarrow{\pi} = (\pi_1, \ldots, \pi_Q) \\ b \leftarrow \{0, 1\} \end{array} \right] - \frac{1}{2} \right| \le \epsilon(\lambda) .$$

---

[10] To keep the definitions minimal, we choose to only present the 0-selective pseudo-randomness property since it is the security notion considered in our results.

3.5   Reductions

Definition 11. *For a VUF* vuf *and a NICA* NICA, *we say a Turing machine* $\mathcal{B}$ *is a* $(t_\mathcal{B}, \epsilon_\mathcal{B}, r, Q, \epsilon_\mathcal{A})$-**reduction** *from breaking* NICA *to breaking the weak selective unpredictability of* vuf, *if for any* $\mathcal{A}$ *that* $(t_\mathcal{A}, Q, \epsilon_\mathcal{A})$-*breaks the weak selective unpredicability of* vuf, *the TM* $\mathcal{B}^\mathcal{A}$ $(t_\mathcal{B} + rt_\mathcal{A}, \epsilon_\mathcal{B})$-*breaks* NICA *making at most* r *oracle queries*[11] *to* $\mathcal{A}$.

4   Proof Size

4.1   Classes of VUFs over Pairing-Friendly Groups

In the following, we introduce the class of VUFs that we want to discuss. Informally speaking, we consider VUFs whose verification algorithm only verifies group membership and pairing equations over the proof, evaluation value, and verification key. We further require that the verification algorithm is *consecutive*, i.e., it first verifies the first element of the proof, then the second, then the third, and so on and at the end of its execution it verifies that the evaluation value is correct. This class of VUFs covers many existing VUFs, we refer to Fig. 1 for an overview of which VUFs are consecutively verifiable.

In this section, we want to show that the evaluation function of VUFs that have such a natural verification algorithm can be expressed as a target group element where the exponent is a rational function in the discrete logarithms of the verification key element and that, informally speaking, the degree of the rational function can be bounded as exponential in the size of the proof. We begin by giving a formal definition of what we consider a set of pairing equations.

Definition 12 (Pairing Equations). *Let* $E \subset \mathbb{Z}_p[X_1, \ldots, X_m]$. *We call* E *a set of **pairing equations** for a pairing group* $\mathcal{G}$ *with public parameters* $\Pi = (p, \mathsf{pp}_\mathbb{G}, \mathsf{pp}_{\mathbb{G}_T}, \circ, \circ_\mathsf{T}, e, \phi(1)) \xleftarrow{\$} \mathsf{GrpGen}(1^\lambda)$ *over variables* $\overrightarrow{X} = X_1, \ldots, X_m$ *with target indicator*[12] *set* $T \subset \{1, \ldots, m\}$ *if the following hold:*

1. $\max_{f \in E}(\deg f) \leq 2$,
2. *for all* $i \in T$ *and* $f \in E$ *it holds that if* X_i *appears in a monomial* m *of* f, *then* $m = c \cdot X_i$ *for some* $c \in \mathbb{Z}_p$.

We describe the evaluation *of a finite set of pairing equations* E *on input* $\mathbf{x}_1, \ldots, \mathbf{x}_m$ *as follows:*

- *We check that the input is a set of group elements* $(\mathbf{x}_1, \ldots \mathbf{x}_m)$, *i.e.,* $\mathbf{x}_i \in \mathbb{G}$ *or* $\mathbf{x}_i \in \mathbb{G}_T$ *for all* i, *and output* $\perp$ *if otherwise.*
- *For each* $i \in [m]$, *we check if* $i \in T \iff \mathbf{x}_i \in \mathbb{G}_T$ *and output* $\perp$ *if otherwise.*

---

[11] Because our weak selective unpredictability is a non-interactive game, there are no concurrency issues.

[12] This set indicates which verification key elements are in the target group. Hence, their exponents should only occur linearly, while source group exponents can occur quadratically.

- *For $f = \left(\sum_{m \in M_f} m \right) \in E$ where M_f is the set of monomials of f, we compute $\mathbf{f}(\overrightarrow{\mathbf{x}}) := \prod_{m \in M_f} \mathbf{m}(\overrightarrow{\mathbf{x}})$ where $\mathbf{m}(\overrightarrow{\mathbf{x}})$ are computed as follows:*
  - *if $m = c \cdot X_i \cdot X_j$ for some $i, j \notin T$ and $c \in \mathbb{Z}_p$, compute $\mathbf{m}(\overrightarrow{\mathbf{x}}) := e(\mathbf{x}_i, \mathbf{x}_j)^c$,*
  - *if $m = c \cdot X_i$ for some $i \notin T$ and some $c \in \mathbb{Z}_p$ and if $\mathbf{x}_i \in \mathbb{G}$, compute $\mathbf{m}(\overrightarrow{\mathbf{x}}) := e(\mathbf{x}_i, \mathbf{g})^c$ where $\mathbf{g} = \phi(1)$ is the fixed generator of $\mathbb{G}$ as given in the group parameters Π. If $i \in T$ and $\mathbf{x}_i \in \mathbb{G}_T$ compute $\mathbf{m}(\overrightarrow{\mathbf{x}}) := \mathbf{x}_i^c$,*
  - *if $m = c$ for $c \in \mathbb{Z}_p$, compute $\mathbf{m}(\overrightarrow{\mathbf{x}}) := e(\mathbf{g}, \mathbf{g})^c$.*
- *We denote by $E(\overrightarrow{\mathbf{x}})$ the function that outputs 1 if for all $f \in E$ it holds that $\mathbf{f}(\overrightarrow{\mathbf{x}}) = e(\mathbf{g}, \mathbf{g})^0$ (if $E = \emptyset$ this always holds) and otherwise outputs 0.*

In the following we describe our class of VUFs that have a consecutive verification algorithm.

Definition 13 (Consecutively Verifiable Pairing-Based VUFs). *We say a VUF $\mathsf{vuf} = (\mathsf{Gen}_{\mathsf{vuf}}, \mathsf{Eval}_{\mathsf{vuf}}, \mathsf{Verify}_{\mathsf{vuf}})$ with input space $\mathcal{X}$ is a **consecutively verifiable pairing-based VUF** if the following hold:*

1. *$\mathsf{Gen}_{\mathsf{vuf}}$ takes as input 1^λ. It samples group parameters $\Pi = (p, \mathsf{pp}_{\mathbb{G}}, \mathsf{pp}_{\mathbb{G}_T}, \circ, \circ_T, e, \mathbf{g} := \phi(1)) \overset{\$}{\leftarrow} \mathsf{GrpGen}(1^\lambda)$ and outputs a verification key $\mathsf{vk} = (\Pi, \overrightarrow{\mathbf{v}})$ such that $\overrightarrow{\mathbf{v}}$ consists of elements of $\mathbb{G}$ and $\mathbb{G}_T$ (plus a secret key sk for which we make no further constraints).*
2. *All function values $\mathbf{y}$ consist of values in $\mathbb{G}_T$.*
3. *All proofs consist of κ values in $\mathbb{G} \cup \mathbb{G}_T$.*
4. *For all $x \in \mathcal{X}$ and all $i \in [\kappa + 1]$, there exists a set $E_{i,x}$ of pairing equations that can be efficiently derived from x and the description of vuf. We require that $E_{i,x} \subset \mathbb{Z}_p[V_1, \ldots, V_n, P_1, \ldots, P_i]$ such that there is at least one polynomial of the form $a_{i,x} \cdot P_i + b_{i,x} \in E_{i,x}$ where $a_{i,x}, b_{i,x} \in \mathbb{Z}_p[V_1, \ldots, V_n, P_1, \ldots, P_{i-1}]$. (We note that since the set $E_{i,x}$ consists of pairing equations it holds that $a_{i,x}$ has degree at most 1 and $b_{i,x}$ has degree at most 2.)*
5. *We require that $\mathsf{Verify}_{\mathsf{vuf}}$ on input $(\mathsf{vk} = (\Pi, \overrightarrow{\mathbf{v}}), x, \mathbf{y} =: \pi_{\kappa+1}, \overrightarrow{\pi})$ outputs 1 if and only if the following hold: $\mathsf{GrpVfy}(\Pi) = 1$, all $\mathbf{v}_i$, for $i \in [n]$, and all π_i, for $i \in [\kappa + 1]$, are valid group elements w.r.t. Π, and for all $i \in [\kappa + 1]$ we have $E_{i,x}(\overrightarrow{\mathbf{v}}, \pi_1, \ldots, \pi_i) = 1$.*
6. *We further require that the ideal $(E_{1,x}, \ldots, E_{\kappa+1,x}, a_{1,x} \cdot \ldots \cdot a_{\kappa+1,x})$ (which is generated by the elements of $E_{1,x}, \ldots, E_{\kappa+1,x}$ and the polynomial $a_{1,x} \cdot \ldots \cdot a_{\kappa+1,x}$) contains the constant polynomial 1 (i.e., $(E_{1,x}, \ldots, E_{\kappa+1,x}, a_{1,x} \cdot \ldots \cdot a_{\kappa+1,x}) = \mathbb{Z}_p[V_1, \ldots, V_k, P_1, \ldots, P_{\kappa+1}])$.*

Requirement 4 will be useful in Lemma 2, as it basically means there needs to be at least one equation that contains the current proof element as a linear factor only. This yields in particular that the proof element in question is not a (non-unique) square root of other elements. The last requirement on a consecutively verifiable pairing-based VUF might seem odd, however, as we will see later, it makes sure that there is no tuple $(\mathsf{vk}, x, \mathbf{y}, \pi)$ s.t. any of the a_i can evaluate to zero on the exponents of $(\mathsf{vk}, x, \mathbf{y}, \pi)$.

Remark 11 (On VRFs with multiple output group elements.). We restrict our framework to VRFs with a single group element in the output. For VRFs with δ elements in the output, we propose the following adaption of the definition of consecutive verifiability: For each output element, we add a formal variable $P_{i_1}, \ldots, P_{i_\delta}$ to the polynomial ring. For consecutivity, we require a partial ordering of all $\kappa + \delta$ variables P_i, where the last element is required to be an output value. We further require that the conditions of Definition 13 hold w.r.t. the partial ordering. Such a consecutively verifiable multi-output VRF implies a consecutively verifiable single-output VRF that uses the last output element as its output and puts all other elements into the proof.

As our results apply to VRFs with a single output element, they also apply to VRFs that are obtained from multi-output VRFs through the transformation described above with the proof size adapted accordingly.

We now define the class of VUFs that evaluate a rational function in the exponent. We will show later that a VUF that fulfills Definition 13 and where the number of group elements in the proof is in $O(\log(\lambda))$ also fulfills Definition 14.

Definition 14 (Rational VUFs). *Let $d, n \in \mathsf{poly}(\lambda)$. We say that a VUF* $\mathsf{vuf} = (\mathsf{Gen}_{\mathsf{vuf}}, \mathsf{Eval}_{\mathsf{vuf}}, \mathsf{Verify}_{\mathsf{vuf}})$ *is **rational** of **evaluation degree** d with $n = n_{\mathsf{S}} + n_{\mathsf{T}}$ verification key elements, if the verification key is of the form* $\mathsf{vk} = (\Pi, \overrightarrow{\mathbf{v}})$ *where* $\Pi := (p, \mathsf{pp}_{\mathbb{G}}, \mathsf{pp}_{\mathbb{G}_T}, \circ, \circ_{\mathsf{T}}, e, \mathbf{g} = \phi(1)) \stackrel{\$}{\leftarrow} \mathsf{GrpGen}(1^\lambda)$ *is a certified group description according to Definition 3, and* $\overrightarrow{\mathbf{v}} := (\mathbf{g}^{v_{\mathsf{S},1}}, \ldots, \mathbf{g}^{v_{\mathsf{S},n_{\mathsf{S}}}}, e(\mathbf{g}, \mathbf{g})^{v_{\mathsf{T},1}}, \ldots, e(\mathbf{g}, \mathbf{g})^{v_{\mathsf{T},n_{\mathsf{T}}}}) \in \mathbb{G}^{n_{\mathsf{S}}} \times \mathbb{G}_T^{n_{\mathsf{T}}}$.

Further, we require for a rational VUF of evaluation degree d that for each $x \in \mathcal{X}$ there are coprime polynomials $\sigma_x, \rho_x \in \mathbb{Z}_p[V_1, \ldots, V_n]$ of total degree at most d s.t. we have for all vk, *all π and all $\mathbf{y} \in \mathbb{G}_T$*

$$\mathsf{Verify}_{\mathsf{vuf}}(\mathsf{vk}, x, \mathbf{y}, \pi) = 1 \implies \rho_x(v_1, \ldots, v_n) \neq 0 \text{ and } \mathbf{y} = e(\mathbf{g}, \mathbf{g})^{\frac{\sigma_x(v_1, \ldots, v_n)}{\rho_x(v_1, \ldots, v_n)}} \quad (6)$$

where $(v_1, \ldots, v_n) = (v_{\mathsf{S},1}, \ldots, v_{\mathsf{S},n_{\mathsf{S}}}, v_{\mathsf{T},1}, \ldots, v_{\mathsf{T},n_{\mathsf{T}}})$ are the exponents of vk.

We require that – given x and a description of vuf *– one can efficiently compute descriptions of σ_x and ρ_x, e.g. as coefficient vectors.*

Definition 15 (Rational Univariate VUFs). *Let $d, n, d_f \in \mathsf{poly}(\lambda)$ and let $f_1, \ldots, f_n : \mathbb{Z}_p \to \mathbb{Z}_p$ be n efficiently computable polynomials of degree at most d_f. Let* $\mathsf{vuf} = (\mathsf{Gen}_{\mathsf{vuf}}, \mathsf{Eval}_{\mathsf{vuf}}, \mathsf{Verify}_{\mathsf{vuf}})$ *be a rational VUF **evaluation degree** d with $n = n_{\mathsf{S}} + n_{\mathsf{T}}$ verification key elements as in Definition 14. We say* vuf *is a rational **univariate** VUF of **internal degree** d_f relative to $f_1, \ldots, f_n$, iff for all* vk, *all $x \in \mathcal{X}$, all π and all $\mathbf{y} \in \mathbb{G}_T$ a successful verification* $\mathsf{Verify}_{\mathsf{vuf}}(\mathsf{vk}, x, \mathbf{y}, \pi) = 1$ *implies the existence of an "effective secret key" s, i.e.,*

$$\exists s \in \mathbb{Z}_p \text{ s.t. } \overrightarrow{\mathbf{v}} = (\mathbf{g}^{f_1(s)}, \ldots, \mathbf{g}^{f_{n_{\mathsf{S}}}(s)}, e(\mathbf{g}, \mathbf{g})^{f_{n_{\mathsf{S}}+1}(s)}, \ldots, e(\mathbf{g}, \mathbf{g})^{f_n(s)}), \quad (7)$$

thus $\mathbf{y} = e(\mathbf{g}, \mathbf{g})^{\frac{\sigma_x(f_1(s), \ldots, f_n(s))}{\rho_x(f_1(s), \ldots, f_n(s))}} = \mathbf{g}^{\widetilde{\sigma}_x(s)/\widetilde{\rho}_x(s)}$ *where σ_x and ρ_x are defined in Definition 14, and $\widetilde{\sigma}_x(s) = \sigma_x(f_1(s), \ldots, f_n(s))$ and $\widetilde{\rho}_x(s) = \rho_x(f_1(s), \ldots, f_n(s))$. Note that $\deg(\widetilde{\sigma}_x), \deg(\widetilde{\rho}_x) \leq d \cdot d_f$.*

Remark 12. In particular, the popular VRF of Dodis & Yampolskiy [16] is a rational univariate VUF with $n = d = d_f = 1$ (if extended by a certified group description).

4.2 From Consecutively Verifiable Pairing-Based VUFs to Rational VUFs

We now turn to proving that the evaluation outputs of consecutively verifiable pairing-based VUFs can be expressed through rational functions in the exponents.

Lemma 2. *Let* $\mathsf{vuf} = (\mathsf{Gen}_{\mathsf{vuf}}, \mathsf{Eval}_{\mathsf{vuf}}, \mathsf{Verify}_{\mathsf{vuf}})$ *be a pairing-based consecutively verifiable VUF with proofs of size κ and a verification key of size n.*

Then, vuf *is a rational VUF of evaluation degree at most $4^{\kappa+1}$ over n variables.*

We refer the reader to the full version [12] for the proof.

5 Algebraic Attacks on Rational VUFs

In this section we prove that the unpredictability of rational univariate VUFs cannot be based algebraically on some non-interactive computational assumptions. To this end, for any algebraic reduction from the NICA to the unpredictability of the VUF, we give a meta-reduction that internally runs the reduction and supplies it with an adversary for the unpredictability of the VUF. This meta-reduction finds a non-zero, low-degree, univariate *target polynomial* that contains the reduction's *effective* secret key as a root. Because the target polynomial has low (polynomial) degree and is non-zero, the meta-reduction can simply factor it and test each of its polynomially many roots against the reduction's verification key. Using the previously obtained secret key the meta-reduction can predict the reduction's challenge image.

Theorem 1. *Let p be a superpolynomial group order. Let* NICA *be a non-interactive computational assumption of size $q \in \mathsf{poly}(\lambda)$. Let $n, d, d_f \in \mathsf{poly}(\lambda)$ and let $f_1, \ldots, f_n \in \mathbb{Z}_p[S]$ be some polynomials of degree at most d_f. Let* vuf *be a rational univariate VUF of evaluation degree d and internal degree d_f over n variables relative to the polynomials $f_1, \ldots, f_n$.*

If there exists an algebraic $(t_\mathcal{B}, \epsilon_\mathcal{B}, r, Q, 1/(Q+1))$-reduction $\mathcal{B}$ from NICA *to the weak Q-selective unpredictability of* vuf *s.t. $Q \geq q^2 + 1$ and $r \in \mathsf{poly}(\lambda)$, then there exists an adversary $\mathcal{M}$ that $(t_\mathcal{M}, \epsilon_\mathcal{M})$-breaks* NICA *with $\epsilon_\mathcal{M} \geq \epsilon_\mathcal{B} - 2^{-\lambda}$ and $t_\mathcal{M} \leq t_\mathcal{B} + \mathsf{poly}(\lambda)$.*

We refer the reader to the full version [12] for the proof.

Remark 13. Indeed, Theorem 1 can be applied if the input space $\mathcal{X}$ is only of polynomial size for a suitable definition of weak selective unpredictiability. Here, one has to make sure that the challenge preimage is not contained in the Q many query preimages, otherwise the adversary could predict trivially.

Corollary 1. *If the reduction in Theorem 1 is efficient, then* NICA *is efficiently solvable. In other words,* $t_\mathcal{B}/\epsilon_\mathcal{B} \in \text{poly}(\lambda) \implies t_\mathcal{M}/\epsilon_\mathcal{M} \in \text{poly}(\lambda)$.

We move on to our next result.

Theorem 2. *Let* $p = p(\lambda)$ *be a superpolynomial group order. Let* NICA *be some univariate DLog-hard assumption according to Definition 7 with* $l_1, l_2, d_{\text{NICA}} \in \text{poly}(\lambda)$, *and polynomials* $r_1, \ldots, r_{l_1}, t_1, \ldots, t_{l_2} \in \mathbb{Z}_p[S]$ *of degree at most* d_{NICA}. *Let* $n, d, r \in \text{poly}(\lambda)$. *Let* vrf *be a rational VRF of evaluation degree* d *with* n *verification key elements s.t.* $\forall x \in \mathcal{X} : \sigma_x(\overrightarrow{V}) = V_1$.[13]

If there exists an algebraic $(t_\mathcal{B}, \epsilon_\mathcal{B}, r, 0, 1)$-*reduction* $\mathcal{B}$ *(that forwards its group description as part of the verification key) from* NICA *to the 0-selective pseudo-randomness of* vrf, *then there exists an adversary* $\mathcal{M}$ *that* $(t_\mathcal{M}, \epsilon_\mathcal{M})$-*breaks* NICA *with* $\epsilon_\mathcal{M} \geq \epsilon_\mathcal{B} - 2^{-\lambda}$ *and* $t_\mathcal{M} \leq t_\mathcal{B} + \text{poly}(l_2, d_{\text{NICA}}, d, \log p, r) = t_\mathcal{B} + \text{poly}(\lambda)$.

We refer the reader to the full version [12] for the proof.

6 Generic Attacks on Parametrized Rational VUFs

Finally, we show the impossibility of algebraic and generic black-box reductions of the hardness of Uber-assumptions to the security of parametrized rational VUFs. Rational VUFs can be seen as a strong generalization of the VUFs of Dodis & Yampolskiy [16].

Definition 16. *A VUF* vuf = $(\text{Gen}_{\text{vuf}}, \text{Eval}_{\text{vuf}}, \text{Verify}_{\text{vuf}})$ *is called* **parametrized rational** *of evaluation degree* $d_{\text{vuf}} = d_{\text{vuf}}(\lambda)$, *if there are polynomials* $\sigma, \rho \in \mathbb{Z}_p[V_{S,1}, \ldots, V_{S,n_1}, V_{T,1}, \ldots, V_{T,n_2}, X]$ *of total degree* d_{vuf} *s.t. the following things hold:*

1. *The set of possible inputs of* vuf *is* $\mathcal{X} = \mathbb{Z}_p$.
2. *For each generator* $\mathbf{h} \in \mathbb{G}$ *and each tuple* $(\text{vk}, x, \mathbf{y}, \pi)$ *accepted by* $\text{Verify}_{\text{vuf}}$ *we have*

$$\rho(\overrightarrow{v_S}, \overrightarrow{v_T}, x) \neq 0 \quad and \quad \mathbf{y} = \mathbf{g}_T^{\sigma(\overrightarrow{v_S}, \overrightarrow{v_T}, x)/\rho(\overrightarrow{v_S}, \overrightarrow{v_T}, x)}.$$

where $\overrightarrow{v_S}$ *resp.* $\overrightarrow{v_T}$ *denote the exponents of the elements* $\text{vk}_{S,1}, \ldots, \text{vk}_{S,n_1}$ *resp.* $\text{vk}_{T,1}, \ldots, \text{vk}_{T,n_2}$ *relative to the basis* $\mathbf{h}$ *resp.* $e(\mathbf{h}, \mathbf{h})$.

We will now introduce our notion of Uber-assumptions, which is a generalization of the notion of Boyen [10].

Definition 17 (Computational Uber-Assumptions). *We call a non-interactive computational assumption* NICA *an* **Uber-assumption** *if there is a polynomial bound* $t = t(\lambda)$ *and a set of sparse polynomials* $f_{A_1}, \ldots, f_{A_{q_1}}, f_{B_1}, \ldots, f_{B_{q_2}} \in \mathbb{Z}_p[Z_1, \ldots, Z_t]$ *that can be computed efficiently s.t. the distributions of challenge samples of* NICA *is identical to the output of the following algorithm:*

---

[13] Essentially, the first verification key element $\mathbf{h} := \mathbf{v}_1$ is the new generator relative to which the VRF is evaluated.

1. **draw** *a generator* $\mathbf{g}$ *of* $\mathbb{G}$
2. **draw** $(z_1, \ldots, z_t) \xleftarrow{\$} \mathbb{Z}_p^t$
3. **set** $a_1 := f_{A_1}(z_1, \ldots, z_t), \ldots, a_{q_1} := f_{A_{q_1}}(z_1, \ldots, z_t)$
4. **set** $b_1 := f_{B_1}(z_1, \ldots, z_t), \ldots, b_{q_2} := f_{B_{q_2}}(z_1, \ldots, z_t)$
5. **return** $(\mathbf{g}, \mathbf{g}^{a_1}, \ldots, \mathbf{g}^{a_{q_1}}, e(\mathbf{g}, \mathbf{g})^{b_1}, \ldots, e(\mathbf{g}, \mathbf{g})^{b_{q_2}})$

Let $d_{\mathsf{NICA}} = \max\{\deg f_{A_1}, \ldots, \deg f_{A_{q_1}}, \deg f_{B_1}, \ldots, \deg f_{B_{q_2}}\}$. We call d_{NICA} the *degree* of NICA and $q = 1 + q_1 + q_2$ the *size* of NICA.

We can now state the formal version of Theorem 3.

Theorem 3. *Let* vuf *be a parametrized rational VUF of evaluation degree* $d_{\mathsf{vuf}} \in O(1)$. *Let* NICA *be an Uber-assumption of degree* $d_{\mathsf{NICA}} \in \mathsf{poly}(\lambda)$ *and of size* $q \leq \sqrt{\log\log(w)}$ *for some* $w \in \mathsf{poly}(\lambda)$.

If NICA *is hard and* $Q > 2 \cdot (1 + \log\log w) \cdot w^{2\log(d_{\mathsf{vuf}}+1)}$, *then there is no generic reduction that can transform an adversary for the weak* Q-*selective unpredictability of* vuf *to a* NICA *solver.*

A full and exhaustive proof of Theorem 3 is given in the full version of this paper [12, Section 6].

In a nutshell, the idea of the proof is to see that, since the reduction is algebraic and generic, the algebraic explanations of each group element give a ring morphism that maps representations of group elements to polynomials in the variables $Z_1, \ldots, Z_t$ of the Uber-Assumption NICA. For each $x \in \mathbb{Z}_p$ queried by the adversary, this ring morphism must be chosen in such a way by the reduction s.t. a system $\mathcal{S}_x$ of polynomial equalities is fulfilled. Since vuf is parametrized of constant degree, we have that $\mathcal{S}_x$ depends itself polynomially on x. Therefore, if $\mathcal{S}_x$ is satisfiable for too many $x \in \mathbb{Z}_p$ it must be satisfiable for each $x \in \mathbb{Z}_p$ and a solution for $\mathcal{S}_{x_0}$ can be computed by the meta-reduction by mere linear algebra. Therefore, the meta-reduction can predict the image to the challenge query x_0 on its own if it can ask for too many queries.

References

1. Abdalla, M., Catalano, D., Fiore, D.: Verifiable random functions from identity-based key encapsulation. In: Joux, A. (ed.) EUROCRYPT 2009. LNCS, vol. 5479, pp. 554–571. Springer, Heidelberg (2009). https://doi.org/10.1007/978-3-642-01001-9_32
2. Au, M.H., Susilo, W., Mu, Y.: Practical compact e-cash. In: Pieprzyk, J., Ghodosi, H., Dawson, E. (eds.) ACISP 2007. LNCS, vol. 4586, pp. 431–445. Springer, Heidelberg (2007). https://doi.org/10.1007/978-3-540-73458-1_31
3. Bauer, B., Fuchsbauer, G., Loss, J.: A classification of computational assumptions in the algebraic group model. In: Micciancio, D., Ristenpart, T. (eds.) CRYPTO 2020. LNCS, vol. 12171, pp. 121–151. Springer, Cham (2020). https://doi.org/10.1007/978-3-030-56880-1_5

4. Belenkiy, M., Chase, M., Kohlweiss, M., Lysyanskaya, A.: Compact e-cash and simulatable VRFs revisited. In: Shacham, H., Waters, B. (eds.) Pairing 2009. LNCS, vol. 5671, pp. 114–131. Springer, Heidelberg (2009). https://doi.org/10.1007/978-3-642-03298-1_9

5. Bitansky, N.: Verifiable random functions from non-interactive witness-indistinguishable proofs. In: Kalai, Y., Reyzin, L. (eds.) TCC 2017. LNCS, vol. 10678, pp. 567–594. Springer, Cham (2017). https://doi.org/10.1007/978-3-319-70503-3_19

6. Blum, M., Micali, S.: How to generate cryptographically strong sequences of pseudo random bits. In: 23rd FOCS, pp. 112–117. IEEE Computer Society Press (1982). https://doi.org/10.1109/SFCS.1982.72

7. Boneh, D., Venkatesan, R.: Breaking RSA may not be equivalent to factoring. In: Nyberg, K. (ed.) EUROCRYPT 1998. LNCS, vol. 1403, pp. 59–71. Springer, Heidelberg (1998). https://doi.org/10.1007/BFb0054117

8. Boneh, D., Boyen, X., Goh, E.-J.: Hierarchical identity based encryption with constant size ciphertext. In: Cramer, R. (ed.) EUROCRYPT 2005. LNCS, vol. 3494, pp. 440–456. Springer, Heidelberg (2005). https://doi.org/10.1007/11426639_26

9. Boneh, D., Montgomery, H.W., Raghunathan, A.: Algebraic pseudorandom functions with improved efficiency from the augmented cascade. In: Al-Shaer, E., Keromytis, A.D., Shmatikov, V. (eds.) ACM CCS 2010, pp. 131–140. ACM Press (2010). https://doi.org/10.1145/1866307.1866323

10. Boyen, X.: The uber-assumption family. In: Galbraith, S.D., Paterson, K.G. (eds.) Pairing 2008. LNCS, vol. 5209, pp. 39–56. Springer, Heidelberg (2008). https://doi.org/10.1007/978-3-540-85538-5_3

11. Brakerski, Z., Goldwasser, S., Rothblum, G.N., Vaikuntanathan, V.: Weak verifiable random functions. In: Reingold, O. (ed.) TCC 2009. LNCS, vol. 5444, pp. 558–576. Springer, Heidelberg (2009). https://doi.org/10.1007/978-3-642-00457-5_33

12. Brandt, N., Hofheinz, D., Kastner, J., Ünal, A.: The price of verifiability: Lower bounds for verifiable random functions. Cryptology ePrint Archive, Paper 2022/762 (2022). https://eprint.iacr.org/2022/762

13. Coron, J.-S.: On the exact security of full domain hash. In: Bellare, M. (ed.) CRYPTO 2000. LNCS, vol. 1880, pp. 229–235. Springer, Heidelberg (2000). https://doi.org/10.1007/3-540-44598-6_14

14. Coron, J.-S.: Optimal security proofs for PSS and other signature schemes. In: Knudsen, L.R. (ed.) EUROCRYPT 2002. LNCS, vol. 2332, pp. 272–287. Springer, Heidelberg (2002). https://doi.org/10.1007/3-540-46035-7_18

15. Dodis, Y.: Efficient construction of (distributed) verifiable random functions. In: Desmedt, Y.G. (ed.) PKC 2003. LNCS, vol. 2567, pp. 1–17. Springer, Heidelberg (2003). https://doi.org/10.1007/3-540-36288-6_1

16. Dodis, Y., Yampolskiy, A.: A verifiable random function with short proofs and keys. In: Vaudenay, S. (ed.) PKC 2005. LNCS, vol. 3386, pp. 416–431. Springer, Heidelberg (2005). https://doi.org/10.1007/978-3-540-30580-4_28

17. Fiore, D., Schröder, D.: Uniqueness is a different story: impossibility of verifiable random functions from trapdoor permutations. In: Cramer, R. (ed.) TCC 2012. LNCS, vol. 7194, pp. 636–653. Springer, Heidelberg (2012). https://doi.org/10.1007/978-3-642-28914-9_36

18. Fleischhacker, N., Jager, T., Schröder, D.: On tight security proofs for Schnorr signatures. J. Cryptol. 32(2), 566–599 (2019). https://doi.org/10.1007/s00145-019-09311-5

19. Fuchsbauer, G., Kiltz, E., Loss, J.: The algebraic group model and its applications. In: Shacham, H., Boldyreva, A. (eds.) CRYPTO 2018. LNCS, vol. 10992, pp. 33–62. Springer, Cham (2018). https://doi.org/10.1007/978-3-319-96881-0_2

20. Goldreich, O., Levin, L.A.: A hard-core predicate for all one-way functions. In: 21st ACM STOC, pp. 25–32. ACM Press (1989). https://doi.org/10.1145/73007.73010

21. Goldreich, O., Goldwasser, S., Micali, S.: How to construct random functions (extended abstract). In: 25th FOCS, pp. 464–479. IEEE Computer Society Press (1984). https://doi.org/10.1109/SFCS.1984.715949

22. Goldwasser, S., Ostrovsky, R.: *Invariant* signatures and non-interactive zero-knowledge proofs are equivalent. In: Brickell, E.F. (ed.) CRYPTO 1992. LNCS, vol. 740, pp. 228–245. Springer, Heidelberg (1993). https://doi.org/10.1007/3-540-48071-4_16

23. Goyal, R., Hohenberger, S., Koppula, V., Waters, B.: A generic approach to constructing and proving verifiable random functions. In: Kalai, Y., Reyzin, L. (eds.) TCC 2017. LNCS, vol. 10678, pp. 537–566. Springer, Cham (2017). https://doi.org/10.1007/978-3-319-70503-3_18

24. Hofheinz, D., Jager, T.: Verifiable random functions from standard assumptions. In: Kushilevitz, E., Malkin, T. (eds.) TCC 2016. LNCS, vol. 9562, pp. 336–362. Springer, Heidelberg (2016). https://doi.org/10.1007/978-3-662-49096-9_14

25. Hohenberger, S., Waters, B.: Constructing verifiable random functions with large input spaces. In: Gilbert, H. (ed.) EUROCRYPT 2010. LNCS, vol. 6110, pp. 656–672. Springer, Heidelberg (2010). https://doi.org/10.1007/978-3-642-13190-5_33

26. Jager, T.: Verifiable random functions from weaker assumptions. In: Dodis, Y., Nielsen, J.B. (eds.) TCC 2015. LNCS, vol. 9015, pp. 121–143. Springer, Heidelberg (2015). https://doi.org/10.1007/978-3-662-46497-7_5

27. Jarecki, S., Shmatikov, V.: Handcuffing big brother: an abuse-resilient transaction escrow scheme. In: Cachin, C., Camenisch, J.L. (eds.) EUROCRYPT 2004. LNCS, vol. 3027, pp. 590–608. Springer, Heidelberg (2004). https://doi.org/10.1007/978-3-540-24676-3_35

28. Katsumata, S.: On the untapped potential of encoding predicates by arithmetic circuits and their applications. In: Takagi, T., Peyrin, T. (eds.) ASIACRYPT 2017. LNCS, vol. 10626, pp. 95–125. Springer, Cham (2017). https://doi.org/10.1007/978-3-319-70700-6_4

29. Katz, J., Zhang, C., Zhou, H.-S.: An analysis of the algebraic group model. Cryptology ePrint Archive, Report 2022/210 (2022). http://eprint.iacr.org/2022/210

30. Kohl, L.: Hunting and gathering – verifiable random functions from standard assumptions with short proofs. In: Lin, D., Sako, K. (eds.) PKC 2019. LNCS, vol. 11443, pp. 408–437. Springer, Cham (2019). https://doi.org/10.1007/978-3-030-17259-6_14

31. Kurosawa, K., Nojima, R., Phong, L.T.: Relation between verifiable random functions and convertible undeniable signatures, and new constructions. In: Susilo, W., Mu, Y., Seberry, J. (eds.) ACISP 2012. LNCS, vol. 7372, pp. 235–246. Springer, Heidelberg (2012). https://doi.org/10.1007/978-3-642-31448-3_18

32. Liang, B., Li, H., Chang, J.: Verifiable random functions from (leveled) multilinear maps. In: Reiter, M., Naccache, D. (eds.) CANS 2015. LNCS, vol. 9476, pp. 129–143. Springer, Cham (2015). https://doi.org/10.1007/978-3-319-26823-1_10

33. Liskov, M.: Updatable zero-knowledge databases. In: Roy, B. (ed.) ASIACRYPT 2005. LNCS, vol. 3788, pp. 174–198. Springer, Heidelberg (2005). https://doi.org/10.1007/11593447_10

34. Lysyanskaya, A.: Unique signatures and verifiable random functions from the DH-DDH separation. In: Yung, M. (ed.) CRYPTO 2002. LNCS, vol. 2442, pp. 597–612. Springer, Heidelberg (2002). https://doi.org/10.1007/3-540-45708-9_38

35. Maurer, U.: Abstract models of computation in cryptography. In: Smart, N.P. (ed.) Cryptography and Coding 2005. LNCS, vol. 3796, pp. 1–12. Springer, Heidelberg (2005). https://doi.org/10.1007/11586821_1

36. Micali, S., Reyzin, L.: Soundness in the public-key model. In: Kilian, J. (ed.) CRYPTO 2001. LNCS, vol. 2139, pp. 542–565. Springer, Heidelberg (2001). https://doi.org/10.1007/3-540-44647-8_32

37. Micali, S., Rivest, R.L.: Micropayments revisited. In: Preneel, B. (ed.) CT-RSA 2002. LNCS, vol. 2271, pp. 149–163. Springer, Heidelberg (2002). https://doi.org/10.1007/3-540-45760-7_11

38. Micali, S., Rabin, M.O., Vadhan, S.P.: Verifiable random functions. In: 40th FOCS, pp. 120–130. IEEE Computer Society Press (1999). https://doi.org/10.1109/SFFCS.1999.814584

39. Naor, M., Reingold, O.: Number-theoretic constructions of efficient pseudo-random functions. In: 38th FOCS, pp. 458–467. IEEE Computer Society Press (1997). https://doi.org/10.1109/SFCS.1997.646134

40. Nechaev, V.I.: Complexity of a determinate algorithm for the discrete logarithm. Math. Notes 55(2), 165–172 (1994)

41. Niehues, D.: Verifiable random functions with optimal tightness. In: Garay, J.A. (ed.) PKC 2021. LNCS, vol. 12711, pp. 61–91. Springer, Cham (2021). https://doi.org/10.1007/978-3-030-75248-4_3

42. Paillier, P., Vergnaud, D.: Discrete-log-based signatures may not be equivalent to discrete log. In: Roy, B. (ed.) ASIACRYPT 2005. LNCS, vol. 3788, pp. 1–20. Springer, Heidelberg (2005). https://doi.org/10.1007/11593447_1

43. Roşie, R.: Adaptive-secure VRFs with shorter keys from static assumptions. In: Camenisch, J., Papadimitratos, P. (eds.) CANS 2018. LNCS, vol. 11124, pp. 440–459. Springer, Cham (2018). https://doi.org/10.1007/978-3-030-00434-7_22

44. Schwartz, J.T.: Fast probabilistic algorithms for verification of polynomial identities. J. ACM 27(4), 701–717 (1980). ISSN 0004-5411. https://doi.org/10.1145/322217.322225.

45. Shoup, V.: Lower bounds for discrete logarithms and related problems. In: Fumy, W. (ed.) EUROCRYPT 1997. LNCS, vol. 1233, pp. 256–266. Springer, Heidelberg (1997). https://doi.org/10.1007/3-540-69053-0_18

46. Yamada, S.: Asymptotically compact adaptively secure lattice IBEs and verifiable random functions via generalized partitioning techniques. In: Katz, J., Shacham, H. (eds.) CRYPTO 2017. LNCS, vol. 10403, pp. 161–193. Springer, Cham (2017). https://doi.org/10.1007/978-3-319-63697-9_6

47. Yao, A.C.C.: Theory and applications of trapdoor functions (extended abstract). In: 23rd FOCS, pp. 80–91. IEEE Computer Society Press (1982). https://doi.org/10.1109/SFCS.1982.45

48. Zhandry, M.: To label, or not to label (in generic groups). Cryptology ePrint Archive, Report 2022/226 (2022). http://eprint.iacr.org/2022/226

Bet-or-Pass: Adversarially Robust Bloom Filters

Moni Naor$^{(\boxtimes)}$ and Noa Oved

Department of Computer Science and Applied Mathematics,
Weizmann Institute of Science, Rehovot, Israel
{moni.naor,noa.oved}@weizmann.ac.il

Abstract. A *Bloom filter* is a data structure that maintains a succinct and probabilistic representation of a set $S \subseteq U$ of elements from a universe U. It supports approximate membership queries. The price of the succinctness is allowing some error, namely false positives: for any $x \notin S$, it might answer 'Yes' but with a small (*non-negligible*) probability.

When dealing with such data structures in adversarial settings, we need to define the correctness guarantee and formalize the requirement that bad events happen infrequently and those false positives are appropriately distributed. Recently, several papers investigated this topic, suggesting different robustness definitions.

In this work we unify this line of research and propose several robustness notions for Bloom filters that allow the adaptivity of queries. The goal is that a robust Bloom filter should behave like a random biased coin even against an adaptive adversary. The robustness definitions are expressed by the type of test that the Bloom filter should withstand. We explore the relationships between these notions and highlight the notion of *Bet-or-Pass* as capturing the desired properties of such a data structure.

1 Introduction

A *Bloom filter* is a data structure that maintains a succinct representation of a set $S \subseteq U$ of elements from a universe U. It supports an approximate version of membership queries: for any $x \in S$, the Bloom filter must answer 'Yes' while for any $x \in U \setminus S$, it should answer 'No', but is allowed to have a small error probability[1] (at most ε), and answer 'Yes'. That is, it admits false positives but not false negatives.

The small memory required by the construction of Bloom filters (as opposed to storing S precisely) and the fast query time make Bloom filters extremely attractive in various applications. This comes at the price of a certain rate of false positive - elements not in the set declared as being in the set. False positives

---

[1] The precise meaning of this probability is the subject of this paper.

Research supported in part by grants from the Israel Science Foundation (no.2686/20), by the Simons Foundation Collaboration on the Theory of Algorithmic Fairness. Moni Naor is the incumbent of the Judith Kleeman Professorial Chair.

E. Kiltz and V. Vaikuntanathan (Eds.): TCC 2022, LNCS 13748, pp. 777–808, 2022.
https://doi.org/10.1007/978-3-031-22365-5_27

can affect performance, e.g., they can incur unnecessary disk access, lead to spam emails that are not marked as spam, and allow misspelled words. Therefore, the false positive rate is the main correctness metric that interests us. It is important to note that the false positive rate cannot be negligible if we wish to save space[2].

When we are dealing with a data structure such as Bloom filters, with a *non-negligible* false-positive rate the question is how should we define the correctness guarantee: what does it mean to see bad events infrequently, i.e., how can we claim the data structure behaves "nicely". (In contrast, in most of cryptography a "bad" event happens with only negligible probability and the definition of security is that we aren't likely to see it at all). One way to define the correctness is by first fixing a sequence of inputs (equivalently, the queries) and then show an upper bound on the false positive rate. However, this is not sufficient in many scenarios, especially when the queries are chosen adaptively, based on previous queries' responses.

This work proposes several robustness notions for Bloom filters that allow adaptivity and capture adversaries with different goals, using different evaluation metrics. The robustness definitions are formalized as tests to the Bloom filter. We investigate the relationships between these notions and propose one notion as the most desirable one to define robust Bloom filters.

There are many variants of Bloom filters, for instance, where the Bloom filter is initially empty and the set S is defined via insert queries, or where some extra information is attached to each element and we wish to retrieve this information in case the element is in the set. In this work we concentrate on the case where the set S is fixed and the queries are adaptively chosen. Our definitions are relevant to the other variants as well, and as far as we can see, so are the relationships we found. In addition, the question of defining the resiliency of a data structure with non-negligible failure faced with an adaptive adversary is relevant to other data structures, and our results may apply to them as well.

Robust Bloom Filters. The correctness of Bloom filters was mainly analyzed under the assumption that we first fix a query x and then compute the error probability over the internal randomness. We refer to this as the *static analysis*. One might ask what happens when an adversary chooses the next query based on the response of previous ones? Does the error probability remain the same? Those questions motivated the analysis of Bloom filters in adversarial settings, where an adversary chooses her queries adaptively.

We refer to a Bloom filter as robust if it satisfies some correctness guarantee under adaptive adversarial settings. Our *wishful thinking* is that a "robust" Bloom filter should behave like a truly unpredictable biased coin; that is, each query is false positive with probability at most ε regardless of the result of previous queries. Indeed, this is the case in the static settings. However, it is not true and more complex to formalize when considering a sequence of (mostly adaptively) chosen queries. One reason this is not true is that seeing the response on

---

[2] The lower bound on memory requirements of a Bloom filter is $n \log 1/\varepsilon$ where n is the size of the set S and ε is the error probability.

previous inputs might leak some information about the internal state of the data structure or the random bits used. This, in turn, can be used by an adversary that, for example, wants to increase the false-positive rate.

An example to demonstrate an adaptive attack is when using Bloom filters in Web cache sharing (see [12]). When a proxy gets a request for a web page, it first checks if the page is available in its cache, and only then does it search for the web page on another proxy cache. As a final resort, it requests the web page from the Web. Therefore, proxies must know the cache's content of other proxies. For such a scheme to be effective, proxies do not transfer the exact contents of their caches but instead periodically broadcast Bloom filters that represent it. If a proxy wants to know if another proxy has a page in its cache, it checks the corresponding Bloom filter. In case of false positives, a proxy may request a page from another proxy, only to find that this proxy does not have that page. In this case, a delay is caused. In the static analysis, one would set the error to be small such that cache misses rarely happen. However, an adversary requesting for web pages can time the result of the proxy, and learn the responses of the Bloom filters. In turn, this might enable her to find false positives and cause unsuccessful cache access, which leads to an overload. Note that the adversary cannot repeat a false positive since the proxy will save it in its cache once a web page is requested. A similar example was presented in [23].

1.1   Our Contributions

We explore old and new notions of *robustness* for Bloom filters and study the relationships between them. The precise definitions are given in Sect. 3. Our definitions aim to capture the idea that a robust Bloom filter should behave like a random biased coin even for an adaptive adversary. We highlight the notion of *Bet-or-Pass* as capturing the desired properties of such a data structure. First, as we shall see, it gives us the strongest guarantee we can (currently) imagine. Second, it is not too strong: there is a Bloom filter satisfying this notion (one based on a construction in [23]). Finally, it is relatively convenient to check whether a suggested construction of a Bloom filter satisfies the definition.

Following the work of Naor and Yogev [23] we define robustness tests in the form of a game with an adversary. The adversary chooses the set S and adaptively queries the Bloom filter. The goal of the adversary differs between tests. Naor and Yogev defined that following the adaptive queries, the adversary **must** output a never-queried before element x^*, which she thinks is a false positive. They said that an adversary wins if x^* is a false positive. They wanted the probability of an adversary to win (equivalently- make the Bloom filter fail the test) to be at most ε. We refer to the security notion of Naor and Yogev as the *Always-Bet (AB) test*.

We define a new test, extending the AB test. First, we allow the adversary to *pass*, meaning she does not have to provide any output. This gives the adversary more flexibility and defines a more robust test. In addition, we define an adversary's profit: if she outputs (bets on) an element x^* which is indeed a false positive, she is rewarded; otherwise, she "pays". If she chooses to pass, her profit is zero. Our profit definition gives rise to a new metric to evaluate Bloom filters: we set the payments so that a random guess with probability ε has an expected profit of 0. We say that an adversary makes the Bloom filter fail in the *Bet-or-Pass (BP) test* if her expected profit is noticeably larger than 0. In this case, the Bloom filter is not BP test resilient, (not robust under the BP test).

The AB and the BP tests consider a one-time challenge, x^*. We also consider tests with a "continuous" flavor; those tests examine the false positive rate in the entire sequence of adaptive queries and look for "anomalies". We propose a new family of tests following our original desire to require a robust Bloom filter to behave like a truly unpredictable biased coin. Informally, it tests whether a sequence generated by the output of a Bloom filter on adaptively selected queries "looks like" a biased random coin to any efficient observer (that examines some property of the sequence). Since there can be elements that are always true negatives and we are only interested in cases where an adversary *increases* the false positive rate, we consider *monotone observers* only - observers that test a monotone property of the sequence. In other words, observers that are sensitive to the addition of false positives and not the reduction of ones. If a Bloom filter does not fail in all monotone tests, we say it is *monotone test* resilient. We then analyze a special case of the monotone test: we look at the expected number of false positives. We say that a Bloom filter is *expected count test* resilient if for all adversaries the expected number of false positive in t queries is at most the expected number of ones in a sequence of t independent biased coin tosses.

Finally, we emphasize why adaptive queries are interesting by introducing a test we call *the semi-adaptive prediction test*. In this test, the adversary commits to a set of queries Q (non-adaptive) before getting access to query the Bloom filter. The adversary aims to find a false positive element from Q that was not queried yet (the adaptive part). A Bloom filter is a semi-adaptive prediction resilient if no adversary can find a false positive element from Q with a probability of at least ε.

Relationships. We explore the relationships between the different definitions (see Fig. 1). We prove that a Bloom filter that is BP test resilient is also AB test resilient. On the other hand, we show that a Bloom filter that is AB test resilient is not necessarily BP test resilient. This suggests that the BP test is a more robust notion than the AB test. We support this idea by showing that *BP test resilience implies monotone test resilience*[3] while a Bloom filter that is AB test resilient is not necessarily monotone test resilient. However, we show that AB test resilience, in turn, implies expected count test and semi-adaptive prediction resilience. We also demonstrate that the expected count test and semi-adaptive prediction are weak notions: we construct Bloom filters that satisfy those notions and fail the AB test. Finally, we show that monotone test resilience implies expected count test resilience, supporting that the expected count is indeed a special case of monotone test. We conclude that being resilient to the BP test guarantees the

---

[3] This is reminiscent of the fact that in pseudorandomness the next-bit-test implies all efficient tests.

desired robust properties and suggests it is the correct way to define a robust Bloom filter.

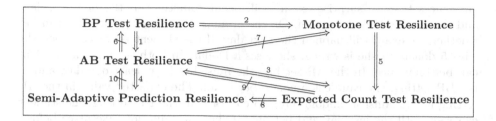

Fig. 1. The relationships between the different definitions.

BP as a Natural Notion of Robustness. Does the BP test capture the desired behavior of a Bloom filter as a random (biased) coin? At first glance, the skeptical reader might think that the option of passing is strange[4]. However, given that BP test resilience implies monotone test resilience, we can get some intuition why this is indeed the case. The idea is that when a Bloom filter fails in the monotone test, we can use the monotone distinguisher to know when to bet. This means that when a Bloom filter's behavior is distinguishable from a random coin, an adversary can exploit that to guess a false positive element with a high probability (higher than a random guess).

Our work explores what it means to be a robust Bloom filter. When trying to suggest a definition, we aim to achieve three requirements: First, the definition is sufficient, i.e., it captures the idea that a robust Bloom filter should behave like a random biased coin. Second, it's not too strong, i.e., there exists a construction of a Bloom filter satisfying this property. Lastly, it is easy to use, i.e., it is formalized as a **simple** test for a Bloom filter. The BP test resilience definition satisfies **all** these requirements, suggesting it is a natural notion of robustness.

Finally, we give an example to directly motivate the BP definition. Consider a system containing k different components, each using a Bloom filter to store some set (e.g., k web proxies with a Bloom filter holding their cache content). Further, assume that the system as a whole can withstand a certain false positive rate, denoted by epsilon. Suppose that there exists an adversary that, with noticeable probability, can find a false positive element with high probability (greater than epsilon) and knows to indicate when it happens. We can use this adversary in all the k components simultaneously in the following way: we locate k' components with a corresponding false positive element. We then query all those k' elements at about the same time. This results in a short period with a high false positive rate in the system, which can cause a denial of service. Note that the other notions fail to capture this attack.

---

[4] An analogy is situation in the casino game of blackjack, where at a certain point in the game the participants may have a small advantage over the house, as more cards are exposed (followed via "card counting"), and may choose to start betting then or to increase their bets.

The Surprise Exam and the AB and BP Notions. We can demonstrate the difference between the AB and BP notions by thinking of these variants wrt the famous surprise exam (or unexpected hanging) paradox [11]. Suppose a teacher announces that a "surprise exam" will occur sometime in the next six days and choose the date at random. On the evening of each day, a student can bet whether the exam will happen the next day. If the student is correct, then she wins 5 dollars; if she is wrong, she loses a Dollar. In both settings the student can bet only once. In the AB setting, she must bet in at least one day, and in the BP setting, she can decide not to bet at all. The expected value in the AB setting is 0 (against a random day). In contrast, in the BP setting, the student can wait until the last day and bet only if the exam did not take place before. In this case, she **knows** the exam is on the last day and has a strictly positive expectation (5/6). If the teacher does not chooses a day at random, but with some other distribution, then we need a more sophisticated strategy, but it is doable.

Computational Assumptions and One-Way Functions. Naor and Yogev [23] proved existential equivalence between Bloom filters that are AB test resilient (against a computationally bounded adversary) and one-way functions[5]. We refer to it as the equivalence result. We ask whether this equivalence still holds given a Bloom filter that is BP test resilient. The simpler direction shows that a Bloom filter that is BP test resilient implies the existence of one way function (we get it immediately by the implication of the BP test on the AB test). Showing the other direction is a little bit more challenging. We show a modification of the construction of Bloom filter from [23] that is based on the existence of one-way functions and prove it is BP test resilient. This, in turn, show the desired equivalence.

In the full version of this paper, we also ask whether weaker notions of robustness imply one-way functions. We show that if one-way functions do not exist, then any non-trivial[6] Bloom filter fails the expected count test the semi-adaptive prediction test.

1.2 Related Work

The first work to consider adaptive adversaries that choose queries based on the response of the Bloom filter is by Naor and Yogev [23]. They defined an adversarial model for Bloom filters through a game with an adversary. The adversary has only oracle access to the Bloom filter and cannot see its internal randomness. She can adaptively query the filter, and her goal is to find a never-queried-before false-positive element. We continue this line of research by introducing

---

[5] One-way functions are functions that, informally speaking, are easy to compute but hard to invert.

[6] Non-trivial Bloom filters are Bloom filters that require less space than the amount of space required to explicitly store the set.

new adversarial models, suggesting new ways to evaluate the Bloom filter performance. Naor and Yogev also presented a tight connection between Bloom filters in their model and one-way functions, which we extend to our settings.

Following [23], Clayton, Patton, and Shrimpton [8] analyzed Bloom filters, as well as other data structures such as counting Bloom filters and count-min sketches, in adversarial settings. They analyzed the probability of getting some predefined number of false-positive elements in a sequence of adaptive queries (as opposed to the probability of finding one never-queried before false-positive element). This type of analysis is similar to our expected count test.

Another move towards adaptivity was made by Bender et al. [2]. Similarly to [23], they indicated that the bound of false-positive probability only applies to a single fixed query, and a sequence of queries can have a much larger false positive rate (simply by repeating a false positive query). Their main concern was when an adversary *repeats* a false positive query (unlike Naor and Yogev, which did not allow repeating queries). To deal with this type of attack, they defined an *adaptive filter*: a filter that adapts to false positives, which means that even for an element that was queried and returned as a false positive, repeating it results in a false positive rate of at most ε. Their analysis assumes that the adversary could not find a never-queried-before element that is a false positive with probability greater than ε when using the result of previous queries. Their assumption can be achieved using the constructions in [23]. Therefore, their work is orthogonal to Naor and Yogev (and ours), since their concern is dealing with repeated queries and does not handle the issue of using adaptivity to find never-queried false positives. Repeated queries were also discussed by Mitzenmacher et al. [21] (adaptive cuckoo filter), and by Lee et al. [18] (telescoping adaptive filter (TAF)).

The problem of defining correctness in adaptive settings was also investigated in the streaming algorithms literature, where there is a growing interest in *adversarial* streaming algorithms. These algorithms preserve their efficiency and correctness even if the stream is chosen adaptively by an adversary that observes the algorithm's output (and therefore can depend on the internal randomness of the algorithm). Hardt and Woodruff [15] showed that linear sketches are inherently non-robust to adaptively chosen inputs and cannot be used to compute the Euclidean norm of its input (while they are primarily used for this reason in the static setting). Kaplan et al. [17] introduced a streaming problem that shows a gap between adversarial and oblivious streaming in the space complexity requirement. On the positive side, Ben-Eliezer et al. [1] presented generic compilers that transform a non-robust streaming algorithm into a robust one in various scenarios. Hassidim et al. [16] and Woodruff and Zhou [28] continued their work suggesting better overhead.

1.3   Open Problems

Our work leaves open several interesting directions. The direct one is whether Monotone Test Resilience implies BP Test Resilience (recall that we show the other direction), or whether the two notions are separable. Are the techniques of

Bender et al. [2] compatible with our results? Namely, can we have a robust BP secure Bloom filter against repetition? Another interesting avenue concerns the idea of allowing to output "don't know" (pass). To better capture the bit-security of decision games, Micciancio and Walter permitted an adversary to output a bot and redefined the advantage of the adversary conditioning on not outputting a bot (Def. 9 in [20]). Outputting a bot is very similar to pass in the BP test, and allowing pass and redefining the advantage gives a better notion. One wonders if there is a connection between these two definitions and if our definition can be applied in a more general setting (e.g., defining better bit-security for general decision games). It seems that knowing you don't know is significant in both cases. The definitions are related but not identical. For instance, in our case, the probability of the "secret bit" being 0 or 1 does not equal $1/2$ (the probability of it being 1, a false positive element, is ϵ). In addition, our game is asymmetrical: there is a difference between the bits 0 and 1 (we are only interested in the adversary outputting 1). We believe that it can be applied in a more general setting, but more work needs to be done to determine that.

2   Model and Problem Definition

For a universe $U = [u]$ we are given a subset $S \subset U$ of n elements. The set can either be fixed throughout the lifetime of the Bloom filter or can be formed via insert queries. As mentioned, we consider in this work the case where the set S is fixed; however, our results can be extended to other settings.

Following the work of [23], we model a Bloom filter $\mathbf{B} = (\mathbf{B}_1, \mathbf{B}_2)$ as a data structure consisting of two parts: a setup algorithm $\mathbf{B}_1$ and a query algorithm $\mathbf{B}_2$. The setup algorithm is randomized, gets a set S as input, and outputs a compressed representation of S, denoted by M. The query algorithm $\mathbf{B}_2$, can be randomized, is given a compressed representation of a set S, and answers membership queries. It gets an element $x \in U$ and outputs 0 or 1, indicating whether x belongs to S or not (and may be wrong for $x \notin S$). For simplicity of notation, we consider a probabilistic query algorithm that cannot change the set representation. However, our results also apply to Bloom filters that can change the set representation.

If $x \notin S$ and $\mathbf{B}_2(\mathbf{B}_1(S), x) = 1$ we say that x is a *false positive*. The main evaluation metric of a Bloom filter is the false positive rate.

Definition 1 (Bloom Filter). *Let $\boldsymbol{B} = (\boldsymbol{B}_1, \boldsymbol{B}_2)$ be a pair of probabilistic polynomial time algorithms such that $\boldsymbol{B}_1$ gets as input a set S and outputs a representation M, and $\boldsymbol{B}_2$ gets as input a representation M and a query element $x \in U$ and outputs a response to the query. We say that $\boldsymbol{B}$ is an (n, ε)-Bloom filter if for all sets S of size n in a suitable universe U it holds that:*

1. *Completeness: For any $x \in S$ we have that $\Pr[\boldsymbol{B}_2(\boldsymbol{B}_1(S, x)) = 1] = 1$*
2. *Soundness: For any $x \notin S$ we have that $\Pr[\boldsymbol{B}_2(\boldsymbol{B}_1(S, x)) = 1] \leq \varepsilon$,*

where the probabilities are over the setup algorithm $\boldsymbol{B}_1$ and query algorithm $\boldsymbol{B}_2$.

From here on, we always assume that $\mathbf{B}$ has this format and sometimes write $\mathbf{B}(S, x)$ instead of $\mathbf{B}_2(\mathbf{B}_1(S), x)$.

The Adaptive Game. Definition 1 considers a single fixed input element x, and the probability is taken over the randomness of the Bloom filter (and not over the choice of x, for example). This is a weak guarantee that we want to strengthen. We consider a sequence of t inputs $x_1, \ldots, x_t$ that is not fixed but chosen adaptively by an adversary.

Defining adaptivity requires specifying what information is made available to the adversary to adapt. Here, we allow the adversary to see the responses of previous queries before choosing the next one. We formalize this by defining a game $\mathsf{AdaptiveGame}_{A,t}(\lambda)$ where λ is a security parameter (see below). In this game, we consider a polynomial-time adversary $\mathcal{A} = (\mathcal{A}_1, \mathcal{A}_2)$ that consists of two parts: $\mathcal{A}_1$ chooses the set S, and $\mathcal{A}_2$ gets as input the set S and oracle access to the query algorithm (initialized with M) and perform adaptive queries. $\mathcal{A}_2$ aims to achieve a different goal in each robustness definition in order to make the Bloom filter fail the game (equivalently, the test). We measure the ability of $\mathcal{A}$ to make the Bloom filter fail with respect to her and the Bloom filter randomness.

To handle a computationally bounded adversary, we add a *security parameter* λ, which is given to the setup phase of the Bloom filter and the adversary as an input (acts as a key length). We now view the running time of the adversary, as well as her probability to make the Bloom filter fail, as functions of λ. Moreover, it enables the running time of the Bloom filter to be polynomial in λ and hence the false positive probability ε can be a function of λ.

We use the notation negl for any function $\mathsf{negl}: \mathbb{N} \to \mathbb{R}^+$ satisfying that for every positive polynomial $p(\cdot)$ there is an N such that for all integers $n > N$ it holds that $\mathsf{negl}(n) < \frac{1}{p(n)}$. Such functions are called *negligible*.

Definition 2. *The Adaptive Game* $\mathsf{AdaptiveGame}_{A,t}(\lambda)$:

1. The adversary $\mathcal{A}_1$ is given input $1^{\lambda + n \log u}$ and outputs a set $S \subset U$ of size n.
2. $\boldsymbol{B}_1$ is given input $(1^{\lambda + n \log u}, S)$ and builds a representation M.
3. The adversary $\mathcal{A}_2$ is given input $(1^{\lambda + n \log u}, S)$ and oracle access to $\boldsymbol{B}_2(M, \cdot)$ and performs at most t adaptive queries $x_1, \ldots, x_t$ to $\boldsymbol{B}_2(M, \cdot)$.

We assume wlog that $x_i \notin S$ for all $i \in [t]$, since Bloom filters admit false positives, but not false negatives, and also, $\mathcal{A}_2$ is given as input the set S. Therefore a queried element can be either false positive or true negative.

Definition 3 (A Test for Bloom Filters). *Let $\boldsymbol{B}$ be an (n, ε)-Bloom filter. For a security parameter λ, an (n, t, ε)-$\mathsf{Test}(\lambda)_{A,t}$ start with an adaptive game $\mathsf{AdaptiveGame}_{A,t}(\lambda)$ with an adversary $\mathcal{A}$. The test is defined by a function that given the transcript of the game (including the set S) decides 'succeed' or 'fail'.*

We say that a Bloom filter is *resilient for some test* (or family of tests) if the probability that any adversary makes it fail the test is upper bounded by some value. This term is formalized for each test in Sect. 3.

The Role of t. The parameter t indicates the number of queries the adversary performs. When t is not known in advance and unbounded, the adversaries must be computationally bounded given the equivalence result of [23] (see Sect. 1.1). However, when t is known in advance, the adversary does not have to be computationally bounded: Naor and Yogev presented a construction of a Bloom filter that is AB test resilient against computationally *unbounded* adversary using $O(n \log \frac{1}{\varepsilon} + t)$ bits of memory.

Inspired by Def. 2.5 in [23] we say that if $\mathbf{B}$ is resilient for any polynomial number of queries, it is *strongly resilient*.

Definition 4 (Strongly Resilient). *For a security parameter λ, we say that $\mathbf{B}$ is an (n, ε)-strongly $\mathsf{Test}(\lambda)_{\mathcal{A},t}$ resilient, if for any polynomial $p(\cdot)$ and $t \leq p(\lambda, n)$ it holds that $\mathbf{B}$ is an (n, t, ε)-$\mathsf{Test}(\lambda)_{\mathcal{A},t}$ resilient.*

An essential property of a Bloom filter is its memory size. Bloom filters are used because their memory size is smaller than an explicit representation of the set. We say that a Bloom filter uses m bits of memory if the largest representation for all sets S of size n is at most m. Carter et al. [7] showed that in order to construct a Bloom filter for sets of size n and error rate ε one must use (roughly) $m \geq n \log \frac{1}{\varepsilon}$ bits of memory (as opposed to $n \log u$ bits needed to answer **exact** membership queries). We can write this as $\varepsilon \geq 2^{-\frac{m}{n}}$ which leads us to the following definition:

Definition 5 (Minimal Error (Def. 2.7 in [23])). *Let $\mathbf{B}$ be an (n, ε)-Bloom filter that uses m bits of memory. We say that $\varepsilon_0 = 2^{-\frac{m}{n}}$ is the minimal error of $\mathbf{B}$.*

A simple construction of a robust Bloom filter can be achieved by storing S precisely, and then there are no false positives for an adversary to find. The disadvantage of this solution is that it requires a large memory, while Bloom filters aim to reduce the memory size. Similarly, a Bloom filter with a substantially low false-positives rate is robust. We are interested in a robust non-trivial Bloom filter. Roughly speaking, a non-trivial Bloom filter is a Bloom filter with ε substantially far from 0 and 1 and a large universe (compared to the memory size, so it will not be possible to store the set explicitly). For convenience, we use the definition of [23].

Definition 6 (Non-trivial Bloom Filter (Def. 2.8 in [23])). *Let $\mathbf{B}$ be an (n, ε)-Bloom filter that uses m bits of memory and let ε_0 be the minimal error of $\mathbf{B}$. We say that $\mathbf{B}$ is non-trivial if for all constants $a > 0$ it holds that $u > \frac{a \cdot m}{\varepsilon_0^2}$ and there exists polynomials $p_1(\cdot), p_2(\cdot)$ such that $\frac{1}{p_1(n)} < \varepsilon_0 \leq \varepsilon < 1 - \frac{1}{p_2(n)}$.*[7]

---

[7] If ε is negligible in n, then any polynomial-time adversary has only a negligible chance of finding any false positive. In that case, we can transform any adaptive adversary into a non-adaptive adversary since it knows the answers already. The same argument appears in [6] as Lemma 4. A similar claim applies to the requirement that ε will be substantially far from 1.

Let λ be the security parameter. It holds that $n = poly(\lambda)$.[8] Therefore we get that ε_0 cannot be too small and ε cannot be too large. I.e.

$$\frac{1}{q_1(\lambda)} \leq \varepsilon_0 \leq \varepsilon \leq 1 - \frac{1}{q_2(\lambda)}, \tag{1}$$

for some polynomials $q_1(\cdot)$ and $q_2(\cdot)$.

2.1   Prediction and Pseudorandomness

Pseudorandomness captures the idea that an object can "look" completely random even though it is far from random, since it was generated from a much shorter seed. One approach to defining it formally is via *indistinguishability*: Let Dist be a distribution on t-bit strings. We say that Dist is pseudorandom if it is infeasible for any polynomial-time algorithm to *distinguish* (in a non negligibly better way than guessing) whether it is given a string sampled according to Dist or whether it is given a uniform t-bit string. This means that pseudorandomness is a computational relaxation of true randomness.

The definition above introduces many tests: each polynomial-time algorithm (distinguisher) serves as a single test. An example of such a test is an algorithm D that returns '1' if the input string's first bit is 0. Therefore, the first bit of a string sampled from Dist should be equal to 0 with probability very close to $1/2$, since the first bit of a string sampled from a uniform distribution equals 0 with probability exactly $1/2$. Otherwise, D can distinguish between the two distributions.

An alternative approach to defining pseudorandomness is having a **single** type of test, *the next bit test*. In this test, a probabilistic polynomial-time algorithm is given a prefix of bits. It aims to *predict* the next bit of the source with a probability of success significantly greater than $1/2$ (this is the Blum-Micali definition [5]).

As Yao [29] showed, these two definitions are equivalent and the infeasability of predicting some bit of a given source can serve as a test for randomness. We show something of a similar nature. Consider a Bloom filter, an attacker and the sequence of bits representing whether a false positive occurred or not on a sequence of queries. Since the probability of a false positive is at most ε, we deal with a non-uniform output distribution. We want this distribution to be indistinguishable from a random independent biased sequence. This means that the false positive events are random independent events even in the case of adaptive queries. We formalize it in the monotone test.

Similar to the result in pseudorandomness, we want to define a prediction test that implies the monotone test. Our starting point is the natural extension of the next bit test for biased bits. This test requires that no observer succeeds in predicting the bits of the source with a probability greater than the bias. However, Schrift and Shamir [27] showed that the natural extension is no longer

---

[8] Since we want the adversary to run in polynomial time in the security parameter.

a universal test for independence. Therefore, we choose a different approach that draws inspiration from the world of gambling.

There are tight connections between gambling and knowledge of a sequence. Cover and Thomas ([9] Chap. 6) used gambling to express the ability to predict. They investigated the relationship between information theory and gambling. They looked at a horse race and presented two equivalent ways to describe the odds. We show one of them, which is referred to as b−to−1: the gambler will pay 1 dollar after the race if his horse loses, and pick up b dollars after the race if his horse wins. They looked at the gambler's wealth, which he wishes to maximize. We use their gambling methodology to define a robust Bloom filter. We let an adversary bet on a false positive: she outputs an element that she believes is a false positive. She gets rewarded if her output element is a false positive, while she is penalized if she outputs a true negative. We allow the adversary to pass, meaning she does not have to bet. In this case, she does not gain or lose any value. She wishes to maximize her wealth as well. We formalize it in the Bet-or-Pass Test and show it implies the monotone test.

3   Defining Robust Bloom Filters

3.1   Background

We have a data structure, Bloom filter, with a non-negligible rate of false positives, denoted by ε. We want to claim it performs well. We can think of the Bloom filter response to a sequence of queries as a sequence of independently biased coin tosses (with bias ε to 1). This is mostly the case when an adversary performs non-adaptive queries; she chooses her queries without seeing the response of the Bloom filter on previous queries. In that case, she gets a false positive (equivalently, one as a response) with probability at most ε in each query. Our *wishful thinking* is that a Bloom filter behaves like a truly unpredictable biased coin even when an adversary sees the response of the Bloom filter on previous queries. Meaning it performs well (robust) even in adaptive settings. However, this wish is a bit complex to formalize. Still, we suggest robustness definitions that try to capture this idea.

Our definition of robust Bloom filter comes in several flavors, depending on whether the adversary aims to find a never-queried-before false-positive element or increase the false-positive rate; what the evaluation metric is, and depending on the information available to the adversary. We discuss each of these choices in turn.

Adaptive vs. Non-adaptive Queries. When discussing adaptivity, we refer to the settings where an adversary can choose the next query based on the response of the Bloom filter on previous ones.

Our wish that a robust Bloom filter behaves like a truly unpredictable biased coin can be hard to meet, even in the non-adaptive case. False-positive elements are not necessarily random independent events, e.g., if the universe is divided into pairs, and both the elements in each pair are either positive or negatives.

However, the problem is more serious when discussing the adaptive case. In the above example, an adversary can query one element in each pair and query the other only if the first one is positive, resulting in a higher false-positive rate.

Therefore, we consider adaptive settings when defining robust Bloom filters: the adversary can adaptively query the filter. Nevertheless, we also analyze the non-adaptive settings and, more precisely, the ability of an adversary to predict a false positive element in the case of non-adaptive queries. We analyze the non-adaptive settings to understand the significance of seeing the responses of the Bloom filter.

One-Time Challenge vs. "Continuous" Challenge. We consider both a one-time challenge and a continuous challenge; By one-time challenge, we refer to tests in which an adversary performs t adaptive queries, and her goal is to find **one** never-queried-before false positive.

Some Bloom filter applications are sensitive to clusters of false positives, e.g. when Bloom filters are used to hold the content of a cache. An adversary that finds many false positives can cause unsuccessful cache access for almost every query, resulting in a Denial of Service (DoS) attack. Motivated by this, we also consider "continuous" tests, which examine the false-positive rate in a sequence of t adaptive queries.

3.2 Robustness in All Shapes and Forms

We will describe five definitions of robustness for Bloom filters capturing various aspects of robustness. For each definition we outline a **test** for the Bloom filter. If the Bloom filter is resilient wrt the test against all adversaries, then we say that it is robust under the corresponding definition. In each of these tests, the adversary performs t queries with a different challenge to achieve, which gives rise to a different type of robust Bloom filter. The difference between the definitions is the goal of the adversary and what she has access to, summarized in Table 1.

The conclusion of this investigation into the various notions of robustness is that the most desired notion is Bet-or-Pass.

The Always-Bet (AB) Test. Our starting point is the definition of [23]: the adversary participates in an adaptive game $\mathsf{AdaptiveGame}_{\mathcal{A},t}(\lambda)$ and then outputs an element x^* that was not queried before (and does not belong to S), which she believes is a false positive. The robustness is defined by the probability that the element is indeed a false positive.

The AB Test $\mathsf{ABTest}_{\mathcal{A},t}(\lambda)$

1. $\mathcal{A}$ participate in $\mathsf{AdaptiveGame}_{\mathcal{A},t}(\lambda)$ (Definition 2).
2. $\mathcal{A}$ outputs x^*.
3. The result of the test is 1 if $x^* \notin S \cup \{x_1, \ldots, x_t\}$ and $\mathbf{B}_2(M, x^*) = 1$, and 0 otherwise. If $\mathsf{ABTest}_{\mathcal{A},t}(\lambda) = 1$, we say that $\mathcal{A}$ made the Bloom filter fail.

Table 1. A table comparing the settings and the adversary goal within different robustness definitions.

Test name	Queries	Adversary goal
Always-Bet	Adaptive	Find a never-queried-before false positive element
Bet-or-Pass	Adaptive	Bet on a never-queried-before false positive element or pass
Monotone	Adaptive	Find an event that happens more frequently (non-negligibly) than a truly random coin tosses
Expected Count	Adaptive	Find more than $\varepsilon \cdot t$ false positive in expectation
Semi-Adaptive Prediction	**Non**-Adaptive	Find a false positive among the queries chosen beforehand

Definition 7 (Always-Bet (AB) Test). *Let $B = (B_1, B_2)$ be an (n, ε)-Bloom filter. We say that B is an (n, t, ε)-Always-Bet (AB) test resilient if for any probabilistic polynomial-time adversary $\mathcal{A} = (\mathcal{A}_1, \mathcal{A}_2)$ there exists a negligible function* negl *such that[9]:*

$$\Pr[\mathsf{ABTest}_{\mathcal{A},t}(\lambda) = 1] \leq \varepsilon + \mathsf{negl}(\lambda),$$

where the probabilities are taken over the internal randomness of B and $\mathcal{A}$.

The Bet-or-Pass (BP) Test. The adversary in the AB-test (Definition 7) **must** output a challenge element x^*. We suggest a definition that allows the adversary to pass; the adversary does not have to output an element. We define an adversary's *profit*: she gets rewarded if her output element is a false positive, while she is penalized if she outputs a true negative. She does not gain or lose any value when she chooses to pass. We use the expected profit to define the robustness: we want the expected profit to be 0. More formally, the adversary participate in an $\mathsf{AdaptiveGame}_{\mathcal{A},t}(\lambda)$. She outputs (b, x^*) where $x^* \notin S \cup \{x_1, \ldots, x_t\}$ is the challenge and $b \in \{0, 1\}$ indicates whether she chooses to bet ($b = 1$) or to pass ($b = 0$). If she passes, x^* is ignored and can be a random element.

The BP Test $\mathsf{BPTest}_{\mathcal{A},t}(\lambda)$

1. $\mathcal{A}$ participate in $\mathsf{AdaptiveGame}_{\mathcal{A},t}(\lambda)$ (Definition 2).
2. $\mathcal{A}$ outputs (b, x^*).
3. $\mathcal{A}$'s profit $C_{\mathcal{A}}$ is defined as:

$$C_{\mathcal{A}} = \begin{cases} \frac{1}{\varepsilon}, & \text{if } x^* \text{ is a false positive and } b = 1, \\ -\frac{1}{1-\varepsilon}, & \text{if } x^* \text{ is \textbf{not} a false positive and } b = 1, \\ 0, & \text{if } b = 0. \end{cases}$$

---

[9] In [23] resilience to this test is simply referred to as adversarial resilient Bloom filter.

Definition 8 (Bet-or-Pass (BP) Test). *Let $B = (B_1, B_2)$ be an (n, ε)-Bloom filter. We say that B is an (n, t, ε)-Bet-or-Pass (BP) test resilient if for every probabilistic polynomial-time adversary $\mathcal{A} = (\mathcal{A}_1, \mathcal{A}_2)$ participating in* BPTest$_{\mathcal{A}, t}(\lambda)$, *there exits a negligible function* negl *such that:*

$$\mathbb{E}[C_\mathcal{A}] \leq \mathsf{negl}(\lambda).$$

The expectation is taken over the internal randomness of B and $\mathcal{A}$.

Note that the expected profit of an adversary outputting a random guess with probability at most ε to be a false positive is at most 0:

$$\mathbb{E}[C_\mathcal{A}] = \underbrace{\Pr[x^* \text{ is FP } \wedge\ b = 1]}_{\leq \varepsilon} \cdot \frac{1}{\varepsilon} - \underbrace{\Pr[x^* \text{ is \textbf{not} FP } \wedge\ b = 1]}_{\geq 1 - \varepsilon} \cdot \frac{1}{1 - \varepsilon} \leq 0$$

The BP test allows an adversary to pass (although if she wants any chance to make the Bloom filter fail, the probability she passes must be noticeably far from 1). Adding the pass option suggests that the BP test is a stronger requirement and more robust notion than the AB test: consider a Bloom filter that behaves "nicely" in most cases except for a few bad cases. The probability of occurrence of the bad cases is negligible. Then this Bloom filter is AB test resilient. However, it is not BP test resilient. For the BP test, an adversary can become "active" (bets) only when she observes the occurrence of some bad cases. Given such bad cases, her success probability is not negligible.

We support this intuition by showing that BP test resilience implies AB test resilience, while the other direction does not necessarily hold. In addition, we consider another family of tests: **the monotone tests**, which resilience to them is implied by the BP test but not by the AB test.

One may note two differences between the AB and BP tests: the adversary must always provide a candidate false positive in the AB test, while it is optional in the BP test. In addition, they differ in the robustness metric: the probability of outputting a false positive vs. the expected profit. However, for the adversaries that always output element with $b = 1$ we show that the robustness metric is equivalent (in Claim 1 below), meaning that allowing the adversary the option to pass is the actual difference between the two.

Let $\mathcal{A}$ be an adversary performing ABTest$_{\mathcal{A}, t}(\lambda)$ (Definition 7). We can think of it as an adversary performing BPTest$_{\mathcal{A}, t}(\lambda)$ (Definition 8) with $b = 1$ always. Therefore her expected profit is:

$$\mathbb{E}[C_\mathcal{A}] = \Pr[x^* \text{ is FP}] \cdot \frac{1}{\varepsilon} - \Pr[x^* \text{ is \textbf{not} FP}] \cdot \frac{1}{1 - \varepsilon}$$

Claim 1. Let $\mathcal{A}$ be an adversary in BPTest$_{\mathcal{A}, t}(\lambda)$ game that always sets $b = 1$. Then there exists a negligible function negl_1 such that $\Pr[x^* \text{ is FP}] \leq \varepsilon + \mathsf{negl}_1(\lambda)$ iff there exists a negligible function negl_2 such that $\mathbb{E}[C_\mathcal{A}] \leq 0 + \mathsf{negl}_2(\lambda)$.

Proof. Let $\mathcal{A}$ be an adversary in the $\mathsf{BPTest}_{\mathcal{A},t}(\lambda)$ game that always sets $b = 1$. Assume that there exists a negligible function negl_1 such that

$$\Pr[x^* \text{ is FP}] \leq \varepsilon + \mathsf{negl}_1(\lambda).$$

Then,

$$
\begin{aligned}
\mathbb{E}[C_{\mathcal{A}}] &= \Pr[x^* \text{ is FP}] \cdot \frac{1}{\varepsilon} - \Pr[x^* \text{ is not FP}] \cdot \frac{1}{1-\varepsilon} \\
&\leq (\varepsilon + \mathsf{negl}_1(\lambda)) \cdot \frac{1}{\varepsilon(1-\varepsilon)} - \frac{1}{1-\varepsilon} \\
&= \frac{\mathsf{negl}_1(\lambda)}{\varepsilon(1-\varepsilon)} \\
&\leq \mathsf{negl}_2(\lambda),
\end{aligned}
$$

for some negligible function negl_2. The last inequality follows from Inequality (1). Now, assume that there exists a negligible function negl_2 such that

$$\mathbb{E}[C_{\mathcal{A}}] \leq \mathsf{negl}_2(\lambda).$$

Therefore,

$$\mathbb{E}[C_{\mathcal{A}}] = \Pr[x^* \text{ is FP}] \cdot \frac{1}{\varepsilon} - \Pr[x^* \text{ is \textbf{not} FP}] \cdot \frac{1}{1-\varepsilon} \leq \mathsf{negl}_2(\lambda)$$

$$\Pr[x^* \text{ is FP}] \cdot \frac{1}{\varepsilon(1-\varepsilon)} \leq \frac{1}{1-\varepsilon} + \mathsf{negl}_2(\lambda)$$

$$\boxed{\Pr[x^* \text{ is FP}] \leq \varepsilon + \underbrace{\varepsilon(1-\varepsilon)}_{\leq 0.5} \cdot \mathsf{negl}_2(\lambda) \leq \varepsilon + \mathsf{negl}_1(\lambda)},$$

for some negligible function negl_1, as desired.

Monotone Efficient Tests. Recall our desire ("wishful thinking") that a "robust" Bloom filter should behave like a truly unpredictable biased coin; It is not clear for both the AB and BP tests whether they satisfy this wish. To treat it more formally we consider monotone tests. A monotone test consists of $\mathsf{AdaptiveGame}_{\mathcal{A},t}(\lambda)$ as before, but now we are not interested in any specific output element. The test examines the response of the Bloom filter on t adaptive queries performed by an adversary $\mathcal{A}$. Continuing the idea of biased coin tosses, we would like to think of false positives as random independent events with a probability smaller or equal to ε. We compare the Bloom filter response on a sequence of t adaptive queries to a sequence of independent biased bits of length t with bias ε (probability of 1 is ε).

In this test, we consider monotone functions. Informally, a monotone function is a function that can only increase when we flip a 0 in the input string to 1:

Definition 9 (Monotone Function). *Let* $t \in \mathbb{N}$*. We say that a function* $f\colon \{0,1\}^t \to \{0,1\}$ *is* monotone *if for every pair of neighboring strings* $x, x' \in \{0,1\}^t$ *that are equal in all locations except in one index* $1 \leq i \leq t$*, i.e.* $x_j = x'_j$ *for all* $j \neq i$ *and* $x_i = 0$ *and* $x'_i = 1$*, we have that* $f(x) = 1$ *implies that* $f(x') = 1$*.*

The probability of a false positive can be less than ε, though this is hardly damaging. We are interested in clusters of false positives. This is what the **monotone** property aims to model.

Let $f\colon \{0,1\}^t \to \{0,1\}$ be a monotone function and D_f a polynomial time algorithm computing f. We consider distinguishers of the form D_f.

We now present the formal definition. The fundamental realization is that a robust Bloom filter should be resilient to *all (efficient) monotone tests*. That is, for any efficient monotone test (or distinguisher) D, the probability that D returns 1, when given the Bloom filter responses on a sequence of adaptively selected queries, should be close (from below) to the probability that D returns 1 when given an independent biased sequence of the same length and with bias ε.

Definition 10 (Monotone Test Resilient). *Let* $B = (B_1, B_2)$ *be an* (n, ε)*-Bloom filter. We say that* B *is* (n, l, ε)*-monotone test resilient if for every monotone probabilistic polynomial-time algorithm (distinguisher)* $D\colon \{0,1\}^t \to \{0,1\}$ *and every probabilistic polynomial-time adversary* $\mathcal{A} = (\mathcal{A}_1, \mathcal{A}_2)$ *participating in an* AdaptiveGame$_{\mathcal{A},t}(\lambda)$ *there exits a negligible function* negl *such that:*

$$\Pr_{S \in G_{\mathcal{A}}} [D(S) = 1] - \Pr_{S_\varepsilon \in B_\varepsilon} [D(S_\varepsilon) = 1] \leq \mathsf{negl}(\lambda)$$

where $G_{\mathcal{A}}$ *is the distribution of the Bloom filter outcomes on* $\mathcal{A}$*'s* t *queries and* B_ε *is a distribution of independent biased sequence of length* t *with bias* ε*.*

Note the similarity and differences with the notion of cryptographic pseudorandomness (see Goldreich [13]). In our setting we consider only *monotone* polynomial-time tests (whereas in the notion of cryptographic pseudorandomness *all* polynomial-time tests are considered) and we look at the difference between the probabilities without an absolute value (whereas there the absolute value should be negligible).

We give examples for relevant monotone tests. The first one is the **FP's count distinguisher**, denoted by D_w for some $w < t$. Let $s \in \{0,1\}^t$. We define,

$$D_w(s) = \begin{cases} 1, & \text{if } \#1 \text{ in } s \text{ is greater than } w, \\ 0, & \text{otherwise.} \end{cases}$$

D_w outputs 1 iff the number of ones (equivalently, false-positive elements) is greater than w. D is monotone. Another example is a **Cluster distinguisher** that outputs 1 iff the sequence contains w consecutive ones. Indeed, this definition captures if a cluster of false positives is found in a Bloom filter response since the probability of finding a cluster of "1" is negligible in a bias coin tosses.

The Expected Count Test. We use $\mathsf{AdaptiveGame}_{\mathcal{A},t}(\lambda)$. Similar to the monotone test, we are not interested in any output. Inspired by Clayton et al. [8], and as a special case of the monotone test, we look at the number of false positive elements that an adversary finds during her t adaptive queries. Let $\mathcal{A}$ be an adversary participating in $\mathsf{AdaptiveGame}_{\mathcal{A},t}(\lambda)$ (Definition 2). Let $Q = \{x_1, \ldots, x_t\}$ be the queries performed by $\mathcal{A}$. Denote the number of false positive queries by $\#\mathsf{FP}_t := |\{x_i \mid \mathbf{B}_2(M, x_i) = 1 \text{ and } x_i \in Q \setminus S\}|$.[10] We want to upper bound the expected number of false positives queries. Formally,

Definition 11 (Expected Count Test). *Let* $B = (B_1, B_2)$ *be an* (n, ε)-*Bloom filter. We say that* B *is* (n, t, ε)-*expected count test resilient if for any probabilistic polynomial-time adversary* $\mathcal{A} = (\mathcal{A}_1, \mathcal{A}_2)$ *participating in* $\mathsf{AdaptiveGame}_{\mathcal{A},t}(\lambda)$ *there exists a negligible function* negl *such that:*

$$\mathbb{E}[\#\mathsf{FP}_t] \leq \varepsilon \cdot t + \mathsf{negl}(\lambda),$$

where the expectation is taken over the internal randomness of B *and* $\mathcal{A}$.

The Semi-Adaptive Prediction Test. Finally, we define a semi-adaptive test: the adversary chooses the queries in advance (non-adaptively) and needs to find a false positive element using oracle access to the Bloom filter (adaptively). This test allows us to evaluate the "power" of adaptive queries.

We formalize this by defining a game, $\mathsf{SemiAdaptiveGame}_{\mathcal{A},t}(\lambda)$. This is done in a fashion similar to $\mathsf{AdaptiveGame}_{\mathcal{A},t}(\lambda)$: we consider a polynomial-time adversary $\mathcal{A} = (\mathcal{A}_1, \mathcal{A}_2)$ that consists of two parts: $\mathcal{A}_1$ chooses the set S and commits to t distinct queries $x_1, \ldots, x_t$, and $\mathcal{A}_2$ gets as input the set S, the queries $x_1, \ldots, x_t$ and oracle access to the query algorithm (initialized with M). $\mathcal{A}_2$ aims to find a false positive element among the t queries without querying this element explicitly.

The semi-adaptive game $\mathsf{SemiAdaptiveGame}_{\mathcal{A},t}(\lambda)$:

1. The adversary $\mathcal{A}_1$ is given input $1^{\lambda + n \log u}$ and outputs a set $S \subset U$ of size n and t distinct queries $x_1, \ldots, x_t$.[11]
2. $\mathbf{B}_1$ is given input $(1^{\lambda + n \log u}, S)$ and builds a representation M.
3. The adversary $\mathcal{A}_2$ is given input $(1^{\lambda + n \log u}, S, (x_1, \ldots, x_t))$ and oracle access to $\mathbf{B}_2(M, \cdot)$. For $i \in [t]$:
   (a) $\mathcal{A}_2$ chooses one of the following: bet on x_i to be a false positive **or** query $\mathbf{B}_2(M, x_i)$. If $\mathcal{A}_2$ choose to bet, then $x^* \leftarrow x_i$ and the game is stopped. Else, she continues.
4. $x^* \leftarrow x_t$
5. The result of the game is 1 if $x^* \notin S$ and $\mathbf{B}_2(M, x^*) = 1$, and 0 otherwise. If $\mathsf{SemiAdaptiveGame}_{\mathcal{A},t}(\lambda) = 1$, we say that $\mathcal{A}$ made the Bloom filter fail.

---

[10] Note that we count the number of false positives without duplicates to not over-credit the adversary.

[11] For convenience, we treat the set of queries as an ordered set. The order can be determined by the adversary when she queries $\mathbf{B}_2$.

Definition 12 (Semi-Adaptive Prediction Resilient). *Let* $B = (B_1, B_2)$ *be an* (n, ε)-*Bloom filter. We say that* B *is an* (n, t, ε)-*semi adaptive prediction resilient Bloom filter if for every probabilistic polynomial-time adversary* $\mathcal{A} = (\mathcal{A}_1, \mathcal{A}_2)$ *there exits a negligible function* negl *such that:*

$$\Pr\left[\mathsf{SemiAdaptiveGame}_{\mathcal{A},t}(\lambda) = 1\right] \leq \varepsilon + \mathsf{negl}(\lambda).$$

Note that we allow the adversary to repeat queries in all the mentioned above definitions, though repeated queries are not counted. We are only interested in its ability to find "fresh" false positive elements, as opposed to [2] where the Bloom filter false-positive rate has to be at most ϵ even if an adversary repeat the same query t times. The latter guarantee forces the Bloom filter to update its internal state after each query, while in our case, it is unnecessary but allowed.

4 Relationships Between the Various Notions of Robustness

In Sect. 3 we defined five different robustness tests. This section shows the relationships between them: which test gives us the most robust Bloom filter and which are the weakest tests. As we shall see, the most desirable notion for a robust Bloom filter is that of Bet-or-Pass. This notion satisfies our desired three requirements: first, it is sufficient, meaning it satisfies the security requirements. Second, it is not too strong: we present a construction of a Bloom filter satisfying the Bet-or-Pass definition. Finally, it is easy to use: it is formalized as a simple test for a Bloom filter.

4.1 Implications

We begin by showing which definition implies which (see Fig. 2). All the implications are true in the strong way; that is if Test_1 implies Test_2 then a Bloom filter is strongly Test_1 resilient is also strongly Test_2 resilient. We present our results considering a polynomial-time adversary; however, they also apply against unbounded adversaries if t is known in advance.

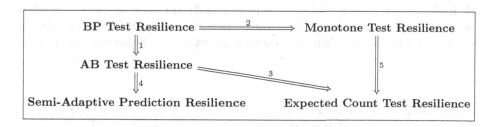

Fig. 2. Tests' implications

The BP Test

Theorem 1. *Let $0 < \varepsilon < 1$ and $n \in \mathbb{N}$. Let $\boldsymbol{B}$ be an (n, ε)-strongly BP test resilient Bloom filter. Then $\boldsymbol{B}$ is an (n, ε)-strongly AB test resilient Bloom filter.*

Proof. Appears in the proof of Claim 1.

Theorem 2. *Let $0 < \varepsilon < 1$ and $n \in \mathbb{N}$. Let $\boldsymbol{B}$ be an (n, ε)-strongly BP test resilient Bloom filter. Then $\boldsymbol{B}$ is also (n, ε)-strongly monotone test resilient.*

Proof. Suppose, towards contradiction, that $\boldsymbol{B}$ is not an (n, ε)-strongly monotone test resilient Bloom filter. There exists a monotone probabilistic polynomial-time test D and probabilistic polynomial-time adversary $\mathcal{A}$ performing $t \leq poly(\lambda, n)$ queries such that D distinguish $G_{\mathcal{A}}$, the vector indicating whether a false positive occurred or not, from the biased independent sequence B_ε; that is, for some polynomial p and infinitely many λ's,

$$\Pr_{S \in G_{\mathcal{A}}} [D(S) = 1] - \Pr_{S_\varepsilon \in B_\varepsilon} [D(S_\varepsilon) = 1] \geq \frac{1}{p(\lambda)} \tag{2}$$

For each λ satisfying Eq. (2), recall that $t \leq q(\lambda)$ for some polynomial q. We define $t + 1$ hybrids. The i-th hybrid $(i = 0, 1, \ldots, t)$, denoted H^i_λ, consists of the i-bit long prefix of $G_{\mathcal{A}}$ followed by the $(t - i)$-bit long suffix of B_ε.

Claim 2. There exists $i^* \in \{1, \ldots, t\}$ such that

$$\Pr_{S \in H^{i^*}_\lambda} [D(S) = 1] - \Pr_{S \in H^{i^*-1}_\lambda} [D(S) = 1] \geq \frac{1}{p(\lambda) \cdot t}. \tag{3}$$

Proof. The proof is immediate by Eq. (2), the pigeonhole principle and the definition of the hybrids. In particular, we use the fact that $H^t_\lambda = G_{\mathcal{A}}$ and $H^0_\lambda = B_\varepsilon$.

We now define an adversary $\mathcal{A}_{BP}$ for the BP test. For simplicity of the analysis, we assume that $\mathcal{A}_{BP}$ knows i^*. The idea is that monotonicity implies that an adversary can know when to bet. $\mathcal{A}_{BP}$ produce a $(i^* - 1)$-bit long prefix using $\mathcal{A}$'s queries and a $(t - i^* - 1)$-bit long suffix that contains random biased bits. Then, she gives the distinguisher the concatenated sequence twice: one time when there is 0 in the i^*-th index and one time where there is 1. If the distinguisher is sensitive to this change, then $\mathcal{A}_{BP}$ chooses to bet on x_{i^*}. Otherwise, she passes.

Adversary $\mathcal{A}_{BP}$

1. Set $i = i^*$
2. Run $\mathcal{A}$ for $i - 1$ queries $x_1, \ldots, x_{i-1}$. For each $j \in [i - 1]$ let $y_j = \boldsymbol{B}(S, x_j)$.
3. Select $r_{i+1}, \ldots, r_t$ independently with bias ε in $\{0, 1\}$ ($\Pr[r_j = 1] = \varepsilon$).
4. If $D(y_1, \ldots, y_{i-1}, 1, r_{i+1}, \ldots, r_t) \neq D(y_1, \ldots, y_{i-1}, 0, r_{i+1}, \ldots, r_t)$, then bet $b = 1$ and output $\mathcal{A}$'s ith query x_i.
5. Else, pass: $b = 0$ (meaning the adversary does not bet in any round)

To analyze the success of $\mathcal{A}_{BP}$ define two sets of sequences from $\{0,1\}^{t-1}$. The first one is BET_i which is defined as

$$\{y_1,\ldots,y_{i-1},r_{i+1},\ldots,r_t | D(y_1,\ldots,y_{i-1},1,r_{i+1},\ldots,r_t) \neq D(y_1,\ldots,y_{i-1},0,r_{i+1},\ldots,r_t)\}$$

and the second one is ONE_i which is defined as

$$\{y_1,\ldots,y_{i-1},r_{i+1},\ldots,r_t | D(y_1,\ldots,y_{i-1},1,r_{i+1},\ldots,r_t) = D(y_1,\ldots,y_{i-1},0,r_{i+1},\ldots,r_t) = 1\}.$$

By the monotonicity of D we have that if

$$D(y_1,\ldots,y_{i-1},1,r_{i+1},\ldots,r_t) \neq D(y_1,\ldots,y_{i-1},0,r_{i+1},\ldots,r_t),$$

then $D(y_1,\ldots,y_{i-1},1,r_{i+1},\ldots,r_t) = 1$ and $D(y_1,\ldots,y_{i-1},0,r_{i+1},\ldots,r_t) = 0$. Using this notation we have:

$$\Pr_{S \in H_\lambda^{i*}}[D(S) = 1] = \Pr[y_1,\ldots,y_{i*-1},r_{i*+1},\ldots,r_t \in \mathsf{BET}_{i*} \wedge x_{i*} \text{ is FP}]$$

$$+ \Pr[y_1,\ldots,y_{i*-1},r_{i*+1},\ldots,r_t \in \mathsf{ONE}_{i*}]$$

and,

$$\Pr_{S \in H_\lambda^{i*-1}}[D(S) = 1] = \varepsilon \cdot \Pr[y_1,\ldots,y_{i*-1},r_{i*+1},\ldots,r_t \in \mathsf{BET}_{i*}]$$

$$+ \Pr[y_1,\ldots,y_{i*-1},r_{i*+1},\ldots,r_t \in \mathsf{ONE}_{i*}],$$

where the probabilities are over the internal randomness of $\mathbf{B}$ and $\mathcal{A}$ and the biased coin flips. Combining the above with Eq. (3) we get:

$$\frac{1}{p(\lambda) \cdot t} \leq \Pr_{S \in H_\lambda^{i*}}[D(S) = 1] - \Pr_{S \in H_\lambda^{i*-1}}[D(S) = 1]$$

$$= \Pr[y_1,\ldots,y_{i*-1},r_{i*+1},\ldots,r_t \in \mathsf{BET}_{i*} \wedge x_{i*} \text{ is FP}]$$

$$- \varepsilon \cdot \Pr[y_1,\ldots,y_{i*-1},r_{i*+1},\ldots,r_t \in \mathsf{BET}_{i*}].$$

Hence we get that the probability that $\mathcal{A}_{BP}$ bets is non-negligible:

$$\Pr[b = 1] = \Pr[y_1,\ldots,y_{i*-1},r_{i*+1},\ldots,r_t \in \mathsf{BET}_{i*}] \geq \frac{1}{p(\lambda) \cdot t \cdot (1 - \varepsilon)},$$

and the probability that $\mathcal{A}_{BP}$ outputs a false positive element, when she bets, is noticeably greater than ε:

$$\Pr[x_{i*} \text{ is FP} \mid b = 1] = \Pr[x_{i*} \text{ is FP} \mid y_1,\ldots,y_{i*-1},r_{i*+1},\ldots,r_t \in \mathsf{BET}_{i*}]$$

$$= \frac{\Pr[x_{i*} \text{ is FP} \wedge y_1,\ldots,y_{i*-1},r_{i*+1},\ldots,r_t \in \mathsf{BET}_{i*}]}{\Pr[y_1,\ldots,y_{i*-1},r_{i*+1},\ldots,r_t \in \mathsf{BET}_{i*}]}$$

$$\geq \frac{1}{p(\lambda) \cdot t} + \varepsilon.$$

Therefore the expected profit of $\mathcal{A}_{BP}$ is noticeably greater then 0, as desired.

The AB Test

Theorem 3. *Let $0 < \varepsilon < 1$ and $n \in \mathbb{N}$. Let $\boldsymbol{B}$ be an (n, ε)-strongly AB test resilient Bloom filter. Then $\boldsymbol{B}$ is also (n, ε)-expected count test resilient.*

Proof. Let $0 < \varepsilon < 1$, $n \in \mathbb{N}$ and let $\boldsymbol{B}$ be an (n, ε)-strongly AB test resilient Bloom filter. Assume, for contradiction, that $\boldsymbol{B}$ is not an (n, ε)-strongly expected count test resilient. Meaning there exists a PPT adversary $\mathcal{A}$ that makes at most $t \leq poly(\lambda, n)$ queries, a polynomial $p(\cdot)$ such that for infinitely many λ's

$$\mathbb{E}[\#\mathsf{FP}_t] \geq \varepsilon \cdot t + \frac{1}{p(\lambda)}.$$

For convenience we assume that the queries were distinct. We use $\mathcal{A}$ to build an adversary $\mathcal{A}'$ that causes $\boldsymbol{B}$ to fail in the (n, t, ε)-AB test.

Adversary $\mathcal{A}'$

1. Choose a random number $j \in [t]$.
2. Runs $\mathcal{A}$ for $j - 1$ queries using oracle access to $\boldsymbol{B}$.
3. Output x_j.

Observe that

$$\mathbb{E}[\#\mathsf{FP}_t] = \mathbb{E}\left[\sum_{i=1}^{t} \mathbb{1}_{\{x_i \text{ is FP}\}}\right] = \sum_{i=1}^{t} \Pr[x_i \text{ is FP}].$$

Then,

$$\Pr[\mathsf{ABTest}_{\mathcal{A}', t}(\lambda) = 1] = \frac{\sum_{i=1}^{t} \Pr[x_i \text{ is FP}]}{t} \geq \varepsilon + \frac{1}{p(\lambda)t} \geq \varepsilon + \frac{1}{q(\lambda)},$$

for some polynomial $q(\cdot)$, where in the last inequality we used the fact that $t \leq poly(\lambda, n)$.

Theorem 4. *Let $0 < \varepsilon < 1$ and $n \in \mathbb{N}$. Let $\boldsymbol{B}$ be an (n, ε)-strongly AB test resilient Bloom filter. Then $\boldsymbol{B}$ is an (n, ε)-strongly semi-adaptive prediction resilient.*

Proof. Immediate by definition: semi-adaptive prediction resilience is a special case of the AB test with non-adaptive queries.

Monotone Tests

Theorem 5. *Let $0 < \varepsilon < 1$ and $n \in \mathbb{N}$. Let $\boldsymbol{B}$ be an (n, ε)-strongly monotone test resilient Bloom filter. Then $\boldsymbol{B}$ is an (n, ε)-strongly expected count test resilient.*

Proof. Let $0 < \varepsilon < 1$, $n \in \mathbb{N}$ and let $\mathbf{B}$ be an (n, ε)-strongly monotone test resilient Bloom filter. Assume, for contradiction, that $\mathbf{B}$ is not an (n, ε)-strongly expected count test resilient. Meaning there exists a PPT adversary $\mathcal{A}$ that makes at most $t \leq poly(\lambda, n)$ queries , a polynomial $p(\cdot)$ such that for infinitely many λ's

$$\mathbb{E}[\#\mathsf{FP}_t] \geq \varepsilon \cdot t + \frac{1}{p(\lambda)}.$$

Therefore, there must exist $1 \leq j \leq t$ s.t. for infinitely many λ's

$$\Pr[x_j \text{ is FP}] \geq \varepsilon + \frac{1}{p(\lambda)t} \geq \varepsilon + \frac{1}{q(\lambda)}.$$

where in the right inequality we used the fact that $t \leq poly(\lambda, n)$. For every $j \in [t]$, we define a monotone test,

$$D_j = \begin{cases} 1, & \text{if the } j\text{-th index in the sequence is 1,} \\ 0, & \text{else.} \end{cases}$$

We show that $\mathbf{B}$ fails the test D_j, meaning it is not an (n, ε)-strongly monotone test resilient Bloom filter. Indeed,

$$\Pr_{S \in G_{\mathcal{A}}}[D_j(S) = 1] - \Pr_{S_\varepsilon \in B_\varepsilon}[D_j(S_\varepsilon) = 1] \geq \varepsilon + \frac{1}{q(\lambda)} - \varepsilon = \frac{1}{q(\lambda)},$$

as desired.

4.2   Separations

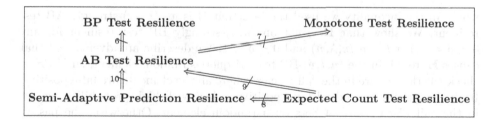

Fig. 3. Tests' separations

We now show the separations between the various notions, as described in Fig. 3; that is, to show a separation between Test_1 and Test_2 we present a construction of a Bloom filter that is strongly Test_1 resilient but is not strongly Test_2 resilient.

AB Test

Theorem 6. *Let $0 < \varepsilon < 1$ and $n \in \mathbb{N}$, then for any $0 < \delta < 1$ and for large enough u:*

1. *Assuming the existence of one-way functions, then there exists a non-trivial Bloom filter $\mathbf{B}$ that is an (n, ε)-strongly AB test resilient and is not an (n, δ)-strongly BP test resilient.*
2. *If t is known in advance, then there exists a non-trivial Bloom filter $\mathbf{B}$ that is an (n, t, ε)-AB test resilient and is not an (n, t, δ)-BP test resilient.*

Proof. Let $0 < \varepsilon < 1$, $0 < \varepsilon_1 < \varepsilon$, $n \in \mathbb{N}$. First, assume that t is unknown and unbounded. To have an (n, ε_1)-strongly AB test resilient Bloom filter, we need to use Naor and Yogev construction that uses one-way functions-using that, and we have a Bloom filter $\mathbf{B}$ that is an (n, ε_1)-strongly AB test resilient. Let $\varepsilon_2 = \frac{\varepsilon - \varepsilon_1}{1 - \varepsilon_1}$. We consider the following Bloom filter $\mathbf{B}'$:

$$\mathbf{B}'(S, \cdot) \equiv \begin{cases} 1, & \text{w.p. } \varepsilon_2, \\ \mathbf{B}(S, \cdot), & \text{w.p. } 1 - \varepsilon_2. \end{cases}$$

That is, in the setup phase $\mathbf{B}'$ flips a coin with bias ε_2 to decide whether it always answers 1 (regardless of the input) or always answers as $\mathbf{B}$. We use the notation "$\equiv$" to denote the result of that coin toss. Let $\varepsilon = \varepsilon_2 + (1 - \varepsilon_2) \cdot \varepsilon_1$. The probability of false positive in $\mathbf{B}'$ equals ε; meaning $\mathbf{B}'$ is an (n, ε)-Bloom filter. Moreover, for all $t \leq poly(\lambda, n)$, $\mathbf{B}'$ is resilient to the (n, t, ε)-AB test:

$$\begin{aligned} \Pr[\mathsf{ABTest}_{\mathcal{A}, t}(\lambda) = 1] &= \Pr[x^* \text{ is } false\, positive] \\ &= \Pr\big[\mathbf{B}'(S, \cdot) \equiv 1 \vee \mathbf{B}'(S, x^*) \equiv \mathbf{B}(S, x^*) = 1\big] \\ &\leq \varepsilon_2 + \varepsilon_1 \cdot (1 - \varepsilon_2) = \varepsilon, \end{aligned}$$

where in the inequality we used the fact that $\mathbf{B}$ is an (n, ε_1)-strongly AB test resilient. We show that $\mathbf{B}$ is not an (n, δ)-strongly BP test resilient for any $0 < \delta < 1$. Let $t \leq poly(\lambda, n)$ and $0 < \delta < 1$. We describe an adversary $\mathcal{A}$ that causes $\mathbf{B}'$ to fail in the (n, t, δ)-BP test. $\mathcal{A}$ queries random elements in $U \setminus S$ to check whether we are in the "all 1" case where all the elements are false positive. If all the queries are indeed false positives, then with high probability, we are in the "all 1" case and $\mathcal{A}$ bets on a random element. Otherwise, she passes. Formally,

Adversary $\mathcal{A}$

1. Choose a random set $S \subset U$ of size n.
2. For $i \in [t]$:
   (a) Query independent random elements $x_i \in U \setminus S$.
3. If for all $i \in [t]$: $\mathbf{B}'(S, x_i) = 1$ (i.e., all the queried elements are false positive), choose a random element x^* and output $(b = 1, x^*)$ (**bet**).
4. Otherwise, set $b = 0$ (**pass**).

First, note that the probability that $\mathcal{A}$ bets is non-negligible:

$$\Pr[\mathcal{A} \text{ bets}] \geq \Pr[\mathcal{A} \text{ bets} \mid \mathbf{B}' \equiv 1] \cdot \Pr[\mathbf{B}' \equiv 1] \geq 1 \cdot \varepsilon_2.$$

Now, assume that $\mathcal{A}$ chooses to bet (i.e., all the queries in step 2 are false-positive elements). Consider the following three cases:

1. We are in the "all 1" case. In this case, the profit is $1/\delta$.
2. We are not in the "all 1" case, and the false positive rate is greater or equal to δ. In this case, the profit is non-negative.
3. Otherwise, the profit is negative, but this happens with probability at most δ^t (which is a very small probability for sufficiently large t)[12].

Summing up the above cases, we get that the expected profit of $\mathcal{A}$ is noticeably greater than zero[13], meaning $\mathbf{B}$ is not an (n, δ)-strongly BP test resilient.

If t is known in advance, we use Naor and Yogev construction of Bloom filter that is resilient to the (n, t, ε_1)-AB test against unbounded adversaries. The above proof holds for this specific t.

Theorem 7. *Let $0 < \varepsilon < 1$ and $n \in \mathbb{N}$, then for any $0 < \delta < 1$ and for large enough u:*

1. *Assuming the existence of one-way functions, then there exists a non-trivial Bloom filter $\mathbf{B}$ that is an (n, ε)-strongly AB test resilient and is not an (n, δ)-strongly monotone test resilient.*
2. *If t is known in advance, then there exists a non-trivial Bloom filter $\mathbf{B}$ that is an (n, t, ε)-AB test resilient and is not an (n, t, δ)-monotone test resilient.*

Proof. Let $0 < \varepsilon < 1$, $0 < \varepsilon_1 < \varepsilon$ and $n \in \mathbb{N}$. We use the Bloom filter $\mathbf{B}'$ defined in the proof of Theorem 6. We show that $\mathbf{B}'$ is not monotone test resilient for any $0 < \delta < 1$ by proving it fails the **FP's count distinguisher**, denoted by D_w (for some $w < t$). Recall,

$$D_w = \begin{cases} 1, & \text{if } \#1 \text{ in the input sequence is greater than } w, \\ 0, & \text{otherwise.} \end{cases}$$

We define the adversary $\mathcal{A}$ as follow:

Adversary $\mathcal{A}$

1. Choose a random set $S \subset U$ of size n.
2. For $i \in [t]$:

---

[12] Any (n, ε) Bloom filter is robust when the number of queries is small: if t is much less than $1/\varepsilon$ then we do not expect the adversary to see any false positives, and hence we can consider the queries as chosen in advance. Therefore, if t is not large enough, it is not interesting.

[13] We want $\delta^t < \varepsilon_2$ leading to $u > t > \log_\delta \varepsilon_2$.

(a) Query independent random elements $x_i \in U \setminus S$.

Observe that with probability at least ε_2 $\mathcal{A}$ can achieve as many false positives as she wants (w.p. ε_2 all the queries are false positives). Meaning for any $t \leq poly(\lambda, n)$ we have

$$\Pr_{S \in G_{\mathcal{A}}} [D_{t-1}(S) = 1] = \Pr[\#FP_t > t - 1] \geq \varepsilon_2.$$

On the other hand, for any $0 < \delta < 1$:

$$\Pr_{S_\delta \in B_\delta} [D_{t-1}(S_\delta) = 1] = \delta^t$$

Therefore,

$$\Pr_{S \in G_{\mathcal{A}}} [D_{t-1}(S) = 1] - \Pr_{S_\delta \in B_\delta} [D_{t-1}(S_\delta) = 1] \geq \varepsilon_2 - \delta^t \geq \frac{1}{p(\lambda)},$$

for some polynomial $p(\cdot)$ and sufficiently large t.

Expected Count Test

Theorem 8. *Let $0 < \varepsilon < 1$ and $n \in \mathbb{N}$, then for any $0 < \delta < 1$ and for large enough u: There exists a Bloom filter B that is an (n, ε)-strongly expected count test resilient, and is not an (n, δ)-strongly semi-adaptive prediction resilient.*

Proof. Let $0 < \varepsilon < 1$, $n \in \mathbb{N}$ and a set S of size n. Let $\varepsilon_1 \leq \frac{\varepsilon}{2-\varepsilon}$ s.t. $\frac{1}{\varepsilon_1} \in \mathbb{N}$. We partition the universe into disjoint blocks of size $b := \frac{1}{\varepsilon_1}$. Let B be a Bloom filter that stores the set S explicitly (we can modify the construction to work for non-trivial Bloom filters as well). We add "synthetic" false-positive elements to B in the following way: each block has exactly one false positive element (resulting in a false positive probability of ε_1 for random queries). In order to determine which element is positive in each set, we use a pseudorandom function[14] PRF. The PRF gets as input the block name and outputs the positive element in the block.

As we shall see, the resulting Bloom filter B is an (n, ε)-strongly expected count test resilient. We first claim that the best strategy for an adversary in order to increase the expected number of false positives is querying each block until she finds the false positive. Consider an adversary $\mathcal{A}$ following this strategy and focus on one block. The expected number of queried elements until finding the false positive is $\frac{b+1}{2}$. Assume $\mathcal{A}$ queries t' blocks (where $t' \gg b$). The false positive rate in this sequence is (with high probability):

$$\frac{t'}{t' \cdot \frac{b+1}{2}} = \frac{2}{b+1} = \frac{2\varepsilon_1}{1+\varepsilon_1} = \varepsilon.$$

---

[14] A pseudorandom function (PRF) is a keyed function F such that F_k (for key k chosen uniformly at random) is indistinguishable from a truly random function given only oracle access to the function. See Goldreich [13].

Now, consider an adversary $\mathcal{A}'$ that uses a different strategy, i.e., she queries blocks and might move on to another block before finding the false positive. Let $\mathcal{A}''$ be an adversary that follows $\mathcal{A}'$'s strategy with a slight change: every time $\mathcal{A}'$ moves on to another block before finding the false-positive, $\mathcal{A}''$ continues querying this block until she finds the false positive. Intuitively, it is better to keep querying an "open" block since we are left with fewer elements. Formally, let us look at all the queries $\mathcal{A}''$ added when continuing querying a block. They are divided into blocks of size at most $b - 1$. Hence, the false-positive rate in these added queries, similarly to the above computation, is at least $2\varepsilon_1 > \varepsilon$. Now, consider the rest of $\mathcal{A}'$'s queries. They either contain blocks that a false positive was found in them or blocks with no false positive. As shown above, the expected number of queried elements before finding a false positive is $\frac{b+1}{2}$. Assume that there are t_1 blocks that a false positive was found in them and t_2 blocks with no false positive. In each block, we query at least one element hence the false positive rate in these queries is at most

$$\frac{t_1}{t_1 \cdot \frac{b+1}{2} + t_2} < \frac{t_1}{t_1 \cdot \frac{b+1}{2}} = \varepsilon.$$

Since $2\varepsilon_1 > \varepsilon$, we get that $\mathcal{A}$ can only improve the expected number of false positives of $\mathcal{A}'$, as desired.

We conclude that the expected number of false positives in t queries is at most εt, as desired.

On the other hand, $\mathbf{B}$ is not an (n, ε)-strongly semi-adaptive prediction resilient. Let $\mathcal{A}$ be an adversary querying $p(\lambda)$ blocks, for some polynomial $p(\cdot)$; that is, she performs $t = p(\lambda) \cdot \frac{1}{\varepsilon_1}$ queries. She acts as follows: she queries each block separately. When she gets the response of the Bloom filter on an entire block except for one element and does not see any false positive, she bets on the remaining element. Therefore,

$$\Pr\left[\mathsf{SemiAdaptiveGame}_{\mathcal{A},t}(\lambda) = 1\right] = 1 - (1 - \varepsilon_1)^t \geq 1 - \frac{1}{q(\lambda)} \geq \delta + \frac{1}{s(\lambda)},$$

for any $0 < \delta < 1$, sufficiently large λ and some polynomials $q(\cdot), s(\cdot)$.

Theorem 9. *Let $0 < \varepsilon < 1$ and $n \in \mathbb{N}$, then for any $0 < \delta < 1$ and for large enough u: There exists a Bloom filter $\mathbf{B}$ that is an (n, ε)-strongly expected count test resilient , and is not an (n, δ)-strongly AB test resilient.*

Proof. Follows from the proof of Theorem 8.

Semi-adaptive Prediction Resilient

Theorem 10. *Let $0 < \varepsilon < 1$ and $n \in \mathbb{N}$, then for any $0 < \delta < 1$ and for large enough u:*

1. *Assuming the existence of one-way functions, there exists a non-trivial Bloom filter $\mathbf{B}$ that is an (n, ε)-strongly semi-adaptive prediction resilient and is not an (n, δ)-strongly AB test resilient.*

2. *If t is known in advance and sufficiently large, there exists a non-trivial Bloom filter **B** that is an (n, t, ε)-semi-adaptive prediction resilient and is not an (n, t, δ)-AB test resilient.*

The proof appears in the full version and is omitted due to space limitations.

4.3   Conclusions

We showed that if a Bloom filter is resilient to the BP test, it is resilient to all monotone tests. At the same time, this does not necessarily hold for a Bloom filter that is resilient to the AB test, demonstrating that the AB test can miss "bad" events such as clusters of false positives. We also proved that the BP test implies the AB test. Altogether we highlight the notion of *Bet-or-Pass* as capturing the desired properties of a robust Bloom filter.

5   Computational Assumptions and One-Way Functions

5.1   Constructions of BP Resilient Filters Using One-Way Functions

What we know so far:

$$\text{BP Test Resilience} \xLeftarrow[\text{We showed}]{\;\;\Longrightarrow\;\;}\!\!\!\!\!/\;\; \text{AB Test Resilience} \xLeftarrow[\Longleftarrow]{[23]} \text{OWF}$$

The black arrows are existential equivalence and the blue arrows are definition implication (with the same parameters) or separation. Therefore, if one-way functions do not exist, any non-trivial Bloom filter fails the BP test. We show that the existence of one-way functions also implies BP test resilient Bloom filters. For that, we show a construction of a Bloom filter that is strongly BP test resilient using one-way functions.

Pseudorandom Functions. A pseudorandom function (PRF) is an efficiently computable, keyed function F that is indistinguishable from a truly random function (given only oracle access to the function). A pseudorandom permutation (PRP) is a pseudorandom function such that F is a permutation and can be both efficiently computable and efficiently invertible.

We can construct pseudorandom function from any (length-doubling) pseudorandom generators [14], which in turn can be based on one-way functions. In addition, we can obtain a pseudorandom permutations from pseudorandom functions (i.e., using Luby-Rackoff construction [19,22]).

Constructing BP Test Resilient Bloom Filters. Our starting point is the transformation presented by Naor and Yogev. Assuming the existence of one-way functions they showed that any Bloom filter could be efficiently transformed into an (n, ε)-strongly AB test resilient Bloom filter using approximately the same amount of memory. The idea is simple: adding a layer of a pseudorandom permutation. That is, on input x, we compute a pseudorandom permutation of x and send it to the original Bloom filter. The main idea is that we make the queries look random by applying a pseudorandom permutation. Therefore an adversary has no significant advantage in choosing the queries adaptively. Note that the correctness properties remain when using the permutation. We ask if the above transformation also yields an (n, ε)-strongly BP test resilient Bloom filter. However, unlike the AB test, the BP test allows an adversary to pass. This gives rise to two potential attacks:

1. Assume that with some non-negligible probability, all the elements in the universe (excluding the set S) are false positives (e.g., the Bloom filter presented in separation Theorem 6). Applying a pseudorandom permutation, in that case, will make no difference; the adversary presented in separation Theorem 6 can still make this Bloom filter to fail the BP test even after adding the PRP layer.

2. The universe is of polynomial size, i.e., $|u| = poly(\lambda)$ and there exists an attacker that knows the exact number of false positives in the universe (this is not an unreasonable property of some constructions). In this case, the attack includes the adversary querying the entire universe U except for one element x^*. Based on the number of false positives she has seen so far, she knows with high probability if x^* is a false positive or not and chooses to bet or pass accordingly.

Therefore, we cannot use the transformation of Naor and Yogev when constructing a BP test resilient Bloom filter.[15]

Apart from the above mentioned transformation, Naor and Yogev presented a construction of a Bloom filter $\mathbf{B}$ that is an (n, t, ε)-AB test resilient against an *unbounded adversary and a given number t of queries*, for any $n, t \in \mathbb{N}$ and $0 < \varepsilon < 1/2$. As we shall see, this construction is actually also good for the BP-test (when the adversary is limited to t queries), i.e. $\mathbf{B}$ is also an (n, t, ε)-BP test resilient for any $n, t \in \mathbb{N}$ and $0 < \varepsilon < 1/2$.

We use this construction with a slight change to yield a Bloom filter $\mathbf{B}'$ against a *computationally bounded adversary when t is not necessarily known and can be unbounded*.

We start by presenting Naor and Yogev's construction (which in turn builds on Carter et al. [7]). They suggested to use a Cuckoo Hashing implementation of dictionary [25,26] to store the set. Roughly speaking, Cuckoo Hashing consists of two tables T_1 and T_2 and two hash functions h_1 and h_2. Each element x is stored in either $T_1[h_1(x)]$ or $T_2[h_2(x)]$. Instead of storing x in those locations, the value of an unpredictable (in the sense described below) function g at point x (i.e. $g(x)$) is stored at either $T_1[h_1(x)]$ or $T_2[h_2(x)]$ (see Fig. 4). When doing a lookup of x the values stored in $T_1[h_1(x)]$ and $T_2[h_2(x)]$ are retrieved and compared to $g(x)$ and a yes is returned iff at least one of them is equal to $g(x)$. The range of g should be about $\frac{2}{\varepsilon}$.

---

[15] It may be possible to modify the transformation to yield a BP test resilient Bloom filter; for instance, we can test if we are in case 1 and reselect the random bits or combat case 2 by adding as noise false positives. We will explore it in future work.

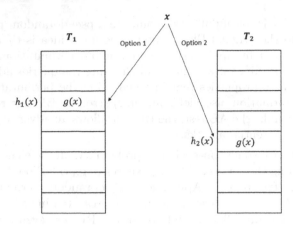

Fig. 4. Bloom filter via cuckoo hashing

For the function $g: U \mapsto V$, they used a very high independence function. More formally, they used a family G of hash functions satisfying that on any set of k inputs, it behaves like a truly random function with high probability (based on the work of [24], and [10]). Note that the guarantee of the function still holds even when the set of queries is chosen adaptively, as shown by Berman et al. [3]. To reduce the memory size further, they use the family G slightly differently. Let $\ell = O\left(\log \frac{1}{\varepsilon}\right)$, and set $k = O\left(\frac{t}{\ell}\right)$. They chose a family G of functions g_i that outputs a single bit (i.e., $V = \{0, 1\}$) and defined g to be the concatenation of ℓ independent g_i functions. Given a query x, they compare $g(x)$ to the appropriate entries, bit by bit. If the first two bits are equal, they continue to the next bit in a cyclic order. Consider an adversary performing t queries. Naor and Yogev showed that even though the adversary performs t queries, each of the ℓ different functions g_i takes part in at most $O(t/\ell) = k$ queries (with high probability). Hence, each function g_i still "looks" random on the queried elements. Therefore, we get a Bloom filter $\mathbf{B}$ that is AB test resilient for t queries and uses $O\left(n \log \frac{1}{\varepsilon} + t\right)$ bits of memory.

The security of the scheme is based on the randomness properties of g. Even if all the values in the tables that have ever been used are known to the adversary (including the functions h_1 and h_2), the value of $g(x)$ is unknown and is uniform in its range. Therefore the probability that it is equal to the value stored in $T_1[h_1(x)]$ or $T_2[h_2(x)]$ is at most $2 \cdot (1/2)^\ell \leq \varepsilon/2$. Transforming from exact k-wise independence to almost k-wise independence adds an error probability of $\varepsilon/2$. Thus, the probability that x is a false positive is at most ε. This proves that the construction is AB test resilient.

But this also means that there is no hint that a success is coming, i.e. that for the queried x the value $g(x)$ is going to be equal to the values stored in locations $h_1(x)$ and $h_2(x)$. The only possible problem could be that more than $O(t/\ell) = k$ queries involve some g_i, but this happens with probability exponentially small in k. So we conclude that we can use this for the BP-test as well. Therefore, we get the following corollary:

Corollary 1. *For any $n, t \in \mathbb{N}$, universe of size $u \in \mathbb{N}$ and $0 < \varepsilon < 1/2$ there exists an (n, t, ε)-BP test resilient Bloom filter (against unbounded adversaries and t known in advance) that uses $O\left(n \log \frac{1}{\varepsilon} + t\right)$ bits of memory. In fact, let B be a Bloom filter as described above. Then for any constant $0 < \varepsilon < 1/2$, B is an (n, t, ε)-BP test resilient Bloom filter against unbounded adversaries, that uses m bits of memory where $m = O\left(n \log \frac{1}{\varepsilon} + t\right)$.*

Note that t needs to be known in advance in this construction (to set k and choose appropriate G).

To get a Bloom filter B' that is an (n, ε)-strongly BP test resilient, we will modify this construction a bit. The idea is simple: for the function g, we use a family of pseudorandom functions. Now, we do not need to set k and the view of g remains random and unpredictable on any set of queried elements (of any size). If the resulting Bloom filter is not a BP-test resilient, then this test can be used to distinguish the PRF from a truly random function. We conclude with the following theorem that we have just proved:

Theorem 11. *Assuming the existence of one-way functions, then for any $n \in \mathbb{N}$, universe of size $n < u \in \mathbb{N}$, and $0 < \varepsilon < 1/2$ there exists a Bloom filter that is an (n, ε)-strongly BP test resilient and uses $O\left(n \log \frac{1}{\varepsilon} + \lambda\right)$ bits of memory. In fact, let B' be a Bloom filter as constructed above. Then for any constant $0 < \varepsilon < 1/2$, B' is an (n, ε)-strongly BP test resilient and uses $O\left(n \log \frac{1}{\varepsilon} + \lambda\right)$ bits of memory.*

Note that it is not known whether replacing the hash functions with a PRF in the standard construction of Bloom filters (i.e. the one in the style of Bloom's original one [4]) results in a Bloom filter that is BP test resilient.

Acknowledgment. We would like to thank the anonymous reviewers for their insightful comments and suggestions.

References

1. Ben-Eliezer, O., Jayaram, R., Woodruff, D.P., Yogev, E.: A framework for adversarially robust streaming algorithms. SIGMOD Rec. **50**(1), 6–13 (2021)
2. Bender, M.A., Farach-Colton, M., Goswami, M., Johnson, R., McCauley, S., Singh, S.: Bloom filters, adaptivity, and the dictionary problem. In: FOCS, pp. 182–193. IEEE Computer Society (2018)
3. Berman, I., Haitner, I., Komargodski, I., Naor, M.: Hardness-preserving reductions via cuckoo hashing. J. Cryptol. **32**(2), 361–392 (2019)
4. Bloom, B.H.: Space/time trade-offs in hash coding with allowable errors. Commun. ACM **13**(7), 422–426 (1970)
5. Blum, M., Micali, S.: How to generate cryptographically strong sequences of pseudo-random bits. SIAM J. Comput. **13**(4), 850–864 (1984)
6. Boyle, E., LaVigne, R., Vaikuntanathan, V.: Adversarially robust property-preserving hash functions. In: ITCS. LIPIcs, vol. 124, pp. 16:1–16:20. Schloss Dagstuhl - Leibniz-Zentrum für Informatik (2019)

7. Carter, L., Floyd, R.W., Gill, J., Markowsky, G., Wegman, M.N.: Exact and approximate membership testers. In: STOC, pp. 59–65. ACM (1978)
8. Clayton, D., Patton, C., Shrimpton, T.: Probabilistic data structures in adversarial environments. In: CCS, pp. 1317–1334. ACM (2019)
9. Cover, T.M., Thomas, J.A.: Elements of Information Theory, 2nd edn. Wiley, Hoboken (2006)
10. Dietzfelbinger, M., Woelfel, P.: Almost random graphs with simple hash functions. In: STOC, pp. 629–638. ACM (2003)
11. Earman, J.: A user's guide to the surprise exam paradoxes, July 2021. http://philsci-archive.pitt.edu/19303/
12. Fan, L., Cao, P., Almeida, J.M., Broder, A.Z.: Summary cache: a scalable wide-area web cache sharing protocol. IEEE/ACM Trans. Netw. $8(3)$, 281–293 (2000)
13. Goldreich, O.: The Foundations of Cryptography - Volume 1: Basic Techniques. Cambridge University Press, Cambridge (2001)
14. Goldreich, O., Goldwasser, S., Micali, S.: How to construct random functions. J. ACM $33(4)$, 792–807 (1986)
15. Hardt, M., Woodruff, D.P.: How robust are linear sketches to adaptive inputs? In: STOC, pp. 121–130. ACM (2013)
16. Hassidim, A., Kaplan, H., Mansour, Y., Matias, Y., Stemmer, U.: Adversarially robust streaming algorithms via differential privacy. In: NeurIPS (2020)
17. Kaplan, H., Mansour, Y., Nissim, K., Stemmer, U.: Separating adaptive streaming from oblivious streaming using the bounded storage model. In: Malkin, T., Peikert, C. (eds.) CRYPTO 2021. LNCS, vol. 12827, pp. 94–121. Springer, Cham (2021). https://doi.org/10.1007/978-3-030-84252-9_4
18. Lee, D.J., McCauley, S., Singh, S., Stein, M.: Telescoping filter: a practical adaptive filter. In: ESA. LIPIcs, vol. 204, pp. 60:1–60:18. Schloss Dagstuhl - Leibniz-Zentrum für Informatik (2021)
19. Luby, M., Rackoff, C.: How to construct pseudorandom permutations from pseudorandom functions. SIAM J. Comput. $17(2)$, 373–386 (1988)
20. Micciancio, D., Walter, M.: On the bit security of cryptographic primitives. In: Nielsen, J.B., Rijmen, V. (eds.) EUROCRYPT 2018, Part I. LNCS, vol. 10820, pp. 3–28. Springer, Cham (2018). https://doi.org/10.1007/978-3-319-78381-9_1
21. Mitzenmacher, M., Pontarelli, S., Reviriego, P.: Adaptive cuckoo filters. ACM J. Exp. Algorithmics 25, 1–20 (2020)
22. Naor, M., Reingold, O.: On the construction of pseudorandom permutations: Luby-Rackoff revisited. J. Cryptol. $12(1)$, 29–66 (1999)
23. Naor, M., Yogev, E.: Bloom filters in adversarial environments. ACM Trans. Algorithms $15(3)$, 35:1–35:30 (2019). (prelim version Crpyto 2015)
24. Pagh, A., Pagh, R.: Uniform hashing in constant time and optimal space. SIAM J. Comput. $38(1)$, 85–96 (2008)
25. Pagh, R.: Cuckoo hashing. In: Kao, M.-Y. (ed.) Encyclopedia of Algorithms, pp. 212–215. Springer, Boston (2008). https://doi.org/10.1007/978-0-387-30162-4_97
26. Pagh, R., Rodler, F.F.: Cuckoo hashing. J. Algorithms $51(2)$, 122–144 (2004)
27. Schrift, A.W., Shamir, A.: On the universality of the next bit test. In: Menezes, A.J., Vanstone, S.A. (eds.) CRYPTO 1990. LNCS, vol. 537, pp. 394–408. Springer, Heidelberg (1991). https://doi.org/10.1007/3-540-38424-3_29
28. Woodruff, D.P., Zhou, S.: Tight bounds for adversarially robust streams and sliding windows via difference estimators. CoRR abs/2011.07471 (2020)
29. Yao, A.C.: Theory and applications of trapdoor functions (extended abstract). In: FOCS, pp. 80–91. IEEE Computer Society (1982)

Author Index

Printed in the United States
by Baker & Taylor Publisher Services